Keith D.G. Johnson   Wheatley 1964.

TYPES OF LITERATURE

GINN
LITERATURE SERIES
Edward J. Gordon
SENIOR AUTHOR

INTRODUCTION TO LITERATURE
THE STUDY OF LITERATURE
UNDERSTANDING LITERATURE
TYPES OF LITERATURE
AMERICAN LITERATURE
ENGLISH LITERATURE

ROBERT A. BENNETT

San Diego Public Schools

VERDA EVANS

Cleveland Public Schools

TYPES OF LITERATURE

EDWARD J. GORDON

Yale University

Consulting Editor, HARRY L. WALEN
Needham (Massachusetts) High School

GINN AND COMPANY

BOSTON, NEW YORK, CHICAGO, ATLANTA, DALLAS, PALO ALTO,

TORONTO

ROBERT A. BENNETT is specialist in language arts for the San Diego City Schools and was formerly consultant in secondary curriculum to the Minneapolis Public Schools. He has been active in the NCTE, serving as chairman of the Advisory Board of the *English Journal,* chairman of the Secondary Section, and member of the Executive Committee.

VERDA EVANS is Directing Supervisor of English for the Cleveland Public Schools. She is a member of the Commission on English of the College Entrance Examination Board, has served as cochairman of the NCTE Committee on Supervision in Big Cities and States and as cochairman of the 1964 NCTE Convention, and is coauthor of a high school workbook-handbook language series.

EDWARD J. GORDON, associate professor of English at Yale University, is director of Yale's Office of Teacher Training. He was English department head at Germantown Friends School in Philadelphia before going to Yale and has given courses on the teaching of English at Newton Junior College, Harvard, and Yale. He has been chairman of and the motivating force behind the annual Yale Conferences on the teaching of English, a director of the School and College Conference on English, a director of NCTE, coeditor of *Essays on the Teaching of English,* and editor of a high school edition of *Huckleberry Finn.*

HARRY L. WALEN, formerly directing editor of secondary school English at Ginn and Company, is now principal of Needham (Massachusetts) High School. He is president of the New England Association of Teachers of English and has served as a director of the NCTE.

Grateful acknowledgment is due to the following publishers, authors, and other holders of copyright material for permission to use selections from their publications.

Acknowledgments

MRS. GEORGE BAMBRIDGE: "The Benefactors," by Rudyard Kipling, from *The Years Between.*
ERNEST BENN LIMITED: "Trifles," by Susan Glaspell.
LURTON BLASSINGAME: "A Favor for Lefty," by Charles Einstein. Reprinted by permission of the author. Copyright Crowell-Collier, 1956.
BRANDT & BRANDT: "By the Waters of Babylon," by Stephen Vincent Benét. From *Selected Works of Stephen Vincent Benét.* Holt, Rinehart and Winston, Inc. Copyright, 1937, by Stephen Vincent Benét. Reprinted by permission of Brandt & Brandt. "You Can't Do That," by John P. Marquand. Copyright 1935 by The Curtis Publishing Company. Reprinted by permission of Brandt & Brandt.
JONATHAN CAPE LIMITED: "The Sniper," from *Spring Sowing,* by Liam O'Flaherty.
CHATTO & WINDUS LTD.: "The Bet," from *The School Mistress and Other Stories,* by Anton Tchehov, translated by Constance Garnett.
MARCHETTE CHUTE: "Getting at the Truth," from *Saturday Review.*
THE CITADEL PRESS: "The Damned Thing," by Ambrose Bierce.
MISS D. E. COLLINS: "A Defence of Detective Stories," by G. K. Chesterton, from *The Defendant.*
CURTIS BROWN, LTD.: "I'll Take the High Road Commission," in *Family Reunion,* by Ogden Nash. Reprinted by permission of the author. Copyright 1931, 1933, 1935, 1936, 1938, 1940, 1942, 1949, 1950 by Ogden Nash.
J. M. DENT & SONS, LTD.: "A Defence of Detective Stories," by G. K. Chesterton, from *The Defendant.* Quotations from "Preface to *The Nigger of the Narcissus*" and "A Familiar Preface," by Joseph Conrad; "The Secret Sharer," from *'Twixt Land and Sea,* by Joseph Conrad.
DODD, MEAD & COMPANY: "Trifles," by Susan Glaspell. Reprinted by permission of Dodd, Mead & Company from *Plays* by Susan Glaspell. Copyright 1920, 1948 by Susan Glas-

The illustrations in this book are the work of the following artists:
Marjorie Auerbach Polly Bolian Don Bolognese Anthony D'Adamo R. J. Lee Don Madden Tom O'Sullivan Susan Perl Norman Pomerantz David Stone Eric von Schmidt Emil Weiss Ed Young

Preface

Reading literature is important to the high school student, for literature has the capacity to acquaint the student with his cultural heritage, to enlarge the possibilities for the student's own growth, and, not least, to give enjoyment. But for literature to function in these ways, the student must know *how* to read. Reading a work of literature is not merely recognizing printed words on a page, but rather it is experiencing an artistic whole expressed through many factors working together in a complex way. The purpose of *Types of Literature* is to enable the student to see for himself how a literary work operates, how its various parts work together to produce meaning.

This book has been arranged by types of literature—the short story, the drama, the essay and biography, the novel, the poem—in order to provide an intensive study of each form. A general introduction to the genre under consideration begins each unit. Within a unit, headnotes discuss one or two literary concepts illustrated by each selection. The short-story unit, for example, proceeds from consideration of basic aspects of the form, such as characterization and point of view, to more difficult concepts, such as irony and symbolism. Each selection is accompanied by questions designed to follow up the concepts discussed in the headnote, to reinforce concepts introduced earlier in the book, and to explore the work as a whole. Vocabulary exercises and composition suggestions are frequently given and are always related to the specific selection they accompany. Where appropriate, oral activity suggestions are also provided.

The illustrations in the book were chosen to enhance the student's appreciation of literature, not merely for their eye appeal or usefulness as fillers. Because poetry should create its own images and ideas, the lyric poems have not been illustrated.

Various supplementary aids appear at the end of the book. Biographical sketches of each author in the book are arranged alphabetically, beginning on page 692. Each sketch includes the titles of major works by that author, and may thus be used as a reference for further reading. Definitions of the literary terms used in this book (and of additional terms some teachers may have occasion to introduce) follow the author biographies. These definitions provide a ready reference for the student and also refer him to pages on which particular terms are discussed at length. An extensive glossary of difficult words that the student will begin to encounter fairly frequently in his reading is also provided. Words rarely encountered, proper names, and allusions are footnoted in the text.

Through reading the selections in this book in conjunction with the unit introductions, the reading headnotes, the questions following each selection, and the supplementary materials, the student should be able to increase his understanding and enjoyment of all types of literature.

Contents

The Novel

Poetry

Julius Caesar

The Short Story

The Sniper*

Liam O'Flaherty

THE LONG June twilight faded into night. Dublin lay enveloped in darkness but for the dim light of the moon that shone through fleecy clouds, casting a pale light as of approaching dawn over the streets and the dark waters of the Liffey. Around the beleaguered Four Courts the heavy guns roared. Here and there through the city, machine guns and rifles broke the silence of the night, spasmodically, like dogs barking on lone farms. Republicans and Free Staters were waging civil war.

On a roof top near O'Connell Bridge, a Republican sniper lay watching. Beside him lay his rifle and over his shoulders were slung a pair of field glasses. His face was the face of a student, thin and ascetic, but his eyes had the cold gleam of the fanatic. They were deep and thoughtful, the eyes of a man who is used to looking at death.

He was eating a sandwich hungrily. He had eaten nothing since morning. He had been too excited to eat. He finished the sandwich, and, taking a flask of whisky from his pocket, he took a short draught. Then he returned the flask to his pocket. He paused for a moment, considering whether he should risk a smoke. It was dangerous. The flash might be seen in the darkness, and there were enemies watching. He decided to take the risk.

Placing a cigarette between his lips, he struck a match, inhaled the smoke hurriedly and put out the light. Almost immediately, a bullet flattened itself against the parapet of the roof. The sniper took another whiff and put out the cigarette. Then he swore softly and crawled away to the left.

Cautiously he raised himself and peered over the parapet. There was a flash and a bullet whizzed over his head. He dropped immediately. He had seen the flash. It came from the opposite side of the street.

He rolled over the roof to a chimney stack in the rear, and slowly drew himself up behind it, until his eyes were level with the top of the parapet. There was nothing to be seen—just the dim outline of the opposite housetop against the blue sky. His enemy was under cover.

Just then an armored car came across the bridge and advanced slowly up the street. It stopped on the opposite side of the street, fifty yards ahead. The sniper could hear the dull panting of the motor. His heart beat faster. It was an enemy car. He wanted to fire, but he knew it was useless. His bullets would never pierce the steel that covered the gray monster.

Then round the corner of a side street came an old woman, her head covered by a tattered shawl. She began to talk to the man in the turret of the car. She was pointing to the roof where the sniper lay. An informer.

* From *Spring Sowing*, by Liam O'Flaherty. Reprinted by permission of Harcourt, Brace & World, Inc.

The turret opened. A man's head and shoulders appeared, looking toward the sniper. The sniper raised his rifle and fired. The head fell heavily on the turret wall. The woman darted toward the side street. The sniper fired again. The woman whirled round and fell with a shriek into the gutter.

Suddenly from the opposite roof a shot rang out and the sniper dropped his rifle with a curse. The rifle clattered to the roof. The sniper thought the noise would wake the dead. He stopped to pick the rifle up. He couldn't lift it. His forearm was dead. "I'm hit," he muttered.

Dropping flat onto the roof, he crawled back to the parapet. With his left hand he felt the injured right forearm. The blood was oozing through the sleeve of his coat. There was no pain—just a deadened sensation, as if the arm had been cut off.

Quickly he drew his knife from his pocket, opened it on the breastwork of the parapet, and ripped open the sleeve. There was a small hole where the bullet had entered. On the other side there was no hole. The bullet had lodged in the bone. It must have fractured it. He bent the arm below the wound. The arm bent back easily. He ground his teeth to overcome the pain.

Then taking out his field dressing, he ripped open the packet with his knife. He broke the neck of the iodine bottle and let the bitter fluid drip into the wound. A paroxysm of pain swept through him. He placed the cotton wadding over the wound and wrapped the dressing over it. He tied the ends with his teeth.

Then he lay still against the parapet, and, closing his eyes, he made an effort of will to overcome the pain.

In the street beneath all was still. The armored car had retired speedily

over the bridge, with the machine gunner's head hanging lifeless over the turret. The woman's corpse lay still in the gutter.

The sniper lay still for a long time nursing his wounded arm and planning escape. Morning must not find him wounded on the roof. The enemy on the opposite roof covered his escape. He must kill that enemy and he could not use his rifle. He had only a revolver to do it. Then he thought of a plan.

Taking off his cap, he placed it over the muzzle of his rifle. Then he pushed the rifle slowly upward over the parapet, until the cap was visible from the opposite side of the street. Almost immediately there was a report, and a bullet pierced the center of the cap. The sniper slanted the rifle forward. The cap slipped down into the street. Then catching the rifle in the middle, the sniper dropped his left hand over the roof and let it hang, lifelessly. After a few moments he let the rifle drop to the street. Then he sank to the roof, dragging his hand with him.

Crawling quickly to the left, he peered up at the corner of the roof. His ruse had succeeded. The other sniper, seeing the cap and rifle fall, thought that he had killed his man. He was now standing before a row of chimney pots, looking across, with his head clearly silhouetted against the western sky.

The Republican sniper smiled and lifted his revolver above the edge of the parapet. The distance was about fifty yards—a hard shot in the dim light, and his right arm was paining him like a thousand devils. He took a steady aim. His hand trembled with eagerness. Pressing his lips together, he took a deep breath through his nostrils and fired. He was almost deafened with the report and his arm shook with the recoil.

Then when the smoke cleared he peered across and uttered a cry of joy. His enemy had been hit. He was reeling over the parapet in his death agony. He struggled to keep his feet, but he was slowly falling forward, as if in a dream. The rifle fell from his grasp, hit the parapet, fell over, bounded off the pole of a barber's shop beneath and then clattered on the pavement.

Then the dying man on the roof crumpled up and fell forward. The body turned over and over in space and hit the ground with a dull thud. Then it lay still.

The sniper looked at his enemy falling and he shuddered. The lust of battle died in him. He became bitten by remorse. The sweat stood out in beads on his forehead. Weakened by his wound and the long summer day of fasting and watching on the roof, he revolted from the sight of the shattered mass of his dead enemy. His teeth chattered, he began to gibber to himself, cursing the war, cursing himself, cursing everybody.

He looked at the smoking revolver in his hand, and with an oath he hurled it to the roof at his feet. The revolver went off with the concussion and the bullet whizzed past the sniper's head. He was frightened back to his senses by the shock. His nerves steadied. The cloud of fear scattered from his mind and he laughed.

Taking the whisky flask from his pocket, he emptied it at a draught. He felt reckless under the influence of the spirit. He decided to leave the roof now and look for his company commander, to report. Everywhere around was quiet. There was not much danger in going through the streets. He picked up his revolver and put it in his pocket. Then he crawled down through the skylight to the house underneath.

When the sniper reached the laneway on the street level, he felt a sudden curiosity as to the identity of the enemy sniper whom he had killed. He decided that he was a good shot, whoever he was. He wondered did he know him. Perhaps he had been in his own company before the split in the army. He decided to risk going over to have a look at him. He peered around the corner into O'Connell Street. In the upper part of the street there was heavy firing, but around here all was quiet.

The sniper darted across the street. A machine gun tore up the ground around him with a hail of bullets, but he escaped. He threw himself face downward beside the corpse. The machine gun stopped.

Then the sniper turned over the dead body and looked into his brother's face.

Introduction to the Short Story

THE SIXTEEN SHORT STORIES in this unit, beginning with O'Flaherty's gripping "The Sniper" and ending with Benét's thoughtful and disturbing "By the Waters of Babylon," have been chosen because in each story the author has accomplished what he set out to do.

A well-written short story is an ordered structure. It does not simply flow out of the author's mind; it must be carefully constructed. A bright light is thrown on certain carefully selected aspects of the characters' lives; significant events are planned; certain details are selected and others rejected. The various parts of the short story—character, plot, theme, setting—are related to each other in a way that brings unity to the story and creates a single impression on the reader's mind. Each writer tells his story in his own way, but he works within the framework of an orderly structure.

Reading a short story, as well as writing one, calls for certain skills. To be a good reader, you must learn to recognize what an author is trying to do in a story and to judge how well he accomplishes his aims. To help you learn these things, each story in this unit (with the exception of the introductory and concluding selections) is preceded by a headnote discussing one or two of its more important features. By considering these headnotes and the questions that follow each selection, you will not only be better able to read short stories critically, but you will also see how the authors have put their stories together.

"The Sniper," which introduces the short story unit, is a good illustration of how an author constructs a story, relating its various elements to one another so as to produce suspense and to make clear their significance. Character and action are two essential elements of all stories—without at least one character no story could exist and without action the character would have little interest or meaning to the reader. In "The Sniper," you know almost nothing about the central character—not his background or the circumstances that brought him to this particular roof, not even his name. Such details are unimportant for O'Flaherty's purpose. What is important are the sniper's actions and feelings as a man engaged in war—a civil war. You see his excitement, the "lust of battle," later his revolt at the dead body of his enemy; you see him eating a sandwich, smoking a cigarette, shooting an old woman. And finally occurs the twist of the last sentence. Is it merely a shock ending, or is O'Flaherty commenting on the hate and death necessarily involved in war when he writes, "the sniper . . . looked into his brother's face"? If you see how O'Flaherty has selected certain actions and details which make the total meaning of the story clear—ones which define for the reader how war makes men act—you are well on your way to understanding a key principle of all stories.

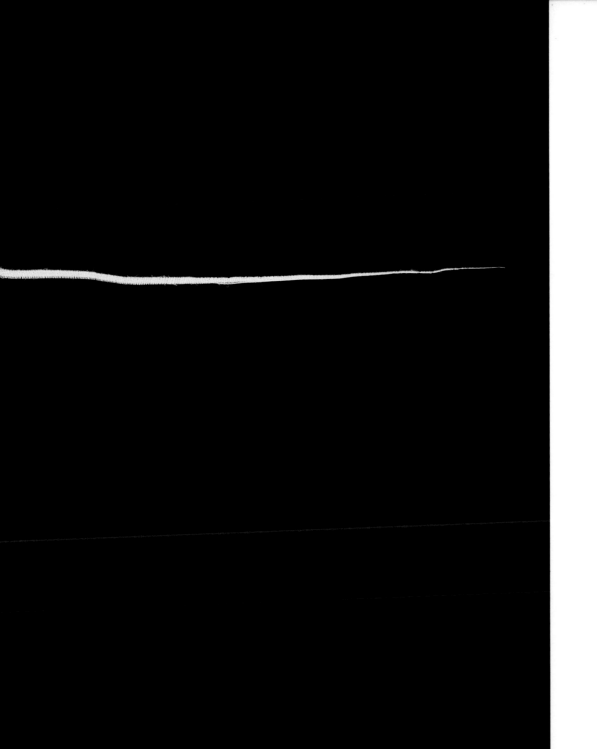

Note also that O'Flaherty dramatizes what he has to say. He does not write an essay or treatise on war; he writes about a specific person and what he does. He involves the reader by making him experience what the sniper experiences. In every good short story you will see the same process—the writer dramatizes observations about people; he gives shape and color to his ideas about the meaning of experience.

The other sixteen stories in this unit have been divided into two groups. The stories in the first group are ones in which the situation related in the story is the dominating interest. The author's purpose is to make the reader wonder how the situation will turn out and perhaps what the characters are like. Such stories may be sad or humorous; they may contain a great deal of action or very little; the people in them may strike the reader as real or simply as puppets. In some of them you will find a close relationship between the characters of the persons involved and the action—each partly causing and partly resulting from the other.

The second group of stories goes further than this. The situation is still important as a means of arousing interest, but in addition the particular incidents and the people dealt with have a significance beyond themselves. To a greater or lesser degree, each sets forth for the reader some portion of truth about human beings, their relations to one another and to forces outside themselves.

Every short story, of course, is put together in its own special way, but one characteristic common to all stories is plot. By plot is meant the series of incidents by which the conflicts, or problems, of a story are developed and finally resolved. Early in every story some kind of question is raised in the perceptive reader's mind. The writer may begin simply by introducing a character who catches the reader's interest. Just as in real life most people like to know what happens to anyone who is of interest to them (a friend, an enemy, a movie star, an athlete), so the reader is curious about what will happen to the short story character. To maintain this curiosity, the writer must then develop some kind of situation that makes the reader wonder how the character will be affected.

The situation must involve conflict of some kind—the character may have to make a decision or he may have to fight or outwit an enemy. In a story with a psychological slant, the reader may simply be curious to find out what makes a character tick, what makes him behave in the way he does. In still other stories, the interest of the reader may center in finding out the meaning of what happens to the character.

Whatever emphasis a story has, however, it should present at least one character about whom the reader wants to find out something. The various episodes, or actions, by which the author shows what he considers of interest in that character's life make up the plot of the story. In a good short story, each development in the plot should seem to be a logical result of something that occurred earlier in the story. In particular, the end of the story—the final resolution of the conflict—

6

should seem logical; otherwise, the whole story will be unconvincing.

As you read the following stories, allow yourself to respond to what the author is trying to do. If the story is a good one, everything in it is important—the scene with which the writer chose to open, the descriptions of setting he decided to include, the person he chose to tell the story. Discovering how the stories in this unit are put together as well as what they say should help you to find new areas of enjoyment in all your reading.

Reading "Early Marriage"

Richter, who sets many of his stories and novels against the westward movement in America, uses a dangerous journey in "Early Marriage" both to arouse suspense and to reveal the characters of the Putman family, early settlers in the Southwest. In some stories, action (or plot) dominates the characters, so that the reader is most interested in what the characters do and in what happens to them. In others, character dominates plot, the main interest being in what the characters are like, why they behave as they do, and how they change.

"Early Marriage" is a fairly equal balance of these two elements. As you read, note how the author shows you what the characters are like—that is, his *characterization*. The chief method of characterizing people in short stories is through their actions. This is true not only of major actions, although these often reveal character most clearly, but also of such little actions as a character's walk, his glancing at himself in a mirror, his crushing an insect—all the little actions that in life itself create the image of an individual. What the characters in a story say, how they say it, and what others say of them also contribute to the reader's knowledge of them. One means by which a reader often comes to know characters in a story more intimately than he knows people in real life is through the author's being able to tell what a character thinks and feels but does not put into words.

The first nine paragraphs of "Early Marriage" introduce the major characters and give the background from which the story's plot develops. The part of a story that explains the characters and the situation previous to the main action is called the *exposition*. Although exposition frequently occurs at the beginning of a story, it need not do so. Richter, for example, provides additional exposition late in "Early Marriage" through the device of having Nancy Belle think back to her first meeting with Stephen. In this story as in many others, the exposition provides the reader with much of his knowledge about the characters.

Early Marriage

Conrad Richter

This western in which not a single shot is fired carries as much suspense as violent tales that echo and re-echo with gunfire. You will find this story of a teen-age girl carrying out her plans for her wedding in sharp contrast to the wedding stories carried in today's society pages. Which contributes more to this contrast—the character of the girl or the character of the country?

FOR TWO DAYS the leathery face of Asa Putman had been a document in cipher to anyone who could read the code. Since Saturday but one traveler had passed his solitary post, a speck of adobe and picket corrals lost on the vast, sandy stretch of the Santa Ana plain. Far as the eye could see from his doorway, the rutted El Paso trail, unfenced, gutterless, innocent of grading, gravel, culverts, or telephone poles, imprinted only by iron tires, the hoofs of horses and oxen, sheep and cattle, and the paw of the loping lobo wolf, lay with dust unraised.

Ordinarily, there were freighters with cracking whips and trailers rumbling on behind. Army trains to and from the forts set up their tents for the night beyond the springs. The private coaches of Santa Fe and Colorado merchants, of cattle kings and Government officials, stopped long enough for the Putman children to admire the ladies, the magnificent woodwork, and the luxurious cushions inside. Trail herds of gaunt red steers bawled for the water in the earthen tank, and pairs and companies of horsemen rode up and down.

But since Saturday not even a solitary buckboard from the far settlements in the Cedar country had called for supplies or letters. Only a girl from the Blue Mesa had ridden in for her and her neighbors' mail. She had eaten dinner with the Putmans, refused to stay overnight and started her long ride home.

A stranger from the East would have spoken about the stillness, the deadly waiting, and asked uneasily why Uncle Gideon hadn't come as promised. But in the Putman household it was not mentioned.

Asa deliberately busied himself about the post, filling the bin beneath the counter with navy beans and green coffee, leafing through the packet of letters in the drawer, and making a long rite out of feeding the occupants of the picket corrals—four horses of which were fresh for the next stage.

Rife, just turned fifteen, carried water and gathered cow chips in an old hide dragged by a rope to his saddle horn. Ignacita, the Mexican housekeeper, spat sharply on her heavy irons in the torrid kitchen and kept glancing over her shoulder and out of the open door and windows.

And Nancy Belle, going on seventeen, packed and repacked the high, iron-bound trunk that her father had bought for her at Santa Fe and sang softly to herself in the way that women sang fifty and sixty years ago.

Saturday she was being married at Gunstock, two hundred miles away— five days' journey in a wagon, four in a saddle or buckboard.

For six months she had thought of little else. The almanac fell apart at June as naturally as her mother's Bible did at the Twenty-third Psalm. So often had she run her finger down the page that anyone might tell from the worn line of type the very day she and Stephen Dewee would be man and wife. The Dewees lived four hundred miles west across the territory in the Beaverhead country. She and Stephen were taking a mountain ranch near his people, and for the wedding they had compromised on Gunstock, nearly equidistant from both families and convenient to friends scattered up and down the Rio Grande.

She had lighted a candle in the dusk, when a figure appeared reluctantly in her doorway. Asa Putman had never been at ease in his daughter's bedroom. A tall, rawhide man in an unbuttoned, sagging vest, he was visibly embarrassed by any furnishings that suggested refinement. Invariably he kept his hat on in the house. He had it on now, a flat top and a flat brim, not so much like the Western hats you see now. Nancy Belle knew that her mother's people had never forgiven him for bringing his young wife and their two small children to this lonely post, at the mercy of outlaws and the worse Apaches.

Tonight she could see that something bothered him. He gave her a sidewise glance, so sharp and characteristic.

"I don't expect, Nancy Belle, you could put off your weddin'?"

The girl stood quietly gazing at him with a face like the tintype of her mother. But under her sedate gray dress, with tight waist and full skirts to the instep, she had frozen. She looked much older than her years. Her air of gentlefolk and her wide-apart gray eyes came from her mother. But the chin, tipped up with resolute fearlessness, was her father's.

"No, Papa!" Her two clear words held all the steady insistence of the desert.

"I figured how you'd feel," he nodded, avoiding her eyes. "I just wanted to put it up to you. I'd 'a' covered the *jornada*[1] on foot to be on time at my own weddin', but I didn't have to count on Gideon to hold me up."

"Are you telling me, Papa, that you can't go to Gunstock tomorrow?" Her voice remained quiet, but a coldness had seized her. Of all the people she had visualized at her wedding, the one next to Stephen she could least spare was the tall, grave figure of her father

"I reckon I kind of can't, Nancy Belle," he said soberly. "Rife could tend to the stage all right and do the feedin'. But they's men come to this post no boy can handle." He shifted his position. "I figured once on closin' up the post till I got back. But the stage is comin' and the mail. And the freighters count on me for feed and grub. Then I got to protect my own property and the mail and freight for the Cedar country that's in the storage room."

"I know," Nancy Belle said steadily. "I can get to Gunstock all right."

Far back in her father's assaying eyes, she fancied she saw a glint of pride.

"You're pretty nigh a woman now, Nancy Belle. And Rife's a good slice of a man. It's a straight trail to the Rio Grande, once you turn at the old post. Both you and Rife's been over it before. Of course, I'd like to be at the weddin', but the boy can tell me about it." He went to the window. "Rife!" he called.

1 **jornada** (hôr nä′də): a long stretch of desert region.

Nancy Belle's brother came in presently. A slight boy, with his father's blue eyes, he seldom made a fuss over anything, even when he shot a stray duck on the tank or when they braked down the last cedar hill into Santa Fe with all the open doors of the plaza shops in sight. And when his father told him now, he showed neither enthusiasm nor regret—merely straightened.

"Sure. I can take you, Nancy Belle," he said.

Something pulled under his sister's tight basque.[2] She remembered the long miles they would have in the wagon, the camps at lonely places, the ugly shadow ever hovering over the outposts of this frontier country, and the blight that, since Saturday, seemed to have fallen on the trail. Her eyes swam. Now, at the last minute, she yielded.

"If you'll let me ride, Papa, I'll wait another day for Uncle Gideon," she promised.

Her father's eyes moved to the ruffled red calico curtains at the shadeless windows.

"I don't hardly count on Gideon comin' any more, Nancy Belle. Besides, it's too long in the saddle to Gunstock—especially for a girl to get married. You'd be plumb wore out, and you wouldn't have your trunk. You couldn't get dressed for your weddin'."

He turned thoughtfully and went out, Rife close behind. Nancy Belle could hear her father's tones, slow and grave, coming from near one of the picket corrals.

It was too far to catch the words; but when they came in, she saw that her brother's features looked a little pale under the tan.

"You better get some sleep, Nancy Belle," her father said. "You and Rife are startin' before daylight. If Gideon comes, I'll ride after."

They had scarcely gone from the room when Ignacita came in from the kitchen, her black eyes glittering over a pile of freshly starched white in her arms.

"Nancy Belle, *chinita!*"[3] she whispered, plucking at the girl's sleeve. "You don't say to your *papacito*[4] I talk to you! I have promise I don't scare you. But I can't see you go so far in the wildness alone, *pobrecita!*[5] Sometimes people go safe from one place to the other, oh, *si!*[6] But sometimes, *chinita*, they don't come back! You have not the oldness like Ignacita. Ay, I tell you these old eyes have see men and women quartered from a tree like sheep or maybe tied over a stove like I don't have the words to say to you."

Nancy Belle did not answer except to lay, one by one, the ironed pieces in her trunk—a bride's muslin underwear trimmed with red and blue feather stitching; long petticoats stiffly flounced with ruffles, and nightgowns long in the sleeve and high in the neck, with ruffles at wrist and throat. The Mexican woman went on hoarsely. The girl folded away her winter's cashmere dress, buttoned up the front and with a white fichu.[7] She unwrapped and wrapped again in crumpled white tissue the red slippers the old gentleman on the stage had sent her as a wedding present from Philadelphia.

When Ignacita had left, she opened her keepsake box covered with colored shells. The mirror on the inside lid

---

2 **basque** (băsk): a fitted waist.

3 **chinita** (shē nē′tə): dearie.
4 **papacito** (pä′pä sē′tō): papa dear.
5 **pobrecita** (pō′brə sē′tə): poor little thing.
6 **sí** (sē): yes.
7 **fichu** (fĭsh′ōō): an ornamental three-cornered cape.

turned back a face as calm as the little golden clouds that hung of an evening over the east to catch the desert sunset. But after she had undressed and put on her nightdress, for a long time she was aware of the soft pound of her heart faintly swaying the bed on its rawhide springs.

At the first sound of Ignacita's hand on the kitchen stove, Nancy Belle sprang out of bed. She dressed on the brown pool of burro skin, the only carpet on her adobe floor. Through the west window she could see the morning star burning like a brilliant candle. It hung, she told herself, over Gunstock and the Beaverhead, where Stephen, at this moment, in their new log ranch house, lay thinking about her.

They ate in the kitchen by lamplight. She had never been so conscious of every detail—the great white cups and saucers, the familiar steel knives, the homy smell of the scorched paper lamp shade, the unreadable eyes of her father, Rife, and Ignacita.

Asa Putman himself carried out the trunk. There was already hay in the wagon, a gunny sack of oats, food in a canned-tomato box and utensils in another, a water keg, bed roll tied in a wagon sheet, an ax, a bridle, and her own sidesaddle, made to order over a man's tree. Her eyes caught the gleam of a rifle leaning up against the seat in the lantern light. Tethered to the rear of the wagon stood her saddle mare, Fancy, with pricked-up ears. She was going along to their new ranch home. Nancy Belle felt that she was still among intimate things, but outside the little circle of light lay darkness and the unknown.

When she said good-by to her father, he kissed her—something he had not done for years.

"You haven't changed your mind, Nancy Belle?" he asked.

She climbed quickly up over the wheel to the spring seat of the wagon before he might see that she was crying. Rife swung up like a monkey on the other side and pushed the rifle into the crevice behind the seat cushion. The lines tautened and the wagon lurched.

"*Dios*[8] go with you safe to your husband, Nancy Belle!" she heard Ignacita cry after her.

The morning star had set. They moved into a world of silent blackness. Nancy Belle could not see how the horses remained on the trail. When she looked back, the only light in all these square miles of black, unfriendly earth was the yellow window of her father's post.

It was almost a vision, golden and far away, like all beautiful things. She didn't trust herself to look again.

Two hours later the wagon was a lonely speck of boat rocking in an illimitable sage-green sea beneath the sun. The canvas wagon sheet fastened over the bows was a kind of sail, and eastward the sandy water did not stop rolling till it washed up at the foot of the faintly blue ramparts of the distant Espiritu Range.

Just before they turned west on the cross trail to the Rio Grande, a heavy wagon with a yoke of oxen in front and a cow behind toiled round the crumbling adobe walls of the old, abandoned post house. A bearded man and a thin woman with a white face sat on the seat. She held a baby in her arms, and three black-eyed children peered from under the wagon sheet.

The bearded man saluted and stopped his willing team. Rife did likewise. The woman spoke first. Her tongue was swift and slightly acid.

"You better turn around and follow us if you want to save your hair!" she called. "Yesterday a sheepherder told us he saw—"

A sharp word from the bearded man caused her to relapse into sullen silence. He asked Rife where he might be going, then climbed down to the trail and said he wanted to talk to him a little. The boy followed reluctantly behind his wagon. Nancy Belle could hear the bearded man's tones coming slow and grave like her father's, while the woman made silent and horribly expressive lip language.

Rife came back, walking stiffly. The bearded man climbed up beside the woman.

"They got to go on," he told her in a low tone, then saluted with his whip. "Good luck, boy! And you, miss!"

Rife raised his whip in stiff acknowledgment. The wagons creaked apart. Nancy Belle saw in front of her the trail to the Rio Grande, little more than a pair of wheel tracks, that lost itself on the lonely plain. Rife seemed relieved that she did not ask what the bearded man had said. But it was enough for her not to be able to forget the woman's fearful signs and mouthings and the horror in the curious eyes of the staring children.

Sister and brother talked very little. Nancy Belle saw her brother's eyes keep sweeping the country, scanning the horizons. Bunches of bear grass that might have been feathers pinioned his blue gaze, and clumps of cane cactus that seemed to hold pointing gun barrels. At arroyos thick with chamiso[9] and Apache plume[10] she could see his feet tighten on the footboard. Once he

9 **chamiso** (chə mē′sō): a semidesert shrub.
10 **Apache plume:** an evergreen shrub of the southwestern United States, so called because of its showy, plumed fruits.

8 **Dios:** God.

pulled out the rifle, but it was only a herd of antelopes moving across the desert page.

They camped for the night when the sun was still high. Nancy Belle asked no questions as the boy drove far off the trail into a grassy *cañada*.[11] She sang softly to herself as she fried the salt side bacon and put the black coffeepot to boil.

Rife hobbled Anton .Chico and the Bar X horse and staked out Fancy close to the wagon.

She pretended not to notice when, before dark, he poured earth on the fire till not a spark or wisp of smoke remained. Out of one eye she watched him climb the side of the *cañada* and stand long minutes sweeping the country from the ridge, a slight, tense figure against the sullen glow of the sunset.

"It's all right," he said when he came down. "You can go to bed."

"What's all right?" she asked him.

"The horses," he said, turning away, and Nancy Belle felt a stab of pain that so soon this boy must bear a man's responsibilities and tell a man's lies.

She prayed silently on her blankets spread on the hay in the wagon box, and lay down with her head on the sidesaddle, her unread Testament in her hand. She heard Rife unroll his camp bed on the ground beneath the wagon. It was all very strange and hushed without her father. Just to feel the Testament in her hand helped to calm her and to remember the day at the post when she had first met Stephen.

Her father had never let her come in contact with the men of the trail. Always, at the first sign of dust cloud on the horizon, he would tell both children to heap up the chip box, fill the water buckets and carry saddles and bridles into the house. But this day Asa Putman and Rife had gone to Fort Sumner. And to Nancy Belle, Uncle Gideon could seldom say no.

It had been a very hot day. She had been sitting in the shade of the earthen bank of the tank, moving her bare feet in the cool water, watching the ripples in the hot south wind. The leaves of the cottonwoods clashed overhead, and she heard nothing until she looked up, and there was a young man on a bluegray horse with dust clinging to his hat brim and mustache. His eyes were direct as an eagle's. Firm lines modeled his lean face. But what she noticed most at the time was the little bow tie on his dark shirt.

Instantly she had tucked her bare, wet legs under her red dress. Her face burned with shame, but the young stranger talked to her about her father coolly, as if she, a girl of fifteen, had not been caught barefooted. Then he did what in her mind was a noble thing. When Uncle Gideon came out, he magnificently turned his back for her to run into the house and pull on shoes and stockings.

She thought of Stephen constantly next day and the next. She had grown a little used to the journey without her father now—the still, uncertain nights under the wagon sheet, sitting, lying, listening, waiting; the less uncertain days with the sun on the endless spaces; her never-quiet perch on the high spring seat under the slanted bow; the bumps, creaks, and lumberings of the wagon; the sand sifting softly over the red, turning wheels; all afternoon the sun in their faces; ahead the far haze and heat waves in which were still lost Gunstock and the Rio Grande. Almost she had forgotten the bearded man with the oxen and the curious, detached horror in the eyes of his children.

11 cañada (kä nyä′də): small canyon; glen.

Since morning of the third day their progress had been slower. The trail seemed level, except for the heavy breathing of the horses. But when Nancy Belle glanced back she could see the steady grade they had been climbing. Abruptly, in mid-afternoon, she found that the long, blue Espiritu Range had disappeared, vanished behind a high pine-clad hill which was its southernmost beginning. It was like the lizard that swallowed itself, a very real lizard. At this moment they were climbing over the lizard's tail.

"Cedars!" Rife said briefly, pointing with the whip to dark sprawling growths ahead.

"You breathe deep up here!" Nancy Belle drank in the light air.

Rife took a sniff, but his blue eyes never ceased to scan the high, black-thatched hill under whose frowning cliff they must pass.

"Soon we can see the Gunstock Mountains," Nancy Belle said.

"And Martin Cross's cabin," Rife nodded. "It's the last water to the Rio Grande."

"He's a nice old man," Nancy Belle ventured casually. "It would be nice to camp by his cabin tonight and talk."

The boy inclined his head. After a few moments he started to whistle softly. At the first cedar Nancy Belle leaped off the moving wagon and climbed back with an evergreen branch. The twig, crushed in her hand, smelled like some store in Santa Fe.

They gained the summit. A breeze was sweeping here from the southwest, and the horses freshened. But Rife had suddenly stopped whistling and Nancy Belle's sprig of cedar lay on her lap. The frowning cliff of the pine-clad hill was still there. But Martin Cross's cabin had turned to a desolate mound of ashes. As they stared, a gust of wind sent wisps of smoke scurrying from the mound, and a red eye opened to watch them from the embers. Nancy Belle felt an uncontrollable twitching in the hair roots at the base of her scalp.

Where Martin Cross's eastbound wheel tracks met the trail, Rife reluctantly halted the horses and wet his air-dried lips.

"The water keg's dry, and the horses. If papa was here, he'd drive over."

"I'm the oldest." Nancy Belle found her voice steady. "I'll ride over. There might be something we can do."

The boy rose quickly. His eyes seemed to remember something his father had said.

"You can drive the wagon over if I wave."

He had thrown her the lines and slipped back through the canvas-covered tunnel of wagon box, picking up Fancy's bridle and the rifle. Barebacked he rode toward the smoldering ashes at the foot of that frowning hill. The chestnut mare's tail and mane streamed like something gold in the wind.

When she looked back to the trail, her eyes were pinioned by a light object in the wheel track ahead of the Bar X horse. It was a long gray feather. Instantly she told herself that it had come from some wild turkey Martin Cross had shot, and yet never had air anywhere become so suddenly horrible and choking as in this canyon.

Rife did not signal her to drive over. She saw him come riding back at full speed. The mare was snorting. As he stopped her at the wagon, her chestnut head kept turning back toward what had once been a cabin. Rife slipped the lead rope about her neck and climbed into the seat with the rifle in his hands.

"The water—you wouldn't want it!"

he said thickly. His cheeks, she noticed, were the color of *yeso*.[12]

"Rife"—Nancy Belle touched his arm when she had driven down the canyon —"what did you see at the cabin?"

The boy sat deaf and rigid beside her, eyes staring straight ahead. She saw that his young hands were still tortured around the barrel of his rifle.

Far down on the pitch-dark mesa she stopped the horses in the trail and listened. There were no stars, not a sound but the flapping of the wagon sheet in the wind and the clank of coffeepot and water bucket under the wagon. Half standing on the footboard, she guided the team off the trail in the intense blackness. Her swift hands helped the trembling boy stake out the mare and hobble the team. They did not light a lantern. Rife declined to eat. Nancy Belle chewed a few dry mouthfuls.

12 yeso (yā′sō): whitewash.

The wind came drawing out of the blackness with a great draft. It hissed through the grass, sucked and tore at the wagon sheet, and whistled through the spokes and brake rigging. Rife did not take his bed roll under the wagon tonight. He drew the ends of the wagon sheet together and lay down in the wagon box near his sister. For a long time they were silent. When she heard his heavy breathing, she lifted the rifle from his chest.

The storm grew. Sand began pelting against the canvas and sifted into the wagon box. An invisible cloud of choking dust found its way into eyes, mouth, ears, and lungs. Nancy Belle laid down the rifle a moment to pull a blanket over the face of the boy. He tossed and muttered pitifully, but he slept on.

Magically the rain, when it came, stopped the sand and dust. The girl drank in the clean-washed air. At daylight she slipped out to the ground.

The mesa, stretching away in the early light, touched here and there with feathers of mist, would have been beautiful except for a sharp new loneliness. The horses were gone!

At her exclamation, Rife appeared from the wagon box. His shame at having slept through the night was quickly overshadowed by their misfortune.

Together they found where Fancy's stake had been pulled out and dragged. Yards farther on they could tell by Anton Chico's tracks that his hobbles had parted.

Nancy Belle made her brother come back to the wagon and stuff his pockets with cold biscuits and antelope jerky. She said she would have a hot breakfast ready when he returned. The horses, perhaps, were just down in some draw where they had drifted with the wind.

When he had gone with the rifle, she filled the coffeepot from a clearing water hole in the nearest arroyo. She fried potatoes and onions in the long-handled skillet. And when he did not come, she set fresh biscuits in the Dutch oven.[13] Each biscuit held a square of salt side bacon in its top, and as it baked, the fat oozed down and incased it in a kind of glazed tastiness.

At noon she thought she heard a shot. Nowhere could she see him on the endless sweep of mesa. By late afternoon she was still alone. She read her Testament and wondered how many women over the world had read it in hours like this. Sitting in the shadow of the wagon, facing the direction in which he had gone, she looked up every few minutes. But all her eyes could find were cloud shadows racing across the lonely face of the mesa. All she could

hear were the desolate cries from the unseen lark sparrows.

Darkness, stillness settled down on the empty land. She climbed back into the wagon and sat on the chuck box, hands rigid on her knees. Again and again she convinced herself that the horses could not have been driven off or she would have seen the drivers' tracks. When wild, sharp barks shattered the stillness and set wires jerking in her limbs, she talked to herself steadily, but a little meaninglessly, of the post—on and on as the darkness was filled with the ringing and counter-ringing of shrill, cracked yappings—not long tones like a dog's, but incredibly short syllables rising, rising in a mad eternal scale and discord.

"I wish Papa had given me two of the chairs," she repeated. "Mamma said they were post oak from Texas. She said they had got white from scrubbing. I liked the laced rawhide seats with the hair left on. It made them soft to sit on. The seats in the parlor were black. And the ones in the kitchen were red. But I liked the brockle[14] one in my room best."

The insane din around the wagon had become terrific. There were only two or three of the animals, Nancy Belle guessed, but they threw their voices and echoes together to make a score.

"When I was little I liked to go in the storage room," her voice went on, scarcely intelligible to her own ears. "It was dark and cool, and smelled of burlap and kerosene and whisky, and sweetish with brown sugar. I can see the fat sacks of green coffee. And the round tins of kerosene had boards on the side. The flour sacks were printed: 'Rough and Ready' in red letters.

13 **Dutch oven:** a small iron kettle for baking. 14 **brockle:** likely to break.

SHORT STORY

Mamma once used to make our underwear out of the sacking. I can smell the salt side bacon in the gunny sacks."

She could tell from the sounds that one of the animals was running insanely back and forth near the wagon tongue. She had never noticed before that they yelped both when breathing in and out. Suddenly came silence. It warned her. Instinctively she felt for the ax.

"Nancy Belle!" a boy's far, anxious voice called from the darkness.

She hallooed and leaned out over the tailboard. Three shadowy forms were coming across the mesa in the starlight. Never had horses looked so good.

"Were you scared?" Rife greeted. "Anything bother you?"

"Nothing," Nancy Belle said. "Just coyotes."

"I had to give Fancy her head after it got dark." He slid wearily to the ground. "She brought us straight back to the wagon."

Nancy Belle had wanted to put her arms around her brother. Now she hugged the mare instead. Rife ate fresh biscuits and a tin plate of cold potatoes. He drank several tin cups of coffee. Nancy Belle had slipped the oats-laden gunny-sack morrals[15] over the horses' heads.

"I had to walk halfway to the mountain," Rife said.

"Just help hitch up; then you can sleep all night," she promised.

It rained again heavily toward midnight. Flashes of lightning lit the drenched plain. For minutes at a time, quivering fingers of blue phosphorescence stood on the ears of the toiling horses. At dawn Nancy Belle still held the reins as the mud-splashed wagon crawled through a world bathed in early purple splendor.

Four days they had been crossing a hundred and seventy miles of desolate plain. Now the end waited in sight. To the west lay a land broken and tumbled by a mighty hand. Hill shouldered hill and range peered over range, all indescribably violet except where peaks tipped by the unseen sun were far-off flaming towers of copper.

It was a new land, her promised land, Stephen's land, Nancy Belle told herself, where nobody burned cow chips, but snapping cedar and pine, where cold water ran in the wooded canyons, and the eye, weary of one flat circle the horizon round, had endless geometric designs to refresh the retina.

She sang softly as the wagon lumbered to the edge of a long, shallow valley, brown and uninhabited, running north and south, and desolate except for a winding ribbon that was white with sky and narrowly bordered with green.

"Rife!" Nancy Belle cried. "The Rio Grande!"

An hour afterwards they pulled out of the sun into the shade of the long cottonwood bosque.[16] Nancy Belle wasn't singing now. Where she remembered wide sandbars glistening with sky and tracked by waterfowl, a chocolate-red flood rolled. Where had been the island, tops of tule[17] and scrub willow swung to and fro with the current.

Anton Chico and the Bar X horse stopped of their own accord in the trail, ears pricked forward at the swirling brown wash. While Rife turned the three horses loose to graze, Nancy Belle silently fried bacon and made coffee. When she had washed skillet and tin dishes in the river, the boy had wired

16 bosque (bōs'kä): woods or a thinly inhabited district.
17 tule: bulrushes that grow on overflowed land in the Southwest.

15 morrals: nose bags.

CONRAD RICHTER

the wagon box to the brake rigging. Now he was tying securely one end of his rope to the center of the coupling pole under the wagon. The other end she knew he would fasten to the inadequate upper horn of the sidesaddle.

"I wouldn't mind the river if I just had my own saddle," he mourned.

They hitched up the team silently. Rife cinched the sidesaddle on Fancy and straddled it, the single stirrup useless to a man. Nancy Belle climbed into the wagon and picked up the lines. The other bank looked as far away as the Espiritu Range from the post. She wanted to say something to her brother —some last word, in case they didn't make it. But all she did was cluck her tongue to the horses.

Gingerly, one slow foot at a time, the team moved down the trail into the water.

"Give 'em their heads!" Rife called from the right rear.

Nancy Belle held a rein in each hand. The red channel water came to the wagon tongue, covered it, reached the horses' bellies. The team wanted to stop. Nancy Belle swung her whip, a stick tipped with a long rawhide lash. The wagon went on. The collars of both horses kept dipping, but never entirely out of sight. Still barely wading, the slow team reached the firmer footing of the island.

Two-thirds of the river still rolled in front of the wagon. The west bank did not seem to have grown much closer, but the east bank behind them had moved far away. The team had to be whipped into the violent current. The water churned white through the wagon wheels. Suddenly both horses appeared to stumble and drop out of sight. Their heads came up wildly, spray blowing from their nostrils. The muddy water hid their legs, but by their bobbing mo-

tions Nancy Belle knew that they were swimming.

"Keep 'em pointed up the river!" Rife shouted.

Already she felt the wagon floating. It swung downstream with the current; then Rife's rope from Fancy's saddle snubbed it. The team was snorting with every breath. The Bar X horse swam high in the water, his withers and part of his back out of the chocolate current. But all she could see of Anton Chico were his nose and ears.

Down between her ankles she saw water in the wagon box. She thought of the hemstitched sheets at the bottom of her trunk, the towels and pillowcases crocheted with shell lace. Her blue velvet corduroy dress was probably wet already, and all the cunning print aprons with dust caps to match. River water couldn't hurt the little yellow creamer, sugar bowl, and covered butter dish that had been her mother's. And the gingham dresses could be washed. What worried her were her wedding dress and the keepsake box, especially the tintypes, one of which was Rife in a child's suit edged with black braid, his brand-new hat on his knee.

An older Rife was shouting something behind her now. She couldn't catch the words. Then she found what it was. The neck and withers of Anton Chico raised suddenly out of the water and both horses were scrambling up the steep bank below the ford. Only quick work with the lines saved the wagon from turning over. Safe and blowing on the high bank, the dripping horses shook themselves like puppies.

Nancy Belle couldn't go on until she had opened the trunk and appraised the damage. Rife unsaddled Fancy and drove on with the refreshed team. Behind his slight back in the wagon box, the girl changed to her blue velvet cor-

duroy, which was hardly wet at all. Then she combed her hair and rolled into a cranny of her trunk the old felt hat that had been too large for her father.

A half-dozen riders met the wagon some miles down the Gunstock Canyon. All of them, Nancy Belle noticed, carried guns. Stephen wore a new white shirt and a gray hat with curled brim she had not seen before. He stood in his stirrups and swung her down in front of him on the saddle, where he kissed her. She had never felt his lips press into such a straight line.

"Papa couldn't come," she said. "So Rife brought me."

She felt Stephen's rigid arm around her.

"We just got in from the Beaverhead ourselves."

"He means they never get any news out in the Beaverhead or he'd 'a' come further east to meet you!" Uncle Billy Williams put in. He had a lovable, squeaky voice. "The Apaches been breakin' loose again. Funny you didn't hear anything over in your country."

Nancy Belle gave him an inscrutable look with her gray eyes. Uncle Billy pulled out his bandanna and blew his nose.

"They got my old friend Judge Hower and his wife and kid in a buggy on the Upper Espiritu. The man that found what they did to 'em, they say, cried like a baby."

"That's all right, Uncle Billy," Stephen said in a gentle voice.

Nancy Belle glanced at Rife. Her brother's face looked gray, the eyes staring as when he had ridden in the late afternoon sunlight from the smoking ashes of Martin Cross's cabin.

Nearly fifty people, gathered in the big parlor upstairs at the hotel, greeted Nancy Belle. An old man whose young black eyes twinkled out of a bearded face said he was glad to see that she had her "hair on straight." Rife stopped with the trunk before driving to the livery, and Stephen's mother showed Nancy Belle to a room to dress.

The guests stopped talking when she came into the parlor in her white wedding dress. Her basque came to a point in the front and back. It fitted like a glove. The silk underskirt came to her instep, and the ruffled overskirt to her knees. She had parted her hair from side to side and brushed the bangs down on her forehead. She felt very lightheaded. The wagon still seemed to be jerking under her.

She glimpsed Rife gazing at her, a rapt expression in his reticent blue eyes. She was glad to see that he had brushed his hair. The brass swinging lamp had been lighted and the dark woodwork of the parlor festooned with evergreen branches. White streamers from the wall met in a papier-mâché bell in one corner. She noticed two children peering eagerly from the dark hall.

Stephen came to her, very straight in a long coat and stand-up collar with a black tie. He led her up beneath the papier-mâché bell. In a sibilant, church-like whisper, the Gunstock preacher made sure of her full name. Then he coughed and began the ceremony. He had a deep voice, but Nancy Belle didn't hear all of the service. Her mind kept going back to a tall, grave man in a lonely adobe post on the wide Santa Ana plain. And after she had said: "I do," her lips moved, but she was not praying for Stephen, her husband.

Understanding the Story

1. What are the Putmans worrying about when the story opens? How does the fact that no one speaks openly about it add to the suspense of the story?
2. How does Asa's direct question to his daughter about postponing her trip and her direct answer reveal their deep affection for each other?
3. Although no direct reference is made to Nancy Belle's mother, we know many things about her. Recall several references that suggest the kind of woman she was.
4. Compare and contrast the way Asa, Rife, and Ignacita show their concern about the proposed journey. What do we learn about their characters from these reactions?
5. Although the focus of the story is on Nancy Belle, the story also shows the growth of fifteen-year-old Rife from "a good slice of a man" to a man. Find some instances that show Rife's youthfulness and several that show his maturity.
6. Why does Nancy Belle talk about the oak chair of her mother's and of the flour sacks in the old storage room while she waits for Rife to return from looking for the horses?

7. What do you learn of Stephen's character from his quiet closing of Uncle Billy's conversation about the Indian massacres?
8. How do the husband and wife whom Nancy Belle and Rife meet on the El Paso trail contribute to the tension of the story? What other incidents or details are used to build tension?
9. Setting is frequently used to create the atmosphere of an incident, as when a ghost story is set against a dark night or a deserted house. At what points in this story is the setting used to suit the action or mood of the characters?

Developing Language Skills

Find several specific instances that reveal Nancy Belle's appreciation of and concern for her young brother as he faces dangerous responsibilities on their trip. Using three of these references, write a paragraph showing her growth as a person.

Reading "The Waltz"

Every story must be told from some point of view. "The Waltz" is told by the main character, and thus uses the *first person point of view*. The author has used the technique of recording the thoughts that supposedly go through a character's mind as the action progresses.

An author's choice of the person to tell a story is something readers are rarely conscious of, but it is possibly the most important factor in making any story what it is. "Early Marriage," for example, if told by the father would become an entirely different story—not simply a slightly different version of the story printed here.

In "The Waltz" the main character is not described; what the reader learns of her comes from the way in which she thinks and the kind of things she thinks, plus the dialogue that is recorded. In explaining the use of dialogue and a character's thoughts in her writing, Dorothy Parker says, "My stories make themselves stories by telling themselves through what people say." Miss Parker is ruthless and complete; when her characters finish talking, there is nothing left to say. It is important to remember in her stories that a character's thoughts and conversation are not only a means of describing action but also a means of character revelation.

CONRAD RICHTER

The Waltz

Dorothy Parker

Dorothy Parker is both one of the gayest and one of the most cynical writers of recent times. "The Waltz," which is often presented as a dramatic monologue (a performance or dramatic reading of a story or poem), represents Miss Parker's most effective storytelling device. You may not like Miss Parker's hypocritical heroine, but you will not forget her.

WHY, *thank you so much. I'd adore to.*

I don't want to dance with him. I don't want to dance with anybody. And even if I did, it wouldn't be him. He'd be well down among the last ten. I've seen the way he dances; it looks like something you do on Saint Walpurgis Night.[1] Just think, not a quarter of an hour ago, here I was sitting, feeling so sorry for the poor girl he was dancing with. And now *I'm* going to be the poor girl. Well, well. Isn't it a small world?

And a peach of a world, too. A true little corker. Its events are so fascinatingly unpredictable, are not they? Here I was, minding my own business, not doing a stitch of harm to any living soul. And then he comes into my life, all smiles and city manners, to sue me for the favor of one memorable mazurka.[2] Why, he scarcely knows my name, let alone what it stands for. It stands for Despair, Bewilderment, Futility, Degradation, and Premeditated Murder, but little does he wot. I don't wot his name, either; I haven't any idea what it is. Jukes,[3] would be my guess from the look in his eyes. How do you do, Mr. Jukes? And how is that dear little brother of yours, with the two heads?

Ah, now why did he have to come around me, with his low requests? Why can't he let me lead my own life? I ask so little—just to be left alone in my quiet corner of the table, to do my evening brooding over all my sorrows. And he must come, with his bows and his scrapes and his may-I-have-this-ones. And I had to go and tell him that I'd adore to dance with him. I cannot understand why I wasn't struck right down dead. Yes, and being struck dead would look like a day in the country, compared to struggling out a dance with this boy. But what could I do? Everyone else at the table had got up to dance, except him and me. There was I, trapped. Trapped like a trap in a trap.

What can you say, when a man asks you to dance with him? . . . Oh, yes, *do* let's dance together—it's so nice to meet a man who isn't a scaredy-cat about catching my beriberi. No. There was nothing for me to do, but say I'd adore to. Well, we might as well get it over with. All right, Cannonball, let's run out on the field. You won the toss; you can lead.

---

1 **Saint Walpurgis Night:** in German folklore a wild revel of witches and demons held the eve of May Day.

2 **mazurka:** Polish dance.
3 **Jukes:** the name of one family in a famous study of two families which had intermarried for generations and whose history showed a high incidence of disease, delinquency, and poverty.

Why, I think it's more of a waltz, really. Isn't it? We might just listen to the music a second. Shall we? Oh, yes, it's a waltz. Mind? Why, I'm simply thrilled. I'd love to waltz with you.

I'd love to waltz with you. I'd love to waltz with you. I'd love to have my tonsils out, I'd love to be in a midnight fire at sea. Well, it's too late now. We're getting under way. *Oh.* Oh, dear. Oh, dear, dear, dear. Oh, this is even worse than I thought it would be. I suppose that's the one dependable law of life—everything is always worse than you thought it was going to be. Oh, if I had any real grasp of what this dance would be like, I'd have held out for sitting it out. Well, it will probably amount to the same thing in the end. We'll be sitting it out on the floor in a minute, if he keeps this up.

I'm so glad I brought it to his attention that this is a waltz they're playing. Heaven knows what might have happened, if he had thought it was something fast; we'd have blown the sides right out of the building. Why does he always want to be somewhere that he isn't? Why can't we stay in one place just long enough to get acclimated? It's this constant rush, rush, rush, that's the curse of American life. That's the reason that we're all of us so—*Ow!* For heaven's sake, don't *kick*, you idiot; this is only second down. Oh, my shin. My poor, poor shin, that I've had ever since I was a little girl!

Oh, no, no, no. Goodness, no. It didn't hurt the least little bit. And anyway it was my fault. Really it was. Truly. Well, you're just being sweet, to say that. It really was all my fault.

I wonder what I'd better do—kill him this instant, with my naked hands, or wait and let him drop in his traces. Maybe it's best not to make a scene. I guess I'll just lie low, and watch the pace get him. He can't keep this up indefinitely—he's only flesh and blood. Die he must, and die he shall, for what he did to me. I don't want to be of the oversensitive type, but you can't tell me that kick was unpremeditated. Freud[4] says there are no accidents. I've led no cloistered life, I've known dancing partners who have spoiled my slippers and torn my dress; but when it comes to kicking, I am Outraged Womanhood. When you kick me in the shin, *smile.*

Maybe he didn't do it maliciously. Maybe it's just his way of showing his high spirits. I suppose I ought to be glad that one of us is having such a good time. I suppose I ought to think myself lucky if he brings me back alive. Maybe it's captious to demand of a practically strange man that he leave your shins as he found them. After all, the poor boy's doing the best he can. Probably he grew up in the hill country, and never had no larnin'. I bet they had to throw him on his back to get shoes on him.

Yes, it's lovely, isn't it? It's simply lovely. It's the loveliest waltz. Isn't it? Oh, I think it's lovely, too.

Why, I'm getting positively drawn to the Triple Threat here. He's my hero. He has the heart of a lion, and the sinews of a buffalo. Look at him— never a thought of the consequences, never afraid of his face, hurling himself into every scrimmage, eyes shining, cheeks ablaze. And shall it be said that I hung back? No, a thousand times no. What's it to me if I have to spend the next couple of years in a plaster cast? Come on, Butch, right through them! Who wants to live forever?

Oh. Oh, dear. Oh, he's all right,

4 **Freud** (froid)**:** famous European psychologist.

thank goodness. For a while I thought they'd have to carry him off the field. Ah, I couldn't bear to have anything happen to him. I love him. I love him better than anybody in the world. Look at the spirit he gets into a dreary, commonplace waltz; how effete the other dancers seem, beside him. He is youth and vigor and courage, he is strength and gaiety and—*Ow!* Get off my instep, you hulking peasant! What do you think I am, anyway—a gangplank? *Ow!*

No, of course it didn't hurt. Why, it didn't a bit. Honestly. And it was all my fault. You see, that little step of yours—well, it's perfectly lovely, but it's just a tiny bit tricky to follow at first. Oh, did you work it up yourself? You really did? Well, aren't you amazing! Oh, now I think I've got it. Oh, I think it's lovely. I was watching you do it when you were dancing before. It's awfully effective when you look at it.

It's awfully effective when you look at it. I bet I'm awfully effective when you look at me. My hair is hanging along my cheeks, my skirt is swaddled about me, I can feel the cold damp of my brow. I must look like something out of the "Fall of the House of Usher."[5] This sort of thing takes a fearful toll of a woman my age. And he worked up his little step himself, he with his degenerate cunning. And it was just a tiny bit tricky at first, but now I think I've got it. Two stumbles, slip, and a twenty-yard dash; yes. I've got it. I've got several other things, too, including a split shin and a bitter heart. I hate this creature I'm chained to. I hated him the moment I saw his leering, bestial face. And here I've been locked

in his noxious embrace for the thirty-five years this waltz has lasted. Is that orchestra never going to stop playing? Or must this obscene travesty of a dance go on until hell burns out?

Oh, they're going to play another encore. Oh, goody. Oh, that's lovely. Tired? I should say I'm not tired. I'd like to go on like this forever.

I should say I'm not tired. I'm dead, that's all I am. Dead, and in what a cause! And the music is never going to stop playing, and we're going on like this, Double-Time Charlie and I, throughout eternity. I suppose I won't care any more, after the first hundred thousand years. I suppose nothing will matter then, not heat nor pain nor broken heart nor cruel, aching weariness. Well. It can't come too soon for me.

I wonder why I didn't tell him I was tired. I wonder why I didn't suggest going back to the table. I could have said let's just listen to the music. Yes, and if he would, that would be the first bit of attention he has given it all evening. George Jean Nathan[6] said that the lovely rhythms of the waltz should be listened to in stillness and not be accompanied by strange gyrations of the human body. I think that's what he said. I think it was George Jean Nathan. Anyhow, whatever he said and whoever he was and whatever he's doing now, he's better off than I am. That's safe. Anybody who isn't waltzing with this Mrs. O'Leary's cow[7] I've got here is having a good time.

Still if we were back at the table, I'd probably have to talk to him. Look at him—what could you say to a thing like

---

5 **"Fall of the House of Usher":** a gloomy short story by Edgar Allan Poe.

6 **George Jean Nathan:** American editor and drama critic.

7 **Mrs. O'Leary's cow:** A cow belonging to a Mrs. O'Leary was blamed for kicking over a lantern in 1871, causing the great Chicago fire.

that! Did you go to the circus this year, what's your favorite kind of ice cream, how do you spell cat? I guess I'm as well off here. As well off as if I were in a cement mixer in full action.

I'm past all feeling now. The only way I can tell when he steps on me is that I can hear the splintering of bones. And all the events of my life are passing before my eyes. There was the time I was in a hurricane in the West Indies, there was the day I got my head cut open in the taxi smash, there was the night the drunken lady threw a bronze ash tray at her own true love and got me instead, there was that summer that the sailboat kept capsizing. Ah, what an easy, peaceful time was mine, until I fell in with Swifty, here. I didn't know what trouble was, before I got drawn into this *danse macabre*.[8] I think my mind is beginning to wander. It almost seems to me as if the orchestra were stopping. It couldn't be, of course; it could never, never be. And yet in my ears there is a silence like the sound of angel voices. . . .

Oh, they've stopped, the mean things. They're not going to play any more. Oh, darn. Oh, do you think they would? Do you really think so, if you gave them twenty dollars? Oh, that would be lovely. And look, do tell them to play this same thing. I'd simply adore to go on waltzing.

8 **danse macabre** (dȧns mȧ kȧ′br): dance of death.

Understanding the Story

1. What is the difference between the italicized and unitalicized sections of the story? In what ways is each necessary to the complete story?
2. How does the technique of recording the character's thoughts contribute to the effectiveness of the story? How would it differ in effect if the girl related her experience and feelings to a girl friend after the dance?
3. Notice how the girl picks up a key word from her gushing, enthusiastic remarks to her partner and repeats it with a different meaning in her savage inner thoughts. Find several instances of this transitional, or connecting, device.
4. Find two vivid comparisons by which the girl describes the way the boy dances.
5. Find several uses of football terminology. Why are they humorous in relation to the situation of this story?
6. Do you feel that the boy is as conceited as the girl presents him, or are we getting a distorted picture of him through her point of view? Support your answer with quotations.

Developing Language Skills

Do you find your own thoughts or actions at any time mirrored in the situation and language of this story? See how you can use the methods employed by Dorothy Parker to express your own feelings.

Boys: Assume you have taken a very unathletic girl to her first football game. Write a page of dialogue which gives both your actual words to her and your unspoken thoughts. Your spoken words can be set off simply by quotation marks, or by italics (underlining) as in "The Waltz."

Girls: Assume you are chatting with a friend about a new dress she is wearing that you consider an unfortunate choice. Write a page of dialogue which gives both your spoken comments to her and your unspoken thoughts.

Reading "Snake Dance"

"The Waltz" and "Snake Dance" contain several similarities of technique. The story in each is related from the point of view of one person. In each, dialogue is an important means of showing what is happening, even though each author uses the words of only the main character. In neither does the author comment directly upon any character. Rather, the reader is allowed to draw his own conclusions about the people in the stories.

In "The Waltz," however, the thoughts of the main character are given, and it is through these thoughts that the reader learns about the feelings of the girl. It is also through these thoughts that the reader has to figure out why she acts as she does. In contrast, "Snake Dance" does not use the main character's thoughts. The reader learns about the feelings of the boy in it through description of his actions, facial expressions, and tone of voice. For example, near the opening we are told "He fished nervously in his pocket for a pack of cigarettes. . . ." and "He glanced at his watch and scowled." Note that the author does *not* directly tell the reader "He was nervous" or "He was worried about the time." He uses an *objective* approach—one in which the reader infers the feelings and thoughts of all characters from factual description of their words and behavior.

"Snake Dance" also uses a different kind of point of view than "The Waltz" does. Corey Ford has chosen the *third person limited point of view* to tell this brief episode. *Third person* means that the author writes, "*He* glanced at *his* watch"; whereas *first person* would mean that this sentence was written, "*I* glanced at *my* watch." *Limited* indicates that Corey Ford limits himself to telling what one of his characters could know.

Snake Dance

Corey Ford

This slight story has an emotional impact that will give you a warm feeling toward Jerry, who is playing a much harder role than the one he reports to his mother. Notice how the author's telling of the story directs a sympathetic spotlight on his main character.

"HELLO. That you, Mom? . . . Oh, I'm sorry, operator, I thought I was connected with . . . No, I'm trying to get long-distance . . . What? Center-ville, Ohio, twelve ring five, I told that other operator . . . What? . . . I *am* holding it."

He fished nervously in his pocket for a pack of cigarettes, pulled one ciga-rette out of the pack with his thumb and forefinger, and stuck it swiftly between his lips. He glanced at his watch and scowled. The game had been over for a half hour. The snake dance would be coming down the street this way any minute now. With his free hand he tore a match from the paper safe, and propped the telephone receiver for a moment between shoulder and ear while he struck the match on the flap. As he put the match to the tip of the cigarette, a thin voice rasped vaguely inside the receiver, and he whipped out the match.

"Hello. Mom? . . . Oh, I'm sorry," he mumbled. "How much?" He took a handful of silver from his pocket and began to drop the coins into the slot of the pay telephone. He could hear someone speaking above the echoing re-verberations inside the phone.

"What? Oh, Mom? Hello, Mom. This is Jerry. I say, this is—Can you hear me now? . . . Sure, I can hear you fine . . . Sure, I'm all right. I'm fine. And you? . . . That's fine.

"Mom"—and his voice seemed to falter for a fraction of a second. Then: "How is he? Is there any change?"

There was a tiny silence.

"Oh." His voice was a little duller when he spoke again. "I see. Yeh. This afternoon, eh? And that other specialist, he said the same thing? Um-hmm . . . Oh, sure, sure. No, of course, Mom, there's nothing to worry about. No, I'm not worried; I only just called to find out if there was any change, that was all. . . . Did they say if he could ever—I mean, can he move his arms any yet?" He gulped. "Well, that doesn't mean anything, really . . . No, of course, all those things take time. Sure, a year, or maybe even less . . . What?"

He took a second cigarette out of his pocket and thrust it between his lips nervously. He lit it from the stub of the first one and ground out the stub beneath his heel.

"What money? Oh, you mean I sent you last week? Now, Mom," impa-tiently, "I told you all about that al-ready in the letter, didn't I? . . . Sure it's a scholarship. I got it for playing football. And so naturally I didn't need all that money you and Pop had been saving up for me to go to college, and so I just thought maybe, with Pop being laid up now for a while and all . . .

"Where? Why, right here." He frowned. "No, this isn't exactly a dormitory; it's—I live here in the fraternity house, you see. Sure I'm in a fraternity. It's the one Pop wanted me to join, too, tell him . . . No, honest, Mom, it doesn't cost me a cent for my room. It's on account of my football."

He opened the folding door a little. He thought he could hear the band in the distance.

"Who, me? Homesick? Not so you'd notice it." He laughed. "I'm having the time of my life here. Everybody's so swell. I know practically everybody here at Dover already. They even all call me by my first name. Say, if you don't think I'm sitting pretty, you ought to see my fraternity house here." He gazed out through the glass door of the phone booth.

"Every night the fellows sit around and we drink beer and chew the fat till . . . Oh, no. No, Mom. Just beer. Or usually we just go down to Semple's for a milk shake . . . No, that's only the drugstore . . . No." He smiled slowly. "I promised you I wouldn't drink, Mom."

In the distance now he could hear the sound of the band approaching.

"Well, Mom, I gotta hang up now. The gang'll be here in a minute. We're having a celebration after the game today. We played Alvord—took 'em sixteen to nothing. . . . Sure I did, the whole game; you oughta seen me in there. I made two touchdowns. Everybody's going down to Semple's after the game, and I gotta be ready, because of course they'll all want me to be there too. Can you hear the band now?"

It was growing louder, and the eager voices in the snake dance could be heard above the brasses, chanting the score of the game in time with the band.

"Now, listen, Mom. One other little thing before they get here. Mom, see, I'm going to be sending you about ten or twelve dollars or so each week from now on until Pop is better. . . . No, Mom. Heck, I got plenty. Sure, they always fix you up with a soft job if you're a good enough player. The alumni do it. . . . Here they are now. Hear them?"

The band had halted outside. Someone led a cheer.

"That's for me, Mom. . . . Sure. Didn't I practically win the game for them today? Hear that?" He kicked open the door of the phone booth.

He held the receiver toward the open door of the phone booth. They were calling, "Jerry!" "Hey, Jerry, hang up on that babe!"

"Hear that, Mom? Now good-by. And look, by the way, if you should ever happen to see Helen," he added carelessly, "tell her I'm sorry I couldn't ask her up to the freshman dance like I'd planned, but with the football season and my scholarship and all—Tell her, Mom. She—she didn't answer my last letter. O.K., Mom. Tell Pop everything's O.K., see? Now don't worry . . . 'By."

He replaced the receiver slowly on the hook and stared at the mouthpiece a moment. As he opened the door and stepped out of the booth, he could see his reflection for a moment in the tall mirror behind the soda fountain—the familiar white cap, the white jacket with "Semple's" stitched in red letters on the pocket. The crowd was lined along the soda fountain, shouting, "Jerry!" "Milk shake, Jerry!"

Understanding the Story

1. Where does the story take place?
2. What is a snake dance? How does it enter into the story?
3. What do you find out about the members of Jerry's family, their relationship to each other, and their financial problems?
4. How does the author let you know that Jerry is a college student?
5. Why are the students calling Jerry's name while he is in the telephone booth? How does Jerry explain their doing so to his mother?
6. Jerry obviously lies to his mother over the telephone. What are his motives?
7. How do the references to Helen emphasize the difficulty of the role Jerry is playing?
8. Imagine that the author had used the first person point of view, having Jerry tell his own story. Explain why, in your judgment, this would be a more effective or less effective device than the author's choice of the third person limited point of view.

Building Vocabulary Skills

1. What is the difference between formal and colloquial language? (If you do not know, handbooks of grammar or composition, as well as a dictionary, will be helpful.)
2. Why does Corey Ford have his hero use colloquial English?
3. Express orally in formal language the paragraph that begins, "Who, me? Homesick?" How does the effect differ from that of the author's version?

Developing Language Skills

Write a short essay that (1) shows the clues throughout the story which prepare the reader for the final surprise paragraph, and (2) defends or criticizes the author's use of the surprise ending to achieve his effect.

Reading "The Cop and the Anthem"

"The Cop and the Anthem" uses the third person point of view in a different way than "Snake Dance." Although both report actions of the main character (the story begins, for example, with the statement "On his bench in Madison Square, Soapy moved uneasily"), "The Cop and the Anthem" also shows the reader Soapy's thoughts and feelings. Toward the story's end, for instance, O. Henry writes that Soapy's "heart responded thrillingly to this novel mood." By including thoughts and feelings, O. Henry uses a *subjective* approach to his main character, in contrast to the *objective* approach in "Snake Dance."

He adopts an *ironic tone* toward Soapy and the events of the story. *Irony,* one of O. Henry's favorite devices, may take several forms in a story. Here he uses *irony of situation,* in which a situation comes out just the opposite from what was anticipated, to dramatize Soapy's confident plans and their disastrous outcomes. He also uses *verbal irony,* describing Soapy in elegant language that contrasts greatly with the kind of language that Soapy himself would use or that would normally be used of him. Even the title of the collection of stories about middle- and lower-class New Yorkers, *The Four Million,* from which this selection is taken, contrasts ironically with the term *The Four Hundred,* used to refer to New York's exclusive list of society leaders.

The Cop and
The Anthem

O. Henry

If you have ever had a carefully worked out scheme fail completely, you will sympathize with Soapy as his confidently laid plans fail one after another. O. Henry often wrote of those whose plans never quite work out, and here he draws a sympathetic picture of the frustrated Soapy, who is moving uneasily on his bench in Central Park as the story opens.

ON HIS BENCH in Madison Square, Soapy moved uneasily. When wild geese honk high of nights, and when women without sealskin coats grow kind to their husbands, and when Soapy moves uneasily on his bench in the park, you may know that winter is near at hand.

A dead leaf fell in Soapy's lap. That was Jack Frost's card. Jack is kind to the regular denizens of Madison Square, and gives fair warning of his annual call. At the corners of four streets he hands his pasteboard[1] to the North Wind, footman of the mansion of All Outdoors, so that the inhabitants thereof may make ready.

Soapy's mind became cognizant of the fact that the time had come for him to resolve himself into a singular Committee of Ways and Means to provide against the coming rigor. And therefore he moved uneasily on his bench.

The hibernatorial[2] ambitions of Soapy were not of the highest. In them there were no considerations of Mediterranean cruises, of soporific Southern skies or drifting in the Vesuvian Bay.[3] Three months on the Island[4] was what his soul craved. Three months of assured

1 **pasteboard:** slang word for a calling card.
2 **hibernatorial:** an adjective coined from *hibernate,* meaning "to pass the winter in close quarters."
3 **Vesuvian Bay:** the bay near Mt. Vesuvius and east of Naples, Italy.
4 **Island:** abbreviation for Blackwell's Island, once the site of a city workhouse; now known as Welfare Island.

board and bed and congenial company, safe from Boreas[5] and bluecoats, seemed to Soapy the essence of things desirable.

For years the hospitable Blackwell's had been his winter quarters. Just as his more fortunate fellow New Yorkers had bought their tickets to Palm Beach and the Riviera each winter, so Soapy had made his humble arrangements for his annual hegira[6] to the Island. And now the time was come. On the previous night three Sabbath newspapers, distributed beneath his coat, about his ankles and over his lap, had failed to repulse the cold as he slept on his bench near the spurting fountain in the ancient square. So the Island loomed big and timely in Soapy's mind. He scorned the provisions made in the name of charity for the city's dependents. In Soapy's opinion the Law was more benign than Philanthropy. There was an endless round of institutions, municipal and eleemosynary,[7] on which he might set out and receive lodging and food accordant with the simple life. But to one of Soapy's proud spirit the gifts of charity are encumbered. If not in coin you must pay in humiliation of spirit for every benefit received at the hands of philanthropy. As Caesar had his Brutus, every bed of charity must have its toll of a bath, every loaf of bread its compensation of a private and personal inquisition. Wherefore it is better to be a guest of the law, which though conducted by rules, does not meddle unduly with a gentleman's private affairs.

Soapy, having decided to go to the Island, at once set about accomplishing his desire. There were many easy ways of doing this. The pleasantest was to dine luxuriously at some expensive restaurant; and then, after declaring insolvency, be handed over quietly and without uproar to a policeman. An accommodating magistrate would do the rest.

Soapy left his bench and strolled out of the square and across the level sea of asphalt, where Broadway and Fifth Avenue flow together. Up Broadway he turned, and halted at a glittering café, where are gathered together nightly the choicest products of the grape, the silkworm and the protoplasm.

Soapy had confidence in himself from the lowest button of his vest upward. He was shaven, and his coat was decent and his neat black, ready-tied four-in-hand had been presented to him by a lady missionary on Thanksgiving Day. If he could reach a table in the restaurant unsuspected, success would be his. The portion of him that would show above the table would raise no doubt in the waiter's mind. A roasted mallard duck, thought Soapy, would be about the thing—with a bottle of Chablis,[8] and then Camembert,[9] a demitasse and a cigar. One dollar for the cigar would be enough. The total would not be so high as to call forth any supreme manifestation of revenge from the café management; and yet the meal would leave him filled and happy for the journey to his winter refuge.

But as Soapy set foot inside the restaurant door the headwaiter's eye fell upon his frayed trousers and decadent shoes. Strong and ready hands turned him about and conveyed him in silence and haste to the sidewalk and

---

5 **Boreas:** from Greek mythology; the god of the north wind.

6 **hegira** (hǐ jī′rə): (also spelled *hejira*) the flight of Mohammed from Mecca; hence, any flight or journey for safety.

7 **eleemosynary** (ĕl′ə mŏs′ə nĕr′ĭ): supported, or dependent, on charity.

8 **Chablis** (shăb′lĭ): a dry, white Burgundy wine.

9 **Camembert** (kăm′əm bâr′): a kind of rich, creamy cheese made in the vicinity of Camembert, France.

averted the ignoble fate of the menaced mallard.

Soapy turned off Broadway. It seemed that his route to the coveted island was not to be an epicurean one. Some other way of entering limbo must be thought of.

At a corner of Sixth Avenue electric lights and cunningly displayed wares behind plate glass made a shopwindow conspicuous. Soapy took a cobblestone and dashed it through the glass. People came running around the corner, a policeman in the lead. Soapy stood still, with his hands in his pockets, and smiled at the sight of brass buttons.

"Where's the man that done that?" inquired the officer excitedly.

"Don't you figure out that I might have had something to do with it?" said Soapy, not without sarcasm, but friendly, as one greets good fortune.

The policeman's mind refused to accept Soapy even as a clue. Men who smash windows do not remain to parley with the law's minions. They take to their heels. The policeman saw a man halfway down the block running to catch a car. With drawn club he joined in the pursuit. Soapy, with disgust in his heart, loafed along, twice unsuccessful.

On the opposite side of the street was a restaurant of no great pretensions. It catered to large appetites and modest purses. Its crockery and atmosphere were thick; its soup and napery thin. Into this place Soapy took his accusive shoes and telltale trousers without challenge. At a table he sat and consumed beefsteak, flapjacks, doughnuts and pie. And then to the waiter he betrayed the fact that the minutest coin and himself were strangers.

"Now, get busy and call a cop," said Soapy. "And don't keep a gentleman waiting."

"No cop for youse," said the waiter, with a voice like butter cakes and an eye like the cherry in a Manhattan cocktail. "Hey, Con!"

Neatly upon his left ear on the callous pavement two waiters pitched Soapy. He arose, joint by joint, as a carpenter's rule opens, and beat the dust from his clothes. Arrest seemed but a rosy dream. The Island seemed very far away. A policeman who stood before a drugstore two doors away laughed and walked down the street.

Five blocks Soapy traveled before his courage permitted him to woo capture again. This time the opportunity presented what he fatuously termed to himself a "cinch." A young woman of a modest and pleasing guise was standing before a show window gazing with sprightly interest at its display of shaving mugs and inkstands, and two yards from the window a large policeman of severe demeanor leaned against a water plug.

It was Soapy's design to assume the role of the despicable and execrated "masher." The refined and elegant appearance of his victim and the contiguity of the conscientious cop encouraged him to believe that he would soon feel the pleasant official clutch upon his arm that would insure his winter quarters on the right little, tight little isle.

Soapy straightened the lady missionary's ready-made tie, dragged his shrinking cuffs into the open, set his hat at a killing cant and sidled toward the young woman. He made eyes at her, was taken with sudden coughs and "hems," smiled, smirked and went brazenly through the impudent and contemptible litany of the "masher." With half an eye Soapy saw that the policeman was watching him fixedly. The young woman moved away a few steps, and again bestowed her absorbed

attention upon the shaving mugs. Soapy followed, boldly stepping to her side, raised his hat and said:

"Ah there, Bedelia! Don't you want to come and play in my yard?"

The policeman was still looking. The persecuted young woman had but to beckon a finger and Soapy would be practically en route for his insular haven. Already he imagined he could feel the cozy warmth of the station house. The young woman faced him and, stretching out a hand, caught Soapy's coat sleeve.

"Sure, Mike," she said joyfully, "if you'll blow me to a pail of suds. I'd have spoke to you sooner, but the cop was watching."

With the young woman playing the clinging ivy to his oak, Soapy walked past the policeman overcome with gloom. He seemed doomed to liberty.

At the next corner he shook off his companion and ran. He halted in the district where by night are found the lightest streets, hearts, vows and librettos. Women in furs and men in greatcoats moved gaily in the wintry air. A sudden fear seized Soapy that some dreadful enchantment had rendered him immune to arrest. The thought brought a little of panic upon it, and when he came upon another policeman lounging grandly in front of a transplendent theater he caught at the immediate straw of "disorderly conduct."

On the sidewalk Soapy began to yell drunken gibberish at the top of his harsh voice. He danced, howled, raved and otherwise disturbed the welkin.[10]

The policeman twirled his club, turned his back to Soapy and remarked to a citizen.

"'Tis one of them Yale lads celebratin' the goose egg they give to the

10 welkin: sky.

Hartford College. Noisy; but no harm. We've instructions to lave them be."

Disconsolate, Soapy ceased his unavailing racket. Would never a policeman lay hands on him? In his fancy the Island seemed an unattainable Arcadia. He buttoned his thin coat against the chilling wind.

In a cigar store he saw a well-dressed man lighting a cigar at a swinging light. His silk umbrella he had set by the door on entering. Soapy stepped inside, secured the umbrella and sauntered off with it slowly. The man at the cigar light followed hastily.

"My umbrella," he said, sternly.

"Oh, is it?" sneered Soapy, adding insult to petit larceny. "Well, why don't you call a policeman? I took it. Your umbrella! Why don't you call a cop? There stands one on the corner."

The umbrella owner slowed his steps. Soapy did likewise, with a presentiment that luck would again run against him. The policeman looked at the two curiously.

"Of course," said the umbrella man— "that is—well, you know how these mistakes occur—I—if it's your umbrella I hope you'll excuse me—I picked it up this morning in a restaurant—If you recognize it as yours, why—I hope you'll—"

"Of course it's mine," said Soapy, viciously.

The ex-umbrella man retreated. The policeman hurried to assist a tall blonde in an opera cloak across the street in front of a street car that was approaching two blocks away.

Soapy walked eastward through a street damaged by improvements. He hurled the umbrella wrathfully into an excavation. He muttered against the men who wear helmets and carry clubs. Because he wanted to fall into their clutches, they seemed to regard him as a king who could do no wrong.

At length Soapy reached one of the avenues to the east where the glitter and turmoil was but faint. He set his face down this toward Madison Square, for the homing instinct survives even when the home is a park bench.

But on an unusually quiet corner Soapy came to a standstill. Here was an old church, quaint and rambling and gabled. Through one violet-stained window a soft light glowed, where, no doubt, the organist loitered over the keys, making sure of his mastery of the coming Sabbath anthem. For there drifted out to Soapy's ears sweet music that caught and held him transfixed against the convolutions of the iron fence.

The moon was above, lustrous and serene; vehicles and pedestrians were few; sparrows twittered sleepily in the eaves—for a little while the scene might have been a country churchyard. And the anthem that the organist played cemented Soapy to the iron fence, for he had known it well in the days when his life contained such things as mothers and roses and ambitions and friends and immaculate thoughts and collars.

The conjunction of Soapy's receptive state of mind and the influences about the old church wrought a sudden and wonderful change in his soul. He viewed with swift horror the pit into which he had tumbled, the degraded days, unworthy desires, dead hopes, wrecked faculties and base motives that made up his existence.

And also in a moment his heart responded thrillingly to this novel mood. An instantaneous and strong impulse moved him to battle with his desperate fate. He would pull himself out of the mire; he would make a man of himself again; he would conquer the evil that had taken possession of him. There was time; he was comparatively young yet; he would resurrect his old eager ambitions and pursue them without faltering. Those solemn but sweet organ notes had set up a revolution in him. Tomorrow he would go into the roaring downtown district and find work. A fur importer had once offered him a place as driver. He would find him tomorrow and ask for the position. He would be somebody in the world. He would—

Soapy felt a hand laid on his arm. He looked quickly around into the broad face of a policeman.

"What are you doin' here?" asked the officer.

"Nothin'," said Soapy.

"Then come along," said the policeman.

"Three months on the Island," said the Magistrate in the Police Court the next morning.

Understanding the Story

1. How does O. Henry suggest in his opening paragraphs that winter is near? How does his way of doing so help to set the mood of the story?
2. Find three references to landmarks that identify the city in which the story takes place.
3. What is Soapy thinking about as he moves uneasily on his park bench? What does he want? How does he plan to bring it about?
4. What practical considerations does Soapy make in laying his plans to be arrested? What characteristics of Soapy do these plans reveal?
5. Irony of situation depends upon a reversal of some kind. What kind of reversals occur in the events of this story? What is the most important reversal?
6. The events that befall Soapy are not the only ironies in this story. What is ironic in the character of the young woman Soapy tries to annoy and of the man whose umbrella he takes?
7. How does O. Henry's use of big words to describe little plans make the story ironic? Find examples of this use of irony.
8. Why does Soapy prefer jail to a charitable institution? Is O. Henry criticizing Soapy or Society? Explain.
9. How does O. Henry keep you from taking Soapy's problems or his plans too seriously?
10. How would the reader's attitude toward Soapy and his problems change if the story were told in the first person from Soapy's point of view? How would the language in the story change?

Building Vocabulary Skills

Find as close synonyms as possible for each italicized word in the following sentences. What do the italicized words have in common? Why does O. Henry use this kind of word?
1. "The *hibernatorial* ambitions of Soapy were not of the highest."
2. "In Soapy's opinion the Law was more *benign* than *Philanthropy*."
3. "The head waiter's eye fell upon his frayed trousers and *decadent* shoes."
4. "It was Soapy's design to assume the role of the *despicable* and *execrated* 'masher.'"
5. "It seemed that his route to the coveted Island was not to be an *epicurean* one."

Developing Language Skills

O. Henry frequently bases his stories on irony. For instance, another of his stories tells of a poor young couple at Christmastime. The husband sells his watch to buy a beautiful hair comb for his wife; his wife sells her hair to a wigmaker to buy a watch chain for her husband.

Write a brief story that ends ironically. Make your characters and their actions realistic and believable, since an improbable story will not provide effective irony.

Reading "A Favor for Lefty"

The *tone* of a story results from the attitude of the author toward his characters and, in a way, his attitude toward his readers. The tone of O. Henry in "The Cop and the Anthem," for example, was ironic, while Dorothy Parker in "The Waltz" adopted a humorous, even slightly cynical, tone. It is as important for a reader to grasp a story's tone as it is to hear a person's tone of voice in conversation: otherwise, one may misread a whole story, just as missing a note of humor, sarcasm, or seriousness in a voice may cause one to misinterpret what is said. Einstein's delightful, straight-faced reporting of the incidents leading up to his surprise ending gives "A Favor for Lefty" its force.

A Favor
for Lefty

Charles Einstein

Many families have an Uncle Leon who attempts to live up to family expectations but never quite succeeds. Uncle Leon's honesty in giving a full accounting of his difficulties provides the right climate for the ironic ending.

IN OUR FAMILY, we have an expression —"Do a favor for Lefty"—that, like the private sayings you have in your own family, is very hard to translate so outsiders will understand. Even today, a generation later, I am not qualified as, say, my father, to use this expression with its exact nuance and meaning (though I have used it time and time again) because I wasn't there when it happened. I was five years old, and five-year-olds don't go to funerals.

What happened was that Mr. Ghiblikian, who lived across the street from us in Boston, died. He died of old age. He was in his eighties, and he had had a long and a full life, and he died peacefully. My grandfather and my father and my Uncle Leon all went to the funeral parlor for the services, and they went in two cars. This was because Uncle Leon had bought a new car the day before, and he insisted on driving

it every chance he got. My grandfather refused to drive anywhere in a car that had Uncle Leon behind the wheel, so Grandfather went with my father; and Uncle Leon went in his own car, a trifle bitterly.

"Why won't you go in the same car with me?" he'd asked Grandfather.

"Because you don't look at the road when you drive," Grandfather said.

"I have to look for the signs," Uncle Leon said.

"You can't drive and look for signs at the same time," my grandfather said, and that was that.

Funeral services were held for Mr. Ghiblikian at one of the largest chapels in Boston, and after that all the cars got in line to follow the hearse to the cemetery. My father and my grandfather got back from the burial before Uncle Leon, and they were both upset about something. From their conversation, often recounted, I have been able to reconstruct at least dimly what had happened.

"He did what you told him," my father said. "He stopped looking for signs and kept his eye on the road."

"So he got lost and never showed up at the cemetery!" Grandfather shouted. "A fine time to stop looking for signs!"

"Look," my father said. "There was a whole crowd of mourners. One more wasn't missed. And of the three of us —you and me and Leon—Leon knew Mr. Ghiblikian the least. It isn't as if he was as close to him as you were."

It was not typical of my father to stick up for Uncle Leon this way, but in later years I have understood that Grandfather was upset over the death of his friend and that my father was trying to soothe him.

He wasn't too successful. "Signs!" my grandfather shouted. "Signs! He didn't even have to look for signs! All he had to do was stay in line in the parade"—"parade" was not the right word for a funeral procession, but my grandfather did not know the right word and meant nothing disrespectful, and my father, wisely, did not correct him—"and he couldn't miss!"

"Maybe he had a flat tire," my father said.

"Brand-new car!" my grandfather bellowed. "It goes two miles, a flat tire?"

"He might have run over a nail."

"So while he's looking for signs he'll look for nails too!"

There was the sound of a key in the door. My Uncle Leon came in and found himself looking down the barrel of an accusing finger.

"You!" my grandfather bellowed at him.

My father said, "Leon, what happened?"

"It's hard to explain," Uncle Leon said.

"It's hard to explain," my grandfather said, in savage mimicry. "Your brother and I, we were at a funeral today. Where were you?"

"At a funeral," Leon said.

"You saw them bury Ghiblikian?" my grandfather asked doubtfully.

"No. I saw them bury somebody else."

"Who?"

"I don't know."

"I may hit him," my grandfather said to my father.

"It's very simple," Uncle Leon said. "I mean, it's not simple, but the way it worked out there wasn't anything else I could do." He looked appealingly at my father. "You know how the cars got jammed up on Beacon Street a few blocks away from the chapel?"

My father nodded, looking carefully at my grandfather.

"Well, I guess I got in the wrong lane," Uncle Leon said. "The traffic started to move, and a cop waved me on through a light, and I saw I was right behind one of the chapel limousines, and right in front of the limousine was a hearse from the same chapel, so naturally I thought I'd moved up in the line and was following Mr. Ghiblikian's hearse." He shrugged. "Nobody told me where the cemetery was, anyway, so I had no way of knowing I was following a different hearse to a different cemetery."

"Seems only yesterday," my grandfather said to him, "you came home from the school saying, 'Papa, I got an A in American history.' What brains have you got? How come you ever got an A in anything?"

"There was just nothing I could do," Uncle Leon said. "The traffic was heavy, and I didn't recognize the people in the car behind me, but Mr. Ghiblikian knew a lot of people I didn't know, so that didn't mean anything; and you couldn't tell who was riding in the limousine in front of me. So"—he took a deep breath—"it wasn't till we turned in the cemetery gate and stopped at the graveside that I realized."

My father said, "Realized that you were at the wrong funeral?"

"Realized that I was the only car in that procession, besides the hearse and the limousine. I got out of the car and there was nobody behind me. And all there was in the limousine up ahead was the widow and the minister and a man from the funeral parlor."

My grandfather stared at him. "So?"

"So what could I do?" Leon said plaintively, "I can't say I'm sorry, good-by. I was in the presence of the dead. The minister came up and shook my hand. I had to stay where I was."

Nobody said anything for a time.

Then Uncle Leon broke the silence. "The minister said his few words, and then it was over, and you know what happened? The widow came up and kissed me on the cheek. And you know what she said? She said, 'I know you don't want to tell me who you are, but you did my husband a favor, coming here today. I want to thank you,' she said."

And that was Uncle Leon's story, and that way it stood until the following morning, when the papers came and there was a little item that said:

Smalltime racketeer Lefty Brown, fatally wounded in a holdup attempt last Thursday, was buried at Fair View Cemetery yesterday, all but unmourned. Cemetery officials said only the widow, *Mrs. Frances Brown, and an unidentified escort accompanied the body to its final resting place. . . .*

It all checked out. That unidentified escort was my Uncle Leon, and I guess the widow must have thought he was some hoodlum or other, which is why she told him she wouldn't ask his name. And since that time we have this expression in our family—"Do a favor for Lefty." It is by no means a sardonic or sarcastic saying, but implies instead something unplanned but nonetheless warm: something that means some unexpected happiness or some unexpected direction, something that deals with fate. It is like the expressions you have come to have in your own family— there's no describing them or explaining them to outsiders. You know how it is.

Understanding the Story

1. At what point in the story does the title acquire significance? What is its meaning?
2. Who tells the story and how does the point of view add to the effect of the story?
3. What tone does the author use in this story? (Consider the feelings he reveals toward the family and the incident.)
4. How does the choice of the funeral of a neighbor who died of old age give the author freedom to write a humorous story about a funeral?
5. How does Charles Einstein prepare the reader to accept Uncle Leon's explanation of getting into the wrong funeral procession?
6. What do you learn about Father and Grandfather in the paragraph in which Grandfather refers to the funeral procession as a parade?

Developing Language Skills

1. Discuss with your family or invent in line with this story the origin of a phrase, saying, or joke that has meaning to members of your family but to no one else. Write a brief account of the circumstances which led up to the birth of one of these sayings, ending the account (if possible) with a surprise twist. Conclude by giving the family interpretation or use of the story.

2. Tone depends on factors such as the person speaking (or writing), to whom he is speaking, the occasion, and the subject. A change in tone may show itself through changes in the way a person phrases his thoughts as well as through changes in the quality of his voice. Write an essay of at least three paragraphs in which you examine how and why your tone changes in different situations. (For example, how is the tone in which you greet a friend different from that in which you greet the school principal?)

Reading "The Damned Thing"

Bierce's focus in this story is much more on the situation (that is, on what happens) than on his characters as people. As a result, his tone as shown in his attitude toward his characters is largely one of detachment.

To produce a sense of drama without involving the reader's sympathies strongly with any one character, Bierce has used three different viewpoints. The opening section is written in the third person: it is told as though the author had been present but invisible at the scene and were now describing it and his conclusions about it to his readers. He does not take us into the thoughts or feelings of the men present, but limits himself to what a witness of the scene could actually have observed.

In the second section, Bierce switches to a character's point of view by having a witness read an account he has written to a coroner's jury. He then changes, in effect, to the point of view of the dead man by concluding with entries from his diary. In this way, Bierce concentrates the reader's interest on *what* happened, not on the individuals involved.

The Damned Thing

Ambrose Bierce

Ambrose Bierce persuades the reader to believe a story that is unbelievable. He does it by presenting down-to-earth characters and carefully reported evidence. His characters, all common-sense citizens, raise the questions you might raise and accept the answers you find yourself accepting. Bierce's love of shock is shown in the opening scene, which is a coroner's inquest in an isolated cabin lighted by a solitary tallow candle.

I

ONE DOES NOT ALWAYS EAT WHAT IS ON THE TABLE

BY THE LIGHT of a tallow candle which had been placed on one end of a rough table a man was reading something written in a book. It was an old account book, greatly worn; and the writing was not, apparently, very legible, for the man sometimes held the page close to the flame of the candle to get a stronger light on it. The shadow of the book would then throw into obscurity a half of the room, darkening a number of faces and figures; for besides the reader, eight other men were present. Seven of them sat against the rough log walls, silent, motionless, and the room being small, not very far from the table. By extending an arm any one of them could have touched the eighth man, who lay on the table, face upward, partly covered by a sheet, his arms at his sides. He was dead.

The man with the book was not reading aloud, and no one spoke; all seemed to be waiting for something to occur; the dead man only was without expectation. From the blank darkness outside came in, through the aperture that served for a window, all the ever unfamiliar noises of night in the wilderness —the long nameless note of a distant coyote; the stilly pulsing thrill of tireless insects in trees; strange cries of night birds, so different from those of the birds of day; the drone of great blundering beetles, and all that mysterious chorus of small sounds that seem always to have been but half heard when they have suddenly ceased, as if conscious of an indiscretion. But nothing of all this was noted in that company; its members were not overmuch addicted to idle interest in matters of no practical importance; that was obvious in every line of their rugged faces—obvious even in the dim light of the single candle. They were evidently men of the vicinity—farmers and woodsmen.

The person reading was a trifle different; one would have said of him that he was of the world, worldly, albeit there was that in his attire which attested a certain fellowship with the organisms of his environment. His coat would hardly have passed muster in San Francisco; his footgear was not of urban origin, and the hat that lay by him on the floor (he was the only one uncovered) was such that if one had consid-

ered it as an article of mere personal
adornment he would have missed its
meaning. In countenance the man was
rather prepossessing, with just a hint of
sternness; though that he may have assumed or cultivated, as appropriate to
one in authority. For he was a coroner.
It was by virtue of his office that he had
possession of the book in which he was
reading; it had been found among the
dead man's effects—in his cabin, where
the inquest was now taking place.

When the coroner had finished reading he put the book into his breast
pocket. At that moment the door was
pushed open and a young man entered.
He, clearly, was not of mountain birth
and breeding: he was clad as those who
dwell in cities. His clothing was dusty,
however, as from travel. He had, in
fact, been riding hard to attend the inquest.

The coroner nodded; no one else
greeted him.

"We have waited for you," said the
coroner. "It is necessary to have done
with this business tonight."

The young man smiled. "I am sorry
to have kept you," he said. "I went
away, not to evade your summons, but
to post to my newspaper an account of
what I suppose I am called back to relate."

The coroner smiled.

"The account that you posted to your
newspaper," he said, "differs, probably,
from that which you will give here under oath."

"That," replied the other, rather hotly
and with a visible flush, "is as you
please. I used manifold paper and
have a copy of what I sent. It was not
written as news, for it is incredible, but
as fiction. It may go as a part of my
testimony under oath."

"But you say it is incredible."

"That is nothing to you, sir, if I also
swear that it is true."

The coroner was apparently not greatly affected by the young man's manifest resentment. He was silent for a time, his eyes upon the floor. The men about the sides of the cabin talked in whispers, but seldom withdrew their gaze from the face of the corpse. Presently the coroner lifted his eyes and said: "We will resume the inquest."

The men removed their hats. The witness was sworn.

"What is your name?" the coroner asked.

"William Harker."

"Age?"

"Twenty-seven."

"You knew the deceased, Hugh Morgan?"

"Yes."

"You were with him when he died?"

"Near him."

"How did that happen—your presence, I mean?"

"I was visiting him at this place to shoot and fish. A part of my purpose, however, was to study him and his odd, solitary way of life. He seemed a good model for a character in fiction. I sometimes write stories."

"I sometimes read them."

"Thank you."

"Stories in general—not yours."

Some of the jurors laughed. Against a somber background humor shows high lights. Soldiers in the intervals of battle laugh easily, and a jest in the death chamber conquers by surprise.

"Relate the circumstances of this man's death," said the coroner. "You may use any notes or memoranda that you please."

The witness understood. Pulling a manuscript from his breast pocket he held it near the candle and turning the leaves until he found the passage that he wanted began to read.

II

WHAT MAY HAPPEN IN A FIELD OF WILD OATS

". . . The sun had hardly risen when we left the house. We were looking for quail, each with a shotgun, but we had only one dog. Morgan said that our best ground was beyond a certain ridge that he pointed out, and we crossed it by a trail through the *chaparral*.[1] On the other side was comparatively level ground, thickly covered with wild oats. As we emerged from the *chaparral* Morgan was but a few yards in advance. Suddenly we heard, at a little distance to our right and partly in front, a noise as of some animal thrashing about in the bushes, which we could see were violently agitated.

"'We've started a deer,' I said. 'I wish we had brought a rifle.'

"Morgan, who had stopped and was intently watching the agitated *chaparral*, said nothing, but had cocked both barrels of his gun and was holding it in readiness to aim. I thought him a trifle excited, which surprised me, for he had a reputation for exceptional coolness, even in moments of sudden and imminent peril.

"'O, come,' I said. 'You are not going to fill up a deer with quail-shot, are you?'

"Still he did not reply; but catching a sight of his face as he turned it slightly toward me I was struck by the intensity of his look. Then I understood that we had serious business in hand and my first conjecture was that we had 'jumped' a grizzly. I advanced to Morgan's side, cocking my piece as I moved.

"The bushes were now quiet and the sounds had ceased, but Morgan was as attentive to the place as before.

1 chaparral (chăp'ə răl'): dense thicket of stiff or thorny shrub.

"'What is it? What the devil is it?' I asked.

"'That Damned Thing!' he replied, without turning his head. His voice was husky and unnatural. He trembled visibly.

"I was about to speak further, when I observed the wild oats near the place of the disturbance moving in the most inexplicable way. I can hardly describe it. It seemed as if stirred by a streak of wind, which not only bent it, but pressed it down—crushed it so that it did not rise; and this movement was slowly prolonging itself directly toward us.

"Nothing that I had ever seen had affected me so strangely as this unfamiliar and unaccountable phenomenon, yet I am unable to recall any sense of fear. I remember—and tell it here because, singularly enough, I recollected it then—that once in looking carelessly out of an open window I momentarily mistook a small tree close at hand for one of a group of larger trees at a little distance away. It looked the same size as the others, but being more distinctly and sharply defined in mass and detail seemed out of harmony with them. It was a mere falsification of the law of aerial perspective, but it startled, almost terrified me. We so rely upon the orderly operation of familiar natural laws that any seeming suspension of them is noted as a menace to our safety, a warning of unthinkable calamity. So now the apparently causeless movement of the herbage and the slow, undeviating approach of the line of disturbance were distinctly disquieting. My companion appeared actually frightened, and I could hardly credit my senses when I saw him suddenly throw his gun to his shoulder and fire both barrels at the agitated grain! Before the smoke of the discharge had cleared away I heard a loud savage cry—a scream like that of a wild animal—and flinging his gun upon the ground Morgan sprang away and ran swiftly from the spot. At the same instant I was thrown violently to the ground by the impact of something unseen in the smoke—some soft, heavy substance that seemed thrown against me with great force.

"Before I could get upon my feet and recover my gun, which seemed to have been struck from my hands, I heard Morgan crying out as if in mortal agony, and mingling with his cries were such hoarse, savage sounds as one hears from fighting dogs. Inexpressibly terrified, I struggled to my feet and looked in the direction of Morgan's retreat; and may Heaven in mercy spare me from another sight like that! At a distance of less than thirty yards was my friend, down upon one knee, his head thrown back at a frightful angle, hatless, his long hair in disorder and his whole body in violent movement from side to side, backward and forward. His right arm was lifted and seemed to lack the hand—at least, I could see none. The other arm was invisible. At times, as my memory now reports this extraordinary scene, I could discern but a part of his body; it was as if he had been partly blotted out—I cannot otherwise express it—then a shifting of his position would bring it all into view again.

"All this must have occurred within a few seconds, yet in that time Morgan assumed all the postures of a determined wrestler vanquished by superior weight and strength. I saw nothing but him, and him not always distinctly. During the entire incident his shouts and curses were heard, as if through an enveloping uproar of such sounds of rage and fury as I had never heard from the throat of man or brute!

"For a moment only I stood irreso-

44

lute, then throwing down my gun I ran forward to my friend's assistance. I had a vague belief that he was suffering from a fit, or some form of convulsion. Before I could reach his side he was down and quiet. All sounds had ceased, but with a feeling of such terror as even these awful events had not inspired I now saw again the mysterious movement of the wild oats, prolonging itself from the trampled area about the prostrate man toward the edge of a wood. It was only when it had reached the wood that I was able to withdraw my eyes and look at my companion. He was dead."

III

A Man Though Naked May Be
in Rags

The coroner rose from his seat and stood beside the dead man. Lifting an edge of the sheet he pulled it away, exposing the entire body, altogether naked and showing in the candlelight a clay-like yellow. It had, however, broad maculations[2] of bluish black, obviously caused by extravasated[3] blood from contusions. The chest and sides looked as if they had been beaten with a bludgeon. There were dreadful lacerations; the skin was torn in strips and shreds.

The coroner moved round to the end of the table and undid a silk handkerchief which had been passed under the chin and knotted on the top of the head. When the handkerchief was drawn away it exposed what had been the throat. Some of the jurors who had risen to get a better view repented their curiosity and turned away their faces. Witness Harker went to the open window and leaned out across the sill, faint and sick. Dropping the handkerchief upon

2 **maculations**: discolorations.
3 **extravasated** (ĭk străv′ə sā′tĭd): forced out.

the dead man's neck the coroner stepped to an angle of the room and from a pile of clothing produced one garment after another, each of which he held up a moment for inspection. All were torn, and stiff with blood. The jurors did not make a closer inspection. They seemed rather uninterested. They had, in truth, seen all this before; the only thing that was new to them being Harker's testimony.

"Gentlemen," the coroner said, "we have no more evidence, I think. Your duty has been already explained to you; if there is nothing you wish to ask you may go outside and consider your verdict."

The foreman rose—a tall, bearded man of sixty, coarsely clad.

"I should like to ask one question, Mr. Coroner," he said. "What asylum did this yer last witness escape from?"

"Mr. Harker," said the coroner, gravely and tranquilly, "from what asylum did you last escape?"

Harker flushed crimson again, but said nothing, and the seven jurors rose and solemnly filed out of the cabin.

"If you have done insulting me, sir," said Harker, as soon as he and the officer were left alone with the dead man, "I suppose I am at liberty to go?"

"Yes."

Harker started to leave, but paused, with his hand on the door latch. The habit of his profession was strong in him—stronger than his sense of personal dignity. He turned about and said:

"The book that you have there—I recognize it as Morgan's diary. You seemed greatly interested in it; you read in it while I was testifying. May I see it? The public would like—"

"The book will cut no figure in this matter," replied the official, slipping it into his coat pocket; "all the entries in it were made before the writer's death."

As Harker passed out of the house the jury re-entered and stood about the table, on which the now covered corpse showed under the sheet with sharp definition. The foreman seated himself near the candle, produced from his breast pocket a pencil and scrap of paper and wrote rather laboriously the following verdict, which with various degrees of effort all signed:

"We, the jury, do find that the remains come to their death at the hands of a mountain lion, but some of us thinks, all the same, they had fits."

IV

AN EXPLANATION FROM THE TOMB

In the diary of the late Hugh Morgan are certain interesting entries having, possibly, a scientific value as suggestions. At the inquest upon his body the book was not put in evidence; possibly the coroner thought it not worth while to confuse the jury. The date of the first of the entries mentioned cannot be ascertained; the upper part of the leaf is torn away; the part of the entry remaining follows:

". . . would run in a half-circle, keeping his head turned always toward the center, and again he would stand still, barking furiously. At last he ran away into the brush as fast as he could go. I thought at first that he had gone mad, but on returning to the house found no other alteration in his manner than what was obviously due to fear of punishment.

"Can a dog see with his nose? Do odors impress some cerebral center with images of the thing that emitted them? . . .

"Sept. 2.—Looking at the stars last night as they rose above the crest of the ridge east of the house, I observed them successively disappear—from left to right. Each was eclipsed but an instant, and only a few at the same time, but along the entire length of the ridge all that were within a degree or two of the crest were blotted out. It was as if something had passed along between me and them; but I could not see it, and the stars were not thick enough to define its outline. Ugh! I don't like this." . . .

Several weeks' entries are missing, three leaves being torn from the book.

"Sept. 27.—It has been about here again—I find evidences of its presence every day. I watched again all last night in the same cover, gun in hand, double-charged with buckshot. In the morning the fresh footprints were there, as before. Yet I would have sworn that I did not sleep—indeed, I hardly sleep at all. It is terrible, insupportable! If these amazing experiences are real I shall go mad; if they are fanciful I am mad already.

"Oct. 3.—I shall not go—it shall not drive me away. No, this is *my* house, *my* land. God hates a coward. . . .

"Oct. 5.—I can stand it no longer; I have invited Harker to pass a few weeks with me—he has a level head. I can judge from his manner if he thinks me mad.

"Oct. 7.—I have the solution of the mystery; it came to me last night—suddenly, as by revelation. How simple—how terribly simple!

"There are sounds that we cannot hear. At either end of the scale are notes that stir no chord of that imperfect instrument, the human ear. They are too high or too grave.[4] I have observed a flock of blackbirds occupying an entire treetop—the tops of several trees—and all in full song. Suddenly—in a moment—at absolutely the same in-

4 **grave:** low in pitch.

stant—all spring into the air and fly away. How? They could not all see one another—whole treetops intervened. At no point could a leader have been visible to all. There must have been a signal of warning or command, high and shrill above the din, but by me unheard. I have observed, too, the same simultaneous flight when all were silent, among not only blackbirds, but other birds—quail, for example, widely separated by bushes—even on opposite sides of a hill.

"It is known to seamen that a school of whales basking or sporting on the surface of the ocean, miles apart, with the convexity[5] of the earth between, will sometimes dive at the same instant

5 convexity: arched form.

—all gone out of sight in a moment. The signal has been sounded—too grave for the ear of the sailor at the masthead and his comrades on the deck—who nevertheless feel its vibrations in the ship as the stones of a cathedral are stirred by the bass of the organ.

"As with sounds, so with colors. At each end of the solar spectrum the chemist can detect the presence of what are known as 'actinic' rays. They represent colors—integral colors in the composition of light—which we are unable to discern. The human eye is an imperfect instrument; its range is but a few octaves of the real 'chromatic scale.' I am not mad; there are colors that we cannot see.

"And, God help me! the Damned Thing is of such a color!"

Understanding the Story

1. To what does the title refer?
2. Explain this comment: Bierce's first paragraph could be stage directions for the opening scene in a melodrama.
3. Where does the inquest take place? Why was it held at night? What elements of the setting contribute to the atmosphere of the story?
4. Note the titles of the section headings. What is their tone? Does their tone differ from the tone of the story itself?
5. What is the attitude of the coroner toward the newspaperman? What evidence do you find for this in the story?
6. What might lead the coroner to accept Harker's statement that his testimony is both incredible and true?
7. Why does Harker read his testimony to the jury instead of giving it from memory? What question does the foreman of the jury ask the coroner after hearing Harker's testimony?
8. What is the verdict of the members of the jury? Why did they give it?
9. Why didn't the coroner read the diary to the jury?
10. How do parts one and three of the story help you to accept parts two and four?

AMBROSE BIERCE

1. Contrast in a paragraph the physical appearance of the coroner with that of the newspaperman, showing how their different personalities are reflected in their appearances.
2. Plan a panel of three students in which one member presents the coroner's point of view toward Morgan's death and the inquest; another, Harker's; and the third, the jury's.

The following three stories may be regarded as transitions between the group you have already read and the more complex group which concludes this unit. At first you may not notice a sharp difference between these stories and the preceding ones, for all writers must try to do certain things in a short story: invent a plot that has suspense, create believable or at least interesting characters, and provide a suitable setting. You might note as you read, however, that the relationship between action and character becomes more important in the following stories. The authors are not simply concerned with making the reader believe that their characters would act as they do, but are apt to make the point of a story depend on the fact that different kinds of inner character lead to certain types of action. Creating interesting situations is still a purpose of the authors, but you will see that they also choose situations which exemplify basic conflicts of many human beings. In other words, these stories begin to add to the goal of entertainment that of serious exploration of human life and character.

Reading "The Heyday of the Blood"

One of the best ways to make anything stand out clearly is to contrast it with something quite different. Dorothy Canfield Fisher has used *contrast* in the following story as a means of focusing attention on the important quality possessed by Gran'ther. How has she created this contrast? Her technique may be compared to that of painting a portrait against a contrasting light or dark background. Her real subject is a character sketch of an old man, but she sets this sketch against the background of a young man who has quite a different attitude toward life than does the old man. By doing this, she has created more than a character sketch; through the contrast, she has brought into the foreground an attitude which she obviously believes essential to leading a full life.

The Heyday of the Blood

Dorothy Canfield Fisher

This story about a worried young man and an exuberant great-grandfather illustrates the wholesome spirit of Dorothy Canfield Fisher's writings. "Live while you live" was not only Gran'ther Pendleton's motto but also the author's. Although Mrs. Fisher chose a small Vermont town as the center of her busy universe, she left it often to travel the length and breadth of the world.

THE OLDER PROFESSOR looked up at the assistant, fumbling fretfully with a pile of papers. "Farrar, what's the *matter* with you lately?" he said sharply.

The younger man started, "Why . . . why . . ." the brusqueness of the other's manner shocked him suddenly into confession. "I've lost my nerve, Professor Mallory, that's what's the matter with me. I'm frightened to death," he said melodramatically.

"What *of?*" asked Mallory, with a little challenge in his tone.

The floodgates were open. The younger man burst out in exclamations, waving his thin, nervous, knotted fingers, his face twitching as he spoke. "Of myself . . . no, not myself, but my body! I'm not well . . . I'm getting

worse all the time. The doctors don't make out what is the matter . . . I don't sleep . . . I worry . . . I forget things, I take no interest in life . . . the doctors intimate a nervous breakdown ahead of me . . . and yet I rest . . . I rest . . . more than I can afford to! I never go out. Every evening I'm in bed by nine o'clock. I take no part in college life beyond my work, for fear of the nervous strain. I've refused to take charge of that summer school in New York, you know, that would be such an opportunity for me . . . if I could only sleep! But though I never do anything exciting in the evening . . . heavens! what nights I have. Black hours of seeing myself in a sanitarium, dependent on my brother! I never . . . why, I'm in hell . . . that's what the matter with me, a perfect hell of ignoble terror!"

He sat silent, his drawn face turned to the window. The older man looked at him speculatively. When he spoke it was with a cheerful, casual quality in his voice which made the other look up at him surprised.

"You don't suppose those great friends of yours, the nerve specialists, would object to my telling you a story, do you? It's very quiet and unexciting. You're not too busy?"

"Busy! I've forgotten the meaning of the word! I don't dare to be!"

"Very well, then; I mean to carry you back to the stony little farm in the Green Mountains, where I had the extreme good luck to be born and raised. You've heard me speak of Hillsboro; and the story is all about my great-grandfather, who came to live with us when I was a little boy."

"Your great-grandfather?" said the other incredulously. "People don't remember their great-grandfathers!"

"Oh, yes, they do, in Vermont. There

was my father on one farm, and my grandfather on another, without a thought that he was no longer young, and there was 'Gran'ther' as we called him, eighty-eight years old and just persuaded to settle back, let his descendants take care of him, and consent to be an old man. He had been in the War of 1812—think of that, you mushroom!—and had lost an arm and a good deal of his health there. He had lately begun to get a pension of twelve dollars a month, so that for an old man he was quite independent financially, as poor Vermont farmers look at things; and he was a most extraordinary character, so that his arrival in our family was quite an event.

"He took precedence at once of the oldest man in the township, who was only eighty-four and not very bright. I can remember bragging at school about Gran'ther Pendleton, who'd be eighty-nine come next Woodchuck Day, and could see to read without glasses. He had been ailing all his life, ever since the fever he took in the war. He used to remark triumphantly that he had now outlived six doctors who had each given him but a year to live; 'and the seventh is going downhill fast, so I hear!' This last was his never-failing answer to the attempts of my conscientious mother and anxious, dutiful father to check the old man's reckless indifference to any of the rules of hygiene.

"They were good disciplinarians with their children, and this naughty old man, who would give his weak stomach frightful attacks of indigestion by stealing out to the pantry and devouring a whole mince pie because he had been refused two pieces at the table—this rebellious, unreasonable, whimsical old madcap[1] was an electric element in our

1 madcap: reckless person.

quiet, orderly life. He insisted on going to every picnic and church sociable, where he ate recklessly of all the indigestible dainties he could lay his hands on, stood in drafts, tired himself to the verge of fainting away by playing games with the children, and returned home, exhausted, animated, and quite ready to pay the price of a day in bed, groaning and screaming out with pain as heartily and unaffectedly as he had laughed with the pretty girls the evening before.

"The climax came, however, in the middle of August, when he announced his desire to go to the county fair, held some fourteen miles down the valley from our farm. Father never dared let Gran'ther go anywhere without himself accompanying the old man, but he was perfectly sincere in saying that it was not because he could not spare a day from the haying that he refused pointblank to consider it. The doctor who had been taking care of Gran'ther since he came to live with us said that it would be crazy to think of such a thing. He added that the wonder was that Gran'ther lived at all, for his heart was all wrong, his asthma was enough to kill a young man, and he had no digestion; in short, if Father wished to kill his old grandfather, there was no surer way than to drive fourteen miles in the heat of August to the noisy excitement of a county fair.

"So Father for once said 'No,' in the tone that we children had come to recognize as final. Gran'ther grimly tied a knot in his empty sleeve—a curious, enigmatic mode of his to express strong emotion—put his one hand on his cane, and his chin on his hand, and withdrew himself into that incalculable distance from the life about him where very old people spend so many hours.

"He did not emerge from this until

one morning toward the middle of fair-week, when all the rest of the family were away—Father and the bigger boys on the far-off upland meadows haying, and Mother and the girls off blackberry-ing. I was too little to be of any help, so I had been left to wait on Gran'ther, and to set out our lunch of bread and milk and huckleberries. We had not been alone half an hour when Gran'ther sent me to extract, from under the mattress of his bed, the wallet in which he kept his pension money. There was six dollars and forty-three cents—he counted it over carefully, sticking out his tongue like a schoolboy doing a sum, and when he had finished he began to laugh and snap his fingers and sing out in his high, cracked old voice:

"'We're goin' to go a skylarkin'! Little Jo Mallory is going to the county fair with his Gran'ther Pendleton, an' he's goin' to have more fun than ever was in the world, and he——'

"'But, Gran'ther, Father said we mustn't!' I protested, horrified.

"'But I say we *shall!* I was your gre't-gran'ther long before he was your feyther, and anyway I'm here and he's not—so, *march!* Out to the barn!'

"He took me by the collar, and, executing a shuffling fandango[2] of triumph, he pushed me ahead of him to the stable, where old white Peggy, the only horse left at home, looked at us amazed.

"'But it'll be twenty-eight miles, and Peg's never driven over eight!' I cried, my old-established world of rules and orders reeling before my eyes.

"'Eight—and—twenty-eight!
But I—am—*eighty*-eight!'

"Gran'ther improvised a sort of whooping chant of scorn as he pulled the harness from the peg. 'It'll do her

2 fandango: a lively Spanish dance.

good to drink some pink lemonade—old Peggy! An' if she gits tired comin' home, I'll git out and carry her part way myself!'

"His adventurous spirit was irresistible. I made no further objection, and we hitched up together, I standing on a chair to fix the checkrein, and Gran'ther doing wonders with his one hand. Then, just as we were—Gran'ther in a hickory shirt, and with an old hat flapping over his wizened face, I bare-legged, in ragged old clothes—so we drove out of the grassy yard, down the steep, stony hill that led to the main valley road, and along the hot, white turnpike, deep with the dust which had been stirred up by the teams on their way to the fair. Gran'ther sniffed the air jubilantly, and exchanged hilarious greetings with the people who constantly overtook old Peg's jogging trot. Between times he regaled me with spicy stories of the hundreds of thousands—they seemed no less numerous to me then—of county fairs he had attended in his youth. He was horrified to find that I had never been even to one.

"'Why, Joey, how old be ye? 'Most eight, ain't it? When I was your age I had run away and been to two fairs an' a hangin'.'

"'But didn't they lick you when you got home?' I asked shudderingly.

"'You *bet* they did!' cried Gran'ther with gusto.

"I felt the world changing into an infinitely larger place with every word he said.

"'Now, this is somethin' *like!*' he exclaimed, as we drew near to Granville and fell into a procession of wagons all filled with country people in their best clothes, who looked with friendly curiosity at the little, shriveled cripple, his face shining with perspiring animation, and at the little boy beside him, his

DOROTHY CANFIELD FISHER

bare feet dangling high above the floor of the battered buckboard, overcome with the responsibility of driving a horse for the first time in his life, and filled with such a flood of new emotions and ideas that he must have been quite pale."

Professor Mallory leaned back and laughed aloud at the vision he had been evoking—laughed with so joyous a relish in his reminiscences that the drawn, impatient face of his listener relaxed a little. He drew a long breath, he even smiled a little absently.

"Oh, that was a day!" went on the professor, still laughing and wiping his eyes. "Never will I have such another! At the entrance to the grounds Gran'ther stopped me while he solemnly untied the knot in his empty sleeve. I don't know what kind of hairbrained vow he had tied up in it, but with the little ceremony disappeared every trace of restraint, and we plunged head over

ears into the saturnalia[3] of delights that was an old-time county fair.

"People had little cash in those days, and Gran'ther's six dollars and forty-three cents lasted like the widow's cruse of oil. We went to see the fat lady, who, if she was really as big as she looked to me then, must have weighed at least a ton. My admiration for Gran'-ther's daredevil qualities rose to infinity when he entered into free-and-easy talk with her, about how much she ate, and could she raise her arms enough to do up her own hair, and how many yards of velvet it took to make her gorgeous, gold-trimmed robe. She laughed a great deal at us, but she was evidently touched by his human interest, for she confided to him that it was not velvet at all, but furniture covering; and when we went away she pressed on us a bag of peanuts. She said she had more pea-

3 **saturnalia** (săt′ər nā′lĭ ə): festival; riotous merry-making and indulgence.

nuts than she could eat—a state of un-bridled opulence which fitted in for me with all the other superlatives of that day.

"We saw the dog-faced boy, whom we did not like at all; Gran'ther express-ing, with a candidly outspoken cyni-cism, his belief that 'them whiskers was glued to him.' We wandered about the stock exhibit, gazing at the monstrous oxen, and hanging over the railings where the prize pigs lived to scratch their backs. In order to miss nothing, we even conscientiously passed through the Woman's Building, where we were very much bored by the serried[4] ranks of preserve jars.

"'Sufferin' Hezekiah!' cried Gran'ther irritably. 'Who cares how gooseberry jel *looks*. If they'd give a felly a taste, now——'

"This reminded him that we were hungry, and we went to a restaurant under a tent, where, after taking stock of the wealth that yet remained of Gran'ther's hoard, he ordered the most expensive things on the bill of fare."

Professor Mallory suddenly laughed out again. "Perhaps in heaven, but cer-tainly not until then, shall I ever taste anything so ambrosial[5] as that fried chicken and coffee ice cream! I have not lived in vain that I have such a memory back of me!"

This time the younger man laughed with the narrator, settling back in his chair as the professor went on:

"After lunch we rode on the merry-go-round, both of us, Gran'ther clinging desperately with his one hand to his red camel's wooden hump, and crying out shrilly to me to be sure and not lose his cane. The merry-go-round had just come in at that time, and Gran'ther had

never experienced it before. After the first giddy flight we retired to a lemon-ade stand to exchange impressions, and finding that we both alike had fallen completely under the spell of the new sensation, Gran'ther said that we 'sh'd keep on a-ridin' till we'd had enough! King Solomon couldn't tell when we'd ever git a chance again!' So we re-turned to the charge, and rode and rode and rode, through blinding clouds of happy excitement, so it seems to me now, such as I was never to know again. The sweat was pouring off from us, and we had tried all the different animals on the machine before we could tear ourselves away to follow the crowd to the race track.

"We took reserved seats, which cost a quarter apiece, instead of the un-shaded ten-cent benches, and Gran'ther began at once to pour out to me a flood of horse talk and knowing race-track aphorisms,[6] which finally made a young fellow sitting next to us laugh super-ciliously.[7] Gran'ther turned on him heatedly.

"'I bet-che fifty cents I pick the win-ner in the next race!' he said sportily.

"'Done!' said the other, still laughing.

"Gran'ther picked a big black mare, who came in almost last, but he did not flinch. As he paid over the half dollar he said: 'Everybody's likely to make mistakes about *some* things; King Solomon was a fool in the head about womenfolks! I bet-che a dollar I pick the winner in *this* race!' and 'Done!' said the disagreeable young man, still laughing. I gasped, for I knew we had only eighty-seven cents left, but Gran'-ther shot me a command to silence out of the corner of his eyes, and announced that he bet on the sorrel gelding.

---

4 **serried:** orderly.
5 **ambrosial:** divine; delightful.

6 **aphorisms** (ăf'ə rĭz'əmz): general truths; sayings.
7 **superciliously** (soo'pər sĭl'ĭ əs lĭ): contemptuously.

"If I live to be a hundred and break the bank at Monte Carlo three times a week," said Mallory, shaking his head reminiscently, "I could not know a tenth part of the frantic excitement of that race or of the mad triumph when our horse won. Gran'ther cast his hat upon the ground, screaming like a steam calliope with exultation as the sorrel swept past the judges' stand ahead of all the others, and I jumped up and down in an agony of delight which was almost more than my little body could hold.

"After that we went away, feeling that the world could hold nothing more glorious. It was five o'clock, and we decided to start back. We paid for Peggy's dinner out of the dollar we had won on the race—I say 'we,' for by that time we were welded into one organism—and we still had a dollar and a quarter left. 'While ye're about it, always go the whole hog!' said Gran'ther, and we spent twenty minutes in laying out that money in trinkets for all the folks at home. Then, dusty, penniless, laden with bundles, we bestowed our exhausted bodies and our uplifted hearts in the old buckboard, and turned Peg's head toward the mountains. We did not talk much during that drive, and though I thought at the time only of the carnival of joy we had left, I can now recall every detail of the trip—how the sun sank behind Indian Mountain, a peak I had known before only through distant views; then, as we journeyed on, how the stars came out above Hemlock Mountain—our own home mountain behind our house, and later, how the fireflies filled the darkening meadows along the river below us, so that we seemed to be floating between the steady stars of heaven and their dancing, twinkling reflection in the valley.

"Gran'ther's dauntless spirit still surrounded me. I put out of mind doubts of our reception at home, and lost myself in delightful ruminatings on the splendors of the day. At first, every once in a while, Gran'ther made a brief remark, such as, ' 'Twas the hindquarters of the sorrel I bet on. He was the only one in the hull kit and bilin' of 'em that his quarters didn't fall away'; or, 'You needn't tell *me* that them Siamese twins ain't unpinned every night as separate as you and me!' But later on, as the damp evening air began to bring on his asthma, he subsided into silence, only broken by great gasping coughs.

"These were heard by the anxious, heartsick watchers at home, and, as old Peg stumbled wearily up the hill, Father came running down to meet us. ' Where you be'n?' he demanded, his face pale and stern in the light of his lantern. 'We be'n to the county fair!' croaked Gran'ther with a last flare of triumph, and fell over sideways against me. Old Peg stopped short, hanging her head as if she, too, were at the limit of her strength. I was frightfully tired myself, and frozen with terror of what Father would say. Gran'ther's collapse was the last straw. I began to cry loudly, but Father ignored my distress with an indifference which cut me to the heart. He lifted Gran'ther out of the buckboard, carrying the unconscious little old body into the house without a glance backward at me. But when I crawled down to the ground, sobbing and digging my fists into my eyes, I felt Mother's arms close around me.

" 'Oh, poor, naughty little Joey!' she said. 'Mother's bad, dear little boy!' "

Professor Mallory stopped short.

"Perhaps that's something else I'll know again in heaven," he said soberly, and waited a moment before he went on: "Well, that was the end of our day. I was so worn out that I fell asleep over my supper, in spite of the excitement in the house about sending for a doctor for Gran'ther, who was, so one of my awe-struck sisters told me, having some kind of 'fits.' Mother must have put me to bed, for the next thing I remember, she was shaking me by the shoulder and saying, 'Wake up, Joey. Your great-grandfather wants to speak to you. He's been suffering terribly all night, and the doctor think's he's dying.'

"I followed her into Gran'ther's room, where the family was assembled about the bed. Gran'ther lay drawn up in a ball, groaning so dreadfully that I felt a chill like cold water at the roots of my hair; but a moment or two after I came in, all at once he gave a great sigh and relaxed, stretching out his legs and laying his arms down on the coverlid. He looked at me and attempted a smile.

"'Well, it was wuth it, warn't it, Joey?' he said gallantly, and closed his eyes peacefully to sleep."

"Did he die?" asked the younger professor, leaning forward eagerly.

"Die? Gran'ther Pendleton? Not much! He came tottering down to breakfast the next morning, as white as an old ghost, with no voice left, his legs trembling under him, but he kept the whole family an hour and a half at the table, telling them in a loud whisper all about the fair, until Father said really he would have to take us to the one next year. Afterward he sat out on the porch watching old Peg graze around the yard. I thought he was in one of his absent-minded fits, but when I came out, he called me to him, and setting his lips to my ear, he whispered:

"'An' the seventh is a-goin' down-hill fast, so I hear!' He chuckled to himself over this for some time, wagging his head feebly, and then he said: 'I tell ye, Joey, I've lived a long time, and I've larned a lot about the way folks is made. The trouble with most of 'em is, they're 'fraid-cats! As Jeroboam Warner used to say—he was in the same rigiment with me in 1812—the only way to manage this business of livin' is to give a whoop and let her rip! If ye just about half-live, ye just the same as half-die; and if ye spend yer time half-dyin', some day ye turn in and die all over, without rightly meanin' to at all—just a kind o' bad habit ye've got yerself inter.' Gran'ther fell into a meditative silence for a moment. 'Jeroboam, he said that the evenin' before the battle of Lundy's Lane, and he got killed the next day. Some live, and some die; but folks that live all over die happy, anyhow! Now I tell you what's my motto, an' what I've lived to be eighty-eight on——"

Professor Mallory stood up and, towering over the younger man, struck one hand into the other as he cried: "This was the motto he told me: 'Live while you live, and then die and be done with it!'"

Understanding the Story

1. What does the title of the story mean? What are some other titles that would suit this story?
2. Find evidence in the first six paragraphs proving that Professor Mallory is a better psychologist than his colleague's nerve specialists.
3. What was Professor Mallory's motive in telling his story?
4. Why does the young assistant ask, "Did he die?"
5. Did Gran'ther have to live to give the story of the trip to the fair its points? Why?

6. Throughout the story Gran'ther expresses in various forms the motto given in the last paragraph, "Live while you live, and then die and be done with it." One example is "While you're about it, always go the whole hog." Find other expressions in the story that suggest the same thing. Add some of your own that are used today.

Building Vocabulary Skills

1. Use the word *heyday* in connection with the football season or a student election.
2. Supply antonyms for the italicized words in the following expressions from the story:
   (a) "a state of unbridled *opulence*"
   (b) "with a *candidly* outspoken cynicism"
3. Supply synonyms for the italicized words in the following expressions from the story:
   (a) "taste anything so *ambrosial* as that fried chicken"
   (b) "race-track *aphorisms*"
   (c) "a young fellow laughed *superciliously*"

Developing Language Skills

1. In two paragraphs or in a brief talk, contrast either (a) the way Jerry (in "Snake Dance") handles his problems with the way the young assistant of this story meets his, or (b) Soapy's attitude toward his problems (in "The Cop and the Anthem") with the young professor's attitude toward his worries in this story.
2. Plan a television interview with Gran'ther following his day at the fair. The questions of the interviewer and the replies of Gran'ther should be designed to bring out Gran'ther's philosophy of life.

Reading "You Can't Do That"

Like "The Heyday of the Blood," this story involves a *contrast* between characters. Marquand uses this device not only to emphasize his concept of honesty and integrity, but also as the very basis for the plot of the story. The conflict upon which the plot is built results from the contrasting values of young John March and of Captain Griggs.

A priceless cloak of red and yellow feathers with which Marquand opens "You Can't Do That" and to which he returns in the last sentences represents the values of John March and is one of the chief means in this story of providing a sense of *unity*. At the beginning, the author presents the cloak as a rare treasure; he then moves into his actual story which shows why John March and his descendants treasure the cloak. After finishing the story, briefly scan the opening description of the cloak. What does the description of the cloak now suggest other than just its value as an heirloom?

SHORT STORY

You Can't Do That

John P. Marquand

"You Can't Do That" takes the reader back to the days of the New England sailing ships in the early 19th-century when schooners and clipper ships sailed the seven seas to bring treasures to the ports of Salem and Boston. This story of how an American sailing family cemented a friendship with a powerful chief of an exotic island concerns Hawaii, now the fiftieth state of the Union.

SINCE THE YEAR 1806, a cloak of red-and-yellow feathers has hung in the hallway of the March house on the Ridge, with a helmet made from the same plumage suspended above it. These two articles have always held the same position on the wall, except for such times as they have been put away in camphor to protect them from the moths. The cloak was brought there by John March and indicates very accurately the first venture of the March ships in the fur-and-sandalwood trade with China. It was hung there by John March when he returned as supercargo[1] on the brig *Polly*, Moses March, owner, and Elihu Griggs,

1 **supercargo:** a person on a merchant ship who is in charge of the cargo and represents the shipowner in all transactions.

master. A single glance at that cloak in the shady, spacious hallway of that square Federalist house is startling to anyone who is even remotely familiar with the curiosities of the South Seas.

It hangs there, an alien object, and yet, through association, somehow strangely suitable to a house like the old March house in a New England seaport town. Granted that its presence there is known to many scholars, familiarity cannot avert a shock of surprise at a sight of that vivid garment, for it is one of the most beautiful objects ever conceived by the mind or executed by the hand of man. It is strange, too, to realize that if that cloak and the helmet above it were sold today, their price would probably equal the March profits in their precarious trade of another century. It is a long fine cloak—and the Marches have always been careful of everything they have laid their hands on—one of the best of the hundred and some odd feather garments which are known to be extant today, and there will never be another made. The o-o which supplied those yellow feathers, only one beneath each wing, a shy bird which once fluttered through the crimson-blossomed Ohia and the tree-fern forests of the Hawaiian mountains, is virtually extinct, and the bird that wore the red plumage is in hardly a better case. He is vanishing from the face of this earth like the genial race whose ancestors collected and attached those feathers to their delicate base of fiber netting in a manner so admired by Captain Cook. Granted that the labor which went into the making of that garment is beyond all accurate calculation, the result was worth it. The reds and yellows are nearly as vivid as when the coat was new. They glisten there in the hallway, jewel-like, with a depth of luster and lacy velvet texture that is more vital than inanimate. On an evening when the lights are lit, John March's cloak glows like flame and there is an element of awe in its splendor.

This is not odd, for it was intended to indicate greatness. The red lozenge pattern upon the yellow, marks it as belonging not alone to one of the *Alii*[2] but to a Hawaiian chief of a royal lineage that was very near to kingship. Its size and the amount of yellow is a sufficient indication of its former owner's greatness. If the shadow of a commoner were to touch the shadow of the man who wore it, that commoner would suffer death, for the man who wore it was sublimated in the complicated feudal ritual of his islands into a being more than human. The feather kahili[3] was carried behind him; an attendant bore his calabash[4] of koa wood to preserve his spittle, his nail parings and his fallen hair, so that they might not fall into the hands of enemies whose kahunas, or witch doctors, might use them in fatal incantations. When the man who wore that cloak walked abroad, the populace assumed a prone position on pain of death. Some trace of the majesty of its first owner's presence still seems to linger about that feather cloak, incongruously, in a New England town.

The cloak was owned by the chieftain Kualai, as his name is spelled, probably incorrectly, in the March letter books and the log of the brig *Polly*, since there were no missionaries then to bring order to the Hawaiian phonetics —no missionaries, no mosquitoes, no red ants to kill the kou trees, no colds, and no disease. Kualai ruled his share of the Kona coast on what is now known as the Big Island, under the protection of the great king Kamehameha in the days when John March was young. In Kualai's youth he had been one of the king's best warriors; in the war exercises he could evade six spears thrown at him simultaneously from varying directions; and he could trace his descent from one of the gods who had sailed with his attendants from the south.

Kualai gave his cloak and helmet to young John March when the *Polly* anchored in a bay on the Kona coast to exchange Yankee notions for sandalwood before proceeding to Canton. There is no doubt that John March valued the gift, for it is mentioned in his will. The clause reads:

Item, the Feather Cloak that was given me by my friend Kualai on my first voyage to the Sandwich Islands, and the feather hat that goes with it, I leave to my daughter, Polly March, and I ask her to guard it carefully.

John March sailed other seas before he died and brought back other curious things, but there is every reason why the cloak should have had a value to him which was more than intrinsic; and his descendants have never sold that cloak because of the reason why it was given him, a reason that is closely connected with honor and integrity. John March was a shrewd trader, but he was an honest man.

In the New England harbor town which was the home port for the March ships, a voyage around the world was not an unusual matter when John March was young. As long as John March could remember, his town had been a port of travelers, although a part of it was cast in the narrow mold of puritanical tradition. When John March was young, no music was allowed in the white church with the rooster on its spire where merchants

---

2 **alii** (ä lē′ē): Hawaiian word for royalty.
3 **kahili** (kä hē′lē): Hawaiian symbol of authority, a pole with a cluster of feathers at one end.
4 **calabash** (kăl′ə băsh′): basket, usually made from a gourd or dried fruit of the calabash tree.

and clerks and shipwrights and returned mariners listened for three hours each Sunday to discourses on original sin. Not even the note of a pipe was allowed, to indicate the pitch for the singing of the psalms, because such a concession was considered an encouragement to idolatrous worship. Yet in such surroundings of a Sunday one could see from the square box of the March pew a distinctly cosmopolitan congregation, for the world across the seas was closer to the town in those days than it has ever been since. Nearly every man and boy and most of the women in the pews and the Reverend Thomas himself, who thundered forth his nasal sermon while the sands ran from his hourglass on the pulpit, knew their geography as well as they knew the intricacies of their catechism. They could talk familiarly of the Baltic ports and of St. Eustatius and St. Kitts.[5] There were plenty who knew the ivory factories and the slave pens on the Grain Coast and the anchorages along Fernando Po.[6] There were plenty who had seen the sand upon the lead from soundings off Madagascar. The weather off Cape Horn was common talk. A restless, burning energy that made the town a lively place, except on Saturday nights and Sunday, had driven others to the factories at Canton. The townspeople were familiar with nearly every world port where money could be gained, for the town lived from shipping. One had to go, of necessity, a long way to make money then, what with European wars and privateers and orders in council and blockades. It was a time for gambling with lives and ships, a time of huge losses and huge gains, and no one could judge which until the ships came in.

It seemed hardly more than a piece of everyday business to John March when his father called him into the square parlor of the March house on the Ridge. It was an evening in April; a bright, fresh fire was burning in the parlor, and the candles were lighted on the mahogany table in the center of the room. Moses March and a man whom John March had never seen before were seated somewhat stiffly by the table with a punch bowl between them. When John March saw the punch, he knew that they were discussing important business, for his father, particularly in his later years, was abstemious with liquor. Moses March had not changed much since John March could remember him. His brown hair, done in a queue,[7] was heavily streaked with gray, and the shrewd lines around his eyes and mouth were deeper and more pronounced. There was an added stoop to his lanky shoulders, but his eyes were as bright as ever and his voice was vibrant, without any quaver of age.

"John," said Moses March, nodding at his guest, "this here is Captain Griggs from Boston. Captain Griggs, he's been sailing for the Perkinses in the fur trade."

In many ways it seemed to John March that Captain Griggs was a younger replica of his father. The captain had the same bony facial contours and the same slouch to his shoulders. When he spoke he had the same flat voice, but his eyes were different—more mobile and less steady. The captain raised a hand before his tight-lipped mouth and coughed, then he rose from his chair with a creaking of his joints, a

---

5 St. Eustatius (ū stā′shĭ əs) **and St. Kitts:** islands of the West Indies.
6 Fernando Po: island, Spanish Guiana.

7 queue (kū): a braid of hair worn hanging down behind.

tall, somber man who might have been a deacon in a church. His eyes met John's and looked away toward some invisible object on the floor, then darted back and looked away again.

"Pleased to meet you," he said. . . . "I compliment you, Mr. March; he's handy looking, that's a fact."

"He's kind of peaked," said Moses March, "but John here's almighty quick at figures."

There was a silence. Captain Griggs ladled himself a fresh tumbler of punch, drank it at a gulp and said, "He needs to be. It pays to be sharp, don't it, Mr. March?"

Moses March smiled in faint embarrassment. He had never been able to acquire a manner with his captains, nor to stop undue familiarity.

"Yes," he said, "I guess so. . . . John, Captain Griggs is taking out the *Polly.* You're sailing with him, supercargo."

John March looked at Captain Griggs again. The captain was staring intently at a lemon peel in the bottom of his glass. The news was entirely unexpected.

"Where to, Father?" he asked.

"Where you haven't been, son," said Moses March, "but you've heard the talk, I guess. Up along the northwest coast for sea otter, trading with the savages, then to these new islands you've heard Enoch Mayo talk about, to put aboard sandalwood, then the whole cargo sold at Canton for tea. The *Polly,* she's sailing the end of the month. You'll start in working over the cargo tomorrow. Your mother, she'll get your things packed."

John March nodded without speaking, and he showed no emotion. It was not the first time that his father had surprised him, because it was one of his father's maxims never to talk about

what he proposed to do until he was ready. His father was always reaching for something new; his mind was always working. Probably he had been pondering over the matter all winter, and now, as though he were speaking about arrangements for hauling firewood, he was making plans to send one of his vessels where a March ship had never gone before.

It was strange to think that while he sat there, a homely, uncouth man, his mind could reach around the world and back. His life had never seemed so plain or matter-of-fact. The order of the March house, each piece of furniture exactly in its place, had never seemed so perfect as when he spoke of that voyage. That literal order of the letter books and the columns in the ledger were all a part of the business. There was no expression of doubt, because they all knew by then that a ship could go wherever there was water.

Captain Griggs ladled himself another tumbler of punch and blew his nose on a long blue handkerchief which seemed to have imparted some of its own color to his nose. Not having been asked to sit down, John March stood examining his new captain, comparing him with other seafaring men whom he had met. The captain was evidently a heavy and competent drinker and no doubt a capable master, but behind his lantern jaws and his high narrow forehead there were hidden convolutions[8] of character beyond John March's grasp. He only knew that by the time the voyage ended he would know the captain like a book. At the present time, all John March could do was to stand staring at the pictures of his own imagination, striving to conjure up the sights which he and Captain Griggs would

8 convolutions: twists.

see. Captain Griggs was staring at him moodily across the brim of his glass.

"He'll do. He'll fill out," he said. "He'll be aft[9] with the mate and me, of course. Does he know navigation, sir?"

"Yes," said Moses March, "he ain't a fool, but I hadn't aimed to make him a sailor. He'll handle this business ashore when I get through."

Captain Griggs nodded in a melancholy way. "I hope he ain't squeamish," he said. "He'll see some rough sights, like as not. We have a saying on the coast 'You hang your conscience on the Horn.'"

"Yes," said Moses March, "I've heard it, but you, captain, I'd like for you to keep your conscience on your ship."

"God bless you, sir," Captain Griggs said quickly, "no owner's ever complained of me. I'm always in my owner's interest. It's just dealing with these here savages, I mean. They've killed

crews on the coast and they're murdering thieves on the islands." He rose stiffly. "You'll be satisfied, Mr. March. You'll be pleased as punch with me. There ain't no tricks in the trade that I don't know thereabouts. Four four-pounders and a bow chaser[10] will be enough, and the grapeshot and plenty of small arms, and thanking you, I'll pick my own mate, and now I'll be under way, and I'll wish you a very good evening, and you, mister"—he nodded to John March.

When the captain was gone, Moses March called to John March again.

"John," he said, "set down. You've been to the Baltic; you've been to the Indies, and I'd proposed keeping you ashore, but I want for you to learn this trade when it's still new." Moses March paused and rubbed his jaw. "I hear tell there's money in it, and we're going where there's money."

9 **aft:** near or in the stern of a vessel.

10 **chaser:** cannon.

"Yes, sir," said John March.

"It seems," his father continued, staring at the fire, "as how these savages put aboard furs, and these other savages put aboard sandalwood, for nothing more than notions and novelties in trading goods. Well, I got 'em for you; you and Griggs can get the rest. He'll try hard. He has his money and more than the usual prerequisites."

"Yes, sir," said John March.

"And sandalwood and furs are worth a mint of money in Canton."

"Yes, sir," said John March.

"You know about it, do you?"

"Yes, sir," said John March, "I've heard 'em talking."

His father smiled. "That's right," he said; "listen to 'em talk, but keep your own mouth shut. Have you anything to say?"

John March thought a moment. He had a number of things to say, but he kept them to himself. "No," he said, "I can obey orders, I guess. You know what you're doing, I guess, Father."

Moses March stroked his chin slowly, and then he asked a sudden question: "How did you like Griggs?"

"He looks too sharp to me," John March said, "but I guess we'll get along."

"Yes," said Moses March, "he's sharp, but maybe that's all right. But mind you watch him, John. I'm sharp, but I guess I'm honest. Mind you watch him."

Even when he was three thousand miles away from town and farther than that by water, something of the town was always with him. The *Polly* was a part of the town because she had been built in the yards by the river, a good tight brig of two hundred and fifty tons. The crew was a part of the town, because most of the men before the mast had been born within its limits. The

sense of the nearness of things he knew gave John March a certain peace when everything else was strange. The emptiness of the Pacific coast, the incredible size of its fir trees, the frowning menace of its mountains, would have oppressed him if it had not been for that sense of home. As it was, everyone stood together and behaved, in order to keep reputations intact when they got home.

John March was used to work. He was satisfactory to Captain Griggs and he was treated well, because he was the owner's son. Once they began bartering for furs off the northwest coast, there was no doubt that the captain knew his business, and John March admired in silence the way the captain worked. Martin Sprague, the mate, knew his business, too, in caring for the ship. The men were armed; there was a sharp lookout day and night. The fourpounders were loaded with grapeshot, and the matches were kept burning. Only a definite number of the painted dugout canoes of the Indians were allowed alongside and only a certain number of savages were permitted on deck to trade. There were very few ships off the coast that year, so that the selection of pelts was particularly fine. Sea-otter pelts came aboard in great quantity in exchange for powder, shot, nails, muskets, beads and blankets. It was a pretty sight to see the captain read faces and weigh the desire to sell. He seemed to have an intuitive sense of when to bargain and when to buy immediately.

"If there's any trade goods left after the islands," he said, "we'll stand back here again and use 'em up. It's a pity to see this fine fur wasting here. I wish we had six ships."

John March could feel the excitement as small goods turned suddenly into a valuable cargo. It was better than any figuring in the countinghouse to see the fur pelts come aboard and to estimate their probable value in a Chinese port.

"Yes, sir," said Captain Griggs, "it seems a pity to haul off and leave this. We ought to buy the villages out and to the devil with the islands and the wood."

They were in the cabin at the time, the captain and Sprague, the mate, a heavy muscular man, and John March, a thin, blond boy.

"Mr. Sprague," said the captain, "pass the rum. What do you think, mister? Shall we do all the trading here and simply water at the islands?"

Martin Sprague rubbed the palm of his left hand over the knuckles of his right. "I never seen trading so easy," he said. "Yes, sir, I think I should."

Then John March spoke up; it was the first time on the voyage that he'd made a positive statement. "We can't," he said.

Captain Griggs set down his glass and scowled. "Young man," he said, "I'm surprised at you. You ought to know better. You do know better. You've behaved yourself fine up till now, my boy. You've done your duty, and more, and I shall be pleased to report favorably to your father if you continue, but there's two things for you to get inside your head. The first is, you were sent here to learn to trade. You don't know this business, and don't you forget it. The second is, I'm captain, and this brig goes where I tell it to. I'm sorry to be obliged to tell you straight."

John March did not shift his position at the table. He knew that he was young and that he was green. He had interrupted solely from a conscientious sense inherited from his race. It had come over him that he was a representative of the March family and of the March cargo. Now that the eyes of the two older men were upon him, he found himself stammering, because he was shy in those days, but his hesitation only made him the more determined to speak out.

"Captain," he said, "I understand what you say. This is your ship, of course, but you are under owner's orders, just as I am. A portion of these trade goods was allotted for furs and the rest for sandalwood. The owner's orders are to stop and trade at the Sandwich Islands.[11] There may be more profit here, but we are to establish relations there. We may send out another ship."

Captain Griggs leaned half across the table. "Young man," he inquired, "are you insinuating I'm not looking after owner's interests? Because if you are, I will not tolerate it. I'm thinking of my owner all the time, and a sight better than you are, maybe. We'll make for the islands tomorrow, and there's an end to that, but if there's any trade goods left when we're through there, why, then, with your kind permission, we'll come back here. I hope that satisfies you."

"Yes," said John March, "it does, and I ask your pardon, captain."

Mr. Sprague rose. "I must be up with the watch," he said, "if you'll excuse me, sir. . . . Will you come with me, Mr. March?"

It was a fine night on deck, clear, with bright stars and a faint, quivering circle of the northern lights. The night was cool, without a breath of wind. The ship with her own small lights was like an insignificant fragment of a dis-

11 Sandwich Islands: The Hawaiian Islands, as they are known today, were called the Sandwich Islands by Captain Cook in honor of his patron, Lord Sandwich.

tant world anchored there in space. The mate took out his pipe and tinder box. There was a flash of spark as he expertly hit the flint against the steel, and then the tinder glowed.

"Johnny March," he said, "I've kind of got to like you. Now you listen to what I say. This kind of spark's all right, but not the kind that you were striking in the cabin. You leave the old man be. He's as good a master as there is, and he's honest with the owners, and that's all we have to care for. I've sailed with Griggs before. I don't need to tell you that a master's king aboard his ship, and you know it makes 'em queer. I've never seen a skipper yet who liked to be crossed. You better leave him be."

"Yes, sir," said John March.

"And listen, Johnny," the mate said, "the islands are a fine place. You'll like the islands. The islands are like heaven, pretty near. The captain will take you ashore, of course, to make the bargain. You'll see plenty of funny sights, but keep your mouth shut, Johnny, except to say 'yes, sir' to the captain. We've got a long way yet to go."

"Yes, sir," said John March.

"That's right," said Sprague, "that's right. I like a tight-lipped boy."

It was said in the forecastle of the *Polly*, just as it was said aft, that Johnny March was taciturn. As a supercargo he had no fixed duties in working the ship, and few knew much about him except that he was March's son. They only saw him as a thin, brown-faced, gray-eyed boy with yellow hair who made no trouble or complaint. They did not know the impression which strange sights made upon him, because he was studiously silent on that voyage to the islands, hardly ever venturing a remark, only answering courteously when addressed. No one on the *Polly*

knew—and perhaps it was just as well—that his thoughts were poetic, because there was no room for poetry on a Yankee trading brig.

The evening before they sighted land, he had a sense of the land's nearness. The banks of clouds off the port bow as the sun went down were pink and gold and were more like land clouds than sea clouds. The *Polly* was moving in the steady breath of the trades and the setting sun struck the bellying sails forward, making their colors soft and golden. The only sounds were the creaking of wood, the straining of ropes and the splash of waves on the bow. He had seen many evenings like that one, but subtly this was different. There was a mystery in the warmth of the air, an intangible unreality in the cloud banks. Captain Griggs came and stood beside him, smelling strongly of rum.

"Mr. Sprague," he said, "you've got everything locked up, I hope. To-morrow we'll be overrun by thieves and their women. Clew up[12] the courses and continue under topsails. Set a watch up in the crosstree, and keep an eye out for breakers. We must not get in too close tonight. . . . And, Mr. March——"

"Yes, sir," said John.

"You and I will go ashore."

"Yes, sir," said Johnny March, and then he cleared his throat: "How will we speak to them, sir?"

"You'll soon learn, boy," said Captain Griggs. "You've got a lot to learn. These islands have kings, or chiefs, and the chiefs will have someone who can speak trading English. The sandalwood is up in the mountains. It will be the property of the king, or chief. We will agree to purchase so many

12 **clew up:** haul or furl.

64

piculs[13] and he'll send his people to cut it. The chief will come aboard to see our goods, and we will make a bargain for the cargo, payable when the wood is safe aboard, you understand. There's no need to make our crew work when the chief will make his people load it. The islanders are handy men on ships. We'll go to see the chief, and we'll make the chief a present. Break out that clock that strikes the hour, and two cutlasses. That will be enough, and maybe"—Captain Griggs paused and hesitated—"three yards of bright print calico; he ought to like it—paper's all they dress in."

"Yes, sir," said Johnny March. "Did you say that they dressed in paper?"

The hard lines of the captain's face wrinkled into an indulgent smile.

"Young man," he said, "it's a fact they dress in paper, when they dress at all, which isn't often. The women, they pound it out of the bark of a tree. They have nothing else on the islands, or almost nothing. Will you come below for a glass of rum?"

"No, thank you, sir," said Johnny March. "I'll stay on deck—that is, if you don't mind."

The sun had dipped out of sight behind a bank of clouds, and then suddenly the light was gone. Without a prelude of dusk, the dark came over them like a warm black garment. It seemed only a second before, that the sky had been red and gold. Then, in another second, the sky was a void of darkness, filled with the trade wind and with stars. He stood for a while listening to the wind singing through the ropes, and then he went below. It was still dark when John March was awakened by a long-drawn-out call and

by Mr. Sprague's voice shouting, "Where away?" and he knew that they had come in sight of land. Once he was up on deck the topsails were slatting sleepily, and off the starboard bow there was a glow in the sky like fire.

"We've hit it to a second, sir," the mate was saying to Captain Griggs. "Yonder's the volcano; we're in the lee of the mountains."

Captain Griggs was a shadow in the starlight. It was too dark to see his face, but his voice was satisfied. "A pretty piece of navigating," he said, "if I do say so, mister. There'll be an inshore breeze by dawn and then we'll make the bay." He sniffed the air. "We can't be far from land," he said, "but there's no use heaving lead. It shelves off here as deep as hell. There'll be an inshore breeze with dawn."

"Is that a light yonder, sir?" asked Johnny March.

Near the horizon there was a twinkling, glimmering point.

"Your eyesight's good," the captain said. "Yes, that will be a fire. We're close to land."

The dawn came as suddenly as the dark, in a swift rush of light as though a hand had snatched away a veil, and John March saw the land. It was a solemn sight to see land which seemed to have risen out of nowhere. Off the bows of the *Polly* was a mountain, black and green, that rose in a gradual slope up into snow and clouds. The coast was dark from volcanic rock which made ugly black gashes between green forests. Close to the water's edge there was a fringe of palms and beeches between black lava headlands. The sea was smooth and calm, and streaked with violet; the air was as soft as the air of spring at home, and was subtly laden with the smells of land. All the colors were soft in a faint, early morning haze.

---

13 piculs (pĭk'ŭlz): Oriental unit of weight, about one hundred and thirty pounds.

The black rocks merged into reds and purples. The greens of the upland forest blended subtly from shades of silver to emerald, and Captain Griggs was right, a soft breeze was filling the sails, moving the *Polly* gently along the coast.

"That's where the sandalwood comes from," Mr. Sprague was saying, "up yonder in the mountains. The coast hereabouts is the favorite place of the kings. Do you see the stone walls and the yellow thatch of the houses of the villages? The chiefs own straight from the tops of the mountains to the sea. How do you like it, son?"

The question made John March tongue-tied. "I think it's very handsome, sir," he said, "a very pleasant island."

The *Polly* was moving under topsails into a small bay. It opened out before them, a smooth amphitheater of water, surrounded by high cliffs. "Yonder's where the kings are buried," the mate said; "they scrape the flesh off their bones and tie them up in paper cloth and put them there in caves with their canoes."

At the head of the bay, John March could see a beach fringed with tall palm trees, the leaves of which moved idly in the breeze, and he could see the thatch of houses beneath them. There was a dark crowd of people on the beach, pushing canoes into the water, log dugouts, balanced by an outrigger and manned by naked paddlers. Captain Griggs was wearing clean linen and a black broadcloth coat, although the day was hot.

"Mister," he said, "we'll anchor. Let go falls[14] and clew up lower topsails and order the stern boat cleared."

By the time the anchor struck the water, the *Polly* was surrounded by

14 falls: tackle used to lower a ship's boat.

canoes and the water was full of swimmers who were pulling themselves up the anchor chain, smiling and laughing; men and women as beautiful as statues, their straight dark hair glistening with the water. Captain Griggs stared at his visitors sourly from the quarter-deck.

"They've got the minds of children," he said; "the chief's man should be here."

As Captain Griggs finished speaking, a native pushed his way through the crowd at the waist and walked aft; evidently a man of importance, because the crowd gave way respectfully. He wore a pair of sailor's cast-off trousers, and his skin was lighter than the others'. His voice rose above the babel of strange words in English.

"Mr. Captain," he called out, "I am Kualai's man."

"Who's he?" asked Captain Griggs. "The chief?"

The other nodded, bobbing his head up and down, still smiling. "Yes," he said, "yes, yes. And he sends me because I speak English good. I've been a sailor on a Boston boat. I speak English very good. Kualai sends me to say *aloha*. He is glad to see you. He asks you will you trade for wood?"

"Yes," said Captain Griggs, "we're here for wood. What's your name?"

"Moku," said the native. "Billy Adams Moku. Kualai ask what name."

The captain nodded condescendingly. "Captain Griggs," he said, "brig *Polly*. Moses March, owner. We're carrying very fine calicoes, ironware, tinware, lead and copper, and even a few muskets. Has your chief got wood?"

Moku nodded. "The wood is coming down. Kualai he will see you." He pointed to a laden canoe. "Kualai sends you food."

Captain Griggs looked at the canoe carefully as it drew alongside. "Very

SHORT STORY

good," he said. "When will he see me?"

"Now," said Moku. "He waits on the shore."

"Mister," the captain called, "have the stern boat lowered. Mr. March and I will go ashore, and, Mr. March, give that man a pocketknife, and bring along the presents."

The dark sand of the beach at the head of the bay seemed insecure under John March's feet, since he had been so long on the water. In the sunshine like a warm June day at home, every sight and sound was new. The crowd of natives standing on the beach drew back from them shyly and smiled, but their tongues kept chattering busily; commenting, probably, on the way these strangers looked. The chief's man walked first, then Captain Griggs, non-chalant and cool, and then John March behind him. They walked along a path beneath a grove of coconut palms and beneath large broad-leafed trees such as he had never seen. They were threading their way through a settlement of houses made of dried grass, past small gardens enclosed between walls of black volcanic rock. His memory of that day always brought back living green against dark rock, and dark smiling faces and red hibiscus flowers. In his memory of the place a soft breeze was always blowing and there was always a strange dry rattle from the leaves of the coconut palms. There was a group of larger houses not far back from the beach which evidently belonged to a man of importance. Natives were busying themselves about a fire in a pit, women and children were staring from open doorways. There was an open pavilion near the center of this group of buildings and the chief's man led them toward it. Seated in a Cantonese armchair under the pavilion was one of the largest men that John March

had ever seen. He was middle-aged, and so corpulent that the chair seemed to creak beneath his weight. A single look at his face was enough to indicate that he was the ruler, Kualai, of whom the man had spoken. The face was set in benign lines that could only have come upon it through suave and complete authority. It was all that was necessary to indicate his rank, but he also had the exterior show of office. He was wearing a yellow-and-red cloak of feathers, dazzlingly bright, which fell below his waist, and an attendant stood behind him holding a large stick which bore a tuft of colored feathers on the end. Moku stopped dead still at the entrance of the pavilion, and the great man rose from his chair and stepped slowly forward, gracefully, in spite of his heavy paunch. It was plain that he had seen other white men and knew something of their manners, because he smiled graciously and held out his right hand. At the same time he spoke melodiously in a language that was all vowels, so that his words sounded like rippling water.

"What's he saying?" asked Captain Griggs.

"Kualai," Moku translated, "he say he's, oh, very glad to see you."

"Well, I guess we're glad to see him too," said Captain Griggs as he shook hands. Then John March saw that Kualai was looking at him.

"He wants to know," said Moku, "who is the other man?"

"Tell him he's the son of the man who owns the vessel," said Captain Griggs.

"He wants to know," said Moku, "is he a chief's son?"

"Tell him yes," said Captain Griggs.

"He would like," said Moku, "to feel his hair. He would like to know if it is real."

"Take off your hat," said Captain

Griggs, "and let him feel your hair. Don't be afraid of him. He won't hurt you."

"All right," said Johnny March. He felt very much like a child as he walked toward Kualai, for the man, now that he was standing, must have been close to seven feet in height. His skin was glistening with coconut oil. He was stretching out his arm. He touched Johnny March's hair gently and then he pulled it softly. Johnny March looked up at him and smiled, and Kualai smiled back.

"Break out the presents," said Captain Griggs, "bow to him and put 'em on the ground."

Kualai's face lighted up at the sight of the clock when John March held it toward him. It was evident that he had never seen such a mechanism—a battered ship's chronometer whose useful days were over. He touched it gingerly and imitated its sound.

"Tick-tick," he said, and John March nodded and repeated after him, "Tick-tick." That interchange of words always seemed to him ridiculous, but somehow there was an exchange of thought with the words which made them friends.

"He asks you to stay and eat," said Moku. "He will come on the ship tomorrow and see the goods, and he asks the young man to stay with him until the trade is over, to sleep inside his house."

Captain Griggs muttered something beneath his breath, and then he said, "March, you'd better stay."

"Yes, sir," said John March, "I'd be very glad to stay." He turned to Moku. "Tell him I'll be glad."

Then Moku spoke again: "Kualai says he will trade with the young man."

"All right," said Captain Griggs, "as long as I'm there too. And tell him"— Captain Griggs' eyes shifted toward the bay and back—"you tell him I want the wood measured on the beach and put aboard by his people. Tell him my men are tired." And then he drew a bottle of rum from his pocket and added plaintively: "Ain't we had enough of this? Let's everybody have a drink, and bring on the dancing girls."

Some half-perceptible change in Captain Griggs' voice made John March turn to watch him. The captain's face was bleak and impassive, but his eyes were shifting from point to point, from the chief to John March, then away to the matting on the ground, then to the houses of the settlement. John March knew him well enough by then to know that the captain was turning over in his mind some thought which he wished entirely to conceal.

"Ah," he said suddenly, "here comes some wood"—and he nodded toward a path which led upward to the mountains.

A dozen men and women were staggering down the path in single file, each bearing a burden of long sticks, and John March knew from hearsay that these were the chief's people, who had been sent to the upland forests where the sandalwood grew. The chief called out an order, which Moku ran to obey, and a few moments later a pile of the sandalwood lay on the matting before his chair, a heap of sticks which varied in size from a few inches to a foot in diameter. The bark had been stripped off, leaving a heavy wood of deep yellow which verged on orange. Captain Griggs ripped out his clasp knife, whittled at the sticks and sniffed the shavings.

"It ain't bad," he said; "in fact, it's prime."

He was right that the wood was fine, since sandalwood was plentiful in the islands then, when the trade was new,

and John March did not suspect that he would live to see the time when hardly a stick would be left standing on the entire island group. Captain Griggs stood there, staring at the pile of wood, apparently lost in thought.

"Tell him we'll pay him well for it," he said, and his voice was soft and almost kindly, "once he lands it on the deck."

But all the while John March was sure that Captain Griggs was concealing some other thought.

It took nearly two weeks to collect the wood and measure it, a space of time which moved in a peculiar series of days and nights, but it was strange to John March how soon the life there grew familiar. Though he could hardly understand a word which was spoken, though nearly every sight and sound in those two weeks was new, he became aware immediately of certain human values. Kualai in his way was a cultivated man of gentle breeding, who had developed his own taste for the arts, and qualities of understanding which were the same on that isolated island as they were elsewhere. He would sit for hours of an evening watching interpretive dances and listening to his minstrels sing of the exploits of his ancestors. He had a good eye for patterns in the tapa cloth, and a nice skill in various games of chance, which he played daily with his choice companions, but, above all, he had a sense of hospitality. He lost no occasion to make John March feel politely that he was a welcome guest. He took him fishing in his war canoe; he took him to the caves and the lava rocks; he took him to watch the young men perform feats of strength; he was even careful that John March's privacy should not be disturbed unduly. When he came aboard the *Polly*, he kept John March beside him. He was greatly pleased with the calico and nails and lead and copper in the trading cargo, but he went through the intricacies of the bargain in a detached way, like a gentleman. In those days trading was easy on the islands, before the chiefs were glutted with material possessions.

"He say he want you to be happy," Moku said, the last time Kualai came aboard; "he wants you to come again."

"Tell him we're happy," said Captain Griggs. "He understands when all the wood's aboard that we'll give out the goods."

Moku nodded. "He understands," he said; "he knows you're good men."

Captain Griggs coughed slightly. "I shall want Mr. March back with me," he said, "tomorrow morning. . . . Mr. March, you come here; I want to speak with you in the cabin."

It occurred to John March, when they were in the cabin, that it was the first time since they had been on the islands that he and Captain Griggs had been alone. Captain Griggs rubbed his long hands together and poured himself a glass of rum.

"Young man," he said, "you've done fine. You've kept that old heathen happy, and that's all we needed—to keep him happy—and now we're all finished shipshape. We'll get the wood stowed tonight"—Captain Griggs smiled happily —"and tomorrow they can come and take off their goods, but I want you aboard first, understand?"

"Yes, sir," said John March, "but there's one thing I don't see. I don't see why you haven't put the goods ashore before this, sir."

Captain Griggs poured himself a second tumbler of rum.

"Young man," he said, "when you take a few more voyages you'll under-

stand you can't trust natives. How do you know we'd get the wood if we put the goods ashore?"

"Because Kualai's honest," John March said.

Captain Griggs looked thoughtfully at the ceiling. "Maybe," he said, "and maybe not. Anyways, we've got the wood. You come aboard tomorrow." And Captain Griggs smiled genially, but even when he smiled, John March had a suspicion that something had been left unsaid, that there was some thought in the captain's mind of which he had not spoken.

Mr. Sprague came up to get him the next morning, carrying a bundle of small presents and perspiring in the heat of the early sun.

"Say good-by to the chief," he said. "The captain's orders are to leave right now. You're to stay aboard until we sail. The quarter boat's waiting at the beach."

John March was sorry, now that it was time to go. He walked to Kualai and held out his hand. "Thank you very much," he said, and the interpreter, Moku, gave him back the chief's answer:

"He say for you to come back soon."

The canoes were gathering about the *Polly* already, by the time he reached the beach. He and Mr. Sprague sat in the stern sheets of the quarter boat while two men rowed, helped by a light breeze offshore.

It was only when they were halfway out that John March was aware of something disturbing.

"Look," he said; "they're setting the lower topsails!"

"Yes," said Mr. Sprague shortly, "so they are. We've got a fair breeze, haven't we?"

"But it'll take a good six hours to put off those goods," said Johnny March.

Mr. Sprague put a heavy hand on his knee and smiled. "Don't you worry, boy," he said. "Captain Griggs will see about those goods."

They were beside the companion ladder by that time, and even John March was puzzled, but nothing more. He was not aware of Captain Griggs' idea until he was on the poop, then he saw that the tarpaulins were off the guns and that men were beside them with matches, and then he saw that the decks were clear and that the sandalwood and the trade goods were all back in the hold. Captain Griggs grinned at him.

"Safe and sound," he said. "You've done very well, Mr. March; your father will be very pleased, I think. . . . Mister, you can man the capstan now."

John March found himself stammering: "But what about the goods, captain? We haven't put the goods ashore."

"No, boy," said Captain Griggs, "we ain't, and we ain't going to. What's the use when we've got the wood aboard? Those goods are going to go for skins."

Even then John March did not entirely understand him. "But you can't do that," he said; "we owe the chief the goods."

"Listen, boy," said Captain Griggs; "this ain't like home. There're plenty of other chiefs, and plenty of other islands. Let 'em come and get the goods, and I'll blow 'em out of water. There ain't no law out here. Now you be quiet, boy."

For a moment John March found it impossible to speak. Now that the whole matter was completely clear, he knew that he should have suspected long ago what must have been in the back of the captain's mind. Captain Griggs proposed sheer robbery, but he would not have called it that. He would have called it a clever piece of business in a place where there was no law.

"You see," Captain Griggs was saying, "it isn't as though they were like us, Mr. March. More fools they, that's all."

Then John March found his voice. "Captain," he said, "this is a March ship. You don't leave until you've set those goods on shore. We don't do things that way, captain. You can't——"

Captain Griggs turned toward him quickly.

"That'll be enough from you," he said. "Who says I can't? I'm trying to make a profit on this voyage. I can, and I will, and I'm taking full responsibility. If you don't like it, get below."

John March's tongue felt dry and parched as he tried to speak. Even in that short while a hundred things were happening. The fore-and-aft staysails and the lower topsails were set by then, and the call came from forward, "Hawser short!" A glance toward the beach was enough to show him that the islanders were aware of the captain's trick. Men were running toward the water. He could hear the beating of a drum. Men in canoes were gesticulating and shouting. Men with spears and clubs and slings were hurrying to the beach.

"Break out anchor, mister," shouted Captain Griggs, "and stand by them guns! Forward there, pass out the small arms! By God, we'll show 'em!"

"Captain," said John March suddenly. He knew there was only one thing to do as he spoke. "If you go, you'll leave me here. I'm going back ashore."

Captain Griggs looked at him and laughed. "They'll kill you back ashore," he said. "Look at 'em on the beach."

John March spoke with difficulty. "You and I are different sorts of men," he said. "You can either set those goods ashore, or I'm going."

"May I inquire," said Captain Griggs, "how you're going to go? Keep your mouth shut, boy!"

In the haste of getting under way, the quarter boat was still drifting alongside, and the captain must have perceived John March's intention from his glance.

He made a lunge at John March, but John March broke away, and then he went on the bulwarks.

"Get ahold of that damned fool!" shouted Captain Griggs. "Lay ahold of him!"

Two of the crew ran toward him and he jumped crashing into the quarter boat. "Get in there after him!" Captain Griggs was shouting. "Don't let him go!"

And then John March cut the painter[15] and the quarter boat was drifting from the side.

"You damned fool!" shouted Captain Griggs. "You hear my orders! Come back here or they'll kill you, March!"

15 painter: rope.

Once the boat was drifting from the side, John March was amazed at himself. His anger and his lack of fear amazed him. He was standing amidships in the quarter boat, shouting back at Captain Griggs.

"I'd rather be killed ashore," he shouted, "than stay aboard with you!" Then he picked up the oars and began to row ashore, slowly, because the boat was heavy for a single man to handle.

"You hear me?" Captain Griggs was shouting. "Stay there and be damned to you!"

John March saw that the anchor was aweigh and the *Polly* was standing slowly out to the open sea. His back was to the beach as he pulled toward it, but he heard the shouting and the beating of the drums. It must have been his anger at Captain Griggs that did not make him afraid, or an assurance within himself that he was right and Captain Griggs was wrong. A glance astern of the quarter boat as he strained at the oars showed him the *Polly* standing out to sea, but he did not look over his shoulder toward the beach. He did not look until the bottom of the quarter boat grated on the sand, then he shipped his oars carefully and stepped ashore. He found himself surrounded by shouting men who waved their spears and their fists in his face, but somehow they were not so real to him as the reality which lay inside himself. He only realized later that a single gesture of fear might have meant his death, but then he was so involved in his own preoccupation and with the single desire which was in him that he walked calmly enough across the beach toward the palm trees and the thatched houses; the crowd in front of him gave way as he walked, and then followed on his heels. He was taking the path to Kualai's house, and the shouting around him died away as he drew near it.

Then he saw Kualai walking toward him in the feather cloak which he had worn the first day they had met, carrying a light throwing spear in his right hand. Kualai was shouting something to him—obviously, a question which he could not understand—and Moku was standing near him.

"Tell Kualai," John March said, "that I come from honest people. Tell him that I have come here to stay until he is paid for his wood." He saw Kualai listening intently to his answer, and then Kualai raised his right arm and drove his spear into the earth.

"He says you are his son," Moku said. "He asks you: Will you please to shake his hand?"

The reaction from what he had done came over him when Kualai grasped his hand. He knew the harsh and accurate consequences of his action then, as the smells and sounds of that Polynesian village came over him like a wave. Captain Griggs had left him, and every vestige of home was gone. He was a stranger among savages, and he might be there forever, for anything he knew, yet even then he knew that he had done the only proper thing. Suddenly he found that he was homesick, because the chief was kind.

"Ask him if I can be alone," he said. "Tell him I want to be alone."

He was given a house of his own that night, next to where the chief slept. He was given a pile of woven mats for his bed and a piece of tapa cloth to cover him. He was given baked pig and sweet potatoes and the gray paste made from the taro root, called poi, for his evening meal, and mullet from Kualai's fish pond. He was as comfortable as he could have hoped to be that night. For a moment when he was awakened early the next morning, he thought he was at home, until he saw the rafters and the thatch above him. Moku was standing near him in his ragged sailor breeches and Kualai himself was bending his head, just entering the door.

"Wake up!" Moku was saying. "The ship is back!"

John March sat up on his bed of mats and rubbed his arm across his face. Although he spoke to Moku, his eyes were on Kualai.

"The ship?" he asked. "What ship?"

"Your ship," said Moku. "She come back, and now the captain, he unloads the goods."

John March stood up. He had no great capacity for showing emotion.

"Ask Kualai if he is satisfied," he said.

Moku nodded. "He says 'yes, very much,'" he said, and Kualai nodded back. "He asks for you to stay a long time—always."

"Thank him, please," said John March, "but tell him, it's my ship. Tell him I must go to see that the goods are right."

"Kualai," Moku answered, "says he will go with you to the beach."

Mr. Sprague had landed in the longboat by the time they had reached the shore, and the beach was already covered with bolts of calico and small goods and ironware and lead and copper. Mr. Sprague nodded to John March formally, as though nothing had happened. "The captain sends his compliments," he said, "and asks you to come aboard, so that he can resume the voyage." And then Sprague grinned, and added, "It's lucky for you, John March, that you're the owner's son."

John March looked at the goods upon the shore. "You can thank the captain from me for coming back," he answered. "You can tell him that I hope we both can forget what has happened, but the complete consignment is not landed yet. I'll stay here until the list is checked."

"You're an accurate man," said Sprague.

John March nodded. "I've been taught to be," he said, and he stayed there on the beach until every item was verified. Then he turned to Kualai and his interpreter.

"Tell the chief," he said, "that I believe that everything is right. Ask his pardon for the delay, but tell him our house will make any mistakes correct. Thank him, and tell him that I am going."

Moku spoke quickly in the musical language of the islands while Kualai stood, looking first at John March, and then at the ship that brought him. After Kualai had listened, he stood silently for a moment. Then he smiled and spoke swiftly. He raised a hand and took off his feather helmet, and one of his men very carefully removed his feather cloak from his shoulders.

"He says there will always be wood for you," said Moku; "he asks you to take his coat."

Understanding the Story

1. What does the author's long and detailed introduction of the cloak accomplish? What are several ways in which he makes you realize the importance of the cloak?

2. What is John's job as supercargo? What is his position in relation to Captain Griggs?

3. What did Captain Griggs imply when he said, "We have a saying on the coast: 'You hang your conscience on the Horn'"? Interpret the answer of John's father: "I've heard it, but you, captain, I'd like for you to keep your conscience on the ship."

4. How does Marquand suggest the character of Captain Griggs during the interview with the Marches?

5. What was the reason for John's first disagreement with the captain?

6. Can you find characteristics that John and Kualai have in common in spite of their differences in race, language, and age?

SHORT STORY

7. Why did it take courage in spite of being the owner's son for John to defy the captain and return to the island?
8. What does the cloak symbolize to the natives?
9. Why does Kualai give John the cloak? What does it symbolize to John?

Building Vocabulary Skills

What do the following sentences tell you about the person being described? Consult the dictionary if the meaning of the italicized word is not clear.
1. "He's kind of *peaked*. . . ."
2. ". . . behind his lantern jaws and his high, narrow forehead there were hidden *convolutions* of character. . . ."
3. ". . . Johnny March was *taciturn*."
4. "The face was set in *benign* lines. . . ."

Developing Language Skills

1. Write a short essay showing specific ways in which the author prepared the reader for John's decision to return to the island when he learned that the natives had not been paid.
2. If your family has some possession that stands for something very special, write a short piece describing the object and giving its background.

Reading "The Third Level"

A *fantasy* is just like any other story except that it couldn't possibly have happened. However, once the reader agrees to accept this make-believe world, he should expect and insist that everything else in the story be realistic, consistent, and believable. A phrase in a poem by Marianne Moore summarizes this necessity: "imaginary gardens with real toads in them."

Contrast is an important part of this fantasy—contrast, not of characters this time, but of one world with another kind of world. Indeed, in most fantasies that are more than adventure stories, the point lies in the contrast between the real world we know and the fantastic, imaginary world invented by the author. As you read "The Third Level," ask yourself (1) what the difference is between the two worlds presented, and (2) why the characters react to each as they do.

Probably what will make this story most memorable for you is its *surprise ending*. Every detail that precedes the ending is preparation for it. The same thing is true in "A Favor for Lefty." In both stories the authors seem to have worked backward in building honest foundations for their surprise endings, which are integral parts of both stories.

JOHN P. MARQUAND

75

The Third Level

Jack Finney

If you have ever found your way through the two levels of Grand Central Station in New York City, you will have a special feeling for Charley who one day finds himself on a third *level, one that is gas-lit and manned by ticket sellers with green eyeshades and sideburns. If you have yet to visit this famous station, remembering this story will give your first trip special zest.*

THE PRESIDENTS of the New York Central and the New York, New Haven and Hartford railroads will swear on a stack of timetables that there are only two. But I say there are three, because I've *been* on the third level at Grand Central Station. Yes, I've taken the obvious step: I talked to a psychiatrist friend of mine, among others. I told him about the third level at Grand Central Station, and he said it was a waking-dream wish fulfillment. He said I was unhappy. That made my wife kind of mad, but he explained that he meant the modern world is full of insecurity, fear, war, worry and all the rest of it, and that I just want to escape. Well, who doesn't? Everybody I know wants to escape, but they don't wander down into any third level at Grand Central Station.

But that's the reason, he said, and my friends all agreed. Everything points to it, they claimed. My stamp collecting, for example; that's a "temporary refuge from reality." Well, maybe, but my grandfather didn't need any refuge from reality; things were pretty nice and peaceful in his day, from all I hear, and he started my collection. It's a nice collection, too, blocks of four of practically every U.S. issue, first-day covers, and so on. President Roosevelt collected stamps, too, you know.

Anyway, here's what happened at Grand Central. One night last summer I worked late at the office. I was in a hurry to get uptown to my apartment so I decided to take the subway from Grand Central because it's faster than the bus.

Now, I don't know why this should have happened to me. I'm just an ordinary guy named Charley, thirty-one years old, and I was wearing a tan gabardine suit and a straw hat with a fancy band; I passed a dozen men who looked just like me. And I wasn't trying to escape from anything; I just wanted to get home to Louisa, my wife.

I turned into Grand Central from Vanderbilt Avenue, and went down the steps to the first level, where you take trains like the Twentieth Century. Then I walked down another flight to the second level, where the suburban trains leave from, ducked into an arched doorway heading for the subway—and got lost. That's easy to do. I've been in and out of Grand Central hundreds of times, but I'm always bumping into new doorways and stairs and corridors. Once I got into a tunnel about a mile long and came out in the lobby of the Roosevelt Hotel. Another time I came up in an office building on Forty-sixth Street, three blocks away.

Sometimes I think Grand Central is

growing like a tree, pushing out new corridors and staircases like roots. There's probably a long tunnel that nobody knows about feeling its way under the city right now, on its way to Times Square, and maybe another to Central Park. And maybe—because for so many people through the years Grand Central *has* been an exit, a way of escape—maybe that's how the tunnel I got into . . . But I never told my psychiatrist friend about that idea.

The corridor I was in began angling left and slanting downward and I thought that was wrong, but I kept on walking. All I could hear was the empty sound of my own footsteps and I didn't pass a soul. Then I heard that sort of hollow roar ahead that means open space and people talking. The tunnel turned sharp left; I went down a short flight of stairs and came out on the third level at Grand Central Station. For just a moment I thought I was back on the second level, but I saw the room was smaller, there were fewer ticket windows and train gates, and the information booth in the center was wood and old-looking. And the man in the booth wore a green eyeshade and long black sleeve protectors. The lights were dim and sort of flickering. Then I saw why; they were open-flame gaslights.

There were brass spittoons on the floor, and across the station a glint of light caught my eye; a man was pulling a gold watch from his vest pocket. He snapped open the cover, glanced at his watch, and frowned. He wore a derby hat, a black four-button suit with tiny lapels, and he had a big, black, handlebar mustache. Then I looked around and saw that everyone in the station was dressed like eighteen-ninety-something; I never saw so many beards, sideburns and fancy mustaches in my life.

A woman walked in through the train gate; she wore a dress with leg-of-mutton sleeves and skirts to the top of her high-buttoned shoes. Back of her, out on the tracks, I caught a glimpse of a locomotive, a very small Currier & Ives[1] locomotive with a funnel-shaped stack. And then I knew.

To make sure, I walked over to a newsboy and glanced at the stack of papers at his feet. It was *The World;* and *The World* hasn't been published for years. The lead story said something about President Cleveland. I've found that front page since, in the Public Library files, and it was printed June 11, 1894.

I turned toward the ticket windows knowing that here—on the third level at Grand Central—I could buy tickets that would take Louisa and me anywhere in the United States we wanted to go. In the year 1894. And I wanted two tickets to Galesburg, Illinois.

Have you ever been there? It's a wonderful town still, with big old frame houses, huge lawns, and tremendous trees whose branches meet overhead and roof the streets. And in 1894, summer evenings were twice as long, and people sat out on their lawns, the men smoking cigars and talking quietly, the women waving palm-leaf fans, with the fireflies all around, in a peaceful world. To be back there with the first World War still twenty years off, and World War II over forty years in the future . . . I wanted two tickets for that.

The clerk figured the fare—he glanced at my fancy hatband, but he figured the fare—and I had enough for two coach tickets, one way. But when I counted out the money and looked up, the clerk was staring at me. He nodded at the

---

1 **Currier-Ives:** 19th-century lithographers specializing in American history and manners.

bills. "That ain't money, mister," he said, "and if you're trying to skin[2] me you won't get very far," and he glanced at the cash drawer beside him. Of course the money was old-style bills, half again as big as the money we use nowadays, and different-looking. I turned away and got out fast. There's nothing nice about jail, even in 1894.

And that was that. I left the same way I came, I suppose. Next day, during lunch hour, I drew three hundred dollars out of the bank, nearly all we had, and bought old-style currency (that *really* worried my psychiatrist friend). You can buy old money at almost any coin dealer's, but you have to pay a premium. My three hundred dollars bought less than two hundred in old-style bills, but I didn't care; eggs were thirteen cents a dozen in 1894.

But I've never again found the corridor that leads to the third level at Grand Central Station, although I've tried often enough.

Louisa was pretty worried when I told her all this, and didn't want me to look for the third level any more, and after a while I stopped; I went back to my stamps. But now we're *both* looking, every week end, because now we have proof that the third level is still there. My friend Sam Weiner disappeared! Nobody knew where, but I sort of suspected because Sam's a city boy, and I used to tell him about Galesburg—I went to school there—and he always said he liked the sound of the place. And that's where he is, all right. In 1894.

Because one night, fussing with my stamp collection, I found—Well, do you know what a first-day cover is? When a new stamp is issued, stamp collectors buy some and use them to mail

2 **skin:** cheat.

envelopes to themselves on the very first day of sale; and the postmark proves the date. The envelope is called a first-day cover. They're never opened; you just put blank paper in the envelope.

That night, among my oldest first-day covers, I found one that shouldn't have been there. But there it was. It was there because someone had mailed it to my grandfather at his home in Galesburg; that's what the address on the envelope said. And it had been there since July 18, 1894—the postmark showed that—yet I didn't remember it at all. The stamp was a six-cent, dull brown, with a picture of President Garfield. Naturally, when the envelope came to Granddad in the mail, it went right into his collection and stayed there —till I took it out and opened it.

The paper inside wasn't blank. It read:

> 941 Willard Street
> Galesburg, Illinois
> July 18, 1894

Charley:

I got to wishing that you were right. Then I got to believing you were right. And, Charley, it's true; I found the third level! I've been here two weeks, and right now, down the street at the Dalys', someone is playing a piano, and they're all out on the front porch singing "Seeing Nelly Home." And I'm invited over for lemonade. Come on back, Charley and Louisa. Keep looking till you find the third level! It's worth it, believe me!

The note is signed *Sam.*

At the stamp and coin store I go to, I found out that Sam bought eight hundred dollars' worth of old-style currency. That ought to set him up in a nice little hay, feed and grain business; he always said that's what he really wished he could do, and he certainly can't go back to his old business. Not in Galesburg, Illinois, in 1894. His old business? Why, Sam was my psychiatrist.

Understanding the Story

1. How does Charley's psychiatrist interpret Charley's story of being on a nonexistent third level at Grand Central Station?
2. How does Charley's answer make him appear as a solid citizen not given to visiting imaginary places?
3. Explain why Charley doesn't tell his psychiatrist about thinking that Grand Central grows like a tree and offers people different kinds of exits.
4. Find several details in Charley's description of the third level that are especially effective in catching the flavor of the 1890's.
5. Why does Charley decide to buy tickets for Galesburg, Illinois?
6. How does the stamp collection help to give the story unity?
7. How does this first-person story differ in the way it is told from Dorothy Parker's "The Waltz"?

JACK FINNEY

Building Vocabulary Skills

How do the following words or phrases help to make the third level of Grand Central Station seem real? Explain each term.

brass spittoons
a black four-button suit with tiny lapels
handle-bar mustache
sideburns
leg-of-mutton sleeves
Currier & Ives locomotive with a funnel-shaped stack

Developing Language Skills

1. Reread Charley's description of entering Grand Central Station. Write a paragraph describing with specific details a public building you have seen. Try to imitate Charley's conversational tone.
2. Imagine that, like Sam the psychiatrist, you have escaped to your own ideal world. In a brief composition told from the first person point of view, describe your arrival in this place. Tell enough about its appearance, the people in it, and their way of life so that your idea of the perfect place is made clear.

Reading "The Necklace"

De Maupassant quickly relates in a few opening paragraphs the essential nature of his main character and the kind of life she lives. As you read the rest of this brief story, note how everything that follows —Mme. Loisel's reactions to a social invitation, her handling of her husband, her borrowing jewelry—depends on this first understanding of her character.

De Maupassant faced the problem of covering many years time in "The Necklace." The *pace* of the story—the speed at which it moves— thus varies greatly at different points. De Maupassant skillfully combines summary (the fastest way of telling a story) with conversation (one of the slowest, although most effective, ways of developing character and action).

These variations in pace are climaxed by the sudden *surprise ending,* an unexpected turn at the end of a story. In the case of inferior stories, such an ending is frequently a kind of trick. No logical connection exists between the kind of characters or earlier events in the story and the unexpected twist at the end. Thus, although the end may amuse or startle the reader on a first reading, it has no particular significance. In a good story, a surprise ending has both dramatic effectiveness and significance in relation to what precedes it. Looking back over "The Necklace" in the light of the ending, decide whether the conclusion illuminates the meaning of Mme. Loisel's life or whether it is simply an ironic twist unrelated to the rest of the story.

The Necklace

Guy de Maupassant

De Maupassant's ability to tell a complex story in a clear, uncluttered fashion is illustrated in "The Necklace." In a few precise paragraphs he draws a picture of a selfish, vain woman and then proceeds to present impersonally the disaster that overtakes her and her husband. The connection between Mme. Loisel's character and the events of her life makes a meaningful point for everyone.

SHE WAS ONE of those pretty and charming girls who are sometimes, as if by a mistake of destiny, born in a family of clerks. She had no dowry, no expectations, no means of being known, understood, loved and married by a rich and distinguished man; and she let herself be married to a junior clerk at the Ministry of Public Instruction.

She dressed plainly because she could not afford to dress otherwise, but she was as unhappy as though she had really fallen from her proper station; since with women there is neither caste nor rank, their beauty, grace, and charm serve for family and birth. Natural fineness, instinct for what is elegant, and suppleness of wit are the only aristocracy, and make women of the people the equals of the greatest ladies.

She suffered ceaselessly, feeling herself born for all the delicacies and all the luxuries. She suffered from the poverty of her apartment, the shabby look of the walls, the worn-out chairs, the ugly curtains. All these things, which another woman of her rank would never have noticed, tortured her and made her angry. The sight of the little Breton peasant who did her humble housework aroused in her sad regrets and desperate thoughts.

She dreamed of silent antechambers hung with Oriental tapestry, lit by tall bronze candelabra, and of two great footmen in knee breeches who sleep in big armchairs, made drowsy by the heavy warmth of the stove. She thought of the drawing rooms fitted up with ancient silk, of the delicate cabinets holding priceless curiosities, and of dainty perfumed drawing rooms made for talks at five o'clock with intimate friends, with men famous and sought after, whom all women envy and whose attention they all desire.

When she sat down to dinner before the round table covered with a tablecloth that had been used three days, opposite her husband, who uncovered the soup tureen and declared with an enchanted air, "Ah, the good *pot-au-feu!*[1] I don't know anything better than that," she thought of dainty dinners, of shining silverware, of tapestry which peopled the walls with ancient personages and with strange birds flying in the midst of a fairy forest; she thought of delicious dishes served on marvelous plates, and of the whispered gallantries which one listened to with a sphinxlike smile all the while eating the pink flesh of a trout or the wings of a quail.

---

1 **pot-au-feu** (pô tō fœ′): boiled beef and vegetables.

She had no dresses, no jewels, nothing. And she loved nothing but that; she felt made for that. She would so have liked to please, to be envied, to be charming, to be sought after.

She had a friend, a former schoolmate at the convent, who was rich and whom she did not like to go to see any more, because she suffered so much when she came back.

But one evening her husband returned home with a triumphant air, holding a large envelope in his hand.

"Here," said he. "Here is something for you."

She tore the paper sharply, and drew out an engraved card on which these words appeared:

The Minister of Public Instruction and Mme. Georges Ramponeau Request the Honor of M. and Mme. Loisel's Company at the Palace of the Ministry on Monday Evening, January 18th.

Instead of being delighted, as her husband hoped, she threw the invitation on the table with disdain, murmuring, "What do you want me to do with that?"

"But, my dear, I thought you would be glad. You never go out, and this is such a fine opportunity. I went to a lot of trouble to get it. Everyone wants to go; it is an important occasion, and few invitations are being given to clerks. The whole official world will be there."

She looked at him with irritation and said impatiently, "And what do you expect me to put on my back?"

He had not thought of that; he stammered, "Why, the dress you go to the theater in. It looks very well to me."

He stopped, distracted, seeing that his wife was crying. Two great tears descended slowly from the corners of her eyes toward the corners of her mouth. He stammered, "What's the matter? What's the matter?"

But, by a violent effort, she had conquered her grief, and she replied, with a calm voice, while she dried her wet cheeks. "Nothing. Only I have no dress, and therefore I can't go to this ball. Give your card to some colleague whose wife has a better wardrobe than I."

He was in despair. He resumed, "Come, let us see, Mathilde. How much would it cost, a suitable dress, which you could use on other occasions, something very simple?"

She reflected several seconds, making her calculations and wondering also what sum she could ask without drawing on herself an immediate refusal and a frightened exclamation from the economical clerk.

Finally she replied, hesitatingly, "I don't know exactly, but I think I could manage it with four hundred francs."

He had grown a little pale, because he was laying aside just that amount to buy a gun and treat himself to a little shooting next summer on the plain of Nanterre, with friends who went there to shoot larks on Sundays.

But he said, "Very well. I will give you four hundred francs. And try to have a pretty dress."

The day of the ball drew near, and Mme. Loisel seemed sad, uneasy, anxious. Her dress was ready, however.

Her husband said to her one evening, "What is the matter? Come, you've been so strange these last three days."

And she answered, "It annoys me not to have a single jewel, not a single stone, nothing to put on. I shall look like a peasant. I should almost rather not go at all."

He resumed, "You might wear natural flowers. It's very stylish at this time of the year. For ten francs you can get two or three magnificent roses."

She was not convinced. "No, there's nothing more humiliating than to look poor among other women who are rich."

But her husband cried, "How stupid you are! Go look up your friend Mme. Forestier, and ask her to lend you some jewels. You know her well enough to do that."

She uttered a cry of joy. "It's true. I never thought of it."

The next day she went to see her friend and told her of her problem.

Mme. Forestier went to a cabinet with a glass door, took out a large jewel box, brought it back, opened it, and said to Mme. Loisel, "Choose, my dear."

She saw first of all some bracelets, then a pearl necklace, then a Venetian cross, gold, and precious stones of admirable workmanship. She tried on the ornaments before the glass; hesitated; could not make up her mind. She kept asking, "Haven't you anything else?"

"Why, yes. Keep looking. I don't know what you have in mind."

All of a sudden she discovered, in a black satin box, a superb necklace of diamonds, and her heart began to beat with an immoderate desire. Her hands trembled as she picked it up. She fastened it around her throat, outside her high-necked dress, and remained lost in ecstasy at the sight of herself.

Then she asked, hesitating, filled with anguish, "Can you lend me that, only that?"

"Why, yes, certainly."

She kissed her friend warmly, then fled with her treasure.

The day of the ball arrived. Mme. Loisel was a great success. She was prettier than them all, elegant, gracious, smiling, and ecstatic with joy. All the men looked at her, asked her name, and tried to be introduced. All the attachés[2] of the cabinet wanted to waltz with her. She was noticed by the minister himself.

She danced with abandon, with passion, intoxicated with pleasure, forgetting all in the triumph of her beauty, in the glory of her success, in a sort of cloud of happiness composed of all this homage, of all this admiration, of all these awakened desires, and of that sense of complete victory which is so sweet to woman's heart.

She took her leave about four o'clock in the morning. Her husband had been sleeping since midnight in a little deserted anteroom with three other gentlemen whose wives were having a very good time.

He threw over her shoulders the wraps which he had brought, modest wraps of common life, whose poverty contrasted with the elegance of the ball dress. She felt this and wanted to escape so as not to be noticed by the other women, who were wrapping themselves in costly furs.

Loisel held her back. "Wait a bit. You will catch cold outside. I will go and call a cab."

But she would not listen to him, and hurried down the stairs. When they were in the street they did not find a carriage; and they began to look for one, hailing the cabmen whom they saw at a distance.

They went down toward the Seine[3] in despair, shivering with cold. At last they found on the quay[4] one of those ancient nocturnal carriages which, exactly as if they were ashamed to show

their misery during the day, are never seen round Paris until after nightfall.

It took them to their door in the Rue des Martyrs,[5] and once more, sadly, they climbed the stairs. All was ended for her. And as for him, he reflected that he must be at the ministry by ten o'clock.

She removed the wraps, which covered her shoulders, before the glass, to see herself once more in all her glory. But suddenly she uttered a cry. She no longer had the necklace around her neck!

Her husband, already half undressed, demanded, "What is the matter with you?"

She turned toward him wildly. "I have—I have—I've lost Mme. Forestier's necklace."

He stood up appalled. "What! . . . How? . . . Impossible!"

And they looked in the folds of her dress, in the folds of her cloak, in her pockets, everywhere. They did not find it.

He asked, "You're sure you had it on when you left the ball?"

"Yes, I felt it in the vestibule of the Ministry."

"But if you had lost it in the street we should have heard it fall. It must be in the cab."

"Yes. Probably. Did you take his number?"

"No. And you, didn't you notice it?"

"No."

They looked at one another in dismay. At last Loisel put on his clothes. "I shall go back on foot," said he, "over our whole route to see if I can't find it."

And he went out. Crumpled in a chair in her ball dress, she was without strength to go to bed, overwhelmed, without fire, without a thought.

---

2 **attachés** (ăt′ə shāz′): members of an embassy staff.
3 **Seine** (sān): river that runs through Paris.
4 **quay** (kē): paved landing bank alongside a navigable body of water.

5 **Rue des Martyrs:** Street of the Martyrs.

Her husband came back about seven o'clock. He had found nothing.

He went to police headquarters, to the newspaper offices, to offer a reward; he went to the cab companies—everywhere, in fact, that offered him the least suspicion of hope.

She waited all day, benumbed in the face of this terrible calamity. Loisel returned at night with a hollow, pale face; he had discovered nothing.

"You must write to your friend," said he, "that you have broken the clasp of her necklace and that you are having it repaired. That will give us time to turn round."

She wrote at his dictation.

At the end of a week they had lost all hope.

And Loisel, who had aged five years, declared, "We must consider how to replace the necklace."

The next day they took the box which had contained it and went to the jeweler whose name was inside. He consulted his books.

"It was not I, Madame, who sold that necklace; I furnished only the jewel case."

Then they went from jeweler to jeweler, searching for a necklace like the other, consulting their memories, both of them sick with chagrin and anguish.

They found in a shop at the Palais Royal a string of diamonds which seemed to them exactly like the one they were looking for. It was worth forty thousand francs. They could have it for thirty-six thousand.

They begged the jeweler not to sell it for three days. And they made a bargain that he should buy it back for thirty-four thousand francs in case they found the other one before the end of February.

Loisel had eighteen thousand francs which his father had left him. He would borrow the rest.

He borrowed, asking a thousand francs of one, five hundred of another, five louis here, three louis there. He gave notes, took up ruinous obligations, dealt with usurers[6] and all kinds of lenders. He compromised all the rest of his life, risked his signature without even knowing if he could make it good; and, frightened by the uncertainties of the future, by the black misery that was about to fall upon him, by the prospect of all the physical privations and of all the moral tortures which he was to suffer, he went to buy the new necklace, putting down upon the merchant's counter thirty-six thousand francs.

When Mme. Loisel took back the necklace, Mme. Forestier said to her with a chilly manner, "You should have returned it sooner. I might have needed it."

She did not open the case, as her friend had so much feared. If she had detected the substitution, what would she have thought? What would she have said? Would she not have taken Mme. Loisel for a thief?

Mme. Loisel now knew the horrible existence of the needy. She took the part suddenly thrust upon her, however, heroically. The dreadful debt must be paid. She would pay it. They dismissed their servant; they changed their lodgings, they rented living quarters in an attic.

She came to know what heavy housework meant, and the dreary, degrading tasks of the kitchen. She washed the dishes, using her rosy nails on the greasy pots and pans. She washed the dirty linen, the shirts, and the dishcloths, which she dried on a line; she carried the garbage down to the street

6 usurers: unscrupulous money lenders.

every morning, and carried up water, stopping for breath at every landing. And, dressed like a woman of the people, she went to the fruit dealer, the grocer, the butcher, her basket on her arm, bargaining, insulted, defending her miserable money sou[7] by sou.

Every month they had to pay off some notes, renew others, obtain more time.

Her husband worked in the evening, keeping the accounts in order for a merchant, and late at night he often copied manuscripts for five sous a page.

And this life lasted ten years.

At the end of ten years they had paid everything—everything, with the rates of usury and the accumulations of the compound interest.

Mme. Loisel looked old now. She had become the plain woman of poor households—strong and hard and rough. With frowsy hair, skirts askew, and red hands she talked loud as she washed the floor with great swishes of water. But sometimes, when her husband was at the office, she sat down near the window and she thought of that gay evening of long ago, of that ball where she had been so beautiful and so admired.

What would have happened if she had not lost that necklace? Who knows? Who knows? How strange life is, and how changeful! How little a thing is needed to save us or ruin us!

But one Sunday, having gone to take a walk in the Champs-Elysées[8] to refresh herself from the labors of the week, she suddenly perceived a woman who was leading a child. It was Mme. Forestier, still young, still beautiful, still charming. Mme. Loisel felt moved. Should she speak to her? Yes, certainly. And, now that she had paid, she was going to tell her all about it. Why not?

She approached her.

"Good day, Jeanne."

The other, astonished to be familiarly addressed by this plain-looking woman, did not recognize her and stammered, "But—Madame! I do not know—You must be mistaken."

"No. I am Mathilde Loisel."

Her friend uttered a cry of dismay. "Oh, my poor Mathilde! How changed you are!"

"Yes, I have had many hard days since I saw you, many miserable days—and all because of you!"

"Of me! How can that be?"

"You remember the diamond necklace that you lent me to wear to a ball?"

"Yes. Well?"

"Well, I lost it."

"What do you mean? You brought it back to me."

"I brought you back another just like it. And for ten years we have been paying for it. You can understand that it was not easy for us, who had nothing. At last it is ended, and I am content."

Mme. Forestier had stopped. "You say that you bought a necklace of diamonds to replace mine?"

"Yes. You never noticed it, then! They were very like." And she smiled with a joy which was proud and naïve.

Mme. Forestier, strongly moved, took her two hands.

"Oh, my poor Mathilde! My necklace was paste![9] It was worth at most five hundred francs!"

---

7 sou (sōō): a French coin worth about one cent.
8 Champs-Elysées (shäN zĕ lē zĕ'): chief avenue in Paris.

9 paste: a lead-glass composition used to make imitation stones.

86   SHORT STORY

Understanding the Story

1. What are Mme. Loisel's characteristics as described by de Maupassant in the first five paragraphs of the story? What are her values?

2. What effect do Mme. Loisel's values have upon her reactions and decisions during the course of the story?

3. How does M. Loisel contrast with his wife? What desire dominates his actions and suggestions at the beginning of the story?

4. The decision not to tell Mme. Forestier about the loss of the necklace originates with M. Loisel. In your opinion, what is his motive for suggesting this course of action? Is it more logical for the suggestion to be made by him or by his wife? Why?

5. The ten years between the replacement of the necklace and the discovery that the original was paste is covered very quickly. The Loisels' life during this time is very different from their previous one. What are some details by which the author enables the reader to imagine very specifically what the Loisels' new life is like?

6. Actions and objects in literature are often symbolic. (See Literary Terms.) That is, they come to stand for ideas or qualities beyond the literal level of meaning. When the necklace first appears in this story, the reader attaches no meaning to it beyond what it actually is—a piece of jewelry. By the end of the story, however, the role that the necklace has played in Mme. Loisel's life should cause the reader to attach a wider significance to it.

   How is Mme. Loisel's instinctive choice of the paste necklace over the other pieces of jewelry symbolic of her character? What does the necklace itself symbolize?

7. Is the ending of this story a trick ending used only for the sake of the surprise, or is the ending justified by what de Maupassant wanted to say about his characters and their lives? (Consider, for example, whether the events leading up to the ten years of drudgery were in any way caused by Mme. Loisel's character or if they were the result of nothing but coincidence. Does the ending provide any comment on Mme. Loisel's character or life?)

8. Outwardly, Mme. Loisel obviously changes during the course of the story. Does her inward character change at all? What evidence do you find for your answer in the story?

9. De Maupassant tells this story quite impersonally. He does not directly approve of or condemn his characters. Do you find any ways in the story by which he influences your feelings or opinions about the characters and their actions?

10. Explain the statement: The reader feels pity but no real compassion for Mme. Loisel and her ten years of wasted life.

Developing Language Skills

1. Read the following sentences from the story and then write several paragraphs telling whether in your judgment Mme. Loisel was lost or saved by the loss of the necklace:

> What would have happened if she had not lost that necklace? Who knows? Who knows? How strange life is, and how changeful! How little a thing is needed to save us or ruin us!

Before you write, consider Mme. Loisel's attitude toward life as the story opens, her reaction to her bad luck, and her acceptance of ten years of drudgery. Use quotations and evidence from the story to support your judgment.

2. Select three stories from this unit which cover varying time spans. ("The Waltz," for example, covers only a few minutes, while "Early Marriage" covers several days.) Describe how the amount of time to be covered affects the way each author has told his story. Consider, for instance, whether the story varies its pace, how it does so, and how changes in pace can indicate the relative importance of events in a story.

Reading "The Bet"

"The Bet" contains a technical problem similar to one in "The Necklace." Chekhov must cover in a few pages a span of fifteen years. Like de Maupassant, he employs the technique of varying summaries of a character or of long periods of time with scenes that develop through conversation, but he recounts the fifteen years preceding the final scene through a *flashback*. This is a technique by which events occurring before the main action of a story are told through a character's mind flashing back to the past. "The Bet" opens on "a dark autumn night," and a banker is thinking back to events which occurred fifteen years before and which explain his present situation.

In this story, you will find that contrast is one of the major methods used to develop theme. The central idea emerges to a great extent through the contrasting of characters, of ideas, of values, and of kinds of freedom. Be alert to these contrasts as you read.

The Bet

Anton Chekhov

This story opens with an old banker recalling a ridiculous bet he had made with a young lawyer fifteen years ago at a gay party, and it closes with the tragic change in the two men. "The Bet," a psychological study of what happens in the mind of a sensitive man under unusual circumstances, reflects Chekhov's interest in the inner lives of human beings. The whole story is an irony in which everything the banker and the lawyer had been so certain of fifteen years before turns out quite differently than they had expected.

I

IT WAS a dark autumn night. The old banker was walking up and down his study and remembering how, fifteen years before, he had given a party one autumn evening. There had been many clever men there, and there had been interesting conversations. Among other things had talked of capital punishment. The majority of the guests, among whom were many journalists and intellectual men, disapproved of the death penalty. They considered that form of punishment out of date, immoral, and unsuitable for Christian States. In the opinion of some of them the death penalty ought to be replaced everywhere by imprisonment for life.

"I don't agree with you," said their host the banker. "I have not tried either the death penalty or imprisonment for life, but if one may judge *a priori*,[1] the death penalty is more moral and more humane than imprisonment for life. Capital punishment kills a man at once, but lifelong imprisonment kills him slowly. Which executioner is the more humane, he who kills you in a few minutes or he who drags the life out of you in the course of many years?"

"Both are equally immoral," observed one of the guests, "for they both have the same object—to take away life. The State is not God. It has not the right to take away what it cannot restore when it wants to."

Among the guests was a young lawyer, a young man of five-and-twenty. When he was asked his opinion, he said:

"The death sentence and the life sentence are equally immoral, but if I had to choose between the death penalty and imprisonment for life, I would certainly choose the second. To live anyhow is better than not at all."

A lively discussion arose. The banker, who was younger and more nervous in those days, was suddenly carried away by excitement; he struck the table with his fist and shouted at the young man:

"It's not true! I'll bet you two millions[2] you wouldn't stay in solitary confinement for five years."

"If you mean that in earnest," said the young man, "I'll take the bet, but I would stay not five but fifteen years."

1 **a priori** (ā prī ōr′ī): through reasoning alone, and not through experience.
2 **millions:** refers to rubles valued at about fifty cents in American money in pre-Revolutionary Russia.

"Fifteen? Done!" cried the banker. "Gentlemen, I stake two millions!"

"Agreed! You stake your millions and I stake my freedom!" said the young man.

And this wild, senseless bet was carried out! The banker, spoilt and frivolous, with millions beyond his reckoning, was delighted at the bet. At supper he made fun of the young man, and said:

"Think better of it, young man, while there is still time. To me two millions are a trifle, but you are losing three or four of the best years of your life. I say three or four, because you won't stay longer. Don't forget either, you unhappy man, that voluntary confinement is a great deal harder to bear than compulsory. The thought that you have the right to step out in liberty at any moment will poison your whole existence in prison. I am sorry for you."

And now the banker, walking to and fro, remembered all this, and asked himself: "What was the object of that bet? What is the good of that man's losing fifteen years of his life and my throwing away two millions? Can it prove that the death penalty is better or worse than imprisonment for life? No, no. It was all nonsensical and meaningless. On my part it was the caprice of a pampered man, and on his part simple greed for money. . . ."

Then he remembered what followed that evening. It was decided that the young man should spend the years of his captivity under the strictest supervision in one of the lodges in the banker's garden. It was agreed that for fifteen years he should not be free to cross the threshold of the lodge, to see human beings, to hear the human voice, or to receive letters and newspapers. He was allowed to have a musical in-strument and books, and was allowed to write letters, to drink wine, and to smoke. By the terms of the agreement, the only relations he could have with the outer world were by a little window made purposely for that object. He might have anything he wanted—books, music, wine, and so on—in any quantity he desired by writing an order, but could only receive them through the window. The agreement provided for every detail and every trifle that would make his imprisonment strictly solitary, and bound the young man to stay there *exactly* fifteen years, beginning from twelve o'clock of November 14, 1870, and ending at twelve o'clock of November 14, 1885. The slightest attempt on his part to break the conditions, if only two minutes before the end, released the banker from the obligation to pay him two millions.

For the first year of his confinement, as far as one could judge from his brief notes, the prisoner suffered severely from loneliness and depression. The sounds of the piano could be heard continually day and night from his lodge. He refused wine and tobacco. Wine, he wrote, excites the desires, and desires are the worst foes of the prisoner; and besides, nothing could be more dreary than drinking good wine and seeing no one. And tobacco spoilt the air of his room. In the first year the books he sent for were principally of a light character; novels with a complicated love plot, sensational and fantastic stories, and so on.

In the second year the piano was silent in the lodge, and the prisoner asked only for the classics. In the fifth year music was audible again, and the prisoner asked for wine. Those who watched him through the window said that all that year he spent doing nothing but eating and drinking and lying on his bed, frequently yawning and angrily talking to himself. He did not read books. Sometimes at night he would sit down to write; he would spend hours writing, and in the morning tear up all that he had written. More than once he could be heard crying.

In the second half of the sixth year the prisoner began zealously studying languages, philosophy, and history. He threw himself eagerly into these studies —so much so that the banker had enough to do to get him the books he ordered. In the course of four years some six hundred volumes were procured at his request. It was during this period that the banker received the following letter from his prisoner:

"My dear Jailer, I write you these lines in six languages. Show them to people who know the languages. Let them read them. If they find not one mistake I implore you to fire a shot in the garden. That shot will show me that my efforts have not been thrown away. The geniuses of all ages and of all lands speak different languages, but the same flame burns in them all. Oh, if you only knew what unearthly happiness my soul feels now from being able to understand them!" The prisoner's desire was fulfilled. The banker ordered two shots to be fired in the garden.

Then after the tenth year, the prisoner sat immovably at the table and read nothing but the Gospel. It seemed strange to the banker that a man who in four years had mastered six hundred learned volumes should waste nearly a year over one thin book easy of comprehension. Theology and histories of religion followed the Gospels.

In the last two years of his confinement the prisoner read an immense quantity of books quite indiscrimi-nately.[3] At one time he was busy with the natural sciences, then he would ask for Byron or Shakespeare. There were notes in which he demanded at the same time books on chemistry, and a manual of medicine, and a novel, and some treatise on philosophy or theology. His reading suggested a man swimming in the sea among the wreckage of his ship, and trying to save his life by greedily clutching first at one spar and then at another.

II

The old banker remembered all this, and thought:

"Tomorrow at twelve o'clock he will regain his freedom. By our agreement I ought to pay him two millions. If I do pay him, it is all over with me: I shall be utterly ruined."

Fifteen years before, his millions had been beyond his reckoning; now he was afraid to ask himself which were greater, his debts or his assets. Desperate gambling on the Stock Exchange, wild speculation, and the excitability which he could not get over even in advancing years, had by degrees led to the decline of his fortune, and the proud, fearless, self-confident millionaire had become a banker of middling rank, trembling at every rise and fall in his investments. "Cursed bet!" muttered the old man, clutching his head in despair. "Why didn't the man die? He is only forty now. He will take my last penny from me, he will marry, will enjoy life, will gamble on the Exchange; while I shall look at him with envy like a beggar, and hear from him every day the same sentence: 'I am indebted to you for the happiness of my life, let me help you!' No, it is too much! The one means of being saved from bank-

3 **indiscriminately:** unselectively.

ruptcy and disgrace is the death of that man!"

It struck three o'clock, the banker listened; everyone was asleep in the house, and nothing could be heard outside but the rustling of the chilled trees. Trying to make no noise, he took from a fireproof safe the key of the door which had not been opened for fifteen years, put on his overcoat, and went out of the house.

It was dark and cold in the garden. Rain was falling. A damp cutting wind was racing about the garden, howling and giving the trees no rest. The banker strained his eyes, but could see neither the earth nor the white statues, nor the lodge, nor the trees. Going to the spot where the lodge stood, he twice called the watchman. No answer followed. Evidently the watchman had sought shelter from the weather, and was now asleep somewhere either in the kitchen or in the greenhouse.

"If I had the pluck to carry out my intention," thought the old man, "suspicion would fall first upon the watchman."

He felt in the darkness for the steps and the door, and went into the entry of the lodge. Then he groped his way into a little passage and lighted a match. There was not a soul there. There was a bedstead with no bedding on it, and in the corner there was a dark cast-iron stove. The seals on the door leading to the prisoner's rooms were intact.

When the match went out the old man, trembling with emotion, peeped through the little window. A candle was burning dimly in the prisoner's room. He was sitting at the table. Nothing could be seen but his back, the hair on his head, and his hands. Open books were lying on the table, on the two easy chairs, and on the carpet near the table.

Five minutes passed and the prisoner did not once stir. Fifteen years' imprisonment had taught him to sit still. The banker tapped at the window with his finger, and the prisoner made no movement whatever in response. Then the banker cautiously broke the seals off the door and put the key in the keyhole. The rusty lock gave a grating sound and the door creaked. The banker expected to hear at once footsteps and a cry of astonishment, but three minutes passed and it was as quiet as ever in the room. He made up his mind to go in.

At the table a man unlike ordinary people was sitting motionless. He was a skeleton with the skin drawn tight over his bones, with long curls like a woman's, and a shaggy beard. His face was yellow with an earthy tint in it, his cheeks were hollow, his back long and narrow, and the hand on which his shaggy head was propped was so thin and delicate that it was dreadful to look at it. His hair was already streaked with silver, and seeing his emaciated,[4] aged-looking face, no one would have believed that he was only forty. He was asleep. . . . In front of his bowed head there lay on the table a sheet of paper on which there was something written in fine handwriting.

"Poor creature!" thought the banker, "he is asleep and most likely dreaming of the millions. And I have only to take this half-dead man, throw him on the bed, stifle him a little with the pillow, and the most conscientious expert would find no sign of a violent death. But let us first read what he has written here. . . ."

The banker took the page from the table and read as follows:

"Tomorrow at twelve o'clock I regain

---

4 emaciated (ĭ mā′shĭ ā′tĭd): very thin.

my freedom and the right to associate with other men, but before I leave this room and see the sunshine, I think it necessary to say a few words to you. With a clear conscience I tell you, as before God, who beholds me, that I despise freedom and life and health, and all that in your books is called the good things of the world.

"For fifteen years I have been intently studying earthly life. It is true I have not seen the earth nor men, but in your books I have drunk fragrant wine, I have sung songs, I have hunted stags and wild boars in the forests, have loved women. . . . Beauties as ethereal as clouds, created by the magic of your poets and geniuses, have visited me at night, and have whispered in my ears wonderful tales that have set my brain in a whirl. In your books I have climbed to the peaks of Elburz and Mont Blanc, and from there I have seen the sun rise and have watched it at evening flood the sky, the ocean, and the mountaintops with gold and crimson. I have watched from there the lightning flashing over my head and cleaving the storm clouds. I have seen green forests, fields, rivers, lakes, towns. I have heard the singing of the sirens, and the strains of the shepherds' pipes; I have touched the wings of comely devils who flew down to converse with me of God. . . . In your books I have flung myself into the bottomless pit, performed miracles, slain, burned towns, preached new religions, conquered whole kingdoms. . . .

"Your books have given me wisdom. All that the unresting thought of man has created in the ages is compressed into a small compass in my brain. I know that I am wiser than all of you.

"And I despise your books, I despise wisdom and the blessings of this world. It is all worthless, fleeting, illusory, and deceptive, like a mirage. You may be proud, wise, and fine, but death will wipe you off the face of the earth as though you were no more than mice burrowing under the floor, and your posterity, your history, your immortal geniuses will burn or freeze together with the earthly globe.

"You have lost your reason and taken the wrong path. You have taken lies for truth, and hideousness for beauty. You would marvel if, owing to strange events of some sorts, frogs and lizards suddenly grew on apple and orange trees instead of fruit, or if roses began to smell like a sweating horse; so I marvel at you who exchange heaven for earth. I don't want to understand you.

"To prove to you in action how I despise all that you live by, I renounce the two millions of which I once dreamed as of paradise and which now I despise. To deprive myself of the right to the money I shall go out from here five hours before the time fixed, and so break the compact. . . ."

When the banker had read this he laid the page on the table, kissed the strange man on the head, and went out of the lodge, weeping. At no other time, even when he had lost heavily on the Stock Exchange, had he felt so great a contempt for himself. When he got home he lay on his bed, but his tears and emotion kept him for hours from sleeping.

Next morning the watchmen ran in with pale faces, and told him they had seen the man who lived in the lodge climb out of the window into the garden, go to the gate, and disappear. The banker went at once with the servants to the lodge and made sure of the flight of his prisoner. To avoid arousing unnecessary talk, he took from the table the writing in which the millions were renounced, and when he got home locked it up in the fireproof safe.

Understanding the Story

1. What was the actual bet that gives the story its title?

2. What evidence in the opening paragraphs supports or disproves the old banker's comments as he looks back on the dinner party, "On my part, it was the caprice of a well-fed man; on the lawyer's, pure greed of gold"?

3. The idea of freedom is continually present in "The Bet." After answering the following questions, state in your own words the theme (or central idea) that emerges from the various discussions and actions involving freedom.

    (a) How does the idea of freedom enter the discussion at the banker's dinner party? What does freedom mean to the men who are present? What value do they place upon it?

    (b) With what words does the young lawyer describe the bet at the dinner party? How does Chekhov describe such a bet immediately afterward?

    (c) In the light of the kind of life the banker is leading, explain the irony in his statement made at the party. "Capital punishment kills a man at once, but lifelong imprisonment kills him slowly." Is the banker himself an entirely free man?

    (d) What kind of freedom, unknown to most men, do the terms of the bet give the prisoner? How do the lawyer and banker contrast with one another in terms of the freedom each possesses or lacks?

    (e) What does the lawyer do with his time during his years of imprisonment? What developments in his thinking are indicated by the various stages of activity and reading he goes through?

    (f) Reread the prisoner's letter. From the second paragraph on, whom is he addressing when he writes *you*? What does he say in the letter about freedom? What are his reasons for regarding it as he does?

    (g) In what way is the bet symbolic of the lives that many (perhaps all) men lead?

4. As the banker visits the lawyer's room the night before the bet ends, how does the setting parallel the banker's state of mind?

5. How do you account for the banker's actions as described in the last sentence of the story?

Building Vocabulary Skills

1. Choose the correct word or phrases in the following sentences:

    (a) Was the capricious banker *unpredictable* or *daring?*

    (b) When the lawyer read indiscriminately, did he read *all kinds of books* or *without stopping?*

    (c) Was the frivolous banker *trifling in his interests* or *overweight physically?*

(d) Does ethereal beauty refer to *earthly qualities* or *spiritual qualities?*

2. Use the term *a priori* in a way that makes its meaning clear in a
   brief paragraph concerning the relative values of death and life
   imprisonment as punishment. See footnote for meaning of the term.

Developing Language Skills

1. Write two or three paragraphs on one of the following:
   (a) Given the story up to the last paragraph, what other ways could
       the story have ended? Would other endings be logical? Would
       they be sufficiently motivated?
   (b) In what ways are the banker and lawyer alike at the time the bet
       was made? In what ways do they differ? How do they contrast
       with one another at the end of the fifteen years?

2. Panel discussion: What ideas on society are represented in this
   story?

Reading "The Pack"

Galsworthy states his theme in the opening paragraph and then develops it through an experience recounted by one of his characters.
The *theme* of a story is its meaning or significance and should not be
confused with the moral of a story. Every story has a theme (although
it may not be directly stated as it is in "The Pack"), but not every story
has a moral. A moral is a lesson taught by a story, whereas a theme is
simply an idea, an observation about people or life, illustrated by a
story. "The Cop and the Anthem," for example, contains no moral,
but it does contain the theme of an individual's plans frequently having
ironic outcomes.

Galsworthy always keeps the focus of this story on the theme. Although you learn interesting facts about undergraduates in an English
university, the setting is merely background for Galsworthy's theme.
The same underlying idea could be developed in any neighborhood,
school, or playground in the world.

The Pack

John Galsworthy

Have you ever been deliberately bumped or pushed by a group of boys in the corridor or on the street? Have you ever done the bumping or pushing? If you have had any experiences of this sort, "The Pack" has a special message for you.

"It's only," said H., "when men run in packs that they lose their sense of decency. At least that's my experience. Individual man—I'm not speaking of savages—is more given to generosity than meanness, rarely brutal, inclines in fact to be a gentleman. It's when you add three or four more to him that his sense of decency, his sense of personal responsibility, his private standards, go by the board. I am not at all sure that he does not become the victim of a certain infectious fever. Something physical takes place, I fancy . . . I happen to be a trustee, with three others, and we do a deal of cheeseparing[1] in the year, which as private individuals we should never dream of."

"That's hardly a fair example," said D., "but on the whole, I quite agree. Single man is not an angel; collective man is a bit of a brute."

The discussion was carried on for several minutes, and then P., who had not yet spoken, said: "They say a pinch of illustration is worth a pound of argument. When I was at the 'Varsity[2] there was a man at the same college with me called Chalkcroft, the son of a high ecclesiastic,[3] a perfectly harmless, well-mannered individual, who had the misfortune to be a Radical, or, as some even thought, a Socialist—anyway, he wore a turndown collar, a green tie, took part in Union[4] debates on the shady side, and no part in college festivities. He was, in fact, a 'smug'[5]—a man, as you know, who, through some accident of his early environment, incomprehensibly fails to adopt the proper view of life. He was never drunk, not even pleasantly, played no games connected with a ball, was believed to be afraid of a horse or a woman, took his exercise in long walks with a man from another college, or solitarily in a skiff upon the river; he also read books, and was prepared to discuss abstract propositions. Thus, in one way or another he disgusted almost every self-respecting undergraduate. Don't imagine, of course, that his case was unusual; we had many such at M—— in my time; but about this Chalkcroft there was an unjustifiable composure, a quiet sarcasm, which made him conspicuously intolerable. He was thought to be a 'bit above himself,' or, rather, he did not seem conscious, as any proper 'smug' should, that he was a bit below his fellows; on the contrary, his figure, which was slim, and slightly stooping, passed in and about college with serene assurance; his pale face with its traces of reprehensible whisker, wore a faint

1 **cheeseparing:** miserly economizing.

2 **'Varsity:** university.
3 **ecclesiastic:** clergyman.
4 **Union:** the name of a debating club at Oxford.
5 **smug:** plodding student; a grind.

smile above his detested green tie; besides, he showed no signs of that poverty which is, of course, some justification to 'smugs' for their lack of conformity. And as a matter of fact, he was *not* poor, but had some of the best rooms in college, which was ever a remembered grievance against him. For these reasons, then," went on P., "it was decided one evening to bring him to trial. This salutary[6] custom had originated in the mind of a third year man named Jefferies, a dark person with a kind of elephantlike unwieldiness in his nose and walk, a biting, witty tongue, and very small eyes with a lecherous[7] expression. He is now a Scottish baronet. This gentleman in his cups had quite a pretty malice, and a sense of the dignity of the law. Wandering of a night in the quadrangles,[8] he never had any difficulty in gathering a troop of fellows in search of distraction, or animated by public and other spirits; and, with them whooping and crowing at his heels, it was his beneficial practice to enter the rooms of any person, who for good and sufficient reasons merited trial, and thereupon to conduct the same with all the ceremony due to the dispensation of British justice. I had attended one of these trials before, on a chuckleheaded youth whose buffoonery was really offensive. The ceremony was funny enough, nor did the youth seem to mind, grinning from ear to ear, and ejaculating continually, 'Oh! I say, Jefferies!'

"The occasion of which I am going to speak now was a different sort of affair altogether. We found the man Chalkcroft at home, reading before his fire by the light of three candles. The room was paneled in black oak, and the yellow candle flames barely lit up the darkness as we came whooping in.

"'Chalkcroft,' said Jefferies, 'we are going to try you.' Chalkcroft stood up and looked at us. He was in a Norfolk jacket, with his customary green tie, and his face was pale.

"He answered: 'Yes, Jefferies? You forgot to knock.'

"Jefferies put out his finger and thumb and delicately plucked Chalkcroft's tie from out of his waistcoat.

"'You wear a green tie, sir,' he said.

"Chalkcroft went the color of the ashes in the grate; then, slowly, a white-hot glow came into his cheeks.

"'Don't look at me, sir,' said Jefferies; 'look at the jury!' and he waved his hand at us. 'We are going to try you for—' He specified an incident of a scabrous[9] character which served as the charge on all such humorous occasions, and was likely to be peculiarly offensive to 'smugs' who are usually, as you know, what is called 'pi.'[10]

"We yelped, guffawed, and settled ourselves in chairs; Jefferies perched himself on a table and slowly swung his thin legs; he always wore very tight trousers. His little black eyes gleamed greedily above his unwieldy nose. Chalkcroft remained standing.

"It was then," pursued P., "that I had my first qualm. The fellow was so still and pale and unmoved; he looked at me, and, when I tried to stare back, his eyes passed me over, quiet and contemptuous. And I remember thinking: 'Why are we all here—we are not a bit the kind of men to do this sort of thing?' And really we were not. With the exception of Jefferies, who was, no doubt, at times inhabited by a devil, and one Anderson, a little man in a long coat,

---

6 **salutary:** healthy (used here ironically).
7 **lecherous:** lustful.
8 **quadrangles:** yards surrounded on four sides by buildings.

9 **scabrous:** risqué; improper.
10 **pi:** English school slang for *pious.*

with a red nose and very long arms, always half-drunk—a sort of desperate character, and long since, of course, a schoolmaster—there wasn't one of us, who, left to himself, would have entered another man's rooms unbidden (however unpopular he might be, however much of a 'smug'), and insulted him to his face. There was Beal, a very fair, rather good-looking man, with bowed legs and no expression to speak of, known as Boshy Beal; Dunsdale, a heavy, long-faced, freckled person, prominent in every college disturbance, but with a reputation for respectability; Horden (called Jos), a big, clean-cut Kentish man with nice eyes, and fists like hammers; Stickland, fussy, with mild habits; Sevenoax, now in the House of Lords; little Holingbroke, the cox; and my old schoolfellow, Fosdyke, whose dignity even then would certainly have forbidden his presence had he not previously dined. Thus, as you see, we were all or nearly all from the 'best' schools in the country, in the 'best' set at M——, and naturally, as individuals, quite—oh! quite—incapable of an ungentlemanlike act.

"Jefferies appointed Anderson gaoler, Dunsdale Public Prosecutor, no one counsel for the defense, the rest of us jury, himself judge, and opened the trial. He was, as I have said, a witty young man, and, dangling his legs, fastening his malevolent black eyes on Chalkcroft, he usurped the functions of us all. The nature of the charge precludes me from recounting to you the details of the trial, and, in fact, I have forgotten them, but as if he were standing here before us, I remember, in the dim glow of those three candles, Chalkcroft's pale, unmoved, ironic face; his unvarying, 'Yes, Jefferies'; his one remonstrance: 'Are you a gentleman, Jefferies?' and our insane laughter at the answer: 'No, sir, a by-our-Lady judge.'

As if he were standing here before us I remember the expression on his face at the question: 'Prisoner, are you guilty—yes or no?' the long pause, the slow, sarcastic: 'As you like, Jefferies.' As if he were standing here before us I remember his calm and his contempt. He was sentenced to drink a tumbler of his own port without stopping; whether the sentence was carried out I cannot tell you; for with one or two more I slipped away.

"The next morning I had such a sense of discomfort that I could not rest till I had sent Chalkcroft a letter of apology.

I caught sight of him in the afternoon walking across the quad with his usual pale assurance, and in the evening I received his answer. It contained, at the end, this sentence: 'I feel sure you would not have come if it hadn't been for the others.' It has occurred to me since that he may have said the same thing to us all—for anything I know, we may all of us have written."

There was a silence. Then H. said: "The Pack! Ah! What secondhand devil is it that gets into us when we run in packs?"

Understanding the Story

1. What is a likely setting for the opening conversation?
2. Find two or three statements that repeat the idea of the opening sentence: "It's only . . . when men run in packs that they lose their sense of decency."
3. What leads P. to tell his story?
4. Why was Chalkcroft considered a "smug" by other students?
5. In what ways did Chalkcroft infuriate his colleagues by not conforming as a "smug"?
6. Where does this statement of P.'s occur in the story?

   "Thus, as you see, we were all or nearly all from the 'best' schools in the country, in the 'best' set at M——, and naturally, as individuals, quite—oh! quite—incapable of an ungentlemanlike act."

   What is P.'s tone as he makes the statement? What point is he making through the information it contains?
7. What is the theme of the story?
8. How is the presentation of this story like that of "The Heyday of the Blood"? Is it exactly the same?

Building Vocabulary Skills

Choose from the following phrases those that describe Chalkcroft and those that refer to Jefferies:

biting, witty tongue
quiet and contemptuous
unwieldy nose

unmoved, ironic face
malevolent black eyes
unjustifiable composure
usual pale assurance

Developing Language Skills

1. What evidence in the story do you find concerning the age of the men discussing the pack?
2. Paragraph 3 states: ". . . it was his [Jefferies's] beneficial practice to enter the rooms of any person, who for good and sufficient reasons merited trial, and thereupon to conduct the same with all the ceremony due to the dispensation of British justice." What is the tone of the speaker? To what extent does he intend his words to be understood literally?
3. What descriptive phrases in paragraph 3 influence your attitude toward Chalkcroft? toward Jefferies? What kind of attitude toward each is created by the phrases you list?
4. Write one paragraph describing a person in which you use descriptive phrases chosen in order to create some definite attitude toward that person. (For example, consider the difference in attitude shown by "His sparkling blue eyes looked straight at you" instead of "His glittering blue eyes fixed on you in a snakelike gaze.")

Reading "All Gold Canyon"

Jack London brings out the theme of this story by contrasting a quiet, peaceful canyon setting with the activities and conflicts of two human beings who enter it. Although London's men (he seldom writes about women) are hardbitten and down-to-earth, his settings are often romantic. In "All Gold Canyon" he becomes almost lyrical as he shows the canyon to the reader from his point of view rather than from a character's. In fact, his method of describing the canyon ("The walls leaned together. . . . The air was drowsy . . . the stream grown garrulous") gives it an almost human personality.

An author may use *setting* to accomplish various goals. Sometimes description of time, place, weather, furnishings—elements of setting—may simply be included because they help to give a sense of reality and credibility to a plot through their concreteness. At other times, the setting may emphasize the mood of a character (just as a rainy day may bring out or strengthen a feeling of sadness in people), or it may be appropriate to the events that are occurring in a story (as in the description of the stormy night in "The Bet"). At still other times, the setting may have important effects upon actions of characters (as the solitary and dangerous El Paso country does in "Early Marriage").

All Gold Canyon

Jack London

"All Gold Canyon" concerns, as do many of London's stories, a strong man fighting for his life. The miner in the story is based on the partner of London's gold-rush days in California and the Klondike, and the setting depicts one aspect of the West that London knew and loved. Indeed, you will find that the intrusion of human beings into the setting—rather than the conflict between human beings—is the real basis for the story.

IT WAS the green heart of the canyon, where the walls swerved back from the rigid plan and relieved their harshness of line by making a little sheltered nook and filling it to the brim with sweetness and roundness and softness. Here all things rested. Even the narrow stream ceased its turbulent downrush long enough to form a quiet pool. Knee-deep in the water, with drooping head and half-shut eyes, drowsed a red-coated, many-antlered buck.

On one side, beginning at the very lip of the pool, was a tiny meadow, a cool, resilient surface of green that extended to the base of the frowning wall. Beyond the pool a gentle slope of earth ran up and up to meet the opposing wall. Fine grass covered the slope—grass that was spangled with flowers, with here and there patches of color—orange and purple and golden. Below, the canyon was shut in. There was no view. The walls leaned together abruptly, and the canyon ended in a chaos of rocks, moss-covered and hidden by a green screen of vines and creepers and boughs of trees. Up the canyon rose far hills and peaks, the big foothills, pine-covered and remote. And far beyond, like clouds upon the border of the sky, towered minarets of white, where the Sierra's eternal snows flashed austerely the blazes of the sun.

There was no dust in the canyon. The leaves and flowers were clean and virginal. The grass was young velvet. Over the pool three cottonwoods sent their snowy fluffs fluttering down the quiet air. On the slope the blossoms of the wine-wooded manzanita filled the air with springtime odors, while the leaves, wise with experience, were already beginning their vertical twist against the coming aridity of summer. In the open spaces on the slope, beyond the farthest shadow reach of the manzanita, poised the mariposa lilies, like so many flights of jeweled moths suddenly arrested and on the verge of trembling into flight again. Here and there that woods harlequin, the madrone, permitting itself to be caught in the act of changing its pea-green trunk to madder red, breathed its fragrance into the air from great clusters of waxen bells. Creamy white were these bells, shaped like lilies of the valley, with the sweetness of perfume that is of the springtime.

There was not a sigh of wind. The air was drowsy with its weight of perfume. It was a sweetness that would have been cloying had the air been heavy and humid. But the air was sharp and thin. It was as starlight transmuted into atmosphere, shot through and warmed by sunshine, and flower-drenched with sweetness.

An occasional butterfly drifted in and out through the patches of light and shade. And from all about rose the low and sleepy hum of mountain bees—feasting sybarites[1] that jostled one another good-naturedly at the board, nor found time for rough discourtesy. So quietly did the little stream drip and ripple its way through the canyon that it spoke only in faint and occasional gurgles. The voice of the stream was as a drowsy whisper, ever interrupted by dozings and silences, ever lifted again in the awakenings.

The motion of all things was a drifting in the heart of the canyon. Sunshine and butterflies drifted in and out among the trees. The hum of the bees and the whisper of the stream were a drifting of sound. And the drifting sound and drifting color seemed to weave together in the making of a delicate and intangible fabric which was the spirit of the place. It was a spirit of peace that was not of death but of smooth-pulsing life, of quietude that was not silence, of movement that was not action, of repose that was quick with existence without being violent with struggle and travail. The spirit of the place was the spirit of the peace of the living, somnolent[2] with the easement and content of prosperity, and undisturbed by rumors of far wars.

The red-coated, many-antlered buck acknowledged the lordship of the spirit of the place and dozed knee-deep in the cool, shaded pool. There seemed no flies to vex him, and he was languid with rest. Sometimes his ears moved when the stream awoke and whispered;

1 sybarites (sĭb′ə rīts′): those devoted to pleasure.
2 somnolent: drowsy.

but they moved lazily, with foreknowledge that it was merely the stream grown garrulous at discovery that it had slept.

But there came a time when the buck's ears lifted and tensed with swift eagerness for sound. His head was turned down the canyon. His sensitive, quivering nostrils scented the air. His eyes could not pierce the green screen through which the stream rippled away, but to his ears came the voice of a man. It was a steady, monotonous, singsong voice. Once the buck heard the harsh clash of metal upon rock. At the sound he snorted with a sudden start that jerked him through the air from water to meadow, and his feet sank into the young velvet, while he pricked his ears and again scented the air. Then he stole across the tiny meadow, pausing once and again to listen, and faded away out of the canyon like a wraith, soft-footed and without sound.

The clash of steel-shod soles against the rocks began to be heard, and the man's voice grew louder. It was raised in a sort of chant and became distinct with nearness, so that the words could be heard:

"Tu'n around an' tu'n yo' face
Untoe them sweet hills of grace
    (D' pow'rs of sin yo' am scornin'!).
Look about an' look aroun',
Fling yo' sin-pack on d' groun'
    (Yo' will meet wid d' Lord in d' mornin'!)."

A sound of scrambling accompanied the song, and the spirit of the place fled away on the heels of the red-coated buck. The green screen was burst asunder, and a man peered out at the meadow and the pool and the sloping sidehill. He was a deliberate sort of man. He took in the scene with one embracing glance, then ran his eyes over the details to verify the general impression. Then, and not until then, did he open his mouth in vivid and solemn approval: "Smoke of life an' snakes of purgatory! Will you just look at that! Wood an' water an' grass an' a sidehill! A pocket[3] hunter's delight an' a cayuse's paradise! Cool green for tired eyes! Pink pills for pale people ain't in it. A secret pasture for prospectors and a resting place for tired burros, by damn!"

He was a sandy-complexioned man in whose face geniality and humor seemed the salient[4] characteristics. It was a mobile face, quick-changing to inward mood and thought. Thinking was in him a visible process. Ideas chased across his face like wind flaws across the surface of a lake. His hair, sparse and unkempt of growth, was as indeterminate and colorless as his complexion. It would seem that all the color of his frame had gone into his eyes, for they were startlingly blue. Also, they were laughing and merry eyes, within them much of the naïveté and wonder of the child; and yet, in an unassertive way, they contained much of calm self-reliance and strength of purpose founded upon self-experience and experience of the world.

From out the screen of vines and creepers he flung ahead of him a miner's pick and shovel and gold pan. Then he crawled out himself into the open. He was clad in faded overalls and black cotton shirt, with hobnailed brogans on his feet, and on his head a hat whose shapelessness and stains advertised the rough usage of wind and rain and sun and camp smoke. He stood erect, seeing wide-eyed the secrecy of the scene and sensuously inhaling the warm, sweet breath of the canyon garden through nostrils that dilated and quivered with delight. His eyes narrowed to laughing slits of blue, his face wreathed itself in joy, and his mouth curled in a smile as he cried aloud: "Jumping dandelions and happy hollyhocks, but that smells good to me! Talk about your attar o' roses an' cologne factories! They ain't in it!"

He had the habit of soliloquy. His quick-changing facial expressions might tell every thought and mood, but the tongue, perforce, ran hard after, repeating, like a second Boswell.[5]

The man lay down on the lip of the pool and drank long and deep of its water. "Tastes good to me," he murmured, lifting his head and gazing across the pool at the sidehill, while he wiped his mouth with the back of his hand. The sidehill attracted his attention. Still lying on his stomach, he studied the hill formation long and carefully. It was a practiced eye that traveled up the slope to the crumbling canyon wall and back and down again to the edge of the pool. He scrambled to his feet and favored the sidehill with a second survey.

"Looks good to me," he concluded, picking up his pick and shovel and gold pan. He crossed the stream below the pool, stepping agilely from stone to stone. Where the sidehill touched the water he dug up a shovelful of dirt and put it into the gold pan. He squatted down, holding the pan in his two hands and partly immersing it in the stream. Then he imparted to the pan a deft circular motion that sent the water sluicing in and out through the dirt and gravel. The larger and the lighter particles worked to the surface, and these, by a skillful dipping movement of the pan, he spilled out and over the

---

3 **pocket:** bed or cavity.
4 **salient:** noticeable; outstanding.

5 **Boswell:** James Boswell, a famous biographer.

edge. Occasionally, to expedite matters, he rested the pan and with his fingers raked out the large pebbles and pieces of rock.

The contents of the pan diminished rapidly until only fine dirt and the smallest bits of gravel remained. At this stage he began to work very deliberately and carefully. It was fine washing, and he washed fine and finer, with a keen scrutiny and delicate and fastidious touch. At last the pan seemed empty of everything but water; but with a quick semicircular flirt[6] that sent the water flying over the shallow rim into the stream, he disclosed a layer of black sand on the bottom of the pan. So thin was this layer that it was like a streak of paint. He examined it closely. In the midst of it was a tiny golden speck. He dribbled a little water in over the depressed edge of the pan. With a

6 flirt: quick toss.

quick flirt he sent the water sluicing across the bottom, turning the grains of black sand over and over. A second tiny golden speck rewarded his effort.

The washing had now become very fine—fine beyond all need of ordinary placer mining. He worked the black sand, a small portion at a time, up the shallow rim of the pan. Each small portion he examined sharply, so that his eyes saw every grain of it before he allowed it to slide over the edge and away. Jealously, bit by bit, he let the black sand slip away. A golden speck, no larger than a pin point, appeared on the rim, and by his manipulation of the water it returned to the bottom of the pan. And in such fashion another speck was disclosed, and another. Great was his care of them. Like a shepherd he herded his flock of golden specks so that not one should be lost. At last, of the pan of dirt nothing remained but his golden herd. He counted it, and then, after all his labor, sent it flying out of the pan with one final swirl of water.

But his blue eyes were shining with desire as he rose to his feet. "Seven," he muttered aloud, asserting the sum of the specks for which he had toiled so hard and which he had so wantonly thrown away. "Seven," he repeated, with the emphasis of one trying to impress a number on his memory.

He stood still a long while, surveying the hillside. In his eyes was a curiosity, new aroused and burning. There was an exultance about his bearing and a keenness like that of a hunting animal catching the fresh scent of game.

He moved down the stream a few steps and took a second panful of dirt.

Again came the careful washing, the jealous herding of the golden specks, and the wantonness with which he sent them flying into the stream when he had counted their number.

"Five," he muttered, and repeated, "five."

He could not forbear another survey of the hill before filling the pan farther down the stream. His golden herds diminished. "Four, three, two, two, one," were his memory tabulations as he moved down the stream. When but one speck of gold rewarded his washing, he stopped and built a fire of dry twigs. Into this he thrust the gold pan and burned it till it was blue-black. He held up the pan and examined it critically. Then he nodded approbation. Against such a color background he could defy the tiniest yellow speck to elude him.

Still moving down the stream, he panned again. A single speck was his reward. A third pan contained no gold at all. Not satisfied with this, he panned three times again, taking his shovels of dirt within a foot of one another. Each pan proved empty of gold, and the fact, instead of discouraging him, seemed to give him satisfaction. His elation increased with each barren washing, until he arose, exclaiming jubilantly, "If it ain't the real thing, may God knock off my head with sour apples!"

Returning to where he had started operations, he began to pan up the stream. At first his golden herds increased—increased prodigiously. "Fourteen, eighteen, twenty-one, twenty-six," ran his memory tabulations. Just above the pool he struck his richest pan— thirty-five colors.

"Almost enough to save," he remarked regretfully, as he allowed the water to sweep them away.

The sun climbed to the top of the sky. The man worked on. Pan by pan he went up the stream, the tally of results steadily decreasing.

"It's just booful, the way it peters out," he exulted when a shovelful of dirt contained no more than a single speck of gold.

And when no specks at all were found in several pans, he straightened up and favored the hillside with a confident glance.

"Ah, ha! Mr. Pocket!" he cried out, as though to an auditor hidden somewhere above him beneath the surface of the slope. "Ah, ha! Mr. Pocket! I'm a-comin', I'm a-comin', an' I'm shorely gwine to get yer! You heah me, Mr. Pocket? I'm gwine to get yer as shore as punkins ain't cauliflowers!"

He turned and flung a measuring glance at the sun poised above him in the azure of the cloudless sky. Then he went down the canyon, following the line of shovel holes he had made in filling the pans. He crossed the stream below the pool and disappeared through the green screen. There was little opportunity for the spirit of the place to return with its quietude and repose, for the man's voice, raised in ragtime song, still dominated the canyon with possession.

After a time, with a greater clashing of steel-shod feet on rock, he returned. The green screen was tremendously agitated. It surged back and forth in the throes of a struggle. There was a loud grating and clanging of metal. The man's voice leaped to a higher pitch and was sharp with imperativeness. A large body plunged and panted. There was a snapping and ripping and rending, and amid a shower of falling leaves a horse burst through the screen. On its back was a pack, and from this trailed broken vines and torn creepers. The animal gazed with astonished eyes at the scene into which it had been precipitated, then dropped its head to the grass and began contentedly to graze. A second horse scrambled into view, slipping once on the mossy rocks and regaining equilibrium when its hoofs sank into the yielding surface of the meadow. It was riderless, though on its back was a high-horned Mexican saddle, scarred and discolored by long usage.

The man brought up the rear. He threw off pack and saddle, with an eye to camp location, and gave the animals their freedom to graze. He unpacked his food and got out frying pan and coffeepot. He gathered an armful of dry wood, and with a few stones made a place for his fire.

"My!" he said, "but I've got an appetite. I could scoff iron filings an' horseshoe nails an' thank you kindly, ma'am, for a second helpin'."

He straightened up, and while he reached for matches in the pocket of his overalls his eyes traveled across the pool to the sidehill. His fingers had clutched the matchbox, but they re-

laxed their hold and the hand came out empty. The man wavered perceptibly. He looked at his preparations for cooking and he looked at the hill.

"Guess I'll take another whack at her," he concluded, starting to cross the stream.

"They ain't no sense in it, I know," he mumbled apologetically. "But keepin' grub back an hour ain't goin' to hurt none, I reckon."

A few feet back from his first line of test pans he started a second line. The sun dropped down the western sky, the shadows lengthened, but the man worked on. He began a third line of test pans. He was crosscutting the hillside, line by line, as he ascended. The center of each line produced the richest pans, while the ends came where no colors showed in the pan. And as he ascended the hillside the lines grew perceptibly shorter. The regularity with which their length diminished served to indicate that somewhere up the slope the last line would be so short as to have scarcely length at all, and that beyond could come only a point. The design was growing into an inverted V. The converging sides of this V marked the boundaries of the gold-bearing dirt.

The apex of the V was evidently the man's goal. Often he ran his eye along the converging sides and on up the hill, trying to divine the apex—the point where the gold-bearing dirt must cease. Here resided "Mr. Pocket," for so the man familiarly addressed the imaginary point above him on the slope, crying out: "Come down out o' that, Mr. Pocket! Be right smart an' agreeable, an' come down!"

"All right," he would add later, in a voice resigned to determination. "All right, Mr. Pocket. It's plain to me I got to come right up an' snatch you out bald-headed. An' I'll do it! I'll do it!" he would threaten still later.

Each pan he carried down to the water to wash, and as he went higher up the hill the pans grew richer, until he began to save the gold in an empty baking-powder can which he carried carelessly in his hip pocket. So engrossed was he in his toil that he did not notice the long twilight of oncoming night. It was not until he tried vainly to see the gold colors in the bottom of the pan that he realized the passage of time. He straightened up abruptly. An expression of whimsical wonderment and awe overspread his face as he drawled, "Gosh darn my buttons! if I didn't plum forget dinner!"

He stumbled across the stream in the darkness and lighted his long-delayed fire. Flapjacks and bacon and warmed-over beans constituted his supper. Then he smoked a pipe by the smoldering coals, listening to the night noises and watching the moonlight stream through the canyon. After that he unrolled his bed, took off his heavy shoes, and pulled the blankets up to his chin. His face showed white in the moonlight, like the face of a corpse. But it was a corpse that knew its resurrection, for the man rose suddenly on one elbow and gazed across at his hillside.

"Good night, Mr. Pocket," he called sleepily. "Good night."

He slept through the early gray of morning until the direct rays of the sun smote his closed eyelids, when he awoke with a start and looked about him until he had established the continuity of his existence and identified his present self with the days previously lived.

To dress he had merely to buckle on his shoes. He glanced at his fireplace and at his hillside, wavered, but fought down the temptation and started the fire.

"Keep yer shirt on, Bill; keep yer shirt on," he admonished himself. "What's the good of rushin'? No use in gettin' all het up an' sweaty. Mr. Pocket'll wait for you. He ain't a-runnin' away before you can get yer breakfast. Now, what you want, Bill, is something fresh in yer bill o' fare. So it's up to you to go an' get it."

He cut a short pole at the water's edge and drew from one of his pockets a bit of line and a draggled fly that had once been a royal coachman.[7]

"Mebbe they'll bite in the early morning," he muttered as he made his first cast into the pool. And a moment later he was gleefully crying: "What'd I tell you, eh? What'd I tell you?"

He had no reel, nor any inclination to waste time, and by main strength, and swiftly, he drew out of the water a flashing ten-inch trout. Three more, caught in rapid succession, furnished his breakfast. When he came to the stepping-stones on his way to his hillside, he was struck by a sudden thought, and paused.

"I'd just better take a hike downstream a ways," he said. "There's no tellin' what cuss may be snoopin' around."

But he crossed over on the stones, and with a "I really oughter take that hike," the need of the precaution passed out of his mind and he fell to work.

At nightfall he straightened up. The small of his back was stiff from stooping toil, and as he put his hand behind him to soothe the protesting muscles, he said: "Now what d'ye think of that, by damn? I clean forgot my dinner again! If I don't watch out, I'll sure be degeneratin' into a two-meal-a-day crank."

"Pockets is the damnedest things I

7 **royal coachman:** artificial fly.

ever see for makin' a man absent-minded," he communed that night, as he crawled into his blankets. Nor did he forget to call up the hillside, "Good night, Mr. Pocket! Good night!"

Rising with the sun and snatching a hasty breakfast, he was early at work. A fever seemed to be growing in him, nor did the increasing richness of the test pans allay this fever. There was a flush in his cheek other than that made by the heat of the sun, and he was oblivious to fatigue and the passage of time. When he filled a pan with dirt, he ran down the hill to wash it; nor could he forbear running up the hill again, panting and stumbling profanely, to refill the pan.

He was now a hundred yards from the water, and the inverted V was assuming definite proportions. The width of the pay dirt steadily decreased, and the man extended in his mind's eye the sides of the V to their meeting place far up the hill. This was his goal, the apex of the V, and he panned many times to locate it.

"Just about two yards above that manzanita bush an' a yard to the right," he finally concluded.

Then the temptation seized him. "As plain as the nose on your face," he said as he abandoned his laborious cross-cutting and climbed to the indicated apex. He filled a pan and carried it down the hill to wash. It contained no trace of gold. He dug deep, and he dug shallow, filling and washing a dozen pans, and was unrewarded even by the tiniest golden speck. He was enraged at having yielded to the temptation, and cursed himself blasphemously and pridelessly. Then he went down the hill and took up the cross-cutting.

"Slow an' certain, Bill; slow an' certain," he crooned. "Short cuts to for-tune ain't in your line, an' it's about time you know it. Get wise, Bill; get wise. Slow an' certain 's the only hand you can play; so go to it, an' keep to it, too."

As the crosscuts decreased, showing that the sides of the V were converging, the depth of the V increased. The gold trace was dipping into the hill. It was only at thirty inches beneath the surface that he could get colors in his pan. The dirt he found at twenty-five inches from the surface, and at thirty-five inches, yielded barren pans. At the base of the V, by the water's edge, he had found the gold colors at the grass roots. The higher he went up the hill, the deeper the gold dipped. To dig a hole three feet deep in order to get one test pan was a task of no mean magnitude; while between the man and the apex intervened an untold number of such holes to be dug. "An' there's no tellin' how much deeper it'll pitch," he sighed, in a moment's pause, while his fingers soothed his aching back.

Feverish with desire, with aching back and stiffening muscles, with pick and shovel gouging and mauling the soft brown earth, the man toiled up the hill. Before him was the smooth slope, spangled with flowers and made sweet with their breath. Behind him was devastation. It looked like some terrible eruption breaking out on the smooth skin of the hill. His slow progress was like that of a slug, befouling beauty with a monstrous trail.

Though the dipping gold trace increased the man's work, he found consolation in the increasing richness of the pans. Twenty cents, thirty cents, fifty cents, sixty cents, were the values of the gold found in the pans, and at nightfall he washed his banner pan, which gave him a dollar's worth of gold dust from a shovelful of dirt.

"I'll just bet it's my luck to have some inquisitive cuss come buttin' in here on my pasture," he mumbled sleepily that night as he pulled the blankets up to his chin.

Suddenly he sat upright. "Bill!" he called sharply. "Now, listen to me, Bill; d'ye hear! It's up to you, tomorrow mornin', to mosey round an' see what you can see. Understand? Tomorrow morning, an' don't you forget it!"

He yawned and glanced across at his sidehill. "Good night, Mr. Pocket," he called.

In the morning he stole a march on the sun, for he had finished breakfast when its first rays caught him, and he was climbing the wall of the canyon where it crumbled away and gave footing. From the outlook at the top he found himself in the midst of loncliness. As far as he could see, chain after chain of mountains heaved them-

selves into his vision. To the east his eyes, leaping the miles between range and range and between many ranges, brought up at last against the white-peaked Sierras—the main crest, where the backbone of the Western world reared itself against the sky. To the north and south he could see more distinctly the cross systems that broke through the main trend of the sea of mountains. To the west the ranges fell away, one behind the other, diminishing and fading into the gentle foothills that, in turn, descended into the great valley which he could not see.

And in all that mighty sweep of earth he saw no sign of man nor of the handiwork of man, save only the torn bosom of the hillside at his feet. The man looked long and carefully. Once, far down his own canyon, he thought he saw in the air a faint hint of smoke. He looked again and decided that it was the purple haze of the hills made dark by a convolution[8] of the canyon wall at its back.

"Hey, you, Mr. Pocket!" he called down into the canyon. "Stand out from under! I'm a-comin', Mr. Pocket! I'm a-comin'!"

The heavy brogans on the man's feet made him appear clumsy-footed, but he swung down from the giddy height as lightly and airily as a mountain goat. A rock, turning under his foot on the edge of the precipice, did not disconcert him. He seemed to know the precise time required for the turn to culminate in disaster, and in the meantime he utilized the false footing itself for the momentary earth contact necessary to carry him on into safety. Where the earth sloped so steeply that it was impossible to stand for a second upright, the man did not hesitate. His foot pressed the impossible surface for but a fraction of the fatal second and gave him the bound that carried him onward. Again, where even the fraction of a second's footing was out of the question, he would swing his body past by a moment's handgrip on a jutting knob of rock, a crevice, or a precariously rooted shrub. At last, with a wild leap and yell, he exchanged the face of the wall for an earth slide and finished the descent in the midst of several tons of sliding earth and gravel.

His first pan of the morning washed out over two dollars in coarse gold. It was from the center of the V. To either side the diminution in the values of the pans was swift. His lines of crosscutting holes were growing very short. The converging sides of the inverted V were only a few yards apart. Their meeting point was only a few yards above him. But the pay streak was dipping deeper and deeper into the earth. By early afternoon he was sinking the test holes five feet before the pans could show the gold trace.

For that matter, the gold trace had become something more than a trace; it was a placer mine[9] in itself, and the man resolved to come back, after he had found the pocket, and work over the ground. But the increasing richness of the pans began to worry him. By later afternoon the worth of the pans had grown to three and four dollars. The man scratched his head perplexedly and looked a few feet up the hill at the manzanita bush that marked approximately the apex of the V. He nodded his head and said oracularly: "It's one o' two things, Bill; one o' two things. Either Mr. Pocket's spilled himself all out an' down the hill, or else Mr. Pocket's that damned rich you maybe won't be able to carry him all away with you. And that'd be terrible, wouldn't it, now?" He chuckled at contemplation of so pleasant a dilemma.

Nightfall found him by the edge of the stream, his eyes wrestling with the gathering darkness over the washing of a five-dollar pan.

"Wisht I had an electric light to go on working," he said.

He found sleep difficult that night. Many times he composed himself and closed his eyes for slumber to overtake him; but his blood pounded with too strong desire, and as many times his eyes opened and he murmured wearily, "Wisht it was sun-up."

Sleep came to him in the end, but his eyes were open with the first paling of the stars, and the gray of dawn caught him with breakfast finished and climbing the hillside in the direction of the secret abiding place of Mr. Pocket.

The first crosscut the man made,

---

8 convolution: a winding; twist.

9 placer mine: superficial deposit of gold.

there was space for only three holes, so narrow had become the pay streak and so close was he to the fountainhead of the golden stream he had been following for four days.

"Be ca'm, Bill; be ca'm," he admonished himself as he broke ground for the final hole where the sides of the V had at last come together in a point.

"I've got the almighty cinch on you, Mr. Pocket, an' you can't lose me," he said many times as he sank the hole deeper and deeper.

Four feet, five feet, six feet, he dug his way down into the earth. The digging grew harder. His pick grated on broken rock. He examined the rock. "Rotten quartz" was his conclusion as, with the shovel, he cleared the bottom of the hole of loose dirt. He attacked the crumbling quartz with the pick, bursting the disintegrating rock asunder with every stroke.

He thrust his shovel into the loose mass. His eye caught a gleam of yellow. He dropped the shovel and squatted suddenly on his heels. As a farmer rubs the clinging earth from fresh-dug potatoes, so the man, a piece of rotten quartz held in both hands, rubbed the dirt away.

"Sufferin' Sardanapolis!" he cried. "Lumps an' chunks of it! Lumps an' chunks of it!"

It was only half rock he held in his hand. The other half was virgin gold. He dropped it into his pan and examined another piece. Little yellow was to be seen, but with his strong fingers he crumbled the rotten quartz away till both hands were filled with glowing yellow. He rubbed the dirt away from fragment after fragment, tossing them into the gold pan. It was a treasure hole. So much had the quartz rotted away that there was less of it than there was of gold. Now and again he found a piece to which no rock clung—a piece that was all gold. A chunk where the pick had laid open the heart of the gold glittered like a handful of yellow jewels, and he cocked his head at it and slowly turned it around and over to observe the rich play of the light upon it.

"Talk about yer Too Much Gold diggin's!" the man snorted contemptuously. "Why, this diggin' 'd make it look like thirty cents. This diggin' is All Gold. An' right here an' now I name this yere canyon 'All Gold Canyon,' b' gosh!"

Still squatting on his heels, he continued examining the fragments and tossing them into the pan. Suddenly there came to him a premonition of danger. It seemed a shadow had fallen upon him. But there was no shadow. His heart had given a great jump up into his throat and was choking him. Then his blood slowly chilled and he felt the sweat of his shirt cold against his flesh.

He did not spring up nor look around. He did not move. He was considering the nature of the premonition he had received, trying to locate the source of the mysterious force that had warned him, striving to sense the imperative presence of the unseen thing that threatened him. There is an aura of things hostile, made manifest by messengers too refined for the senses to know; and this aura he felt, but knew not how he felt it. His was the feeling as when a cloud passes over the sun. It seemed that between him and life had passed something dark and smothering and menacing, a gloom, as it were, that swallowed up life and made for death—his death.

Every force of his being impelled him to spring up and confront the unseen danger, but his soul dominated the panic, and he remained squatting on his heels, in his hands a chunk of gold. He did not dare to look around, but he knew by now that there was something behind him and above him. He made believe to be interested in the gold in his hand. He examined it critically, turned it over and over, and rubbed the dirt from it. And all the time he knew that something behind him was looking at the gold over his shoulder.

Still feigning interest in the chunk of gold in his hand, he listened intently, and he heard the breathing of the thing behind him. His eyes searched the ground in front of him for a weapon, but they saw only the uprooted gold, worthless to him now in his extremity. There was his pick, a handy weapon on occasion; but this was not such an occasion. The man realized his predicament. He was in a narrow hole that was seven feet deep. His head did not come to the surface of the ground. He was in a trap.

He remained squatting on his heels. He was quite cool and collected; but his mind, considering every factor, showed him only his helplessness. He continued rubbing the dirt from the quartz fragments and throwing the gold into the pan. There was nothing else for him to do. Yet he knew that he would have to rise up, sooner or later, and face the danger that breathed at his back. The minutes passed, and with the passage of each minute he knew that by so much he was nearer the time when he must stand up, or else—and his wet shirt went cold against his flesh again at the thought—or else he might receive death as he stooped there over his treasure.

Still he squatted on his heels, rubbing dirt from gold and debating in just what manner he should rise up. He might rise up with a rush and claw his way out of the hole to meet whatever threatened on the even footing above ground; or he might rise up slowly and carelessly, and feign casually to discover the thing that breathed at his back. His instinct and every fighting fiber of his body favored the mad, clawing rush to the surface. His intellect, and the craft thereof, favored the slow and cautious meeting with the thing that menaced and that he could not see. And while he debated, a loud, crashing noise burst on his ear. At the same instant he received a stunning blow on the left side of the back, and from the point of impact felt a rush of flame through his flesh. He sprang up in the air, but halfway to his feet collapsed. His body crumpled in like a leaf withered in sudden heat, and he came down, his chest across his pan of gold, his face in the dirt and rock, his legs tangled and twisted because of the restricted space at the bottom of the hole. His legs twitched convulsively several times. His body was shaken as with a mighty ague. There was a slow expansion of the lungs, accompanied by a deep sigh. Then the air was slowly, very slowly, exhaled, and his body as slowly flattened itself down into inertness.

Above, revolver in hand, a man was peering down over the edge of the hole. He peered for a long time at the prone and motionless body beneath him. After a while the stranger sat down on the edge of the hole so that he could see into it, and rested the revolver on his knee. Reaching his hand into a pocket, he drew out a wisp of brown paper. Into this he dropped a few crumbs of tobacco. The combination became a cigarette, brown and squat, with the ends turned in. Not once did he take his eyes from the body at the bottom of the hole. He lighted the cigarette and drew its smoke into his

lungs with a caressing intake of the breath. He smoked slowly. Once the cigarette went out and he relighted it. And all the while he studied the body beneath him.

In the end he tossed the cigarette stub away and rose to his feet. He moved to the edge of the hole. Spanning it, a hand resting on each edge, and with the revolver still in the right hand, he muscled his body down into the hole. While his feet were yet a yard from the bottom he released his hands and dropped down.

At the instant his feet struck bottom he saw the pocket miner's arm leap out, and his own legs knew a swift, jerking grip that overthrew him. In the nature of the jump his revolver hand was above his head. Swiftly as the grip had flashed about his legs, just as swiftly he brought the revolver down. He was still in the air, his fall in process of completion, when he pulled the trigger. The explosion was deafening

in the confined space. The smoke filled the hole so that he could see nothing. He struck the bottom on his back, and like a cat's the pocket miner's body was on top of him. Even as the miner's body passed on top the stranger crooked in his right arm to fire; and even in that instant the miner, with a quick thrust of elbow, struck his wrist. The muzzle was thrown up, and the bullet thudded into the dirt of the side of the hole.

The next instant the stranger felt the miner's hand grip his wrist. The struggle was now for the revolver. Each man strove to turn it against the other's body. The smoke in the hole was clearing. The stranger, lying on his back, was beginning to see dimly. But suddenly he was blinded by a handful of dirt deliberately flung into his eyes by his antagonist. In that moment of shock his grip on the revolver was broken. In the next moment he felt a smashing darkness descend upon his brain, and in the midst of the darkness even the darkness ceased.

But the pocket miner fired again and again, until the revolver was empty. Then he tossed it from him and, breathing heavily, sat down on the dead man's legs.

The miner was sobbing and struggling for breath. "Measly skunk!" he panted; "a-campin' on my trail an' lettin' me do the work, an' then shootin' me in the back!"

He was half crying from anger and exhaustion. He peered at the face of the dead man. It was sprinkled with loose dirt and gravel, and it was difficult to distinguish the features.

"Never laid eyes on him before," the miner concluded his scrutiny. "Just a common an' ordinary thief, damn him! An' he shot me in the back! He shot me in the back!"

He opened his shirt and felt himself, front and back, on his left side.

"Went clean through, and no harm done!" he cried jubilantly. "I'll bet he aimed all right, all right; but he drew the gun over when he pulled the trigger—the cuss! But I fixed 'm! Oh, I fixed 'm!"

His fingers were investigating the bullet hole in his side, and a shade of regret passed over his face. "It's goin' to be stiff," he said. "An' it's up to me to get mended an' get out o' here."

He crawled out of the hole and went down the hill to his camp. Half an hour later he returned, leading his pack horse. His open shirt disclosed the rude bandages with which he had dressed his wounds. He was slow and awkward with his left-hand movements, but that did not prevent his using the arm.

The bight[10] of the pack rope under

10 bight: middle part or loop in a rope.

the dead man's shoulders enabled him to heave the body out of the hole. Then he set to work gathering up his gold. He worked steadily for several hours, pausing often to rest his stiffening shoulder and to exclaim: "He shot me in the back, the measly skunk! He shot me in the back!"

When his treasure was quite cleaned up and wrapped securely into a number of blanket-covered parcels, he made an estimate of its value.

"Four hundred pounds, or I'm a Hottentot," he concluded. "Say two hundred in quartz an' dirt; that leaves two hundred pounds of gold. Bill! Wake up. Two hundred pounds of gold! Forty thousand dollars! An' it's yourn —all yourn!"

He scratched his head delightedly and his fingers blundered into an unfamiliar groove. They quested along it for several inches. It was a crease through his scalp where the second bullet had plowed.

He walked angrily over to the dead man.

"You would, would you?" he bullied. "You would, eh? Well, I fixed you good an' plenty, an' I'll give you decent burial, too. That's more 'n you'd have done for me."

He dragged the body to the edge of the hole and toppled it in. It struck the bottom with a dull crash, on its side, the face twisted up to the light. The miner peered down at it.

"An' you shot me in the back!" he said accusingly.

With pick and shovel he filled the hole. Then he loaded the gold on his horse. It was too great a load for the animal, and when he had gained his camp he transferred part of it to his saddle horse. Even so, he was compelled to abandon a portion of his outfit—pick and shovel and gold pan, extra food and cooking utensils, and divers odds and ends.

The sun was at the zenith when the man forced the horses at the screen of vines and creepers. To climb the huge boulders the animals were compelled to uprear and struggle blindly through the tangled mass of vegetation. Once the saddle horse fell heavily, and the man removed the pack to get the animal on his feet. After it started on its way again the man thrust his head out from among the leaves and peered up at the sidehill.

"The measly skunk!" he said, and disappeared.

There was a ripping and tearing of vines and boughs. The trees surged back and forth, marking the passage of the animals through the midst of them. There was a clashing of steel-shod hoofs on stone, and now and again an oath or a sharp cry of command. Then the voice of the man was raised in song:

"Tu'n around an' tu'n yo' face
Untoe them sweet hills of grace
  (D' pow'rs of sin yo' am scornin'!).
Look about an' look aroun',
Fling yo' sin-pack on d' groun'
  (Yo' will meet wid d' Lord in d' mornin'!)."

The song grew faint and fainter, and through the silence crept back the spirit of the place. The stream once more drowsed and whispered; the hum of the mountain bees rose sleepily. Down through the perfume-weighted air fluttered the snowy fluffs of the cottonwoods. The butterflies drifted in and out among the trees, and over all blazed the quiet sunshine. Only remained the hoof marks in the meadow and the torn hillside to mark the boisterous trail of the life that had broken the peace of the place and passed on.

Understanding the Story

1. What is the theme of London's story? What is he saying about nature or about man? Upon what evidence in the story do you base your answer?
2. What mood is established by the opening description of the canyon? How does it change with the miner's arrival? Find specific words used by the author that contrast the disappearance of the buck with the arrival of the man.
3. Explain what London tells about the miner in this paragraph: "He stood still a long while, surveying the hillside. In his eyes was a curiosity, new aroused and burning. There was an exultance about his bearing and a keenness like that of a hunting animal catching the fresh scent of game."
4. How does the author let you know what the miner is thinking? Why is this device more effective than an author's summary of the miner's thoughts would be?
5. What two conflicts does Bill face in the story? What characteristics enable him to win both encounters?
6. What examples of foreshadowing (hints of what is going to happen) can you find that make the appearance of the attacker seem natural?
7. How does the author present the attacker so that you have no regret or pity when he is killed?

JACK LONDON

8. How does the miner react to the intruder's attack? Does he have any twinges of conscience at any time because of killing a man? Do you blame him for the killing as you read the story? How do you account for these reactions?
9. How do the last two paragraphs help to give the story unity?

Building Vocabulary Skills

Find a phrase or synonym giving the meaning that the italicized words have in the story:

1. *turbulent* downrush (p. 101, col. 1)
2. *resilient* surface (p. 101, col. 1)
3. *languid* with rest (p. 102, col. 1)
4. *intangible* fabric (p. 102, col. 1)
5. stream grown *garrulous* (p. 102, col. 2)
6. *indeterminate* and colorless (p. 103, col. 1)
7. habit of *soliloquy* (p. 103, col. 2)
8. *wavered* perceptibly (p. 106, col. 2)
9. memory *tabulations* (p. 105, col. 1)
10. *whimsical* wonderment (p. 107, col. 1)
11. *perceptibly* shorter (p. 106, col. 2)
12. *continuity* of his existence (p. 107, col. 2)
13. *apex* of the V (p. 106, col. 2)
14. no *mean* magnitude (p. 108, col. 2)
15. *premonition* of danger (p. 111, col. 2)
16. *aura* of things hostile (p. 111, col. 2)

Developing Language Skills

Select a scene which, to you, conveys some definite effect, such as eerieness, loneliness, or wildness. Through careful selection of details and choice of words, describe this scene in one or two paragraphs so as to make clear the effect of the scene.

Reading "A Mystery of Heroism"

To write a convincing story, an author must reveal the purposes and impulses that determine the behavior of his characters. These various purposes, impulses, and desires are what make up a character's *motivation*. In some stories the motives for a character's action are obvious. In "All Gold Canyon," for example, the miner has two clear motives: one to find the pocket of gold and the other to save his life. In "A Mystery of Heroism," however, a major point of the story is that the main character does not know why he acts as he does. Nevertheless, Crane makes the soldier's behavior and his uncertainty wholly believable. In daily life we often see people perform actions that result partly from desires of which they are not conscious, or perhaps from the excitement and confusion of events around them, or even from the need simply to do something rather than remain inactive. Although Private Collins remains as confused about his motives at the end of this story as at the beginning, the reader should have a clearer understanding than the young soldier of the motives that led to his apparently unexplainable actions.

A Mystery of Heroism

Stephen Crane

Crane's short story "A Mystery of Heroism" is similar to his famous novel The Red Badge of Courage, *in that it concerns a common soldier in the War Between the States and reports his confusions and fears. This selection illustrates Crane's effective selection of realistic details and his skillful choice of words to convey these details in giving his impression of a battle scene.*

THE DARK UNIFORMS of the men were so coated with dust from the incessant wrestling of the two armies that the regiment almost seemed a part of the clay bank which shielded them from the shells. On the top of the hill a battery was arguing in tremendous roars with some other guns, and to the eye of the infantry,[1] the artillerymen, the guns, the caissons,[2] the horses, were distinctly outlined upon the blue sky. When a piece was fired, a red streak as round as a log flashed low in the heavens, like a monstrous bolt of lightning. The men of the battery wore white duck trousers, which somehow emphasized their legs; and when they ran and crowded in little groups at the bidding of the shouting officers, it was more impressive than usual to the infantry.

Fred Collins, of A Company, was saying: "Thunder! I wisht I had a drink. Ain't there any water round here?" Then somebody yelled, "There goes th' bugler!"

As the eyes of half the regiment swept in one machinelike movement there was an instant's picture of a horse in a great convulsive leap of a death wound and a rider leaning back with a crooked arm and spread fingers before his face. On the ground was the crimson terror of an exploding shell, with fibers of flame that seemed like lances. A glittering bugle swung clear of the rider's back as fell headlong the horse and the man. In the air was an odor as from a conflagration.

Sometimes they of the infantry looked down at a fair little meadow which spread at their feet. Its long, green grass was rippling gently in a breeze.

1 **infantry:** foot soldiers.
2 **caissons** (kā′sənz): ammunition wagons for artillery.

Beyond it was the gray form of a house half torn to pieces by shells and by the busy axes of soldiers who had pursued firewood. The line of an old fence was now dimly marked by long weeds and by an occasional post. A shell had blown the well-house to fragments. Little lines of gray smoke ribboning upward from some embers indicated the place where had stood the barn.

From beyond a curtain of green woods there came the sound of some stupendous scuffle, as if two animals of the size of islands were fighting. At a distance there were occasional appearances of swift-moving men, horses, batteries, flags, and, with the crashing of infantry volleys were heard, often, wild and frenzied cheers. In the midst of it all Smith and Ferguson, two privates of A Company, were engaged in a heated discussion, which involved the greatest questions of the national existence.

The battery on the hill presently engaged in a frightful duel. The white legs of the gunners scampered this way and that way, and the officers redoubled their shouts. The guns, with their demeanors of stolidity and courage, were typical of something infinitely self-possessed in this clamor of death that swirled around the hill.

One of a "swing" team[3] was suddenly smitten quivering to the ground, and his maddened brethren dragged his torn body in their struggle to escape from this turmoil and danger. A young soldier astride one of the leaders swore and fumed in his saddle, and furiously jerked at the bridle. An officer screamed out an order so violently that his voice broke and ended the sentence in a falsetto[4] shriek.

The leading company of the infantry regiment was somewhat exposed, and the colonel ordered it moved more fully under the shelter of the hill. There was the clank of steel against steel.

A lieutenant of the battery rode down and passed them, holding his right arm carefully in his left hand. And it was as if this arm was not at all a part of him, but belonged to another man. His sober and reflective charger[5] went slowly. The officer's face was grimy and perspiring, and his uniform was tousled as if he had been in direct grapple with an enemy. He smiled grimly when the men stared at him. He turned his horse toward the meadow.

Collins, of A Company, said: "I wisht I had a drink. I bet there's water in that there ol' well yonder!"

"Yes; but how you goin' to git it?"

For the little meadow which intervened was now suffering a terrible onslaught of shells. Its green and beautiful calm had vanished utterly. Brown earth was being flung in monstrous handfuls. And there was a massacre of the young blades of grass. They were being torn, burned, obliterated. Some curious fortune of the battle had made this gentle little meadow the object of the red hate of the shells, and each one as it exploded seemed like an imprecation[6] in the face of a maiden.

The wounded officer who was riding across this expanse said to himself, "Why, they couldn't shoot any harder if the whole army was massed here!"

A shell struck the gray ruins of the house, and as, after the roar, the shattered wall fell in fragments, there was a noise which resembled the flapping of shutters during a wild gale of winter. Indeed, the infantry paused in the

---

3 **"swing" team:** battery horses used to move gun carriages into position.
4 **falsetto** (fôl sĕt′ō): high, artificial voice.

5 **charger:** horse trained to charge.
6 **imprecation:** curse.

shelter of the bank appeared as men standing upon a shore contemplating a madness of the sea. The angel of calamity had under its glance the battery upon the hill. Fewer white-legged men labored about the guns. A shell had smitten one of the pieces, and after the flare, the smoke, the dust, the wrath of this blow were gone, it was possible to see white legs stretched horizontally upon the ground. And at that interval to the rear, where it is the business of battery horses to stand with their noses to the fight awaiting the command to drag their guns out of the destruction or into it or wheresoever these incomprehensible humans demanded with whip and spur—in this line of passive and dumb spectators, whose fluttering hearts yet would not let them forget the iron laws of man's control of them—in this rank of brute-soldiers there had been relentless and hideous carnage. From the ruck[7] of bleeding and prostrate horses, the men of the infantry could see one animal raising its stricken body with its forelegs, and turning its nose with mystic and profound eloquence toward the sky.

Some comrades joked Collins about his thirst. "Well, if yeh want a drink so bad, why don't yeh go git it!"

"Well, I will in a minnet, if yeh don't shut up!"

A lieutenant of artillery floundered his horse straight down the hill with as great concern as if it were level ground. As he galloped past the colonel of the infantry, he threw up his hand in swift salute. "We've got to get out of that," he roared angrily. He was a black-bearded officer, and his eyes, which resembled beads, sparkled like those of an insane man. His jumping horse sped along the column of infantry.

7 **ruck:** multitude.

The fat major, standing carelessly with his sword held horizontally behind him and with his legs far apart, looked after the receding horseman and laughed. "He wants to get back with orders pretty quick, or there'll be no batt'ry left," he observed.

The wise young captain of the second company hazarded to the lieutenant colonel that the enemy's infantry would probably soon attack the hill, and the lieutenant colonel snubbed him.

A private in one of the rear companies looked out over the meadow, and then turned to a companion and said, "Look there, Jim!" It was the wounded officer from the battery, who some time before had started to ride across the meadow, supporting his right arm carefully with his left hand. This man had encountered a shell apparently at a time when no one perceived him, and he could now be seen lying face downward with a stirruped foot stretched across the body of his dead horse. A leg of the charger extended slantingly upward precisely as stiff as a stake. Around this motionless pair the shells still howled.

There was a quarrel in A Company. Collins was shaking his fist in the faces of some laughing comrades. "Dern yeh! I ain't afraid t' go. If yeh say much, I will go!"

"Of course, yeh will! You'll run through that there medder, won't yeh?"

Collins said, in a terrible voice, "You see now!" At this ominous threat his comrades broke into renewed jeers.

Collins gave them a dark scowl and went to find his captain. The latter was conversing with the colonel of the regiment.

"Captain," said Collins, saluting and standing at attention—in those days all trousers bagged at the knees—"captain,

I want t' get permission to go git some water from that there well over yonder!"

The colonel and the captain swung about simultaneously and stared across the meadow. The captain laughed. "You must be pretty thirsty, Collins?"

"Yes, sir, I am."

"Well—ah," said the captain. After a moment, he asked, "Can't you wait?"

"No, sir."

The colonel was watching Collins's face. "Look here, my lad," he said, in a pious sort of a voice—"look here, my lad"—Collins was not a lad—"don't you think that's taking pretty big risks for a little drink of water?"

"I dunno," said Collins uncomfortably. Some of the resentment toward his companions, which perhaps had forced him into this affair, was beginning to fade. "I dunno wether 'tis."

The colonel and the captain contemplated him for a time.

"Well," said the captain finally.

"Well," said the colonel, "if you want to go, why, go."

Collins saluted. "Much obliged t' yeh."

As he moved away the colonel called after him. "Take some of the other boys' canteens with you an' hurry back now."

"Yes, sir, I will."

The colonel and the captain looked at each other then, for it had suddenly occurred that they could not for the life of them tell whether Collins wanted to go or whether he did not.

They turned to regard Collins, and as they perceived him surrounded by gesticulating comrades, the colonel said: "Well, by thunder! I guess he's going."

Collins appeared as a man dreaming. In the midst of the questions, the advice, the warnings, all the excited talk of his company mates, he maintained a curious silence.

They were very busy in preparing him for his ordeal. When they inspected him carefully it was somewhat like the examination that grooms give a horse before a race; and they were amazed, staggered by the whole affair. Their astonishment found vent in strange repetitions.

"Are yeh sure a-goin'?" they demanded again and again.

"Certainly I am," cried Collins, at last furiously.

He strode sullenly away from them. He was swinging five or six canteens by their cords. It seemed that his cap would not remain firmly on his head, and often he reached and pulled it down over his brow.

There was a general movement in the compact column. The long animal-like thing moved slightly. Its four hundred eyes were turned upon the figure of Collins.

"Well, sir, if that ain't th' derndest thing! I never thought Fred Collins had the blood in him for that kind of business."

"What's he goin' to do, anyhow?"

"He's goin' to that well there after water."

"We ain't dyin' of thirst, are we? That's foolishness."

"Well, somebody put him up to it, an' he's doin' it."

"Say, he must be a desperate cuss."

When Collins faced the meadow and walked away from the regiment, he was vaguely conscious that a chasm, the deep valley of all prides, was suddenly between him and his comrades. It was provisional,[8] but the provision was that he return as a victor. He had blindly been led by quaint emotions, and laid himself under an obligation to walk squarely up to the face of death.

8 **provisional:** conditional.

But he was not sure that he wished to make a retraction, even if he could do so without shame. As a matter of truth, he was sure of very little. He was mainly surprised.

It seemed to him supernaturally strange that he had allowed his mind to maneuver his body into such a situation. He understood that it might be called dramatically great.

However, he had no full appreciation of anything, excepting that he was actually conscious of being dazed. He could feel his dulled mind groping after the form and color of this incident. He wondered why he did not feel some keen agony of fear cutting his sense like a knife. He wondered at this, because human expression had said loudly for centuries that men should feel afraid of certain things, and that all men who did not feel this fear were phenomena[9]—heroes.

He was, then, a hero. He suffered that disappointment which we would all have if we discovered that we were ourselves capable of those deeds which we most admire in history and legend. This, then, was a hero. After all, heroes were not much.

No, it could not be true. He was not a hero. Heroes had no shames in their lives, and, as for him, he remembered borrowing fifteen dollars from a friend and promising to pay it back the next day, and then avoiding that friend for ten months. When at home his mother had aroused him for the early labor of his life on the farm, it had often been his fashion to be irritable, childish, diabolical; and his mother had died since he had come to the war.

He saw that, in this matter of the well, the canteens, the shells, he was an intruder in the land of fine deeds.

9 **phenomena** (fĭ nŏm′ə nə): exceptional persons.

He was now about thirty paces from his comrades. The regiment had just turned its many faces toward him.

From the forest of terrific noises there suddenly emerged a little uneven line of men. They fired fiercely and rapidly at distant foliage on which appeared little puffs of white smoke. The spatter of skirmish firing was added to the thunder of the guns on the hill. The little line of men ran forward. A color sergeant fell flat with his flag as if he had slipped on ice. There was hoarse cheering from this distant field.

Collins suddenly felt that two demon fingers were pressed into his ears. He could see nothing but flying arrows, flaming red. He lurched from the shock of this explosion, but he made a mad rush for the house, which he viewed as a man submerged to the neck in a boiling surf might view the shore. In the air, little pieces of shell howled and the earthquake explosions drove him insane with the menace of their roar. As he ran the canteens knocked together with a rhythmical tinkling.

As he neared the house, each detail of the scene became vivid to him. He was aware of some bricks of the vanished chimney lying on the sod. There was a door which hung by one hinge.

Rifle bullets called forth by the insistent skirmishers came from the far-off bank of foliage. They mingled with the shells and the pieces of shells until the air was torn in all directions by hootings, yells, howls. The sky was full of fiends who directed all their wild rage at his head.

When he came to the well, he flung himself face downward and peered into its darkness. There were furtive silver glintings some feet from the surface. He grabbed one of the canteens and, unfastening its cap, swung it down by the cord. The water flowed slowly in with an indolent gurgle.

And now as he lay with his face turned away he was suddenly smitten with the terror. It came upon his heart like the grasp of claws. All the power faded from his muscles. For an instant he was no more than a dead man.

The canteen filled with a maddening slowness, in the manner of all bottles. Presently he recovered his strength and addressed a screaming oath to it. He leaned over until it seemed as if he intended to try to push water into it with his hands. His eyes as he gazed down into the well shone like two pieces of metal and in their expression was a great appeal and a great curse. The stupid water derided him.

There was the blaring thunder of a shell. Crimson light shone through the swift-boiling smoke and made a pink reflection on part of the wall of the well. Collins jerked out his arm and canteen with the same motion that a man would use in withdrawing his head from a furnace.

He scrambled erect and glared and hesitated. On the ground near him lay the old well bucket, with a length of rusty chain. He lowered it swiftly into the well. The bucket struck the water and then, turning lazily over, sank. When, with hand reaching tremblingly over hand, he hauled it out, it knocked often against the walls of the well and spilled some of its contents.

In running with a filled bucket, a man can adopt but one kind of gait. So through this terrible field over which screamed practical angels of death Collins ran in the manner of a farmer chased out of a dairy by a bull.

His face went staring white with anticipation—anticipation of a blow that would whirl him around and down. He would fall as he had seen other men

122

fall, the life knocked out of them so suddenly that their knees were no more quick to touch the ground than their heads. He saw the long blue line of the regiment, but his comrades were standing looking at him from the edge of an impossible star. He was aware of some deep wheel ruts and hoofprints in the sod beneath his feet.

The artillery officer who had fallen in this meadow had been making groans in the teeth of the tempest of sound. These futile cries, wrenched from him by his agony, were heard only by shells, bullets. When wild-eyed Collins came running, this officer raised himself. His face contorted and blanched from pain, he was about to utter some great beseeching cry. But suddenly his face straightened and he called: "Say, young man, give me a drink of water, will you?"

Collins had no room amid his emotions for surprise. He was mad from the threats of destruction.

"I can't!" he screamed, and in his reply was a full description of his quaking apprehension. His cap was gone and his hair was riotous. His clothes made it appear that he had been dragged over the ground by the heels. He ran on.

The officer's head sank down and one elbow crooked. His foot in its brass-bound stirrup still stretched over the body of his horse and the other leg was under the steed.

But Collins turned. He came dashing back. His face had now turned gray and in his eyes was all terror. "Here it is! here it is!"

The officer was as a man gone in drink. His arm bent like a twig. His head drooped as if his neck were of willow. He was sinking to the ground, to lie face downward.

Collins grabbed him by the shoulder. "Here it is. Here's your drink. Turn over. Turn over, man, for God's sake!"

With Collins hauling at his shoulder, the officer twisted his body and fell with his face turned toward that region where lived the unspeakable noises of the swirling missiles. There was the faintest shadow of a smile on his lips as he looked at Collins. He gave a sigh, a little primitive breath like that from a child.

Collins tried to hold the bucket steadily, but his shaking hands caused the water to splash all over the face of the dying man. Then he jerked it away and ran on.

The regiment gave him a welcoming roar. The grimed faces were wrinkled in laughter.

His captain waved the bucket away. "Give it to the men!"

The two genial, skylarking young lieutenants were the first to gain possession of it. They played over it in their fashion.

When one tried to drink the other teasingly knocked his elbow. "Don't, Billie! You'll make me spill it," said the one. The other laughed.

Suddenly there was an oath, the thud of wood on the ground, and a swift murmur of astonishment among the ranks. The two lieutenants glared at each other. The bucket lay on the ground empty.

Understanding the Story

1. The opening of the story describes a battle scene. Read the first paragraphs carefully and decide from whose point of view the scene is described. Where does this point of view shift and why?
2. Each of the first ten or so paragraphs is like a scene flashed before the reader. There is almost no transition from one paragraph to the next. What are the only elements these scenes have in common with each other? What is the effect of presenting them in such a disconnected manner?
3. What impression do you have of the men's attitude toward the battle up to the paragraph beginning "There was a quarrel in Company A"? What evidence do you find for your answer in the story? Is the author's attitude the same as the men's? Explain your answer.
4. What remarks by Collins's comrades and superiors prepare you for his mixed feelings when he finds himself actually started on his dangerous errand?
5. What motivates Collins to make his dangerous trip? He has several chances to stop without losing face, but he does not. What are some of the forces that may have led him to make the journey?
6. As Collins starts his trip, why does he feel he must be a hero? What are the reasons for his deciding he cannot be a hero?
7. Does Crane intend the reader to regard Collins as a hero or not? What is the significance of the title "A Mystery of Heroism"?
8. Both London's strong character, Bill the miner, and Crane's weak character, Private Collins, accomplish what they set out to do. What are the chief differences in their situations?
9. The spilling of the bucket of water may be regarded as a symbolic action. As a symbol, what might it represent?

Developing Language Skills

1. Reread the three paragraphs on page 121 that begin "He was, then, a hero . . ." and close with Collins's thoughts when he decides that he is "an intruder in the land of fine deeds." Write two paragraphs agreeing or disagreeing with his decision that he is not a hero. Begin by defining your own idea of what a hero is.
2. An author's choice of words and of phrasing is important in giving to a scene the interpretation he wants it to have. Write one or two paragraphs explaining what effect the choice of words or the manner of phrasing given below has upon "A Mystery of Heroism" as a war story. (For example, how do they indicate that the men see the battle? What aspects of war do they bring out?)
   (a) "Some curious fortune of the battle had made this little meadow the object of the red hate of the shells. . . ." "This man had encountered a shell apparently. . . ." "Rifle bullets called forth by the insistent skirmishers came from the far-off bank of foliage."

(b) "The white legs of the gunners scampered this way and that way. . . ." ". . . a battery was arguing in tremendous roars with some other guns. . . ." "The battery on the hill presently engaged in a frightful duel."

(c) The fact that Crane, especially in the first part of the story, generally refers to "the men," "the two armies," "the regiment," "a rider," "the infantry," etc., rather than identifying individuals or sides.

Reading "The Leader of the People"

In "A Mystery of Heroism" you were asked to consider the motivation of Private Collins. *Motivation* is again a key to meaning in "The Leader of the People." You need to consider *why* Jody, the boy upon whom Steinbeck focuses attention, acts as he does and feels as he does. And to fully understand Jody's motivation, you will also need to ask why his father and his grandfather behave as they do. As in life itself, only when you become aware of the desires and the purposes of people can you explain the meaning of their actions.

In "The Leader of the People," small details, as well as larger actions, build up the character of each person and make him convincing to the reader. For example, what is suggested by the dog's stiffening at Carl's approach? by Jody's self-conscious use of profanity?

Steinbeck is skillful not only in his interweaving of plot and character, but also in his unobtrusive use of *symbolism* to bring out his theme. A *symbol* in a short story may be an action, an object, sometimes even a character or a part of the setting which expands in meaning beyond the actual part it has in the plot. At the opening of this story, Jody forms plans for going on a mouse hunt: he wants to kill all the mice living in an old haystack. As the story progresses, this mouse hunt gradually becomes a symbol of the longing most people have to assert their power and to possess authority; the reader also sees that it symbolizes the destructive use of such power. As you read, note the lines that explain why Jody wants to go on a mouse hunt, that show Grandfather's opinion of it, and that show Jody's changing feelings about it. Through this symbol, Steinbeck comments on the subject of authority and leadership—a subject central to the main events of the story—and shows the reader the nature of the choice Jody makes at the end of the story.

The Leader of the People

John Steinbeck

"The Leader of the People," told from the viewpoint of a young boy, is one of a group of short stories about ranch life in California's Salinas Valley. In this story, a proud old pioneer who lives in his memories and talks too much of his early feats is humiliated in the presence of Jody, his young grandson, by Jody's impatient, somewhat insensitive father. The boy's reactions to the conflict between his father and grandfather indicate to the reader what kind of boy he is and what he is likely to become as a mature man.

ON SATURDAY AFTERNOON Billy Buck, the ranch-hand, raked together the last of the old year's haystack and pitched small forkfuls over the wire fence to a few mildly interested cattle. High in the air small clouds like puffs of cannon smoke were driven eastward by the March wind. The wind could be heard whishing in the brush on the ridge crests, but no breath of it penetrated down into the ranch-cup.

The little boy, Jody, emerged from the house eating a thick piece of buttered bread. He saw Billy working on the last of the haystack. Jody tramped down scuffing his shoes in a way he had been told was destructive to good shoe-leather. A flock of white pigeons flew out of the black cypress tree as Jody passed, and circled the tree and landed again. A half-grown tortoise-shell cat leaped from the bunkhouse porch, galloped on stiff legs across the road, whirled and galloped back again. Jody picked up a stone to help the game along, but he was too late, for the cat was under the porch before the stone could be discharged. He threw the stone into the cypress tree and started the white pigeons on another whirling flight.

Arriving at the used-up haystack, the boy leaned against the barbed wire fence. "Will that be all of it, do you think?" he asked.

The middle-aged ranch-hand stopped his careful raking and stuck his fork into the ground. He took off his black hat and smoothed down his hair. "Nothing left of it that isn't soggy from ground moisture," he said. He replaced his hat and rubbed his dry leathery hands together.

"Ought to be plenty mice," Jody suggested.

"Lousy with them," said Billy. "Just crawling with mice."

"Well, maybe, when you get all through, I could call the dogs and hunt the mice."

"Sure, I guess you could," said Billy Buck. He lifted a forkful of the damp ground-hay and threw it into the air. Instantly three mice leaped out and burrowed frantically under the hay again.

Jody sighed with satisfaction. Those plump, sleek, arrogant mice were doomed. For eight months they had lived and multiplied in the haystack. They had been immune from cats, from traps, from poison and from Jody. They had grown smug in their security, overbearing and fat. Now the time of disaster had come; they would not survive another day.

Billy looked up at the top of the hills that surrounded the ranch. "Maybe you better ask your father before you do it," he suggested.

"Well, where is he? I'll ask him now."

"He rode up to the ridge ranch after dinner. He'll be back pretty soon."

Jody slumped against the fence post. "I don't think he'd care."

As Billy went back to his work he said ominously, "You'd better ask him anyway. You know how he is."

Jody did know. His father, Carl Tiflin, insisted upon giving permission for anything that was done on the ranch, whether it was important or not. Jody sagged farther against the post until he was sitting on the ground. He looked up at the little puffs of wind-driven cloud. "Is it like to rain, Billy?"

"It might. The wind's good for it, but not strong enough."

"Well, I hope it don't rain until after I kill those damn mice." He looked over his shoulder to see whether Billy had noticed the mature profanity. Billy worked on without comment.

Jody turned back and looked at the side-hill where the road from the outside world came down. The hill was washed with lean March sunshine. Silver thistles, blue lupins and a few poppies bloomed among the sage bushes. Halfway up the hill Jody could see Doubletree Mutt, the black dog, digging in a squirrel hole. He paddled for a while and then paused to kick bursts of dirt out between his hind legs, and he dug with an earnestness which belied the knowledge he must have had that no dog had ever caught a squirrel by digging in a hole.

Suddenly, while Jody watched, the black dog stiffened, and backed out of the hole and looked up the hill toward the cleft in the ridge where the road came through. Jody looked up too. For a moment Carl Tiflin on horseback stood out against the pale sky and then he moved down the road toward the house. He carried something white in his hand.

The boy started to his feet. "He's got a letter," Jody cried. He trotted away toward the ranch house, for the letter would probably be read aloud and he wanted to be there. He reached the house before his father did, and ran in. He heard Carl dismount from his creaking saddle and slap the horse on the side to send it to the barn where Billy would unsaddle it and turn it out.

Jody ran into the kitchen. "We got a letter!" he cried.

His mother looked up from a pan of beans. "Who has?"

"Father has. I saw it in his hand."

Carl strode into the kitchen then, and Jody's mother asked, "Who's the letter from, Carl?"

He frowned quickly. "How did you know there was a letter?"

She nodded her head in the boy's direction. "Big-Britches Jody told me."

Jody was embarrassed.

His father looked down at him contemptuously. "He is getting to be a Big-Britches," Carl said. "He's minding everybody's business but his own. Got his big nose into everything."

Mrs. Tiflin relented a little. "Well, he hasn't enough to keep him busy. Who's the letter from?"

Carl still frowned on Jody. "I'll keep him busy if he isn't careful." He held out a sealed letter. "I guess it's from your father."

Mrs. Tiflin took a hairpin from her

head and slit open the flap. Her lips pursed judiciously. Jody saw her eyes snap back and forth over the lines. "He says," she translated, "he says he's going to drive out Saturday to stay for a little while. Why, this is Saturday. The letter must have been delayed." She looked at the postmark. "This was mailed day before yesterday. It should have been here yesterday." She looked up questioningly at her husband, and then her face darkened angrily. "Now what have you got that look on you for? He doesn't come often."

Carl turned his eyes away from her anger. He could be stern with her most of the time, but when occasionally her temper arose, he could not combat it.

"What's the matter with you?" she demanded again.

In his explanation there was a tone of apology Jody himself might have used. "It's just that he talks," Carl said lamely. "Just talks."

"Well, what of it? You talk yourself."

"Sure I do. But your father only talks about one thing."

"Indians!" Jody broke in excitedly. "Indians and crossing the plains!"

Carl turned fiercely on him. "You get out, Mr. Big-Britches! Go on, now! Get out!"

Jody went miserably out the back door and closed the screen with elaborate quietness. Under the kitchen window his shamed, downcast eyes fell upon a curiously shaped stone, a stone of such fascination that he squatted down and picked it up and turned it over in his hands.

The voices came clearly to him through the open kitchen window. "Jody's damn well right," he heard his father say. "Just Indians and crossing the plains. I've heard that story about how the horses got driven off about a thousand times. He just goes on and

on, and he never changes a word in the things he tells."

When Mrs. Tiflin answered her tone was so changed that Jody, outside the window, looked up from his study of the stone. Her voice had become soft and explanatory. Jody knew how her face would have changed to match the tone. She said quietly, "Look at it this way, Carl. That was the big thing in my father's life. He led a wagon train clear across the plains to the coast, and when it was finished, his life was done. It was a big thing to do, but it didn't last long enough. Look!" she continued, "it's as though he was born to do that, and after he finished it, there wasn't anything more for him to do but think about it and talk about it. If there'd been any farther west to go, he'd have gone. He's told me so himself. But at last there was the ocean. He lives right by the ocean where he had to stop."

She had caught Carl, caught him and entangled him in her soft tone.

"I've seen him," he agreed quietly. "He goes down and stares off west over the ocean." His voice sharpened a little. "And then he goes up to the Horseshoe Club in Pacific Grove, and he tells people how the Indians drove off the horses."

She tried to catch him again. "Well, it's everything to him. You might be patient with him and pretend to listen."

Carl turned impatiently away. "Well, if it gets too bad, I can always go down to the bunkhouse and sit with Billy," he said irritably. He walked through the house and slammed the front door after him.

Jody ran to his chores. He dumped the grain to the chickens without chasing any of them. He gathered the eggs from the nests. He trotted into the house with the wood and interlaced it so carefully in the wood-box that two armloads seemed to fill it to overflowing.

His mother had finished the beans by now. She stirred up the fire and brushed off the stove-top with a turkey wing. Jody peered cautiously at her to see whether any rancor toward him remained. "Is he coming today?" Jody asked.

"That's what his letter said."

"Maybe I better walk up the road to meet him."

Mrs. Tiflin clanged the stove-lid shut. "That would be nice," she said. "He'd probably like to be met."

"I guess I'll just do it then."

Outside, Jody whistled shrilly to the dogs. "Come on up the hill," he commanded. The two dogs waved their tails and ran ahead. Along the roadside the sage had tender new tips. Jody tore off some pieces and rubbed them on his hands until the air was filled with the sharp wild smell. With a rush the dogs leaped from the road and yapped into the brush after a rabbit. That was the last Jody saw of them, for when they failed to catch the rabbit, they went back home.

Jody plodded on up the hill toward the ridge top. When he reached the little cleft where the road came through, the afternoon wind struck him and blew up his hair and ruffled his shirt. He looked down on the little hills and ridges below and then out at the huge green Salinas Valley. He could see the white town of Salinas far out in the flat and the flash of its windows under the waning sun. Directly below him, in an oak tree, a crow congress had convened. The tree was black with crows all cawing at once.

Then Jody's eyes followed the wagon road down from the ridge where he stood, and lost it behind a hill, and picked it up again on the other side.

On that distant stretch he saw a cart slowly pulled by a bay horse. It disappeared behind the hill. Jody sat down on the ground and watched the place where the cart would reappear again. The wind sang on the hilltops and the puff-ball clouds hurried eastward.

Then the cart came into sight and stopped. A man dressed in black dismounted from the seat and walked to the horse's head. Although it was so far away, Jody knew he had unhooked the check-rein, for the horse's head dropped forward. The horse moved on, and the man walked slowly up the hill beside it. Jody gave a glad cry and ran down the road toward them. The squirrels bumped along off the road, and a road-runner flirted its tail and raced over the edge of the hill and sailed out like a glider.

Jody tried to leap into the middle of his shadow at every step. A stone rolled under his foot and he went down. Around a little bend he raced, and there, a short distance ahead, were his grandfather and the cart. The boy dropped from his unseemly running and approached at a dignified walk.

The horse plodded stumble-footedly up the hill and the old man walked beside it. In the lowering sun their giant shadows flickered darkly behind them. The grandfather was dressed in a black broadcloth suit and he wore kid congress gaiters[1] and a black tie on a short, hard collar. He carried his black slouch hat in his hand. His white beard was cropped close and his white eyebrows overhung his eyes like moustaches. The blue eyes were sternly merry. About the whole face and figure there was a granite dignity, so that every motion seemed an impossible thing. Once at

---

1 kid congress gaiters: soft leather shoes with elastic insertions at the side.

rest, it seemed the old man would be stone, would never move again. His steps were slow and certain. Once made, no step could ever be retraced; once headed in a direction, the path would never bend nor the pace increase nor slow.

When Jody appeared around the bend, Grandfather waved his hat slowly in welcome, and he called, "Why, Jody! Come down to meet me, have you?"

Jody sidled near and turned and matched his step to the old man's step and stiffened his body and dragged his heels a little. "Yes, sir," he said. "We got your letter only today."

"Should have been here yesterday," said Grandfather. "It certainly should. How are all the folks?"

"They're fine, sir." He hesitated and then suggested shyly, "Would you like to come on a mouse hunt tomorrow, sir?"

"Mouse hunt, Jody?" Grandfather chuckled. "Have the people of this generation come down to hunting mice? They aren't very strong, the new people, but I hardly thought mice would be game for them."

"No, sir. It's just play. The haystack's gone. I'm going to drive out the mice to the dogs. And you can watch, or even beat the hay a little."

The stern, merry eyes turned down on him. "I see. You don't eat them, then. You haven't come to that yet."

Jody explained, "The dogs eat them, sir. It wouldn't be much like hunting Indians, I guess."

"No, not much—but then later, when the troops were hunting Indians and shooting children and burning teepees, it wasn't much different from your mouse hunt."

They topped the rise and started down into the ranch-cup, and they lost the sun from their shoulders. "You've grown," Grandfather said. "Nearly an inch, I should say."

"More," Jody boasted. "Where they mark me on the door, I'm up more than an inch since Thanksgiving even."

Grandfather's rich throaty voice said, "Maybe you're getting too much water and turning to pith and stalk. Wait until you head out, and then we'll see."

Jody looked quickly into the old man's face to see whether his feelings should be hurt, but there was no will to injure, no punishing nor putting-in-your-place light in the keen blue eyes. "We might kill a pig," Jody suggested.

"Oh, no! I couldn't let you do that. You're just humoring me. It isn't the time and you know it."

"You know Riley, the big boar, sir?"

"Yes. I remember Riley well."

"Well, Riley ate a hole into that same haystack, and it fell down on him and smothered him."

"Pigs do that when they can," said Grandfather.

"Riley was a nice pig, for a boar, sir. I rode him sometimes, and he didn't mind."

A door slammed at the house below them, and they saw Jody's mother standing on the porch waving her apron in welcome. And they saw Carl Tiflin walking up from the barn to be at the house for the arrival.

The sun had disappeared from the hills by now. The blue smoke from the house chimney hung in flat layers in the purpling ranch-cup. The puff-ball clouds, dropped by the falling wind, hung listlessly in the sky.

Billy Buck came out of the bunkhouse and flung a wash basin of soapy water on the ground. He had been shaving in mid-week, for Billy held Grandfather in reverence, and Grandfather said that Billy was one of the few men of the new generation who had not gone soft. Although Billy was in middle age, Grandfather considered him a boy.

Now Billy was hurrying toward the house too.

When Jody and Grandfather arrived, the three were waiting for them in front of the yard gate.

Carl said, "Hello, sir. We've been looking for you."

Mrs. Tiflin kissed Grandfather on the side of his beard, and stood still while his big hand patted her shoulder. Billy shook hands solemnly, grinning under his straw moustache. "I'll put up your horse," said Billy, and he led the rig away.

Grandfather watched him go, and then, turning back to the group, he said as he had said a hundred times before, "There's a good boy. I knew his father, old Mule-tail Buck. I never knew why they called him Mule-tail except he packed mules."

Mrs. Tiflin turned and led the way into the house. "How long are you going to stay, Father? Your letter didn't say."

"Well, I don't know. I thought I'd stay about two weeks. But I never stay as long as I think I'm going to."

In a short while they were sitting at the white oilcloth table eating their supper. The lamp with the tin reflector hung over the table. Outside the dining-room windows the big moths battered softly against the glass.

Grandfather cut his steak into tiny pieces and chewed slowly. "I'm hungry," he said. "Driving out here got my appetite up. It's like when we were crossing. We all got so hungry every night we could hardly wait to let the meat get done. I could eat about five pounds of buffalo meat every night."

"It's moving around does it," said Billy. "My father was a government packer. I helped him when I was a kid. Just the two of us could about clean up a deer's ham."

"I knew your father, Billy," said Grandfather. "A fine man he was. They called him Mule-tail Buck. I don't know why except he packed mules."

"That was it," Billy agreed. "He packed mules."

Grandfather put down his knife and fork and looked around the table. "I remember one time we ran out of meat—" His voice dropped to a curious low singsong, dropped into a tonal groove the story had worn for itself. "There was no buffalo, no antelope, not even rabbits. The hunters couldn't even shoot a coyote. That was the time for the leader to be on the watch. I was the leader, and I kept my eyes open. Know why? Well, just the minute the people began to get hungry they'd start slaughtering the team oxen. Do you believe that? I've heard of parties that just ate up their draft cattle. Started from the middle and worked toward the ends. Finally they'd eat the lead pair, and then the wheelers. The leader of a party had to keep them from doing that."

In some manner a big moth got into the room and circled the hanging kerosene lamp. Billy got up and tried to clap it between his hands. Carl struck with a cupped palm and caught the moth and broke it. He walked to the window and dropped it out.

"As I was saying," Grandfather began again, but Carl interrupted him. "You'd better eat some more meat. All the rest of us are ready for our pudding."

Jody saw a flash of anger in his mother's eyes. Grandfather picked up his knife and fork. "I'm pretty hungry, all right," he said. "I'll tell you about that later."

When supper was over, when the family and Billy Buck sat in front of the fireplace in the other room, Jody anxiously watched Grandfather. He saw the signs he knew. The bearded head leaned forward; the eyes lost their sternness and looked wonderingly into the fire; the big lean fingers laced themselves on the black knees. "I wonder," he began, "I just wonder whether I ever told you how those thieving Piutes drove off thirty-five of our horses."

"I think you did," Carl interrupted. "Wasn't it just before you went up into the Tahoe country?"

Grandfather turned quickly toward his son-in-law. "That's right. I guess I must have told you that story."

"Lots of times," Carl said cruelly, and he avoided his wife's eyes. But he felt the angry eyes on him, and he said, "'Course I'd like to hear it again."

Grandfather looked back at the fire. His fingers unlaced and laced again. Jody knew how he felt, how his insides were collapsed and empty. Hadn't Jody been called a Big-Britches that very afternoon? He arose to heroism and opened himself to the term Big-Britches again. "Tell about Indians," he said softly.

Grandfather's eyes grew stern again. "Boys always want to hear about Indians. It was a job for men, but boys want to hear about it. Well, let's see. Did I ever tell you how I wanted each wagon to carry a long iron plate?"

Everyone but Jody remained silent. Jody said, "No. You didn't."

"Well, when the Indians attacked, we always put the wagons in a circle and fought from between the wheels. I thought that if every wagon carried a long plate with rifle holes, the men could stand the plates on the outside of the wheels when the wagons were in the circle and they would be protected. It would save lives and that would make up for the extra weight of the iron. But of course the party wouldn't do it. No

party had done it before and they couldn't see why they should go to the expense. They lived to regret it, too."

Jody looked at his mother, and knew from her expression that she was not listening at all. Carl picked at a callus on his thumb and Billy Buck watched a spider crawling up the wall.

Grandfather's tone dropped into its narrative groove again. Jody knew in advance exactly what words would fall. The story droned on, speeded up for the attack, grew sad over the wounds, struck a dirge at the burials on the great plains. Jody sat quietly watching Grandfather. The stern blue eyes were detached. He looked as though he were not very interested in the story himself.

When it was finished, when the pause had been politely respected as the frontier of the story, Billy Buck stood up and hitched his trousers. "I guess I'll turn in," he said. Then he faced Grandfather. "I've got an old powder horn and a cap and ball pistol down to the bunkhouse. Did I ever show them to you?"

Grandfather nodded slowly. "Yes, I think you did, Billy. Reminds me of a pistol I had when I was leading the people across." Billy stood politely until the little story was done, and then he said, "Good night," and went out of the house.

Carl Tiflin tried to turn the conversation then. "How's the country between here and Monterey? I've heard it's pretty dry."

"It is dry," said Grandfather. "There's not a drop of water in the Laguna Seca. But it's a long pull from '87. The whole country was powder then, and in '61 I believe all the coyotes starved to death. We had fifteen inches of rain this year."

"Yes, but it all came too early. We could do with some now." Carl's eyes fell on Jody. "Hadn't you better be getting to bed?"

Jody stood up obediently. "Can I kill the mice in the old haystack, sir?"

"Mice? Oh! Sure, kill them all off. Billy said there isn't any good hay left."

Jody exchanged a secret and satisfying look with Grandfather. "I'll kill every one tomorrow," he promised.

Jody lay in his bed and thought of the impossible world of Indians and buffaloes, a world that had ceased to be forever. He wished he could have been living in the heroic time, but he knew he was not of heroic timber. No one living now, save possibly Billy Buck, was worthy to do the things that had been done. A race of giants had lived then, fearless men, men of a staunchness unknown in this day. Jody thought of the wide plains and of the wagons moving across like centipedes. He thought of Grandfather on a huge white horse, marshaling the people. Across his mind marched the great phantoms, and they marched off the earth and they were gone.

He came back to the ranch for a moment, then. He heard the dull rushing sound that space and silence make. He heard one of the dogs, out in the doghouse, scratching a flea and bumping his elbow against the floor with every stroke. Then the wind arose again and the black cypress groaned and Jody went to sleep.

He was up half an hour before the triangle sounded for breakfast. His mother was rattling the stove to make the flames roar when Jody went through the kitchen. "You're up early," she said. "Where are you going?"

"Out to get a good stick. We're going to kill the mice today."

"Who is 'we'?"

"Why, Grandfather and I."

"So you've got him in it. You always

like to have someone in with you in case there's blame to share."

"I'll be right back," said Jody. "I just want to have a good stick ready for after breakfast."

He closed the screen door after him and went out into the cool blue morning. The birds were noisy in the dawn and the ranch cats came down from the hill like blunt snakes. They had been hunting gophers in the dark, and although the four cats were full of gopher meat, they sat in a semi-circle at the back door and mewed piteously for milk. Doubletree Mutt and Smasher moved sniffing along the edge of the brush, performing the duty with rigid ceremony, but when Jody whistled, their heads jerked up and their tails waved. They plunged down to him, wriggling their skins and yawning. Jody patted their heads seriously, and moved on to the weathered scrap pile. He selected an old broom handle and a short piece of inch-square scrap wood. From his pocket he took a shoelace and tied the ends of the sticks loosely together to make a flail. He whistled his new weapon through the air and struck the ground experimentally, while the dogs leaped aside and whined with apprehension.

Jody turned and started down past the house toward the old haystack ground to look over the field of slaughter, but Billy Buck, sitting patiently on the back steps, called to him, "You better come back. It's only a couple of minutes till breakfast."

Jody changed his course and moved toward the house. He leaned his flail against the steps. "That's to drive the mice out," he said. "I'll bet they're fat. I'll bet they don't know what's going to happen to them today."

"No, nor you either," Billy remarked philosophically, "nor me, nor anyone."

Jody was staggered by this thought. He knew it was true. His imagination twitched away from the mouse hunt. Then his mother came out on the back porch and struck the triangle, and all thoughts fell in a heap.

Grandfather hadn't appeared at the table when they sat down. Billy nodded at his empty chair. "He's all right? He isn't sick?"

"He takes a long time to dress," said Mrs. Tiflin. "He combs his whiskers and rubs up his shoes and brushes his clothes."

Carl scattered sugar on his mush. "A man that's led a wagon train across the plains has got to be pretty careful how he dresses."

Mrs. Tiflin turned on him. "Don't do that, Carl! Please don't!" There was more of threat than of request in her tone. And the threat irritated Carl.

"Well, how many times do I have to listen to the story of the iron plates, and the thirty-five horses? That time's done. Why can't he forget it, now it's done?" He grew angrier while he talked, and his voice rose. "Why does he have to tell them over and over? He came across the plains. All right! Now it's finished. Nobody wants to hear about it over and over."

The door into the kitchen closed softly. The four at the table sat frozen. Carl laid his mush spoon on the table and touched his chin with his fingers.

Then the kitchen door opened and Grandfather walked in. His mouth smiled tightly and his eyes were squinted. "Good morning," he said, and he sat down and looked at his mush dish.

Carl could not leave it there. "Did— did you hear what I said?"

Grandfather jerked a little nod.

"I don't know what got into me, sir. I didn't mean it. I was just being funny."

Jody glanced in shame at his mother, and he saw that she was looking at Carl, and that she wasn't breathing. It was an awful thing that he was doing. He was tearing himself to pieces to talk like that. It was a terrible thing to him to retract a word, but to retract it in shame was infinitely worse.

Grandfather looked sidewise. "I'm trying to get right side up," he said gently. "I'm not being mad. I don't mind what you said, but it might be true, and I would mind that."

"It isn't true," said Carl. "I'm not feeling well this morning. I'm sorry I said it."

"Don't be sorry, Carl. An old man doesn't see things sometimes. Maybe you're right. The crossing is finished. Maybe it should be forgotten, now it's done."

Carl got up from the table. "I've had enough to eat. I'm going to work. Take your time, Billy!" He walked quickly out of the dining-room. Billy gulped the rest of his food and followed soon after. But Jody could not leave his chair.

"Won't you tell any more stories?" Jody asked.

"Why, sure I'll them them, but only when—I'm sure people want to hear them."

"I like to hear them, sir."

"Oh! Of course you do, but you're a little boy. It was a job for men, but only little boys like to hear about it."

Jody got up from his place. "I'll wait outside for you, sir. I've got a good stick for those mice."

He waited by the gate until the old man came out on the porch. "Let's go down and kill the mice now," Jody called.

"I think I'll just sit in the sun, Jody. You go kill the mice."

"You can use my stick if you like."

"No, I'll just sit here a while."

Jody turned disconsolately away, and walked down toward the old haystack. He tried to whip up his enthusiasm with thoughts of the fat juicy mice. He beat the ground with his flail. The dogs coaxed and whined about him, but he could not go. Back at the house he could see Grandfather sitting on the porch, looking small and thin and black.

Jody gave up and went to sit on the steps at the old man's feet.

"Back already? Did you kill the mice?"

"No, sir. I'll kill them some other day."

The morning flies buzzed close to the ground and the ants dashed about in front of the steps. The heavy smell of sage slipped down the hill. The porch boards grew warm in the sunshine.

Jody hardly knew when Grandfather started to talk. "I shouldn't stay here, feeling the way I do." He examined his strong old hands. "I feel as though the crossing wasn't worth doing." His eyes moved up the side-hill and stopped on a motionless hawk perched on a dead limb. "I tell those old stories, but they're not what I want to tell. I only know how I want people to feel when I tell them.

"It wasn't Indians that were important, nor adventures, nor even getting out here. It was a whole bunch of people made into one big crawling beast. And I was the head. It was westering² and westering. Every man wanted something for himself, but the big beast that was all of them wanted only westering. I was the leader, but if I hadn't been there, someone else would have been the head. The thing had to have a head.

"Under the little bushes the shadows were black at white noonday. When we saw the mountains at last, we cried —all of us. But it wasn't getting here that mattered, it was movement and westering.

"We carried life out here and set it down the way those ants carry eggs. And I was the leader. The westering was as big as God, and the slow steps that made the movement piled up and piled up until the continent was crossed.

"Then we came down to the sea, and it was done." He stopped and wiped his eyes until the rims were red. "That's what I should be telling instead of stories."

When Jody spoke, Grandfather started and looked down at him. "Maybe I could lead the people some day," Jody said.

The old man smiled. "There's no place to go. There's the ocean to stop you. There's a line of old men along the shore hating the ocean because it stopped them."

"In boats I might, sir."

"No place to go, Jody. Every place is taken. But that's not the worst—no, not the worst. Westering has died out of the people. Westering isn't a hunger any more. It's all done. Your father is right. It is finished." He laced his fingers on his knee and looked at them.

Jody felt very sad. "If you'd like a glass of lemonade I could make it for you."

Grandfather was about to refuse, and then he saw Jody's face. "That would be nice," he said. "Yes, it would be nice to drink a lemonade."

Jody ran into the kitchen where his mother was wiping the last of the breakfast dishes. "Can I have a lemon to make a lemonade for Grandfather?"

His mother mimicked— "And another lemon to make a lemonade for you."

"No, ma'am. I don't want one."

---

2 **westering:** moving westward.

"Jody! You're sick!" Then she stopped suddenly. "Take a lemon out of the cooler," she said softly. "Here, I'll reach the squeezer down to you."

Understanding the Story

1. What kind of person is Jody at the beginning of the story? Support your answer with details from the story. (For example, what do Jody's rushing ahead of his father to tell his mother about the letter and his saying *damn* in front of Billy reveal?)
2. Before Carl first speaks in the story, what details indicate certain aspects of his character? What do his comments on Jody's telling about the letter reveal about Carl? How does his treatment of Jody differ from Grandfather's?
3. Point out several incidents in which Steinbeck contrasts Jody with his father. Point out others in which he contrasts Grandfather with Carl. How do these persons differ? Do these contrasts represent differences in generations or in persons? Support your answer with evidence from the story.
4. When Jody first goes to meet Grandfather and mentions the mouse hunt to him, to what does Grandfather compare the hunt? What is symbolized by Jody's rejection of the mouse hunt at the end of the story?
5. Although this story contains an obvious conflict between Carl and Grandfather, Jody is really the center of the story. In the beginning, we are shown that Jody wants to feel "big," that he wants to be thought of as mature. What are some of his actions that are simply childish efforts to be grown-up? What are some of his actions that show real evidence of maturity?
6. What qualities does Steinbeck show are possessed by a mature person in "The Leader of the People"?
7. What is the significance of Jody's mother's changing her teasing comment at the end of the story to, "Here, I'll reach the squeezer down to you"?
8. Who is the leader of the people? Explain.

Developing Language Skills

1. Write a paragraph sketch of Carl Tiflin based on the following three incidents: Carl's first appearance on horseback, Carl's killing of the moth at dinner, and Carl's final exit following his awkward and embarrassing apology at the breakfast table.
2. In an essay, discuss the nature of the conflict between Carl and Grandfather. What is the conflict? What does each man represent in the story? What is Steinbeck showing through this conflict? Pay special attention to Grandfather's talk with Jody at the end of the story when he begins, "I feel as though the crossing wasn't worth doing."

JOHN STEINBECK

A review of the short-story unit, based on Benét's "By the Waters of Babylon," follows the story. One part of the review asks you to apply your knowledge of the literary techniques explained in earlier stories of the unit to this particular selection. All the questions emphasize the importance of building your own literary standards.

By the Waters of Babylon

Stephen Vincent Benét

THE NORTH and the west and the south are good hunting ground, but it is forbidden to go east. It is forbidden to go to any of the Dead Places except to search for metal and then he who touches the metal must be a priest or the son of a priest. Afterwards, both the man and the metal must be purified. These are the rules and the laws; they are well made. It is forbidden to cross the great river and look upon the place that was the Place of the Gods—this is most strictly forbidden. We do not even say its name though we know its name. It is there that spirits live, and demons—it is there that there are the ashes of the Great Burning. These things are forbidden—they have been forbidden since the beginning of time.

My father is a priest; I am the son of a priest. I have been in the Dead Places near us, with my father—at first, I was afraid. When my father went into the house to search for the metal, I stood by the door and my heart felt small and weak. It was a dead man's house, a spirit house. It did not have the smell of man, though there were old bones in a corner. But it is not fitting that a priest's son should show fear. I looked at the bones in the shadow and kept my voice still.

Then my father came out with the metal—a good, strong piece. He looked at me with both eyes but I had not run away. He gave me the metal to hold—I took it and did not die. So he knew that I was truly his son and would be a priest in my time. That was when I was very young—nevertheless, my brothers would not have done it, though they are good hunters. After that, they gave me the good piece of meat and the warm corner by the fire. My father watched over me—he was glad that I should be a priest. But when I boasted or wept without a reason, he punished me more strictly than my brothers. That was right.

After a time, I myself was allowed to go into the dead houses and search for metal. So I learned the ways of those houses—and if I saw bones, I was no longer afraid. The bones are light and old—sometimes they will fall into dust if you touch them. But that is a great sin.

I was taught the chants and the spells—I was taught how to stop the running of blood from a wound and many secrets. A priest must know many secrets —that was what my father said. If the hunters think we do all things by chants and spells, they may believe so—it does not hurt them. I was taught how to read in the old books and how to make the old writings—that was hard and took a long time. My knowledge made me happy—it was like a fire in my heart. Most of all, I liked to hear of the Old Days and the stories of the gods. I asked myself many questions that I could not answer, but it was good to ask them. At night, I would lie awake and listen to the wind—it seemed to me that it was the voice of the gods as they flew through the air.

We are not ignorant like the Forest People—our women spin wool on the wheel, our priests wear a white robe. We do not eat grubs from the tree, we have not forgotten the old writings, although they are hard to understand. Nevertheless, my knowledge and my lack of knowledge burned in me—I wished to know more. When I was a man at last, I came to my father and said, "It is time for me to go on my journey. Give me your leave."

He looked at me for a long time, stroking his beard, then he said at last, "Yes. It is time." That night, in the house of the priesthood, I asked for and received purification. My body hurt but my spirit was a cool stone. It was my father himself who questioned me about my dreams.

He bade me look into the smoke of the fire and see—I saw and told what I saw. It was what I have always seen—a river, and, beyond it, a great Dead Place and in it the gods walking. I have always thought about that. His eyes were stern when I told him—he was no longer my father but a priest. He said, "This is a strong dream."

"It is mine," I said, while the smoke waved and my head felt light. They were singing the Star song in the outer chamber and it was like the buzzing of bees in my head.

He asked me how the gods were dressed and I told him how they were dressed. We know how they were dressed from the book, but I saw them as if they were before me. When I had finished, he threw the sticks three times and studied them as they fell.

"This is a very strong dream," he said. "It may eat you up."

"I am not afraid," I said and looked at him with both eyes. My voice sounded thin in my ears but that was because of the smoke.

He touched me on the breast and the forehead. He gave me the bow and the three arrows.

"Take them," he said. "It is forbidden to travel east. It is forbidden to cross the river. It is forbidden to go to the Place of the Gods. All these things are forbidden."

"All these things are forbidden," I said, but it was my voice that spoke and not my spirit. He looked at me again.

"My son," he said. "Once I had young dreams. If your dreams do not eat you up, you may be a great priest. If they eat you, you are still my son. Now go on your journey."

I went fasting, as is the law. My body hurt but not my heart. When the dawn came, I was out of sight of the village. I prayed and purified myself, waiting for a sign. The sign was an eagle. It flew east.

Sometimes signs are sent by bad spirits. I waited again on the flat rock, fasting, taking no food. I was very still —I could feel the sky above me and the earth beneath. I waited till the sun was beginning to sink. Then three deer passed in the valley, going east—they did not wind me or see me. There was a white fawn with them—a very great sign.

I followed them, at a distance, waiting for what would happen. My heart was troubled about going east, yet I knew that I must go. My head hummed with my fasting—I did not even see the panther spring upon the white fawn. But, before I knew it, the bow was in my hand. I shouted and the panther lifted his head from the fawn. It is not easy to kill a panther with one arrow but the arrow went through his eye and into his brain. He died as he tried to spring—he rolled over, tearing at the ground. Then I knew I was meant to go east—I knew that was my journey. When the night came, I made my fire and roasted meat.

It is eight suns' journey to the east and a man passes by many Dead Places. The Forest People are afraid of them but I am not. Once I made my fire on the edge of a Dead Place at night and, next morning, in the dead house, I found a good knife, little rusted. That was small to what came afterward but it made my heart feel big. Always when I looked for game, it was in front of my arrow, and twice I passed hunting parties of the Forest People without their knowing. So I knew my magic was strong and my journey clean, in spite of the law.

Toward the setting of the eighth sun, I came to the banks of the great river. It was half-a-day's journey after I had left the god-road—we do not use the god-roads now for they are falling apart into great blocks of stone, and the forest is safer going. A long way off, I had seen the water through trees but the trees were thick. At last, I came out upon an open place at the top of a cliff. There was the great river below, like a giant in the sun. It is very long, very wide. It could eat all the streams we know and still be thirsty. Its name is Ou-dis-sun, the Sacred, the Long. No man of my tribe had seen it, not even my father, the priest. It was magic and I prayed.

Then I raised my eyes and looked south. It was there, the Place of the Gods.

How can I tell what it was like—you do not know. It was there, in the red light, and they were too big to be houses. It was there with the red light upon it, mighty and ruined. I knew that in another moment the gods would see me. I covered my eyes with my hands and crept back into the forest.

Surely, that was enough to do, and live. Surely it was enough to spend the night upon the cliff. The Forest People themselves do not come near. Yet, all through the night, I knew that I should have to cross the river and walk in the places of the gods, although the gods ate me up. My magic did not help me at all and yet there was a fire in my bowels, a fire in my mind. When the sun rose, I thought, "My journey has been clean. Now I will go home from my journey." But, even as I thought so, I knew I could not. If I went to the Place of the Gods, I would surely die, but, if I did not go, I could never be at peace with my spirit again. It is better to lose one's life than one's spirit, if one is a priest and the son of a priest.

Nevertheless, as I made the raft, the tears ran out of my eyes. The Forest People could have killed me without fight, if they had come upon me then, but they did not come. When the raft was made, I said the sayings for the dead and painted myself for death. My heart was cold as a frog and my knees like water, but the burning in my mind would not let me have peace. As

I pushed the raft from the shore, I began my death song—I had the right. It was a fine song.

"I am John, son of John," I sang. "My
    people are the Hill People. They
    are the men.
I go into the Dead Places but I am not
    slain.
I take the metal from the Dead Places
    but I am not blasted.
I travel upon the god-roads and am not
    afraid. E-yah! I have killed the
    panther, I have killed the fawn!
E-yah! I have come to the great river.
    No man has come there before.
It is forbidden to go east, but I have
    gone, forbidden to go on the great
    river, but I am there.
Open your hearts, you spirits, and hear
    my song.
    Now I go to the Place of the Gods,
    I shall not return.
My body is painted for death and my
    limbs weak, but my heart is big as
    I go to the Place of the Gods!"

All the same, when I came to the Place of the Gods, I was afraid, afraid. The current of the great river is very strong—it gripped my raft with its hands. That was magic, for the river itself is wide and calm. I could feel evil spirits about me, in the bright morning; I could feel their breath on my neck as I was swept down the stream. Never have I been so much alone—I tried to think of my knowledge, but it was a squirrel's heap of winter nuts. There was no strength in my knowledge any more and I felt small and naked as a new-hatched bird —alone upon the great river, the servant of the gods.

Yet, after a while, my eyes were opened and I saw. I saw both banks of the river—I saw that once there had been god-roads across it, though now they were broken and fallen like broken vines. Very great they were, and wonderful and broken—broken in the time of the Great Burning when the fire fell out of the sky. And always the current took me nearer to the Place of the Gods, and the huge ruins rose before my eyes.

I do not know the customs of rivers —we are the People of the Hills. I tried to guide my raft with the pole but it spun around. I thought the river meant to take me past the Place of the Gods and out into the Bitter Water of the legends. I grew angry then—my heart felt strong. I said aloud, "I am a priest and the son of a priest!" The gods heard me—they showed me how to paddle with the pole on one side of the raft. The current changed itself— I drew near to the Place of the Gods.

When I was very near, my raft struck and turned over. I can swim in our lakes—I swam to the shore. There was a great spike of rusted metal sticking out into the river—I hauled myself up upon it and sat there, panting. I had saved my bow and two arrows and the knife I found in the Dead Place but that was all. My raft went whirling downstream toward the Bitter Water. I looked after it, and thought if it had trod me under, at least I would be safely dead. Nevertheless, when I had dried my bowstring and restrung it, I walked forward to the Place of the Gods.

It felt like ground underfoot; it did not burn me. It is not true what some of the tales say, that the ground there burns forever, for I have been there. Here and there were the marks and stains of the Great Burning, on the ruins, that is true. But they were old marks and old stains. It is not true either, what some of our priests say, that it is an island covered with fogs and enchantments. It is not. It is a great Dead Place—greater than any Dead Place we know. Everywhere in it there are god-roads, though most are cracked and broken. Everywhere there are the ruins of the high towers of the gods.

How shall I tell what I saw? I went carefully, my strung bow in my hand, my skin ready for danger. There should have been the wailings of spirits and the shrieks of demons, but there were not. It was very silent and sunny where I had landed—the wind and the rain and the birds that drop seeds had done their work—the grass grew in the cracks of the broken stone. It is a fair island—no wonder the gods built there. If I had come there, a god, I also would have built.

How shall I tell what I saw? The towers are not all broken—here and there one still stands, like a great tree in a forest, and the birds nest high. But the towers themselves look blind, for the gods are gone. I saw a fish hawk, catching fish in the river. I saw a little dance of white butterflies over a great heap of broken stones and columns. I went there and looked about me—there was a carved stone with cut-letters, broken in half. I can read letters but I could not understand these. They said UBTREAS. There was also the shattered image of a man or a god. It had been made of white stone and he wore his hair tied back like a woman's. His name was ASHING, as I read on the cracked half of a stone. I thought it wise to pray to ASHING, though I do not know that god.

How shall I tell what I saw? There was no smell of man left, on stone or metal. Nor were there many trees in that wilderness of stone. There are many pigeons, nesting and dropping in the towers—the gods must have loved them, or, perhaps, they used them for sacrifices. There are wild cats that roam the god-roads, green-eyed, unafraid of man. At night they wail like demons but they are not demons. The wild dogs are more dangerous, for they hunt in a pack, but them I did not meet till later. Everywhere there are the carved stones, carved with magical numbers or words.

I went North—I did not try to hide myself. When a god or a demon saw me, then I would die, but meanwhile I was no longer afraid. My hunger for knowledge burned in me—there was so much that I could not understand. After a while, I knew that my belly was hungry. I could have hunted for my meat, but I did not hunt. It is known that the gods did not hunt as we do— they got their food from enchanted boxes and jars. Sometimes these are still found in the Dead Places—once, when I was a child and foolish, I opened such a jar and tasted it and found the food sweet. But my father found out and punished me for it strictly, for, often, that food is death. Now, though, I had long gone past what was forbidden, and I entered the likeliest towers, looking for the food of the gods.

I found it at last in the ruins of a great temple in the mid-city. A mighty temple it must have been, for the roof was painted like the sky at night with its stars—that much I could see, though the colors were faint and dim. It went down into great caves and tunnels—perhaps they kept their slaves there. But when I started to climb down, I heard the squeaking of rats, so I did not go —rats are unclean, and there must have been many tribes of them, from the squeaking. But near there, I found food, in the heart of a ruin, behind a door that still opened. I ate only the fruits from the jars—they had a very sweet taste. There was drink, too, in bottles of glass—the drink of the gods was strong and made my head swim. After I had eaten and drunk, I slept on the top of a stone, my bow at my side.

When I woke, the sun was low. Looking down from where I lay, I saw a dog sitting on his haunches. His tongue was hanging out of his mouth; he looked as if he were laughing. He was a big dog, with a gray-brown coat, as big as a wolf. I sprang up and shouted at him but he did not move—he just sat there as if he were laughing. I did not like that. When I reached for a stone to throw, he moved swiftly out of the way of the stone. He was not afraid of me; he looked at me as if I were meat. No doubt I could have killed him with an arrow, but I did not know if there were others. Moreover, night was falling.

I looked about me—not far away there was a great, broken god-road, leading North. The towers were high enough, but not so high, and while many of the dead-houses were wrecked, there were some that stood. I went toward this god-road, keeping to the heights of the ruins, while the dog followed. When I had reached the god-road, I saw that there were others behind him. If I had slept later, they would have come upon me asleep and torn out my throat. As it was, they were sure enough of me; they did not hurry. When I went into the dead-house, they kept watch at the entrance—doubtless they thought they would have a fine hunt. But a dog cannot open a door and I knew, from the books, that the gods did not like to live on the ground but on high.

I had just found a door I could open when the dogs decided to rush. Ha! They were surprised when I shut the door in their faces—it was a good door, of strong metal. I could hear their foolish baying beyond it but I did not stop to answer them. I was in darkness—I found stairs and climbed. There were many stairs, turning around till my head was dizzy. At the top was another door—I found the knob and opened it. I was in a long small chamber—on one side of it was a bronze door that could not be opened, for it had no handle. Perhaps there was a magic word to open it but I did not have the word. I turned to the door in the opposite side of the wall. The lock of it was broken and I opened it and went in.

Within, there was a place of great riches. The god who lived there must have been a powerful god. The first room was a small anteroom—I waited there for some time, telling the spirits of the place that I came in peace and not as a robber. When it seemed to me that they had had time to hear me, I went on. Ah, what riches! Few, even, of the windows had been broken—it was all as it had been. The great windows that looked over the city had not been broken at all though they were dusty and streaked with many years. There were coverings on the floors, the colors not greatly faded, and the chairs were soft and deep. There were pictures upon the walls, very strange, very wonderful—I remember one of a bunch of flowers in a jar—if you came close to it, you could see nothing but bits of color, but if you stood away from it, the flowers might have been picked yesterday. It made my heart feel strange to look at this picture—and to look at the figure of a bird, in some hard clay, on a table and see it so like our birds. Everywhere there were books and writings, many in tongues that I could not read. The god who lived there must have been a wise god and full of knowledge. I felt I had right there, as I sought knowledge also.

Nevertheless, it was strange. There was a washing-place but no water—perhaps the gods washed in air. There was a cooking-place but no wood, and though there was a machine to cook food, there was no place to put fire in it. Nor were there candles or lamps—there were things that looked like lamps but they had neither oil nor wick. All these things were magic, but I touched them and lived—the magic had gone out of them. Let me tell one thing to show. In the washing-place, a thing said "Hot" but it was not hot to the touch—another thing said "Cold" but it was not cold. This must have been a strong magic but the magic was gone. I do not understand—they had ways—I wish that I knew.

It was close and dry and dusty in their house of the gods. I have said the magic was gone but that is not true—it had gone from the magic things but it had not gone from the place. I felt the spirits about me, weighing upon me. Nor had I ever slept in a Dead Place before—and yet, tonight, I must sleep there. When I thought of it, my tongue felt dry in my throat, in spite of my wish for knowledge. Almost I would have gone down again and faced the dogs, but I did not.

I had not gone through all the rooms when the darkness fell. When it fell, I went back to the big room looking over the city and made fire. There was a place to make fire and a box with wood in it, though I do not think they cooked there. I wrapped myself in a floor-covering and slept in front of the fire—I was very tired.

Now I tell what is very strong magic. I woke in the midst of the night. When I woke, the fire had gone out and I was cold. It seemed to me that all around me there were whisperings and voices. I closed my eyes to shut them out. Some will say that I slept again, but I do not think that I slept. I could feel the spirits drawing my spirit out of my body as a fish is drawn on a line.

Why should I lie about it? I am a priest and the son of a priest. If there are spirits, as they say, in the small Dead Places near us, what spirits must there not be in that great Place of the Gods? And would not they wish to speak? After such long years? I know that I felt myself drawn as a fish is drawn on a line. I had stepped out of my body—I could see my body asleep in front of the cold fire, but it was not I. I was drawn to look out upon the city of the gods.

It should have been dark, for it was night, but it was not dark. Everywhere there were lights—lines of light—circles and blurs of light—ten thousand torches would not have been the same. The sky itself was alight—you could barely see the stars for the glow in the sky. I thought to myself "This is strong magic" and trembled. There was a roaring in my ears like the rushing of rivers. Then my eyes grew used to the light and my ears to the sound. I knew that I was seeing the city as it had been when the gods were alive.

That was a sight indeed—yes, that was a sight: I could not have seen it in the body—my body would have died. Everywhere went the gods, on foot and in chariots—there were gods beyond number and counting and their chariots blocked the streets. They had turned night to day for their pleasure—they did not sleep with the sun. The noise of their coming and going was the noise of many waters. It was magic what they could do—it was magic what they did.

I looked out of another window—the great vines of their bridges were mended and the god-roads went East and West. Restless, restless, were the gods and always in motion! They burrowed tunnels under rivers—they flew in the air. With unbelievable tools they did giant works—no part of the earth was safe from them, for, if they wished for a thing, they summoned it from the other side of the world. And always, as they labored and rested, as they feasted and made love, there was a drum in their ears—the pulse of the giant city, beating and beating like a man's heart.

Were they happy? What is happiness to the gods? They were great, they were mighty, they were wonderful and terrible. As I looked upon them and their magic, I felt like a child—but a little more, it seemed to me, and they would pull down the moon from the sky. I saw them with wisdom beyond wisdom and knowledge beyond knowledge. And yet not all they did was well done—even I could see that—and yet their wisdom could not but grow until all was peace.

Then I saw their fate come upon them and that was terrible past speech. It came upon them as they walked the streets of their city. I have been in the fights with the Forest People—I have seen men die. But this was not like that. When gods war with gods, they use weapons we do not know. It was fire falling out of the sky and a mist that poisoned. It was the time of the Great Burning and the Destruction. They ran about like ants in the streets of their city—poor gods, poor gods! Then the towers began to fall. A few escaped—yes, a few. The legends tell it. But, even after the city had become a Dead Place, for many years the poison was still in the ground. I saw it happen, I saw the last of them die. It was

darkness over the broken city and I wept.

All this, I saw. I saw it as I have told it, though not in the body. When I woke in the morning, I was hungry, but I did not think first of my hunger for my heart was perplexed and confused. I knew the reason for the Dead Places but I did not see why it had happened. It seemed to me it should not have happened, with all the magic they had. I went through the house looking for an answer. There was so much in the house I could not understand—and yet I am a priest and the son of a priest. It was like being on one side of the great river, at night, with no light to show the way.

Then I saw the dead god. He was sitting in his chair, by the window, in a room I had not entered before and, for the first moment, I thought that he was alive. Then I saw the skin on the back of his hand—it was like dry leather. The room was shut, hot and dry—no doubt that had kept him as he was. At first I was afraid to approach him—then the fear left me. He was sitting looking out over the city—he was dressed in the clothes of the gods. His age was neither young nor old—I could not tell his age. But there was wisdom in his face and great sadness. You could see that he would have not run away. He had sat at his window, watching his city die—then he himself had died. But it is better to lose one's life than one's spirit—and you could see from the face that his spirit had not been lost. I knew, that, if I touched him, he would fall into dust—and yet, there was something unconquered in the face.

That is all of my story, for then I knew he was a man—I knew then that they had been men, neither gods nor demons. It is a great knowledge, hard to tell and believe. They were men—

they went a dark road, but they were men. I had no fear after that—I had no fear going home, though twice I fought off the dogs and once I was hunted for two days by the Forest People. When I saw my father again, I prayed and was purified. He touched my lips and my breast, he said, "You went away a boy. You come back a man and a priest." I said, "Father, they were men! I have been in the Place of the Gods and seen it! Now slay me, if it is the law—but still I know they were men."

He looked at me out of both eyes. He said, "The law is not always the same shape—you have done what you have done. I could not have done it in my time, but you come after me. Tell!"

I told and he listened. After that, I wished to tell all the people but he showed me otherwise. He said, "Truth is a hard deer to hunt. If you eat too much truth at once, you may die of the truth. It was not idly that our fathers forbade the Dead Places." He was right—it is better the truth should come little by little. I have learned that, being a priest. Perhaps, in the old days, they ate knowledge too fast.

Nevertheless, we make a beginning. It is not for the metal alone we go to the Dead Places now—there are the books and the writings. They are hard to learn. And the magic tools are broken—but we can look at them and wonder. At least, we make a beginning. And, when I am chief priest we shall go beyond the great river. We shall go to the Place of the Gods—the place newyork—not one man but a company. We shall look for the images of the gods and find the god ASHING and the others—the gods Licoln and Biltmore and Moses. But they were men who built the city, not gods or demons. They were men. I remember the dead man's face. They were men who were here before us. We must build again.

Review of the Short Story

1. The literary terms listed below are introduced in the reading skills headnotes preceding the stories you have read. Although an author may have used several of these techniques in his writing, one was singled out for special emphasis in each story.

   To refresh your memory on the use of the various terms, turn to the stories named after each term and read the headnote immediately preceding each story. Some headnotes deal with elements common to all stories—such as characterization, tone, setting. Others deal with a special technique found in only certain stories—such as the surprise ending or symbolism. Analyze "By the Waters of Babylon," showing how the elements common to all stories were handled by Benét and what special techniques he employed.

   (a) *Characterization* "Early Marriage," "The Leader of the People"
   (b) *Contrast* "The Heyday of the Blood," "You Can't Do That," "The Third Level"
   (c) *Exposition* "Early Marriage"

(d) *Fantasy*	"The Third Level"
(e) *Irony*	"The Cop and the Anthem"
(f) *Motivation*	"A Mystery of Heroism," "The Leader of the People"
(g) *Point of View*	"The Waltz," "Snake Dance," "The Cop and the Anthem," "The Damned Thing"
(h) *Setting*	"All Gold Canyon"
(i) *Surprise Ending*	"The Necklace," "The Third Level"
(j) *Symbol*	"The Leader of the People"
(k) *Theme*	"The Pack"
(l) *Tone*	"A Favor for Lefty"

2. After reading "By the Waters of Babylon," write a Reading Skills headnote of not more than one hundred words introducing the term *allusion* and showing its use in the story. (Reading Psalm 137 will help you explain the allusion made in the title of the story.)

3. Excluding "By the Waters of Babylon," select three stories from this unit that have particularly significant titles in view of their themes. Explain the relation of the title to the meaning of the story.

4. Give a brief report or write a short essay on two stories in which you feel the main character's motivation is well developed. Using specific evidence from the stories, explain what the motivation of each character was for his actions, and why you consider it convincing.

5. Choose one of the stories listed below and write about three hundred words pointing out how the *way* the story was told was important in creating just the right effect: "The Waltz," "The Heyday of the Blood," or "The Damned Thing." Consider such questions as:

   (a) Who tells the story? Could the same story have been told or the same effect created if another point of view had been used?

   (b) How was the necessary background for understanding the story introduced? How did the author explain what the situation was?

   (c) At what point in the story is the element of suspense introduced? That is, where are questions first raised in the readers mind? How is this done?

   (d) Is contrast used? For what purpose is it used?

   (e) Does the author tell you as much about the characters as you need to know? How does he tell you what they are like?

Drama

The Curtain Rises

THE HOUSE LIGHTS DIM and the curtain rises on the magical world of theater. Into the spotlight will step the play's characters, and through these characters you will experience love, anger, sorrow, and happiness. Because drama has that extra dimension of flesh and blood, their struggles will become yours.

Experience with drama is not all new to you. For years you have viewed motion picture and television dramas or listened to radio plays or to recordings of plays. A number of you may have acted in neighborhood, church, and school shows; some of you may have seen professional stage plays. In this unit you will study carefully the play script that forms the basis of dramatic presentations. If you are familiar with the playwright's technique, all forms of drama will have more meaning and enjoyment for you.

The term *drama* comes to our language from a Greek word meaning "to do" or "to act." Drama involves not merely action, but purposeful action. The one essential ingredient of the dramatic is *conflict:* a struggle between men, between opposing ideas, or between man and nature that sparks the interest of the audience in the resolution of the play. The outcome of the conflict gives the drama its meaning.

A playwright usually presents at least one character to whom an audience reacts sympathetically. The resulting emotional involvement can be extremely strong. Indeed, there is a story of a Western small-town cowboy who, in the early days of motion pictures, got so upset when a film hero seemed almost trapped by the movie villains that he pulled out his gun and fired at the badmen's screen images, shouting to the hero that he would help him. While actually seeing and hearing a performance causes the fullest projection of one's feelings into a play, reading can give the same experience. When you read Webster's appeal to the jury in "The Devil and Daniel Webster," perhaps you will feel the power drama can have over emotions.

What the characters in a play say—the dialogue—is the backbone of drama. Although it is aided by action, the dialogue carries the triple burden of telling the play's story, revealing what the characters are like, and creating the mood or feeling that the playwright wants the reader to experience.

As you read the plays in this unit, you will study some of the techniques used by successful dramatists. An understanding of character and plot development in "Trifles," of the metaphorical statement of theme in "The Golden Doom," and of the creation of the unworldly atmosphere in "The Devil and Daniel Webster" are all essential to your discovery of the meaning of these plays. Through critically reading play scripts, not only will you increase your enjoyment of reading and seeing plays, but also you will be better able to evaluate their worth as dramatic literature.

Reading "Trifles"

Plays were written to be heard and seen on a stage. In studying drama you must assume a dual role as both reader and viewer. If you want to capture the total impression the playwright created, you should imagine the setting, the characters, and the action as you read. In the play "Trifles" the stark setting is a farmhouse kitchen. It will help you to visualize the action of the characters if, as you read the author's description of the scene, you draw a floor plan that indicates the position of furniture, doors, windows, etc. Begin your plan by drawing a stage similar to the one shown below.

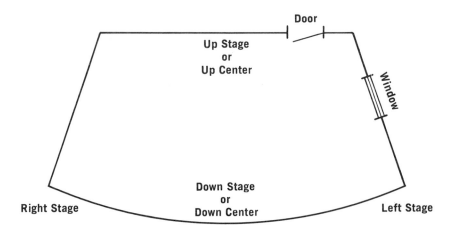

As you read the play, you will want to do more than just imagine the characters' movements; you will want to visualize their appearance. Note the author's opening description of the scene. Which man is the youngest, which woman the thinner? How much do you know about the personalities of the five characters before the first one speaks?

As you read the play, each character will more fully reveal the type of person he is. As in short stories, *characterization* is an essential element of the total work. The dramatist must present each character in such a way that his reader will understand the person's temperament and the individual characteristics that make him different from others. He must make a character's behavior consistent, and the reasons for the character's actions—his motivation—must be believable to the reader. What a character says, how he behaves, and what other characters say about him are three ways a playwright has of developing a character's personality.

In the play "Trifles" the audience never sees the two characters most important to the story. Yet note how the playwright is able to create persons you know and understand without bringing them on stage.

150

Trifles

Susan Glaspell

Murder, while not pleasant subject matter, has frequently been the basis for suspense-filled plots in literature. It is treated in a somewhat unusual way in "Trifles," which concerns the unraveling of the clues to a murder mystery. At the end of the play, the solution has been revealed but not put into actual words. You will need to read alertly to reach the correct conclusions: the casual opening conversation, for instance, is more important than it may at first appear.

CHARACTERS
SHERIFF (Mr. Peters)
COUNTY ATTORNEY
MR. HALE
MRS. PETERS
MRS. HALE

SCENE: *The kitchen in the now abandoned farmhouse of* **JOHN WRIGHT,** *a gloomy kitchen, and left without having been put in order—unwashed pans under the sink, a loaf of bread outside the breadbox, a dish towel on the table —other signs of incompleted work. At the rear the outer door opens and the* **SHERIFF** *comes in followed by the* **COUNTY ATTORNEY** *and* **HALE.** *The* **SHERIFF** *and* **HALE** *are men in middle life, the* **COUNTY ATTORNEY** *is a young man; all are much bundled up and go at once to the stove. They are followed by the two women— the* **SHERIFF's WIFE** *first; she is a slight wiry woman, a thin nervous face.* **MRS. HALE** *is larger and would ordinarily be called more comfortable looking, but she is disturbed now and looks fearfully about as she enters. The women have come in slowly, and stand close together near the door.*

COUNTY ATTORNEY (*rubbing his hands*). This feels good. Come up to the fire, ladies.

MRS. PETERS (*after taking a step forward*). I'm not—cold.

SHERIFF (*unbuttoning his overcoat and stepping away from the stove as if to mark the beginning of official business*). Now, Mr. Hale, before we move things about, you explain to Mr. Henderson just what you saw when you came here yesterday morning.

COUNTY ATTORNEY. By the way, has anything been moved? Are things just as you left them yesterday?

SHERIFF (*looking about*). It's just the same. When it dropped below zero last night I thought I'd better send Frank out this morning to make a fire for us—no use getting pneumonia with a big case on, but I told him not to touch anything except the stove—and you know Frank.

COUNTY ATTORNEY. Somebody should have been left here yesterday.

SHERIFF. Oh—yesterday. When I had to send Frank to Morris Center for that man who went crazy—I want you to know I had my hands full yesterday. I knew you could get back from Omaha by today and as long as I went over everything here myself—

COUNTY ATTORNEY. Well, Mr. Hale, tell just what happened when you came here yesterday morning.

HALE. Harry and I had started to town with a load of potatoes. We came along the road from my place and as I got here I said, "I'm going to see if I can't get John Wright to go in with me in a party telephone." I spoke to Wright about it once before and he put me off, saying folks talked too much anyway, and all he asked was peace and quiet—I guess you know about how much he talked himself; but I thought maybe if I went to the house and talked about it before his wife, though I said to Harry that I didn't know as what his wife wanted made much difference to John—

COUNTY ATTORNEY. Let's talk about that later, Mr. Hale. I do want to talk about that, but tell now just what happened when you got to the house.

HALE. I didn't hear or see anything; I knocked at the door, and still it was all quiet inside. I knew they must be up, it was past eight o'clock. So I knocked again, and I thought I heard somebody say, "Come in." I wasn't sure, I'm not sure yet, but I opened the door—this door (*indicating the door by which the two women are still stand-*

ing) and there in that rocker—(*pointing to it*) sat Mrs. Wright.

(*They all look at the rocker.*)

COUNTY ATTORNEY. What—was she doing?

HALE. She was rockin' back and forth. She had her apron in her hand and was kind of—pleating it.

COUNTY ATTORNEY. And how did she—look?

HALE. Well, she looked queer.

COUNTY ATTORNEY. How do you mean—queer?

HALE. Well, as if she didn't know what she was going to do next. And kind of done up.

COUNTY ATTORNEY. How did she seem to feel about your coming?

HALE. Why, I don't think she minded —one way or other. She didn't pay much attention. I said, "How do, Mrs. Wright, it's cold, ain't it?" And she said, "Is it?"—and went on kind of pleating at her apron. Well, I was surprised; she didn't ask me to come up to the stove, or to set down, but just sat there, not even looking at me, so I said, "I want to see John." And then she— laughed. I guess you would call it a laugh. I thought of Harry and the team outside, so I said a little sharp: "Can't I see John?" "No," she says, kind o' dull like. "Ain't he home?" says I. "Yes," says she, "he's home." "Then why can't I see him?" I asked her, out of patience. "'Cause he's dead," says she. "*Dead?*" says I. She just nodded her head, not getting a bit excited, but rockin' back and forth. "Why—where is he?" says I, not knowing what to say. She just pointed upstairs—like that (*himself pointing to the room above*). I got up, with the idea of going up there. I walked from there to here—then I says, "Why, what did he die of?" "He died of a rope round his neck," says she, and just went on pleatin' at her apron. Well, I went out and called Harry. I thought I might—need help. We went upstairs and there he was lyin'—

COUNTY ATTORNEY. I think I'd rather have you go into that upstairs, where you can point it all out. Just go on now with the rest of the story.

HALE. Well, my first thought was to get that rope off. It looked . . . (*Stops, his face twitches.*) . . . but Harry, he went up to him, and he said, "No, he's dead all right, and we'd better not touch anything." So we went back down stairs. She was still sitting that same way. "Has anybody been notified?" I asked. "No," says she, unconcerned. "Who did this, Mrs. Wright?" said Harry. He said it businesslike—and she stopped pleatin' of her apron. "I don't know," she says. "You don't *know?*" says Harry. "No," says she. "Weren't you sleepin' in the bed with him?" says Harry. "Yes," says she, "but I was on the inside." "Somebody slipped a rope round his neck and strangled him and you didn't wake up?" says Harry. "I didn't wake up," she said after him. We must 'a looked as if we didn't see how that could be, for after a minute she said, "I sleep sound." Harry was going to ask her more questions but I said maybe we ought to let her tell her story first to the coroner, or the sheriff, so Harry went fast as he could to Rivers' place, where there's a telephone.

COUNTY ATTORNEY. And what did Mrs. Wright do when she knew that you had gone for the coroner?

HALE. She moved from that chair to this one over here (*pointing to a small chair in the corner*) and just sat there with her hands held together and looking down. I got a feeling that I ought to make some conversation, so I said I had come in to see if John wanted to put in a telephone, and at that she started to laugh, and then she stopped and looked at me—scared. (*The* COUNTY ATTORNEY, *who has had his notebook out, makes a note.*) I dunno, maybe it wasn't scared. I wouldn't like to say it was. Soon Harry got back, and then Dr. Lloyd came, and you, Mr. Peters, and so I guess that's all I know that you don't.

COUNTY ATTORNEY (*looking around*). I guess we'll go upstairs first—and then out to the barn and around there. (*To the* SHERIFF.) You're convinced that there was nothing important here—nothing that would point to any motive.

SHERIFF. Nothing here but kitchen things.

> (*The* COUNTY ATTORNEY, *after again looking around the kitchen, opens the door of a cupboard closet. He gets up on a chair and looks on a shelf. Pulls his hand away, sticky.*)

COUNTY ATTORNEY. Here's a nice mess.

> (*The women draw nearer.*)

MRS. PETERS (*to the other woman*). Oh, her fruit; it did freeze. (*To the* LAWYER.) She worried about that when it turned so cold. She said the fire'd go out and her jars would break.

SHERIFF. Well, can you beat the women! Held for murder and worryin' about her preserves.

COUNTY ATTORNEY. I guess before we're through she may have something more serious than preserves to worry about.

HALE. Well, women are used to worrying over trifles.

> (*The two women move a little closer together.*)

COUNTY ATTORNEY (*with the gallantry of a young politician*). And yet, for all their worries, what would we do without the ladies? (*The women do not unbend. He goes to the sink, takes a dipperful of water from the pail and pouring it into a basin, washes his hands. Starts to wipe them on the roller towel, turns it for a cleaner place.)* Dirty towels! *(Kicks his foot against the pans under the sink.)* Not much of a housekeeper, would you say, ladies?

MRS. HALE *(stiffly)*. There's a great deal of work to be done on a farm.

COUNTY ATTORNEY. To be sure. And yet *(with a little bow to her)* I know there are some Dickson county farmhouses which do not have such roller towels.

(He gives it a pull to expose its full length again.)

MRS. HALE. Those towels get dirty awful quick. Men's hands aren't always as clean as they might be.

COUNTY ATTORNEY. Ah, loyal to your sex, I see. But you and Mrs. Wright were neighbors. I suppose you were friends, too.

MRS. HALE *(shaking her head)*. I've not seen much of her of late years. I've not been in this house—it's more than a year.

COUNTY ATTORNEY. And why was that? You didn't like her?

MRS. HALE. I liked her all well enough. Farmers' wives have their hands full, Mr. Henderson. And then—

COUNTY ATTORNEY. Yes—?

MRS. HALE *(looking about)*. It never seemed a very cheerful place.

COUNTY ATTORNEY. No—it's not cheerful. I shouldn't say she had the home-making instinct.

MRS. HALE. Well, I don't know as Wright had, either.

COUNTY ATTORNEY. You mean that they didn't get on very well?

MRS. HALE. No, I don't mean anything. But I don't think a place'd be any cheerfuller for John Wright's being in it.

COUNTY ATTORNEY. I'd like to talk more of that a little later. I want to get the lay of things upstairs now.

(He goes to the left, where three steps lead to a stair door.)

SHERIFF. I suppose anything Mrs. Peters does'll be all right. She was to take in some clothes for her, you know, and a few little things. We left in such a hurry yesterday.

COUNTY ATTORNEY. Yes, but I would like to see what you take, Mrs. Peters, and keep an eye out for anything that might be of use to us.

MRS. PETERS. Yes, Mr. Henderson.

(The women listen to the men's steps on the stairs, then look about the kitchen.)

MRS. HALE. I'd hate to have men coming into my kitchen, snooping around and criticizing.

(She arranges the pans under sink which the LAWYER had shoved out of place.)

MRS. PETERS. Of course it's no more than their duty.

MRS. HALE. Duty's all right, but I guess that deputy sheriff that came out to make the fire might have got a little of this on. *(Gives the roller towel a pull.)* Wish I'd thought of that sooner. Seems mean to talk about her for not having things slicked up when she had to come away in such a hurry.

MRS. PETERS *(who has gone to a small table in the left rear corner of the room, and lifted one end of a towel that covers a pan)*. She had bread set.

(Stands still.)

MRS. HALE *(eyes fixed on a loaf of bread beside the breadbox, which is on a low shelf at the other side of the room). (Moves slowly toward it.)* She was going to put this in there. *(Picks up loaf, then abruptly drops it. In a manner of returning to familiar things.)* It's a shame about her fruit. I wonder if it's all gone. (*Gets up on the chair and looks.*) I think there's some here that's all right, Mrs. Peters. Yes—here; (*holding it toward the window*) this is cherries, too. (*Looking again.*) I declare I believe that's the only one. (*Gets down, bottle in her hand. Goes to the sink and wipes it off on the outside.*) She'll feel awful bad after all her hard work in the hot weather. I remember the afternoon I put up my cherries last summer.

(*She puts the bottle on the big kitchen table, center of the room. With a sigh, is about to sit down in the rocking chair. Before she is seated realizes what chair it is; with a slow look at it, steps back. The chair which she has touched rocks back and forth.*)

MRS. PETERS. Well, I must get those things from the front room closet. (*She goes to the door at the right, but after looking into the other room, steps back.*) You coming with me, Mrs. Hale? You could help me carry them.

(*They go in the other room; reappear,* MRS. PETERS *carrying a dress and skirt,* MRS. HALE *following with a pair of shoes.*)

MRS. PETERS. My, it's cold in there.

(*She puts the clothes on the big table, and hurries to the stove.*)

MRS. HALE (*examining the skirt*). Wright was close. I think maybe that's why she kept so much to herself. She didn't even belong to the Ladies Aid. I suppose she felt she couldn't do her part, and then you don't enjoy things when you feel shabby. She used to wear pretty clothes and be lively, when she was Minnie Foster, one of the town girls singing in the choir. But that— oh, that was thirty years ago. This all you was to take in?

MRS. PETERS. She said she wanted an apron. Funny thing to want, for there isn't much to get you dirty in jail, goodness knows. But I suppose just to make her feel more natural. She said they was in the top drawer in this cupboard. Yes, here. And then her little shawl that always hung behind the door. (*Opens stair door and looks.*) Yes, here it is.

(*Quickly shuts door leading upstairs.*)

MRS. HALE (*abruptly moving toward her*). Mrs. Peters?

MRS. PETERS. Yes, Mrs. Hale?

MRS. HALE. Do you think she did it?

MRS. PETERS (*in a frightened voice*). Oh, I don't know.

MRS. HALE. Well, I don't think she did. Asking for an apron and her little shawl. Worrying about her fruit.

MRS. PETERS (*starts to speak, glances up, where footsteps are heard in the room above*). (*In a low voice.*) Mr. Peters says it looks bad for her. Mr. Henderson is awful sarcastic in a speech and he'll make fun of her sayin' she didn't wake up.

MRS. HALE. Well, I guess John Wright didn't wake when they was slipping that rope under his neck.

MRS. PETERS. No, it's strange. It must have been done awful crafty and still. They say it was such a—funny way to kill a man, rigging it all up like that.

MRS. HALE. That's just what Mr. Hale said. There was a gun in the house. He says that's what he can't understand.

MRS. PETERS. Mr. Henderson said coming out that what was needed for the case was a motive; something to show anger, or—sudden feeling.

MRS. HALE (*who is standing by the table*). Well, I don't see any signs of anger around here. (*She puts her hand on the dish towel which lies on the table, stands looking down at table, one half of which is clean, the other half messy.) It's wiped to here. (Makes a move as if to finish work, then turns and looks at loaf of bread outside the breadbox. Drops towel. In that voice of coming back to familiar things.) Wonder how they are finding things upstairs. I hope she had it a little more red-up up there. You know, it seems kind of *sneaking*. Locking her up in town and then coming out here and trying to get her own house to turn against her!

Mrs. Peters. But Mrs. Hale, the law is the law.

Mrs. Hale. I s'pose 'tis. (*Unbuttoning her coat.*) Better loosen up your things, Mrs. Peters. You won't feel them when you go out.

> (**Mrs. Peters** *takes off her fur tippet, goes to hang it on hook at back of room, stands looking at the under part of the small corner table.*)

Mrs. Peters. She was piecing a quilt.

> (*She brings the large sewing basket and they look at the bright pieces.*)

Mrs. Hale. It's log cabin pattern. Pretty, isn't it? I wonder if she was goin' to quilt it or just knot it?

> (*Footsteps have been heard coming down the stairs. The* **Sheriff** *enters followed by* **Hale** *and the* **County Attorney.**)

Sheriff. They wonder if she was going to quilt it or just knot it!

> (*The men laugh, the women look abashed.*)

County Attorney (*rubbing his hands over the stove*). Frank's fire didn't do much up there, did it? Well, let's go out to the barn and get that cleaned up.

> (*The men go outside.*)

Mrs. Hale (*resentfully*). I don't know as there's anything so strange, our takin' up our time with little things while we're waiting for them to get the evidence. (*She sits down at the big table smoothing out a block with decision.*) I don't see as it's anything to laugh about.

Mrs. Peters (*apologetically*). Of course they've got awful important things on their minds.

> (*Pulls up a chair and joins* **Mrs. Hale** *at the table.*)

Mrs. Hale (*examining another block*). Mrs. Peters, look at this one. Here, this is the one she was working on, and look at the sewing! All the rest of it has been so nice and even. And look at this! It's all over the place! Why, it looks as if she didn't know what she was about!

> (*After she has said this they look at each other, then start to glance back at the door. After an instant* **Mrs. Hale** *has pulled at a knot and ripped the sewing.*)

Mrs. Peters. Oh, what are you doing, Mrs. Hale?

Mrs. Hale (*mildly*). Just pulling out a stitch or two that's not sewed very good. (*Threading a needle.*) Bad sewing always made me fidgety.

Mrs. Peters (*nervously*). I don't think we ought to touch things.

Mrs. Hale. I'll just finish up this end. (*Suddenly stopping and leaning forward.*) Mrs. Peters?

Mrs. Peters. Yes, Mrs. Hale?

Mrs. Hale. What do you suppose she was so nervous about?

Mrs. Peters. Oh—I don't know. I don't know as she was nervous. I sometimes sew awful queer when I'm just tired. (**Mrs. Hale** *starts to say something, looks at* **Mrs. Peters,** *then goes on sewing.*) Well I must get these things wrapped up. They may be

through sooner than we think. (*Putting apron and other things together.*) I wonder where I can find a piece of paper, and string.

MRS. HALE. In that cupboard, maybe.

MRS. PETERS (*looking in cupboard*). Why, here's a bird cage. (*Holds it up.*) Did she have a bird, Mrs. Hale?

MRS. HALE. Why, I don't know whether she did or not—I've not been here for so long. There was a man around last year selling canaries cheap, but I don't know as she took one; maybe she did. She used to sing real pretty herself.

MRS. PETERS (*glancing around*). Seems funny to think of a bird here. But she must have one, or why would she have a cage? I wonder what happened to it.

MRS. HALE. I s'pose maybe the cat got it.

MRS. PETERS. No, she didn't have a cat. She's got that feeling some people have about cats—being afraid of them. My cat got in her room and she was real upset and asked me to take it out.

MRS. HALE. My sister Bessie was like that. Queer, ain't it?

MRS. PETERS (*examining the cage*). Why, look at this door. It's broke. One hinge is pulled apart.

MRS. HALE (*looking too*). Looks as if someone must have been rough with it.

MRS. PETERS. Why, yes.

(*She brings the cage forward and puts it on the table.*)

MRS. HALE. I wish if they're going to find any evidence they'd be about it. I don't like this place.

MRS. PETERS. But I'm awful glad you came with me, Mrs. Hale. It would be lonesome for me sitting here alone.

MRS. HALE. It would, wouldn't it? (*Dropping her sewing.*) But I tell you what I do wish, Mrs. Peters. I wish I had come over sometimes when *she* was here. I—(*looking around the room*)—wish I had.

Mrs. Peters. But of course you were awful busy, Mrs. Hale—your house and your children.

Mrs. Hale. I could've come. I stayed away because it weren't cheerful—and that's why I ought to have come. I—I've never liked this place. Maybe because it's down in a hollow and you don't see the road. I dunno what it is, but it's a lonesome place and always was. I wish I had come over to see Minnie Foster sometimes. I can see now—

(*Shakes her head.*)

Mrs. Peters. Well, you mustn't reproach yourself, Mrs. Hale. Somehow we just don't see how it is with other folks until—something comes up.

Mrs. Hale. Not having children makes less work—but it makes a quiet house, and Wright out to work all day, and no company when he did come in. Did you know John Wright, Mrs. Peters?

Mrs. Peters. Not to know him; I've seen him in town. They say he was a good man.

Mrs. Hale. Yes—good, he didn't drink, and kept his word as well as most, I guess, and paid his debts. But he was a hard man, Mrs. Peters. Just to pass the time of day with him—(*Shivers.*) Like a raw wind that gets to the bone. (*Pauses, her eye falling on the cage.*) I should think she would 'a wanted a bird. But what do you suppose went with it?

Mrs. Peters. I don't know, unless it got sick and died.

(*She reaches over and swings the broken door, swings it again; both women watch it.*)

Mrs. Hale. You weren't raised round here, were you? (Mrs. Peters *shakes her head.*) You didn't know—her?

Mrs. Peters. Not till they brought her yesterday.

Mrs. Hale. She—come to think of it, she was kind of like a bird herself—real sweet and pretty, but kind of timid and—fluttery. How—she—did—change. (*Silence; then as if struck by a happy thought and relieved to get back to everyday things.*) Tell you what, Mrs. Peters, why don't you take the quilt in with you? It might take up her mind.

Mrs. Peters. Why, I think that's a real nice idea, Mrs. Hale. There couldn't possibly be any objection to it, could there? Now, just what would I take? I wonder if her patches are in here—and her things.

(*They look in the sewing basket.*)

Mrs. Hale. Here's some red. I expect this has got sewing things in it. (*Brings out a fancy box.*) What a pretty box. Looks like something somebody would give you. Maybe her scissors are in here. (*Opens box. Suddenly puts her hand to her nose.*) Why—(Mrs. Peters *bends nearer, then turns her face away.*) There's something wrapped up in this piece of silk.

Mrs. Peters. Why, this isn't her scissors.

Mrs. Hale (*lifting the silk*). Oh, Mrs. Peters—its—

(Mrs. Peters *bends closer.*)

Mrs. Peters. It's the bird.

Mrs. Hale (*jumping up*). But, Mrs. Peters—look at it! It's neck! Look at its neck! It's all—other side *to*.

Mrs. Peters. Somebody—wrung—its —neck.

(*Their eyes meet. A look of growing comprehension, of horror. Steps are heard outside.* Mrs. Hale *slips box under quilt pieces, and sinks into her chair. Enter* Sheriff *and* County Attorney. Mrs. Peters *rises.*)

COUNTY ATTORNEY (*as one turning from serious things to little pleasantries*). Well, ladies, have you decided whether she was going to quilt it or knot it?

MRS. PETERS. We think she was going to—knot it.

COUNTY ATTORNEY. Well, that's interesting, I'm sure. (*Seeing the bird cage.*) Has the bird flown?

MRS. HALE (*putting more quilt pieces over the box*). We think the—cat got it.

COUNTY ATTORNEY (*preoccupied*). Is there a cat?

(MRS. HALE *glances in a quick covert way at* MRS. PETERS.)

MRS. PETERS. Well, not *now*. They're superstitious, you know. They leave.

COUNTY ATTORNEY (*to* SHERIFF PETERS, *continuing an interrupted conversation*). No sign at all of anyone having come from the outside. Their own rope. Now let's go up again and go over it piece by piece. (*They start upstairs.*) It would have to have been someone who knew just the—

(MRS. PETERS *sits down. The two women sit there not looking at one another, but as if peering into something and at the same time holding back. When they talk now it is in the manner of feeling their way over strange ground, as if afraid of what they are saying, but as if they cannot help saying it.*)

MRS. HALE. She liked the bird. She was going to bury it in that pretty box.

MRS. PETERS (*in a whisper*). When I was a girl—my kitten—there was a boy took a hatchet, and before my eyes—and before I could get there—(*Covers her face an instant.*) If they hadn't held me back I would have—(*Catches herself, looks upstairs where steps are heard, falters weakly*)—hurt him.

MRS. HALE (*with a slow look around her*). I wonder how it would seem never to have had any children around. (*Pause.*) No, Wright wouldn't like the bird—a thing that sang. She used to sing. He killed that, too.

MRS. PETERS (*moving uneasily*). We don't know who killed the bird.

MRS. HALE. I knew John Wright.

MRS. PETERS. It was an awful thing was done in this house that night, Mrs. Hale. Killing a man while he slept, slipping a rope around his neck that choked the life out of him.

MRS. HALE. His neck. Choked the life out of him.

(*Her hand goes out and rests on the bird cage.*)

MRS. PETERS (*with rising voice*). We don't know who killed him. We don't *know*.

MRS. HALE (*her own feeling not interrupted*). If there'd been years and years of nothing, then a bird to sing to you, it would be awful—still, after the bird was still.

MRS. PETERS (*something within her speaking*). I know what stillness is. When we homesteaded in Dakota, and my first baby died—after he was two years old, and me with no other then—

MRS. HALE (*moving*). How soon do you suppose they'll be through, looking for the evidence?

MRS. PETERS. I know what stillness is. (*Pulling herself back.*) The law has got to punish crime, Mrs. Hale.

MRS. HALE (*not as if answering that*). I wish you'd seen Minnie Foster when she wore a white dress with blue ribbons and stood up there in the choir and sang. (*A look around the room.*) Oh, I *wish* I'd come over here once in a while! That was a crime! That was a crime! Who's going to punish that?

MRS. PETERS (looking upstairs). We mustn't—take on.

MRS. HALE. I might have known she needed help! I know how things can be—for women. I tell you, it's queer, Mrs. Peters. We live close together and we live far apart. We all go through the same things—it's all just a different kind of the same thing. (Brushes her eyes, noticing the bottle of fruit, reaches out for it.) If I was you I wouldn't tell her her fruit was gone. Tell her it ain't. Tell her it's all right. Take this in to prove it to her. She— she may never know whether it was broke or not.

MRS. PETERS (takes the bottle, looks about for something to wrap it in; takes petticoat from the clothes brought from the other room, very nervously begins winding this around the bottle. In a false voice). My, it's a good thing the men couldn't hear us. Wouldn't they just laugh! Getting all stirred up over a little thing like a—dead canary. As if that could have anything to do with —with—wouldn't they laugh!

(The men are heard coming down stairs.)

MRS. HALE (under her breath). Maybe they would—maybe they wouldn't.

COUNTY ATTORNEY. No, Peters, it's all perfectly clear except a reason for do- ing it. But you know juries when it comes to women. If there was some definite thing. Something to show— something to make a story about—a thing that would connect up with this strange way of doing it—

(The women's eyes meet for an instant. Enter HALE from outer door.)

HALE. Well, I've got the team around. Pretty cold out there.

COUNTY ATTORNEY. I'm going to stay here a while by myself. (To the SHER- IFF.) You can send Frank out for me,

can't you? I want to go over every- thing. I'm not satisfied that we can't do better.

SHERIFF. Do you want to see what Mrs. Peters is going to take in?

(The LAWYER goes to the table, picks up the apron, laughs.)

COUNTY ATTORNEY. Oh, I guess they're not very dangerous things the ladies have picked out. (Moves a few things about, disturbing the quilt pieces which cover the box. Steps back.) No, Mrs. Peters doesn't need supervising. For that matter, a sheriff's wife is mar- ried to the law. Ever think of it that way, Mrs. Peters?

MRS. PETERS. Not—just that way.

SHERIFF (chuckling). Married to the law. (Moves toward the other room.) I just want you to come in here a min- ute, George. We ought to take a look at these windows.

COUNTY ATTORNEY (scoffingly). Oh, windows!

SHERIFF. We'll be right out, Mr. Hale.

(HALE goes outside. The SHERIFF follows the COUNTY ATTORNEY into the other room. Then MRS. HALE rises, hands tight together, looking intensely at MRS. PETERS, whose eyes make a slow turn, finally meeting MRS. HALE's. A moment MRS. HALE holds her, then her own eyes point the way to where the box is concealed. Suddenly MRS. PETERS throws back quilt pieces and tries to put the box in the bag she is wear- ing. It is too big. She opens box, starts to take bird out, can- not touch it, goes to pieces, stands there helpless. Sound of a knob turning in the other room. MRS. HALE snatches the box and puts it in the pocket of her big coat. Enter COUNTY ATTORNEY and SHERIFF.)

COUNTY ATTORNEY (*facetiously*). Well, Henry, at least we found out that she was not going to quilt it. She was going to—what is it you call it, ladies?

MRS. HALE (*her hand against her pocket*). We call it—knot it, Mr. Henderson.

CURTAIN

Understanding the Play

1. As the curtain goes up, how does the author tell you why these people are here?
2. The opening conversation of the play is primarily expository—that is, it gives background information that is necessary to an understanding of the rest of the play. What is this information? How is its relation made to seem natural?
3. How does the author get the men off stage? Why does she do so?
4. Although Mr. and Mrs. Wright are never on stage, they are central to the play's plot. How does the author create characters that the audience does not meet? Why is it important that the audience know about these two characters?
5. How does Mr. Wright contrast with his wife?
6. Why are Mrs. Peters and Mrs. Hale more important than the men to the play's plot? In what way are these women different from each other, and in what way are they similar? Since they are on stage for the entire play, other characters are not free to talk about them. How does the playwright reveal to the audience the personalities of these two women?
7. What does the author accomplish by having Mrs. Hale a long-time inhabitant of the area, and Mrs. Peters a newcomer?
8. Can you reconstruct what happened and why it happened? Prove what you say by referring to the clues in the play.
9. In naming the play "Trifles" the author underscores the basic irony of the play. Read examples from the play of the men chiding the women for their interest in trifles. Why are the lines ironic?

SUSAN GLASPELL

161

Developing Language Skills

1. "Trifles" presents two law-abiding women who deliberately withhold important evidence in a murder case. Plan a panel in which
the members identify from the play the reasons for the women's
decision not to report the evidence they discover. The members
should also tell why they approve or disapprove of this decision.

2. A writer frequently uses "trifles"—apparently insignificant details—
to reveal the character of a person he is describing. The kind of
clothes a person wears or the items he stops to look at in a store
window or the title of a book he is carrying—all these trifling details and others like them tell a great deal about a person.

   Write three or four paragraphs in which you suggest as clearly
as you can what some person is like through the use of revealing details. Imagine that you are describing someone you have seen only
once (for example, on a train or in a store). A good way to approach
this assignment would be actually to observe someone in such a
situation and to note the "trifles" that usually go unobserved.

Reading "The Golden Doom"

Authors frequently express their meaning through a *comparison* of
two essentially different things. In the play *Julius Caesar*, Antony at
Caesar's funeral says, "I . . ./Show you sweet Caesar's wounds, poor
poor dumb mouths, /And bid them speak for me." Here Shakespeare
compares the sword wounds in Caesar's side to silent mouths. The
reader senses the relationship: as lips encircle a mouth so blood sur-
rounds Caesar's wounds. To Antony's audience, these "dumb mouths"
speak far more eloquently of Caesar's harsh treatment at the hands of
the conspirators than Antony can with words.

An entire play can also use this comparative technique, in the sense
that the action of the play is like other situations in life. "The Golden
Doom," for example, is more than the tale of a king who sacrifices his
crown to the stars. The Chief Prophet says to the King, "If you sacrifice your crown which is pride, . . . you may still reign in your kingdom though humble and uncrowned." What does Dunsany say about
the relationship between pride and power? Do the children, King,
counselor, and other characters represent certain universal attitudes
and qualities? Understanding how the characters or actions in a literary work may be like people or actions in different situations is essential
to a full understanding of your reading.

The Golden Doom

Lord Dunsany

"The Golden Doom" takes you to a strange land where a purple bird foretells a king's death. In this play you will discover that in drama, as in other forms of literature, the author has an artistic purpose. It may be to create a mood, to arouse an emotion, or to relate some truth or understanding about human experience. This purpose is achieved if the play has the effect on its audience that the dramatist intended. In drama the purpose is given form through the speech and action of the characters. When you have read the play, consider its meaning to you. You will discover that the playwright's task is quite different from that of an author of a novel; the dramatist must relate meaning primarily through action and dialogue. He must use the words of characters within the play to state his interpretation of events. Often his meaning cannot be directly stated, but only implied. Therefore, the reader of a play must be alert in inferring meaning from a study of the dialogue and action.

CHARACTERS

THE KING   FIRST PROPHET
CHAMBERLAIN   SECOND PROPHET
CHIEF PROPHET   FIRST SENTRY
GIRL   SECOND SENTRY
BOY   STRANGER
SPIES   ATTENDANTS

SCENE: *Outside the King's great door in Zericon.*

TIME: *Some while before the fall of Babylon.*

Two Sentries pace to and fro, then halt, one on each side of the great door.

FIRST SENTRY. The day is deadly sultry.

SECOND SENTRY. I would that I were swimming down the Gyshon, on the cool side. under the fruit trees.

FIRST SENTRY. It is like to thunder or the fall of a dynasty.

SECOND SENTRY. It will grow cool by nightfall. Where is the King?

FIRST SENTRY. He rows in the golden barge with ambassadors or whispers with captains concerning future wars. The stars spare him!

SECOND SENTRY. Why do you say "the stars spare him"?

FIRST SENTRY. Because if a doom from the stars fall suddenly on a king it swallows up his people and all things round about him, and his palace falls and the walls of his city and citadel, and the apes come in from the woods and the large beasts from the desert, so that you would not say that a king had been there at all.

SECOND SENTRY. But why should a doom from the stars fall on the King?

FIRST SENTRY. Because he seldom placates them.

SECOND SENTRY. Ah! I have heard that said of him.

FIRST SENTRY. Who are the stars that a man should scorn them? Should they that rule the thunder, the plague and the earthquake withhold these things save for much prayer? Always ambassadors are with the King, and his commanders, come in from distant lands, prefects[1] of cities and makers of the laws, but never the priests of the stars.

SECOND SENTRY. Hark! Was that thunder?

FIRST SENTRY. Believe me, the stars are angry.

(*Enter a* STRANGER. *He wanders toward the* KING's *door, gazing about him.*)

SENTRIES (*lifting their spears at him*). Go back! Go back!

STRANGER. Why?

FIRST SENTRY. It is death to touch the King's door.

STRANGER. I am a stranger from Thessaly.

FIRST SENTRY. It is death even for a stranger.

STRANGER. Your door is strangely sacred.

FIRST SENTRY. It is death to touch it.

(*The* STRANGER *wanders off.*)

(*Enter two* CHILDREN *hand in hand.*)

BOY (*to the* SENTRY). I want to see the King to pray for a hoop.

(*The* SENTRY *smiles.*)

BOY (*pushes the door; to* GIRL). I cannot open it. (*To the* SENTRY.) Will it do as well if I pray to the King's door?

SENTRY. Yes, quite as well. (*Turns to talk to the other* Sentry.) Is there anyone in sight?

SECOND SENTRY (*shading his eyes*). Nothing but a dog, and he far out on the plain.

FIRST SENTRY. Then we can talk awhile and eat bash.

BOY. King's door, I want a little hoop.

(*The* SENTRIES *take a little bash between finger and thumb from pouches and put that wholly forgotten drug to their lips.*)

GIRL (*pointing*). My father is a taller soldier than that.

BOY. My father can write. He taught me.

GIRL. Ho! Writing frightens nobody. My father is a soldier.

BOY. I have a lump of gold. I found it in the stream that runs down to Gyshon.

GIRL. I have a poem. I found it in my own head.

BOY. Is it a long poem?

GIRL. No. But it would have been only there were no more rhymes for sky.

BOY. What is your poem?

GIRL. I saw a purple bird
　　Go up against the sky
And it went up and up
　　And round about did fly.

BOY. I saw it die.

GIRL. That doesn't scan.[2]

---

1 **prefects:** high officials.

2 **doesn't scan:** does not contain the same number of accents and syllables as the girl's poem.

DRAMA

Boy. Oh, that doesn't matter.

Girl. Do you like my poem?

Boy. Birds aren't purple.

Girl. My bird was.

Boy. Oh!

Girl. Oh, you don't like my poem!

Boy. Yes, I do.

Girl. No, you don't; you think it horrid.

Boy. No. I don't.

Girl. Yes, you do. Why didn't you say you liked it? It is the only poem I ever made.

Boy. I do like it. I do like it.

Girl. You don't, you don't!

Boy. Don't be angry. I'll write it on the door for you.

Girl. You'll write it?

Boy. Yes, I can write it. My father taught me. I'll write it with my lump of gold. It makes a yellow mark on the iron door.

Girl. Oh, do write it! I would like to see it written like real poetry.

(The **Boy** *begins to write. The* **Girl** *watches.)*

First Sentry. You see, we'll be fighting again soon.

Second Sentry. Only a little war. We never have more than a little war with the hill-folk.

First Sentry. When a man goes to fight, the curtains of the gods wax thicker than ever before between his eyes and the future; he may go to a great or to a little war.

Second Sentry. There can only be a little war with the hill-folk.

First Sentry. Yet sometimes the gods laugh.

Second Sentry. At whom?

First Sentry. At kings.

Second Sentry. Why have you grown uneasy about this war in the hills?

First Sentry. Because the King is powerful beyond any of his fathers, and has more fighting men, more horses, and wealth that could have ransomed his father and his grandfather and dowered their queens and daughters; and every year his miners bring him more from the opal mines and from the turquoise quarries. He has grown very mighty.

SECOND SENTRY. Then he will the more easily crush the hill-folk in a little war.

FIRST SENTRY. When kings grow very mighty the stars grow very jealous.

BOY. I've written your poem.

GIRL. Oh, have you really?

BOY. Yes, I'll read it to you. (*He reads.*)

> I saw a purple bird
>   Go up against the sky
> And it went up and up
>   And round about did fly.
>   I saw it die.

GIRL. It doesn't scan.

BOY. That doesn't matter.

(*Enter furtively a* SPY, *who crosses stage and goes out. The* SENTRIES *cease to talk.*)

GIRL. That man frightens me.

BOY. He is only one of the King's spies.

GIRL. But I don't like the King's spies. They frighten me.

BOY. Come on, then, we'll run away.

SENTRY (*noticing the children again*). Go away, go away! The King is coming, he will eat you.

(*The* BOY *throws a stone at the* SENTRY *and runs out. Enter another* SPY, *who crosses the stage. Enter third* SPY, *who notices the door. He examines it and utters an owl-like whistle. No. 2 comes back. They do not speak. Both whistle. No. 3 comes. All examine the door. Enter the* KING *and his* CHAMBERLAIN. *The* KING *wears a purple robe. The* SENTRIES *smartly transfer their*

spears to their left hands and return their right arms to their right sides. They then lower their spears until their points are within an inch of the ground, at the same time raising their right hands above their heads. They stand for some moments thus. Then they lower their right arms to their right sides, at the same time raising their spears. In the next motion they take their spears into their right hands and lower the butts to the floor, where they were before, the spears slanting forward a little. Both* SENTRIES *must move together precisely.*)

FIRST SPY (*runs forward to the* KING *and kneels, abasing his forehead to the floor*). Something has written on the iron door.

CHAMBERLAIN. On the iron door!

KING. Some fool has done it. Who has been here since yesterday?

FIRST SENTRY (*shifts his hand a little higher on his spear, brings the spear to his side and closes his heels all in one motion; he then takes one pace backward with his right foot; then he kneels on his right knee; when he has done this he speaks, but not before*). Nobody, Majesty, but a stranger from Thessaly.

KING. Did he touch the iron door?

FIRST SENTRY. No, Majesty; he tried to, but we drove him away.

KING. How near did he come?

FIRST SENTRY. Nearly to our spears, Majesty.

KING. What was his motive in seeking to touch the iron door?

FIRST SENTRY. I do not know, Majesty.

KING. Which way did he go?

FIRST SENTRY (*pointing left*). That way, Majesty, an hour ago.

(*The King whispers with one of his* SPIES, *who stoops and examines the ground and steals away. The* SENTRY *rises.*)

KING (*to his two remaining* SPIES). What does this writing say?

A SPY. We cannot read, Majesty.

KING. A good spy should know everything.

SECOND SPY. We watch, Majesty, and we search out, Majesty. We read shadows, and we read footprints, and whispers in secret places. But we do not read writing.

KING (*to the* CHAMBERLAIN). See what it is.

CHAMBERLAIN (*goes up and reads*). It is treason, Majesty.

KING. Read it.

CHAMBERLAIN.

I saw a purple bird
 Go up against the sky,
And it went up and up
And round about did fly.
 I saw it die.

FIRST SENTRY (*aside*). The stars have spoken.

KING (*to the* SENTRY). Has anyone been here but the stranger from Thessaly?

SENTRY (*kneeling as before*). Nobody, Majesty.

KING. You saw nothing?

FIRST SENTRY. Nothing but a dog far out upon the plain and the children of the guard at play.

KING (*to the* SECOND SENTRY). And you?

SECOND SENTRY (*kneeling*). Nothing, Majesty.

CHAMBERLAIN. That is strange.

KING. It is some secret warning.

CHAMBERLAIN. It is treason.

KING. It is from the stars.

CHAMBERLAIN. No, no, Majesty. Not from the stars, not from the stars. Some man has done it. Yet the thing should be interpreted. Shall I send for the prophets of the stars?

(*The* KING *beckons to his* SPIES. *They run up to him.*)

KING. Find me some prophet of the stars. (*Exeunt* SPIES.) I fear that we may go no more, my chamberlain, along the winding ways of unequaled Zericon, nor play dahoori with the golden balls. I have thought more of my people than of the stars and more of Zericon than of windy Heaven.

CHAMBERLAIN. Believe me, Majesty, some idle man has written it and passed by. Your spies shall find him, and then his name will be soon forgotten.

KING. Yes, yes. Perhaps you are right, though the sentries saw no one. No doubt some beggar did it.

CHAMBERLAIN. Yes, Majesty, some beggar has surely done it. But look, here come two prophets of the stars. They shall tell us that this is idle.

(*Enter two* PROPHETS *and a* BOY *attending them. All bow deeply to the* KING. *The two* SPIES *steal in again and stand at back.*)

KING. Some beggar has written a rhyme on the iron gate, and as the ways of rhyme are known to you I desired you, rather as poets than as prophets, to say whether there was any meaning in it.

CHAMBERLAIN. 'Tis but an idle rhyme.

FIRST PROPHET (*bows again and goes up to door*). (*He glances at the writing.*) Come hither, servant of those that serve the stars.

(ATTENDANT *approaches.*)

FIRST PROPHET. Bring hither our golden cloaks, for this may be a matter for rejoicing; and bring our green cloaks also, for this may tell of young new beautiful things with which the stars will one day gladden the King; and bring our black cloaks also, for it may be a doom. (*Exit the* **Boy**; *the* **Prophet** *goes up to the door and reads solemnly.*) The stars have spoken.

(*Re-enter* **Attendant** *with cloaks.*)

King. I tell you that some beggar has written this.

First Prophet. It is written in pure gold. (*He dons the black cloak over body and head.*)

King. What do the stars mean? What warning is it?

First Prophet. I cannot say.

King (*to* **Second Prophet**). Come you then and tell us what the warning is.

Second Prophet (*goes up to the door and reads*). The stars have spoken. (*He cloaks himself in black.*)

King. What is it? What does it mean?

Second Prophet. We do not know, but it is from the stars.

Chamberlain. It is a harmless thing; there is no harm in it, Majesty. Why should not birds die?

King. Why have the prophets covered themselves in black?

Chamberlain. They are a secret people and look for inner meanings. There is no harm in it.

King. They have covered themselves in black.

Chamberlain. They have not spoken of any evil thing. They have not spoken of it.

King. If the people see the prophets covered in black they will say that the stars are against me and believe that my luck has turned.

Chamberlain. The people must not know.

King. Some prophet must interpret to us the doom. Let the chief prophet of the stars be sent for.

Chamberlain (*going toward left exit*). Summon the chief prophet of the stars that look on Zericon.

Voices Off. The chief prophet of the stars. The chief prophet of the stars.

Chamberlain. I have summoned the chief prophet, Majesty.

King. If he interpret this aright I will put a necklace of turquoises round his neck with opals from the mines.

Chamberlain. He will not fail. He is a very cunning interpreter.

King. What if he covers himself with a huge black cloak and does not speak and goes muttering away, slowly with bended head, till our fear spreads to the sentries and they cry aloud?

Chamberlain. This is no doom from the stars, but some idle scribe hath written it in his insolence upon the iron door, wasting his hoard of gold.

King. Not for myself I have a fear of doom, not for myself; but I inherited a rocky land, windy and ill-nurtured, and nursed it to prosperity by years of peace and spread its boundaries by years of war. I have brought up harvests out of barren acres and given good laws unto naughty towns, and my people are happy, and lo, the stars are angry!

Chamberlain. It is not the stars, it is not the stars, Majesty, for the prophets of the stars have not interpreted it. Indeed, it was only some reveler wasting his gold.

(*Meanwhile enter* **Chief Prophet** *of the stars that look on Zericon.*)

King. Chief Prophet of the Stars that look on Zericon, I would have you interpret the rhyme upon yonder door.

Chief Prophet (*goes up to the door and reads*). It is from the stars.

King. Interpret it and you shall have great turquoises round your neck, with opals from the mines in the frozen mountains.

Chief Prophet (*cloaks himself like the others in a great black cloak*). Who

should wear purple in the land but a King, or who go up against the sky but he who has troubled the stars by neglecting their ancient worship? Such a one has gone up and up increasing power and wealth, such a one has soared above the crowns of those that went before him, such a one the stars have doomed, the undying ones, the illustrious.

(*A pause.*)

KING. Who wrote it?

CHIEF PROPHET. It is pure gold. Some god has written it.

CHAMBERLAIN. Some god?

CHIEF PROPHET. Some god whose home is among the undying stars.

FIRST SENTRY (*aside to the* SECOND SENTRY). Last night I saw a star go flaming earthward.

KING. Is this a warning or is it a doom?

CHIEF PROPHET. The stars have spoken.

KING. It is, then, a doom?

CHIEF PROPHET. They speak not in jest.

KING. I have been a great King—Let it be said of me "The stars overthrew him, and they sent a god for his doom." For I have not met my equal among kings that man should overthrow me; and I have not oppressed my people that man should rise up against me.

CHIEF PROPHET. It is better to give worship to the stars than to do good to man. It is better to be humble before the gods than proud in the face of your enemy though he do evil.

KING. Let the stars hearken yet and I will sacrifice a child to them—I will sacrifice a girl child to the twinkling stars and a male child to the stars that blink not, the stars of the steadfast eyes. (*To his* SPIES.) Let a boy and girl be brought for sacrifice. (*Exit a* SPY *to the right looking at footprints.*) Will you accept this sacrifice to the god

LORD DUNSANY

that the stars have sent? They say that the gods love children.

CHIEF PROPHET. I may refuse no sacrifice to the stars nor to the gods whom they send. (*To the other* PROPHETS.) Make ready the sacrificial knives.

(*The* PROPHETS *draw knives and sharpen them.*)

KING. Is it fitting that the sacrifice take place by the iron door where the god from the stars has trod, or must it be in the temple?

CHIEF PROPHET. Let it be offered by the iron door. (*To the other* PROPHETS.) Fetch hither the altar stone.

(*The owl-like whistle is heard off right. The* THIRD SPY *runs crouching toward it. Exit.*)

KING. Will this sacrifice avail to avert the doom?

CHIEF PROPHET. Who knows?

KING. I fear that even yet the doom will fall.

CHIEF PROPHET. It were wise to sacrifice some greater thing.

KING. What more can a man offer?

CHIEF PROPHET. His pride.

KING. What pride?

CHIEF PROPHET. Your pride that went up against the sky and troubled the stars.

KING. How shall I sacrifice my pride to the stars?

CHIEF PROPHET. It is upon your pride that the doom will fall, and will take away your crown and will take away your kingdom.

KING. I will sacrifice my crown and reign uncrowned amongst you, so only I save my kingdom.

CHIEF PROPHET. If you sacrifice your crown which is your pride, and if the stars accept it, perhaps the god that they sent may avert the doom and you may still reign in your kingdom though humbled and uncrowned.

KING. Shall I burn my crown with spices and with incense or cast it into the sea?

CHIEF PROPHET. Let it be laid here by the iron door where the god came who wrote the golden doom. When he comes again by night to shrivel up the city or to pour an enemy in through the iron door, he will see your cast-off pride and perhaps accept it and take it away to the neglected stars.

KING (*to the* CHAMBERLAIN). Go after my spies and say that I make no sacrifice. (*Exit the* CHAMBERLAIN *to the right; the* KING *takes off his crown.*) Good-by, my brittle glory; kings have sought you; the stars have envied you. (*The stage grows darker.*)

CHIEF PROPHET. Even now the sun has set who denies the stars, and the day is departed wherein no gods walk abroad. It is near the hour when spirits roam the earth and all things that go unseen, and the faces of the abiding stars will be soon revealed to the fields. Lay your crown there and let us come away.

KING (*lays his crown before the iron door; then to the* SENTRIES). Go! And let no man come near the door all night.

THE SENTRIES (*kneeling*). Yes, Majesty.

(*They remain kneeling until after the* KING *has gone.* KING *and the* CHIEF PROPHET *walk away.*)

CHIEF PROPHET. It was your pride. Let it be forgotten. May the stars accept it. (*Exeunt left.*)

(*The* SENTRIES *rise.*)

FIRST SENTRY. The stars have envied him!

SECOND SENTRY. It is an ancient crown. He wore it well.

FIRST SENTRY. May the stars accept it.

SECOND SENTRY. If they do not accept it what doom will overtake him?

FIRST SENTRY. It will suddenly be as though there were never any city of Zericon nor two sentries like you and me standing before the door.

SECOND SENTRY. Why! How do you know?

FIRST SENTRY. That is ever the way of the gods.

SECOND SENTRY. But it is unjust.

FIRST SENTRY. How should the gods know that?

SECOND SENTRY. Will it happen to-night?

FIRST SENTRY. Come! we must march away. (*Exeunt right.*)

(*The stage grows increasingly darker. Re-enter the* CHAMBER-LAIN *from the right. He walks across the stage and goes out to the left. Re-enter* SPIES *from the right. They cross the stage, which is now nearly dark.*)

BOY (*enters from the right, dressed in white, his hands out a little, crying*).

King's door, King's door, I want my little hoop. (*He goes up to the King's door. When he sees the King's crown there, he utters a satisfied*) O-oh! (*He takes it up, puts it on the ground, and, beating it before him with the scepter, goes out by the way that he entered.*)

(*The great door opens; there is light within; a furtive* SPY *slips out and sees that the crown is gone. Another* SPY *slips out. Their crouching heads come close together.*)

FIRST SPY (*hoarse whisper*). The gods have come!

(*They run back through the door and the door is closed. It opens again and the* KING *and the* CHAMBERLAIN *come through.*)

KING. The stars are satisfied.

CURTAIN

Understanding the Play

1. Lord Dunsany wrote of this play: "It is just a simple story, though of a far country. Any ironies in it are clear enough to be seen." What is the basic irony that underlies the entire plot of the play? In what way is the ending ironic? What is Dunsany satirizing through the irony?

2. In this play, Dunsany has created the atmosphere of a fairy tale or fantasy rather than that of historical realism. What are some specific actions or lines of dialogue that contribute to this atmosphere?

3. At first the King is inclined to take a rational view of the verse on the iron door. What lines that he speaks show this view of the matter?

4. The King finally accepts the verse as a doom from the stars. Although this is partly accounted for by the general superstition of the land in which the play is set, what evidence is there in the King's speeches that his own sense of guilt partly leads to his final interpretation? What does he feel guilty about?

5. The kind of superstitious beliefs held by the characters of this play would not be shared by most readers of the play. Is Dunsany merely satirizing a situation few of his readers will encounter? Or are the beliefs held by his characters and their reactions to what happens parallels to beliefs and reactions still widely found in modern civilizations? What are the parallels?

Developing Vocabulary Skills

A good author's choice of words is not haphazard. He uses the particular words he does because they help to create the effect he wants. Dunsany, for example, created the atmosphere of a fairy tale partly through the kind of words he used. This is most obvious in the case of four words he made up: the proper names *Zericon* and *Gyshon* and the words *bash* and *dahoori*. These suggest a faraway place and have an Oriental, somewhat mysterious ring to them. The very fact that *bash* and *dahoori* have no actual meaning adds to the sense of fantasy.

This suggestive quality is possessed by many real words. When a word suggests qualities and ideas that are not a part of its actual definition, it has connotative meaning. *Rose*, for example, can suggest beauty or passion, although these qualities have nothing to do with its actual definition.

What connotations do the italicized words in the following sentences have? That is, what qualities, ideas, or emotions do they suggest apart from their dictionary meanings? As a help in answering, consider why the italicized word in each sentence is better than the alternatives put in parentheses after the sentence.

1. "It is like to *thunder* or the fall of a dynasty." (p. 163)
   (*a loud noise* or *lightning*)

2. "He . . . *whispers* with captains concerning future wars." (p. 163)
   (*confers*)

3. "I saw a *purple* bird
   Go up against the sky" (p. 167)
   (*little* or *brown*)

4. "I have thought more of my people than of the stars and more of Zericon than of *windy* Heaven." (p. 167)
   (*great* or *beautiful*)

5. " . . . bring our *black* cloaks also, for it may be a doom." (p. 167)
   (*brown* or *red*)

6. "It is an *ancient* crown." (p. 170)
   (*old*).

Developing Language Skills

Write a paragraph in which you explain your interpretation of the meaning of the play. Base your conclusions upon evidence from the play.

Reading "The Devil and Daniel Webster"

The *atmosphere* of a literary selection is the mood or feeling created by the author. The playwright, through all the dramatic techniques available to him, seeks to create an audience response that will be in harmony with the action of the play. Thus, through elements of the setting (such as bright lights and gay colors for lighthearted comedy; a somber stage scene for sadness; thunder, lightning, and shadows for mystery and suspense; soft lights and colors for love and romance) the viewer is led to expect certain situations to develop.

Atmosphere is also created through the dialogue and action of the play. Early in "The Devil and Daniel Webster" Jabez asks his bride Mary if she is happy. Mary replies, "Yes. So happy, I'm afraid. . . . I suppose it happens to every girl—just for a minute. It's like spring turning into summer. You want it to be summer. But the spring was sweet. I'm sorry. Forgive me. It just came and went, like something cold. As if we'd been too lucky." Through these lines the gay atmosphere of the wedding party is changed to one in which the reader expects the entrance of evil. When Webster arrives and pays his respects "to a most charming lady and her very fortunate spouse," he is interrupted twice, once by the twang of a fiddlestring breaking and again by a discordant squeak from the fiddle. By these sounds an atmosphere of fearful expectancy is created, and the audience is made aware that trouble is approaching.

Another technique used by Benét to establish atmosphere is the short rhythmic speeches of the wedding guests at the opening of the play. The directions suggest that the conversation "follow the tune of the dance music." As the curtain rises, the audience immediately senses from this stylized, and thus unrealistic, dialogue that the events of the play may be strange or unnatural.

Lighting and sound effects are used to establish the atmosphere when Scratch's black box is opened: "The lights wink and there is a clap of thunder"; and again when Scratch summons the jury: "There is a clap of thunder and a flash of light. The stage blacks out completely. All that can be seen is the face of Scratch, lit with a ghastly green light. . . ." As you read "The Devil and Daniel Webster," note the effect of these theatrical devices on your feelings. To what extent is your mood in harmony with the actions of the play? How well are you led to expect the type of events that are to occur?

STEPHEN VINCENT BENÉT

The Devil and Daniel Webster°

Stephen Vincent Benét

Jabez Stone in this play is an American version of Faust, whose story is the basis for several famous works. The Faust story had its source in a German magician, Dr. Johann Faust, who after his death in 1540 became a legendary figure when an account of his life and "abominable deeds" was published. The play Doctor Faustus, written by the English playwright Christopher Marlowe in the 16th century, retells this legend, ending with the devil dragging Faustus off to Hell. Goethe, a 19th century German writer, contributed further to the myth in his monumental drama Faust. His version adds this new theme: that in spite of any compact between the devil and man, as long as man attempts to reach higher goals in life, the devil cannot win his soul. This legend and theme inspired Stephen Vincent Benét to write about an American Faust in "The Devil and Daniel Webster."

CHARACTERS

JABEZ STONE	KING PHILIP
MARY STONE	TEACH
DANIEL WEBSTER	WALTER BUTLER
MR. SCRATCH	SIMON GIRTY
THE FIDDLER	DALE
JUSTICE HATHORNE	MEN and WOMEN of Cross Corners,
JUSTICE HATHORNE'S CLERK	New Hampshire

SCENE: JABEZ STONE'S *farmhouse.*
TIME: *1841.*

The scene is the main room of a New Hampshire farmhouse in 1841, a big comfortable room that hasn't yet developed the stuffiness of a front parlor. A door, right, leads to the kitchen—a door, left, to the outside. There is a fireplace, right. Windows, in center, show a glimpse of summer landscape. Most of the furniture has been cleared away for the dance which follows the wedding of JABEZ *and* MARY STONE, *but there is a settle or bench by the fireplace, a table, left, with some wedding presents upon it, at least three chairs by the table, and a cider barrel on which the* FIDDLER *sits, in front of the table. Near the table, against the side wall, there is a cupboard where there are glasses and a jug. There is a clock.*

A country wedding has been in progress—the wedding of JABEZ *and* MARY STONE. *He is a husky young farmer, around twenty-eight or thirty. The bride is in her early twenties. He is dressed in stiff, store clothes but not ridiculously—they are of good quality and he looks important. The bride is in a simple white or cream wedding dress and may carry a small, stiff bouquet of country flowers.*

Now the wedding is over and the guests are dancing. The FIDDLER *is perched on the cider barrel. He plays and calls square-dance figures. The guests include the recognizable types of a small New England town, doctor, lawyer, storekeeper, old maid, schoolteacher, farmer, etc. There is an air of prosperity and hearty country mirth about the whole affair.*

At rise, JABEZ *and* MARY *are up left center, receiving the congratulations of a few last guests who talk to them and pass on to the dance. The others are dancing. There is a buzz of conversation that follows the tune of the dance music.*

FIRST WOMAN. Right nice wedding.

FIRST MAN. Handsome couple.

SECOND WOMAN (*passing through crowd with dish of oyster stew*). Oysters for supper!

SECOND MAN (*passing cake*). And layer cake—layer cake——

AN OLD MAN (*hobbling toward cider barrel*). Makes me feel young again! Oh, by jingo!

AN OLD WOMAN (*pursuing him*). Henry, Henry, you've been drinking cider!

FIDDLER. Set to your partners! Dosy-do!

WOMEN. Mary and Jabez.

MEN. Jabez and Mary.

A WOMAN. Where's the State Senator?

A MAN. Where's the lucky bride?

(*With cries of "Mary—Jabez—strike it up, fiddler—make room for the bride and groom," the* CROWD *drags* MARY *and* JABEZ, *pleased but embarrassed, into the center of the room and* MARY *and* JABEZ *do a little solo dance, while the* CROWD *claps, applauds and makes various remarks.*)

A MAN. Handsome steppers!

A WOMAN. She's pretty as a picture.

A SECOND MAN. Cut your pigeon-wing,[1] Jabez!

THE OLD MAN. Young again, young again, that's the way I feel! (*He tries to cut a pigeon-wing himself.*)

THE OLD WOMAN. Henry, Henry, careful of your rheumatiz!

A THIRD WOMAN. Makes me feel all teary—seeing them so happy.

(*The solo dance ends, the music stops for a moment.*)

THE OLD MAN (*gossiping to a neighbor*). Wonder where he got it all—

---

1 **pigeon-wing:** a fancy dancing step in which the two legs are kicked together while the dancer is jumping in the air.

Stones was always poor.

His Neighbor. Ain't poor now—makes you wonder just a mite.

A Third Man. Don't begrudge it to him—but I wonder where he got it.

The Old Man (*starting to whisper*). Let me tell you something——

The Old Woman (*quickly*). Henry, Henry, don't you start to gossip. (*She drags him away.*)

Fiddler (*cutting in*). Set to your partners! Scratch for corn!

(*The dance resumes, but as it does so, the* **Crowd** *chants back and forth.*)

Women. Gossip's got a sharp tooth.

Men. Gossip's got a mean tooth.

Women. She's a lucky woman. They're a lucky pair.

Men. That's true as gospel. But I wonder where he got it.

Women. Money, land and riches.

Men. Just came out of nowhere.

Women and **Men** (*together*). Wonder where he got it all.—But that's his business.

Fiddler. Left and right—grand chain!

(*The dance rises to a pitch of ecstasy with the final figure—the fiddle squeaks and stops. The dancers mop their brows.*)

First Man. Whew! Ain't danced like that since I was knee-high to a grasshopper!

Second Man. Play us "The Portland Fancy," fiddler!

Third Man. No, wait a minute, neighbor. Let's hear from the happy pair! Hey, Jabez!

Fourth Man. Let's hear from the State Senator!

(*They crowd around* **Jabez** *and push him up on the settle.*)

Old Man. Might as well. It's the last time he'll have the last word!

Old Woman. Now, Henry Banks, you ought to be ashamed of yourself!

Old Man. Told you so, Jabez!

The Crowd. Speech!

Jabez (*embarrassed*). Neighbors—friends—I'm not much of a speaker—spite of your 'lecting me to State Senate——

The Crowd. That's the ticket, Jabez. Smart man, Jabez. I voted for ye. Go ahead, Senator, you're doing fine.

Jabez. But we're certainly glad to have you here—me and Mary. And we want to thank you for coming and——

A Voice. Vote the Whig[2] ticket!

Another Voice. Hooray for Daniel Webster!

Jabez. And I'm glad Hi Foster said that, for those are my sentiments, too. Mr. Webster has promised to honor us with his presence here tonight.

The Crowd. Hurray for Dan'l! Hurray for the greatest man in the U. S.!

Jabez. And when he comes, I know we'll give him a real New Hampshire welcome.

The Crowd. Sure we will—Webster forever—and down with Henry Clay!

Jabez. And meanwhile—well, there's Mary and me (*takes her hand*)—and, if you folks don't have a good time, well, we won't feel right about getting married at all. Because I know I've been lucky—and I hope she feels that way, too. And, well, we're going to be happy or bust a trace![3] (*He wipes his brow to terrific applause. He and* **Mary** *look at each other.*)

A Woman (*in kitchen doorway*). Come and get the cider, folks!

(*The* **Crowd** *begins to drift away—a few to the kitchen—a few toward the door that leads to the outside. They furnish a shifting background to the next little*

---

2 Whig: a political party formed about 1834 in opposition to the Democrats.
3 trace: a strap on a harness for attaching a horse to a vehicle.

scene, where **Mary** *and* **Jabez** *are left alone by the fireplace.*)

Jabez. Mary.

Mary. Mr. Stone.

Jabez. Mary.

Mary. My husband.

Jabez. That's a big word, husband.

Mary. It's a good word.

Jabez. Are you happy, Mary?

Mary. Yes. So happy, I'm afraid.

Jabez. Afraid?

Mary. I suppose it happens to every girl—just for a minute. It's like spring turning into summer. You want it to be summer. But the spring was sweet. (*Dismissing the mood.*) I'm sorry. Forgive me. It just came and went, like something cold. As if we'd been too lucky.

Jabez. We can't be too lucky, Mary. Not you and me.

Mary (*rather mischievously*). If you say so, Mr. Stone. But you don't even know what sort of housekeeper I am.

And Aunt Hepsy says——

Jabez. Bother your Aunt Hepsy! There's just you and me and that's all that matters in the world.

Mary. And you don't know something else——

Jabez. What's that?

Mary. How proud I am of you. Ever since I was a little girl. Ever since you carried my books. Oh, I'm sorry for women who can't be proud of their men. It must be a lonely feeling.

Jabez (*uncomfortably*). A man can't always be proud of everything, Mary. There's some things a man does, or might do—when he has to make his way.

Mary (*laughing*). I know—terrible things—like being the best farmer in the county and the best State Senator——

Jabez (*quietly*). And a few things, besides. But you remember one thing, Mary, whatever happens. It was all for you. And nothing's going to happen. Because he hasn't come yet—and he would have come if it was wrong.

MARY. But it's wonderful to have Mr. Webster come to us.

JABEZ. I wasn't thinking about Mr. Webster. (*He takes both her hands.*) Mary, I've got something to tell you. I should have told you before, but I couldn't seem to bear it. Only, now that it's all right, I can. Ten years ago——

A VOICE (*from off stage*). Dan'l! Dan'l Webster!

> (**JABEZ** *drops* **MARY'S** *hands and looks around. The* **CROWD** *begins to mill and gather toward the door. Others rush in from the kitchen.*)

ANOTHER VOICE. Black Dan'l! He's come!

ANOTHER VOICE. Three cheers for the greatest man in the U. S.!

ANOTHER VOICE. Three cheers for Daniel Webster!

> (*And, to the cheering and applause of the crowd,* **DANIEL WEBSTER** *enters and stands for a moment upstage, in the familiar pose, his head thrown back, his attitude leonine. He stops the cheering of the crowd with a gesture.*)

WEBSTER. Neighbors—old friends—it does me good to hear you. But don't cheer me—I'm not running for President this summer. (*A laugh from the* **CROWD**.) I'm here on a better errand—to pay my humble respects to a most charming lady and her very fortunate spouse.

> (*There is the twang of a fiddle-string breaking.*)

FIDDLER. 'Tarnation! Busted a string!

A VOICE. He's always bustin' strings.

> (**WEBSTER** *blinks at the interruption but goes on.*)

WEBSTER. We're proud of State Senator Stone in these parts—we know what he's done. Ten years ago he started out with a patch of land that was mostly rocks and mortgages and now—well, you've only to look around you. I don't know that I've ever seen a likelier farm, not even at Marshfield—and I hope, before I die, I'll have the privilege of shaking his hand as Governor of this State. I don't know how he's done it—I couldn't have done it myself. But I know this—Jabez Stone wears no man's collar. (*At this statement there is a discordant squeak from the fiddle and* **JABEZ** *looks embarrassed.* **WEBSTER** *knits his brows.*) And what's more, if I know Jabez, he never will. But I didn't come here to talk politics—I came to kiss the bride. (*He does so among great applause. He shakes hands with* **JABEZ**.) Congratulations, Stone—you're a lucky man. And now, if our friend in the corner will give us a tune on his fiddle——

> (*The* **CROWD** *presses forward to meet the great man. He shakes hands with several.*)

A MAN. Remember me, Mr. Webster? Saw ye up at the State House at Concord.

ANOTHER MAN. Glad to see ye, Mr. Webster. I voted for ye ten times.

> (**WEBSTER** *receives their homage politely, but his mind is still on music.*)

WEBSTER (*a trifle irritated*). I said, if our friend in the corner would give us a tune on his fiddle——

FIDDLER (*passionately, flinging the fiddle down*). Hell's delight—excuse me, Mr. Webster. But the very devil's got into that fiddle of mine. She was doing all right up to just a minute ago. But now I've tuned her and tuned her and she won't play a note I want.

> (*And, at this point,* **MR. SCRATCH** *makes his appearance. He has*

entered, unobserved, and mixed with the crowd while all eyes were upon DANIEL WEBSTER. *He is, of course, the devil—a New England devil, dressed like a rather shabby attorney but with something just a little wrong in clothes and appearance. For one thing, he wears black gloves on his hands. He carries a large black tin box, like a botanist's collecting box, under one arm. Now he slips through the crowd and taps the* FIDDLER *on the shoulder.*)

SCRATCH (*insinuatingly*). Maybe you need some rosin on your bow, fiddler?

FIDDLER. Maybe I do and maybe I don't. (*Turns and confronts the stranger.*) But who are you? I don't remember seeing you before.

SCRATCH. Oh, I'm just a friend—a humble friend of the bridegroom's. (*He walks toward* JABEZ. *Apologetically.*) I'm afraid I came in the wrong way, Mr. Stone. You've improved the place so much since I last saw it that I hardly knew the front door. But, I assure you, I came as fast as I could.

JABEZ (*obviously shocked*). It—it doesn't matter. (*With a great effort.*) Mary—Mr. Webster—this is a—a friend of mine from Boston—a legal friend. I didn't expect him today but——

SCRATCH. Oh, my dear Mr. Stone— an occasion like this—I wouldn't miss it for the world. (*He bows.*) Charmed, Mrs. Stone. Delighted, Mr. Webster. But—don't let me break up the merriment of the meeting. (*He turns back toward the table and the* FIDDLER.)

FIDDLER (*with a grudge, to* SCRATCH). Boston lawyer, eh?

SCRATCH. You might call me that.

FIDDLER (*tapping the tin box with his bow*). And what have you got in that big tin box of yours? Law papers?

SCRATCH. Oh—curiosities for the most part. I'm a collector, too.

FIDDLER. Don't hold much with Boston curiosities, myself. And you know about fiddling too, do you? Know all about it?

SCRATCH. Oh—— (*A deprecatory shrug.*)

FIDDLER. Don't shrug your shoulders at me—I ain't no Frenchman. Telling me I needed more rosin!

MARY (*trying to stop the quarrel*). Isaac—please——

FIDDLER. Sorry, Mary—Mrs. Stone. But I been playing the fiddle at Cross Corners weddings for twenty-five years. And now here comes a stranger from Boston and tells me I need more rosin!

SCRATCH. But, my good friend——

FIDDLER. Rosin indeed! Here—play it yourself then and see what you can make of it! (*He thrusts the fiddle at* SCRATCH. *The latter stiffens, slowly lays his black collecting box on the table, and takes the fiddle.*)

SCRATCH (*with feigned embarrassment*). But really, I—— (*He bows toward* JABEZ.) Shall I—Mr. Senator?

(JABEZ *makes a helpless gesture of assent.*)

MARY (*to* JABEZ). Mr. Stone—Mr. Stone—are you ill?

JABEZ. No—no—but I feel—it's hot——

WEBSTER (*chuckling*). Don't you fret, Mrs. Stone. I've got the right medicine for him. (*He pulls a flask from his pocket.*) Ten-year-old Medford, Stone —I buy it by the keg down at Marshfield. Here—— (*He tries to give some of the rum to* JABEZ.)

JABEZ. No—(*he turns*)—Mary—Mr. Webster—— (*But he cannot explain. With a burst.*) Oh, let him play—let him play! Don't you see he's bound to? Don't you see there's nothing we can do?

(*A rustle of discomfort among the guests.* SCRATCH *draws the bow across the fiddle in a horrible discord.*)

FIDDLER (*triumphantly*). I told you so, stranger. The devil's in that fiddle!

SCRATCH. I'm afraid it needs special tuning. (*Draws the bow in a second discord.*) There—that's better. (*Grinning.*) And now for this happy—this very happy occasion—in tribute to the bride and groom—I'll play something appropriate—a song of young love——

MARY. Oh, Jabez—Mr. Webster—stop him! Do you see his hands? He's playing with gloves on his hands.

(WEBSTER *starts forward, but, even as he does so,* SCRATCH *begins to play and all freeze as* SCRATCH *goes on with the extremely inappropriate song that follows. At first his manner is oily and mocking—it is not till he reaches the line "The devil took the words away" that he really becomes terrifying and the crowd starts to be afraid.*)

SCRATCH (*accompanying himself fantastically*).

Young William was a thriving boy.
(Listen to my doleful tale.)
Young Mary Clark was all his joy.
(Listen to my doleful tale.)

He swore he'd love her all his life.
She swore she'd be his loving wife.

But William found a gambler's den
And drank with livery-stable[4] men.

He played the cards, he played the dice.
He would not listen to advice.

And when in church he tried to pray,
The devil took the words away.
(SCRATCH, *still playing, starts to march across the stage.*)

The devil got him by the toe
And so, alas, he had to go.

"Young Mary Clark, young Mary Clark,
I now must go into the dark."
(*These last two verses have been directed at* JABEZ. SCRATCH *continues, now turning on* MARY.)
Young Mary lay upon her bed.
"Alas my Will-i-am is dead."

He came to her a bleeding ghost——
(*He rushes at* MARY *but* WEBSTER *stands between them.*)

WEBSTER. Stop! Stop! You miserable wretch—can't you see that you're frightening Mrs. Stone? (*He wrenches the fiddle out of* SCRATCH'S *hands and tosses it aside.*) And now, sir—out of this house!

SCRATCH (*facing him*). You're a bold man, Mr. Webster. Too bold for your own good, perhaps. And anyhow, it wasn't my fiddle. It belonged to—— (*He wheels and sees the* FIDDLER *tampering with the collecting box that has been left on the table.*) Idiot! What are you doing with my collecting box? (*He rushes for the* FIDDLER *and chases him round the table, but the* FIDDLER *is just one jump ahead.*)

FIDDLER. Boston lawyer, eh? Well, I don't think so. I think you've got something in that box of yours you're afraid to show. And, by jingo—— (*He throws open the lid of the box. The lights wink and there is a clap of thunder. All eyes stare upward. Something has flown out of the box. But what?* FIDDLER, *with relief.*) Why, 'tain't nothing but a moth.

---

4 **livery-stable:** place that hires out horses and vehicles.

MARY. A white moth—a flying thing.

WEBSTER. A common moth—*telea polyphemus*——

THE CROWD. A moth—just a moth—a moth——

FIDDLER (*terrified*). But it ain't. It ain't no common moth! I seen it! And it's got a death's-head on it! (*He strikes at the invisible object with his bow to drive it way.*)

VOICE OF THE MOTH. Help me, neighbors! Help me!

WEBSTER. What's that? It wails like a lost soul.

MARY. A lost soul.

THE CROWD. A lost soul—lost—in darkness—in the darkness.

VOICE OF THE MOTH. Help me, neighbors!

FIDDLER. It sounds like Miser Stevens.

JABEZ. Miser Stevens!

THE CROWD. The Miser—Miser Stevens—a lost soul—lost.

FIDDLER (*frantically*). It sounds like Miser Stevens—and you had him in your box. But it can't be. He ain't dead.

JABEZ. He ain't dead—I tell you he ain't dead! He was just as spry and mean as a woodchuck Tuesday.

THE CROWD. Miser Stevens—soul of Miser Stevens—but he ain't dead.

SCRATCH (*dominating them*). Listen! (*A bell off stage begins to toll a knell, slowly, solemnly.*)

MARY. The bell—the church bell—the bell that rang at my wedding.

WEBSTER. The church bell—the passing bell.

JABEZ. The funeral bell.

THE CROWD. The bell—the passing bell—Miser Stevens—dead.

VOICE OF THE MOTH. Help me, neighbors, help me! I sold my soul to the devil. But I'm not the first or the last. Help me. Help Jabez Stone!

SCRATCH. Ah, would you! (*He catches the moth in his red bandanna, stuffs it back into his collecting box, and shuts the lid with a snap.*)

VOICE OF THE MOTH (*fading*). Lost—lost forever, forever. Lost, like Jabez Stone.

(*The* **CROWD** *turns on* **JABEZ**. *They read his secret in his face.*)

THE CROWD. Jabez Stone—Jabez Stone—answer us—answer us.

MARY. Tell them, dear—answer them—you are good—you are brave—you are innocent.

(*But the* **CROWD** *is all pointing hands and horrified eyes.*)

THE CROWD. Jabez Stone—Jabez Stone. Who's your friend in black, Jabez Stone? (*They point to* **SCRATCH.**)

WEBSTER. Answer them, Mr. State Senator.

THE CROWD. Jabez Stone—Jabez Stone. Where did you get your money, Jabez Stone?

(**SCRATCH** *grins and taps his collecting box.* **JABEZ** *cannot speak.*)

JABEZ. I—I—— (*He stops.*)

THE CROWD. Jabez Stone—Jabez Stone. What was the price you paid for it, Jabez Stone?

JABEZ (*looking around wildly*). Help me, neighbors! Help me!

(*This cracks the built-up tension and sends the* **CROWD** *over the edge into fanaticism.*)

A WOMAN'S VOICE (*high and hysterical*). He's sold his soul to the devil! (*She points to* **JABEZ.**)

OTHER VOICES. To the devil!

THE CROWD. He's sold his soul to the devil! The devil himself! The devil's playing the fiddle! The devil's come for his own!

JABEZ (*appealing*). But, neighbors—I didn't know—I didn't mean—oh, help me!

THE CROWD (*inexorably*). He's sold his soul to the devil!

SCRATCH (*grinning*). To the devil!

THE CROWD. He's sold his soul to the devil! There's no help left for him, neighbors! Run, hide, hurry, before we're caught! He's a lost soul—Jabez Stone—he's the devil's own! Run, hide, hasten! (*They stream across the stage like a flurry of bats, the cannier[5] picking up the wedding presents they have given to take along with them.*)

(**MR. SCRATCH** *drives them out into the night, fiddle in hand, and follows them.* **JABEZ** *and* **MARY** *are left with* **WEBSTER.** **JABEZ** *has sunk into a chair, beaten, with his head in his hands.* **MARY** *is trying to comfort him.* **WEBSTER** *looks at them for a moment and shakes his head, sadly. As he crosses to exit to the porch, his hand drops for a moment on* **JABEZ'S** *shoulder, but* **JABEZ** *makes no sign.* **WEBSTER** *exits.* **JABEZ** *lifts his head.*)

MARY (*comforting him*). My dear—my dear——

JABEZ. I—it's all true, Mary. All true. You must hurry.

MARY. Hurry?

JABEZ. Hurry after them—back to the village—back to your folks. Mr. Webster will take you—you'll be safe with Mr. Webster. You see, it's all true and he'll be back in a minute. (*With a shudder.*) The other one. (*He groans.*) I've got until twelve o'clock. That's the contract. But there isn't much time.

MARY. Are you telling me to run away from you, Mr. Stone?

JABEZ. You don't understand, Mary. It's true.

MARY. We made some promises to each other. Maybe you've forgotten them. But I haven't. I said, it's for

---

5 **cannier:** thriftier; shrewder.

better or worse. It's for better or worse. I said, in sickness or in health. Well, that covers the ground, Mr. Stone.

JABEZ. But, Mary, you must—I command you.

MARY. "For thy people shall be my people and thy God my God." (*Quietly.*) That was Ruth, in the Book. I always liked the name of Ruth—always liked the thought of her. I always thought—I'll call a child Ruth, some time. I guess that was just a girl's notion. (*She breaks.*) But, oh, Jabez—why?

JABEZ. It started years ago, Mary. I guess I was a youngster then—guess I must have been. A youngster with a lot of ambitions and no way in the world to get there. I wanted city clothes and a big white house—I wanted to be State Senator and have people look up to me. But all I got on the farm was a crop of stones. You could work all day and all night but that was all you got.

MARY (*softly*). It was pretty—that hill farm, Jabez. You could look all the way across the valley.

JABEZ. Pretty? It was fever and ague —it was stones and blight. If I had a horse, he got colic—if I planted garden-truck, the woodchucks ate it. I'd lie awake nights and try to figure out a way to get somewhere—but there wasn't any way. And all the time you were growing up, in the town. I couldn't ask you to marry me and take you to a place like that.

MARY. Do you think it's the place makes the difference to a woman? I'd —I'd have kept your house. I'd have stroked the cat and fed the chickens and seen you wiped your shoes on the mat. I wouldn't have asked for more. Oh, Jabez—why didn't you tell me?

JABEZ. It happened before I could. Just an average day—you know—just an average day. But there was a mean

east wind and a mean small rain. Well, I was plowing, and the share broke clean off on a rock where there hadn't been any rock the day before. I didn't have money for a new one—I didn't have money to get it mended. So I said it and I said loud, "I'll sell my soul for about two cents," I said. (*He stops.* **MARY** *stares at him.*) Well, that's all there is to it, I guess. He came along that afternoon—that fellow from Boston —and the dog looked at him and ran away. Well, I had to make it more than two cents, but he was agreeable to that. So I pricked my thumb with a pin and signed the paper. It felt hot when you touched it, that paper. I keep remembering that. (*He pauses.*) And it's all come true and he's kept his part of the bargain. I got the riches and I've married you. What shall I do?

MARY. Let us run away! Let us creep and hide!

JABEZ. You can't run away from the devil—I've seen his horses. Miser Stevens tried to run away.

MARY. Let us pray—let us pray to the God of Mercy that He redeem us.

JABEZ. I can't pray, Mary. The words just burn in my heart.

MARY. I won't let you go! I won't! There must be someone who could help us. I'll get the judge and the squire——

JABEZ. Who'll take a case against old Scratch? Who'll face the devil himself and do him brown?[6] There isn't a lawyer in the world who'd dare do that.

(**WEBSTER** *appears in the doorway.*)

WEBSTER. Good evening, neighbors. Did you say something about lawyers——

MARY. Mr. Webster!

JABEZ. Dan'l Webster! But I thought——

6 **to do him brown:** to swindle him.

WEBSTER. You'll excuse me for leaving you for a moment. I was just taking a stroll on the porch, in the cool of the evening. Fine summer evening, too.

JABEZ. Well, it might be, I guess, but that kind of depends on the circumstances.

WEBSTER. H'm. Yes. I happened to overhear a little of your conversation. I gather you're in trouble, Neighbor Stone.

JABEZ. Sore trouble.

WEBSTER (*delicately*). Sort of law case, I understand.

JABEZ. You might call it that, Mr. Webster. Kind of a mortgage case, in a way.

MARY. Oh, Jabez!

WEBSTER. Mortgage case. Well, I don't generally plead now, except before the Supreme Court, but this case of yours presents some very unusual features and I never deserted a neighbor in trouble yet. So, if I can be of any assistance——

MARY. Oh, Mr. Webster, will you help him?

JABEZ. It's a terrible lot to ask you. But—well, you see, there's Mary. And, if you could see your way to it——

WEBSTER. I will.

MARY (*weeping with relief*). Oh, Mr. Webster!

WEBSTER. There, there, Mrs. Stone. After all, if two New Hampshire men aren't a match for the devil, we might as well give the country back to the Indians. When is he coming, Jabez?

JABEZ. Twelve o'clock. The time's getting late.

WEBSTER. Then I'd better refresh my memory. The—er—mortgage was for a definite term of years?

JABEZ. Ten years.

WEBSTER. And it falls due——?

JABEZ. Tonight. Oh, I can't see how I came to be such a fool!

WEBSTER. No use crying over spilt milk, Stone. We've got to get you out of it, now. But tell me one thing. Did you sign this precious document of your own free will?

JABEZ. Yes, it was my own free will. I can't deny that.

WEBSTER. H'm, that's a trifle unfortunate. But we'll see.

MARY. Oh, Mr. Webster, can you save him? Can you?

WEBSTER. I shall do my best, madam. That's all you can ever say till you see what the jury looks like.

MARY. But even you, Mr. Webster—oh, I know you're Secretary of State—I know you're a great man—I know you've done wonderful things. But it's different—fighting the devil!

WEBSTER (*towering*). I've fought John C. Calhoun, madam. And I've fought Henry Clay. And, by the great shade of Andrew Jackson, I'd fight ten thousand devils to save a New Hampshire man!

JABEZ. You hear, Mary?

MARY. Yes. And I trust Mr. Webster. But—oh, there must be some way that I can help!

WEBSTER. There is one, madam, and a hard one. As Mr. Stone's counsel, I must formally request your withdrawal.

MARY. No.

WEBSTER. Madam, think for a moment. You cannot help Mr. Stone—since you are his wife, your testimony would be prejudiced. And frankly, madam, in a very few moments this is going to be no place for a lady.

MARY. But I can't—I can't leave him—I can't bear it!

JABEZ. You must go, Mary. You must.

WEBSTER. Pray, madam—you can help us with your prayers. Are the prayers of the innocent unavailing?

MARY. Oh, I'll pray—I'll pray. But a woman's more than a praying machine, whatever men think. And how do I know?

WEBSTER. Trust me, Mrs. Stone.

(MARY *turns to go, and, with one hand on* JABEZ's *shoulder, as she moves to the door, says the following prayer:*)

MARY.

Now may there be a blessing and a light betwixt thee and me, forever.

For, as Ruth unto Naomi, so do I cleave unto thee.

Set me as a seal upon thy heart, as a seal upon thine arm, for love is strong as death.

Many waters cannot quench love, neither can the floods drown it.

As Ruth unto Naomi, so do I cleave unto thee.

The Lord watch between thee and me when we are absent, one from the other.

Amen. Amen. (*She goes out.*)

WEBSTER. Amen.

JABEZ. Thank you, Mr. Webster. She ought to go. But I couldn't have made her do it.

WEBSTER. Well, Stone—I know ladies —and I wouldn't be surprised if she's still got her ear to the keyhole. But she's best out of this night's business. How long have we got to wait?

JABEZ (*beginning to be terrified again*). Not long—not long.

WEBSTER. Then I'll just get out the jug, with your permission, Stone. Somehow or other, waiting's wonderfully shorter with a jug. (*He crosses to the cupboard, gets out jug and glasses, pours himself a drink.*) Ten-year-old Medford. There's nothing like it. I saw an inchworm take a drop of it once and he stood right up on his hind legs and bit a bee. Come—try a nip.

JABEZ. There's no joy in it for me.

WEBSTER. Oh, come, man, come! Just because you've sold your soul to the devil, that needn't make you a tee-totaler. (*He laughs and passes the jug to* JABEZ *who tries to pour from it. But at that moment the clock whirs and begins to strike the three-quarters, and* JABEZ *spills the liquor.*)

JABEZ. Oh!

WEBSTER. Never mind—it's a nervous feeling, waiting for a trial to begin. I remember my first case——

JABEZ. 'Tain't that. (*He turns to* WEBSTER.) Mr. Webster—Mr. Webster— harness your horses and get away from this place as fast as you can!

WEBSTER (*placidly*). You've brought me a long way, neighbor, to tell me you don't like my company.

JABEZ. I've brought you the devil's own way. I can see it all, now. He's after both of us—him and his damn collecting box! Well, he can have me, if he likes—I don't say I relish it but I made the bargain. But you're the whole United States! He can't get you, Mr. Webster—he mustn't get you!

WEBSTER. I'm obliged to you, Neighbor Stone. It's kindly thought of. But there's a jug on the table and a case in hand. And I never left a jug or a case half-finished in my life. (*There is a knock at the door.* JABEZ *gives a cry.*) Ah, I thought your clock was a trifle slow, Neighbor Stone. Come in!

(SCRATCH *enters from the night.*)

SCRATCH. Mr. Webster! This *is* a pleasure!

WEBSTER. Attorney of record for Jabez Stone. Might I ask your name?

SCRATCH. I've gone by a good many. Perhaps Scratch will do for the evening. I'm often called that in these regions. May I? (*He sits at the table and pours a drink from the jug. The liquor steams as it pours into the glass while* JABEZ *watches, terrified.* SCRATCH *grins, toasting* WEBSTER *and* JABEZ *silently in the liquor. Then he becomes businesslike. To* WEBSTER.) And now I call upon you, as a law-abiding citizen, to assist me in taking possession of my property.

WEBSTER. Not so fast, Mr. Scratch. Produce your evidence, if you have it.
    (SCRATCH *takes out a black pocket-book and examines papers.*)

SCRATCH. Slattery—Stanley—Stone. (*Takes out a deed.*) There, Mr. Webster. All open and aboveboard and in due and legal form. Our firm has its reputation to consider—we deal only in the one way.

WEBSTER (*taking deed and looking it over*). H'm. This appears—I say, it appears—to be properly drawn. But, of course, we contest the signature. (*Tosses it back, contemptuously.*)

SCRATCH (*suddenly turning on* JABEZ *and shooting a finger at him*). Is that your signature?

JABEZ (*wearily*). You know it is.

WEBSTER (*angrily*). Keep quiet, Stone. (*To* SCRATCH.) But that is a minor matter. This precious document isn't worth the paper it's written on. The law permits no traffic in human flesh.

SCRATCH. Oh, my dear Mr. Webster! Courts in every State in the Union have held that human flesh is property and recoverable. Read your Fugitive Slave Act. Or, shall I cite Brander versus McRae?

WEBSTER. But, in the case of the State of Maryland versus Four Barrels of Bourbon——

SCRATCH. That was overruled, as you know, sir. North Carolina versus Jenkins and Co.

WEBSTER (*unwillingly*). You seem to have an excellent acquaintance with the law, sir.

SCRATCH. Sir, that is no fault of mine. Where I come from, we have always gotten the pick of the Bar.

WEBSTER (*changing his note, heartily*). Well, come now, sir. There's no need to make hay and oats of a trifling matter when we're both sensible men. Surely we can settle this little difficulty out of court. My client is quite prepared to offer a compromise. (SCRATCH *smiles.*) A very substantial compromise. (SCRATCH *smiles more broadly, slowly shaking his head.*) Hang it, man, we offer ten thousand dollars! (SCRATCH *signs "No."*) Twenty thousand—thirty —name your figure! I'll raise it if I have to mortgage Marshfield!

SCRATCH. Quite useless, Mr. Webster. There is only one thing I want from you—the execution of my contract.

WEBSTER. But this is absurd. Mr. Stone is now a State Senator. The property has greatly increased in value!

SCRATCH. The principle of *caveat emptor*[7] still holds, Mr. Webster. (*He yawns and looks at the clock.*) And now, if you have no further arguments to adduce—I'm rather pressed for time —— (*He rises briskly as if to take* JABEZ *into custody.*)

WEBSTER (*thundering*). Pressed or not, you shall not have this man. Mr. Stone is an American citizen and no American citizen may be forced into the service of a foreign prince. We fought England for that, in '12, and we'll fight all hell for it again!

SCRATCH. Foreign? And who calls me a foreigner?

WEBSTER. Well, I never yet heard of the dev—of your claiming American citizenship?

SCRATCH. And who with better right? When the first wrong was done to the first Indian, I was there. When the

7 **caveat emptor** (kā′vē ăt′ ĕmp′tôr): Let the purchaser beware.

first slaver put out for the Congo, I stood on her deck. Am I not in your books and stories and beliefs, from the first settlements on? Am I not spoken of, still, in every church in New England? 'Tis true, the North claims me for a Southerner and the South for a Northerner, but I am neither. I am merely an honest American like yourself—and of the best descent—for, to tell the truth, Mr. Webster, though I don't like to boast of it, my name is older in the country than yours.

WEBSTER. Aha! Then I stand on the Constitution! I demand a trial for my client!

SCRATCH. The case is hardly one for an ordinary jury—and indeed, the lateness of the hour——

WEBSTER. Let it be any court you choose, so it is an American judge and an American jury. Let it be the quick or the dead, I'll abide the issue.

SCRATCH. The quick or the dead! You have said it! (*He points his finger at the place where the jury is to appear. There is a clap of thunder and a flash of light. The stage blacks out completely. All that can be seen is the face of* SCRATCH, *lit with a ghastly green light as he recites the invocation that summons the* JURY. *As, one by one, the important* JURYMEN *are mentioned, they appear.*)

I summon the jury Mr. Webster demands.
From churchyard mold and gallows grave,

Brimstone pit and burning gulf,
I summon them!
Dastard,[8] liar, scoundrel, knave,
I summon them! Appear!
There's Simon Girty,[9] the renegade,
The haunter of the forest glade
Who joined with Indian and wolf
To hunt the pioneer.
The stains upon his hunting shirt
Are not the blood of the deer.
There's Walter Butler,[10] the loyalist,
Who carried a firebrand in his fist
Of massacre and shame.
King Philip's [11]eye is wild and bright
They slew him in the great Swamp Fight,
But still, with terror and affright,
The land recalls his name.
Blackbeard Teach,[12] the pirate fell,
Smeet[13] the strangler, hot from hell,
Dale,[14] who broke men on the wheel,
Morton,[15] of the tarnished steel,
I summon them, I summon them
From their tormented flame!
Quick or dead, quick or dead,
Broken heart and bitter head,
True Americans, each one,
Traitor and disloyal son,
Cankered earth and twisted tree,
Outcasts of eternity,
Twelve great sinners, tried and true,
For the work they are to do!
I summon them, I summon them!
Appear, appear, appear!

(*The* JURY *has now taken its place in the box*—WALTER BUTLER *in the place of foreman. They are eerily lit and so made-up as to*

8 **Dastard:** a mean coward.
9 **Simon Girty:** Indian scout and renegade (1741-1818) who aided the British during the Revolutionary War by stirring up the Indians against the colonists.
10 **Walter Butler:** Loyalist (1752?-1781) who spread fire and horror through New York's Mohawk Valley during the Revolutionary War.
11 **King Philip:** Indian chief (d. 1676) who led an uprising against the early white settlers in New England.

12 **Blackbeard Teach:** pirate (d. 1718) who operated among the West Indies and was known for his cruelty.
13 **Smeet:** Reverend John Smeet, a strangler.
14 **Dale:** an early governor of Virginia (d. 1619), known for his severity.
15 **Morton:** Thomas Morton, a British adventurer, who was disliked by the Pilgrims because of his religious beliefs and rival fur trade with the Indians, and who was sent back to England in 1628 on charges of selling arms to the Indians.

STEPHEN VINCENT BENÉT

suggest the unearthly. They sit stiffly in their box. At first, when one moves, all move, in stylized gestures. It is not till the end of **WEBSTER's** speech that they begin to show any trace of humanity. They speak rhythmically, and, at first, in low, eerie voices.)

JABEZ (seeing them, horrified). A jury of the dead!

JURY. Of the dead!

JABEZ. A jury of the damned!

JURY. Of the damned!

SCRATCH. Are you content with the jury, Mr. Webster?

WEBSTER. Quite content. Though I miss General Arnold from the company.

SCRATCH. Benedict Arnold is engaged upon other business. Ah, you asked for a justice, I believe. (He points his finger and **JUSTICE HATHORNE**, a tall, lean, terrifying Puritan, appears, fol-

lowed by his **CLERK**.) Justice Hathorne is a jurist of experience. He presided at the Salem witch trials. There were others who repented of the business later. But not he, not he!

HATHORNE. Repent of such notable wonders and undertakings? Nay, hang them, hang them all! (He takes his place on the bench.)

(The **CLERK**, an ominous little man with clawlike hands, takes his place. The room has now been transformed into a courtroom.)

CLERK (in a gabble of ritual). Oyes, oyes, oyes.[16] All ye who have business with this honorable court of special session this night, step forward!

HATHORNE (with gavel). Call the first case.

CLERK. The World, the Flesh and the Devil versus Jabez Stone.

HATHORNE. Who appears for the plaintiff?

16 **Oyes** (ō′yĕs): hear (a word used in court ritual).

SCRATCH. I, Your Honor.

HATHORNE. And for the defendant?

WEBSTER. I.

JURY. The case—the case—he'll have little luck with this case.

HATHORNE. The case will proceed.

WEBSTER. Your Honor, I move to dismiss this case on the grounds of improper jurisdiction.

HATHORNE. Motion denied.

WEBSTER. On the grounds of insufficient evidence.

HATHORNE. Motion denied.

JURY. Motion denied—denied. Motion denied.

WEBSTER. I will take an exception.

HATHORNE. There are no exceptions in this court.

JURY. No exceptions—no exceptions in this court. It's a bad case, Daniel Webster—a losing case.

WEBSTER. Your Honor——

HATHORNE. The prosecution will proceed——

SCRATCH. Your Honor—gentlemen of the jury. This is a plain, straightforward case. It need not detain us long.

JURY. Detain us long—it will not detain us long.

SCRATCH. It concerns one thing alone —the transference, barter and sale of a certain piece of property, to wit, his soul, by Jabez Stone, farmer, of Cross Corners, New Hampshire. That transference, barter or sale is attested by a deed. I offer that deed in evidence and mark it Exhibit A.

WEBSTER. I object.

HATHORNE. Objection denied. Mark it Exhibit A.

(SCRATCH *hands the deed—an ominous and impressive document —to the* CLERK *who hands it to* HATHORNE. HATHORNE *hands it back to the* CLERK *who stamps it. All very fast and with mechanical gestures.*)

JURY. Exhibit A—mark it Exhibit A. (SCRATCH *takes the deed from the* CLERK *and offers it to the* JURY, *who pass it rapidly among them, hardly looking at it, and hand it back to* SCRATCH.) We know the deed—the deed—it burns in our fingers—we do not have to see the deed. It's a losing case.

SCRATCH. It offers incontestable evidence of the truth of the prosecution's claim. I shall now call Jabez Stone to the witness stand.

JURY (*hungrily*). Jabez Stone to the witness stand, Jabez Stone. He's a fine, fat fellow, Jabez Stone. He'll fry like a battercake, once we get him where we want him.

WEBSTER. Your Honor, I move that this jury be discharged for flagrant and open bias!

HATHORNE. Motion denied.

WEBSTER. Exception.

HATHORNE. Exception denied.

JURY. His motion's always denied. He thinks himself smart and clever— lawyer Webster. But his motion's always denied.

WEBSTER. Your Honor! (*He chokes with anger.*)

CLERK (*advancing*). Jabez Stone to the witness stand!

JURY. Jabez Stone—Jabez Stone.

(WEBSTER *gives* JABEZ *an encouraging pat on the back, and* JABEZ *takes his place in the witness stand, very scared.*)

CLERK (*offering a black book*). Do you solemnly swear—testify—so help you—and it's no good for we don't care what you testify?

JABEZ. I do.

SCRATCH. What's your name?

JABEZ. Jabez Stone.

SCRATCH. Occupation?

JABEZ. Farmer.

SCRATCH. Residence?

JABEZ. Cross Corners, New Hampshire.

(*These three questions are very fast and mechanical on the part of* SCRATCH. *He is absolutely sure of victory and just going through a form.*)

JURY. A farmer—he'll farm in hell—we'll see that he farms in hell.

SCRATCH. Now, Jabez Stone, answer me. You'd better, you know. You haven't got a chance and there'll be a cooler place by the fire for you.

WEBSTER. I protest! This is intimidation! This mocks all justice!

HATHORNE. The protest is irrelevant, incompetent and immaterial. We have our own justice. The protest is denied.

JURY. Irrelevant, incompetent and immaterial—we have our own justice—oh, ho, Daniel Webster! (*The* JURY'S *eyes fix upon* WEBSTER *for an instant, hungrily.*)

SCRATCH. Did you or did you not sign this document?

JABEZ. Oh, I signed it! You know I signed it. And, if I have to go to hell for it, I'll go!

(*A sigh sweeps over the* JURY.)

JURY. One of us—one of us now—we'll save a place by the fire for you, Jabez Stone.

SCRATCH. The prosecution rests.

HATHORNE. Remove the prisoner.

WEBSTER. But I wish to cross-examine—I wish to prove——

HATHORNE. There will be no cross-examination. We have our own justice. You may speak, if you like. But be brief.

JURY. Brief—be very brief—we're weary of earth—incompetent, irrelevant and immaterial—they say he's a smart man, Webster, but he's lost his case tonight—be very brief—we have our own justice here.

(WEBSTER *stares around him like a baited bull. Can't find words.*)

MARY'S VOICE (*from off stage*). Set me as a seal upon thy heart, as a seal upon thine arm, for love is strong as death——

JURY (*loudly*). A seal!—ha, ha—a burning seal!

MARY'S VOICE. Love is strong——

JURY (*drowning her out*). Death is stronger than love. Set the seal upon Daniel Webster—the burning seal of the lost. Make him one of us—one of the damned—one with Jabez Stone!

(*The* JURY'S *eyes all fix upon* WEBSTER. *The* CLERK *advances as if to take him into custody. But* WEBSTER *silences them all with a great gesture.*)

WEBSTER. Be still!

I was going to thunder and roar. I shall not do that.

I was going to denounce and defy. I shall not do that.

You have judged this man already with your abominable justice. See that you defend it. For I shall not speak of this man.

You are demons now, but once you were men. I shall speak to every one of you.

Of common things I speak, of small things and common.

The freshness of morning to the young, the taste of food to the hungry, the day's toil, the rest by the fire, the quiet sleep.

These are good things.

But without freedom they sicken, without freedom they are nothing.

Freedom is the bread and the morning and the risen sun.

It was for freedom we came in the boats and the ships. It was for freedom we came.

It has been a long journey, a hard one, a bitter one.

But, out of the wrong and the right, the sufferings and the starvations, there is a new thing, a free thing.

The traitors in their treachery, the wise in their wisdom, the valiant in their courage—all, all have played a part.

It may not be denied in hell nor shall hell prevail against it.

Have you forgotten this? (*He turns to the* JURY.) Have you forgotten the forest?

GIRTY (*as in a dream*). The forest, the rustle of the forest, the free forest.

WEBSTER (*to* KING PHILIP). Have you forgotten your lost nation?

KING PHILIP. My lost nation—my fires in the wood—my warriors.

WEBSTER (*to* TEACH). Have you forgotten the sea and the way of ships?

TEACH. The sea—and the swift ships sailing—the blue sea.

JURY. Forgotten—remembered—forgotten yet remembered.

WEBSTER. You were men once. Have you forgotten?

JURY. We were men once. We have not thought of it nor remembered. But we were men.

WEBSTER.

Now here is this man with good and evil in his heart.

Do you know him? He is your brother. Will you take the law of the oppressor and bind him down?

It is not for him that I speak. It is for all of you.

There is sadness in being a man but it is a proud thing, too.

There is failure and despair on the journey—the endless journey of mankind.

We are tricked and trapped—we stumble into the pit—but, out of the pit, we rise again.

No demon that was ever foaled can know the inwardness of that—only men—bewildered men.

They have broken freedom with their hands and cast her out from the nations—yet shall she live while man lives.

She shall live in the blood and the heart—she shall live in the earth of this country—she shall not be broken.

When the whips of the oppressors are broken and their names forgotten and destroyed,

I see you, mighty, shining, liberty, liberty! I see free men walking and talking under a free star.

God save the United States and the men who have made her free.

The defense rests.

JURY (*exultantly*). We were men—we were free—we were men—we have not forgotten—our children—our children shall follow and be free.

HATHORNE (*rapping with gavel*). The jury will retire to consider its verdict.

BUTLER (*rising*). There is no need. The jury has heard Mr. Webster. We find for the defendant, Jabez Stone!

JURY. Not guilty!

SCRATCH (*in a screech, rushing forward*). But, Your Honor——

(*But, even as he does so, there is a flash and a thunderclap, the stage blacks out again, and when the lights come on,* JUDGE *and* JURY *are gone. The yellow light of dawn lights the windows.*)

JABEZ. They're gone and it's morning—Mary, Mary!

MARY (*in doorway*). My love—my dear. (*She rushes to him.*)

(*Meanwhile* SCRATCH *has been collecting his papers and trying to sneak out. But* WEBSTER *catches him.*)

WEBSTER. Just a minute, Mr. Scratch. I'll have that paper first, if you please. (*He takes the deed and tears it.*) And, now, sir, I'll have *you!*

SCRATCH. Come, come, Mr. Webster. This sort of thing is ridic—ouch—is ri-

diculous. If you're worried about the costs of the case, naturally, I'd be glad to pay.

WEBSTER. And so you shall! First of all, you'll promise and covenant never to bother Jabez Stone or any other New Hampshire man from now till doomsday. For any hell we want to raise in this State, we can raise ourselves, without any help from you.

SCRATCH. Ouch! Well, they never did run very big to the barrel but—ouch—I agree!

WEBSTER. See you keep to the bargain! And then—well, I've got a ram named Goliath. He can butt through an iron door. I'd like to turn you loose in his field and see what he could do to you. (SCRATCH *trembles.*) But that would be hard on the ram. So we'll just call in the neighbors and give you a shivaree.[17]

17 **shivaree:** a mock serenade with kettles, tin horns, etc.

SCRATCH. Mr. Webster—please—oh—

WEBSTER. Neighbors! Neighbors! Come in and see what a long-barreled, slab-sided, lantern-jawed, fortune-telling note-shaver I've got by the scruff of the neck! Bring on your kettles and your pans! (*A noise and murmur outside.*) Bring on your muskets and your flails!

JABEZ. We'll drive him out of New Hampshire!

MARY. We'll drive old Scratch away!
(*The* CROWD *rushes in, with muskets, flails, brooms, etc. They pursue* SCRATCH *around the stage, chanting.*)

THE CROWD.
We'll drive him out of New Hampshire!
We'll drive old Scratch away!
Forever and a day, boys,
Forever and a day!
(*They finally catch* SCRATCH *between two of them and fling him out of the door, bodily.*)

DRAMA

A MAN. Three cheers for Dan'l Webster!

ANOTHER MAN. Three cheers for Daniel Webster! He's licked the devil!

WEBSTER (*moving to center stage, and joining* JABEZ's *hands and* MARY's). And whom God hath joined let no man put asunder. (*He kisses* MARY *and turns, dusting his hands.*) Well, that job's done. I hope there's pie for breakfast, Neighbor Stone.

(*And, as some of the women, dancing, bring in pies from the kitchen*)

CURTAIN

Understanding the Play

1. Benét must create an atmosphere in which the story's elements of fantasy will be accepted by the audience. What are some of the techniques he uses that lead the reader to accept the devil's appearance?
2. What is contained in the black box? Why can a moth speak?
3. Why was Webster at Jabez's home? Why did he agree to take a seemingly hopeless case after Jabez warns him to leave?
4. What characteristic favorable to Scratch's cause was possessed by each member of the jury? What characteristic favorable to Webster's cause?
5. Why did Webster decide not to "thunder and roar" at the jury? What did he do instead?
6. What theme does Benét develop in the following passage from Webster's speech to the jury?

> There is failure and despair on the journey—the endless journey
> of mankind.
> We are tricked and trapped—we stumble into the pit—but, out
> of the pit, we rise again.

Why does Benét introduce this theme early in the play with Jabez's speech to Mary, "There's some things a man does, or might do—when he has to make his own way"?
7. What evidence is there that Webster's victory over Scratch is complete?
8. Stephen Vincent Benét was a poet as well as a writer of short stories and a dramatist. Some scenes in this play are written in poetic form and some in prose. Which scenes are written in poetic form? Why did he choose poetry for these scenes?

Developing Language Skills

If you watch television programs frequently or attend many American movies, you may have noticed that more often than not they tend to have happy endings. "The Devil and Daniel Webster" too, unlike many treatments of the Faust legend, has a happy ending—Jabez is not punished; the devil is not triumphant. Some readers have felt that the happy ending, as typified in this story, reflects the optimism of Americans and a belief that all difficulties can be overcome or escaped, but that it is not always the most logical ending for a story.

Write one paragraph in which you explain whether or not you consider the ending of "The Devil and Daniel Webster" logical in view of the characters involved and the events up to the happy conclusion. Use specific evidence from the play to justify your opinion.

Developing Oral Reading Skills

Plays are meant to be heard rather than read silently. Some professional acting groups give very exciting performances without costumes, scenery, or actions simply by reading from lecterns or while seated on stools on an empty stage. Your class might divide into about five production teams with five to eight students in each group to give this type of performance. After selecting a scene from one of the plays you have just read, choose the person in each group who would make the best director for your scene. It will be his responsibility to cast each part and to suggest ways of making each character believable. A narrator's part may need to be written to show how the scene fits into the context of the entire play. During rehearsals of your scene, pay strict attention to the director. Play production is fun when a good presentation is prepared, but whether amateur or professional it demands constant attention and perfect discipline from every member of the production team.

Reading "The Winslow Boy"

Dramaturgy is the art of writing and producing plays. In the one-act plays you have just read, you have discovered much about this art. As you read the final play in this unit, a full-length play, notice the organizational structure the playwright uses in developing his plot: exposition, complication, crisis, resolution. *Exposition* is the part of a play which explains who the characters are, where they are, and in what situation the audience finds them. The *complication* is the introduction of problems that must be solved by the characters. Each successive problem becomes more important and more intense until the moment of greatest suspense and tension is reached. It is here at the *crisis* of the play that an alert audience can see the direction of the play's conclusion. Following the crisis of a play, there remain a series of less intense problems to be worked out. The working out of these problems until the final outcome is reached is known as the *resolution* of the play. As a whole, these elements make up the system of actions that is known as the *plot* of the play.

The action of a play is not necessarily confined to just physical action. Often the problems presented must be solved in the minds of the characters. An audience should, therefore, observe changes and developments within characters as well as the progress of the situation.

The main story or plot is usually the only one in a short play. In a full-length play, however, the dramatist has time to develop subplots in which minor characters have serious problems to solve. Although the play is entitled *The Winslow Boy*, you will discover that the father is the chief character in the main plot and that Catherine is the main character in the subplot. The main plot of a play allows the dramatist to state his theme through the dialogue and actions of the characters most involved in the play's central conflict; the subplot enables him to approach his theme from the point of view of other characters with different problems. It may serve as a comparison that clarifies the main theme or as a parallel that reinforces it.

Just as a novel is typically divided into parts or chapters, the action of a play is divided into *acts*. The majority of modern full-length plays have three acts, musical plays usually have two, plays written earlier in this century typically have four, and Shakespearean plays have five. Although *The Winslow Boy* is a full-length modern play, it is divided into two acts. Its length, however, is equal to that of most three-act plays. *Scenes* are used within an act by a playwright to show a change in place or in time. Usually the curtain is lowered or the stage is darkened for a few seconds to indicate the change in scene. If more time is required for costume, make-up, or scenery changes, the time between scenes must be lengthened. An *episode* is a part of a scene in which no major character enters or leaves. The entrance or exit of a major character usually denotes a *transition* between episodes. Note the act, scene, and episode divisions as you read *The Winslow Boy*.

TERENCE RATTIGAN   **195**

The Winslow Boy°

Terence Rattigan

Mystery story fans know that circumstantial evidence—accounts of actions surrounding an event—can make an innocent person appear to be guilty. The story of someone accused of a crime and believed guilty by all but a few because of circumstantial evidence is a familiar situation in literature. In The Winslow Boy *you will meet a boy who finds himself in such a situation. The members of his family face the problem of making great personal sacrifices if they are to vindicate his honor. The theme of the play is developed by presenting characters who have different attitudes toward the boy's innocence and different ideas about the reasonableness of making sacrifices in order to defend him. As these characters come into conflict with each other, contrasting value systems are thrown into sharp relief. The case of Winslow versus the King is a stirring affirmation of the play's key line, "Let Right be done!"*

CHARACTERS

RONNIE WINSLOW
VIOLET
ARTHUR WINSLOW
GRACE WINSLOW
DICKIE WINSLOW
CATHERINE WINSLOW
JOHN WATHERSTONE
DESMOND CURRY
MISS BARNES
FRED, *the photographer*
SIR ROBERT MORTON

The action passes in the drawing room of a house in Kensington, and extends over two years of a period which, though unspecified, may be taken as preceding the war of 1914-1918.

ACT I

Scene 1: A Sunday morning in July.
Scene 2: An evening in April. Nine months later.

ACT II

Scene 1: An evening in January. Nine months later.
Scene 2: An afternoon in June. Five months later.

ACT I

SCENE 1

The drawing room of a house in Court-field Gardens, South Kensington, at some period not long before the war of 1914-18. The furnishings betoken solid but not undecorative upper middle-class comfort. It is a Sunday morning in July. Church bells are heard. As the curtain rises they fade. **RONNIE,** *a boy of about fourteen, is staring with wide, unblinking eyes at a portrait of himself on the piano. He is dressed in the uniform of an Osborne[1] naval cadet. There is something rigid and tense in his attitude, and his face is blank and without expression. He turns and wanders aimlessly across to the fireplace. There is a sound from the hall. He looks despairingly round as though contemplating flight.* **VIOLET,** *an elderly maid, enters up* C. *She carries a tray with a cigarette box, ashtrays and match box on it. At the sight of* **RON-NIE** *she stops in the doorway in astonishment.*

VIOLET. Master Ronnie!

RONNIE (*with ill-managed sang-froid[2]*). Hullo, Violet.

VIOLET (*moving down to table* R.C.). Why, good gracious! We weren't expecting you back till Tuesday. (*She puts tray on table.*)

RONNIE. Yes, I know.

VIOLET (*moving to* R. *of* **GRACE'S** *chair* L. *of* C.). Why ever didn't you let us know you were coming, you silly boy? Your mother should have been at the station to meet you. The idea of a child like you wandering all over London by yourself. I never did!

How ever did you get in? By the garden, I suppose—— (*She moves to table* R. C.)

RONNIE. No. The front door. I rang and cook opened it.

VIOLET. Where's your trunk and your tuckbox?[3] (*She puts cigarette box, matches and one ashtray on table.*)

RONNIE. Upstairs. The taximan carried them up——

VIOLET. Taximan? You took a taxi? (**RONNIE** *nods.*) All by yourself? Well, I don't know what little boys are coming to, I'm sure. What your father and mother will say, I don't know——

RONNIE. Where are they, Violet?

VIOLET. Church, of course.

RONNIE (*vacantly*). Oh, yes. It's Sunday, isn't it? (*He moves toward table* R. C.)

VIOLET (*crossing to fireplace* L. *with two ashtrays*). What's the matter with you? What have they been doing to you at Osborne? (*She puts ashtrays on mantelpiece.*)

RONNIE (*turning to her, sharply*). What do you mean?

VIOLET. They seem to have made you a bit soft in the head, or something. (*She fusses with cushions in armchair down* L.) Well—I suppose I'd better get your unpacking done—Mr. Dickie's been using your chest of drawers for all his dress clothes and things. I'll just clear 'em out and put 'em on his bed—that's what I'll do. (*She straightens up and turns to* **RONNIE.**) He can find room for 'em somewhere else.

RONNIE (*taking step toward* **GRACE'S** *chair*). Shall I help you?

VIOLET (*scornfully*). I know *your* help. With *your* help I'll be at it all day. No, you just wait down here for your mother and father. (*She crosses*

---

1 Osborne: a British Royal Naval Academy from 1903 to 1921.

2 sang-froid (säN frwà´): coolness; composure.

3 tuckbox: box in which schoolboys are sent food, such as cake and candy, from home.

to table R. C., *and picks up tray.)* They'll be back in a minute. (RONNIE *nods and turns hopelessly to fireplace.* VIOLET *looks at his retreating back, puzzled.)* Well?

RONNIE *(turning).* Yes?

VIOLET. Don't I get a kiss or are you too grown-up for that now? *(She moves to C.)*

RONNIE. Sorry, Violet. *(He goes up to her and is enveloped in her ample bosom.)*

VIOLET. That's better. My, what a big boy you're getting! *(She holds him at arm's length and inspects him.)* Quite the little naval officer, aren't you?

RONNIE *(smiling forlornly).* Yes. That's right.

VIOLET. Well, well, I must be getting on—— (VIOLET *releases him and goes out up C. Closes door.* RONNIE *resumes his attitude of utter dejection. Takes out of his pocket a letter in a sealed envelope. After a second's hesitation, he opens it, and reads contents. The perusal appears to increase his misery. He takes two or three quick steps toward U. C. hall door. Then stops, uncertainly. Sound of voices in hall.* RONNIE, *with a strangled sob, runs to window R. and out into garden. Door up C. opens.* ARTHUR WINSLOW, RONNIE's *father, enters, a man of about sixty with a rather deliberately cultured patriarchal air. He carries a prayer book and is leaning heavily on a stick. He makes for fireplace, sitting in his armchair, followed by* RONNIE's *mother,* GRACE. *She is about ten years younger and has the faded remnants of prettiness. She, too, carries a prayer book.)*

GRACE *(entering U. C.).* But he's so old, dear. From the back of the church you really can't hear a word he says. *(She comes above table R. C., and puts down her prayer book on it.* CATH-ERINE, RONNIE's *sister, enters U. C. She is approaching thirty and has an air of masculinity about her which is at odd variance with her mother's intense femininity. She carries a handbag. She makes for armchair down L.* DICKIE, RONNIE's *brother, follows her in. He is an Oxford[4] undergraduate, large, noisy and cheerful. He hovers up C.)*

ARTHUR. He's a good man, Grace.

GRACE. But what's the use of being good, if you're inaudible?

CATHERINE. A problem in ethics for you, Father. *(She takes book from small table in extreme down L. corner, sits on arm of armchair rear and reads.* ARTHUR, *at fireplace, looks round at open French windows.)*

ARTHUR. There's a draught, Grace.

GRACE. Oh, dear—it's coming on to rain. *(She moves to settee down L. of piano, taking off her hat and coat. Puts them on settee.)*

DICKIE. I'm on Mother's side. The old boy's so doddery now he can hardly finish the course at all. I timed him today. It took him seventy-five seconds dead from a flying start to reach the pulpit, and then he needed the whip coming round the bend. I call that pretty bad going.

ARTHUR. I'm afraid I don't think that's very funny, Richard.

DICKIE. Oh, don't you, Father?

ARTHUR. Doddery though Mr. Jackson may seem now, I very much doubt if, when he was at Oxford, he failed in his pass mods.[5]

DICKIE *(coming down below table R. C.; aggrieved).* Dash it—Father—you promised not to mention that again this vac[6]—— *(He sits on downstage edge of table.)*

---

4 **Oxford:** British university.
5 **pass mods:** first public examination leading to a college degree.
6 **vac:** vacation.

GRACE. You did, you know, Arthur.

ARTHUR. There was a condition to my promise—if you remember—that Dickie should provide me with reasonable evidence of his intentions to work. (GRACE *takes tin of cigarettes from desk* R. *and fills box on table* R. C.)

DICKIE. Well, haven't I, Father? Didn't I stay in all last night—a Saturday night—and work?

ARTHUR. You stayed in, Dickie. I would be the last to deny that.

GRACE. You *were* making rather a noise, dear, with that old gramophone[7] of yours. I really can't believe you could have been doing much work with that going on all the time.

DICKIE. Funnily enough, Mother, it helps me to concentrate.

ARTHUR. Concentrate on what?

DICKIE. Work, of course.

ARTHUR. That wasn't exactly what you appeared to be concentrating on when I came down to fetch a book— sleep, may I say—having been rendered out of the question, by the hideous sounds emanating from this room.

DICKIE. Edwina and her brother just looked in on their way to the Grahams' dance—they only stayed a minute.

GRACE. What an idiotic girl that is! Oh, sorry, Dickie—I was forgetting. You're rather keen on her, aren't you?

ARTHUR. You would have had ample proof of that fact, Grace, if you had seen them in the attitude in which I found them last night.

DICKIE. We were practicing the Bunny Hug.

GRACE. The what, dear?

DICKIE. The Bunny Hug. It's the new dance.

CATHERINE (*helpfully*). It's like the Turkey Trot—only more dignified. (*She sits in chair by down* R. *table.*)

GRACE. Oh, I thought that was the Tango.

DICKIE. No. More like a Fox Trot, really. Something between a Boston Glide and a Kangaroo Hop.

ARTHUR. We appear to be straying from the point. Whatever animal was responsible for the posture I found you in has little to do with the fact that to my certain knowledge you have not yet done one single stroke of work so far this vacation.

DICKIE. Oh. Well, I do work awfully fast, you know—once I get down to it.

ARTHUR. Indeed? That assumption can hardly be based on experience, I take it.

DICKIE. Dash it, Father! (*He rises and crosses to desk* R.) You are laying in to me, this morning. (*He sits on stool by desk.*)

ARTHUR. I think it's time you found out, Dickie, that I'm not spending two hundred pounds a year keeping you at Oxford, merely that you may make a lot of useless friends and learn to dance the Bunny Hop. (GRACE *moves to desk and replaces cigarette tin.*)

DICKIE. Hug, Father.

ARTHUR. The exact description of the obscenity is immaterial.

GRACE (*patting* DICKIE *on head*). Father's quite right, you know, dear. You really have been going the pace a bit, this vac.

DICKIE. Yes, I know, Mother—but the season's nearly over now.

GRACE (*looking to piano* U. R. *at* RONNIE's *portrait; with a sigh*). I wish you were as good about work as Ronnie.

DICKIE (*hotly*). I like that. That's a bit thick, I must say. All Ronnie ever has to do with his footling[8] little homework is to add two and two, while I——

---

7 gramophone: phonograph.

8 footling: useless.

ARTHUR. Ronnie, may I remind you, is at least proving a good deal more successful in adding two and two than you were at his age.

DICKIE (*rising and crossing to* C.; *now furious*). Oh yes, *I* know. *I* know. *He* got into Osborne and *I* failed. That's going to be brought up again.

GRACE. Nobody's bringing it up, dear.

DICKIE. Oh, yes they are. It's going to be brought up against me all my life. Ronnie's the good little boy, I'm the bad little boy. You've just stuck a couple of labels on us that nothing on earth is ever going to change.

GRACE. Don't be so absurd, dear——

DICKIE. It's not absurd. It's quite true. Isn't it, Kate? (CATHERINE *looks up*.)

CATHERINE. I'm sorry, Dickie. I haven't been listening. Isn't what quite true?

DICKIE. That in the eyes of Mother and Father nothing that Ronnie does is ever wrong, and nothing that I do is ever right? (CATHERINE *rises and crosses* L., *with her book, to below* GRACE's *chair. She faces* DICKIE *a moment before she speaks. She leaves her handbag on chair*.)

CATHERINE. If I were you, Dickie, dear, I'd go and have a nice lie-down before lunch.

DICKIE (*after pause*). Perhaps you're right. (*He goes toward door up* C.)

ARTHUR. If you're going to your room, I suggest you take that object with you. (*He points to gramophone on desk down* R. CATHERINE *sits in* GRACE's *chair* L. *and reads*.) It's out of place in a drawing room. (DICKIE, *with an air of hauteur,*[9] *crosses to desk* R., *picks up gramophone and carries it to door up* C.) It might help you to concentrate on the work you're going to do this afternoon. (DICKIE *stops at door, then turns slowly*.)

DICKIE (*with dignity*). That is out of the question, I'm afraid.

ARTHUR. Indeed? Why?

DICKIE. I have an engagement with Miss Gunn.

ARTHUR. On a Sunday afternoon? You're escorting her to the National Gallery, no doubt?

DICKIE. No. The Victoria and Albert Museum. (DICKIE *goes out with as much dignity as is consistent with the carrying of a very bulky gramophone.* ARTHUR *picks up* Punch[10] *from table by his chair and sits in chair*.)

GRACE. How stupid of him to say that about labels. (*She turns and goes toward French window.*) There's no truth in it at all—is there, Kate?

CATHERINE (*deep in her book*). No, Mother.

GRACE. Oh, dear, it's simply pelting. (*She turns from window and crosses to* CATHERINE.) What are you reading, Kate?

CATHERINE. Len Rogers' Memoirs.

GRACE. Who's Len Rogers?

CATHERINE. A Trades Union leader.

GRACE. Does John know you're a radical?

CATHERINE. Oh, yes.

GRACE. And a suffragette?[11]

CATHERINE. Certainly.

GRACE (*with a smile*). And he still wants to marry you?

CATHERINE. He seems to.

GRACE. Oh, by the way, I've told him to come early for lunch—so that he can have a few words with Father first.

CATHERINE. Good idea. (*To* ARTHUR.) I hope you've been primed,

---

9 **hauteur** (hō tûr´): pride.

10 **Punch:** a famous British humorous weekly magazine.

11 **suffragette** (sŭf´rə jĕt´): one who worked for the right of women to vote.

have you, Father? (*She rises, leaves her book in chair and goes to* ARTHUR.)

ARTHUR. What's that?

CATHERINE (*sitting on* R. *arm of* AR-THUR's *chair*). You know what you're going to say to John, don't you? You're not going to let me down and forbid the match, or anything, are you? Because I warn you, if you do, I shall elope.

ARTHUR (*taking her hand*). Never fear, my dear. I'm far too delighted at the prospect of getting you off our hands at last.

CATHERINE (*smiling*). I'm not sure I like that "at last."

GRACE. Do you love him, dear?

CATHERINE. John? Yes, I do.

GRACE. You're such a funny girl. You never show your feelings much, do you? You don't behave as if you were in love.

CATHERINE. How does one behave as if one is in love?

ARTHUR. One doesn't read Len Rogers. One reads Byron.[12]

CATHERINE. I do both.

ARTHUR. An odd combination.

CATHERINE. A satisfying one.

GRACE. I meant—you don't talk about him much, do you?

CATHERINE. No. I suppose I don't.

GRACE (*sighing*). I don't think you modern girls have the feelings our generation did. It's this New Woman attitude.

CATHERINE (*rising and facing* GRACE). Very well, Mother. I love John in every way that a woman can love a man, and far, far more than he loves me. Does that satisfy you?

GRACE (*embarrassed*). Well, really, Kate, darling—I didn't ask for anything quite like that—— (*To* ARTHUR.)

What are you laughing at, Arthur?

ARTHUR (*chuckling*). One up to the New Woman.

GRACE. Nonsense. (*She turns and goes toward French window.*) She misunderstood me, that's all. (*At window.*) Just look at the rain! (*She turns to* CATHERINE.) Kate, darling, does Desmond know about you and John?

CATHERINE. I haven't told him. (*She picks up her book.*) On the other hand, if he hasn't guessed, he must be very dense.

ARTHUR. He *is* very dense.

GRACE. Oh, no. He's quite clever, if you really get under his skin.

ARTHUR. Oddly enough, I've never had that inclination. (CATHERINE *smiles. She crosses downstage to* R. *desk.*)

GRACE (*moving to settee*). I think he's a dear. (*She turns toward* CATHERINE.) Kate, darling, you *will* be kind to him, won't you? (*She picks up her coat and hat.*)

CATHERINE (*patiently*). Yes, Mother. Of course I will.

GRACE. Poor Desmond! He's really a very good sort—— (*She breaks off suddenly and stares out of French window.*) Hello! There's someone in our garden. (*She crosses to window.*)

CATHERINE (*going to window*). Where?

GRACE (*pointing*). Over there, do you see?

CATHERINE. No.

GRACE. He's just gone behind that bush. It was a boy, I think. Probably Mrs. Williamson's awful little Dennis.

CATHERINE (*turning into room*). Well, whoever it is must be getting terribly wet. (*She puts her book on desk.*)

GRACE. Why can't he stick to his own garden? (*A sound of voices outside in hall.*) Is that John?

---

12 **Byron:** popular romantic British poet of the 19th century.

CATHERINE. It sounded like it. (*They both listen for a moment.*)

GRACE. Yes. It's John. (*To* CATHERINE.) Quick! In the dining room!

CATHERINE. All right. (*She dashes across to door up* L.)

GRACE. Here! You've forgotten your bag. (*She darts to chair down* L., *picks up bag and takes it to* CATHERINE *at door.* CATHERINE *takes bag and goes out* U. L. *into dining room.*)

ARTHUR (*startled*). What on earth is going on?

GRACE (*in a stage whisper*). We're leaving you alone with John. When you've finished, cough or something.

ARTHUR (*testily*). What do you mean, or something?

GRACE. I know. Knock on the floor with your stick—three times. Then we'll come in.

ARTHUR. You don't think that might look a trifle coincidental?

GRACE. Sh! (GRACE *disappears into dining room. At same moment* VIOLET *enters up* C.)

VIOLET (*announcing*). Mr. Watherstone. (JOHN WATHERSTONE *comes in. He is a man of about thirty, dressed in an extremely well-cut morning coat*[13] *and striped trousers, an attire which, though excused by church parade, we may well feel has been donned for this occasion. He moves down* L. *of* GRACE's *chair to* ARTHUR. VIOLET *goes out* U. C.)

ARTHUR. How are you, John? I'm very glad to see you.

JOHN. How do you do, sir?

ARTHUR. Will you forgive me not getting up? My arthritis has been troubling me rather a lot lately.

JOHN. I'm very sorry to hear that, sir. Catherine told me it was better.

---

13 **morning coat:** a coat that tapers off from the front waistline to the coattails.

ARTHUR. It was, for a time. Now it's worse again. Do you smoke? (*He indicates cigarette box on table* R. C.)

JOHN. Yes, sir. I do. (*He crosses to table.*) Thank you. (*He takes cigarette and adds hastily*) In moderation, of course.

ARTHUR (*with a faint smile*). Of course. (*A pause while* JOHN *lights cigarette.* ARTHUR *watches him.*) Well, now. I understand you wish to marry my daughter.

JOHN. Yes, sir. That's to say, I've proposed to her and she's done me the honor of accepting me.

ARTHUR. I see. I trust when you corrected yourself, your second statement wasn't a denial of your first? (JOHN *looks puzzled.*) I mean, you do *really* wish to marry her?

JOHN. Of course, sir.

ARTHUR. Why, of course? There are plenty of people about who don't wish to marry her.

JOHN. I meant, of course, because I proposed to her.

ARTHUR. That, too, doesn't necessarily follow. However, we don't need to quibble. We'll take the sentimental side of the project for granted. As regards the more practical aspect, perhaps you won't mind if I ask you a few rather personal questions. (*He waves* JOHN *to sit in* GRACE's *chair.*)

JOHN (*sitting*). Naturally not, sir. It's your duty.

ARTHUR. Quite so. Now your income: are you able to live on it?

JOHN. No, sir. I'm in the regular army.

ARTHUR. Yes, of course.

JOHN. But my army pay is supplemented by an allowance from my father.

ARTHUR. So I understand. Now your father's would be, I take it, about twenty-four pounds a month.

JOHN (*surprised*). Yes, sir, that's exactly right.

ARTHUR. So that your total income—with your subaltern's[14] pay and allowances plus the allowance from your father, would be, I take it, about four hundred and twenty pounds a year.

JOHN (*more surprised*). Again, exactly the figure.

ARTHUR. Well, well. It all seems perfectly satisfactory. I really don't think I need delay my congratulations any longer. (*He extends his hand.* JOHN *rises and gratefully takes* ARTHUR's *hand.*)

JOHN. Thank you, sir, very much.

ARTHUR. I must say, it was very good of you to be so frank and informative.

JOHN. Not at all.

ARTHUR. Your answers to my questions deserve an equal frankness from me about Catherine's own affairs. I'm afraid she's not—just in case you thought otherwise—the daughter of a rich man.

JOHN. I didn't think otherwise, sir.

ARTHUR. Good. Well, now—— (*He suddenly cocks his head on one side and listens. There is the sound of a gramophone playing "Hitchey-Koo" from somewhere upstairs.*) Would you be so good as to touch the bell? (JOHN *crosses to fireplace and rings bell. It is heard distantly. He turns and stands with his back to fireplace.*) Thank you. Well, now, continuing about my own financial affairs. The Westminster Bank pays me a small pension—three hundred and fifty, to be precise—and my wife has about two hundred a year of her own. Apart from that we have nothing, except such savings as I've been able to make during my career at the bank—the interest from which raises my total income to about eight hundred pounds per annum. (VIOLET *comes in up* C.)

VIOLET. You rang, sir?

ARTHUR. Yes, Violet, my compliments to Mr. Dickie and if he doesn't stop that cacophonous[15] hullabaloo at once, I'll throw him and his infernal machine into the street.

VIOLET. Yes, sir. What was that word again? Cac-something——

ARTHUR. Never mind. Say anything you like, only stop him.

VIOLET. Well, sir, I'll do my best, but you know what Master Dickie's like with his blessed old ragtime.

ARTHUR. Yes, Violet, I do.

VIOLET. I could say you don't think it's quite nice on a Sunday.

ARTHUR. (*roaring*). You can say I don't think it's quite nice on any day. Just stop him making that confounded din, that's all.

VIOLET. Yes, sir. (VIOLET *goes out* U. C.)

ARTHUR (*apologetically*). Our Violet has no doubt already been explained to you?

JOHN. I don't think so. Is any explanation necessary?

ARTHUR. I fear it is. She came to us direct from an orphanage a very long time ago, as a sort of under-between maid on probation, and in that capacity she was quite satisfactory; but I'm afraid, as parlormaid, she has developed certain marked eccentricities in the performance of her duties—due, no doubt, to the fact that she has never fully known what they were. Well, now, where were we? Ah, yes. I was telling you about my sources of income, was I not?

JOHN. Yes, sir.

---

14 **subaltern** (sŭb ŏl′tərn): an officer below the rank of captain.

15 **cacophonous** (kə kŏf′ə nəs): disagreeable sounding.

ARTHUR. Now, in addition to the ordinary expenses of life, I have to maintain two sons—one at Osborne, and the other at Oxford—neither of whom, I'm afraid, will be in a position to support themselves for some time to come—one, because of his extreme youth and the other because of—er—other reasons. (*Gramophone record stops suddenly.*) So, you see, I am not in a position to be very lavish as regards Catherine's dowry.

JOHN. No, sir, I quite see that.

ARTHUR. I propose to settle on her one sixth of my total capital—which, worked out to the final fraction, is exactly eight hundred and thirty-three pounds six and eightpence. But let us deal in round figures and say eight hundred and fifty pounds.

JOHN. I call that very generous, sir.

ARTHUR. Not as generous as I would have liked, I'm afraid. However—as my wife would say—beggars can't be choosers.

JOHN. Exactly, sir.

ARTHUR. Well, then, if you're agreeable to that arrangement, I don't think there's anything more we need discuss.

JOHN. No, sir.

ARTHUR. Splendid. (*A pause. ARTHUR takes his stick and raps it, with an air of studied unconcern, three times on floor. They wait. Nothing happens.*)

JOHN (*crossing above table* R. C.). Pretty rotten weather, isn't it?

ARTHUR. Yes. Vile. (*He raps again. A pause. Again nothing happens.*) Would you care for another cigarette?

JOHN. No, thank you, sir. I'm still smoking. (*ARTHUR takes up stick to rap again, then thinks better of it. He struggles out of his chair and goes slowly but firmly to door up* L. *He throws open door. In apparent surprise.*) Well, imagine that! My wife and daughter are in here, of all places.

Come in, Grace. Come in, Catherine. John's here. (*GRACE comes in. CATHERINE follows.*)

GRACE (*crossing ARTHUR*). Why, John —how nice! (*JOHN steps forward and they meet* C. *They shake hands.*) My, you do look a swell! Doesn't he, Kate, darling?

CATHERINE (*between ARTHUR and GRACE*). Quite, indeed. (*A pause.*)

GRACE (*unable to repress herself— coyly*). Well?

ARTHUR. Well, what?

GRACE. How did your little talk go?

ARTHUR (*testily*). I understood you weren't supposed to know we were having a little talk.

GRACE. Oh, you are infuriating! Is everything all right, John? (*JOHN nods, smiling.*) Oh, I'm so glad. I really am.

JOHN. Thank you, Mrs. Winslow.

GRACE. May I kiss you? After all, I'm practically your mother now.

JOHN. Yes. Of course. (*JOHN allows himself to be kissed, ARTHUR crosses up* C., *comes down between* JOHN *and* GRACE.)

ARTHUR (*to* JOHN). While I, by the same token, am practically your father, but if you will forgive me——

JOHN (*smiling*). Certainly, sir.

ARTHUR. Grace, I think we might allow ourselves a little modest celebration at luncheon. Will you find me the key of the cellars? (*ARTHUR turns and goes out door up* C.)

GRACE (*following him*). Yes, dear. (*She turns at door; coyly.*) I don't suppose you two will mind being left alone for a few minutes, will you? (*GRACE follows ARTHUR out.*)

CATHERINE. Was it an ordeal?

JOHN. I was scared to death.

CATHERINE. My poor darling—— (*She goes quickly to him. They kiss.*)

JOHN. The annoying thing was that I had a whole lot of neatly turned phrases ready for him and he wouldn't let me use them.

CATHERINE. Such as? (JOHN *brings her down* C.)

JOHN. Oh—how proud and honored I was by your acceptance of me, and how determined I was to make you a loyal and devoted husband—and to maintain you in the state to which you were accustomed—all that sort of thing. All very sincerely meant.

CATHERINE. Anything about loving me a little?

JOHN (*lightly*). That I thought we could take for granted. So did your father, incidentally. (*He leans against edge of table* R. C.)

CATHERINE. I see. (*She gazes at him.*) Goodness, you do look smart!

JOHN. Not bad, is it? Poole's.

CATHERINE. What about *your* father? How did he take it?

JOHN. All right.

CATHERINE. I bet he didn't.

JOHN. Oh, yes. He's been wanting me to get married for years. Getting worried about grandchildren, I suppose. (JOHN *holds out his hand to her.* CATHERINE *takes it and goes to him.*)

CATHERINE. He disapproves of me, doesn't he?

JOHN. Oh, no. Whatever makes you think that?

CATHERINE. He has a way of looking at me through his monocle that shrivels me up.

JOHN. He's just being a colonel, darling, that's all. All colonels look at you like that. Anyway, what about the way your father looks at me! Tell me, are all your family as scared of him as I am?

CATHERINE. Dickie is, of course; and Ronnie, though he doesn't need to be. Father worships him. I don't know about Mother being scared of him. Sometimes perhaps. I'm not—ever.

JOHN. You're not scared of anything, are you?

CATHERINE. Oh, yes. Heaps of things.

JOHN. Such as?

CATHERINE (*with a smile*). Oh . . . They're nearly all concerned with you. (RONNIE *looks cautiously in at French windows. He now presents a very bedraggled and woebegone appearance, with his uniform wringing wet, and his damp hair over his eyes.*)

JOHN. You might be a little more explicit . . .

RONNIE (*in a low voice*). Kate! (CATHERINE *turns and sees him.*)

CATHERINE (*amazed*). Ronnie! What on earth——

RONNIE. Where's Father? (*He stands just inside French windows.*)

CATHERINE. I'll go and tell him—— (*She makes a slight move toward door.*)

RONNIE (*urgently*). No, don't; please, Kate, don't! (CATHERINE *stops up* C., *puzzled.*)

CATHERINE. What's the trouble, Ronnie? (RONNIE, *trembling on the edge of tears, does not answer.* JOHN *rises and breaks* C. *He looks slightly puzzled. As she goes to* RONNIE.) You're wet through. You'd better go and change.

RONNIE. No.

CATHERINE (*gently*). What's the trouble, darling? You can tell me. (RONNIE *looks at* JOHN.) You know John Watherstone, Ronnie. You met him last holidays, don't you remember? (RONNIE *remains silent, obviously reluctant to talk in front of a comparative stranger.*)

JOHN (*tactfully*). I'll disappear. (*He moves to door up* C.)

CATHERINE (*pointing to door up* L.). In there, do you mind? (JOHN *goes out* U. L. *quietly up* L. RONNIE *crosses below table* R. C.) Now, darling, tell me.

What is it? Have you run away? (RONNIE, *his back to her, shakes his head, evidently not trusting himself to speak. She comes down to him.*) What is it, then? (RONNIE *pulls out letter from his pocket and slowly hands it to her She reads it quietly.*) Oh, no!

RONNIE (*turning to her*). I didn't do it. (CATHERINE *rereads letter in silence.*) Kate, I didn't. Really, I didn't.

CATHERINE (*abstractedly*). No, darling. (*She seems uncertain what to do.*) This letter is addressed to Father. Did you open it?

RONNIE. Yes.

CATHERINE. You shouldn't have done that——

RONNIE. I was going to tear it up. Then I heard you come in from church and ran into the garden—I didn't know what to do——

CATHERINE (*still distracted*). Did they send you up alone?

RONNIE. They sent a Petty Officer[16] up with me. He was supposed to wait and see Father, but I sent him away. (*Indicating letter.*) Kate—shall we tear it up now?

CATHERINE. No, darling.

RONNIE. We could tell Father term had ended two days sooner——

CATHERINE. No, darling.

RONNIE. I didn't do it, Kate, really I didn't—— (DICKIE *comes in up* C. *He does not seem surprised to see* RONNIE.)

DICKIE (*coming down* C., *cheerfully*). Hello, Ronnie, old lad. How's everything? (RONNIE *turns away from him.*)

CATHERINE (*to* DICKIE). You knew he was here?

DICKIE. Oh, yes. His trunks and things are all over our room. Trouble?

CATHERINE. Yes.

16 **Petty Officer:** a noncommissioned junior officer in the Navy.

DRAMA

DICKIE. I'm sorry. (*He crosses to desk* R., *examines some gramophone records.*)

CATHERINE. You stay here with him. I'll find Mother.

DICKIE. All right. (CATHERINE *goes out up* C. *A pause.*) What's up, old chap?

RONNIE. Nothing.

DICKIE. Come on—tell me.

RONNIE. It's all right.

DICKIE. Have you been sacked? (RONNIE *nods.*) Bad luck. What for?

RONNIE. I didn't do it.

DICKIE (*reassuringly*). No, of course you didn't.

RONNIE. Honestly, I didn't.

DICKIE. That's all right, old chap. No need to go on about it. I believe you.

RONNIE. You don't.

DICKIE. Well, I don't know what it is they've sacked you for, yet——

RONNIE (*in a low voice*). Stealing.

DICKIE (*evidently relieved*). Oh, is that all? I didn't know they sacked chaps for *that*, these days.

RONNIE. I didn't do it.

DICKIE. Why, good heavens, at school we used to pinch[17] everything we could jolly well lay our hands on. All of us. (*As he speaks he quietly approaches* RONNIE.) I remember there was one chap—Carstairs his name was—captain of cricket, believe it or not—absolutely nothing was safe with him—nothing at all. Pinched a squash racket of mine once, I remember—— (*He puts his arm on* RONNIE'S *shoulder.*) Believe me, old chap, pinching's nothing. Nothing at all. I say—you're a bit damp, aren't you?

RONNIE. I've been out in the rain.

DICKIE. You're shivering a bit, too, aren't you? Oughtn't you to go and change? I mean, we don't want you catching pneumonia——

RONNIE. I'm all right. (GRACE *comes in up* C. CATHERINE *follows.* GRACE *comes quickly to* RONNIE. *He sees her, turns away from* DICKIE *and runs into her arms.*)

GRACE. There, darling! It's all right, now. (RONNIE *begins to cry quietly, his head buried in her dress.*)

RONNIE (*his voice muffled*). I didn't do it, Mother.

GRACE. No, darling. Of course you didn't. We'll go upstairs now, shall we, and get out of these nasty wet clothes?

RONNIE. Don't tell Father.

GRACE. No, darling. Not yet. I promise. Come along, now. (*She leads him up* C. *toward door.*) Your new uniform, too. What a shame! (GRACE *and* RONNIE *go out up* C.)

DICKIE. I'd better go and keep *cave*[18] for them. Ward off the old man if he looks like going upstairs. (*He goes to door up* C. CATHERINE *nods.*) I say—who's going to break the news to him eventually? I mean, someone'll have to.

CATHERINE. Don't let's worry about that now.

DICKIE. Well, you can count me out. In fact, I don't want to be within a thousand miles of that explosion. (DICKIE *goes out up* C. CATHERINE *moves to door up* L. *and opens it.*)

CATHERINE (*calling*). John. (*She leaves door open and comes down to fireplace.* JOHN *comes in.*)

JOHN (*entering*). Bad news? (*He comes down by* ARTHUR'S *chair.* CATHERINE *nods.*) That's rotten for you. I'm awfully sorry.

CATHERINE (*violently*). How can people be so cruel?

---

17 **pinch:** steal.

18 **cave** (kā′vē): a Latin term, meaning literally "beware." Here, "guard."

JOHN (*uncomfortably*). Expelled, I suppose? (JOHN *gets his answer from* CATHERINE'S *silence, while she recovers herself.*)

CATHERINE. How little imagination some people have! Why should they torture a child of that age, John? What's the point of it?

JOHN. What's he supposed to have done?

CATHERINE. Stolen some money.

JOHN. Oh.

CATHERINE. Ten days ago, it said in the letter. Why on earth didn't they let us know? Just think what that poor little creature has been going through these last ten days down there, entirely alone, without anyone to look after him, knowing what he had to face at the end of it! And then, finally, they send him up to London with a Petty Officer. Is it any wonder he's nearly out of his mind?

JOHN. It does seem pretty heartless, I know——

CATHERINE. Heartless? It's cold, calculated—inhumanity. How I'd love to have that Commanding Officer here for just two minutes. I'd—I'd——(*She crosses below* JOHN *and turns up* C.)

JOHN (*gently*). Darling—it's quite natural you should feel angry about it, but you must remember, he's not really at school. He's in the Service.[19]

CATHERINE. What difference does that make?

JOHN. Well, they have ways of doing things in the Service which may seem to an outsider horribly brutal, but at least they're always scrupulously fair. You can take it from me, that there must have been a very full inquiry before they'd take a step of this sort.

What's more, if there's been a delay of ten days, it would only have been in order to give the boy a better chance to clear himself—— (*He pauses.* CATHERINE *is silent. She turns away and moves above table* R. C.) I'm sorry, Catherine darling. I'd have done better to keep my mouth shut. (*He crosses to her.*)

CATHERINE. No. What you said was perfectly true——

JOHN. It was tactless of me to say it, though. I'm sorry.

CATHERINE (*lightly*). That's all right.

JOHN. Forgive me? (*Lays his arm on her shoulder.*)

CATHERINE. Nothing to forgive.

JOHN. Believe me, I'm awfully sorry. (*He pauses.*) How will your father take it?

CATHERINE (*simply*). It might kill him—— (*Sound of voices in hall.*) Oh, heavens! We've got Desmond to lunch. I'd forgotten——

JOHN. Who?

CATHERINE (*crossing above* JOHN *to door up* C.). Desmond Curry—our family solicitor.[20] Oh, Lord! (*In a hasty whisper.*) Darling—be polite to him, won't you?

JOHN. Why? Am I usually so rude to your guests?

CATHERINE. No, but he doesn't know about us yet——

JOHN. Who does?

CATHERINE (L. *of door; still in a whisper*). Yes, but he's been in love with me for years—it's a family joke—— (VIOLET *comes in up* C.)

VIOLET (*announcing*). Mr. Curry. (DESMOND CURRY *comes in up* C. *A man of about forty-five, with the figure of an athlete gone to seed. He has a mildly furtive manner, rather as if he*

---

19 **He's in the Service:** As a student in the Royal Naval Academy, he was under military rather than civilian laws.

20 **solicitor:** a person admitted to practice law in any court.

had just absconded with his firm's petty cash, and hopes no one is going to be too angry about it. JOHN, *when he sees him, cannot repress a faint smile at the thought of him loving* CATHERINE. VIOLET *goes out.*)

CATHERINE. Hullo, Desmond. (*They shake hands.*) I don't think you know John Watherstone——

DESMOND. No—but, of course, I've heard a lot about him—— (*He turns to* JOHN.)

JOHN. How do you do? (JOHN *wipes the smile off his face, as he meets* CATHERINE's *glance. He and* DESMOND *shake hands. A pause.*)

DESMOND. Well, well, well. I trust I'm not early?

CATHERINE. No. Dead on time, Desmond—as always.

DESMOND. Capital. Capital. (*Another pause.*)

JOHN
CATHERINE } (*together*). { Pretty ghastly, this rain. Tell me, Desmond.

JOHN. I'm so sorry.

CATHERINE. It's quite all right. I was only going to ask how you did in your cricket[21] match yesterday, Desmond?

DESMOND. Not too well, I'm afraid. My shoulder's still giving me trouble—— (*Another pause. At length.*) Well, well. I hear I'm to congratulate you both——

CATHERINE. Desmond—you know?

DESMOND. Violet told me, just now—in the hall. Yes—I must congratulate you both.

CATHERINE. Thank you so much, Desmond.

JOHN. Thank you.

DESMOND. Of course, it's quite ex-

---

21 **cricket:** an outdoor game played with ball, bats, and wickets.

pected, I know. Quite expected. Still, it was rather a surprise, hearing it like that—from Violet in the hall.

CATHERINE. We were going to tell you, Desmond, dear. It was only official this morning, you know. In fact, you're the first person to hear it.

DESMOND. Am I? Am I, indeed? Well, I'm sure you'll both be very happy.

JOHN
CATHERINE } (*murmuring together*). { Thank you, Desmond. Thank you.

DESMOND. Only this morning? Fancy. (GRACE *comes in up* C.)

GRACE (*coming between* DESMOND *and* CATHERINE). Hello, Desmond, dear.

DESMOND. Hello, Mrs. Winslow.

GRACE (*to* CATHERINE). I've got him to bed—— (CATHERINE *drops down below table* R. C. *and sits in chair* R. *of it.* JOHN *follows her and stands below table. They both take cigarettes.*)

CATHERINE. Good.

DESMOND. Nobody ill, I hope?

GRACE. No, no. Nothing wrong at all—— (ARTHUR *comes in up* C. *He carries a bottle under his arm and has a corkscrew.*)

ARTHUR. Grace, when did we last have the cellars seen to?

GRACE (*breaking up* L.). I can't remember, dear.

ARTHUR. Well, they're in a shocking condition. (*He turns and shuts door.*) Hello, Desmond. How are you? You're not looking well.

DESMOND. Am I not? I've strained my shoulder, you know.

ARTHUR. Well, why do you play these ridiculous games of yours? Resign yourself to the onrush of middle age, and abandon them, my dear Desmond. (*He moves to fireplace. Prepares to draw cork.*)

DESMOND. Oh, I could never do that. Not give up cricket. Not altogether.

JOHN (*making conversation*). Are you any relation of D. W. H. Curry who used to play for Middlesex?

DESMOND (*whose moment has come*). I *am* D. W. H. Curry.

GRACE (*coming down to her chair*). Didn't you know we had a great man in the room? (*She sits.*)

JOHN. Gosh! Curry of Curry's match?

DESMOND. That's right. (*He comes down* C.)

JOHN. Hat trick[22] against the Players in—what year was it?

DESMOND. 1895. At Lord's.[23]

JOHN. Gosh! Do you know you used to be a schoolboy hero of mine?

DESMOND. Did I? Did I, indeed?

JOHN. Yes. I had a signed photograph of you.

DESMOND. Yes, I used to sign a lot once, for schoolboys, I remember.

ARTHUR. Only for schoolboys, Desmond? (*He rings bell.*)

DESMOND. I fear so—yes. Girls took no interest in cricket in those days.

JOHN. Gosh! D. W. H. Curry—in person. Well, I'd never have thought it.

DESMOND (*sadly*). I know. Very few people would nowadays.

CATHERINE (*quickly*). Oh, John didn't mean that, Desmond.

DESMOND. I fear he did. (*Pats his protuberant stomach.*) This is the main trouble. Too much office work and too little exercise, I fear.

ARTHUR. Nonsense. Too much exercise and too little office work. (VIOLET *comes in up* C.)

VIOLET. You rang, sir?

ARTHUR. Yes, Violet. Bring some glasses, would you?

VIOLET. Very good, sir. (VIOLET *goes out up* C.)

ARTHUR. I thought we'd try a little of the Madeira[24] before luncheon—we're celebrating, you know, Desmond— (GRACE *furtively indicates* DESMOND. *He adds hastily*)—my wife's fifty-fourth birthday.

GRACE. Arthur! Really!

CATHERINE. It's all right, Father, Desmond knows——

DESMOND. Yes, indeed. It's wonderful news, isn't it? I'll most gladly drink a toast to the—er—to the——

ARTHUR (*politely*). Happy pair, I think, is the phrase that is eluding you.

DESMOND. Well, as a matter of fact, I was looking for something new to say.

ARTHUR (*murmuring*). A forlorn quest, my dear Desmond.

GRACE (*protestingly*). Arthur, really! You mustn't be so rude.

ARTHUR. I meant, naturally, that no one—with the possible exception of Voltaire—could find anything new to say about an engaged couple—— (DICKIE *opens door up* C. *He allows* VIOLET *to enter with tray of glasses, then follows her in.* VIOLET *comes to table by* ARTHUR's *chair and puts tray on it.*) Ah, my dear Dickie—just in time for a glass of Madeira in celebration of Kate's engagement to John—— (*He begins to pour the wine.*)

DICKIE. Oh, is that all finally spliced up now? (*He crosses above table to* CATHERINE *and kisses her; then crosses below her to* JOHN, *shakes hands.*)

ARTHUR. Quite so. I should have added just now—with the possible exception of Voltaire and Dickie Wins-

---

22 Hat trick: the performance of a bowler who dismisses three batsmen with consecutive balls in cricket, formerly rewarded by the gift of a new hat from his club.
23 Lord's: a famous cricket field and club in London.

24 Madeira (mə dĭr′ə): wine made on the island of Madeira located in the Atlantic, north of the Canary Islands.

DRAMA

low. (*To* VIOLET.) Take these round, will you, Violet? (*General buzz of conversation.* VIOLET *takes tray first to* GRACE, *then to* CATHERINE, *then to* JOHN. ARTHUR *puts bottle on table at his* R.)

CATHERINE. Are we allowed to drink our own healths? (DICKIE *takes a glass.*)

ARTHUR. I think it's permissible.

GRACE. No. It's bad luck. (VIOLET *offers glass to* DESMOND.)

JOHN. We defy augury. Don't we, Kate?

GRACE. You mustn't say that, John, dear. I know. You can drink each other's healths. That's all right. (VIOLET *goes to* ARTHUR.)

ARTHUR. Are my wife's superstitious terrors finally allayed? Good. (*He takes a drink.* VIOLET *moves above* ARTHUR'S *chair. Puts bottle on tray and tray on table, toasting.*) Catherine and John. (*All drink—*CATHERINE *and* JOHN *to each other.* VIOLET *lingers, smiling. Seeing* VIOLET.) Ah, Violet! We mustn't leave you out. You must join this toast.

VIOLET. Well—thank you, sir. (AR-THUR *pours her out a glass.*) Not too much, sir, please. Just a sip.

ARTHUR. Quite so. (*He holds out glass.*) Your reluctance would be more convincing if I hadn't noticed you'd brought an extra glass——

VIOLET (*taking glass from* ARTHUR). Oh, I didn't bring it for myself, sir. I brought it for Master Ronnie—— (*She extends her glass.*) Miss Kate and Mr. John. (*She takes a sip.*)

ARTHUR. You brought an extra glass for Master Ronnie, Violet?

VIOLET (*mistaking his bewilderment*). Well—I thought you might allow him just a sip, sir. Just to drink the toast. He's that grown-up these days. (DES-MOND *is staring gloomily into his glass.*

Others are frozen with apprehension.)

ARTHUR. Master Ronnie isn't due back from Osborne until Tuesday, Violet.

VIOLET. Oh, no, sir. He's back already. Came back unexpectedly this morning, all by himself.

ARTHUR. No, Violet. That isn't true. Someone has been playing a joke.

VIOLET. Well, I saw him in here with my own two eyes, sir, as large as life just before you come in from church— and then I heard Mrs. Winslow talking to him in his room——

ARTHUR. Grace—what does this mean?

CATHERINE (*rising and crossing to* C. *between* GRACE *and* DESMOND; *instinctively taking charge*). All right, Violet. You can go——

VIOLET. Yes, Miss. (VIOLET *goes out up* C.)

ARTHUR (*to* CATHERINE). Did *you* know Ronnie was back?

CATHERINE. Yes——

ARTHUR. And you, Dickie?

DICKIE. Yes, Father.

ARTHUR. Grace?

GRACE (*helplessly*). We thought it best you shouldn't know—for the time being. Only for the time being, Arthur.

ARTHUR (*slowly*). Is the boy ill? (*No one answers.* ARTHUR *looks from one face to another in bewilderment.*) Answer me, someone! Is the boy very ill? Why must I be kept in the dark like this? Surely I have the right to know. If he's ill I must be with him——

CATHERINE (*steadily*). No, Father. He's not ill. (*She takes a step closer to* GRACE. ARTHUR *suddenly realizes the truth from the tone of her voice.*)

ARTHUR. Will someone tell me what has happened, please? (GRACE *looks at* CATHERINE *with helpless inquiry.* CATHERINE *nods.* GRACE *takes letter from her dress.*)

GRACE (*timidly*). He brought this letter for you—Arthur.

ARTHUR. Read it to me, please——

GRACE. Arthur—not in front of——

ARTHUR. Read it to me, please. (GRACE *again looks at* CATHERINE *for advice, and again receives a nod.* ARTHUR *is sitting with head bowed.* GRACE *begins to read.*)

GRACE. "Confidential. I am commanded by My Lord's Commissioners of the Admiralty to inform you that they have received a communication from the Commanding Officer of the Royal Naval College at Osborne, reporting the theft of a five-shilling[25] postal order at the College on the 7th instant, which was afterwards cashed at the post office. Investigation of the circumstances of the case leaves no other conclusion possible than that the postal order was taken by your son, Cadet Ronald Arthur Winslow. My Lords deeply regret that they must therefore request you to withdraw your son from the College." It's signed by someone—I can't quite read his name —— (*She turns away quickly to hide her tears.* CATHERINE *puts a comforting hand on her shoulder.* ARTHUR *has not changed his attitude. A pause. The gong sounds in hall outside.*)

ARTHUR (*at length*). Desmond—be so good as to call Violet. (DESMOND *goes up* C., *opens door and steps into hall. Gong stops. He returns at once and holds door.* VIOLET *enters.*) Violet, ask Master Ronnie to come down and see me.

GRACE (*rising*). Arthur—he's in bed.

ARTHUR. You told me he wasn't ill.

GRACE. He's not at all well.

ARTHUR. Do as I say, Violet.

VIOLET. Very good, sir. (VIOLET *goes out up* C., *closing door.*)

ARTHUR. Perhaps the rest of you would go in to luncheon? Grace, would you take them in?

GRACE (*hovering*). Arthur—don't you think——

ARTHUR (*ignoring her*). Dickie, will you decant that bottle of claret I brought up from the cellar?

DICKIE. Yes, Father. (*Puts his empty glass on table* R. C.)

ARTHUR. I put it on the sideboard in the dining room.

DICKIE (*crossing below* JOHN *and up* C. *to door up* L.). Yes, Father. (DICKIE *goes out up* L.)

ARTHUR. Will you go in, Desmond? And John? (DESMOND *and* JOHN *move to door up* L. *and go out.* CATHERINE *follows them to door and waits.* GRACE *is still hovering.*)

GRACE. Arthur?

ARTHUR. Yes, Grace?

GRACE. Please don't—please don't—— (*She stops, uncertainly.*)

ARTHUR. What mustn't I do?

GRACE. Please don't forget he's only a child—— (ARTHUR *does not answer her.*)

CATHERINE. Come on, Mother. (GRACE *goes up to* CATHERINE *at door. She looks back at* ARTHUR. *He has still not altered his position and is ignoring her. She goes into dining room up* L., *followed by* CATHERINE. ARTHUR *does not move after they are gone. After an appreciable pause there comes a timid knock on door up* C.)

ARTHUR. Come in. (RONNIE *appears in doorway. He is in a dressing gown. He stands on threshold.*) Come in and shut the door. (RONNIE *closes door behind him.*) Come over here. (RONNIE *walks slowly to his father, who gazes at him steadily for some time, without speaking. At length.*) Why aren't you in your uniform?

RONNIE (*murmuring*). It got wet.

ARTHUR. How did it get wet?

RONNIE. I was out in the garden in the rain.

ARTHUR. Why?

RONNIE (*reluctantly*). I was hiding.

ARTHUR. From me? (RONNIE *nods.*) Do you remember once, you promised me that if ever you were in trouble of any sort you would come to me first?

RONNIE. Yes, Father.

ARTHUR. Why didn't you come to me now? Why did you have to go and hide in the garden?

RONNIE. I don't know, Father.

ARTHUR. Are you so frightened of me? (RONNIE *does not reply.* ARTHUR *gazes at him a moment, then holds up letter.*) In this letter it says you stole a postal order. (RONNIE *opens his mouth to speak.* ARTHUR *stops him.*) Now I don't want you to say a word until you've heard what *I've* got to say. If you did it, you must tell me. I shan't be angry with you, Ronnie—provided you tell me the truth. But if you tell me a lie, I shall know it, because a lie between you and me can't be hidden. I shall know it, Ronnie—so remember that before you speak. (*He pauses.*) Did you steal this postal order?

RONNIE (*with hesitation*). No, Father. I didn't. (ARTHUR *takes step towards him.*)

ARTHUR (*staring into his eyes*). Did you steal this postal order?

RONNIE. No, Father. I didn't. (ARTHUR *continues to stare into his eyes for a second, then relaxes.*)

ARTHUR. Go on back to bed. (RONNIE *goes gratefully to door up* C.) And in future I trust that a son of mine will at least show enough sense to come in out of the rain.

RONNIE. Yes, Father. (RONNIE *goes out.* ARTHUR *crosses down* R. *to desk. He picks up phone on desk.*)

ARTHUR (*into phone*). Hullo. Are you there? (*Speaks very distinctly.*) I want to put a trunk call[26] through, please. A trunk call. . . . Yes. . . . The Royal Naval College, Osborne. . . . That's right. . . . Replace receiver? Certainly. (*He replaces receiver and then, after a moment's meditation, turns and crosses briskly up* L. *and goes out into dining room up* L.)

QUICK CURTAIN

---

26 **trunk call:** long-distance.

Understanding the Play

1. The play opens with Ronnie on stage. What impression does the audience receive from his actions? What does Rattigan accomplish by opening this way rather than with the family's return from church?

2. Exposition is an important element of the preceding scene. What information is given in the opening conversation between Violet and Ronnie? What questions does this information immediately raise?

What facts are learned about the lives of Dickie and Catherine in the conversation that follows the family's entrance onto the stage? How does the author suggest during the conversation that Catherine may have to face problems with John at some time?

Assuming that this is a carefully written play, all the information that is given in the first scene presumably is included for some purpose. What do you learn about the family finances in this act? How is the inclusion of the information made to seem natural? Presuming the information is given for a reason, what does its inclusion suggest to the alert reader?

3. Character revelation is also an important element of this scene. As the characters are introduced in turn, what do you learn about the kind of person each is?

4. Contrasts between characters are an essential feature of this play. What contrast between Ronnie and Dickie is built up? How do John and Catherine contrast with each other in their reactions to the letter about Ronnie? How do Arthur and Grace contrast with each other in their reactions to Ronnie's expulsion?

5. In a play of several acts or scenes, each one usually leads up to and closes with a moment of tension or excitement. What is the most dramatic moment of the preceding scene?

6. With what questions is the audience left at the end of the scene?

Building Vocabulary Skills

This play was written by an Englishman and concerns an English family. As you read the first scene, you may have noticed some differences between British and American usages and word meanings. "Solicitor," for example, is used when Americans would have said "lawyer." What other differences between American and British usage can you locate in this play?

ACT I

Scene 2

Same, nine months later. About six o'clock, a spring evening. Dickie *is winding up his gramophone which, somehow or other, appears to have found its way back into the drawing room and is now on piano. A pile of books and an opened notebook on desk provide evidence of interrupted labors.* Dickie *has a book in one hand. He starts gramophone and it emits a scratchy and muffled rendering of "Alexander's Ragtime Band."* Dickie *listens for a few seconds with evident appreciation, then essays a little* pas seul,[1] *at same time reading book.* Catherine *comes in up* c. *She is in evening dress, and carries a cloak, gloves, bag and scarf.* Dickie *goes to gramophone and stops it. He puts book on piano.*

Dickie. Hullo? Do you think the old man can hear this upstairs?

Catherine. I shouldn't think so. I couldn't. (*She puts her things on chair* L. *of door.*)

Dickie. Soft needle and an old sweater down the horn. Is the doctor still with him? (*He changes record.* Catherine *nods.*) What's the verdict, do you know?

Catherine. I heard him say Father needed a complete rest—— (*She moves down to fireplace.*)

Dickie. Don't we all?

Catherine (*indicating books on desk*). It doesn't look as if *you* did. (*She looks at her hair in mirror.*) He said he ought to go to the country and forget all his worries.

Dickie. Fat chance there is of that, I'd say.

Catherine. I know. (*She picks up her bag.*)

Dickie. I say, you look a treat. New dress?

Catherine (*turning to him*). Is it likely? No, it's an old one I've had done up.

Dickie. Where are you going to?

Catherine. Daly's. Dinner first—at the Cri'. (*She takes a step down* c.)

Dickie. Nice. You wouldn't care to take me along with you, I suppose?

Catherine. You suppose quite correctly.

Dickie. John wouldn't mind.

Catherine. I dare say not. I would.

Dickie. I wish I had someone to take me out. In your new feminine world do you suppose women will be allowed to do some of the paying?

Catherine. Certainly.

Dickie. Really? Then the next time you're looking for someone to chain themselves to Mr. Asquith,[2] you can jolly well call on me.

Catherine (*laughing*). Edwina might take you out if you gave her the hint. She's very rich——

Dickie. If I gave Edwina a hint of that sort I wouldn't see her this side of Doomsday.

Catherine. You sound a little bitter, Dickie, dear.

Dickie. Oh, no. Not bitter. Just realistic. (Violet *comes in up* c. *with evening paper on salver.*) Good egg! The *Star!* . . . (*He moves to* c. *and makes a grab for it.* Catherine *makes a grab for it, and gets it before* Dickie. *She comes down to back of table* R. c. *with it.* Dickie *follows and cranes his neck over her shoulder.*)

Violet. You won't throw it away, will you, Miss? If there's anything in

---

1 essays a little pas seul: tries a dance step.

2 Mr. Asquith: British statesman and Prime Minister during World War I.

it again, cook and I would like to read it, after you. (CATHERINE *is hastily turning over pages.*)

CATHERINE (*placing her bag on table*). No. That's all right, Violet. (VIOLET *goes out.*) Here it is. (DICKIE *sits on chair* R. *of table.*) "The Osborne Cadet." There are two more letters. "Sir—I am entirely in agreement with your correspondent, Democrat, concerning the scandalously highhanded treatment by the Admiralty of the case of the Osborne Cadet. The efforts of Mr. Arthur Winslow to secure a fair trial for his son have evidently been thwarted at every turn by a soulless oligarchy[3]——"

DICKIE. Soulless oligarchy! That's rather good.

CATHERINE. "It is high time private and peaceful citizens of this country awoke to the increasing encroachment of their ancient freedom by the new despotism of Whitehall.[4] The Englishman's home was once said to be his castle. It seems it is rapidly becoming his prison. Your obedient servant, Libertatis Amator."[5]

DICKIE. Good for old Amator!

CATHERINE. The other's from "Perplexed." "Dear Sir—I cannot understand what all the fuss is about in the case of the Osborne Cadet. Surely, we have more important matters to get ourselves worked up about than a fourteen-year-old boy and a five-shilling postal order." Silly old fool!

DICKIE. How do you know he's old? (*He rises.*)

CATHERINE. Isn't it obvious? "With the present troubles in the Balkans and a certain major European Power rapidly outbuilding our Navy, the Admiralty might be forgiven if it stated that it had rather more urgent affairs to deal with than Master Ronnie Winslow's little troubles. A further inquiry before the judge advocate of the Fleet has now fully confirmed the original findings that the boy was guilty. I sincerely trust that this will finally end this ridiculous and sordid little storm in a teacup. I am, Sir, etc., Perplexed." (*A pause.*)

DICKIE (*reading over her shoulder*). "This correspondence must now cease. —Editor." Damn!

CATHERINE. Oh dear! (*She sits in chair* L. *of table.*) How hopeless it seems sometimes.

DICKIE. Yes, it does, doesn't it? (*He pauses. Thoughtfully.*) You know, Kate—don't give me away to the Old Man, will you?—but the awful thing is, if it hadn't been my own brother I think I might quite likely have seen Perplexed's point.

CATHERINE. Might you?

DICKIE. Well, I mean—looking at it from every angle and all that—it does seem rather a much ado about damn all. I mean to say—a mere matter of pinching. (*Bitterly.*) And it's all so beastly expensive. . . . Let's cheer ourselves up with some music. (*He turns up to gramophone and sets it going.*)

CATHERINE (*listening to record*). Is that what it's called?

DICKIE. Come and practice a few steps. (CATHERINE *rises and joins* DICKIE *above table. They dance, in the manner of the period, with arms fully outstretched and working up and down, pump-handle style. Surprised.*) I say! Jolly good!

CATHERINE. Thank you, Dickie.

DICKIE. Who taught you? John, I suppose.

CATHERINE. No. I taught John, as it happens——

---

3 **oligarchy** (ŏl′ə gär′kĭ): state ruled by the few.
4 **Whitehall**: the British imperial government.
5 **Libertatis Amator**: lover of liberty.

DICKIE. Feminism—even in love? (CATHERINE nods, smiling. They continue to dance. After a pause.) When's the happy date now?

CATHERINE. Postponed again.

DICKIE. Oh, no! Why?

CATHERINE. His father's gone abroad for six months.

DICKIE. Why pay any attention to that old—(he substitutes word) gentleman?

CATHERINE. I wouldn't—but John does—so I have to. (Something in her tone makes DICKIE stop dancing and gaze at her seriously.)

DICKIE. I say—nothing wrong, is there? (CATHERINE shakes head, smiling, but not too emphatically.) I mean —you're not going to be left on the altar rails or anything, are you?

CATHERINE. Oh, no. I'll get him past the altar rails, if I have to drag him there.

DICKIE. Do you think you might have to?

CATHERINE. Quite frankly, yes.

DICKIE. Competition?

CATHERINE. Not yet. Only—differences of opinion. (They resume dancing.)

DICKIE. I see. Well, take some advice from an old hand, will you?

CATHERINE. Yes, Dickie.

DICKIE. Suppress your opinions. Men don't like 'em in their lady friends, even if they agree with 'em. And if they don't—it's fatal. Pretend to be half-witted, like Edwina, then he'll adore you.

CATHERINE. I know. I do, sometimes, and then I forget. Still, you needn't worry. If there's ever a clash between what I believe and what I feel, there's not much doubt about which will win.

DICKIE. That's the girl! Of course, I don't know why you didn't fall in love with Ramsay Macdonald.[6] . . . (ARTHUR comes in up C. He is walking with more difficulty than when we last saw him. DICKIE and CATHERINE hastily stop dancing. They have finished down R. DICKIE moves quickly up R. and turns off gramophone.)

CATHERINE (moving up C. to ARTHUR; quickly). It was entirely my fault, Father. I enticed Dickie from his work to show me a few dance steps.

ARTHUR. Oh? I must admit I am surprised you succeeded. (He moves to fireplace.)

DICKIE (getting off subject). What did the doctor say, Father?

ARTHUR. He said, if I remember his exact words, that we weren't quite as well as when we last saw each other. (He turns at fireplace.) That information seems expensive at a guinea.[7] (He sees paper.) Oh, is that the Star? Let me see it, please. (CATHERINE moves quickly to table and crosses to ARTHUR with paper. ARTHUR sits in his chair.) John will be calling for you here, I take it? (DICKIE takes his book from piano, moves down R. and sits at desk.)

CATHERINE. Yes, Father.

ARTHUR. It might be better, perhaps, if you didn't ask him in. This room will shortly be a clutter of journalists, solicitors, barristers, and other impedimenta.

CATHERINE (examining her hair in mirror over fireplace). Is Sir Robert Morton coming to see you here?

ARTHUR (reading papers). I could hardly go and see him, could I? (A short pause. DICKIE, in deference to his father's presence, continues to work. ARTHUR reads the Star. CATHERINE glances at herself in mirror, then wanders to door up C.)

6 **Ramsay MacDonald:** a liberal leader of the time who was supported by the Suffragettes.
7 **guinea:** about $5.25 then.

CATHERINE. I must go and do something about my hair.

DICKIE. What's the matter with your hair?

CATHERINE. Nothing, except I don't like it very much. (CATHERINE *goes out up* C. DICKIE *opens two more books with a busy air.* ARTHUR *finishes reading paper and stares moodily into space.*)

ARTHUR (*at length*). I wonder if I could sue "Perplexed"?

DICKIE. It might be a way of getting the case into court.

ARTHUR. On the other hand, he has not been libelous. Merely base. (*He throws paper away from him, and regards* DICKIE *thoughtfully.* DICKIE, *feeling his father's eye on him, is elaborately industrious. At length, politely*) Do you mind if I disturb you for a moment?

DICKIE (*pushing books away*). No, Father.

ARTHUR. I want to ask you a question, but before I do, I must impress on you the urgent necessity for an absolutely truthful answer.

DICKIE. Naturally.

ARTHUR. Naturally means by nature, and I'm afraid I have not yet noticed that it has invariably been your nature to answer my questions truthfully.

DICKIE (*rising*). Oh. (*He crosses to* ARTHUR.) Well, I will this one, Father. I promise.

ARTHUR. Very well. (*He stares at him for a moment.*) What do you suppose one of your bookmaker friends would lay in the way of odds against your getting a degree? (*A pause.*)

DICKIE. Oh. Well, let's think. Say—about evens.

ARTHUR. Hm. I rather doubt if at that price your friend would find many takers.

DICKIE. Well—perhaps seven to four against.

ARTHUR. I see. And what about the odds against your eventually becoming a civil servant?

DICKIE. Well—a bit steeper, I suppose.

ARTHUR. Exactly. Quite a bit steeper. (*A pause.*)

DICKIE. You don't want to have a bet, do you?

ARTHUR. No, Dickie. I'm not a gambler. And that's exactly the trouble. Unhappily, I'm no longer in a position to gamble two hundred pounds a year on what you yourself admit is an outside chance.

DICKIE. Not an outside chance, Father. A good chance.

ARTHUR. Not good enough, Dickie, I'm afraid—with things as they are at the moment. Definitely not good enough. I fear my mind is finally made up. (*A long pause.*)

DICKIE. You want me to leave Oxford —is that it?

ARTHUR. I'm afraid so, Dickie.

DICKIE. Oh. (*He turns away, unable to face* ARTHUR.) Straight away?

ARTHUR. No. You can finish your second year.

DICKIE. And what then?

ARTHUR. I can get you a job in the bank.

DICKIE (*quietly*). Oh, Lord!

ARTHUR (*after pause, rather apologetically*). It'll be quite a good job, you know. Luckily, my influence in the bank still counts for something.

DICKIE (*turning to* ARTHUR). Father— if I promised you—I mean, *really* promised you—that from now on I'll work like a—— (ARTHUR *shakes head slowly.*) It's the case, I suppose?

ARTHUR. It's costing me a lot of money.

DICKIE. I know. It must be. Still, couldn't you—I mean, isn't there any way—— (ARTHUR *again shakes head. As he turns away again.*) Oh, Lord!

ARTHUR. I'm afraid this is rather a shock for you. I'm sorry.

DICKIE. What? No. No, it isn't, really. I've been rather expecting it as a matter of fact—especially since I hear you are hoping to brief Sir Robert Morton. Still, I can't say but what it isn't a bit of a slap in the face—— (*Front doorbell rings.*)

ARTHUR. There is a journalist coming to see me. Do you mind if we talk about this some other time?

DICKIE (*crossing slowly to desk*). No. Of course not, Father. (*He begins forlornly to gather his books.*)

ARTHUR (*with a half-smile*). I should leave those there, if I were you.

DICKIE. Yes. I will. Good idea. (*He goes to door up* C.)

ARTHUR (*politely*). Tell me—how is your friend Miss Edwina Gunn these days?

DICKIE (*turning and coming down to* C.). Very well, thanks awfully.

ARTHUR. You don't suppose she'd mind if you took her to the theater—or gave her a little present, perhaps?

DICKIE. Oh, I'm sure she wouldn't.

ARTHUR (*taking coin purse from waistcoat pocket*). I'm afraid I can only make it a couple of sovereigns.[8] (*He extracts two coins.*)

DICKIE (*crossing to* ARTHUR *and taking them*). Thanks awfully, Father.

ARTHUR. With what's left over, you can always buy something for yourself.

DICKIE. Oh. Well, as a matter of fact, I don't suppose there will be an awful lot left over. Still, it's jolly decent of you. I say, Father—I think I could do with a little spot of something. Would you mind?

8 sovereigns: coins worth about $5.00 then.

ARTHUR. Of course not. You'll find the decanter in the dining room.

DICKIE. Thanks awfully. (*He moves up toward door up* L.)

ARTHUR. I must thank you, Dickie, for bearing what must have been a very unpleasant blow with some fortitude.

DICKIE (*uncomfortably*). Oh, rot, Father! (DICKIE *goes out up* L. ARTHUR *sighs deeply.* VIOLET *comes in up* C.)

VIOLET (*announcing proudly*). The *Daily News!* (MISS BARNES *comes in, a rather untidily dressed woman of about forty, with a gushing manner.* ARTHUR *rises.*)

MISS BARNES. Mr. Winslow? So good of you to see me. (*Comes down to* ARTHUR.)

ARTHUR. How do you do?

MISS BARNES (*simpering*). You're surprised to see a lady reporter? I know. Everyone is. And yet why not? What could be more natural?

ARTHUR. What, indeed? Pray sit down—— (MISS BARNES *sits in* GRACE's *chair.*)

MISS BARNES. My paper usually sends me out on stories which have a special appeal to women—stories with a little heart, you know, like this one—a father's fight for his little son's honor. . . . (ARTHUR *winces visibly.*)

ARTHUR. I venture to think this case has rather wider implications than that. . . .

MISS BARNES. Oh, yes. The political angle. I know. Very interesting, but not *quite* my line of country. Now what I'd really like to do is to get a nice picture of you and your little boy together. I've brought my assistant and camera. They're in the hall. Where is your little boy?

ARTHUR. My son is arriving from school in a few minutes. His mother has gone to the station to meet him.

MISS BARNES (*making note*). From school? How interesting. So you got a school to take him? I mean, they didn't mind the unpleasantness?

ARTHUR. No.

MISS BARNES. And why is he coming back this time?

ARTHUR. He hasn't been expelled again, if that is what you're implying. He is coming to London to be examined by Sir Robert Morton, whom we are hoping to brief——

MISS BARNES. Sir Robert Morton! (*She whistles appreciatively.*) Well!

ARTHUR. Exactly.

MISS BARNES (*doubtingly*). But do you *really* think he'll take a little case like this?

ARTHUR (*explosively*). It is not a little case, madam——

MISS BARNES. No, no. Of course not. But still—Sir Robert Morton!

ARTHUR. I understand that he is the best advocate[9] in the country. He is certainly the most expensive——

MISS BARNES. Oh, yes. I suppose if one is prepared to pay his fee one can get him for almost *any* case.

ARTHUR. Once more, madam—this is *not* almost any case——

MISS BARNES. No, no. Of course not. Well now, perhaps you wouldn't mind giving me a few details. When did it all start?

ARTHUR. Nine months ago. The first thing I knew of the charge was when my son arrived home with a letter from the Admiralty informing me of his expulsion. I telephoned Osborne to protest, and was referred by them to the Lords of the Admiralty. My solicitors then took the matter up and demanded from the Admiralty the fullest possible inquiry. For weeks we were ignored, then met with a blank refusal, and only

finally got reluctant permission to view the evidence.

MISS BARNES (*indifferently*). Really?

ARTHUR. My solicitors decided that the evidence was highly unsatisfactory, and fully justified the reopening of proceedings. We applied to the Admiralty for a Court Martial. They ignored us. We applied for a civil trial. They ignored us again.

MISS BARNES. They ignored you?

ARTHUR. Yes. But after tremendous pressure had been brought to bear—letters to the papers, questions in the House, and other means open to private citizens of this country—the Admiralty eventually agreed to what they called an independent inquiry.

MISS BARNES (*vaguely*). Oh, good!

ARTHUR. It was not good, madam. At that independent inquiry, conducted by the Judge Advocate of the Fleet—against whom I am saying nothing, mind you—my son—a child of fourteen, was not represented by counsel, solicitors or friends. What do you think of that?

MISS BARNES. Fancy!

ARTHUR. You may well say "fancy."

MISS BARNES. And what happened at the inquiry?

ARTHUR. Inevitably he was found guilty again, and thus branded for the second time before the world as a thief and a forger——

MISS BARNES (*her attention wandering*). What a shame!

ARTHUR. I need hardly tell you, madam, that I am not prepared to let the matter rest there. I shall continue to fight this monstrous injustice with every weapon and every means at my disposal. Now it happens I have a plan. . . . (*He sits in his chair.*)

MISS BARNES (*staring at French window*). Oh, what charming curtains! (*She rises.*) What are they made of?

9 advocate: lawyer who pleads in a law court.

(*She crosses to window, examines heavy curtains.* ARTHUR *sits for a moment in paralyzed silence.*)

ARTHUR (*at length*). Madam—I fear I have no idea. (*Sound of voices in hall.*)

MISS BARNES (*leaving curtains, brightly*). Ah! Do I hear the poor little chap himself? (RONNIE *comes in up* C., *boisterously, followed by* GRACE. *He is evidently in the highest of spirits.*)

RONNIE. Hullo, Father! (*He runs to* ARTHUR.)

ARTHUR. Hullo, Ronnie. (GRACE *crosses up* R. *toward window and greets* MISS BARNES.)

RONNIE (*excitedly*). I say, Father—Mr. Moore says I'm to tell you I needn't come back till Monday, if you like—so that gives me three whole days. (*He sits against* L. *arm of chair.*)

ARTHUR. Mind my leg!

RONNIE. Sorry, Father.

ARTHUR (*kissing* RONNIE *on forehead*). How are you, my boy? (*He puts* L. *arm round* RONNIE.)

RONNIE. Oh, I'm absolutely tophole,[10] Father. Mother says I've grown an inch.

MISS BARNES (*crossing downstage to* C.). Ah! Now that's exactly the way I'd like to take my picture. Would you hold it, Mr. Winslow? (*She goes to door up* C. *and calls.*) Fred! Come in now, will you?

RONNIE (*in a sibilant whisper*). Who's she? (FRED *enters up* C. *He is a listless photographer, complete with apparatus.*)

FRED (*gloomily*). 'Afternoon, all.

MISS BARNES (*coming down* C.). That's the pose I suggest. (FRED *comes down to* MISS BARNES, *looks briefly at* ARTHUR *and* RONNIE.)

FRED. Yes. It'll do. (*He begins to*

10 **tophole**: topnotch.

set up apparatus down C. Moves GRACE'S *chair and chair* L. *of table.* ARTHUR *continues to hold* RONNIE *close against him in pose suggested. He turns his head to* GRACE.)

ARTHUR. Grace, dear, this lady is from the *Daily News.* She is extremely interested in your curtains.

GRACE (*delighted*). Oh, really? How nice! (*She moves to window.*)

MISS BARNES. Yes, indeed. (*She moves to window.*) I was wondering what they were made of.

GRACE. ⎫
RONNIE. ⎬ (*together*).

Well, it's an entirely new material, you know. I'm afraid I don't know what it's called, but I got them at Barker's last year. Apparently it's a sort of mixture of wild silk and . . .

Father, are we going to be in the *Daily News?*

ARTHUR. It appears so.

MISS BARNES. ⎫
RONNIE. ⎬ (*together*).

(*Now genuinely busy with her pencil and pad*). Just a second, Mrs. Winslow. I'm afraid my shorthand isn't very good. I must just get that down.

Oh, good! They get the *Daily News* in the school library, and everyone's bound to see it.

FRED. Quite still, please. (*Everybody looks at* FRED. FRED *takes photograph.*) All right, Miss Barnes. (*Gathers up his apparatus.*)

MISS BARNES (*engrossed with* GRACE). Thank you, Fred. (*She crosses to* L. C. *to* ARTHUR.) Good-by, Mr. Winslow, and the very best of good fortune in your inspiring fight. (FRED *goes out up* C. GRACE *crosses to* C., *turns to* RONNIE.) Good-by, little chap. Remember—the darkest hour is just before the dawn. (*She turns up* C. *to* GRACE.) Well, it was very good of you to tell me all that, Mrs. Winslow. I'm sure our readers will be most interested. (*She moves up to door.*)

RONNIE. What's she talking about? (MISS BARNES *goes out up* C. GRACE *follows her out.*)

ARTHUR. The case, I imagine.

RONNIE (*crossing to piano*). Oh, the case! Father, do you know the train had fourteen coaches? (*Plays with gramophone.*)

ARTHUR. Did it indeed?

RONNIE. Yes. All corridor.

ARTHUR. Remarkable.

RONNIE. Of course, it was one of the very biggest expresses—I walked all the way down it from one end to the other.

ARTHUR. I had your half-term report, Ronnie.

RONNIE (*suddenly silenced by perturbation*). Oh, yes?

ARTHUR. On the whole it was pretty fair.

RONNIE. Oh, good.

ARTHUR. I'm glad you seem to be settling down so well—very glad indeed. (GRACE *comes in up* C.)

GRACE. What a charming woman, Arthur! (RONNIE *moves down* R.)

ARTHUR. Charming. I trust you gave her full details about our curtains?

GRACE (*coming down to table* R. C.). Oh, yes. I told her everything. (*She replaces chair* L. *of table.*)

ARTHUR (*wearily*). I'm so glad.

GRACE. I do think women reporters are a good idea. (*Moves to her chair and straightens it.*)

RONNIE (*crossing to* ARTHUR; *excitedly*). I say, Father—will it be all right for me to stay till Monday? I mean, I won't be missing any work—only Divinity—— (*He jogs his father's leg again.*)

ARTHUR. Mind my leg!

RONNIE. Oh, sorry, Father! Is it bad?

ARTHUR. Yes, it is. (*To* GRACE.) Grace, take him upstairs and get him washed. Sir Robert will be here in a few minutes.

GRACE (*to* RONNIE). Come on, darling. (*She goes to door and opens it.*)

RONNIE. All right. (*As he goes to door up* C.) I say, do you know how long the train took? A hundred and twenty-three miles in two hours and fifty-two minutes. Violet! Violet! I'm back. (RONNIE *goes out up* C. *chattering shrilly.* GRACE *closes door after him and comes down to* ARTHUR.)

GRACE. Did the doctor say anything, dear?

ARTHUR. A great deal—but very little to the purpose.

GRACE. Violet says he left an ointment for your back. Four massages a day. Is that right?

ARTHUR. Something of the kind.

GRACE. I think you'd better have one now, hadn't you, Arthur?

ARTHUR. No.

GRACE. But, dear, you've got plenty of time before Sir Robert comes, and if you don't have one now you won't be able to have another before you go to bed.

ARTHUR. Precisely.

GRACE. But really, Arthur, it does seem awfully silly to spend all this money on doctors if you're not even going to do what they say——

ARTHUR (*impatiently*). All right, Grace. All right. All right. (*He rises.*)

GRACE. Thank you, dear. (*Turns upstage.* CATHERINE *comes in up* C.)

CATHERINE. Ronnie's back, judging by the noise——

GRACE (*examining* CATHERINE). I must say that old frock has come out very well. John'll never know it isn't brand new. . . .

CATHERINE (*up* C.). He's late, curse him.

ARTHUR. Grace, go on up and attend to Ronnie and prepare the witches' brew for me. I'll come up when you're ready.

GRACE. Very well, dear. (*To* CATHERINE.) Yes, that does look good. I must say Mme. Dupont's a treasure. (GRACE *goes out up* C. CATHERINE *comes down to table* R. C. *She picks up her bag.*)

ARTHUR (*wearily*). Oh, Kate, Kate! Are we both mad, you and I? (*He moves to* C.)

CATHERINE (*searching in her bag*). What's the matter, Father? (*Closes her bag and puts it down on table.*)

ARTHUR. I don't know. I suddenly feel suicidally inclined. (*Bitterly.*) A father's fight for his little boy's honor. Special appeal to all women. Photo inset of Mrs. Winslow's curtains. Is there any hope for the world?

CATHERINE (*going to him, smiling*). I think so, Father.

ARTHUR. Shall we drop the whole thing, Kate?

CATHERINE (*taking a step back*). I don't consider that a serious question, Father.

ARTHUR (*slowly*). You realize that if we go on, your marriage settlement must go?

CATHERINE (*lightly*). Oh, yes. I gave that up for lost weeks ago. (*She turns back to table, takes cigarette and lights it.*)

ARTHUR. Things are all right between you and John, aren't they?

CATHERINE. Oh, yes, Father, of course. Everything's perfect.

ARTHUR. I mean—it won't make any difference between you, will it?

CATHERINE. Good heavens, no!

ARTHUR. Very well, then. Let us pin our faith to Sir Robert Morton. (CATHERINE *is silent.* ARTHUR *looks at her as if he had expected an answer, then nods.*) I see I'm speaking only for myself in saying that.

CATHERINE (*lightly*). You know what I think of Sir Robert Morton, Father. Don't let's go into it again now. It's too late, anyway.

ARTHUR. It's not too late. He hasn't accepted the brief[11] yet.

CATHERINE (*shortly*). Then I'm rather afraid I hope he never does. And that has nothing to do with my marriage settlement, either. (*A pause.* ARTHUR *looks angry for a second, then subsides.*)

ARTHUR (*mildly*). I made inquiries about that fellow you suggested—I am told he is not nearly as good an advocate as Morton.

CATHERINE (*looking out of window*). He's not nearly so fashionable.

ARTHUR (*doubtfully*). I want the best——

CATHERINE. The best in this case certainly isn't Morton.

ARTHUR. Then why does everyone say he is?

CATHERINE (*moving to* ARTHUR; *roused*). Because if one happens to be a large monopoly attacking a trade union or a Tory[12] paper libeling a Labor leader, he *is* the best. But it utterly defeats me how you or anyone else could expect a man of his record to have even a tenth of his heart in a case where the boot is entirely on the other foot.

ARTHUR. Well, I imagine if his heart isn't in it, he won't accept the brief.

CATHERINE. He might still. It depends what there is in it for him. Luckily there isn't much——

ARTHUR (*bitterly*). There is a fairly substantial check.

CATHERINE. He doesn't want money.

---

11 brief: law case.
12 Tory: British conservative political party.

He must be a very rich man.

ARTHUR. What does he want, then?

CATHERINE. Anything that advances his interests. (*She turns away and moves below table* R. C. ARTHUR *shrugs shoulders.*)

ARTHUR (*after pause*). I believe you are prejudiced because he spoke against women's suffrage.

CATHERINE. I am. I'm prejudiced because he is always speaking against what is right and just. Did you read his speech in the House on the Trades Disputes Bill?

GRACE (*off, calling*). Arthur! Arthur! (*A pause.*)

ARTHUR (*smiling*). Oh, well—in the words of the Prime Minister, let us wait and see! (*Turns and goes up* C. *At door he turns back to* CATHERINE.) You're my only ally, Kate. Without you I believe I should have given up long ago.

CATHERINE. Rubbish.

ARTHUR. It's true. Still, you must sometimes allow me to make my own decisions. I have an instinct about Morton. (CATHERINE *does not reply. Doubtfully.*) We'll see which is right —my instinct or your reason, eh? (AR- THUR *goes out up* C.)

CATHERINE (*half to herself*). I'm afraid we will. (*She realizes it is getting dark and moves swiftly to door up* C. *She switches on lights, then crosses up to window.* DICKIE *enters from up* L. *door.*)

DICKIE (*bitterly*). Hullo, Kate! (*He closes door.*)

CATHERINE (*closing curtains*). Hullo, Dickie. (*She turns to him.* DICKIE *crosses mournfully to door up* C. *She crosses to* DICKIE *up* C.) What's the matter? Edwina jilted you or something?

DICKIE. Haven't you heard? (CATH- ERINE *shakes her head.*) I'm being scratched from the Oxford Stakes at the end of the year.

CATHERINE. Oh, Dickie! I'm awfully sorry.

DICKIE. Did you know it was in the wind?

CATHERINE. I knew there was a risk —— (*She breaks away to up* R. C.)

DICKIE. You might have warned a fellow. I fell plumb into the old man's trap. My gosh, I could just about murder that little brother of mine. (*Bitterly.*) What's he have to go about pinching postal orders for? And why the hell does he have to get himself nabbed doing it? Silly little blighter![13] (DICKIE *goes out gloomily up* C. *He leaves door open. Front doorbell rings.* CATHERINE *imagines it is* JOHN *and quickly picks up her bag and goes to door up* C.)

CATHERINE (*going into hall; calling*). All right, Violet. It's only Mr. Wather- stone. I'll answer it. (CATHERINE *turns back into room. She picks up cloak, gloves and scarf from chair* L. *of door, then goes out up* C. *She closes door. Sound of voices in hall.* CATHERINE *enters up* C. *As she enters.*) I'm so sorry. I was expecting a friend. (DES- MOND *and* SIR ROBERT MORTON *follow her in.* DESMOND *carries brief case.* SIR ROBERT *is a man in the early forties; tall, thin, cadaverous and immensely elegant. He wears long overcoat and carries his hat. He looks rather a fop and his supercilious expression bears out this view.* CATHERINE *comes down* C. *Drops cloak, scarf and gloves over* GRACE'S *chair and continues to fire- place.* SIR ROBERT *passes* DESMOND *and comes to chair* L. *of the table* R. C.) Won't you sit down, Sir Robert? My father won't be long. (SIR ROBERT *bows slightly, and sits down on chair*

---

13 **blighter:** British slang for "chap" or "fellow."

L. *of table, still in his overcoat.*) Won't you sit here. (*She indicates* ARTHUR's *chair.*) It's far more comfortable.

SIR ROBERT. No, thank you.

DESMOND (*at* SIR ROBERT's L. *elbow, fussing*). Sir Robert has a most important dinner engagement, so we came a little early.

CATHERINE. I see.

DESMOND. I'm afraid he can only spare us a very few minutes of his most valuable time this evening. Of course, it's a long way for him to come—so far from his chambers[14]—and very good of him to do it, too, if I may say so. . . . (*He bows to* SIR ROBERT, *who bows slightly back.*)

CATHERINE. I know. I can assure you we're very conscious of it. (SIR ROBERT *gives her a quick look, and a faint smile.*)

DESMOND. Perhaps I had better advise your father of our presence——

CATHERINE. Yes, do, Desmond. You'll find him in his bedroom—having his leg rubbed.

DESMOND. Oh, I see. (DESMOND *goes out up* C. *A pause.*)

CATHERINE. Is there anything I can get you, Sir Robert? A whisky and soda, or a brandy?

SIR ROBERT. No, thank you.

CATHERINE. Will you smoke?

SIR ROBERT. No, thank you.

CATHERINE (*holding up her cigarette*). I hope you don't mind me smoking?

SIR ROBERT. Why should I?

CATHERINE. Some people find it shocking.

SIR ROBERT (*indifferently*). A lady in her own home is surely entitled to behave as she wishes. (*A pause.*)

CATHERINE. Won't you take your coat off, Sir Robert?

SIR ROBERT. No, thank you.

CATHERINE. You find it cold in here? I'm sorry.

SIR ROBERT. It's perfectly all right. (*Conversation languishes again.* SIR ROBERT *looks at his watch.*)

CATHERINE. What time are you dining?

SIR ROBERT. Eight o'clock.

CATHERINE. Far from here?

SIR ROBERT. Devonshire House.

CATHERINE. Oh. Then of course, you mustn't on any account be late.

SIR ROBERT. No. (*Another pause.*)

CATHERINE. I suppose you know the history of this case, do you, Sir Robert?

SIR ROBERT (*examining his nails*). I believe I have seen most of the relevant documents.

CATHERINE. Do you think we can bring the case into court by a collusive action?[15]

SIR ROBERT. I really have no idea——

CATHERINE. Curry and Curry seem to think that might hold——

SIR ROBERT. Do they? They are a very reliable firm. (CATHERINE *is on verge of losing her temper.*)

CATHERINE (*after a pause*). I'm rather surprised that a case of this sort should interest you, Sir Robert.

SIR ROBERT. Are you?

CATHERINE. It seems such a very trivial affair, compared to most of your great forensic[16] triumphs. (SIR ROBERT *does not reply.*) I was in court during your cross-examination of Len Rogers, in the Trades Union embezzlement case.

SIR ROBERT. Really?

CATHERINE. It was masterly.

SIR ROBERT. Thank you.

CATHERINE. I suppose you heard that he committed suicide—a few months ago?

---

14 **chambers:** law office.

15 **a collusive action:** charge there had been a secret agreement with intent to defraud.
16 **forensic:** argumentative; rhetorical.

SIR ROBERT. Yes. I had heard.

CATHERINE. Many people believed him innocent, you know.

SIR ROBERT. So I understand. (*After a faint pause.*) As it happens, however, he was guilty. (GRACE *comes in hastily up* C.)

GRACE (*coming down* C.). Sir Robert? My husband's so sorry to have kept you, but he's just coming. (SIR ROBERT *rises. He and* GRACE *shake hands.*)

SIR ROBERT. It's perfectly all right. How do you do?

CATHERINE. Sir Robert is dining at Devonshire House, Mother.

GRACE. Oh, really? Oh, then you have to be punctual, of course, I do see that. It's the politeness of princes, isn't it? (*She crosses downstage to lamp by desk and switches it on.*)

SIR ROBERT. So they say.

GRACE. In this case, the other way round, of course. Ah, I think I hear my husband on the stairs. I hope Catherine entertained you all right?

SIR ROBERT (*with a faint bow to* CATHERINE). Very well, thank you. (ARTHUR *comes in up* C. DESMOND *follows him in.*)

ARTHUR (*coming down* C.). Sir Robert? I am Arthur Winslow.

SIR ROBERT. How do you do?

ARTHUR. I understand you are rather pressed for time. (DESMOND *comes above table* R. C.)

GRACE. Yes. He's dining at Devonshire House. (*She moves round end of table to* DESMOND.)

ARTHUR. Are you, indeed? My son should be down in a minute. I expect you will wish to examine him. (GRACE *takes cigarette box and ashtray from table. She crosses upstage and puts them on mantelpiece.*)

SIR ROBERT (*indifferently*). Just a few questions. I fear that is all I will have time for this evening.

ARTHUR. I am rather sorry to hear that. He has made the journey especially from school for this interview and I was hoping that by the end of it, I should know definitely yes or no if you would accept the brief. (GRACE *sits in armchair down* L.)

DESMOND (*pacifically*). Well, perhaps Sir Robert would consent to finish his examination some other time? (*He opens his brief case on table and takes out documents.*)

SIR ROBERT. It might be arranged.

ARTHUR. Tomorrow?

SIR ROBERT. Tomorrow is impossible. I am in court all the morning, and in the House of Commons for the rest of the day. (*Carelessly.*) If a further examination should prove necessary it will have to be some time next week.

ARTHUR. I see. Will you forgive me if I sit down? (*Moves to his chair and sits.*) Curry has been telling me you think it might be possible to proceed by Petition of Right. (SIR ROBERT *sits* L. *of table.*)

CATHERINE. What's a Petition of Right?

DESMOND. Well—granting the assumption that the Admiralty, as the Crown, can do no wrong——

CATHERINE (*murmuring*). I thought that was exactly the assumption we refused to grant?

DESMOND. In law, I mean. Now a subject can sue the Crown, nevertheless, by Petition of Right, redress[17] being granted as a matter of grace—and the custom is for the Attorney-General —on behalf of the King—to endorse the Petition, and allow the case to come to court. (*He moves documents along table in front of* SIR ROBERT.)

SIR ROBERT. It is interesting to note that the exact words he uses on such

17 redress (rē′drĕs): amends.

occasions are: Let Right be done.

ARTHUR. Let Right be done. I like that phrase, sir.

SIR ROBERT. It has a certain ring about it—has it not? (*Languidly.*) Let Right be done. (RONNIE *comes in up* C. *He is in an Eton suit,*[18] *looking very spick and span.*)

ARTHUR. This is my son, Ronald. Ronnie, this is Sir Robert Morton.

RONNIE (*coming down* C.). How do you do, sir? (*Shakes hands with* SIR ROBERT.)

ARTHUR. He is going to ask you a few questions. You must answer them all truthfully—as you always have. (*Begins to struggle out of his chair.*) I expect you would like us to leave——

SIR ROBERT. No, provided, of course, that you don't interrupt. (*To* CATHERINE.) Miss Winslow, will you sit down, please? (CATHERINE *sits on pouffe*[19] *by fireplace. To* RONNIE.) Will you stand at the table, facing me? (RONNIE *moves round table and stands above chair* R. *of it.*) That's right. (DESMOND *crosses behind* SIR ROBERT *to* L. C. *He faces* RONNIE *across table and begins examination very quietly.*) How old are you?

RONNIE. Fourteen and seven months.

SIR ROBERT. You were, then, thirteen and ten months old when you left Osborne; is that right?

RONNIE. Yes, sir.

SIR ROBERT. Now I would like you to cast your mind back to July 7th of last year. Will you tell me in your own words exactly what happened to you on that day?

RONNIE. All right. Well, it was a half-holiday, so we didn't have any work after dinner——

SIR ROBERT. Dinner?

RONNIE. Yes. At one o'clock. Until Prep. at seven——

SIR ROBERT. Prep. at seven?

RONNIE. Yes. Just before dinner I went to the Chief Petty Officer and asked him to let me have fifteen and six out of what I had in the College Bank——

SIR ROBERT. Why did you do that?

RONNIE. I wanted to buy an air pistol.

SIR ROBERT. Which cost fifteen and six?

RONNIE. Yes, sir.

SIR ROBERT. And how much money did you have in the College Bank at the time?

RONNIE. Two pounds three shillings.

ARTHUR. So you see, sir, what incentive could there possibly be for him to steal five shillings?

SIR ROBERT (*coldly*). I must ask you to be good enough not to interrupt me, sir. (*To* RONNIE.) After you had withdrawn the fifteen and six, what did you do?

RONNIE. I had dinner.

SIR ROBERT. Then what?

RONNIE. I went to the locker-room and put the fifteen and six in my locker.

SIR ROBERT. Yes. Then?

RONNIE. I went to get permission to go down to the post office. Then I went to the locker-room again, got out my money, and went down to the post office.

SIR ROBERT. I see. Go on.

RONNIE. I bought my postal order——

SIR ROBERT. For fifteen and six?

RONNIE. Yes. Then I went back to college. Then I met Elliott minor,[20] and he said: "I say, isn't it rot? Someone's broken into my locker and

---

18 Eton suit: suit with a short coat and a large turnover collar.

19 pouffe: a piece of furniture, usually circular, with cushioned seats.

20 Elliott minor: the younger of two Elliott boys in the same school.

pinched a postal order. I've reported it to the P.O."[21]

Sir Robert. Those were Elliott minor's exact words?

Ronnie. He might have used another word for rot——

Sir Robert. I see. Continue——

Ronnie. Well then, just before Prep., I was told to go along and see Commander Flower. The woman from the post office was there, and the Commander said: "Is this the boy?" and she said, "It might be. I can't be sure. They all look so much alike."

Arthur. You see? She couldn't identify him. (Sir Robert *glares at* Arthur.)

Sir Robert (*to* Ronnie). Go on.

Ronnie. Then she said: "I only know that the boy who bought a postal order for fifteen and six was the same boy that cashed one for five shillings." So the Commander said: "Did you buy a postal order for fifteen and six?" And I said, "Yes," and then they made me write Elliott minor's name on an envelope, and compared it to the signature on the postal order—then they sent me to the sanatorium, and ten days later I was sacked—I mean—expelled.

Sir Robert. I see. (*He rises. Quietly.*) Did you cash a postal order belonging to Elliott minor for five shillings?

Ronnie. No, sir.

Sir Robert. Did you break into his locker and steal it?

Ronnie. No, sir. (Dickie *enters up* C. *Stands furtively in doorway, not knowing whether to come in or go out.*)

Sir Robert. And that is the truth, the whole truth, and nothing but the truth?

Ronnie. Yes, sir. (Arthur *waves* Dickie *impatiently to come and stand behind his chair.*)

21 P.O.: petty officer.

Sir Robert. Right. When the Commander asked you to write Elliott's name on an envelope, how did you write it? With Christian name or initials?

Ronnie. I wrote: "Charles K. Elliott."

Sir Robert. Charles K. Elliott. Did you by any chance happen to see the forged postal order in the Commander's office?

Ronnie. Oh, yes. The Commander showed it to me.

Sir Robert. Before or after you had written Elliott's name on the envelope?

Ronnie. After.

Sir Robert. After. And did you happen to see how Elliott's name was written on the postal order?

Ronnie. Yes, sir. The same.

Sir Robert. The same? Charles K. Elliott?

Ronnie. Yes, sir.

Sir Robert. When you wrote on the envelope—what made you choose that particular form?

Ronnie. That was the way he usually signed his name.

Sir Robert. How did you know?

Ronnie. Well—he was a friend of mine——

Sir Robert. That is no answer. How did you know?

Ronnie. I'd seen him sign things.

Sir Robert. What things?

Ronnie. Oh—ordinary things.

Sir Robert. I repeat—what things?

Ronnie (*reluctantly*). Bits of paper.

Sir Robert. Bits of paper? And why did he sign his name on bits of paper?

Ronnie. I don't know.

Sir Robert. You do know. Why did he sign his name on bits of paper?

Ronnie. He was practicing his signature.

Sir Robert. And you saw him?

Ronnie. Yes.

SIR ROBERT. Did he know you saw him?

RONNIE. Well—yes——

SIR ROBERT. In other words, he showed you exactly how he wrote his signature?

RONNIE. Yes. I suppose he did.

SIR ROBERT. Did you practice writing it yourself?

RONNIE. I might have done.

SIR ROBERT. What do you mean, you might have done? Did you, or did you not?

RONNIE. Yes.

ARTHUR (*sharply*). Ronnie! You never told me that.

RONNIE. It was only for a joke——

SIR ROBERT. Never mind whether it was for a joke or not. The fact is, you practiced forging Elliott's signature.

RONNIE. It wasn't forging——

SIR ROBERT. What do you call it, then?

RONNIE. Writing.

SIR ROBERT. Very well. Writing. Whoever stole the postal order and cashed it also *wrote* Elliott's signature, didn't he?

RONNIE. Yes.

SIR ROBERT. And, oddly enough, in the exact form in which you had earlier been practicing *writing* his signature.

RONNIE (*indignantly*). I say! Which side are you on?

SIR ROBERT (*snarling*). Don't be impertinent! (*He consults a document.*) Are you aware that the Admiralty sent up the forged postal order to Mr. Ridgley-Pearce—the greatest handwriting expert in England?

RONNIE. Yes.

SIR ROBERT. And you know that Mr. Ridgley-Pearce affirmed that there was no doubt that the signature on the postal order and the signature you wrote on the envelope were by one and the same hand?

RONNIE. Yes.

SIR ROBERT. And you still say that you didn't forge that signature?

RONNIE. Yes, I do.

SIR ROBERT. In other words, Mr. Ridgley-Pearce doesn't know his job?

RONNIE. Well, he's wrong, anyway.

SIR ROBERT. When you went into the locker-room after lunch, were you alone?

RONNIE. I don't remember.

SIR ROBERT. I think you do. Were you alone in the locker-room?

RONNIE. Yes.

SIR ROBERT. And you knew which was Elliott's locker?

RONNIE. Yes. Of course.

SIR ROBERT. Why did you go in there at all?

RONNIE. I've told you. To put my fifteen and six away.

SIR ROBERT. Why?

RONNIE. I thought it would be safer.

SIR ROBERT. Why safer than your pocket?

RONNIE. I don't know.

SIR ROBERT. You had it in your pocket at dinnertime. Why this sudden fear for its safety?

RONNIE (*plainly rattled*). I tell you I don't know——

SIR ROBERT. It was rather an odd thing to do, wasn't it? The money was perfectly safe in your pocket. Why did you suddenly feel yourself impelled to put it away in your locker?

RONNIE (*almost shouting*). I don't know.

SIR ROBERT. Was it because you knew you would be alone in the locker-room at that time?

RONNIE. No.

SIR ROBERT. Where was Elliott's locker in relation to yours?

RONNIE. Next to it but one.

SIR ROBERT. Next but one. What time did Elliott put his postal order in his locker?

RONNIE. I don't know. I didn't even know he had a postal order in his locker. I didn't know he had a postal order at all.

SIR ROBERT. Yet you say he was a great friend of yours——

RONNIE. He didn't tell me he had one.

SIR ROBERT. How very secretive of him. (*Makes note on document.*) What time did you go to the locker-room?

RONNIE. I don't remember.

SIR ROBERT. Was it directly after dinner?

RONNIE. Yes, I think so.

SIR ROBERT. What did you do after leaving the locker-room?

RONNIE. I've told you. I went for permission to go to the post office.

SIR ROBERT. What time was that?

RONNIE. About a quarter past two.

SIR ROBERT. Dinner is over at a quarter to two. Which means that you were alone in the locker-room for half an hour?

RONNIE. I wasn't there all that time——

SIR ROBERT. How long were you there?

RONNIE. About five minutes.

SIR ROBERT. What were you doing for the other twenty-five?

RONNIE. I don't remember.

SIR ROBERT. It's odd that your memory is so good about some things and so bad about others——

RONNIE. Perhaps I waited outside the C.O.'s[22] office.

SIR ROBERT (*with searing sarcasm*). Perhaps you waited outside the C.O.'s office. And perhaps no one saw you there, either?

RONNIE. No. I don't think they did.

SIR ROBERT. What were you thinking

22 C.O.'s: Commanding Officer's.

about outside the C.O.'s office for twenty-five minutes?

RONNIE (*wildly*). I don't even know if I was there. I can't remember. Perhaps I wasn't there at all.

SIR ROBERT. No. Perhaps you were still in the locker-room rifling Elliott's locker——

ARTHUR (*indignantly*). Sir Robert, I must ask you——

SIR ROBERT. Quiet! (RONNIE *makes a slight move in to table.*)

RONNIE. I remember now. I remember. Someone did see me outside the C.O.'s office. A chap called Casey. I remember I spoke to him.

SIR ROBERT. What did you say?

RONNIE. I said: "Come down to the post office with me. I'm going to cash a postal order."

SIR ROBERT (*triumphantly*). *Cash* a postal order!

RONNIE. I mean get.

SIR ROBERT. You said "cash." Why did you say "cash" if you meant get?

RONNIE. I don't know.

SIR ROBERT. I suggest "cash" was the truth.

RONNIE. No, no. It wasn't. It wasn't really. You're muddling me.

SIR ROBERT. You seem easily muddled. How many other lies have you told?

RONNIE. None. Really I haven't.

SIR ROBERT (*bending forward malevolently*). I suggest your whole testimony is a lie.

RONNIE. No! It's the truth.

SIR ROBERT. I suggest there is barely one single word of truth in anything you have said either to me, or to the judge advocate, or to the Commander. I suggest that you broke into Elliott's locker, that you stole the postal order for five shillings belonging to Elliott, and you cashed it by means of forging his name.

RONNIE (*wailing*). I didn't. I didn't.

SIR ROBERT. I suggest that you did it for a joke, meaning to give Elliott the five shillings back, but that when you met him and he said he had reported the matter that you got frightened and decided to keep quiet.

RONNIE. No, no, no. It isn't true.

SIR ROBERT. I suggest that by continuing to deny your guilt you are causing great hardship to your own family, and considerable annoyance to high and important persons in this country——

CATHERINE (*on her feet*). That's a disgraceful thing to say!

ARTHUR (*rising*). I agree.

SIR ROBERT (*leaning forward and glaring at* RONNIE *with utmost venom*). I suggest that the time has at last come for you to undo some of the misery you have caused by confessing to us all now that you are a forger, a liar and a thief. (GRACE *rises.*)

RONNIE (*in tears*). I'm not! I'm not! I'm not! I didn't do it. (GRACE *crosses swiftly down to* RONNIE *and envelops him.*)

ARTHUR. This is outrageous, sir. (DESMOND *crosses above* SIR ROBERT *to table and collects documents.* JOHN *enters up* C., *dressed in evening clothes.*)

JOHN. Kate, dear, I'm late. I'm terribly sorry—— (*He stops short as he takes in the scene.* RONNIE *is sobbing hysterically on his mother's breast.* ARTHUR *and* CATHERINE *are glaring indignantly at* SIR ROBERT, *who is engaged in putting his papers together.*)

SIR ROBERT (*to* DESMOND). Can I drop you anywhere? My car is at the door.

DESMOND. Er—no—I thank you.

SIR ROBERT (*carelessly*). Well, send all this stuff round to my chambers tomorrow morning, will you?

DESMOND. But—but will you need it now?

SIR ROBERT. Oh, yes. The boy is plainly innocent. I accept the brief. (SIR ROBERT *bows to* ARTHUR *and* CATHERINE *and walks languidly to door past the bewildered* JOHN, *to whom he gives a polite nod as he goes out.* RONNIE *continues to sob hysterically.*)

QUICK CURTAIN

Understanding the Play

1. Nine months pass between scenes 1 and 2. How does the playwright quickly tell the audience what has happened during them? What is the information he gives?
2. Conflict is an essential ingredient of drama. What conflicting attitudes toward Ronnie's case are introduced by the expository material at the beginning of this scene?
3. How does the author reveal that the family is hard pressed financially? What additional conflict is introduced by this information?
4. How is the lady reporter characterized? What function does she serve in the play?
5. What does the reader learn about Sir Robert Morton before he comes on stage? What parts of the information about him are opinion? What parts are fact?
6. As a result of the attitude held by various other characters toward Sir Robert and of his conduct of Ronnie's examination, what attitude do you as a reader have toward him? What kind of man do you believe him to be and what evidence do you find in this scene for your opinions?
7. What doubtful points are there in Ronnie's story as he tells it to Sir Robert?
8. In what way is the closing of this scene parallel to the close of scene 1?
9. With what question(s) is the audience left at the end of this scene?

Developing Language Skills

1. Have a panel of three explain the contrasting attitudes of Catherine, Dickie, and Ronnie toward the importance of the case as revealed in the preceding scene. The panel should use specific lines from the play to illustrate the attitude of each.
2. One of Rattigan's main tasks in using Ronnie's expulsion from school as the cause of the many conflicts in this play is to make the incident seem important enough to have the consequences that it does. If the audience feels, as some of the characters in the play do, that it is merely a trivial incident of no significance, then the point of the whole play is lost.
    Write a paragraph in which you consider how the playwright introduces this problem and how he deals with it during Act I.

ACT II

SCENE 1

Same. Nine months later. An evening in January, about ten-thirty. ARTHUR *is sitting in his armchair reading aloud from evening paper. Listening to him are* RONNIE *and* GRACE, *though neither seems to be doing so with much concentration.* RONNIE *is sitting in armchair down* L., *finding it hard to keep his eyes open and* GRACE, *sitting in her chair, darning, has evidently other and, to her, more important matters on her mind. The only light in the room comes from fire, and lamp above* ARTHUR'S *chair.*

ARTHUR (*reading*). "–the Admiralty, during the whole of this long-drawn-out dispute, have at no time acted hastily or ill-advisedly, and it is a matter of mere histrionic hyperbole[1] for the Right Honorable and learned gentleman opposite to characterize the conduct of my department as that of callousness so inhuman as to amount to deliberate malice towards the boy Winslow. Such unfounded accusations I can well choose to ignore. (An Honorable Member: "You can't.") Honorable Members opposite may interrupt as much as they please, but I repeat—there is nothing whatever that the Admiralty has done, or failed to do, in the case of this cadet for which I, as First Lord, need to apologize. (Further Opposition interruptions.)" (*He stops reading and looks up.*) I must say it looks as if the First Lord's having rather a rough passage—— (ARTHUR *breaks off, noticing* RONNIE'S *head has fallen back on cushions and he is asleep. At*

RONNIE.) I trust my reading isn't keeping you awake. (*No answer.*) I say I trust my reading isn't keeping you awake! (*Again no answer. Helplessly.*) Grace!

GRACE. My poor sleepy little lamb! It's long past his bedtime, Arthur.

ARTHUR. Grace, dear—at this very moment your poor sleepy little lamb is the subject of a very violent and heated debate in the House of Commons. I should have thought, in the circumstances, it might have been possible for him to contrive to stay awake for a few minutes past his bedtime——

GRACE. I expect he's over-excited —— (ARTHUR *and* GRACE *both look at the tranquilly oblivious form.*)

ARTHUR. A picture of over-excitement. (*Sharply.*) Ronnie! Ronnie! (*No answer.*) Ronnie!

RONNIE (*opening his eyes*). Yes, Father?

ARTHUR. I am reading the account of the debate. Would you like to listen, or would you rather go to bed?

RONNIE. Oh, I'd like to listen, of course, Father. I was listening, too, only I had my eyes shut——

ARTHUR. Very well. (*He reads.*) "The First Lord continued amid further interruptions: the chief point of criticism against the Admiralty appears to center in the purely legal question of the Petition of Right brought by Mr. Arthur Winslow and the Admiralty's demurrer[2] thereto. Sir Robert Morton has made great play with his eloquent reference to the liberty of the individual menaced, as he puts it, by the new despotism of bureaucracy—and I was as moved as any Honorable Member opposite by his resonant use of the words: "Let Right be done"—the time-

---

1 **histrionic hyperbole** (hĭ pûr′bə lē′): theatrical overstatement.

2 **demurrer** (dĭ mûr′ər): a legal plea objecting to the case proceeding further.

honored phrase with which, in his opinion, the Attorney-General should, without question, have endorsed Mr. Winslow's Petition of Right. Nevertheless, the matter is not nearly as simple as he appears to imagine. Cadet Ronald Winslow was a servant of the Crown, and has therefore no more right than any other member of His Majesty's forces—to sue the Crown in open court. To allow him to do so—would undoubtedly raise the most dangerous precedents. There is no doubt whatever in my mind that in certain cases private rights may have to be sacrificed for the public good——" (*He looks up.*) And what other excuse, pray, did Charles I make for ship money?[3] (RONNIE, *after a manful attempt to keep his eyes open by self-pinchings and other devices, has once more succumbed to oblivion. Sharply.*) Ronnie! Ronnie! (RONNIE *stirs, turns over, slides more comfortably into cushions.*) Would you believe it!

GRACE. He's dead tired. I'd better take him up to his bed——

ARTHUR. No, if he must sleep, let him sleep there.

GRACE. Oh, but he'd be much more comfy in his little bed——

ARTHUR. I dare say; but the debate continues and until it's ended the cause of it all will certainly not make himself comfy in his little bed. (VIOLET *comes in up* C.)

VIOLET (*to* ARTHUR). There are three more reporters in the hall, sir. Want to see you very urgently. Shall I let them in?

ARTHUR. No. Certainly not. I issued a statement yesterday. Until the debate is over I have nothing more to say.

3 Charles I . . . ship money: a tax levied by Charles I for the protection of the English coast and considered unfair by many people.

VIOLET. Yes, sir. That's what I told them, but they wouldn't go.

ARTHUR. Well, make them. Use force, if necessary.

VIOLET. Yes, sir. And shall I cut some sandwiches for Miss Catherine, as she missed her dinner?

GRACE. Yes, Violet. Good idea.

VIOLET. Yes, ma'am. (VIOLET *goes out up* C. *As she closes door, to unseen persons in hall.*) No. No good. No more statements.

ARTHUR. Grace, dear——

GRACE. Yes?

ARTHUR. I fancy this might be a good opportunity of talking to Violet.

GRACE (*quite firmly*). No, dear.

ARTHUR. Meaning that it isn't a good opportunity? Or meaning that you have no intention at all of ever talking to Violet?

GRACE. I'll do it one day, Arthur. Tomorrow, perhaps. Not now.

ARTHUR. I believe you'd do better to grasp the nettle. Delay only adds to your worries——

GRACE (*bitterly*). My worries? What do you know about my worries? (*She rises with darning work in her hand.*)

ARTHUR. A good deal, Grace. But I feel they would be a lot lessened if you faced the situation squarely.

GRACE. It's easy for you to talk, Arthur. You don't have to do it.

ARTHUR. I will, if you like.

GRACE. No, dear. (*She picks up workbasket on pouffe and goes up to workbasket by door, into which she puts smaller basket and darning work.*)

ARTHUR. If you explain the dilemma to her carefully—if you even show her the figures I jotted down for you yesterday—I venture to think you won't find her unreasonable.

GRACE. It won't be easy for her to find another place.

234   DRAMA

ARTHUR. We'll give her an excellent reference.

GRACE. That won't alter the fact that she's never been properly trained as a parlormaid and—well—you know yourself how we're always having to explain her to people. No, Arthur, I don't mind how many figures she's shown, it's a brutal thing to do. (*Comes down to* ARTHUR'S R.)

ARTHUR. Facts are brutal things.

GRACE (*a shade hysterically*). Facts? I don't think I know what facts are any more—— (*Turns away toward* C.)

ARTHUR. The facts at this moment are that we have a half of the income we had a year ago and we're living at nearly the same rate. However you look at it that's bad economics——

GRACE (*turning to him*). I'm not talking about economics, Arthur—I'm talking about ordinary, common or garden facts—things we took for granted a year ago and which now don't seem to matter any more.

ARTHUR. Such as?

GRACE (*moving to* ARTHUR *with rising voice*). Such as a happy home and peace and quiet and an ordinary respectable life, and some sort of future for us and our children. In the last year you've thrown all that overboard, Arthur. There's your return for it, I suppose—(*She indicates headline in paper.*)—and it's all very exciting and important, I'm sure, but it doesn't bring back any of the things that we've lost —— (RONNIE *stirs in his sleep. She lowers her voice.*) I can only pray to God that you know what you're doing. (*She turns to pouffe and picks up two pieces of underwear.*)

ARTHUR (*after a pause; rising*). I know exactly what I'm doing, Grace. I'm going to publish my son's innocence before the world, and for that end I am not prepared to weigh the cost.

GRACE (*taking step toward* ARTHUR). But the cost may be out of all proportion——

ARTHUR. It may be. That doesn't concern me. I hate heroics, Grace, but you force me to say this. An injustice has been done. I am going to set it right, and there is no sacrifice in the world I am not prepared to make in order to do so.

GRACE (*with sudden violence*). Oh, I wish I could see the sense of it all! (*Points to* RONNIE.) He's perfectly happy, at a good school, doing very well. No one need ever have known about Osborne, if you hadn't gone and shouted it out to the whole world. As it is, whatever happens now, he'll go through the rest of his life as the boy in that Winslow case—the boy who stole that postal order——

ARTHUR (*grimly*). The boy didn't steal that postal order.

GRACE (*wearily*). What's the difference? When millions are talking and gossiping about him a "did" or a "didn't" hardly matters. The Winslow boy is bad enough. You talk about sacrificing everything for him; but when he's grown up he won't thank you for it, Arthur—even though you've given your life to—publish his innocence, as you call it. (ARTHUR *makes an impatient gesture.*) Yes, Arthur—your life. You talk gaily about arthritis and a touch of gout and old age and the rest of it, but you know as well as any of the doctors what really is the matter with you. (*Nearly in tears.*) You're destroying yourself, Arthur, and me and your family besides—and for what, I'd like to know? I've asked you and Kate to tell me a hundred times—but you never can. For what, Arthur?

ARTHUR (*quietly*). For justice, Grace.

GRACE. That sounds very noble. Are you sure it's true? Are you sure it isn't

just plain pride and self-importance and sheer brute stubbornness?

ARTHUR (*putting a hand out to her*). No, Grace. I don't think it is. I really don't think it is——

GRACE. No. This time I'm not going to cry and say I'm sorry, and make it all up again. I can stand anything if there is a reason for it. But for no reason at all, it's unfair to ask so much of me. It's unfair. . . . (GRACE *breaks down, moves swiftly to door up* C. *and goes out.* RONNIE *opens his eyes.* ARTHUR *makes a move as though he is about to follow* GRACE.)

RONNIE. What's the matter, Father?

ARTHUR (*turning up* C.). Your mother is a little upset.

RONNIE (*drowsily*). Why? Aren't things going well?

ARTHUR. Oh, yes. (*Murmuring.*) Very well. Very well, indeed. (RONNIE *contentedly closes his eyes again.* ARTHUR *comes down to his chair and*

sits. *Gently.*) You'd better go to bed now, Ronnie. You'll be more comfortable. (*He sees* RONNIE *is asleep again. Leans forward and makes as if to wake him, then shrugs shoulders and sits back.* VIOLET *comes in up* C. *with sandwiches on a plate, and letter on a salver. She puts sandwiches on table* R. C.; *then crosses to* ARTHUR, *hands him letter.* ARTHUR *puts it down on table beside him without opening it.* VIOLET *turns up* C.) Thank you, Violet. Oh, Violet——

VIOLET (*turning up* C. *placidly*). Yes, sir?

ARTHUR. How long have you been with us?

VIOLET. Twenty-four years come April, sir.

ARTHUR. As long as that?

VIOLET. Yes, sir. Miss Kate was that high when I first came (*She indicates a small child.*) and Mr. Dickie hadn't even been thought of——

236

ARTHUR. I remember your coming to us, now. I remember it well. What do you think of this case, Violet?

VIOLET. A fine old rumpus that is, and no mistake.

ARTHUR. It is, isn't it? A fine old rumpus.

VIOLET. There was a bit in the *Evening News.* Did you read it, sir?

ARTHUR. No. What did it say?

VIOLET. Oh, about how it was a fuss about nothing and a shocking waste of the Government's time, but how it was a good thing all the same because it could only happen in England——

ARTHUR. There seems to be a certain lack of logic in that argument——

VIOLET. Well, perhaps they put it a bit different, sir. Still, that's what it said all right. And when you think it's all because of our Master Ronnie I have to laugh about it sometimes, I really do. Wasting the Government's time at his age! I never did. Well, wonders will never cease.

ARTHUR. I know. Wonders will never cease.

VIOLET. Well—would that be all, sir?

ARTHUR (*after slight pause*). Yes, Violet. That'll be all. (VIOLET *opens door up* C. *and comes face to face with* CATHERINE.)

CATHERINE. Good evening, Violet.

VIOLET. Good evening, Miss. (CATHERINE *comes in.* VIOLET *switches on lights, then goes out, shutting door.*)

CATHERINE (*coming down to* ARTHUR). Hullo, Father. (*She kisses him. Indicates* RONNIE.) An Honorable Member described *that* this evening as a piteous little figure, crying aloud to humanity for justice and redress. I wish he could see him now.

ARTHUR (*testily*). It's long past his bedtime. What's happened? Is the debate over?

CATHERINE (*going up* R. *and putting*

cloak *and gloves on settee*). As good as. The First Lord gave an assurance that in future there would be no inquiry at Osborne or Dartmouth[4] without informing the parents first. That seemed to satisfy most Members——

ARTHUR. But what about our case? Is he going to allow us a fair trial?

CATHERINE. Apparently not.

ARTHUR. But that's iniquitous. I thought he would be forced to——

CATHERINE. I thought so, too. The House evidently thought otherwise.

ARTHUR. Will there be a division?[5]

CATHERINE. There may be. If there is the Government will win.

ARTHUR. What is the motion?

CATHERINE. (*Coming down to table* R. C.) To reduce the First Lord's salary by a hundred pounds. (*With a faint smile.*) Naturally, no one really wants to do that. (*She sees sandwiches.*) Are those for me?

ARTHUR. Yes. (CATHERINE *starts to eat sandwiches.*) So we're back where we started, then?

CATHERINE. It looks like it.

ARTHUR. The debate has done us no good at all?

CATHERINE. It's aired the case a little, perhaps. A few more thousand people will say to each other at breakfast tomorrow: "That boy ought to be allowed a fair trial." (*She sits in chair* L. *of table.*)

ARTHUR. What's the good of that, if they can't make themselves heard?

CATHERINE. I think they can—given time.

ARTHUR. Given time? (*He pauses.*) But didn't Sir Robert make any protest when the First Lord refused a trial?

CATHERINE. Not a verbal protest. Something far more spectacular and dramatic. He'd had his feet on the

4 **Dartmouth:** another British naval college.
5 **division:** vote.

Treasury table and his hat over his eyes, during most of the First Lord's speech—and suddenly got up very deliberately, glared at the First Lord, threw a whole bundle of notes on the floor, and stalked out of the House. It made a magnificent effect. If I hadn't known I could have sworn he was genuinely indignant——

ARTHUR. Of course he was genuinely indignant. So would any man of feeling be.

CATHERINE. Sir Robert, Father dear, is not a man of feeling. I don't think any emotion at all can stir that fishy heart——

ARTHUR. Except, perhaps, a single-minded love of justice.

CATHERINE. Nonsense. A single-minded love of Sir Robert Morton.

ARTHUR. You're very ungrateful to him, considering all he's done for us these last months—— (CATHERINE *rises and turns up* C.)

CATHERINE. I'm not ungrateful, Father. He's been wonderful—I admit it freely. No one could have fought a harder fight.

ARTHUR. Well, then——

CATHERINE. It's only his motives I question. At least I don't question them at all. I know them.

ARTHUR. What are they?

CATHERINE. First—publicity—you know—"Look at me, the staunch defender of the little man"—and then second—a nice popular stick to beat the Government with. Both very useful to an ambitious man. Luckily for him we've provided them. (*Comes down a step.*)

ARTHUR. Luckily for us, too, Kate.

CATHERINE. Oh, I agree. But don't fool yourself about him, Father, for all that. The man is a fish, a hard, cold-blooded, supercilious, sneering fish. (VIOLET *enters up* C.)

VIOLET (*announcing*). Sir Robert Morton. (CATHERINE *chokes over her sandwich. Moves above chair* L. *of table.* SIR ROBERT *comes in up* C.)

SIR ROBERT. Good evening. (*He comes down* C.)

CATHERINE (*still choking*). Good evening.

SIR ROBERT. Something gone down the wrong way?

CATHERINE. Yes.

SIR ROBERT. May I assist? (*He pats her on back.*)

CATHERINE. Thank you.

SIR ROBERT (*to* ARTHUR). Good evening, sir. I thought I would call, and give you an account of the day's proceedings, but I see your daughter has forestalled me.

CATHERINE. Did you know I was in the gallery?

SIR ROBERT (*gallantly*). In such a charming hat, how could I have missed you?

ARTHUR. It was very good of you to call, sir, nevertheless.

SIR ROBERT (*seeing* RONNIE). Ah. The *casus belli*[6]—dormant—— (ARTHUR *rises and stretches across to wake* RONNIE.) No, no, I beg of you. Please do not disturb his innocent slumbers.

CATHERINE. *Innocent* slumbers?

SIR ROBERT. Exactly. Besides, I fear since our first encounter he is, rather pardonably, a trifle nervous of me.

CATHERINE (*sitting* L. *of table*). Will you betray a technical secret, Sir Robert? What happened in that first examination to make you so sure of his innocence?

SIR ROBERT. Three things. First of all, he made far too many damaging admissions. A guilty person would have been much more careful—much more on his guard. Secondly, I laid

6 casus belli (kā′səs bĕl′ī): reason for war.

him a trap; and thirdly, left him a loop-hole. Anyone who was guilty would have fallen into the one and darted through the other. He did neither.

CATHERINE. The trap was to ask him suddenly what time Elliott put the postal order in his locker. Wasn't it?

SIR ROBERT. Yes.

ARTHUR. And the loophole?

SIR ROBERT. I then suggested to him that he had stolen the postal order for a joke—which, had he been guilty he would surely have admitted to as being the lesser of two evils.

CATHERINE. I see. It was very cleverly thought out.

SIR ROBERT (*with a little bow*). Thank you.

ARTHUR. May we offer you some refreshment, Sir Robert? A whisky and soda?

SIR ROBERT. No, thank you. Nothing at all. (*Sits in* GRACE'*s chair and puts one foot on pouffe.*)

ARTHUR. My daughter has told me of your demonstration during the First Lord's speech. She described it as—magnificent.

SIR ROBERT (*with glance at* CATHERINE). Did she? That was good of her. It's a very old trick, you know. I've done it, many times in the Courts. It's nearly always surprisingly effective —— (CATHERINE *catches her father's eye and nods triumphantly. To* CATHERINE.) Was the First Lord at all put out by it—did you notice?

CATHERINE. How could he have failed to be? (*She rises and crosses to* ARTHUR.) I wish you could have seen it, Father—it was—— (*She notices letter on table beside* ARTHUR *and snatches it up with a sudden gesture. She examines envelope.*) When did this come?

ARTHUR. A few minutes ago. Do you know the writing?

CATHERINE. Yes. (*She puts letter back on table.*)

ARTHUR. Whose is it?

CATHERINE. I shouldn't bother to read it, if I were you. (ARTHUR *looks at her, puzzled, then takes up letter.*)

ARTHUR (*to* SIR ROBERT). Will you forgive me?

SIR ROBERT. Of course. (ARTHUR *opens letter and begins to read.* CATHERINE *watches him for a moment; then sits on arm of his chair and turns with a certain forced liveliness to* SIR ROBERT.)

CATHERINE. Well, what do you think the next step should be?

SIR ROBERT. I have already been considering that, Miss Winslow—I believe that perhaps the best plan would be to renew our efforts to get the Director of Public Prosecutions to act.

CATHERINE (*with one eye on her father*). But do you think there's any chance of that?

SIR ROBERT. Oh, yes. In the main it will chiefly be a question of making ourselves a confounded nuisance——

CATHERINE. We've certainly done that quite successfully so far, thanks to you ——

SIR ROBERT (*suavely*). Ah. That is perhaps the only quality I was born with—the ability to make myself a confounded nuisance. (*He, too, has his eyes on* ARTHUR, *sensing something amiss.* ARTHUR *finishes reading letter.*)

CATHERINE (*with false vivacity*). Father—Sir Robert thinks we might get the Director of Public Prosecutions to act.

ARTHUR. What?

SIR ROBERT. We were discussing how to proceed with the case——

ARTHUR. The case? (*He stares a little blankly, from the one to the other.*) Yes. We must think of that, mustn't we? (*He pauses.*) How to proceed with the case? (*To* SIR ROBERT, *abruptly.*) I'm afraid I don't think, all things considered, that much purpose would be served by going on—— (*He hands letter to* CATHERINE. SIR ROBERT *stares blankly at* ARTHUR. CATHERINE *crosses up* R., *reading letter.*)

SIR ROBERT (*with sudden change of tone*). Of course we must go on.

ARTHUR (*in a low voice*). It is not for you to choose, sir. The choice is mine.

SIR ROBERT (*harshly*). Then you must reconsider it. To give up now would be insane.

ARTHUR. Insane? My sanity has already been called in question tonight —for carrying the case as far as I have.

SIR ROBERT. Whatever the contents of that letter—or whatever has happened to make you lose heart, I insist that we continue the fight——

ARTHUR. Insist? We? It is my fight —my fight alone—and it is for me alone to judge when the time has come to give up.

SIR ROBERT (*violently*). Give up? But why give up? In Heaven's name, man, why? (*Rises and faces* ARTHUR.)

ARTHUR (*slowly*). I have made many sacrifices for this case. Some of them I had no right to make, but I made them, none the less. But there is a limit, and I have reached it. I am sorry, Sir Robert. More sorry, perhaps, than you are, but the Winslow case is now closed.

SIR ROBERT. Balderdash![7] (*He turns away and crosses down* R. ARTHUR *looks surprised at this unparliamentary expression.* CATHERINE *has read, and reread, the letter, and now breaks silence in a calm, methodical voice.*)

CATHERINE. My father doesn't mean what he says, Sir Robert.

SIR ROBERT. I'm glad to hear it.

7 **Balderdash:** nonsense.

CATHERINE. Perhaps I should explain that this letter——

ARTHUR. No, Kate.

CATHERINE. Sir Robert knows so much about our family affairs, Father, I don't see it will matter much if he learns a little more. (*To* SIR ROBERT.) This letter is from a certain Colonel Watherstone who is the father of the man I'm engaged to. We've always known he was opposed to the case, so it really comes as no surprise. In it he says that our efforts to discredit the Admiralty in the House of Commons today have resulted merely in our making the name of Winslow a nationwide laughing-stock. I think that's his phrase. (*She consults letter.*) Yes. That's right. "A nationwide laughing-stock."

SIR ROBERT. I don't care for his English——

CATHERINE. It's not very good, is it? He goes on to say that unless my father will give him a firm undertaking to drop this "whining and reckless agitation"—I suppose he means the case—he will exert every bit of influence he has over his son to prevent his marrying me.

SIR ROBERT. I see. An ultimatum.

CATHERINE. Yes—but a pointless one.

SIR ROBERT. He has no influence over his son?

CATHERINE. Oh, yes. A little, naturally. But his son is of age, and his own master——

SIR ROBERT. Is he dependent on his father for money?

CATHERINE. He gets an allowance. But he can live perfectly well—we both can live perfectly well—without it. (SIR ROBERT *stares hard at* CATHERINE, *then turns abruptly and crosses to* ARTHUR.)

SIR ROBERT. Well, sir?

ARTHUR. I'm afraid I can't go back on what I have already said. I will give you a decision in a few days——

SIR ROBERT. Your daughter seems prepared to take the risk—— (CATHERINE *comes down to table and takes cigarette.*)

ARTHUR. I am not. Not, at least, until I know how great a risk it is——

SIR ROBERT (*turning to* CATHERINE). How do you estimate the risk, Miss Winslow? (CATHERINE, *for all her bravado, is plainly scared. She is engaged in lighting cigarette as* SIR ROBERT *asks his question.*)

CATHERINE (*after a pause*). Negligible. (SIR ROBERT *stares at her again. Feeling his eyes on her,* CATHERINE *returns his glance defiantly. A pause.*)

SIR ROBERT (*returning abruptly to his languid manner*). I see. May I take a cigarette, too? (*He crosses to table* R. C.)

CATHERINE. Yes, of course. I thought you didn't smoke.

SIR ROBERT. Only occasionally. (*He takes cigarette. To* ARTHUR.) I really must apologize to you, sir, for speaking to you as I did, just now. It was unforgivable.

ARTHUR. Not at all. You were upset at giving up the case—and, to be frank, I liked you for it——

SIR ROBERT (*with deprecating gesture*). It has been rather a tiring day. The House of Commons is a peculiarly exhausting place, you know. Too little ventilation and far too much hot air— I really am most truly sorry.

ARTHUR (*dismissing matter*). Please. (*He sits in his chair.*)

SIR ROBERT (*carelessly*). Of course, you must decide about the case as you wish. (*To* CATHERINE.) That really is a most charming hat, Miss Winslow——

CATHERINE. I'm glad you like it.

SIR ROBERT. It seems decidedly wrong to me that a lady of your political persuasion should be allowed to adorn herself with such a very femi-nine allurement. It really looks so awfully like trying to have the best of both worlds——

CATHERINE. I'm not a militant, you know, Sir Robert. I don't go about breaking shop windows with a hammer or pouring acid down pillar boxes.[8]

SIR ROBERT (*languidly*). I am truly glad to hear it. Both those activities would be highly unsuitable in that hat—— (CATHERINE *glares at him, but suppresses an angry retort. She moves to chair* R. *of table and sits.*) I have never yet fully grasped what active steps you do take to propagate your cause, Miss Winslow?

CATHERINE (*shortly*). I'm an organizing secretary at the West London Branch of the Women's Suffrage Association.

SIR ROBERT. Indeed? Is the work hard?

CATHERINE. Very.

SIR ROBERT. But not, I should imagine, particularly lucrative.

CATHERINE. The work is voluntary and unpaid.

SIR ROBERT (*murmuring*). Dear me! What sacrifices you young ladies seem prepared to make for your convictions —— (VIOLET *enters up* C.)

VIOLET (*to* CATHERINE). Mr. Watherstone is in the hall, Miss. Says he would like to have a word with you in private—most particular—— (*A pause.*)

CATHERINE. Oh. (*She rises.*) I'll come out to him——

ARTHUR. No. See him in here. (*He begins to struggle out of his chair.*) You wouldn't mind coming to the dining room, would you, Sir Robert, for a moment?

SIR ROBERT. Not in the least.

CATHERINE. All right, Violet. (*She moves up* R. C.)

---

8 pillar boxes: public boxes for collecting mail.

VIOLET (*speaking into hall*). Will you come in, sir? (JOHN *comes in, looking depressed and anxious.* CATHERINE *greets him with a smile, which he returns only halfheartedly. This exchange is lost on* ARTHUR, *who has his back to them, but not on* SIR ROBERT. VIOLET *goes out and shuts door.*)

CATHERINE. Hullo, John.

JOHN. Hullo. (*To* ARTHUR.) Good evening, sir.

ARTHUR (*turning upstage, moving toward door up* L.). Good evening. (*He continues to dining room, opens door, and switches on light.*)

CATHERINE. I don't think you've met Sir Robert Morton.

JOHN. No. I haven't. How do you do, sir? (SIR ROBERT *moves up between* CATHERINE *and* JOHN; *they shake hands.*)

SIR ROBERT. How do you do? (*He sizes him up quickly, then crosses up* L. *to* ARTHUR.) I think you promised me a whisky and soda. (*Turns to* JOHN.) May I offer my very belated congratulations?

JOHN. Congratulations? Oh, yes. Thank you. (ARTHUR *and* SIR ROBERT *go out into dining room up* L. *A pause.* CATHERINE *is watching* JOHN *with an anxious expression.* JOHN *moves down* L. *to* RONNIE.) Is he asleep?

CATHERINE. Yes. (*She takes off her hat and drops it on settee.*)

JOHN (*still looking at* RONNIE). Sure he's not shamming?

CATHERINE. Yes.

JOHN (*after a pause*). My father's written your father a letter.

CATHERINE. I know. I've read it.

JOHN. Oh!

CATHERINE. Did you?

JOHN. Yes. He showed it to me. (*A pause.* JOHN *is carefully not looking at* CATHERINE.) Well, what's his answer?

CATHERINE. My father? I don't suppose he'll send one.

JOHN. You think he'll ignore it?

CATHERINE. Isn't that the best answer to blackmail?

JOHN (*muttering*). It was highhanded of the old man, I admit.

CATHERINE. Highhanded?

JOHN. I tried to get him not to send it.

CATHERINE. I'm glad.

JOHN. The trouble is—he's perfectly serious.

CATHERINE. I never thought he wasn't.

JOHN. If your father does decide to go on with the case, I'm very much afraid he'll do everything he threatens.

CATHERINE. Forbid the match?

JOHN. Yes.

CATHERINE (*almost pleadingly*). Isn't that rather an empty threat, John?

JOHN (*slowly*). Well, there's always the allowance.

CATHERINE (*dully*). Yes, I see. There's always the allowance——

JOHN. I tell you, Kate, darling, this is going to need careful handling; otherwise we'll find ourselves in the soup.

CATHERINE. Without your allowance would we be in the soup?

JOHN. And without your settlement? My dear old girl, of course we would. Dash it all, I can't even live on my pay as it is, but with two of us——

CATHERINE. I've heard it said that two can live as cheaply as one.

JOHN. Don't you believe it. Two can live as cheaply as two, and that's all there is to it.

CATHERINE (*moving slowly downstage*). Yes, I see. I didn't know. (*She sits on chair* L. *of table.*)

JOHN (*moving* C. *to her*). Unlike you, I have a practical mind, Kate. I'm sorry, but it's no use dashing blindly ahead without thinking of these things first. The problem has got to be faced.

CATHERINE. I'm ready to face it, John. What do you suggest?

JOHN (cautiously). Well—I think you should consider very carefully before you take the next step.

CATHERINE. I can assure you we will, John. The question is—what is the next step——? (JOHN turns GRACE's chair round and sits on arm.)

JOHN. Well—this is the way I see it. I'm going to be honest now. I hope you don't mind——

CATHERINE. No. I should welcome it.

JOHN. Your young brother over there pinches or doesn't pinch a five bob postal order. For over a year you and your father fight a magnificent fight on his behalf, and I'm sure everyone admires you for it.

CATHERINE. Your father hardly seems to.

JOHN. Well, he's a diehard, like these old admirals you've been up against. I meant ordinary reasonable people like myself. But now look—you've had two inquiries, the Petition of Right case which the Admiralty had thrown out of court, and the Appeal. And now, good heavens, you've had the whole damned House of Commons getting themselves worked up into a frenzy about it. Surely, darling, that's enough for you? Surely, the case can end there?

CATHERINE (slowly). Yes. I suppose the case can end there. (Rises and crosses to fireplace.)

JOHN (pointing to RONNIE). He won't mind.

CATHERINE. No. I know he won't.

JOHN. Look at him! (He gazes down at RONNIE.) Perfectly happy and content. Not a care in the world. How do you know what's going on in his mind? How can you be so sure he didn't do it?

CATHERINE (also gazing down at RONNIE). I'm not so sure he didn't do it.

JOHN (rising, appalled). Then why in Heaven's name have you and your father spent all this time and money trying to prove his innocence?

CATHERINE (quietly). His innocence or guilt aren't important to me. They are to my father. Not to me. I believe he didn't do it; but I may be wrong. To prove that he didn't do it, is of hardly more interest to me than the identity of the college servant, or whoever it was, who did it. All that I care about is that people should know that a Government department has ignored a fundamental human right and that it should be forced to acknowledge it. That's all that's important to me, John, but it is terribly important.

JOHN. But, darling, after all those long noble words, it does really resolve itself to a question of a fourteen-year-old boy and a five bob postal order, doesn't it?

CATHERINE. Yes, it does. (Continues to gaze down at RONNIE.)

JOHN (reasonably). Well now, look. There's a European war blowing up, there's a coal strike on, there's a fair chance of civil war in Ireland, and there's a hundred and one other things on the horizon at the moment that I think you genuinely could call important. And yet, with all that on its mind, the House of Commons takes a whole day to discuss him—(Pointing to RONNIE.) and his bally postal order. Surely you must see that's a little out of proportion—— (He pauses. CATHERINE raises her head slowly.)

CATHERINE (with some spirit). All I know is, John, that if ever the time comes when the House of Commons has so much on its mind that it can't find time to discuss a Ronnie Winslow and his bally postal order, this country will be a far poorer place than it is now. (*She moves toward* JOHN. *Wearily.*) But you needn't go on, John, dear. You've said quite enough. I entirely see your point of view. (*She sits in* GRACE'S *chair.*)

JOHN (*breaking away* R.). I don't know whether you realize that all this publicity you're getting is making the name of Winslow a bit of a—well——

CATHERINE (*steadily*). A nationwide laughing-stock, your father said.

JOHN (*sitting on edge of table below* L. *chair*). Well, that's putting it a bit steep. But people do find the case a bit ridiculous, you know. I mean, I get chaps coming up to me in the mess all the time and saying: "It is true you're going to marry the Winslow girl? You'd better be careful. You'll find yourself up in front of the House of Lords for pinching the Adjutant's bath." Things like that. They're not awfully funny——

CATHERINE. That's nothing. They're singing a verse about us at the Alhambra——

"Winslow one day went to Heaven
And found a poor fellow in quod.[9]
The fellow said I didn't do it,
So naturally Winslow sued God."

JOHN (*coming off table*). Well, darling—you see——

CATHERINE. Yes, I see. (*Quietly.*) Do you want to marry me, John?

JOHN. What?

CATHERINE. I said, do you want to marry me?

JOHN. Well, of course I do. You know I do. We've been engaged for over a year now. Have I ever wavered before?

CATHERINE. No, never before.

JOHN (*correcting himself*). I'm not wavering now. Not a bit—— I'm

9 **quod** (kwŏd): prison.

only telling you what I think is the best course for us to take.

CATHERINE. But isn't it already too late? Even if we gave up the case, would you still want to marry—the Winslow girl?

JOHN. All that would blow over in no time.

CATHERINE (*slowly*). And we'd have the allowance——

JOHN. Yes. We would.

CATHERINE. And that's so important——

JOHN (*moving to her; quietly*). It is, darling. I'm sorry, but you can't shame me into saying it isn't.

CATHERINE. I didn't mean to shame you——

JOHN. Oh, yes, you did. I know that tone of voice.

CATHERINE (*humbly*). I'm sorry. (JOHN *sits on arm of* CATHERINE'S *chair.*)

JOHN (*confidently*). Well, now—what's the answer?

CATHERINE (*slowly*). I love you, John, and want to be your wife.

JOHN. Well, then, that's all I want to know. Darling! I was sure nothing so stupid and trivial could possibly come between us. (*He kisses her. She responds wearily. Telephone rings. After pause* CATHERINE *releases herself. She rises and crosses to desk.* JOHN *rises and turns upstage.*)

CATHERINE (*lifting receiver*). Hullo. . . . Yes. . . . Will you wait a minute? (*Crosses up* L. *to dining room door, opens it, and calls:*) Sir Robert! Someone wants you on the telephone. (SIR ROBERT *enters from dining room.*)

SIR ROBERT. Thank you. I'm sorry to interrupt.

CATHERINE. You didn't. We'd finished our talk. (SIR ROBERT *looks at her inquiringly. She gives him no sign. He crosses upstage to phone.*)

SIR ROBERT (*noticing sandwiches*).

How delicious. May I help myself? (*He takes one and continues to desk.*)

CATHERINE. Do.

SIR ROBERT (*into telephone*). Hullo. . . . Yes, Michael. . . . F. E.? I didn't know he was going to speak. . . . I see. . . . Go on. (*Voice on phone speaks for some time. SIR ROBERT listens with closed eyelids, munching sandwich. ARTHUR appears in dining room doorway. At length.*) Thank you, Michael. (*He hangs up receiver and moves above table* R. C. *To* ARTHUR.) There has been a most interesting development in the House.

ARTHUR. What?

SIR ROBERT. My secretary tells me that a barrister friend of mine who, quite unknown to me, was interested in the case, got on his feet shortly after nine-thirty and delivered one of the most scathing denunciations of a Government department ever heard in the House. (*To* CATHERINE.) What a shame we missed it—his style is quite superb——

ARTHUR. What happened?

SIR ROBERT. The debate revived, of course, and the First Lord, who must have felt himself fairly safe, suddenly found himself under attack from all parts of the House. It appears that rather than risk a division he has this moment given an undertaking that he will instruct the Attorney-General to endorse our Petition of Right. The case of Winslow versus Rex[10] can now therefore come to court. (*A pause.* ARTHUR *and* CATHERINE *stare at him unbelievingly.*) Well, sir, what are my instructions?

ARTHUR (*slowly*). The decision is no longer mine. You must ask my daughter.

SIR ROBERT (*to* CATHERINE). What are my instructions, Miss Winslow? (*He takes another sandwich.* CATHERINE *looks down at sleeping* RONNIE. ARTHUR *watches her intensely.* SIR ROBERT, *munching sandwich, also looks at her.*)

CATHERINE (*in a flat voice*). Do you need my instructions, Sir Robert? Aren't they already on the Petition? Doesn't it say, "Let Right be done"?

JOHN (*furiously*). Kate! (*No answer.*) Good night. (*JOHN goes out up* C. SIR ROBERT, *with languid speculation, watches him go.*)

SIR ROBERT (*his mouth full*). Well, then—we must endeavor to see that it is. (*Front door is heard to slam.*)

QUICK CURTAIN

10 Rex: the King.

Understanding the Play

1. What is the subject of the debate between Grace and Arthur at the opening of Act II? What is its purpose within the play?
2. What different ideas does each have of justice? Are both right, or does Rattigan present one as right and the other as wrong?
3. The subplot concerning Catherine and John forms much of the interest in the preceding scene. How does Rattigan connect the subplot with the main one?

4. In talking to John, Catherine says "His [Ronnie's] innocence or guilt aren't important to me." What are her reasons for deciding the case should be continued? How are her father's reasons for wanting the case to go on different?
5. Sir Robert appears very anxious to continue with the case in this scene. Are you given the reasons for his anxiousness? How do you interpret his motives?
6. When John arrives, Catherine says "I'll come out to him—" However, her father, although he can walk only with difficulty, insists that she see John in the drawing room, while he and Sir Robert leave. What is Rattigan's reason for having him do so?

Developing Language Skills

Motivation—a character's reasons for action—is very important to a play. Select one of the following characters—Grace, Arthur, Catherine, or John—and write one paragraph in which you explain the character's reasons for wanting the case continued or dropped. Support your explanation by evidence from the play.

ACT II

SCENE 2

Same, five months later. A stiflingly hot afternoon in June nearly two years less one month since RONNIE's *dismissal from Osborne. The French window stands open, and a wheelchair has been placed just inside.* ARTHUR's *chair has been removed and in its place now stands* GRACE's *chair. A bowl of roses is on table above fireplace.* GRACE's *hat, bag and gloves are on settee. When curtain rises, stage is empty and phone is ringing insistently. After a few seconds,* DICKIE's *voice can be heard, calling from direction of hall—* "Mother"—"Violet," *to which he gets no reply. He enters up* C., *carrying suitcase, evidently very hot, his straw hat pushed on to back of his head and panting from his exertions. He wears a neat, dark blue suit, a sober tie and stiff collar.*

DICKIE (*in doorway*). Anybody about? (*He puts down suitcase by door and crosses to desk. Into phone.*) Hullo. . . . No, not Senior—Junior . . . I don't know where he is. . . . *Daily Mail?* . . . No, I'm the brother . . . elder brother— that's right. . . . Well, I'm in the banking business. . . . That's right. Following in father's footsteps. . . . My views on the case? Well, I—I—er—I don't know I have any, except, I mean, I hope we win and all that. . . . No, I haven't been in court. I've only just arrived from Reading. . . . Reading. . . . Yes. That's where I work. . . . Yes, I've come up for the last two days of the trial. Verdict's expected tomorrow, isn't it? . . . Twenty-two, last March. . . . Seven years older. . . . No. He was thirteen when it happened, but now he's fifteen. . . . Well, I suppose if I'm anything I'm a sort of a Liberal-Conservative. . . . Single. . . . No. No immediate prospects. I say, is this at all interesting to you?

. . . Well, a perfectly ordinary kid, just like any other—makes a noise, does fretwork, doesn't wash and all that. . . . Doesn't wash. . . . (*Alarmed.*) I say, don't take that too literally. I mean he does, sometimes. . . . Yes, all right. Good-by. . . . (*Hangs up receiver; crosses above table to door up* C., *picks up suitcase and goes out leaving door wide open. Phone rings again. Drops suitcase in hall and comes into room again.* GRACE *enters up* L.)

GRACE (*crossing down to desk*). Oh, hullo, darling. (DICKIE *stops up* C.) When did you get here? (*She picks up receiver. Into phone.*) Everyone out. (*Hangs up receiver, crosses to* DICKIE *and embraces him.*) You're thinner. I like your new suit.

DICKIE. Straight from Reading's Savile Row.[1] Off the peg[2] at thirty-seven and six. (*He points to phone.*) I say—does that go on all the time?

GRACE. All blessed day. The last four days it simply hasn't stopped.

DICKIE (*breaking toward fireplace*). I had to fight my way in through an army of reporters and people——

GRACE. Yes, I know. (*She follows him a step.*) You didn't say anything, I hope, Dickie dear. It's better not to say a word——

DICKIE. I don't think I said anything much. . . . (*Carelessly.*) Oh, yes, I did say that I personally thought he did it.

GRACE (*horrified*). Dickie! You didn't! (DICKIE *smiles at her.*) Oh, I see. It's a joke. You mustn't say things like that, even in fun, Dickie, dear—— (*She goes to door up* C. *and closes it.*)

DICKIE. How's it all going?

GRACE. I don't know. (*She comes a little down* C.) I've been there all four

days now and I've hardly understood a word that's going on. Kate says the judge is against us, but he seems a charming old gentleman to me. (*Faintly shocked.*) Sir Robert's so rude to him —— (*Phone rings. She crosses to desk, lifts receiver, automatically says:*) Nobody in. (*And hangs up. She goes to French window and calls:*) Arthur! Lunch! I'll come straight down. Dickie's here. (DICKIE *moves to fireplace. She turns back into room and crosses downstage to* C.) Kate takes the morning session, then she comes home and relieves me with Father, and I go to the court in the afternoons, so you can come with me as soon as she's in.

DICKIE. Will there be room for me?

GRACE. Oh, yes. They reserve places for the family. You never saw such crowds in all your life. And such excitement. Cheers and applause and people being turned out. It's thrilling —you'll love it, Dickie.

DICKIE. Well—if I don't understand a word——

GRACE. Oh, that doesn't matter. (*She moves up to settee and puts on hat and gloves.*) They all get so terribly worked up—you find yourself getting worked up, too. Sir Robert and the Attorney-General go at each other hammer and tongs—you wait and hear them—all about Petitions and demurrers and prerogatives and things. Nothing to do with Ronnie at all—seems to me——

DICKIE. How did Ronnie get on in the witness box?

GRACE. Two days he was cross-examined. Two whole days. Imagine it, the poor little pet. I must say he didn't seem to mind much. He said two days with the Attorney-General wasn't nearly as bad as two minutes with Sir Robert. Kate says he made a very good impression with the jury——

---

1 **Savile Row:** London's exclusive tailor shops. (He is making fun of the shops in Reading.)
2 **Off the peg:** ready-made suit.

DICKIE. How is Kate, Mother?

GRACE. Oh, all right. You heard about John, I suppose——

DICKIE. Yes. That's what I meant. How has she taken it?

GRACE. You never can tell with Kate. She never lets you know what she's feeling. We all think he's behaved very badly—— (ARTHUR *appears at window. He is walking very groggily.*) Arthur! (*She goes to him.*) You shouldn't have come up those steps by yourself.

ARTHUR. I had little alternative.

GRACE. I'm sorry, dear. I was talking to Dickie. (*She helps* ARTHUR *into wheelchair.*)

ARTHUR. Oh, hullo, Dickie. How are you? (*He works chair to corner of desk.* GRACE *puts* ARTHUR'S *stick by side of piano.*)

DICKIE (*crossing to* ARTHUR, *shaking hands*). Very well, thank you, Father.

ARTHUR. I've been forced to adopt this ludicrous form of propulsion. I apologize. You look very well. A trifle thinner, perhaps——

DICKIE. Hard work, Father.

ARTHUR. Or late hours.

DICKIE. You can't keep late hours in Reading.

ARTHUR. You could keep late hours anywhere. I've had quite a good report about you from Mr. Lamb.

DICKIE. Good egg! He's a decent old stick, the old baa-lamb. I took him racing last Saturday. Had the time of his life and lost his shirt.

ARTHUR. Did he? I have no doubt that, given the chance, you'll succeed in converting the entire Reading branch of the Westminster Bank into a book-making establishment. Mr. Lamb says you've joined the Territorials.[3]

---

3 **Territorials:** members of the Territorial Reserve, a British army defense unit.

DICKIE. Yes, Father.

ARTHUR. Why have you done that?

DICKIE. Well, from all accounts there is a fair chance of a bit of a scrap quite soon. If there is I don't want it to be all over before I can get in on it——

ARTHUR. If there is what you call a scrap you'll do far better to stay in the bank.

DICKIE. Oh, no, Father. I mean, the bank's all right—but still—a chap can't help looking forward to a bit of a change—I can always go back to the bank afterward—— (*Phone rings.* AR-THUR *takes receiver off and puts it down on desk.*)

GRACE (*coming behind* ARTHUR). Oh, no, dear, you can't do that. (*She propels* ARTHUR *to* C. DICKIE *moves above table* R. C.)

ARTHUR. Why not?

GRACE. It annoys the exchange.

ARTHUR. I prefer to annoy the exchange than have the exchange annoy me. Catherine's late. She was in at half-past one yesterday. (GRACE *turns* ARTHUR *to face downstage. She stands to his* R.)

GRACE. Perhaps they're taking the lunch interval later today.

ARTHUR. Lunch interval? This isn't a cricket match. (*He looks at her.*) Nor, may I say, is it a matinee at the Gaiety. Why are you wearing that highly unsuitable get-up?

GRACE. Don't you like it, dear? I think it is Mme. Dupont's best.

ARTHUR. Grace—your son is facing a charge of theft and forgery——

GRACE. Oh, dear! It's so difficult! I simply can't be seen in the same old dress, day after day! (*A thought strikes her.*) I tell you what, Arthur. I'll wear my black coat and skirt tomorrow—for the verdict.

ARTHUR (*glares at her, helplessly, then turns his chair toward door up* L.).

Did you say my lunch was ready? (DICKIE *rushes up* L. *to open door.*)

GRACE. Yes, dear. (*She pushes* AR-THUR *up* L.) It's only cold. I did the salad myself. Violet and cook are at the trial.

DICKIE. Is Violet still with you? She was under sentence last time I saw you——

GRACE. She's been under sentence for the last six months, poor thing—only she doesn't know it. Neither your father nor I have the courage to tell her——

ARTHUR (*stopping at door*). I have the courage to tell her.

GRACE. It's funny that you don't, then, dear.

ARTHUR. I will.

GRACE (*hastily*). No, no, you mustn't. When it's to be done, I'll do it.

ARTHUR. You see, Dickie? These taunts of cowardice are daily flung at my head; but should I take them up I'm forbidden to move in the matter. Such is the logic of women. (ARTHUR *wheels himself out up* L. *door.* DICKIE, *who has been holding door open, closes it after him.*)

DICKIE. How *is* he? (GRACE *shakes her head quietly. She moves down to fireplace.*) Will you take him away after the trial?

GRACE. He's promised to go into a nursing home.

DICKIE. Do you think he will?

GRACE. How do I know? He'll probably find some new excuse.

DICKIE. But surely, if he loses this time, he's lost for good, hasn't he?

GRACE (*slowly*). So they say, Dickie, dear—I can only hope it's true.

DICKIE. How did you keep him away from the trial?

GRACE. Kate and Sir Robert together. He wouldn't listen to me or the doctor.

DICKIE (*crossing up* R. C.). Poor old

Mother! You must have been having a pretty rotten time of it, one way and another——

GRACE. I've said my say, Dickie. He knows what I think. Not that he cares. He never has—all his life. Anyway, I've given up worrying. He's always said he knew what he was doing. It's my job to try and pick up the pieces, I suppose. (CATHERINE *enters up* C.)

CATHERINE. Lord! The heat! (*She closes door.*) Mother, can't you get rid of those reporters——? Hullo, Dickie.

DICKIE (*moving to her*). Hullo, Kate. (*Embraces her.*)

CATHERINE. Come to be in at the death? (*She moves a step down* C.)

DICKIE. Is that what it's going to be?

CATHERINE. Looks like it. I could cheerfully strangle that old brute of a judge, Mother. He's dead against us.

GRACE. Oh, dear!

CATHERINE. Sir Robert's very worried. He said the Attorney-General's speech made a great impression on the jury. I must say it was very clever. To listen to him yesterday you would have thought that a verdict for Ronnie would simultaneously cause a mutiny in the Royal Navy and triumphant jubilation in Berlin. (*Door opens slightly and* ARTHUR *appears in opening in his wheelchair.* DICKIE *rushes across and opens door wider.*)

ARTHUR. You're late, Catherine. (*He wheels himself to* C.)

CATHERINE. I know, Father, I'm sorry. There was such a huge crowd outside as well as inside the court that I couldn't get a cab. And I stayed to talk to Sir Robert. (GRACE *moves in to* L. C. DICKIE *comes down behind* GRACE *and sits on arm of chair down* L.)

GRACE (*pleased*). Is there a bigger crowd even than yesterday, Kate?

CATHERINE. Yes, Mother, far bigger.

ARTHUR. How did it go this morning?

CATHERINE. Sir Robert finished his cross-examination of the postmistress. I thought he'd demolish her completely. She admitted she couldn't identify Ronnie in the Commander's office. She admitted she couldn't be sure of the time he came in. She admitted that she was called away to the telephone while he was buying his fifteen-and-six postal order, and that all Osborne cadets looked alike to her in their uniforms, so that it might quite easily have been another cadet who cashed the five shillings. It was a brilliant cross-examination. So gentle and quiet. He didn't bully her, or frighten her—he just coaxed her into tying herself into knots. Then when he'd finished the Attorney-General asked her again whether she was absolutely positive that the same boy that bought the fifteen-and-six postal order also cashed the five shilling one. She said, "Yes." She was quite, quite sure because Ronnie was such a good-looking little boy that she had specially noticed him. She hadn't said that in her examination-in-chief. I could see those twelve good men and true nodding away to each other. I believe it undid the whole of that magnificent cross-examination.

ARTHUR. If she thought him so especially good-looking, why couldn't she identify him the same evening?

CATHERINE. Don't ask me, Father. Ask the Attorney-General. I'm sure he has a beautifully reasonable answer.

DICKIE. Ronnie good-looking! What utter rot! She must be lying, that woman.

GRACE. Nonsense, Dickie! I thought he looked very well in the box yesterday, didn't you, Kate?

CATHERINE. Yes, Mother.

ARTHUR. Who else gave evidence for the other side?

CATHERINE. The Commander, the Chief Petty Officer, and one of the boys at the College.

ARTHUR. Anything very damaging?

CATHERINE. Nothing that we didn't expect. The boy showed obviously that he hated Ronnie and was torn to shreds by Sir Robert. The Commander scored, though. He's an honest man and genuinely believes Ronnie did it.

GRACE (moving C. and facing CATHERINE). Did you see anybody interesting in court, dear?

CATHERINE. Yes, Mother. John Watherstone.

GRACE. John? I hope you didn't speak to him, Kate.

CATHERINE. Of course I did.

GRACE. Kate, how could you! What did he say?

CATHERINE. He wished us luck.

GRACE. What impertinence! The idea of John Watherstone coming calmly up in court to wish you luck—I think it's the most disgraceful, cold-blooded——

ARTHUR. Grace—you will be late for the resumption.

GRACE. Oh, will I? Are you ready, Dickie?

DICKIE (rising). Yes, Mother. (Picks up his hat.)

GRACE. You don't think that nice, gray suit of yours you paid so much money for——?

ARTHUR. What time are they resuming, Kate?

CATHERINE. Two o'clock.

ARTHUR. It's twenty past two now.

GRACE. Oh, dear! We'll be terribly late. Kate—that's your fault. Arthur, you must finish your lunch—(DICKIE goes to door up C.)

ARTHUR. Yes, Grace.

GRACE. Promise, now.

ARTHUR. I promise.

GRACE (to herself). I wonder if Violet will remember to pick up those onions.

(*She goes up* C. *to door.*) Perhaps I'd better do it on the way back from the Court. (*To* DICKIE.) Now, Dickie, when you get to the front door put your head down like me, and just charge through them all. (DICKIE *holds door open.*)

ARTHUR. Why don't you go out by the garden?

GRACE. I wouldn't like to risk tearing this dress getting through that hedge. Come on, Dickie. I always shout: "I'm the maid and don't know nothing," so don't be surprised.

DICKIE. Right-oh, Mother. (GRACE *and* DICKIE *go out. A pause.*)

ARTHUR. Are we going to lose this case, Kate? (CATHERINE *quietly shrugs shoulders.*) It's our last chance.

CATHERINE. I know.

ARTHUR (*with sudden violence*). We've got to win it. (CATHERINE *does not reply.*) What does Sir Robert think?

CATHERINE. He seems very worried.

ARTHUR (*thoughtfully*). I wonder if you were right, Kate. I wonder if we could have had a better man?

CATHERINE. No, Father, we couldn't have had a better man.

ARTHUR. You admit that now, do you?

CATHERINE. Only that he's the best advocate in England and for some reason—prestige, I suppose—he seems genuinely anxious to win this case. I don't go back on anything else I've ever said about him.

ARTHUR. The papers said that he began today by telling the judge he felt ill and might have to ask for an adjournment. I trust he won't collapse

———

CATHERINE. He won't. It was just another of those brilliant tricks of his that he's always boasting about. It got him the sympathy of the Court and

possibly—— No, I won't say that——

ARTHUR. Say it.

CATHERINE (*slowly*). Possibly provided him with an excuse if he's beaten.

ARTHUR. You don't like him, do you?

CATHERINE (*indifferently*). There's nothing in him to like or dislike, Father. I admire him. (DESMOND *appears at window. He stands just inside room.* CATHERINE *and* ARTHUR *turn and see him.*)

DESMOND. I trust you do not object to me employing this rather furtive entry? The crowds at the front door are most alarming, so I came through the garden.

ARTHUR. Come in, Desmond. Why have you left the court? (DESMOND *comes down to stool at desk. Puts hat and umbrella on stool.*)

DESMOND. My partner will be holding the fort. He is perfectly competent, I promise you——

ARTHUR. I'm glad to hear it.

DESMOND. I wonder if I might see Catherine alone. I have a matter of some urgency to communicate to her

———

ARTHUR. Oh. Do you wish to hear this urgent matter, Kate?

CATHERINE. Yes, Father.

ARTHUR. Very well. I shall go and finish my lunch. (*He wheels his chair up* L. *to up* L. *door.*)

DESMOND (*flying to help*). Allow me.

ARTHUR. Thank you. I can manage this vehicle without assistance. Perhaps you wouldn't mind opening the door. (DESMOND *opens door up* L. ARTHUR *goes out.* CATHERINE *moves above table to chair* R. *of it and sits.*)

DESMOND (*closing door and turning to* CATHERINE). I fear I should have warned you of my visit. Perhaps I have interrupted? (*He moves to* C.)

CATHERINE. No, Desmond. Please sit down. (DESMOND *sits* L. *of table.*)

DESMOND. Thank you. I'm afraid I have only a very short time. I must get back to court for the cross-examination of the Judge Advocate.

CATHERINE. Yes, Desmond. Well?

DESMOND. I have a taxi-cab waiting at the end of the street.

CATHERINE (*smiling*). How very extravagant of you, Desmond.

DESMOND (*also smiling*). Yes. But it shows you how rushed this visit must necessarily be. The fact of the matter is—it suddenly occurred to me during the lunch adjournment that I had better see you today——

CATHERINE (*her thoughts far distant*). Why?

DESMOND. I have a question to put to you, Kate, which, if I had postponed putting until after the verdict, you might—who knows—have thought had been prompted by pity—if we had lost. Or—if we had won, your reply might—again who knows—have been influenced by gratitude. Do you follow me, Kate?

CATHERINE. Yes, Desmond. I think I do.

DESMOND. Ah. Then possibly you have some inkling of what the question is I have to put to you?

CATHERINE. Yes, I think I have.

DESMOND (*a trifle disconcerted*). Oh.

CATHERINE. I'm sorry, Desmond. I ought, I know, to have followed the usual practice in such cases, and told you I had no inkling whatever.

DESMOND. No, no. Your directness and honesty are two of the qualities I so much admire in you. I'm glad you have guessed. It makes my task the easier——

CATHERINE (*in matter-of-fact voice*). Will you give me a few days to think it over?

DESMOND. Of course. Of course.

CATHERINE. I need hardly tell you how grateful I am, Desmond.

DESMOND (*a trifle bewildered*). There is no need, Kate, no need at all—— (*Rises and moves above table.*)

CATHERINE. You mustn't keep your taxi waiting.

DESMOND (*fiercely*). Oh, bother my taxi! (*Recovering himself.*) Forgive me, Kate, but you see I know very well what your feelings for me really are.

CATHERINE (*gently*). You do, Desmond?

DESMOND. Yes, Kate. I know quite well they have never amounted to much more than a sort of—well—shall we say, friendliness? A warm friendliness, I hope. Yes, I think perhaps we can definitely say, warm. But no more than that. That's true, isn't it?

CATHERINE (*quietly*). Yes, Desmond.

DESMOND. I know, I know. Of course, the thing is that even if I proved the most devoted and adoring husband that ever lived—which, I may say—if you give me the chance, I intend to be—your feelings for me would never—could never—amount to more than that. When I was younger it might, perhaps, have been a different story. When I played cricket for England—— (DESMOND *notices faintest expression of pity that has crossed* CATHERINE's *face. Apologetically.*) And of course, perhaps even that would not have made so much difference. Perhaps you feel I cling too much to my past athletic prowess. I feel it myself, sometimes—but the truth is I have not much else to cling to save that and my love for you. The athletic prowess is fading, I'm afraid, with the years, and the stiffening of the muscles—but my love for you will never fade.

CATHERINE (*smiling*). That's very charmingly said, Desmond.

DESMOND. Don't make fun of me, Kate, please. I meant it. Every word. (*Clears his throat and moves above chair L. of table.*) However, let us take a more mundane approach and examine the facts. Fact One. You don't love me and never can. Fact Two. I love you, always have and always will. That is the situation—and it is a situation which, after most careful consideration, I am fully prepared to accept. I reached this decision some months ago, but thought at first it would be better to wait until this case, which is so much on all our minds, should be over. Then at lunch today I determined to anticipate the verdict tomorrow, and let you know what was in my mind at once. No matter what you feel or don't feel for me—no matter what you feel for anyone else, I want you to be my wife. (*A pause.* CATHERINE *rises and moves above table.*)

CATHERINE. I see. Thank you, Desmond. That makes everything much clearer.

DESMOND. There is much more that I had meant to say, but I shall put it in a letter.

CATHERINE. Yes, Desmond, do.

DESMOND. Then I may expect your answer in a few days?

CATHERINE. Yes, Desmond.

DESMOND (*suddenly crossing down R.*). I must get back to court. (*Collects his hat, umbrella and gloves.*) How did you think it went this morning?

CATHERINE. I thought the postmistress restored the Admiralty's case with that point about Ronnie's looks

———

DESMOND. Oh, no, no, no. (*Moves above chair R. of table.*) Not at all. There is still the overwhelming fact that she couldn't identify him. What a brilliant cross-examination, was it not?

CATHERINE. Brilliant.

DESMOND. He is a strange man, Sir Robert. At times, so cold and distant and—and——

CATHERINE. Fishlike.

DESMOND. Fishlike, exactly. And yet he has a real passion about this case. A real passion. I happen to know—of course this must on no account go any further—but I happen to know that he has made a very, very great personal sacrifice in order to bring it to court.

CATHERINE. Sacrifice? What? Of another brief?

DESMOND. No, no. That would be no sacrifice to him. No—he was offered —you really promise to keep this to yourself?

CATHERINE. My dear Desmond, whatever the Government offered him can't be as startling as all that; he's in the Opposition.

DESMOND. As it happens it was quite startling, and a most graceful compliment, if I may say so, to his performance as Attorney-General under the last government.

CATHERINE. What was he offered, Desmond?

DESMOND. The appointment of Lord Chief Justice. He turned it down simply in order to be able to carry on with the case of Winslow versus Rex. Strange are the ways of men, are they not? Good-by, my dear.

CATHERINE. Good-by, Desmond. (*Offers her hand.* DESMOND *takes it and, overcome with emotion, kisses it.* DESMOND *goes out quickly through French window.* CATHERINE *looks after him, in deep thought, with a puzzled, strained expression. It does not look as though it were* DESMOND *she was thinking of. Door up L. opens and* ARTHUR *peeps round.*)

ARTHUR. May I come in now?

CATHERINE. Yes, Father. He's gone.

ARTHUR. I'm rather tired of being gazed at from the street, while eating my mutton, as though I were an animal at the zoo.

CATHERINE (slowly). I've been a fool, Father. (Comes to fireplace.)

ARTHUR. Have you, my dear?

CATHERINE. An utter fool.

ARTHUR. In default of further information, I can only repeat, have you, my dear?

CATHERINE. There's no further information. I'm under a pledge of secrecy.

ARTHUR. Oh. What did Desmond want?

CATHERINE. To marry me.

ARTHUR. I trust the folly you were referring to wasn't your acceptance of him?

CATHERINE (smiling). No, Father. Would it be such folly, though?

ARTHUR. Lunacy.

CATHERINE. Oh, I don't know. He's nice and he's doing very well as a solicitor.

ARTHUR. Neither very compelling reasons for marrying him.

CATHERINE. Seriously, I shall have to think it over.

ARTHUR. Think it over, by all means. But decide against it.

CATHERINE. I'm nearly thirty, you know.

ARTHUR. Thirty isn't the end of life.

CATHERINE. It might be—for an unmarried woman, with not much looks.

ARTHUR. Rubbish. (CATHERINE shakes her head.) Better far to live and die an old maid than to marry Desmond.

CATHERINE. Even an old maid must eat.

ARTHUR. I am leaving you and your mother everything, you know.

CATHERINE (quietly). Everything?

ARTHUR. There is still a little left. (He pauses.) Did you take my suggestion as regards your Woman's Suffrage Association?

CATHERINE. Yes, Father.

ARTHUR. You demanded a salary?

CATHERINE. I asked for one.

ARTHUR. And they're going to give it to you, I trust.

CATHERINE. Yes, Father. Two pounds a week.

ARTHUR (angrily). That's insulting.

CATHERINE. No. It's generous. It's all they can afford. We're not a very rich organization, you know.

ARTHUR. You'll have to think of something else.

CATHERINE. What else? Darning socks? That's about my only other accomplishment.

ARTHUR. There must be something useful you can do.

CATHERINE. You don't think the work I am doing at the W. S. A. is useful? (ARTHUR is silent.) You may be right. But it's the only work I'm fitted for, all the same. (She pauses.) No, Father. (Moves to pouffe.) The choice is quite simple. Either I marry Desmond and settle down into quite a comfortable and not really useless existence—or I go on for the rest of my life earning two pounds a week in the service of a hopeless cause. (Sits on pouffe.)

ARTHUR. A hopeless cause? I've never heard you say that before.

CATHERINE. I've never felt it before. (ARTHUR is silent.) John's going to get married next month.

ARTHUR. Did he tell you?

CATHERINE. Yes. He was very apologetic.

ARTHUR. Apologetic!

CATHERINE. He didn't need to be. It's a girl I know slightly. She'll make him a good wife.

ARTHUR. Is he in love with her?

CATHERINE. No more than he was with me. Perhaps, even, a little less.

ARTHUR. Why is he marrying her so soon after—after——?

CATHERINE. After jilting me? Because he thinks there's going to be a war. If there is his regiment will be among the first to go overseas. Besides, his father approves strongly. She's a General's daughter. Very, very suitable.

ARTHUR. Poor Kate! (*Pauses, takes her hand slowly.*) How I've messed up your life, haven't I?

CATHERINE. No, Father. Any messing-up that's been done has been done by me.

ARTHUR. I'm so sorry, Kate. I'm so sorry.

CATHERINE. Don't be, Father. We both knew what we were doing.

ARTHUR. Did we?

CATHERINE. I think we did.

ARTHUR. Yet our motives seem to have been different all along—yours and mine, Kate. Can we both have been right?

CATHERINE. I believe we can. I believe we have been.

ARTHUR. And yet they've always been so infernally logical, our opponents, haven't they?

CATHERINE. I'm afraid logic has never been on our side.

ARTHUR. Brute stubbornness—a selfish refusal to admit defeat. That's what your mother thinks have been our motives——

CATHERINE. Perhaps she's right. Perhaps that's all they have been.

ARTHUR. But perhaps brute stubbornness isn't such a bad quality in the face of injustice?

CATHERINE. Or in the face of tyranny. (*She pauses. The cry of a* NEWSPAPER BOY *can be heard faintly outside.*) If you could go back, Father, and choose again—would your choice be different?

ARTHUR. Perhaps.

CATHERINE. I don't think so.

ARTHUR. I don't think so, either.

CATHERINE. I still say we both knew what we were doing. And we were right to do it.

ARTHUR (*kissing top of her head*). Dear Kate, thank you. (*A silence.* NEWSPAPER BOY *can be heard dimly shouting from street outside.*) You aren't going to marry Desmond, are you?

CATHERINE (*with a smile*). In the words of the Prime Minister, Father, wait and see.

ARTHUR (*listening*). What's that boy shouting, Kate?

CATHERINE. Only—"Winslow Case—Latest."

ARTHUR. It didn't sound to me like "Latest." (CATHERINE *rises and crosses down toward window. Suddenly we hear it quite plainly:* "*Winslow Case Result! Winslow Case Result!*") Result?

CATHERINE. There must be some mistake. (VIOLET *enters, with broad smile, in fever of excitement.*)

VIOLET. Oh, sir! Oh, sir!

ARTHUR (*backing his chair round to face up* R.). What happened?

VIOLET. Oh, Miss Kate, what a shame you missed it! Just after they come back from lunch, and Mrs. Winslow she wasn't there neither, nor Master Ronnie. The cheering and the shouting and the carrying-on—you never heard anything like it in all your life— and Sir Robert standing there at the table with his wig on crooked and the tears running down his face—running down his face they were, and not able to speak because of the noise. Cook and me, we did a bit of crying too; we just couldn't help it—you couldn't, you know. Oh, it was lovely. We did enjoy ourselves. And then cook had her hat knocked over her eyes by the man behind who was cheering and waving his arms about something

chronic and shouting about liberty—you would have laughed, Miss, to see her, she was that cross—but she didn't mind really, she was only pretending, and we kept on cheering and the judge kept on shouting, but it wasn't any good because even the jury joined in, and some of them climbed out of the box to shake hands with Sir Robert. And then outside in the street it was just the same—you couldn't move for the crowd and you'd think they'd all gone mad the way they were carrying on. Some of them were shouting, "Good old Winslow," and singing, "For he's a jolly good fellow," and cook had her hat knocked off again. Oh, it was lovely! (*To* Arthur.) Well, sir, you must be feeling nice and pleased, now it's all over?

Arthur. Yes, Violet, I am.

Violet. That's right, I always said it would come all right in the end, didn't I?

Arthur. Yes, you did.

Violet. Two years all but one month it's been, now, since Master Ronnie came back that day. Fancy.

Arthur. Yes.

Violet. I don't mind telling you, sir, I wondered sometimes whether you and Miss Kate weren't just wasting your time carrying on the way you have. Still, you couldn't have felt that if you'd been in court today. (*Turns to go, then stops.*) Oh, sir, Mrs. Winslow asked me to remember most particular to pick up some onions from the greengrocer, but in the excitement I'm afraid——

Catherine. That's all right, Violet. I think Mrs. Winslow is picking them up herself, on her way back.

Violet. I see, Miss. Poor Madam, what a sell for her when she gets to the court and finds it's all over. Well, sir, congratulations, I'm sure.

Arthur. Thank you, Violet. (Violet *goes out up* c. *After pause.*) It would appear, then, that we've won.

CATHERINE (*going to* ARTHUR). Yes, Father, it would appear that we've won. (*She breaks down and cries, her head on her father's lap.*)

ARTHUR (*slowly*). I would have liked to have been there. (*A pause.* VIOLET *enters up* C.)

VIOLET (*announcing*). Sir Robert Morton. (CATHERINE *jumps up hastily and dabs her eyes as she crosses to window.* SIR ROBERT *enters up* C. VIOLET *goes out.*)

SIR ROBERT (*coming down* C.). I thought you might like to hear the actual terms of the Attorney-General's statement—— (*He pulls out scrap of paper.*) So I jotted it down for you. (*He reads:*) "I say now, on behalf of the Admiralty, that I accept the declaration of Ronald Arthur Winslow that he did not write the name on the postal order, that he did not take it and that he did not cash it, and that consequently he was innocent of the charge which was brought against him two years ago. I make that statement without any reservation of any description, intending it to be a complete acceptance of the boy's statements." (*Folds paper and hands it to* ARTHUR.)

ARTHUR. It is rather hard for me to find the words I should speak to you.

SIR ROBERT. Pray do not trouble yourself to search for them. Let us take these rather tiresome and conventional expressions of gratitude for granted, shall we? Now, on the question of damages and costs. I fear we shall find the Admiralty rather niggardly. You are likely still to be left considerably out of pocket. However, doubtless we can apply a slight spur to the First Lord's posterior in the House of Commons.

ARTHUR. Please, sir—no more trouble —I beg. Let the matter rest here. (*Indicates piece of paper.*) That is all I have ever asked for.

SIR ROBERT (*turning to* CATHERINE). A pity you were not in court, Miss Winslow. The verdict appeared to cause quite a stir.

CATHERINE. So I heard. Why did the Admiralty throw up the case?

SIR ROBERT. It was a foregone conclusion, once the handwriting expert had been discredited, not for the first time in legal history—I knew we had a sporting chance and no jury in the world would have convicted on the postmistress's evidence.

CATHERINE. But this morning you seemed so depressed.

SIR ROBERT. Did I? The heat in the courtroom was very trying, you know. Perhaps I was a little fatigued—— (VIOLET *enters up* C.)

VIOLET (*to* ARTHUR). Oh, sir, the gentlemen at the front door say, please would you make a statement? They say they won't go away until you do.

ARTHUR. Very well, Violet. Thank you.

VIOLET. Yes, sir. (VIOLET *goes out.*)

ARTHUR (*to* SIR ROBERT). What shall I say? (SIR ROBERT *moves behind* ARTHUR's *chair to help him.*)

SIR ROBERT (*indifferently*). I hardly think it matters. Whatever you say will have little bearing on what they write.

ARTHUR. What shall I say, Kate?

CATHERINE. You'll think of something, Father. (SIR ROBERT *pushes chair up* C.)

ARTHUR (*sharply*). No! I decline to meet the Press in this ridiculous chariot. (*To* CATHERINE.) Get me my stick!

CATHERINE (*protestingly*). Father— you know what the doctor——

ARTHUR. Get me my stick! (CATHERINE *goes to piano and gets his stick. She and* SIR ROBERT *help him out of chair.*) I could say: "I am happy to have lived long enough to have seen justice done to my son——"

CATHERINE. It's a little gloomy, Father. You're going to live for ages yet—— (*They help him to door,* SIR ROBERT *on his* R., CATHERINE *on his* L.)

ARTHUR. Am I? Wait and see. I could say: "This victory is not mine. It is the people who have triumphed—as they always will triumph—over despotism." How does that strike you, sir? A trifle pretentious, perhaps.

SIR ROBERT. Perhaps. I should say it none the less. It will be very popular.

ARTHUR. Ha! Perhaps I had better say what I really feel, which is merely: "Thank God we beat 'em." (ARTHUR *goes out up* C. CATHERINE *closes door.*)

SIR ROBERT. Miss Winslow, might I be rude enough to ask you for a little of your excellent whisky?

CATHERINE. Of course. (CATHERINE *goes into dining room.* SIR ROBERT, *left alone, droops his shoulders wearily. Comes down* C. *and subsides into chair* L. *of table. When* CATHERINE *enters with whisky he straightens his shoulders instinctively, but does not rise.*)

SIR ROBERT. That is very kind. Perhaps you would forgive me not getting up? The heat in that courtroom was really so infernal. (*Takes glass from her and drains it quickly.*)

CATHERINE (*noticing his hand is trembling slightly*). Are you feeling all right, Sir Robert?

SIR ROBERT. Just a slight nervous reaction—that is all. Besides, I have not been feeling myself all day. I told the judge so this morning, if you remember, but I doubt if he believed me. He thought it was a trick. What suspicious minds people have, have they not?

CATHERINE. Yes.

SIR ROBERT (*handing her back the glass*). Thank you. (CATHERINE *crosses*

to fireplace and puts glass on mantel. Turns slowly back to face SIR ROBERT *as if nerving herself for an ordeal.*)

CATHERINE. Sir Robert, I'm afraid I have a confession and an apology to make to you.

SIR ROBERT (*sensing what is coming*). My dear young lady—I am sure the one is rash and the other superfluous. I would far rather hear neither——

CATHERINE (*with a smile*). I am afraid you must. This is probably the last time I shall see you, and it is a better penance for me to say this than to write it. I have entirely misjudged your attitude to this case, and if in doing so I have ever seemed to you either rude or ungrateful, I am sincerely and humbly sorry.

SIR ROBERT (*indifferently*). My dear Miss Winslow, you have never seemed to me either rude or ungrateful. And my attitude to this case has been the same as yours—a determination to win at all costs. Only—when you talk of gratitude—you must remember that those costs were not mine but yours.

CATHERINE. Weren't they yours also, Sir Robert?

SIR ROBERT. I beg your pardon?

CATHERINE. Haven't you, too, made a very special sacrifice for the case?

SIR ROBERT (*after pause*). The robes of that office would not have suited me.

CATHERINE. Wouldn't they?

SIR ROBERT (*with venom*). And what is more, I fully intend to report Curry to the Law Society. (*Rises and turns upstage.*)

CATHERINE. Please don't. He did me a great service by telling me——

SIR ROBERT. Well, I must ask you never to divulge it to another living soul, and even to forget it yourself.

CATHERINE. I shall never divulge it. I'm afraid I can't promise to forget it myself.

SIR ROBERT. Very well! (*Moves toward her.*) If you choose to endow an unimportant incident with romantic significance, you are perfectly at liberty to do so. I must go.

CATHERINE. Why are you always at such pains to prevent people knowing the truth about you, Sir Robert?

SIR ROBERT. Am I indeed?

CATHERINE. You know you are. Why?

SIR ROBERT. Perhaps because *I* do not know the truth about myself.

CATHERINE. That is no answer.

SIR ROBERT. My dear Miss Winslow, are you cross-examining me?

CATHERINE. On this point, yes. Why are you so ashamed of your emotions?

SIR ROBERT. Because, as a lawyer, I must necessarily distrust them.

CATHERINE. Why?

SIR ROBERT. To fight a case on emotional grounds is the surest way of losing it. Emotions muddy the issue. Cold, clear logic—and buckets of it— should be the lawyer's only equipment.

CATHERINE. Was it cold clear logic that made you weep today at the verdict?

SIR ROBERT (*after slight pause*). Your maid, I suppose, told you that? It doesn't matter. It will be in the papers tomorrow, anyway. (*Fiercely.*) Very well, then, if you must have it, here it is: I wept today because right had been done.

CATHERINE. Not justice?

SIR ROBERT. No. Not justice. Right. It is not hard to do justice—very hard to do right. Unfortunately, while the appeal of justice is intellectual, the appeal of right appears, for some odd reason, to induce tears in court. That is my answer and my excuse. And now, may I leave the witness box?

CATHERINE. No. One last question. How can you reconcile your support of Winslow against the Crown with your political beliefs?

SIR ROBERT. Very easily. No one party has a monopoly of concern for individual liberty. On that issue all parties are united.

CATHERINE. I don't think so.

SIR ROBERT. You don't?

CATHERINE. No. Not all parties. Only some people from all parties.

SIR ROBERT. That is a wise remark. We can only hope then, that those "some people" will always prove enough people. You would make a good advocate.

CATHERINE. Would I?

SIR ROBERT (*playfully*). Why do you not canalize your feministic impulses towards the law-courts, Miss Winslow, and abandon the lost cause of Women's Suffrage?

CATHERINE. Because I don't believe it *is* a lost cause.

SIR ROBERT. No? Are you going to continue to pursue it?

CATHERINE. Certainly.

SIR ROBERT. You will be wasting your time.

CATHERINE. I don't think so.

SIR ROBERT. A pity. In the House of Commons in days to come I shall make a point of looking up at the Gallery in the hope of catching a glimpse of you in that provocative hat. (*Enter* RONNIE *up* C.)

RONNIE (*coming down* R. *of* SIR ROBERT). I say, Sir Robert, I'm most awfully sorry. I didn't know anything was going to happen.

SIR ROBERT. Where were you?

RONNIE. At the pictures. I'm most awfully sorry. I say—we won, didn't we?

SIR ROBERT. Yes, we won. Well, good-by, Miss Winslow. Shall I see you in the House, then, one day? (*He offers his hand.*)

CATHERINE (*shaking his hand with a smile*). Yes, Sir Robert. One day. But not in the Gallery. Across the floor.[4]

SIR ROBERT (*with a faint smile*). Perhaps. Good-by. (*He turns to go.*)

SLOW CURTAIN

[4] **Across the floor:** on the floor of Parliament (as a woman member of the opposition party).

Understanding the Play

1. How does the author fill the audience in on what has been happening since the end of the first scene in Act II? In your own words, sum up the situation as scene 2 opens.
2. If Catherine had accepted Desmond's proposal in this scene, would the action have been sufficiently motivated? What are the reasons that might lead to her accepting him? On the basis of what you have learned about her character during the play and of her statements during this scene, do you think it probable that she will eventually marry him?
3. Contrast Violet's report of the victory with Sir Robert's. What different purpose is served by each?
4. How does Catherine's opinion of Sir Robert change as the play progresses? What causes the change of opinion?
5. What is the central conflict of the entire play? How does it relate to the often repeated line "Let Right be done"? Can you think of any situations in contemporary life which involve similar conflicts?
6. Would the meaning of this play be any different if the trial had been lost? Or is the point Rattigan wished to make the same whether or not Winslow wins his case?
7. Character, as has been frequently stated, is revealed by actions. In the course of the entire play, what action by each of the following persons—Arthur Winslow, Catherine, Desmond, Sir Robert, and John—do you consider the most significant in revealing his or her character? What does each action you name reveal about the person?

Developing Language Skills

1. Which of the following questions do you believe more accurately states the central problem of the entire play: Is Ronnie innocent or guilty? or Will Ronnie win a court trial for the charge made against him? Write two or three paragraphs stating your position and the reasons for it.
2. Near the end of the play, Sir Robert says that not *justice* but *right* had been done. In one paragraph show how Sir Robert differentiates between the two terms.
3. In a panel discussion, show the sacrifices that had to be made to win the case by each of the following characters: Arthur, Grace, Dickie,

Catherine, Sir Robert. Conclude the presentation by discussing whether or not the victory was worth their sacrifices.

4. The following lines are spoken when the Winslow family first appears on stage in Act I:

> ARTHUR. He's a good man, Grace.
> GRACE. But what's the use of being good, if you're inaudible?
> CATHERINE. A problem in ethics for you, Father.

The lines concern their minister. What bearing do the lines have on the rest of the play—the problems that arise and the decisions the characters have to make?

Developing Oral Reading Skills

Divide into four groups. Each group plan an oral reading from a different scene from the play to give to the class. Present the four readings in the order that they occur in the play.

The Curtain Falls

When the final curtain of a play falls, you will have only begun to experience the impact of the play. You might first think back over the plot. The following questions will help you to build standards for evaluating a play: Did the story hold your interest? Did the conflict seem real or did it seem artificial and unimportant? Did the plot structure build to a climax? Was the conclusion an inevitable result of the play's action?

You may also remember some striking lines from the play. Was the dialogue true to the characters? Did it reveal their personalities? Did the dialogue advance the action of the plot?

Because drama presents people so directly, you will remember the characters of a play long after you have seen or read it. Were the characters of more than one dimension? Did they have both good and bad qualities? Were the motivations, or reasons, for their actions believable? What did you learn about people and the way they act from the play?

Finally, you should consider the themes dealt with in the play. What is the play about? How does it apply to the life around you? Can the action of the characters be interpreted as a comment on human behavior? Was the theme an outgrowth of the conflict rather than a tagged-on moral preachment in the dialogue? Is the theme universally significant—that is, will it have meaning in other times and in other places?

In answering these questions, you will not only discover the meaning of the play but also will find yourself evaluating its worth as literature.

TERENCE RATTIGAN

Essay and Biography

Introduction to the Essay

THE ESSAY changes style and emphasis as the world changes and reflects variations in the mood and temper of the times. As a result, it is impossible to define the essay exactly, for the word has come to cover a variety of prose forms. Essays differ from short stories and drama in that an essayist usually reflects on or explains ideas, experiences, and people, whereas the short story writer or dramatist creates from his imagination a world of characters who act out experiences and ideas for the reader. The essay form is as old as the Greek philosopher Plato, who lived four hundred years before the birth of Christ, and as new as the editorial in tomorrow's newspaper. About the only statement that applies to all essays is that they are short compositions dealing with a limited subject.

Frequently a distinction is made between two major kinds of essays: the informal and the formal. The *formal essay* (represented by two selections on language at the end of this unit) usually has a serious purpose, is logically organized, and tends to be informative and analytical. Critical essays and serious discussions in such areas as history and philosophy are generally examples of the formal essay. The *informal essay* is much more personal in its approach to its subject matter —which may be anything at all. In organization, it may appear to ramble—although the author generally covers precisely what he intends to and uses the rambling structure to obtain a casual, conversational effect. Style (which includes such elements as diction, tone, and arrangement of subject matter) is extremely important in the writing of informal essays, for good ones are more a result of *how* the writer expresses himself than *what* he expresses. The reader of an informal, or personal, essay must feel that the writer is an interesting and entertaining person. Indeed, the effect should be much like that of a good conversationalist on his hearers.

The originator of the informal essay (the type which makes up most of this unit) is generally regarded as Montaigne, a French philosopher and writer. In 1580, he published a collection of writings called *Essais*, which was the first use of this word as the name for a literary form. The word itself means "attempts" or "tries" and was used to indicate that the discussions were not complete, formally organized treatments of an idea but were partial attempts to cover a subject. Early essays were fairly serious in intent and often were concerned with making some moral or educational point. They have changed a great deal through the years, however. Many are now whimsical or satirical. Some use dialogue and story, so that they are almost indistinguishable from the short story. Others might best be termed character sketches.

For several decades the personal essay, sometimes called "the little old lady in lavender," has been losing ground to tougher-minded writing that relies on satire and argument to tell its story in magazines such

as *Harper's* and *The Atlantic Monthly*. In spite of this trend, magazines such as *The New Yorker* and *Esquire* continue to publish delightful informal essays that have little of the old lady in lavender about
them.

In this unit, you will read essays dealing with a wide variety of subjects and using a number of approaches to their subjects. Three divisions within the unit—description, narration, and exposition—indicate
three major approaches used by essayists. Learning how successful
writers make their descriptions compelling, their reports readable, and
their criticism clear should help you to become better readers and
better writers. From James Thurber's hilarious account of family life
to Paul Gallico's reporting the demands of professional sports is a long
jump—but one that proves the infinite possibilities of the essay form.

The Descriptive Essay

*In a descriptive essay the writer recreates and shares his impression
of persons, places, or experiences by giving concrete details. Thus,
the writers of the following essays make it possible for the reader to
see the rocky coast of Maine, to feel the violence of a cyclone, to "fly
blind" in a Model T, and to watch spring arriving from the southern
tip of the Atlantic Coast to the northernmost corner of New England.*

Reading "The Lobstering Man"

Many of Coffin's distinguishing marks—short sentences, images, direct statements—appear in the first two paragraphs of "The Lobstering
Man." Coffin uses few subordinating words; he makes strong, unqualified statements. He does not say his lobstermen *could;* he says
his lobstermen *did*. He occasionally uses figures of speech to turn
abstract ideas into sharply etched pictures. ("They bob in the boats
close up to the stars. . . . and come home powdered with the stars
of frozen spray.") Coffin's lobsterman becomes the symbol not only
of the State of Maine but of hard work, courage, and integrity as well.

264

The Lobstering Man

Robert P. Tristram Coffin

Whether Coffin is locating Maine on the map by saying it is "the state of us that gets the sun first in our blue eyes" or explaining why a lobster turns red in boiling water, he paints an unforgettable picture of Maine's blue waters and her bronzed lobstermen. Of lobstering Coffin writes, "Lobstering is a stand-up job, good for the back, good for the mind." Of lobstering men he says, "A man has to be half iron and the other half granite to get along, if he is a lobsterman." Coffin makes his readers proud that Maine is part of America and that lobstering is one of America's earliest traditions.

BY THE PINE—which is really a spruce, if I know my evergreens—on the Great Seal of the State of Maine, stand a farmer and a sailor. They ought to be one man. Of course, the farmer is a sort of sop to the few Maine men who don't have a reach of the ocean in their front-dooryard. He is only the left-hand half of a man. Most Maine farmers are as much on the sea as on the land. So the sailor's dress should be the state dress. Now most of the sailors of Maine go after lobsters. These ar-mored crustaceans[1] are Maine's top catch. So, in all fairness, the lobstering man is the Great Seal of the most eastern of these United States, the state of us that gets the sun first in our blue eyes.

A lobstering man is a good man to have as a symbol of anybody's republic. He is not only, in most cases, a dyed-in-the-wool Republican and all wool and a yard wide in his civic sense, but he is also a master-craftsman, a tough man physically, a master of weather on three levels, master of his own boat and soul, and a strong character! He has to be all these things if he wants to make his living off lobsters, and live. The poor lobstermen die young, or else go off and run somebody's railroad or corporation.

THE MAN

Lobsters are hard fish to take. They have become harder and harder as civilization has advanced and learned to enjoy them as its tastiest dish and as lobsters have become fewer in number. Anciently, they lined the beaches in shoals after a no'theaster; but now they are taking to deeper and deeper water. A man has to reach down into twelve fathoms or more to get his hands on the best of them. He has to send all the brains he possesses down on a slender warp[2] and into a subtle house of wood and rigged cord.

No other fishing has so many angles to it as lobstering. It takes a carpenter, a weaver, a meteorologist,[3] a sailor, a good Yankee guesser, a judge of human nature and fish nature—which often coincide if the man and the fish live to-

---

1 **crustaceans:** shellfish.
2 **warp:** rope.
3 **meteorologist:** an expert in weather and climate.

gether a long time—an athlete, and a Job,[4] to bring this horny dekapod[5] up from the deep. But when a man tips a ladleful of pink lobster stew, gilded with melted butter, into his mouth, he is glad he was all these men rolled together. Or when he runs his index finger around a lobster's body-shell, red from boiling, and brings it out loaded down with jade-green tomalley, caviar[6] of Maine, and licks his finger!

Of course the lobsterer eats lobster at least once a day, even though it is a kind of drinking of his pearls. Lobsters are the coast man's money crop. All the others, potatoes, cows, beans and boys, cordwood, proverbs, and philosophy, are just subsistence crops. This man, by the bye, makes out with a very fine subsistence! The fisherman-farmer makes his bank money out of his traps. He may drag in a small fortune in herring on a moonlit July night, or seine[7] up a college education for his son in a good smelt season. Yet these are special windfalls. By and large, season in, season out, it is lobsters he lives by. They are his steady income. As they grow scarcer and more popular, the price per pound goes up, the man lengthens his string, digs deeper and deeper into the ocean, and brings up his hot dollars from the cold water. So he keeps even.

THE TRAP

The coast man takes his income in a trap. The lobster trap is a work of art and genius. It is about the only fish-trap that cannot be turned out by machines in factories on assembly lines.

It must remain a handcraft thing. That makes for security and stability in this machine-ridden world. The thing is too intricate, and the lobster too temperamental, to invite mass production. The air may finally be full of plastic planes and the earth groan with synthetic automobiles; but Old Man Ocean is too corrosive and salt to be fooled by substitutes for honest old hard work and hand-work, hemp, tar, and wood.

The trap is a product of the seasons, too. The three arches of it are of spruce, cut in the Fall and cured through the Winter. On these, in the Spring, laths[8] are nailed with galvanized nails, and a lath door opens in the side and buttons with three hand-whittled pine buttons a man has carried in his pants till they are like bone. The two ends to the trap are nets of tarred twine. The nets taper, as they go in towards each other like two funnels, and end in iron rings, stayed, by intricate cords, in mid-air in the middle of the trap.

These nets, the lobster-heads, are woven through the Winter from a hook in back of the cookstove. The lobsterman's wife often is better at weaving these than her husband. So a woman may enter into this art. The heads are knit with a needle of white pine, always hand-whittled, the length of a small boy's breeches, and as lovely an object of art as any artist could ask for. It is like the dart in a Greek egg-and-dart[9] border at its end, but has a second, smaller arrowhead inside, concentric[10] with the outer. This needle colors like bronze with the use of years. Like the weather-vane arrow and the wooden coot[11] with his uptilted smile and the

4 **Job:** a character in the Old Testament noted for his patience.
5 **horny dekapod:** lobster. *Dekapod* means "having ten feet."
6 **caviar:** a delicacy prepared from fish eggs.
7 **seine:** net.

8 **laths** (lăthz): thin strips of wood.
9 **egg-and-dart:** a kind of pattern.
10 **concentric:** having a center in common.
11 **coot:** northern ducklike bird.

feather at his tail, plucked from the hat of the fisherman's wife, this piece of Maine whittling belongs with the lions of Assyria and Greek vases in the museums.

The iron rings at the nets' small, inner ends have to be just the right circumference for a middle-aged lobster to climb through, putting his left, or clam-crusher, claw through first, then his clam-digging right claw after, next, his stickpin emerald eyes, and lastly pulling in the whole of his broiler plate body. This is, if he is a right-handed lobster. One-third of all lobsters are left-handed, so of course they go into the lure vice versa, putting the dominant limb first, as among our uncles and aunts. One-third is a higher proportion of left-handedness than among us humans. And as left-handedness is a sign of culture and evolutionary meliorism,[12] you can see where we stand!—Three or four million years behind the lobsters!

The big lobsters have to be sacrificed and let go free. One would eat all the bait at one gulp. And the female produces eggs in geometric proportion to her age. Age increases her beauty and charm, unlike the case with Helen of Troy; she grows worth her weight in platinum. So catching a twelve-year-old matron would be matricide[13] in a heinous form, and would soon empty the sea of all lobsters. By the way, if all the eggs produced by a twelve-year-old lobster matured, I believe it would take only a small handful of years before lobsters would fill up the whole ocean and leave no room for the water. That's where traps come in. We are really doing a good turn eating the lobster, both for the lobster and the ocean, not to mention ourselves!

THE LOBSTER

Lobsters are long-lived and grow large. As a boy, I saw the uncle of mine who was the perennial failure among all my uncles pull up a trap with a lobster in it the size of myself. The lobster had broken the head of the trap in. He smiled at us. He filled the whole trap. My uncle saw his fortune made. Then the warp broke. The lobster went smiling back into the deep. My uncle sat down so hard he went through the boat's seat and loosened three boards in the boat's bottom with his. He had a large bottom, as most uncles who are failures have.

There used to be a lobster mounted on a board in a restaurant in Portland over a yardstick's length long. One bite of his claw could have taken off a man's hand. One of my family, an admiral in His Majesty's Navy, though Latin-School and Boston-bred, used to correspond with Commodore Hull of the American Navy and plead with him to send him over to England a lobster such as Sir Isaac had known as a boy in Boston Bay, a ninety-pounder! Commodore Hull finally obliged with a big lobster, the length of a man. The British Admiral was delighted. A showman offered him a big price for it, but Sir Isaac gave it to a lady friend of his. He was rather disappointed though; the lobster seemed a kind of runt to give to a lady for a valentine.

Deep out in the dark Gulf of Maine, crustaceans the size of Tritons[14] must crawl, as octogenarians,[15] and delve out scallops as big as dinner plates, crushing them in their claws like so much tissue, eat high, and remain uncaught and merry. Their ladies, the size of

12 **meliorism:** betterment.
13 **matricide:** killing of one's mother.

14 **Tritons:** sea gods with the head and upper body of a man and the tail of a fish.
15 **octogenarians:** eighty-year-olds.

ROBERT P. TRISTRAM COFFIN

mermaids, sport with the pearls from big mussels. They smile in scorn at the slant-mouthed sharks sliding deadly over above.

TRAP SETTING

There is a birch-wood button on the top of the middle arch in the trap. This is where the bait cord is stayed. The cord has an iron needle, which is strung through the gills or bodies of the bait, and the bait is then hung down inside the trap, midway between the two hooped entrances. The trap has a flat double bottom, and between the double laths here flat rocks are shoved in, to keep the trap down on the bottom and topside up. So a mason's touch is called for. The warp is made fast to the top of the arch on one end. It bears, on the end of its fifteen or twenty fathoms of length, a buoy,[16] painted

the family's two colors, to float on the bay, with the family's license number burned into the wood, and the *paterfamilias's*[17] name scrolled by his jackknife in a handsome flourish upon it.

A good man can run up, say, fifty traps in a Spring, if he has two or three little sons, as he should have, with mouths full of galvanized nails ready for him to use and eyes brimming blue with worship, to egg him on, to hand him things, drawknife or hammer. But the trap is begun in the Fall, with a sharp eye and a sharp ax in the spruce-woods, when the man picks out the right-grained branches that are already half lobster-bows on the tree. And it goes on through the Winter in the flying of the wooden needle at the lobster-heads.

An average good lobsterman, middle-aged, with a quiverful of wiry sons to spell him, will run to about one hun-

16 **buoy** (boi): an anchored floating object used as a marker.

18 **rose hips**: the bright-colored fruit of the rose.

ESSAY

dred and forty traps fishing regularly. But I know two octogenarians, with white hair but tough as new ten-penny nails, with all their sons gone inland and become white-haired bank-presidents or poets, who fish one hundred and fifty. Below one hundred traps, laziness sets in, and it is a losing game. Above two hundred, the lobstering man enters the capitalist class and ceases to count, has to hire assistants, has no time for whittling, sons, or human nature. One hundred and fifty traps is safe.

It is good to see my octogenarian friends coming home with their white hair against the evergreens. They stand up slim and straight in their dories, backing-water with their oars. You would swear they were twenty. They are a sight to see in a Maine dawn. Their cheeks are like rose hips.[18] Their eyes are a blue that even Maine sky cannot get. All the people around love them. The young men like to have them around. And the women. Any day is a better day that starts out with their old blue eyes crinkled up deep with the early, low light.

Once the traps are made, the lobstering man has only just begun. It is the fishing of the traps that makes the artist out of him. He sets his traps in a circle, from his own doorstep, if he is on bold water—and he better be—out into the Atlantic and loops back to his landing, so he won't have to be loafing rowing back. Work in a circle, from home to home. All this is, if his grandfather before him had the sense to own this particular circle of the sea. If not, the man may have to go miles from his cove and cut a new swath in the ocean. And he will row through forests of traps to get to his freehold. You can't own the Atlantic, but Maine lobstermen own pretty good circles of it, and woe be to any who come within. Certain men belong to certain reefs, and a shotgun may warn off an intruder. And when sound fails, lead steps in.

Of course the fisherman has to know the right bottom for lobsters. Along reefs is the best. A hard and rugged bottom, not mud. A lobster likes rockweed to live in. The fisherman has to know the ocean floor like his own kitchen's. He has to know it a long ways out. For in Winter he has to move his traps into deep water. When the bays freeze, the lobster, who is a Republican of Republicans, like his hunter above him, and a stickler for keeping the same temperature, goes out deep and keeps warm and serene. He also moves about from week to week in other seasons. He has his picnic grounds and his trysting places, his places to dine. You have to know where to find him. He is current and tasty meat in every month but July. Then he sheds his whole shell, down to his smallest legs and fringes on them, and while doing so becomes soft and tasteless, so you will have to leave him alone. You throw him back when he is shedding.

THE RULES OF THE GAME

You have to throw him back if he's a she, too, and has the brown eggs under the wide flanges of his tail. This for the sake of lobsters' perpetuity. You have to throw him back into the ocean also if he is less than four and a half inches along his back body-shell from the tip of his thorned Roman nose to the bottom of his hard jacket. The lobsterman has a gauge in his boat that length. But he never uses it. He can tell at a glance which smaller ones must

---

17 paterfamilias: father.

go over the side, he can tell in the night by a touch. He knows the "shorts" instantly when he opens the trap's door and takes the many crabs out by their rear, smallest claws, picks up each starfish and tears it asunder, and comes at last to the one or two good lobsters that are in each trap. Again and again, every lobster goes over. The starfish he tears carefully into fives, so they can't sprout legs again, because starfish are death on his bait, they suck all the goodness in it up through their harpy-like[19] mouths. Maybe a "count" lobster is left. The man picks him up with thumb and forefinger, just at the joining of his claws to the back shell, so the shears the lobster sweeps about cannot carve him up, fishes a pine plug out of his rear pants-pocket, wedges both claws to by shoving the wood deep into the joints of the jaws.

The lobsterman is obliged by law to throw the short lobsters back into the sea. Every tenth fisherman along the Maine coast is a warden. But he doesn't need to be. Most of the men who fish are honest as the day is long. They know which side their bread is buttered on. They know they must live on lobsters, and lobsters must live if *they* want to. So they throw the little fellows back and let them get their growth. They keep their best crop going, for their sons will be lobstering men after them.

You must not pull another man's traps. It is as simple as that. It is also as bronze as the Ten Commandments. The Eleven. For not pulling another man's lobster traps is the only commandment the coast men have added to the lot that Moses staggered down Sinai with. I know a man who does.

But he has only one eye. And buckshot rattles in his wily bones when he sits gingerly down. There may well be sudden death on a fine morning. More than one water-thief has died of lead-poisoning. The high islands make good ambushes. You may see a man lying flat on a headland for hours, watching the dots of his lobster buoys with his three-diameter eyes, and a shining gun beside him. Oh, the good lobstering man—and he's mostly good, if he wants to bring up his family and live—will forgive boys out for a lark, or a Summer resident hungry for just one meal of lobster, and not schooled well in the hard coast honesty. He will smile and shake his head when he pulls his traps and finds them empty over and over, and the doors unbuttoned. But he will not put up with a man who makes a business of theft and should know better.

BAIT

Bait is a crucial matter. The best is the smelliest. The lobster likes his fish good and dead, the longer, the better. I know that the best lobstering men drive their trucks all the way to Portland or Jonesport to get the leavings of the trawlers[20] which have grown ripe[21] on the wharves. They come home smelling to heaven. When they go out to the traps, their bait tubs scent up the bay. Yet when they come in, their boats are clean as a whistle, and the men's hands smell as sweet as the bayberry along the shore. A lobstering man, if he is good, keeps his boat fresh as a daisy. He is a clean man. And ripe-baiters bring home their tubs running over with lobsters and get rid of

---

19 harpy: mythological creature that seized the food of its victims.

20 trawlers: fishing crafts.
21 ripe: spoiled; rotten.

the ripeness somehow on the way in the wind.

For all the bait smells, a lobster trap fishing is a fine and delicate business. The idea is that the lobster—who won't come too far from his love or his nap or his favorite scenery of waving kelp and seaweed—smells the aroma of defunct fish, stops digging for clams, and comes with his hundred paddles going like lace and sees the strange sudden hostel of laths and arches. He touches it with his antennae. He sees the stairway of net going up to the door. He sees a whole boiled dinner hanging ready. Mince pie and tea all turned out! He goes up the stairs cautiously. Puts in big-claw after big-claw, and squeezes through the opening. He takes the feast in both arms and hangs and feeds on its fatness. When he is done, being a creature fond of his comfort, he dozes and does little worrying. He stays there radiating good will. He is in no hurry to leave. Who knows, maybe more old fish may sprout on that needle! He paddles about.

Then suddenly his restaurant stands on end, rises, and travels up fast. The lobster, alarmed, tries to find the door. But he misses that small circle, swims into the trap's corners, tries again, misses. The blue world is growing dangerous and green. He darts about frantic. Then the green world bursts open, and he is out in a breathless bubble of a universe. A giant upright lobster opens his house at the side, takes him back of his claws. He tries to bite the creature. But the creature thrusts a splinter into the jaws of his scissors, and throws him down on a mountain of cousins and aunts with whom he does not care to have even a nodding acquaintance, on others he has not even been introduced to. He is hopping, hopping mad. He tries to flap

his way free, but his tail beats in vain on utter emptiness. He sulks on the mountain of strangers. Then he is put back in water, but it is only a small square of the Atlantic, a slatted and dreary prison. Fish are thrown to him. But he has no appetite, he aches for freedom. Then he is taken out, by George! carried in a net elsewhither, and in the green flower of his life, rankling with rage at the indecorum of it all, cold with the sea, he is plunged into boiling water. No wonder he comes out of the kettle red!

The good lobstering man pulls once a day. The shiftless, every other, and he comes home empty for his pains. For lobsters, after their dinner's digested, *can*, when unhurried, find the way out of prison. The lobstering man pulls at the ebb, so he will have the least length of the warps to take in and the least bending of his back at the labor. The good man goes out at dawn, and then through his weeks follows the moon late into twilight, till he catches the low tide at sun-up again. He lives on a slide rule and keeps no regular hours. But his wife keeps the pot of black tea always on the back of the stove and a slab or two of apple pie always ready for him.

The man goes in his gasoline boat, cuts the switch as he comes up to his first buoy, catches the rope with his gaff[22] where he stands near the stern, heaves up a leg on the gunwale,[23] fetches a pull, keeps the rope taut, and hand-over-hand pulls her in fast. The trap breaks water, he heaves it up on the rail, opens the door, takes out the welter of crabs biting one another into knots, throws out the "shorts," saves the one or two "counts," and plugs them. Then

22 **gaff:** barbed spear or hook.
23 **gunwale:** upper edge of the side of a boat.

he baits up again, dowses the trap over, throws out the warp in loops, cranks up his engine, and chugs on to the next one. So around his whole circle of a day's work, bucking the tide, bucking the wind and weather, and always with that cloud of white and gray seagulls, screaming for bait scraps, hovering around him.

HAZARDS OF LOBSTERING

Lobstering is a stand-up job, good for the back, good for the mind. All day the man stands to it, and when he gets back home, he seems to have forgotten how to sit, and eats his cold pie and hot tea standing. I am beginning to believe that many of the lobstering men I know have no hinge in the middle at all. I've never caught them sitting.

Lobstering is an all-weather job, too, and the fisherman is wet as often as he is dry. He learns to keep perpendicular in his never-horizontal boat, and he grows so shaped to the roll of the sea that he walks on land in the way he stands in a boat. Winter and Summer he goes out, he toughens, he browns, his face takes on the color of weather. Sun or snow, sleet or shine, he looks them all in the face, and his face shows it and grows handsome. His high-nosed reach-boat cuts the waves, and he stands and steers by the rope where it passes the engine.

Alone in the boat, day in, day out, year in, year out, in blue shine and white fog, and under the walking death of the hail. Some day, maybe, he will not come back. The waves will come whitening in, but not he. He knows that. It gives a gleam to his eyes. A wave bigger than the others, a lurch to the boat. He will go. Often he is a man who never has learned to swim. What use, with a boat gone on, and miles of freezing ocean around? He will go. And the boat will run aimless till the engine dies. But his boat will be picked up. His son will inherit his boat. Things will come out all right in the end.

The wall between warm life and cold death is very thin out there where the reefs whiten in the January sun and the whole ocean leans suddenly in, with buoys and boat leaning with it, against the toothed shore, and if that small spark in the spray there fails . . . The small life of fire in the engine may flicker out, and the heavy boat lie and roll helpless, and a wave lift it to the ragged rocks. The man stoops over his engine and protects the faint spark from the drenching scud with his aching and buffeted body. A clumsy move, a misstep, a skipped spark, and it can be the cold dark of the ocean floor for good for him. And crabs that feast on a face. He knows it. That is why the man is so sure and beautiful on his feet, ties the knot so quick and true with his hands. There are only his muscles and quick brain to keep the five quarts of blood warm in him in the cold, hating inertia of the infinite power he rolls through. He is captain and crew and master of his life alone. The arrogant way he stands and the quiet way he speaks and looks show it.

One bitter, zero Winter day, on Penobscot, a lobsterman's propeller fouled[24] in his lobster warp. The rope wound right on tight as the string on a top. The man was tethered in his own boat, on the open sea, to sure death. His own boat had nailed him to the sea. There was only one thing to do. The man did it. He stripped off his clothes, went over the rail with his jackknife, and cut the fouled warp away from the

24 **fouled:** tangled.

bronze under the water. Then he came up sputtering to the knife-edged wind, dragged himself aboard, cranked her up, put on what clothes he could with his numbed hands, and came home to double pneumonia, but, through that, to life.

A man has to be half iron and the other half granite to get along, if he is a lobsterman. It is lucky both substances come thick along the Maine coast. And the hard business pays good dividends. In hard cash. But in hard manhood also.

DIVIDENDS OF LOBSTERING

The man is his own boss. He makes his own hours. He builds and runs his own boat, alone. That is something. He makes and owns most of his own gear. He depends on himself. He gets a lot of good air into him, deep. He gets to know loneliness well. It is a solitary calling he follows, but he learns to get along well with his thoughts. That is a thing most men never do. He is a three-dimensional man in this world that is becoming so two-dimensional. He knows air, water, earth, well. His things are handmade. He is his own boat-builder, carpenter. He knows all the weathers, good and bad. I know one lobstering man who goes out in his boat to sit for half an hour in every good sunset that comes along. The lobstering man has time for things. He has learned how to look around the corners of time and space and see what it is going to be like ahead. He spots death lurking under a narrow reef on a mean low tide. His eyes get so they can look a long way off and see the squall, the fog coming, and from that it is only a step to seeing what ideas will be coming also.

This lobstering man is a sight for sore eyes or the eyes of an artist. He looks clean, and he looks good. He wears a cap long in the visor to keep the coast sun out of his eyes. He wears hip boots, and sheds light from his oilskins. His face gets the color of white-pine panels in old houses. The maps of old Decembers and Junes are lined out on his neck. His hands, from handling the traps, grow to looking like anchors. He is a good man to anchor to, if you want to get things done. He stands very straight, even at eighty. He may squint at his eyes, but he can see a smart distance. He walks with a roll, as suits his long boots, but he gets to a place fast. He looks especially handsome in the wind; but he goes well with his Eden-like dawns and the Apocalyptic[25] sunsets, too. A lot of light comes out of him as well as out of his background. A lot of artists follow him up and down the coast and paint him. He goes well in oils, having his oilskins and having his solidity on him. Winslow Homer got him down in the fogs. N. C. Wyeth got him down in the amber light of his sunset, backing-water up to a cove with sides like a rainbow. My friend, Steve Etnier,[26] gets his hard angles into the razor-sharp light of an August noon. Steve has one of him for his skipper and cook, boatswain, major prophet, and general manager. In his empire hung over the Kennebec's[27] wicked mouth, Steve needs him.

Lobstering men fit naturally into paintings. For they live and breathe and have their being in the midst of free-running azures and salty siennas[28] all their time. They are the men who see the most sunrises and sunsets over wide water. They pass through fog and come out beaded with beauty in the sun. They bob in the boats close up to the stars. They are out in every kind of wind. They stand through snowsqualls and come home powdered with the stars of frozen spray. They run along silver roadways to the moon. They are silhouetted much against headlands. They toss along laces of evergreens, over laces of surf. They and their white and green and black boats are always out where colors are clear and the waves fill the world with sparkle.

From being so much in the weather, the lobstering man gets a face like bronze. He gets to standing bronze-like in his body, too. He never puts on fat, he moves about so much. Leaning against the wind, he grows lean himself. He is cut right down to essential muscle and bone, as he would put it, to "withing." He would look fine in bronze.

And he does. One of the best of his kind has got into a statue. He is Elroy Johnson, of Bailey's Island, lobsterman, and he went to the last World's Fair, the one in New York, in bronze. He went as the typical Down East lobstering man. Elroy is one of the few men who have gone into bronze while still alive and working. Most of us have to wait till we are dead. Elroy is about the best lobsterman along the whole coast. I am glad he is a friend of mine. The World's Fair didn't hurt him any, either. He looks a lot like Will Rogers —easy to look at and very American. He talks the way Will Rogers used to, too. Maine coast men are very easy on their words, softer-spoken than Southerners. They are good men to put the baby to sleep when they talk, they are so gentle and deep in their speaking.

So now the world knows how a lobstering man looks. A bronze, lean man. The world ought to be proud to know him.

25 **Apocalyptic:** referring to the end of the world.
26 **Homer, Wyeth, Etnier:** American artists.
27 **Kennebec** (kĕn'ə bĕk'): river in Maine.
28 **siennas:** brownish-yellows or orange-reds.

Understanding the Essay

1. What character traits of the lobstermen lead Coffin to declare near the opening of the essay: "A lobstering man is a good man to have as a symbol of anybody's republic"?

2. In Coffin's references to sons of lobstermen who have gone inland "to run somebody's railroad or corporation" or become "white-haired bank presidents or poets" there is an indirect comparison with lobstermen. What differences does Coffin see between lobstermen and these other kinds of men? Which men does he prefer?

3. How is Coffin's reference to the lobster gauge both a professional and a personal compliment to lobstermen?

4. How does Coffin support his statement "Not pulling another man's lobster traps is the only commandment the coast men have added to the lot that Moses staggered down Sinai with"?

5. "The Lobstering Man" is essentially a descriptive essay. How does Coffin introduce some element of action to add to its vitality? What are one or two specific instances of his doing so?

6. Close examination of a small section of Coffin's essay reveals much about the techniques he has used throughout it. Reread the section entitled "The Trap" and answer the following questions:

   (a) What kind of sentence does Coffin most frequently use? (Simple? Compound? Complex?) Why is it suited to this essay?

   (b) What are some instances of his using comparisons or figures of speech to make a description clearer?

   (c) Coffin's subject is a fairly technical one in this section. What are some phrases or details he uses that create a conversational, even humorous, effect rather than a formal, technical one?

   (d) Coffin rarely states his own values directly in this essay, yet the reader can tell what many of them are. What are some sentences in this section which indicate Coffin's values? What are these values?

7. Coffin's style is colloquial and direct. However, he often uses difficult, "big" words that we usually associate with more formal contexts. For example, he writes that "left-handedness is a sign of culture and evolutionary meliorism." Find several other examples of Coffin's using such words. What is the effect of using them?

Building Vocabulary Skills

Report to the class on the source of the following allusions:

1. ". . . it is a kind of drinking of his pearls."
2. ". . . this piece of Maine whittling belongs with the lions of Assyria and Greek vases in the museums."
3. "It is also as bronze as the Ten Commandments."

Developing Language Skills

Take any of the following for your topic sentence and expand it into a paragraph. Take details from the essay but use your own words.

1. "A lobstering man is a good man to have as a symbol of anybody's republic."
2. The world of the lobsterman is full of danger.
3. "The lobstering man has time for things. He has learned how to look around the corners of time and space and see what it is going to be like ahead."

Reading "The Elements"

Saint-Exupéry explains at the opening of his essay the difficulty of writing descriptions of terrifying experiences. He writes that a cyclone was "much the most brutal and overwhelming experience I ever underwent; and yet beyond a certain point I do not know how to convey its violence except by piling one adjective on another, so that in the end I should convey no impression at all—unless perhaps that of an embarrassing taste for exaggeration." He uses several methods to overcome this difficulty. One is simply a balancing of sentences—long sentences contrasting with short, explosive fragments of sentences. This device makes the short sentences very emphatic, so that they drive home the sense of danger. Another device is repetition, which again emphasizes and creates a sense of emotional intensity—"I must straighten out. Straighten out. Straighten out." Similes and metaphors are used—partly for the sake of vividness, but more for that of making an unfamiliar experience clear by comparison to familiar things. And a last important device is personification. By speaking of the elements as human beings, Saint-Exupéry creates a dramatic conflict that otherwise would be missing.

The Elements[*]

Antoine de Saint-Exupéry[1]

This excerpt from Wind, Sand and Stars *describes a violent encounter with a cyclone over Argentina in the nineteen-twenties. This event occurred early in Saint-Exupéry's career when he was pioneering strange and perilous routes.*

WHEN JOSEPH CONRAD described a typhoon he said very little about towering waves, or darkness, or the whistling of the wind in the shrouds. He knew better. Instead, he took his reader down into the hold of the vessel, packed with emigrant coolies, where the rolling and the pitching of the ship had ripped up and scattered their bags and bundles, burst open their boxes, and flung their humble belongings into a crazy heap. Family treasures painfully collected in a lifetime of poverty, pitiful mementoes so alike that nobody but their owners could have told them apart, had lost their identity and lapsed into chaos, into anonymity, into an amorphous[2] magma.[3] It was this human drama that Conrad described when he painted a typhoon.

Every airline pilot has flown through tornadoes, has returned out of them to the fold—to the little restaurant in Toulouse[4] where we sat in peace under the watchful eye of the waitress—and there, recognizing his powerlessness to convey what he has been through, has given up the idea of describing hell. His descriptions, his gestures, his big words would have made the rest of us smile as if we were listening to a little boy bragging. And necessarily so. The cyclone of which I am about to speak was, physically, much the most brutal and overwhelming experience I ever underwent; and yet beyond a certain point I do not know how to convey its violence except by piling one adjective on another, so that in the end I should convey no impression at all—unless perhaps that of an embarrassing taste for exaggeration.

It took me some time to grasp the fundamental reason for this powerlessness, which is simply that I should be trying to describe a catastrophe that never took place. The reason why writers fail when they attempt to evoke horror is that horror is something invented after the fact, when one is recreating the experience over again in the memory. Horror does not manifest itself in the world of reality. And so, in beginning my story of a revolt of the elements which I myself lived through I have no feeling that I shall write something which you will find dramatic.

I had taken off from the field at Trelew and was flying down to Comodoro-Rivadavia, in the Patagonian Argen-

---

1 Pronounced äN twȧn′də säN tĕg zY pĕ rē′.
2 amorphous (ə môr′fəs): shapeless.
3 magma: mixture.

4 Toulouse (tōō lōōz′): city in southern France.

tine.[5]   Here the crust of the earth is as dented as an old boiler.   The high-pressure regions over the Pacific send the winds past a gap in the Andes into a corridor fifty miles wide through which they rush to the Atlantic in a strangled and accelerated buffeting that scrapes the surface of everything in their path.   The sole vegetation visible in this barren landscape is a plantation of oil derricks looking like the after-effects of a forest fire.   Towering over the round hills on which the winds have left a residue of stony gravel, there rises a chain of prow-shaped, saw-toothed, razor-edged mountains stripped by the elements down to the bare rock.

For three months of the year the speed of these winds at ground level is up to a hundred miles an hour.   We who flew the route knew that once we had crossed the marshes of Trelew and had reached the threshold of the zone they swept, we should recognize the winds from afar by a gray-blue tint in the atmosphere at the sight of which we would tighten our belts and shoulder-straps in preparation for what was coming.   From then on we had an hour of stiff fighting and of stumbling again and again into invisible ditches of air. This was manual labor, and our muscles felt it pretty much as if we had been carrying a longshoreman's load.   But it lasted only an hour.   Our machines stood up under it.   We had no fear of wings suddenly dropping off.   Visibility was generally good, and not a problem. This section of the line was a stint, yes; it was certainly not a drama.

But on this particular day I did not like the color of the sky.

The sky was blue.   Pure blue.   Too pure.   A hard blue sky that shone over the scraped and barren world while the fleshless vertebrae of the mountain chain flashed in the sunlight.   Not a cloud.   The blue sky glittered like a new-honed knife.   I felt in advance the vague distaste that accompanies the prospect of physical exertion.   The purity of the sky upset me.   Give me a good black storm in which the enemy is plainly visible.   I can measure its extent and prepare myself for its attack. I can get my hands on my adversary. But when you are flying very high in clear weather the shock of a blue storm is as disturbing as if something collapsed that had been holding up your ship in the air.   It is the only time when a pilot feels that there is a gulf beneath his ship.

Another thing bothered me.   I could see on a level with the mountain peaks not a haze, not a mist, not a sandy fog, but a sort of ash-colored streamer in the sky.   I did not like the look of that scarf of filings scraped off the surface of the earth and borne out to sea by the wind. I tightened my leather harness as far as it would go and I steered the ship with one hand while with the other I hung on to the longeron[6] that ran along-side my seat.   I was still flying in re-markably calm air.

Very soon came a slight tremor.   As every pilot knows, there are secret little quiverings that foretell your real storm. No rolling, no pitching.   No swing to speak of.   The flight continues hori-zontal and rectilinear.[7]   But you have felt a warning drum on the wings of your plane, little intermittent rappings scarcely audible and infinitely brief, little cracklings from time to time as if there were traces of gunpowder in the air.

---

5 **Patagonian Argentine:** a tableland in the south-ern Argentine.

6 **longeron** (lŏn′jə rən): part of the framing of the fuselage.

7 **rectilinear:** in a straight line.

And then everything round me blew up.

Concerning the next couple of minutes I have nothing to say. All that I can find in my memory is a few rudimentary notions, fragments of thoughts, direct observations. I cannot compose them into a dramatic recital because there was no drama. The best I can do is to line them up in a kind of chronological order.

In the first place, I was standing still. Having banked right in order to correct a sudden drift, I saw the landscape freeze abruptly where it was and remain jiggling on the same spot. I was making no headway. My wings had ceased to nibble into the outline of the earth. I could see the earth buckle, pivot—but it stayed put. The plane was skidding as if on a toothless cogwheel.

Meanwhile I had the absurd feeling that I had exposed myself completely to the enemy. All those peaks, those crests, those teeth that were cutting into the wind and unleashing its gusts in my direction, seemed to me so many guns pointed straight at my defenseless person. I was slow to think, but the thought did come to me that I ought to give up altitude and make for one of the neighboring valleys where I might take shelter against a mountainside. As a matter of fact, whether I liked it or not I was being helplessly sucked down towards the earth.

Trapped this way in the first breaking waves of a cyclone about which I learned, twenty minutes later, that at sea level it was blowing at the fantastic rate of one hundred and fifty miles an hour, I certainly had no impression of tragedy. Now, as I write, if I shut my eyes, if I forget the plane and the flight and try to express the plain truth about what was happening to me, I find that I felt weighed down, I felt like a porter carrying a slippery load, grabbing one object in a jerky movement that sent another slithering down, so that, overcome by exasperation, the porter is tempted to let the whole load drop. There is a kind of law of the shortest distance to the image, a psychological law by which the event to which one is subjected is visualized in a symbol that represents its swiftest summing up: I was a man who, carrying a pile of plates, had slipped on a waxed floor and let his scaffolding of porcelain crash.

I found myself imprisoned in a valley. My discomfort was not less, it was greater. I grant you that a down current has never killed anybody, that the expression "flattened out by a down current" belongs to journalism and not to the language of flyers. How could air possibly pierce the ground? But here I was in a valley at the wheel of a ship that was three-quarters out of my control. Ahead of me a rocky prow swung to left and right, rose suddenly high in the air for a second like a wave over my head, and then plunged down below my horizon.

Horizon? There was no longer a horizon. I was in the wings of a theater cluttered up with bits of scenery. Vertical, oblique, horizontal, all of plane geometry was awhirl. A hundred transversal[8] valleys were muddled in a jumble of perspectives. Whenever I seemed about to take my bearings a new eruption would swing me round in a circle or send me tumbling wing over wing and I would have to try all over again to get clear of all this rubbish. Two ideas came into my mind. One was a discovery: for the first time I understood the cause of certain accidents in the mountains when

8 transversal: crisscross.

no fog was present to explain them. For a single second, in a waltzing landscape like this, the flyer had been unable to distinguish between vertical mountainsides and horizontal planes. The other idea was a fixation: The sea is flat: I shall not hook anything out at sea.

I banked—or should I use that word to indicate a vague and stubborn jockeying through the east-west valleys? Still nothing pathetic to report. I was wrestling with chaos, was wearing myself out in a battle with chaos, struggling to keep in the air a gigantic house of cards that kept collapsing despite all I could do. Scarcely the faintest twinge of fear went through me when one of the walls of my prison rose suddenly like a tidal wave over my head. My heart hardly skipped a beat when I was tripped up by one of the whirling eddies of air that the sharp ridge darted into my ship. If I felt anything unmistakably in the haze of confused feelings and notions that came over me each time one of these powder magazines blew up, it was a feeling of respect. I respected that sharp-toothed ridge. I respected that peak. I respected that dome. I respected that transversal valley opening out into my valley and about to toss me God knew how violently as soon as its torrent of wind flowed into the one on which I was being borne along.

What I was struggling against, I discovered, was not the wind but the ridge itself, the crest, the rocky peak. Despite my distance from it, it was the wall of rock I was fighting with. By some trick of invisible prolongation, by the play of a secret set of muscles, this was what was pummeling me. It was against this that I was butting my head. Before me on the right I recognized the peak of Salamanca, a perfect cone which, I knew, dominated the sea. It cheered me to think I was about to escape out to sea. But first I should have to wrestle with the gale off that peak, try to avoid its down-crushing blow. The peak of Salamanca was a giant. I was filled with respect for the peak of Salamanca.

There had been granted me one second of respite. Two seconds. Something was collecting itself into a knot, coiling itself up, growing taut. I sat amazed. I opened astonished eyes. My whole plane seemed to be shivering, spreading outward, swelling up. Horizontal and stationary it was, yet lifted before I knew it fifteen hundred feet straight into the air in a kind of apotheosis.[9] I who for forty minutes had not been able to climb higher than two hundred feet off the ground was suddenly able to look down on the enemy. The plane quivered as if in boiling water. I could see the wide waters of the ocean. The valley opened out into this ocean, this salvation.—And at that very moment, without any warning whatever, half a mile from Salamanca, I was suddenly struck straight in the midriff by the gale off that peak and sent hurtling out to sea.

There I was, throttle wide open, facing the coast. At right angles to the coast and facing it. A lot had happened in a single minute. In the first place, I had not flown out to sea. I had been spat out to sea by a monstrous cough, vomited out of my valley as from the mouth of a howitzer.[10] When, what seemed to me instantly, I banked in order to put myself where I wanted to be in respect of the coastline, I saw that the coastline was a mere blur, a characterless strip of blue; and I was five miles out to sea. The mountain range stood up like a crenelated[11] fortress against the pure sky while the cyclone crushed me down to the surface of the waters. How hard that wind was blowing I found out as soon as I tried to climb, as soon as I became conscious of my disastrous mistake: throttle wide open, engines running at my maximum, which was one hundred and fifty miles an hour, my plane hanging sixty feet over the water, I was unable to budge. When a wind like this one attacks a tropical forest it swirls through the branches like a flame, twists them into corkscrews, and uproots giant trees as if they were radishes. Here, bounding off the mountain range, it was leveling out the sea.

Hanging on with all the power in my engines, face to the coast, face to that wind where each gap in the teeth of the range sent forth a stream of air like a long reptile, I felt as if I were clinging to the tip of a monstrous whip that was cracking over the sea.

In this latitude the South American continent is narrow and the Andes are not far from the Atlantic. I was struggling not merely against the whirling winds that blew off the east-coast range, but more likely also against a whole sky blown down upon me off the peaks of the Andean chain. For the first time in four years of airline flying I began to worry about the strength of my wings. Also, I was fearful of bumping the sea—not because of the down currents which, at sea level, would necessarily provide me with a horizontal air mattress, but because of the helplessly acrobatic positions in which this wind was buffeting me. Each time that I was tossed I became afraid that I might

9 **apotheosis** (ə pŏth'ĭ ō'sĭs): deification.
10 **howitzer** (hou'ĭt sər): a short cannon.

11 **crenelated**: notched; battlemented.

be unable to straighten out. Besides, there was a chance that I should find myself out of fuel and simply drown. I kept expecting the gasoline pumps to stop priming, and indeed the plane was so violently shaken up that in the half-filled tanks as well as in the gas lines the gasoline was sloshing round, not coming through, and the engines, instead of their steady roar, were sputtering in a sort of dot-and-dash series of uncertain growls.

I hung on, meanwhile, to the controls of my heavy transport plane, my attention monopolized by the physical struggle and my mind occupied by the very simplest thoughts. I was feeling practically nothing as I stared down at the imprint made by the wind on the sea. I saw a series of great white puddles, each perhaps eight hundred yards in extent. They were running towards me at a speed of one hundred and fifty miles an hour where the down-surging windspouts broke against the surface of the sea in a succession of horizontal explosions. The sea was white and it was green—white with the whiteness of crushed sugar and green in puddles the color of emeralds. In this tumult one wave was indistinguishable from another. Torrents of air were pouring down upon the sea. The winds were sweeping past in giant gusts as when, before the autumn harvests, they blow a great flowing change of color over a wheatfield. Now and again the water went incongruously transparent between the white pools, and I could see a green and black sea-bottom. And then the great glass of the sea would be shattered anew into a thousand glittering fragments.

It seemed hopeless. In twenty minutes of struggle I had not moved forward a hundred yards. What was more, with flying as hard as it was out

here five miles from the coast, I wondered how I could possibly buck the winds along the shore, assuming I was able to fight my way in. I was a perfect target for the enemy there on shore. Fear, however, was out of the question. I was incapable of thinking. I was emptied of everything except the vision of a very simple act. I must straighten out. Straighten out. Straighten out.

There were moments of respite, nevertheless. I dare say those moments themselves were equal to the worst storms I had hitherto met, but by comparison with the cyclone they were moments of relaxation. The urgency of fighting off the wind was not quite so great. And I could tell when these intervals were coming. It was not I who moved toward those zones of relative calm, those almost green oases clearly painted on the sea, but they that flowed toward me. I could read clearly in the waters the advertisement of a habitable province. And with each interval of repose the power to feel and to think was restored to me. Then, in those moments, I began to feel I was doomed. Then was the time that little by little I began to tremble for myself. So much so that each time I saw the unfurling of a new wave of the white offensive I was seized by a brief spasm of panic which lasted until the exact instant when, on the edge of that bubbling caldron, I bumped into the invisible wall of wind. That restored me to numbness again.

Up! I wanted to be higher up. The next time I saw one of those green zones of calm it seemed to me deeper than before and I began to be hopeful of getting out. If I could climb high enough, I thought, I would find other currents in which I could make some headway. I took advantage of the truce to essay a swift climb. It was hard. The enemy had not weakened. Three hundred feet. Six hundred feet. If I could get up to three thousand feet I was safe, I said to myself. But there on the horizon I saw again that white pack unleashed in my direction. I gave it up. I did not want them at my throat again; I did not want to be caught off balance. But it was too late. The first blow sent me rolling over and over and the sky became a slippery dome on which I could not find a footing.

One has a pair of hands and they obey. How are one's orders transmitted to one's hands?

I had made a discovery that horrified me: my hands were numb. My hands were dead. They sent me no message. Probably they had been numb a long time and I had not noticed it. The pity was that I had noticed it, had raised the question. That was serious.

Lashed by the wind, the wings of the plane had been dragging and jerking at the cables by which they were controlled from the wheel, and the wheel in my hands had not ceased jerking a single second. I had been gripping the wheel with all my might for forty minutes, fearful lest the strain snap the cables. So desperate had been my grip that now I could not feel my hands.

What a discovery! My hands were not my own. I looked at them and decided to lift a finger: it obeyed me. I looked away and issued the same order: now I could not feel whether the finger had obeyed or not. No message had reached me. I thought: "Suppose my hands were to open: how would I know it?" I swung my head round and looked again: my hands were still locked round the wheel. Nevertheless,

I was afraid. How can a man tell the difference between the sight of a hand opening and the decision to open that hand, when there is no longer an exchange of sensations between the hand and the brain? How can one tell the difference between an image and an act of the will? Better stop thinking of the picture of open hands. Hands live a life of their own. Better not offer them this monstrous temptation. And I began to chant a silly litany which went on uninterruptedly until this flight was over. A single thought. A single image. A single phrase tirelessly chanted over and over again: "I shut my hands. I shut my hands. I shut my hands." All of me was condensed into that phrase and for me the white sea, the whirling eddies, the saw-toothed range ceased to exist. There was only "I shut my hands." There was no danger, no cyclone, no land unattained. Somewhere there was a pair of rubber hands which, once they let go the wheel, could not possibly come alive in time to recover from the tumbling drop into the sea.

I had no thoughts. I had no feelings except the feeling of being emptied out. My strength was draining out of me and so was my impulse to go on fighting. The engines continued their dot-and-dash sputterings, their little crashing noises that were like the intermittent cracklings of a ripping canvas. Whenever they were silent longer than a second I felt as if a heart had stopped beating. There! that's the end. No, they've started up again.

The thermometer on the wing, I happened to see, stood at twenty below zero, but I was bathed in sweat from head to foot. My face was running with perspiration. What a dance! Later I was to discover that my storage batteries had been jerked out of their steel flanges[12] and hurtled up through the roof of the plane. I did not know then, either, that the ribs on my wings had come unglued and that certain of my steel cables had been sawed down to the last thread. And I continued to feel strength and will oozing out of me. Any minute now I should be overcome by the indifference born of utter weariness and by the mortal yearning to take my rest.

What can I say about this? Nothing. My shoulders ached. Very painfully. As if I had been carrying too many sacks too heavy for me. I leaned forward. Through a green transparency I saw sea-bottom so close that I could make out all the details. Then the wind's hand brushed the picture away.

In an hour and twenty minutes I had succeeded in climbing to nine hundred feet. A little to the south—that is, on my left—I could see a long trail on the surface of the sea, a sort of blue stream. I decided to let myself drift as far down as that stream. Here where I was, facing west, I was as good as motionless, unable either to advance or retreat. If I could reach that blue pathway, which must be lying in the shelter of something not the cyclone, I might be able to move in slowly to the coast. So I let myself drift to the left. I had the feeling, meanwhile, that the wind's violence had perhaps slackened.

It took me an hour to cover the five miles to shore. There in the shelter of a long cliff I was able to finish my journey south. Thereafter I succeeded in keeping enough altitude to fly inland to the field that was my destination. I was able to stay up at nine hundred feet. It was very stormy, but nothing

like the cyclone I had come out of. That was over.

On the ground I saw a platoon of soldiers. They had been sent down to watch for me. I landed near by and we were a whole hour getting the plane into the hangar. I climbed out of the cockpit and walked off. There was nothing to say. I was very sleepy. I kept moving my fingers, but they stayed numb. I could not collect my thoughts enough to decide whether or not I had been afraid. Had I been afraid? I couldn't say. I had witnessed a strange sight. What strange sight? I couldn't say. The sky was blue and the sea was white. I felt I ought to tell someone about it since I was back from so far away! But I had no grip on what I had been through. "Imagine a white sea . . . very white . . . whiter still." You cannot convey things to people by piling up adjectives, by stammering.

You cannot convey anything because there is nothing to convey. My shoulders were aching. My insides felt as if they had been crushed in by a terrible weight. You cannot make drama out of that, or out of the cone-shaped peak of Salamanca. That peak was charged like a powder magazine; but if I said so people would laugh. I would myself. I respected the peak of Salamanca. That is my story. And it is not a story.

There is nothing dramatic in the world, nothing pathetic, except in human relations. The day after I landed I might get emotional, might dress up my adventure by imagining that I who was alive and walking on earth was living through the hell of a cyclone. But that would be cheating, for the man who fought tooth and nail against that cyclone had nothing in common with the fortunate man alive the next day. He was far too busy.

---

12 flanges (flăn′jəz): protective rims.

I came away with very little booty indeed, with no more than this meager discovery, this contribution: How can one tell an act of the will from a simple image when there is no transmission of sensation?

I could perhaps succeed in upsetting you if I told you some story of a child unjustly punished. As it is, I have involved you in a cyclone, probably without upsetting you in the least. This is no novel experience for any of us. Every week men sit comfortably at the cinema and look on at the bombardment of some Shanghai or other, some Guernica,[13] and marvel without a trace of horror at the long fringes of ash and soot that twist their slow way into the sky from those man-made volcanoes. Yet we all know that together with the grain in the granaries, with the heritage of generations of men, with the treasures of families, it is the burning flesh of children and their elders that, dissipated in smoke, is slowly fertilizing those black cumuli.

The physical drama itself cannot touch us until some one points out its spiritual sense.

13 Guernica (gĕr nē′kä): a Spanish town that was bombed and destroyed by German planes in April, 1937. It has become a symbol of the brutality of war.

Understanding the Essay

1. What is the purpose of the opening paragraph on Conrad's description of a typhoon? What points does Saint-Exupéry make about effective writing in this essay?
2. At what point in the essay does Saint-Exupéry first begin to build suspense by introducing the idea of impending danger?
3. What techniques of writing are illustrated in the following quotations?
   (a) "The sky was blue. Pure blue. Too pure. A hard blue sky that shone over the scraped and barren world while the fleshless vertebrae of the mountain chain flashed in the sunlight. Not a cloud. The blue sky glittered like a new-honed knife."
   (b) "The enemy had not weakened. . . . on the horizon I saw again that white pack unleashed in my direction."
   (c) "I was a man who, carrying a pile of plates, had slipped on a waxed floor and let his scaffolding of porcelain crash."
   Find additional examples in the essay of the techniques illustrated above.
4. In the third paragraph, Saint-Exupéry writes: "Horror does not manifest itself in the world of reality." Judging by the last six paragraphs, what does he mean by this statement? How does it relate to the experience he describes?

Building Vocabulary Skills

Supply synonyms that are not figures of speech for the italicized words that are used as metaphors:

"Conrad *painted*"
"*saw-toothed, razor-edged* mountains"
"stubborn *jockeying*"
"*spat* out to sea"
"*vomited* out of my valley"
Why are the author's words more effective?

Developing Language Skills

1. Find examples from the essay of two of the following techniques: simile and metaphor, repetition, personification, balancing of short and long sentences. Then write two paragraphs explaining what Saint-Exupéry achieves by the use of these two techniques. Use the examples you have found to make clear your explanation.
2. Compare Coffin's account of the dangers of lobstering with Saint-Exupéry's account of his experiences in the cyclone. Which appeals to you more and why? Base your answer on specific incidents, such as Coffin's account of the lobsterman on Penobscot Bay who had to fight for his life when his propeller caught in his lobster warp in contrast to Saint-Exupéry's account of losing feeling in his hands. Consider if the differing roles of the authors—one a participant and one an observer—affect your reaction.

Reading "The Return of the Elvers"

The first part of Teale's essay uses the casual tone of the traveler interested in the southern home of northern robins and the hillsides of dogwood that he and his wife enjoy as they move northward with spring. The second half of the essay reveals the impassioned naturalist who reviews in sharp detail the 20th-century scientific detective work that uncovered the strange life pattern of the baby eels. Notice how Teale's specific details back up his general comments.

ESSAY

The Return of the Elvers

Edwin Way Teale

"Dingy with soot, snowdrifts had melted into slush and were freezing again" that dreary February day when the Teales left their New York home and headed south to carry out their dreams of meeting spring under southern skies and following it north. "Spring advances up the United States at the average rate of about fifteen miles a day," reports Mr. Teale. Following this unusual timetable, the Teales traveled 17,000 miles from February to June and saw spring return in twenty-three different states, beginning in the Everglades of Florida and ending in the White Mountains of New Hampshire. After working east from the escarpment of the Blue Ridge to the Coastal Plains, the Teales saw the fabulous return of the baby eels reported in this selection.

THE NEXT MORNING, before breakfast, we opened a book that would have fascinated Charles Dickens. It was the Statesville Telephone Directory.

In a pocket notebook, Dickens used to jot down unusual names for later use in his novels. As we leafed through the directory we seemed to be going over one of these notebooks. Here

were fresh and original names. They stirred the imagination. We amused ourselves, as we drove east that day, by conjuring up characters Dickens might have fitted to such names as Herman Goforth, J. C. Turnipseed, Bess Gant, R. E. Nooe, Peggy Snipes, C. Moose, Laura Jolly, and J. C. Dayvault.

For the next few days our route zigzagged over the Piedmont.[1] We crossed the cedar-bordered Yadkin River, in Randolph County, where hundreds of thousands of northern robins sometimes concentrate in winter. We paused beside a sunken meadow that spread away for half a mile in one vast, brilliant tapestry of spring—red and blue and yellow wildflowers intermingling, with the bright scarlet of the painted cup predominating. Near Concord, North Carolina, we passed our first spring swarm of honeybees. It enveloped a roadside sign, with parts of the cluster descending the post like drippings of yellow wax.

All one day we ran through localized spring showers. Sometimes the rain came down the concrete to meet us, the line of its advancing front as clearly defined as though it were a breaking wave. We could see before us huge raindrops pounding the concrete, the highway glistening with running water, while we rode on dry and dusty pavement. There would be one measurable moment when we were out of the shower, then in it—the great drops drumming on the roof and hood of the car, the windshield streaming with such quantities of water that one end of the arc of the swinging rubber wipers was blurred while the other end was being wiped clean. For several miles we would be enveloped in the deluge.

[1] **Piedmont:** a tract of high level land between the Atlantic Coast and the Appalachian Mountains.

Then it would pass. We would speed for a time along wet pavements; then we would be beyond the storm and the highway would be dry again. Five times in a hundred miles we plunged into such rainstorms. Each time the sensation was like diving head first into an advancing wave.

As we worked east, from the escarpment[2] of the Blue Ridge to the fall line where rivers drop off the Piedmont onto the Coastal Plain, we watched leaves expanding as though we were watching a lapse-time movie. Traveling downhill, we were advancing in the spring. As we proceeded, the same kinds of trees were clothed in larger leaves.

Near Southern Pines the flat and sandy fields lay under a haze of delicate pastel shadings of red and blue where sorrel and toadflax intermingled. Masses of blue lupines rose beside the road; and beneath the long-leaf pines, where giant cones and foot-long fallen needles carpeted the ground, bird's-foot violets lifted thousands of flowers. Farther north, as we neared Chapel Hill to spend two days with our friends, Dr. and Mrs. Raymond Adams, whole hillsides were white with dogwood.

There after weeks associated with swamps and caves and mountaintops, we suddenly found ourselves at lunches, giving speeches, caught up in civilized routine once more. We visited bird-feeding stations. We were shown wildflower gardens. We attended meetings. We looked up Richard L. Weaver, of the American Nature Study Society, and accepted an invitation to join an outing of the North Carolina Bird Club, at Beaufort on the coast. We examined Dr. Adams's extensive collection of Thoreau[3] material and

2 **escarpment:** steep cliff.
3 **Thoreau** (thôr′ō): Henry David Thoreau (1817-1862), American writer and naturalist.

when Walter Harding arrived for dinner, in a dripping green raincoat during a spring hailstorm, we held an impromptu reunion of the Thoreau Society. In Chapel Hill we met old friends and made new ones. There we also met Heine.

Heine was the Adams's engaging dachshund. At eleven, Heine was as old, proportionately, as a man of seventy-five. Several times a day he would be overcome by wheezing fits of coughing. We noticed that these occurred most often when Dr. Adams was talking. The next summer, at Walden Pond, in Massachusetts, when various speakers addressed the Thoreau Society at the occasion of marking Thoreau's hutsite, Heine was in the audience. He remained perfectly quiet until Dr. Adams began to speak; then he was attacked by violent coughing. This was, perhaps, his manner of attracting notice. For pets employ a legion stratagems in bidding for attention.

A Carolina spring heat wave was beginning the morning we left Chapel Hill for Beaufort. Highways shimmered before us. Dragonflies tilted wildly in the heated air. And all across the Coastal Plain, in lowland stretches, the waxy yellow and red flowers of pitcher plants shone in the glaring sunshine. North Carolina is the longest state, east and west, this side of the Mississippi. We had traversed its length, from one end to the other, when we reached the sea at the U.S. Fish and Wildlife research station at Beaufort.

Out of the confusion of meetings and field trips the following day we recall especially the song of a Macgillivray's seaside sparrow and the bright red mud dauber nests formed from dust of disintegrating bricks at old Fort Macon. We met Mrs. Cecil Appleberry, of Wilmington, who promised to show us the natural history of the Cape Fear region, and Charlotte Hilton Green, whose nature column in the Raleigh *News and Observer* has stimulated widespread interest in the North Carolina outdoors. We heard of an albino white-throated sparrow which could be identified only by its song and a female cardinal that battled its reflection in a window like a male robin redbreast at mating time. We also heard of the oddest pet of our experience.

John Pearson, one of the research scientists at the laboratory, told us of his adventures with a pet baby eel which he kept for five years in a glass jar. Whenever he made a trip away from home, the jar and its occupant went along. During the day the eel buried itself in sand at the bottom of the container. There it remained until Pearson came home. The vibrations of his footfalls were sufficient to arouse it. It would pop out of the sand and dart to the surface to be fed. Sometimes it would thrust fully a fourth of its body above the surface reaching for bits of shrimp or fish held at the end of a pair of tweezers. As long as titbits were offered it continued to gorge itself. On one inland trip, when seafood was difficult to get, Pearson fed it small fragments of beefsteak. Soon after this feast the pet eel died. Beef is more fibrous, harder to digest, than fish and is believed to have been the cause of death.

On the back of an envelope Pearson sketched a map. We followed it the next day as we drove south toward Wilmington. Turning off the main highway near Newport, we ran over the pale, anemic sand of a dirt road through pine flats, past a prison camp, into a pocket of crested flycatchers,[4] under

nighthawks hunting in the sunshine, and came at last to a wooden bridge below a log dam. The little stream that flowed beneath it was partly choked by boulders and fallen limbs. Its water was the color of root beer. This was the lonely setting for a fabulous event of spring.

Below us, as we looked down, the water fanned out over shoals of light sand tinted amber by the flow. Soon we became aware of little threads of life, hardly as long as a little finger, hardly thicker than a darning needle, moving upstream, wriggling across the shallows, fighting the current. One after the other, a dozen crossed the little sand bar and disappeared into the deeper, darker pool above. These slender creatures were elvers, baby eels, ending a year-and-a-half journey, a journey that had carried them 10,000,000 times their own length across the open sea. Now, so close to their goal, they were traveling by day as well as by night, in brilliant sunshine as well as under the cover of darkness.

We leaned on the rail of the bridge and, with the sun warm on our backs, stared down at this parade from the sea. A procession of elvers, head to tail, was following the sinuous[5] edge of the sand bar. Now a single baby eel was deflected into an aquatic merry-go-round where the water swirled lazily in a shallow depression about the size of a dinner plate. Three times it made a circuit of this miniature lagoon, swimming faster and faster apparently sensing something was wrong. Bursting from this cul-de-sac,[6] it turned, as though on rails, upstream, nosing head on into the current. The nervous system of the elver, during its spring mi-

5 **sinuous:** winding.
6 **cul-de-sac** (kŭl′də săk′)**:** a passage with only one outlet.

4 **flycatchers:** kind of bird.

gration inland, seems set like an automatic pilot. The wriggling creature instinctively tries to keep the pressure on both sides of its body equal and in consequence swims head on into flowing water.

All up the coast, on that spring day, baby eels, millions and billions of baby eels, were streaming inland from the sea. They were mounting rivers and creeks and brooks. They were fighting their way up torrents, wriggling over spray-drenched rocks around waterfalls, threading their way into lakes and ponds and reservoirs, penetrating to the headwaters of all the infinitely branched water lanes leading to the sea. No course was too roundabout. No path was too difficult. They were climbing tumbling brooks to reach mountain lakes, working into the depths of the Great Dismal Swamp, even penetrating the aqueducts and mains[7] of the

7 aqueducts and mains: large water pipes.

water supply systems of the largest seaboard cities.

For weeks the "eel-fare," as the English term this return of the elvers, had been going on. We stared down with a feeling of awe and respect at these diminutive travelers, so tenacious of purpose, so unwearied by travel. Only the sides of the log dam upstream had to be surmounted and their long journey would be at an end. In the pond behind the barricade they would reach the headwaters of the stream. Sometimes at night, below this dam, John Pearson had told us, the elvers piled up in a squirming mass, temporarily blocked by the log wall ahead of them. It was the final obstacle in an odyssey of obstacles.

Near the edge of the stream, swirls and swifter currents had scoured away the sediment, so that the amber water slid over clear white sand. A chain of such lighter spots, with the sediment dark between them, extended for a dozen feet or so upstream. Each little eel that wriggled across such a spot stood out against its lighter background. Once a parade of elvers passed along the chain of sand spots, appearing and disappearing, becoming successively visible and invisible like forms stealing at dusk before a series of lighted windows.

Sometimes the little migrants speeded up; sometimes they slowed down; sometimes they nosed into quiet nooks and rested. But hour after hour the intermittent procession continued. It wound in and out among the waving flags of green scum that fluttered from submerged branches. It passed beneath whirligig beetles, spinning unheeding on the surface, beneath the shadow of a green-tinted dragonfly that darted and hovered over the stream, through golden meshes of sunlight reflected from the ripples.

This upstream journey was the reverse of the movement that had carried adult eels down this very ravine the autumn before. Migrating to the sea to breed and die, they had traveled by night and rested by day and had ridden with the current instead of opposing it. The Chinook salmon of the Northwest migrates into streams, returns to fresh water to spawn.[8] The eel reverses the procedure. It migrates to the sea, from fresh water to salt. Otherwise it remains sterile. Only in the abysses of the ocean is it able to reproduce its kind.

The breeding eels that had slipped down the stream the autumn before had been well layered with fat. As summer had merged with autumn, they had ceased to eat. Their bodies had lost their color, had taken on a silvery sheen. All along the Atlantic seaboard of North America, all along the coast of Europe, other silver eels had begun their last journey. On cool autumn nights, eels hurrying to the sea sometimes crawl for a mile or more across dewy meadows to reach streams that will carry them to salt water. Away from the coast, they all turn south, swimming day after day and week after week in the direction of the Sargasso Sea.[9]

For centuries silver eels disappeared and baby eels reappeared and no man knew the events that took place between. Aristotle[10] believed that eels were sexless, that new eels came into being spontaneously in the sea. His opinion prevailed for centuries. Leeuwenhoek, the pioneer Dutch microscopist, mistook parasites[11] for young eels and announced that the creatures gave birth to living young. Sir Thomas Browne reported—as a "strange yet well attested" fact—"the production of eeles in the backs of living cods and perches." Thus science progressed from misconception to misconception until very recent times. Less than half a century has passed since one of the great detectives of science, the Danish ichthyologist, Johannes Schmidt, filled in the blank between the disappearance of the silver eels and the appearance of the elvers. Only the experiments of Karl von Frisch, in the realm of the language of the honeybee, have in modern times rivaled these patient researches of Schmidt.

In his quaint book, *Vegetable Statics*, published in 1727, Stephen Hales wisely observes: "Hardly do we guess

8 spawn: lay eggs.

9 **Sargasso** (sär găs′ō) **Sea:** a region in the Atlantic, northeast of the West Indies.
10 **Aristotle:** Greek philosopher (384-322 B.C.) interested in science.
11 **parasites:** animals or plants that live on or within other organisms.

aright at the things that are upon earth; and with labor do we find the things that are before us." With what labor did Schmidt unravel the mystery of the baby eels!

Year after year he put to sea. He was hunting for a needle in a haystack and the haystack was as big as the ocean. His cruises of investigation ranged from America to Egypt, from Iceland to the Canary Islands and the West Indies. For nearly two decades he kept doggedly at a seemingly hopeless task. One of his research ships, the *Margrethe*, was wrecked on a West Indian island. But slowly his accumulating information drew him closer to the solution of this riddle of great antiquity.

In May, 1904, on the research steamer *Thor*, Schmidt hauled in a Petersen's young-fish trawl and found in it the first baby eel ever taken in the open Atlantic. What followed afterwards, Schmidt described in 1923, in *The Philosophical Transactions of the Royal Society of London*. Other baby eels were pulled from the sea. Those near the European coast were larger than those farther out and farther south. Reasoning that the younger the eel the smaller it would be, Schmidt followed smaller and smaller clues into the region of the Sargasso Sea. There, four years in succession, he found minute larvae,[12] less than ten millimeters long. The center of the breeding area, he concluded, lies approximately equidistant from Bermuda and the Leeward Isles.

Here the brown Sargassum weed drifts above the greatest abyss of the Atlantic Ocean. Four miles of water separate the surface and the floor of the sea. It is here that the outward journey of the adult eels is ended. Here they find the right conditions of temperature and depth for spawning. One female will scatter as many as 100,000 eggs in the water. The silver eels breed and die and leave behind a myriad spherical eggs floating in the sea.

These eggs are "bathypelagic." That is, they drift at considerable depths in the ocean. In February the eggs begin to hatch, often a thousand feet below the surface. From them emerge minute larvae, from seven to fifteen millimeters long. They are flattened vertically into the shape of a willow leaf standing on its edge. They are crystal clear. Colorless blood is pumped through colorless bodies. The only pigment they contain is found in the dark pin points of their eyes.

Slowly these larvae work upward through the darkness and the crushing pressure of the depths. In swimming, they undulate from side to side. When at rest, they maintain their balance by curling up like a loosely coiled watchspring. Biting with minute needle-teeth, they feed on microscopic fare, such as little spheres of algae. As they near the surface they begin drifting with the ocean currents, starting the long, unhurried trek that carries them north. Both American and European eels spawn west of longitude 50 degrees. While most of the billions of eggs released by American eels are to the west of the billions of eggs released by European eels, there is a common overlapping area where the eggs of both float side by side. Side by side the eels hatch out, one destined from the beginning for life in North American waters and the other for a home on the continent of Europe.

Instinct, planted in their tiny, transparent bodies, leads them across hun-

---

12 larvae (lär′vē): early form of any animal that changes its form when it becomes an adult.

ESSAY

dreds or thousands of miles of watery waste to their respective destinations. The backbone of a baby eel is a kind of ticket revealing its destination to the scientist with a microscope. By counting the vertebrae he can predict infallibly whether it will eventually turn east or west. From the time they hatch, North American eels have from 104 to 110 vertebrae, never more. European eels have from 111 to 118, never fewer. Thus a single vertebra divides the two. If a baby eel has 110 vertebrae, it is destined to turn toward America; if it has 111, it will veer away toward Europe. The journey of the European eel, which matures less quickly, takes three years; that of the American eel only a little more than one. On the Pacific coast of America there are no eels except Lampreys.[13] However on the Oriental side of the Pacific eels are found. They too disappear into the sea in autumn.

Swimming northward in the Atlantic both European and American elvers engage in an ocean odyssey attended by many dangers. The procession of elvers below our North Carolina bridge was made up of the survivors who had safely run the gantlet of fish and jellyfish and squid, of enemies innumerable. At the age of six months, the American eels are about one inch long. European eels are hardly half as long. At that time the two can be told apart at a glance, by size alone.

Strangely enough, during generations while the mystery of the eel's spawning ground remained unsolved, scientists were familiar with the baby eels themselves. They had been pickled in alcohol, examined through microscopes, minutely described, and given the scientific name of *Leptocephelus*—all the

while the scientists assuming they were examining another species of small tropical fish, never suspecting that they held in their hands the key to the great riddle.

People who see adult eels pour down to the sea in fall and baby eels appear from the sea in spring assume the latter are the progeny of the former. Instead there is always a lapse of a generation between. The elvers we were seeing were the children of the adults that had gone downstream two autumns before. Each year the silver eels, swimming southward through the ocean to breed and die, pass the elvers, in numbers beyond imagining, working northward. The life of the eel begins and ends in a journey through the sea.

By the time it is one year old the young eel is in wintery seas off the North American coast. Here an amazing change begins. Its knife-blade body shrinks. It contracts both vertically and longitudinally. It assumes the form of a slender, transparent rod. It is known, now, as a glass eel. In this transformation, it loses weight as well as size. A glass eel sometimes weighs only one-third as much as it did in its *Leptocephelus* form.

The earliest days of spring find the transparent elvers moving in across the Continental Shelf toward estuaries and inlets.[14] One of the many mysteries that remain in connection with their return is the manner in which they distribute themselves along the coast. Tagged Chinook salmon return, after five years in the sea, to the very brook where they were born. Their instinctive return to their birthplace distributes them throughout the watercourses of the Northwest. But how are the

14 **estuaries and inlets:** narrow strips of water extending into a body of land from a river, ocean, or lake.

13 **Lampreys** (lăm′prĭz): eel-like water animals.

eels spread along the length of the eastern coast? Why do they not pile up with too many in the South, too few in the North? Do they, like the salmon, carry an instinctive chart within their bodies, guiding them back to certain streams? Probably not. For, while the salmon are returning where they have been before, the eels are entering a new world when they approach the shore. Perhaps some hatch earlier than others or ride north in swifter currents, thus lengthening their journey before instinct turns them toward the land. Whatever the cause, the eels, in their infinite numbers, are distributed all along the seaboard from the sluggish, lowland streams of the rice country to rocky brooks in Maine.

All the rivers are in spring flood, all the tides are at spring high, when the elvers throng in toward the surf. They wait until the tides subside from their highest crests; wait, usually, until some night of warm spring rain. Then they pour into the estuaries. They drive head on into the current and, with fresh water around them for the first time in their lives, wriggle upstream.

By now they are no longer transparent. Beginning with small darkened cells along their backbones, pigmentation has spread across their backs. This darkened upper surface of their bodies provides needed camouflage in a new realm of many enemies. Herons, kingfishers, pickerel, bass, older eels, all gorge themselves on the moving hordes of elvers. Those which survive, which find themselves in the quiet upper reaches of rivers and brooks, in lakes and ponds—sometimes as high as 8000 feet above sea level—feed and grow for at least eight years before they reach maturity. The females, larger than the males, may attain a length of five feet and a weight of twenty pounds before, in silver dress, they begin the last long journey that rounds out their lives.

We talked in low, almost awed voices, of all the strange life history of the eel as we stared down at those little travelers passing beneath us, so close to journey's end. Their minute bodies were equipped with instincts we could but dimly comprehend, instincts that had guided them north, that had swung their course to the west, that had brought them, at a time of high spring tides, close to shore. Their movement across the coastal shallows was a tide within a tide, a tide of incoming life, a greater tide, dependent upon stronger forces than the attraction of the moon, upon the invisible, all-mysterious forces of instinct.

Understanding the Essay

1. How does the first third of this essay differ from the rest in selection and treatment of subject matter? What writing technique shows up in both parts of the essay in statements like "we watched leaves expanding as though we were watching a lapse-time movie" (first part) and "It [the eel] assumes the form of a slender, transparent rod" (last part)?

2. Is the paragraph about John Pearson and his pet eel an effective transition between the first part of the essay and the rest of it? Why or why not?

3. Why does Teale give in such detail the various theories concerning the reproduction of eels advanced by Aristotle, Leeuwenhoek, and Sir Thomas Browne?

4. How did the Danish ichthyologist Johannes Schmidt establish the fact that eels breed in the Sargasso Sea?

5. In what way does Teale's last paragraph return the essay to the tone and viewpoint of the first part of the essay?

Reading "Farewell, My Lovely"

Homespun metaphors and word pictures right out of the Sears Roebuck catalogue combine to show the reader a fabulous creation of an era long gone. The authors say "the old Ford practically *was* the American scene" and then proceed to furnish proof that it was not only the American scene but a gay, reckless, and incredible scene that can never be recaptured. They endow their creation with human qualities, writing "A Ford was born naked as a baby," and give it a rosy afterglow with the Ruby Safety Reflector and Moto Wings. No one could put a Model T together from reading this "tribute of the sigh that is not a sob," but no one will forget the car "like a horse, rolling the bit on its tongue." Through their casual comments in parentheses—"I didn't like these, I remember" or "That's what I was always told, anyway"—the authors keep the reader interested in those who drove the Model T. Never for a minute, however, does their focus leave the car itself, "the miracle God had wrought."

LEE STROUT WHITE

Farewell, My Lovely!*

(An aging male kisses an old flame goodbye, circa 1936)

Lee Strout White

Richard Lee Strout and E. B. White teamed up in 1936 as Lee Strout White to produce the following extravagant tribute to the Model T, Henry Ford's horseless carriage that flourished from 1909 until 1927. More than fifteen million of these cars were sold in their short eighteen-year history. They are collector's items today. Strout has not revealed how he fell in love with Ford's famous "flivver," but E. B. White speaks from firsthand experience. The summer after White was graduated from Cornell, he and a friend drove an old Model T to the West Coast.

I SEE by the new Sears Roebuck catalogue that it is still possible to buy an axle for a 1909 Model T Ford, but I am not deceived. The great days have faded, the end is in sight. Only one page in the current catalogue is devoted to parts and accessories for the Model T; yet everyone remembers springtimes when the Ford gadget section was larger than men's clothing, almost as large as household furnishings. The last Model T was built in 1927, and the car is fading from what scholars call the American scene—which is an understatement, because to a few million people who grew up with it, the old Ford practically *was* the American scene.

It was the miracle God had wrought. And it was patently the sort of thing that could only happen once. Mechanically uncanny, it was like nothing that had ever come to the world before. Flourishing industries rose and fell with it. As a vehicle, it was hard-working, commonplace, heroic; and it often seemed to transmit those qualities to the persons who rode in it. My own generation identifies it with Youth, with its gaudy, irretrievable excitements; before it fades into the mist, I would like to pay it the tribute of the sigh that is not a sob, and set down random entries in a shape somewhat less cumbersome than a Sears Roebuck catalogue.

The Model T was distinguished from all other makes of cars by the fact that its transmission was of a type known as planetary—which was half metaphysics, half sheer friction. Engineers accepted the word "planetary" in its epicyclic[1] sense, but I was always conscious that

1 epicyclic: In ancient astronomy, an *epicycle* was the circle in which a planet moved. This circle moved at the same time around another larger circle. To an engineer, *epicyclic* would mean "operating by bands, wheels, or pulleys designed to travel around the circumference of another part, which may also be moving."

it also meant "wandering," "erratic." Because of the peculiar nature of this planetary element, there was always, in Model T, a certain dull rapport[2] between engine and wheels, and even when the car was in a state known as neutral, it trembled with a deep imperative and tended to inch forward. There was never a moment when the bands were not faintly egging the machine on. In this respect it was like a horse, rolling the bit on its tongue, and country people brought to it the same technique they used with draft animals.

Its most remarkable quality was its rate of acceleration. In its palmy days the Model T could take off faster than anything on the road. The reason was simple. To get under way, you simply hooked the third finger of the right hand around a lever on the steering column, pulled down hard, and shoved your left foot forcibly against the low-speed pedal. These were simple, positive motions; the car responded by lunging forward with a roar. After a few seconds of this turmoil, you took your toe off the pedal, eased up a mite on the throttle, and the car, possessed of only two forward speeds, catapulted directly into high with a series of ugly jerks and was off on its glorious errand. The abruptness of this departure was never equalled in other cars of the period. The human leg was (and still is) incapable of letting in a clutch with anything like the forthright abandon that used to send Model T on its way. Letting in a clutch is a negative, hesitant motion, depending on delicate nervous control; pushing down the Ford pedal was a simple, country motion—an expansive act, which came as natural as kicking an old door to make it budge.

The driver of the old Model T was a man enthroned. The car, with top up, stood seven feet high. The driver sat on top of the gas tank, brooding it with his own body. When he wanted gasoline, he alighted, along with everything else in the front seat; the seat was pulled off, the metal cap unscrewed, and a wooden stick thrust down to sound the liquid in the well. There were always a couple of these sounding sticks kicking around in the ratty sub-cushion regions of a flivver. Refuelling was more of a social function then, because the driver had to unbend, whether he wanted to or not. Directly in front of the driver was the windshield—high, uncompromisingly erect. Nobody talked about air resistance, and the four cylinders pushed the car through the atmosphere with a simple disregard of physical law.

There was this about a Model T: the purchaser never regarded his purchase as a complete, finished product. When you bought a Ford, you figured you had a start—a vibrant, spirited framework to which could be screwed an almost limitless assortment of decorative and functional hardware. Driving away from the agency, hugging the new wheel between your knees, you were already full of creative worry. A Ford was born naked as a baby, and a flourishing industry grew up out of correcting its rare deficiencies and combatting its fascinating diseases. Those were the great days of lily-painting. I have been looking at some old Sears Roebuck catalogues, and they bring everything back so clear.

First you bought a Ruby Safety Reflector for the rear, so that your posterior would glow in another car's brilliance. Then you invested thirty-nine cents in some radiator Moto Wings, a popular ornament which gave the Peg-

2 rapport: sympathetic understanding.

LEE STROUT WHITE

asus[3] touch to the machine and did something godlike to the owner. For nine cents you bought a fan-belt guide to keep the belt from slipping off the pulley.

You bought a radiator compound to stop leaks. This was as much a part of everybody's equipment as aspirin tablets are of a medicine cabinet. You bought special oil to prevent chattering, a clamp-on dash light, a patching outfit, a tool box which you bolted to the running board, a sun visor, a steering-column brace to keep the column rigid, and a set of emergency containers for gas, oil, and water—three thin, disc-like cans which reposed in a case on the running board during long, important journeys—red for gas, gray for water, green for oil. It was only a beginning. After the car was about a year old, steps were taken to check the alarming disintegration. (Model T was full of tumors, but they were benign.) A set of anti-rattlers (ninety-eight cents) was a popular panacea.[4] You hooked them on to the gas and spark rods, to the brake pull rod, and to the steering-rod connections. Hood silencers, of black rubber, were applied to the fluttering hood. Shock-absorbers and snubbers gave "complete relaxation." Some people bought rubber pedal pads, to fit over the standard metal pedals. (I didn't like these, I remember.) Persons of a suspicious or pugnacious turn of mind bought a rear-view mirror; but most Model T owners weren't worried by what was coming from behind because they would soon enough see it out in front. They rode in a state of cheerful catalepsy.[5] Quite a large mu-

tinous clique among Ford owners went over to a foot accelerator (you could buy one and screw it to the floor board), but there was a certain madness in these people, because the Model T, just as she stood, had a choice of three foot pedals to push, and there were plenty of moments when both feet were occupied in the routine performance of duty and when the only way to speed up the engine was with the hand throttle.

Gadget bred gadget. Owners not only bought ready-made gadgets, they invented gadgets to meet special needs. I myself drove my car directly from the agency to the blacksmith's, and had the smith affix two enormous iron brackets to the port running board to support an army trunk.

People who owned closed models builded along different lines: they bought ball grip handles for opening doors, window anti-rattlers, and de-luxe flower vases of the cut-glass anti-splash type. People with delicate sensibilities garnished their car with a device called the Donna Lee Automobile Dissemina-tor—a porous vase guaranteed, according to Sears, to fill the car with a "faint clean odor of lavender." The gap between open cars and closed cars was not as great then as it is now: for $11.95, Sears Roebuck converted your touring car into a sedan and you went forth renewed. One agreeable quality of the old Fords was that they had no bumpers, and their fenders softened and wilted with the years and permitted the driver to squeeze in and out of tight places.

Tires were 30 x 3½, cost about twelve dollars, and punctured readily. Everybody carried a Jiffy patching set, with a nutmeg grater to roughen the tube before the goo was spread on. Everybody was capable of putting on a patch, expected to have to, and did have to.

3 **Pegasus:** a winged horse in Greek mythology. Often a symbol of poetry.
4 **panacea:** cure-all.
5 **catalepsy:** abnormal condition of muscular rigidity.

ESSAY

During my association with Model T's, self-starters were not a prevalent[6] accessory. They were expensive and under suspicion. Your car came equipped with a serviceable crank, and the first thing you learned was how to Get Results. It was a special trick, and until you learned it (usually from another Ford owner, but sometimes by a period of appalling experimentation) you might as well have been winding up an awning. The trick was to leave the ignition switch off, proceed to the animal's head, pull the choke (which was a little wire protruding through the radiator) and give the crank two or three nonchalant upward lifts. Then, whistling as though thinking about something else, you would saunter back to the driver's cabin, turn the ignition on, return to the crank, and this time, catching it on the down stroke, give it a quick spin with plenty

of That. If this procedure was followed, the engine almost always responded—first with a few scattered explosions, then with a tumultuous gunfire, which you checked by racing around to the driver's seat and retarding the throttle. Often, if the emergency brake hadn't been pulled all the way back, the car advanced on you the instant the first explosion occurred and you would hold it back by leaning your weight against it. I can still feel my old Ford nuzzling me at the curb, as though looking for an apple in my pocket.

In zero weather, ordinary cranking became an impossibility, except for giants. The oil thickened, and it became necessary to jack up the rear wheels, which, for some planetary reason, eased the throw.

The lore and legend that governed the Ford were boundless. Owners had their own theories about everything;

6 prevalent: widespread.

LEE STROUT WHITE

299

they discussed mutual problems in that wise, infinitely resourceful way old women discuss rheumatism. Exact knowledge was pretty scarce, and often proved less effective than superstition. Dropping a camphor ball into the gas tank was a popular expedient;[7] it seemed to have a tonic effect on both man and machine. There wasn't much to base exact knowledge on. The Ford driver flew blind. He didn't know the temperature of his engine, the speed of his car, the amount of his fuel, or the pressure of his oil (the old Ford lubricated itself by what was amiably described as the "splash system"). A speedometer cost money and was an extra, like a windshield-wiper. The dashboard of the early models was bare save for an ignition key; later models, grown effete,[8] boasted an ammeter[9] which pulsated alarmingly with the throbbing of the car. Under the dash was a box of coils, with vibrators which you adjusted, or thought you adjusted. Whatever the driver learned of his motor, he learned not through instruments but through sudden developments. I remember that the timer was one of the vital organs about which there was ample doctrine. When everything else had been checked, you "had a look" at the timer. It was an extravagantly odd little device, simple in construction, mysterious in function. It contained a roller, held by a spring, and there were four contact points on the inside of the case against which, many people believed, the roller rolled. I have had a timer apart on a sick Ford many times. But I never really knew what I was up to— I was just showing off before God.

There were almost as many schools of thought as there were timers. Some people, when things went wrong, just clenched their teeth and gave the timer a smart crack with a wrench. Other people opened it up and blew on it. There was a school that held that the timer needed large amounts of oil; they fixed it by frequent baptism. And there was a school that was positive it was meant to run dry as a bone; these people were continually taking it off and wiping it. I remember once spitting into a timer; not in anger, but in a spirit of research. You see, the Model T driver moved in the realm of metaphysics.[10] He believed his car could be hexed.

One reason the Ford anatomy was never reduced to an exact science was that, having "fixed" it, the owner couldn't honestly claim that the treatment had brought about the cure. There were too many authenticated cases of Fords fixing themselves—restored naturally to health after a short rest. Farmers soon discovered this, and it fitted nicely with their draft-horse philosophy: "Let 'er cool off and she'll snap into it again."

A Ford owner had Number One Bearing constantly in mind. This bearing, being at the front end of the motor, was the one that always burned out, because the oil didn't reach it when the car was climbing hills. (That's what I was always told, anyway.) The oil used to recede and leave Number One dry as a clam flat; you had to watch that bearing like a hawk. It was like a weak heart—you could hear it start knocking, and that was when you stopped to let her cool off. Try as you would to keep the oil supply right, in

7 **expedient:** way of getting immediate results.
8 **effete:** soft through over-refinement.
9 **ammeter:** instrument measuring strength of battery.

10 **metaphysics:** the supernatural (now obsolete in this sense).

ESSAY

the end Number One always went out. "Number One Bearing burned out on me and I had to have her replaced," you would say, wisely; and your companions always had a lot to tell about how to protect and pamper Number One to keep her alive.

Sprinkled not too liberally among the millions of amateur witch doctors who drove Fords and applied their own abominable cures were the heaven-sent mechanics who could really make the car talk. These professionals turned up in undreamed-of spots. One time, on the banks of the Columbia River in Washington, I heard the rear end go out of my Model T when I was trying to whip it up a steep incline onto the deck of a ferry. Something snapped; the car slid backward into the mud. It seemed to me like the end of the trail. But the captain of the ferry, observing the withered remnant, spoke up.

"What's got her?" he asked.

"I guess it's the rear end," I replied, listlessly. The captain leaned over the rail and stared. Then I saw that there was a hunger in his eyes that set him off from other men.

"Tell you what," he said, carelessly, trying to cover up his eagerness, "let's pull her up onto the boat, and I'll help you fix her while we're going back and forth on the river."

We did just this. All that day I plied between the towns of Pasco and Kennewick, while the skipper (who had once worked in a Ford garage) directed the amazing work of resetting the bones of my car.

Springtime in the heyday of the Model T was a delirious season. Owning a car was still a major excitement, roads were still wonderful and bad. The Fords were obviously conceived in madness: any car which was capable of going from forward into reverse without any perceptible mechanical hiatus[11] was bound to be a mighty challenging thing to the human imagination. Boys used to veer them off the highway into a level pasture and run wild with them, as though they were cutting up with a girl. Most everybody used the reverse pedal quite as much as the regular foot brake—it distributed the wear over the bands and wore them all down evenly. That was the big trick, to wear all the bands down evenly, so that the final chattering would be total and the whole unit scream for renewal.

The days were golden, the nights were dim and strange. I still recall with trembling those loud, nocturnal[12] crises when you drew up to a signpost and raced the engine so the lights would be bright enough to read destinations by. I have never been really planetary since. I suppose it's time to say goodbye. Farewell, my lovely!

11 hiatus: pause.
12 nocturnal: at night.

Understanding the Essay

1. What tone do the authors establish in the first two paragraphs? Find several sentences that express their feeling toward their subject.
2. Find the four major divisions of the essay between the introduction and the conclusion. Tell in three or four words what each section discusses.

3. Why is "complete relaxation" (p. 298, col. 1, used in referring to the shock absorbers) in quotation marks?
4. What effect do the authors secure by capitalizing words and phrases ordinarily not capitalized?
5. Find several examples of the authors' referring to the Model T as a person by assigning it human characteristics or frailties.
6. Why has this essay been termed "a love letter to an automobile"?

Developing Language Skills

1. On p. 297, col. 2, White writes: "Those were the great days of lily-painting." The origin of the phrase *painting the lily* is probably in the lines from Shakespeare's *King John:* "To paint the lily,/To throw a perfume on the violet."
   (*a*) What would you judge the meaning of the phrase to be from these two uses of it?
   (*b*) How does White's statement apply to the Model T?
   (*c*) Use the word *lily-painting* in connection with a school personality or activity.
2. Explain to the class the meaning of *period piece* and show why this selection could be classified as a period piece.
3. Write an essay, in the manner of "Farewell, My Lovely!" on some piece of machinery you know well (such as an old radio, a bike, or a car). Try to use the same elegance of manner and diction used in the above essay to get a comic effect.

The Narrative Essay

In the narrative essay, the writer reports events, real or imagined, that enable him to communicate an idea or make a comment on life. Something happens in the narrative essay—whether it be a series of unbelievable and thoroughly delightful tantrums of the family dog or a vivid retelling of dramatic moments in a career of sports reporting.

Reading "The Dog That Bit People"

Thurber is a writer who gets his best effects from quiet understatements that hang in the air. He is not a man to nail down a phrase or cap a story with a punch line. Instead, he tells his story in an apparently straightforward manner broken by furtive, half-apologetic side comments that seem irrelevant but actually produce much of the story's humor. Another Thurber device is the use of only slightly related incidents, beginning and ending abruptly and tied together by the repetition of a word or phrase.

The Dog That Bit People[*]

James Thurber

This story about the family dog is from My Life and Hard Times, *which Thurber says is based on "the little perils of routine living." The real humor of this story and others about the Thurber family is the matter-of-fact way members of the family accept the preposterous things that happen regularly in their Columbus, Ohio, household. Critic Clifton Fadiman says that James Thurber plays two roles as a writer, the Sane Innocent and the Confused Innocent. He adds, "Actually, Mr. Thurber is never confused and never innocent."*

PROBABLY NO ONE MAN should have as many dogs in his life as I have had, but there was more pleasure than distress in them for me except in the case of an Airedale named Muggs. He gave me more trouble than all the other fifty-four or five put together, although my moment of keenest embarrassment was the time a Scotch terrier named Jeannie, who had just had six puppies in the clothes closet of a fourth floor apartment in New York, had the unexpected seventh and last at the corner of Eleventh Street and Fifth Avenue during a walk she had insisted on taking. Then, too, there was the prize winning French poodle, a great big black poodle —none of your little, untroublesome white miniatures—who got sick riding in the rumble seat of a car with me on her way to the Greenwich Dog Show. She had a red rubber bib tucked around her throat and, since a rainstorm came up when we were halfway through the Bronx, I had to hold over her a small green umbrella, really more of a parasol. The rain beat down fearfully and suddenly the driver of the car drove into a big garage, filled with mechanics. It happened so quickly that I forgot to put the umbrella down and I will always remember, with sickening distress, the look of incredulity mixed with hatred that came over the face of the particular hardened garage man that came over to see what we wanted, when he took a look at me and the poodle. All garage men, and people of that intolerant stripe, hate poodles with their curious hair cut, especially the pom-poms that you got to leave on their hips if you expect the dogs to win a prize.

But the Airedale, as I have said, was the worst of all my dogs. He really wasn't my dog, as a matter of fact: I came home from a vacation one summer to find that my brother Roy had bought him while I was away. A big, burly, choleric[1] dog, he always acted as if he thought I wasn't one of the family. There was a slight advantage in being one of the family, for he didn't bite the family as often as he bit strangers. Still, in the years that we had him he bit everybody but mother, and he made a pass at her once but missed. That was

1 **choleric** (kŏl′ər ĭk)**:** easily angered.

during the month when we suddenly had mice, and Muggs refused to do anything about them. Nobody ever had mice exactly like the mice we had that month. They acted like pet mice, almost like mice somebody had trained. They were so friendly that one night when mother entertained at dinner the Friraliras, a club she and my father had belonged to for twenty years, she put down a lot of little dishes with food in them on the pantry floor so that the mice would be satisfied with that and wouldn't come into the dining room. Muggs stayed out in the pantry with the mice, lying on the floor, growling to himself—not at the mice, but about all the people in the next room that he would have liked to get at. Mother slipped out into the pantry once to see how everything was going. Everything was going fine. It made her so mad to see Muggs lying there, oblivious of the mice—they came running up to her—that she slapped him and he slashed at her, but didn't make it. He was sorry immediately, mother said. He was always sorry, she said, after he bit someone, but we could not understand how she figured this out. He didn't act sorry.

Mother used to send a box of candy every Christmas to the people the Airedale bit. The list finally contained forty or more names. Nobody could understand why we didn't get rid of the dog. I didn't understand it very well myself, but we didn't get rid of him. I think that one or two people tried to poison Muggs—he acted poisoned once in a while—and old Major Moberly fired at him once with his service revolver near the Seneca Hotel in East Broad Street—but Muggs lived to be almost eleven years old and even when he could hardly get around he bit a Congressman who had called to see my father on business. My mother had never liked the Con-

gressman—she said the signs of his horoscope showed he couldn't be trusted (he was Saturn with the moon in Virgo[2])—but she sent him a box of candy that Christmas. He sent it right back, probably because he suspected it was trick candy. Mother persuaded herself it was all for the best that the dog had bitten him, even though father lost an important business association because of it. "I wouldn't be associated with such a man," mother said. "Muggs could read him like a book."

We used to take turns feeding Muggs to be on his good side, but that didn't always work. He was never in a very good humor, even after a meal. Nobody knew exactly what was the matter with him, but whatever it was it made him irascible, especially in the mornings. Roy never felt very well in the morning, either, especially before breakfast, and once when he came downstairs and found that Muggs had moodily chewed up the morning paper he hit him in the face with a grapefruit and then jumped up on the dining room table, scattering dishes and silverware and spilling the coffee. Muggs's first free leap carried him all the way across the table and into a brass fire screen in front of the gas grate but he was back on his feet in a moment and in the end he got Roy and gave him a pretty vicious bite in the leg. Then he was all over it; he never bit anyone more than once at a time. Mother always mentioned that as an argument in his favor; she said he had a quick temper but that he didn't hold a grudge. She was forever defending him. I think she liked him because he wasn't well. "He's not strong," she would say, pityingly, but that was inaccurate; he may not have been well but he was terribly strong.

2 Saturn . . . Virgo: signs of the zodiac.

One time my mother went to the Chittenden Hotel to call on a woman mental healer who was lecturing in Columbus on the subject of "Harmonious Vibrations." She wanted to find out if it was possible to get harmonious vibrations into a dog. "He's a large tan-colored Airedale," mother explained. The woman said that she had never treated a dog but she advised my mother to hold the thought that he did not bite and would not bite. Mother was holding the thought the very next morning when Muggs got the iceman but she blamed that slip-up on the iceman. "If you didn't think he would bite you, he wouldn't," mother told him. He stomped out of the house in a terrible jangle of vibrations.

One morning when Muggs bit me slightly, more or less in passing, I reached down and grabbed his short stumpy tail and hoisted him into the air. It was a foolhardy thing to do and the last time I saw my mother, about six months ago, she said she didn't know what possessed me. I don't either, except that I was pretty mad. As long as I held the dog off the floor by his tail he couldn't get at me, but he twisted and jerked so, snarling all the time, that I realized I couldn't hold him that way very long. I carried him to the kitchen and flung him onto the floor and shut the door on him just as he crashed against it. But I forgot about the backstairs. Muggs went up the backstairs and down the frontstairs and had me cornered in the living room. I managed to get up onto the mantelpiece above the fireplace, but it gave way and came down with a tremendous crash throwing a large marble clock, several vases, and myself heavily to the floor. Muggs was so alarmed by the racket that when I picked myself up he had disappeared. We couldn't find him any-

where, although we whistled and shouted, until old Mrs. Detweiler called after dinner that night. Muggs had bitten her once, in the leg, and she came into the living room only after we assured her that Muggs had run away. She had just seated herself when, with a great growling and scratching of claws, Muggs emerged from under a davenport where he had been quietly hiding all the time, and bit her again. Mother examined the bite and put arnica[3] on it and told Mrs. Detweiler that it was only a bruise. "He just bumped you," she said. But Mrs. Detweiler left the house in a nasty state of mind.

Lots of people reported our Airedale to the police but my father held a municipal office at the time and was on friendly terms with the police. Even so, the cops had been out a couple of times—once when Muggs bit Mrs. Rufus Sturtevant and again when he bit Lieutenant-Governor Malloy—but mother told them that it hadn't been Muggs's fault but the fault of the people who were bitten. "When he starts for them, they scream," she explained, "and that excites him." The cops suggested that it might be a good idea to tie the dog up, but mother said that it mortified him to be tied up and that he wouldn't eat when he was tied up.

Muggs at his meals was an unusual sight. Because of the fact that if you reached toward the floor he would bite you, we usually put his food plate on top of an old kitchen table with a bench alongside the table. Muggs would stand on the bench and eat. I remember that my mother's Uncle Horatio, who boasted that he was the third man up Missionary Ridge,[4] was splutteringly

3 arnica: medicine for treating bruises.
4 Missionary Ridge: Battle in the War Between the States, fought in 1863 near Chattanooga, Tennessee.

indignant when he found out that we fed the dog on a table because we were afraid to put his plate on the floor. He said he wasn't afraid of any dog that ever lived and that he would put the dog's plate on the floor if we would give it to him. Roy said that if Uncle Horatio had fed Muggs on the ground just before the battle he would have been the first man up Missionary Ridge. Uncle Horatio was furious. "Bring him in! Bring him in now!" he shouted. "I'll feed the —— on the floor!" Roy was all for giving him a chance, but my father wouldn't hear of it. He said that Muggs had already been fed. "I'll feed him again!" bawled Uncle Horatio. We had quite a time quieting him.

In his last year Muggs used to spend practically all of his time outdoors. He didn't like to stay in the house for some reason or other—perhaps it held too many unpleasant memories for him. Anyway, it was hard to get him to come

in and as a result the garbage man, the iceman, and the laundryman wouldn't come near the house. We had to haul the garbage down to the corner, take the laundry out and bring it back, and meet the iceman a block from home. After this had gone on for some time we hit on an ingenious arrangement for getting the dog in the house so that we could lock him up while the gas meter was read, and so on. Muggs was afraid of only one thing, an electrical storm. Thunder and lightning frightened him out of his senses (I think he thought a storm had broken the day the mantelpiece fell). He would rush into the house and hide under a bed or in a clothes closet. So we fixed up a thunder machine out of a long narrow piece of sheet iron with a wooden handle on one end. Mother would shake this vigorously when she wanted to get Muggs into the house. It made an excellent imitation of thunder, but I suppose it

306

was the most roundabout system for running a household that was ever devised. It took a lot out of mother.

A few months before Muggs died, he got to "seeing things." He would rise slowly from the floor, growling low, and stalk stiff-legged and menacing toward nothing at all. Sometimes the Thing would be just a little to the right or left of a visitor. Once a Fuller Brush salesman got hysterics. Muggs came wandering into the room like Hamlet following his father's ghost. His eyes were fixed on a spot just to the left of the Fuller Brush man, who stood it until Muggs was about three slow, creeping paces from him. Then he shouted. Muggs wavered on past him into the hallway grumbling to himself but the Fuller man went on shouting. I think mother had to throw a pan of cold water on him before he stopped. That was the way she used to stop us boys when we got into fights.

Muggs died quite suddenly one night. Mother wanted to bury him in the family lot under a marble stone with some such inscription as "Flights of angels sing thee to thy rest" but we persuaded her it was against the law. In the end we just put up a smooth board above his grave along a lonely road. On the board I wrote with an indelible pencil "Cave Canem."[5] Mother was quite pleased with the simple classic dignity of the old Latin epitaph.

5 Cave Canem: Beware the Dog.

Understanding the Essay

1. Why could this story have been called "Mother and the Dog That Bit People"?
2. Explain how the following techniques add to the effect of the story:
   (a) Matter-of-fact reporting of unbelievable occurrences,
   (b) Abrupt switch from one incident to another,
   (c) The quiet endings with few punch lines,
   (d) The use of side comments that have no apparent connection with the story.
3. Why is Mother Thurber's pleasure over "the simple classic dignity of the old Latin epitaph" on the dog's headstone a perfect ending for Thurber's delightful characterization of his extraordinary mother?

Reading "A Dissertation upon Roast Pig"

This essay divides into two parts. The first is a tall story about Bo-Bo and his father; the second is a series of extravagant tributes on the pleasures of good food. Lamb uses exaggeration throughout the essay, both in the invented tale of Bo-Bo and in the language with which he rhapsodizes on roast pig. An appreciation of Lamb's essay depends on the reader's receptivity to the personality Lamb creates for his speaker—a person who digresses, assumes a simple air but can use learned language, truly loves such things as roast pig yet can see the humor in his own absorption in them, is widely read, and (his strongest characteristic) invites the reader to share his own attitude of humor and good will.

JAMES THURBER

A Dissertation¹ Upon Roast Pig

Charles Lamb

Charles Lamb, one of the best English essayists of the 19th century, wrote this whimsical piece entitled "A Dissertation upon Roast Pig" to amuse, employing humor that is gentle rather than cutting. Read this story carefully because it is one of the pieces most frequently referred to in all of literature.

MANKIND, says a Chinese manuscript, which my friend M. was obliging enough to read and explain to me, for the first seventy thousand ages ate their meat raw, clawing or biting it from the living animal, just as they do in Abyssinia to this day. This period is not obscurely hinted at by their great Confucius² in the second chapter of his Mundane Mutations, where he designates a kind of golden age by the term Cho-fang, literally the Cooks' holiday. The manuscript goes on to say, that the art of roasting, or rather broiling (which I take to be the elder brother) was accidentally discovered in the manner following. The swineherd, Ho-ti, having gone out into the woods one morning,

as his manner was, to collect mast³ for his hogs, left his cottage in the care of his eldest son Bo-Bo, a great lubberly boy, who being fond of playing with fire, as younkers⁴ of his age commonly are, let some sparks escape into a bundle of straw, which kindling quickly, spread the conflagration over every part of their poor mansion, till it was reduced to ashes. Together with the cottage (a sorry antediluvian⁵ makeshift of a building, you may think it), what was of much more importance, a fine litter of new-farrowed pigs, no less than nine in number, perished. China pigs have been esteemed a luxury all over the East from the remotest periods that we read of. Bo-Bo was in the utmost consternation, as you may think, not so much for the sake of the tenement, which his father and he could easily build up again with a few dry branches, and the labor of an hour or two, at any time, as for the loss of the pigs. While he was thinking what he should say to his father, and wringing his hands over the smoking remnants of one of those untimely sufferers, an odor assailed his nostrils, unlike any scent which he had before experienced. What could it proceed from?—not from the burnt cottage —he had smelt that smell before—indeed this was by no means the first accident of the kind which had occurred through the negligence of this unlucky young firebrand. Much less did it resemble that of any known herb, weed, or flower. A premonitory moistening at the same time overflowed his nether⁶ lip. He knew not what to think. He next stooped down to feel the pig, if there were any signs of life in it. He burnt

---

1 **Dissertation:** formal, scholarly discussion.
2 **Confucius:** Chinese philosopher and teacher (551-478 B.C.).
3 **mast:** acorns or beechnuts.
4 **younkers:** youngsters.
5 **antediluvian:** before the Flood described in the Bible.
6 **nether:** lower.

his fingers, and to cool them he applied them in his booby fashion to his mouth. Some of the crumbs of the scorched skin had come away with his fingers, and for the first time in his life (in the world's life indeed, for before him no man had known it) he tasted—*crackling!*[7] Again he felt and fumbled at the pig. It did not burn him so much now, still he licked his fingers from a sort of habit. The truth at length broke into his slow understanding, that it was the pig that smelt so, and the pig that tasted so delicious; and, surrendering himself up to the new-born pleasure, he fell to tearing up whole handfuls of the scorched skin with the flesh next it, and was cramming it down his throat in his beastly fashion, when his sire entered amid the smoking rafters, armed with retributory cudgel, and finding how affairs stood, began to rain blows upon the young rogue's shoulders, as thick as hailstones, which Bo-Bo heeded not any more than if they had been flies. The tickling pleasure, which he experienced in his lower regions, had rendered him quite callous to any inconveniences he might feel in those remote quarters. His father might lay on, but he could not beat him from his pig, till he had fairly made an end of it, when, becoming a little more sensible of his situation, something like the following dialogue ensued.

"You graceless whelp, what have you got there devouring? Is it not enough that you have burnt me down three houses with your dog's tricks, and be hanged to you, but you must be eating fire, and I know not what—what have you got there, I say?"

"O father, the pig, the pig, do come and taste how nice the burnt pig eats."

[7] **crackling:** crisply browned layer of fat just under the skin of a young pig.

The ears of Ho-ti tingled with horror. He cursed his son, and he cursed himself that ever he should beget a son that should eat burnt pig.

Bo-Bo, whose scent was wonderfully sharpened since morning, soon raked out another pig, and fairly rending it asunder, thrust the lesser half by main force into the fists of Ho-ti, still shouting out "Eat, eat, eat the burnt pig, Father, only taste—O Lord,"—with such-like barbarous ejaculations, cramming all the while as if he would choke.

Ho-ti trembled in every joint while he grasped the abominable thing, wavering whether he should not put his son to death for an unnatural young monster, when the crackling scorching his fingers, as it had done his son's, and applying the same remedy to them, he in his turn tasted some of its flavor, which, make what sour mouths he would for a pretense, proved not altogether displeasing to him. In conclusion (for the manuscript here is a little tedious) both father and son fairly sat down to the mess, and never left off till they had despatched all that remained of the litter.

Bo-Bo was strictly enjoined not to let the secret escape, for the neighbours would certainly have stoned them for a couple of abominable wretches, who could think of improving upon the good meat which God had sent them. Nevertheless, strange stories got about. It was observed that Ho-ti's cottage was burnt down now more frequently than ever. Nothing but fires from this time forward. Some would break out in broad day, others in the nighttime. As often as the sow farrowed, so sure was the house of Ho-ti to be in a blaze; and Ho-ti himself, which was the more remarkable, instead of chastising his son, seemed to grow more indulgent to him than ever. At length they were watched, the terrible mystery discovered, and father and son summoned to take their trial at Pekin,[8] then an inconsiderable assize town.[9] Evidence was given, the obnoxious food itself produced in court, and verdict about to be pronounced, when the foreman of the jury begged that some of the burnt pig, of which the culprits stood accused, might be handed into the box. He handled it, and they all handled it, and burning their fingers, as Bo-Bo and his father had done before them, and nature prompting to each of them the same remedy, against the face of all the facts, and the clearest charge which judge had ever given—to the surprise of the whole court, townsfolk, strangers, reporters, and all present—without leaving the box, or any manner of consultation whatever, they brought in a simultaneous verdict of Not Guilty.

The judge, who was a shrewd fellow, winked at the manifest iniquity of the decision; and, when the court was dismissed, went privily,[10] and bought up all the pigs that could be had for love or money. In a few days his lordship's town house was observed to be on fire. The thing took wing, and now there was nothing to be seen but fires in every direction. Fuel and pigs grew enormously dear all over the district. The insurance offices one and all shut up shop. People built slighter and slighter every day, until it was feared that the very science of architecture would in no long time be lost to the world. Thus this custom of firing houses continued, till in process of time, says my manuscript, a sage arose, like our Locke,[11] who made a discovery, that the flesh of

8 **Pekin:** now Peiping, a principal city of China.
9 **assize town:** a town in which a court sits.
10 **privily:** secretly.
11 **Locke:** John Locke (1632–1704), English philosopher.

310

swine, or indeed of any other animal, might be cooked (*burnt*, as they called it) without the necessity of consuming a whole house to dress it. Then first began the rude form of a gridiron.[12] Roasting by the string, or spit, came in a century or two later, I forget in whose dynasty. By such slow degrees, concludes the manuscript, do the most useful, and seemingly the most obvious arts, make their way among mankind.——

Without placing too implicit faith in the account above given, it must be agreed, that if a worthy pretext for so dangerous an experiment as setting houses on fire (especially in these days) could be assigned in favour of any culinary object, that pretext and excuse might be found in ROAST PIG.

Of all the delicacies in the whole *mundus edibilis*,[13] I will maintain it to be the most delicate—*princeps obsoniorum*.[14]

I speak not of your grown porkers—things between pig and pork—those hobbydehoys—but a young and tender suckling—under a moon old—guiltless as yet of the sty—with no original speck of the *amor immunditiae*,[15] the hereditary failing of the first parent, yet manifest—his voice as yet not broken, but something between a childish treble, and a grumble—the mild forerunner, or *praeludium*,[16] of a grunt.

He must be roasted. I am not ignorant that our ancestors ate them seethed, or boiled—but what a sacrifice of the exterior tegument![17]

There is no flavor comparable, I will contend, to that of the crisp, tawny, well-watched, not over-roasted, *crack-ling*, as it is well called—the very teeth are invited to their share of the pleasure at this banquet in overcoming the coy, brittle resistance—with the adhesive oleaginous—O call it not fat—but an indefinable sweetness growing up to it —the tender blossoming of fat—fat cropped in the bud—taken in the shoot —in the first innocence—the cream and quintessence of the child pig's yet pure food——the lean, no lean, but a kind of animal manna—or, rather, fat and lean (if it must be so) so blended and running into each other, that both together make but one ambrosian result, or common substance.

Behold him, while he is doing—it seemeth rather a refreshing warmth, than a scorching heat, that he is so passive to. How equably[18] he twirleth round the string!—Now he is just done. To see the extreme sensibility of that tender age, he hath wept out his pretty eyes—radiant jellies—shooting stars[19]—

See him in the dish, his second cradle, how meek he lieth!—wouldst thou have had this innocent grow up to the grossness and indocility which too often accompany maturer swinehood? Ten to one he would have proved a glutton, a sloven, an obstinate, disagreeable animal—wallowing in all manner of filthy conversation—from these sins he is happily snatched away—

Ere sin could blight, or sorrow fade,
Death came with timely care[20]—

his memory is odoriferous—no clown curseth, while his stomach half rejecteth, the rank bacon—no coal-heaver bolteth him in reeking sausages—he hath a fair

---

12 **gridiron**: grated cooking utensil.
13 *mundus edibilis*: world of eatables.
14 *princeps obsoniorum*: chief of delicacies.
15 *amor immunditiae*: love of dirt.
16 *praeludium*: prelude.
17 **tegument**: skin.

18 **equably**: tranquilly; evenly.
19 **shooting stars**: reference to an old belief that shooting stars dropped jellylike substances on the earth.
20 **Ere . . . care**: from Coleridge's "Epitaph on an Infant."

sepulcher in the grateful stomach of the judicious epicure—and for such a tomb might be content to die.

He is the best of Sapors.[21] Pineapple is great. She is indeed almost too transcendent—a delight, if not sinful, yet so like to sinning, that really a tender-conscienced person would do well to pause—too ravishing for mortal taste, she woundeth and excoriateth[22] the lips that approach her—like lovers' kisses, she biteth—she is a pleasure bordering on pain from the fierceness and insanity of her relish—but she stoppeth at the palate—she meddleth not with the appetite—and the coarsest hunger might barter her consistently for a mutton chop.

Pig—let me speak his praise—is no less provocative of the appetite, than he is satisfactory to the criticalness of the censorious palate. The strong man may batten[23] on him, and the weakling refuseth not his mild juices.

Unlike to mankind's mixed characters, a bundle of virtues and vices, inexplicably intertwisted, and not to be unraveled without hazard, he is—good throughout. No part of him is better or worse than another. He helpeth, as far as his little means extend, all around. He is the least envious of banquets. He is all neighbors' fare.

I am one of those, who freely and ungrudgingly impart a share of the good things of this life which fall to their lot (few as mine are in this kind) to a friend. I protest I take as great an interest in my friend's pleasures, his relishes, and proper satisfactions, as in mine own. "Presents," I often say, "endear Absents." Hares, pheasants, partridges, snipes, barndoor chickens (those "tame villatic fowl"),[24] capons, plovers, brawn, barrels of oysters, I dispense as freely as I receive them. I love to taste them, as it were, upon the tongue of my friend. But a stop must be put somewhere. One would not, like Lear,[25] "give every thing." I make my stand upon pig. Methinks it is an ingratitude to the Giver of all good flavors, to extradomiciliate, or send out of the house, slightingly, (under pretext of friendship, or I know not what) a blessing so particularly adapted, predestined, I may say, to my individual palate—It argues an insensibility.

I remember a touch of conscience in this kind at school. My good old aunt, who never parted from me at the end of a holiday without stuffing a sweetmeat, or some nice thing, into my pocket, had dismissed me one evening with a smoking plum cake, fresh from the oven. In my way to school (it was over London Bridge) a gray-headed old beggar saluted me (I have no doubt at this time of day that he was a counterfeit). I had no pence to console him with, and in the vanity of self-denial, and the very coxcombry[26] of charity, schoolboylike, I made him a present of —the whole cake! I walked on a little, buoyed up, as one is on such occasions, with a sweet soothing of self-satisfaction; but before I had got to the end of the bridge, my better feelings returned, and I burst into tears, thinking how ungrateful I had been to my good aunt, to go and give her good gift away to a stranger, that I had never seen before, and who might be a bad man for aught I knew; and then I thought of the pleasure my aunt would be taking in think-

---

21 **Sapors:** flavors.
22 **excoriateth:** chafes; makes sore.
23 **batten:** grow fat.

24 **tame villatic fowl:** a phrase from Milton's *Samson Agonistes. Villatic* means "village."
25 **Lear:** Shakespeare's *King Lear,* who gave his kingdom to his daughters.
26 **coxcombry:** vanity.

ing that I—I myself, and not another—would eat her nice cake—and what should I say to her the next time I saw her—how naughty I was to part with her pretty present—and the odor of that spicy cake came back upon my recollection, and the pleasure and the curiosity I had taken in seeing her make it, and her joy when she sent it to the oven, and how disappointed she would feel that I had never had a bit of it in my mouth at last—and I blamed my impertinent spirit of almsgiving, and out-of-place hypocrisy of goodness, and above all I wished never to see the face again of that insidious,[27] good-for-nothing, old gray impostor.

Our ancestors were nice[28] in their method of sacrificing these tender victims. We read of pigs whipped to death with something of a shock, as we hear of any other obsolete custom. The age of discipline is gone by, or it would be curious to inquire (in a philosophical light merely) what effect this process might have toward intenerating and dulcifying[29] a substance, naturally so mild and dulcet as the flesh of young pigs. It looks like refining a violet. Yet we should be cautious, while we condemn the inhumanity, how we censure the wisdom of the practice. It might impart a gusto—

I remember an hypothesis, argued upon by the young students, when I was at St. Omer's,[30] and maintained with much learning and pleasantry on both sides, "Whether, supposing that the flavor of a pig who obtained his death by whipping (per flagellationem extremam[31]) superadded a pleasure upon the palate of a man more intense than any possible suffering we can conceive in the animal, is man justified in using that method of putting the animal to death?" I forget the decision.

His sauce should be considered. Decidedly, a few bread crumbs, done up with his liver and brains, and a dash of mild sage. But, banish, dear Mrs. Cook, I beseech you, the whole onion tribe. Barbecue your whole hogs to your palate, steep them in shallots,[32] stuff them out with plantations of the rank and guilty garlic; you cannot poison them, or make them stronger than they are—but consider, he is a weakling —a flower.

27 insidious: wily.
28 nice: discriminating.
29 intenerating and dulcifying: making tender and sweet.

30 St. Omer's: an early Jesuit college in northern France. (Lamb did not attend it.) Rather meaningless questions, learnedly phrased, were often debated in the past at such colleges.
31 per flagellationem extremam: by beating to death.
32 shallots: small onions.

Understanding the Essay

1. What kind of writing does the word *dissertation* suggest? How does Lamb's title, "A Dissertation upon Roast Pig," set the tone for the entire essay, even though the first part tells the story of Bo-Bo and the last part gives Lamb's views on the joys of eating?
2. Why does Lamb use a serious, semihistorical approach to the fantastic tale of Bo-Bo and his father?
3. What does the paragraph (in the last third of the essay) that begins "I am one of those who freely and ungrudgingly" reveal about the "I" in the story?

4. How does the apparently aimless account of the speaker's giving his aunt's plum cake to the beggar fit into the essay?
5. Turn to Lamb's description of the "young and tender suckling." Select several descriptive phrases that appeal to your sense of taste or smell.
6. Why does Lamb use Latin phrases? What is their effect?

Building Vocabulary Skills

Make sure that you understand the meaning of the italicized words in the excerpts given below; then rewrite the sentences using substitute words or phrases (synonyms) for the italicized words. What characteristic do the italicized words have in common?
1. "A *premonitory* moistening at the same time overflowed his nether lip."
2. "Bo-Bo, whose scent was wonderfully sharpened since morning, soon raked out another pig, and fairly *rending it asunder*, thrust the lesser half by main force into the fists of Ho-ti."
3. "Bo-Bo was strictly *enjoined* not to let the secret escape. . . ."
4. "At length they were watched, the terrible mystery discovered, and father and son summoned to take their trial at Pekin, then an *inconsiderable* assize town."
5. "The judge . . . winked at the *manifest iniquity* of the decision. . . ."

Developing Language Skills

1. Explain Lamb's pun, "Presents endear Absents."
2. What does Lamb mean when he says, "It looks like refining a violet"? How is this reference similar to the phrase "lily-painting" in "Farewell, My Lovely"?
3. After making sure that you understand the meaning of *anachronism,* find several anachronisms in Lamb's story of Bo-Bo. Why are they used?

Reading "Lincoln Speaks at Gettysburg"

Carl Sandburg's training as an editorial writer on the Chicago *Daily News* shows up in the clear objective reporting of the first three sections of this selection. In these, he covers the political climate surrounding Lincoln's acceptance of a not-too-gracious invitation to speak at Gettysburg, the actual ceremonies at Gettysburg, and the newspaper coverage of the dedication. The last section is a tiny jewel of an essay which evokes the timeless, rather than historical, significance of the Gettysburg Address. Note how Sandburg interweaves the words of the Address with symbolic descriptions of the clock and the changing seasons.

Lincoln Speaks at Gettysburg[*]

Carl Sandburg

Carl Sandburg wrote The War Years *in an attic in his home among the sand dunes of Michigan. He took over the attic complete with a stove, a cot, a lot of bookshelves, a typewriter, and a crackerbox. "If Grant and Sherman could run campaigns from crackerboxes so could I," he said. That he was able to do so is proved by his four-volume work on Lincoln of such broad comprehension that it is "a biography not only of Lincoln but of the Civil War as well." Sandburg says that his purpose in writing the work was "to restore Lincoln to the common people to whom he belongs."*

A PRINTED INVITATION came to Lincoln's hands notifying him that on Thursday, November 19, 1863, exercises would be held for the dedication of a National Soldiers' Cemetery at Gettysburg. The same circular invitation had been mailed to Senators, Congressmen, the governors of Northern States, members of the Cabinet, by the commission of Pennsylvanians who had organized a corporation through which Maine, New Hampshire, Vermont, Massachusetts, Rhode Island, Maryland, Connecticut, New York, New Jersey, Pennsylvania, Delaware, West Virginia, Ohio, Indiana, Illinois, Michigan, Wisconsin, and Minnesota were to share the cost of a decent burying-ground for the dust and bones of the Union and Confederate dead.

In the helpless onrush of the war, it was known, too many of the fallen had lain as neglected cadavers rotting in the open fields or thrust into so shallow a resting place that a common farm plow caught in their bones. Now by order of Governor Curtin of Pennsylvania seventeen acres had been purchased on Cemetery Hill, where the Union center stood its colors on the second and third of July, and plots of soil had been allotted each State for its graves.

The sacred and delicate duties of orator of the day had fallen on Edward Everett. An eminent cultural figure, perhaps foremost of all distinguished American classical orators, he was born in 1794, had been United States Senator, Governor of Massachusetts, member of Congress, Secretary of State under Fillmore, Minister to Great Britain, Phi Beta Kappa poet at Harvard, professor of Greek at Harvard, president of Harvard. . . .

Serene, suave, handsomely venerable in his sixty-ninth year, a prominent specimen of Northern upper-class distinction, Everett was a natural choice of the Pennsylvania commissioners, who sought an orator for a solemn national occasion. When in September they notified him that the date of the occasion would be October 23, he replied that he would need more time for preparation, and the dedication was postponed till November 19.

Lincoln meanwhile, in reply to the printed circular invitation, sent word to the commissioners that he would be present at the ceremonies. This made it necessary for the commissioners to consider whether the President should be asked to deliver an address when present. Clark E. Carr of Galesburg, Illinois, representing his State on the Board of Commissioners, noted that the decision of the Board to invite Lincoln to speak was an afterthought. "The question was raised as to his ability to speak upon such a grave and solemn occasion. . . . Besides, it was said that, with his important duties and responsibilities, he could not possibly have the leisure to prepare an address. . . . In answer . . . it was urged that he himself, better than any one else, could determine as to these questions, and that, if he were invited to speak, he was sure to do what, under the circumstances, would be right and proper."

And so on November 2 David Wills of Gettysburg, as the special agent of Governor Curtin and also acting for the several States, by letter informed Lincoln that the several States having soldiers in the Army of the Potomac who were killed, or had since died at hospitals in the vicinity, had procured grounds for a cemetery and proper burial of their dead. "These grounds will be consecrated and set apart to this sacred purpose by appropriate ceremonies on Thursday, the 19th instant. I am authorized by the Governors of the various States to invite you to be present and participate in these ceremonies, which will doubtless be very imposing and solemnly impressive. It is the desire that after the oration, you, as Chief Executive of the nation, formally set apart these grounds to their sacred use by a few appropriate remarks."

Mr. Wills proceeded farther as to the solemnity of the occasion, and when Lincoln had finished reading the letter he understood definitely that the event called for no humor and that a long speech was not expected from him. "The invitation," wrote Clark E. Carr, "was not settled upon and sent to Mr. Lincoln until the second of November, more than six weeks after Mr. Everett had been invited to speak, and but little more than two weeks before the exercises were held." . . .

Lamon noted that Lincoln wrote part of his intended Gettysburg address at Washington, covered a sheet of foolscap paper with a memorandum of it, and before taking it out of his hat and reading it to Lamon he said that it was not at all satisfactory to him, that he was afraid he would not do himself credit nor come up to public expectation. He had been too busy to give it the time he would like to. . . .

Various definite motives besides vague intuitions may have guided Lincoln in his decision to attend and speak even though half his Cabinet had sent formal declinations in response to the printed circular invitations they had all received. Though the Gettysburg dedication was to be under interstate auspices, it had tremendous national significance for Lincoln because on the platform would be the State governors whose co-operation with him was of vast importance. Also a slander and a libel had been widely mouthed and printed that on his visit to the battlefield of Antietam nearly a year before he had laughed obscenely at his own funny stories and called on Lamon to sing a cheap comic song. Perhaps he might go to Gettysburg and let it be seen how he demeaned himself on a somber landscape of sacrifice. . . .

Fifteen thousand, some said 30,000 or 50,000, people were on Cemetery Hill for the exercises [on November 19] when the procession from Gettysburg arrived afoot and horseback representing the United States Government, the army and navy, governors of States, mayors of cities, a regiment of troops, hospital corps, telegraph-company representatives, Knights Templar, Masonic Fraternity, Odd Fellows, and other benevolent associations, the press, fire departments, citizens of Pennsylvania and other States. They were scheduled to start at ten o'clock and at that hour of the clock Lincoln in a black suit, high silk hat, and white gloves came out of the Wills residence and mounted a horse. A crowd was on hand and he held a reception on horseback. At eleven the parade began to move. The President's horse seemed small for him, as some looked at it. Clark E. Carr, just behind the President, believed he noticed that the President sat erect and looked majestic to begin with and then got to thinking so that his body leaned forward, his arms hung limp, and his head bent far down. . . .

The march of the procession of military and civic bodies began. "Mr. Lincoln was mounted upon a young and beautiful chestnut horse, the largest in the Cumberland Valley," wrote Lieutenant Cochrane. This seemed the first occasion that anyone had looked at the President mounted with a feeling that just the right horse had been picked to match his physical length. "His towering figure surmounted by a high silk hat made the rest of us look small," thought Cochrane. . . .

The march was over in fifteen minutes. But Mr. Everett, the orator of the day, had not arrived. Bands played till noon. Mr. Everett arrived. . . .

Benjamin B. French, officer in charge of buildings in Washington, introduced the Honorable Edward Everett, orator of the day, who rose, bowed low to Lincoln, saying, "Mr. President." Lincoln responded, "Mr. Everett."

The orator of the day then stood in silence before a crowd that stretched to limits that would test his voice. Beyond and around were the wheat fields, the meadows, the peach orchards, long slopes of land, and five and seven miles farther the contemplative blue ridge of a low mountain range. His eyes could sweep them as he faced the audience. He had taken note of it in his prepared and rehearsed address. "Overlooking these broad fields now reposing from the labors of the waning year, the mighty Alleghanies dimly towering before us, the graves of our brethren beneath our feet, it is with hesitation that I raise my poor voice to break the eloquent silence of God and Nature. But the duty to which you have called me must be performed;—grant me, I pray you, your indulgence and your sympathy." Everett proceeded, "It was appointed by law in Athens," and gave an extended sketch of the manner in which the Greeks cared for their dead who fell in battle. He spoke of the citizens assembled to consecrate the day. "As my eye ranges over the fields whose sods were so lately moistened by the blood of gallant and loyal men, I feel, as never before, how truly it was said of old that it is sweet and becoming to die for one's country."

Northern cities would have been trampled in conquest but for "those who sleep beneath our feet," said the orator. He gave an outline of how the war began, traversed[1] decisive features

1 traversed: reviewed.

of the three days' battles at Gettysburg, discussed the doctrine of State sovereignty and denounced it, drew parallels from European history, and came to his peroration[2] quoting Pericles[3] on dead patriots: "The whole earth is the sepulcher of illustrious men." The men of nineteen sister States had stood side by side on the perilous ridges. "Seminary Ridge, the Peach-Orchard, Cemetery, Culp, and Wolf Hill, Round Top, Little Round Top, humble names, henceforward dear and famous,—no lapse of time, no distance of space, shall cause you to be forgotten." He had spoken for an hour and fifty-seven minutes, some said a trifle over two hours, repeating almost word for word an address that occupied nearly two newspaper pages, as he had written it and as it had gone in advance sheets to many newspapers.

Everett came to his closing sentence without a faltering voice: "Down to the latest period of recorded time, in the glorious annals of our common country there will be no brighter page than that which relates THE BATTLES OF GETTYSBURG." It was the effort of his life and embodied the perfections of the school of oratory in which he had spent his career. His erect form and sturdy shoulders, his white hair and flung-back head at dramatic points, his voice, his poise, and chiefly some quality of inside goodheartedness, held most of his audience to him, though the people in the front rows had taken their seats three hours before his oration closed.

The Baltimore Glee Club sang an ode written for the occasion by Benjamin B. French, who had introduced Everett to the audience. . . .

Having read Everett's address, Lincoln knew when the moment drew near for him to speak. He took out his own manuscript from a coat pocket, put on his steel-bowed glasses, stirred in his chair, looked over the manuscript, and put it back in his pocket. The Baltimore Glee Club finished. The specially chosen Ward Hill Lamon[4] rose and spoke the words "The President of the United States," who rose, and holding in one hand the two sheets of paper at which he occasionally glanced, delivered the address in his high-pitched and clear-carrying voice. The *Cincinnati Commercial* reporter wrote, "The President rises slowly, draws from his pocket a paper, and, when commotion subsides, in a sharp, unmusical treble voice, reads the brief and pithy remarks." Hay wrote in his diary, "The President, in a firm, free way, with more grace than is his wont,[5] said his half dozen words of consecration." Charles Hale of the *Boston Advertiser*, also officially representing Governor Andrew of Massachusetts, had notebook and pencil in hand, took down the slow-spoken words of the President, as follows:

Fourscore and seven years ago, our fathers brought forth upon this continent a new nation, conceived in liberty and dedicated to the proposition that all men are created equal.

Now we are engaged in a great civil war, testing whether that nation—or any nation, so conceived and so dedicated—can long endure.

We are met on a great battlefield of that war. We are met to dedicate a portion of it as the final resting place of those who have given their lives that that nation might live.

It is altogether fitting and proper that we should do this.

2 **peroration:** concluding part of a speech.
3 **Pericles:** a statesman of ancient Athens.

4 **Ward Hill Lamon:** Lincoln's law partner in Danville, Illinois. When Lincoln became President, he chose Lamon as his private secretary. Lamon later wrote a book entitled *Recollections of Abraham Lincoln.*
5 **wont** (wŭnt): custom.

ESSAY

But, in a larger sense, we cannot dedicate, we cannot consecrate, we cannot hallow, this ground. The brave men, living and dead, who struggled here, have consecrated it, far above our power to add or to detract.

The world will very little note nor long remember what we say here; but it can never forget what they did here.

It is for us, the living, rather, to be dedicated, here, to the unfinished work that they have thus far so nobly carried on. It is rather for us to be here dedicated to the great task remaining before us; that from these honored dead we take increased devotion to that cause for which they here gave the last full measure of devotion; that we here highly resolve that these dead shall not have died in vain; that the nation shall, under God, have a new birth of freedom, and that government of the people, by the people, for the people, shall not perish from the earth.

The *New York Tribune* and many other newspapers indicated "[Applause.]" at five places in the address

CARL SANDBURG

and "[Long continued applause.]" at the end. The applause, however, according to most of the responsible witnesses, was formal and perfunctory,[6] a tribute to the occasion, to the high office, to the array of important men of the nation on the platform, by persons who had sat as an audience for three hours. Ten sentences had been spoken in five minutes, and some were surprised that it should end before the orator had really begun to get his outdoor voice.

A photographer had made ready to record a great historic moment, had bustled about with his dry plates, his black box on a tripod, and before he had his head under the hood for an exposure, the President had said "by the people, for the people" and the nick of time was past for a photograph. . . .

The *New York Times* reporter gave

6 **perfunctory:** mechanical.

319

his summary of the program by writing: "The opening prayer by Reverend Mr. Stockton was touching and beautiful, and produced quite as much effect upon the audience as the classic sentences of the orator of the day. President Lincoln's address was delivered in a clear loud tone of voice, which could be distinctly heard at the extreme limits of the large assemblage. It was delivered (or rather read from a sheet of paper which the speaker held in his hand) in a very deliberate manner, with strong emphasis, and with a most businesslike air."

The *Philadelphia Press* man, John Russell Young, privately felt that Everett's speech was the performance of a great actor whose art was too evident, that it was "beautiful but cold as ice." The *New York Times* man noted: "Even while Mr. Everett was delivering his splendid oration, there were as many people wandering about the fields, made memorable by the fierce struggles of July, as stood around the stand listening to his eloquent periods. They seem to have considered, with President Lincoln, that it was not what was *said* here, but what was *done* here, that deserved their attention. . . . In wandering about these battlefields, one is astonished and indignant to find at almost every step of his progress the carcasses of dead horses which breed pestilence in the atmosphere. I am told that more than a score of deaths have resulted from this neglect in the village of Gettysburg the past summer; in the house in which I was compelled to seek lodgings, there are now two boys sick with typhoid fever attributed to this cause. Within a stone's throw of the whitewashed hut occupied as the headquarters of General Meade, I counted yesterday no less than ten carcasses of dead horses, lying on the ground where

they were struck by the shells of the enemy."

The audience had expected, as the printed program stipulated, "Dedicatory Remarks, by the President of the United States." No eloquence was promised. Where eloquence is in flow the orator must have time to get tuned up, to expatiate and expand while building toward his climaxes, it was supposed. The *New York Tribune* man and other like observers merely reported the words of the address with the one preceding sentence: "The dedicatory remarks were then delivered by the President." These reporters felt no urge to inform their readers about how Lincoln stood, what he did with his hands, how he moved, vocalized, or whether he emphasized or subdued any parts of the address. Strictly, no address as such was on the program from him. He was down for just a few perfunctory "dedicatory remarks."

According to Lamon, Lincoln himself felt that about all he had given the audience was ordinary garden-variety dedicatory remarks, for Lamon wrote that Lincoln told him just after delivering the speech that he had regret over not having prepared it with greater care. "Lamon, that speech won't *scour*. It is a flat failure and the people are disappointed." On the farms where Lincoln grew up as a boy when wet soil stuck to the mold board of a plow they said it didn't "scour."

The near-by *Patriot and Union* of Harrisburg took its fling: "The President succeeded on this occasion because he acted without sense and without constraint in a panorama that was gotten up more for the benefit of his party than for the glory of the nation and the honor of the dead. . . . We pass over the silly remarks of the President; for the credit of the nation we are willing that the veil of oblivion shall be dropped over them and that they shall no more be repeated or thought of."

The *Chicago Times* held that "Mr. Lincoln did most foully traduce the motives of the men who were slain at Gettysburg" in his reference to "a new birth of freedom," the *Times* saying, "They gave their lives to maintain the old government, and the only Constitution and Union." He had perverted history, misstated the cause for which they died, and with "ignorant rudeness" insulted the memory of the dead, the *Times* alleged: "Readers will not have failed to observe the exceeding bad taste which characterized the remarks of the President and Secretary of State at the dedication of the soldiers' cemetery at Gettysburg. The cheek of every American must tingle with shame as he reads the silly, flat, and dish-watery utterances of the man who has to be pointed out to intelligent foreigners as the President of the United States. And neither he nor Seward could refrain, even on that solemn occasion, from spouting their odious abolition doctrines. The readers of THE TIMES ought to know, too, that the valorous President did not dare to make this little journey to Gettysburg without being escorted by a bodyguard of soldiers. For the first time in the history of the country, the President of the United States, in traveling through a part of his dominions, on a peaceful, even a religious mission, had to be escorted by a bodyguard of soldiers . . . it was fear for his own personal safety which led the President to go escorted as any other military despot might go." In the pronouncement of a funeral sermon Mr. Lincoln had intruded an "offensive exhibition of boorishness and vulgarity," had alluded to tribal differences that an Indian orator eulogizing dead warriors would have omitted, "which he knew would excite unnecessarily the bitter prejudices of his hearers." Therefore the *Chicago Times* would inquire, "Is Mr. Lincoln less refined than a savage?"

A Confederate outburst of war propaganda related to Lincoln and the Gettysburg exercises was set forth in a *Richmond Examiner* editorial, and probably written by its editor, Edward A. Pollard, taking a day off from his merciless and occasionally wild-eyed criticism of President Jefferson Davis of the Confederacy. And the *Chicago Times*, which seldom let a day pass without curses on Lincoln for his alleged suppression of free speech and a free press, reprinted in full the long editorial from the *Examiner*. "The dramatic exhibition at Gettysburg is in thorough keeping with Yankee character, suited to the usual dignity of their chosen chief," ran part of the editorial scorn. "Stage play, studied attitudes, and effective points were carefully elaborated and presented to the world as the honest outpourings of a nation's heart. In spite of shoddy contracts, of universal corruption, and cruel thirst for southern blood, these people have ideas . . . have read of them in books . . . and determined accordingly to have a grand imitation of them. . . . Mr. Everett was equal to the occasion. He 'took down his Thucydides,'[7] and fancied himself a Pericles commemorating the illustrious dead. The music, the eloquence, the bottled tears and hermetically sealed[8] grief, prepared for the occasion, were all properly brought out in honor of the heroes, whom they crimp[9] in Ireland,

---

7 **Thucydides** (thōō sǐd′ə dēz′): historian of ancient Greece.
8 **hermetically sealed:** airtight.
9 **crimp:** secure for military service by force or trickery.

inveigle[10] in Germany, or hunt down in the streets of New York.

"So far the play was strictly classic. To suit the general public, however, a little admixture of the more irregular romantic drama was allowed. A vein of comedy was permitted to mingle with the deep pathos of the piece. This singular novelty, and deviation from classic propriety, was heightened by assigning this part to the chief personage. Kings are usually made to speak in the magniloquent language supposed to be suited to their elevated position. On the present occasion Lincoln acted the clown."

This was in the customary tone of the *Chicago Times* and relished by its supporting readers. Its rival, the *Chicago Tribune*, however, had a reporter who telegraphed (unless some editor who read the address added his own independent opinion) a sentence: "The dedicatory remarks of President Lincoln will live among the annals of man."

The *Cincinnati Gazette* reporter added after the text of the address, "That this was the right thing in the right place, and a perfect thing in every respect, was the universal encomium."[11]

The American correspondent of the London *Times* wrote that "the ceremony was rendered ludicrous by some of the sallies of that poor President Lincoln. . . . Anything more dull and commonplace it would not be easy to produce."

Count Gurowski, the only man ever mentioned by Lincoln to Lamon as his possible assassin, wrote in a diary, "Lincoln spoke, with one eye to a future platform and to re-election."

The *Philadelphia Evening Bulletin* said thousands who would not read the elaborate oration of Mr. Everett would read the President's few words "and not many will do it without a moistening of the eye and a swelling of the heart." The *Detroit Advertiser and Tribune* said Mr. Everett had nobly told the story of the battle, "but he who wants to take in the very spirit of the day, catch the unstudied pathos that animates a sincere but simple-minded man, will turn from the stately periods[12] of the professed orator to the brief speech of the President." The *Providence Journal* reminded readers of the saying that the hardest thing in the world is to make a good five-minute speech: "We know not where to look for a more admirable speech than the brief one which the President made at the close of Mr. Everett's oration. . . . Could the most elaborate and splendid oration be more beautiful, more touching, more inspiring, than those thrilling words of the President? They had in our humble judgment the charm and power of the very highest eloquence." . . .

The *Springfield Republican* had veered from its first opinion that Lincoln was honest but "a Simple Susan." Its comment ran: "Surpassingly fine as Mr. Everett's oration was in the Gettysburg consecration, the rhetorical honors of the occasion were won by President Lincoln. His little speech is a perfect gem; deep in feeling, compact in thought and expression, and tasteful and elegant in every word and comma. Then it has the merit of unexpectedness in its verbal perfection and beauty. We had grown so accustomed to homely and imperfect phrase in his productions that we had come to think it was the law of his utterance. But this shows he can talk handsomely as well as act sensibly. Turn back and read it over, it will re-

---

10 inveigle (ĭn vē′gəl): win through deception.
11 encomium: high praise.

12 periods: sentences.

pay study as a model speech. Strong feelings and a large brain were its parents—a little painstaking its *accoucheur*."[13] . . .

Everett's opinion of the speech he heard Lincoln deliver was written in a note to Lincoln the next day and was more than mere courtesy: "I should be glad if I could flatter myself that I came as near to the central idea of the occasion in two hours as you did in two minutes." Lincoln's immediate reply was: "In our respective parts yesterday, you could not have been excused to make a short address, nor I a long one. I am pleased to know that, in your judgment, the little I did say was not entirely a failure."

At Everett's request Lincoln wrote with pen and ink a copy of his Gettysburg Address, which manuscript was auctioned at a Sanitary Fair in New York for the benefit of soldiers. At the request of George Bancroft, the historian, he wrote another copy for a Soldiers' and Sailors' Fair at Baltimore. He wrote still another to be lithographed as a facsimile in a publication, *Autographed Leaves of Our Country's Authors*. For Mr. Wills, his host at Gettysburg, he wrote another. The first draft, written in Washington, and the second one, held while delivering it, went into John Hay's hands to be eventually presented to the Library of Congress.

After the ceremonies at Gettysburg Lincoln lunched with Governor Curtin, Mr. Everett, and others at the Wills home, held a reception that had not been planned, handshaking nearly an hour, looking gloomy and listless but brightening sometimes as a small boy or girl came in line, and stopping one tall man for remarks as to just how high up he reached. At five o'clock he attended a patriotic meeting in the Presbyterian church, walking arm-in-arm with old John Burns, and listening to an address by Lieutenant Governor-elect Anderson of Ohio. At six-thirty he was on the departing Washington train. In the dining car his secretary John Hay ate with Simon Cameron and Wayne MacVeagh. Hay had thought Cameron and MacVeagh hated each other, but he noted: "I was more than usually struck by the intimate jovial relations that existed between men that hate and detest each other as cordially as do these Pennsylvania politicians."

The ride to Washington took until midnight. Lincoln was weary, talked little, stretched out on one of the side seats in the drawing room and had a wet towel laid across his eyes and forehead.

He had stood that day, the world's foremost spokesman of popular government, saying that democracy was yet worth fighting for. He had spoken as one in mist who might head on deeper yet into mist. He incarnated[14] the assurances and pretenses of popular government, implied that it could and might perish from the earth. What he meant by "a new birth of freedom" for the nation could have a thousand interpretations. The taller riddles of democracy stood up out of the address. It had the dream touch of vast and furious events epitomized[15] for any foreteller to read what was to come. He did not assume that the drafted soldiers, substitutes, and bounty-paid privates had died willingly under Lee's shot and shell, in deliberate consecration of themselves to the Union cause. His ca-

---

13 *accoucheur* (ăk′o͞o shûr′): one who brought it to birth; delivered it.

14 **incarnated:** made real in the flesh.
15 **epitomized** (ĭ pĭt′ə mīzd): summarized.

dences[16] sang the ancient song that where there is freedom men have fought and sacrificed for it, and that freedom is worth men's dying for. For the first time since he became President he had on a dramatic occasion declaimed, howsoever it might be read, Jefferson's proposition which had been a slogan of the Revolutionary War—"All men are created equal"—leaving no other inference than that he regarded the Negro slave as a man. His outwardly smooth sentences were inside of them gnarled and tough with the enigmas of the American experiment.

Back at Gettysburg the blue haze of the Cumberland Mountains had dimmed till it was a blur in a nocturne.[17] The moon was up and fell with a bland golden benevolence on the new-made graves of soldiers, on the sepulchers of old settlers, on the horse carcasses of which the onrush of war had not yet permitted removal. The *New York Herald* man walked amid them and ended the story he sent his paper: "The air, the trees, the graves are silent. Even the relic hunters are gone now. And the soldiers here never wake to the sound of reveille."

In many a country cottage over the land, a tall old clock in a quiet corner told time in a tick-tock deliberation. Whether the orchard branches hung with pink-spray blossoms or icicles of sleet, whether the outside news was seedtime or harvest, rain or drouth, births or deaths, the swing of the pendulum was right and left and right and left in a tick-tock deliberation. The face and dial of the clock had known the eyes of a boy who listened to its tick-tock and learned to read its minute and hour hands. And the boy had seen years measured off by the swinging pendulum, and grown to man size, had gone away. And the people in the cottage knew that the clock would stand there and the boy never again come into the room and look at the clock with the query, "What is the time?"

In a row of graves of the Unidentified the boy would sleep long in the dedicated final resting place at Gettysburg. Why he had gone away and why he would never come back had roots in some mystery of flags and drums, of national fate in which individuals sink as in a deep sea, of men swallowed and vanished in a man-made storm of smoke and steel.

The mystery deepened and moved with ancient music and inviolable[18] consolation because a solemn Man of Authority had stood at the graves of the Unidentified and spoken the words "We cannot consecrate—we cannot hallow—this ground. The brave men, living and dead, who struggled here, have consecrated it far above our poor power to add or detract. . . . From these honored dead we take increased devotion to that cause for which they gave the last full measure of devotion."

To the backward and forward pendulum swing of a tall old clock in a quiet corner they might read those cadenced words while outside the windows the first flurry of snow blew across the orchard and down over the meadow, the beginnings of winter in a gun-metal gloaming to be later arched with a star-flung sky.

---

16 **cadences** (kā′dən səz): rhythms.
17 **nocturne**: night scene.

18 **inviolable** (ĭn vī′ə lə bəl): secure against violation.

ESSAY

Understanding the Essay

1. What does Sandburg establish through his factual account of Lincoln's invitation to speak at Gettysburg?
2. Find several reasons that Lincoln may have accepted the carefully worded belated invitation to speak at the Gettysburg ceremonies when lesser men were ignoring the occasion.
3. How do Lincoln and Edward Everett contrast with each other?
4. How does Lieutenant Cochrane's remark concerning Lincoln's appearance on horseback at Gettysburg foreshadow the ultimate recognition of the quality of his speech?
5. How does Sandburg's comment, "Ten sentences had been spoken in five minutes, and some were surprised that it should end before the orator had really begun to get his outdoor voice," explain in part the lukewarm reaction of the crowd?
6. What does Lincoln's comment to his friend and secretary, "Lamon, that speech won't *scour*," reveal about Lincoln's opinion of the importance of the occasion?
7. What do the excerpts from the newspaper editorials reveal about Civil War newspapers? Which of the conflicting newspaper reports of the speech included here is closest to the opinion held today?
8. What is Sandburg's evaluation of the speech as shown in the last eight paragraphs of this selection?
9. Although the last sentence of the essay seems to be purely descriptive, it also contains Sandburg's final comment on the Gettysburg Address. What is this comment? (Consider: Who are the *they* referred to? Why is the detail of the swinging pendulum included? How does the phrase *gun-metal gloaming* refer to the historical situation? What is implied by the concluding phrase—"to be later arched with a star-flung sky"?)

Developing Language Skills

1. The last eight paragraphs of Sandburg's account differ from the rest of the piece in tone, choice of words, and emotional appeal. This short critical piece carries Sandburg's opinion. Write one paragraph explaining Sandburg's reasons for believing that the Gettysburg Address is both a great political speech and a great human document, using quotations from this selection to support your explanation.
2. Find several places in which the text of Lincoln's address as taken down by Charles Hale of the *Boston Advertiser* differs from the official version. Why is the official version stronger?

Gallico develops his main theme—the importance of the sports writer's knowing what he is talking about—through the selection of sharp details and his choice of picture words. His special quality is making the reader feel as well as see an event. He writes easily and convincingly of the "tough skin of the water" in high diving and of "the sharp tingling of the skin from head to foot, followed by a sudden amazing sharpness of vision" when a motor quits in a plane two or three thousand feet up. He uses figures of speech as naturally as he does the names of the champions whose moments of glory and defeat he covered.

The Feel

Paul Gallico

If you are inclined to boo the receiver when he drops the football in the end zone, you may change your mind after you read "The Feel." Paul Gallico's curiosity as a cub reporter drove him to try every sport that he covered for his paper, from billiards to boxing, to get "the feel" of it. His feel must have been the right one because he was the highest-paid sports writer in the world when he left newspaper work in his late thirties to turn to free-lance writing.

A CHILD WANDERING through a department store with its mother, is admonished over and over again not to touch things. Mother is convinced that the child only does it to annoy or because it is a child, and usually hasn't the vaguest inkling of the fact that Junior is "touching" because he is a little blotter soaking up information and knowledge, and "feel" is an important adjunct[1] to seeing. Adults are exactly the same, in a measure, as you may ascertain when some new gadget or article is produced for inspection. The average person says: "Here, let me see that," and holds out his hand. He doesn't mean "see," because he is already seeing it. What he means is that he wants to get it into his hands and feel it so as to become better acquainted.

I do not insist that a curiosity and capacity for feeling sports is necessary to be a successful writer, but it is fairly obvious that a man who has been tapped on the chin with five fingers wrapped up in a leather boxing glove and propelled by the arm of an expert knows more about that particular sensation than one who has not, always provided he has the gift of expressing himself. I once inquired of a heavyweight prizefighter by the name of King Levinsky, in a radio interview, what it felt like to be hit on the chin by Joe Louis, the

1 adjunct: addition; accessory.

King having just acquired that experience with rather disastrous results. Levinsky considered the matter for a moment and then reported: "It don't feel like nuttin'," but added that for a long while afterwards he felt as though he were "in a transom."

I was always a child who touched things and I have always had a tremendous curiosity with regard to sensation. If I knew what playing a game felt like, particularly against or in the company of experts, I was better equipped to write about the playing of it and the problems of the men and women who took part in it. And so, at one time or another, I have tried them all, football, baseball, boxing, riding, shooting, swimming, squash, handball, fencing, driving, flying, both land and sea planes, rowing, canoeing, skiing, riding a bicycle, ice-skating, roller-skating, tennis, golf, archery, basketball, running, both the hundred-yard dash and the mile, the high jump and shot put, badminton, angling, deep-sea, stream-, and surfcasting, billiards and bowling, motorboating and wrestling, besides riding as a passenger with the fastest men on land and water and in the air, to see what it felt like. Most of them I dabbled in as a youngster going through school and college, and others, like piloting a plane, squash, fencing, and skiing, I took up after I was old enough to know better, purely to get the feeling of what they were like.

None of these things can I do well, but I never cared about becoming an expert, and besides, there wasn't time. But there is only one way to find out accurately human sensations in a ship two or three thousand feet up when the motor quits, and that is actually to experience that gone feeling at the pit of the stomach and the sharp tingling of the skin from head to foot, followed by a sudden amazing sharpness of vision, clear-sightedness, and coolness that you never knew you possessed as you find the question of life or death completely in your own hands. It is not the "you" that you know, but somebody else, a stranger, who noses the ship down, circles, fastens upon the one best spot to sit down, pushes or pulls buttons to try to get her started again, and finally drops her in, safe and sound. And it is only by such experience that you learn likewise of the sudden weakness that hits you right at the back of the knees after you have climbed out and started to walk around her and that comes close to knocking you flat as for the first time since the engine quit its soothing drone you think of destruction and sudden death.

Often my courage has failed me and I have funked completely, such as the time I went up to the top of the thirty-foot Olympic diving-tower at Jones Beach, Long Island, during the competitions, to see what it was like to dive from that height, and wound up crawling away from the edge on hands and knees, dizzy, scared, and a little sick, but with a wholesome respect for the boys and girls who hurled themselves through the air and down through the tough skin of the water from that awful height. At other times sheer ignorance of what I was getting into has led me into tight spots such as the time I came down the Olympic ski run from the top of the Kreuzeck,[2] six thousand feet above Garmisch-Partenkirchen,[3] after having been on skis but once before in snow and for the rest had no more than a dozen lessons on an indoor artificial slide in a New York department store.

2 **Kreuzeck:** ski area in Bavarian Alps.
3 **Garmisch-Partenkirchen:** town in foothills of Bavarian Alps where Olympic ski competition is held.

At one point my legs, untrained, got so tired that I couldn't stem (brake) any more, and I lost control and went full tilt and all out, down a three-foot twisting path cut out of the side of the mountain, with a two-thousand-foot abyss on the left and the mountain itself on the right. That was probably the most scared I have ever been, and I scare fast and often. I remember giving myself up for lost and wondering how long it would take them to retrieve my body and whether I should be still alive. In the meantime the speed of the descent was increasing. Somehow I was keeping my feet and negotiating turns, how I will never know, until suddenly the narrow patch opened out into a wide, steep stretch of slope with a rise at the other end, and *that* part of the journey was over.

By some miracle I got to the bottom of the run uninjured, having made most of the trip down the icy, perpendicular slopes on the flat of my back. It was the thrill and scare of a lifetime, and to date no one has been able to persuade me to try a jump. I know when to stop. After all, I am entitled to rely upon my imagination for something. But when it was all over and I found myself still whole, it was also distinctly worth while to have learned what is required of a ski runner in the breakneck *Abfahrt* or downhill race, or the difficult *slalom.*[4] Five days later, when I climbed laboriously (still on skis) halfway up that Alp and watched the Olympic downhill racers hurtling down the perilous, ice-covered, and nearly perpendicular *Steilhang,*[5] I knew that I was looking at a great group of athletes who, for one thing, did not know the meaning of the word *fear.* The slope was studded with small pine trees and rocks, but half

4 slalom (slä′lŏm): downhill skiing race over a zigzag course.
5 Steilhang: ski run in Bavarian Alps.

ESSAY

of the field gained precious seconds by hitting that slope all out, with complete contempt for disaster rushing up at them at a speed often better than sixty miles an hour. And when an unfortunate Czech skidded off the course at the bottom of the slope and into a pile of rope and got himself snarled up as helpless as a fly in a spider's web, it was a story that I could write from the heart. I had spent ten minutes getting myself untangled after a fall, *without* any rope to add to the difficulties. It seems that I couldn't find where my left leg ended and one more ski than I had originally donned seemed to be involved somehow. Only a person who has been on those fiendish runners knows the sensation.

It all began back in 1922 when I was a cub sports-writer and consumed with more curiosity than was good for my health. I had seen my first professional prizefights and wondered at the curious behavior of men under the stress of blows, the sudden checking and the beginning of a little fall forward after a hard punch, the glazing of the eyes and the loss of locomotor[6] control, the strange actions of men on the canvas after a knockdown as they struggled to regain their senses and arise on legs that seemed to have turned into rubber. I had never been in any bad fist fights as a youngster, though I had taken a little physical punishment in football, but it was not enough to complete the picture. Could one think under those conditions?

I had been assigned to my first training-camp coverage, Dempsey's at Saratoga Springs, where he was preparing for his famous fight with Luis Firpo. For days I watched him sag a spar boy with what seemed to be no more than a light cuff on the neck, or pat his face with what looked like no more than a caressing stroke of his arm, and the fellow would come all apart at the seams and collapse in a useless heap, grinning vacuously[7] or twitching strangely. My burning curiosity got the better of prudence and a certain reluctance to expose myself to physical pain. I asked Dempsey to permit me to box a round with him. I had never boxed before, but I was in good physical shape, having just completed a four-year stretch as a galley slave in the Columbia eight-oared shell.[8]

When it was over and I escaped through the ropes, shaking, bleeding a little from the mouth, with rosin dust on my pants and a vicious throbbing in my head, I knew all that there was to know about being hit in the prize-ring. It seems that I had gone to an expert for tuition. I knew the sensation of being stalked and pursued by a relentless, truculent[9] professional destroyer whose trade and business it was to injure men. I saw the quick flash of the brown forearm that precedes the stunning shock as a bony, leather-bound fist lands on cheek or mouth. I learned more (partly from photographs of the lesson, viewed afterwards, one of which shows me ducked under a vicious left hook, an act of which I never had the slightest recollection) about instinctive ducking and blocking than I could have in ten years of looking at prizefights, and I learned, too, that as the soldier never hears the bullet that kills him, so does the fighter rarely, if ever, see the punch that tumbles blackness over him like a mantle, with a tearing rip as though the roof of

---

6 **locomotor:** relating to movement.

7 **vacuously:** stupidly.
8 **galley slave in the Columbia eight-oared shell:** member of the Columbia University rowing crew.
9 **truculent** (trŭk′yə lənt): savage.

his skull were exploding, and robs him of his senses.

There was just that—a ripping in my head and then sudden blackness, and the next thing I knew, I was sitting on the canvas covering of the ring floor with my legs collapsed under me, grinning idiotically. How often since have I seen that same silly, goofy look on the faces of dropped fighters—and understood it. I held onto the floor with both hands, because the ring and the audience outside were making a complete clockwise revolution, came to a stop, and then went back again counter-clockwise. When I struggled to my feet, Jack Kearns, Dempsey's manager, was counting over me, but I neither saw nor heard him and was only conscious that I was in a ridiculous position and that the thing to do was to get up and try to fight back. The floor swayed and rocked beneath me like a fishing dory in an off-shore swell, and it was a welcome respite when Dempsey rushed into a clinch, held me up, and whispered into my ear: "Wrestle around a bit, son, until your head clears." And then it was that I learned what those little love-taps to the back of the neck and the short digs to the ribs can mean to the groggy pugilist more than half knocked out. It is a murderous game, and the fighter who can escape after having been felled by a lethal blow has my admiration. And there, too, I learned that there can be no sweeter sound than the bell that calls a halt to hostilities.

From that afternoon on, also, dated my antipathy for the spectator at prize-fights who yells: "Come on, you bum, get up and fight! Oh, you big quitter! Yah yellow, yah yellow!" Yellow, eh? It is all a man can do to get up after being stunned by a blow, much less fight back. But they do it. And how a man is able to muster any further interest in

a combat after being floored with a blow to the pit of the stomach will always remain to me a miracle of what the human animal is capable of under stress.

Further experiments were less painful, but equally illuminating. A couple of sets of tennis with Vinnie Richards taught me more about what is required of a top-flight tournament tennis-player than I could have got out of a dozen books or years of reporting tennis matches. It is one thing to sit in a press box and write caustically[10] that Brown played uninspired tennis, or Black's court covering was faulty and that his frequent errors cost him the set. It is quite another to stand across the net at the back of a service court and try to get your racket on a service that is so fast that the ear can hardly detect the interval between the sound of the server's bat hitting the ball and the ball striking the court. Tournament tennis is a different game from week-end tennis. For one thing, in average tennis, after the first hard service has gone into the net or out, you breathe a sigh of relief, move up closer and wait for the cripple to come floating over. In big-time tennis second service is practically as hard as the first, with an additional twist on the ball.

It is impossible to judge or know anything about the speed of a forehand drive hit by a champion until you have had one fired at you, or, rather, away from you, and you have made an attempt to return it. It is then that you first realize that tennis is played more with the head than with the arms and the legs. The fastest player in the world cannot get to a drive to return it if he hasn't thought correctly, guessed its di-

10 caustically: cuttingly.

rection, and anticipated it by a fraction of a second.

There was golf with Bob Jones and Gene Sarazen and Tommy Armour, little Cruickshank and Johnny Farrell, and Diegel and other professionals; and experiments at trying to keep up in the water with Johnny Weissmuller, Helene Madison, and Eleanor Holm, attempts to catch football passes thrown by Benny Friedman. Nobody actually plays golf until he has acquired the technical perfection to be able to hit the ball accurately, high, low, hooked or faded and placed. And nobody knows what real golf is like until he has played around with a professional and seen him play, not the ball, but the course, the roll of the land, the hazards, the wind, and the texture of the greens and the fairways. It looks like showmanship when a top-flight golfer plucks a handful of grass and lets it flutter in the air, or abandons his drive to march two hundred yards down to the green and look over the situation. It isn't. It's golf. The average player never knows or cares whether he is putting with or across the grain of a green. The professional *always* knows. The same average player standing on the tee is concentrated on getting the ball somewhere on the fairway, two hundred yards out. The professional when preparing to drive is actually to all intents and purposes playing his *second* shot. He means to place his drive so as to open up the green for his approach. But you don't find that out until you have played around with them when they are relaxed and not competing, and listen to them talk and plan attacks on holes.

Major-league baseball is one of the most difficult and precise of all games, but you would never know it unless you went down on the field and got close to it and tried it yourself. For instance, the distance between pitcher and catcher is a matter of twenty paces, but it doesn't seem like enough when you don a catcher's mitt and try to hold a pitcher with the speed of Dizzy Dean or Dazzy Vance. Not even the sponge that catchers wear in the palm of the hand when working with fast-ball pitchers, and the bulky mitt are sufficient to rob the ball of shock and sting that lames your hand unless you know how to ride with the throw and kill some of its speed. The pitcher, standing on his little elevated mound, looms up enormously over you at that short distance, and when he ties himself into a coiled spring preparatory to letting fly, it requires all your self-control not to break and run for safety. And as for the things they can do with a baseball, those major-league pitchers . . . ! One way of finding out is to wander down on the field an hour or so before game-time when there is no pressure on them, pull on the catcher's glove, and try to hold them.

I still remember my complete surprise the first time I tried catching for a real curve-ball pitcher. He was a slim, spidery left-hander of the New York Yankees, many years ago, by the name of Herb Pennock. He called that he was going to throw a fast breaking curve and warned me to expect the ball at least two feet outside the plate. Then he wound up and let it go, and that ball came whistling right down the groove for the center of the plate. A novice, I chose to believe what I saw and not what I heard, and prepared to catch it where it was headed for, a spot which of course it never reached, because just in front of the rubber, it swerved sharply to the right and passed nearly a yard from my glove. I never had a chance to catch it. That way, you learn about the mysterious drop, the ball that sails down the alley chest high but which you must be prepared to catch around your ankles because of the sudden dip it takes at the end of its passage as though someone were pulling it down with a string. Also you find out about the queer fade-away, the slow curve, the fast in- and out-shoots that seem to be timed almost as delicately as shrapnel, to burst, or rather break, just when they will do the most harm—namely, at the moment when the batter is swinging.

Facing a big-league pitcher with a bat on your shoulder and trying to hit his delivery is another vital experience in gaining an understanding of the game about which you are trying to write vividly. It is one thing to sit in the stands and scream at a batsman: "Oh, you bum!" for striking out in a pinch, and another to stand twenty yards from that big pitcher and try to make up your mind in a hundredth of a second whether to hit at the offering or not, where to swing and when, not to mention worrying about protecting yourself from the consequences of being struck by the ball that seems to be heading straight for your skull at an appalling rate of speed. Because, if you are a big-league player, you cannot very well afford to be gun-shy and duck away in panic from a ball that swerves in the last moment and breaks perfectly over the plate, while the umpire calls: "Strike!" and the fans jeer. Nor can you afford to take a crack on the temple from the ball. Men have died from that. It calls for undreamed-of niceties of nerve and judgment, but you don't find that out until you have stepped to the plate cold a few times during batting practice or in training quarters, with nothing at stake but the acquisition of experience, and see what a fine case

of the jumping jitters you get. Later on, when you are writing your story, your imagination, backed by the experience, will be able to supply a picture of what the batter is going through as he stands at the plate in the closing innings of an important game, with two or three men on base, two out, and his team behind in the scoring, and fifty thousand people screaming at him.

The catching and holding of a forward pass for a winning touchdown on a cold, wet day always make a good yarn, but you might get an even better one out of it if you happen to know from experience about the elusive qualities of a hard, soggy, mud-slimed football rifled through the air, as well as something about the exquisite timing, speed, and courage it takes to catch it on a dead run, with two or three 190-pound men reaching for it at the same time or waiting to crash you as soon as your fingers touch it.

Any football coach during a light practice will let you go down the field and try to catch punts, the long, fifty-yard spirals and the tricky, tumbling end-over-enders. Unless you have had some previous experience, you won't hang on to one out of ten, besides knocking your fingers out of joint. But if you have any imagination, thereafter you will know that it calls for more than negligible[11] nerve to judge and hold that ball and even plan to run with it, when there are two husky ends bearing down at full speed, preparing for a head-on tackle.

In 1932 I covered my first set of National Air Races, in Cleveland, and immediately decided that I had to learn how to fly to find out what that felt like. Riding as a passenger isn't flying. Being up there all alone at the controls of

11 **negligible** (nĕg′lə jə bəl): so little as to be disregarded.

a ship is. And at the same time began a series of investigations into the "feel" of the mechanized sports to see what they were all about and the qualities of mentality, nerve, and physique they called for from their participants. These included a ride with Gar Wood in his latest and fastest speedboat, *Miss America X*, in which for the first time he pulled the throttle wide open on the Detroit River straightaway; a trip with the Indianapolis Speedway driver Cliff Bergere, around the famous brick raceway; and a flip with Lieutenant Al Williams, one time U. S. Schneider Cup race pilot.

I was scared with Wood, who drove me at 127 miles an hour, jounced, shaken, vibrated, choked with fumes from the exhausts, behind which I sat hanging on desperately to the throttle bar, which after a while got too hot to hold. I was on a plank between Wood and his mechanic, Johnson, and thought that my last moment had come. I was still more scared when Cliff Bergere hit 126 on the Indianapolis straightaways in the tiny racing car in which I was hopelessly wedged, and after the first couple of rounds quite resigned to die and convinced that I should. But I think the most scared I have ever been while moving fast was during a ride I took in the cab of a locomotive on the straight, level stretch between Fort Wayne, Indiana, and Chicago, where for a time we hit 90 miles per hour, which of course is no speed at all. But nobody who rides in the comfortable Pullman coaches has any idea of the didoes[12] cut up by a locomotive in a hurry, or the thrill of pelting through a small town, all out and wide open, including the crossing of some thirty or forty frogs[13] and switches, all of which must be set right. But that wasn't sport. That was just plain excitement.

12 **didoes:** tricks.
13 **frogs:** devices at railroad intersections to keep cars on the right tracks.

I have never regretted these researches. Now that they are over, there isn't enough money to make me do them again. But they paid me dividends, I figured. During the great Thompson Speed Trophy race for land planes at Cleveland in 1935, Captain Roscoe Turner was some eight or nine miles in the lead in his big golden, low-wing, speed monoplane. Suddenly, coming into the straightaway in front of the grandstands, buzzing along at 280 miles an hour like an angry hornet, a streamer of thick, black smoke burst from the engine cowling[14] and trailed back behind the ship. Turner pulled up immediately, using his forward speed to gain all the altitude possible, turned and got back to the edge of the field, still pouring out that evil black smoke. Then he cut his switch, dipped her nose down, landed with a bounce and a bump, and rolled up to the line in a perfect stop. The crowd gave him a great cheer as he climbed out of the oil-spattered machine, but it was a cheer of sympathy because he had lost the race after having been so far in the lead that had he continued he could not possibly have been overtaken.

14 cowling: metal covering over the engine.

There was that story, but there was a better one too. Only the pilots on the field, all of them white around the lips and wiping from their faces a sweat not due to the oppressive summer heat, knew that they were looking at a man who from that time on, to use their own expression, was living on borrowed time. It isn't often when a Thompson Trophy racer with a landing speed of around eighty to ninety miles an hour goes haywire in the air, that the pilot is able to climb out of the cockpit and walk away from his machine. From the time of that first burst of smoke until the wheels touched the ground and stayed there, he was a hundred-to-one shot to live. To the initiated, those dreadful moments were laden with suspense and horror. Inside that contraption was a human being who any moment might be burned to a horrible, twisted cinder, or smashed into the ground beyond all recognition, a human being who was cool, gallant, and fighting desperately. Every man and woman on the field who had ever been in trouble in the air was living those awful seconds with him in terror and suspense. I, too, was able to experience it. That is what makes getting the "feel" of things distinctly worth while.

Understanding the Essay

1. In the first paragraph how does Gallico explain the meaning of his title, "The Feel"?
2. How does the idea of the first paragraph lead into that of the second? What is the main idea of paragraph 2? How does the anecdote about Levinsky relate to it?
3. After reading the first sentence of the second paragraph, in which Gallico presents the main idea of his story, find other places in which he says the same thing in different ways.
4. What are Gallico's reasons for not becoming an expert in the sports he tried?

5. How do Gallico's title and the first two paragraphs supply unity to the whole essay? What, if any, principle of organization do you find in the rest of the essay?
6. How does Gallico avoid antagonizing the reader when he reports his exploits? That is, how does he avoid dramatizing himself or sounding conceited?
7. Why is this statement true?—Gallico could end his essay at almost any point by merely adding the last sentence of the story to the end of any experience he is reporting.

Building Vocabulary Skills

Study the replacements for the *italicized* words in the following phrases. Then explain to the class the differences in meaning between Gallico's words and the substitutes. Use a dictionary if needed.
1. "feel is an important *adjunct* to seeing" (addition)
2. "since the engine quit its soothing *drone*" (throb)
3. "*hurtling* down the *perilous*" (skiing . . . dangerous)
4. "timed almost as *delicately* as shrapnel" (carefully)
5. "elusive qualities of a *mud-slimed* football" (muddy)

Developing Language Skills

1. Gallico is skillful in making the reader see and hear as well as feel an experience. Choose one or two experiences he recounts and point out the words and phrases he uses that appeal to the senses.
2. Write an essay developing one of the following statements:
    "Tournament tennis is a very different game from week-end tennis."
    "None of these things can I do well but I never cared about becoming an expert, and besides, there wasn't time."

The Expository Essay

In an expository essay, the writer explains a subject, using definition, example, comparison or contrast, and logical reasoning as methods of development. His purpose may be to clarify an idea, to analyze a problem or work of art, or to report on some event or topic.

Although argument is often regarded as a separate form from exposition, the two have many features in common and are combined in this unit. Argumentative writing seeks to convince the reader of the truth of an idea or of the rightness of a proposal. The words, examples, and authorities chosen are intended to convince the reader of something. At the same time, the writer must use such expository techniques as definition and example to make his argument.

As you read the following six essays, you will see that the desire to persuade the reader of some point is present in each. The approaches vary widely, however, from parody to scholarly discussion.

Although definitions are ordinarily formal statements, Charles Brooks shows that they can be personal and informal as he points out the differences between wit and humor. He makes much use of contrast ("Wit wears silk, but humor in homespun endures the wind") and illustration to make clear his definitions. He also relies heavily on metaphors and similes to dramatize his many comparisons and contrasts.

On the Difference Between Wit and Humor

Charles S. Brooks

Charles Brooks, an unpredictable essayist, is hard to classify. He is close kin to Charles Lamb in that much of the pleasure of reading him is in the whimsical way he expresses his random thoughts. Nevertheless, Brooks does have a destination and he reaches it swiftly in spite of seeming to saunter toward it.

I AM NOT SURE that I can draw an exact line between wit and humor. Perhaps the distinction is so subtle that only those persons can decide who have long white beards. But even an ignorant man, so long as he is clear of Bedlam,[1] may have an opinion.

I am quite positive that of the two, humor is the more comfortable and more livable quality. Humorous persons, if their gift is genuine and not a mere shine upon the surface, are always agreeable companions and they sit through the evening best. They have pleasant mouths turned up at the corners. To these corners the great Master of marionettes[2] has fixed the strings and he holds them in his nimblest fingers to twitch them at the slightest jest. But the mouth of a merely witty man is hard and sour until the moment of its discharge. Nor is the flash from a witty man always comforting, whereas a humorous man radiates a general pleasure and is like another candle in the room.

I admire wit, but I have no real liking for it. It has been too often employed against me, whereas humor is always an ally. It never points an impertinent finger into my defects. Humorous persons do not sit like explosives on a fuse. They are safe and easy comrades. But a wit's tongue is as sharp as a donkey driver's stick. I may gallop the faster for its prodding, yet the touch behind is too persuasive for any comfort.

1 **Bedlam:** a mental institution.
2 **Master of marionettes:** God.

Wit is a lean creature with sharp inquiring nose, whereas humor has a kindly eye and comfortable girth. Wit, if it be necessary, uses malice to score a point—like a cat it is quick to jump—but humor keeps the peace in an easy chair. Wit has a better voice in a solo, but humor comes into the chorus best. Wit is as sharp as a stroke of lightning, whereas humor is diffuse like sunlight. Wit keeps the season's fashions and is precise in the phrases and judgments of the day, but humor is concerned with homely eternal things. Wit wears silk, but humor in homespun endures the wind. Wit sets a snare, whereas humor goes off whistling without a victim in its mind. Wit is sharper company at table, but humor serves better in mischance and in the rain. When it tumbles wit is sour, but humor goes uncomplaining without its dinner. Humor laughs at another's jest and holds its sides, while wit sits wrapped in study for a lively answer. But it is a workaday world in which we live, where we get mud upon our boots and come weary to the twilight—it is a world that grieves and suffers from many wounds in these years of war: and therefore as I think of my acquaintance, it is those who are humorous in its best and truest meaning rather than those who are witty who give the more profitable companionship.

And then, also, there is wit that is not wit. As someone has written:

Nor ever noise for wit on me could
    pass,
When thro' the braying I discerned
    the ass.

I sat lately at dinner with a notoriously witty person (a really witty man) whom our hostess had introduced to provide the entertainment. I had read many of his reviews of books and plays, and while I confess their wit and brilliancy, I had thought them to be hard and intellectual and lacking in all that broader base of humor which aims at truth. His writing—catching the bad habit of the time—is too ready to proclaim a paradox and to assert the unusual, to throw aside in contempt the valuable haystack in a fine search for a paltry needle. His reviews are seldom right—as most of us see the right—but they sparkle and hold one's interest for their perversity[3] and unexpected turns.

In conversation I found him much as I had found him in his writing—although, strictly speaking, it was not a conversation, which requires an interchange of word and idea and is turn about. A conversation should not be a market where one sells and another buys. Rather, it should be a bargaining back and forth, and each person should be both merchant and buyer. My rubber plant for your victrola, each offering what he has and seeking his deficiency. It was my friend B—— who fairly put the case when he said that he liked so much to talk that he was willing to pay for his audience by listening in his turn.

But this was a speech and a lecture. He loosed on us from the cold spigot of his intellect a steady flow of literary allusion—a practice which he professes to hold in scorn—and wit and epigram.[4] He seemed torn from the page of Meredith.[5] He talked like ink. I had believed before that only people in books could talk as he did, and then only when their author had blotted and scratched their performance for a seventh time before he sent it to the printer. To me it was an entirely new

3 **perversity:** contrariness.
4 **epigram:** pointed comment concisely expressed.
5 **Meredith:** George Meredith (1828-1909), English novelist and poet.

experience, for my usual acquaintances are good common honest daytime woolen folk and they seldom average better than one bright thing in an evening.

At first I feared that there might be a break in his flow of speech which I should be obliged to fill. Once, when there was a slight pause—a truffle was engaging him—I launched a frail remark; but it was swept off at once in the renewed torrent. And seriously it does not seem fair. If one speaker insists—to change the figure—on laying all the cobbles of a conversation, he should at least allow another to carry the tarpot and fill in the chinks. When the evening was over, although I recalled two or three clever stories, which I shall botch in the telling, I came away tired and dissatisfied, my tongue dry with disuse.

Now I would not seek that kind of man as a companion with whom to be becalmed in a sailboat, and I would

not wish to go to the country with him, least of all to the North Woods or any place outside of civilization. I am sure that he would sulk if he were deprived of an audience. He would be crotchety at breakfast across his bacon. Certainly for the woods a humorous man is better company, for his humor in mischance comforts both him and you. A humorous man—and here lies the heart of the matter—a humorous man has the high gift of regarding an annoyance in the very stroke of it as another man shall regard it when the annoyance is long past. If a humorous person falls out of a canoe he knows the exquisite jest while his head is still bobbing in the cold water. A witty man, on the contrary, is sour until he is changed and dry: but in a week's time when company is about, he will make a comic story of it.

My friend A—— with whom I went once into the Canadian woods has genuine humor, and no one can be a more satisfactory comrade. I do not recall that he said many comic things, and at bottom he was serious as the best humorists are. But in him there was a kind of joy and exaltation that lasted throughout the day. If the duffle were piled too high and fell about his ears, if the dinner was burned or the tent blew down in a driving storm at night, he met these mishaps as though they were the very things he had come north to get, as though without them the trip would have lacked its spice. This is an easy philosophy in retrospect but hard when the wet canvas falls across you and the rain beats in. A—— laughed at the very moment of disaster as another man will laugh later in an easy chair. I see him now swinging his ax for firewood to dry ourselves when we were spilled in a rapids; and again, while pitching our tent on a sandy beach when another storm had drowned us. And there is a certain cry of his (dully, *Wow!* on paper) expressive to the initiated of all things gay, which could never issue from the mouth of a merely witty man.

Real humor is primarily human—or divine, to be exact—and after that the fun may follow naturally in its order. Not long ago I saw Louis Jouvet of the French Company play Sir Andrew Ague-Cheek.[6] It was a most humorous performance of the part, and the reason is that the actor made no primary effort to be funny. It was the humanity of his playing, making his audience love him first of all, that provoked the comedy. His long thin legs were comi-

cal and so was his drawling talk, but the very heart and essence was this love he started in his audience. Poor fellow! how delightfully he smoothed the feathers in his hat! How he feared to fight the duel! It was easy to love such a dear silly human fellow. A merely witty player might have drawn as many laughs, but there would not have been the catching at the heart.

As for books and the wit or humor of their pages, it appears that wit fades, whereas humor lasts. Humor uses permanent nutgalls.[7] But is there anything more melancholy than the wit of another generation? In the first place, this wit is intertwined with forgotten circumstance. It hangs on a fashion—on the style of a coat. It arose from a forgotten bit of gossip. In the play of words the sources of the pun are lost. It is like a local jest in a narrow coterie,[8] barren to an outsider. Sydney Smith[9] was the most celebrated wit of his day, but he is dull reading now. Blackwood's[10] at its first issue was a witty daring sheet, but for us the pages are stagnant. I suppose that no one now laughs at the witticisms of Thomas Hood.[11] Where are the wits of yesteryear? Yet the humor of Falstaff[12] and Lamb[13] and Fielding[14] remains and is a reminder to us that humor, to be real, must be founded on humanity and on truth.

6 Sir Andrew Ague-Cheek (ā′gū chēk′): comic character in Shakespeare's *Twelfth Night*.

7 nutgalls: growths on an oak tree.
8 coterie (kō′tə rī): clique or set.
9 Sydney Smith: English clergyman and essayist (1771-1845).
10 Blackwood's: Scottish literary magazine.
11 Thomas Hood: English poet (1799-1845).
12 Falstaff: comic Shakespearean character.
13 Lamb: Charles Lamb; see his essay in this unit.
14 Fielding: Henry Fielding (1707-1754), English novelist.

CHARLES S. BROOKS

Understanding the Essay

1. What general distinction between wit and humor does the author make in the second paragraph?
2. What are the chief methods Brooks uses to develop the difference between wit and humor?
3. Give two or three examples of each method.
4. On the basis of Brooks's distinctions, is the tone of his essay witty or humorous? Find evidence in the essay to support your answer.

Building Vocabulary Skills

In the following list of words, mark those used to refer to humor with *H* and those to wit with *W*:

chorus	homespun	lecture	scorn
comfortable	humanity	lightning	sharp
companionship	impertinent	livable	silk
easy	intellectual	malice	snare
exaltation	jest	pleasant	solo
explosive	joy	precise	sour
genuine	kindly	prodding	sunlight
homely	lean	radiates	uncomplaining

Write a paragraph showing how the listing of the words describing wit and those describing humor support the author's statement "that of the two, humor is the more comfortable and more livable quality."

Developing Language Skills

Discuss the following quotations to determine whether they classify as wit or humor according to Brooks's definition. Look for specific statements in his essay to support your judgments. Enjoying the discussion should be as important as agreeing on the answers.

1. "Well, if I called the wrong number, why did you answer the phone?" (James Thurber)
2. "Thrusting my nose firmly between his teeth, I threw him heavily to the ground on top of me." (Mark Twain)
3. "She ran the whole gamut of emotions from A to B." (Dorothy Parker)
4. "What this country needs is a good five-cent nickel." (F. P. Adams)
5. "She is intolerable, but that is her only fault." (Charles Talleyrand)
6. "A cynic is a man who knows the price of everything and the value of nothing." (Oscar Wilde)
7. "A gentleman is one who never hurts anyone's feelings unintentionally." (Oscar Wilde)
8. "I can resist everything but temptation." (Oscar Wilde)
9. "Youth is a wonderful thing; what a crime to waste it on children." (G. B. Shaw)

In this essay, Chesterton makes sweeping statements about detective stories and then backs up his declarations with concrete examples and specific allusions. He delights in startling his readers and dramatizing his views with paradoxical statements (a *paradox* is a statement which contains apparently contradictory ideas, both of which are true upon examination), such as describing "burglars and footpads" (street thieves) as "placid old conservatives."

A Defense of Detective Stories

G. K. Chesterton

As the creator of a series of detective stories starring Father Brown, gentle priest and official investigator, Chesterton speaks with the voice of authority in this defense of the detective story. He also lives up to his reputation as a man who liked to be "on the other side" of a question. Instead of defending the detective story in the usual way as harmless escape reading, he defends it as the only form of popular literature that expresses the mystery and poetry of modern city life.

IN ATTEMPTING to reach the genuine psychological reason for the popularity of detective stories, it is necessary to rid ourselves of many mere phrases. It is not true, for example, that the populace prefer bad literature to good, and accept detective stories because they are bad literature. The mere absence of artistic subtlety does not make a book popular. Bradshaw's Railway Guide contains few gleams of psychological comedy, yet it is not read aloud uproariously on winter evenings. If detective stories are read with more exuberance than railway guides, it is certainly because they are more artistic. Many good books have fortunately been popular; many bad books, still more fortunately, have been unpopular. A good detective story would probably be even more popular than a bad one. The trouble in this matter is that many people do not realize that there is such a thing as a good detective story; it is to them like speaking of a good devil. To write a story about a burglary is, in their eyes, a sort of spiritual manner of committing it. To persons of somewhat weak sensibility this is natural enough; it must be confessed that many detective stories are as full of sensational crime as one of Shakespeare's plays.

There is, however, between a good detective story and a bad detective story as much, or, rather more, difference than there is between a good epic and a bad one. Not only is a detective story a perfectly legitimate form of art, but it has certain definite and real advantages as an agent of the public weal.[1]

The first essential value of the detective story lies in this, that it is the earliest and only form of popular literature in which is expressed some sense of the poetry of modern life. Men lived among mighty mountains and eternal forests for ages before they realized that they were poetical; it may reasonably be inferred that some of our descendants may see the chimney pots as rich a purple as the mountain peaks, and find the lampposts as old and natural as the trees. Of this realization of a great city itself as something wild and obvious the detective story is certainly the *Iliad*.[2] No one can have failed to notice that in these stories the hero or the investigator crosses London with something of the loneliness and liberty of a prince in a tale of elfland, that in the course of that incalculable journey the casual omnibus assumes the primal colors of a fairy ship. The lights of the city begin to glow like innumerable goblin eyes, since they are the guardians of some secret, however crude, which the writer knows and the reader does not. Every twist of the road is like a finger pointing to it; every fantastic skyline of chimney pots seems wildly and derisively signaling the meaning of the mystery.

This realization of the poetry of London is not a small thing. A city is, properly speaking, more poetic even than a countryside, for while Nature is a chaos of unconscious forces, a city is a chaos of conscious ones. The crest of the flower or the pattern of the lichen[3] may or may not be significant symbols. But there is no stone in the street and no brick in the wall that is not actually a deliberate symbol—a message from some man, as much as if it were a tele-

gram or a post card. The narrowest street possesses, in every crook and twist of its intention, the soul of the man who built it, perhaps long in his grave. Every brick has as human a hieroglyph[4] as if it were a graven brick of Babylon;[5] every slate on the roof is as educational a document as if it were a slate covered with addition and subtraction sums. Anything which tends, even under the fantastic form of the minutiae[6] of Sherlock Holmes, to assert this romance of detail in civilization, to emphasize this unfathomably human character in flints and tiles, is a good thing. It is good that the average man should fall into the habit of looking imaginatively at ten men in the street even if it is only on the chance that the eleventh might be a notorious thief. We may dream, perhaps, that it might be possible to have another and higher romance of London, that men's souls have stranger adventures than their bodies, and that it would be harder and more exciting to hunt their virtues than to hunt their crimes. But since our great authors (with the admirable exception of Stevenson[7]) decline to write of that thrilling mood and moment when the eyes of the great city, like the eyes of a cat, begin to flame in the dark, we must give fair credit to the popular literature which, amid a babble of pedantry[8] and preciosity,[9] declines to regard the present as prosaic or the common as commonplace. Popular art in all ages has been interested in contemporary manners and costume; it dressed the groups around the Crucifixion in the garb of Floren-

---

1 **weal:** welfare.
2 *Iliad:* a Greek epic poem about the Trojan war.
3 **lichen** (lī′kən): mosslike plant.

4 **hieroglyph:** a character in the picture writing of the ancients.
5 **Babylon:** ancient city in southwestern Asia.
6 **minutiae** (mĭ nū′shĭ ē′): small details.
7 **Stevenson:** Robert Louis Stevenson (1850-1894), Scottish author.
8 **pedantry:** display of knowledge.
9 **preciosity** (prĕsh′ĭ ŏs′ə tĭ): overcareful refinement of speech.

ESSAY

tine gentlefolk or Flemish burghers.[10] In the last century it was the custom for distinguished actors to present Macbeth in a powdered wig and ruffles. How far we are ourselves in this age from such conviction of the poetry of our own life and manners may easily be conceived by anyone who chooses to imagine a picture of Alfred the Great[11] toasting the cakes dressed in tourist's knickerbockers, or a performance of *Hamlet* in which the Prince appeared in a frock coat, with a crape band round his hat. But this instinct of the age to look back, like Lot's wife,[12] could not go on forever. A rude, popular[13] literature of the romantic possibilities of the modern city was bound to arise. It has arisen in the popular detective stories, as rough and refreshing as the ballads of Robin Hood.

There is, however, another good work that is done by detective stories. While it is the constant tendency of the Old Adam[14] to rebel against so universal

10 **burghers:** townsmen.
11 **Alfred the Great:** King of England who lived 849-901.
12 **Lot's wife:** Biblical character said to have been turned into a pillar of salt because she looked back when fleeing the city.
13 **popular:** of the common people.
14 **Old Adam:** human tendency to sin.

and automatic a thing as civilization, to preach departure and rebellion, the romance of police activity keeps in some sense before the mind the fact that civilization itself is the most sensational of departures and the most romantic of rebellions. By dealing with the unsleeping sentinels who guard the outposts of society, it tends to remind us that we live in an armed camp, making war with a chaotic world, and that the criminals, the children of chaos, are nothing but the traitors within our gates. When the detective in a police romance stands alone, and somewhat fatuously fearless amid the knives and fists of a thieves' kitchen, it does certainly serve to make us remember that it is the agent of social justice who is the original and poetic figure, while the burglars and footpads are merely placid old cosmic conservatives, happy in the immemorial respectability of apes and wolves. The romance of the police force is thus the whole romance of man. It is based on the fact that morality is the most dark and daring of conspiracies. It reminds us that the whole noiseless and unnoticeable police management by which we are ruled and protected is only a successful knight-errantry.

Understanding the Essay

1. Which (there are several) of the following ideas, in Chesterton's opinion, account for the "genuine psychological reason for the popularity of the detective story"?
   (*a*) The populace prefer bad literature to good.
   (*b*) The detective story expresses some of the poetry of modern life.
   (*c*) The detective story is more interesting than Bradshaw's Railway Guide.
   (*d*) The detective story dramatizes the streets and bricks of the city.
   (*e*) Most great authors decline to write about everyday city life.
   (*f*) The detective or investigator is often a kind of Robin Hood.
   (*g*) Agents of the law fearlessly guard the outposts of society.
   (*h*) The romance of the police force is the whole romance of man.

2. How does the following excerpt from the first paragraph prepare the reader to consider detective stories as worthy of discussion?

> A good detective story would probably be more popular than a bad one. The trouble in this matter is that many people do not realize that there is such a thing as a good detective story; it is to them like speaking of a good devil. . . . it must be confessed that many detective stories are as full of sensational crime as one of Shakespeare's plays.

3. Find examples of ways in which Chesterton says the detective story expresses the poetry of modern life, especially city life.
4. Explain: "Every brick has as human a hieroglyph as if it were a graven brick of Babylon; every slate on the roof is as educational a document as if it were a slate covered with addition and subtraction sums."

Developing Language Skills

1. Plan a panel of three or four to explain the following allusions and Chesterton's use of them:

Shakespeare's plays	Flemish burghers
the *Iliad*	*Macbeth*
Babylon	Alfred the Great
Sherlock Holmes	*Hamlet*
Stevenson	Lot's wife
Florentine gentlefolk	Robin Hood

2. Choose specific examples to support or attack Chesterton's statement, "A city is, properly speaking, more poetic even than a countryside, for while Nature is a chaos of unconscious forces, a city is a chaos of conscious ones." Write two or three paragraphs based on these examples and developing your own viewpoint.

Reading "You, Too, Can Write the Casual Style"

Whyte organizes his essay around twelve carefully chosen devices which all develop one general idea. Capitalization of words that have no right to capitalization except in the author's mind has become a Whyte trademark. Other trademarks are a high-brow vocabulary, including jargon (language special to one group) and common words with special current meanings, and a general tone of sophisticated irony. In this article, his use of the style he is poking fun at makes the whole essay a parody (overstated imitation) of the Casual Style.

You, Too, Can Write the Casual Style

William H. Whyte, Jr.

If you remember that the pseudonym under which this experienced, worldly-wise author writes occasionally is Otis Binet Stanford, *a combination of three well-known standardized intelligence tests that you have probably taken, you will easily recognize his humorous intent in this essay. Published originally in* Harper's Magazine, *the article compliments its readers by assuming they will not take it at face value. As you read, share the author's tongue-in-cheek attitude and be alert to sentences which express an attitude actually opposite to the writer's real opinions.*

A REVOLUTION has taken place in American prose. No longer the short huffs and puffs, the unqualified word, the crude gusto of the declarative sentence. Today the fashion is to write casually.

The Casual Style is not exactly new. Originated in the early twenties, it has been refined and improved and refined again by a relatively small band of writers, principally for *The New Yorker*,[1] until now their mannerisms have become standards of sophistication. Everybody is trying to join the club. Newspaper columnists have forsaken the beloved metaphors of the sports page for the Casual Style, and one of the quickest ways for an ad man to snag an award from other ad men is to give his copy the low-key, casual pitch; the copy shouldn't sing these days—it should whisper. Even Dr. Rudolf Flesch,[2] who has been doing so much to teach people how to write like other people, is counseling his followers to use the Casual Style. Everywhere the ideal seems the same: be casual.

But how? There is very little down-to-earth advice. We hear about the rapier-like handling of the bromide,[3] the keen eye for sham and pretension, the exquisite sense of nuance, the unerring ear for the vulgate.[4] But not much about actual technique. The layman, as a consequence, is apt to look on the Casual Style as a mandarin dialect[5] which he fears he could never master.

Nonsense. The Casual Style is within everyone's grasp. It has now become so perfected by constant polishing that its devices may readily be identified, and they change so little that their use need be no more difficult for the novice than for the expert. (That's not quite all there is to it, of course. Some apparently casual writers, Thurber and E. B. White, among others, rarely use the devices.)

The subject matter, in the first place, is not to be ignored. Generally speaking, the more uneventful it is, or the more pallid the writer's reaction to it, the better do form and content marry.

---

1 *The New Yorker*: sophisticated weekly magazine.

2 **Dr. Rudolph Flesch:** author of such books as *The Art of Plain Talk* and *How To Write Better*.
3 **bromide:** commonplace.
4 **vulgate:** colloquial speech.
5 **mandarin dialect:** official language. Earlier phrase meant the Chinese dialect used by the official classes.

Take, for example, the cocktail party at which the writer can show how bored everyone is with everyone else, and how utterly fatuous they all are anyhow. Since a non-casual statement—*e.g.,*[6] "The party was a bore"—would destroy the reason for writing about it at all, the Casual Style here is not only desirable but mandatory.[7]

Whatever the subject, however, twelve devices are the rock on which all else is built. I will present them one by one, illustrating them with examples from such leading casual stylists as Wolcott Gibbs, John Crosby, John McCarten, and (on occasion) this magazine's "Mr. Harper." If the reader will digest what follows, he should be able to dash off a paragraph indistinguishable from the best casual writing being done today.

(1) *Heightened Understatement.* Where the old-style writer would say, "I don't like it," "It is not good," or something equally banal, the casual writer says it is *"something less than good."* He avoids direct statement and strong words—except, as we will note, where he is setting them up to have something to knock down. In any event, he qualifies. "Somewhat" and "rather," the bread-and-butter words of the casual writer, should become habitual with you; similarly with such phrases as "I suppose," "it seems to me," "I guess," or "I'm afraid." "Elusive" or "elude" are good, too, and if you see the word "charm" in a casual sentence you can be pretty sure that "eludes me," or "I find elusive," will not be far behind.

(2) *The Multiple Hedge.* Set up an ostensibly[8] strong statement, and then, with your qualifiers, shoot a series of alternately negative and positive charges into the sentence until finally you neutralize the whole thing. Let's take, for example, the clause, "certain names have a guaranteed nostalgic magic." Challenge enough here; the names not only have magic, they have guaranteed magic. A double hedge reverses the charge. "Names which have, *I suppose* [hedge 1], a guaranteed nostalgic magic, *though there are times that I doubt it* [hedge 2]. . . ."

We didn't have to say they were guaranteed in the first place, of course, but without such straw phrases we wouldn't have anything to construct a hedge on and, frequently, nothing to write at all. The virtue of the hedge is that by its very negating effect it makes any sentence infinitely expansible. Even if you have so torn down your original statement with one or two hedges that you seem to have come to the end of the line, you have only to slip in an anti-hedge, a strengthening word (*e.g.,* "definitely," "unqualified," etc.), and begin the process all over again. Witness the following quadruple hedge: "I found Mr. Home entertaining *from time to time* [hedge 1] on the ground, *I guess* [hedge 2], that the singular idiom and unearthly detachment of the British upper classes have *always* [anti-hedge] seemed *reasonably* [hedge 3] droll to me, *at least in moderation* [hedge 4]." The art of plain talk, as has been pointed out, does not entail[9] undue brevity.

If you've pulled hedge on hedge and the effect still remains too vigorous, simply wipe the slate clean with a cancellation clause at the end. "It was all exactly as foolish as it sounds," says Wolcott Gibbs, winding up some 570 casual words on a subject, "and I wouldn't give it another thought."

---

6 *e.g.: exempli gratia,* for example.
7 **mandatory:** required.
8 **ostensibly:** apparently.

9 **entail:** necessarily involve.

(3) *Narcissizing*[10] *Your Prose.* The casual style is nothing if not personal; indeed, you will usually find in it as many references to the writer as to what he's supposed to be talking about. For you do not talk about the subject; you talk about its impact on you. With the reader peering over your shoulder, you look into the mirror and observe your own responses as you run the entire range of the casual writer's emotions. You may reveal yourself as, in turn, listless ("the audience seemed not to share my boredom"); insouciant[11] ("I was really quite happy with it"); irritated ("The whole thing left me tired and cross"); comparatively gracious ("Being in a comparatively gracious mood, I won't go into the details I didn't like"); or hesitant ("I wish I could say that I could accept his hypothesis").

(4) *Preparation for the Witticism.* When the casual writer hits upon a clever turn of phrase or a nice conceit,[12] he uses this device to insure that his conceit will not pass unnoticed. Suppose, for example, you have thought of something to say that is pretty darn good if you say so yourself. The device, in effect, is to say so yourself. If you want to devastate a certain work as "a study of vulgarity in high places," don't say this flat out. Earlier in the sentence prepare the reader for the drollery ahead with something like "what I am tempted to call," or "what could best be described as" or "If it had to be defined in a sentence, it might well be called. . . ."

Every writer his own claque.[13]

(5) *Deciphered Notes Device; or Cute-Things-I-Have-Said.* In this one you are your own stooge as well. You feed yourself lines. By means of the slender fiction that you have written something on the back of an envelope or the margin of a program, you catch yourself good-humoredly trying to decipher these shrewd, if cryptic,[14] little jottings. *Viz.:*[15] "Their diagnoses are not nearly as crisp as those I find in my notes"; ". . . sounds like an inadequate description, but it's all I have on my notes, and it may conceivably be a very high compliment."

(6) *The Kicker.* An echo effect. "My reactions [included] an irritable feeling that eleven o'clock was past Miss Keim's bedtime,"—and now the Kicker—*"not to mention my own."* This type of thing practically writes itself. "She returns home. She should never have left home in the first place. —— ——— —."*

* "And neither should I."

(7) *Wit of Omission.* By calling attention to the fact that you are not going to say it, you suggest that there is something very funny you could say if only you wanted to. "A thought occurred to me at this point," you may say, when otherwise stymied,[16] "but I think we had better not go into *that.*"

(8) *The Planned Colloquialism.* The casual writer savors colloquialisms. This is not ordinary colloquial talk—nobody is more quickly provoked than the casual writer by ordinary usage. It is, rather, a playful descent into the vulgate. Phrases like "darn," "awfully," "as all getout," "mighty," and other folksy idioms are ideal. The less you would be likely to use the word normally yourself the more pointed the effect. Contrast is what you are after, for it is the

---

10 **Narcissizing** (när′sĭ sī′zĭng): filling with excessive self-love or conceit.
11 **insouciant** (ĭn sōō′sĭ ənt): unbothered.
12 **conceit:** witty expression of an idea.
13 **claque** (klăk): group of flattering admirers.

14 **cryptic:** mysterious.
15 **Viz.:** *videlicet,* namely.
16 **stymied:** blocked.

WILLIAM H. WHYTE, JR.

347

facetious[17] interplay of language levels —a blending, as it were, of the East Fifties[18] and the Sticks—that gives the Casual Style its off-hand charm.

(9) *Feigned*[19] *Forgetfulness.* Conversation gropes; it is full of "what I really meant was" and "maybe I should have added," backings and fillings and second thoughts of one kind or another. Writing is different; theoretically, ironing out second thoughts beforehand is one of the things writers are paid to do. In the Casual Style, however, it is exactly this exposure of the writer composing in public that makes it so casual. For the professional touch, then, ramble, rebuke yourself in print ("what I really meant, I guess"), and if you have something you feel you should have said earlier, don't say it earlier, but say later that you guess you should have said it earlier.

(10) *The Subject-Apologizer, or Pardon-Me-for-Living.* The Casual Stylist must always allow for the possibility that his subject is just as boring to the reader as it is to him. He may forestall this by seeming to have stumbled on it by accident, or by using phrases like: "If this is as much news to you as it is to me," or "This, in case you've been living in a cave lately, is. . . ."

(11) *The Omitted Word.* This all began modestly enough the day a *New Yorker* writer dropped the articles "the" and "a" from the initial sentence of an anecdote (*e.g.*, "Man we know told us"; "Fellow name of Brown"). Now even such resolutely low-brow writers as Robert Ruark affect it, and they are applying it to any part of speech anywhere in the sentence. You can drop a pronoun ("Says they're shaped like pyramids";) verb ("You been away from soap opera the last couple of weeks?"); or preposition ("Far as glamour goes . . .").

(12) *The Right Word.* In the lexicon[20] of the casual writer there are a dozen or so adjectives which in any context have, to borrow a phrase, a guaranteed charm. Attrition[21] is high— "brittle," "febrile," "confected," for example, are at the end of the run. Ten, however, defy obsolescence: *antic, arch, blurred, chaste, chill, crisp, churlish, disheveled, dim, disembodied.*

They are good singly, but they are even better when used in tandem; *c.f.,*[22] "In an arch, antic sort of way"; "In an arch, blurred sort of way;" "In an arch, crisp sort of way." And so on.

Finally, the most multi-purpose word of them all: "altogether." Frequently it is the companion of "charming" and "delightful," and in this coupling is indispensable to any kind of drama criticism. It can also modify the writer himself (*e.g.*, "Altogether, I think . . ."). Used best, however, it just floats, unbeholden to any other part of the sentence.

Once you have mastered these twelve devices, you too should be able to write as casually as all getout. At least it seems to me, though I may be wrong, that they convey an elusive archness which the crisp literary craftsman, in his own dim sort of way, should altogether cultivate these days. Come to think of it, the charm of the Casual Style is something less than clear to me, but we needn't go into *that*. Fellow I know from another magazine says this point of view best described as churlish. Not, of course, that it matters.

---

17 facetious (fə sē′shəs)**:** humorous; witty.
18 East Fifties: section of New York City, representing sophistication here.
19 Feigned (fānd)**:** pretended.
20 lexicon: dictionary.
21 attrition: wearing out.
22 c.f.: *confer,* compare.

Understanding the Essay

1. What is Whyte's attitude toward the revolution in American prose that he refers to in his first sentence? What are some of the forces he identifies with this revolution? What is his attitude toward them?
2. How does the author's capitalization of "Casual Style" help to set the ironic tone of the essay?
3. What do the comments about the "beloved metaphors of the sports page" and Dr. Rudolph Flesch's "teaching people how to write like other people" suggest about Whyte's attitude toward such influences?
4. How does the sentence in parentheses about James Thurber and E. B. White make a distinction between casual writing and Casual Style as identified by Whyte?
5. What does Whyte say about the subject matter most suitable for the Casual Style?
6. In the last paragraph Whyte uses many of the techniques he has described in the essay. Locate as many examples of these techniques as you can. Identify each technique by the name that Whyte gave it in the essay.
7. How does Whyte tell his readers that he is opposed to the Casual Style without saying so directly?

Developing Language Skills

1. Following the advice in the three paragraphs under *The Multiple Hedge*, device #2, write a short paper giving your *qualified* (in the sense Mr. Whyte uses the word) opinion on a current school issue.
2. Make a report to the class on the Casual Style using excerpts from *The New Yorker* to prove or disprove Mr. Whyte's point.

Reading "The Cliché Expert Reveals Himself in His True Colors"

You may have a friend who never studies late but "burns the midnight oil" and who is never calm but rather "cool as a cucumber." The first few times these and similar expressions (known as clichés) were used, they were fresh and unexpected. However, constant use has dulled their imagery and made them stale and expected. *Cliché* comes from the French word for a block, or plate, used in printing. In the same way that the block prints the same thing over and over, a cliché is an expression used over and over until it loses all originality and freshness.

Humorist Frank Sullivan uses irony in the following essay to attack the problem of triteness. His questioner, by pretending to seek information, exposes the Cliché Expert, who—although proud of his ability to use clichés—unintentionally reveals his own silliness and superficiality.

WILLIAM H. WHYTE, JR.   349

The Cliché Expert Reveals Himself in His True Colors

Frank Sullivan

Talking in dull, commonplace phrases makes an individual a bore. The stimulating person speaks in fresh, exact language, while the bore relies on trite, overworked phrases. He makes his offense worse (he would say "adds insult to injury") by offering his clichés as though they were unexpected and rather clever things to say.

Q: Mr. Arbuthnot, would you mind telling us today how you happened to become a cliché expert? Was it easy?

A: Easy! Don't make me laugh, Mr. Crouse. It was an uphill climb. A cliché novitiate[1] is no bed of roses, and if anyone ever tells you it is, do you know how I want you to take his statement?

Q: How?

A: With a grain of salt. I shall tell you about my career, since you insist, and as a special treat, I shall describe it to you entirely in terms of the seesaw cliché.

Q: The seesaw cliché?

A: You'll see what I mean. Before I made my mark as a cliché expert, I had my ups and downs. Sometimes, when everything was at sixes and sevens, it almost seemed as though my dearest ambitions were going to wrack and ruin. I had moments when I was almost tempted to believe that everything was a snare and a delusion. Even my own flesh and blood discouraged me, in spite of the fact that I was their pride and joy . . . You aren't listening, Mr. Crouse.

Q: Yes I am. I just closed my eyes because the light hurt. You were saying that your own kith and kin discouraged you.

A: I didn't say kith and kin, but it doesn't matter. For a considerable period of time it was nip and tuck whether I would sink or swim. If I had not been hale and hearty, and well equipped for a rough-and-tumble struggle, I wouldn't have come through. But I kept at it, hammer and tongs. I gave 'em tit for tat . . . Mr. Crouse, you *are* asleep.

Q: No, I'm not, Mr. Arbuthnot. You were saying you went after your goal hard and fast.

A: I did. I eschewed[2] wine, woman, and song—

Q: Ah, but wine, woman, and song is not a seesaw cliché, Mr. Arbuthnot.

A: Yes it is, too. Woman is standing in the middle, balancing. I worked morning, noon, and night, and kept to the straight and narrow. The consequence was that in the due course of time—

Q: And tide?

A: Please! In the due course of time things began to come my way by fits and starts, and a little later by leaps and bounds. Now, I'm fine and dandy.

---

1 novitiate (nō vǐsh′ǐ ǐt): training period.

2 eschewed (ĕs chōōd′): stayed away from.

Q: High, wide, and handsome, eh?

A: I wish I had said that, Mr. Crouse.

Q: You—

A: Will, Oscar.[3] Had you there, Mr. Crouse, didn't I, ha ha! When I started I was free, white, and twenty-one. Now I'm fat, fair, and forty, and I venture to predict that no man, without regard to race, creed, or color, is a better master of the cliché than your servant—your *humble* servant—Magnus Arbuthnot.[4] So much for my life story in terms of the seesaw cliché.

Q: It certainly is an interesting story, Mr. Arbuthnot—by and large.

A: Well, in all due modesty, I suppose it is, although sometimes, to tell you the truth, I think there is neither rhyme nor reason to it.

Q: Where were you born, Mr. Arbuthnot?

A: In the altogether.

Q: I see. How?

A: On the impulse of the moment.

Q: And when?

A: In the nick of time.

Q: It is agreeable to find a man so frank about himself, Mr. Arbuthnot.

A: Why not? You asked me a question. You know what kind of question it was?

Q: Impertinent?

A: Oh, my dear man, no.

Q: Personal?

A: Civil. You asked me a civil question. I answered you by telling you the truth. I gave it to you, if I may be permitted to say so, straight from the shoulder. I revealed myself to you in my—

Q: True colors?

A: Ah, someone told you. Rather, someone *went* and told you.

Q: Were you ever in love, Mr. Arbuthnot, or am I out of order in asking that?

A: Not at all. I have had my romances.

Q: How nice.

A: Ah, you wouldn't say so if you knew what kind of romances they were.

Q: What kind were they?

A: Blighted romances, all of 'em. I kept trying to combine single blessedness with wedded bliss. It didn't work. I had a sweetheart in every port, and I worshiped the ground they walked on, each and every one of them. This ground amounts to a matter of 18,467 acres, as of my latest blighted romance.

Q: Hm! You must have been quite a pedestrian.

A: Well, those are the figures when the tide was out; only 16,468 acres at the neap.[5] I was land-poor at the end. And you take the advice of a sadder—

Q: And a wiser man.

A: That's what I was going to say. And never trust the weaker sex, or you'll have an awakening. You seem to be so smart, interrupting me all the while, maybe you can tell me what kind of awakening.

Q: Awakening? Awakening? I'm afraid you have me.

A: Rude awakening.

Q: Oh, of course. Now, I don't think your story would be complete, Mr. Arbuthnot, without some statement from you regarding your material circumstances. Are you well-to-do, or are you—

A: Hard pressed for cash? No, I'm solvent. I'm well paid.

3 **Will, Oscar:** from an anecdote concerning Oscar Wilde, a famous English wit of the late 19th century. Evidently many of his stories and witty remarks were ones he stole from others and passed off as his own. On one occasion, John Sargent (a painter) made a clever remark, and Wilde, who was present, told him: "I wish I had said that." "You will, Oscar," Sargent replied.
4 **Magnus Arbuthnot:** The Great Arbuthnot.

5 **neap:** high tide during the first and third quarters of the moon.

Q: You mean you get a handsome salary?

A: I prefer to call it a princely stipend. You know what kind of coin I'm paid in?

Q: No. What?

A: Coin of the realm. Not that I give a hoot for money. You know how I refer to money?

Q: As the root of all evil?

A: No, but you have a talking point there. I call it lucre—filthy lucre.

Q: On the whole, you seem to have a pretty good time, Mr. Arbuthnot.

A: Oh, I'm not complaining. I'm as snug as a bug in a rug. I'm clear as crystal—when I'm not dull as dishwater. I'm cool as a cucumber, quick as a flash, fresh as a daisy, pleased as Punch, good as my word, regular as clockwork, and I suppose at the end of my declining years, when I'm gathered to my ancestors, I'll be dead as a doornail.

Q: *Eh bien! C'est la vie!*[6]

A: *Mais oui, mon vieux.*[7] I manage. I'm the glass of fashion and the mold of form. I have a finger in every pie, all except this finger. I use it for pointing with scorn. When I go in for malice, it is always malice aforethought. My nods are significant. My offers are standing. I am at cross-purposes and in dire straits. My motives are ulterior, my circles are vicious, my retainers are faithful, and my hopefuls are young. My suspicions are sneaking, my glee is fiendish, my stories are likely. I am drunk.

Q: Drunk?

A: Yes, with power. You know where?

Q: Where?

A: Behind the throne. I am emotional. My mercies are tender, and when I cry, I cry quits. I am lost in thought and up in arms. I am a square shooter with my trusty revolver. My courage is vaunted and my shame is crying, but I don't care—a rap. I have been in the depths of despair, when a watery grave in the briny deep seemed attractive. Eventually I want to marry and settle down, but the woman I marry must be clever.

Q: Clever?

A: With the needle.

Q: Well, I'd certainly call you a man who had led a full life, Mr. Arbuthnot, and a likable chap, too.

A: Yes, I'm a peach of a fellow. I'm a diamond in the rough, all wool and a yard wide. I'm too funny for words and too full for utterance. I'm a gay dog, and I like to trip the light fantastic and burn the candle at both ends with motley throngs of boon companions. I may be foolish but my folly is at least sheer.

Q: I think you certainly have run—

A: I certainly have. The entire gamut of human emotions. I know the facts of life. I'm afraid I've got to go now, Mr. Crouse. I'm due back at my abode. Do you know what kind of abode I live in?

Q: Humble, Mr. Arbuthnot?

A: Certainly not. Palatial! Goodby, my little periwinkle!

---

6 *Eh bien! C'est la vie!* Well! That's life!
7 *Mais oui, mon vieux:* But of course, old man.

8 gamut (găm′ət): range.

ESSAY

Understanding the Essay

1. What is a cliché expert?
2. Why is the title an appropriate one?
3. How does use of the question and answer method contribute to the effectiveness of the essay?
4. What is a seesaw cliché, as the term is used in this essay?
5. What character does Sullivan give to Mr. Crouse, the interviewer? What attitude does Mr. Crouse apparently have toward clichés? Give two or three instances from the essay from which you formed your opinion.

Developing Language Skills

1. Humorist Gelett Burgess in his essay "Are You a Bromide?" says: "The Bromide has no salt nor spice nor savor—but he is the bread of society, the veriest staff of life." What does he mean?
2. Although clichés are generally to be avoided, they sometimes are used effectively. For example, Dorothy Parker in "The Waltz" used many clichés (such as "And a peach of a world, too") to reveal the character of the speaker. Or a magazine like *Time* may turn a cliché into a satirical comment as when it described a Congressman as "more concerned about whether the shad were running down in Fredericksburg than about the pretty kettle of fish on Capitol Hill."

    Spend some time listening to the conversations around you and in reading magazines and newspapers, noting the clichés you come across. Then write two paragraphs, giving a few examples of clichés that were effective and of ones that were merely trite. Explain what caused the difference in effect.

The Argumentative Essay

You will discover two views of our language in the arguments by Wilson Follett and Bergen Evans over the merits of two dictionaries, both published by the G. and C. Merriam Company of Springfield, Massachusetts, twenty-seven years apart. The *Webster's New International Dictionary, Second Edition*, was published in 1934, and the *Webster's Third New International Dictionary* was published in 1961. The Second Edition has served in the past as the authoritative reference for writers, editors, teachers, and students, who have consulted it to solve problems of language. The latest of these unabridged dictionaries took three hundred scholars twenty-seven years to complete.

Follett believes that the Second International was written as a dictionary should be written and that the Third International should have followed this pattern; Evans maintains that the Third International is a modern, scientific work that is preferable to the earlier "horse-and-buggy" editions. The two writers disagree on the purpose a dictionary should serve, and they forcefully argue for their opposite points of

FRANK SULLIVAN   353

view. Follett maintains in his essay that dictionary makers have a responsibility to be authorities on using English well, but Evans maintains that the dictionary's job is to describe how language *is* used, not
how it *should* be used.

Reading "Sabotage in Springfield"

Although it may never have occurred to you to get angry or to feel
strongly one way or another over a dictionary, Wilson Follett's feelings
about the publication of a dictionary are immediately communicated
to the reader. Indeed, one need read no farther than the accusation in
the title to know the author's aroused opinion. Follett's formal and
learned language is the appropriate vehicle for his conservative argument. The large number of hard words is an indication of this writer's
preference for a formal style, and the frequent use of emotionally
charged words communicates the high feelings that run throughout
the magazine article. The emotional slant and formal language are
both well illustrated in his sweeping statement: "In fine, the anxiously
awaited work that was to have crowned cisatlantic linguistic scholarship with a particular glory turns out to be a scandal and a disaster."
"Cisatlantic linguistic scholarship" is a real mouthful, and "scandal
and a disaster" are pretty strong words to describe a dictionary.

A number of perhaps unfamiliar terms related to the subject of language appear in the following essays. Some of these are listed below:
it will help you to familiarize yourself with them before reading the
essays.

1. *barbarism:* an expression that is not considered standard.
2. *citation:* a quotation. In dictionary-making, a citation is a quotation taken down as an example of how a word is used.
3. *colloquial:* correct in conversation or on informal occasions; not
   acceptable in formal speech.
4. *dialect:* a form of a language common in a certain locality, and
   usually differing somewhat from the standard form of the language.
   It would be considered correct in the locality where it is spoken.
5. *etymology* (ĕt'ə mŏl'ə jĭ): the origin of a word.
6. *lexicography* (lĕk'sə kŏg'rə fĭ): the art or process of dictionary-
   making.
7. *linguistic:* relating to language.
8. *locution:* a particular manner of expressing something (as "a strange
   locution").
9. *neologism* (nĭ ŏl'ə jĭz'əm): a new word or expression.
10. *obsolete:* no longer in use.
11. *philology* (fĭ lŏl'ə jĭ): the study of language.
12. *solecism* (sŏl'ə sĭz'əm): words combined ungrammatically.
13. *usage:* the customary use of a term.

Sabotage in Springfield

Wilson Follett

"Why have a Dictionary at all if any-thing goes?" This comment from an editorial assistant sums up Mr. Follett's many grievances against Webster's Third New International Dictionary. *Mr. Follett is an angry man who bit-terly attacks the premise that the job of a dictionary is to record language as it is being used today. He declares that the scholars responsible for the diction-ary have abandoned their responsibility to those who turn to the unabridged dictionary to see how language should be used.*

I

OF DICTIONARIES, as of newspapers, it might be said that the bad ones are too bad to exist, the good ones too good not to be better. No dictionary of a living language is perfect or ever can be, if only because the time required for com-pilation, editing, and issuance is so great that shadows of obsolescence are falling on parts of any such work before it ever gets into the hands of a user. Preparation of *Webster's Third New International Dictionary of the English Language* began intensively in the Springfield establishment of G. & C.

Merriam Company in 1936, but the century was nine months into its seventh decade before any outsider could have his first look at what had been accomplished. His first look is, of course, incompetent to acquaint him with the merits of the new work; these no one can fully discover without months or years of everyday use. On the other hand, it costs only minutes to find out that what will rank as the great event of American linguistic history in this decade, and perhaps in this quarter century, is in many crucial particulars a very great calamity.

Why should the probable and possi-ble superiorities of the Third New In-ternational be so difficult to assess,[1] the shortcomings so easy? Because the superiorities are special, departmental, and recondite,[2] the shortcomings gen-eral and within the common grasp. The new dictionary comes to us with a claim of 100,000 new words or new defi-nitions. These run almost overwhelm-ingly to scientific and technological terms or meanings that have come into existence since 1934, and especially to words classified as ISV (belonging to the international scientific vocabulary). No one person can possibly use or even comprehend all of them; the coverage in this domain, certainly impressive to the nonspecialist, may or may not com-mand the admiration of specialists. It is said that historians of the graphic arts[3] and of architecture were displeased with the 1934 Webster, both for its omissions and for some definitions of what it included in their fields. Its 1961 successor may have disarmed their reservations; only they can pronounce.

---

1 **assess:** judge the value of.
2 **recondite** (rĕk'ən dīt'): so scholarly as to be hid-den.
3 **graphic arts:** such arts as painting, drawing, and engraving.

But all of us may without brashness form summary judgments about the treatment of what belongs to all of us —the standard, staple, traditional language of general reading and speaking, the ordinary vocabulary and idioms of novelist, essayist, letter writer, reporter, editorial writer, teacher, student, advertiser; in short, fundamental English. And it is precisely in this province that Webster III has thrust upon us a dismaying assortment of the questionable, the perverse, the unworthy, and the downright outrageous.

Furthermore, what was left out is as legitimate a grievance to the ordinary reader as anything that has been put in. Think—if you can—of an unabridged dictionary from which you cannot learn who Mark Twain was (though **mark twain** is entered as a leadsman's cry), or what were the names of the apostles, or that the Virgin was Mary the mother of Jesus of Nazareth, or what and where the District of Columbia is!

The disappointment and the shock are intensified, of course, because of the unchallenged position earned by the really unabridged immediate predecessor of this strange work. *Webster's New International Dictionary*, Second Edition (1934), consummated[4] under the editorship of William Allan Neilson, at once became the most important reference book in the world to American writers, editors, teachers, students, and general readers—everyone to whom American English was a matter of serious interest. What better could the next revision do than extend the Second Edition in the direction of itself, bring it up to date, and correct its scattering of oversights and errata?[5]

The 1934 dictionary had been, heaven knows, no citadel of conservatism, no last bastion of puristical[6] bigotry. But it had made shrewd reports on the status of individual words; it had taken its clear, beautifully written definitions from fit uses of an enormous vocabulary by judicious users; it had provided accurate, impartial accounts of the endless guerrilla war between grammarian and antigrammarian and so given every consultant the means to work out his own decisions. Who could wish the forthcoming revision any better fortune than a comparable success in applying the same standards to whatever new matter the new age imposed?

Instead, we have seen a century and a third of illustrious history largely jettisoned;[7] we have seen a novel dictionary formula improvised, in great part out of snap judgments and the sort of theoretical improvement that in practice impairs; and we have seen the gates propped wide open in enthusiastic hospitality to miscellaneous confusions and corruptions. In fine, the anxiously awaited work that was to have crowned cisatlantic[8] linguistic scholarship with a particular glory turns out to be a scandal and a disaster. Worse yet, it plumes itself on its faults and parades assiduously[9] cultivated sins as virtues without precedent.

II

EXAMINATION cannot proceed far without revealing that Webster III, behind its front of passionless objectivity, is in truth a fighting document. And the

---

6 **puristical:** overconcerned with the purity of language.
7 **jettisoned:** thrown overboard.
8 **cisatlantic:** on this side of the Atlantic (that is, American).
9 **assiduously** (ə sĭj′o͞o əs lĭ): diligently; very carefully.

4 **consummated:** completed.
5 **errata** (ĭ rä′tə): errors of printers or writers that appear in a published work.

enemy it is out to destroy is every obstinate vestige of linguistic punctilio,[10] every surviving influence that makes for the upholding of standards, every criterion for distinguishing between better usages and worse. In other words, it has gone over bodily to the school that construes traditions as enslaving, the rudimentary principles of syntax[11] as crippling, and taste as irrelevant. This revolution leaves it in the anomalous[12] position of loudly glorifying its own ancestry—which is indeed glorious —while tacitly[13] sabotaging the principles and ideals that brought the preceding Merriam-Webster to its unchallengeable pre-eminence. The Third New International is at once a resounding tribute of lip service to the Second and a wholesale repudiation of it—a sweeping act of apology, contrition, and reform.

The right-about-face is, of course, particularly evident in the vocabulary approved. Within a few days of publication the new dictionary was inevitably notorious for its unreserved acceptance as standard of *wise up, get hep* (it uses the second as a definition of the first), *ants in one's pants, one for the book, hugeous, nixie, passel, hepped up* (with *hepcat* and *hepster*), *anyplace, someplace,* and so forth. These and a swarm of their kind it admits to full canonical[14] standing by the suppression of such qualifying status labels as *colloquial, slang, cant, facetious,* and *substandard.* The classification *colloquial* it abolishes outright: "it is impossible to know whether a word out of context is colloquial or not." Of *slang* it makes a chary occasional use despite a similar

reservation: "No word is invariably slang, and many standard words can be given slang connotations or used so inappropriately as to become slang." *Cornball* is ranked as slang, *corny* is not.

The overall effect signifies a large-scale abrogation[15] of one major responsibility of the lexicographer. He renounces it on the curious ground that helpful discriminations are so far beyond his professional competence that he is obliged to leave them to those who, professing no competence at all, have vainly turned to him for guidance. If some George Ade[16] of the future, aspiring to execute a fable in slang, were to test his attempt by the status labels in Webster III, he would quickly discover with chagrin that he had expressed himself almost without exception in officially applauded English. With but slight exaggeration we can say that if an expression can be shown to have been used in print by some jaded reporter, some candidate for office or his speech writer, some potboiling minor novelist, it is well enough credentialed for the full blessing of the new lexicography.

This extreme tolerance of crude neologisms and of shabby diction generally, however, is but one comparatively trifling aspect of the campaign against punctilio. We begin to sound its deeper implications when we plunge into the definitions and the copious examples that illustrate and support them. Under the distributive pronoun *each* we find, side by side: "(each of them is to pay his own fine) (each of them are to pay their own fine)." Where could anyone look for a neater, more succinct[17]

---

10 **punctilio:** careful attention to good form.
11 **syntax:** sentence structure.
12 **anomalous:** irregular; inconsistent.
13 **tacitly** (tăs'ĭt lĭ): silently.
14 **canonical:** approved by authority.

15 **abrogation:** abolishment.
16 **George Ade:** an American humorist (1886-1944) who wrote stories in a slangy language.
17 **succinct** (sək sĭngkt'): brief.

WILSON FOLLETT

way to outlaw the dusty dogma that a pronoun should agree in number with its antecedent? Here is the same maneuver again under another distributive, *everybody:* "usu. referred to by the third person singular (everybody is bringing his own lunch) but sometimes by a plural personal pronoun (everybody had made up their minds)." Or try *whom* and *whomever:* "(a . . . recruit whom he hoped would prove to be a crack salesman) (people . . . whom you never thought would sympathize) . . . (I go out to talk to whomever it is) . . . (he attacked whomever disagreed with him)." It is, then, all right to put the subject of a finite verb in the accusative case—"esp. after a preposition or a verb of which it might mistakenly be considered the object."

III

SHALL we look into what our dictionary does with a handful of the more common solecisms, such as a publisher might introduce into a cooked-up test for would-be copy editors? Begin with *center around* (or *about*). It seems obvious that expressions derived from Euclidean geometry should make Euclidean sense. A center is a point; it is what things are around, not what is around them; they center *in* or *on* or *at* the point. The Second Edition defined the Great White Way as "That part of Broadway . . . centering about Times Square"—patently an oversight. Is it the same oversight that produces, in the Third: "heresy . . . 3: a group or school of thought centering around a particular heresy"? We look up *center* itself, and, lo: "(a story to tell, centered around the political development of a great state) . . . (more scholarship than usual was centered around the main

problems)," followed by several equivalent specimens.

Here is *due to.* First we come on irreproachable definitions, irreproachably illustrated, of *due* noun and *due* adjective, and we think we are out of the woods. Alas, they are followed by the manufacture of a composite[18] preposition, *due to,* got up solely to extenuate[19] such abominations as "the event was canceled due to inclement weather." An adjective can modify a verb, then. And here is a glance at that peculiarly incriminating redundancy[20] of the slipshod writer, *equally as:* "equally opposed to Communism as to Fascism." The intolerable *hardly than* or *scarcely than* construction is in full favor: "hardly had the birds dropped than she jumped into the water and retrieved them." The sequence *different than* has the double approbation of editorial use and a citation: conjunctive *unlike* means "in a manner that is different than," and a passage under *different* reads "vastly different in size than it was twenty-five years ago." Adjectival *unlike* and conjunctive *unlike* both get illustrations that implicitly commend the unanchored and grammarless modifier: "so many fine men were outside the charmed circle that, unlike most colleges, there was no disgrace in not being a club man"; "unlike in the gasoline engine, fuel does not enter the cylinder with air on the intake stroke."

This small scattering should not end without some notice of that darling of the advanced libertarians, *like* as a conjunction, first in the meaning of *as,* secondly (and more horribly) in that of *as if.* Now, it is well known to the linguistic historian that *like* was so used

---

18 composite (kəm pŏz′ĭt)**:** compound.
19 extenuate: excuse.
20 redundancy: using more words than necessary to express an idea.

ESSAY

for a long time before and after Langland.[21] But it is as well known that the language rather completely sloughed off this usage; that it has long been no more than a regional colloquialism, a rarely seen aberration[22] among competent writers, or an artificially cultivated irritant among defiant ones. *The Saturday Evening Post*, in which *like* for *as* is probably more frequent than in any other painstakingly edited magazine, has seldom if ever printed that construction except in reproducing the speech or tracing the thoughts of characters to whom it might be considered natural. The arguments for *like* have been merely defensive and permissive. Not for centuries has there been any real pressure of authority on a writer to use *like* as a conjunction—until our Third New International Dictionary decided to exert its leverage.

How it is exerted will appear in the following: "(impromptu programs where they ask questions much like I do on the air) . . . (looks like they can raise better tobacco) (looks like he will get the job) (wore his clothes like he was . . . afraid of getting dirt on them) (was like he'd come back from a long trip) (acted like she felt sick) . . . (sounded like the motor had stopped) . . . (the violin now sounds like an old masterpiece should) (did it like he told me to) . . . (wanted a doll like she saw in the store window) . . . (anomalies like just had occurred)."

By the processes represented in the foregoing and countless others for which there is no room here, the latest Webster whittles away at one after another of the traditional controls until there is little or nothing left of them. The controls, to be sure, have often enough been overvalued and overdone by pedants and purists, by martinets[23] and bigots; but more often, and much more importantly, they have worked as aids toward dignified, workmanlike, and cogent uses of the wonderful language that is our inheritance. To erode and undermine them is to convert the language into a confusion of unchanneled, incalculable williwaws,[24] a capricious wind blowing whithersoever it listeth. And that, if we are to judge by the total effect of the pages under scrutiny—2720 of them and nearly 8000 columns of vocabulary, all compact in Times roman[25]—is exactly what is wanted by the patient and dedicated saboteurs in Springfield. They, if they keep their ears to the ground, will hear many echoes of the despairing cry already wrung from one editorial assistant on a distinguished magazine that still puts its faith in standards: "Why have a Dictionary at all if anything goes?"

IV

THE DEFINITIONS are reinforced, it will have been conveyed, with copious citations from printed sources. These citations occupy a great fraction of the total space. They largely account for the reduction in the number of entries (from 600,000 to 450,000) and for the elimination of the Gazetteer, the Biographical Dictionary, and the condensed key to pronunciation and symbols that ran across the bottoms of facing pages—all very material deprivations. Some 14,000 authors, we are told, are represented in the illustrative quotations—"mostly from the mid-twentieth century."

---

21 Langland: an English poet of the 14th century.
22 aberration: wandering from the normal or right.

23 martinets: strict disciplinarians.
24 williwaws: sudden gusts of wind.
25 Times roman: a style of type.

Can some thousands of authors truly worth space in a dictionary ever be found in any one brief period? Such a concentration can hardly fail to be, for the purposes of a dictionary, egregiously[26] overweighted with the contemporary and the transient. Any very short period, such as a generation, is a period of transition in the history of English, and any great mass of examples drawn primarily from it will be disproportionately focused on transitional and ephemeral[27] elements. To say that recording English *as we find it today* is precisely the purpose of a new dictionary is not much of a retort. For the bulk of the language that we use has come down to us with but minor, glacially slow changes from time out of mind, and a worthy record of it must stand on a much broader base than the fashions of yesterday.

It is, then, a mercy that among the thousands of scraps from recent authors, many of them still producing, we can also find hundreds from Shakespeare, the English Bible, Fielding, Dickens, Hawthorne, Melville, Henry James, Mark Twain, and so on. But the great preponderance of latter-day prose, little of it worth repeating and a good deal of it hardly worth printing in the first place, is likely to curtail by years the useful life of the Third New International.

So much is by the way. When we come to the definitions proper we face something new, startling, and formidable in lexicography. The definitions, all of them conformed to a predetermined rhetorical pattern, may be products of a theory—Gestaltist,[28] perhaps?

—of how the receiving mind works. The pattern, in the editor's general preface, is described as follows: "The primary objective of precise, sharp defining has been met through development of a new dictionary style based upon completely analytical one-phrase definitions throughout the book. Since the headword in a definition is intended to be modified only by structural elements restrictive in some degree and essential to each other, the use of commas either to separate or to group has been severely limited, chiefly to elements in apposition or in series. The new defining pattern does not provide for a predication which conveys further expository comment."

This doctrine of the strictly unitary definition is of course formulated and applied in the interest of a logical integrity and a simplification never before consistently attained by lexical definitions. What it produces, when applied with the rigor here insisted on, is in the first place some of the oddest prose ever concocted by pundits.[29] A typical specimen, from the definition of the simplest possible term: "**rabbit punch . . . :** a short chopping blow delivered to the back of the neck or the base of the skull with the edge of the hand opposite the thumb that is illegal in boxing." When the idea, being not quite so simple, requires the one-phrase statement of several components, the definition usually turns out to be a great unmanageable and unpunctuated blob of words strung out beyond the retentive powers of most minds that would need the definition at all. Both theory and result will emerge clearly enough from a pair of specimens, the first dealing with a familiar everyday noun, the second with a mildly technical one:

26 egregiously (ĭ grē′jəs lĭ): conspicuously, for bad qualities.
27 ephemeral (ĭfĕm′ər əl): short-lived.
28 Gestaltist: relating to a school of psychology which sees things in patterns or wholes rather than as separate and unrelated.

29 pundits: learned teachers.

groan . . . **1**: a deep usu. inarticulate and involuntary often strangled sound typically abruptly begun and ended and usu. indicative of pain or grief or tension or desire or sometimes disapproval or annoyance

kymograph . . . **1**: a recording device including an electric motor or clockwork that drives a usu. slowly revolving drum which carries a roll of plain or smoked paper and also having an arrangement for tracing on the paper by means of a stylus a graphic record of motion or pressure (as of the organs of speech, blood pressure, or respiration) often in relation to particular intervals of time.

About these typical definitions as prose, there is much that any good reader might well say. What must be said is that the grim suppression of commas is a mere crotchet. It takes time to read such definitions anyway; commas in the right places would speed rather than slow the reading and would clarify rather than obscure the sense, so that the unitary effect—largely imaginary at best—would be more helped than hurt. In practice, the one-phrase design without further expository predication lacks all the asserted advantages over a competently written definition of the free conventional sort; it is merely more difficult to write, often impossible to write well, and tougher to take in. Compare the corresponding definitions from the Second Edition:

groan . . . A low, moaning sound; usually, a deep, mournful sound uttered in pain or great distress; sometimes, an expression of strong disapprobation; as, the remark was received with *groans*.

kymograph . . . **a** An automatic apparatus consisting of a motor revolving a drum covered with smoked paper, on which curves of pressure, etc., may be traced.

V

EVERYONE professionally concerned with the details of printed English can be grateful to the new Webster for linking the parts of various expressions that have been either hyphenated compounds or separate words—*highlight, highbrow* and *lowbrow, overall, wisecrack, lowercase* and *uppercase*, and so on. Some of the unions now recognized were long overdue; many editors have already got them written into codes of house usage. But outside this small province the new work is a copy editor's despair, a propounder of endless riddles.

What, for example, are we to make of the common abbreviations *i.e.* and *e.g.*? The first is entered in the vocabulary as **ie** (no periods, no space), the second as **e g** (space, no periods). In the preliminary list, "Abbreviations Used in This Dictionary," both are given the customary periods. (Oddly, the list translates its *i.e.* into "that is," but merely expands *e.g.* into "exempli gratia.") Is one to follow the vocabulary or the list? What point has the seeming inconsistency?

And what about capitalization? All vocabulary entries are in lowercase except for such abbreviations as ARW (air raid warden), MAB (medical advisory board), and PX (post exchange). Words possibly inviting capitalization are followed by such injunctions as *cap, usu cap, sometimes not cap, usu cap 1st A, usu cap A&B.* (One of the small idiosyncrasies is that "usu.," the most frequent abbreviation, is given a period when roman, denied it when italic.) From **america**, adjective—all proper nouns are excluded—to **american yew** there are over 175 consecutive entries that require such injunctions; would it not have been simpler and more economical to capitalize the entries? A flat *"cap,"* of course, means "always capitalized." But how often is "usually," and when is "sometimes"? We get dictionaries expressly that they may settle such problems for us. This dictionary seems to make a virtue of leaving them in flux, with the explanation that many matters are subjective and that the individual must decide them for himself—a curious abrogation of authority in a work extolled as "more useful and authoritative than any previous dictionary."

The rock-bottom practical truth is that the lexicographer cannot abrogate his authority if he wants to. He may think of himself as a detached scientist reporting the facts of language, declining to recommend use of anything or abstention from anything; but the myriad[30] consultants of his work are not going to see him so. He helps create, not a book of fads and fancies and private opinions, but a Dictionary of the English Language. It comes to every reader under auspices that say, not "Take it or leave it," but rather something like this: "Here in 8000 columns is a definitive[31] report of what a synod[32] of the most trustworthy American experts consider the English language to be in the seventh decade of the 20th century. This is your language; take it and use it. And if you use it in conformity with the principles and practices here exemplified, your use will be the most accurate attainable by any American of this era." The fact that the compilers disclaim authority and piously refrain from judgments is meaningless: the work itself, by virtue of its inclusions and exclusions, its mere existence, is a whole universe of judgments, received by millions as the Word from on high.

And there we have the reason why it is so important for the dictionary maker to keep his discriminations sharp, why it is so damaging if he lets them get out of working order. Suppose he enters a new definition for no better reason than that some careless, lazy, or uninformed scribbler has jumped to an absurd conclusion about what a word means or has been too harassed to run down the word he really wanted. This new definition is going to persuade tens of thousands that, say, *cohort*, a word of multitude, means one associate or crony "(he and three alleged housebreaking cohorts were arraigned on attempted burglary charges)" or that the vogue word *ambivalence*, which denotes simultaneous love and hatred of someone or something, means "continual oscillation between one thing and its opposite (novels . . . vitiated by an ambivalence between satire and sentimentalism)." To what is the definer contributing if not to subversion and decay? To the swallower of the definition it never occurs that he can have drunk corruption from a well that he has every reason to trust as the ultimate in purity. Multiply him by the number of people simultaneously influenced, and the resulting figure by the years through which the influence continues, and a great deal of that product by the influences that will be disseminated through speech and writing and teaching, and you begin to apprehend the scope of the really enormous disaster that can and will be wrought by the lexicographer's abandonment of his responsibility.

30 **myriad**: an indefinitely large number.
31 **definitive**: complete.
32 **synod** (sĭn′əd): assembly; council.

Understanding the Essay

1. How soon does Follett's strong feeling against the Third Edition become apparent? What key word in the opening paragraph represents the author's view of the new dictionary?
2. What is the strength in the argument that "it costs only minutes" to judge the dictionary a "calamity"? the weakness?
3. What has been sabotaged? To answer this question refer to the discussion in the last section of the article.
4. In paragraph 3, Section I, you are encouraged to agree with the author in forming a quick judgment about the treatment of certain matters in the dictionary. Is this paragraph a logically sound one? Explain the reasons for your answer.
5. At the beginning of the essay, the author refers to the dictionary as a "fighting document." What does the author mean by this expression? How does this view of the dictionary justify the tone of the essay?
6. What small commendation of the dictionary is conceded in the opening paragraph of Section V? How does this faint praise either weaken or strengthen Follett's argument?
7. What view of the dictionary makers are you expected to accept when the author says (Section V, paragraph 4) that they "*piously* refrain from judgments"? Explain how the word *piously* is emotionally charged.
8. In the last paragraph we are told that the dictionary makers have contributed to "subversion." How is this word at the end of the essay related to a word in the title? How does this choice of diction make the essay more effective?
9. How does the conclusion about the lexicographer's responsibility relate to the title of the article? What does Mr. Follett consider the dictionary maker's responsibility to be? Where does he summarize the responsibility?

Building Vocabulary Skills

1. The word *sabotage* has an interesting etymology. Look this word up in a dictionary (Follett would prefer you to use Webster's Second International), and report to the class on the history of the word.
2. Explain the meaning of the prefix *cis-* in the word *cisatlantic*.
3. Almost any person who is trying to persuade others to adopt a certain opinion uses some emotionally charged language. For example, words like *reactionary*, *conservative*, *liberal*, and *radical* are frequently used in political speeches and writing. These words generally call forth strong reactions from anyone concerned with politics, although the precise reaction depends largely on the individual viewpoint of a hearer or reader. For the most part, no one likes to be called a reactionary or a radical—although, strangely enough, the same people might well approve of historical figures who actually

were reactionaries or radicals. However, the connotations—that is, the associations—of the words make them into what are called *loaded* or *slanted* terms: ones people react to emotionally.

Other terms call forth emotional reactions, not because of their associations, but because of their meanings. When something is called *good* or *bad, kind* or *cruel,* the speaker or writer is expressing an emotional as well as an intellectual reaction. If the speaker is convincing, his emotional reaction is often transferred to his audience through these words.

Follett uses a number of emotionally charged words in his essay—indeed, the word *sabotage* in the title is an example of such a word. People are against sabotage before they read this essay: if the writer can successfully associate the idea of sabotage with *Webster's Third New International Dictionary,* his readers will be against that dictionary also.

Find other examples of such emotionally charged words in the essay and explain what emotional state each conveys.

Reading "But What's a Dictionary For?"

Bergen Evans adopts a sometimes breezy style to refute the conservative opposition to the Third International. In contrast to Wilson Follett's formality, Evans's defense of the dictionary is written with a sense of humor. A humorous remark may sometimes get nearer the truth and be more devastating in an argument than a high sounding, perhaps pompous, remark. Evans tweaks the noses of a number of influential publications, including *The New York Times* and *Life* magazine, which criticized the dictionary. The article, published five months later than Follett's in the same magazine, is principally concerned with taking on the more formal Mr. Follett. Look for examples of Evans's light touch, and decide for yourself whether he is successful in his defense of the dictionary and whether he demolishes opposition with his thrusts of humor.

But What's a Dictionary For?

Bergen Evans

Mr. Evans position is that the dictionary neither snickers nor denounces. It records. He finds the Third International a modern scientific work to which readers may turn to find out how the language is used today, not how it should be used. He takes to task reviewers whose criticisms show that they "seem unable to read the Third International and unwilling to read the Second."

I

THE STORM of abuse in the popular press that greeted the appearance of *Webster's Third New International Dictionary* is a curious phenomenon. Never has a scholarly work of this stature been attacked with such unbridled fury and contempt. An article in the *Atlantic* viewed it as a "disappointment," a "shock," a "calamity," "a scandal and a disaster." *The New York Times*, in a special editorial, felt that the work would "accelerate the deterioration" of the language and sternly accused the editors of betraying a public trust. The *Journal* of the American Bar Association saw the publication as "deplor-able," "a flagrant example of lexicographic irresponsibility," "a serious blow to the cause of good English." *Life* called it "a non-word deluge," "monstrous," "abominable," and "a cause for dismay." They doubted that "Lincoln could have modeled his Gettysburg Address" on it—a concept of how things get written that throws very little light on Lincoln but a great deal on *Life*.

What underlies all this sound and fury? Is the claim of the G. & C. Merriam Company, probably the world's greatest dictionary maker, that the preparation of the work cost $3.5 million, that it required the efforts of three hundred scholars over a period of twenty-seven years, working on the largest collection of citations ever assembled in any language—is all this a fraud, a hoax?

So monstrous a discrepancy in evaluation requires us to examine basic principles. Just what's a dictionary for? What does it propose to do? What does the common reader go to a dictionary to find? What has the purchaser of a dictionary a right to expect for his money?

Before we look at basic principles, it is necessary to interpose two brief statements. The first of these is that a dictionary is concerned with words. Some dictionaries give various kinds of other useful information. Some have tables of weights and measures on the flyleaves. Some list historical events, and some, home remedies. And there's nothing wrong with their so doing. But the great increase in our vocabulary in the past three decades compels all dictionaries to make more efficient use of their space. And if something must be eliminated, it is sensible to throw out these extraneous things and stick to words.

Yet wild wails arose. *The Saturday Review* lamented that one can no longer find the goddess Astarte under a separate heading—though they point out that a genus of mollusks[1] named after the goddess is included! They seemed to feel that out of sheer perversity the editors of the dictionary stooped to mollusks while ignoring goddesses and that, in some way, this typifies modern lexicography. Mr. Wilson Follett, folletizing (his mental processes demand some special designation) in the *Atlantic*, cried out in horror that one is not even able to learn from the Third International "that the Virgin was Mary, the mother of Jesus"!

The second brief statement is that there has been even more progress in the making of dictionaries in the past thirty years than there has been in the making of automobiles. The difference, for example, between the much-touted[2] Second International (1934) and the much-clouted Third International (1961) is not like the difference between yearly models but like the difference between the horse and buggy and the automobile. Between the appearance of these two editions a whole new science related to the making of dictionaries, the science of descriptive linguistics, has come into being.

Modern linguistics gets its charter from Leonard Bloomfield's *Language* (1933). Bloomfield, for thirteen years professor of Germanic philology at the University of Chicago and for nine years professor of linguistics at Yale, was one of those inseminating[3] scholars who can't be relegated[4] to any department and don't dream of accepting established categories and procedures just because they're established. He was as much an anthropologist[5] as a linguist, and his concepts of language were shaped not by Strunk's *Elements of Style* but by his knowledge of Cree Indian dialects.

The broad general findings of the new science are:

1. All languages are systems of human conventions, not systems of natural laws. The first—and essential—step in the study of any language is observing and setting down precisely what happens when native speakers speak it.

2. Each language is unique in its pronunciation, grammar, and vocabulary. It cannot be described in terms of logic or of some theoretical, ideal language. It cannot be described in terms of any other language, or even in terms of its own past.

3. All languages are dynamic rather than static, and hence a "rule" in any language can only be a statement of contemporary practice. Change is constant—and normal.

4. "Correctness" can rest only upon usage, for the simple reason that there is nothing else for it to rest on. And all usage is relative.

From these propositions it follows that a dictionary is good only insofar as it is a comprehensive and accurate description of current usage. And to be comprehensive it must include some indication of social and regional associations.

New dictionaries are needed because English has changed more in the past two generations than at any other time in its history. It has had to adapt to extraordinary cultural and technological changes, two world wars, unparalleled

---

1 mollusks: shellfish.
2 much-touted: much publicly praised.
3 inseminating scholars: scholars whose work is original and influential.
4 relegated (rĕl′ə gā′təd): dismissed; banished.

5 anthropologist (ăn′thrə pŏl′ə jĭst): one who studies human beings, their environment and culture.

changes in transportation and communication, and unprecedented movements of populations.

More subtly, but pervasively,[6] it has changed under the influence of mass education and the growth of democracy. As written English is used by increasing millions and for more reasons than ever before, the language has become more utilitarian[7] and more informal. Every publication in America today includes pages that would appear, to the purist of forty years ago, unbuttoned gibberish. Not that they are; they simply show that you can't hold the language of one generation up as a model for the next.

It's not that you mustn't. You *can't*. For example, in the issue in which *Life* stated editorially that it would follow the Second International, there were over forty words, constructions, and meanings which are in the Third International but not in the Second. The issue of *The New York Times* which hailed the Second International as the authority to which it would adhere and the Third International as a scandal and a betrayal which it would reject used one hundred and fifty-three separate words, phrases, and constructions which are listed in the Third International but not in the Second and nineteen others which are condemned in the Second. Many of them are used many times, more than three hundred such uses in all. *The Washington Post*, in an editorial captioned "Keep Your Old Webster's," says, in the first sentence, "don't throw it away," and in the second, "hang on to it." But the old Webster's labels *don't* "colloquial" and doesn't include "hang on to," in this sense, at all.

In short, all of these publications are written in the language that the Third International describes, even the very editorials which scorn it. And this is no coincidence, because the Third International isn't setting up any new standards at all; it is simply describing what *Life, The Washington Post,* and *The New York Times* are doing. Much of the dictionary's material comes from these very publications, the *Times,* in particular, furnishing more of its illustrative quotations than any other newspaper.

And the papers have no choice. No journal or periodical could sell a single issue today if it restricted itself to the American language of twenty-eight years ago. It couldn't discuss half the things we are interested in, and its style would seem stiff and cumbrous. If the editorials were serious, the public—and the stockholders—have reason to be grateful that the writers on these publications are more literate than the editors.

II

AND so back to our questions: what's a dictionary for, and how, in 1962, can it best do what it ought to do? The demands are simple. The common reader turns to a dictionary for information about the spelling, pronunciation, meaning, and proper use of words. He wants to know what is current and respectable. But he wants—and has a right to—the truth, the full truth. And the full truth about any language, and especially about American English today, is that there are many areas in which certainty is impossible and simplification is misleading.

Even in so settled a matter as spelling, a dictionary cannot always be absolute. *Theater* is correct, but so is

---

6 pervasively: spread throughout.
7 utilitarian: characterized by usefulness.

theatre. And so are *traveled* and *travelled, plow* and *plough, catalog* and *catalogue,* and scores of other variants. The reader may want a single certainty. He may have taken an unyielding position in an argument, he may have wagered in support of his conviction and may demand that the dictionary "settle" the matter. But neither his vanity nor his purse is any concern of the dictionary's; it must record the facts. And the fact here is that there are many words in our language which may be spelled, with equal correctness, in either of two ways.

So with pronunciation. A citizen listening to his radio might notice that James B. Conant, Bernard Baruch, and Dwight D. Eisenhower pronounce *economics* as ECKuhnomiks, while A. Whitney Griswold, Adlai Stevenson, and Herbert Hoover pronounce it EEKuhnomiks. He turns to the dictionary to see which of the two pronunciations is "right" and finds that they are both acceptable.

Has he been betrayed? Has the dictionary abdicated its responsibility? Should it say that one *must* speak like the president of Harvard or like the president of Yale, like the thirty-first President of the United States or like the thirty-fourth? Surely it's none of its business to make a choice. Not because of the distinction of these particular speakers; lexicography, like God, is no respecter of persons. But because so widespread and conspicuous a use of two pronunciations among people of this elevation shows that there *are* two pronunciations. Their speaking establishes the fact which the dictionary must record.

Among the "enormities" with which *Life* taxes the Third International is its listing of "the common mispronunciation" *heighth*. That it is labeled a "dialectal variant" seems, somehow, to compound the felony. But one hears the word so pronounced, and if one professes to give a full account of American English in the 1960's, one has to take some cognizance[8] of it. All people do not possess *Life's* intuitive perception that the word is so "monstrous" that even to list it as a dialect variation is to merit scorn. Among these, by the way, was John Milton, who, in one of the greatest passages in all literature, besought the Holy Spirit to raise him to the "highth" of his great argument. And even the *Oxford English Dictionary* is so benighted as to list it, in full boldface, right alongside of *Height* as a variant that has been in the language since at least 1290.

Now there are still, apparently, millions of Americans who retain, in this as in much else, some of the speech of Milton. This particular pronunciation seems to be receding, but the *American Dialect Dictionary* still records instances of it from almost every state on the Eastern seaboard and notes that it is heard from older people and "occasionally in educated speech," "common with good speakers," "general," "widespread."

Under these circumstances, what is a dictionary to do? Since millions speak the word this way, the pronunciation can't be ignored. Since it has been in use as long as we have any record of English and since it has been used by the greatest writers, it can't be described as substandard or slang. But it is heard now only in certain localities. That makes it a dialectal pronunciation, and an honest dictionary will list it as such. What else can it do? Should it do?

8 **cognizance:** notice.

THE average purchaser of a dictionary uses it most often, probably, to find out what a word "means." As a reader, he wants to know what an author intended to convey. As a speaker or writer, he wants to know what a word will convey to his auditors. And this, too, is complex, subtle, and forever changing.

An illustration is furnished by an editorial in *The Washington Post* (January 17, 1962). After a ringing appeal to those who "love truth and accuracy" and the usual bombinations[9] about "abdication of authority" and "barbarism," the editorial charges the Third International with "pretentious and obscure verbosity"[10] and specifically instances its definition of "so simple an object as a door."

The definition reads:

a movable piece of firm material or a structure supported usu. along one side and swinging on pivots or hinges, sliding along a groove, rolling up and down, revolving as one of four leaves, or folding like an accordion by means of which an opening may be closed or kept open for passage into or out of a building, room, or other covered enclosure or a car, airplane, elevator, or other vehicle.

Then follows a series of special meanings, each particularly defined and, where necessary, illustrated by a quotation.

Since, aside from roaring and admonishing the "gentlemen from Springfield" that "accuracy and brevity are virtues," the *Post's* editorial fails to explain what is wrong with the definition, we can only infer from "so simple" a thing that the writer takes the plain, downright, man-in-the-street attitude that a door is a door and any damn fool knows that.

But if so, he has walked into one of lexicography's biggest booby traps: the belief that the obvious is easy to define. Whereas the opposite is true. Anyone can give a fair description of the strange, the new, or the unique. It's the commonplace, the habitual, that challenges definition, for its very commonness compels us to define it in uncommon terms. Dr. Johnson was ridiculed on just this score when his dictionary appeared in 1755. For two hundred years his definition of a network as "any thing reticulated or decussated, at equal distances, with interstices between the intersections" has been good for a laugh. But in the merriment one thing is always overlooked: no one has yet come up with a better definition! Subsequent dictionaries defined it as a mesh and then defined a mesh as a network. That's simple, all right.

Anyone who attempts sincerely to state what the word *door* means in the United States of America today can't take refuge in a log cabin. There has been an enormous proliferation[11] of closing and demarking devices and structures in the past twenty years, and anyone who tries to thread his way through the many meanings now included under *door* may have to sacrifice brevity to accuracy and even have to employ words that a limited vocabulary may find obscure.

Is the entrance to a tent a door, for instance? And what of the thing that seals the exit of an airplane? Is this a door? Or what of those sheets and jets of air that are now being used, in place of old-fashioned oak and hinges, to

---

9 **bombinations:** dronings; buzzings.
10 **verbosity:** wordiness.

11 **proliferation:** rapid production of new quantities.

screen entrances and exits. Are they doors? And what of those accordion-like things that set off various sections of many modern apartments? The fine print in the lease takes it for granted that they are doors and that spaces demarked by them are rooms—and the rent is computed on the number of rooms.

Was I gypped by the landlord when he called the folding contraption that shuts off my kitchen a door? I go to the Second International, which the editor of the *Post* urges me to use in preference to the Third International. Here I find that a door is

The movable frame or barrier of boards, or other material, usually turning on hinges or pivots or sliding, by which an entranceway into a house or apartment is closed and opened; also, a similar part of a piece of furniture, as in a cabinet or bookcase.

This is only forty-six words, but though it includes the cellar door, it excludes the barn door and the accordion-like thing.

So I go on to the Third International. I see at once that the new definition is longer. But I'm looking for accuracy, and if I must sacrifice brevity to get it, then I must. And, sure enough, in the definition which raised the *Post's* blood pressure, I find the words "folding like an accordion." The thing *is* a door, and my landlord is using the word in one of its currently accepted meanings.

We don't turn to a work of reference merely for confirmation. We all have words in our vocabularies which we have misunderstood, and to come on the true meaning of one of these words is quite a shock. All our complacency and self-esteem rise to oppose the discovery. But eventually we must accept the humiliation and laugh it off as best we can.

Some, often those who have set themselves up as authorities, stick to their error and charge the dictionary with being in a conspiracy against them. They are sure that their meaning is the only "right" one. And when the dictionary doesn't bear them out they complain about "permissive" attitudes instead of correcting their mistake.

The New York Times and *The Saturday Review* both regarded as contemptibly "permissive" the fact that one meaning of one word was illustrated by a quotation from Polly Adler. But a rudimentary knowledge of the development of any language would have told them that the underworld has been a far more active force in shaping and enriching speech than all the synods that have ever convened. Their attitude is like that of the patriot who canceled his subscription to the *Dictionary of American Biography* when he discovered that the very first volume included Benedict Arnold!

The ultimate of "permissiveness," singled out by almost every critic for special scorn, was the inclusion in the Third International of *finalize*. It was this, more than any other one thing, that was given as the reason for sticking to the good old Second International—that "peerless authority on American English," as the *Times* called it. But if it was such an authority, why didn't they look into it? They would have found *finalize* if they had.

And why shouldn't it be there? It exists. It's been recorded for two generations. Millions employ it every day. Two Presidents of the United States —men of widely differing cultural backgrounds—have used it in formal statements. And so has the Secretary-General of the United Nations, a man of unusual linguistic attainments. It isn't permitting the word but omitting it that would break faith with the reader. Because it is exactly the sort of word we want information about.

To list it as substandard would be to imply that it is used solely by the ignorant and the illiterate. But this would be a misrepresentation: President Kennedy and U Thant are highly educated men, and both are articulate and literate. It isn't even a freak form. On the contrary, it is a classic example of a regular process of development in English, a process which has given us such thoroughly accepted words as *generalize, minimize, formalize,* and *verbalize.* Nor can it be dismissed on logical grounds or on the ground that it is a mere duplication of *complete.* It says something that *complete* doesn't say and says it in a way that is significant in the modern bureaucratic world: one usually *completes* something which he has initiated but *finalizes* the work of others.

One is free to dislike the word. I don't like it. But the editor of a dictionary has to examine the evidence for a word's existence and seek it in context to get, as clearly and closely as he can, the exact meaning that it conveys to those who use it. And if it is widely used by well-educated, literate, reputable people, he must list it as a standard word. He is not compiling a volume of his own prejudices.

IV

AN INDIVIDUAL's use of his native tongue is the surest index to his position within his community. And those who turn to a dictionary expect from it some statement of the current status of a word or a grammatical construction. And it is with the failure to assume this function that modern lexicography has been most fiercely charged. The charge is based on a naïve assumption that simple labels can be attached in all instances. But they can't. Some words are standard in some constructions and not in others. There may be as many shades of status as of meaning, and modern lexicography instead of abdicating this function has fulfilled it to a degree utterly unknown to earlier dictionaries.

Consider the word *fetch,* meaning to "go get and bring to." Until recently a standard word of full dignity ("Fetch me, I pray thee, a little water in a vessel"—I Kings 17:10), it has become slightly tainted. Perhaps the command latent[12] in it is resented as undemocratic. Or maybe its use in training dogs to retrieve has made some people feel that it is an undignified word to apply to human beings. But, whatever the reason, there is a growing uncertainty about its status, and hence it is the sort of word that conscientious people look up in a dictionary.

Will they find it labeled "good" or "bad"? Neither, of course, because either applied indiscriminately would be untrue. The Third International lists nineteen different meanings of the verb *to fetch.* Of these some are labeled "dialectal," some "chiefly dialectal," some "obsolete," one "chiefly Scottish," and two "not in formal use." The primary meaning—"to go after and bring back"—is not labeled and hence can be accepted as standard, accepted with the more assurance because the many shades of labeling show us that the word's status has been carefully considered.

On grammatical questions the Third International tries to be equally exact and thorough. Sometimes a construction is listed without comment, meaning that in the opinion of the editors it is unquestionably respectable. Some-

12 **latent** (lā'tənt): hidden.

times a construction carries the comment "used by speakers and writers on all educational levels though disapproved by some grammarians." Or the comment may be "used in substandard speech and formerly also by reputable writers." Or "less often in standard than in substandard speech." Or simply "dial."

And this very accurate reporting is based on evidence which is presented for our examination. One may feel that the evidence is inadequate or that the evaluation of it is erroneous. But surely, in the face of classification so much more elaborate and careful than any known heretofore, one cannot fly into a rage and insist that the dictionary is "out to destroy . . . every vestige of linguistic punctilio . . . every criterion for distinguishing between better usages and worse."

Words, as we have said, are continually shifting their meanings and connotations and hence their status. A word which has dignity, say, in the vocabulary of an older person may go down in other people's estimation. Like *fetch*. The older speaker is not likely to be aware of this and will probably be inclined to ascribe the snickers of the young at his speech to that degeneration of manners which every generation has deplored in its juniors. But a word which is coming up in the scale—like *jazz*, say, or, more recently, *crap*—will strike his ear at once. We are much more aware of offenses given us than of those we give. And if he turns to a dictionary and finds the offending word listed as standard—or even listed, apparently—his response is likely to be an outburst of indignation.

But the dictionary can neither snicker nor fulminate.[13] It records. It will offend many, no doubt, to find the expression *wise up*, meaning to inform or to become informed, listed in the Third International with no restricting label. To my aging ears it still sounds like slang. But the evidence—quotations from the *Kiplinger Washington Letter* and *The Wall Street Journal*—convinces me that it is I who am out of step, lagging behind. If such publications have taken to using *wise up* in serious contexts, with no punctuational indication of irregularity, then it is obviously respectable. And finding it so listed and supported, I can only say that it's nice to be informed and sigh to realize that I am becoming an old fogy. But, of course, I don't have to use it (and I'll be damned if I will! "Let them smile, as I do now, At the old forsaken bough Where I cling").

In part, the trouble is due to the fact that there is no standard for standard. Ideas of what is proper to use in serious, dignified speech and writing are changing—and with breathtaking rapidity. This is one of the major facts of contemporary American English. But it is no more the dictionary's business to oppose this process than to speed it up.

Even in our standard speech some words are more dignified and some more informal than others, and dictionaries have tried to guide us through these uncertainties by marking certain words and constructions as "colloquial," meaning "inappropriate in a formal situation." But this distinction, in the opinion of most scholars, has done more harm than good. It has created the notion that these particular words are inferior, when actually they might be the best possible words in an informal statement. And so—to the rage of many reviewers—the Third International has dropped this label. Not all labels, as angrily charged, but only this one out

---

13 **fulminate** (fŭl′mə nāt′): thunder; denounce.

of a score. And the doing so may have been an error, but it certainly didn't constitute "betrayal" or "abandoning of all distinctions." It was intended to end a certain confusion.

In all the finer shades of meaning, of which the status of a word is only one, the user is on his own, whether he likes it or not. Despite *Life's* artless assumption about the Gettysburg Address, nothing worth writing is written *from* a dictionary. The dictionary, rather, comes along afterwards and describes what *has been* written.

Words in themselves are not dignified, or silly, or wise, or malicious. But they can be used in dignified, silly, wise, or malicious ways by dignified, silly, wise, or malicious people. *Egghead,* for example, is a perfectly legitimate word, as legitimate as *highbrow* or *longhaired.* But there is something very wrong and very undignified, by civilized standards, in a belligerent dislike for intelligence and education. *Yak* is an amusing word for persistent chatter. Anyone could say, "We were just yakking over a cup of coffee," with no harm to his dignity. But to call a Supreme Court decision *yakking* is to be vulgarly insulting and so, undignified. Again, there's nothing wrong with *confab* when it's appropriate. But when the work of a great research project, employing hundreds of distinguished scholars over several decades and involving the honor of one of the greatest publishing houses in the world, is described as *confabbing* (as *The New York Times* editorially described the preparation of the Third International), the use of this particular word asserts that the lexicographers had merely sat around and talked idly. And the statement becomes undignified—if not, indeed, slanderous.

The lack of dignity in such statements is not in the words, nor in the diction-aries that list them, but in the hostility that deliberately seeks this tone of expression. And in expressing itself the hostility frequently shows that those who are expressing it don't know how to use a dictionary. Most of the reviewers seem unable to read the Third International and unwilling to read the Second.

The *American Bar Association Journal,* for instance, in a typical outburst ("a deplorable abdication of responsibility"), picked out for special scorn the inclusion in the Third International of the word *irregardless.* "As far as the new Webster's is concerned," said the *Journal,* this meaningless word "is just as legitimate as any other word in the dictionary." Thirty seconds spent in examining the book they were so roundly condemning would have shown them that in it *irregardless* is labeled "nonstand"—which means "nonstandard," which means "not conforming to the usage generally characteristic of educated native speakers of the language." Is that "just as legitimate as any other word in the dictionary"?

The most disturbing fact of all is that the editors of a dozen of the most influential publications in America today are under the impression that *authoritative* must mean *authoritarian.* Even the "permissive" Third International doesn't recognize this identification—editors' attitudes being not yet, fortunately, those of the American people. But the Fourth International may have to.

The new dictionary may have many faults. Nothing that tries to meet an ever-changing situation over a terrain as vast as contemporary English can hope to be free of them. And much in it is open to honest, and informed, disagreement. There can be linguistic objection to the eradication of proper names. The removal of guides to pronunciation from the foot of every page may not have been worth the valuable space it saved. The new method of defining words of many meanings has disadvantages as well as advantages. And of the half million or more definitions, hundreds, possibly thousands, may seem inadequate or imprecise. To some (of whom I am one) the omission of the label "colloquial" will seem meritorious; to others it will seem a loss.

But one thing is certain: anyone who solemnly announces in the year 1962 that he will be guided in matters of English usage by a dictionary published in 1934 is talking ignorant and pretentious nonsense.

Understanding the Essay

1. Contrast what Bergen Evans says that a dictionary is for with what Follett says that a dictionary is for.

2. What tone does Evans establish in his title? How does his language in the title establish this tone? Why would Evans's title, which is consistent with the body of his essay, be inappropriate for Follett's essay?

3. How did Evans have an advantage in his argument with Follett?

4. Evans labels Follett's article on the dictionary "abuse." Is the abuse deserved or not? After completing both essays, explain your judgment.

5. How does Evans make fun of *Life* magazine in the last sentence in the opening paragraph?

6. For what purpose does Evans refer to Bloomfield's scientific work on language?

7. At the beginning of Section II, Evans returns to the question posed in the title. Summarize his answer to the question. How does Evans's explanation of a dictionary's responsibility differ from Follett's?

8. Why does the author dwell on the definition of the word *door*?

9. How does Evans justify the dictionary's treatment of the word *finalize*? How would Follett probably feel about this word?

10. Evans says about the function of a dictionary: "It records." How does this two-word statement dramatize the difference between Evans and Follett?

11. How does Evans back up the statement that "Most of the reviewers seem unable to read the Third International and unwilling to read the Second"?

12. The controversy between the two camps has been said to be between those who think a dictionary should *prescribe* and those who think it should *describe*. Which camp is each of the two men in?

Building Vocabulary Skills

1. What is the literary allusion in the phrase "sound and fury" in the second paragraph? When you have looked up the context of this phrase in *Macbeth* (Act V, scene v), explain how the phrase becomes more meaningful as Evans uses it.
2. What generalization can you make in comparing the language of the two essays by Evans and Follett? (For one thing, you probably found more unfamiliar words in Follett's writing.)
3. Look up and report to the class on the meanings of the words *authoritative* and *authoritarian*. What does Evans mean when he writes: "The most disturbing fact of all is that the editors of a dozen of the most influential publications in America today are under the impression that *authoritative* must mean *authoritarian*"?
4. Why does Evans coin the word *folletizing*? Why does he think that Mr. Follett's "mental processes demand some special designation"? Look up the word *bowdlerize* and explain how the origin of the word is similar to that of *folletize*.

Developing Language Skills

1. Explain how Evans's use of "much-touted" and "much-clouted" makes for more effective expression.
2. *Analogy* is a technique frequently used in argument. It is a comparison between two things—such as situations, periods of time, or actions —and is used primarily for two purposes. First, by showing what was true in one instance, an arguer may seek to convince his audience that the same is true of the situation he is arguing about. Or, secondly, he may compare the situation under discussion to some similar one that is more familiar in order to make a point clearer. For example, the proverb "As the twig is bent, so the tree shall grow" is used as an analogy to the growth of a human being: it is used both to prove and to make clear a point. An analogy may be a false one: the likenesses between the things being compared may not justify the comparison. Whenever you come across an analogy that is being used to make a point, you should ask if the two things involved are logically comparable and if the conclusion drawn from the comparison is a sound one.

   What analogy does Evans use in Section I, paragraph 6? Is it a sound analogy? Is it backed up by factual information in the rest of the article?
3. Write an essay of several paragraphs in which you develop your own views on the superiorities and weaknesses of the two dictionaries discussed by Follett and Evans. If Webster's Second Edition and Third New International are available, use contrasting entries in them as specific illustrations for your points. If they are not available, use the contrasting entries from them which follow for your examples.

Listed below are several parallel entries from *Webster's New International Dictionary, Second Edition* and *Webster's Third New International Dictionary*. Some words listed may have other meanings than those given; however, the definition quoted is the complete one for the sense in which a word is being defined. Study of these definitions may help you to form your own opinion on the merits of each.

SECOND INTERNATIONAL

bomb (bŏm; 277; bŭm, *given by the older orthoepists, as Walker and Smart, is still used by some*), *n.* [F. *bombe*, fr. It. *bomba* bombshell, fr. L. *bombus* a noise, fr. Gr. *bombos* a deep hollow sound.] **1.** *Mil.* A projectile, containing a high-explosive charge, which is propelled at low velocities by a mortar or other thrower. Cf. SHELL.
2. Any similar missile or device; as, a dynamite *bomb*.
3. A small war vessel with bomb-throwing mortars.
4. A vessel, as a steel cylinder, for compressed gases.
5. The combustion chamber of a bomb calorimeter.
6. *Geol.* A mass of viscous lava projected by explosion from a volcano and rounded by passage through the air.
7. *Whaling.* An explosive head on a harpoon or lance.

get around. *Colloq.* **a** = *get about*, above. **b** To circumvent, as by persuasion; to evade; as, to *get around* a law.

high'–brow' (hī'brou'), *n.* One who has a high brow, or forehead; hence, one who is intellectual or learned; esp., one who assumes, or appears to assume, an attitude of intellectual superiority.

Highboy, c. 1700, with turned Legs and plain and scrolled Stretchers.

rabbit punch. *Boxing.* A short chopping blow delivered to the back of the neck or the base of the skull when the body of the adversary is bent forward.

than (thăn; 71), *conj.* [ME. *than, thon, then, thanne, thonne, thenne,* than, then, fr. AS. *thanne, thonne.*]
2. Short for: **a** *Obs. Rather than.* **b** *Archaic. Other, or otherwise, than.*
3. *Dial.* When; — used after *scarcely, hardly.*

tout (to͞ot), *v. t. & i.* To toot, or proclaim loudly.

THIRD INTERNATIONAL

¹**bomb** \'bäm; *sometimes esp South and chiefly archaic* 'bəm\ *n* -s [F *bombe*, fr. It *bomba*, prob. fr. L *bombus* deep hollow sound, fr. Gk *bombos*; of imit. origin like ON *bumba* drum, Lith *bambéti* to hum, buzz, Alb *bumbulii* it is thundering] **1 :** a projectile or other device carrying an explosive charge fused to detonate under certain conditions (as upon impact or through a timing contrivance) and that is hurled (as by a mortar), dropped (as from an aircraft), or merely set into position at a given point (as dynamite) with varying effects (as concussion, or fire-flinging, or the release of gases) depending upon the type used ⟨spangle ∼*s* for fireworks displays⟩; *also* **:** any container (as of propaganda leaflets or food) designed to be dropped from aircraft in the manner of an aerial bomb **2 :** a vessel (as a steel cylinder) for compressed gases: as **a :** a pressure vessel for conducting chemical experiments at high temperature and high pressure **b :** a small manually operated dispenser that releases a substance stored under pressure (as an insecticide, a fire-extinguishing liquid, or paint) in the form of a vapor, spray, or gas **3 :** the combustion chamber of a bomb calorimeter **4 :** a mass of lava exploded from a volcanic vent and shaped while viscous by passage through the air into a rounded form ranging from a few inches to many feet in diameter **5 :** an explosive head on a harpoon **6 :** BOMBE **7 :** a lead-lined container for radioactive material used esp. in the radiation treatment of cancer ⟨a cobalt ∼⟩ **8 :** BOMB-SHELL 2

get around **1 :** to get the better of **:** CIRCUMVENT ⟨a small group of aggressive citizens has managed to *get around*.. the largest, richest, most powerful international combine in the history of the world —Fred Smith⟩ **2 :** to escape the force of **:** EVADE ⟨there is no *getting around* it: meaning implies convention —J.M.Barzun⟩

¹**highbrow** \'∗,∗\ *n* [¹*high* + *brow*] **:** a person who possesses or has pretensions to strong intellectual interests or superiority **:** one who regards aloofly or contemptuously manifestations of mass culture **:** EGGHEAD ⟨∼*s* . . . despise soap operas and are repelled by the success stories in popular magazines —W. O.Aydelotte⟩ ⟨∼*s* who believe that . . . art is for art's sake —A.J.Toynbee⟩

¹**rabbit punch** *n* [fr. the manner in which a rabbit is stunned prior to being killed and butchered] **:** a short chopping blow delivered to the back of the neck or the base of the skull with the edge of the hand opposite the thumb that is illegal in boxing
²**rabbit punch** *vt* **:** to strike with a rabbit punch

than \thən, then, (;)than, *rapid* **2 :** rather than — usu used only after *prefer, preferable,* and *preferably,* and sometimes considered substandard even there ⟨I preferred to be cal'ed a coward ∼ fight —John Reed⟩ **3 :** other than ⟨we have no alternative ∼ to follow the sense of our own experience —K.L. Patton⟩ **4 :** WHEN ⟨had barely left the lift at the bottom ∼ the lift bell started to ring —David Masters⟩ — used esp. after *scarcely* and *hardly* ⟨hardly had the birds dropped ∼ she jumped into the water and retrieved them —G.G.Carter⟩

tout \'taut *also* 'tüt, *usu* -d-+V\ *vt* -ED/-ING/-s [alter. (perh. influenced by ¹*tout*) of ³*toot*] **:** to proclaim loudly **:** overly publicize **:** BALLYHOO ⟨∼*ed* as the world's most elaborate suburban shopping development —*Wall Street Jour.*⟩ ⟨work is ∼*ed* as the basic virtue —H.H.Mansfield⟩

ESSAY

Introduction to Biography

EVEN THOUGH the biography section is part of the larger essay unit, it has a personality of its own. With the exception of Marchette Chute's essay, which is concerned with the many difficulties the biographer encounters in "getting at the truth," all of the biographies pay tribute to a person or an event. In a way, Miss Chute also pays tribute as she reports the obstacles faced by honest biographers as they attempt to report the truth.

Jesse Stuart, looking back at his childhood, calls upon the unspoiled, proud memories of a young boy as he pays tribute to his father. John Dos Passos uses the lives of the Wright brothers to dramatize a historical event that changed the lives of all of us.

Edward Weeks pays double tribute, to a writer who is a fiery woman of great courage and to a literary magazine that has been and is unusually helpful to new authors. Weeks uses excerpts from letters and books to create a memorable picture of a rewarding partnership. Gilbert Highet, through selection and arrangement of material, pays tribute to a famous American by dramatizing the events surrounding several significant Christmas seasons in his subject's life. John Galsworthy's "Reminiscences of Conrad" combines literary evaluation with personal memories to relate its story of the thirty-one-year friendship between two literary giants.

All of these biographers are professional writers and, with the exception of Dos Passos and Highet, also had a personal relationship to their subjects that gives their writing authority. Dos Passos and Highet treat their subjects with the imagination of the literary artist, developing the characters they see behind the historical facts. Each biographical essay, as Marchette Chute writes in the following essay, is an attempt to get at the truth—the truth about another's life or one's own past.

Reading "Getting at the Truth"

"Getting at the Truth" is an essay that convincingly supports its general statements through the use of examples. Miss Chute's transitional words and phrases (the repetition of a key word or a statement such as "Here is a small example") provide an orderly framework for developing the general idea of her opening paragraph. She makes few points, but she makes them clearly and gives each point generous support. She uses the "self-willed flamingo" in *Alice in Wonderland* as an image for the various facts that face the biographer and force him to investigate further before fitting them into a book.

Getting at
the Truth

Marchette Chute

Marchette Chute's convincing examples of the many not-quite-truthful ways facts can be used may make you hesitate the next time you find yourself telling a personal experience or reporting an argument with a friend.

THIS IS A rather presumptuous title for a biographer to use, since truth is a very large word. In the sense that it means the reality about a human being it is probably impossible for a biographer to achieve. In the sense that it means a reasonable presentation of all the available facts it is more nearly possible, but even this limited goal is harder to reach than it appears to be. A biographer needs to be both humble and cautious when he remembers the nature of the material he is working with, for a historical fact is rather like the flamingo that Alice in Wonderland tried to use as a croquet mallet. As soon as she got its neck nicely straightened out and was ready to hit the ball, it would turn and look at her with a puzzled expression, and any biographer knows that what is called a "fact" has a way of doing the same.

Here is a small example. When I was writing my forthcoming biography,

"Ben Jonson[1] of Westminster," I wanted to give a paragraph or two to Sir Philip Sidney,[2] who had a great influence on Jonson. No one thinks of Sidney without thinking of chivalry, and to underline the point I intended to use a story that Sir Fulke Greville told of him. Sidney died of gangrene, from a musket shot that shattered his thigh, and Greville says that Sidney failed to put on his leg armor while preparing for battle because the marshal of the camp was not wearing leg armor and Sidney was unwilling to do anything that would give him a special advantage.

The story is so characteristic both of Sidney himself and of the misplaced high-mindedness of late Renaissance chivalry that I wanted to use it, and since Sir Fulke Greville was one of Sidney's closest friends the information seemed to be reliable enough. But it is always well to check each piece of information as thoroughly as possible and so I consulted another account of Sidney written by a contemporary, this time a doctor who knew the family fairly well. The doctor, Thomas Moffet, mentioned the episode but he said that Sidney left off his leg armor because he was in a hurry.

The information was beginning to twist in my hand and could no longer be trusted. So I consulted still another contemporary who had mentioned the episode, to see which of the two he agreed with. This was Sir John Smythe, a military expert who brought out his book a few years after Sidney's death. Sir John was an old-fashioned conservative who advocated the use of heavy armor even on horseback, and he deplored the current craze for leaving off

1 **Ben Jonson:** English dramatist, (1573?-1637).
2 **Sir Philip Sidney:** English statesman and author, (1554-1586).

378

leg protection, "the imitating of which . . . cost that noble and worthy gentleman Sir Philip Sidney his life."

So here I was with three entirely different reasons why Sidney left off his leg armor, all advanced by careful writers who were contemporaries of his. The flamingo had a legitimate reason for looking around with a puzzled expression.

The only thing to do in a case like this is to examine the point of view of the three men who are supplying the conflicting evidence. Sir Fulke Greville was trying to prove a thesis: that his beloved friend had an extremely chivalric nature. Sir John Smythe also was trying to prove a thesis: that the advocates of light arming followed a theory that could lead to disaster. Only the doctor, Thomas Moffet, was not trying to prove a thesis. He was not using his own explanation to reinforce some point he wanted to make. He did not want anything except to set down on paper what he believed to be the facts; and since we do not have Sidney's own explanation of why he did not put on leg armor, the chances are that Dr. Moffet is the safest man to trust.

For Moffet was without desire. Nothing can so quickly blur and distort the facts as desire—the wish to use the facts for some purpose of your own—and nothing can so surely destroy the truth. As soon as the witness wants to prove something he is no longer impartial and his evidence is no longer to be trusted.

The only safe way to study contemporary testimony is to bear constantly in mind this possibility of prejudice and to put almost as much attention on the writer himself as on what he has written. For instance, Sir Anthony Weldon's description of the Court of King James is lively enough and often used as source material; but a note from the publisher admits that the pamphlet was issued as a warning to anyone who wished to "side with this bloody house" of Stuart. The publisher, at any rate, did not consider Weldon an impartial witness. At about the same time Arthur Wilson published his history of Great Britain, which contained an irresistibly vivid account of the agonized death of the Countess of Somerset. Wilson sounds reasonably impartial; but his patron[3] was the Earl of Essex, who had good reason to hate that particular countess, and there is evidence that he invented the whole scene to gratify his patron.

Sometimes a writer will contradict what he has already written, and in that case the only thing to do is to investigate what has changed his point of view. For instance, in 1608 Captain John Smith issued a description of his capture by Powhatan, and he made it clear that the Indian chief had treated him with unwavering courtesy and hospitality. In 1624 the story was repeated in Smith's "General History of Virginia," but the writer's circumstances had changed. Smith needed money, "having a prince's mind imprisoned in a poor man's purse," and he wanted the book to be profitable. Powhatan's daughter, the princess Pocahontas, had recently been in the news, for her visit to England had aroused a great deal of interest among the sort of people that Smith hoped would buy his book. So Smith supplied a new version of the story, in which the once-hospitable Powhatan would have permitted the hero's brains to be dashed out if Pocahontas had not saved his life. It was the second story that achieved fame, and of course it may have been true. But it is impossible to trust it because the desire of the writer

3 **patron:** one who supports or aids an artist. (The nobility frequently acted as patrons of the arts in the past.)

is so obviously involved; as Smith said in his prospectus,[4] he needed money and hoped that the book would give "satisfaction."

It might seem that there was an easy way for a biographer to avoid the use of this kind of prejudiced testimony. All he has to do is to construct his biography from evidence that cannot be tampered with—from parish records, legal documents, bills, accounts, court records, and so on. Out of these solid gray blocks of impersonal evidence it should surely be possible to construct a road that will lead straight to the truth and that will never bend itself to the misleading curve of personal desire.

This might be so if the only problem involved were the reliability of the material. But there is another kind of desire that is much more subtle, much more pervasive, and much more dangerous than the occasional distortions of fact that contemporary writers may have permitted themselves to make; and this kind of desire can destroy the truth of a biography even if every individual fact in it is as solid and as uncompromising as rock. Even if the road is built of the best and most reliable materials it can still curve away from the truth because of this other desire that threatens it: the desire of the biographer himself.

A biographer is not a court record or a legal document. He is a human being, writing about another human being, and his own temperament, his own point of view, and his own frame of reference are unconsciously imposed upon the man he is writing about. Even if the biographer is free from Captain Smith's temptation—the need for making money—and wants to write nothing but the literal truth, he is still handi-capped by the fact that there is no such thing as a completely objective human being.

An illustration of what can happen if the point of view is sufficiently strong is the curious conclusion that the 19th-century biographers reached about William Shakespeare. Shakespeare joined a company of London actors in 1594, was listed as an actor in 1598 and 1603, and was still listed as one of the "men actors" in the company in 1609. Shortly before he joined this company Shakespeare dedicated two narrative poems to the Earl of Southampton, and several years after Shakespeare died his collected plays were dedicated to the Earl of Pembroke. This was his only relationship with either of the two noblemen, and there is nothing to connect him with them during the fifteen years in which he belonged to the same acting company and during which he wrote nearly all his plays.

But here the desire of the biographers entered in. They had been reared in the strict code of 19th-century gentility[5] and they accepted two ideas without question. One was that there are few things more important than an English lord; the other was that there are few things less important than a mere actor. They already knew the undeniable fact that Shakespeare was one of the greatest men who ever lived; and while they could not go quite so far as to claim him as an actual member of the nobility, it was clear to them that he must have been the treasured friend of both the Earl of Southampton and the Earl of Pembroke and that he must have written his plays either while basking in their exalted company or while he was roaming the green countryside by the

---

4 **prospectus:** preliminary statement describing a forthcoming book.

5 **gentility:** refinement.

waters of the river Avon. (It is another basic conviction of the English gentleman that there is nothing so inspiring as nature.) The notion that Shakespeare had spent all these years as the working member of a company of London actors was so abhorrent that it was never seriously considered. It could not be so; therefore it was not.

These biographers did their work well. When New South Wales built its beautiful memorial library to Shakespeare, it was the coat of arms of the Earl of Southampton that alternated with that of royalty in dignified splendor over the bookshelves. Shakespeare had been re-created in the image of desire, and desire will always ignore whatever is not relevant to its purpose. Because the English gentlemen did not like Shakespeare's background it was explained away as though it had never existed, and Shakespeare ceased to be an actor because so lowly a trade was not suited to so great a man.

All this is not to say that a biography should be lacking in a point of view. If it does not have a point of view it will be nothing more than a kind of expanded article for an encyclopedia—a string of facts arranged in chronological order with no claim to being a real biography at all. A biography must have a point of view and it must have a frame of reference. But it should be a point of view and a frame of reference implicit in[6] the material itself and not imposed upon it.

It might seem that the ideal biographical system, if it could be achieved, would be to go through the years of research without feeling any kind of emotion. The biographer would be a kind of fact-finding machine and then suddenly, after his years of research, a kind of total vision would fall upon him and he would transcribe it in his best and most persuasive English for a waiting public. But research is fortunately not done by machinery, nor are visions likely to descend in that helpful manner. They are the product not only of many facts but also of much thinking, and it is only when the biographer begins to get emotional in his thinking that he ought to beware.

It is easy enough to make good resolutions in advance, but a biographer cannot altogether control his sense of excitement when the climax of his years of research draws near and he begins to see the pieces fall into place. Almost without his volition, A, B, and D fit together and start to form a pattern, and it is almost impossible for the biographer not to start searching for C. Something turns up that looks remarkably like C, and with a little trimming of the edges and the ignoring of one very slight discrepancy it will fill the place allotted for C magnificently.

It is at this point that the biographer ought to take a deep breath and sit on his hands until he has had time to calm down. He has no real, fundamental reason to believe that his discovery is C, except for the fact that he wants it to be. He is like a man looking for a missing piece in a difficult jigsaw puzzle, who has found one so nearly the right shape that he cannot resist the desire to jam it into place.

If the biographer had refused to be tempted by his supposed discovery of C and had gone on with his research, he might have found not only the connecting, illuminating fact he needed but much more besides. He is not going to look for it now. Desire has blocked the way. And by so much his biography will fall short of what might have been the truth.

6 implicit (ĭm plĭs′ĭt) in: involved in the nature of.

It would not be accurate to say that a biographer should be wholly lacking in desire. Curiosity is a form of desire. So is the final wish to get the material down on paper in a form that will be fair to the reader's interest and worthy of the subject. But a subconscious desire to push the facts around is one of the most dangerous things a biographer can encounter, and all the more dangerous because it is so difficult to know when he is encountering it.

The reason Alice had so much trouble with her flamingo is that the average flamingo does not wish to be used as a croquet mallet. It has other purposes in view. The same thing is true of a fact, which can be just as self-willed as a flamingo and has its own kind of stubborn integrity. To try to force a series of facts into a previously desired arrangement is a form of misuse to which no self-respecting fact will willingly submit itself. The best and only way to treat it is to leave it alone and be willing to follow where it leads, rather than to press your own wishes upon it.

To put the whole thing into a single sentence: you will never succeed in getting at the truth if you think you know, ahead of time, what the truth ought to be.

Understanding the Essay

1. What sentence in the opening paragraph is a summary of the essay?
2. In order to prove her main point, Marchette Chute offers three contradictory theories on Sidney's death. Why did she decide to choose one theory?
3. As the essay goes on, what distinction is being made between fact and prejudice? What is meant here by source material?
4. How does Marchette Chute prove that "the desire of the biographer himself" may also distort truth?
5. What is meant by the statement that a biography should have "a point of view and a frame of reference implicit in the material itself and not imposed upon it"?
6. How are the temptations of a biographer like those of a man doing a jigsaw puzzle?
7. Has the author demonstrated that a historical fact is like Alice's flamingo? State the reasons for your answer.

Developing Language Skills

Write a paragraph illustrating the truth of the last sentence of the essay. Begin your paragraph with the sentence: "You will never succeed in getting at the truth if you think you know, ahead of time, what the truth ought to be." Then go on to prove this statement with two examples taken from the essay.

BIOGRAPHY

Jesse Stuart has a knack of revealing the character and background of his relatives and neighbors through the language of the Kentucky hills. Using dialogue, he reveals their sense of justice and their respect for the rights of the individual. Drawing on his childhood memories, Stuart reconstructs his father's conversations with his family and neighbors, creating a memorable picture of Mick Stuart.

God's Oddling [1]

Jesse Stuart

This story concerns Mick Stuart's fight to save the first home the family had ever owned. Jesse Stuart says of God's Oddling, *the book about his father from which this selection was taken, "This is the one book I have wanted most to write all my life."*

WE MOVED from farm to farm always hoping we could get enough ahead so we could buy a farm of our own. But in those early years when I was a boy, we couldn't earn enough above the family's need to think about buying a piece of land. When we found seedling apple-tree sprouts along the road, seedling peach-tree sprouts or plum sprouts, we would dig them up, carry them to our rented land and set them out. When we got ready to move to another farm, we'd dig up our seedling fruit trees and take them with us. We'd set them out again on the land we had rented. Soon our trees were getting too big to dig up and take along.

"We ought to buy land, Mick," Mom said. "If we don't, look what we are going to lose. It will be like it was once before. We'll have to move away and leave a lot of our trees or buy a new wagon to haul them on. What we would pay for a new wagon would make a payment on a piece of land—one big enough to hold our dead and give us space to set our trees. If we could find a piece of land without a house on it, we could buy it cheaper. We can build a house. We can cut logs for the walls, rive[2] boards for the roof, and pick up stones for the chimney."

"There's only one more place in this Hollow," Pa said. "It's 50 acres without a house on it. It is a place nobody will have. I can buy it for six dollars an acre, for the heirs are wanting to sell it to keep from paying taxes on it. There's not a fence on it, there's not a building on it, and not an acre of ground cleared. There's not a fruit tree nor a graveyard on it. It has good timber, plenty of rocks, and little runlets of cool water. But $300 is a lot of money to pay for it."

"But we can buy it," Mom said. "We can sell two cows and make the first payment. If we don't, we're going to lose our trees."

"You are right," Pa said.

1 **Oddling:** a person who stands out as different from those about him.

2 **rive:** split.

"And I study[3] about the two boys we have buried on Pap's farm," Mom said. "They are all right there so long as he owns the land. But he may not always own it. When he loses it, I'll worry a lot."

"This is the farm that suits my pocket-book," Pa said, after we had gone over every acre of it. "It has plenty of good water. It has everything I want. Just one thing wrong. Do you know what it is?"

"Not a building on it," I said. "This farm is a wilderness of trees."

Pa stood wiping his red face with a blue bandanna and holding on to his mattock handle. I was carrying the long-handle shovel across my shoulder. We had been over the old Jack Sinnett farm where he had dug holes three feet deep, feeling and sifting the dirt through his fingers, smelling and observing it closely. I had shoveled the dirt back in the holes he had dug on the hilltops, the little ridges, and down in the valleys. We had tested each of the fifty acres on this hilly farm.

"We can conquer the wilderness all right," he said. "We can build a house on it. But this is not what's wrong. There's not a wagon road leading to this farm."

"How did the Sinnetts get out when they lived here?" I asked.

"There's the old road, see," he said, pointing to a winding scar of yellow earth up a rugged slope with tall timber on either side. "That used to be a county road. That was fifty years ago. That's not even a footpath now. And it's been fenced in."

"Then you won't buy this farm?" I said.

"Yes, I'll buy it," he replied quickly. "Any place I can buy has to have a fault so it will sell cheap. That's the only reason I'll be able to buy this one. We'll buy it and do something about a road later."

That afternoon Pa contracted the land. He came home smoking a cigar instead of chewing home-grown Burley tobacco. He walked proudly. We knew that he had bought the land and that he had made the first payment with the two cows. But we had two cows left and we would soon have two more, for we never sold a heifer calf. We held on to them like we held trees.

In March, 1920, we moved to Uncle Martin Hilton's farm. It joined our 50 acres. Uncle Frank Sparks moved us up W-Hollow.[4] The road was so rough the wagonload of plunder[5] nearly turned over. Once we had to put poles under the wagon. The mules got down on their knees and pulled.

"Frank, just as soon as I make another payment on this place," my father said, "I'm going to build a house. I'm not going to live on Martin's place any longer than I can get me a house built of my own. And I'm going to build it right here."

The jolt wagon rolled over the place where he said he was going to build. We crossed through the sand gap and moved around the side of the hill until we reached a log house surrounded by plum and beech, unloaded our furniture and set up the cookstove. Mom cooked a meal for us. We were hungry and tired.

"The first thing to build on our farm is a barn," Pa said. "I've always liked good barns. They come before good houses, to my way of seeing. We need the cows on our own land so we can

---

3 **study**: worry; think.

4 **W-Hollow**: a valley in Greenup County, Kentucky, where Jesse Stuart lives today.
5 **plunder**: family possessions.

get their droppings to enrich the land. A lot of our land is awful poor. It's sassafras, pine, and sawbrier land. And God knows that's the poorest land in the world."

"I'll tell you what I'll do, Mitch, since I know you want a barn," Uncle Martin Hilton said. "I'll give you the Calihan house for a barn if you'll move it across the hill. People are all the time wanting to rent it; I don't have enough land for myself."

We tore the house down. Then we had an old-fashioned neighborhood "barn-raising," invited the men in from the farms near us, threw up the logs in a single day and put the rafters on the barn.

"We have a place for the cows and the horse; now we must build a house for ourselves," Pa said one night at the supper table. "A barn is the foundation of a farm."

When we cleared an acre of land where our barn stood, the sawbriers were so thick we had to cut them with a scythe from around the scrubby oaks and pines before we could get close to the trees to chop them down. We crated the chickens and hauled them to the new barn. We turned them loose to live. "They'll have to scratch for a livin' this spring," Mom lamented. "Next spring we'll have corn to feed them."

There was a hollow north of the place where we planned to build our house. The treetops where the big timber had been cut were so thick one could step from top to top and never have to set his foot on the ground. Sawbriers, black-locust sprouts, and wild grapevines grew among these. It was a wilderness a man had to fight his way through, and often get down and crawl before he could go from one end of the

hollow to another. We raked the leaves from the ridge road that surrounded the hollow in the shape of a horseshoe. The leaves were dry. We set fire at the ring's edge around the top of the hill and fired from the bottom. The two rings of fire met. The land was loamy, clean and soft. We did not plow it. We just double-furrowed it and planted it. We put beans in the hills of corn and planted pumpkins by the rotted stumps.

We cleared a garden first, then truck patches, then we cleared ground for corn and tobacco. We carried leaves from under the trees in the wooded section to our fields and turned the leaves under for fertilizer. When a ditch started in one of our fields, we knew it would get deeper and many ditches would start. My father never heard of the word *erosion* but he knew what erosion was. His was one of the best ways to stop it, too. He filled the ditch with brush, turned the tips uphill and the branches caught the wash that came down the ditch. If the brush was slow to work, which it seldom was, he filled the ditch with fodder. And this was sure to stop it. Very seldom did we use rock, for the water washed around the rocks and over them.

My father made our fifty acres one of the prettiest little farms in our county. He never hurt his land, for he cared for it like it was a living thing. He was careful never to "overcrop" any field. He farmed our hills three years and then he sowed the land in grass. He planted our corn in the dark of the moon[6] so it would not grow tall and would ear well. He planted our potatoes in the light of the moon so they would grow near the top of the ground and be easy to dig. He planted our

6 **dark of the moon:** moonless period of a month.

beans when the signs were in the arms so they would grow long. The moon and the almanac told him when to plant and when to reap. Maybe it was foolish, but he raised good crops on thin earth. We had to make "every edge of the ax cut that would" so we could live. We did live and we bought the land about us. We got three-thirds of our crops instead of two-thirds, since we owned our land. And we could farm as we pleased. Our hearts were in our land. Parts of our hearts were buried in the land that we had rented.

"We have the crop planted, son," Pa said. "Now you, Sophia, and Sal will have to raise it. I must hunt work and make payments on the land." I was introduced to a big horse and cutter-plow in "new ground." Often the handles of the plow jolted my ribs when the plow point struck a stump burned off under the ground. But I plowed the corn, and Sophia and Mom hoed it and cut the weeds. Heavy rains fell. Our corn shot up from the fresh loam like bullets from a gun.

Then Pa got a job on the Chesapeake & Ohio railroad section. It was the best job he ever had. He owned land now, and he was going to work on the railroad section to pay for it. This was in 1921, and I was fourteen years old. My grandfather, Nathan Hilton, had come to live with us, and he was seventy-five years of age. He had cut timber and farmed most of his life. Grandpa and I planned to build the house while Pa worked on the section to pay for the land no one else dared to buy because it didn't have a road.

"We can pay for the land, build a house, and make a road," Pa said one evening at the supper table, after he had walked five miles across the mountain from the railroad section where he had worked ten hours for $2.84 a day.

"All we've got to do is stick together and work."

In the spring of 1921, Grandpa and I started building our house. We cut oaks on this farm and scored and hewed them into logs to build the walls. Then we sawed down straight, unblemished oaks that we split into bolts and rove into clapboard shingles to make a roof.

In September we had a "house-raising" and invited all the neighbors. The men came to help start the building of the house and their wives came to help Mom cook. I remember twenty-nine men came. I remember the big table filled with good food the women set for us. I remember how they waited on the table and how we ate.

But Grandfather Hilton and I (with the aid of a carpenter to build the foundation, put in the windows, and hang the doors) actually built the house. It took us from July until December. I remember the sweat and curses that went into that house better than anybody else unless it is Grandpa. He was seventy-six then and I was fifteen. He would get mad and throw his tools over the hill and I would have to go and get them. The hard thing for us was to make two stone masons out of two supposed-to-be-carpenters. Grandpa changed the plans of the house to suit himself. He said if he was to build it he had the right to make it the way he pleased. He wanted to build a chimney in the center of the house.

"I've just been thinkin' about blastin' that big rock out there where you used to lay on your back and shoot squirrels," Grandpa said while we worked on the house. "I can get enough rock out'n that big rock to build a chimney to this house."

Grandpa meant a place where men had quarried sandstone for chimneys.

We went to this sandstone, drilled a hole in it, and dynamited. We picked down the stones and smoothed them off with dull axes. Then we hauled these quarried stones into the floorless house. We used a block and tackle to lift them up on the chimney. Sometimes four strands of new rope would snap like shoestrings and the stone would fall. We would get new rope and do it over again. Two of us erected the chimney. It was work, too. Though the house was unfinished we moved into it in November. We were glad to leave the place where we had been living. Just before we made this last move my mother gave birth to her seventh child, a girl, Glennis Juanita.

Grandpa was a 220-pound, broad-shouldered man, powerful with a double-bitted ax, sledge hammer, a maul and a crosscut saw. He nearly worked me to death building this six-room house. We were granted permission by one of our neighbors to drive our mule team across his land to haul our house plunder to our new home. But we were granted permission to haul over his land just one time, that was to move in. We couldn't move out again.

Mom was able to move after the birth of her last child. And we were all anxious to move. We loaded the old spring wagon for the last time. Uncle Frank Sparks helped us again. "It's the seventh time I've moved you in the last fourteen years," he said. "You've lived in purt' nigh every house on this creek and you ain't got beyond the bounds of these hills yet."

"Frank, you won't move me again until I'm dead and in my coffin," Pa said. "I'm on this farm to stay. It is my own land. It is a wilderness but it is mine. I've got a good barn and I've got a good family to work. I'll have a fine farm here some day."

We moved to where we live today, a

place back in the hills. We began to work on land of our own. There was a great difference, too. My father would say: "I've spent my strength on other men's land. Now I am old and I've got land of my own." We cleared the thickets. We farmed them two years. Then we sowed them in grass. We set fruit trees on the south hill slope. We set strawberries in new land. We put improvements on the place that was a wilderness before we moved there.

Home at last. And it was good to have a home. It was a place where wind blew off the pine-tree tops and passed over our house. We smelled pine fragrance in the winter wind there. It was a lonely place. It was desolate. But it was home. And it was good to have a home on a little piece of land where one could bury his own dead. It was good to hear the chickens cackle and see the wrens coming back each year to build in the smokehouse. It was good to hear the martins building in a box in early spring. And best of all it was good to see the hollyhocks blooming in the front yard.

We had just moved onto our farm when Jake Timmins walked down the path to the barn where Pa and I were nailing planks on a barn stall. Pa stood with a nail in one hand and his hatchet in the other while I stood holding the plank. We watched this small man with a beardy face walk toward us. He took short steps and jabbed his sharpened sourwood cane into the ground as he hurried down the path.

"Wonder what he's after?" Pa asked as Jake Timmins came near the barn.

"Don't know," I said.

"Howdy, Mick," Jake said as he leaned on his cane and looked over the new barn that we had built.

"Howdy, Jake," Pa grunted. We had heard how Jake Timmins had taken men's farms. Pa was nervous when he spoke, for I watched the hatchet shake in his hand.

"I see you're still a-putting improvements on yer barn," Jake said.

"A-tryin' to get it fixed for winter," Pa told him.

"I'd advise ye to stop now, Mick," he said. "Jist want to be fair with ye so ye won't go ahead and do a lot of work fer me fer nothing."

"How's that, Jake?" Pa asked.

"Ye've built yer barn on my land, Mick," he said with a little laugh.

"Ain't you a-joking, Jake?" Pa asked him.

"Nope, this is my land by rights," he told Pa as he looked our new barn over. "I hate to take this land with this fine barn on it, but it's mine and I'll haf to take it."

"I'm afraid not, Jake," Pa said. "I've been around here since I was a boy. I know where the lines run. I know that ledge of rocks with that row of oak trees a-growing on it is the line!"

"No it hain't, Mick," Jake said. "If it goes to court, ye'll find out. The line runs from that big dead chestnut up there on the knoll, straight across this holler to the top of the knoll up there where the twin hickories grow."

"But that takes my barn, my meadow, my garden," Pa said. "That takes ten acres of the best land I have. It almost gets my house!"

The hatchet quivered in Pa's hand and his lips trembled when he spoke.

"Tim Mennix sold ye land that belonged to me," Jake said.

"But you ought to a-said something about it before I built my house and barn on it," Pa told Jake fast as the words would leave his mouth.

"Sorry, Mick," Jake said, "but I must

be a-going. I've given ye fair warning that ye air a-building on my land!"

"But I bought this land," Pa told him. "I'm a-goin' to keep it."

"I can't hep that," Jake told Pa as he turned to walk away. "Don't tear this barn down fer it's on my property!"

"Don't worry, Jake," Pa said. "I'm not a-tearing this barn down. I'll be a-feeding my cattle in it this winter!"

Jake Timmins walked slowly up the path the way he had come. Pa and I stood watching him as he stopped and looked our barn over; then he looked at our garden that we had fenced and he looked at the new house that we had built.

"I guess he'll be a-claiming the house too," Pa said.

And just as soon as Jake Timmins crossed the ledge of rocks that separated our farms Pa threw his hatchet to the ground and hurried from the barn.

"Where are you a-going, Pa?" I asked.

"To see Tim Mennix."

"Can I go too?"

"Come along," he said.

We hurried over the mountain path toward Tim Mennix's shack. He lived two miles from us. Pa's brogan shoes rustled the fallen leaves that covered the path. October wind moaned among the leafless treetops. Soon as we reached the shack we found Tim cutting wood near his woodshed.

"What's the hurry, Mick?" Tim asked Pa who stood wiping sweat from his face with his blue bandanna.

"Jake Timmins is a-tryin' to take my land," Pa told Tim.

"Ye don't mean it?"

"I do mean it," Pa said. "He's just been to see me and he said the land where my barn, garden, and meadow were belonged to him. Claims about ten acres of the best land I got. I told

him I bought it from you and he said it didn't belong to you to sell."

"That ledge of rocks and the big oak trees that grow along the backbone of the ledge has been the line fer seventy years," Tim said. "But lissen, Mick, when Jake Timmins wants a piece of land, he takes it."

"People told me he's like that," Pa said. "I was warned against buying my farm because he's like that. People said he'd steal all my land if I lived beside him ten years."

"He'll have it before then, Mick," Tim Mennix told Pa in a trembling voice. "He didn't have but an acre to start from. That acre was a bluff where three farms jined and no one fenced it in because it was worthless and they didn't want it. He had a deed made fer this acre and he's had forty lawsuits when he set his fences over on other people's farms and took their land, but he goes to court and wins every time."

"I'll have the County Surveyor, Finn Madden, to survey my lines," Pa said.

"That won't hep any," Tim told Pa. "There's been more people kilt over the line fences that he's surveyed than has been kilt over any other one thing in this county. Surveyor Finn Madden's a good friend to Jake."

"But he's the County Surveyor," Pa said. "I'll haf to have him."

"Jake Timmins is a dangerous man," Tim Mennix warned Pa. "He's dangerous as a loaded double-barrel shotgun with both hammers cocked."

"I've heard that," Pa said. "I don't want any trouble. I'm a married man with a family."

When we reached home, we saw Jake upon the knoll at the big chestnut tree sighting across the hollow to the twin hickories on the knoll above our house. And as he sighted across the hollow, he walked along and drove stakes into the ground. He set one stake in our front yard, about five feet from the corner of our house. Pa started out on him once but Mom wouldn't let him go. Mom said let the law settle the dispute over the land.

And that night Pa couldn't go to sleep. I was awake and heard him a-walking the floor. I knew that Pa was worried, for Jake was the most feared man among our hills. He had started with one acre and now had over four hundred acres that he had taken from other people.

Next day Surveyor Finn Madden and Jake ran a line across the hollow just about on the same line that Jake had surveyed with his own eyes. And while Surveyor Finn Madden looked through the instrument, he had Jake set the stakes and drive them into the ground with a poleax. They worked at the line all day. And when they had finished surveying the line, Pa went up on the knoll at the twin hickories behind our house and asked Surveyor Finn Madden if his line was right.

"Surveyed it right with the deed," he told Pa. "Tim Mennix sold you land that didn't belong to him."

"Looks like this line would've been surveyed before I built my barn," Pa said.

"Can't see why it wasn't," he told Pa. "Looks like you're a-losing the best part of your farm, Mick."

Then Surveyor Finn Madden, a tall man with a white beard, and Jake Timmins went down the hill together.

"I'm not so sure that I'm a-losing the best part of my farm," Pa said. "I'm not a-goin' to sit down and take it! I know Jake's a land thief and it's time his stealing land is stopped."

"What are you a-goin' to do, Pa?" I asked.

"Don't know," he said.

"You're not a-goin' to hurt Jake over the land, are you?"

He didn't say anything but he looked at the two men as they turned over the ledge of rocks and out of sight.

"You know Mom said the land wasn't worth hurting anybody over," I said.

"But it's my land," Pa said.

That night Pa walked the floor, and Mom got out of bed and talked to him and made him go to bed. The next day Sheriff Eif Whiteapple served a notice on Pa to keep his cattle out of the barn that we had built. The notice said that the barn belonged to Jake Timmins. Jake ordered us to put our chickens up, to keep them off his garden when it was our garden. He told us not to let anything trespass on his land and his land was on the other side of the stakes. We couldn't even walk in part of our yard.

"He'll have the house next if we don't do something about it," Pa said.

Pa walked around our house in a deep study. He was trying to think of something to do about it. Mom talked to him. She told him to get a lawyer and fight the case in court. But Pa said something had to be done to prove that the land belonged to us, though we had a deed for our land in our trunk. And before Sunday came, Pa dressed in his best clothes.

"Where're you a-going, Mick?" Mom asked.

"A-goin' to see Uncle Mel," he said. "He's been in a lot of line-fence fights and he could give me some good advice!"

"We hate to stay here and you gone, Mick," Mom said.

"Just don't step on property Jake laid claim to until I get back," Pa said. "I'll be back soon as I can. Some time next week you can look for me."

Pa went to West Virginia to get

Uncle Mel. And while he was gone, Jake Timmins hauled wagonloads of hay and corn to the barn that we had built. He had taken over as if it were his own and as if he would always have it. We didn't step beyond the stakes where Surveyor Finn Madden had surveyed. We waited for Pa to come. And when Pa came, Uncle Mel came with him carrying a long-handled double-bitted ax and a turkey[7] of clothes across his shoulder. Before they reached the house, Pa showed Uncle Mel the land Jake Timmins had taken.

"Land hogs air pizen as copperhead snakes," Uncle Mel said, then he fondled his long white beard in his hand. Uncle Mel was eighty-two years old, but his eyes were keen as sharp-pointed briers and his shoulders were broad and his hands were big and rough. He had been a timber cutter all his days and he was still a-cuttin' timber in West Virginia at the age of eighty-two. "He can't do this to ye, Mick!"

Uncle Mel was madder than Pa when he looked over the new line that they had surveyed from the dead chestnut on one knoll to the twin hickories on the other knoll.

"Anybody would know the line wouldn't go like that," Uncle Mel said. "The line would follow the ridge."

"Looks that way to me too," Pa said.

"He's a-stealin' yer land, Mick," Uncle Mel said. "I'll hep ye get yer land back. He'll never beat me. I've had to fight too many squatters a-tryin' to take my land. I know how to fight 'em with the law."

That night Pa and Uncle Mel sat before the fire and Uncle Mel looked over Pa's deed. Uncle Mel couldn't read very well and when he came to a word he couldn't read, I told him what it was.

"We'll haf to have a court order first, Mick," Uncle Mel said. "When we get the court order, I'll find the line."

I didn't know what Uncle Mel wanted with a court order, but I found out after he got it. He couldn't chop on a line tree[8] until he got an order from the court. And soon as Pa got the court order and gathered a group of men for witnesses, Uncle Mel started work on the line fence.

"Sixteen rods[9] from the dead chestnut due north," Uncle Mel said, and we started measuring sixteen rods due north.

"That's the oak tree, there," Uncle Mel said. It measured exactly sixteen rods from the dead chestnut to the black oak tree.

"Deed said the oak was blazed," Uncle Mel said, for he'd gone over the deed until he'd memorized it. "See the scar, men," Uncle Mel said.

"But that was done seventy years ago," Pa said.

"Funny about the testimony of trees," Uncle Mel told Pa. Tim Mennix, Orbie Dorton, and Dave Sperry were there too. "The scar will allus stay on the outside of a tree well as on the inside. The silent trees will keep their secrets."

Uncle Mel started chopping into the tree. He swung his ax over his shoulder and bit out a slice of wood every time he struck. He cut a neat block into the tree until he found a dark place deep inside the tree.

"Come, men, and look," Uncle Mel said. "Look at that scar. It's as pretty a scar as I ever seen in the heart of a tree!"

---

7 **turkey:** a lumberman's kit.

8 **line tree:** tree marking property line.
9 **rod:** a measure 16½ feet in length.

And while Uncle Mel wiped sweat with his blue bandanna from his white beard, we looked at the scar.

"It's a scar, all right," Tim Mennix said, since he had been a timber cutter most of his life and knew a scar on a tree.

"Think that was cut seventy years ago," Orbie Dorton said. "That's when the deed was made and the old survey was run."

"We'll see if it's been seventy years ago," Uncle Mel said as he started counting the rings in the tree. "Each ring is a year's growth."

We watched Uncle Mel pull his knife from his pocket, open the blade, and touch each ring with his knife-blade point as he counted the rings across the square he had chopped into the tree. Uncle Mel counted exactly seventy rings from the bark to the scar.

"Ain't it the line tree, boys?" Uncle Mel asked.

392

"Can't be anything else," Dave Sperry said.

And then Uncle Mel read the deed, which called for a mulberry thirteen rods due north from the black oak. We measured to the mulberry and Uncle Mel cut his notch to the scar and counted the rings. It was seventy rings from the bark to the scar. Ten more rods we came to the poplar the deed called for, and he found the scar on the outer bark and inside the tree. We found every tree the deed called for but one, and we found its stump. We surveyed the land from the dead chestnut to the twin hickories. We followed it around the ledge.

"We have the evidence to take to court," Uncle Mel said. "I'd like to bring the jurymen right here to this line fence to show 'em."

"I'll go right to town and put this thing in court," Pa said.

"I'll go around and see the men that

have lost land to Jake Timmins," Uncle Mel said. "I want 'em to be at the trial."

Before our case got to court, Uncle Mel had shown seven of our neighbors how to trace their lines and get their land back from Jake Timmins. And when our trial was called, the courthouse was filled with people who had lost land and who had disputes with their neighbors over line fences, attending the trial to see if we won. Jake Timmins, Surveyor Finn Madden, and their lawyer, Henson Stapleton, had produced their side of the question before the jurors and we had lawyer Sherman Stone and our witnesses to present our side, while all the landowners Jake Timmins had stolen land from listened to the trial. The foreman of the jury asked that the members of the jury be taken to the line fence.

"Now here's the way to tell where a line was blazed on saplings seventy years ago," Uncle Mel said, as he showed them the inner mark on the line oak; then he showed them the outward scar. Uncle Mel took them along the line fence and showed them each tree that the deed called for, all but the one that had fallen.

"It's plain as the nose on your face," Uncle Mel would say every time he explained each line tree. "Too many land thieves in this county and a county surveyor the Devil won't have in hell."

After Uncle Mel had explained the line fence to the jurors, they followed Sheriff Whiteapple and his deputies back to the courtroom. Pa went with them to get the decision. Uncle Mel waited at our house for Pa to return.

"That land will belong to Mick," Uncle Mel told us. "And the hay and corn in that barn will belong to him."

When Pa came home, there was a smile on his face.

"It's yer land, ain't it, Mick?" Uncle Mel asked.

"It's still my land," Pa said, "and sixteen men are now filing suits to recover their land. Jake Timmins won't have but an acre left."

"Remember the hay and corn he put in yer barn is yourn," Uncle Mel said. Uncle Mel got up from his chair, stretched his arms. Then he said, "I must be a-gettin' back to West Virginia to cut timber. If ye have any more land troubles, write me."

We tried to get Uncle Mel to stay longer. But he wouldn't stay. He left with his turkey of clothes and his long-handled, double-bitted ax across his shoulder. We waved good-by to him as he walked slowly down the path and out of sight on his way to West Virginia.

Understanding the Biography

1. What title might you give to this selection which would sum up what it is about?
2. What were the chief reasons that Jesse's mother wanted Mick to buy a farm, and what do they reveal about her as a person?
3. How does Jesse present a realistic picture of his tenant-farmer father without making him appear a failure as a person?
4. How does the account of Mick's planting corn in the dark of the moon and potatoes in the light of the moon add to the reader's understanding of him?

JESSE STUART

5. What qualities of the Stuart family are revealed in the account of Jesse and Grandfather building the house in W-Hollow?
6. How does the paragraph preceding Jake Timmins's arrival increase the tension his appearance created?
7. Why is Jesse's account of Uncle Mel's method of surveying more effective than if he had summarized it?
8. As far as Jake Timmins is concerned, how is the result of his effort to seize the Stuart's land ironic?

Developing Language Skills

In explaining the title of his book, Jesse Stuart said:

> The title of this book, *God's Oddling*, comes from something my father used to call my brother and me. For years he used to call me "oddling" because I had gone away to school and become a writer, and because I didn't smoke the tobacco we grew or drink the mountain liquor brewed nearby. . . . It was just before he died that I thought my father was one of God's oddlings, not me. He was a proud, independent man, who always made his own decisions and went his own way. He was a very gentle man, too. He was an oddling, all right.

Write a paragraph beginning: Mick Stuart was a proud, independent man, who always made his own decisions and went his own way. Then go on to prove the statement by citing a few examples from the selection. Be specific enough in your examples so that a reader could point to the section of the essay you are citing. Remember that you are proving that the father is proud and independent; offer evidence to prove each characteristic.

Reading "The Campers at Kitty Hawk"

This selection, which is really the biography of an event, represents one of the unusual devices used by Dos Passos to establish the background for his unflattering view of social and economic life in America following World War I in his trilogy *USA*. *The Big Money*, from which this story is taken, is the third novel in the trilogy and covers the Booming Twenties. Dos Passos adds a heroic quality to this biography of the Wright brothers by using varied typographical devices and unusual writing forms. He sets some of his paragraphs in italics, frequently omits the ordinary punctuation, and breaks up his long and complex sentences into patterns resembling free verse. This unusual arrangement of sentences and paragraphs adds force and stature to the simple lives and great achievement of Wilbur and Orville Wright.

The Campers at Kitty Hawk

John Dos Passos

Dos Passos' imaginative story of the Wright brothers, who made the first practical airplane flight in the world in their homemade plane from Kill Devil Hill on the dunes of Kitty Hawk, North Carolina, is a moving tribute to American dreamers and doers.

On December seventeenth, nineteen hundred and three, Bishop Wright of the United Brethren onetime editor of the *Religious Telescope*[1] received in his frame house on Hawthorn Street in Dayton, Ohio, a telegram from his boys Wilbur and Orville who'd gotten it into their heads to spend their vacations in a little camp out in the dunes of the North Carolina coast tinkering with a homemade glider they'd knocked together themselves. The telegram read:

SUCCESS FOUR FLIGHTS THURSDAY MORNING ALL AGAINST TWENTYONE MILE WIND STARTED FROM LEVEL WITH ENGINEPOWER ALONE AVERAGE SPEED THROUGH AIR THIRTYONE MILES LONGEST FIFTYSEVEN SECONDS INFORM PRESS HOME CHRISTMAS

The figures were a little wrong because the telegraph operator misread Orville's hasty penciled scrawl
  but the fact remains
  that a couple of young bicycle mechanics from Dayton, Ohio
  had designed constructed and flown
  for the first time ever a practical airplane.

After running the motor a few minutes to heat it up I released the wire that held the machine to the track and the machine started forward into the wind. Wilbur ran at the side of the machine holding the wing to balance it on the track. Unlike the start on the 14th made in a calm the machine facing a 27 mile wind started very slowly. . . .

1 *Religious Telescope:* national church magazine of the Evangelical United Brethren.

Wilbur was able to stay with it until it lifted from the track after a forty-foot run. One of the lifesaving men snapped the camera for us taking a picture just as it reached the end of the track and the machine had risen to a height of about two feet. . . . The course of the flight up and down was extremely erratic, partly due to the irregularities of the air, partly to lack of experience in handling this machine. A sudden dart when a little over a hundred and twenty feet from the point at which it rose in the air ended the flight. . . . This flight lasted only 12 seconds but it was nevertheless the first in the history of the world in which a machine carrying a man had raised itself by its own power into the air in full flight, had sailed forward without reduction of speed and had finally landed at a point as high as that from which it started.

A little later in the day the machine was caught in a gust of wind and turned over and smashed, almost killing the coastguardsman who tried to hold it down;
 it was too bad
 but the Wright brothers were too happy to care
 they'd proved that the damn thing flew.

When these points had been definitely established we at once packed our goods and returned home knowing that the age of the flying machine had come at last.

They were home for Christmas in Dayton, Ohio, where they'd been born in the seventies of a family who had been settled west of the Alleghenies since eighteen fourteen, in Dayton, Ohio, where they'd been to grammarschool and highschool and joined their father's church and played baseball and hockey and worked out on the parallel bars and the flying swing and sold newspapers and built themselves a printingpress out of odds and ends from the junkheap and flown kites and tinkered with mechanical contraptions and gone around town as boys doing odd jobs to turn an honest penny.

 The folks claimed it was the bishop's bringing home a helicopter, a fiftycent mechanical toy made of two fans worked by elastic bands that was supposed to hover in the air, that had got his two youngest boys hipped on the subject of flight

 so that they stayed home instead of marrying the way the other boys did, and puttered all day about the house picking up a living with jobprinting,

 bicyclerepair work,

 sitting up late nights reading books on aerodynamics.

 Still they were sincere churchmembers, their bicycle business was prosperous, a man could rely on their word. They were popular in Dayton.

In those days flyingmachines were the big laugh of all the cracker-barrel philosophers. Langley's[2] and Chanute's[3] unsuccessful experiments had been jeered down with an I-told-you-so that rang from coast to coast. The Wrights' big problem was to find a place secluded enough to carry on their experiments without being the horselaugh of the countryside. Then they had no money to spend;

they were practical mechanics; when they needed anything they built it themselves.

They hit on Kitty Hawk,
on the great dunes and sandy banks that stretch south towards Hatteras[4] seaward of Albemarle Sound,[5]
a vast stretch of seabeach
empty except for a coastguard station, a few fishermen's shacks and the swarms of mosquitoes and the ticks and chiggers in the crabgrass behind the dunes
and overhead the gulls and swooping terns, in the evening fish-hawks and cranes flapping across the saltmarshes, occasionally eagles
that the Wright brothers followed soaring with their eyes
as Leonardo[6] watched them centuries before
straining his sharp eyes to apprehend
the laws of flight.

Four miles across the loose sand from the scattering of shacks, the Wright brothers built themselves a camp and a shed for their gliders. It was a long way to pack their groceries, their tools, anything they happened to need; in summer it was hot as blazes, the mosquitoes were hell;
but they were alone there
and they'd figured out that the loose sand was as soft as anything they could find to fall in.

There was a glider[7] made of two planes and a tail in which they lay flat on their bellies and controlled the warp of the planes by shimmying their hips, taking off again and again all day from a big dune named Kill Devil Hill,
they learned to fly.

Once they'd managed to hover for a few seconds
and soar ever so slightly on a rising aircurrent
they decided the time had come
to put a motor in their biplane.

---

2 Langley: Sam P. Langley (1834-1906), U.S. pioneer in aeronautics.
3 Chanute: Octave Chanute (1832-1910), U.S. pioneer in glider experimentation.
4 Hatteras: Cape Hatteras, a promontory off the east coast of North Carolina.
5 Albemarle Sound: an inlet on the northeast coast of North Carolina.
6 Leonardo: Leonardo da Vinci (1452-1519), Italian artist and scientist, who was much interested in principles of flying.
7 glider: a motorless, heavier-than-air craft operating by the action of air currents.

JOHN DOS PASSOS

Back in the shop in Dayton, Ohio, they built an airtunnel,[8] which is their first great contribution to the science of flying, and tried out model planes in it.

They couldn't interest any builders of gasoline engines so they had to build their own motor.

It worked; after that Christmas of nineteen three the Wright brothers weren't doing it for fun any more; they gave up their bicycle business, got the use of a big old cowpasture belonging to the local banker for practice flights, spent all the time when they weren't working on their machine in promotion, worrying about patents, infringements, spies, trying to interest government officials, to make sense out of the smooth involved heartbreaking remarks of lawyers.

In two years they had a plane that would cover twentyfour miles at a stretch round and round the cowpasture.

People on the interurban car used to crane their necks out of the windows when they passed along the edge of the field, startled by the clattering pop pop of the old Wright motor and the sight of the white biplane like a pair of ironingboards one on top of the other chugging along a good fifty feet in the air. The cows soon got used to it.

___

8 air tunnel: a tunnel-like chamber through which air is forced and in which scale models of airplanes can be tested to determine the effects of wind pressure. Now known as a wind tunnel.

BIOGRAPHY

As the flights got longer
the Wright brothers got backers,
engaged in lawsuits,
lay in their beds at night sleepless with the whine of phantom millions, worse than the mosquitoes at Kitty Hawk.
In nineteen seven they went to Paris,
allowed themselves to be togged out in dress suits and silk hats,
learned to tip waiters
talked with government experts, got used to gold braid and post-ponements and vandyke beards[9] and the outspread palms of politicos. For amusement
they played diabolo in the Tuileries[10] gardens.

They gave publicized flights at Fort Myers, where they had their first fatal crackup, St. Petersburg, Paris, Berlin; at Pau[11] they were all the rage,
such an attraction that the hotelkeeper
wouldn't charge them for their room.
Alfonso of Spain[12] shook hands with them and was photographed sitting in the machine,
King Edward[13] watched a flight,
the Crown Prince insisted on being taken up,
the rain of medals began.

They were congratulated by the Czar
and the King of Italy and the amateurs of sport, and the society climbers and the papal titles,
and decorated by a society for universal peace.

Aeronautics became the sport of the day.
The Wrights don't seem to have been very much impressed by the upholstery and the braid and the gold medals and the parades of plush horses,
they remained practical mechanics
and insisted on doing all their own work themselves,
even to filling the gasolinetank.

In nineteen eleven they were back on the dunes
at Kitty Hawk with a new glider.

---

9 **vandyke beards:** small pointed beards popular in Europe at the turn of the century.
10 **Tuileries:** formerly a royal residence.
11 **Pau:** a winter resort in southwest France.
12 **Alfonso of Spain:** Alfonso XIII (1886-1941), King of Spain from 1902 until deposed in 1931.
13 **King Edward:** Edward VII (1841-1910), King of England 1901-1910.

Orville stayed up in the air for nine and a half minutes, which remained a long time the record for motorless flight.

The same year Wilbur died of typhoid fever in Dayton.

In the rush of new names: Farman, Blériot, Curtiss, Ferber, Esnault-Peltrie, Delagrange;[14]

in the snorting impact of bombs and the whine and rattle of shrapnel and the sudden stutter of machineguns after the motor's been shut off overhead,

and we flatten into the mud

and make ourselves small cowering in the corners of ruined walls,

the Wright brothers passed out of the headlines

but not even headlines or the bitter smear of newsprint or the choke of smokescreen and gas or chatter of brokers on the stockmarket or barking of phantom millions or oratory of brasshats laying wreaths on new monuments

can blur the memory

of the chilly December day

two shivering bicycle mechanics from Dayton, Ohio,

first felt their homemade contraption

whittled out of hickory sticks,

gummed together with Arnstein's bicycle cement,

stretched with muslin they'd sewn on their sister's sewingmachine in their own backyard on Hawthorn Street in Dayton, Ohio,

soar into the air

above the dunes and the wide beach

at Kitty Hawk.

14 Farman . . . Delagrange: all pioneers in flying.

Understanding the Biography

1. Why is the date, December 17, 1903, a good way to open this story?
2. How does Dos Passos use typographical devices to identify direct statements by the Wright brothers? factual information concerning them? his own sweeping version of their progress and difficulties?
3. What image of the Wright brothers does Dos Passos establish in his first paragraph? Does he keep this image throughout the entire piece? Show several instances in the latter part of the story that support your answer.
4. How does the use of colloquial expressions ("gotten it into their heads" and "tinkering with a homemade glider they'd knocked together themselves") help to establish the personalities of the Wright brothers?
5. What final image of the Wright brothers does Dos Passos present in the last eleven lines? How does this final description contrast with the preceding ten lines? What is the point of the contrast?

Developing Language Skills

1. Select a newspaper or magazine account of an invention or unusual event and rewrite it in verse form similar to that used by Dos Passos in this story. Attach the original story to your version.
2. Find a straight prose account of the Wright brothers and report to the class on the differences between it and Dos Passos' version.

Reading "Agnes Newton Keith"

Edward Weeks, editor of *The Atlantic Monthly* magazine, in this selection from *In Friendly Candor*, his volume of essays about authors with whom he has worked, not only shows how a perceptive editor works with a new author whose manuscript excites his interest but also builds up, step by step, the unforgettable figure of a courageous, spirited woman. Jesse Stuart creates the figure of his father from personal memories, but Editor Weeks has to build his character from a series of letters, a manuscript for a book, and a very few personal meetings. Utilizing all these sources, Mr. Weeks quotes from Mrs. Keith's letter to him, from his suggestions to her, and from the manuscript itself to bring this intelligent and charming woman alive for the reader. The reader will learn quickly that if he wants to follow the thread of the story he will have to be alert to the author's many switches from commentary to quoted material.

Agnes Newton Keith

Edward Weeks

A manila envelope with exotic postage stamps brought to an editor's office an unusual view of a faraway land.

THE *Atlantic* is more receptive to unknown writers than any other magazine I can think of in America. The truth is that we need young writers quite as much as they need us. Their unsolicited manuscripts come to us "over the transom," tossed in and uninvited, and always one—sometimes as many as six— will be found in any issue.

In the autumn of 1937 a manila envelope with bizarre stamps reached my desk. The letter accompanying the manuscript began: "I enclose the account of Saudin, a young Murut[1] of North Borneo,[2] who visited America. I was recently engaged in the struggle with home mail when Saudin arrived back at our home in Sandakan after his visit to the United States. Saudin and our 'boy,' Arusap, are brother Muruts from the same village and Saudin has always been accustomed to weekend in our back-quarters when in the vicinity of Sandakan. When Arusap inter-

rupted my mail to tell me that Saudin had returned from my country with news of its strange doings we called him in, and my husband and I spent all morning listening to his naïve but not unwise comments about what he had seen." And it ended, "I am an American woman married to an Englishman in Civil Service, the Conservator of Forests for British North Borneo." The author signed herself Agnes Newton Keith.

Saudin, it appeared, had taken care of the wild animals the Martin Johnsons[3] had captured in Borneo and were shipping back to the States; at the end of the voyage he had passed several months in New York City, wandering about with an "IF LOST RETURN TO ——" tag on his collar and marveling at the behavior of American women who in the dead of winter "did not wear many clothes except around their necks, where they wore the skin of animals."

When he was asked what he liked best of all in New York, he said "the red electric signs that run like streams of fire," and he added, "Mr. Johnson took me to eat at a place where you put money in a hole and take out a plate of food. I think this place was very cunning indeed, because the hole to receive a ten-cent piece was so small that you could not put in a five-cent piece, and the hole for a five-cent piece did not answer if you put in a one-cent piece." Saudin's experiences, so shrewd and innocent, were related in Malay to Mrs. Keith and her husband, and her translation was a happy discovery for the *Atlantic*.

It took six weeks for my letter of acceptance to reach Sandakan and by return post came a second manuscript

---

1 **Murut** (mōō′rōōt): tribal name in North Borneo.
2 **North Borneo:** an island in the Malay archipelago.

3 **Martin Johnsons:** famed American husband and wife explorers.

accompanied by this message: "Saudin visits us occasionally, and I give him news of America. His natural niceness has not been spoiled by his travels. He does not work energetically, but why should he? His bank account will last him a lifetime, as a Murut spends money. His store clothes have been much admired. A few years ago the popular picture postal card in Borneo was Mensaring, the Murut Chief, in loin cloth. Now it is Any Murut in Saudin's borrowed New York suit." The letter went on: "The natives of this country are a saddening, maddening, lovable, heartbreaking lot. They are a gentle and courteous people, yet one from whom the zest of life seems to have been taken since the ancient rite of Headhunting has been banned by Government . . ."

I held up the publication of this second paper, since it gave me the definite hope that we had the makings of a book here and I knew that the serial would be more effective when the volume was finished. Instead of acceptance, I sent her the announcement of an *Atlantic* $5000 Award which we were offering for the best book of nonfiction to reach us by February, 1939, and I added this encouragement:

. . . What I want you to do is to tell the story of your daily life in North Borneo so that any stay-at-home here or in England might read it with an active sense of participation. Sandakan, you say, is "ultra-conventional English." Well, so it may be to your experienced eye, but from the evidence I have seen thus far in your narratives, there are trimmings which would set your headquarters apart from most other outposts of England. The book should begin, then, with a friendly account of your headquarters, how long you have been in Sandakan, the scope of your husband's activity, the nature of your

compound and its staff, and once having defined your daily orbit,[4] you will be free to take up the strangers who interrupt your routine—Usip and Abanawas—and equally free to write about those excursions to Sulu Sea or that longer jaunt up the Kinabatangan River . . . I want you —"Agnes Newton Keith" as you sign yourself—to be the connecting link, and thus your presence in every chapter is required, whether as referee, partisan, or merely an observer.

"To journey together is happiness," she had once written—indeed, this was to be the theme of the book—and she gave me fascinating itineraries of the journeys she made with her husband: "We plan to leave here in three weeks for a trip into Interior North Borneo. From the border of Dutch Borneo we will go in native canoes up the Kalabakang River to its headwaters, then cross the watershed on foot, and come down the rapids of the Kinabatangan River in small native boats. This country is the last stronghold of the headhunters, and has not been visited by white men since about 1880, at which time a punitive expedition was directed against the headhunters for their activities. We will see natives who have had no contact with civilization, living their own way of life. I can see material for stories which should come from the trip in time. Might a more direct journal form of the trip also be acceptable? No white woman has been in the part of the country I mention. I do not mention this from the Adventuring White Woman point of view, because all the initiative in these trips is my husband's and I just go along. But I do find in comparing notes with men that I see different things in the native villages from what the men see."

4 orbit: round of duties.

Of course I wanted the journal of that trip for the book, and I wanted other more homely details too. Where did she go for a hair-do in Sandakan? (To the Chinese, she replied.) How did Harry protect his rare books on botany from the damp heat? (They had built an inner room, she said, which could seal off the effect of the rains.) How many Europeans were there in Sandakan and what was the attitude toward the Eurasians and the other racial groups on this, the third largest island in the world? This was deliberate needling, but I was eager to have her finish the book for the contest, and I was not sure she could make it in the intervening year for she seemed to be laboring under difficulties, whether from the heat or illness I could not determine.

Her manuscript arrived in the closing days, and as the outer wrapping with the gay, even more exotic stamps was removed, here was a mound of white paper bound up in a sarong of striking brown and blue design. (We were to reproduce that lovely pattern later for the binding.) The top page bore the title *Land Below the Wind* and beneath the last page, separated by tissue, were pencil sketches of Sandakan, the houseboys, the affectionate apes who were the family pets, a tent in a dripping jungle and the author propped up in a cot, writing underneath an open umbrella—casual drawings which conveyed so surely, often humorously, what Agnes wanted the reader to see.

The title was beautifully euphonious,[5] but whatever did it mean? *Land Below the Wind*, we were told, was the translation of the Malay name for Borneo. The use of the southwest monsoon[6] for trading led the ancient navigators to divide Southern Asia into lands "to its windward"[7] and others "to its leeward."[8] Borneo, in the latter group, was thus the "land below the wind." This point being clarified, the judges went on to read.

As I have indicated, this was a book of episodes, some of them laid in Sandakan, which was the capital of North Borneo, others deep in the forests or in remote native villages. When Harry went on his official expeditions, Agnes went with him, eager, protesting and usually vulnerable. The trip to Timbun Mata Island held moments of "immoderate joy." "On the other hand," as she says, "there were also the leeches, pigticks, mosquitoes, sand flies, and red ants, and the night when our palm leaf hut blew away in a changing monsoon, and had to be reassembled leaf by leaf from the jungle." Some of the episodes were better than others, and the time sequence was not always clear; what bound the book together was Agnes's ability to make do under any conditions, her extraordinary sympathy for the common lot of mankind, no matter what color the skin, and the trust and fidelity which the Keiths reposed in each other. Of the three finalists, *Land Below the Wind* was the most absorbing and refreshing; it was different from any other book we had ever published, and I was elated when it won the Award by a vote of 6 to 1.

All this time I had envisioned Mrs. Keith as a short sturdy little woman in a felt cloche[9] and heavy tweeds, an image derived from my concept of those who dwelt in the periphery[10] of the Empire. The Keiths flew to America for a six months' leave in June of 1939;

5 **euphonious** (ū fō′nĭ əs): smooth-sounding.
6 **monsoon:** a periodic wind.

7 **windward:** the side toward the wind.
8 **leeward:** the side sheltered from the wind.
9 **cloche** (klôsh): helmet-shaped hat.
10 **periphery** (pə rĭf′ə rĭ): outskirts.

Harry stopped off at Victoria, British Columbia, to see his ninety-year-old mother, and Agnes after a family reunion came East for the *Atlantic* reception, the press interviews, and the Prize. When she stepped off the plane at the Boston airport I had my first sight of that slender, long-legged Californian whose high cheekbones and dark almond eyes reminded me instantly of Queen Nefertiti,[11] and I could tell from the admiring glances of the reporters and from the way people turned to look at her in the restaurant that we had here one of a kind.

On this first visit to Boston she spent the mornings working with me on the manuscript as we fitted it together chronologically, and the afternoons in her room inking in her drawings. She bought a trousseau[12] of new clothes, for she and Harry were planning to spend the late summer and early autumn at Oxford where he was to take a refresher course. Bit by bit she pieced together for me the mosaic of their background. They had met at the University of California where Agnes was majoring in English and where Harry Keith in his thorough English way was soaking up everything he could learn about the tropical rain forests and the agriculture of the Pacific. After her graduation Agnes went to work as a cub reporter for the San Francisco *Examiner*. Here she did well until one bright Saturday noon, as she left the building, she was attacked by a dope addict with a two-foot iron pipe who had made up his mind to kill the first person to emerge from the *Examiner* doors. He very nearly succeeded. The concussion with its aftermath of blinding headaches

(these were what interrupted her writing) invalided her for nearly three years. When she was at last well enough to travel, she went abroad with her brother Alfred, an engineer who had just graduated from the California Institute of Technology, and it was on this trip that she again encountered Harry Keith, once of Berkeley, now a young forester, home on his first leave after four years in North Borneo. Their attraction for each other, which was irresistible, and their determination to marry hastened her recovery. Her family was dubious that she could stand up to the demands of the life in the tropics, but Agnes seemed to thrive on the prospect. She went out to Borneo as a bride with the eagerness of an American, uninhibited by the traditions of colonial civil service. The headaches had lost their hold, she told me, and as she was caught up in the adventure of her new life her writing became obligatory.

The exhilaration of the Atlantic Award was the high point, for the Keiths never did get to Oxford. The outbreak of the war cut short their holiday; they were recalled to Sandakan and Agnes took back with her in her trunk the *Atlantic* trousseau, much of which she was never to wear.

The success of *Land Below the Wind*, which we first serialized in the *Atlantic* and which was then chosen by the Book-of-the-Month Club, I reported to her long distance. The royalties we arranged to pay her over a series of years, for she had serious misgivings about the future, but the first check assisted in the arrival of Henry George Keith II, who was born in Sandakan on April 5, 1940. "The producing of young George," she wrote me, "who spent his pre-natal days traveling by plane, by bus and motor, by train and by ship, through war zones and blackouts, in a violently un-

---

11 **Queen Nefertiti:** Egyptian queen of the first half of the 14th century B.C., noted for her beauty.
12 **trousseau:** in this sense, a complete wardrobe.

orthodox manner much disapproved of by consulting obstetricians, has about monopolized my creative energies for this last year. However I have literary hopes for the future now that young George has his toes dug firmly into life on his own account."

From the first Agnes had no illusions about the Japanese invasion, and after the fall of Singapore she was under pressure to return to America with her baby. Instead she built up a lifesaving kit of drugs for George, Harry and herself, and in an article which reached me shortly before Pearl Harbor she foretold how the three of them might retreat by canoe into the interior to hide away with friendly natives in the jungle until the Japanese had been driven off. We published the paper, "Before Invasion: A Letter from North Borneo," in the *Atlantic* for February, 1942, and the week after it appeared Agnes and Harry and George were prisoners of the Japa-

nese; when the Japs landed, the Keiths like the other officials were at their posts.

For three and a half years they survived in separate prison camps, Agnes and baby George with the other white women and children, Harry with the other males from Sarawak[13] and Dutch Borneo. What happened to them during their long ordeal we were not to know until later: the humiliation and the filth, the bodily depletion due to malnutrition, the spirit-cracking degradation of captivity, and the torture (at one time the Japanese questioned her for several days, and during this episode they broke her collarbone, dislocated and strained her left arm, and broke a rib) could hardly be imagined by us who were free. Three times the curtain was lifted by prisoner-of-war postcards from the Imperial Japanese

13 **Sarawak** (sə rä′wäk)**:** section of British North Borneo.

BIOGRAPHY

Army, the first to her mother, the other two to me:

Xmas Day, 1944

Dear Ted:

Quote Sherman reference war.[14] What about Red Cross? Resources this country limited. Our one hope peace soon. All three ragged, tired, homesick, but surviving. Love,

AGNES & HARRY & GEORGE KEITH
Internment Camp, Borneo

May 18, 1945

Meet husband occasionally. Health moderate. George fine, energetic. My new professions: truck gardening, white wing, privy engineering.

Fed up with war. "Hope deferred . . ."[15] etc. Love,

AGNES, HARRY, GEORGE KEITH
Internment Camp, Borneo

On the eleventh of that September they were liberated by the 9th Australian Army Division after Sandakan had been burned by the Japs and reduced to rubble. This is what Agnes wrote me as they waited for the prison gates to open.

Kuching, Internment Camp
Sept. 11, 1945

Dear Ted:

At last! Peace & freedom! We hope to be completely free in a few hours time, as the Nipponese are expected to evacuate Kuching at 12 noon today. There are no words to express our feelings. War is Hell—Peace is Heaven. Thank God, Thank God, the end has come. We have been fed by parachute from Australian Red Cross for 2 weeks now. I have put on almost a pound a day. Harry is also improving in strength. George is fine. Ate his first piece of bread & butter with terrific excitement. First parachute dropped

bread. We showed it to children with wonder. "That's BREAD!" Children had all forgotten what it was.

There is a GOOD story here. I long for time & paper to finish it. I have much material & notes, etc. Of course much difficulty in hiding everything while under Nip. rule. When I arrive U. S. shall CONCENTRATE. Home soon as possible. Nobody knows yet. Love to you—

AGNES & GEORGE KEITH

The Japanese commandant of their camp, for whom at the close Agnes had pity, committed hara-kiri;[16] the prisoners—Agnes was down to 87 pounds—were fed and doctored; Agnes eventually wangled them a passage by plane to Manila and thence by Army transport to Seattle.

So the Keiths came home. Six years had elapsed since they had last seen California. Agnes's mother had died while they were captive; Jean their daughter had grown up into a life of her own; she and Agnes's beloved brother Alfred were there to greet them; and there was a second happy reunion with Harry's mother, whose age was now edging up to the century mark but who had been holding on indomitably until her son's return. It was a small family circle contracted even further by Alfred's tragic death from a heart attack within the month of their return. Griefstricken, the Keiths went to the hospital for the treatment and surgery they had so long needed.

In October with her strength building up Agnes again flew into Boston bringing with her the notes for a new book written on tissue and other scraps of paper which she had hidden in George's stuffed panda and in the tins which she buried. She was much thinner and the strain she had lived through had left its

---

14 Quote . . . war: This refers to a well-known statement, "War is hell," made by W. T. Sherman, the Civil War general.
15 Hope deferred: the beginning of "Hope deferred maketh the heart sick" (Proverbs 13:12).

16 hara-kiri (hä′rə kĭr′ĭ): suicide.

mark, but the eyes still held the same eagerness and luster and her spirit was intact. Her fingernails which she had lost through malnutrition were only beginning to grow in and her fingertips were so sensitive that she could not type for more than an hour each day. She stayed with my associates Dudley and Jeannette Cloud, and her cogitating was done in a quiet room they put at her disposal. At the office we had plenty to talk about, for the manuscript pages she had brought with her, occasionally and very naturally, went into excessive detail. There were passages that read like overstatements and the fact that they had actually happened as she said did not lessen my criticism that they lacked the power to convince. Agnes was quite aware of this herself and of something deeper: she was writing against war, not against individual cruelty, and she summed this up when she said, "All I want is to forget talk of revenge, and get down to the basic fact that as long as we countenance the great atrocity of war, it is ridiculous to protest at personal atrocity." So we sifted and read aloud and tried by the eye, now modifying, now letting the stark realities stand until the pages spoke for her as she intended, and with magnanimity.

Three Came Home as it emerged that autumn is a unique book. No other woman in any country has so perfectly preserved the undaunted will and the compassion of the spirit in defeat. The last page of the book is the most eloquent, and it should be quoted for those who have not read it:

I know now the value of freedom. In all of my life before I had existed as a free woman, and didn't know it.

This is what freedom means to me. The right to live with, to touch and to love, my husband and my children. The right to look about me without fear of seeing people beaten. The capacity to work for ourselves and our children.

The possession of a door, and a key with which to lock it. Moments of silence. A place in which to weep, with no one to see me doing so.

The freedom of my eyes to scan the face of the earth, the mountains, trees, fields, and sea, without barbed wire across my vision. The freedom of my body to walk with the wind, and no sentry to stop me. Opportunity to earn the food to keep me strong. The ability to look each month at a new moon without asking, How many more times must this beauty shine on my captivity?

I will never give up these rights again. There may be more to life than these things. But there is no life without them.

I must also quote the beginning and the end of a letter which she wrote me on her return to Victoria in November, 1946.

Dear Ted,

I am wanting to thank you for all that you and the *Atlantic* family did for me in Boston—but I find that I just can't do it. Unless you know what *I* was before you can't possibly know what you did for me.

My secretary, who had typed out my original almost illegible diaries for me, has been reading the typescript sent from Boston of the finished manuscript. She is pleased with me—and disappointed with the book; she says the starkness and terror are gone from both of us. That's what Boston did; took the starkness and terror out of me, and made of the facts a readable book. I hope I haven't sacrificed too many principles by the way. And if I have—well, it's something to be a human being again . . .

My dear Ted, again thank you for my pleasure in Boston. To come home to the *Atlantic*, the only home and family in my own country that I now have, was everything that a homecoming should be—and something to remember dearly when I am again in exile.

And for your help on my book I also am at a loss to thank you sufficiently.

As it proved Harry Keith was actually back in Sandakan and hard at work less than six months after his release from the Kuching prison. The compulsion which took him there Agnes explained in a letter written shortly before his departure. The book could not go to press until we had received her final additions, and the last of the illustrations, and here is her accounting for the delay:

Harry may go at any moment. Just waiting for the High Commissioner at Ottawa to get him a seat on the next push-bike to the orient. Fortunately, there do not seem to be many boats, planes, submarines going to Borneo just now. How wonderful if there was never another one!

As soon as Harry goes I will get down to work. But at the moment—well, one must live sometimes. It will appear ridiculous to anybody else that two middle-aged persons can be madly in love, but there you are. There is nothing like prison life to make married life seem good. After 3½ years with 280 females I center all my affections on your sex.

I guess the reason Harry is going back is because he is English. If you see his face when somebody remarks philosophically that England is finished, and the British Empire a thing of the past, then you know.

Also in Borneo we had many Asiatic friends who risked their lives, sometimes gave their lives, to help us. We can get no news of these people now. Harry wants to ascertain their fates, and help those whom he can help. Those are his reasons for going—But as for me, I couldn't possibly go for any reason yet. I just become ill at the thought.

Agnes followed Harry out to the East in July of 1947 after the publication of *Three Came Home,* and after she had spoken at Irita Van Doren's Book and Author Luncheon with an intensity which moved and stilled that vast audience. She went with dread. Harry had flown up to Hong Kong to meet her, and when she went ashore with him, her nerve came back.

I arrived at Sandakan on September 2, having left Victoria on June 26. Coming back here with Harry, after a month of happiness together, subdued the ghosts of my past, and it wasn't as bad as I feared. We have a glorious location for our shack, surrounded by sky and Sulu Sea on the very top of a hill, and I like it.

To my surprise I find that the tropical beauty, the wildness, and the primitive people of Borneo enthrall me again. So much so that I want to write another book . . .

In 1950, after four years of reconstruction, the three Keiths came home on leave. Agnes brought with her the manuscript of her new book, *White Man Returns,* and after perusing it in Boston I flew out to Seattle where we spent one forty-hour day in a bedroom of a Seattle hotel with Harry stretched out and drowsing beside us while at the desk Agnes and I went through it page by page.

There was need for haste and not only for the book. The Korean War had broken out and North Borneo had been calling for Harry to come back immediately. It was a wrenching decision, and most of all for Harry who had been considering the possibility of teaching in a school of forestry. This, of course, would hold the trio together. If they went, it would reopen scars which were just healing; it would force them to leave George at home alone in Canada for schooling; and it would expose them to the new hostility which was breaking out in "Asia for the Asians," a hostility which had already resulted in the assassination of a British official known to them both.

At the day's end we dined on "New York T-bone steaks," which always seem such an absurd item for a Western restaurant, and afterwards they escorted me to the airport. As we waited for my flight to be announced Agnes drew me apart. We stood there looking at the Indian gewgaws and Alaskan souvenirs which were on display and suddenly I noticed that there were tears in her eyes. "Ted," she said, "we are going, and I am very afraid. If anything should happen to us, will you please look after George?" The eyes and the pressure of hands can only acknowledge a trust like that.

Two years later at the behest of the United Nations the Keiths moved on to the Philippines to take part there in the reconstruction and the revival led so magnificently by Magsaysay. Their extended tour of duty there opened up still another window on the Pacific, and it was here that Agnes wrote *Bare Feet in the Palace,* growing out of her living knowledge of the Philippines. Today, still under orders from the United Nations, the Keiths, with George as a young assistant, are in Libya,[17] where for three years they have been devoting their skill and energies to the problems of that impecunious[18] but hopeful and developing country.

This is a century when in America it has been fashionable to deride colonialism and those who bore any part of the white man's burden. The dedication of the Keiths and their heart-testing decision to go back when they could so understandably have retired from the field is unselfishness beyond the call of duty. The Keiths have been doing in the Southwest Pacific what Dr. Schweitzer has been doing in Lambaréné, and what Barbara Ward[19] and her husband, Sir Robert Jackson, have been doing in Ghana—devoting their skill, their encouragement, and their farsightedness to the faith that what men hold in common is so much more important than that which divides them.

17 **Libya:** in North Africa.
18 **impecunious** (ĭm′pə kū′nĭ əs): poor.
19 **Barbara Ward:** writer and journalist, particularly concerned with international subjects.

Understanding the Biography

1. How does the first paragraph prepare you for the story and also explain the role *The Atlantic Monthly* magazine plays in contemporary literature?
2. What purposes do the author's frequent quotations from Agnes Keith's letters and book serve in this essay?
3. What argument does Agnes Keith give supporting her suggestion that her comments on a jungle trip with her husband might be worth publishing?
4. What qualities of Mrs. Keith are revealed in her prisoner-of-war postcards from the Japanese prison at Kuching?
5. What is her attitude toward her personal sufferings during her imprisonment?
6. In the last paragraph of the essay what great tribute does Editor Weeks pay the Keiths and others who are spending their lives in foreign service?

Developing Language Skills

1. Discuss the qualities of the Keiths that Editor Weeks says make "a powerful book out of a series of episodes of uneven quality and uncertain time sequence."
2. Write a paraphrase of the freedoms that Agnes Keith names in the last page of her book *Three Came Home* and that Editor Weeks reprints in his essay.
3. Although Editor Weeks is writing about Agnes Newton Keith, what does this essay reveal about him? Write a paragraph pointing out his professional help (such as his specific questions about everyday life in Borneo) and his personal help that went beyond his concerns as an editor.

Reading "The Old Gentleman"

Gilbert Highet is remarkably successful in telling his story from the viewpoint of the old gentleman himself. The author seems to be using "the cool, comprehensive gaze which every visitor remembered" as he looks over some sixty Christmases. Highet uses two narrative techniques, the building of suspense and the flashback, to give his characterization the appeal of a short story. He not only withholds the identity of the old gentleman for a third of the essay, but he also develops suspense about the specific events connected with each of the Christmases recalled. His use of the flashback, a device that moves events backward in time instead of following a chronological order, requires close attention from the reader and adds to the essay's interest.

EDWARD WEEKS

The Old Gentleman

Gilbert Highet

This tribute to a famous American by a 20th-century, Scottish-born American brings "The Old Gentleman" warmly and vividly to life. The selection is taken from Gilbert Highet's volume of essays People, Places, and Books.

THE OLD GENTLEMAN was riding round his land. He had retired several years ago, after a busy career; but farming was what he liked, and he knew that the best way to keep farms prosperous was to supervise them in person. So, although he was approaching seventy, he rode round his property for four or five hours, several days each week. It was not easy for him, but it was not difficult either. He never thought whether a thing was easy or difficult. If it ought to be done, it would be done. Besides, he had always been strong. Although his hair was white and his eyes were dimming, he stood a good six feet and weighed 210 pounds. He rose at four every morning. It was December now, Christmas was approaching, snow was in the air, frost and snow on the ground. This month he had been away from home on a toilsome but necessary trip; and in the hard weather he had been able to ride over his farms

very seldom. Still, he liked to see them whenever he could. The land was quiet; yet a deal of work remained to be done.

There was much on the old gentleman's mind. His son[1] had come home from college in some kind of disturbance and uneasiness, unwilling to go back again. Perhaps he should be sent elsewhere—to Harvard, or William and Mary? Perhaps he should have a private tutor? . . . Meanwhile, in order to teach him habits of quiet and undistracted industry, "I can [the old gentleman wrote to a friend], and I believe I do, keep him in his room a certain portion of the twenty-four hours." But even so, nothing would substitute for the boy's own will power, which was apparently defective. The grandchildren,[2] too, were sometimes sick, because they were spoiled. Not by their grandmother, but by their mother. The old gentleman's wife never spoiled anyone: indeed, she wrote to Fanny to warn her, saying emphatically, "I am sure there is nothing so pernisious as over charging the stomack of a child."

He thought hard and long about the state of the nation. Although he had retired from politics, he was often consulted, and he kept closely in touch. One advantage of retirement was that it gave him time to think over general principles. Never an optimist, he could usually see important dangers some time before they appeared to others. This December, as he rode over the stiff clods under the pale sky, he was thinking over two constant threats to his country. One was the danger of disputes between the separate States and the central government. (Congress had

1 **son:** an adopted son, the child of his stepson (who had died).
2 **grandchildren:** the two older children of his stepson.

just passed a law designed to combat sedition, and two of the States had immediately denounced it as unconstitutional. This could lead only to disaster.) The other problem was that respectable men were not entering public life. They seemed to prefer to pursue riches, to seek their private happiness, as though such a thing were possible if the nation itself declined. The old gentleman decided to write to Mr. Henry, whom he considered a sound man, and urge him to re-enter politics: he would surely be elected if he would consent to stand;[3] and then, with his experience, he could do much to bridge the gap between the federal government and the States.

The old gentleman stopped his horse. With that large, cool, comprehensive gaze which every visitor always remembered, he looked round the land. It was doing better. Five years ago his farms had been almost ruined by neglect and greed. During his long absence the foremen had cropped them too hard and omitted to cultivate and fertilize, looking for quick and easy profits. Still, even before retiring, he had set about restoring the ground to health and vigor: first, by feeding the soil as much as possible, all year round; second by "a judicious succession of crops"; and third, most important of all, by careful regularity and constant application. As he put it in a letter, "To establish good rules, and a regular system, is the life and the soul of every kind of business." Now the land was improving every year. It was always a mistake to expect rapid returns. To build up a nation and to make a farm out of the wilderness, both needed long, steady, thoughtful, determined application; both were the work of the will.

3 consent to stand: a term (still used in England) meaning to run for office.

Long ago, when he was only a boy, he had copied out a set of rules to help in forming his manners and his character—in the same careful way as he would lay out a new estate or survey a recently purchased tract of land. The last of the rules he still remembered. *Keep alive in your breast that little spark of celestial fire called Conscience.* Some of the philosophers said that the spark from heaven was reason, the power of the intellect, which we share with God. The old gentleman did not quarrel with them, but he did not believe them. He knew that the divine fire in the spirit was the sense of duty, the lawfulness which orders the whole universe, the power of which a young poet then alive was soon to write

> Thou dost preserve the stars from wrong;
> And the most ancient heavens, through Thee, are fresh and strong.

His mind turned back over his long and busy life. He never dreamed or brooded, but he liked to note things down, to plan them and record them. Now, on this cold December day, he could recall nearly every Christmas he had ever spent: sixty at least. Some were peaceful, some were passed in deadly danger, many in war, some in strange lonely places, some in great assemblies, some in happiness and some in anguish of soul, none in despair.

One of the worst was Christmas Day of twenty-one years before. That was early in the war, a bad time. It snowed four inches on Christmas. His men were out in the open, with no proper quarters. Although he started them on building shelters, an aggressive move by the enemy made them stand to arms and interrupt all other work for nearly a week. And they had no decent uniforms, no warm coats, no strong shoes, no regular supplies, two days without meat, three days without bread, almost a quarter of his entire force unfit for duty. He was receiving no supplies from the government, and he was actually meeting opposition from the locals. They had sent up a protest against keeping the troops in service during the winter. Apparently they thought you could raise an army whenever you needed one—not understanding that this little force was the only permanent barrier between them and foreign domination. He had replied with crushing energy to that protest. In a letter to the President of Congress, he wrote:

I can assure those gentlemen that it is a much easier and less distressing thing to draw remonstrances in a comfortable room by a good fire side than to occupy a cold, bleak hill, and sleep under frost and snow without clothes or blankets. However, although they seem to have little feeling for the naked and distressed soldiers, I feel superabundantly for them, and from my soul I pity those miseries which it is neither in my power to relieve or prevent.

He ended with his well-known, strongly and gracefully written signature, G. WASHINGTON.

The year before that, 1776, things had been nearly as bad—the same difficulty about uniforms and supplies. Late in December he wrote earnestly from his camp, "For godsake hurry with the clothing as nothing will contribute more to facilitate the recruiting service than warm & comfortable clothing to those who engage . . . The Commissary informs me that he cannot prevail on the millers to grind; & that the troops in consequence are like to suffer for want

of flour . . . This must be remedied by fair or other means." However, his chief concern then was not supplies, nor discipline, nor defense, but attack. On Christmas Day, long before dawn, he was crossing the Delaware River at McKonkey's Ferry, with a striking force of over two thousand men. He spent Christmas morning marching to Trenton. Next day he attacked Colonel Rahl and his Hessians. Half of them were sleeping off their Christmas liquor, and nearly all were paralyzed with drowsiness and astonishment. Hungry and hopeful, the Americans burst in on them like wolves among fat cattle. The surprise was complete. The victory, prepared on Christmas Day, was the first real success of the war.

Two winters later at Christmas time, Washington was in Philadelphia to discuss the plans for next year's campaign with a Congressional committee. People were very civil; they called him the Cincinnatus[4] of America; and some of them made an effort to take the war seriously. But many did not. He would rather have been in winter quarters with his men. A few days before Christmas 1778 he wrote to Mr. Harrison that, as far as he could see, most people were sunk in "idleness, dissipation, and extravagance . . . Speculation, peculation,[5] and an insatiable thirst for riches seem to have got the better of every other consideration and almost of every order of men."

Year after year he was in winter quarters at Christmas time, usually in a simple farmhouse, "neither vast nor commodious," in command of a starving and bankrupt army. In 1781, after York-

4 **Cincinnatus:** Roman general and statesman about 519 B.C. He accepted a plea to act as dictator when Rome was in serious danger and retired to private life when the danger was over.
5 **peculation:** misuse of public moneys.

town, things were a trifle better, and he had dinner with his wife and family at Mr. Morris's in Philadelphia amid general rejoicing. But the following Christmas was the blackest ever. He had thought of asking for leave, to look after his "long neglected private concerns"; but the army was very close to mutiny, which would have meant the final loss of the war and the probable collapse of the entire nation. It was not only the enlisted men now, it was the officers: they were preparing to make a formal protest to Congress with a list of their grievances; and only the personal influence of Washington himself, only his earnest pleading and his absolute honesty and selflessness, kept the little force in being through that winter.

Yet by Christmas the next year, in 1783, it was all over. Washington said farewell to his officers, and then, on December 23rd, he resigned his commission. His formal utterance still stands, grave as a monument:

Happy in the confirmation of our Independence and Sovereignty, and pleased with the opportunity afforded the United States of becoming a respectable nation, I resign, with satisfaction, the appointment I accepted with diffidence: a diffidence in my abilities to accomplish so arduous a task, which, however, was superceded by a confidence in the rectitude of our cause, the support of the supreme power of the Union, and the patronage of Heaven.

So he said. And the President of Congress replied, in terms which, although still balanced and baroque,[6] are more emotional and almost tender:

We join you in commending the interests of our dearest country to the Almighty God, beseeching him to dispose the hearts and minds of its citizens, to improve the

opportunity afforded them of becoming a happy and respectable nation. And for you, we address to him our earnest prayers, that a life so beloved may be fostered with all his care; that your days may be happy as they have been illustrious; and that he will finally give you that reward which this world cannot give.

Next day Washington left for Mount Vernon, and spent Christmas 1783 at home in peace.

Some years passed. December was always busy. Washington was on horseback nearly every day, riding round his place, directing the operations which kept the land alive and fed all those who lived on it, ditching, threshing, hog-killing, repairing walls, lifting potatoes, husking corn. And it was a poor December when he did not have at least half a dozen days' hunting, though in that thickly wooded country he often lost his fox and sometimes hounds too. For Christmas after Christmas in the eighties, his diary shows him living the life of a peaceful squire, and on the day itself usually entertaining friends and relatives. On Christmas Eve 1788, Mr. Madison stayed with him, and was sent on to Colchester next day in Washington's carriage.

Again a change. Christmas 1789 saw him as the first President of the United States, living in New York, the capital of the Union, and receiving formal calls from diplomats and statesmen. In the forenoon he attended St. Paul's Chapel; in the afternoon Mrs. Washington received visitors, "not numerous, but respectable"; and next day Washington rode out to take his exercise. (He and Theodore Roosevelt were probably the finest horsemen of all our Presidents; those who knew him best liked to think of him on horseback, the most graceful

6 baroque: elaborate.

rider in the country.) But for years thereafter his exercise was cut short and his days were swallowed up in the constant crowding of business. He rarely saw his land and seldom visited his home. His Christmases were formal and public; brilliant, but not warm; not holidays.

But now, after his final retirement, he had time to look back on earlier Christmases. Some of them were very strange. Christmas of 1751 he had spent at sea. His elder brother Lawrence, frail and overworked, sailed to Barbados[7] for a winter cruise, and George accompanied him. On November 3rd, they landed at Bridgetown, and were invited to dine next day with Major Clarke, O.C. British forces. Washington observed gravely to his diary: "We went,—myself with some reluctance, as the smallpox was in his family." Less than two weeks later Washington was down with smallpox, which kept him in bed for nearly a month; but he recovered with very few marks. By December 25th he and his brother were sailing back, past the Leeward Islands. As he liked to do all through his life, he noted the weather ("fine, clear and pleasant with moderate sea") and the situation ("latitude 18°30′"); and, with a youthful exuberance which he soon lost, he adds: "We dined on a fat Irish goose, Beef, &ca &ca, and drank a health to our absent friends."

Five years later, he was a colonel engaged in one of the wars that helped to make this continent Anglo-Saxon instead of Latin: the war to keep the French, pressing downward along the Ohio from Canada and upward along the Mississippi from New Orleans, from

encircling the British colonies in an enclave[8] along the coast and cutting them off forever from the wealth of the plains, the rivers, and the distant, fabulous Pacific. Those two Christmases Washington could recall as a time of profound depression, filled with the things he hated most: anarchic competition and anarchic indiscipline. He commanded a Virginia regiment; and Captain Dagworthy of the Maryland troops at Fort Cumberland would not supply him. He despised drunkenness and slack soldiering; and he would not tolerate the attempts by the liquor trade to batten on his troops and run local elections by handing out free liquor. His enemies beat him temporarily, not by bending his will, but by wrecking his health. Christmas 1757 saw him on leave after a physical collapse which looked very like an attack of consumption, involving hemorrhage, fever, and a certain hollowness of the chest which never quite left him. He bore up as well as he could under the barrage of slander which his enemies poured in upon him, including the foulest of all, that he was accepting graft; but he had been ill for months when he finally broke down. (Years later, when he was appointed Commander-in-Chief, he was offered a regular salary, but refused to accept it. Instead, he asked Congress to pay his expenses; he kept the accounts scrupulously; and he presented them without extras at the end of the war. Slanders are always raised about great men; but this one slander was never leveled at Washington again.)

He looked back beyond that to one of the hardest Christmases in his memory. That was the Christmas of 1753, when he was only twenty-one. Governor Din-

---

7 Barbados: an island in the West Indies.

8 enclave: an area enclosed within foreign territory.

BIOGRAPHY

widdie had determined to stop the encirclement of Virginia. The French were building forts on the Ohio, and arresting traders from the British colonies who penetrated that territory. Soon there would be nothing westward except a ring of hostile Indians supported by arrogant French officers. Isolated by land, the colonies could later have been cut off by sea, too, and the seed would have withered almost before it struck firm root.

The governor commissioned young Major Washington to make his way to the French fort, to deliver a letter from him to the French commandant, and to bring back both a reply and an estimate of the situation. He did; but he was very nearly killed. Not by the French. Or not directly. They merely told him that they were absolutely determined to take possession of the Ohio territory, and returned a diplomatic but unsatisfactory reply to the governor's letter.

Still, Major Washington had at least the substance of a good intelligence report, for he had inspected the fort and his men had observed how many canoes the French were building. He had only to return. The French, however, endeavored to persuade him to go up and interview the governor of French Canada; and, that failing, set about bribing the Indians in his party with liquor and guns either to leave him altogether or to delay until the worst of the winter, when travel would be impossible for months. But Washington had a good guide; he was friendly with the Indian chief; and he had a tireless will. He set off on the return journey about the third week in December, when snow was already falling heavily mixed with rain. Six days were spent on a river full of ice. The canoes began to give out. The horses foundered. The rest of the party went more and more slowly. Major Washington "put himself in In-

GILBERT HIGHET

417

dian walking dress" and pushed on, on foot. On Christmas Day he was making his way toward the Great Beaver Creek. Next day he left the entire party to follow with horses, money, and baggage, and set out alone with the guide, Christopher Gist.

Next day a lone Indian who pretended to know the territory, but who was evidently a French agent, spent some hours leading the two men off their route, and finally shot at the young officer from close range. Gist would have killed him; but Washington would not allow it: they kept him for several hours, and then let him go. Then they pressed on eastward. They had to cross the swollen, ice-jammed Allegheny River. They built a raft; but they could force it only halfway through the roaring current and the hammering ice blocks. That night they spent freezing on an island in midstream. In the morning, they struggled across on the ice, and pressed on again. In his journal the guide recorded that the major was "much fatigued." But still he kept going: eighteen miles a day with a gun and a full pack, over rough territory, threatened by hostile Indians, in mid-December, with snow and rain falling from the sky and lying thick on the ground.

Now, over a period of forty-five years, he looked back on that Christmas. It had been, he remembered, "as fatiguing a journey as it is possible to conceive"— and still a necessary one. It was the first of his many services to his country, to keep it from being surrounded and strangled from without or poisoned from within. And he reflected that it is not necessary to try to be brave, or clever, or generous, or beloved, or even happy. It is necessary simply to do one's duty. All else flows from that. Without that, all else is useless.

Darkness closed in early in these winter days. It was getting toward Christmas of the year 1798. General Charles Pinckney and his lady were expected for Christmas dinner. The old gentleman finished looking over the land, and turned homeward. He paid no heed to the cold.

Understanding the Biography

1. What are the "two constant threats to his country" that the old gentleman thinks about as he rides over his estate?
2. When he looks back on his boyhood and the rules of conduct by which he lived, what does he consider the "spark from heaven"?
3. How does Highet's having Washington remember events and dates in order of their vividness rather than as they happened add to the feeling that the old gentleman actually is telling his own story?
4. What Christmas days does Washington remember?
5. Contrast Washington's Christmases of the middle eighties with those from 1789 to 1797.
6. Reread the last paragraph to determine when these reminiscences take place. What is the effect of the last sentence?
7. How does Highet's opening his flashbacks with the Christmas of 1777 and closing them with the Christmas of 1753 tie in with the rule of conduct that Washington calls to mind early in the essay and refers to again in the next to the last paragraph?

Developing Language Skills

Write a paragraph in which you tell what kind of person Washington was, according to Highet. In your opening sentence name any one of Washington's characteristics that you concluded was a major one from reading this essay; then go on to summarize one of the incidents from the essay that supports your opening sentence.

Reading "Reminiscences of Conrad"

The richness of this chronologically organized selection lies in Galsworthy's choice of details and incidents that add up to a compelling and sympathetic picture of an author whose writing caused the critics of the world to "rub their eyes." Galsworthy's ability to look at both sides of issues and motives is clearly demonstrated in the paragraph that begins, "I saw little of Conrad during the war." In fact, this passage furnishes the key to the deep affection and mutual respect between the two men. Read carefully those sections of the essay dealing with loyalty and fidelity and with Conrad's likes and dislikes to help you better understand Conrad's short novel *The Secret Sharer*, which you will read later.

Reminiscences
of Conrad

John Galsworthy

Opening with a glimpse of a young ship's officer with a peaked beard and a strong foreign accent, Galsworthy affectionately portrays the beginning and growth of a famous literary and personal friendship between himself and Joseph Conrad. Both men were leading English novelists at the turn of the century.

MANY WRITERS knew my dead friend, and will write of him better than I; but no other writer knew him quite so long, or knew him both as sailor and novelist.

It was in March 1893 that I first met Conrad on board the English sailing ship *Torrens* in Adelaide Harbour.[1] He was superintending the stowage of cargo. Very dark he looked in the burning sunlight—tanned, with a peaked brown beard, almost black hair, and dark brown eyes, over which the lids were deeply folded. He was thin, not tall, his arms very long, his shoulders broad, his head set rather forward. He spoke to me with a strong foreign accent. He seemed to me strange on an English ship. For fifty-six days I sailed in his company.

The chief mate bears the main bur-

den of a sailing ship. All the first night he was fighting a fire in the hold. None of us seventeen passengers knew of it till long after. It was he who had most truck with the tail of that hurricane off the Leeuwin,[2] and later with another storm. He was a good seaman, watchful of the weather, quick in handling the ship; considerate with the apprentices —we had a long, unhappy Belgian youth among them, who took unhandily to the sea and dreaded going aloft; Conrad compassionately spared him all he could. With the crew he was popular; they were individuals to him, not a mere gang; and long after he would talk of this or that among them, especially of old Andy the sailmaker: "I liked that old fellow, you know." He was friendly with the young second mate, a cheerful, capable young seaman, very English; and respectful, if faintly ironic, to his whiskered, stout old English captain. I, supposed to be studying navigation for the Admiralty Bar,[3] would every day work out the position of the ship with the captain. On one side of the saloon table we would sit and check our observations with those of Conrad, who from the other side of the table would look at us a little quizzically. For Conrad had commanded ships, and his subordinate position on the *Torrens* was only due to the fact that he was then still convalescent from the Congo experience which had nearly killed him. Many evening watches in fine weather we spent on the poop. Ever the great teller of a tale, he had already nearly twenty years of tales to tell. Tales of ships and storms, of Polish revolution, of his youthful Carlist[4] gun-running

2 **Leeuwin** (lōō′ĭn): cape at the southwest point of Australia.
3 **Admiralty Bar:** department having legal authority over naval affairs.
4 **Carlist:** a supporter of claims of Don Carlos or his heirs to the Spanish throne.

1 **Adelaide Harbour:** port in Australia.

adventure, of the Malay seas,[5] and the Congo; and of men *and* men: all to a listener who had the insatiability of a twenty-five-year-old.

When, seven or eight years later, Conrad, though then in his best period and long acclaimed a great writer by the few, was struggling, year in year out, to keep a roof over him amidst the apathy of the many who afterwards fell over each other to read him in his worst period, I remember urging him to raise the wind by tale-telling in public. He wouldn't, and he was right. Still, so incomparable a *raconteur*[6] must have made a success, even though his audience might have missed many words owing to his strange yet fascinating accent.

On that ship he talked of life, not literature; and it is *not* true that I introduced him to the life of letters. At Cape Town,[7] on my last evening, he asked me to his cabin, and I remember feeling that he outweighed for me all the other experiences of that voyage. Fascination was Conrad's great characteristic—the fascination of vivid expressiveness and zest, of his deeply affectionate heart, and his far-ranging subtle mind. He was extraordinarily perceptive and receptive. . . . He appreciated the super-subtle, the ultra-civilised as completely as he grasped the life and thoughts of simple folk. . . .

Between his voyages in those last days of his sailor's life Conrad used to stay at rooms in Gillingham Street, near Victoria Station.[8] It was there that he read so prodigiously, and there that he suffered from bouts of that lingering Congo fever which dogged his health and fastened a deep, fitful gloom over his spirit. In a letter to me he once said: "I don't say anything of actual bodily pain, for, God is my witness, I care for that less than nothing." He was, indeed, truly stoical, and his naturally buoyant spirit reacted with extreme suddenness. But all the years I knew him—thirty-one—he had to fight for decent health. Such words as "I have been abominably ill—abominably is the right word," occur again and again in his letters, and his creative achievement in a language not native to him, in face of these constant bouts of illness, approaches the marvellous.

It was the sea that, in my view, gave Conrad to the English language. A fortunate accident—for he knew French better than English at that time. He started his manhood, as it were, at Marseilles. In a letter to me (1905) he says: "In Marseilles I did begin life thirty-one years ago. It's the place where the puppy opened his eyes." He was ever more at home with French literature than with English, spoke that language with less accent, liked Frenchmen, and better understood their clearer thoughts. And yet, perhaps, not quite an accident; for after all he had the roving quality which has made the English the great sea nation of the world; and, I suppose, instinct led him to seek in English ships the fullest field of expression for his nature. England, too, was to him the romantic country; it had been enshrined for him, as a boy in Poland, by Charles Dickens, Captain Marryat,[9] Captain Cook,[10] and Franklin, the Arctic explorer. He always spoke of Dick-

---

5 **Malay seas:** seas southeast of Asia.
6 *raconteur* (răk′ŏn tûr′): storyteller.
7 **Cape Town:** seaport capital of the Union of South Africa.
8 **Victoria Station:** railroad station in London.

9 **Captain Marryat:** Frederic Marryat (1792-1848), a captain in the Royal Navy and the author of a series of novels of sea life.
10 **Captain Cook:** James Cook (1728-1779), famous English sea captain who sailed around the world and left records of his principal voyages.

JOHN GALSWORTHY

ens with the affection we have for the writers who captivate our youth.

No one, I take it, ever read the earliest Conrad without the bewildered fascination of one opening eyes on a new world; without, in fact, the feeling he himself describes in that passage of *Youth,* where he wakes up in an open boat in his first Eastern port, and sees "the East looking at him." I doubt if he will ever be surpassed as a creator of what we Westerners term "exotic atmosphere." The Malay coasts and rivers of *Almayer's Folly, An Outcast of the Islands* and the first pages of *The Rescue;* the Congo of *Heart of Darkness;* the Central Southern America of *Nostromo,* with many other land and seascapes, are bits of atmospheric painting *in excelsis.*[11] Only one expression adequately described the sensations of us who read *Almayer's Folly* in 1894. We rubbed our eyes. Conrad was critically accepted from the very start; he never published a book that did not rouse a chorus of praise; but it was twenty years before he was welcomed by the public with sufficient warmth to give him a decent income.

Chance, in 1914—an indifferent Conrad—at last brought him fortune. From that year on to the end his books sold well; yet, with the exception of *The Secret Sharer* and some parts of *Victory,* none of his work in that late period was up to his own exalted mark. Was it natural that popular success should have coincided with the lesser excellence? Or was it simply an example of how long the strange takes to pierce the pickled hide of the reader of fiction? Or, still more simply, the undeniable fact that the reading public is more easily reached than it used to be? . . .

I first re-encountered Conrad some months after that voyage when we paid a visit together to "Carmen"[12] at Covent Garden Opera.[13] "Carmen" was a vice with us both. It was already his fourteenth time of seeing that really dramatic opera. The blare of Wagner[14] left him as cold as it leaves me; but he shared with my own father a curious fancy for Meyerbeer.[15] In June 1910 he wrote: "I suppose I am now the only human being in these islands who thinks Meyerbeer a great composer; and I am an alien at that, and not to be wholly trusted." But music, fond though he was of it, could play no great part in a life spent at sea and, after his marriage in 1895, in the country. He went up to Town[16] but seldom. He wrote always with blood and tears and needed seclusion for it.

A spurt was characteristic of Conrad's endings; he finished most of his books in that way—his vivid nature instinctively staged itself with dramatic rushes. Moreover, all those long early years he worked under the whip-lash of sheer necessity.

A sailor and an artist, he had little sense of money. He was not of those who can budget exactly and keep within it; and anyway he had too little, however neatly budgeted. It is true that his dramatic instinct and his subtlety would take a sort of pleasure in plotting against the lack of money, but it was at best a lugubrious amusement for one who had to whip his brain along when he was tired, when he was ill, when he was almost desperate. Letter after let-

12 "Carmen": opera by Bizet.
13 Covent Garden Opera: theater in London, the principal home in England of English and Italian opera.
14 Wagner (väg′nər): Richard Wagner (1813-1883), German composer. His music is of a dramatic, overwhelming nature.
15 Meyerbeer (mī′ər bār′): Giacomo Meyerbeer (1791-1864), German composer.
16 Town: London.

11 *in excelsis* (ĭn ĕk sĕl′sĭs): of the best.

BIOGRAPHY

ter, talk after talk, unfolded to me the travail of those years. He needed to be the Stoic he really was.

I used to stay with him a good deal from 1895–1905, first at Stanford in Essex and then at Stanford in Kent.[17] He was indefatigably good to me while my own puppy's eyes were opening to literature, and I was still in the early stages of that struggle with his craft which a writer worth his salt never quite abandons.

His affectionate interest was always wholly generous. In his letters to me— two to three hundred—there is not a sentence which breaks, or even jars, the feeling that he cared that one should do good work. There is some valuable criticism, but never any impatience, and no stinting of appreciation or encouragement. He never went back on friendship. The word "loyalty" has been much used by those who write or speak of him. It has been well used. He was always loyal to what he had at heart— to his philosophy, to his work, and to his friends; he was loyal even to his dislikes (not few) and to his scorn. People talk of Conrad as an aristocrat; I think it rather a silly word to apply to him. His mother's family, the Bebrowskis, were Polish landowners; the Korzeniowskis, too, his father's family, came, I think, of landowning stock; but the word aristocrat is much too dry to fit Conrad; he had no touch with "ruling," no feeling for it, except, maybe, such as is necessary to sail a ship; he was first and last the rover and the artist, with such a first-hand knowledge of men and things that he was habitually impatient with labels and pigeonholes, with cheap theorising and word debauchery. He stared life very much in the face, and distrusted those who didn't. Above all,

he had the keen humour which spiflicates[18] all class and catalogues, and all ideals and aspirations that are not grounded in the simplest springs of human nature. He laughed at the clichés of so-called civilisation. His sense of humour, indeed, was far greater than one might think from his work. He had an almost ferocious enjoyment of the absurd. Writing seemed to dry or sardonise his humour. But in conversation his sense of fun was much more vivid; it would leap up in the midst of gloom or worry, and take charge with a shout.

Conrad had six country homes after his marriage, besides two temporary abodes. He wrote jestingly to my wife: "Houses are naturally rebellious and inimical to man." And, perhaps, having lived so much on ships, he really had a feeling of that sort. He certainly grew tired of them after a time.

I best remember Pent Farm at Stanford in Kent—that little, very old, charming, if inconvenient farmhouse, with its great barn beyond the yard, under the lee of the almost overhanging Pent. It was a friendly dwelling where you had to mind your head in connection with beams; and from whose windows you watched ducks and cats and lambs in the meadows beyond. He liked those quiet fields and that sheltering hill. Though he was not what we should call a "lover of nature" in the sense of one who spends long hours lost in the life of birds and flowers, of animals and trees, he could be vividly impressed by the charm and the variety of such things. He was fond, too, of Hudson's[19] books; and no lover of Hudson's work is insensible to nature. . . .

18 spiflicates: destroys.
19 Hudson: W. H. Hudson (1841-1922), an author who was interested in nature and who devoted a great proportion of his writing to birds. *Green Mansions* (1904), set in the South American forest, is a well-known novel by him.

17 Essex and Kent: counties in the southeastern part of England.

JOHN GALSWORTHY

Many might suppose that Conrad would naturally settle by the sea. He never did. He had seen too much of it; like the sailor who when he turns into his bunk takes care that no sea air shall come in, he lived always well inland. The sea was no favourite with one too familiar with its moods. He disliked being labelled a novelist of the sea. He wrote of the sea, as perhaps no one, not even Herman Melville,[20] has written; but dominant in all his writing of the sea is the note of struggle and escape. His hero is not the sea, but man in conflict with that cruel and treacherous element. Ships he loved, but the sea—no. Not that he ever abused it, or talked of it with aversion; he accepted it as he accepted all the inscrutable remorselessness of Nature. It was man's job to confront Nature with a loyal and steady heart—that was Con-

rad's creed, his contribution to the dignity of life. Is there a better? First and last he was interested in men, fascinated by the terrific spectacle of their struggles in a cosmos about which he had no illusions. He was sardonic, but he had none of the cynicism characteristic of small, coldhearted beings.

He customarily laboured in the morning, and often would sit long hours over a single page. In 1906, when he was staying in our London house, he wrote to my wife: "I don't know that I am writing much in the little wooden house" (out in the garden), "but I smoke there religiously for three and a half hours every morning, with a sheet of paper before me and an American fountain-pen in my hand. What more could be expected from a conscientious author, I can't imagine."

In later years, when his enemy, gout, often attacked his writing hand, he was obliged to resort a good deal to dictation of first drafts. I cannot but believe

21 *parvenu* (pär'və nū'): upstart; newcomer.

that his work suffered from that necessity. But there were other and increasing handicaps—the war, which he felt keenly, and those constant bouts of ill-health which dragged at his marvellous natural vitality. I think I never saw Conrad quite in repose. His hands, his feet, his knees, his lips—sensitive, expressive, and ironical—something was always in motion, the dynamo never quite at rest within him. His mind was extraordinarily active and his memory for impressions and people most retentive, so that he stored with wonderful accuracy all the observations of his dark-brown eyes, which were so piercing and yet could be so soft. He had the precious faculty of interest in detail. To that we owe his pictures of scenes and life long past—their compelling verisimilitude, the intensely vivid variety of their composition. The storehouse of his subconscious self was probably as interesting and comprehensive a museum as any in the world. It is from the material in our subconscious minds that we create. Conrad's eyes never ceased snapshotting, and the millions of photographs they took were laid away by him to draw on. Besides, he was not hampered in his natural watchfulness by the preoccupation of an egoistic personality. He was not an egoist; he had far too much curiosity and genuine interest in things and people to be that. I don't mean to say that he had not an interest in himself and a belief in his own powers. His allusions to his work are generally disparaging; but at heart he knew the value of his gifts; and he liked appreciation, especially from those (not many) in whose judgment he had faith. He received more praise, probably, than any other writer of our time; but he never suffered from that *parvenu*[21] dis-

ease, swelled head; and "I," "I," "I" played no part in his talk.

People have speculated on the literary influences that for him were formative. . . . Conrad was a most voracious reader, and he was trilingual. A Slav temperament, a life of duty and adventure, vast varied reading, and the English language—those were the elements from which his highly individual work emerged. Not I, who have so often heard him speak of them, will deny his admiration for Flaubert, de Maupassant, Turgenev, and Henry James,[22] but one has only to read Conrad's first book, *Almayer's Folly*, to perceive that he started out on a path of his own, with a method quite peculiar to himself, involuted[23] to a dangerous degree, perhaps, and I can trace no definite influence on him by any writer. . . . No one could help Conrad. He had to subdue to the purposes of his imagination a language that was not native to him; to work in a medium that was not the natural clothing of his Polish temperament. There were no guides to the desert that he crossed. . . .

I saw little of Conrad during the war.[24] Of whom did one see much? He was caught in Poland at the opening of that business, and it was some months before he succeeded in getting home. Tall words, such as "War to end War," left him, a continental and a realist, appropriately cold. When it was over he wrote: "So I send these few lines to convey to you both all possible good wishes for unbroken felicity in your new home and many years of peace. At the same time I'll confess that neither felicity nor peace inspires me with much confidence. There is an

---

20 **Herman Melville:** American author (1819-1891), best known for his novel *Moby Dick*, the story of a whaling voyage.

22 **Flaubert . . . James:** famous 19th-century writers.
23 **involuted:** involved; complicated.
24 **the war:** World War I.

air of 'the packed valise' about these two divine but unfashionable figures. I suppose the North Pole would be the only place for them, where there is neither thought nor heat, where the very water is stable, and the democratic bawlings of the virtuous leaders of mankind die out into a frozen, unsympathetic silence." Conrad had always a great regard for men of action, for workmen who stuck to their last and did their own jobs well; he had a corresponding distrust of amateur omniscience and handy wise-acres; he curled his lip at political and journalistic protestation; cheap-jackery and clap-trap of all sorts drew from him a somewhat violently expressed detestation. I suppose what he most despised in life was ill-educated theory, and what he most hated, blatancy and pretence. He smelled it coming round the corner and at once his bristles would rise. He was an extremely quick judge of a man. I remember a dinner convoked by me, that he might meet a feminine compatriot of his own married to one who was not a compatriot. The instant dislike he took to the latter individual was so full of electricity that we did not dine in comfort. The dislike was entirely merited. This quick instinct for character and types inimical to him was balanced by equally sure predilections, so that his friendships were always, or nearly always, lasting—I can think of only one exception. He illustrated vividly the profound truth that friendship is very much an affair of nerves, grounded in instinct rather than in reason or in circumstance, the outcome of a sort of deep affinity which prevents jarring. His Preface to the *Life of Stephen Crane*[25] supplies all the evi-

dence we need of Conrad's instantaneous yet lasting sympathy with certain people; and of his instant antipathy to others. It contains also the assurance that after he became a writer he "never kept a diary and never owned a notebook"—a statement which surprised no one who knew the resources of his memory and the brooding nature of his creative spirit.

"Genius" has somewhere been defined as the power to make much out of little. In *Nostromo* Conrad made a continent out of just a sailor's glimpse of a South American port, some twenty years before. In *The Secret Agent* he created an underworld out of probably as little actual experience. On the other hand, we have in *The Nigger*, in *Youth* and *Heart of Darkness* the raw material of his own life transmuted into the gold of fine art. People—and there are such—who think that writers like Conrad, if there be any, can shake things from their sleeve, would be staggered if they could have watched the pain and stress of his writing life. In his last letter to me but one, February 1924, he says: "However, I have begun to work a little —on my runaway novel. I call it 'runaway' because I've been after it for two years (*The Rover* is a mere interlude) without being able to overtake it. The end seems as far as ever! It's like a chase in a nightmare—weird and exhausting. Your news that you have finished a novel brings me a bit of comfort. So there are novels that *can* be finished—then why not mine? Of course I see 'fiction' advertised in the papers— heaps of it. But published announcements seem to me mere phantasms . . . I don't believe in their reality." There are dozens of such allusions to almost despairing efforts in his letters. He must, like all good workmen, have had his hours of compensation; but if ever a

25 *Life of Stephen Crane*: a book by Thomas Beer, with an introduction by Joseph Conrad.

man worked in the sweat of spirit and body it was Conrad. That is what makes his great achievement so inspiring. He hung on to his job through every kind of weather, mostly foul. He never shirked. In an age more and more mechanical, more and more given to short cuts and the line of least resistance, the example of his life's work shines out; its instinctive fidelity, his artist's desire to make the best thing he could. Fidelity! Yes, that is the word which best sums up his life and work.

The last time I saw Conrad—about a year ago—I wasn't very well, and he came and sat in my bedroom, full of affectionate solicitude. It seems, still, hardly believable that I shall not see him again. His wife tells me that a sort of homing instinct was on him in the last month of his life, that he seemed sometimes to wish to drop everything and go back to Poland. Birth calling to Death—no more than that, perhaps, for he loved England, the home of his wandering, of his work, of his last long landfall.

If to a man's deserts is measured out the quality of his rest, Conrad shall sleep well.

1924.

Understanding the Biography

1. How would you describe Galsworthy's attitude toward Conrad? Give three or four specific lines from the selection that support your answer.
2. What facts do you learn about Conrad in Galsworthy's second and third paragraphs?
3. Why is Galsworthy traveling on a sailing ship? Is he younger or older than Conrad?
4. Find Galsworthy's support for his statement, "Fascination was Conrad's great characteristic."
5. Why did the young Polish lad, who knew French before he knew English, choose England for his adopted country and English as his language (according to Galsworthy)?
6. What point is Galsworthy making when he quotes the sentence from Conrad's *Youth* in which the young Conrad awakens in an open boat in his first Eastern port and finds "the East looking at him"?
7. Does Galsworthy consider Conrad a novelist who wrote about the sea or a novelist who used the sea as background? How does he support his opinion?
8. What qualities of Conrad does Galsworthy mention in accounting for Conrad's highly individual work?

9. What kind of men did Conrad admire? What kind did he dislike?

10. Galsworthy's reminiscences include physical descriptions of Conrad, personal observations of his actions and conversation, reaction of other people to Conrad, excerpts from his letters, references to his literary achievement and the obstacles that he faced, and personal tributes. Choose three passages, each using a different method of characterization, that you consider especially effective in revealing Conrad's personality. What do they reveal about him and what methods of characterization do they use?

Building Vocabulary Skills

1. Look back at the context in which the following phrases are used. Explain the meaning of each quotation.

   (a) "raise the wind" (p. 421)

   (b) "we rubbed our eyes" (p. 422)

   (c) "an indifferent Conrad" (p. 422)

   (d) "the pickled hide of the reader of fiction" (p. 422)

   (e) " 'Carmen' was a vice with us both." (p. 422)

2. In this tribute of a writer to a fellow writer, Galsworthy reveals his own character as well as that of Conrad.

   > . . . he was first and last the rover and the artist, with such a first-hand knowledge of men and things that he was habitually impatient with *labels* and *pigeonholes*, with *cheap theorising* and *word debauchery*. He stared life very much in the face, and distrusted those who didn't. Above all, he had the keen humour which *spiflicates all class and catalogues*, and all ideals and aspirations that are not grounded in the simplest springs of human nature. *He laughed at the clichés of so-called civilisation.*

   What do the italicized statements reveal of Conrad? of Galsworthy?

Developing Language Skills

1. Galsworthy says of Conrad's talent for friendship: "He illustrated vividly the profound truth that friendship is very much an affair of nerves, grounded in instinct rather than in reason or in circumstances." How does he support this statement? Do you agree with the comment in general? Why or why not? Answer these questions in two or three well-organized paragraphs.

2. What trait is Galsworthy emphasizing in the following statement? "Tall words, such as 'War to end War,' left him, a continental and a realist, appropriately cold." What is Galsworthy's attitude toward this trait? How is Galsworthy using the word *continental* in his statement?

3. What is the subject of the *if* clause in Galsworthy's final sentence? What is the meaning of *deserts*? Restate this tribute in a sentence beginning with the main clause. Is this sentence the best over-all summary of Conrad? If not, which statement would you choose?
4. In her essay "Getting at the Truth," Marchette Chute wrote:

> . . . this is not to say that a biography should be lacking in a point of view. If it does not have a point of view it will be nothing more than a kind of expanded article for an encyclopedia—a string of facts arranged in chronological order with no claim to being a real biography at all. A biography must have a point of view. . . .

Select one of the biographical essays you have read and write an essay of three or four paragraphs in which you discuss the author's point of view toward his subject. What are the points he wishes to make about his subject? How does he make them? Is he objective in his approach? Use specific statements from the biography to support your general ideas.

The Novel

Introduction to The Secret Sharer

THE CONRAD CENTENNIAL in 1957 brought new and deserved attention to the works of this Polish-English writer who created not only the spell of faraway places but also the drama of man's search for identity and confidence in an indifferent or even hostile world. *The Secret Sharer,* written in 1909 but not published until 1912, carries both these Conrad trademarks in its compact story of a young captain's ordeal in the Gulf of Siam on board a British sailing ship.

Although there is some disagreement among critics on whether *The Secret Sharer* is a short novel or a long short story, there is no disagreement about its excellence. For our purposes, *The Secret Sharer* is a short novel that reveals in miniature Conrad's imaginative genius and technical perfection.

Conrad, usually pessimistic about his own writing, said of *The Secret Sharer* in a letter to a friend, "Every word fits, and there's not a single uncertain note. Luck, my boy! Pure luck!" Critics agree that there is not a single uncertain note in the story, but they credit its perfection not to luck but rather to Conrad's painstaking way with words and to his magnificent technique.

Conrad is fascinated with words and their power. In "A Familiar Preface" he declares, "Give me the right word and the right accent and I will move the world."[1] This very love of words has brought attacks from certain critics. They say that Conrad uses three adjectives instead of one, that his sentences are too long and involved, and that he uses too many similes—all of which make for slow reading. These characteristics are found in many of his stories but not in *The Secret Sharer,* a concise, polished work. However, even *The Secret Sharer* should be read slowly, precisely because so much is packed into it.

In another of his famous prefaces Conrad says, "My task which I am trying to achieve is, by the power of the written word to make you hear, to make you feel—it is, before all, to make you *see*."[2] In *The Secret Sharer,* Conrad makes you hear the light footfall of the steward, makes you feel the captain's terror at the footfall, and makes you see the furtive exchange of glances between the two officers after a strange order or unusual action of the captain.

Conrad limits his novels to one significant phase or segment of life or character and reveals it by carefully selected experiences. A great difference between Conrad's type of novel and more loosely constructed ones is in the management of plot. A Conrad novel sacrifices the freedom and sweep that Dickens, for example, has, in order to secure a tighter, more disciplined effect. In his effort to focus attention on the young

---

[1] Joseph Conrad, "A Familiar Preface," *A Conrad Argosy,* Introduction by William McFee (Doubleday, Doran and Co., New York, 1942), p. 665.
[2] *Ibid.,* "Preface to *The Nigger of the 'Narcissus',*" p. 82.

captain's inner conflict and development, Conrad eliminates all unnecessary information. Throughout *The Secret Sharer*, the relationship between the captain and the fugitive dominates the outward, adventure-tale aspects of the story.

The qualities of restraint and discipline in Conrad's work were ones evidently commented upon by critics of his own time. In the preface to an autobiographical work, he once wrote:

> It seems to me that in one, at least, authoritative quarter of criticism I am suspected of a certain unemotional, grim acceptance of facts. . . .
>
> My answer is that . . . there are some of us to whom an open display of sentiment is repugnant. . . .
>
> . . . I have always suspected in the effort to bring into play the extremities of emotions the debasing touch of insincerity. In order to move others deeply we must deliberately allow ourselves to be carried away beyond the bounds of our normal sensibility—innocently enough, perhaps, and of necessity, like an actor who raises his voice on the stage above the pitch of natural conversation—but still we have to do that.[3]

In letters to his friends, Conrad revealed that he disliked being called a novelist of the sea. He uses the sea as background for many of his stories because he knows it so well, but his hero is never the sea. His hero is man in conflict with himself. Conrad never makes the mistake of thinking that interesting adventures of the sea or of anything else will make up for uninteresting characters. His stories are focused on men, usually young men, who encounter personal crises that probe their weaknesses and test their consciences. In Conrad's world, disaster is only a step behind success. Some of his men win their battles; others lose them. But even in defeat, his men achieve a moral victory of sorts. They pass from isolation and insecurity to awareness and recognition of their relationship to the outside world.

Although Conrad bridges the 19th and 20th centuries, his stories, concerned with an outer world of exotic lands and eastern seas and ships that sailed these seas, and an inner world alive with men's fears and loyalties and strengths and weaknesses, belong to the 20th century. *The Secret Sharer* is such a story.

---

[3] *Ibid.*, "A Familiar Preface," pp. 667-668.

The Secret Sharer

Joseph Conrad

ON MY right hand there were lines of fishing stakes resembling a mysterious system of half-submerged bamboo fences, incomprehensible in its division of the domain of tropical fishes, and crazy of aspect as if abandoned forever by some nomad tribe of fishermen now gone to the other end of the ocean; for there was no sign of human habitation as far as the eye could reach. To the left a group of barren islets, suggesting ruins of stone walls, towers, and block-houses, had its foundations set in a blue sea that itself looked solid, so still and stable did it lie below my feet; even the track of light from the westering sun shone smoothly, without that animated glitter which tells of an imperceptible ripple. And when I turned my head to take a parting glance at the tug which had just left us anchored outside the bar, I saw the straight line of the flat shore joined to the stable sea, edge to edge, with a perfect and unmarked closeness, in one leveled floor half brown, half blue under the enormous dome of the sky. Corresponding in their insignificance to the islets of the sea, two small clumps of trees, one on each side of the only fault in the impeccable joint, marked the mouth of the river Meinam we had just left on the first preparatory stage of our homeward journey; and, far back on the inland level, a larger and loftier mass, the grove surrounding the great Paknam pagoda,[1] was the only thing on which the eye could rest from the vain task of exploring the monotonous sweep of the horizon. Here and there gleams as of a few scattered pieces of silver marked the windings of the great river; and on the nearest of them, just within the bar, the tug steaming right into the land became lost to my sight, hull and funnel and masts, as though the impassive earth had swallowed her up without an effort, without a tremor. My eye followed the light cloud of her smoke, now here, now there, above the plain, according to the devious curves of the stream, but always fainter and farther away, till I lost it at last behind the miter-shaped hill of the great pagoda. And then I was left alone with my ship, anchored at the head of the Gulf of Siam.[2]

She floated at the starting point of a long journey, very still in an immense stillness, the shadows of her spars flung far to the eastward by the setting sun. At that moment I was alone on her decks. There was not a sound in her—and around us nothing moved, nothing lived, not a canoe on the water, not a bird in the air, not a cloud in the sky. In this breathless pause at the threshold of a long passage we seemed to be measuring our fitness for a long and arduous enterprise, the appointed task of both our existences to be carried out, far from all human eyes, with only sky and sea for spectators and for judges.

There must have been some glare in the air to interfere with one's sight, be-

1 **pagoda:** an oriental temple.
2 **Gulf of Siam:** an inlet, South China Sea.

cause it was only just before the sun left us that my roaming eyes made out beyond the highest ridge of the principal islet of the group something which did away with the solemnity of perfect solitude. The tide of darkness flowed on swiftly; and with tropical suddenness a swarm of stars came out above the shadowy earth, while I lingered yet, my hand resting lightly on my ship's rail as if on the shoulder of a trusted friend. But, with all that multitude of celestial bodies staring down at one, the comfort of quiet communion with her was gone for good. And there were also disturbing sounds by this time— voices, footsteps forward; the steward flitted along the main deck, a busily ministering spirit; a hand bell tinkled urgently under the poop deck. . . .

I found my two officers waiting for me near the supper table, in the lighted cuddy.[3] We sat down at once, and as I helped the chief mate, I said:

"Are you aware that there is a ship anchored inside the islands? I saw her mastheads above the ridge as the sun went down."

He raised sharply his simple face, overcharged by a terrible growth of whisker, and emitted his usual ejaculations: "Bless my soul, sir! You don't say so!"

My second mate was a round-cheeked, silent young man, grave beyond his years, I thought; but as our eyes happened to meet I detected a slight quiver on his lips. I looked down at once. It was not my part to encourage sneering on board my ship. It must be said, too, that I knew very little of my officers. In consequence of certain events of no particular significance, except to myself, I had been appointed

3 cuddy: cabin in afterpart of ship used as officers' dining room.

to the command only a fortnight before. Neither did I know much of the hands forward. All these people had been together for eighteen months or so, and my position was that of the only stranger on board. I mention this because it has some bearing on what is to follow. But what I felt most was my being a stranger to the ship; and if all the truth must be told, I was somewhat of a stranger to myself. The youngest man on board (barring the second mate), and untried as yet by a position of the fullest responsibility, I was willing to take the adequacy of the others for granted. They had simply to be equal to their tasks; but I wondered how far I should turn out faithful to that ideal conception of one's own personality every man sets up for himself secretly.

Meantime the chief mate, with an almost visible effect of collaboration on the part of his round eyes and frightful whiskers, was trying to evolve a theory of the anchored ship. His dominant trait was to take all things into earnest consideration. He was of a painstaking turn of mind. As he used to say, he "liked to account to himself" for practically everything that came in his way, down to a miserable scorpion he had found in his cabin a week before. The why and the wherefore of that scorpion —how it got on board and came to select his room rather than the pantry (which was a dark place and more what a scorpion would be partial to), and how on earth it managed to drown itself in the inkwell of his writing desk— had exercised him infinitely. The ship within the islands was much more easily accounted for; and just as we were about to rise from the table he made his pronouncement. She was, he doubted not, a ship from home lately arrived. Probably she drew too much water to cross the bar except at the top of spring tides. Therefore she went into that natural harbor to wait for a few days in preference to remaining in an open roadstead.[4]

"That's so," confirmed the second mate, suddenly, in his slightly hoarse voice. "She draws over twenty feet. She's the Liverpool ship *Sephora* with a cargo of coal. Hundred and twenty-three days from Cardiff."[5]

We looked at him in surprise.

"The tugboat skipper told me when he came on board for your letters, sir," explained the young man. "He expects to take her up the river the day after tomorrow."

After thus overwhelming us with the extent of his information he slipped out of the cabin. The mate observed regretfully that he "could not account for that young fellow's whims." What prevented him telling us all about it at once, he wanted to know.

I detained him as he was making a move. For the last two days the crew had had plenty of hard work, and the night before they had very little sleep. I felt painfully that I—a stranger—was doing something unusual when I directed him to let all hands turn in without setting an anchor watch. I proposed to keep on deck myself till one o'clock or thereabouts. I would get the second mate to relieve me at that hour.

"He will turn out the cook and the steward at four," I concluded, "and then give you a call. Of course at the slightest sign of any sort of wind we'll have the hands up and make a start at once."

He concealed his astonishment. "Very well, sir." Outside the cuddy he put his head in the second mate's door to inform him of my unheard-of caprice to take a five hours' anchor watch on myself. I heard the other raise his voice incredulously: "What? The captain himself?" Then a few more murmurs, a door closed, then another. A few moments later I went on deck.

My strangeness, which had made me sleepless, had prompted that unconventional arrangement, as if I had expected in those solitary hours of the night to get on terms with the ship of which I knew nothing, manned by men of whom I knew very little more. Fast alongside a wharf, littered like any ship in port with a tangle of unrelated things, invaded by unrelated shore people, I had hardly seen her yet properly. Now, as she lay cleared for sea, the stretch of her main deck seemed to me very fine under the stars. Very fine, very roomy for her size, and very inviting. I descended the poop[6] and paced the waist, my mind picturing to myself the coming passage through the Malay Archipelago,[7] down the Indian Ocean, and up the Atlantic. All its phases were familiar enough to me, every characteristic, all the alternatives which were likely to face me on the high seas—everything! . . . except the novel responsibility of command. But I took heart from the reasonable thought that the ship was like other ships, the men like other men, and that the sea was not likely to keep any special surprises expressly for my discomfiture.[8]

Arrived at that comforting conclusion, I bethought myself of a cigar and went below to get it. All was still down there. Everybody at the after end of the ship was sleeping profoundly. I

---

4 **roadstead:** a protected place near shore where ships can ride at anchor.
5 **Cardiff:** Welsh seaport.

6 **poop:** a raised deck at the stern (rear of ship).
7 **Archipelago** (är'kə pĕl'ə gō'): large expanse of water scattered with islands.
8 **discomfiture:** frustration; embarrassment.

came out again on the quarterdeck, agreeably at ease in my sleeping suit on that warm breathless night, barefooted, a glowing cigar in my teeth, and, going forward, I was met by the profound silence of the fore end of the ship. Only as I passed the door of the forecastle I heard a deep, quiet, trustful sigh of some sleeper inside. And suddenly I rejoiced in the great security of the sea as compared with the unrest of the land, in my choice of that untempted life presenting no disquieting problems, invested with an elementary moral beauty by the absolute straightforwardness of its appeal and by the singleness of its purpose.

The riding light[9] in the fore-rigging burned with a clear, untroubled, as if symbolic, flame, confident and bright in the mysterious shades of the night. Passing on my way aft along the other side of the ship, I observed that the rope side ladder, put over, no doubt, for the master of the tug when he came to fetch away our letters, had not been hauled in as it should have been. I became annoyed at this, for exactitude in small matters is the very soul of discipline. Then I reflected that I had myself peremptorily[10] dismissed my officers from duty, and by my own act had prevented the anchor watch being formally set and things properly attended to. I asked myself whether it was wise ever to interfere with the established routine of duties even from the kindest of motives. My action might have made me appear eccentric. Goodness only knew how that absurdly whiskered mate would "account" for my conduct, and what the whole ship thought of that informality of their new captain. I was vexed with myself.

Not from compunction[11] certainly but, as it were mechanically, I proceeded to get the ladder in myself. Now a side ladder of that sort is a light affair and comes in easily, yet my vigorous tug, which should have brought it flying on board, merely recoiled upon my body in a totally unexpected jerk. What the devil! ... I was so astounded by the immovableness of that ladder that I remained stock-still, trying to account for it to myself like that imbecile mate of mine. In the end, of course, I put my head over the rail.

The side of the ship made an opaque belt of shadow on the darkling glassy shimmer of the sea. But I saw at once something elongated and pale floating very close to the ladder. Before I could form a guess a faint flash of phosphorescent light, which seemed to issue suddenly from the naked body of a man, flickered in the sleeping water with the elusive, silent play of summer lightning in a night sky. With a gasp I saw revealed to my stare a pair of feet, the long legs, a broad livid[12] back immersed right up to the neck in a greenish cadaverous glow. One hand, awash, clutched the bottom rung of the ladder. He was complete but for the head. A headless corpse! The cigar dropped out of my gaping mouth with a tiny plop and a short hiss quite audible in the absolute stillness of all things under heaven. At that I suppose he raised up his face, a dimly pale oval in the shadow of the ship's side. But even then I could only barely make out down there the shape of his black-haired head. However, it was enough for the horrid, frost-bound sensation which had gripped me about the chest to pass off. The moment of vain ex-

---

9 **riding light:** a white light, visible all around the horizon, shown by vessels at anchor.
10 **peremptorily** (pĕr ĕmp′tə rĭ lĭ): authoritatively.

11 **compunction:** a feeling of guilt.
12 **livid** (lĭv′ĭd): ashy-colored.

clamations was past, too. I only
climbed on the spare spar and leaned
over the rail as far as I could, to bring
my eyes nearer to that mystery floating
alongside.

As he hung by the ladder, like a resting swimmer, the sea lightning played
about his limbs at every stir; and he
appeared in it ghastly, silvery, fishlike.
He remained as mute as a fish, too. He
made no motion to get out of the water,
either. It was inconceivable that he
should not attempt to come on board,
and strangely troubling to suspect that
perhaps he did not want to. And my
first words were prompted by just that
troubled incertitude.

"What's the matter?" I asked in my
ordinary tone, speaking down to the
face upturned exactly under mine.

"Cramp," it answered, no louder.
Then slightly anxious, "I say, no need
to call anyone."

"I was not going to," I said.

"Are you alone on deck?"

"Yes."

I had somehow the impression that
he was on the point of letting go the
ladder to swim away beyond my ken—
mysterious as he came. But, for the
moment, this being appearing as if he
had risen from the bottom of the sea
(it was certainly the nearest land to the
ship) wanted only to know the time. I
told him. And he, down there, tentatively:[13]

"I suppose your captain's turned in?"

"I am sure he isn't," I said.

He seemed to struggle with himself,
for I heard something like the low, bitter murmur of doubt. "What's the
good?" His next words came out with
a hesitating effort.

"Look here, my man. Could you call
him out quietly?"

I thought the time had come to declare myself.

13 **tentatively:** uncertainly; experimentally.

"I am the captain."

I heard a "By Jove!" whispered at the level of the water. The phosphorescence flashed in the swirl of the water all about his limbs, his other hand seized the ladder.

"My name's Leggatt."

The voice was calm and resolute. A good voice. The self-possession of that man had somehow induced a corresponding state in myself. It was very quietly that I remarked:

"You must be a good swimmer."

"Yes. I've been in the water practically since nine o'clock. The question for me now is whether I am to let go this ladder and go on swimming till I sink from exhaustion, or—to come on board here."

I felt this was no mere formula of desperate speech, but a real alternative in the view of a strong soul. I should have gathered from this that he was young; indeed, it is only the young who are ever confronted by such clear issues. But at the time it was pure intuition on my part. A mysterious communication was established already between us two —in the face of that silent, darkened tropical sea. I was young, too; young enough to make no comment. The man in the water began suddenly to climb up the ladder, and I hastened away from the rail to fetch some clothes.

Before entering the cabin I stood still, listening in the lobby at the foot of the stairs. A faint snore came through the closed door of the chief mate's room. The second mate's door was on the hook, but the darkness in there was absolutely soundless. He, too, was young and could sleep like a stone. Remained the steward, but he was not likely to wake up before he was called. I got a sleeping suit out of my room and, coming back on deck, saw the naked man from the sea sitting on the main hatch, glimmering white in the darkness, his elbows on his knees and his head in his hands. In a moment he had concealed his damp body in a sleeping suit of the same gray-stripe pattern as the one I was wearing and followed me like my double on the poop. Together we moved right aft,[14] barefooted, silent.

"What is it?" I asked in a deadened voice, taking the lighted lamp out of the binnacle,[15] and raising it to his face.

"An ugly business."

He had rather regular features; a good mouth; light eyes under somewhat heavy, dark eyebrows; a smooth, square forehead; no growth on his cheeks; a small, brown mustache, and a well-shaped, round chin. His expression was concentrated, meditative, under the inspecting light of the lamp I held up to his face; such as a man thinking hard in solitude might wear. My sleeping suit was just right for his size. A well-knit young fellow of twenty-five at most. He caught his lower lip with the edge of white, even teeth.

"Yes," I said, replacing the lamp in the binnacle. The warm, heavy tropical night closed upon his head again.

"There's a ship over there," he murmured.

"Yes, I know. The *Sephora.* Did you know of us?"

"Hadn't the slightest idea. I am the mate of her—" He paused and corrected himself. "I should say I *was.*"

"Aha! Something wrong?"

"Yes. Very wrong indeed. I've killed a man."

"What do you mean? Just now?"

"No, on the passage. Weeks ago. Thirty-nine south. When I say a man—"

---

14 aft: toward or in the rear of a ship.
15 binnacle: box containing ship's compass and lantern.

"Fit of temper," I suggested, confidently.

The shadowy, dark head, like mine, seemed to nod imperceptibly above the ghostly gray of my sleeping suit. It was, in the night, as though I had been faced by my own reflection in the depths of a somber and immense mirror.

"A pretty thing to have to own up to for a Conway boy,"[16] murmured my double, distinctly.

"You're a Conway boy?"

"I am," he said, as if startled. Then, slowly . . . "Perhaps you too—"

It was so; but being a couple of years older I had left before he joined. After a quick interchange of dates a silence fell; and I thought suddenly of my absurd mate with his terrific whiskers and the "Bless my soul—you don't say so" type of intellect. My double gave me an inkling of his thoughts by saying:

"My father's a parson in Norfolk. Do you see me before a judge and jury on that charge? For myself I can't see the necessity. There are fellows that an angel from heaven—— And I am not that. He was one of those creatures that are just simmering all the time with a silly sort of wickedness. Miserable devils that have no business to live at all. He wouldn't do his duty and wouldn't let anybody else do theirs. But what's the good of talking! You know well enough the sort of ill-conditioned snarling cur—"

He appealed to me as if our experiences had been as identical as our clothes. And I knew well enough the pestiferous[17] danger of such a character where there are no means of legal repression. And I knew well enough also that my double there was no homicidal ruffian. I did not think of asking him for details, and he told me the story roughly in brusque, disconnected sentences. I needed no more. I saw it all going on as though I were myself inside that other sleeping suit.

"It happened while we were setting a reefed foresail,[18] at dusk. Reefed foresail! You understand the sort of weather. The only sail we had left to keep the ship running; so you may guess what it had been like for days. Anxious sort of job, that. He gave me some of his cursed insolence at the sheet. I tell you I was overdone with this terrific weather that seemed to have no end to it. Terrific, I tell you—and a deep ship. I believe the fellow himself was half crazed with funk.[19] It was no time for gentlemanly reproof, so I turned round and felled him like an ox. He up and at me. We closed just as an awful sea made for the ship. All hands saw it coming and took to the rigging, but I had him by the throat, and went on shaking him like a rat, the men above us yelling, 'Look out! look out!' Then a crash as if the sky had fallen on my head. They say that for over ten minutes hardly anything was to be seen of the ship—just the three masts and a bit of the forecastle head[20] and of the poop all awash driving along in a smother of foam. It was a miracle that they found us, jammed together behind the forebits. It's clear that I meant business, because I was holding him by the throat still when they picked us up. He was black in the face. It was too much for them. It seems they rushed us aft together, gripped as we were, screaming 'Murder!' like a lot of lunatics, and broke into the cuddy.

---

16 **Conway boy:** graduate of Merchant Marine Training Ship Conway.
17 **pestiferous** (pĕs tĭf'ər əs): spreading harm.
18 **setting a reefed foresail:** hoisting a partly folded sail.
19 **funk:** fear.
20 **forecastle head:** forward part of the ship.

And the ship running for her life, touch and go all the time, any minute her last in a sea fit to turn your hair gray only a-looking at it. I understand that the skipper, too, started raving like the rest of them. The man had been deprived of sleep for more than a week, and to have this sprung on him at the height of a furious gale nearly drove him out of his mind. I wonder they didn't fling me overboard after getting the carcass of their precious shipmate out of my fingers. They had rather a job to separate us, I've been told. A sufficiently fierce story to make an old judge and a respectable jury sit up a bit. The first thing I heard when I came to myself was the maddening howling of that endless gale, and on that the voice of the old man. He was hanging on to my bunk, staring into my face out of his sou'wester.[21]

"'Mr. Leggatt, you have killed a man. You can act no longer as chief mate of this ship.'"

His care to subdue his voice made it sound monotonous. He rested a hand on the end of the skylight to steady himself with, and all that time did not stir a limb, so far as I could see. "Nice little tale for a quiet tea party," he concluded in the same tone.

One of my hands, too, rested on the end of the skylight; neither did I stir a limb, so far as I knew. We stood less than a foot from each other. It occurred to me that if old "Bless my soul —you don't say so" were to put his head up the companion and catch sight of us, he would think he was seeing double, or imagine himself come upon a scene of weird witchcraft; the strange captain having a quiet confabulation[22] by the wheel with his own gray ghost.

I became very much concerned to prevent anything of the sort. I heard the other's soothing undertone.

"My father's a parson in Norfolk," it said. Evidently he had forgotten he had told me this important fact before. Truly a nice little tale.

"You had better slip down into my stateroom now," I said, moving off stealthily. My double followed my movements; our bare feet made no sound; I let him in, closed the door with care, and, after giving a call to the second mate, returned on deck for my relief.

"Not much sign of any wind yet," I remarked when he approached.

"No, sir. Not much," he assented, sleepily, in his hoarse voice, with just enough deference, no more, and barely suppressing a yawn.

"Well, that's all you have to look out for. You have got your orders."

"Yes, sir."

I paced a turn or two on the poop and saw him take up his position face forward with his elbow in the ratlines[23] of the mizzen-rigging before I went below. The mate's faint snoring was still going on peacefully. The cuddy lamp was burning over the table on which stood a vase with flowers, a polite attention from the ships' provision merchant—the last flowers we should see for the next three months at the very least. Two bunches of bananas hung from the beam symmetrically, one on each side of the rudder casing. Everything was as before in the ship—except that two of her captain's sleeping suits were simultaneously in use, one motionless in the cuddy, the other keeping very still in the captain's stateroom.

It must be explained here that my

---

21 sou'wester: sailor's waterproof hat of oilskin.
22 confabulation: informal talk.

23 ratlines (răt′lĭnz): thin ropes that serve as a ladder for climbing the rigging.

cabin had the form of the capital letter L, the door being within the angle and opening into the short part of the letter. A couch was to the left, the bed-place to the right; my writing desk and the chronometers' table faced the door. But anyone opening it, unless he stepped right inside, had no view of what I call the long (or vertical) part of the letter. It contained some lockers surmounted by a bookcase; and a few clothes, a thick jacket or two, caps, oilskin coat, and such like, hung on hooks. There was at the bottom of that part a door opening into my bathroom, which could be entered also directly from the saloon.[24] But that way was never used.

The mysterious arrival had discovered the advantage of this particular shape. Entering my room, lighted strongly by a big bulkhead lamp swung on gimbals[25] above my writing desk, I did not see him anywhere till he stepped out quietly from behind the coats hung in the recessed part.

"I heard somebody moving about, and went in there at once," he whispered.

I, too, spoke under my breath.

"Nobody is likely to come in here without knocking and getting permission."

He nodded. His face was thin and the sunburn faded, as though he had been ill. And no wonder. He had been, I heard presently, kept under arrest in his cabin for nearly seven weeks. But there was nothing sickly in his eyes or in his expression. He was not a bit like me, really; yet, as we stood leaning over my bed-place, whispering side by side, with our dark heads together and our backs to the door, anybody bold enough to open it stealthily would have

been treated to the uncanny sight of a double captain busy talking in whispers with his other self.

"But all this doesn't tell me how you came to hang on to our side ladder," I inquired, in the hardly audible murmurs we used, after he had told me something more of the proceedings on board the *Sephora* once the bad weather was over.

"When we sighted Java Head[26] I had had time to think all those matters out several times over. I had six weeks of doing nothing else, and with only an hour or so every evening for a tramp on the quarter-deck."

He whispered, his arms folded on the side of my bed-place, staring through the open port. And I could imagine perfectly the manner of this thinking out—a stubborn if not a steadfast operation; something of which I should have been perfectly incapable.

"I reckoned it would be dark before we closed with the land," he continued, so low that I had to strain my hearing, near as we were to each other, shoulder touching shoulder almost. "So I asked to speak to the old man. He always seemed very sick when he came to see me—as if he could not look me in the face. You know, that foresail saved the ship. She was too deep to have run long under bare poles. And it was I that managed to set it for him. Anyway, he came. When I had him in my cabin—he stood by the door looking at me as if I had the halter around my neck already—I asked him right away to leave my cabin door unlocked at night while the ship was going through Sunda Straits.[27] There would be the Java coast

24 **saloon:** large cabin (for dining, here).
25 **gimbals:** suspension devices to keep the lamp level regardless of the tilt of the ship.

26 **Java Head:** a point of land reaching into the Java Sea, south of Borneo.
27 **Sunda Straits:** narrow passage between Sumatra and Java.

JOSEPH CONRAD

within two or three miles, off Angier Point. I wanted nothing more. I've had a prize for swimming my second year in the Conway."

"I can believe it," I breathed out.

"God only knows why they locked me in every night. To see some of their faces you'd have thought they were afraid I'd go about at night strangling people. Am I a murdering brute? Do I look it? By Jove! if I had been he wouldn't have trusted himself like that into my room. You'll say I might have chucked him aside and bolted out, there and then—it was dark already. Well, no. And for the same reason I wouldn't think of trying to smash the door. There would have been a rush to stop me at the noise, and I did not mean to get into a confounded scrimmage. Somebody else might have got killed—for I would not have broken out only to get chucked back, and I did not want any more of that work. He refused, looking more sick than ever. He was afraid of the men, and also of that old second mate of his who had been sailing with him for years—a gray-headed old humbug; and his steward, too, had been with him devil knows how long—seventeen years or more—a dogmatic[28] sort of loafer who hated me like poison, just because I was the chief mate. No chief mate ever made more than one voyage in the *Sephora*, you know. Those two old chaps ran the ship. Devil only knows what the skipper wasn't afraid of (all his nerve went to pieces altogether in that hellish spell of bad weather we had)—of what the law would do to him—of his wife, perhaps. Oh, yes! she's on board. Though I don't think she would have meddled. She would have been only too glad to have me out of the ship in any way.

28 dogmatic (dŏg măt′ĭk): opinionated.

The 'brand of Cain'[29] business, don't you see. That's all right. I was ready enough to go off wandering on the face of the earth—and that was price enough to pay for an Abel of that sort. Anyhow, he wouldn't listen to me. 'This thing must take its course. I represent the law here.' He was shaking like a leaf. 'So you won't?' 'No!' 'Then I hope you will be able to sleep on that,' I said, and turned my back on him. 'I wonder that *you* can,' cries he, and locks the door.

"Well, after that, I couldn't. Not very well. That was three weeks ago. We have had a slow passage through the Java Sea; drifted about Carimata for ten days. When we anchored here they thought, I suppose, it was all right. The nearest land (and that's five miles) is the ship's destination; the consul would soon set about catching me; and there would have been no object in bolting to these islets there. I don't suppose there's a drop of water on them. I don't know how it was, but tonight that steward, after bringing me my supper, went out to let me eat it, and left the door unlocked. And I ate it—all there was, too. After I had finished I strolled out on the quarter-deck. I don't know that I meant to do anything. A breath of fresh air was all I wanted, I believe. Then a sudden temptation came over me. I kicked off my slippers and was in the water before I had made up my mind fairly. Somebody heard the splash and they raised an awful hullabaloo. 'He's gone! Lower the boats! He's committed suicide! No, he's swimming.' Certainly I was swimming. It's not so easy for a swimmer

29 brand of Cain: (Genesis 4:8-15). Cain killed his brother Abel, the first murder according to Biblical tradition. God then condemned Cain to wander over the earth and set a mark upon him that he might be recognized, saying anyone who killed Cain should be punished sevenfold.

like me to commit suicide by drowning. I landed on the nearest islet before the boat left the ship's side. I heard them pulling about in the dark, hailing, and so on, but after a bit they gave up. Everything quieted down and the anchorage became as still as death. I sat down on a stone and began to think. I felt certain they would start searching for me at daylight. There was no place to hide on those stony things—and if there had been, what would have been the good? But now I was clear of that ship, I was not going back. So after a while I took off all my clothes, tied them up in a bundle with a stone inside, and dropped them in the deep water on the outer side of that islet. That was suicide enough for me. Let them think what they liked, but I didn't mean to drown myself. I meant to swim till I sank—but that's not the same thing. I struck out for another of these little islands, and it was from that one that I first saw your riding light. Something to swim for. I went on easily, and on the way I came upon a flat rock a foot or two above water. In the daytime, I dare say, you might make it out with a glass from your poop. I scrambled up on it and rested myself for a bit. Then I made another start. That last spell must have been over a mile."

His whisper was getting fainter and fainter, and all the time he stared straight out through the porthole, in which there was not even a star to be seen. I had not interrupted him. There was something that made comment impossible in his narrative, or perhaps in himself; a sort of feeling, a quality, which I can't find a name for. And when he ceased, all I found was a futile whisper: "So you swam for our light?"

"Yes—straight for it. It was something to swim for. I couldn't see any stars low down because the coast was in the way, and I couldn't see the land, either. The water was like glass. One might have been swimming in a confounded thousand-feet deep cistern with no place for scrambling out anywhere; but what I didn't like was the notion of swimming round and round like a crazed bullock before I gave out; and as I didn't mean to go back . . . No. Do you see me being hauled back, stark naked, off one of these little islands by the scruff of the neck and fighting like a wild beast? Somebody would have got killed for certain, and I did not want any of that. So I went on. Then your ladder—"

"Why didn't you hail the ship?" I asked, a little louder.

He touched my shoulder lightly. Lazy footsteps came right over our heads and stopped. The second mate had crossed from the other side of the poop and might have been hanging over the rail, for all we knew.

"He couldn't hear us talking—could he?" My double breathed into my very ear, anxiously.

His anxiety was an answer, a sufficient answer, to the question I had put to him. An answer containing all the difficulty of that situation. I closed the porthole quietly, to make sure. A louder word might have been overheard.

"Who's that?" he whispered then.

"My second mate. But I don't know much more of the fellow than you do."

And I told him a little about myself. I had been appointed to take charge while I least expected anything of the sort, not quite a fortnight ago. I didn't know either the ship or the people. Hadn't had the time in port to look about me or size anybody up. And as to the crew, all they knew was that I was appointed to take the ship home. For the rest, I was almost as much of a stranger on board as himself, I said.

And at the moment I felt it most acutely. I felt that it would take very little to make me a suspect person in the eyes of the ship's company.

He had turned about meantime; and we, the two strangers in the ship, faced each other in identical attitudes.

"Your ladder—" he murmured, after a silence. "Who'd have thought of finding a ladder hanging over at night in a ship anchored out here! I felt just then a very unpleasant faintness. After the life I've been leading for nine weeks, anybody would have got out of condition. I wasn't capable of swimming round as far as your rudder chains. And, lo and behold! there was a ladder to get hold of. After I gripped it I said to myself, 'What's the good?' When I saw a man's head looking over I thought I would swim away presently and leave him shouting—in whatever language it was. I didn't mind being looked at. I —I liked it. And then you speaking to me so quietly—as if you had expected me—made me hold on a little longer. It had been a confounded lonely time—I don't mean while swimming. I was glad to talk a little to somebody that didn't belong to the *Sephora*. As to asking for the captain, that was a mere impulse. It could have been no use, with all the ship knowing about me and the other people pretty certain to be round here in the morning. I don't know—I wanted to be seen, to talk with somebody, before I went on. I don't know what I would have said. . . . 'Fine night, isn't it?' or something of the sort."

"Do you think they will be round here presently?" I asked with some incredulity.

"Quite likely," he said, faintly.

He looked extremely haggard all of a sudden. His head rolled on his shoulders.

"H'm. We shall see then. Meantime get into that bed," I whispered. "Want help? There."

It was a rather high bed-place with a set of drawers underneath. This amazing swimmer really needed the lift I gave him by seizing his leg. He tumbled in, rolled over on his back, and flung one arm across his eyes. And then, with his face nearly hidden, he must have looked exactly as I used to look in that bed. I gazed upon my other self for a while before drawing across carefully the two green serge curtains which ran on a brass rod. I thought for a moment of pinning them together for greater safety, but I sat down on the couch, and once there I felt unwilling to rise and hunt for a pin. I would do it in a moment. I was extremely tired, in a peculiarly intimate way, by the strain of stealthiness, by the effort of whispering and the general secrecy of this excitement. It was three o'clock by now and I had been on my feet since nine, but I was not sleepy; I could not have gone to sleep. I sat there, fagged out, looking at the curtains, trying to clear my mind of the confused sensation of being in two places at once, and greatly bothered by an exasperating knocking in my head. It was a relief to discover suddenly that it was not in my head at all, but on the outside of the door. Before I could collect myself the words "Come in" were out of my mouth, and the steward entered with a tray, bringing in my morning coffee. I had slept, after all, and I was so frightened that I shouted, "This way! I am here, steward," as though he had been miles away. He put down the tray on the table next the couch and only then said, very quietly, "I can see you are here, sir." I felt him give me a keen look, but I dared not meet his eyes just then. He must have wondered why I had drawn the curtains of my bed before going to sleep on the couch. He went out, hooking the door open as usual.

I heard the crew washing decks above me. I knew I would have been told at once if there had been any wind. Calm, I thought, and I was doubly vexed. Indeed, I felt dual more than ever. The steward reappeared suddenly in the doorway. I jumped up from the couch so quickly that he gave a start.

"What do you want here?"

"Close your port, sir—they are washing decks."

"It is closed," I said, reddening.

"Very well, sir." But he did not move from the doorway and returned my stare in an extraordinary, equivocal[30] manner for a time. Then his eyes wavered, all his expression changed, and in a voice unusually gentle, almost coaxingly:

"May I come in to take the empty cup away, sir?"

"Of course!" I turned my back on him while he popped in and out. Then I unhooked and closed the door and even pushed the bolt. This sort of thing could not go on very long. The cabin was as hot as an oven, too. I took a peep at my double, and discovered that he had not moved, his arm was still over his eyes; but his chest heaved; his hair was wet; his chin glistened with perspiration. I reached over him and opened the port.

"I must show myself on deck," I reflected.

Of course, theoretically, I could do what I liked, with no one to say nay to me within the whole circle of the horizon; but to lock my cabin door and take the key away I did not dare. Directly I put my head out of the companion I saw the group of my two officers, the second mate barefooted, the chief mate in long india-rubber boots, near the break of the poop, and the steward halfway down the poop ladder talking to them eagerly. He happened to catch sight of me and dived, the second ran down on the main deck shouting some order or other, and the chief mate came to meet me, touching his cap.

There was a sort of curiosity in his eye that I did not like. I don't know whether the steward had told them that I was "queer" only, or downright drunk, but I know the man meant to have a good look at me. I watched him coming with a smile which, as he got into point-blank range, took effect and froze his very whiskers. I did not give him time to open his lips.

"Square the yards by lifts and braces before the hands go to breakfast."

It was the first particular order I had given on board that ship; and I stayed on deck to see it executed, too. I had felt the need of asserting myself without loss of time. That sneering young cub got taken down a peg or two on that occasion, and I also seized the opportunity of having a good look at the face of every foremast man as they filed past me to go to the after braces. At breakfast time, eating nothing myself, I presided with such frigid dignity that the two mates were only too glad to escape from the cabin as soon as decency permitted and all the time the dual working of my mind distracted me almost to the point of insanity. I was constantly watching myself, my secret self, as dependent on my actions as my own personality, sleeping in that bed, behind the door which faced me as I sat at the head of the table. It was very much like being mad, only it was worse because one was aware of it.

I had to shake him for a solid minute, but when at last he opened his eyes it

30 equivocal (ĭ kwĭv′ə kəl): doubtful.

was in the full possession of his senses, with an inquiring look.

"All's well so far," I whispered. "Now you must vanish into the bathroom."

He did so, as noiseless as a ghost, and I then rang for the steward, and facing him boldly, directed him to tidy up my stateroom while I was having my bath— "and be quick about it." As my tone admitted of no excuses, he said, "Yes sir," and ran off to fetch his dustpan and brushes. I took a bath and did most of my dressing, splashing, and whistling softly for the steward's edification,[31] while the secret sharer of my life stood drawn up bolt upright in that little space, his face looking very sunken in daylight, his eyelids lowered under the stern, dark line of his eyebrows drawn together by a slight frown.

When I left him there to go back to my room the steward was finishing dusting. I sent for the mate and engaged him in some insignificant conversation. It was, as it were, trifling with the terrific character of his whiskers; but my object was to give him an opportunity for a good look at my cabin. And then I could at last shut, with a clear conscience, the door of my stateroom and get my double back into the recessed part. There was nothing else for it. He had to sit still on a small folding stool, half smothered by the heavy coats hanging there. We listened to the steward going into the bathroom out of the saloon, filling the water bottles there, scrubbing the bath, setting things to rights, whisk, bang, clatter—out again into the saloon—turn the key—click. Such was my scheme for keeping my second self invisible. Nothing better could be contrived under the circumstances. And there we sat; I at my writing desk ready to appear busy with some papers, he behind me, out of sight of the door. It would not have been prudent to talk in daytime; and I could not have stood the excitement of that queer sense of whispering to myself. Now and then, glancing over my shoulder, I saw him far back there, sitting rigidly on the low stool, his bare feet close together, his arms folded, his head hanging on his breast—and perfectly still. Anybody would have taken him for me.

I was fascinated by it myself. Every moment I had to glance over my shoulder. I was looking at him when a voice outside the door said:

"Beg pardon, sir."

"Well!" . . . I kept my eyes on him, and so, when the voice outside the door announced, "There's a ship's boat coming our way, sir," I saw him give a start —the first movement he had made for hours. But he did not raise his bowed head.

"All right. Get the ladder over."

I hesitated. Should I whisper something to him? But what? His immobility seemed to have been never disturbed. What could I tell him he did not know already? . . . Finally I went on deck.

II

THE SKIPPER of the *Sephora* had a thin red whisker all round his face, and the sort of complexion that goes with hair of that color; also the particular, rather smeary shade of blue in the eyes. He was not exactly a showy figure; his shoulders were high, his stature but middling—one leg slightly more bandy[32] than the other. He shook hands, looking vaguely around. A spiritless tenacity[33] was his main characteristic, I

---

31 **edification**: benefit.

32 **bandy**: bowed.
33 **tenacity** (tĭ năs′ə tĭ): persistence.

judged. I behaved with a politeness which seemed to disconcert him. Perhaps he was shy. He mumbled to me as if he were ashamed of what he was saying; gave his name (it was something like Archbold—but at this distance of years I hardly am sure), his ship's name, and a few other particulars of that sort, in the manner of a criminal making a reluctant and doleful confession. He had had terrible weather on the passage out—terrible—terrible—wife aboard, too.

By this time we were seated in the cabin and the steward brought in a tray with a bottle and glasses. "Thanks! No." Never took liquor. Would have some water, though. He drank two tumblerfuls. Terrible thirsty work. Ever since daylight had been exploring the islands round his ship.

"What was that for—fun?" I asked, with an appearance of polite interest.

"No!" He sighed. "Painful duty."

As he persisted in his mumbling and I wanted my double to hear every word, I hit upon the notion of informing him that I regretted to say I was hard of hearing.

"Such a young man, too!" he nodded, keeping his smeary blue, unintelligent eyes fastened upon me. What was the cause of it—some disease? he inquired, without the least sympathy and as if he thought that, if so, I'd got no more than I deserved.

"Yes; disease," I admitted in a cheerful tone which seemed to shock him. But my point was gained, because he had to raise his voice to give me his tale. It is not worth while to record that version. It was just over two months since all this had happened, and he had thought so much about it that he seemed completely muddled as to its bearings, but still immensely impressed.

"What would you think of such a thing happening on board your own ship? I've had the *Sephora* for these fifteen years. I am a well-known shipmaster."

He was densely distressed—and perhaps I should have sympathized with him if I had been able to detach my mental vision from the unsuspected sharer of my cabin as though he were my second self. There he was on the other side of the bulkhead,[34] four or five feet from us, no more, as we sat in the saloon. I looked politely at Captain Archbold (if that was his name), but it was the other I saw, in a gray sleeping suit, seated on a low stool, his bare feet close together, his arms folded, and every word said between us falling into the ears of his dark head bowed on his chest.

"I have been at sea now, man and boy, for seven-and-thirty years, and I've never heard of such a thing happening in an English ship. And that it should be my ship. Wife on board, too."

I was hardly listening to him.

"Don't you think," I said, "that the heavy sea which, you told me, came aboard just then might have killed the man? I have seen the sheer weight of a sea kill a man very neatly, by simply breaking his neck."

"Good God!" he uttered, impressively, fixing his smeary blue eyes on me. "The sea! No man killed by the sea ever looked like that." He seemed positively scandalized at my suggestion. And as I gazed at him, certainly not prepared for anything original on his part, he advanced his head close to mine and thrust his tongue out at me so suddenly that I couldn't help starting back.

After scoring over my calmness in this graphic way he nodded wisely. If I had seen the sight, he assured me, I

---

34 **bulkhead:** upright partition.

would never forget it as long as I lived. The weather was too bad to give the corpse a proper sea burial. So next day at dawn they took it up on the poop, covering its face with a bit of bunting; he read a short prayer, and then, just as it was, in its oilskins and long boots, they launched it amongst those mountainous seas that seemed ready every moment to swallow up the ship herself and the terrified lives on board of her.

"That reefed foresail saved you," I threw in.

"Under God—it did," he exclaimed fervently. "It was by a special mercy, I firmly believe, that it stood some of those hurricane squalls."

"It was the setting of that sail which—" I began.

"God's own hand in it," he interrupted me. "Nothing less could have done it. I don't mind telling you that I hardly dared give the order. It seemed impossible that we could touch anything without losing it, and then our last hope would have been gone."

The terror of that gale was on him yet. I let him go on for a bit, then said, casually—as if returning to a minor subject:

"You were very anxious to give up your mate to the shore people, I believe?"

He was. To the law. His obscure tenacity on that point had in it something incomprehensible and a little awful; something, as it were, mystical, quite apart from his anxiety that he should not be suspected of "countenancing[35] any doings of that sort." Seven-and-thirty virtuous years at sea, of which over twenty of immaculate command, and the last fifteen in the *Sephora*, seemed to have laid him under some pitiless obligation.

"And you know," he went on, groping shamefacedly amongst his feelings, "I did not engage that young fellow. His people had some interest with my owners. I was in a way forced to take him on. He looked very smart, very gentlemanly, and all that. But do you know—I never liked him, somehow. I am a plain man. You see, he wasn't exactly the sort for the chief mate of a ship like the *Sephora*."

I had become so connected in thoughts and impressions with the secret sharer of my cabin that I felt as if I, personally, were being given to understand that I, too, was not the sort that would have done for the chief mate of a ship like the *Sephora*. I had no doubt of it in my mind.

"Not at all the style of man. You understand," he insisted, superfluously, looking hard at me.

I smiled urbanely.[36] He seemed at a loss for a while.

"I suppose I must report a suicide."

"Beg pardon?"

"Sui-cide! That's what I'll have to write to my owners directly I get in."

"Unless you manage to recover him before tomorrow," I assented, dispassionately. . . . "I mean, alive."

He mumbled something which I really did not catch, and I turned my ear to him in a puzzled manner. He fairly bawled:

"The land—I say, the mainland is at least seven miles off my anchorage."

"About that."

My lack of excitement, of curiosity, of surprise, of any sort of pronounced interest, began to arouse his distrust. But except for the felicitous[37] pretense of deafness I had not tried to pretend anything. I had felt utterly incapable

---

35 **countenancing:** approving.

36 **urbanely** (ûr bān′lĭ): politely.
37 **felicitous** (fĭ lĭs′ə təs): happily thought of.

THE NOVEL

of playing the part of ignorance properly, and therefore was afraid to try. It is also certain that he had brought some ready-made suspicions with him, and that he viewed my politeness as a strange and unnatural phenomenon. And yet how else could I have received him? Not heartily! That was impossible for psychological reasons, which I need not state here. My only object was to keep off his inquiries. Surlily? Yes, but surliness might have provoked a point-blank question. From its novelty to him and from its nature, punctilious courtesy was the manner best calculated to restrain the man. But there was the danger of his breaking through my defense bluntly. I could not, I think, have met him by a direct lie, also for psychological (not moral) reasons. If he had only known how afraid I was of his putting my feeling of identity with the other to the test! But, strangely enough—(I thought of it only afterward)

—I believe that he was not a little disconcerted[38] by the reverse side of that weird situation, by something in me that reminded him of the man he was seeking—suggested a mysterious similitude to the young fellow he had distrusted and disliked from the first.

However that might have been, the silence was not very prolonged. He took another oblique step.

"I reckon I had no more than a two-mile pull to your ship. Not a bit more."

"And quite enough, too, in this awful heat," I said.

Another pause full of mistrust followed. Necessity, they say, is mother of invention, but fear, too, is not barren of ingenious suggestions. And I was afraid he would ask me point-blank for news of my other self.

"Nice little saloon, isn't it?" I remarked, as if noticing for the first time

38 disconcerted: upset.

JOSEPH CONRAD

449

the way his eyes roamed from one closed door to the other. "And very well fitted out, too. Here, for instance," I continued, reaching over the back of my seat negligently and flinging the door open, "is my bathroom."

He made an eager movement, but hardly gave it a glance. I got up, shut the door of the bathroom, and invited him to have a look round, as if I were very proud of my accommodation. He had to rise and be shown round, but he went through the business without any raptures whatever.

"And now we'll have a look at my stateroom," I declared, in a voice as loud as I dared to make it, crossing the cabin to the starboard side with purposely heavy steps.

He followed me in and gazed around. My intelligent double had vanished. I played my part.

"Very convenient—isn't it?"

"Very nice. Very com . . ." He didn't finish, and went out brusquely as if to escape from some unrighteous wiles of mine. But it was not to be. I had been too frightened not to feel vengeful; I felt I had him on the run, and I meant to keep him on the run. My polite insistence must have had something menacing in it, because he gave in suddenly. And I did not let him off a single item; mate's room, pantry, store-rooms, the very sail locker which was also under the poop—he had to look into them all. When at last I showed him out on the quarter-deck he drew a long, spiritless sigh, and mumbled dismally that he must really be going back to his ship now. I desired my mate, who had joined us, to see to the captain's boat.

The man of whiskers gave a blast on the whistle which he used to wear hanging round his neck, and yelled, "Sephora's away!" My double down there

in my cabin must have heard, and certainly could not feel more relieved than I. Four fellows came running out from somewhere forward and went over the side, while my own men, appearing on deck too, lined the rail. I escorted my visitor to the gangway ceremoniously, and nearly overdid it. He was a tenacious beast. On the very ladder he lingered, and in that unique, guiltily conscientious manner of sticking to the point:

"I say . . . you . . . you don't think that—"

I covered his voice loudly:

"Certainly not. . . . I am delighted. Good-by."

I had an idea of what he meant to say, and just saved myself by the privilege of defective hearing. He was too shaken generally to insist, but my mate, close witness of that parting, looked mystified and his face took on a thoughtful cast. As I did not want to appear as if I wished to avoid all communication with my officers, he had the opportunity to address me.

"Seems a very nice man. His boat's crew told our chaps a very extraordinary story, if what I am told by the steward is true. I suppose you had it from the captain, sir?"

"Yes. I had a story from the captain."

"A very horrible affair—isn't it, sir?"

"It is."

"Beats all these tales we hear about murders in Yankee ships."

"I don't think it beats them. I don't think it resembles them in the least."

"Bless my soul—you don't say so! But of course I've no acquaintance whatever with American ships, not I, so I couldn't go against your knowledge. It's horrible enough for me. . . . But the queerest part is that those fellows seemed to have some idea the man was hidden aboard here. They had really.

Did you ever hear of such a thing?"

"Preposterous—isn't it?"

We were walking to and fro athwart[39] the quarter-deck. No one of the crew forward could be seen (the day was Sunday), and the mate pursued:

"There was some little dispute about it. Our chaps took offense. 'As if we would harbor a thing like that,' they said. 'Wouldn't you like to look for him in our coal hole?' Quite a tiff. But they made it up in the end. I suppose he did drown himself. Don't you, sir?"

"I don't suppose anything."

"You have no doubt in the matter, sir?"

"None whatever."

I left him suddenly. I felt I was producing a bad impression, but with my double down there it was most trying to be on deck. And it was almost as trying to be below. Altogether a nerve-trying situation. But on the whole I felt less torn in two when I was with him. There was no one in the whole ship whom I dared take into my confidence. Since the hands had got to know his story, it would have been impossible to pass him off for anyone else, and an accidental discovery was to be dreaded now more than ever. . . .

The steward being engaged in laying the table for dinner, we could talk only with our eyes when I first went down. Later in the afternoon we had a cautious try at whispering. The Sunday quietness of the ship was against us; the stillness of air and water around her was against us; the elements, the men were against us—everything was against us in our secret partnership; time itself —for this could not go on forever. The very trust in Providence was, I suppose, denied to his guilt. Shall I confess that this thought cast me down very much?

And as to the chapter of accidents which counts for so much in the book of success, I could only hope that it was closed. For what favorable accident could be expected?

"Did you hear everything?" were my first words as soon as we took up our position side by side, leaning over my bed-place.

He had. And the proof of it was his earnest whisper, "The man told you he hardly dared to give the order."

I understood the reference to be to that saving foresail.

"Yes. He was afraid of it being lost in the setting."

"I assure you he never gave the order. He may think he did, but he never gave it. He stood there with me on the break of the poop after the maintopsail blew away, and whimpered about our last hope—positively whimpered about it and nothing else—and the night coming on! To hear one's skipper go on like that in such weather was enough to drive any fellow out of his mind. It worked me up into a sort of desperation. I just took it into my own hands and went away from him, boiling, and—. But what's the use telling you? *You* know! . . . Do you think that if I had not been pretty fierce with them I should have got the men to do anything? Not it! The bosun[40] perhaps? Perhaps! It wasn't a heavy sea—it was a sea gone mad! I suppose the end of the world will be something like that; and a man may have the heart to see it coming once and be done with it—but to have to face it day after day—I don't blame anybody. I was precious little better than the rest. Only—I was an officer of that old coal-wagon, anyhow—"

"I quite understand," I conveyed that sincere assurance into his ear. He was

---

39 athwart (ə thwôrt′): across the length.

40 bosun: petty officer in charge of deck crew.

out of breath with whispering; I could hear him pant slightly. It was all very simple. The same strung-up force which had given twenty-four men a chance, at least, for their lives, had, in a sort of recoil, crushed an unworthy mutinous existence.

But I had no leisure to weigh the merits of the matter—footsteps in the saloon, a heavy knock. "There's enough wind to get under way with, sir." Here was the call of a new claim upon my thoughts and even upon my feelings.

"Turn the hands up," I cried through the door. "I'll be on deck directly."

I was going out to make the acquaintance of my ship. Before I left the cabin our eyes met—the eyes of the only two strangers on board. I pointed to the recessed part where the little camp-stool awaited him and laid my finger on my lips. He made a gesture—somewhat vague—a little mysterious, accompanied by a faint smile, as if of regret.

This is not the place to enlarge upon the sensations of a man who feels for the first time a ship move under his feet to his own independent word. In my case they were not unalloyed. I was not wholly alone with my command; for there was that stranger in my cabin. Or rather, I was not completely and wholly with her. Part of me was absent. That mental feeling of being in two places at once affected me physically as if the mood of secrecy had penetrated my very soul. Before an hour had elapsed since the ship had begun to move, having occasion to ask the mate (he stood by my side) to take a compass bearing of the Pagoda, I caught myself reaching up to his ear in whispers. I say I caught myself, but enough had escaped to startle the man. I can't describe it otherwise than by saying that he shied. A grave, preoccupied manner, as though he were in posses-

sion of some perplexing intelligence, did not leave him henceforth. A little later I moved away from the rail to look at the compass with such a stealthy gait that the helmsman noticed it—and I could not help noticing the unusual roundness of his eyes. These are trifling instances, though it's to no commander's advantage to be suspected of ludicrous eccentricities. But I was also more seriously affected. There are to a seaman certain words, gestures, that should in given conditions come as naturally, as instinctively as the winking of a menaced eye. A certain order should spring on to his lips without thinking; a certain sign should get itself made, so to speak, without reflection. But all unconscious alertness had abandoned me. I had to make an effort of will to recall myself back (from the cabin) to the conditions of the moment. I felt that I was appearing an irresolute commander to those people who were watching me more or less critically.

And, besides, there were the scares. On the second day out, for instance, coming off the deck in the afternoon (I had straw slippers on my bare feet) I stopped at the open pantry door and spoke to the steward. He was doing something there with his back to me. At the sound of my voice he nearly jumped out of his skin, as the saying is, and incidentally broke a cup.

"What on earth's the matter with you?" I asked, astonished.

He was extremely confused. "Beg pardon, sir. I made sure you were in your cabin."

"You see I wasn't."

"No, sir. I could have sworn I had heard you moving in there not a moment ago. It's most extraordinary . . . very sorry, sir."

I passed on with an inward shudder. I was so identified with my secret double that I did not even mention the fact in those scanty, fearful whispers we exchanged. I suppose he had made some slight noise of some kind or other. It would have been miraculous if he hadn't at one time or another. And yet, haggard as he appeared, he looked always perfectly self-controlled, more than calm—almost invulnerable.[41] On my suggestion he remained almost entirely in the bathroom, which, upon the whole, was the safest place. There could be really no shadow of an excuse for anyone ever wanting to go in there, once the steward had done with it. It was a very tiny place. Sometimes he reclined on the floor, his legs bent, his head sustained on one elbow. At others I would find him on the camp-stool, sitting in his gray sleeping suit and with his cropped dark hair like a patient, unmoved convict. At night I would smuggle him into my bed-place, and we would whisper together, with the regular footfalls of the officer of the watch passing and repassing over our heads. It was an infinitely miserable time. It was lucky that some tins of fine preserves were stowed in a locker in my stateroom; hard bread I could always get hold of; and so he lived on stewed chicken, paté de foie gras,[42] asparagus, cooked oysters, sardines—on all sorts of abominable sham delicacies out of tins. My early morning coffee he always drank; and it was all I dared do for him in that respect.

Every day there was the horrible maneuvering to go through so that my room and then the bathroom should be done in the usual way. I came to hate the sight of the steward, to abhor the voice of that harmless man. I felt that it was he who would bring on the disaster of discovery. It hung like a sword over our heads.

The fourth day out, I think (we were then working down the east side of the Gulf of Siam, tack for tack,[43] in light winds and smooth water)—the fourth day, I say, of this miserable juggling with the unavoidable, as we sat at our evening meal, that man, whose slightest movement I dreaded, after putting down the dishes ran upon deck busily. This could not be dangerous. Presently he came down again; and then it appeared that he had remembered a coat of mine which I had thrown over a rail to dry after having been wetted in a shower which had passed over the ship in the afternoon. Sitting stolidly at the head of the table I became terrified at the sight of the garment on his arm. Of course he made for my door. There was no time to lose.

"Steward," I thundered. My nerves were so shaken that I could not govern my voice and conceal my agitation. This was the sort of thing that made my terrifically whiskered mate tap his forehead with his forefinger. I had detected him using that gesture while talking on deck with a confidential air to the carpenter. It was too far to hear a word, but I had no doubt that this pantomime could only refer to the strange new captain.

"Yes, sir," the pale-faced steward turned resignedly to me. It was this maddening course of being shouted at, checked without rhyme or reason, arbitrarily chased out of my cabin, suddenly called into it, sent flying out of his pantry on incomprehensible errands, that accounted for the growing wretchedness of his expression.

41 **invulnerable** (ĭn vŭl′nər ə bəl): unable to be injured.

42 **paté de foie gras** (pä tě′də fwà grä′): a delicacy made of goose liver.

43 **tack for tack**: zigzagging.

"Where are you going with that coat?"

"To your room, sir."

"Is there another shower coming?"

"I'm sure I don't know, sir. Shall I go up again and see, sir?"

"No! never mind."

My object was attained, as of course my other self in there would have heard everything that passed. During this interlude my two officers never raised their eyes off their respective plates; but the lip of that confounded cub, the second mate, quivered visibly.

I expected the steward to hook my coat on and come out at once. He was very slow about it; but I dominated my nervousness sufficiently not to shout after him. Suddenly I became aware (it could be heard plainly enough) that the fellow for some reason or other was opening the door of the bathroom. It was the end. The place was literally not big enough to swing a cat in. My voice died in my throat and I went stony all over. I expected to hear a yell of surprise and terror, and made a movement, but had not the strength to get on my legs. Everything remained still. Had my second self taken the poor wretch by the throat? I don't know what I would have done next moment if I had not seen the steward come out of my room, close the door, and then stand quietly by the sideboard.

Saved, I thought. But, no! Lost! Gone! He was gone!

I laid my knife and fork down and leaned back in my chair. My head swam. After a while, when sufficiently recovered to speak in a steady voice, I instructed my mate to put the ship round at eight o'clock himself.

"I won't come on deck," I went on. "I think I'll turn in, and unless the wind shifts I don't want to be disturbed before midnight. I feel a bit seedy."

"You did look middling bad a little while ago," the chief mate remarked without showing any great concern.

They both went out, and I stared at the steward clearing the table. There was nothing to be read on that wretched man's face. But why did he avoid my eyes I asked myself. Then I thought I should like to hear the sound of his voice.

"Steward!"

"Sir!" Startled as usual.

"Where did you hang up that coat?"

"In the bathroom, sir." The usual anxious tone. "It's not quite dry yet, sir."

For some time longer I sat in the cuddy. Had my double vanished as he had come? But of his coming there was an explanation, whereas his disappearance would be inexplicable. . . . I went slowly into my dark room, shut the door, lighted the lamp, and for a time dared not turn round. When at last I did I saw him standing bolt upright in the narrow recessed part. It would not be true to say I had a shock, but an irresistible doubt of his bodily existence flitted through my mind. Can it be, I asked myself, that he is not visible to other eyes than mine? It was like being haunted. Motionless, with a grave face, he raised his hands slightly at me in a gesture which meant clearly, "Heavens! what a narrow escape!" Narrow indeed. I think I had come creeping quietly as near insanity as any man who has not actually gone over the border. That gesture restrained me, so to speak.

The mate with the terrific whiskers was now putting the ship on the other tack. In the moment of profound silence which follows upon the hands going to their stations I heard on the poop his raised voice: "Hard alee!" and the distant shout of the order repeated

454

on the maindeck. The sails, in that light breeze, made but a faint fluttering noise. It ceased. The ship was coming round slowly; I held my breath in the renewed stillness of expectation; one wouldn't have thought that there was a single living soul on her decks. A sudden brisk shout, "Mainsail haul!" broke the spell, and in the noisy cries and rush overhead of the men running away with the main brace we two, down in my cabin, came together in our usual position by the bed-place.

He did not wait for my question. "I heard him fumbling here and just managed to squat myself down in the bath," he whispered to me. "The fellow only opened the door and put his arm in to hang the coat up. All the same—"

"I never thought of that," I whispered back, even more appalled than before at the closeness of the shave, and marveling at that something unyielding in his character which was carrying him through so finely. There was no agitation in his whisper. Whoever was being driven distracted, it was not he. He was sane. And the proof of his sanity was continued when he took up the whispering again.

"It would never do for me to come to life again."

It was something that a ghost might have said. But what he was alluding to was his old captain's reluctant admission of the theory of suicide. It would obviously serve his turn—if I had understood at all the view which seemed to govern the unalterable purpose of his action.

"You must maroon[44] me as soon as ever you can get amongst these islands off the Cambodje shore," he went on.

"Maroon you! We are not living in a boy's adventure tale," I protested. His scornful whispering took me up.

44 **maroon**: put ashore in a desolate place.

"We aren't indeed! There's nothing of a boy's tale in this. But there's nothing else for it. I want no more. You don't suppose I am afraid of what can be done to me? Prison or gallows or whatever they may please. But you don't see me coming back to explain such things to an old fellow in a wig[45] and twelve respectable tradesmen, do you? What can they know whether I am guilty or not—or of *what* I am guilty, either? That's my affair. What does the Bible say? 'Driven off the face of the earth.' Very well. I am off the face of the earth now. As I came at night so I shall go."

"Impossible!" I murmured. "You can't."

"Can't? . . . Not naked like a soul on the Day of Judgment. I shall freeze on to this sleeping suit. The Last Day is not yet—and . . . you have understood thoroughly. Didn't you?"

I felt suddenly ashamed of myself. I may say truly that I understood—and my hesitation in letting that man swim away from my ship's side had been a mere sham sentiment, a sort of cowardice.

"It can't be done now till next night," I breathed out. "The ship is on the offshore tack[46] and the wind may fail us."

"As long as I know that you understand," he whispered. "But of course you do. It's a great satisfaction to have got somebody to understand. You seem to have been there on purpose." And in the same whisper, as if we two whenever we talked had to say things to each other which were not fit for the world to hear, he added, "It's very wonderful."

We remained side by side talking in our secret way—but sometimes silent or just exchanging a whispered word or two at long intervals. And as usual he stared through the port. A breath of wind came now and again into our faces. The ship might have been moored in dock, so gently and on an even keel she slipped through the water, that did not murmur even at our passage, shadowy and silent like a phantom sea.

At midnight I went on deck, and to my mate's great surprise put the ship round on the other tack. His terrible whiskers flitted round me in silent criticism. I certainly should not have done it if it had been only a question of getting out of that sleepy gulf as quickly as possible. I believe he told the second mate, who relieved him, that it was a great want of judgment. The other only yawned. That intolerable cub shuffled about so sleepily and lolled against the rails in such a slack, improper fashion that I came down on him sharply.

"Aren't you properly awake yet?"

"Yes, sir! I am awake."

"Well, then, be good enough to hold yourself as if you were. And keep a lookout. If there's any current we'll be closing with some islands before daylight."

The east side of the gulf is fringed with islands, some solitary, others in groups. On the blue background of the high coast they seem to float on silvery patches of calm water, arid and gray, or dark green and rounded like clumps of evergreen bushes, with the larger ones, a mile or two long, showing the outlines of ridges, ribs of gray rock under the dark mantle of matted leafage. Unknown to trade, to travel, almost to geography, the manner of life they harbor is an unsolved secret. There must be villages—settlements of fishermen at least—on the largest of

45 **wig:** English judges wear wigs in court.
46 **offshore tack:** headed away from shore.

them, and some communication with the world is probably kept up by native craft. But all that forenoon, as we headed for them, fanned along by the faintest of breezes, I saw no sign of man or canoe in the field of the telescope I kept on pointing at the scattered group.

At noon I gave no orders for a change of course, and the mate's whiskers became much concerned and seemed to be offering themselves unduly to my notice. At last I said:

"I am going to stand right in. Quite in—as far as I can take her."

The stare of extreme surprise imparted an air of ferocity also to his eyes, and he looked truly terrific for a moment.

"We're not doing well in the middle of the gulf," I continued, casually. "I am going to look for the land breezes tonight."

"Bless my soul! Do you mean, sir, in the dark amongst the lot of all them islands and reefs and shoals?"

"Well—if there are any regular land breezes at all on this coast one must get close inshore to find them, mustn't one?"

"Bless my soul!" he exclaimed again under his breath. All that afternoon he wore a dreamy, contemplative appearance which in him was a mark of perplexity. After dinner I went into my stateroom as if I meant to take some rest. There we two bent our dark heads over a half-unrolled chart lying on my bed.

"There," I said. "It's got to be Koh-ring.[47] I've been looking at it ever since sunrise. It has got two hills and a low point. It must be inhabited. And on the coast opposite there is what

47 Koh-ring: small mountainous island off the Gulf of Siam.

looks like the mouth of a biggish river —with some town, no doubt, not far up. It's the best chance for you that I can see."

"Anything. Koh-ring let it be."

He looked thoughtfully at the chart as if surveying chances and distances from a lofty height—and following with his eyes his own figure wandering on the blank land of Cochin-China, and then passing off that piece of paper clean out of sight into uncharted regions. And it was as if the ship had two captains to plan her course for her. I had been so worried and restless running up and down that I had not had the patience to dress that day. I had remained in my sleeping suit, with straw slippers and a soft floppy hat. The closeness of the heat in the gulf had been most oppressive, and the crew were used to see me wandering in that airy attire.

"She will clear the south point as she heads now," I whispered into his ear. "Goodness only knows when, though, but certainly after dark. I'll edge her in to half a mile, as far as I may be able to judge in the dark—"

"Be careful," he murmured, warningly—and I realized suddenly that all my future, the only future for which I was fit, would perhaps go irretrievably to pieces in any mishap to my first command.

I could not stop a moment longer in the room. I motioned him to get out of sight and made my way on the poop. That unplayful cub had the watch. I walked up and down for a while thinking things out, then beckoned him over.

"Send a couple of hands to open the two quarter-deck ports," I said, mildly.

He actually had the impudence, or else so forgot himself in his wonder at such an incomprehensible order, as to repeat:

"Open the quarter-deck ports! What for, sir?"

"The only reason you need concern yourself about is because I tell you to do so. Have them open wide and fastened properly."

He reddened and went off, but I believe made some jeering remark to the carpenter as to the sensible practice of ventilating a ship's quarter-deck. I know he popped into the mate's cabin to impart the fact to him because the whiskers came on deck, as it were by chance, and stole glances at me from below—for signs of lunacy or drunkenness, I suppose.

A little before supper, feeling more restless than ever, I rejoined, for a moment, my second self. And to find him sitting so quietly was surprising, like something against nature, inhuman.

I developed my plan in a hurried whisper.

"I shall stand in as close as I dare and then put her round. I shall presently find means to smuggle you out of here into the sail locker, which communicates with the lobby. But there is an opening, a sort of square for hauling the sails out, which gives straight on the quarter-deck and which is never closed in fine weather, so as to give air to the sails. When the ship's way is deadened in stays[48] and all the hands are aft at the main braces you shall have a clear road to slip out and get overboard through the open quarter-deck port. I've had them both fastened up. Use a rope's end to lower yourself into the water so as to avoid a splash—you know. It could be heard and cause some beastly complication."

He ʼkept silent for a while, then whispered, "I understand."

48 in stays: that moment when a sailing ship is changing tack (direction) and is in a kind of suspended motion.

"I won't be there to see you go," I began with an effort. "The rest . . . I only hope I have understood, too."

"You have. From first to last," and for the first time there seemed to be a faltering, something strained in his whisper. He caught hold of my arm, but the ringing of the supper bell made me start. He didn't, though; he only released his grip.

After supper I didn't come below again till well past eight o'clock. The faint, steady breeze was loaded with dew; and the wet, darkened sails held all there was of propelling power in it. The night, clear and starry, sparkled darkly, and the opaque, lightless patches shifting slowly against the low stars were the drifting islets. On the port bow there was a big one more distant and shadowily imposing by the great space of sky it eclipsed.

On opening the door I had a back view of my very own self looking at a chart. He had come out of the recess and was standing near the table.

"Quite dark enough," I whispered.

He stepped back and leaned against my bed with a level, quiet glance. I sat on the couch. We had nothing to say to each other. Over our heads the officer of the watch moved here and there. Then I heard him move quickly. I knew what that meant. He was making for the companion; and presently his voice was outside my door.

"We are drawing in pretty fast, sir. Land looks rather close."

"Very well," I answered. "I am coming on deck directly."

I waited till he was gone out of the cuddy, then rose. My double moved too. The time had come to exchange our last whispers, for neither of us was ever to hear each other's natural voice.

"Look here!" I opened a drawer and

took out three sovereigns.[49]   Take this, anyhow. I've got six and I'd give you the lot, only I must keep a little money to buy some fruit and vegetables for the crew from native boats as we go through Sunda Straits."

He shook his head.

"Take it," I urged him, whispering desperately. "No one can tell what—"

He smiled and slapped meaningly the only pocket of the sleeping jacket. It was not safe, certainly. But I produced a large old silk handkerchief of mine, and tying the three pieces of gold in a corner, pressed it on him. He was touched, I suppose, because he took it at last and tied it quickly round his waist under the jacket, on his bare skin.

Our eyes met; several seconds elapsed, till, our glances still mingled, I extended my hand and turned the lamp out.

49 sovereigns: British gold coins.

Then I passed through the cuddy, leaving the door of my room wide open. . . . "Steward!"

He was still lingering in the pantry in the greatness of his zeal, giving a rub-up to a plated cruet stand the last thing before going to bed. Being careful not to wake up the mate, whose room was opposite, I spoke in an undertone.

He looked round anxiously. "Sir!"

"Can you get me a little hot water from the galley?"

"I am afraid, sir, the galley fire's been out for some time now."

"Go and see."

He fled up the stairs.

"Now," I whispered, loudly, into the saloon—too loudly, perhaps, but I was afraid I couldn't make a sound. He was by my side in an instant—the double captain slipped past the stairs—through the tiny dark passage . . . a sliding door. We were in the sail locker, scrambling on our knees over the sails. A sudden thought struck me. I saw myself wandering barefooted, bare-headed, the sun beating on my dark poll.[50] I snatched off my floppy hat and tried hurriedly in the dark to ram it on my other self. He dodged and fended off silently. I wonder what he thought had come to me before he understood and suddenly desisted. Our hands met gropingly, lingered united in a steady, motionless clasp for a second. . . . No word was breathed by either of us when they separated.

I was standing quietly by the pantry door when the steward returned.

"Sorry, sir. Kettle barely warm. Shall I light the spirit lamp?"

"Never mind."

I came out on deck slowly. It was now a matter of conscience to shave the land as close as possible—for now he must go overboard whenever the ship was put in stays. Must! There could be no going back for him. After a moment I walked over to leeward and my heart flew into my mouth at the nearness of the land on the bow. Under any other circumstances I would not have held on a minute longer. The second mate had followed me anxiously.

I looked on till I felt I could command my voice.

"She will weather,"[51] I said then in a quiet tone.

"Are you going to try that, sir?" he stammered out incredulously.

I took no notice of him and raised my tone just enough to be heard by the helmsman.

"Keep her good full."

"Good full, sir."

The wind fanned my cheek, the sails slept, the world was silent. The strain of watching the dark loom of the land grow bigger and denser was too much for me. I had shut my eyes—because the ship must go closer. She must! The stillness was intolerable. Were we standing still?

When I opened my eyes the second view started my heart with a thump. The black southern hill of Koh-ring seemed to hang right over the ship like a towering fragment of the everlasting night. On that enormous mass of blackness there was not a gleam to be seen, not a sound to be heard. It was gliding irresistibly toward us and yet seemed already within reach of the hand. I saw the vague figures of the watch grouped in the waist, gazing in awed silence.

"Are you going on, sir?" inquired an unsteady voice at my elbow.

I ignored it. I had to go on.

"Keep her full. Don't check her way. That won't do now," I said warningly.

"I can't see the sails very well," the helmsman answered me, in strange, quavering tones.

Was she close enough? Already she was, I won't say in the shadow of the land, but in the very blackness of it, already swallowed up as it were, gone too close to be recalled, gone from me altogether.

"Give the mate a call," I said to the young man who stood at my elbow as still as death. "And turn all hands up."

My tone had a borrowed loudness reverberated from the height of the land. Several voices cried out together: "We are all on deck, sir."

Then stillness again, with the great shadow gliding closer, towering higher, without a light, without a sound. Such a hush had fallen on the ship that she might have been a bark of the dead

50 poll: head.
51 She will weather: The ship will catch enough breeze to keep from drifting to shore.

THE NOVEL

floating in slowly under the very gate of Erebus.[52]

"My God! Where are we?"

It was the mate moaning at my elbow. He was thunderstruck, and as it were deprived of the moral support of his whiskers. He clapped his hands and absolutely cried out, "Lost!"

"Be quiet," I said sternly.

He lowered his tone, but I saw the shadowy gesture of his despair. "What are we doing here?"

"Looking for the land wind."

He made as if to tear his hair, and addressed me recklessly.

"She will never get out. You have done it, sir. I knew it'd end in something like this. She will never weather, and you are too close now to stay. She'll drift ashore before she's round. O my God!"

I caught his arm as he was raising it

52 Erebus (ĕr′ə bəs): a gloomy area before entering Hades, land of the dead.

to batter his poor devoted head, and shook it violently.

"She's ashore already," he wailed, trying to tear himself away.

"Is she? . . . Keep good full there!"

"Good full, sir," cried the helmsman in a frightened, thin, childlike voice.

I hadn't let go the mate's arm and went on shaking it. "Ready about, do you hear? You go forward"—shake—"and stop there"—shake—"and hold your noise"—shake—"and see these head sheets properly overhauled"—shake, shake—shake.

And all the time I dared not look toward the land lest my heart should fail me. I released my grip at last and he ran forward as if fleeing for dear life.

I wondered what my double there in the sail locker thought of this commotion. He was able to hear everything—and perhaps he was able to understand why, on my conscience, it had to be thus close—no less. My first order.

"Hard alee!" re-echoed ominously under the towering shadow of Koh-ring as if I had shouted in a mountain gorge. And then I watched the land intently. In that smooth water and light wind it was impossible to feel the ship coming-to. No! I could not feel her. And my second self was making now ready to slip out and lower himself overboard. Perhaps he was gone already . . . ?

The great black mass brooding over our very mastheads began to pivot away from the ship's side silently. And now I forgot the secret stranger ready to depart, and remembered only that I was a total stranger to the ship. I did not know her. Would she do it? How was she to be handled?

I swung the mainyard and waited helplessly. She was perhaps stopped, and her very fate hung in the balance, with the black mass of Koh-ring like the gate of the everlasting night towering over her taffrail.[53] What would she do now? Had she way[54] on her yet? I stepped to the side swiftly, and on the shadowy water I could see nothing except a faint phosphorescent flash revealing the glassy smoothness of the sleeping surface. It was impossible to tell—and I had not learned yet the feel of my ship. Was she moving? What I needed was something easily seen, a piece of paper, which I could throw overboard and watch. I had nothing on me. To run down for it I didn't dare. There was no time. All at once my strained, yearning stare distinguished a white object floating within a yard of the ship's side. White on the black water. A phosphorescent flash passed under it. What was that thing? . . . I recognized my own floppy hat. It must have fallen off his head . . . and he

didn't bother. Now I had what I wanted—the saving mark for my eyes. But I hardly thought of my other self, now gone from the ship, to be hidden forever from all friendly faces, to be a fugitive and a vagabond on the earth, with no brand of the curse on his sane forehead to stay a slaying hand . . . too proud to explain.

And I watched the hat—the expression of my sudden pity for his mere flesh. It had been meant to save his homeless head from the dangers of the sun. And now—behold—it was saving the ship, by serving me for a mark to help out the ignorance of my strangeness. Ha! It was drifting forward, warning me just in time that the ship had gathered sternway.

"Shift the helm," I said in a low voice to the seaman standing still like a statue.

The man's eyes glistened wildly in the binnacle light as he jumped round to the other side and spun round the wheel.

I walked to the break of the poop. On the overshadowed deck all hands stood by the forebraces waiting for my order. The stars ahead seemed to be gliding from right to left. And all was so still in the world that I heard the quiet remark "She's round," passed in a tone of intense relief between two seamen.

"Let go and haul."

The foreyards ran round with a great noise, amidst cheery cries. And now the frightful whiskers made themselves heard giving various orders. Already the ship was drawing ahead. And I was alone with her. Nothing! no one in the world should stand now between us, throwing a shadow on the way of silent knowledge and mute affection, the perfect communion of a seaman with his first command.

53 taffrail: rail around the stern (rear) of ship.
54 way: headway; progress.

Walking to the taffrail, I was in time to make out, on the very edge of a darkness thrown by a towering black mass like the very gateway of Erebus—yes, I was in time to catch an evanescent glimpse of my white hat left behind to mark the spot where the secret sharer of my cabin and of my thoughts, as though he were my second self, had lowered himself into the water to take his punishment: a free man, a proud swimmer striking out for a new destiny.

The Story

On an elementary level, *The Secret Sharer* is an adventure story in which a young sea captain befriends a murderer chiefly because the young stranger bears a striking resemblance to himself. As his ship lies motionless waiting for a wind that does not come, he hides the fugitive in his cabin for several days and finally takes the ship dangerously close to an island so the stranger may swim ashore.

This summary raises two questions. Why does the captain risk his career to help the stranger who has no claim on him? Why does he take his ship dangerously close to land on a dark night? These questions can be answered on two levels.

On a moral level, the young captain risks his career in going against the training and tradition of a ship's officer because he feels that the young officer is not a murderer in the usual sense and that he will not be fairly treated by the weak, unimaginative, conventionbound captain of the *Sephora*. Thus, the captain feels morally bound to take the ship dangerously close to shore in order to give the fugitive a better chance to reach land.

On a symbolic level, the story is a study of the psychological reactions and changes in a young man because of the feeling of identity and relationship that he experiences with another. As he faces personal risks in helping the stranger, the captain is also testing himself to see if he has the moral strength to command a ship and a crew that are strange to him. On this level, the captain takes his ship dangerously close to shore not to help Leggatt, who is a strong swimmer and needs no extra help, but to prove that he is in full command of his ship.

When the story opens, the captain is not sure of himself. "If all the truth must be told," he says, "I was somewhat of a stranger to myself." Just before he discovers the fugitive at the rope ladder, the captain is pacing the deck of his becalmed ship trying to gain confidence from observing the serenity of the sea and smoking a cigar. At this moment, his knowledge of the sea is the only thing he is sure of.

During the course of the story, the most important problem for the captain is one he had stated even before the arrival of Leggatt: "I wondered how far I should turn out faithful to that ideal conception of one's own personality every man sets up for himself secretly." In recognizing himself in Leggatt, in his sense of doubleness with this stranger, the question is not merely whether to turn Leggatt over to the authorities or not, but whether to betray himself—his inner conception of himself—or not. The story concerns the captain's search for self-knowledge, his discovery of his own identity. In this sense, *The Secret Sharer* is not a story of the sea at all: it concerns, as the sentence just quoted indicates, the problem of "every man."

When the story ends, Leggatt is striking out bravely on his new destiny, and the captain has lost his sense of insecurity and strangeness as he becomes the captain of his ship to whom orders and command come instinctively. Like Leggatt, he, too, is striking out on a new destiny.

Part I

Understanding the Story—What happened?

1. What do you learn in the first seven paragraphs that help you to understand the young captain's question to himself at the end of the seventh paragraph: "I wondered how far I should turn out faithful to that ideal conception of one's own personality every man sets up for himself"?

   Review these facts to help you in understanding the captain's statement:

   (*a*) Who tells the story?

   (*b*) Where is he when the story opens?

   (*c*) Why is the ship there?

   (*d*) What is the captain's relation to the ship and the crew?

2. What does the reaction of the officers to the captain's unexpected decision to dismiss the crew and take the anchor-watch himself reveal about shipboard discipline and routine?

3. What thought is worrying the young captain as he paces the deck of his ship?

4. How does Conrad keep the ship and the crew in the background as he focuses the story on the young narrator-captain?

5. What is the captain's reaction when he sees the rope ladder over the side of the ship?

6. Point out several unusual aspects of the encounter between Leggatt and the captain.

7. What does Leggatt's telling the captain twice that his father is a parson in Norfolk suggest?

8. What is the shape of the captain's cabin and how does it lend itself to providing hiding space for Leggatt?

9. What fact about ship discipline is the captain counting on as he plans to hide Leggatt in his cabin?
10. What points of identity or likeness do you discover between the captain and Leggatt during their first meeting?
11. What answers do you find to the following questions in Leggatt's account of his killing the seaman?
   (*a*) How and when had Leggatt killed the man?
   (*b*) What was the attitude of the crew and the captain toward Leggatt following the killing?
   (*c*) How did the captain of the *Sephora* contribute to Leggatt's decision to slip overboard and swim until he sank?
   (*d*) How does Leggatt distinguish between committing suicide and swimming until he could not go any farther?

Understanding the Story—Why did these things happen?

(Keep in mind that nothing happens in a novel that the author does not want to have happen. Everything that happens has some significance.)

1. The captain (the speaker of the story) refers to the chief mate's "terrible whiskers" in a rather humorous way and describes him as a man of a "painstaking turn of mind" who likes "to account to himself for practically everything." He presents the second mate as a young man with a tendency to sneer and is annoyed when he detects a "slight quiver on his lips." What relationship between the captain and his officers do such details and the captain's way of describing them indicate? In view of the rest of the plot, why does Conrad want such a relationship?
2. Why does the captain decide to take the five-hour anchor watch himself and order the crew to turn in?
3. Why does Conrad emphasize the young captain's feeling of strangeness toward his ship and his crew? Does this feeling influence the captain's reaction toward the stranger?
4. Explain the irony in the following statement which occurs shortly before the captain's discovery of Leggatt: "And suddenly I rejoiced in the great security of the sea as compared with the unrest of the land, in my choice of that untempted life presenting no disquieting problems, invested with an elementary moral beauty by the absolute straightforwardness of its appeal and by the singleness of its purpose."
5. Why does the captain confide in the stranger his lack of security on his own ship?
6. Why does the captain order the chief mate to "square the yards by lifts and braces before the hands go to breakfast"?
7. Why does the captain say, "It was very much like being mad, only it was worse because one was aware of it," following several suspicious actions on his part after his decision to hide Leggatt?

Part II

Understanding the Story—What happened?

1. Find several of the captain's first impressions of his visitor that help to create the reader's image of him.
2. Compare the *Sephora* captain's version of the crime with Leggatt's version with special reference to:
   (a) the conditions under which the sailor was killed,
   (b) the setting of the reefed topsail,
   (c) the terror of the hurricane,
   (d) the difference between Leggatt as a person and the rest of the ship's company, including the captain.
3. To what does the captain credit the feeling of uneasiness between himself and the *Sephora's* captain during their visit?
4. What does the captain find himself doing when he goes on deck in response to the chief mate's report that there was enough wind to get under way?
5. Review some of the tensest moments that the captain had while hiding Leggatt.
6. What reason does the captain give the chief mate when he says he is taking the ship as close to the shore as he can?
7. What does the captain give Leggatt before he leaves the ship?
8. What is the real reason that the captain takes his ship so close to shore? He tells the mate it is to catch the land breeze; he tells Leggatt that it is to get him as close to shore as possible. What other reason does he have?
9. When the captain in sudden panic realizes that he is in complete charge of the ship and is not sure how she will respond to his handling, what helps him to determine his bearings?
10. What is the reaction of the crew when the ship comes round safely after seeming to head blindly and swiftly in the darkness toward shore?

Understanding the Story—Why did these things happen?

1. Why does the captain pretend to be hard of hearing when he talks with the captain of the *Sephora?* When does he shout at the steward for the same reason?
2. Why does the visiting captain thrust his tongue in the captain's face?
3. Why does the captain insist on showing his visitor every nook and corner of his cabin?
4. Why does the captain feel that he would not be able to lie to his visitor if he asked him directly if Leggatt were on board?
5. Why does the visit of the *Sephora* captain increase the necessity of keeping Leggatt hidden from the officers and crew?
6. Why does Conrad have the steward break the cup?

7. Why does Leggatt say to the captain, "It would never do for me to come to life again"?

8. Why does the captain "put the ship round on the other tack" even in the face of the chief mate's disapproval?

9. Why does the captain order the quarter-deck ports opened? Why does he send the steward to the galley for hot water?

10. Why does the captain's reflection on Leggatt also apply to the captain, "a free man, a proud swimmer striking out for a new destiny"?

General Questions

1. Who is the hero of the story—Leggatt or the captain? Give reasons for your answer.

2. Does the captain tell the story of his secret sharer immediately after it happened or long afterward? How do you know? What does the time at which the experience is related add to the story?

3. How does the captain as the reader sees him at the beginning of the story contrast with the captain as he appears at the end of the story? Why has he changed?

4. Why does Conrad open the story with a long paragraph filled with sensory impressions (sights and sounds) and no action and close the story with a series of short action-filled paragraphs?

5. How do the opening and closing paragraphs give the story unity and focus? On what and whom do they focus attention?

6. Explain the symbolism of the following objects. Remember that a symbol carries its own meaning as well as an additional one on another level. (See Literary Terms.)
   (a) The riding light in the forerigging.
   (b) The captain's cigar.
   (c) The identical sleeping suits.
   (d) The captain's floppy white hat.

7. What characteristics or types of individuals do the following people represent in *The Secret Sharer*?
   (a) The captain of the *Sephora*.
   (b) The young captain.
   (c) Leggatt.

Building Vocabulary Skills

Rewrite the following sentences, substituting a synonym or phrase for each italicized word that will express as precisely as possible its meaning. Try to find the meaning from the sentence, but if you are not certain of the word, consult the dictionary.

1. (p. 434) "He was of a *painstaking* turn of mind."

2. (p. 435) "I heard the other raise his voice *incredulously:* 'What? The captain himself?'"

3. (p. 436) "Then I *reflected* that I had myself *peremptorily* dismissed my officers from duty. . . ."

4. (p. 436) "My action might have made me appear *eccentric*."
5. (p. 437) "And he, down there, *tentatively:* 'I suppose your captain's turned in?'"
6. (p. 439) ". . . he told me the story roughly in *brusque*, disconnected sentences."
7. (p. 445) ". . . I presided with such *frigid* dignity that the two mates were only too glad to escape from the cabin as soon as *decency* permitted. . . ."
8. (p. 446) ". . . I saw him far back there, sitting *rigidly* on the low stool. . . ."
9. (p. 446) "His *immobility* seemed to have been never disturbed."
10. (p. 446) "A *spiritless tenacity* was his main characteristic, I judged."
11. (p. 447) "He was *densely* distressed. . . ."
12. (p. 447) "After *scoring* over my calmness in this *graphic* way he nodded wisely."
13. (p. 448) "His obscure tenacity on this point had in it something *incomprehensible* and a little *awful*. . . ."
14. (p. 449) "He took another *oblique* step."
15. (p. 450) ". . . he drew a long, *spiritless* sigh and mumbled *dismally* that he must really be going back to his ship now."
16. (p. 452) ". . . it's to no commander's advantage to be suspected of *ludicrous eccentricities*."
17. (p. 453) "Sitting *stolidly* at the head of the table I became terrified at the sight of the garment on his arm."
18. (p. 453) "'Yes, sir,' the pale-faced steward turned *resignedly* to me."
19. (p. 454) ". . . I *dominated* my nervousness *sufficiently* not to shout after him."
20. (p. 455) "Whoever was being driven *distracted*, it was not he."
21. (p. 456) "That *intolerable* cub *shuffled* about so sleepily . . . that I came down on him sharply."
22. (p. 459) "He was still *lingering* in the pantry in the greatness of his *zeal*. . . ."

Developing Language Skills

1. Write several paragraphs supporting or denying this statement: Leggatt was not actually guilty of murder.
2. Discuss the captain's reaction after hearing the second version of the killing on the *Sephora*: "It was all very simple. The same strungup force which had given twenty-four men a chance, at least, for their lives, had, in a sort of recoil, crushed an unworthy mutinous existence." Does this comment mean that the captain approves of Leggatt's crime? Does it mean that all crimes that benefit others should not be subject to law? Does the captain set himself up as being higher than the law?
3. Explain to the class the meaning of Leggatt's remark, "No chief mate ever made more than one voyage in the *Sephora*, you know."

Refer to the opening paragraph of Galsworthy's essay on Conrad (p. 420) to understand the duties of a chief mate on a sailing vessel.

4. Write a paragraph showing how this observation of the captain concerning Leggatt as he disappears into the sea could be applied equally to himself as he successfully takes charge of his ship: ". . . a free man, a proud swimmer striking out for a new destiny."

5. Tell why you do or do not accept this statement: The following thoughts of the captain express the beginning and end of the real story—

> I wondered how far I should turn out faithful to that ideal conception of one's own personality every man sets up for himself secretly. [Beginning of story] And I was alone with her. Nothing, no one in the world should stand now between us, throwing a shadow on the way of silent knowledge and mute affection, the perfect communion of a seaman with his first command. [End of story]

6. Write several paragraphs explaining this comment about Conrad's writing in relation to *The Secret Sharer:* "Conrad's heroes are always being tested, not to prove themselves to the world as much as to prove themselves to themselves."

7. Write for thirty minutes in class comparing the captain's search for himself or his struggle to live up to his image of himself in *The Secret Sharer* with that of a man facing the same kind of test in another novel or play you have read.

8. Look up the story of Cain and Abel in Genesis 4:8-16. Explain in two or three paragraphs the relationship of the story to *The Secret Sharer.* In particular, consider the relationship indicated by the following quotations:

> The "brand of Cain" business, don't you see. . . . I was ready enough to go off wandering on the face of the earth. (p. 442)

> I saw myself wandering barefooted, bareheaded, the sun beating on my dark poll. (p. 460)

> . . . to be hidden forever from all friendly faces, to be a fugitive and a vagabond on the earth, with no brand of the curse on his sane forehead to stay a slaying hand . . . too proud to explain. (p. 462)

> . . . had lowered himself into the water to take his punishment. . . . (p. 463)

Poetry

Reading Poetry

A POET tries to convey to you, the reader, an experience he has had. He tries, through many devices, to cause in you an emotion similar to the one he had. And he tries, through the experience he chooses, to say something about what life means to him.

You read poetry better when you know what questions to ask about a poem. You should ask three main questions: *What is the experience being described? How is the poem put together? What does the experience mean?* Other questions are important, but subordinate to these. Let us find some answers in "Crystal Moment" by Robert P. Tristram Coffin.

Crystal Moment

Robert P. Tristram Coffin

Once or twice this side of death
Things can make one hold his breath.

From my boyhood I remember
A crystal moment of September.

A wooded island rang with sounds 5
Of church bells in the throats of hounds.

A buck leaped out and took the tide
With jewels flowing past each side.

With his high head like a tree
He swam within a yard of me. 10

I saw the golden drop of light
In his eyes turned dark with fright.

I saw the forest's holiness
On him like a fierce caress.

Fear made him lovely past belief, 15
My heart was trembling like a leaf.

He leaned towards the land and life
With need upon him like a knife.

In his wake the hot hounds churned,
They stretched their muzzles out and yearned. 20

They bayed no more, but swam and throbbed,
Hunger drove them till they sobbed.

Pursued, pursuers reached the shore
And vanished. I saw nothing more.

So they passed, a pageant such 25
As only gods could witness much.

Life and death upon one tether
And running beautiful together.

In this poem *what the experience is* comes across quite clearly. You can get at it if you ask: What is the occasion of the poem? And who is the speaker in the poem? The poet recalls that as a boy he saw a deer, a buck, being chased by hunters and their dogs. He tries to recapture for us this experience and to set down for us what it was like. He might have merely summarized and said, "I remember hearing dogs baying and then a deer swimming close by me. He reached the woods and disappeared with the dogs close behind." If he had done this, you would have felt little of the excitement and pity which the author wants you to have; in other words, you would not have had the appropriate emotional reaction.

Now, *how is the poem put together?* What makes the statement a poem? The poet wants you to take part in the experience: to see it and to hear it, to sense it. He uses concrete words, carefully chosen because of their connotative value and the emotional response they elicit—words like *crystal* and *jewels*. In a few places, the first four lines and the last four, the author speaks to you with direct statement; but in the rest of the poem he offers a series of images which appeal to your senses of sight and hearing. You, as a reader, must build the picture in your mind.

When the buck swims by with "jewels flowing past each side," what do you see? His head is "like a tree," and you should imaginatively see his antlers. How can an eye be like a "golden drop of light" or how can a heart tremble "like a leaf"? These simple words provide comparisons through which you can share the scene and the experience with the poet. If you keep asking such questions of a poem and can find the answers, you will have mastered one of the key approaches to understanding all poetry.

The words in poetry are like notes of music: they must be heard. When you read aloud a few lines, you will notice that the alternation of accented and unaccented syllables is quite regular. Of course, the poem is not to be read in this monotonous rhythm, but the underlying beat is always there, making up the sound of the poem. In a good oral reading you should put the heavier stresses on the key words in the meaning. The resulting blend of rhythm and meaning will give you a proper reading.

Another device with which you are familiar is rhyme, the repetition of similar sounds. In "Crystal Moment" the rhyme scheme is easily identified—the first line of each couplet (two paired lines) has the same end sound as the second.

> Once or twice this side of *death*
> Things can make one hold his *breath*.

Because the sound is repeated, its echo rings in the mind. The repetition of the sound gives added unity to the poem; it ties together units of thought.

Finally you ask: *What does the experience mean?* Does the poet, through this experience he describes, offer his view of some truth about life? The answer here is "Yes"; Coffin—most directly in the last four lines—expresses his idea that death is always close to all of us. We never know from one day to the next whether life or death will win the race that day.

> Pursued, pursuers reached the shore
> And vanished. I saw nothing more.

The meaning is, of course, more complex than this simplified statement of it, for it grows out of the entire poem. To grasp it fully, you would need to ask such questions as, "Why is the word *beautiful* used in the last line?" and "Why are the hounds pursuing the buck?"

A poem, then, is not something to race through once. In a good poem, the choice of words and the joining of them is the most precise and meaningful handling of language possible in literature. Careful reading and rereading are essential.

In this unit you will study four major aspects of poetry: images, figurative language, rhythm, and sound. The sections dealing with these four aspects each begin with poems that are preceded by comment directing your attention to various techniques and themes. Each section ends with poems without comment, to which you should apply what you have learned in the earlier part of the section. The unit concludes with some examples of light verse and a long narrative poem. If you are interested in the technical aspects of rhythm, you will find a brief explanation on pages 604 to 607.

Images

One of the most striking qualities of good poetry is its power to present with a high degree of accuracy almost indefinable feelings, moods, and reflections. How does it do this?

A distinction between two opposite kinds of language—*concrete* and *abstract*—is helpful in answering the question. An *abstract* term is one which represents an idea or generality. Words such as *architecture* and *justice* are abstractions; so are *modern art, human nature,* and *courage.* Abstractions are very useful, particularly in such areas as philosophy, science, or literary theory, for they have very general references.

Concrete terms, on the other hand, represent things that can be known directly by the senses. Examples of concrete words are *thorn, crowbar, emerald, honey-colored,* and *salty.* A concrete word, unless it names something one has never experienced, will suggest to one's imagination some sensation: a form, a color, an odor, a sound. Poetry tends to use such words frequently, although not exclusively, of course.

Concrete terms tend to evoke stronger reactions than do abstract ones, in the same way that seeing an accident is apt to cause a stronger reaction in an observer than would simply the abstract idea of pain or danger. Most good poets communicate an idea or a sensation or an emotion to a reader by putting the abstraction into concrete terms. It is in this way that the successful poet can cause his readers to share experiences that people usually have difficulty putting into words.

The process is more difficult than it sounds. The poet does not simply use any concrete terms—he must find the right ones, the ones that will recreate for the reader the experience and the ideas that he himself has had. In using concrete language, the poet necessarily produces *images*—representations of sense experiences. One of the most basic techniques you, as a reader, must use in reading poetry is to recreate in your mind the sensations—the sights, sounds, tastes—that a poet's images suggest.

Reading "Aboard at a Ship's Helm" and "The Dismantled Ship"

Whitman avoids expressing his meaning abstractly in the two following poems, but relies primarily on the image of a ship to convey his meaning. As you read each poem, ask yourself what Whitman's attitude is toward the ship he is describing, and what ideas or qualities he associates with the ship.

Aboard at a Ship's Helm

Walt Whitman

Aboard at a ship's helm,
A young steersman steering with care.

Through fog on a sea-coast dolefully ringing,
An ocean-bell—O a warning bell, rocked by the waves.

O you give good notice indeed, you bell by the sea-reefs ring-
ing,   5
Ringing, ringing, to warn the ship from its wreck-place.

For as on the alert O steersman, you mind the loud admonition,
The bows turn, the freighted ship tacking speeds away under her
    gray sails,
The beautiful and noble ship with all her precious wealth speeds
    away gayly and safe.

But O the ship, the immortal ship!   O ship aboard the ship!   10
Ship of the body, ship of the soul, voyaging, voyaging, voyaging.

Understanding the Poem

1. What incident is described in lines 1-9?
2. What words indicate Whitman's attitude toward the ship?
3. In what ways is the "ship of the body, ship of the soul" like the ship
   of lines 1-9?
4. What does Whitman mean by the exclamations of line 10?   Are they
   exclamations of surprise?   fear?   joy?   What causes the particular
   emotion he feels?

The Dismantled Ship

Walt Whitman

In some unused lagoon, some nameless bay,
On sluggish, lonesome waters, anchored near the shore,
An old, dismasted, gray and battered ship, disabled, done,
After free voyages to all the seas of earth, hauled up at last and haw-
    sered tight,
Lies rusting, mouldering.

Understanding the Poem

1. What does line 4 suggest is the most important difference between
   "the dismantled ship" and its former state?
2. From his description, how does Whitman seem to feel toward the
   ship?   (For instance, does he regard it as ugly junk?)

The following poem presents two scenes. Whitman does not state directly the essential difference between the two, but the central idea of the poem results from the contrast between them. As you read, consider how the image of the lecture room differs from that of the stars.

When I Heard the Learn'd Astronomer

Walt Whitman

When I heard the learn'd astronomer,
When the proofs, the figures, were ranged in columns before me,
When I was shown the charts and diagrams, to add, divide, and meas-
ure them,
When I sitting heard the astronomer where he lectured with much
applause in the lecture room,
How soon unaccountable I became tired and sick,
Till rising and gliding out I wandered off by myself,
In the mystical moist night air, and from time to time,
Looked up in perfect silence at the stars.

Understanding the Poem

1. How does the scene in the lecture room contrast with the scene outdoors?
2. What do the stars apparently mean to the astronomer? What is his
reaction to them?
3. How does the speaker of the poem react to the stars?
4. What is the meaning of the contrasts shown in the poem?

Roethke, instead of presenting a single image, lists what is almost a short catalogue of images. Note that he develops this poem through the joining of concrete images with abstract qualities—for example, the concrete word *pencils* with the abstract word *sadness*. In reading the poem, try to discover what all the images have in common and why they are associated with such qualities as *sadness, dolor,* and *misery*.

Dolor

Theodore Roethke

I have known the inexorable sadness of pencils,
Neat in their boxes, dolor of pad and paperweight,
All the misery of manila folders and mucilage,
Desolation in immaculate public places,
Lonely reception room, lavatory, switchboard,   5
The unalterable pathos of basin and pitcher,
Ritual of multigraph, paper clip, comma,
Endless duplication of lives and objects.
And I have seen dust from the walls of institutions,
Finer than flour, alive, more dangerous than silica,   10
Sift, almost invisible, through long afternoons of tedium,
Dripping a fine film on nails and delicate eyebrows,
Glazing the pale hair, the duplicate gray standard faces.

Understanding the Poem

1. What are some possible places in which all the objects named in this poem are found?
2. In what way are the objects named in lines 1-7 like the people of the last lines?
3. Which line best sums up what the poet is saying in the entire poem?
4. What does Roethke mean in line 10 when he describes the dust as "alive, more dangerous than silica"? How can it be alive? Why is it dangerous?

Reading "Auto Wreck"

"Auto Wreck" calls for very careful reading, for it is not at all a simple poem. Shapiro wants to suggest a number of things that can be summed up abstractly—the excitement of an accident, its horror, the sickened feeling of the onlookers, their sense of being jerked out of the ordinary world, and the question of what such an accident means and who is responsible. Summed up in this abstract way, however, his ideas are not too original or emotionally powerful. The poem, with its concrete language and carefully chosen images, is much more moving.

You may notice in reading the poem that it uses two kinds of images: images that are literal (that is, factual) descriptions of the scene of the wreck, and images that help you to imagine the scene and the onlookers' reactions by comparing them to other things. The opening lines provide examples of both. The ambulance's light, for instance, is a "ruby flare"—a literal image describing part of the scene. The ambulance is also described as "Pulsing out red light like an artery"—a figurative image based on a comparison. When figurative descriptions are used, ask yourself why the comparison used is appropriate. What does it suggest beyond the actual appearance of the scene? Why, for example, is "like an artery" a good comparison?

Auto Wreck

Karl Shapiro

Its quick soft silver bell beating, beating,
And down the dark one ruby flare
Pulsing out red light like an artery,
The ambulance at top speed floating down
Past beacons and illuminated clocks   5
Wings in a heavy curve, dips down,
And brakes speed, entering the crowd.
The doors leap open, emptying light;
Stretchers are laid out, the mangled lifted
And stowed into the little hospital.   10
Then the bell, breaking the hush, tolls once,
And the ambulance with its terrible cargo
Rocking, slightly rocking, moves away,
As the doors, an afterthought, are closed.

478

We are deranged, walking among the cops   15
Who sweep glass and are large and composed.
One is still making notes under the light.
One with a bucket douches ponds of blood
Into the street and gutter.
One hangs lanterns on the wrecks that cling,   20
Empty husks of locusts, to iron poles.

Our throats were tight as tourniquets,
Our feet were bound with splints, but now,
Like convalescents intimate and gauche,[1]
We speak through sickly smiles and warn   25
With the stubborn saw of common sense,
The grim joke and the banal[2] resolution.
The traffic moves around with care,
But we remain, touching a wound
That opens to our richest horror.   30
Already old, the question Who shall die?
Becomes unspoken Who is innocent?
For death in war is done by hands;
Suicide has cause and stillbirth, logic;
And cancer, simple as a flower, blooms.   35
But this invites the occult[3] mind,
Cancels our physics with a sneer,
And spatters all we knew of denouement[4]
Across the expedient and wicked stones.

1 gauche (gōsh): awkward.
2 banal: trite.
3 occult: supernatural.
4 denouement (dā′noō mäN′): the outcome or unraveling of a situation. The term is frequently used for the end of plays in which all problems and loose ends are cleared up in the last scene.

Understanding the Poem

1. Who is the speaker in this poem? Where is he?
2. What images are used in lines 1-30 that keep the wreck and its victims in the reader's mind even though the images are figurative descriptions of other parts of the scene?
3. Why does Shapiro use the word *tolls* in line 11?
4. In lines 33-35, Shapiro speaks of other forms of death. How do they differ from the one described in the poem?
5. Line 37 says the accident "Cancels our physics with a sneer." What does the line mean? (Does "physics" refer to what modern man has achieved through his knowledge of science, such as the building of automobiles?)

6. What does the phrase "all we knew of denouement" mean? What ideas did man have about "denouement," or the end of life? How does the accident destroy these ideas?
7. What does "expedient" mean? In what sense are the stones "expedient and wicked"?
8. Shapiro says that the question left in the minds of the onlookers is "Who is innocent?" What do you think he means by this question?

Reading "Thoughts During an Air Raid"

The stories of tragedy and death that appear daily in the news rarely cause much grief in those who read and hear them. Most of us react—perhaps necessarily—with the feeling that such things happen to other people, not to us. "Thoughts During an Air Raid" concerns this reaction; it asks such questions as why people react impersonally to death and what the consequences are for an individual who does react this way.

Spender's subject is an abstract one and in the poem you will find a number of abstract terms. These abstractions, however, are intermixed with concrete detail and with images, which give the poem much of its reality.

Thoughts During an Air Raid

Stephen Spender

Of course, the entire effort is to put oneself
Outside the ordinary range
Of what are called statistics. A hundred are killed
In the outer suburbs. Well, well, one carries on.
So long as this thing "I" is propped up on   5
The girdered bed which seems so like a hearse,
In the hotel bedroom with the wallpaper
Blowing smoke-wreaths of roses, one can ignore
The pressure of those names under the fingers
Indented by lead type on newsprint,   10
In the bar, the marginal wailing wireless.[1]
Yet supposing that a bomb should dive
Its nose right through this bed, with one upon it?
The thought's obscene. Still, there are many
For whom one's loss would illustrate   15

The "impersonal" use indeed. The essential is
That every "one" should remain separate
Propped up under roses, and no one suffer
For his neighbor. Then horror is postponed
Piecemeal for each, until it settles on him   20
That wreath of incommunicable grief
Which is all mystery or nothing.

1 **wireless:** radio (British usage).

Understanding the Poem

1. Where is the speaker in the poem? What is he doing?
2. What is meant by "statistics" in line 3?
3. Why does the bed seem like a hearse?
4. What are "those names" in line 9?
5. What does *obscene* mean? Why is the thought of being killed by a bomb obscene?
6. What meanings does the phrase "the 'impersonal' use" (l. 16) have? Express in your own words the idea of the sentence in which it occurs.
7. Why is it "essential" that "every 'one' should remain separate"? What would happen if every one did not?
8. In the clause "Then horror is postponed/Piecemeal for each," Spender states that, when an individual remains unaffected by the suffering and death of others, he can only postpone realizing the horror of such events. Why is the horror postponed "piecemeal"?
9. In lines 20-21, the poet goes on to say that finally horror "settles on him/That wreath of incommunicable grief." Note that the image of a wreath first appears in line 8, in which we learn that the wallpaper has wreaths of roses on it. The image of roses reappears in line 18: "Propped up under roses." Again we see the scene with the speaker propped up on his hearselike bed with the wallpaper roses around him. But through the wording we also should be reminded of a corpse with flowers laid over it. In line 21 the wreath, which the reader now should associate with the idea of death, settles on the individual who until this point has avoided becoming involved with such catastrophes. He cannot avoid his own death, however, which is an "incommunicable grief" since it cannot be shared with anyone. And Spender indicates in the last line that he is not sure whether death will prove "all mystery or nothing." In either event, one's own death will have to be undergone alone—just as one remained separate from others while alive.

What attitude do you think the poet has toward the impersonal reaction of people to the lives and deaths of others? What are the reasons for your conclusion?

Former Barn Lot

Mark Van Doren

Once there was a fence here,
    And the grass came and tried,
Leaning from the pasture,
    To get inside.

But colt feet trampled it,   5
    Turning it brown;
Until the farmer moved
    And the fence fell down.

Then any bird saw,
    Under the wire,   10
Grass nibbling inward
    Like green fire.

Understanding the Poem

1. What is the speaker in the poem looking at?
2. How can grass lean? How can it nibble "Like green fire"?
3. Is there a conflict in this poem? If so, what is it?

The Fish

Elizabeth Bishop

I caught a tremendous fish
and held him beside the boat
half out of water, with my hook
fast in a corner of his mouth.
He didn't fight.   5
He hadn't fought at all.
He hung a grunting weight,
battered and venerable
and homely. Here and there
his brown skin hung in strips   10
like ancient wallpaper,
and its pattern of darker brown
was like wallpaper:
shapes like full-blown roses
stained and lost through age.   15
He was speckled with barnacles,

fine rosettes of lime,
and infested
with tiny white sea-lice,
and underneath two or three   20
rags of green weed hung down.
While his gills were breathing in
the terrible oxygen
—the frightening gills,
fresh and crisp with blood,   25
that can cut so badly—
I thought of the coarse white flesh
packed in like feathers,
the big bones and the little bones,
the dramatic reds and blacks   30
of his shiny entrails,
and the pink swim-bladder
like a big peony.
I looked into his eyes
which were far larger than mine   35
but shallower, and yellowed,
the irises backed and packed
with tarnished tinfoil
seen through the lenses
of old scratched isinglass.   40
They shifted a little, but not
to return my stare.
—It was more like the tipping
of an object toward the light.
I admired his sullen face,   45
the mechanism of his jaw,
and then I saw
that from his lower lip
—if you could call it a lip—

grim, wet, and weapon-like,   50
hung five old pieces of fishline,
or four and a wire leader
with the swivel still attached,
with all their five big hooks
grown firmly in his mouth.   55
A green line, frayed at the end
where he broke it, two heavier
    lines,
and a fine black thread
still crimped from the strain and
    snap
when it broke and he got away.   60
Like medals with their ribbons
frayed and wavering,
a five-haired beard of wisdom
trailing from his aching jaw.
I stared and stared   65
and victory filled up
the little rented boat,
from the pool of bilge
where oil had spread a rainbow
around the rusted engine   70
to the bailer rusted orange,
the sun-cracked thwarts,[1]
the oarlocks on their strings,
the gunnels[2]—until everything
was rainbow, rainbow, rainbow!   75
And I let the fish go.

1 **thwarts:** the rower's seat.
2 **gunnels:** point in a boat where the topsides
meet the deck.

Understanding the Poem

1. List the various things to which the fish is compared. What kind
   of attitude do they create toward the fish?
2. At the end, when "victory filled up" the boat, the reader is given a
   description of the boat. What kind of boat is it? Judging by the
   choice of words, how do you think the boat impressed the speaker
   at the moment? Why does she describe the boat at this point?
3. How does the image of lines 61-64 help to explain why the speaker
   lets the fish go?

The Runaway

Robert Frost

Once when the snow of the year was beginning to fall,
We stopped by a mountain pasture to say, "Whose colt?"
A little Morgan[1] had one forefoot on the wall,
The other curled at his breast. He dipped his head
And snorted at us. And then he had to bolt.   5
We heard the miniature thunder where he fled,
And we saw him, or thought we saw him, dim and gray,
Like a shadow against the curtain of falling flakes.
"I think the little fellow's afraid of the snow.
He isn't winter-broken. It isn't play   10
With the little fellow at all. He's running away.
I doubt if even his mother could tell him, 'Sakes,
It's only weather.' He'd think she didn't know!
Where is his mother? He can't be out alone."
And now he comes again with clatter of stone,   15
And mounts the wall again with whited eyes
And all his tail that isn't hair up straight.
He shudders his coat as if to throw off flies.
"Whoever it is that leaves him out so late,
When other creatures have gone to stall and bin,   20
Ought to be told to come and take him in."

1 **Morgan:** American breed of horses.

Understanding the Poem

1. What images does Frost offer you in this poem? Into what distinct
   pictures does the poem divide?
2. What comment on fear or loneliness does the poem make?
3. What impression do you receive of the speaker in the poem? What
   gives you this impression?

Barter

Sara Teasdale

Life has loveliness to sell,
   All beautiful and splendid things,
Blue waves whitened on a cliff,
   Soaring fire that sways and sings,
And children's faces looking up   5
Holding wonder like a cup.

Life has loveliness to sell,
   Music like a curve of gold,
Scent of pine trees in the rain,
   Eyes that love you, arms that hold,   10
And for your spirit's still delight,
Holy thoughts that star the night.

Spend all you have for loveliness,
   Buy it and never count the cost;
For one white singing hour of peace   15
   Count many a year of strife well lost,
And for a breath of ecstasy
Give all you have been, or could be.

Understanding the Poem

1. Why is *sell* used in the first line instead of *give?*
2. What are the images which describe the loveliness of life? What
   kind of things do they indicate the speaker values?
3. How is the third stanza different from the first two?
4. Why is the poem called *Barter?*

Figurative Language

One of the major characteristics of poetry (although not of every single poem) is its use of comparison as a way of saying something. You have already seen this quality of poetry in the preceding section: many images are used because there is a similarity between them and the poet's real subject.

Some comparisons are very obvious ones—the similarities between the two things being talked about immediately leap to one's mind. For example, life has so many parallels to a journey that the comparison has been used over and over. Turns in the road and the new scenes encountered may represent the changes that occur in a life; hills and valleys may represent the ups and downs of fortune; crossroads may represent the making of decisions.

If you have done much reading, you may be aware of some other basic comparisons that appear frequently in literature. Two widely used ones are a river as life and night as death. Can you point out the parallels between the two things involved?

When a poet expresses himself through such comparisons, he is using *figurative language*. As the above examples indicate, figurative language frequently uses an image (something concrete, such as a road) to represent an abstraction (such as life). Indeed, it is very difficult to talk for long about any abstract subject without using figurative expressions. The chief difference between the figurative language of poetry and that of ordinary conversation is simply that the former is more original and more carefully chosen. The figures of speech we use every day are usually dead ones—they do not even strike us as different from ordinary language. When we use the expression "the foot of the mountain," for instance, we are using a figure of speech, but it is so common an expression that we do not think of it as one.

In the following poems you will find living figures of speech, however. Through them, the poet is trying to express as precisely as possible just what a certain experience or object or concept is like.

Reading "Dramatic Fragment"

As its title indicates, this is a fragment—the circumstances which caused the speaker to utter the words are unknown; the speaker himself is unknown, as is the person he is addressing. Yet the speaker's state of mind and the general nature of the situation are made quite clear in four short lines.

The chief means by which Stickney shows the speaker's state of mind is through an image presented in the form of a *simile*. A simile is a comparison between two things essentially unlike, but with one (or perhaps several) characteristics in common, and connected by a word such as *like, as,* or *as if.* Some common similes are *black as ink, sly as a fox, shy as a violet*—comparisons so common that their effectiveness as an original or striking way of expression has been lost. Some of the poems in the previous section use similes in ways that make a scene much clearer and more vivid, and which at times suggest the poet's emotions and attitudes toward a situation—for instance, "Our throats were tight as tourniquets" (in "Auto Wreck") and "Like medals with their ribbons/frayed and wavering" (in "The Fish").

Dramatic Fragment

Trumbull Stickney

Sir, say no more.
Within me 't is as if
The green and climbing eyesight of a cat
Crawled near my mind's poor birds.

Understanding the Poem

1. How much do you know about the situation in this poem?
2. What does the simile of lines 3-4 tell about the speaker and what he is experiencing? Could the same thing be said as briefly and effectively in nonfigurative language?
3. The headnote preceding the poem explained why it is called a fragment. Why is it called *dramatic?*

Reading "Apparently with no surprise"

The meaning of this poem develops largely from the use of *personification.* As the term itself indicates, personification is the making of something into a person—objects, animals, or abstractions are spoken of as though they were human beings. Thus, the phrase "happy Flower" in line 2 personifies the flower since happiness is a human emotion, not a flower's. Sometimes personification may be used as a dramatic device. When nature, for example, offers difficulties or dangers, personifying it introduces an element of human conflict that adds to the sense of drama and suspense (as in the essay "The Elements" or in a Walt Disney movie). In the following poem, it also offers the means of putting an abstract thought into concrete terms. The meaning of the poem results from such personifying phrases as "The Frost beheads it" and "The blond Assassin."

"Apparently with no surprise"

Emily Dickinson

Apparently with no surprise
To any happy Flower
The Frost beheads it at its play—
In accidental power—
The blond Assassin passes on—
The Sun proceeds unmoved
To measure off another Day
For an Approving God.

Understanding the Poem

1. If the flower and the frost were really like human beings, what would be surprising about the situation described in lines 1-4?
2. Who is "The blond Assassin"? What connotations does *blond* have which heighten the sense that the situation is a startling, unusual one?
3. What comment is the poet making in lines 6-8? Could the speaker's attitude be described as *unmoved* or as *approving*? If not, what is it?
4. Is the poet reacting only to the death of a flower, or does the poem have a wider application? Explain.

Reading "Prayers of Steel"

Both simile and personification are figures of speech which may be included under the broader term *metaphor*. A metaphor is a comparison of two things having one or more characteristics in common, although in most respects unlike. It does not necessarily introduce the comparison by the words *like* or *as*, nor does it necessarily compare nonliving things to human beings—when it does, the more specific terms *simile* and *personification* are generally used. Some commonly used metaphors are illustrated in these sentences:

The paragraph is a *meaty* one.
His anger *kindled* at the sight.
The *Iron Curtain* is a reality of modern life.

A metaphor may be a single word as in the above sentences, but it can also run throughout a sentence (or even paragraph) as in the following examples:

Enslaved by his habits of thinking, he remained a prisoner of his own mind until a new environment broke down the bars of the past.

The new ideas struck sparks in the minds of enough men so that the few small flames soon grew to a forest fire.

If you examine the common metaphors that occur in conversations, newspapers, and magazines, you will see that frequently they express an idea in fewer words than nonfigurative language could. Or they may be used to make a statement vivid or to add emotional intensity to it.

In the following few poems, metaphors that extend throughout a poem are used. In "Prayers of Steel," Sandburg does not tell you outright what the crowbar or the steel spike or their actions represent. That is, he gives you only one side of the metaphor. You will sense easily enough, though, that he is not primarily talking about steel and the functions it performs; rather, he is using these as metaphors for human actions.

Prayers of Steel

Carl Sandburg

Lay me on an anvil, O God.
Beat me and hammer me into a crowbar.
Let me pry loose old walls.
Let me lift and loosen old foundations.

Lay me on an anvil, O God.
Beat me and hammer me into a steel spike.
Drive me into the girders that hold a skyscraper together.
Take red-hot rivets and fasten me into the central girders.
Let me be the great nail holding a skyscraper through blue
    nights into white stars.

Understanding the Poem

1. What are the two prayers of the steel?
2. What do the old walls and foundations represent?
3. How is the function the steel will perform in the first stanza different from that in the second?

4. What human experiences and actions are expressed metaphorically in this poem? (For example, what is meant by "Lay me on an anvil" or "Drive me into the girders that hold a skyscraper together"?)
5. What is the significance of "through blue nights into white stars"?

Reading "The Coach of Life"

The following poem is again an extended metaphor—a variation on the theme of life as a journey. What parallels does Pushkin see between the two?

The Coach of Life

Alexander Pushkin

Though often somewhat heavy-freighted,
The coach rolls at an easy pace;
And Time, the coachman, grizzly-pated,[1]
But smart, alert—is in his place.

We board it lightly in the morning   5
And on our way at once proceed.
Repose and slothful comfort scorning,
We shout: "Hey, there! Get on! Full speed!"

Noon finds us done with reckless daring,
And shaken up. Now care's the rule.   10
Down hills, through gulleys roughly faring,
We sulk, and cry: "Hey, easy, fool!"

The coach rolls on, no pitfalls dodging.
At dusk, to pains more wonted[2] grown,
We drowse, while to the night's dark lodging   15
Old coachman Time drives on, drives on.

1 **grizzly-pated:** gray-haired.
2 **wonted:** accustomed.

Understanding the Poem

1. What is the coach in this poem? Who is the coachman? Through his descriptions of them, what is Pushkin saying about the things they represent?
2. Whom is Pushkin referring to by "we" in the poem?
3. What changes in time occur during the poem? What do these changes represent?
4. What metaphor is involved in "Down hills, through gulleys"?
5. How do the reactions of the passengers change during the journey? What does each reaction represent?
6. What represents death in the poem? What kind of attitude does Pushkin apparently have toward death, judging by the image he uses to represent it?

Reading "The Ninth of April"

On April 9, 1940, Denmark was invaded by the Germans. Gelsted, a Dane, consistently opposed the Nazis; he expresses in this poem his reaction to the invasion.

Part of the poem is a direct statement about the experience. Much of it, however, uses figurative language to show his thoughts and feelings. As you read, ask yourself what purpose the figures of speech have. For instance, how does speaking of Denmark as a woman dramatize Gelsted's experience? Would an abstract, literal statement of his feelings have the same emotional and dramatic impact?

The Ninth of April

Otto Gelsted

At dawn the dark birds flew
With noisy motors, through
The pale defenseless heavens overhead;
We saw and understood
With our hearts' dearest blood,   5
That we were sentenced to eat slavery's bread.

A day so blue and clear!
The sun we waited for
Shone meaninglessly like a blind man's eye;
Voiceless with despair   10
In the glittering morning air,
Denmark lay down upon the ground to die.

Yet, in that time of fear,
When she lay bleeding there,
And death and deadly night alone had power,   15
We saw and understood,
With our heart's dearest blood,
That we had never loved her till that hour.

Understanding the Poem

1. What are "the dark birds"? Apart from the literal accuracy the
   word *dark* may have as a description, why is it an appropriate word?
2. How is time used to give the poem its organization?
3. Lines 8-9 state "The sun we waited for / Shone meaninglessly like
   a blind man's eye." Why were they waiting for the sun? Why does
   it turn out to be "like a blind man's eye"?
4. What is the experience expressed in the last three lines?

Reading "Peter at Fourteen"

If you are taking Latin, you will probably be familiar with many of
the references in this poem. It is addressed to a boy who is evidently
reading in school Caesar's account of his Gallic conquests, which begins "All Gaul is divided into three parts. . . ." The Belgae and the
Helvetii mentioned in stanza 2 were tribes conquered by Caesar. At
the time Rome was highly civilized, in contrast to the primitive culture
and organization of more northern Europe. However, after Rome fell
and as the Middle Ages advanced (see stanza 6), the Gauls adopted
much of Roman culture, became completely Christian, and built
cathedrals that are among the greatest architectural achievements of
the world.

Although such historical information is important to an understanding of this selection, the poem is not primarily about Caesar, Rome, or
Gaul. Rather, it is about Peter and, as line 7 indicates, the past serves
as a metaphor for his experiences and emotions as an adolescent.

Peter at Fourteen

Constance Carrier

What do you care for Caesar, who yourself
are in three parts divided, and must find,
past daydream and rebellion and bravado,
the final shape and substance of your mind?

What are the Belgae, the Helvetii,   5
to you? I doubt that you will read in them
metaphor of your stand against dominion,
or see as yours their desperate stratagem.

They found their tribal rank, their feuds, their freedom,
obliterated, lost beyond return.   10
It took them years to see that law and order
could teach them things that they might care to learn.

As fiercely individual, as violent
as they, you clutch your values and your views,
fearful that self may not survive absorption.   15
(Who said *to learn* at first is like *to lose?*)

Not courage, no, but nature will betray you.
You will stop fighting, finally, and your pride,
that fed so long upon your independence,
flourish on what convention can provide,   20

till you may grow more Roman than the Romans,
contemptuous of pagan broils and brawls,
and even, mastering your mentors' knowledge,
go on to build cathedrals, like the Gauls.

Understanding the Poem

1. What is Peter like, judging from the poem? Give the lines or phrases upon which you base your answer. What are the three parts into which he is divided?
2. What do the Romans stand for in this poem? the Gauls?
3. What are the parallels between Peter and the Gauls?
4. What does stanza 6 mean?
5. Judging by this poem, what is gained by the growth to civilization or maturity? What is lost?

Reading "A Brook in the City"

We come into contact with many *symbols* in everyday life. The flag is one you are all familiar with. Like all symbols, it is itself an actual thing, but it also stands for something else—a fact we recognize in saying "I pledge allegiance to the flag and to the republic for which it stands." Undoubtedly you are also familiar with the figure of Uncle Sam as a cartoonist's symbol for the United States or its government. The badge of a policeman or the insignia of a soldier are other publicly recognized symbols.

In speaking of symbols, you will find it useful to remember that a symbol, although it represents something else, is also meaningful in itself. For example, the cross is often used as a symbol of Christianity or of such concepts as suffering and sacrifice. However, these meanings that it now symbolizes grew out of an actual cross, an object connected with events which led people to give it symbolic significance.

A literary work may use symbols that the reader is already familiar with, ones whose basic meanings are already established. A writer may also create his own symbols by describing an object or experience in such a way that the reader realizes he is not only talking about that thing itself, but is also using it to stand for other things.

Why does a writer use a symbol instead of making a direct statement about the things it stands for? Partly because, like an image or metaphor, a symbol gives concrete reality to abstract ideas and qualities. Also, a symbol rarely stands for one definite thing; it usually represents a complexity of ideas and qualities, and may also suggest the emotions or attitudes of the author toward what the symbol represents. Its emotional effect upon a reader is generally more powerful than that of a nonsymbolic statement. All of these qualities of symbolism are illustrated in the following sentences, part of an address to a political convention by William Jennings Bryan in 1896 in connection with putting the United States on a gold standard: "You shall not press down upon the brow of labor this crown of thorns. You shall not crucify mankind upon a cross of gold."

As a factual statement about the economic consequences of going on the gold standard, the above lines leave something to be desired. As political oratory (which often resembles a rather crude form of poetry in the techniques it uses), it proved extremely effective.

The symbolism in "A Brook in the City" is not confined to any one line or passage; rather, it pervades the whole poem. As the reader begins the poem, he does not know that the brook in the city is symbolic of anything. Indeed, the first half of the poem contains only the slightest hints that the poet has anything more in mind than describing a certain scene. But from line 13 to the end, the questions the speaker asks and the manner in which he refers to the brook very strongly suggest that the scene represents something more than just itself to him.

A Brook in the City

Robert Frost

The farmhouse lingers, though averse to square
With the new city street it has to wear
A number in. But what about the brook
That held the house as in an elbow-crook?
I ask as one who knew the brook, its strength   5
And impulse, having dipped a finger length
And made it leap my knuckle, having tossed
A flower to try its currents where they crossed.
The meadow grass could be cemented down
From growing under pavements of a town;   10
The apple trees be sent to hearth-stone flame.
Is water wood to serve a brook the same?
How else dispose of an immortal force
No longer needed? Staunch it at its source
With cinder loads dumped down? The brook was thrown   15
Deep in a sewer dungeon under stone
In fetid darkness still to live and run—
And all for nothing it had ever done
Except forget to go in fear perhaps.
No one would know except for ancient maps   20
That such a brook ran water. But I wonder
If from its being kept forever under
The thoughts may not have risen that so keep
This new-built city from both work and sleep.

Understanding the Poem

1. What scene is the speaker looking at?
2. Why does the scene arouse questions in his mind? What are these questions?
3. The poem states that "The brook was thrown / Deep in a sewer dungeon under stone." How does this personification tell you the poet's attitude toward the fate of the brook?
4. What does the last sentence of the poem mean?
5. What larger conflicts and questions are represented by the particular "brook in the city" described in this poem?

The next two poems both describe situations that are symbolic, but the poets do not spell out for the reader what their symbols stand for. There are clues, however. You will need to read the poems carefully and more than once to understand them fully. Remember that, as in all poems using figurative language, one thing is being talked about in terms of another.

The title of "The End of the World" is the only direct indication of what the poem is presumably about. How does MacLeish use symbolism to show what the end of the world might be like?

In "The Circus; or One View of It," a circus man is evidently describing his show. To whom is he addressing himself? Notice the questions that he puts as he talks, particularly the question in lines 26-28. Do they suggest any meaning beyond their surface one?

The End of the World

Archibald MacLeish

Quite unexpectedly as Vasserot[1]
The armless ambidextrian[2] was lighting
A match between his great and second toe
And Ralph the lion was engaged in biting
The neck of Madame Sossman while the drum   5
Pointed, and Teeny was about to cough
In waltz time swinging Jocko by the thumb—
Quite unexpectedly the top blew off:

And there, there overhead, there, there, hung over
Those thousands of white faces, those dazed eyes,   10
There in the starless dark the poise, the hover,
There with vast wings across the canceled skies,
There in the sudden blackness the black pall
Of nothing, nothing, nothing—nothing at all.

---

1 Vasserot: This name and the others used in the poem have been invented by MacLeish.

2 ambidextrian: person capable of using either hand with equal skill. Also, a person who is double-dealing or who sides with two opposite parties.

Understanding the Poem

1. Before tackling the symbolical meaning of this poem, you should be sure you have a firm grasp of the literal happenings in it.
   (a) To whom does the speaker refer first?
   (b) What is strange about this person?
   (c) What is Ralph the lion doing?
   (d) Is Ralph ferocious and angry? frightened? casual?
   (e) What is Teeny doing?
   (f) Who might Jocko be?
   (g) Who are the "thousands of white faces"?
   (h) Where might all these characters be found?
   (i) What happens "Quite unexpectedly"?
2. Up until the last line, what would you expect to be "there"? Why? What evidence is there in the poem for you to expect this?
3. If you were reading this poem aloud, what tone of voice would you use in reading lines 1-8? What effect would you be trying to convey? Why?
4. What tone of voice would you use for lines 9-13? Why?
5. What effect would you try to convey as you read the last line? Why?
6. In view of the title and what it says has happened, what is the impact of the first stanza as you reread it? How might the "thousands of white faces" and the activities described in stanza 1 represent man and his world?
7. What do you think MacLeish is saying about the world and how it will end in this poem? (Be sure there is evidence in the poem to support your answer.)

The Circus; or One View of It

Theodore Spencer

Said the circus man, Oh what do you like
Best of all about my show—
The circular rings, three rings in a row,
With animals going around, around,
Tamed to go running round, around,   5
And around, round, around they go;
Or perhaps you like the merry-go-round,
Horses plunging sedately up,
Horses sedately plunging down,
Going around the merry-go-round;   10

Or perhaps you like the clown with a hoop,
Shouting, rolling the hoop around;
Or the elephants walking around in a ring
Each trunk looped to a tail's loop,
Loosely ambling around the ring;   15
How do you like this part of the show?
Everything's busy and on the go;
The peanut men cry out and sing,
The round fat clown rolls on the ground,
The trapeze ladies sway and swing,   20
The circus horses plunge around
The circular rings, three rings in a row;
Here they come, and here they go.
And here you sit, said the circus man,
Around in a circle to watch my show;   25
Which is show and which is you,
Now that we're here in this circus show,
Do I know? Do you know?
But hooray for the clowns and the merry-go-round,
The painted horses plunging round,   30
The live, proud horses stamping the ground,
And the clowns and the elephants swinging around;
Come to my show; hooray for the show,
Hooray for the circus all the way round!
Said the round exuberant circus man.   35
Hooray for the show! said the circus man.

Understanding the Poem

1. The root meaning of *circus* is "circle" or "ring." Where do you find this meaning suggested in other words or details of the poem?
2. This poem comes from a collection entitled *The Paradox in the Circle*. What ideas might the poet be suggesting through his emphasis on circles and roundness in this particular poem? (Think, for example, of the connotations such expressions as "going round in circles," "caught on a merry-go-round," and "a vicious circle" give to the image of the circle.)
3. Who is the *you* of lines 24 and 26?
4. What relationship is there between the *you* and the show? Are there any spectators at this show?
5. For what might the circus be a symbol? What parallels are there between the two things?

The following three poems are examples of a rather special form of personification—the *fable*. The fable, which more frequently appears as prose, is a story pointing up some truth and usually doing so by making animals talk and act like human beings. Through what the animals say and do, the writer drives home a view of human behavior that is often critical.

Fable

Ralph Waldo Emerson

THE mountain and the squirrel
Had a quarrel,
And the former called the latter "Little Prig";[1]
Bun[2] replied,
"You are doubtless very big;   5
But all sorts of things and weather
Must be taken in together,
To make up a year
And a sphere.
And I think it no disgrace   10
To occupy my place.
If I'm not so large as you,
You are not so small as I,
And not half so spry.
I'll not deny you make   15
A very pretty squirrel track;
Talents differ; all is well and wisely put;
If I cannot carry forests on my back,
Neither can you crack a nut."

1 **Prig:** one who is smug and overparticular.
2 **Bun:** the squirrel.

The Indian Upon God

William Butler Yeats

I passed along the water's edge below the humid trees,
My spirit rocked in evening light, the rushes round my knees,
My spirit rocked in sleep and sighs; and saw the moorfowl pace
All dripping on a grassy slope, and saw them cease to chase
Each other round in circles, and heard the eldest speak: 5
Who holds the world between His bill and made us strong or
    weak
Is an undying moorfowl, and He lives beyond the sky.
The rains are from His dripping wing, the moonbeams from
    His eye.
I passed a little further on and heard a lotus talk:
Who made the world and ruleth it, He hangeth on a stalk,   10
For I am in His image made, and all this tinkling tide
Is but a sliding drop of rain between His petals wide.
A little way within the gloom a roebuck raised his eyes
Brimful of starlight, and he said: *The Stamper of the Skies,*
He is a gentle roebuck; for how else, I pray, could He   15
Conceive a thing so sad and soft, a gentle thing like me?
I passed a little further on and heard a peacock say:
Who made the grass and made the worms and made my feathers
    gay,
He is a monstrous peacock, and He waveth all the night
His languid tail above us, lit with myriad spots of light.   20

1 **roebuck:** a small, graceful deer.

aesop revised by archy[1]

don marquis

a wolf met a spring
lamb drinking
at a stream
and said to her
you are the lamb   5
that muddied this stream
all last year
so that i could not get
a clean fresh drink
i am resolved that   10
this outrage
shall not be enacted again
this season
i am going to kill you
just a moment   15
said the lamb
i was not born last
year so it could not
have been i
the wolf then pulled   20
a number of other
arguments as to why the lamb
should die
but in each case the lamb
pretty innocent that she was   25
easily proved
herself guiltless
well well said the wolf
enough of argument
you are right and i am wrong   30
but i am going to eat
you anyhow
because i am hungry

stop exclamation point
cried a human voice   35
and a man came over
the slope of the ravine
vile lupine marauder
you shall not kill that
beautiful and innocent   40
lamb for i shall save her
exit the wolf
left upper entrance
snarling
poor little lamb   45
continued our human hero
sweet tender little thing
it is well that i appeared
just when i did
it makes my blood boil   50
to think of the fright
to which you have been
subjected in another
moment i would have been
too late come home with me   55
and the lamb frolicked
about her new found friend
gamboling as to the sound
of a wordsworthian tabor[2]
and leaping for joy   60
as if propelled by a stanza
from william blake[3]
these vile and bloody wolves

1 **aesop revised by archy:** Aesop, who lived about the sixth century B.C., was a writer of fables. Archy, an invention of Don Marquis, is a poetic cockroach who writes free verse (see p. 513).

2 **wordsworthian tabor:** an allusion to the following two lines from a well known poem by William Wordsworth (1770-1850), an English poet: "And while the young lambs bound / As to the tabor's sound."

3 **william blake:** an English poet (1757-1827) who often used the lamb as an image or symbol in his poetry. One of his poems is called "The Lamb."

went on our hero
in honest indignation   65
they must be cleared out
of the country
the meads must be made safe
for sheepocracy
and so jollying her along   70
with the usual human hokum
he led her to his home
and the son of a gun
did not even blush when
they passed the mint bed   75
gently he cut her throat
all the while inveighing
against the inhuman wolf
and tenderly he cooked her
and lovingly he sauced her   80
and meltingly he ate her

and piously he said a grace
thanking his gods
for their bountiful gifts to him
and after dinner   85
he sat with his pipe
before the fire meditating
on the brutality of wolves
and the injustice of
the universe   90
which allows them to harry
poor innocent lambs
and wondering if he
had not better
write to the papers   95
for as he said
for god s sake can t
something be done about it
                              archy

Understanding the Poems

1. What point is being made in each of the three preceding poems?
2. Which of the three poems employs irony? How?

Reading "The Eagle That Is Forgotten"

Altgeld is remembered as a man who championed the underprivi-
leged and worked for social and political reform. He was elected governor of Illinois in 1892 and was particularly interested in the cause of
prison reform. Although he was denounced as a radical by conservatives in his own time, Lindsay's view of him in the following poem is
far different.

The Eagle That Is Forgotten

(John P. Altgeld.   Born December 30, 1847; died March 12, 1902)

Vachel Lindsay

Sleep softly . . . eagle forgotten . . . under the stone.
Time has its way with you there, and the clay has its own.

"We have buried him now," thought your foes, and in secret re-
    joiced.
They made a brave show of their mourning, their hatred unvoiced.
They had snarled at you, barked at you, foamed at you day after
    day.   5
Now you were ended.   They praised you, . . . and laid you away.

The others that mourned you in silence and terror and truth,
The widow bereft of her crust, and the boy without youth,
The mocked and the scorned and the wounded, the lame and the
    poor
That should have remembered forever, . . . remember no more.   10

Where are those lovers of yours, on what name do they call
The lost, that in armies wept over your funeral pall?
They call on the names of a hundred high-valiant ones,
A hundred white eagles have risen the sons of your sons,
The zeal in their wings is a zeal that your dreaming began   15
The valor that wore out your soul in the service of man.

Sleep softly, . . . eagle forgotten, . . . under the stone,
Time has its way with you there and the clay has its own.
Sleep on, O brave-hearted, O wise man, that kindled the flame—
To live in mankind is far more than to live in a name,   20
To live in mankind, far, far more . . . than to live in a name.

Understanding the Poem

1. To what are Altgeld's foes compared in line 5? How does this metaphor contrast with that between Altgeld and an eagle?
2. In what ways is the eagle an appropriate metaphor for this poem?
3. What emotion dominates lines 3-6? lines 7-10? lines 13-16? How
   would these be reflected in the tone of voice and the speed with
   which the poem should be read aloud?

Morning at the Window

T. S. Eliot

They are rattling breakfast plates in basement kitchens,
And along the trampled edges of the street
I am aware of the damp souls of housemaids
Sprouting despondently at area gates.

   The brown waves of fog toss up to me
Twisted faces from the bottom of the street,
And tear from a passer-by with muddy skirts
An aimless smile that hovers in the air
And vanishes along the level of the roofs.

Understanding the Poem

1. What metaphor is used in lines 3-4? What is the effect of this metaphor? What kind of feeling does it indicate the speaker has toward people and the morning?
2. What impression of the morning is created by such details as "the trampled edges of the street" and "brown waves of fog"? What other details contribute to this impression?
3. What is the over-all effect of the scene described in this poem?

A Kind of Good-bye

Theodore Spencer

I met an old man near a darkened house,
And he looked in my eyes and spoke of that house,
Said the girl with flame in her voice, in her hair.
"What did he say to you standing there?
What did he say to you, darling, darling?"   5

He said that the house was my own house;
Said the girl with flame in her eyes, in her hair;
That's what he said to me standing there;
That's what he said to me, darling, darling.

He said I'd live all day in that house,   10
He said I'd live all night in that house,
Said the girl with flame in her hands, in her hair;
"And what did you answer him standing there?
What did you answer him, darling, darling?"

I said I hated my darkened house,   15
Said the girl with flame in her skin, in her hair.
That's what I said to him standing there;
That's what I said to him, darling, darling.

But the old man told me to enter that house;
'You are here; we are ready; come into your house;'   20
He told me to enter my darkened house,
Said the girl with flame in her heart, in her hair.
That's what he said to me standing there;
That's what he said to me, darling, darling.

Understanding the Poem

1. Between what two people is the conversation in this poem taking place? What is the relationship between them?
2. "A Kind of Good-bye" is a poem on the borderline between metaphor and symbol. What does the "darkened house" represent? Who is the "old man"?
3. Line 3 is repeated in each stanza with slight variations. What are these variations? What does the flame represent?
4. What experience is the girl describing? Why is the poem called "A Kind of Good-bye"?

In Waste Places

James Stephens

As a naked man I go
Through the desert, sore afraid;
Holding high my head, although
I'm as frightened as a maid.

The lion crouches there! I saw   5
In barren rocks his amber eye!
He parts the cactus with his paw!
He stares at me, as I go by!

He would pad upon my trace
If he thought I was afraid!   10
If he knew my hardy face
Veils the terrors of a maid.

He rises in the night-time, and
He stretches forth! He snuffs the air!
He roars! He leaps along the sand!   15
He creeps! He watches everywhere!

His burning eyes, his eyes of bale
Through the darkness I can see!
He lashes fiercely with his tail!
He makes again to spring at me!   20

I am the lion, and his lair!
I am the fear that frightens me!
I am the desert of despair!
And the night of agony!

Night or day, whate'er befall,   25
I must walk that desert land,
Until I dare my fear, and call
The lion out to lick my hand!

Understanding the Poem

1. Explain in nonmetaphorical language what Stephens is saying in
   stanza 6.

2. Is this poem describing a specific occasion or a general type of experience? How much do you know about what is taking place in the speaker?

Developing Language Skills

Below is an earlier published version of "In Waste Places." Compare the two versions carefully. Then write one or two paragraphs explaining the changes that you consider most significant. Consider whether any changes made a difference (even a slight one) in the meaning of the poem, whether the emotional effect is strengthened by any changes. Where one word has been substituted for another (as *veils* for *hides* and *pad* for *follow*), try to decide why the poet changed the first version (was the meaning of the new word more appropriate? was its sound better? or what?).

As a naked man I go
    Through the desert sore afraid,
Holding up my head, although
    I am as frightened as a maid.

The couching lion there I saw   5
    From barren rocks lift up his eye,
He parts the cactus with his paw,
    He stares at me as I go by.

He would follow on my trace
    If he knew I was afraid,   10
If he knew my hardy face
    Hides the terrors of a maid.

In the night he rises, and
    He stretches forth, he snuffs the air,
He roars and leaps along the sand,   15
    He creeps and watches everywhere.

His burning eyes, his eyes of bale,
    Through the darkness I can see;
He lashes fiercely with his tail,
    He would love to spring at me.   20

I am the lion in his lair,
    I am the fear that frightens me,
I am the desert of despair,
    And the nights of agony.

Night or day, whate'er befall,   25
    I must walk that desert land,
Until I can dare to call
    The lion out to lick my hand.

Rhythm

Sound is a basic element of poetry. You know that sounds you hear around you affect you in different ways: the beat of a jazz band is different from the muffled, slow beat of a drum; the lapping of a brook, from the pounding of ocean surf; the steady insistence of a football cheer, from the slower rhythms of a Bible reading; the sighing of a soft wind in a pine tree, from the battering surge of rain and wind in a storm. These sounds we hear are capable of affecting our feelings—sometimes very strongly. The sound of poetry, too, can change mere words on a page into something alive and meaningful.

The poet has several means of controlling the speed and loudness of lines. He can speed up your reading by using sounds that are easily mouthed, sounds which require little movement of a reader's tongue and lips: words with short vowels and *l*'s and *m*'s, liquid sounds. He can slow you up by using long vowels and hard sounds like *d* and *t*, especially when the latter come close together. Or he may use long words and put in punctuation marks to slow you up. Of course, if your enunciation is poor, if you mutter ("mudder") and say "pija" for *pitcher,* the whole effect will be lost.

The poet also expects you to fit the speed to the sense of the poem. For instance, phrases describing a sad scene usually require a slow reading. Passages describing something like a horse galloping or the rush of a train would call for a rapid rate.

As you read this sentence, you find yourself accenting certain sounds more heavily than others. The resulting beats make an irregular pattern—so irregular that there is no apparent rhythm to it. The poet, however, often regularizes the beat of words: he often arranges his sounds so that they fall in regular patterns of sound. We call this beat his rhythm.

The arrangement of the rhythmic beats is called the meter of the poem. On page 604 you will find a description of some common terms we use to describe the meter of a poem.

Reading "Once by the Pacific"

"Once by the Pacific" has a colloquial ring to its language, yet what the speaker is experiencing has little of the casual quality that the colloquial language suggests. The scene, as the speaker sees it, is a frightening one.

Once you are sure of the meaning expressed through the images and figurative language of the poem, look at its form. You will probably notice first that it is written in *couplets:* units of two lines which rhyme. If you then read aloud a line, listening to its rhythm, you can easily hear that a regular alternation of a lightly accented syllable with a heavily accented one occurs. Using a slanted mark to indicate a heavy (or stressed) accent, we can indicate the stresses that occur in this way:

The sháttered wáter máde a místy dín.

Within this line there are five units, each consisting of an unaccented syllable followed by an accented one. The technical name for such a unit is an *iamb,* or *iambic foot.* The iambic foot is the most common one in English poetry, for its repetition is closest to the usual rhythm of prose English while still maintaining a regular pattern of beats.

If you examine the rest of the poem, you will find that some lines occasionally contain a *foot* (that is, a unit) different from the iamb ("great waves," for example, is a foot in which both syllables are accented). However, the iambic foot is the most frequent one throughout the poem. It is suitable both to the somewhat casual, conversational style and to the description of waves regularly beating against the shore.

Once by the Pacific

Robert Frost

The shattered water made a misty din.
Great waves looked over others coming in,
And thought of doing something to the shore
That water never did to land before.
The clouds were low and hairy in the skies,   5
Like locks blown forward in the gleam of eyes.
You could not tell, and yet it looked as if
The shore was lucky in being backed by cliff,
The cliff in being backed by continent;
It looked as if a night of dark intent   10
Was coming, and not only a night, an age.
Someone had better be prepared for rage.
There would be more than ocean-water broken
Before God's last *Put out the Light* was spoken.

Understanding the Poem

1. Where is the speaker in this poem? What is he looking at?
2. What is the author's feeling toward the sea? Which words suggest his feeling?
3. The author begins with a description of the sea. Where does he end his description and begin commenting on the scene?
4. In addition to describing what he sees at the present time, the poet says that the scene suggests something more. What kind of conflict does the scene suggest? Are any results of the conflict suggested? Refer to specific phrases in the poem in justifying your answers.
5. What does Frost mean by his last two lines?

Reading "The Benefactors"

Although almost all English poetry up to the last hundred years used some regular rhythmic beat, few good poets ever use a rhythmic pattern without varying it at all. Poets can vary a rhythmic pattern in several ways. One method is to vary the number of feet from line to line. Another is to add an extra syllable to a line occasionally (as Frost did, for example, in "Once by the Pacific"). Perhaps the most common method is to shift the accent from where it would usually occur in the pattern of rhythm to a normally unaccented position. Frost did this too, as the following line illustrates:

Someone had better be prepared for rage.

How do you know when an accent shifts from its regular position in a pattern of beats? In the above line, you know because of the normal way in which *someone* is pronounced: the first syllable is always accented most heavily. (You should not accent words differently than you usually do because they appear in a poem.) You can also tell by the importance a word has in a line of poetry whether it should be accented or not. For example, the first word of the following poem is accented even though, according to the rhythmic pattern of the poem, the first syllables of lines are unaccented. The exclamation mark following it indicates its importance and the need for stressing it.

All these techniques for varying a rhythmic pattern are used in "The Benefactors." In reading it, you should be aware of the basic pattern (which is iambic), but you should also avoid a singsong effect through awareness of the variations that occur.

The Benefactors

Rudyard Kipling

Ah! What avails the classic bent
And what the cultured word,
Against the undoctored incident
That actually occurred?

And what is Art whereto we press   5
Through paint and prose and rhyme—
When Nature in her nakedness
Defeats us every time?

It is not learning, grace nor gear,
    Nor easy meat and drink,   10
But bitter pinch of pain and fear
    That makes creation think.

When in this world's unpleasing youth
    Our godlike race began,
The longest arm, the sharpest tooth,   15
    Gave man control of man;

Till, bruised and bitten to the bone
    And taught by pain and fear,
He learned to deal the far-off stone,
    And poke the long, safe spear.   20

So tooth and nail were obsolete
    As means against a foe,
Till, bored by uniform defeat,
    Some genius built the bow.

Then stone and javelin proved as vain   25
    As old-time tooth and nail;
Till, spurred anew by fear and pain,
    Man fashioned coats of mail.

Then was there safety for the rich
    And danger for the poor,   30
Till someone mixed a powder which
    Redressed[1] the scale once more.

1 **redressed:** adjusted again; corrected.

Helmet and armour disappeared
    With sword and bow and pike,
And, when the smoke of battle cleared,   35
    All men were armed alike. . . .

And when ten million such were slain
    To please one crazy king,
Man, schooled in bulk by fear and pain,
    Grew weary of the thing;   40

And, at the very hour designed
    To enslave him past recall,
His tooth-stone-arrow-gun-shy mind
    Turned and abolished all.

All Power, each Tyrant, every Mob   45
    Whose head has grown too large,
Ends by destroying its own job
    And works its own discharge;

And Man, whose mere necessities
    Move all things from his path,   50
Trembles meanwhile at their decrees,
    And deprecates[2] *their wrath!*

2 deprecates: seeks to avert; disapproves of.

Understanding the Poem

1. Paraphrase the first two stanzas.
2. What, stanza by stanza, is the history of man outlined by the poet?
3. What does the poet see as the outcome of the development of weapons?
4. To whom does "their" refer in the last two lines of the poem?
5. Paraphrase the final two stanzas.
6. In what way is the title, "The Benefactors," used ironically?
7. What irregularities can you find in the rhythmic pattern?

Developing Oral Reading Skills

Read aloud a few lines from the poem in a singsong rhythm emphasizing the metric pattern. Reread the same lines in a more natural rhythm in which you use the inflections of normal speech, accenting key words for meaning. The poem should be clearer to your listeners through this second method of reading. The meter still will provide a background rhythmic accompaniment, but will not dominate the meaning.

The following poem uses rhythm in a very different manner from the two preceding ones, for it does not have a regular repeated beat. This lack of a regularly repeated beat is called *free verse.*

The poem does not lack rhythm, however. Repetition of phrasing is one way in which a rhythmic effect is created. And the rhythm of people's speech is consciously imitated throughout: sometimes slow and drawling, sometimes quick-fire and staccato.

They Have Yarns*

Carl Sandburg

They have yarns
Of a skyscraper so tall they had to put hinges
On the two top stories so to let the moon go by,
Of one corn crop in Missouri when the roots
Went so deep and drew off so much water
The Mississippi riverbed that year was dry,
Of pancakes so thin they had only one side,
Of "a fog so thick we shingled the barn and six feet out on the fog,"
Of Pecos Pete straddling a cyclone in Texas and riding it to the west
    coast where "it rained out under him,"
Of the man who drove a swarm of bees across the Rocky Mountains
    and the Desert "and didn't lose a bee,"
Of a mountain railroad curve where the engineer in his cab can touch
    the caboose and spit in the conductor's eye,
Of the boy who climbed a cornstalk growing so fast he would have
    starved to death if they hadn't shot biscuits up to him,
Of the old man's whiskers: "When the wind was with him his whiskers
    arrived a day before he did,"
Of the hen laying a square egg and cackling, "Ouch!" and of hens lay-
    ing eggs with the dates printed on them,
Of the ship captain's shadow: it froze to the deck one cold winter
    night,

Of mutineers on that same ship put to chipping rust with rubber hammers,
Of the sheep counter who was fast and accurate: "I just count their feet and divide by four,"
Of the man so tall he must climb a ladder to shave himself,
Of the runt so teeny-weeny it takes two men and a boy to see him,
Of mosquitoes: one can kill a dog, two of them a man,
Of a cyclone that sucked cookstoves out of the kitchen, up the chimney flue, and on to the next town,
Of the same cyclone picking up wagon tracks in Nebraska and dropping them over in the Dakotas,
Of the hook-and-eye snake unlocking itself into forty pieces, each piece two inches long, then in nine seconds flat snapping itself together again,
Of the watch swallowed by the cow—when they butchered her a year later the watch was running and had the correct time,
Of horned snakes, hoop snakes that roll themselves where they want to go, and rattlesnakes carrying bells instead of rattles on their tails,
Of the herd of cattle in California getting lost in a giant redwood tree that had hollowed out,
Of the man who killed a snake by putting its tail in its mouth so it swallowed itself,
Of railroad trains whizzing along so fast they reach the station before the whistle,
Of pigs so thin the farmer had to tie knots in their tails to keep them from crawling through the cracks in their pens,
Of Paul Bunyan's big blue ox, Babe, measuring between the eyes forty-two ax-handles and a plug of Star tobacco exactly,
Of John Henry's hammer and the curve of its swing and his singing of it as "a rainbow round my shoulder."

"Do tell!"
"I want to know!"
"You don't say so!"
"For the land's sake!"
"Gosh all fishhooks!"
"Tell me some more.
I don't believe a word you say
but I love to listen
to your sweet harmonica
to your chin-music.
Your fish stories hang together
when they're just a pack of lies:
you ought to have a leather medal:
you ought to have a statue
carved of butter: you deserve
a large bouquet of turnips."

"Yessir," the traveler drawled,
"Away out there in the petrified forest
everything goes on the same as usual.
The petrified birds sit in their petrified nests
and hatch their petrified young from petrified eggs."

A high-pressure salesman jumped off the Brooklyn Bridge and was
saved by a policeman. But it didn't take him long to sell the idea
to the policeman. So together they jumped off the bridge.

One of the oil men in heaven started a rumor of a gusher down in hell.
All the other oil men left in a hurry for hell. As he gets to thinking about the rumor he had started he says to himself there might
be something in it after all. So he leaves for hell in a hurry.

"The number 42 will win this raffle, that's my number." And when he
won they asked him whether he guessed the number or had a system. He said he had a system, "I took up the old family album
and there on page 7 was my grandfather and grandmother both
on page 7. I said to myself this is easy for 7 times 7 is the number
that will win and 7 times 7 is 42."

Once a shipwrecked sailor caught hold of a stateroom door and floated
for hours till friendly hands from out of the darkness threw him a
rope. And he called across the night, "What country is this?" and
hearing voices answer, "New Jersey," he took a fresh hold on the
floating stateroom door and called back half-wearily, "I guess I'll
float a little farther."

An Ohio man bundled up the tin roof of a summer kitchen and sent it
to a motor car maker with a complaint of his car not giving service.
In three weeks a new car arrived for him and a letter: "We regret
delay in shipment but your car was received in a very bad order."
A Dakota cousin of this Ohio man sent six years of tin can accumulations to the same works, asking them to overhaul his car. Two
weeks later came a rebuilt car, five old tin cans, and a letter: "We
are also forwarding you five parts not necessary in our new model."
Thus fantasies heard at filling stations in the midwest. Another relates
to a Missouri mule who took aim with his heels at an automobile
rattling by. The car turned a somersault, lit next a fence, ran right
along through a cornfield till it came to a gate, moved onto the
road and went on its way as though nothing had happened. The
mule heehawed with desolation, "What's the use?"
Another tells of a farmer and his family stalled on a railroad crossing,
how they jumped out in time to see a limited express knock it into
flinders, the farmer calling, "Well, I always did say that car was
no shucks in a real pinch."

RHYTHM

When the Masonic Temple in Chicago was the tallest building in the United States west of New York, two men who would cheat the eyes out of you if you gave 'em a chance, took an Iowa farmer to the top of the building and asked him, "How is this for high?" They told him that for $25 they would go down in the basement and turn the building around on its turntable for him while he stood on the roof and saw how this seventh wonder of the world worked. He handed them $25. They went. He waited. They never came back.

This is told in Chicago as a folk tale, the same as the legend of Mrs. O'Leary's cow kicking over the barn lamp that started the Chicago fire, when the Georgia visitor, Robert Toombs, telegraphed an Atlanta crony, "Chicago is on fire, the whole city burning down, God be praised!"

Nor is the prize sleeper Rip Van Winkle and his scolding wife forgotten, nor the headless horseman scooting through Sleepy Hollow

Nor the sunken treasure-ships in coves and harbors, the hideouts of gold and silver sought by Coronado, nor the Flying Dutchman rounding the Cape doomed to nevermore pound his ear nor ever again take a snooze for himself

Nor the sailor's caretaker Mother Carey seeing to it that every seafaring man in the afterworld has a seabird to bring him news of ships and women, an albatross for the admiral, a gull for the deckhand

Nor the sailor with a sweetheart in every port of the world, nor the ships that set out with flying colors and all the promises you could ask, the ships never heard of again,

Nor Jim Liverpool, the riverman who could jump across any river and back without touching land he was that quick on his feet,

Nor Mike Fink along the Ohio and the Mississippi, half wild horse and half cockeyed alligator, the rest of him snags and snapping turtle. "I can outrun, outjump, outshoot, outbrag, outdrink, and outfight, rough and tumble, no holts barred, any man on both sides of the river from Pittsburgh to New Orleans and back again to St. Louis. My trigger finger itches and I want to go redhot. War, famine and bloodshed puts flesh on my bones, and hardship's my daily bread."

Nor the man so lean he threw no shadow: six rattlesnakes struck at him at one time and every one missed him.

Understanding the Poem

1. What are the three major divisions of this poem? What repetitions —of form or content—are used within each division to produce a sense of rhythm and unity?
2. The poem opens with the words "They have yarns." Who is "they"?

3. If you read this poem carefully, it probably left you with the impression that Americans of all times and places have had certain common characteristics. Some characteristics are illustrated by the kind of yarns people tell—for example, they all show a sense of humor. Others are illustrated by the actions and comments of people within the individual yarns—for example, several anecdotes show the ability to sell an idea or product. What are other characteristics illustrated in the poem?

Reading "in Just-"

In the following poem, Cummings uses an even freer poetic form than Sandburg does in "They Have Yarns." He abandons the usual practices of capitalization and punctuation, using capitals primarily for emphasis of a word and using spacing to indicate pauses and separations of thought. By doing this and by creating the images he does, Cummings captures much of the joy and magical sense a child experiences as spring arrives. As you read "in Just-," be aware of how the spacing and line divisions control the rhythm.

"in Just-"*

e. e. cummings

in Just-
spring   when the world is mud-
luscious the little
lame balloonman

whistles   far   and wee

and eddieandbill come
running from marbles and
piracies and it's
spring

when the world is puddle-wonderful

---

the queer
old balloonman whistles
far   and   wee
and bettyandisbel come dancing

from hop-scotch and jump-rope and

it's
spring
and
        the
                goat-footed
balloonMan   whistles
far
and
wee

Understanding the Poem

1. What are some words or phrases that best help to capture a child's reaction to spring?
2. Which lines in this poem should be read fastest? Which slowest? How do you know?
3. What mythological allusion is being made in the description *goat-footed*? Why is it appropriate to the poem?

Stanzas Written on the Road Between Florence and Pisa

George Gordon, Lord Byron

Oh, talk not to me of a name great in story;
The days of our youth are the days of our glory;
And the myrtle[1] and ivy of sweet two-and-twenty
Are worth all your laurels,[2] though ever so plenty.

What are garlands[3] and crowns to the brow that is wrinkled?   5
'Tis but as a dead-flower with May-dew besprinkled.
Then away with all such from the head that is hoary![4]
What care I for the wreaths that can *only* give glory?

---

1 **myrtle:** a fast-growing shrub.
2 **laurels:** leaves which symbolize victory.
3 **garland:** a wreath of flowers, often given to a victor.
4 **hoary:** white or gray with age.

Oh Fame!—if I e'er took delight in thy praises,   10
'Twas less for the sake of thy high-sounding phrases,
Than to see the bright eyes of the dear one discover
She thought that I was not unworthy to love her.

There chiefly I sought thee, *there* only I found thee;
Her glance was the best of the rays that surround thee;   15
When it sparkled o'er aught that was bright in my story,
I knew it was love, and I felt it was glory.

Understanding the Poem

1. In the first two stanzas, what does Byron believe is more important than fame?
2. In the final two stanzas, what does Byron consider the chief value of fame?
3. What pattern of unaccented and accented beats is repeated most often in this poem? Does the rhythm tend to give a lighthearted or a dignified tone to the poem?
4. Do you find the rhythm of the poem appropriate or intrusive? Why?

Reading "Song: To the Men of England"

The following poem, along with others by Shelley, was inspired by political conditions—particularly the occurrence of the Manchester Massacre—in England. On August 16, 1819, a mass meeting was held in St. Peter's Fields, Manchester, to demand the reform of Parliament. An attack, endorsed by the government, was made by the yeomanry upon the peaceable crowd, which contained many women and children, and at least six hundred persons were killed or wounded. The indignation aroused by this event contributed much to the success of the reform movement.

Song

To the Men of England

Percy Bysshe Shelley

Men of England, wherefore plow
For the lords who lay ye low?
Wherefore weave with toil and care
The rich robes your tyrants wear?

Wherefore feed, and clothe, and save,   5
From the cradle to the grave,
Those ungrateful drones who would
Drain your sweat—nay, drink your blood?

Wherefore, Bees of England, forge
Many a weapon, chain, and scourge,   10
That these stingless drones may spoil
The forced produce of your toil?

Have ye leisure, comfort, calm,
Shelter, food, love's gentle balm?
Or what is it ye buy so dear   15
With your pain and with your fear?

The seed ye sow, another reaps;
The wealth ye find, another keeps;
The robes ye weave, another wears;
The arms ye forge, another bears.   20

Sow seed—but let no tyrant reap;
Find wealth—let no impostor heap;
Weave robes—let not the idle wear;
Forge arms—in your defense to bear.

Shrink to your cellars, holes, and cells;   25
In halls ye deck, another dwells.
Why shake the chains ye wrought? Ye see
The steel ye tempered glance on ye.

With plow and spade, and hoe and loom,
Trace your grave, and build your tomb,   30
And weave your winding-sheet, till fair
England be your sepulcher.

Understanding the Poem

1. To which "Men of England" is Shelley speaking?
2. Whom is Shelley referring to when he speaks of the drones? Why does he use the metaphor of a beehive?
3. State the idea expressed in stanza 8 in your own words.
4. In view of the title, would you expect this poem to have a regular rhythm? Why?
5. What does the poet want to accomplish through this poem? Why is a regular rhythm suitable or unsuitable to accomplishing his purpose?

"O what is that sound"

W. H. Auden

O what is that sound which so thrills the ear
    Down in the valley drumming, drumming?
Only the scarlet soldiers, dear,
    The soldiers coming.

O what is that light I see flashing so clear   5
    Over the distance brightly, brightly?
Only the sun on their weapons, dear,
    As they step lightly.

O what are they doing with all that gear,
    What are they doing this morning, this morning?   10
Only their usual manoeuvres, dear,
    Or perhaps a warning.

O why have they left the road down there,
    Why are they suddenly wheeling, wheeling?
Perhaps a change in their orders, dear.   15
    Why are you kneeling?

O haven't they stopped for the doctor's care,
    Haven't they reined their horses, their horses?
Why, they are none of them wounded, dear,
    None of these forces.   20

O is it the parson they want, with white hair,
    Is it the parson, is it, is it?
No, they are passing his gateway, dear,
    Without a visit.

O it must be the farmer who lives so near.   25
    It must be the farmer so cunning, so cunning?
They have passed the farmyard already, dear,
    And now they are running.

O where are you going? Stay with me here!
    Were the vows you swore deceiving, deceiving?   30
No, I promised to love you, dear,
    But I must be leaving.

O it's broken the lock and splintered the door,
    O it's the gate where they're turning, turning;
Their boots are heavy on the floor   35
    And their eyes are burning.

Understanding the Poem

1. What is the situation in this poem? Who are the speakers? Is anything gained or lost by not making the story and its characters more specific?
2. The rhythm in this poem is a heavy one. Using a slant mark to indicate an accented syllable, write out one stanza indicating all the accented syllables.
3. Why is a definite, even heavy rhythm suitable to this poem? What is the effect of the rhythm?

Sound

The sound of a poem is more than its rhythmic beat. The poet's craft also includes the selecting and organizing of matching sounds that help to express his idea or mood.

The most frequent way of matching sounds is through rhyme—in which the last accented vowel of two words and the sounds following that vowel have an identical sound (*ringing, singing*). If the rhyme falls on a single stressed syllable at the end of a line, the rhyme is *masculine;* but if the rhyme includes a stressed syllable followed by one or more unaccented syllables, it is called a *feminine rhyme.* The following lines illustrate both kinds of rhyme.

> From its sources which well
> In the tarn on the fell;
> From its fountains,
> In the mountains,
> Its rills and its gills—

Well and *fell* is a masculine rhyme. *Fountains* and *mountains* is a feminine rhyme. Both rhymes are called *end rhymes* because they occur at the end of a poetic line. *Rills* and *gills* in the final line of the above quotation is an example of *internal rhyme,* a rhyme formed within a line of poetry.

Rhyme may be used to accomplish some specific purpose—such as calling attention to important words by the emphasis rhyme gives them. Primarily, however, it is used simply because the human ear responds to it with pleasure.

Reading "The Cataract of Lodore"

Here, recreated in words, is a sound image of a tiny mountain stream growing in size and speed on its way to a waterfall. You may wish to read the poem silently at first, but do not fail to read it aloud before you attempt to discuss the poet's accomplishment.

Rhyme is used throughout the poem, but you will also discover other linkings of words through sound. *Alliteration* is one such method of linking words that is frequently used in "The Cataract of Lodore." By alliteration is meant the repetition of a sound in closely connected words: for example, South Seas, *d*ead as a *d*oornail, *b*right and *b*reezy. As these examples indicate, alliteration usually occurs at the beginning of words, although it may involve sounds within words too (as in "ba*bb*ling *b*rook").

The Cataract of Lodore

Robert Southey

"How does the Water
Come down at Lodore?"
My little boy asked me
Thus, once on a time;
And moreover he tasked me   5
To tell him in rhyme.
Anon at the word,
There first came one daughter,
And then came another,
To second and third   10
The request of their brother,
And to hear how the Water
Comes down at Lodore,
With its rush and its roar,
As many a time   15
They had seen it before.
So I told them in rhyme,
For of rhymes I had store;
And 'twas in my vocation
For their recreation   20
That so I should sing;
Because I was Laureate[1]
To them and the King.

From its sources which well
In the Tarn on the fell;   25
From its fountains
In the mountains,
Its rills and its gills;
Through moss and through brake,
It runs and it creeps   30
For awhile, till it sleeps
In its own little Lake.
And thence at departing,
Awakening and starting,

---

[1] **Laureate:** Southey was Poet Laureate of England from 1813-1843. The Laureate is appointed by the sovereign.

It runs through the reeds,   35
And away it proceeds,
Through meadow and glade,
In sun and in shade,
And through the wood-shelter,
Among crags in its flurry,   40
Helter-skelter,
Hurry-scurry.
Here it comes sparkling,
And there it lies darkling;
Now smoking and frothing   45
Its tumult and wrath in,
Till in this rapid race
On which it is bent,
It reaches the place
Of its steep descent.   50

The Cataract strong
Then plunges along,
Striking and raging
As if a war waging
Its caverns and rocks among;   55
Rising and leaping,
Sinking and creeping,
Swelling and sweeping,
Showering and springing,
Flying and flinging,   60
Writhing and ringing,
Eddying and whisking,
Spouting and frisking,
Turning and twisting,
Around and around   65
With endless rebound
Smiting and fighting,
A sight to delight in;
Confounding, astounding,
Dizzying and deafening the ear with its sound   70
Collecting, projecting,
Receding and speeding,
And shocking and rocking,
And darting and parting,
And threading and spreading,   75
And whizzing and hissing,
And dripping and skipping,
And hitting and splitting,
And shining and twining,

And rattling and battling,   80
And shaking and quaking,
And pouring and roaring,
And waving and raving,
And tossing and crossing,
And flowing and going,   85
And running and stunning,
And foaming and roaming,
And dinning and spinning,
And dropping and hopping,
And working and jerking,   90
And guggling and struggling,
And heaving and cleaving,
And moaning and groaning;
And glittering and frittering,

And gathering and feathering,   95
And whitening and brightening,
And quivering and shivering,
And hurrying and scurrying,
And thundering and floundering;

Dividing and gliding and sliding,   100
And falling and brawling and sprawling,
And driving and riving and striving,
And sprinkling and twinkling and wrinkling,
And sounding and bounding and rounding,
And bubbling and troubling and doubling,   105
And grumbling and rumbling and tumbling,
And clattering and battering and shattering;

Retreating and beating and meeting and sheeting,
Delaying and straying and playing and spraying,
Advancing and prancing and glancing and dancing,   110
Recoiling, turmoiling and toiling and boiling,
And gleaming and streaming and steaming and beaming,
And rushing and flushing and brushing and gushing,
And flapping and rapping and clapping and slapping,
And curling and whirling and purling and twirling,   115
And thumping and plumping and bumping and jumping,
And dashing and flashing and splashing and clashing;
And so never ending, but always descending,
Sounds and motions forever and ever are blending,
All at once and all o'er, with a mighty uproar,   120
And this way the Water comes down at Lodore.

Understanding the Poem

1. Look at the poem on the page. How is its appearance similar to the course of the mountain stream?
2. What do you believe is the author's purpose in this poem? How well do you think he accomplishes this purpose? Defend your answer by reading aloud from the poem.
3. Locate examples of masculine rhyme, feminine rhyme, end rhyme, internal rhyme, and alliteration in the poem.

Building Vocabulary Skills

Many of the words in this poem were chosen for their sound as well as for their meaning. Locate some words which you believe were chosen more for their sound than for their meaning. Be prepared to defend your selection.

Reading "The Santa-Fé Trail"

"The Santa-Fé Trail" depends for most of its effect upon a very strong, even exaggerated, rhythm and upon a plentiful use of rhyme. In addition to rhyme and alliteration, *onomatopoeia* is also used as a musical device. The term refers to the use of words in which the sound suggests the meaning. Words like *buzz, crack,* and *sigh* are examples of onomatopoeia. Poems that present images concerned with sound are apt to use onomatopoeic words ("The Cataract of Lodore," as well as the following poem, uses it extensively). A poet can go beyond simply using words like *buzz* or *sigh* in creating an onomatopoeic effect. The following lines, for instance, suggest the sound of a horn through repetition of the long "o," although the words by themselves are not onomatopoeic.

> Listen to the gold-horn . . .
> Old-horn . . .
> Cold-horn . . .

In reading the various sections of "The Santa-Fé Trail," try to determine the effect Lindsay wanted to create in each by the sound of his words.

The Santa-Fé Trail (A Humoresque)[1]

Vachel Lindsay

(I asked the old Negro: "What is that bird that sings so well?" He answered: "That is the Rachel-Jane." "Hasn't it another name—lark, or thrush, or the like?" "No. Jus' Rachel-Jane.")

I. In Which a Racing Auto Comes from the East

This is the order of the music of the morning:— *To be sung*
First, from the Far East comes but a crooning. *delicately, to*
The crooning turns to a sunrise singing. *an improvised*
Hark to the *calm*-horn, *balm*-horn, *psalm*-horn. *tune.*
Hark to the *faint*-horn, *quaint*-horn, *saint*-horn   5

Hark to the *pace*-horn, *chase*-horn, *race*-horn. *To be sung or*
And the holy veil of the dawn has gone. *read with*
Swiftly the brazen car comes on. *great speed.*
It burns in the East as the sunrise burns.
I see great flashes where the far trail turns.   10
Its eyes are lamps like the eyes of dragons.
It drinks gasoline from big red flagons.
Butting through the delicate mists of the morning,
It comes like lightning, goes past roaring.
It will hail all the windmills, taunting, ringing,   15
Dodge the cyclones,
Count the milestones,
On through the ranges the prairie-dog tills—
Scooting past the cattle on the thousand hills. . . .
Ho for the tear-horn, scare-horn, dare-horn,   20   *To be read or*
Ho for the *gay*-horn, *bark*-horn, *bay*-horn. *sung in a roll-*
Ho for Kansas land that restores us *ing bass, with*
When houses choke us, and great books bore us! *some delibera-*
Sunrise Kansas, harvesters' Kansas, *tion.*
A million men have found you before us.   25
A million men have found you before us.

---

1 **Humoresque:** a fanciful or humorous work.

I want live things in their pride to remain.
I will not kill one grasshopper vain
Though he eats a hole in my shirt like a door.
I let him out, give him one chance more.   30
Perhaps, while he gnaws my hat in his whim,
Grasshopper lyrics occur to him.

*In an even,
deliberate,
narrative
manner.*

I am a tramp by the long trail's border,
Given to squalor, rags and disorder.
I nap and amble and yawn and look,   35
Write fool-thoughts in my grubby book,
Recite to the children, explore at my ease,
Work when I work, beg when I please,
Give crank-drawings, that make folks stare
To the half-grown boys in the sunset glare,   40
And get me a place to sleep in the hay
At the end of a live-and-let-live day.

I find in the stubble of the new-cut weeds
A whisper and a feasting, all one needs:
The whisper of the strawberries, white and red   45
Here where the new-cut weeds lie dead.

But I would not walk all alone till I die
Without some life-drunk horns going by.
And up round this apple-earth they come
Blasting the whispers of the morning dumb:—   50
Cars in a plain realistic row.
And fair dreams fade
When the raw horns blow.

On each snapping pennant
A big black name:—   55
The careering city
Whence each car came.
They tour from Memphis, Atlanta, Savannah,
Tallahassee and Texarkana.
They tour from St. Louis, Columbus, Manistee,   60
They tour from Peoria, Davenport, Kankakee.
Cars from Concord, Niagara, Boston,
Cars from Topeka, Emporia, and Austin.
Cars from Chicago, Hannibal, Cairo.
Cars from Alton, Oswego, Toledo.   65
Cars from Buffalo, Kokomo, Delphi,
Cars from Lodi, Carmi, Loami.

*Like a train-
caller in a
Union Depot.*

Ho for Kansas, land that restores us
When houses choke us, and great books bore us!
While I watch the highroad   70
And look at the sky,
While I watch the clouds in amazing grandeur
Roll their legions without rain
Over the blistering Kansas plain—
While I sit by the milestone   75
And watch the sky,
The United States
Goes by.

Listen to the iron-horns, ripping, racking.   *To be given*
Listen to the quack-horns, slack and clacking.   80   *very harshly,*
Way down the road, trilling like a toad,   *with a*
Here comes the *dice*-horn, here comes the *vice*-horn,   *snapping ex-*
Here comes the *snarl*-horn, *brawl*-horn, *lewd*-horn,   *plosiveness.*
Followed by the *prude*-horn, bleak and squeaking:—
(Some of them from Kansas, some of them from Kansas.)   85
Here comes the *hod*-horn, *plod*-horn, *sod*-horn,
Nevermore-to-*roam*-horn, *loam*-horn, *home*-horn.
(Some of them from Kansas, some of them from Kansas.)

        Far away the Rachel-Jane   *To be read or*
        Not defeated by the horns   90   *sung, well-nigh*
        Sings amid a hedge of thorns:—   *in a whisper.*
        "Love and life,
        Eternal youth—
        Sweet, sweet, sweet, sweet,
        Dew and glory,   95
        Love and truth,
        Sweet, sweet, sweet, sweet."

WHILE SMOKE-BLACK FREIGHTS ON THE DOUBLE-TRACKED RAILROAD, *Louder and*
DRIVEN AS THOUGH BY THE FOUL FIEND'S OX-GOAD,   *louder, faster*
SCREAMING TO THE WEST COAST, SCREAMING TO THE EAST,   100   *and faster.*
CARRY OFF A HARVEST, BRING BACK A FEAST,
AND HARVESTING MACHINERY AND HARNESS FOR THE BEAST,
THE HAND-CARS WHIZ, AND RATTLE ON THE RAILS,
THE SUNLIGHT FLASHES ON THE TIN DINNER-PAILS.
And then, in an instant, ye modern men,   105   *In a rolling*
Behold the procession once again,   *bass, with*
The United States goes by!   *increasing*
Listen to the iron-horns, ripping, racking,   *deliberation.*
Listen to the *wise*-horn, desperate-to-*advise* horn,   *With a snap-*
Listen to the *fast*-horn, *kill*-horn, *blast*-horn. . . . 110 *ping explosive-*
                                                            ness.
        Far away the Rachel-Jane   *To be sung or*
        Not defeated by the horns   *read well-nigh*
        Sings amid a hedge of thorns:—   *in a whisper.*

Love and life,
Eternal youth,
Sweet, sweet, sweet, sweet,
Dew and glory,
Love and truth.
Sweet, sweet, sweet, sweet.
The mufflers open on a score of cars
With wonderful thunder,
CRACK, CRACK, CRACK,
CRACK-CRACK, CRACK-CRACK,
CRACK, CRACK, CRACK,
Listen to the gold-horn . . .
Old-horn . . .
Cold-horn . . .
And all of the tunes, till the night comes down
On hay-stack, and ant-hill, and wind-bitten town.

Then far in the west, as in the beginning,
Dim in the distance, sweet in retreating,
Hark to the faint-horn, quaint-horn, saint-horn,
Hark to the calm-horn, balm-horn, psalm-horn. . . .

They are hunting the goals that they understand:—
San-Francisco and the brown sea-sand.
My goal is the mystery the beggars win.
I am caught in the web the night-winds spin.
The edge of the wheat-ridge speaks to me.
I talk with the leaves of the mulberry tree.
And now I hear, as I sit all alone
In the dusk, by another big Santa-Fé stone,
The souls of the tall corn gathering round
And the gay little souls of the grass in the ground.
Listen to the tale the cottonwood tells.
Listen to the windmills, singing o'er the wells.
Listen to the whistling flutes without price
Of myriad prophets out of paradise.
Harken to the wonder
That the night-air carries. . . .
Listen . . . to . . . the . . . whisper . . .
Of . . . the . . . prairie . . . fairies
    Singing o'er the fairy plain:—
    "Sweet, sweet, sweet, sweet.
    Love and glory,
    Stars and rain,
    Sweet, sweet, sweet, sweet. . . ."

115

120

125

130

135

140

145

150

155

*To be brawled
in the begin-
ning with a
snapping
explosiveness,
ending in a
languorous
chant.*

*To be sung to
exactly the
same whis-
pered tune as
the first five
lines.*

*This section
beginning
sonorously,
ending in a
languorous
whisper.*

*To the same
whispered tune
as the Rachel-
Jane song—
but very
slowly.*

Understanding the Poem

1. Who is narrating the poem? Where do you discover his identity? What do you find out about the type of person he is?
2. Read from the poem what you *see* in the first 26 lines. What image describes the car's headlights? How is the image continued in the following lines? Read what you *hear* in the same lines.
3. At one point, the speaker says, "Behold the procession once again, / The United States goes by!" What picture do you get of the United States in this poem? Refer to specific lines to justify your answer.
4. The directions Lindsay gives for reading this poem indicate various contrasts he wants to bring out. What are some of the contrasts?
5. Find several lines in which onomatopoeia is used.

Developing Oral Reading Skills

Plan an oral presentation of "The Santa-Fé Trail" by the class. Read aloud by groups or individuals, contrasting the stillness of the morning with the intrusion of the first car and the noise of the highway with the song of Rachel-Jane and the growing stillness of the evening. Some sections may best be read by boys, whereas girls' voices will most effectively re-create the author's mood for other sections. A single narrator might read the lines beginning with "I." Your goal should be to create in vocal sounds what Vachel Lindsay heard along the Santa Fé Trail. Note the marginal directions he has given for a reading of the poem.

Reading "The Mountain Whippoorwill"

Benét's poem is more than the story of Hill-Billy Jim—it is a melodious lyric of the mountain folk. One method by which the poet obtains this melodic quality is through euphonious lines. *Euphony* is the pleasant effect of easily pronounced consonant and vowel combinations, as in line 2 of "The Mountain Whippoorwill": "Sof' win' slewin' thu' the sweet-potato vine." No hard and fast rules determine whether a line is euphonic or not; however, vowels, *l*'s, *m*'s, *w*'s, *v*'s, and *s*'s are letters that tend to produce a melodious effect.

A poet is most likely to strive for euphony when he wants his subject matter to be connected with harmonious sounds—for instance, in describing music, a pleasant voice, a gentle wind, or the lapping of water. He might also use euphonic lines in connection with anything peaceful, beautiful, or delicate, in order to reinforce these qualities through the sounds used to describe them.

The Mountain Whippoorwill

Or, How Hill-Billy Jim Won the Great Fiddlers' Prize

(A Georgia Romance)

Stephen Vincent Benét

Up in the mountains, it's lonesome all the time,
(Sof' win' slewin' thu' the sweet-potato vine).

Up in the mountains, it's lonesome for a child.
(Whippoorwills a-callin' when the sap runs wild).

Up in the mountains, mountains in the fog,   5
Everythin's as lazy as an old houn' dog.

Born in the mountains, never raised a pet,
Don't want nuthin' an' never got it yet.

Born in the mountains, lonesome-born,
Raised runnin' ragged thu' the cockleburrs and corn.   10

Never knew my pappy, mebbe never should.
Think he was a fiddle made of mountain laurelwood.

Never had a mammy to teach me pretty-please.
Think she was a whippoorwill, a-skitin' thu' the trees.

Never had a brother ner a whole pair of pants,   15
But when I start to fiddle, why, yuh got to start to dance!

Listen to my fiddle—Kingdom Come—Kingdom Come!
Hear the frogs a-chunkin' "Jug o' rum, Jug o' rum!"
Hear that mountain-whippoorwill be lonesome in the air,
An' I'll tell yuh how I traveled to the Essex County Fair.   20

Essex County has a mighty pretty fair,
All the smarty fiddlers from the South come there.

Elbows flyin' as they rosin up the bow
For the First Prize Contest in the Georgia Fiddlers' Show.

Old Dan Wheeling, with his whiskers in his ears,
Kingpin fiddler for nearly twenty years.

Big Tom Sargent, with his blue walleye,
An' Little Jimmy Weezer that can make a fiddle cry.

All sittin' roun', spittin' high an' struttin' proud,
(Listen, little whippoorwill, yuh better bug yore eyes!)
Tun-tun-a-tunin' while the jedges told the crowd
Them that got the mostest claps'd win the bestest prize.

Everybody waitin' for the first tweedledee,
When in comes a-stumblin'—hill-billy me!

Bowed right pretty to the jedges an' the rest,
Took a silver dollar from a hole inside my vest,

Plunked it on the table an' said, "There's my callin' card!
An' anyone that licks me—well, he's got to fiddle hard!"

Old Dan Wheeling, he was laughin' fit to holler,
Little Jimmy Weezer said, "There's one dead dollar!"

Big Tom Sargent had a yaller-toothy grin,
But I tucked my little whippoorwill spang underneath my chin,
An' petted it an' tuned it till the jedges said, "Begin!"

Big Tom Sargent was the first in line;
He could fiddle all the bugs off a sweet-potato vine.
He could fiddle down a possum from a mile-high tree.
He could fiddle up a whale from the bottom of the sea.

Yuh could hear hands spankin' till they spanked each other raw,
When he finished variations on "Turkey in the Straw."

Little Jimmy Weezer was the next to play;
He could fiddle all night, he could fiddle all day.

He could fiddle chills, he could fiddle fever,
He could make a fiddle rustle like a lowland river.

He could make a fiddle croon like a lovin' woman.
An' they clapped like thunder when he'd finished strummin'.

Then came the ruck of the bobtailed fiddlers,
The let's go-easies, the fair-to-middlers.

They got their claps an' they lost their bicker,
An' settled back for some more corn-licker.

An' the crowd was tired of their no-count squealing,   60
When out in the center steps Old Dan Wheeling.

He fiddled high and he fiddled low,
(Listen, little whippoorwill; yuh got to spread yore wings!)
He fiddled with a cherrywood bow.
(Old Dan Wheeling's got bee-honey in his strings.)   65

He fiddled the wind by the lonesome moon,
He fiddled a most almighty tune.

He started fiddling like a ghost,
He ended fiddling like a host.

He fiddled north an' he fiddled south,   70
He fiddled the heart right out of yore mouth.

He fiddled here an' he fiddled there.
He fiddled salvation everywhere.

When he was finished, the crowd cut loose,
(Whippoorwill, they's rain on yore breast.)   75
An' I sat there wonderin', "What's the use?"
(Whippoorwill, fly home to yore nest.)

But I stood up pert an' I took my bow,
An' my fiddle went to my shoulder, so.

An'—they wasn't no crowd to get me fazed—   80
But I was alone where I was raised.

Up in the mountains, so still it makes yuh skeered.
Where God lies sleepin' in his big white beard.

An' I heard the sound of the squirrel in the pine,
An' I heard the earth a-breathin' thu' the long nighttime.   85

They've fiddled the rose, an' they've fiddled the thorn,
But they haven't fiddled the mountain-corn.

They've fiddled sinful an' fiddled moral,
But they haven't fiddled the breshwood-laurel.

They've fiddled loud, an' they've fiddled still,   90
But they haven't fiddled the whippoorwill.

I started off with a *dump-diddle-dump,*
(*Oh, hell's broke loose in Georgia!*)
Skunk-cabbage growin' by the bee-gum stump,
(*Whippoorwill, yo're singin' now!*)   95

Oh, Georgia booze is mighty fine booze,
The best yuh ever poured yuh,
But it eats the soles right offen yore shoes,
For Hell's broke loose in Georgia.

My mother was a whippoorwill pert,   100
My father, he was lazy,
But I'm Hell broke loose in a new store shirt
To fiddle all Georgia crazy.

Swing yore partners—up an' down the middle!
Sashay now—oh, listen to that fiddle!   105
Flapjacks flippin' on a red-hot griddle,
An' hell broke loose,
Hell broke loose,
Fire on the mountains—snakes in the grass.
Satan's here a-bilin'—oh, Lordy, let him pass!   110
Go down Moses, set my people free,
Pop goes the weasel thu' the old Red Sea!
Jonah sittin' on a hickory-bough,
Up jumps a whale—an' where's yore prophet now?
Rabbit in the pea-patch, possum in the pot,   115
Try an' stop my fiddle, now my fiddle's gettin' hot!
Whippoorwill, singin' thu' the mountain hush,
Whippoorwill, shoutin' from the burnin' bush,
Whippoorwill, cryin' in the stable-door,
Sing tonight as yuh never sang before!   120
Hell's broke loose like a stompin' mountain-shoat,
Sing till yuh bust the gold in yore throat!
Hell's broke loose for forty miles aroun'
Bound to stop yore music if yuh don't sing it down.
Sing on the mountains, little whippoorwill,   125
Sing to the valleys, an' slap 'em with a hill,
For I'm struttin' high as an eagle's quill,
An' Hell's broke loose,
Hell's broke loose,
Hell's broke loose in Georgia!   130

They wasn't a sound when I stopped bowin',
(*Whippoorwill, yuh can sing no more.*)
But, somewhere or other, the dawn was growin',
(*Oh, mountain whippoorwill!*)

An' I thought, "I've fiddled all night an' lost.   135
Yo're a good hill-billy, but yuh've been bossed."

So I went to congratulate old man Dan,
—But he put his fiddle into my han'—
An' then the noise of the crowd began.

Understanding the Poem

1. Who won the contest? In what line is the winner revealed? How do you know that the result surprised Hill-Billy Jim?
2. A whippoorwill is a bird, but what else is it in this poem? What does Hill-Billy Jim mean by: "Whippoorwill, they's rain on yore breast" and "Whippoorwill, fly home to yore nest"?
3. The poet must create the musical quality of his composition through the sound of his words. What initial consonant sound is repeated to produce such a quality in line 2? Read other examples of alliteration in the poem that help to suggest the sound of the fiddlers' music.
4. Find several instances of euphony in "The Mountain Whippoorwill."
5. Judging from the context, what do the italicized words in the following lines mean:

> Sof' win' *slewin'* thu' the sweet-potato vine. (1.2)
> Think she was a whippoorwill, *a-skittin'* thu' the trees. (1.14)
> They got their claps an' they lost their *bicker*. (1.58)

6. How is the rhythm of this poem like that of a square dance? Why is it an appropriate rhythm?

Reading "Four Preludes on Playthings of the Wind"

Cacophony (the opposite of euphony) is a term used to describe discordant, harsh, unmusical sounds. Such sounds are often difficult to articulate, and thus may have the effect of slowing down a line. Some sounds which have a cacophonic effect when several of them are used within a line are *k*, hard *g* or *c*, *qu*, and sometimes *t*, *d*, *b*, and *p*. Cacophony is often deliberately used by poets in describing disagreeable, ugly, or feared subjects. For example, Sandburg employs cacophony to describe the rats in a destroyed city in the following poem.

Four Preludes on Playthings of the Wind°

Carl Sandburg

"The past is a bucket of ashes."

1

THE woman named Tomorrow
sits with a hairpin in her teeth
and takes her time
and does her hair the way she wants it
and fastens at last the last braid and coil   5
and puts the hairpin where it belongs
and turns and drawls: Well, what of it?
My grandmother, Yesterday, is gone.
What of it?   Let the dead be dead.

2

The doors were cedar   10
and the panels strips of gold
and the girls were golden girls
and the panels read and the girls chanted:
  We are the greatest city,
  the greatest nation: 15
  nothing like us ever was.

The doors are twisted on broken hinges.
Sheets of rain swish through on the wind
  where the golden girls ran and the panels read:
  We are the greatest city,   20
  the greatest nation,
  nothing like us ever was.

3

It has happened before.
Strong men put up a city and got
    a nation together, 25
And paid singers to sing and women
      to warble: We are the greatest city,
        the greatest nation,
        nothing like us ever was.

And while the singers sang 30
and the strong men listened
and paid the singers well
and felt good about it all,
   there were rats and lizards who listened
   . . . and the only listeners left now 35
   . . . are . . . the rats . . . and the lizards.

And there are black crows
crying, "Caw, caw,"
bringing mud and sticks
building a nest 40
    over the words carved
    on the doors where the panels were cedar
    and the strips on the panels were gold
    and the golden girls came singing:
      We are the greatest city, 45
      the greatest nation:
      nothing like us ever was.

The only singers now are crows crying, "Caw, caw,"
And the sheets of rain whine in the wind and doorways.
And the only listeners now are . . . the rats . . . and the lizards. 50

4

    The feet of the rats
    scribble on the door sills;
    the hieroglyphs of the rat footprints
    chatter the pedigrees of the rats
    and babble of the blood 55
    and gabble of the breed
    of the grandfathers and the great-grandfathers
    of the rats.

And the wind shifts
and the dust on a door sill shifts   60
and even the writing of the rat footprints
tells us nothing, nothing at all
about the greatest city, the greatest nation
where the strong men listened
and the women warbled: Nothing like us ever was.   65

Understanding the Poem

1. What is the theme of "Four Preludes on Playthings of the Wind"?
   Compare this with the theme of "By the Waters of Babylon" by
   Stephen Vincent Benét.
2. What images does Sandburg connect with the flourishing city? with
   the destroyed city? Why are the images connected with each appropriate ones?
3. What do you believe is the author's attitude toward the golden city?
   toward the devastated city? What evidence do you find in the poem
   for your answer?
4. Read specific lines or passages which use cacophony. Are there any
   lines which are euphonic?
5. In section 4, the speaker says: "the hieroglyphs of the rat footprints /
   chatter the pedigrees of the rats." What does *hieroglyphs* mean?
   Which meanings apply in this line?

   With what in the preceding parts of the poem do "the hieroglyphs
   of the rat footprints" contrast? What is the point being made by
   the contrast?
6. What does the phrase "playthings of the wind" mean?

Of A' the Airts

Robert Burns

Of a' the airts[1] the wind can blaw
   I dearly like the west,
For there the bonie lassie lives,
   The lassie I lo'e best.
There wild woods grow, and rivers row,   5
   And monie a hill between,
But day and night my fancy's flight
   Is ever wi' my Jean.

---

1 **airts:** directions of the compass.

I see her in the dewy flowers—
   I see her sweet and fair.   10
I hear her in the tunefu' birds—
   I hear her charm the air.
There's not a bonie flower that springs
   By fountain, shaw,[2] or green,
There's not a bonie bird that sings,   15
   But minds me o' my Jean.

2 shaw: small wood or grove.

Understanding the Poem

1. With what does the poet compare his Jean? In what ways is she like these things?
2. Identify two devices of sound used in line 5.
3. Is this poem an example of euphony or cacophony? Point out specific lines and the sounds in them which support your answer. Is the tendency of the poem toward one of these appropriate to its subject or not?

from

Pippa Passes

Robert Browning

The year's at the spring
And day's at the morn;
Morning's at seven;
The hillside's dew-pearled;
The lark's on the wing;
The snail's on the thorn:
God's in his heaven—
All's right with the world!

Understanding the Poem

1. What is the time setting of this poem?
2. What three images does the poet select to describe the scene?
3. Contrast the last image with the first two. What does it contribute to the poem?
4. What is the tone of this lyric?

The Song of Shadows

Walter de la Mare

Sweep thy faint strings, Musician,
    With thy long lean hand;
Downward the starry tapers burn,
    Sinks soft the waning sand;
The old hound whimpers couched in sleep,   5
    The embers smoulder low;
Across the walls the shadows
    Come, and go.

Sweep softly thy strings, Musician,
    The minutes mount to hours;   10
Frost on the windless casement weaves
    A labyrinth of flowers;
Ghosts linger in the darkening air,
    Hearken at the open door;
Music hath called them, dreaming,   15
    Home once more.

Understanding the Poem

1. What is the "waning sand" in line 4?
2. What is a "labyrinth of flowers" in line 12?
3. Which of the devices of sound discussed in this section are used in "The Song of Shadows"? What effects are achieved by these devices in the poem?

Jazz Fantasia[1]

Carl Sandburg

Drum on your drums, batter on your banjoes,
sob on the long cool winding saxophones.
Go to it, O jazzmen.

Sling your knuckles on the bottoms of the happy
tin pans, let your trombones ooze, and go husha-
husha-hush with the slippery sand-paper.

Moan like an autumn wind high in the lonesome treetops, moan soft like you wanted somebody terrible,
cry like a racing car slipping away from a motorcycle
cop, bang-bang! you jazzmen, bang altogether drums,
traps, banjoes, horns, tin cans—make two people fight
on the top of a stairway and scratch each other's eyes
in a clinch tumbling down the stairs.

Can the rough stuff . . . now a Mississippi steamboat
pushes up the night river with a hoo-hoo-hoo-oo . . .
and the green lanterns calling to the high soft stars
. . . a red moon rides on the humps of the low river
hills . . . go to it, O jazzmen.

1 **Fantasia:** a musical selection with no fixed form or style.

Understanding the Poem

1. Which stanza should be read the loudest? Which the softest? Which words or phrases in each stanza provide the basis for your answer?
2. Compare the sound of the last three lines of the third stanza with the first three lines of the last stanza. Which words in these six lines provide the transition between them?
3. What do you believe was the poet's purpose in writing "Jazz Fantasia"? Why did he succeed or fail in achieving this purpose?

"All of us always turning away for solace"

Delmore Schwartz

All of us always turning away for solace

From the lonely room where the self must be honest,
All of us turning from being alone (at best
Boring) because what we want most is to be
Interested,

         play billiards, poking a ball   5
On the table, play baseball, batting a ball
On the diamond, play football, kicking a ball
On the gridiron,
      70,000 applauding.

This amuses, this indeed is our solace: 10
Follow the bouncing ball! O, fellow, follow,
See what is here and clear, one thing repeated,
Bounding, evasive, caught and uncaught, fumbled,
Follow the bouncing ball; and thus you follow,
Fingering closely your breast on the left side,   15

The bouncing ball you turned from for solace.

Understanding the Poem

1. What is "The bouncing ball" of the last line? What does the last line mean?
2. This poem does not rely on a definite scheme of rhythm or rhyme for its unity. Rather, repetition plays a large part in holding the poem together—repetition of letters, syllables, phrasing. For example, note the italicized repetitions of line 1: "*All* of us *al*ways turning away for *so*lace." Examine the poem carefully and see what other examples of repetition you find.
3. The central image of this poem is a bouncing ball. Do you find the rhythm of the poem and its sounds appropriate to this image? Explain your answer.

                                        POETRY

Light Verse

Reading **Ogden Nash**

Diction refers to the selection of words in writing or speaking. Good diction consists in selecting carefully the right word for one's purpose: that is, a word which has both the exact connotative and dictionary meanings one wants. Diction is important in all poetry, for it takes the right word to create the exact feeling or image the poet desires.

In light verse the poet's diction is often determined by his wish to produce a humorous effect. For example, note the rhyming words in the first two of Nash's couplets: "calliope . . . diope" and "talcum . . . walcum." The diction is not proper according to accepted standards, but for Nash's purpose the twisting of words is justified by the effect produced. Although his verse is light, Nash frequently chooses words that normally appear in formal contexts and that we associate with a serious tone (for example, *transcendental*). In such cases, his diction contributes to the humor of a piece by its very unexpectedness.

Pediatric[1] Reflection

Many an infant that screams like a calliope
Could be soothed by a little attention to its diope.

1 **Pediatric:** relating to the branch of medicine dealing with infants and children.

Reflection on Babies

A bit of talcum
Is always walcum.

The Parent

Children aren't happy with nothing to ignore,
And that's what parents were created for.

I'll Take the High Road Commission

In between the route marks
And the shaving rhymes,
Black and yellow markers
Comment on the times.

All along the highway   5
Hear the signs discourse:

MEN
SLOW
WORKING
;
SADDLE   10
CROSSING
HORSE
.

Cryptic crossroad preachers
Proffer good advice,
Helping wary drivers   15
Keep out of Paradise.

Transcontinental sermons,
Transcendental talk:

SOFT
CAUTION   20
SHOULDERS
;
CROSS
CHILDREN
WALK
.

Wisest of the proverbs,   25
Truest of the talk,
Have I found the dictum:

CROSS
CHILDREN
WALK   30
.

When Adam took the highway
He left his sons a guide:
CROSS
CHILDREN
WALK
;

CHEERFUL
CHILDREN
RIDE
.

35

Reading "Very Like a Whale"

"Very Like a Whale" is a spoof on the use of figurative language. By pretending that some well-known metaphors and similes of poetry are meant to be taken as literal comparisons, Nash produces some very ludicrous results.

The title of the poem is taken from the following conversation which occurs in Shakespeare's *Hamlet* (Act III, scene ii). Polonius, an older man, is trying to be very agreeable to Hamlet, who is in a bitter mood and provokes this conversation at Polonius's expense.

HAMLET. Do you see yonder cloud that's almost in shape of a camel?
POLONIUS. By th' mass, and 'tis like a camel indeed.
HAMLET. Methinks it is like a weasel.
POLONIUS. It is backed like a weasel.
HAMLET. Or like a whale.
POLONIUS. Very like a whale.

To appreciate the poem, you also need to know the opening of "The Destruction of Sennacherib" by Byron, the poem that is the subject of Nash's humor. Its first stanza is as follows:

The Assyrian came down like the wolf on the fold,
And his cohorts were gleaming in purple and gold;
And the sheen of their spears was like stars on the sea,
When the blue wave rolls nightly on deep Galilee.

In reading Nash's poem, you will see that the deliberate violation of perfect rhyme and of the expected rhythm provides much of the humorous effect. *Better for* and *metaphor* is the first use of *imperfect rhyme:* words that are almost, but not exactly, similar in their rhyming sounds. And the rhythmic effect becomes funny when Nash includes a line that goes on and on long after the reader, judging by the length of the preceding lines, expects it to end.

Very Like a Whale

One thing that literature would be greatly the better for
Would be a more restricted employment by authors of
    simile and metaphor.
Authors of all races, be they Greeks, Romans, Teutons
    or Celts,
Can't seem just to say that anything is the thing it is
    but have to go out of their way to say that it is like
    something else.
What does it mean when we are told   5
That the Assyrian came down like a wolf on the fold?
In the first place, George Gordon Byron had had enough
    experience
To know that it probably wasn't just one Assyrian, it
    was a lot of Assyrians.
However, as too many arguments are apt to induce
    apoplexy and thus hinder longevity,
We'll let it pass as one Assyrian for the sake of brevity.   10
Now then, this particular Assyrian, the one whose co-
    horts were gleaming in purple and gold,
Just what does the poet mean when he says he came
    down like a wolf on the fold?
In heaven and earth more than is dreamed of in our
    philosophy there are a great many things,[1]
But I don't imagine that among them there is a wolf
    with purple and gold cohorts or purple and gold
    anythings.
No, no, Lord Byron, before I'll believe that this As-   15
    syrian was actually like a wolf I must have some
    kind of proof;
Did he run on all fours and did he have a hairy tail and
    a big red mouth and big white teeth and did he
    say Woof woof?
Frankly I think it very unlikely, and all you were en-
    titled to say, at the very most,
Was that the Assyrian cohorts came down like a lot of
    Assyrian cohorts about to destroy the Hebrew host.

---

1 In . . . things: an allusion to the following lines from *Hamlet:* "There are more things
in heaven and earth, Horatio, / Than are dreamt of in your philosophy" (I, v, 166-167).

But that wasn't fancy enough for Lord Byron, oh dear
    me no, he had to invent a lot of figures of speech
    and then interpolate them,
With the result that whenever you mention Old Testa-   20
    ment soldiers to people they say Oh yes, they're
    the ones that a lot of wolves dressed up in gold and
    purple ate them.
That's the kind of thing that's being done all the time
    by poets, from Homer to Tennyson;
They're always comparing ladies to lilies and veal to
    venison,
And they always say things like that the snow is a white
    blanket after a winter storm.
Oh it is, is it, all right then, you sleep under a six-inch
    blanket of snow and I'll sleep under a half-inch
    blanket of unpoetical blanket material and we'll
    see which one keeps warm,
And after that maybe you'll begin to comprehend dimly   25
What I mean by too much metaphor and simile.

Developing Language Skills

1. Write two paragraphs, explaining in the first the point (or points) you
   believe Ogden Nash is making in "Very Like a Whale" and in the
   second the reasons you believe support or contradict his point(s).
   Be sure your reasons are not merely unsupported opinion, but are
   well-thought-out arguments for or against Nash's points.
2. Write one to three paragraphs analyzing devices Nash uses to produce humor in his poems. Consider his choice of words, his use of
   rhyme and rhythm, his choice and treatment of subject matter.
3. Try writing a humorous couplet in the style of Ogden Nash. Note
   that rhymes of two or three syllables are apt to be more humorous
   than masculine rhymes. Also note that the last phrase or word
   generally provides the humorous punch.

Reviewing Poetic Techniques: Two Poems

Reading "Renascence"

Keeping in mind the various approaches to understanding poetry you have studied in this unit, read the following lyric poem by Edna St. Vincent Millay. "Renascence," published when its author was only twenty, describes an inner experience that is both shattering and creative.

Renascence[1]

Edna St. Vincent Millay

All I could see from where I stood
Was three long mountains and a wood;
I turned and looked another way,
And saw three islands in a bay.
So with my eyes I traced the line   5
Of the horizon, thin and fine,
Straight around till I was come
Back to where I'd started from;
And all I saw from where I stood
Was three long mountains and a wood.   10

Over these things I could not see:
These were the things that bounded me.
And I could touch them with my hand,
Almost, I thought, from where I stand!
And all at once things seemed so small   15
My breath came short, and scarce at all.
But, sure, the sky is big, I said:
Miles and miles above my head.
So here upon my back I'll lie
And look my fill into the sky.   20
And so I looked, and after all,
The sky was not so very tall.
The sky, I said, must somewhere stop . . .
And—sure enough!—I see the top!

---

1 **Renascence** (rĭ năs′əns): a new birth.

The sky, I thought, is not so grand;
I 'most could touch it with my hand!
And reaching up my hand to try,
I screamed, to feel it touch the sky.

I screamed, and—lo!—Infinity   30
Came down and settled over me;
Forced back my scream into my chest;
Bent back my arm upon my breast;
And, pressing of the Undefined
The definition on my mind,   35
Held up before my eyes a glass
Through which my shrinking sight did pass
Until it seemed I must behold
Immensity made manifold;
Whispered to me a word whose sound   40
Deafened the air for worlds around,
And brought unmuffled to my ears
The gossiping of friendly spheres,
The creaking of the tented sky,
The ticking of Eternity.

I saw and heard, and knew at last   45
The How and Why of all things, past,
And present, and forevermore.
The Universe, cleft to the core,
Lay open to my probing sense,
That, sickening, I would fain pluck thence   50
But could not,—nay! but needs must suck
At the great wound, and could not pluck
My lips away till I had drawn
All venom out.—Ah, fearful pawn:[2]
For my omniscience[3] paid I toll   55
In infinite remorse of soul.

All sin was of my sinning, all
Atoning[4] mine, and mine the gall[5]
Of all regret. Mine was the weight
Of every brooded wrong, the hate   60
That stood behind each envious thrust,
Mine every greed, mine every lust.

2 **pawn:** a person of little significance.
3 **omniscience:** knowledge of everything.
4 **atoning:** making up for past sin.
5 **gall:** bitterness.

And all the while, for every grief,
Each suffering, I craved relief
With individual desire;   65
Craved all in vain! And felt fierce fire
About a thousand people crawl;
Perished with each,—then mourned for all!

A man was starving in Capri;
He moved his eyes and looked at me;   70
I felt his gaze, I heard his moan,
And knew his hunger as my own.
I saw at sea a great fog bank
Between two ships that struck and sank;
A thousand screams the heavens smote;[6]   75
And every scream tore through my throat.

No hurt I did not feel, no death
That was not mine; mine each last breath
That, crying, met an answering cry
From the compassion that was I.   80
All suffering mine, and mine its rod;
Mine, pity like the pity of God.

Ah, awful weight!   Infinity
Pressed down upon the finite[7] Me!
My anguished spirit, like a bird,   85
Beating against my lips I heard;
Yet lay the weight so close about
There was no room for it without.
And so beneath the weight lay I
And suffered death, but could not die.   90

Long had I lain thus, craving death,
When quietly the earth beneath
Gave way, and inch by inch, so great
At last had grown the crushing weight,
Into the earth I sank till I   95
Full six feet under ground did lie,
And sank no more,—there is no weight
Can follow here, however great.
From off my breast I felt it roll,
And as it went my tortured soul   100
Burst forth and fled in such a gust
That all about me swirled the dust.

6 **smote:** hit with force.
7 **finite:** having limits.

Deep in the earth I rested now.
Cool is its hand upon the brow
And soft its breast beneath the head   105
Of one who is so gladly dead.
And all at once, and over all
The pitying rain began to fall;
I lay and heard each pattering hoof
Upon my lowly, thatchèd roof,   110
And seemed to love the sound far more
Than ever I had done before.
For rain it hath a friendly sound
To one who's six feet under ground;
And scarce the friendly voice or face,   115
A grave is such a quiet place.

The rain, I said, is kind to come
And speak to me in my new home.
I would I were alive again
To kiss the fingers of the rain,   120
To drink into my eyes the shine
Of every slanting silver line,
To catch the freshened, fragrant breeze
From drenched and dripping apple trees.
For soon the shower will be done,   125
And then the broad face of the sun
Will laugh above the rain-soaked earth
Until the world with answering mirth
Shakes joyously, and each round drop
Rolls, twinkling, from its grass-blade top.   130

How can I bear it, buried here,
While overhead the sky grows clear
And blue again after the storm?
O, multicolored, multiform,
Belovèd beauty over me,   135
That I shall never, never see
Again! Spring-silver, autumn-gold,
That I shall never more behold!—
Sleeping your myriad[8] magics through,
Close-sepulchred[9] away from you!   140
O God, I cried, give me new birth,
And put me back upon the earth!
Upset each cloud's gigantic gourd
And let the heavy rain, down-poured

8 **myriad:** a very great number.
9 **sepulchred:** buried.

In one big torrent, set me free,   145
Washing my grave away from me!

I ceased; and through the breathless hush
That answered me, the far-off rush
Of herald wings came whispering
Like music down the vibrant string   150
Of my ascending prayer, and—crash!
Before the wild wind's whistling lash
The startled storm clouds reared on high
And plunged in terror down the sky!
And the big rain in one black wave   155
Fell from the sky and struck my grave.

I know not how such things can be;
I only know there came to me
A fragrance such as never clings
To aught save happy living things;   160
A sound as of some joyous elf
Singing sweet songs to please himself,
And, through and over everything,
A sense of glad awakening.
The grass, a-tiptoe at my ear,   165

Whispering to me I could hear;
I felt the rain's cool finger tips
Brushed tenderly across my lips,
Laid gently on my sealèd sight,
And all at once the heavy night   170
Fell from my eyes and I could see!—
A drenched and dripping apple tree,
A last long line of silver rain,
A sky grown clear and blue again.
And as I looked a quickening gust   175
Of wind blew up to me and thrust
Into my face a miracle
Of orchard-breath, and with the smell,—
I know not how such things can be!—
I breathed my soul back into me.   180

Ah! Up then from the ground sprang I
And hailed the earth with such a cry
As is not heard save from a man
Who has been dead, and lives again.
About the trees my arms I wound;   185
Like one gone mad I hugged the ground;
I raised my quivering arms on high;
I laughed and laughed into the sky;

Till at my throat a strangling sob
Caught fiercely, and a great heartthrob 190
Sent instant tears into my eyes:
O God, I cried, no dark disguise
Can e'er hereafter hide from me
Thy radiant identity!
Thou canst not move across the grass 195
But my quick eyes will see Thee pass,
Nor speak, however silently,
But my hushed voice will answer Thee.
I know the path that tells Thy way
Through the cool eve of every day; 200
God, I can push the grass apart
And lay my finger on Thy heart!

The world stands out on either side
No wider than the heart is wide;
Above the world is stretched the sky,— 205
No higher than the soul is high.
The heart can push the sea and land
Farther away on either hand;
The soul can split the sky in two,
And let the face of God shine through. 210
But East and West will pinch the heart
That can not keep them pushed apart;
And he whose soul is flat—the sky
Will cave in on him by and by.

Understanding the Poem

1. What were the dimensions of the poet's world in the first part of the poem?
2. What caused the poet her "infinite remorse of soul"?
3. What is the significance of the lines: "Into the earth I sank till I / Full six feet under ground did lie"?
4. Why did the poet wish to be alive again?
5. How was the poet's new life different from her past life?
6. What are the dimensions of the poet's new world?

Reading "Ars Poetica"

Ars Poetica, a Latin phrase, is a traditional term for entitling a philosophy of poetry. Translated, it means "The Art of Poetry." MacLeish's poem is presented here as a conclusion to your study of this unit. How can a poem be *dumb, wordless, motionless in time, equal to, but not true*? Why should a poem *not mean, but be*?

Ars Poetica

Archibald MacLeish

A poem should be palpable[1] and mute
As a globed fruit

Dumb
As old medallions to the thumb

Silent as the sleeve-worn stone   5
Of casement ledges where the moss has grown—

A poem should be wordless
As the flight of birds

       ✿

A poem should be motionless in time
As the moon climbs   10

Leaving, as the moon releases
Twig by twig the night-entangled trees,

Leaving, as the moon behind the winter leaves,
Memory by memory the mind—

A poem should be motionless in time   15
As the moon climbs

       ✿

A poem should be equal to:
Not true

For all the history of grief
An empty doorway and a maple leaf   20

For love
The leaning grasses and two lights above the sea—

A poem should not mean
But be

1 **palpable:** tangible.

Narrative Poetry

Poetry may be classified into three types: narrative, lyric, and dramatic. Most of the poems you have read in this unit are lyric poems, ones concerned with the poet's personal moods and ideas and based on his imaginative reflection on experience. Dramatic poetry, as its name indicates, either is in the form of, or uses some technique of, drama. The author may, for example, relate a story through dialogue, seeking to project the emotions and conflicts of the characters to his audience as a playwright does. Or a poem that emphasizes a situation of conflict might be called dramatic. "O what is that sound" is a short dramatic poem. Narrative poetry also tells a story, but nondramatically. Like a short story, it is constructed around a plot, develops characters and their relationships, and frequently uses description. The narrative poem you will read is "Gareth and Lynette" by Alfred, Lord Tennyson.

Narrative poetry was one of the first literary forms to take shape. The early Greeks epics of Homer, the *Iliad* and the *Odyssey*, are narrative poems about the wanderings and exploits of a hero. One of the oldest pieces of writing in Anglo-Saxon literature is a narrative poem, the story of Beowulf. Since men have always been interested in their past history and gloried in their national heroes, tales of valiant deeds were told around the evening fire by roving minstrels, long before the age of printing. These tales, then as now, stirred men's hearts and gave them a sense of identity with the heroes of physical combats and brave deeds. Each storyteller, seeking to perfect his art, added new and more exciting events to his tale, until today it is often difficult to distinguish between fact and fiction in these old narratives. The storytellers of old were not only interested in entertaining their listeners, but also learned early the possibilities of teaching moral lessons through their verse. Thus, their tales often show the kind of behavior admired in earlier times and the values held by the people of the age. From these stories that once entertained the knights and ladies of the Middle Ages came the folk epics, metrical romances, ballads, and literary epics of our past.

Idylls of the King

One of these folk epics concerned King Arthur and his Knights of the Round Table. Historians generally agree that a Celtic leader by the name of Arturias once lived. About a century after the Roman legions withdrew from England in 410, Arthur struggled to defend Britain against the invading pagan Saxons and their allies. After his death (A.D. 538), his forces were finally pushed back into the Welsh mountains by the invaders, and the social order decayed into a semi-barbaric state. His exploits were first recorded by an early monk and later told and told again by a succession of writers and storytellers.

Geoffrey of Monmouth, the first to describe Arthur's court and his famous teacher, Merlin the magician, was probably the most important. The most famous account of King Arthur was written by Sir Thomas Malory in *Le Morte Darthur* (The Death of Arthur).

In 1485, England's first printer, William Caxton, published a volume called *Le Morte Darthur* in which Sir Thomas Malory drew together the various bright-colored threads of the King Arthur legend. One perfect copy of this book still exists. Malory's version is a racy, readable prose account of the Arthurian legend, the first to be written in colloquial English. This use of colloquial language has had a continuing influence on English literary style.

The story of Arthur, like the stories of such other heroes as Robin Hood and William Tell, grew more fantastic and idealistic with each retelling. The search of King Arthur's knights for the Holy Grail, the cup used by Jesus at the Last Supper according to legend, became symbolic of their quest for purity and righteousness. Arthur, himself representing the human conscience, became the center of a whole cycle of stories.

From the folk epic developed by many people about King Arthur, Alfred Tennyson fashioned a stately literary epic in twelve narrative poems. He had been captivated since his youth by the many accounts of life in Camelot, King Arthur's capital city. After years of reflection and work, Tennyson created from the Arthurian legend a moral allegory entitled *Idylls of the King*. An *idyll* is a narrative which makes use of many descriptive word pictures. Tennyson's *Idylls*, written in a highly ornamental style, are not only pictures of medieval life and the adventures of the Knights of the Round Table, but they are also symbolic images of timeless spiritual truths.

The chief change from the earlier versions of the legend is in the character of King Arthur. Tennyson makes him a high-minded hero who charges that each knight be faithful to one maiden only as he helps to build a noble society based on justice, love, and order. This characterization is in marked contrast to the bloody, romantic Arthur idolized in 9th-century England. Each generation that told the story of Arthur told it in terms of its own dreams and ideals. Tennyson brought his Victorian idealism to his telling of the legend. However, he keeps these major themes that are common to all versions of the fabulous story:

1. Arthur was a brave and noble king who united Britain into a single realm;
2. Guinevere was his beautiful but faithless queen;
3. Merlin, a magician, was Arthur's most trusted adviser;
4. Lancelot was the bravest knight;
5. Gareth was the most determined and starry-eyed of all the candidates for knighthood;
6. Sir Galahad was the most virtuous of the knights.

Both Malory's version and Tennyson's *Idylls* are marked by profound awareness of sin, of human frailty, and of personal responsibility, as well as of deep compassion for the retribution that weak humanity brings upon itself.

Tennyson uses the seasons of the year symbolically, grouping the idylls loosely into spring, summer, autumn, and winter as he tells the story of chivalry beginning in spring, reaching full flower in summer, beginning to wither in autumn, and dying in winter. Although each idyll is a separate story, many of the characters run through the entire epic.

"The Coming of Arthur," which opens the epic of twelve idylls, tells how Arthur subdued the twelve rebellious princes (of whom King Lot of Norway was chief), established his famous court in Camelot, and gathered about him a group of knights dedicated to deeds of daring and chivalry. This idyll also tells of King Arthur's winning Guinevere as his queen.

"The Passing of Arthur," the closing idyll, recounts the sad days in Camelot when the knights forget their vows and quarrel among themselves. The disloyal love of Lancelot and Queen Guinevere and the wicked plotting of Modred (Arthur's nephew) lead to the disintegration of the court. This tale tells of Lancelot going into exile in France, Guinevere entering a convent, and King Arthur dying as his noble dreams come to an end.

In between these two tales Tennyson tells ten adventurous stories. "Gareth and Lynette," second of the idylls, represents Arthur's famous Round Table when its glory is spreading through the land and noble youths from all countries seek to join King Arthur in his endeavors.

In "Gareth and Lynette," set in the springtime, Gareth, the youngest son of Lot and Bellicent, promises his mother Bellicent, who tries to dissuade him from leaving home to enter Arthur's court, that he will conceal his noble name. He also promises her to work in King Arthur's kitchens for a year as a scullery boy to prove his desire to be a knight. Gareth is a proud youth, and his mother hopes that this promise will keep him from the court. Gareth, however, goes to the court and works for twelve humiliating months in the scullery. His life is made particularly difficult by the taunts of Sir Kay, the King's steward, who derisively calls the lad Beaumains because of his large hands. At the end of the year, Beaumains is knighted by Sir Lancelot under his noble name, Gareth, and to prove his worthiness obtains the quest of Lynette, who seeks help from King Arthur and his court to liberate her sister Lyonors, held prisoner in Castle Perilous.

Gareth and Lynette

Alfred, Lord Tennyson

CHARACTERS

LOT, a minor king who fought against King Arthur.
BELLICENT (bĕl'ĭ sənt), Lot's wife, half-sister to King Arthur.
SIR GAWAIN (gä'wān), son of Lot and Bellicent, a Knight of the Round Table.
SIR MODRED (mō'drĭd), brother of Gawain, also a Knight of the Round Table.
GARETH (găr'ĕth), youngest son of Lot and Bellicent.
KING ARTHUR, ruler of the realm; leader of the Knights of the Round Table.
SIR LANCELOT, King Arthur's favorite knight.
SIR KAY, supervisor of the household affairs in King Arthur's court.
LYNETTE, a young damsel whose sister, Lyonors, is held prisoner.
THE BARON, a wealthy landowner.
SIR MORNING-STAR, an evil knight who represents youth.
SIR NOONDAY-SUN, an evil knight who represents middle age.
SIR EVENING-STAR, an evil knight who represents old age.
DEATH, the brother of the three evil knights.

The last tall son of Lot and Bellicent,
And tallest, Gareth, in a showerful spring
Stared at the spate.[1] A slender-shafted Pine
Lost footing, fell, and so was whirled away.
5 "How he went down," said Gareth, "as a false knight
Or evil king before my lance if lance
Were mine to use—O senseless cataract,
Bearing all down in thy precipitancy[2]—
And yet thou art but swollen with cold snows
10 And mine is living blood: thou dost His will.
The Maker's, and not knowest, and I that know,
Have strength and wit, in my good mother's hall
Linger with vacillating obedience,
Prisoned, and kept and coaxed and whistled to—
15 Since the good mother holds me still a child!
Good mother is bad mother unto me!
A worse were better; yet no worse would I.

1 spate : flooded stream.

2 precipitancy : headlong rush.

560

Heaven yield[3] her for it, but in me put force
To weary her ears with one continuous prayer,
20 Until she let me fly discaged to sweep
In ever-highering eagle-circles up
To the great Sun of Glory,[4] and thence swoop
Down upon all things base, and dash them dead,
A knight of Arthur, working out his will,
25 To cleanse the world. Why, Gawain, when he came
With Modred hither in the summertime,
Asked me to tilt[5] with him, the proven knight.
Modred for want of worthier was the judge.
Then I so shook him in the saddle, he said,
30 'Thou hast half prevailed against me,' said so—he—
Tho' Modred biting his thin lips was mute,
For he is always sullen: what care I?"

    And Gareth went, and hovering round her chair
Asked, "Mother, though ye count me still the child,
35 Sweet mother, do ye love the child?" She laughed,
"Thou art but a wild-goose to question it."
"Then, Mother, an[6] ye love the child," he said,
"Being a goose and rather tame than wild,
Hear the child's story." "Yea, my well-beloved,
40 An 'twere but of the goose and golden eggs."

    And Gareth answered her with kindling eyes,
"Nay, nay, good Mother, but this egg of mine
Was finer gold than any goose can lay;
For this an Eagle, a royal Eagle, laid
45 Almost beyond eye-reach, on such a palm
As glitters gilded in thy Book of Hours.[7]
And there was ever haunting round the palm
A lusty youth, but poor, who often saw
The splendor sparkling from aloft, and thought
50 'An I could climb and lay my hand upon it,
Then were I wealthier than a leash of[8] kings.'
But ever when he reached a hand to climb,
One, that had loved him from his childhood, caught
And stayed him, 'Climb not lest thou break thy neck,
55 I charge thee by my love,' and so the boy,
Sweet Mother, neither clomb, nor brake his neck,
But brake his very heart in pining for it,
And passed away."

                To whom the mother said,
"True love, sweet son, had risked himself and climbed,
60 And handed down the golden treasure to him."

ALFRED, LORD TENNYSON

561

3 yield : reward.

4 Sun of Glory : King Arthur.

5 tilt : engage in a contest on horseback using lances.

6 an : if.

7 Book of Hours : prayer book to be used at certain hours of the day.

8 a leash of : three.

And Gareth answered her with kindling eyes,
"Gold? said I gold?—ay then, why he, or she,
Or whosoe'er it was, or half the world
Had ventured—*had* the thing I spake of been
65 Mere gold—but this was all of that true steel,
Whereof they forged the brand[9] Excalibur,[10]
And lightnings played about it in the storm,
And all the little fowl were flurried at it,
And there were cries and clashings in the nest,
70 That sent him from his senses: let me go."

Then Bellicent bemoaned herself and said,
"Hast thou no pity upon my loneliness?
Lo, where thy father Lot beside the hearth
Lies like a log, and all but smoldered out!
75 For ever since when traitor to the King[11]
He fought against him in the Barons' war,
And Arthur gave him back his territory,
His age hath slowly drooped, and now lies there
A yet-warm corpse, and yet unburiable,
80 No more; nor sees, nor hears, nor speaks, nor knows.
And both thy brethren are in Arthur's hall,
Albeit neither loved with that full love
I feel for thee, nor worthy such a love:
Stay therefore thou; red berries charm the bird
85 And thee, mine innocent, the jousts,[12] the wars,
Who never knewest finger-ache, nor pang
Of wrenched or broken limb—an often chance
In those brain-stunning shocks, and tourney-falls,
Frights to my heart; but stay: follow the deer
90 By these tall firs and our fast-falling burns;[13]
So make thy manhood mightier day by day;
Sweet is the chase: and I will seek thee out
Some comfortable bride and fair, to grace
Thy climbing life, and cherish my prone year,[14]
95 Till falling into Lot's forgetfulness
I know not thee, myself, nor anything.
Stay, my best son! ye are yet more boy than man."

Then Gareth, "An ye hold me yet for child,
Hear yet once more the story of the child.
100 For, Mother, there was once a King, like ours;
The prince his heir, when tall and marriageable,
Asked for a bride; and thereupon the King
Set two before him. One was fair, strong, armed—
But to be won by force—and many men

105 Desired her; one, good lack,[15] no man desired.
   And these were the conditions of the King:
   That save he won the first by force, he needs
   Must wed that other, whom no man desired,
   A red-faced bride who knew herself so vile,
110 That evermore she longed to hide herself,
   Nor fronted[16] man or woman, eye to eye—
   Yea—some she cleaved to, but they died of her.
   And one—they called her Fame; and one—O Mother,
   How can ye keep me tethered to you—Shame!
115 Man am I grown, a man's work must I do.
   Follow the deer? follow the Christ, the King,
   Live pure, speak true, right wrong, follow the King—
   Else, wherefore born?"

                         To whom the mother said,
   "Sweet son, for there be many who deem him[17] not,
120 Or will not deem him, wholly proven King—
   Albeit in mine own heart I knew him King,
   When I was frequent with him in my youth,
   And heard him Kingly speak, and doubted him
   No more than he, himself; but felt him mine,
125 Of closest kin to me: yet—wilt thou leave
   Thine easeful biding here, and risk thine all,
   Life, limbs, for one that is not proven King?
   Stay, till the cloud that settles round his birth
   Hath lifted but a little. Stay, sweet son."

130   And Gareth answered quickly, "Not an hour,
   So that ye yield me—I will walk through fire,
   Mother, to gain it—your full leave to go.
   Not proven, who swept the dust of ruined Rome[18]
   From off the threshold of the realm, and crushed
135 The Idolaters,[19] and made the people free?
   Who should be King save him who makes us free?"

       So when the Queen, who long had sought in vain
   To break him from the intent to which he grew,
   Found her son's will unwaveringly one,
140 She answered craftily, "Will ye walk through fire?
   Who walks through fire will hardly heed the smoke.
   Ay, go then, an ye must: only one proof,
   Before thou ask the King to make thee knight,
   Of thine obedience and thy love to me,
   Thy mother—I demand."

ALFRED, LORD TENNYSON

15 good lack : an exclamation.

16 fronted : faced.

17 him : King Arthur.

18 Rome : The Roman armies had abandoned England.
19 crushed the Idolaters : defeated the invading heathen Saxons.

145And Gareth cried,

"A hard one, or a hundred, so I go.
Nay—quick! the proof to prove me to the quick!"

But slowly spake the mother looking at him,
"Prince, thou shalt go disguised to Arthur's hall,
150 And hire thyself to serve for meats and drinks
Among the scullions[20] and the kitchen-knaves,[21]
And those that hand the dish across the bar.
Nor shalt thou tell thy name to anyone.
And thou shalt serve a twelvemonth and a day."

155 For so the Queen believed that when her son
Beheld his only way to glory lead
Low down through villain[22] kitchen-vassalage,[23]
Her own true Gareth was too princely-proud
To pass thereby; so should he rest with her,
160 Closed in her castle from the sound of arms.

Silent awhile was Gareth, then replied,
"The thrall[24] in person may be free in soul,
And I shall see the jousts. Thy son am I,
And since thou art my mother, must obey.
165 I therefore yield me freely to thy will;
For hence will I, disguised, and hire myself
To serve with scullions and with kitchen-knaves;
Nor tell my name to any—no, not the King."

Gareth awhile lingered. The mother's eye
170 Full of the wistful fear that he would go,
And turning toward him wheresoe'er he turned,
Perplexed[25] his outward purpose, till an hour,
When wakened by the wind which with full voice
Swept bellowing through the darkness on to dawn,
175 He rose, and out of slumber calling two
That still had tended on him from his birth,
Before the wakeful mother heard him, went.

The three were clad like tillers of the soil.
Southward they set their faces. The birds made
180 Melody on branch, and melody in mid-air.
The damp hill slopes were quickened into green,
And the live green had kindled into flowers,
For it was past the time of Easterday.

20 scullions : kitchen workers.
21 kitchen-knaves : boys who work in the kitchen.

22 villain : lower class.
23 vassalage : servitude.

24 thrall : slave.

25 Perplexed : interfered with.

So, when their feet were planted on the plain
185 That broadened toward the base of Camelot,[26]
Far off they saw the silver-misty morn
Rolling her smoke about the Royal mount,
That rose between the forest and the field.
At times the summit of the high city flashed;
190 At times the spires and turrets halfway down
Pricked through the mist; at times the great gate shone
Only, that opened on the field below:
Anon,[27] the whole fair city had disappeared.

Then those who went with Gareth were amazed,
195 One crying, "Let us go no further, lord.
Here is a city of Enchanters, built
By fairy Kings." The second echoed him,
"Lord, we have heard from our wise men at home
To Northward, that this King is not the King,
200 But only changeling[28] out of Fairyland,
Who drave the heathen hence by scorcery
And Merlin's glamour."[29] Then the first again,
"Lord, there is no such city anywhere,
But all a vision."

Gareth answered them
205 With laughter, swearing he had glamour enow[30]
In his own blood, his princedom, youth and hopes,
To plunge old Merlin in the Arabian sea;
So pushed them all unwilling toward the gate.
And there was no gate like it under heaven.
210 For barefoot on the keystone, which was lined
And rippled like an ever-fleeting wave,
The Lady of the Lake stood: all her dress
Wept from her sides as water flowing away;
But like the cross her great and goodly arms
215 Stretched under all the cornice and upheld:
And drops of water fell from either hand;
And down from one a sword was hung, from one
A censer,[31] either worn with wind and storm;
And o'er her breast floated the sacred fish;[32]
220 And in the space to left of her, and right,
Were Arthur's wars in weird devices done,
New things and old co-twisted, as if Time
Were nothing, so inveterately,[33] that men
Were giddy gazing there; and over all
225 High on the top were those three Queens,[34] the friends
Of Arthur, who should help him at his need.

ALFRED, LORD TENNYSON

26 Camelot : the city where King Arthur's palace and court were located.

27 Anon : at another time.

28 changeling : a baby secretly exchanged for another.
29 glamour : enchantment.

30 enow : enough.

31 censer : a vessel for burning incense.
32 fish : a traditional symbol for Christ.

33 inveterately : habitually (the word's meaning is unclear here).
34 three Queens : They appear in other *Idylls*, and are said to represent Faith, Hope, and Charity.

Then those with Gareth for so long a space
Stared at the figures, that at last it seemed
The dragon-boughts[35] and elvish emblemings
230 Began to move, seethe, twine and curl: they called
To Gareth, "Lord, the gateway is alive."

And Gareth likewise on them fixed his eyes
So long, that even to him they seemed to move.
Out of the city a blast of music pealed.
235 Back from the gate started the three, to whom
From out thereunder came an ancient man,[36]
Long-bearded, saying, "Who be ye, my sons?"

Then Gareth, "We be tillers of the soil,
Who leaving share[37] in furrow come to see
240 The glories of our King: but these, my men,
(Your city moved so weirdly in the mist)
Doubt if the King be King at all, or come
From Fairyland; and whether this be built
By magic, and by fairy Kings and Queens;
245 Or whether there be any city at all,
Or all a vision: and this music now
Hath scared them both, but tell thou these the truth."

Then that old Seer made answer playing on him
And saying, "Son, I have seen the good ship sail
250 Keel upward and mast downward in the heavens,[38]
And solid turrets topsy-turvy in air:
And here is truth; but an it please thee not,
Take thou the truth as thou hast told it me.
For truly, as thou sayest, a Fairy King
255 And Fairy Queens have built the city, son;
They came from out a sacred mountain-cleft
Toward the sunrise, each with harp in hand,
And built it to the music of their harps.
And as thou sayest it is enchanted, son,
260 For there is nothing in it as it seems
Saving the King; tho' some there be that hold
The King a shadow, and the city real:
Yet take thou heed of him, for, so thou pass
Beneath this archway, then wilt thou become
265 A thrall to his enchantments, for the King
Will bind thee by such vows, as is a shame
A man should not be bound by, yet the which
No man can keep; but, so thou dread to swear,
Pass not beneath this gateway, but abide
270 Without, among the cattle of the field.

35 boughts : coils.

36 an ancient man : Merlin.

37 share : plow.

38 I have seen . . . in the heavens : A reflection of a ship seen in the sky after it had sailed beyond the horizon would be upside down.

ALFRED, LORD TENNYSON

For, an ye heard a music, like enow
They are building still, seeing the city is built
To music, therefore never built at all,
And therefore built for ever."

Gareth spake

275 Angered, "Old Master, reverence thine own beard
That looks as white as utter truth, and seems
Wellnigh as long as thou art statured tall!
Why mockest thou the stranger that hath been
To thee fair-spoken?"

But the Seer replied,

280 "Know ye not then the Riddling of the Bards?
'Confusion, and illusion, and relation,
Elusion, and occasion, and evasion'?
I mock thee not but as thou mockest me,
And all that see thee, for thou art not who
285 Thou seemest, but I know thee who thou art.
And now thou goest up to mock the King,
Who cannot brook[39] the shadow of any lie."

39 brook : endure.

Unmockingly the mocker ending here
Turned to the right, and passed along the plain;
290 Whom Gareth looking after said, "My men,
Our one white lie sits like a little ghost
Here on the threshold of our enterprise.
Let love be blamed for it, not she,[40] nor I:
Well, we will make amends."

40 she : Bellicent.

With all good cheer

295 He spake and laughed, then entered with his twain
Camelot, a city of shadowy palaces
And stately, rich in emblem and the work
Of ancient kings who did their days in stone;[41]
Which Merlin's hand, the Mage[42] at Arthur's court,
300 Knowing all arts, had touched, and everywhere
At Arthur's ordinance, tipped with lessening peak
And pinnacle, and had made it spire to heaven.
And ever and anon a knight would pass
Outward, or inward to the hall: his arms
305 Clashed; and the sound was good to Gareth's ear.
And out of bower[43] and casement[44] shyly glanced
Eyes of pure women, wholesome stars of love;
And all about a healthful people stepped
As in the presence of a gracious king.

41 did their days in stone :
recorded their deeds on
stones and through statues
and monuments.
42 Mage : magician.

43 bower : cottage.
44 casement : window.

³¹⁰   Then into hall Gareth ascending heard
    A voice, the voice of Arthur, and beheld
    Far over heads in that long-vaulted hall
    The splendor of the presence of the King
    Throned, and delivering doom[45]—and looked no more—
³¹⁵   But felt his young heart hammering in his ears,
    And thought, "For this half-shadow of a lie
    The truthful King will doom me when I speak."
    Yet pressing on, though all in fear to find
    Sir Gawain or Sir Modred, saw nor one
³²⁰   Nor other, but in all the listening eyes
    Of those tall knights, that ranged about the throne,
    Clear honor shining like the dewy star
    Of dawn, and faith in their great King, with pure
    Affection, and the light of victory,
³²⁵   And glory gained, and evermore to gain.

    Then came a widow crying to the King,
    "A boon,[46] Sir King! Thy father, Uther, reft[47]
    From my dead lord a field with violence:
    For howsoe'er at first he proffered[48] gold,
³³⁰   Yet, for the field was pleasant in our eyes,
    We yielded not; and then he reft us of it
    Perforce,[49] and left us neither gold nor field."

    Said Arthur, "Whether would ye? gold or field?"
    To whom the woman weeping, "Nay, my lord,
³³⁵   The field was pleasant in my husband's eye."

    And Arthur, "Have thy pleasant field again,
    And thrice the gold for Uther's use thereof,
    According to the years. No boon is here,
    But justice, so thy say be proven true.
³⁴⁰   Accursed, who from the wrongs his father did
    Would shape himself a right!"

                And while she passed,
    Came yet another widow crying to him,
    "A boon, Sir King! Thine enemy, King, am I.
    With thine own hand thou slewest my dear lord,
³⁴⁵   A knight of Uther in the Barons' war,
    When Lot and many another rose and fought
    Against thee, saying thou wert basely born.
    I held with these, and loathe to ask thee aught.
    Yet lo! my husband's brother had my son
³⁵⁰   Thralled[50] in his castle, and hath starved him dead;

45 doom : judgment.

46 boon : favor; request.
47 reft : seized.

48 proffered : offered.

49 Perforce : by force.

50 Thralled : imprisoned.

ALFRED, LORD TENNYSON

569

And standeth seized of that inheritance
Which thou that slewest the sire hast left the son.
So though I scarce can ask it thee for hate,
Grant me some knight to do the battle for me,
355 Kill the foul thief, and wreak[51] me for my son."

51 wreak : avenge.

Then strode a good knight forward, crying to him,
"A boon, Sir King! I am her kinsman, I.
Give me to right her wrong, and slay the man."

Then came Sir Kay, the seneschal,[52] and cried,
360 "A boon, Sir King! even that thou grant her none,
This railer,[53] that hath mocked thee in full hall—
None; or the wholesome boon of gyve[54] and gag."

52 seneschal : supervisor of the household affairs of the court.
53 railer : scolder.
54 gyve : shackle.

But Arthur, "We sit King, to help the wronged
Through all our realm. The woman loves her lord.
365 Peace to thee, woman, with thy loves and hates!
The kings of old had doomed thee to the flames,
Aurelius Emrys[55] would have scourged[56] thee dead,
And Uther slit thy tongue: but get thee hence—
Lest that rough humor[57] of the kings of old
370 Return upon me! Thou that art her kin,
Go likewise; lay him low and slay him not,
But bring him here, that I may judge the right,
According to the justice of the King:
Then, be he guilty, by that deathless King[58]
375 Who lived and died for men, the man shall die."

55 Aurelius Emrys : King Uther's brother, uncle to King Arthur.
56 scourged : whipped.
57 humor : mood.

58 deathless King : Christ.

Then came in hall the messenger of Mark,
A name of evil savor[59] in the land,
The Cornish king. In either hand he bore
What dazzled all, and shone far-off as shines
380 A field of charlock in the sudden sun
Between two showers, a cloth of palest gold,
Which down he laid before the throne, and knelt,
Delivering,[60] that his lord, the vassal king,[61]
Was even upon his way to Camelot;
385 For having heard that Arthur of his grace
Had made his goodly cousin, Tristram, knight,
And, for himself was of the greater state,
Being a king, he trusted his liege-lord[62]
Would yield him this large honor all the more;
390 So prayed him well to accept this cloth of gold,
In token of true heart and fealty.[63]

59 savor : repute.

60 Delivering : saying.
61 vassal king : below the rank of King Arthur.

62 liege-lord : the lord to whom he owes allegiance.

63 fealty : loyalty.

ALFRED, LORD TENNYSON

571

Then Arthur cried to rend the cloth, to rend
In pieces, and so cast it on the hearth.
An oak tree smoldered there. "The goodly knight!
395 What! shall the shield of Mark stand among these?"
For, midway down the side of that long hall
A stately pile—whereof along the front,
Some blazoned,[64] some but carven,[65] and some blank,
There ran a treble range of stony shields—
400 Rose, and high-arching overbrowed the hearth.
And under every shield a knight was named:
For this was Arthur's custom in his hall;
When some good knight had done one noble deed,
His arms were carven only; but if twain
405 His arms were blazoned also; but if none
The shield was blank and bare without a sign
Saving the name beneath; and Gareth saw
The shield of Gawain blazoned rich and bright,
And Modred's blank as death; and Arthur cried
410 To rend the cloth and cast it on the hearth.

"More like are we to reave him of his crown[66]
Than make him knight because men call him king.
The kings we found, ye know we stayed their hands
From war among themselves, but left them kings;
415 Of whom were any bounteous, merciful,
Truth-speaking, brave, good livers, them we enrolled
Among us, and they sit within our hall.
But Mark hath tarnished the great name of king,
As Mark would sully[67] the low state of churl:[68]
420 And, seeing he hath sent us cloth of gold,
Return, and meet, and hold him from our eyes,
Lest we should lap him up in cloth of lead,[69]
Silenced forever—craven[70]—a man of plots,
Craft, poisonous counsels, wayside ambushings—
425 No fault of thine: let Kay the seneschal
Look to thy wants, and send thee satisfied—
Accursed, who strikes nor lets the hand be seen!"

And many another suppliant[71] crying came
With noise of ravage wrought[72] by beast and man,
430 And evermore a knight would ride away.

Last, Gareth leaning both hands heavily
Down on the shoulders of the twain, his men,
Approached between them toward the King, and asked,
"A boon, Sir King (his voice was all ashamed),

64 blazoned : decorated in color with the knight's coat of arms.
65 carven : carved.

66 reave him of his crown : forcibly take his crown away from him.

67 sully : dishonor.
68 churl : a peasant.

69 cloth of lead : used as a coffin in burial.
70 craven : coward.

71 suppliant : entreater.
72 ravage wrought : destruction caused.

435 For see ye not how weak and hungerworn
   I seem—leaning on these? grant me to serve
   For meat and drink among thy kitchen-knaves
   A twelvemonth and a day, nor seek my name.
   Hereafter I will fight."

                                    To him the King,
440 "A goodly youth and worth a goodlier boon!
   But so thou wilt no goodlier, then must Kay,
   The master of the meats and drinks, be thine."

   He rose and passed; then Kay, a man of mien[73]   73 mien : appearance.
   Wan-sallow as the plant that feels itself
   Root-bitten by white lichen,[74]   74 lichen : organism that
                                                        grows on plants or rocks.

445   "Lo ye now!
   This fellow hath broken from some Abbey, where,
   God wot,[75] he had not beef and brewis[76] enow,   75 wot : knows.
   However that might chance! but an he work,   76 brewis : broth.
   Like any pigeon will I cram his crop,
450 And sleeker shall he shine than any hog."

   Then Lancelot standing near, "Sir Seneschal,
   Sleuth-hound thou knowest, and gray, and all the hounds;
   A horse thou knowest, a man thou dost not know:
   Broad brows and fair, a fluent[77] hair and fine,   77 fluent : flowing.
455 High nose, a nostril large and fine, and hands
   Large, fair and fine!—Some young lad's mystery—
   But, or from sheepcot[78] or king's hall, the boy   78 sheepcot : sheepfold.
   Is noble-natured. Treat him with all grace,
   Lest he should come to shame thy judging of him."

460   Then Kay, "What murmurest thou of mystery?
   Think ye this fellow will poison the King's dish?
   Nay, for he spake too fool-like: mystery!
   Tut, an the lad were noble, he had asked
   For horse and armor: fair and fine, forsooth!
465 Sir Fine-face, Sir Fair-hands? but see thou to it
   That thine own fineness, Lancelot, some fine day
   Undo thee not—and leave my man to me."

   So Gareth all for glory underwent
   The sooty yoke of kitchen-vassalage;
470 Ate with young lads his portion by the door,
   And couched at night with grimy kitchen-knaves.
   And Lancelot ever spake him pleasantly,

ALFRED, LORD TENNYSON   573

But Kay the seneschal who loved him not
Would hustle and harry him, and labor him
475 Beyond his comrade of the hearth,[79] and set
To turn the broach,[80] draw water, or hew wood,
Or grosser tasks; and Gareth bowed himself
With all obedience to the King, and wrought
All kind of service with a noble ease
480 That graced the lowliest act in doing it.
And when the thralls had talk among themselves,
And one would praise the love that linked the King
And Lancelot—how the King had saved his life
In battle twice, and Lancelot once the King's—
485 For Lancelot was the first in Tournament,
But Arthur mightiest on the battlefield—
Gareth was glad. Or if some other told,
How once the wandering forester at dawn,
Far over the blue tarns[81] and hazy seas,
490 On Caer-Eryri's[82] highest found the King,
A naked babe, of whom the Prophet spake,
"He passes to the Isle Avilion,[83]
He passes and is healed and cannot die"—
Gareth was glad. But if their talk were foul,
495 Then would he whistle rapid as any lark,
Or carol some old roundelay,[84] and so loud
That first they mocked, but, after, reverenced him.
Or Gareth telling some prodigious[85] tale
Of knights, who sliced a red life-bubbling way
500 Through twenty folds of twisted dragon, held
All in a gap-mouthed circle his good mates
Lying or sitting round him, idle hands,
Charmed; till Sir Kay, the seneschal, would come
Blustering upon them, like a sudden wind
505 Among dead leaves, and drive them all apart.
Or when the thralls had sport among themselves,
So there were any trial of mastery,
He, by two yards in casting bar or stone
Was counted best; and if there chanced a joust,
510 So that Sir Kay nodded him leave to go,
Would hurry thither, and when he saw the knights
Clash like the coming and retiring wave,
And the spear spring, and good horse reel, the boy
Was half beyond himself for ecstasy.

515 So for a month he wrought among the thralls;
But in the weeks that followed, the good Queen,[86]
Repentant of the word she made him swear,
And saddening in her childless castle, sent,

79 comrade of the hearth :
the other kitchen boys.
80 broach : spit for meat.

81 tarns : mountain lakes.
82 Caer-Eryri : Mt. Snow-
don, highest point in Wales.
83 Isle Avilion : mythological island, believed near
an earthly paradise.

84 roundelay : song.

85 prodigious : marvelous.

86 Queen : Bellicent.

Between the increscent and decrescent moon,[87]
520 Arms for her son, and loosed him from his vow.

This, Gareth hearing from a squire of Lot
With whom he used to play at tourney once,
When both were children, and in lonely haunts
Would scratch a ragged oval on the sand,
525 And each at either dash from either end—
Shame never made girl redder than Gareth joy.
He laughed; he sprang. "Out of the smoke, at once
I leap from Satan's foot to Peter's knee[88]—
These news be mine, none other's—nay, the King's—
530 Descend into the city:" whereon he sought
The King alone, and found, and told him all.

"I have staggered thy strong Gawain in a tilt
For pastime; yea, he said it: joust can I.
Make me thy knight—in secret! let my name
535 Be hidden, and give me the first quest, I spring
Like flame from ashes."

Here the King's calm eye
Fell on, and checked, and made him flush, and bow
Lowly, to kiss his hand, who answered him,
"Son, the good mother let me know thee here,
540 And sent her wish that I would yield thee thine.
Make thee my knight? my knights are sworn to vows
Of utter hardihood, utter gentleness,
And, loving, utter faithfulness in love,
And uttermost obedience to the King."

545 Then Gareth, lightly springing from his knees,
"My King, for hardihood I can promise thee.
For uttermost obedience make demand
Of whom ye gave me to, the Seneschal,
No mellow master of the meats and drinks!
550 And as for love, God wot, I love not yet,
But love I shall, God willing."

And the King—
"Make thee my knight in secret? yea, but he,[89]
Our noblest brother, and our truest man,
And one with me in all, he needs must know."

555 "Let Lancelot know, my King, let Lancelot know,
Thy noblest and thy truest!"

ALFRED, LORD TENNYSON

[87] Between . . . moon : at full moon.

[88] from Satan's . . . knee : from hell to the gates of heaven.

[89] he : Lancelot.

And the King—
"But wherefore would ye men should wonder at you?
Nay, rather for the sake of me, their King,
And the deed's sake my knighthood to the deed,
Than to be noised of."

560   Merrily Gareth asked,
"Have I not earned my cake in baking of it?
Let be my name until I make my name!
My deeds will speak: it is but for a day."
So with a kindly hand on Gareth's arm
565 Smiled the great King, and half-unwillingly
Loving his lusty youthhood yielded to him.
Then, after summoning Lancelot privily,
"I have given him the first quest: he is not proven.
Look therefore when he calls for this in hall,
570 Thou get to horse and follow him far away.
Cover the lions on thy shield, and see
Far as thou mayest, he be nor ta'en nor slain."

    Then that same day there passed into the hall
A damsel of high lineage,[90] and a brow
575 May blossom, and a cheek of appleblossom,
Hawk-eyes; and lightly was her slender nose
Tip-tilted like the petal of a flower;
She into hall passed with her page and cried,
    "O King, for thou hast driven the foe without,
580 See to the foe within! bridge, ford, beset
By bandits, everyone that owns a tower
The Lord for half a league.[91] Why sit ye there?
Rest would I not, Sir King, an I were king,
Till even the lonest hold[92] were all as free
585 From cursed bloodshed, as thine altar-cloth
From that blest blood[93] it is a sin to spill."

    "Comfort thyself," said Arthur, "I nor mine
Rest: so my knighthood keep the vows they swore,
The wastest moorland of our realm shall be
590 Safe, damsel, as the center of this hall.
What is thy name? thy need?"

                     "My name?" she said—
"Lynette my name; noble; my need, a knight
To combat for my sister, Lyonors,
A lady of high lineage, of great lands,
595 And comely,[94] yea, and comelier than myself.
She lives in Castle Perilous: a river

90 high lineage : noble birth.

91 half a league : approximately a mile and a half.

92 lonest hold : loneliest castle.

93 blest blood : sacramental wine.

94 comely : beautiful.

Runs in three loops about her living-place;
And o'er it are three passings,[95] and three knights
Defend the passings, brethren, and a fourth
600 And of that four the mightiest, holds her stayed
In her own castle, and so besieges her
To break her will, and make her wed with him:
And but delays his purport[96] till thou send
To do the battle with him, thy chief man
605 Sir Lancelot whom he trusts to overthrow,
Then wed, with glory; but she will not wed
Save whom she loveth, or a holy life.[97]
Now therefore have I come for Lancelot."

Then Arthur mindful of Sir Gareth asked,
610 "Damsel, ye know this Order[98] lives to crush
All wrongers of the Realm. But say, these four,
Who be they? What the fashion of the men?"[99]

"They be of foolish fashion, O Sir King,
The fashion of that old knight-errantry
615 Who ride abroad and do but what they will;
Courteous or bestial from the moment,[100] such
As have nor law nor king; and three of these
Proud in their fantasy call themselves the Day,[101]
Morning-Star, and Noon-Sun, and Evening-Star,
620 Being strong fools; and never a whit[102] more wise
The fourth, who always rideth armed in black,
A huge man-beast of boundless savagery.
He names himself the Night and oftener Death,
And wears a helmet mounted with a skull,
625 And bears a skeleton figured on his arms,
To show that who may slay or scape[103] the three
Slain by himself shall enter endless night.
And all these four be fools, but mighty men,
And therefore am I come for Lancelot."

630 Hereat Sir Gareth called from where he rose,
A head with kindling eye above the throng,
"A boon, Sir King—this quest!" then—for he marked
Kay near him groaning like a wounded bull—
"Yea, King, thou knowest thy kitchen-knave am I.
635 And mighty through thy meats and drinks am I,
And I can topple over a hundred such.
Thy promise, King," and Arthur glancing at him,
Brought down a momentary brow.[104] "Rough, sudden,
And pardonable, worthy to be knight—
640 Go therefore," and all hearers were amazed.

ALFRED, LORD TENNYSON

95 passings : bridges.

96 purport : purpose.

97 a holy life : enter a convent.

98 this Order : the Knights of the Round Table.

99 What the . . . men? : What sort of men?

100 from the moment : depending on their mood.

101 three of these . . . the Day : The three brothers call themselves the Day; their individual names are listed in the next line.
102 whit : bit.

103 scape : escape.

104 Brought down . . . brow : frowned momentarily.

But on the damsel's forehead shame, pride, wrath
Slew the May-white:[105] she lifted either arm,
"Fie on thee, King! I asked for thy chief knight,
And thou hast given me but a kitchen-knave."
645 Then ere a man in hall could stay[106] her, turned,
Fled down the lane of access to the King,
Took horse, descended the slope street, and passed
The weird white gate, and paused without, beside
The field of tourney, murmuring "kitchen-knave."

650   Now two great entries opened from the hall,
At one end one, that gave upon a range
Of level pavement where the King would pace
At sunrise, gazing over plain and wood;
And down from this a lordly stairway sloped
655 Till lost in blowing trees and tops of towers;
And out by this main doorway passed the King.
But one was counter[107] to the hearth, and rose
High that the highest-crested helm[108] could ride
Therethrough nor graze: and by this entry fled
660 The damsel in her wrath, and on to this
Sir Gareth strode, and saw without the door
King Arthur's gift, the worth of half a town,
A warhorse of the best, and near it stood
The two that out of north had followed him:
665 This bare a maiden shield, a casque; that held[109]
The horse, the spear; whereat Sir Gareth loosed
A cloak that dropped from collarbone to heel,
A cloth of roughest web, and cast it down,
And from it like a fuel-smothered fire,
670 That looked half-dead, brake bright, and flashed as those
Dull-coated things, that making slide apart
Their dusk wing-cases, all beneath there burns
A jeweled harness, ere they pass and fly.
So Gareth ere he parted flashed in arms.
675 Then as he donned the helm, and took the shield
And mounted horse and grasped a spear, of grain
Storm-strengthened on a windy site, and tipped
With trenchant[110] steel, around him slowly pressed
The people, while from out of kitchen came
680 The thralls in throng, and seeing who had worked
Lustier[111] than any, and whom they could but love,
Mounted in arm, threw up their caps and cried,
"God bless the King, and all his fellowship!"
And on through lanes of shouting Gareth rode
685 Down the slope street, and passed without the gate.

105 Slew the May-white :
turned the white to red.

106 stay : stop.

107 one was counter : one
entry was opposite.
108 helm : helmet.

109 This bare . . . that
held : One held a shield
without a coat of arms and
a helmet; the other one
held, etc.

110 trenchant : sharp.

111 Lustier : more vigor-
ously.

ALFRED, LORD TENNYSON

So Gareth passed with joy; but as the cur
Plucked from the cur he fights with, ere his cause
Be cooled by fighting, follows, being named,
His owner, but remembers all, and growls
690 Remembering, so Sir Kay beside the door
Muttered in scorn of Gareth whom he used
To harry and hustle.

                            "Bound upon a quest
With horse and arms—the King hath passed his time[112]—
My scullion knave! Thralls to your work again,
695 For an your fire be low ye kindle mine!
Will there be dawn in West and eve in East?
Begone!—my knave!—belike and like enow
Some old head-blow not heeded in his[113] youth
So shook his wits they wander in his prime—
700 Crazed! How the villain lifted up his voice,
Nor shamed to bawl[114] himself a kitchen-knave.
Tut: he was tame and meek enow with me,
Till peacocked up[115] with Lancelot's noticing.
Well—I will after my loud knave, and learn
705 Whether he know me for his master yet.
Out of the smoke he came, and so my lance
Hold, by God's grace, he shall into the mire—
Thence, if the King awaken from his craze,
Into the smoke again."[116]

112 the King . . . his time :
Arthur is getting too old.

113 his : Gareth's.

114 bawl : call.

115 peacocked up : made
proud.

116 Into the smoke again :
back into the kitchen.

                               But Lancelot said,
710 "Kay, wherefore wilt thou go against the King,
For that did never he whereon ye rail,
But ever meekly served the King in thee?
Abide: take counsel; for this lad is great
And lusty, and knowing both of lance and sword."
715 "Tut, tell not me," said Kay, "ye are overfine
To mar stout knaves with foolish courtesies."
Then mounted, on through silent faces rode
Down the slope city, and out beyond the gate.

    But by the field of tourney lingering yet
720 Muttered the damsel, "Wherefore did the King
Scorn me? for, were Sir Lancelot lacked, at least
He might have yielded to me one of those
Who tilt for lady's love and glory here,
Rather than—O sweet heaven! O fie upon him—
His kitchen-knave."

To whom Sir Gareth drew
(And there were none but few goodlier than he)
Shining in arms, "Damsel, the quest is mine.
Lead, and I follow." She thereat, as one
That smells a foul-fleshed agaric in the holt,
730 And deems it carrion of some woodland thing,[117]
Or shrew, or weasel, nipped her slender nose
With petulant thumb and finger, shrilling, "Hence!
Avoid, thou smellest all of kitchen-grease.
And look who comes behind," for there was Kay.
735 "Knowest thou not me? thy master? I am Kay.
We lack thee by the hearth."

> 117 That smells . . . wood-
> land thing : who smells a
> decayed fungus in the wood
> and thinks that it is the
> decaying flesh of some ani-
> mal.

                                    And Gareth to him,
"Master no more! too well I know thee, ay—
The most ungentle knight in Arthur's hall."
"Have at thee then," said Kay: they shocked,[118] and Kay
740 Fell shoulder-slipped,[119] and Gareth cried again,
"Lead, and I follow," and fast away she fled.

> 118 shocked : met violently.
> 119 shoulder-slipped :
> shoulder out of joint.

But after sod and shingle ceased to fly
Behind her, and the heart of her good horse
Was nigh to burst with violence of the beat,
745 Perforce she stayed, and overtaken spoke.

"What doest thou, scullion, in my fellowship?
Deem'st thou that I accept thee aught the more
Or love thee better, that by some device
Full cowardly, or by mere unhappiness,[120]
750 Thou hast overthrown and slain thy master—thou!—
Dishwasher and broach turner, loon![121]—to me
Thou smellest all of kitchen as before."

> 120 unhappiness : accident.

> 121 loon : fool.

"Damsel," Sir Gareth answered gently, "say
Whate'er ye will, but whatsoe'er ye say,
755 I leave not till I finish this fair quest,
Or die therefore."

                              "Ay, wilt thou finish it?
Sweet lord, how like a noble knight he talks!
The listening rogue hath caught the manner of it.
But, knave, anon thou shalt be met with, knave,
760 And then by such a one that thou for all
The kitchen brewis that was ever supped
Shalt not once dare to look him in the face."

ALFRED, LORD TENNYSON

"I shall assay,"[122] said Gareth with a smile
That maddened her, and away she flashed again
765 Down the long avenues of a boundless wood,
And Gareth following was again beknaved.[123]

"Sir Kitchen-knave, I have missed the only way
Where Arthur's men are set along the wood;
The wood is nigh[124] as full of thieves as leaves:
770 If both be slain, I am rid of thee; but yet,
Sir Scullion, canst thou use that spit of thine?
Fight, an thou canst: I have missed the only way."

So till the dusk that followed evensong[125]
Rode on the two, reviler and reviled;
775 Then after one long slope was mounted, saw,
Bowl-shaped, through tops of many thousand pines
A gloomy-gladed hollow slowly sink
To westward—in the deeps whereof a mere,[126]
Round as the red eye of an Eagle-owl,
780 Under the half-dead sunset glared; and shouts
Ascended, and there brake a servingman
Flying from out of the black wood, and crying,
"They have bound my lord to cast him in the mere."
Then Gareth, "Bound am I to right the wronged,
785 But straitlier bound am I to bide with thee."
And when the damsel spake contemptuously,
"Lead, and I follow," Gareth cried again,
"Follow, I lead!" so down among the pines
He plunged; and there, blackshadowed nigh the mere,
790 And mid-thigh-deep in bulrushes and reed,
Saw six tall men haling[127] a seventh along,
A stone about his neck to drown him in it.
Three with good blows he quieted, but three
Fled through the pines; and Gareth loosed the stone
795 From off his neck, then in the mere beside
Tumbled it; oilily bubbled up the mere.
Last, Gareth loosed his bonds and on free feet
Set him, a stalwart Baron, Arthur's friend.

"Well that ye came, or else these caitiff[128] rogues
800 Had wreaked themselves on me; good cause is theirs
To hate me, for my wont[129] hath ever been
To catch my thief, and then like vermin here
Drown him, and with a stone about his neck;
And under this wan[130] water many of them
805 Lie rotting, but at night let go the stone,

122 assay : try.

123 beknaved : called
knave.

124 nigh : nearly.

125 evensong : evening
prayer.

126 mere : small lake.

127 haling : hauling.

128 caitiff : wicked.

129 wont : practice.

130 wan : gloomy.

And rise, and flickering in a grimly light
Dance on the mere. Good now, ye have saved a life
Worth somewhat as the cleanser of this wood
And fain would I reward thee worshipfully.
What guerdon[131] will ye?"

810   Gareth sharply spake,
"None! for the deed's sake have I done the deed,
In uttermost obedience to the King.
But wilt thou yield this damsel harborage?"[132]

    Whereat the Baron saying, "I well believe
815 You be of Arthur's Table," a light laugh
Broke from Lynette, "Ay, truly of a truth,
And in a sort, being Arthur's kitchen-knave!—
But deem not I accept thee aught the more,
Scullion, for running sharply with thy spit
820 Down on a rout of craven[133] foresters.

A thresher with his flail had scattered them.
Nay—for thou smellest of the kitchen still.
But an this lord will yield us harborage,
Well."

          So she spake. A league beyond the wood,
825 All in a full-fair manor and a rich,
His towers where that day a feast had been
Held in high hall, and many a viand[134] left,
And many a costly cate,[135] received the three.
And there they placed a peacock in his pride[136]
830 Before the damsel, and the Baron set
Gareth beside her, but at once she rose.

    "Meseems, that here is much discourtesy,
Setting this knave, Lord Baron, at my side.
Hear me—this morn I stood in Arthur's hall,
835 And prayed the King would grant me Lancelot
To fight the brotherhood of Day and Night—
The last a monster unsubduable
Of any save of him for whom I called—
Suddenly bawls this frontless[137] kitchen-knave,

840 'The quest is mine; thy kitchen-knave am I,
And mighty through thy meats and drinks am I.'
Then Arthur all at once gone mad replies,
'Go therefore,' and so gives the quest to him—
Him—here—a villian fitter to stick swine
845 Than ride abroad redressing women's wrong,
Or sit beside a noble gentlewoman."

ALFRED, LORD TENNYSON

Then half-ashamed and part-amazed, the lord
Now looked at one and now at other, left
The damsel by the peacock in his pride,
850 And, seating Gareth at another board,
Sat down beside him, ate and then began.

"Friend, whether thou be kitchen-knave, or not,
Or whether it be the maiden's fantasy,
And whether she be mad, or else the King,
855 Or both or neither, or thyself be mad,
I ask not: but thou strikest a strong stroke,
For strong thou art and goodly therewithal,
And saver of my life; and therefore now,
For here be mighty men to joust with, weigh
860 Whether thou wilt not with thy damsel back
To crave again Sir Lancelot of the King.
Thy pardon; I but speak for thine avail,[138]
The saver of my life."

                  And Gareth said,
"Full pardon, but I follow up the quest,
865 Despite of Day and Night and Death and Hell."

So when, next morn, the lord whose life he saved
Had, some brief space, conveyed them on their way
And left them with God-speed, Sir Gareth spake,
"Lead, and I follow." Haughtily she replied,

870 "I fly no more: I allow thee for an hour.
Lion and stoat[139] have isled together, knave,
In time of flood. Nay, furthermore, methinks
Some ruth[140] is mine for thee. Back wilt thou, fool?
For hard by here is one will overthrow
875 And slay thee: then will I to court again,
And shame the King for only yielding me
My champion from the ashes of his hearth."

To whom Sir Gareth answered courteously,
"Say thou thy say, and I will do my deed.
880 Allow me for mine hour, and thou wilt find
My fortunes all as fair as hers,[141] who lay
Among the ashes and wedded the King's son."

Then to the shore of one of those long loops
Wherethrough the serpent river coiled, they came.
885 Rough-thicketed were the banks and steep; the stream

138 avail : own advantage.

139 stoat : ermine.

140 ruth : pity.

141 hers : Cinderella's.

Full, narrow; this a bridge of single arc
Took at a leap; and on the further side
Arose a silk pavilion,[142] gay with gold
In streaks and rays, and all Lent lily[143] in hue,
890 Save that the dome was purple, and above,
Crimson, a slender banneret fluttering.
And therebefore the lawless warrior paced
Unarmed, and calling, "Damsel, is this he,
The champion thou hast brought from Arthur's hall?
895 For whom we let thee pass." "Nay, nay," she said,
"Sir Morning-Star. The King in utter scorn
Of thee and thy much folly hath sent thee here
His kitchen-knave: and look thou to thyself:
See that he fall not on thee suddenly,
900 And slay thee unarmed: he is not knight but knave."

Then at his call, "O daughters of the Dawn,
And servants of the Morning-Star, approach,
Arm me," from out the silken curtain-folds
Barefooted and bareheaded three fair girls
905 In gilt and rosy raiment came: their feet
In dewy grasses glistened; and the hair
All over glanced with dewdrop or with gem
Like sparkles in the stone Avanturine.[144]
These armed him in blue arms, and gave a shield
910 Blue also, and thereon the morning star.
And Gareth silent gazed upon the knight,
Who stood a moment, ere his horse was brought,
Glorying;[145] and in the stream beneath him, shone,
Immingled with Heaven's azure waveringly,
915 The gay pavilion and the naked feet,
His arms, the rosy raiment, and the star.

Then she that watched him, "Wherefore stare ye so?
Thou shakest in thy fear: there yet is time:
Flee down the valley before he get to horse.
920 Who will cry shame? Thou art not knight but knave."

Said Gareth, "Damsel, whether knave or knight,
Far liefer[146] had I fight a score of times
Than hear thee so missay me and revile.
Fair words were best for him who fights for thee;
925 But truly foul are better, for they send
That strength of anger through mine arms, I know
That I shall overthrow him."

ALFRED, LORD TENNYSON

142 pavilion : a large tent, often with a rounded or peaked top.
143 Lent lily : the yellow daffodil.

144 Avanturine : rock containing mica.

145 Glorying : showing off.

146 liefer : rather.

                                        And he that bore
The star, being mounted, cried from o'er the bridge,
"A kitchen-knave, and sent in scorn of me!
930 Such fight not I, but answer scorn with scorn.
For this were shame to do him further wrong
Than set him on his feet, and take his horse
And arms, and so return him to the King.
Come, therefore, leave thy lady lightly,[147] knave.   147 lightly : quickly.
935 Avoid:[148] for it beseemeth not a knave   148 Avoid : depart.
To ride with such a lady."

                              "Dog, thou liest.
I spring from loftier lineage than thine own."
He spake; and all at fiery speed the two
Shocked on the central bridge, and either spear
940 Bent but not brake, and either knight at once,
Hurled as a stone from out of a catapult
Beyond his horse's crupper[149] and the bridge,   149 Beyond . . . crupper :
Fell, as if dead; but quickly rose and drew,   behind his horse.
And Gareth lashed so fiercely with his brand
945 He drave his enemy backward down the bridge,
The damsel crying, "Well-stricken, kitchen-knave!"
Till Gareth's shield was cloven;[150] but one stroke   150 cloven : split.
Laid him that clove it groveling on the ground.

        Then cried the fallen, "Take not my life: I yield."
950 And Gareth, "So this damsel ask it of me
Good—I accord it easily as a grace."
She reddening, "Insolent scullion: I of thee?
I bound to thee for any favor asked!"
"Then shall he die."   And Gareth there unlaced
955 His helmet as to slay him, but she shrieked,
"Be not so hardy, scullion, as to slay
One nobler than thyself." "Damsel, thy charge[151]   151 charge : command.
Is an abounding pleasure to me.   Knight,
Thy life is thine at her command.   Arise
960 And quickly pass to Arthur's hall, and say
His kitchen-knave hath sent thee.   See thou crave[152]   152 crave : beg.
His pardon for thy breaking of his laws.
Myself, when I return, will plead for thee.
Thy shield is mine—farewell; and, damsel, thou,
Lead, and I follow."

965   And fast away she fled.
Then when he came upon her, spake, "Methought,
Knave, when I watched thee striking on the bridge
The savor of thy kitchen came upon me

ALFRED, LORD TENNYSON

587

A little faintlier: but the wind hath changed:
970 I scent it twentyfold." And then she sang,
" 'O morning star' (not that tall felon there
Whom thou by sorcery or unhappiness
Or some device, has foully overthrown),
'O morning star that smilest in the blue,
975 O star, my morning dream hath proven true,
Smile sweetly, thou! my love hath smiled on me.'

"But thou begone, take counsel, and away,
For hard by here is one that guards a ford—
The second brother in their fool's parable[153]—
980 Will pay thee all thy wages,[154] and to boot.
Care not for shame: thou art not knight but knave."

To whom Sir Gareth answered, laughingly,
"Parables? Hear a parable of the knave.
When I was kitchen-knave among the rest
985 Fierce was the hearth, and one of my co-mates
Owned a rough dog, to whom he cast his coat,
'Guard it,' and there was none to meddle with it.
And such a coat art thou, and thee the King
Gave me to guard, and such a dog am I,
990 To worry, and not to flee—and—knight or knave—
The knave that doth thee service as full knight
Is all as good, meseems, as any knight
Toward thy sister's freeing."

                                    "Ay, Sir Knave!
Ay, knave, because thou strikest as a knight,
995 Being but knave, I hate thee all the more."

"Fair damsel, you should worship me the more,
That, being but knave, I throw thine enemies."

"Ay, ay," she said, "but thou shalt meet thy match."

So when they touched the second river-loop,
1000 Huge on a huge red horse, and all in mail
Burnished[155] to blinding, shone the Noonday Sun
Beyond a raging shallow. As if the flower,[156]
That blows a globe of after arrowlets,
Ten thousandfold had grown, flashed the fierce shield,
1005 All sun; and Gareth's eyes had flying blots
Before them when he turned from watching him.
He from beyond the roaring shallow roared,

153 fool's parable : idea represented by the brother's attire.

154 pay . . . wages : avenge his brother's defeat.

155 Burnished : polished.

156 flower : dandelion.

"What doest thou, brother, in my marches[157] here?"
And she athwart the shallow shrilled again,
1010 "Here is a kitchen-knave from Arthur's hall
Hath overthrown thy brother, and hath his arms."
"Ugh!" cried the Sun, and vizoring up[158] a red
And cipher[159] face of rounded foolishness,
Pushed horse across the foamings of the ford,
1015 Whom Gareth met midstream: no room was there
For lance or tourney-skill: four strokes they struck
With sword, and these were mighty; the new knight
Had fear he might be shamed; but as the Sun
Heaved up a ponderous arm to strike the fifth,
1020 The hoof of his horse slipped in the stream, the stream
Descended, and the Sun was washed away.

Then Gareth laid his lance athwart the ford:
So drew him home; but he that fought no more,
As being all bone-battered on the rock,
1025 Yielded; and Gareth sent him to the King.
"Myself when I return will plead for thee."
"Lead, and I follow." Quietly she led.
"Hath not the good wind, damsel, changed again?"
"Nay, not a point: nor art thou victor here.
1030 There lies a ridge of slate across the ford;
His horse thereon stumbled—ay, for I saw it.

" 'O Sun' (not this strong fool whom thou, Sir Knave,
Hast overthrown through mere unhappiness),
'O Sun, that wakenest all to bliss or pain,
1035 O moon, that layest all to sleep again,
Shine sweetly: twice my love hath smiled on me.'

"What knowest thou of lovesong or of love?
Nay, nay, God wot, so thou wert nobly born,
Thou hast a pleasant presence. Yea, perchance,—

1040 " 'O dewy flowers that open to the sun,
O dewy flowers that close when day is done,
Blow sweetly: twice my love hath smiled on me.'

"What knowest thou of flowers, except, belike,
To garnish meats with? hath not our good King
1045 Who lent me thee, the flower of kitchendom,
A foolish love for flowers? what stick ye round
The pasty? wherewithal deck the boar's head?
Flowers? nay, the boar hath rosemaries and bay.[160]

ALFRED, LORD TENNYSON

157 marches : territory.

158 vizoring up : closing the face opening on his helmet.
159 cipher : a zero.

160 Flowers . . . and bay : The king's boar is not decorated with flowers but with rosemary and bay (shrubs).

"'O birds, that warble to the morning sky,
1050 O birds that warble as the day goes by,
Sing sweetly: twice my love hath smiled on me.'

"What knowest thou of birds, lark, mavis,[161] merle,[162]
Linnet?[163] what dream ye when they utter forth
May-music growing with the growing light,
1055 Their sweet sun-worship? these be for the snare
(So runs thy fancy) these be for the spit,
Larding and basting. See thou have not now
Larded thy last, except thou turn and fly.
There stands the third fool of their allegory."

1060   For there beyond a bridge of treble bow,[164]
All in a rose-red from the west, and all
Naked it seemed, and glowing in the broad
Deep-dimpled current underneath, the knight,
That named himself the Star of Evening, stood.

1065   And Gareth, "Wherefore waits the madman there
Naked in open dayshine?" "Nay," she cried,
"Not naked, only wrapped in hardened skins
That fit him like his own; and so ye cleave
His armor off him, these will turn the blade."

1070   Then the third brother shouted o'er the bridge,
"O brother-star, why shine ye here so low?
Thy ward[165] is higher up: but have ye slain
The damsel's champion?" and the damsel cried,

"No star of thine, but shot from Arthur's heaven
1075 With all disaster unto thine and thee!
For both thy younger brethren have gone down
Before this youth; and so wilt thou, Sir Star;
Art thou not old?"

                    "Old, damsel, old and hard.
Old, with the might and breath of twenty boys."
1080 Said Gareth, "Old, and over-bold in brag!
But that same strength which threw the Morning Star
Can throw the Evening."

                    Then that other blew
A hard and deadly note upon the horn.
"Approach and arm me!" With slow steps from out
1085 An old storm-beaten, russet, many-stained
Pavilion, forth a grizzled damsel came,

161 mavis : song thrush.

162 merle : European black-bird.

163 Linnet : small finch.

164 treble bow : three spans.

165 ward : watch station.

590

And armed him in old arms, and brought a helm
With but a drying evergreen for crest,
And gave a shield whereon the Star of Even
1090 Half-tarnished and half-bright, his emblem, shone.
But when it glittered o'er the saddle-bow,
They madly hurled together on the bridge;
And Gareth overthrew him, lighted, drew,
There met him drawn, and overthrew him again,
1095 But up like fire he started: and as oft
As Gareth brought him groveling on his knees,
So many a time he vaulted up again;
Till Gareth panted hard, and his great heart,
Foredooming[166] all his trouble was in vain,
1100 Labored within him, for he seemed as one
That all in later, sadder age begins
To war against ill uses[167] of a life,
But these from all his life arise, and cry,
"Thou hast made us lords, and canst not put us down!"
1105 He half despairs; so Gareth seemed to strike
Vainly, the damsel clamoring all the while,
"Well done, knave-knight, well stricken, O good knight-
      knave—
O knave, as noble as any of all the knights—
Shame me not, shame me not. I have prophesied—
1110 Strike, thou art worthy of the Table Round—
His arms are old, he trusts the hardened skin—
Strike—strike—the wind will never change again."
And Gareth hearing ever stronglier smote,
And hewed great pieces of his armor off him,
1115 But lashed in vain against the hardened skin,
And could not wholly bring him under, more
Than loud Southwesterns, rolling ridge on ridge,
The buoy that rides at sea, and dips and springs
Forever; till at length Sir Gareth's brand
1120 Clashed his, and brake it utterly to the hilt.
"I have thee now"; but forth that other sprang,
And, all unknightlike, writhed[168] his wiry arms
Around him, till he felt, despite his mail,
Strangled, but straining even his uttermost
1125 Cast, and so hurled him headlong o'er the bridge
Down to the river, sink or swim, and cried,
"Lead, and I follow."

                          But the damsel said,
"I lead no longer; ride thou at my side;
Thou art the kingliest of all kitchen-knaves.

166 Foredooming : fearing.

167 ill uses : bad habits.

168 writhed : twisted.

ALFRED, LORD TENNYSON

1130   "'O trefoil,[169] sparkling on the rainy plain,
    O rainbow with three colors after rain,
    Shine sweetly: thrice my love hath smiled on me.'

    "Sir—and, good faith, I fain had added Knight,
    But that I heard thee call thyself a knave—
1135 Shamed am I that I so rebuked, reviled,
    Missaid thee; noble I am; and thought the King
    Scorned me and mine; and now thy pardon, friend,
    For thou hast ever answered courteously,
    And wholly bold thou art, and meek withal
1140 As any of Arthur's best, but, being knave,
    Hast mazed my wit:[170] I marvel what thou art."

    "Damsel," he said, "you be not all to blame,
    Saving that you mistrusted our good King
    Would handle scorn, or yield you, asking, one
1145 Not fit to cope[171] your quest. You said your say;
    Mine answer was my deed. Good sooth![172] I hold
    He scarce is knight, yea but half-man, nor meet
    To fight for gentle damsel, he, who lets
    His heart be stirred with any foolish heat
1150 At any gentle damsel's waywardness.
    Shamed? care not! thy foul sayings fought for me:
    And seeing now thy words are fair, methinks
    There rides no knight, not Lancelot, his great self,
    Hath force to quell[173] me."

                    Nigh upon that hour
1155 When the lone hern forgets his melancholy,
    Lets down his other leg, and stretching, dreams
    Of goodly supper in the distant pool,
    Then turned the noble damsel smiling at him,
    And told him of a cavern hard at hand,
1160 Where bread and baken meats and good red wine
    Of Southland, which the Lady Lyonors
    Had sent her coming champion, waited him.

    Anon they passed a narrow comb[174] wherein
    Were slabs of rock with figures, knights on horse
1165 Sculptured, and decked in slowly-waning hues.
    "Sir Knave, my knight, a hermit once was here,
    Whose holy hand hath fashioned on the rock
    The war of Time against the soul of man.
    And yon four fools have sucked their allegory
1170 From these damp walls, and taken but the form.
    Know ye not these?" and Gareth looked and read—

169 trefoil : three-leaf clover.

170 mazed by wit : puzzled me.

171 cope : achieve.

172 sooth : truth.

173 quell : defeat.

174 comb : hollow in the side of a hill.

In letters like to those the vexillary[175]
Hath left crag-carven o'er the streaming Gelt[176]—
"Phosphorus,"[177] then "Meridies"[178]—"Hesperus"[179]—
1175 "Nox"[180]—"Mors,"[181] beneath five figures, armed men,
Slab after slab, their faces forward all,
And running down the Soul, a Shape that fled
With broken wings, torn raiment and loose hair,
For help and shelter to the hermit's cave.
1180 "Follow the faces, and we find it. Look,
Who comes behind?"

                         For one[182]—delayed at first
Through helping back the dislocated Kay
To Camelot, then by what thereafter chanced,
The damsel's headlong error through the wood—
1185 Sir Lancelot, having swum the river-loops—
His blue shield-lions covered—softly drew
Behind the twain, and when he saw the star[183]
Gleam, on Sir Gareth's turning to him, cried,
"Stay, felon knight, I avenge me for my friend."
1190 And Gareth crying pricked[184] against the cry;
But when they closed—in a moment—at one touch
Of that skilled spear, the wonder of the world—
Went sliding down so easily, and fell,
That when he[185] found the grass within his hands
1195 He laughed; the laughter jarred upon Lynette:
Harshly she asked him, "Shamed and overthrown,
And tumbled back into the kitchen-knave,
Why laugh ye? that ye blew your boast in vain?"
"Nay, noble damsel, but that I, the son
1200 Of old King Lot and good Queen Bellicent,
And victor of the bridges and the ford,
And knight of Arthur, here lie thrown by whom
I know not, all through mere unhappiness—
Device and sorcery and unhappiness—
1205 Out, sword; we are thrown!" And Lancelot answered,
    "Prince,
O Gareth—through the mere unhappiness
Of one who came to help thee, not to harm,
Lancelot, and all as glad to find thee whole,
As on the day when Arthur knighted him."

1210   Then Gareth, "Thou—Lancelot!—thine the hand
That threw me? An some chance to mar the boast
Thy brethren of thee make—which could not chance—
Had sent thee down before a lesser spear,
Shamed had I been, and sad—O Lancelot—thou!"

175 vexillary : Roman stand-
ard-bearer.
176 Gelt : a river.
177 Phosphorus : morning
star (Greek).
178 Meridies : midday
(Latin).
179 Hesperus : evening star
(Latin).
180 Nox : night (Latin).
181 Mors : death (Latin).

182 one : Sir Lancelot.

183 star : Gareth has the
defeated knight's armor.

184 pricked : spurred his
horse.

185 he : Gareth.

ALFRED, LORD TENNYSON

1215 Whereat the maiden, petulant, "Lancelot,
Why came ye not, when called? and wherefore now
Come ye, not called? I gloried in my knave,
Who being still rebuked, would answer still
Courteous as any knight—but now, if knight,
1220 The marvel dies, and leaves me fooled and tricked,
And only wondering wherefore played upon:
And doubtful whether I and mine be scorned.
Where should be truth if not in Arthur's hall,
In Arthur's presence? Knight, knave, prince and fool,
I hate thee and forever."

                                        And Lancelot said,
1225 "Blessed be thou, Sir Gareth! knight art thou
To the King's best wish. O damsel, be you wise
To call him shamed, who is but overthrown?
Thrown have I been, nor once, but many a time.
1230 Victor from vanquished issues at the last,
And overthrower from being overthrown.
With sword we have not striven; and thy good horse
And thou are weary; yet not less I felt
Thy manhood through that wearied lance of thine.
1235 Well hast thou done; for all the stream is freed,
And thou hast wreaked his[186] justice on his foes,
And when reviled, hast answered graciously,
And makest merry when overthrown. Prince, Knight,
Hail, Knight and Prince, and of our Table Round!"

186 wreaked his : inflicted
King Arthur's.

1240 And then when turning to Lynette he told
The tale of Gareth, petulantly she said,
"Ay well—ay well—for worse than being fooled
Of others, is to fool one's self. A cave,
Sir Lancelot, is hard by, with meats and drinks
1245 And forage[187] for the horse, and flint for fire.
But all about it flies a honeysuckle.
Seek, till we find." And when they sought and found,
Sir Gareth drank and ate, and all his life
Passed into sleep; on whom the maiden gazed.
1250 "Sound sleep be thine! sound cause to sleep hast thou.
Wake lusty! Seem I not as tender to him
As any mother? Ay, but such a one
As all day long hath rated[188] at her child,
And vexed his day, but blesses him asleep—
1255 Good lord, how sweetly smells the honeysuckle
In the hushed night, as if the world were one
Of utter peace, and love, and gentleness!

187 forage : food.

188 rated : scolded.

ALFRED, LORD TENNYSON

O Lancelot, Lancelot"—and she clapped her hands—
"Full merry am I to find my goodly knave
1260 Is knight and noble. See now, sworn have I,
Else yon black felon[189] had not let me pass,
To bring thee back to do the battle with him.
Thus an thou goest, he[190] will fight thee first;
Who doubts thee victor? so will my knight-knave
1265 Miss the full flower of this accomplishment."

Said Lancelot, "Peradventure he,[191] you name,
May know my shield. Let Gareth, an he will,
Change his for mine, and take my charger, fresh,
Not to be spurred, loving the battle as well
1270 As he that rides him." "Lancelot-like," she said,
"Courteous in this, Lord Lancelot, as in all."

And Gareth, wakening, fiercely clutched the shield;
"Ramp[192] ye lance-splintering lions, on whom all spears
Are rotten sticks! ye seem agape[193] to roar!
1275 Yes, ramp and roar at leaving of your lord!—
Care not, good beasts, so well I care for you.
O noble Lancelot, from my hold on these
Streams virtue—fire—through one that will not shame
Even the shadow of Lancelot under shield.
Hence: let us go."

1280   Silent the silent field
They traversed. Arthur's harp[194] though summer-wan,[195]
In countermotion to the clouds, allured
The glance of Gareth dreaming on his liege.
A star shot: "Lo," said Gareth, "the foe falls!"
1285 An owl whooped: "Hark the victor pealing there!"
Suddenly she that rode upon his left
Clung to the shield that Lancelot lent him, crying,
"Yield, yield him this again: 'tis he must fight:
I curse the tongue that all through yesterday
1290 Reviled thee, and hath wrought on Lancelot now
To lend thee horse and shield: wonders ye have done;
Miracles ye cannot: here is glory enow
In having flung the three: I see thee maimed,
Mangled: I swear thou canst not fling the fourth."

1295   "And wherefore, damsel? tell me all ye know.
You cannot scare me; nor rough face, or voice,
Brute bulk of limb, or boundless savagery
Appal[196] me from the quest."

596

189 black felon : the fourth
evil knight.

190 he : the black knight.

191 Peradventure he : perhaps the black knight.

192 Ramp : spring up.

193 agape : with mouth
opened.

194 Arthur's harp : a single
star or a constellation.
195 summer-wan : not yet
summer.

196 Appal : frighten.

                                        "Nay, Prince," she cried,
      "God wot, I never looked upon the face,
1300 Seeing he never rides abroad by day;
      But watched him have I like a phantom pass
      Chilling the night: nor have I heard the voice.
      Always he made his mouthpiece of a page
      Who came and went, and still reported him
1305 As closing in himself the strength of ten,
      And when his anger tare him, massacring
      Man, woman, lad and girl—yea, the soft babe!
      Some hold that he hath swallowed infant flesh,
      Monster! O Prince, I went for Lancelot first,
1310 The quest is Lancelot's: give him back the shield."

      Said Gareth laughing, "An he fight for this,
      Belike he wins it as the better man:
      Thus—and not else!"

                              But Lancelot on him urged
      All the devisings of their chivalry[197]
1315 When one might meet a mightier than himself;
      How best to manage horse, lance, sword and shield,
      And so fill up the gap where force might fail
      With skill and fineness. Instant[198] were his words.

      Then Gareth, "Here be rules. I know but one—
1320 To dash against mine enemy and to win.
      Yet have I watched thee victor in the joust,
      And seen thy way." "Heaven help thee," sighed Lynette.

      Then for a space, and under cloud that grew
      To thunder-gloom palling[199] all stars, they rode
1325 In converse till she made her palfrey[200] halt,
      Lifted an arm, and softly whispered, "There."
      And all the three were silent seeing, pitched
      Beside the Castle Perilous on flat field,
      A huge pavilion like a mountain peak
1330 Sunder[201] the glooming crimson on the marge,[202]
      Black, with black banner, and a long black horn
      Beside it hanging; which Sir Gareth grasped,
      And so, before the two could hinder him,
      Sent all his heart and breath through all the horn.
1335 Echoed the walls; a light twinkled; anon
      Came lights and lights, and once again he blew;
      Whereon were hollow tramplings up and down
      And muffled voices heard, and shadows passed;

197 devisings of their chivalry : skills of knighthood.

198 Instant : urgent.

199 palling : covering.

200 palfrey : small horse.

201 Sunder : split.

202 marge : edges.

ALFRED, LORD TENNYSON

Till high above him, circled with her maids,
1340 The Lady Lyonors at a window stood,
Beautiful among lights, and waving to him
White hands, and courtesy; but when the Prince
Three times had blown—after long hush—at last—
The huge pavilion slowly yielded up,
1345 Through those black foldings, that which housed therein.
High on a nightblack horse, in nightblack arms,
With white breastbone, and barren ribs of Death,
And crowned with fleshless laughter[203]—some ten steps—
In the half-light—through the dim dawn—advanced
1350 The monster, and then paused, and spake no word.

    But Gareth spake and all indignantly,
"Fool, for thou hast, men say, the strength of ten,
Canst thou not trust the limbs thy God hath given,
But must, to make the terror of thee more,
1355 Trick thyself out in ghastly imageries
Of that which Life hath done with, and the clod,[204]
Less dull than thou, will hide with mantling flowers
As if for pity?" But he spake no word;
Which set the horror higher: a maiden swooned;
1360 The Lady Lyonors wrung her hands and wept,
As doomed to be the bride of Night and Death;
Sir Gareth's head prickled beneath his helm;
And even Sir Lancelot through his warm blood felt
Ice strike, and all that marked[205] him were aghast.

1365   At once Sir Lancelot's charger[206] fiercely neighed,
And Death's dark war horse bounded forward with him.
Then those that did not blink the terror,[207] saw
That Death was cast to ground, and slowly rose.
But with one stroke Sir Gareth split the skull.
1370 Half fell to right and half to left and lay.
Then with a stronger buffet[208] he clove the helm
As throughly as the skull; and out from this
Issued the bright face of a blooming boy
Fresh as a flower new-born, and crying, "Knight,
1375 Slay me not: my three brethren bade me do it,
To make a horror all about the house,
And stay[209] the world from Lady Lyonors.
They never dreamed the passes would be passed."
Answered Sir Gareth graciously to one
1380 Not many a moon his younger, "My fair child,
What madness made thee challenge the chief knight
Of Arthur's hall?" "Fair Sir, they bad me do it.

203 fleshless laughter : a grinning skull.

204 clod : earth.

205 marked : saw.

206 Lancelot's charger : Gareth was riding Lancelot's horse.
207 blink the terror : close their eyes on the black knight.

208 buffet : blow.

209 stay : keep.

ALFRED, LORD TENNYSON

They hate the King, and Lancelot, the King's friend,
They hoped to slay him somewhere on the stream,
1385 They never dreamed the passes could be passed."

Then sprang the happier day from underground;[210]
And Lady Lyonors and her house, with dance
And revel and song, made merry over Death,
As being after all their foolish fears
1390 And horrors only proven a blooming boy.
So large mirth lived and Gareth won the quest.

And he[211] that told the tale in older times
Says that Sir Gareth wedded Lyonors,
But he,[212] that told it later, says Lynette.

210 Then sprang . . . from underground : as plants come to life in the spring after winter's season of death.

211 he : Sir Thomas Malory, who had written an earlier account of Gareth and Lynette.

212 he : Lord Tennyson.

Understanding the Poem

1. What is on Gareth's mind when we first meet him (through l. 32)? What does the pine swept away by a cataract suggest to him?
2. (ll. 33-160) What arguments does Gareth raise with his mother? How does his mother answer each argument? Under what conditions will she let Gareth go? What was the motive behind her proposal?
3. (161-177) Why does Gareth accept his mother's conditions? Why does he leave at night? Who are his companions?
4. (178-183) Gareth begins his journey in the spring of the year. What might the spring symbolize in this poem?
5. (184-274) How is Camelot described? Paraphrase lines 263-270.
6. What does the old man mean by the words "The city is built/To music, therefore never built at all,/And therefore built forever" (272-274)?
7. (270-430) What is meant (l. 316) by the "half-shadow of a lie"? As Gareth comes into the court, various people are making pleas to King Arthur. What is each plea? What do you learn about Arthur as he handles each plea? How is justice being defined here?
8. (431-467) When it is Gareth's turn, how does he avoid telling who he really is? What is Sir Kay's reaction to taking Gareth as his helper? What is Lancelot's reaction to Gareth?
9. (468-531) Describe Gareth's new life. What message does Gareth get from his mother? What is his reaction?
10. (532-572) What agreement do Gareth and Arthur arrive at? What standards does Arthur have for his Knights? What agreement does Arthur make with Lancelot?

11. (573-629) As the "damsel of high lineage" arrives, what do we learn of what she is like? What is her problem? What are the characteristics of the four men who guard her sister? Why does she want Lancelot to accompany her?

12. (630-724) Why does Gareth intervene? What is the damsel's reaction to Arthur's acceptance of Gareth's request? What is Arthur's gift to Gareth? What is Sir Kay's reaction? What is Lancelot's reaction?

13. (725-772) As Gareth starts on his quest, what is the relation between him and the damsel?

14. (773-846) Describe their first adventure. What effect does it have on the damsel?

15. What does the "peacock in his pride" (ll. 829 and 849) suggest?

16. (747-863) What is the Baron's response to Lynette's complaint?

17. (870-882) What is the damsel's last plea to Gareth? What is his response?

18. (883-976) Describe the meeting with Sir Morning-Star. What is the damsel's reaction to the battle?

19. (977-1031) Describe Gareth's encounter with Noonday-Sun, the second guard. What is the damsel's reaction?

20. (1032-1059) How does Lynette's song contrast with her spoken comments? Is there any difference in her attitude toward Gareth since they first set out?

21. (1043-1162) Describe the encounter with the Star of Evening. What comparison is used to describe the battle in lines 1100-1104? How is the damsel changing in her attitude toward Gareth? What has Gareth's attitude been toward her in all these episodes? How is his attitude expressed in lines 1142-1154?

22. (1163-1180) As they arrive at the cave, the damsel explains the carvings. How do they help you to understand the poem as an allegory?

23. (1181-1280) Describe the reunion between Gareth and Lancelot.

24. (1280-1364) How is the damsel reacting to the final battle? How are the setting and the last enemy described?

25. (1365-1385) How does Gareth overcome death?

Techniques of Poetry

1. Which of the figures of speech that you studied in the first part of this unit are employed in each of the following passages?

(a) (20-23)   "Until she let me fly discaged to sweep
In ever-highering eagle-circles up
To the great Sun of Glory, and thence swoop
Down upon all things base, and dash them dead,"

(b) (73-74)   "Lo, where thy father Lot beside the hearth
Lies like a log, and all but smoldered out!"

(c) (182)   "And the live green had kindled into flowers."

(d) (212-213)   "all her dress
Wept from her sides as water flowing away."

(e) (275-276)   " 'Old Master, reverence thine own beard
That looks as white as utter truth. . . .' "

(f) (443-445)   "Kay, a man of mien
Wan-sallow as the plant that feels itself
Root-bitten by white lichen."

(g) (503-505)   "Sir Kay, the seneschal, would come
Blustering upon them, like a sudden wind
Among dead leaves, and drive them all apart."

(h) (535-536)   " 'I spring
Like flame from ashes.' "

(i) (666-673)   "whereat Sir Gareth loosed
A cloak . . . .
And from it like a fuel-smothered fire,
That looked half-dead, brake bright, and flashed
    as those
Dull-coated things, that making slide apart
Their dusk wing-cases, all beneath there burns
A jeweled harness, ere they pass and fly."

(j) (686-691)   "but as the cur
Plucked from the cur he fights with, ere his cause
Be cooled by fighting, follows, being named,
His owner, but remembers all, and growls
Remembering, so Sir Kay beside the door
Muttered in scorn of Gareth. . . ."

2. How do the comparisons involving Sir Kay (*f, g, j*) help to characterize him? How do they help to form the reader's attitude toward
him?
3. What things are being compared in *d* and in *e*? How are the things
being compared alike?
4. What similarities are there in the comparisons involving Gareth
(*a, h, i*)? What reason do they suggest for Tennyson's placing the
story of Gareth second in the *Idylls of the King*, during the time of
Arthur's rising power?
5. Which of the preceding passages use fire as a comparison? What
qualities does fire represent in them?

Developing Language Skills

1. An allegory is a narrative in which certain characters and elements in the setting represent abstract qualities or ideas in order to reveal some truth about human existence. *The Pilgrim's Progress* by John Bunyan, for example, is an allegory in which characters such as Mr. Worldly Wiseman and Faithful and parts of the setting such as Doubting Castle and the Slough of Despond represent the qualities suggested by their names. Plan a panel discussion exploring the allegorical significance of the following elements from "Gareth and Lynette":

Camelot	Morning-Star
Castle Perilous	Noonday-Sun
The three coils of the river	Evening-Star
	The Black Knight

    After class discussion, write a composition in which you state an idea about life contained in "Gareth and Lynette" and show how this idea was developed in the poem.

2. The structure of this poem is still with us in one of America's most persistent art forms—the cowboy story. The common theme of both is that good will overcome evil. If you look closely at the plot of a Western, you will see that it parallels in many ways the Camelot tale you have just read. In either a panel discussion or in a composition, describe the parallels you can find between the two.

Meter

Whenever you talk, you accent some sounds more than others. When the accented sounds occur in a regularly repeated pattern, a rhythmical beat appears. This pattern of beats is called meter.

The process of identifying a poem's meter is *scansion*. The first step in scanning a poem is to determine the pattern of accented and unaccented syllables. In the third line of "Crystal Moment,"

From my *boy*hood *I* remember

a reader must place the accent on the italicized syllables. It is difficult to read the line in any other pattern. This metric pattern in which the accented beat comes first and then is followed by one unaccented beat is called *trochaic* meter.

As is true of many poems, however, the meter of any one line may not be the meter of the entire poem. Reading on in "Crystal Moment," we find that several other lines conform to the following pattern:

A *wood*ed *is*land *rang* with *sounds*.

In these lines the unaccented syllable occurs first and is followed by a single accented syllable. This pattern is called *iambic* meter. It is the closest rhythm to normal speech and is the meter most frequently used in English poetry. The fact that different meters may be used in a poem is not an indication of poetic weakness; a poet often varies his meter to relieve the repetitious pattern or to create a special effect.

Below is a chart of the most common meters in poetry. They are listed in the order of their approximate frequency.

TERM	NUMBER OF SYLLABLES	EXAMPLE	DESCRIPTION
Iambic (ī ăm'bĭk)	2	a *head*	an unaccented syllable followed by an accented syllable
Trochaic (trō kā'ĭk)	2	*mes* sage	an accented syllable followed by an unaccented syllable
Anapestic (ăn'ə pĕs'tĭk)	3	in ter *fere*	two unaccented syllables followed by an accented syllable
Dactylic (dăk tĭl'ĭk)	3	*mem* o ry	an accented syllable followed by two unaccented syllables
Spondee (spŏn'dē)	2	*first-rate*	two accented syllables in succession
Amphibrach (ăm'fə brăk')	3	O *hi* o	an unaccented syllable followed by an accented syllable and another unaccented one
Amphimacer (ăm fĭm'ə sər)	3	*Free*dom *Train*	an accented syllable followed by an unaccented syllable and another accented one

The poet tries to select the pattern that best fits the mood of his poem. Two-syllable patterns—iambic and trochaic—are suitable for serious feelings and also for a conversational effect; on the other hand, the three-syllable patterns—especially the more common anapestic and dactylic—produce a quicker, happier, and lighter effect. The spondee is used as a variation from other meters; its effect generally is to emphasize and slow down.

The second step in scanning a poem is to count the number of times the metric pattern is repeated in each line. In the following lines from "Crystal Moment"—

A *buck* / leaped *out* / and *took* / the *tide* /
With *jew* / els *flow* / ing *past* / each *side*. /

—the *iambic* pattern of an unaccented syllable followed by an accented syllable is repeated four times in each line. Each repetition is called a *foot*. When there are four feet in each line the meter is called *tetrameter*. Thus the complete description of the above lines from "Crystal Moment" would be *iambic tetrameter*.

The names of other meters which are determined by the number of feet (the number of times the metric pattern is repeated) in a line of poetry are listed below:

NUMBER OF FEET IN EACH LINE	TERM
1	Monometer
2	Dimeter
3	Trimeter
4	Tetrameter
5	Pentameter
6	Hexameter
7	Heptameter
8	Octameter

To describe the meter, then, you must use two terms. The first identifies the pattern of accents, and the second tells how many times this pattern is repeated in each line. To indicate a poem's meter, one usually draws a line at the end of each foot and puts a slant mark over accented syllables. Below are a few examples of various meters:

Iambic Pentameter
The shát / tered wát / er máde / a mís / ty dín.

Anapestic Dimeter
From its sóur /ces which wéll
In the tárn/on the féll.

Amphibrachs
Di víd ing / and glíd ing / and slíd ing,
And fáll ing / and bráwl ing / and spráwl ing.

Much poetry, of course, does not use a regular meter. This is particularly true of modern poetry. And poets who do use a regular rhythmic pattern create numerous variations from those which have been described. For instance, pauses created by a period or comma may take the place of a syllable. Or an extra unaccented syllable may be added to the end of a line (see "Stanzas Written on the Road Between Florence and Pisa"). Differences in the way two readers interpret a poem may also result in different accents in a line, each reader accenting the words he considers most important.

Scanning a poem should not be an end in itself. It is simply one more approach to understanding how a poem is put together. The effect the rhythm has on the tone of the poem, its suitability to the subject matter, and the use of variations to relieve monotony or emphasize key words are what you should be aware of.

Samuel Taylor Coleridge once composed the lines on the opposite page to help his son Derwent remember the metrical patterns. Perhaps by memorizing the first half of the poem, you too will be better able to scan the poetry you study.

Metrical Feet

Lesson for a Boy

Trōchĕe[1] trīps frŏm lōng tŏ shōrt;
From long to long in solemn sort
Slōw Spōndēe stālks; strōng fŏot! yet ill able
Ēvĕr tŏ cōme ŭp wĭth Dāctўl trĭsўllăblĕ.
Īambĭcs mārch frŏm shōrt tŏ lōng;—   5
Wĭth ă lēap ănd ă bōund thĕ swĭft Ānăpĕsts thrōng;
One syllable long, with one short at each side,
Ămphībrăchўs hāstes wĭth ă stātelў stride;—
Fĭrst ănd lāst bēĭng lōng, mĭddlĕ shōrt, Ămphĭmācer
Strĭkes hĭs thūndērĭng hōofs lĭke ă prōud hīgh-brĕd Rācer.   10
If Derwent be innocent, steady, and wise,
And delight in the things of earth, water, and skies;
Tender warmth at his heart, with these meters to show it,
With sound sense in his brains, may make Derwent a poet,—
May crown him with fame, and must win him the love   15
Of his father on earth and his Father above.
            My dear, dear child!
Could you stand upon Skiddaw,[2] you would not from its whole ridge
See a man who so loves you as your fond S. T. COLERIDGE.

1 Coleridge uses a long mark (−) for accented syllables and a curved mark (ᵕ) for
unaccented syllables.
2 **Skiddaw:** a mountain in northwest England.

Julius Caesar

adapted from An Introduction to Shakespeare

Marchette Chute

WHEN William Shakespeare was about four years old he had a chance to see his first play.

The acting company came on horseback, bringing a wagon for their costumes and their swords, their feathers and their drums. They went first to the mayor, to ask his permission to put on plays in Stratford, and the mayor for that year happened to be Mr. John Shakespeare, William's father. The mayor not only gave his permission but also arranged for a payment of nine shillings out of the town funds so that the first show could be seen by everyone without charge.

All over England the acting companies stopped their wagons and set up their stages. Sometimes they used town halls, like the one in Stratford, and sometimes large private houses, but usually they acted in the courtyards of the local inns. Every town had at least one inn— Stratford had four—and the actors found that they could build a scaffolding at one end of the innyard and have their penny audience stand in front of it, while the wealthier people leaned out of the upstairs windows and looked down on the stage below.

The actors used the London inns so often that they built permanent scaffoldings at a large inn like the Cross Keys; but even the best of them had disadvantages. It was not easy to collect the entrance money, with so many people coming and going, and there was no way to store the costumes and the properties. Moreover the actors had to share the innyards with the carters, who used them several times a week to pack their freight wagons and meet their customers.

What the actors needed was a theater building, and when Shakespeare was twelve years old a Londoner named James Burbage decided to build one. Burbage was a prominent actor and in his youth he had been trained as a carpenter. To these advantages he added a single-minded, vigorous optimism and a great love of the theater; and with the full support of his lively wife, he set out to build the first theater in England.

There was no building in England, or even in Europe, that Burbage could use as a model, so he had to work out his own design. He made it somewhat like the innyards, with a stage jutting into a courtyard and seats arranged in tiers overhead, and he planned to use the same system of charging a penny for standing room and more for the upstairs seats. But since he wanted everyone to see the stage easily he made the building round, like the great amphitheaters that were being used south of London for bear-baiting, and, like them, he made his building open to the sky. There was a ring of thatch around the outside to protect the seats and the actors' rooms, and there was also a slanting cover over the stage itself. James Burbage was an actor and he knew how much money had been invested in the velvets and satins of the theater costumes.

If James Burbage had planned the wrong design he would have been ruined, and it would have been a long time before anyone else attempted to build a theater in England. But Burbage knew his business, and the theater was an instant success.

The actors had many reasons to be grateful to Burbage. They no longer had to move out for the carters, and they had a large, contented audience safely installed before the show started. They had a storage place for their scripts and their piles of expensive costumes, as well as for their huge clutter of properties that included everything from gilt spears and caldrons to portable castles and tombs, and they also had adequate dressing rooms for the first time in their strenuous lives.

Above all, they had the latest in stage equipment and design, for Burbage had given them five different levels on which to produce their plays. At the lowest level were the trap doors, built into the floor of the stage, and an actor who was playing a devil could crouch on a little platform, be drawn up to the stage level, and leap out with an explosion of fireworks as realistically as though he had just come from the infernal regions. Ghosts could do the same; and if the actors needed a grave or a ditch they could pull the platform up halfway and leave it there, with perhaps a small plaster tree or a bank of imitation moss to show that the scene was taking place outdoors.

The next level was the main stage and here the actors produced all their most important scenes. The jutting front area could be used for coronations and wars and city streets, and behind it was a small inner stage that could be used as a shop or a study. Above this, on the next level, was a balcony which could be used for anything from a mountain to a city wall. If a town was besieged in a play, for instance, the invaders gathered on the main stage and the besieged townsmen fought them off from the balcony.

Just under the roof of his theater, Burbage had installed a series of pulleys, so that if a play called for a goddess to be wafted down from the heavens she could be wafted down with great dignity. Up there, under the roof, a man could also send down thunderbolts, or stuffed birds, or warning hands clutching swords, and he could imitate the

As interest in the drama increased during the 16th century, acting companies frequently used innyards for their productions. They performed the play on a raised platform at one end of the courtyard, while spectators stood on the open ground or on the surrounding balconies.

WILLIAM SHAKESPEARE

rattle of rain or anything else that was called for in the script. There was also room aloft for the musicians, ready with trumpets for the battle scenes or hautboys for coronations, although the musicians were moved about and sometimes even played from under the stage. Anything could be shown in the theater, from a storm at sea to the chariot of the sun, and every year the actors could work out new and astonishing stage effects for their audiences.

Most of Shakespeare's fellow actors had been trained in the profession since childhood but Shakespeare himself entered it comparatively late. When he was eighteen years old he was still in Stratford. And he had apparently intended to settle down there since in the autumn of his eighteenth year he married a woman named Anne Hathaway, who belonged to a well-to-do farming family in a nearby village. There were three children in the next two years, a daughter named Susanna and then twins named Hamnet and Judith.

Stratford was a rather rigid and conservative little town and many young men left it to go up to London. Richard Field, for instance, left Stratford when he was fifteen to become apprenticed to a London printer and within ten years he owned the business. But publishing was a respectable business, while most people were convinced that acting was not; and there must have been many citizens of Stratford who were sorry to see the eldest son of a respected man like John Shakespeare take up so shiftless and vagabond a career.

By the time Shakespeare was twenty-eight years old he was a well-known figure in the London theater. He was attacked by Robert Greene as an actor who dared to write plays and defended by Henry Chettle as a good playwright and an excellent actor. It is not known which of the acting companies in London he was working with at the time, but two years later, in 1594, he joined the Chamberlain's Men and stayed with them until he retired from the stage.

This company gave him the freedom he wanted, as the great range and variety of his work from that time forward bear witness. No one but Shakespeare himself is responsible for the greatness of his plays. But the actors of his company gave him loyal, intelligent support and space in which to experiment, and the penny public of the ordinary London theaters gave him their devoted patronage. The literary men of London looked with contempt upon these "penny knaves," but the approval of the regular theater public was good enough for Shakespeare.

The mayor of London strongly disapproved of young people going to plays and said so frequently. He would have kept them away altogether if he could, but in spite of his position and influence there was nothing he could do to stop them. Young Londoners were determined to go to plays, and they were particularly determined to go to the plays of William Shakespeare.

Shakespeare had settled down with a single acting company, and he stayed with them for the rest of his career; but he had not settled down

During the 16th and 17th centuries, plays and other entertainments were often pro-duced in guild halls or in the great halls of wealthy private homes or schools—sometimes at banquets or during holiday seasons or for other special occasions. For example, in 1594 Shakespeare's Comedy of Errors *was presented at Gray's Inn (home of a legal guild) during the Christmas season.*

WILLIAM SHAKESPEARE

as a writer. He went on experimenting with increasing vigor, trying first one kind of play and then another, and the plays he gave his fortunate company at the rate of two a year had no pattern and no neatness. They began to cover larger and larger areas of human experience, until in the end Shakespeare had brought the whole world into existence on the London stage.

One of the most famous of his plays is *Julius Caesar,* which he wrote about five years after he joined the Chamberlain's Men. *Julius Caesar* is a play about politics; and since politics are made by men, it is a study of why men do things. In this case, it is the problem of why a group of enlightened citizens decide to commit a murder—what drives them to it and what happens afterwards—and Shakespeare understood so well the complication of good intentions and political expediency that can lead to disaster that his play is just as applicable to the 20th century as it was to the 16th.

London audiences knew a good deal about Caesar, since his murder had been a popular subject in amateur theatricals. Some members of the audience might also have read Plutarch's *Lives,* which had recently been translated by an Elizabethan soldier and which contained a brilliant study of Caesar's downfall. But even the best-informed members of the audience must have been startled by what Shakespeare was able to do with the old story.

The central figure in the play is not Caesar, but his friend Brutus who kills him. Brutus feels that the end justifies the means and that since Caesar is a dictator it is necessary to kill him. He clings to the fact that he is only doing evil so that good may come of it, and in the end he plunges the whole country into civil war.

As for Caesar, Shakespeare had never encountered a dictator and yet he knew the type well. He knew the self-hypnosis that drove him to think he was above ordinary human weaknesses, and the rage his friends felt when they saw him behave like a god, when they knew all about his deaf ear and his love of flattery and the other things that made him an ordinary man. Caesar, as long as he is alive, is an ordinary man, with more conceit than most. Caesar murdered is a legend, and Brutus and his friends cannot kill it.

> O Julius Caesar! thou art mighty yet!
> Thy spirit walks abroad and turns our swords . . .

The conspirators have no unifying idea to hold them together once they have killed Caesar, and the quarrel between Brutus and his best friend is a marvelous study of two well-intentioned men who are getting increasingly on each other's nerves. The only man who knows exactly what he wants to do is Antony, and his speech to the Romans over Caesar's dead body is a kind of handbook for all skillful political propagandists.

In Shakespeare's own day, the literary critics did not realize that his wonderful plays would become immortal. It was two actors in his own company, John Heminges and Henry Condell, who had the greatest faith in the future. They were convinced that the reputation of their "friend and fellow" would be safe if only his work could be made available to the ordinary reading public.

. . . It is not our province, who only gather his works and give them to you, to praise him. It is yours that read him . . . Read him, therefore; and again and again; and if then you do not like him, surely you are in manifest danger not to understand him. And so we leave him to other of his friends, whom, if you need, can be your guides; if you need them not, you can lead yourselves and others. And such readers we wish him.

John Heminges
Henry Condell

Their wish was answered. It was such readers he got, and no other writer in the world's history has been loved by so many people or has given so much happiness.

Reading Shakespeare

If William Shakespeare were to step into the 20th century, atomic energy and men in space might not surprise him so much as the fact that scholars study and teach his plays. During his time, Shakespeare's plays were popular with the young people and the shopkeepers as well as with the lords and ladies who attended his theater. Today, they are still read and watched by all ages and kinds of people. Memorable characters and universal themes are two of the qualities that have made Shakespeare's plays so long-lived. Although Shakespeare drew the characters for *Julius Caesar* from the 16th-century English translation of Plutarch's *Lives*, he has greatly expanded upon the materials he found there, making his people come alive through their jealousies, ambitions, and loyalties. In his portrayal of the relationships and conflicts between characters, Shakespeare has developed such universal themes as love of freedom and the relation of men to history.

As you read *Julius Caesar*, you will discover that most of it is written in verse. The basic rhythm is iambic pentameter (see p. 604) and the lines are unrhymed—a kind of poetry known as *blank verse*. However, if you select any passage and study its rhythm, you will find that few lines in it conform exactly to this pattern. They may vary slightly in the basic number of ten syllables per line, and the position of the accents will vary quite a bit. In this manner, Shakespeare avoids a monotonous rhythm and attains a more natural line for speaking. In reading the play—either silently or aloud—you should not assume that the end of a line indicates the end of a sentence or a break in the meaning. Note the punctuation as you would in a regular sentence, and pause where the meaning calls for it.

You will also discover as you read that the play makes use of several *stage conventions*, some of which are seldom practiced today. A stage convention is a custom, or practice, accepted by an audience even though they recognize it as unrealistic. One convention frequently used by Shakespeare in his plays is the *soliloquy*, a speech in which a character gives voice to his inner thoughts. Through the soliloquy, an audience can know what a character is thinking or feeling but would not realistically be likely to say. The *aside* is a similar convention: a character expresses a thought aloud which other characters on the stage supposedly do not hear. Although you cannot tell in reading the play, another convention practiced in Elizabethan times was to have women's parts played by boys.

One problem you, as a high school student, may encounter in reading *Julius Caesar* is the language. Many words used in it have changed their meanings somewhat since Elizabethan times or are no longer used. These words have been footnoted for you. Beliefs of people have also changed somewhat in the last 350 years. Many people in Shakespeare's audience accepted ghosts, witches, signs from the heavens, and other superstitions as realities; all his audience was accustomed to the introduction of such supernatural elements into plays. Indeed, something like the ghost of Caesar (who appears in this play) was regarded as a part of history; it was not Shakespeare's invention.

As you read *Julius Caesar*, then, you should be aware of the context in which it was written and first seen. Three centuries from now, our modern plays will undoubtedly also seem strange in some ways on the surface. The important parts of the play, however, are Shakespeare's understanding of human nature and his probing of what happens when men take it upon themselves to influence history. In these matters, *Julius Caesar* is still relevant to our times.

Julius Caesar and His World

When the play opens, a small group of Romans is concerned over the growing power of the dictator Julius Caesar while the mass of citizens is celebrating his military triumphs. This divided feeling was not new to the Romans. Four hundred years before the birth of Julius Caesar, Rome had become a republic following a successful revolt led by the wealthy Brutus family against the ruling monarch. This new republic was ruled by a Senate made up of wealthy patricians, with two senators elected consuls by the Senate to act as co-rulers. The plebians (common people) gradually won privileges from the Senate to protect their rights, but there remained a law that permitted a dictator to rule in times of emergency. Among the dictators Rome had had in the last four hundred years were Marius, who represented the plebeians, and Sulla, who represented the patricians.

Although Julius Caesar was born to a patrician family, he achieved great popularity with the common people because of the money spent for the recreation and relief of the plebeians during his terms in public office. In 60 B.C. he became a member of a triumvirate (three-man rule) to govern Rome. The other members of the triumvirate were the wealthy landowner Crassus and the military leader Pompey. As a member of the triumvirate, Caesar was made governor of Gaul and was given an army with which he conquered much of what is now France and England. By using the money from his conquests to pay bonuses to his soldiers and to relieve the tax burden of the Roman plebeians, he further increased his popularity.

After Crassus was killed in battle, Pompey, concerned about Caesar's growing popularity, turned to the patricians for support. Caesar was ordered by the Senate to disband his army; instead he invaded Italy and defeated Pompey's forces. Pompey himself was killed in Egypt fleeing from Caesar's armies.

As the play opens in 44 B.C., Caesar has recently returned in triumph from Munda in Spain, where he has defeated the armies of Pompey's two sons. He is now the sole ruler of the Roman Empire, having been voted a dictator for life the year before. The play opens by showing the attitudes various Romans hold concerning Caesar's power.

The Tragedy of Julius Caesar

William Shakespeare

Dramatis Personae.

JULIUS CAESAR (jōōl′yəs sē′zər)
OCTAVIUS CAESAR (ŏk tā′vĭ əs sē′zər)
MARCUS ANTONIUS, usually called Mark Antony (märk ăn′tə nĭ) } Triumvirs after the death of Julius Caesar
M. AEMILIUS LEPIDUS (ē mĭl′ĭ əs lĕp′ĭ dəs)

CICERO (sĭs′ə rō′)
PUBLIUS (pŭb′lĭ əs) } Senators
POPILIUS LENA (pə pĭl′ĭ əs lē′nə)

MARCUS BRUTUS (mär′kəs brōō′təs)
CASSIUS (kăsh′əs)
CASCA (kăs′kə)
TREBONIUS (trə bō′nĭ əs)
LIGARIUS (lĭ gâr′ĭ əs) } Conspirators against Julius Caesar
DECIUS BRUTUS (dē′shəs brōō′təs)
METELLUS CIMBER (mĕ tĕl′ləs sĭm′bər)
CINNA (sĭn′ə)

FLAVIUS (flā′vĭ əs) and MARULLUS (mə rŭl′əs), Tribunes of the People
ARTEMIDORUS (är′tə mə dō′rəs), a Sophist (teacher)
A SOOTHSAYER
CINNA, a poet
Another Poet

LUCILIUS (lōō sĭl′ĭ əs)
TITINIUS (tĭ tĭn′ĭ əs)
MESSALA (mə sā′lə) } friends to Brutus and Cassius
YOUNG CATO (kā′tō)
VOLUMNIUS (və lŭm′nĭ əs)

VARRO (văr′ō)
CLITUS (klĭ′təs)
CLAUDIUS (klô′dĭ əs) } servants to Brutus
STRATO (strā′tō)
LUCIUS (lōō′sⱨəs)
DARDANIUS (där dā′nĭ əs)

PINDARUS (pĭn′dər əs), servant to Cassius
A Servant to Caesar; to Antony; to Octavius
CALPURNIA (kăl pûr′nĭ ə), wife to Caesar
PORTIA (pōr′shə), wife to Brutus
The Ghost of Caesar
Senators, Citizens, Guards, Attendants, etc.

Act I

Scene I. *Rome. A street.*

Enter Flavius, Marullus, *and certain*
Commoners *over the stage.*

Flavius. Hence! home, you idle creatures, get you home!
Is this a holiday?¹ What, know you not,
Being mechanical,² you ought not walk
Upon a laboring day without the sign
5 Of your profession? Speak, what trade art thou?
    Carpenter. Why, sir, a carpenter.
    Marullus. Where is thy leather apron and thy rule?
What dost thou with thy best apparel on?
You, sir, what trade are you?
10   Cobbler. Truly sir, in respect of a fine workman I am but,
as you would say, a cobbler.³
    Marullus. But what trade art thou? Answer me directly.
    Cobbler. A trade, sir, that I hope I may use with a safe
conscience, which is indeed, sir, a mender of bad soles.⁴
15   Marullus. What trade, thou knave? Thou naughty knave,
    what trade?
    Cobbler. Nay, I beseech you, sir, be not out with me. Yet
if you be out, sir, I can mend you.⁵
    Marullus. What mean'st thou by that? Mend me, thou
    saucy fellow?
    Cobbler. Why, sir, cobble you.
20 Flavius. Thou art a cobbler, art thou?
    Cobbler. Truly, sir, all that I live by is with the awl.⁶ I
meddle with no tradesman's matters nor women's matters, but
with all. I am indeed, sir, a surgeon to old shoes. When they
are in great danger, I recover them. As proper men as ever
25 trod upon neat's leather⁷ have gone upon my handiwork.
    Flavius. But wherefore art not in thy shop today?
Why dost thou lead these men about the streets?
    Cobbler. Truly, sir, to wear out their shoes, to get myself
into more work. But indeed, sir, we make holiday to see Caesar
30 and to rejoice in his triumph.
    Marullus. Wherefore rejoice? What conquest brings he
    home?
What tributaries⁸ follow him to Rome
To grace in captive bonds his chariot wheels?
You blocks, you stones, you worse than senseless things!
35 O you hard hearts, you cruel men of Rome!
Knew you not Pompey? Many a time and oft
Have you climbed up to walls and battlements,
To tow'rs and windows, yea, to chimney tops,

---

1 Hence . . . holiday : The people of Rome have left their work to celebrate the triumphant return of Julius Caesar on February 15, 44 B.C.
2 being mechanical : having a trade.

3 cobbler : Two meanings are intended—a clumsy workman and a shoe repairman.
4 soles : a pun playing *soles* with *souls.*

5 I can mend you : He continues the pun by referring to his shoes.

6 awl : a pun playing *awl*, a cobbler's tool, with *all.*

7 neat's leather : cowhide.

8 tributaries : men giving money or services.

Your infants in your arms, and there have sat
40 The livelong day, with patient expectation,
To see great Pompey pass the streets of Rome.
And when you saw his chariot but appear,
Have you not made an universal shout,
That Tiber[9] trembled underneath her banks
45 To hear the replication of your sounds
Made in her concave shores?
And do you now put on your best attire?
And do you now cull out a holiday?
And do you now strew flowers in his way
50 That comes in triumph over Pompey's blood?[10]
Be gone!
Run to your houses, fall upon your knees,
Pray to the gods to intermit[11] the plague
That needs must light on this ingratitude.
55   FLAVIUS. Go, go, good countrymen, and for this fault
Assemble all the poor men of your sort;
Draw them to Tiber banks, and weep your tears
Into the channel, till the lowest stream
Do kiss the most exalted shores[12] of all.
                    (*Exeunt all the* COMMONERS.)
60 See, whe'r their basest metal[13] be not moved.
They vanish tongue-tied in their guiltiness.
Go you down that way towards the Capitol;
This way will I. Disrobe the images
If you do find them decked with ceremonies.[14]
65   MARULLUS. May we do so?
You know it is the feast of Lupercal.[15]
     FLAVIUS. It is no matter. Let no images
Be hung with Caesar's trophies. I'll about
And drive away the vulgar[16] from the streets.
70 So do you too, where you perceive them thick.
These growing feathers plucked from Caesar's wing
Will make him fly an ordinary pitch,[17]
Who else[18] would soar above the view of men[19]
And keep us all in servile fearfulness.   (*Exeunt.*)

Scene II. *Rome. A public place.*

(*Music.*) *Enter* CAESAR, ANTONY (*for the course*),[1] CALPURNIA,
PORTIA, DECIUS, CICERO, BRUTUS, CASSIUS, CASCA; *a great crowd
following, among them a* SOOTHSAYER;[2] *after them,* MARULLUS
          and FLAVIUS.

     CAESAR. Calpurnia.
     CASCA.   Peace, ho! Caesar speaks. (*Music ceases.*)

Side notes:

9 Tiber (tī′bər) : a river near Rome.

10 Pompey's (pŏm′pĭz) blood : Caesar is returning from his victory over Pompey's sons.

11 intermit : postpone.

12 exalted shores : the highest point to which the river rises.

13 basest metal : lowest nature.

14 Disrobe . . . ceremonies: remove the scarfs and ornaments (tokens of triumph) from statues of Caesar which have been placed around the city.

15 feast of Lupercal (loo′pər kăl) : religious celebration for a god of fertility.

16 vulgar : commoners.

17 pitch : height.

18 else : otherwise.

19 above the view of men : as a god.

1 course : race.

2 Soothsayer : fortuneteller.

CAESAR.   Calpurnia.

CALPURNIA. Here, my lord.

CAESAR. Stand you directly in Antonius' way
When he doth run his course. Antonius.

5   ANTONY. Caesar, my lord?

CAESAR. Forget not in your speed, Antonius,
To touch Calpurnia; for our elders say
The barren, touched in this holy chase,
Shake off their sterile curse.[3]

ANTONY.   I shall remember.

10   When Caesar says "Do this," it is performed.

CAESAR. Set on, and leave no ceremony out.   (*Music.*)

SOOTHSAYER. Caesar!

CAESAR. Ha! Who calls?

CASCA. Bid every noise be still. Peace yet again!

(*Music ceases.*)

15   CAESAR. Who is it in the press that calls on me?
I hear a tongue shriller than all the music
Cry "Caesar!" Speak. Caesar is turned to hear.

SOOTHSAYER. Beware the ides of March.

CAESAR.   What man is that?

BRUTUS. A soothsayer bids you beware the ides of March.[4]

20   CAESAR. Set him before me; let me see his face.

CASSIUS. Fellow, come from the throng; look upon Caesar.

CAESAR. What say'st thou to me now? Speak once again.

SOOTHSAYER. Beware the ides of March.

CAESAR. He is a dreamer. Let us leave him. Pass.

(*Sennet.[5] Exeunt all but* BRUTUS *and* CASSIUS.)

25   CASSIUS. Will you go see the order of the course?

BRUTUS. Not I.

CASSIUS. I pray you do.

BRUTUS. I am not gamesome. I do lack some part
Of that quick spirit that is in Antony.

30   Let me not hinder, Cassius, your desires.
I'll leave you.

CASSIUS. Brutus, I do observe you now of late;
I have not from your eyes that gentleness
And show of love as I was wont to have.[6]

35   You bear too stubborn and too strange a hand
Over your friend that loves you.[7]

BRUTUS.   Cassius,
Be not deceived. If I have veiled my look,
I turn the trouble of my countenance
Merely upon myself.[8] Vexed I am

40   Of late with passions of some difference,[9]
Conceptions only proper to myself,[10]
Which give some soil, perhaps, to my behaviors;

3 touch . . . curse : It was believed that a woman touched by a man in the race would be able to have children. Calpurnia and Caesar were childless; thus, Caesar would lack an heir as emperor.

4 ides of March : March 15.

5 Sennet : trumpet fanfare.

6 wont to have : used to have.

7 You bear . . . loves you : You treat your friend too roughly and too much like a stranger.

8 I turn . . . myself : Brutus explains that personal troubles have kept him from appearing friendlier.

9 passions of some difference : conflicting emotions.

10 proper to myself : Brutus again points out that his problems are personal ones.

But let not therefore my good friends be grieved
(Among which number, Cassius, be you one)
45　Nor construe any further my neglect
Than that poor Brutus, with himself at war,
Forgets the shows of love to other men.

　　　CASSIUS. Then, Brutus, I have much mistook your passion;[11]
By means whereof[12] this breast of mine hath buried
50　Thoughts of great value, worthy cogitations.[13]
Tell me, good Brutus, can you see your face?

　　　BRUTUS. No, Cassius; for the eye sees not itself
But by reflection, by some other things.

　　　CASSIUS. 'Tis just.
55　And it is very much lamented, Brutus,
That you have no such mirrors as will turn
Your hidden worthiness into your eye,
That you might see your shadow. I have heard
Where many of the best respect in Rome
60　(Except immortal Caesar), speaking of Brutus
And groaning underneath this age's yoke,[14]
Have wished that noble Brutus had his eyes.

　　　BRUTUS. Into what dangers would you lead me, Cassius,
That you would have me seek into myself
65　For that which is not in me?

　　　CASSIUS. Therefore, good Brutus, be prepared to hear;
And since you know you cannot see yourself
So well as by reflection, I, your glass,
Will modestly discover to yourself
70　That of yourself which you yet know not of.
And be not jealous on[15] me, gentle Brutus.
Were I a common laugher,[16] or did use
To stale with ordinary oaths my love
To every new protester;[17] if you know
75　That I do fawn on men and hug them hard,
And after scandal[18] them; or if you know
That I profess[19] myself in banqueting
To all the rout,[20] then hold me dangerous.

　　　　　　　　　　　　　(Flourish[21] and shout.)
　　　BRUTUS. What means this shouting? I do fear the people
Choose Caesar for their king.
80　　CASSIUS.　　　　　　　Ay, do you fear it?
Then must I think you would not have it so.

　　　BRUTUS. I would not, Cassius; yet I love him well.
But wherefore do you hold me here so long?
What is it that you would impart to me?
85　If it be aught toward the general good,
Set honor in one eye and death i' th' other,
And I will look on both indifferently;

11 mistook your passion : misunderstood your attitude.

12 By means whereof : because of this.

13 worthy cogitations : important thoughts.

14 yoke : Rome's lack of freedom under Caesar.

15 jealous on : suspicious of.

16 laugher : clown.

17 To stale . . . protester : to make easy friends with everyone who professes friendship.

18 scandal : slander.

19 profess : declare my affections.

20 the rout : the crowd.

21 Flourish : a trumpet fanfare.

For let the gods so speed me as I love
The name of honor more than I fear death.

90   CASSIUS. I know that virtue to be in you, Brutus,
As well as I do know your outward favor.22
Well, honor is the subject of my story.
I cannot tell what you and other men
Think of this life; but for my single self,

95 I had as lief not be as live to be
In awe of such a thing as I myself.23
I was born free as Caesar; so were you.
We both have fed as well, and we can both
Endure the winter's cold as well as he.

100 For once, upon a raw and gusty day,
The troubled Tiber chafing with her shores,
Caesar said to me, "Dar'st thou, Cassius, now
Leap in with me into this angry flood
And swim to yonder point?" Upon the word,

105 Accouterd24 as I was, I plungèd in
And bade him follow. So indeed he did.
The torrent roared, and we did buffet it
With lusty sinews, throwing it aside
And stemming it with hearts of controversy.25

110 But ere we could arrive the point proposed,
Caesar cried, "Help me, Cassius, or I sink!"
I, as Aeneas, our great ancestor,
Did from the flames of Troy upon his shoulder
The old Anchises bear, so from the waves of Tiber

115 Did I the tired Caesar.26 And this man
Is now become a god, and Cassius is
A wretched creature and must bend his body27
If Caesar carelessly but nod on him.
He had a fever when he was in Spain,

120 And when the fit was on him, I did mark
How he did shake. 'Tis true, this god did shake.
His coward lips did from their color fly,
And that same eye whose bend doth awe the world
Did lose his luster. I did hear him groan.

125 Ay, and that tongue of his that bade the Romans
Mark him and write his speeches in their books,
Alas, it cried, "Give me some drink, Titinius,"
As a sick girl! Ye gods, it doth amaze me
A man of such a feeble temper should

130 So get the start of the majestic world
And bear the palm28 alone.   (*Shout. Flourish.*)
    BRUTUS. Another general shout?
I do believe that these applauses are
For some new honors that are heaped on Caesar.

22 outward favor : handsome appearance.

23 of such a thing as I myself : another man.

24 Accouterd : dressed.

25 controversy : rivalry.

26 as Aeneas (ĭ nē′əs) . . . tired Caesar : Cassius claims that he saved Caesar from drowning in the river in the same manner that Aeneas, the founder of Rome, rescued his father, Anchises, from the burning Troy.
27 bend his body : bow.

28 palm : The palm is a symbol of victory.

135   CASSIUS. Why, man, he doth bestride the narrow world
      Like a Colossus,[29] and we petty men
      Walk under his huge legs and peep about
      To find ourselves dishonorable graves.
      Men at some time are masters of their fates.
140 The fault, dear Brutus, is not in our stars,[30]
      But in ourselves, that we are underlings.
      "Brutus," and "Caesar." What should be in that "Caesar"?
      Why should that name be sounded more than yours?
      Write them together: yours is as fair a name.
145 Sound them: it doth become the mouth as well.
      Weigh them: it is as heavy. Conjure[31] with 'em:
      "Brutus" will start a spirit as soon as "Caesar."
      Now in the names of all the gods at once,
      Upon what meat doth this our Caesar feed
150 That he is grown so great? Age, thou are shamed!
      Rome, thou hast lost the breed of noble bloods!
      When went there by an age since the great Flood
      But it was famed with more than with one man?
      When could they say (till now) that talked of Rome
155 That her wide walls encompassed but one man?
      Now is it Rome indeed, and room enough,[32]
      When there is in it but one only man!
      O, you and I have heard our fathers say
      There was a Brutus once[33] that would have brooked[34]
160 Th' eternal devil to keep his state in Rome
      As easily as a king.
         BRUTUS. That you do love me I am nothing jealous.[35]
      What you would work me to, I have some aim.[36]
      How I have thought of this, and of these times,
165 I shall recount hereafter. For this present,
      I would not (so with love I might entreat you)
      Be any further moved. What you have said
      I will consider; what you have to say
      I will with patience hear, and find a time
170 Both meet to hear and answer such high things.
      Till then, my noble friend, chew upon this:
      Brutus had rather be a villager
      Than to repute himself a son of Rome
      Under these hard conditions as this time
175 Is like to lay upon us.
      CASSIUS.   I am glad
      That my weak words have struck but thus much show
      Of fire from Brutus.

        Enter CAESAR *and his train.*[37]

      BRUTUS. The games are done, and Caesar is returning.

29 Colossus (kə lŏs′əs) : a huge statue, of the ancient world, that straddled the entrance of the harbor of Rhodes.

30 in our stars : in fate.

31 Conjure : Summon spirits.

32 Rome . . . room enough: a pun; *Rome* and *room* had similar pronunciations.

33 a Brutus once : an earlier Brutus who freed Rome.
34 brooked : endured.

35 nothing jealous : not doubtful.
36 have some aim : can guess.

37 train : followers.

JULIUS CAESAR

CASSIUS. As they pass by, pluck Casca by the sleeve,
180 And he will (after his sour fashion) tell you
What hath proceeded worthy note today.
BRUTUS. I will do so. But look you, Cassius!
The angry spot doth glow on Caesar's brow,
And all the rest look like a chidden[38] train.

185 Calpurnia's cheek is pale, and Cicero
Looks with such ferret[39] and such fiery eyes
As we have seen him in the Capitol,
Being crossed in conference by some senators.
CASSIUS. Casca will tell us what the matter is.
190 CAESAR. Antonius.
ANTONY. Caesar?
CAESAR. Let me have men about me that are fat,
Sleek-headed men, and such as sleep a-nights.
Yond Cassius has a lean and hungry look.
195 He thinks too much. Such men are dangerous.
ANTONY. Fear him not, Caesar; he's not dangerous.
He is a noble Roman, and well given.[40]
CAESAR. Would he were fatter! But I fear him not.
Yet if my name[41] were liable to fear,
200 I do not know the man I should avoid
So soon as that spare Cassius. He reads much,
He is a great observer, and he looks
Quite through the deeds of men. He loves no plays
As thou dost, Antony; he hears no music.
205 Seldom he smiles, and smiles in such a sort
As if he mocked himself and scorned his spirit
That could be moved to smile at anything.
Such men as he be never at heart's ease
Whiles they behold a greater than themselves,
210 And therefore are they very dangerous.
I rather tell thee what is to be feared
Than what I fear; for always I am Caesar.
Come on my right hand, for this ear is deaf,
And tell me truly what thou think'st of him.
        (Sennet. Exeunt CAESAR and his train. CASCA remains.)
215 CASCA. You pulled me by the cloak. Would you speak with
        me?[42]
BRUTUS. Ay, Casca. Tell us what hath chanced today
That Caesar looks so sad,
CASCA. Why, you were with him, were you not?
BRUTUS. I should not then ask Casca what had chanced.
220 CASCA. Why, there was a crown offered him; and being
offered him, he put it by with the back of his hand thus; and
then the people fell a-shouting.
BRUTUS. What was the second noise for?

38 chidden : scolded.

39 ferret : red, like a ferret's.

40 well given : well disposed.
41 my name : I (that is, Caesar).

42 You pulled . . . with me : Note that in this speech and all others Casca speaks in prose.

WILLIAM SHAKESPEARE   625

CASCA. Why, for that too.

225 CASSIUS. They shouted thrice. What was the last cry for?

CASCA. Why, for that too.

BRUTUS. Was the crown offered him thrice?

CASCA. Ay, marry, was't![43] and he put it by thrice, every
time gentler than other; and at every putting-by mine honest
230 neighbors shouted.

CASSIUS. Who offered him the Crown?

CASCA. Why, Antony.

BRUTUS. Tell us the manner of it, gentle Casca.

CASCA. I can as well be hanged as tell the manner of it. It
235 was mere foolery; I did not mark it. I saw Mark Antony offer
him a crown—yet 'twas not a crown neither, 'twas one of these
coronets[44]—and, as I told you, he put it by once; but for all
that, to my thinking, he would fain have had it. Then he offered it to him again; then he put it by again; but to my
240 thinking, he was very loath to lay his fingers off it. And then
he offered it the third time. He put it the third time by; and
still as he refused it, the rabblement hooted, and clapped their
chopt hands, and threw up their sweaty nightcaps, and uttered
such a deal of stinking breath because Caesar refused the
245 crown that it had, almost, choked Caesar; for he swoonded and
fell down at it. And for mine own part, I durst not laugh, for
fear of opening my lips and receiving the bad air.

44 coronets : a kind of crown inferior to those used by kings.

CASSIUS. But soft, I pray you. What, did Caesar swound?

CASCA. He fell down in the market place and foamed at
250 mouth and was speechless.

BRUTUS. 'Tis very like. He hath the falling sickness.[45]

CASSIUS. No, Caesar hath it not; but you, and I,
And honest Casca, we have the falling sickness.

45 falling sickness : epilepsy.

CASCA. I know not what you mean by that,[46] but I am sure
255 Caesar fell down. If the tag-rag people did not clap him and
hiss him, according as he pleased and displeased them, as they
use to do the players in the theater, I am no true man.

46 I know not . . . by that : Casca does not (or at least pretends he does not) understand Cassius's ironic remark.

BRUTUS. What said he when he came unto himself?

CASCA. Marry, before he fell down, when he perceived the
260 common herd was glad he refused the crown, he plucked me
ope his doublet[47] and offered them his throat to cut. An[48] I had
been a man of any occupation, if I would not have taken him
at a word I would I might go to hell among the rogues. And
so he fell. When he came to himself again, he said, if he had
265 done or said anything amiss, he desired their worships to think
it was his infirmity. Three or four wenches where I stood cried
"Alas, good soul!" and forgave him with all their hearts. But
there's no heed to be taken of them. If Caesar had stabbed
their mothers, they would have done no less.

47 doublet : Elizabethan jacket.
48 an : if.

270 BRUTUS. And after that, he came thus sad away?

CASCA. Ay.

CASSIUS. Did Cicero say anything?

CASCA. Ay, he spoke Greek.

CASSIUS. To what effect?

275 CASCA. Nay, an I tell you that, I'll ne'er look you i' th'
face again.[49] But those that understood him smiled at one another and shook their heads; but for mine own part, it was
Greek to me. I could tell you more news too. Marullus and
Flavius, for pulling scarfs off Caesar's images, are put to
280 silence.[50] Fare you well. There was more foolery yet, if I
could remember it.

CASSIUS. Will you sup with me tonight, Casca?

CASCA. No, I am promised forth.

CASSIUS. Will you dine with me tomorrow?

285 CASCA. Ay, if I be alive, and your mind hold, and your
dinner worth eating.

CASSIUS. Good. I will expect you.

CASCA. Do so. Farewell both.   (*Exit.*)

BRUTUS. What a blunt fellow is this grown to be!
290 He was quick mettle[51] when he went to school.

CASSIUS. So is he now in execution
Of any bold or noble enterprise,
However he puts on this tardy form.[52]
This rudeness is a sauce to his good wit,
295 Which gives men stomach to digest his words
With better appetite.

BRUTUS. And so it is. For this time I will leave you.
Tomorrow, if you please to speak with me,
I will come home to you; or if you will,
300 Come home to me, and I will wait for you.

CASSIUS. I will do so. Till then, think of the world.

                                    (*Exit* BRUTUS.)

Well, Brutus, thou art noble; yet I see
Thy honorable mettle may be wrought
From that it is disposed.[53] Therefore it is meet
305 That noble minds keep ever with their likes;
For who so firm that cannot be seduced?
Caesar doth bear me hard;[54] but he loves Brutus.
If I were Brutus now and he were Cassius,
He should not humor[55] me. I will this night,
310 In several hands, in at his windows throw,
As if they came from several citizens,
Writings, all tending to the great opinion
That Rome holds of his name; wherein obscurely
Caesar's ambition shall be glancèd at.[56]
315 And after this let Caesar seat him sure,
For we will shake him, or worse days endure.   (*Exit.*)

49 I'll ne'er . . . again :
Casca could not under-
stand Greek.

50 put to silence : forbidden to take any part in
public affairs.

51 quick mettle : able.

52 tardy form : stupid appearance.

53 Thy honorable . . . it is
disposed : You can be
changed.

54 bear me hard : does not
like me.

55 humor : convince.

56 glancèd at : hinted at.

Scene III. *Rome. A street.*[1]

Thunder and lightning. Enter, from opposite sides, CASCA,
with his sword drawn, and CICERO.

CICERO. Good even, Casca. Brought you Caesar home?
Why are you breathless? and why stare you so?
   CASCA. Are not you moved when all the sway of earth
Shakes like a thing unfirm? O Cicero,
5   I have seen tempests when the scolding winds
Have rived the knotty oaks, and I have seen
Th' ambitious ocean swell and rage and foam
To be exalted with the threat'ning clouds;
But never till tonight, never till now,
10   Did I go through a tempest dropping fire.
Either there is a civil strife in heaven,
Or else the world, too saucy with the gods,
Incenses them to send destruction.
   CICERO. Why, saw you any thing more wonderful?
15   CASCA. A common slave (you know him well by sight)
Held up his left hand, which did flame and burn
Like twenty torches joined; and yet his hand,
Not sensible of fire, remained unscorched.
Besides (I ha' not since put up my sword),
20   Against the Capitol I met a lion,
Who glared upon me, and went surly by
Without annoying me. And there were drawn
Upon a heap[2] a hundred ghastly women,
Transformèd with their fear, who swore they saw
25   Men, all in fire, walk up and down the streets.
And yesterday the bird of night[3] did sit
Even at noonday upon the market place,
Hooting and shrieking. When these prodigies
Do so conjointly meet,[4] let not men say
30   "These are their reasons—they are natural,"
For I believe they are portentous[5] things
Unto the climate[6] that they point upon.
   CICERO. Indeed it is a strange-disposèd time.[7]
But men may construe things after their fashion,
35   Clean from the purpose of the things themselves.[8]
Comes Caesar to the Capitol tomorrow?
   CASCA. He doth; for he did bid Antonius
Send word to you he would be there tomorrow.
   CICERO. Good night then, Casca. This disturbèd sky
Is not to walk in.
40   CASCA.   Farewell, Cicero.   (*Exit* CICERO.)
                  Enter CASSIUS.
   CASSIUS. Who's there?

1 Rome. A street : it is
now a few days later, the
night of March 14.

2 drawn . . . heap : standing close together.

3 bird of night : the owl.

4 conjointly meet : coin-
cide.

5 portentous (pŏr tĕn′təs) :
threatening; foreshadowing
danger.

6 climate : region.

7 strange-disposèd time :
unusual.

8 men may . . . themselves:
Men interpret signs according to their desires rather
than reasoning out their
true meaning.

JULIUS CAESAR

CASCA.   A Roman.

CASSIUS.   Casca, by your voice.

CASCA. Your ear is good. Cassius, what night is this!

CASSIUS. A very pleasing night to honest men.

CASCA. Who ever knew the heavens menace so?

45 CASSIUS. Those that have known the earth so full of faults.
For my part, I have walked about the streets,
Submitting me unto the perilous night,
And, thus unbracèd,[9] Casca, as you see,
Have bared my bosom to the thunder-stone;[10]
50 And when the cross blue lightning seemed to open
The breast of heaven, I did present myself
Even in the aim and very flash of it.

    CASCA. But wherefore did you so much tempt the heavens?
It is the part of men to fear and tremble
55 When the most mighty gods by tokens send
Such dreadful heralds to astonish us.

    CASSIUS. You are dull, Casca, and those sparks of life
That should be in a Roman you do want,
Or else you use not. You look pale, and gaze,
60 And put on fear, and cast yourself in wonder,
To see the strange impatience of the heavens;
But if you would consider the true cause—
Why all these fires, why all these gliding ghosts,
Why birds and beasts, from quality and kind;
65 Why old men fool and children calculate;[11]
Why all these things change from their ordinance,
Their natures, and preformèd faculties,
To monstrous[12] quality—why, you shall find
That heaven hath infused them with these spirits
70 To make them instruments of fear and warning
Unto some monstrous state.
Now could I, Casca, name to thee a man
Most like this dreadful night
That thunders, lightens, opens graves, and roars
75 As doth the lion in the Capitol;
A man no mightier than thyself or me
In personal action, yet prodigious grown[13]
And fearful, as these strange eruptions are.

    CASCA. 'Tis Caesar that you mean. Is it not, Cassius?

80 CASSIUS. Let it be who it is. For Romans now
Have thews and limbs like to their ancestors;
But woe the while! our fathers' minds are dead,
And we are governed with our mothers' spirits;
Our yoke and sufferance show us womanish.

85 CASCA. Indeed, they say the senators tomorrow
Mean to establish Caesar as a king,

9 unbracèd : coat open.

10 thunder-stone : Thunder was believed to release stones from heaven that would destroy whatever they hit.

11 old men . . . calculate : reverse of normal where old men do the thinking and children the playing.

12 monstrous : abnormal.

13 prodigious grown : grown huge.

WILLIAM SHAKESPEARE   629

And he shall wear his crown by sea and land
In every place save here in Italy.

    CASSIUS. I know where I will wear this dagger then;
90 Cassius from bondage will deliver Cassius.14
Therein, ye gods, you make the weak most strong;
Therein, ye gods, you tyrants do defeat.
Nor stony tower, nor walls of beaten brass,
Nor airless dungeon, nor strong links of iron,
95 Can be retentive to the strength of spirit;
But life, being weary of these worldly bars,
Never lacks power to dismiss itself.
If I know this, know all the world besides,
That part of tyranny that I do bear
I can shake off at pleasure.   *(Thunder still.)*
100   CASCA.   So can I.
So every bondman in his own hand bears
The power to cancel his captivity.

    CASSIUS. And why should Caesar be a tyrant then?
Poor man! I know he would not be a wolf
105 But that he sees the Romans are but sheep;
He were no lion, were not Romans hinds.15
Those that with haste will make a mighty fire
Begin it with weak straws. What trash is Rome,
What rubbish and what offal,16 when it serves
110 For the base matter to illuminate
So vile a thing as Caesar! But, O grief,
Where hast thou led me? I, perhaps, speak this
Before a willing bondman.17 Then I know
My answer must be made. But I am armed,
115 And dangers are to me indifferent.

    CASCA. You speak to Casca, and to such a man
That is no fleering18 telltale. Hold, my hand.
Be factious19 for redress of all these griefs,
And I will set this foot of mine as far
As who goes farthest.
120   CASSIUS.   There's a bargain made.
Now know you, Casca, I have moved already
Some certain of the noblest-minded Romans
To undergo with me an enterprise
Of honorable-dangerous consequence;
125 And I do know, by this they stay for me
In Pompey's Porch;20 for now, this fearful night,
There is no stir or walking in the streets,
And the complexion of the element
In favor's like the work we have in hand,
130 Most bloody, fiery, and most terrible.

14 will deliver Cassius : Cassius will kill himself with his dagger rather than become subject to Caesar.

15 hinds : female deer.

16 offal : refuse.

17 willing bondman : Cassius cleverly implies that Casca wants to be a slave to Caesar.

18 fleering : grinning.

19 Be factious : Form a group.

20 Pompey's Porch : the magnificent entrance to Pompey's Theater.

Enter CINNA.

CASCA. Stand close awhile, for here comes one in haste.

CASSIUS. 'Tis Cinna. I do know him by his gait.

He is a friend. Cinna, where haste you so?

CINNA. To find out you. Who's that? Metellus Cimber?

135　CASSIUS. No, it is Casca, one incorporate²¹

To our attempts. Am I not stayed²² for, Cinna?

CINNA. I am glad on't. What a fearful night is this!

There's two or three of us have seen strange sights.

CASSIUS. Am I not stayed for? Tell me.

CINNA.　　　　　　　　　　　　Yes, you are.

140　O Cassius, if you could

But win the noble Brutus to our party—

CASSIUS. Be you content. Good Cinna, take this paper

And look you lay it in the praetor's chair,²³

Where Brutus may but find it. And throw this

145　In at his window. Set this up with wax

Upon old Brutus' statue. All this done,

Repair²⁴ to Pompey's Porch, where you shall find us.

Is Decius Brutus and Trebonius there?

CINNA. All but Metellus Cimber, and he's gone

150　To seek you at your house. Well, I will hie²⁵

And so bestow these papers as you bade me.

CASSIUS. That done, repair to Pompey's Theater.

　　　　　　　　　　　　　　　(*Exit* CINNA.)

Come, Casca, you and I will yet ere day

See Brutus at his house. Three parts of him

155　Is ours already, and the man entire

Upon the next encounter yields him ours.

CASCA. O, he sits high in all the people's hearts;

And that which would appear offense in us,

His countenance, like richest alchemy,

160　Will change to virtue and to worthiness.²⁶

CASSIUS. Him and his worth and our great need of him

You have right well conceited.²⁷ Let us go,

For it is after midnight; and ere day

We will awake him and be sure of him.　　(*Exeunt.*)

21 incorporate : joined.

22 stayed : waited.

23 praetor's (prē′tərz) chair: the chair Brutus sits in as a judge.

24 Repair : come.

25 hie : hurry.

26 like richest . . . worthiness : As alchemy changes base metals into gold, so Brutus will change their murder of Caesar into honorable conduct.

27 conceited : thought; imagined.

WILLIAM SHAKESPEARE

631

The first public theater in London was built by James Burbage in 1576; others appeared soon after. Modeled on the innyard, they were open to the sky and round. Spectators stood around the three open sides of the stage or sat in the balconies (and sometimes on the stage itself). The flying flag indicates to the city that a play is being performed.

632   JULIUS CAESAR

Understanding the Play

ACT I

Scene i

1. What is the situation as the play opens?
2. What does Shakespeare reveal of events previous to the opening of the play through the action of this scene?
3. What does this scene reveal about the people of Rome?
4. What does Flavius mean by his last four lines?

Scene ii

1. What two different interpretations of Caesar are developed in the first twenty-four lines?
2. Why does Shakespeare introduce the Soothsayer into this scene? What is Caesar's reaction to him?
3. Summarize the argument Cassius uses to convince Brutus that Caesar is dangerous to Rome.
4. What attitude does Cassius have toward Caesar? Where is the first indication of this attitude?
5. Contrast Casca at the opening of the scene with Casca at the close. What attitude toward Caesar does this change reveal?
6. Contrast Brutus's and Cassius's feelings toward Caesar.
7. What does Cassius mean in lines 139-141?
8. What attitude does Caesar have toward Cassius? In what lines does he reveal this feeling?
9. What information do we get from Casca about events off stage?
10. What is the meaning of Cassius's last speech?

Scene iii

1. What devices does Shakespeare use in creating the atmosphere of this scene?
2. Contrast the arguments Cassius uses with Casca with the arguments he used with Brutus.
3. Before reading Act II summarize all the events leading up to the ides of March. What do you already know about Caesar, Brutus, Cassius, Casca, and Antony?

Act II

Scene I. *Rome.*

Enter BRUTUS *in his orchard.*[1]

BRUTUS. What, Lucius, ho!
I cannot by the progress of the stars
Give guess how near to day.[2] Lucius, I say!
I would it were my fault to sleep so soundly.
5 When, Lucius, when? Awake, I say! What, Lucius!

Enter LUCIUS.

LUCIUS. Called you, my lord?
BRUTUS. Get me a taper[3] in my study, Lucius.
When it is lighted, come and call me here.
LUCIUS. I will, my lord.   (*Exit.*)
10 BRUTUS. It must be by his death;[4] and for my part,
I know no personal cause to spurn at[5] him,
But for the general.[6] He would be crowned.
How that might change his nature, there's the question.
It is the bright day that brings forth the adder,[7]
15 And that craves wary walking. Crown him—that!
And then I grant we put a sting in him
That at his will he may do danger with.
Th' abuse of greatness is, when it disjoins
Remorse from power.[8] And to speak truth of Caesar,
20 I have not known when his affections swayed
More than his reason. But 'tis a common proof
That lowliness is young ambition's ladder,
Whereto the climber-upward turns his face;
But when he once attains the upmost round,
25 He then unto the ladder turns his back,
Looks in the clouds, scorning the base degrees
By which he did ascend. So Caesar may.
Then lest he may, prevent.[9] And since the quarrel
Will bear no color for the thing he is,
30 Fashion it thus:[10] that what he is, augmented,
Would run to these and these extremities;
And therefore think him as a serpent's egg,
Which, hatched, would as his kind grow mischievous,[11]
And kill him in the shell.

Enter LUCIUS.

35 LUCIUS. The taper burneth in your closet,[12] sir.
Searching the window for a flint, I found
This paper, thus sealed up; and I am sure
It did not lie there when I went to bed.

(*Gives him the letter.*)

1 orchard : The scene is the garden outside the home of Brutus. It is later the same night, just before dawn on March 15.
2 Lines 2-3 indicate that, although the storm has ceased, the sky is a blaze of meteors, and Brutus cannot tell the time (see 1.44).
3 taper : candle.
4 his death : Caesar's death.
5 spurn at : condemn.
6 for the general : for the public's sake.
7 adder : poisonous snake (refers to Caesar's growing power).
8 he may do . . . power : Caesar may forget mercy if he becomes all-powerful.
9 prevent : take measures to stop Caesar.
10 since the quarrel . . . it thus : Since our case cannot be justified by Caesar's actions, we shall explain it thus.
11 would as his . . . mischievous : would, like other snakes, become harmful.
12 closet : study.

Brutus. Get you to bed again; it is not day.

40 Is not tomorrow, boy, the ides of March?

    Lucius. I know not, sir.

    Brutus. Look in the calendar and bring me word.

    Lucius. I will, sir.   *(Exit.)*

    Brutus. The exhalations,[13] whizzing in the air,

45 Give so much light that I may read by them.

              (Opens the letter and reads.)

  "Brutus, thou sleep'st. Awake, and see thyself!

  Shall Rome, etc. Speak, strike, redress!"[14]

  "Brutus, thou sleep'st. Awake!"

  Such instigations have been often dropped

50 Where I have took them up.

  "Shall Rome, etc." Thus must I piece it out:[15]

  Shall Rome stand under one man's awe? What, Rome?

  My ancestors did from the streets of Rome

  The Tarquin drive when he was called a king.

55 "Speak, strike, redress!" Am I entreated

  To speak and strike? O Rome, I make thee promise,

  If the redress will follow, thou receivest

  Thy full petition[16] at the hand of Brutus!

            Enter Lucius.

    Lucius. Sir, March is wasted fifteen days.[17]

                 (Knock within.)

60 **Brutus.** 'Tis good. Go to the gate; somebody knocks.

               (Exit Lucius.*)*

  Since Cassius first did whet me against Caesar,

  I have not slept.

  Between the acting of a dreadful thing

  And the first motion, all the interim is

65 Like a phantasma or a hideous dream.

  The genius and the mortal instruments[18]

  Are then in council, and the state of man,

  Like to a little kingdom, suffers then

  The nature of an insurrection.

            Enter Lucius.

70 **Lucius.** Sir, 'tis your brother[19] Cassius at the door,

  Who doth desire to see you.

    Brutus.   Is he alone?

    Lucius. No, sir, there are moe[20] with him.

    Brutus.   Do you know them?

    Lucius. No, sir. Their hats are plucked about their ears

  And half their faces buried in their cloaks,

75 That by no means I may discover them

  By any mark of favor.[21]

    Brutus.   Let 'em enter.   *(Exit* Lucius.*)*

13 exhalations : meteors.

14 redress : set right.

15 piece it out : The note is incomplete, leaving Brutus to finish the thought. Note that he follows the reasoning that Cassius planted in his mind during Act I.

16 Thy full petition : the full measure of what you ask.

17 March . . . days : It is March 15.

18 genius . . . instruments: the spirit (or inner person) and the body.

19 brother : Cassius was married to Brutus's sister.

20 moe : others.

21 any mark of favor : their appearance.

They are the faction. O conspiracy,
Sham'st thou to show thy dang'rous brow by night,
When evils are most free? O, then by day
80 Where wilt thou find a cavern dark enough
To mask thy monstrous visage? Seek none, conspiracy.
Hide it in smiles and affability!
For if thou path, thy native semblance on,
Not Erebus itself were dim enough
85 To hide thee from prevention.[22]

Enter the conspirators, CASSIUS, CASCA, DECIUS, CINNA,
METELLUS CIMBER, *and* TREBONIUS.

CASSIUS. I think we are too bold upon your rest.
Good morrow, Brutus. Do we trouble you?
BRUTUS. I have been up this hour, awake all night.
Know I these men that come along with you?
90 CASSIUS. Yes, every man of them; and no man here
But honors you; and every one doth wish
You had but that opinion of yourself
Which every noble Roman bears of you.
This is Trebonius.
BRUTUS.   He is welcome hither.
95 CASSIUS. This, Decius Brutus.
BRUTUS.   He is welcome too.
CASSIUS. This, Casca; this, Cinna; and this, Metellus Cim-
   ber.
BRUTUS. They are all welcome.
What watchful cares do interpose themselves
Betwixt your eyes and night?[23]
100 CASSIUS. Shall I entreat a word?   (*They whisper.*)
DECIUS. Here lies the east. Doth not the day break here?
CASCA. No.
CINNA. O, pardon, sir, it doth; and yon gray lines
That fret[24] the clouds are messengers of day.
105 CASCA. You shall confess that you are both deceived.
Here, as I point my sword, the sun arises,
Which is a great way growing on[25] the south,
Weighing the youthful season[26] of the year.
Some two months hence, up higher toward the north
110 He first presents his fire; and the high east
Stands as the Capitol, directly here.[27]
BRUTUS. Give me your hands all over, one by one.
CASSIUS. And let us swear our resolution.
BRUTUS. No, not an oath. If not the face of men,[28]
115 The sufferance[29] of our souls, the time's abuse[30]—
If these be motives weak, break off betimes,[31]

22 if thou path . . . prevention : If you walk with
your natural feelings showing, Hades is not dark
enough to hide you and
keep you from being
stopped.

23 What watchful . . . night:
What problems prevent you
from sleeping?

24 fret : interlace.

25 growing on : toward.
26 youthful season : spring.
27 Lines 105-111 allow Cassius privately to invite Brutus to join the conspiracy.
28 face of men : feelings
and appearance of fellow-
citizens.
29 sufferance : suffering.
30 time's abuse : continual
violation of the Roman constitution.
31 betimes : promptly.

JULIUS CAESAR

And every man hence to his idle bed.
So let high-sighted[32] tyranny range on
Till each man drop by lottery.[33] But if these
120 (As I am sure they do) bear fire enough
To kindle cowards and to steel with valor
The melting spirits of women, then, countrymen,
What need we any spur but our own cause
To prick us to redress? what other bond
125 Than secret Romans that have spoke the word
And will not palter?[34] and what other oath
Than honesty to honesty engaged
That this shall be, or we will fall for it?
Swear priests and cowards and men cautelous,[35]
130 Old feeble carrions[36] and such suffering souls
That welcome wrongs; unto bad causes swear
Such creatures as men doubt; but do not stain
The even virtue[37] of our enterprise,
Nor th' insuppressive mettle[38] of our spirits,
135 To think that or[39] our cause or our performance
Did need an oath; when every drop of blood
That every Roman bears, and nobly bears,
Is guilty of a several bastardy[40]
If he do break the smallest particle
140 Of any promise that hath passed from him.
    CASSIUS. But what of Cicero? Shall we sound him?
I think he will stand very strong with us.
    CASCA. Let us not leave him out.
    CINNA.   No, by no means.
    METELLUS. O, let us have him! for his silver hairs
145 Will purchase us a good opinion
And buy men's voices to commend our deeds.
It shall be said his judgment ruled our hands.
Our youths and wildness shall no whit appear,
But all be buried in his gravity.[41]
150   BRUTUS. O, name him not! Let us not break with him;[42]
For he will never follow anything
That other men begin.
    CASSIUS.   Then leave him out.
    CASCA. Indeed he is not fit.
    DECIUS. Shall no man else be touched but only Caesar?
155   CASSIUS. Decius, well urged. I think it is not meet[43]
Mark Antony, so well beloved of Caesar,
Should outlive Caesar. We shall find of him
A shrewd contriver; and you know, his means,
If he improve[44] them, may well stretch so far
160 As to annoy us all; which to prevent,
Let Antony and Caesar fall together.

WILLIAM SHAKESPEARE   **637**

32 high-sighted : arrogant.
33 by lottery : as his turn comes up.

34 palter : trifle.

35 cautelous : overcautious.
36 carrions : physical wrecks.

37 even virtue : unblemished honor.
38 mettle : courage.
39 To think that or : by thinking that either.

40 bastardy : illegitimacy.

41 gravity : stability and authority.
42 O, name . . . with him : Let us not share our plan with him.

43 meet : suitable.

44 improve : use.

BRUTUS. Our course will seem too bloody, Caius Cassius,
To cut the head off and then hack the limbs,
Like wrath in death and envy afterwards;
165 For Antony is but a limb of Caesar.
Let us be sacrificers, but not butchers, Caius.
We all stand up against the spirit of Caesar,
And in the spirit of men there is no blood.
O that we then could come by Caesar's spirit
170 And not dismember Caesar! But, alas,
Caesar must bleed for it! And, gentle friends,
Let's kill him boldly, but not wrathfully;
Let's carve him as a dish fit for the gods,
Not hew him as a carcass fit for hounds.
175 And let our hearts, as subtle masters do,
Stir up their servants to an act of rage[45]
And after seem to chide 'em. This shall make
Our purpose necessary, and not envious;[46]
Which so appearing to the common eyes,
180 We shall be called purgers,[47] not murderers.
And for Mark Antony, think not of him;
For he can do no more than Caesar's arm
When Caesar's head is off.

CASSIUS. Yet I fear him;
For in the ingrafted[48] love he bears to Caesar—
185 **BRUTUS.** Alas, good Cassius, do not think of him!
If he love Caesar, all that he can do
Is to himself—take thought, and die for Caesar.[49]
And that were much he should;[50] for he is given
To sports, to wildness, and much company.
190 **TREBONIUS.** There is no fear in him. Let him not die;
For he will live, and laugh at this hereafter. *(Clock strikes.)*
BRUTUS. Peace! Count the clock.
CASSIUS. The clock hath stricken three.
TREBONIUS. 'Tis time to part.
CASSIUS. But it is doubtful yet
Whether Caesar will come forth today or no;
195 For he is superstitious grown of late,
Quite from the main opinion he held once
Of fantasy, of dreams, and ceremonies.[51]
It may be these apparent prodigies,[52]
The unaccustomed terror of this night,
200 And the persuasion of his augurers[53]
May hold him from the Capitol today.
DECIUS. Never fear that. If he be so resolved,
I can o'ersway him; for he loves to hear
That unicorns may be betrayed with trees[54]
205 And bears with glasses,[55] elephants with holes,[56]

45 let our . . . rage : Their hearts are not to be angry as their hands perform an act of rage.
46 envious : malicious.
47 purgers : cleaners; purifiers.

48 ingrafted : deep.

49 take thought . . . for Caesar : die of grief.
50 that were much he should : It would be surprising if he should do that.

51 Quite from . . . ceremonies : Until recently Caesar had not believed in omens.
52 apparent prodigies : striking signs.
53 augurers (ô′gər ərz) : fortunetellers.
54 unicorns . . . trees : By dodging behind a tree, a hunter can trick the unicorn into sticking his horn into the trunk.
55 glasses : mirrors used by hunters to distract the bear.
56 holes : deep pits hid by branches and leaves.

JULIUS CAESAR

Lions with toils,[57] and men with flatterers;
But when I tell him he hates flatterers,
He says he does, being then most flattered.
Let me work;
210 For I can give his humor the true bent
And I will bring him to the Capitol.
    CASSIUS. Nay, we will all of us be there to fetch[58] him.
    BRUTUS. By the eighth hour. Is that the uttermost?
    CINNA. Be that the uttermost, and fail not then.
215   METELLUS. Caius Ligarius doth bear Caesar hard,[59]
Who rated[60] him for speaking well of Pompey.
I wonder none of you have thought of him.
    BRUTUS. Now, good Metellus, go along by him.
He loves me well, and I have given him reasons.
220 Send him but hither, and I'll fashion[61] him.
    CASSIUS. The morning comes upon's. We'll leave you,
        Brutus.
And, friends, disperse yourselves; but all remember
What you have said and show yourselves true Romans.
    BRUTUS. Good gentlemen, look fresh and merrily.
225 Let not our looks put on our purposes,
But bear it as our Roman actors do,
With untired spirits and formal constancy.[62]
And so good morrow to you every one.
                    (*Exeunt all but* BRUTUS.)
Boy! Lucius! Fast asleep? It is no matter.
230 Enjoy the honey-heavy dew of slumber.
Thou hast no figures nor no fantasies
Which busy care draws in the brains of men;
Therefore thou sleep'st so sound.
                Enter PORTIA.
    PORTIA.   Brutus, my lord!
    BRUTUS. Portia! What mean you? Wherefore rise you now?
235 It is not for your health thus to commit
Your weak condition to the raw cold morning.
    PORTIA. Nor for yours neither. Y' have ungently,[63] Brutus,
Stole from my bed. And yesternight at supper
You suddenly arose and walked about,
240 Musing and sighing with your arms across;
And when I asked you what the matter was,
You stared upon me with ungentle looks.
I urged you further; then you scratched your head
And too impatiently stamped with your foot.
245 Yet I insisted; yet you answered not,
But with an angry wafture of your hand
Gave sign for me to leave you. So I did,
Fearing to strengthen that impatience

57 toils : nets.	
58 fetch : escort.	
59 bear Caesar hard : does not like Caesar.	
60 rated : reprimanded.	
61 fashion : convince.	
62 Let not . . . constancy : Act as you would normally.	
63 ungently : impolitely.	

Which seemed too much enkindled, and withal[64]
250 Hoping it was but an effect of humor,[65]
Which sometime hath his hour with every man.
It will not let you eat nor talk nor sleep,
And could it work so much upon your shape
As it hath much prevailed on your condition,[66]
255 I should not know you Brutus. Dear my lord,
Make me acquainted with your cause of grief.
    BRUTUS. I am not well in health, and that is all.
    PORTIA. Brutus is wise and, were he not in health,
He would embrace the means to come by it.
260   BRUTUS. Why, so I do. Good Portia, go to bed.
    PORTIA. Is Brutus sick, and is it physical[67]
To walk unbracèd and suck up the humors[68]
Of the dank morning? What, is Brutus sick,
And will he steal out of his wholesome bed
265 To dare the vile contagion of the night,[69]
And tempt the rheumy[70] and unpurgèd[71] air,
To add unto his sickness? No, my Brutus.
You have some sick offense within your mind,
Which by the right and virtue of my place
270 I ought to know of; and upon my knees
I charm you, by my once commended beauty,
By all your vows of love, and that great vow
Which did incorporate and make us one,
That you unfold to me, yourself, your half,
275 Why you are heavy—and what men tonight
Have had resort to you; for here have been
Some six or seven, who did hide their faces
Even from darkness.
    BRUTUS.   Kneel not, gentle Portia.
    PORTIA. I should not need if you were gentle Brutus.
280 Within the bond of marriage, tell me, Brutus,
Is it excepted I should know no secrets
That appertain to you? Am I yourself
But, as it were, in sort or limitation?[72]
To keep with you at meals, comfort your bed,
285 And talk to you sometimes? Dwell I but in the suburbs
Of your good pleasure? If it be no more,
Portia is Brutus' harlot,[73] not his wife.
    BRUTUS. You are my true and honorable wife,
As dear to me as are the ruddy drops
290 That visit my sad heart.
    PORTIA. If this were true, then should I know this secret.
I grant I am a woman; but withal
A woman that Lord Brutus took to wife.
I grant I am a woman; but withal

---

64 withal : at the same time.

65 an effect of humor : your mood.

66 condition : disposition.

67 physical : good for your health.

68 humors : dampness.

69 vile . . . night : Night air was supposed to be poisonous.

70 rheumy : damp.

71 unpurged : not yet purified by the sun's rays.

72 in sort or limitation : in a restricted way.

73 harlot : mistress.

295 A woman well-reputed, Cato's daughter.
Think you I am no stronger than my sex,
Being so fathered and so husbanded?
Tell me your counsels;[74] I will not disclose 'em.
I have made strong proof of my constancy,[75]
300 Giving myself a voluntary wound
Here, in the thigh. Can I bear that with patience,
And not my husband's secrets?
    BRUTUS.   O ye gods,
Render me worthy of this noble wife!   (Knock.)
Hark, hark! One knocks. Portia, go in awhile,
305 And by-and-by thy bosom shall partake
The secrets of my heart.
All my engagements I will construe[76] to thee,
All the charactery[77] of my sad brows.
Leave me with haste.   (Exit PORTIA.)
            Lucius, who's that knocks?

      Enter LUCIUS and CAIUS LIGARIUS.

310   LUCIUS. Here is a sick man that would speak with you.
    BRUTUS. Caius Ligarius, that Metellus spake of.
Boy, stand aside. Caius Ligarius, how?
    CAIUS. Vouchsafe good-morrow from a feeble tongue.
    BRUTUS. O, what a time have you chose out, brave Caius,
315 To wear a kerchief![78] Would you were not sick!
    CAIUS. I am not sick if Brutus have in hand
Any exploit worthy the name of honor.
    BRUTUS. Such an exploit have I in hand, Ligarius,
Had you a healthful ear to hear of it.
320   CAIUS. By all the gods that Romans bow before,
I here discard my sickness! (Throws off his kerchief.) Soul of
    Rome!
Brave son, derived from honorable loins![79]
Thou like an exorcist[80] hast conjured up
My mortified spirit.[81] Now bid me run,
325 And I will strive with things impossible;
Yea, get the better of them. What's to do?
    BRUTUS. A piece of work that will make sick men whole.
    CAIUS. But are not some whole that we must make sick?
    BRUTUS. That must we also. What it is, my Caius,
330 I shall unfold to thee as we are going
To whom it must be done.
    CAIUS.   Set on[82] your foot,
And with a heart new-fired I follow you,
To do I know not what; but it sufficeth
That Brutus leads me on.   (Thunder.)
    BRUTUS.   Follow me then.   (Exeunt.)

74 counsels : secrets.
75 constancy : faithfulness.

76 engagements I will construe : affairs I will explain.
77 charactery : meaning.

78 wear a kerchief : Ligarius, according to the custom of the time, was wearing a kerchief around his head to protect it from draughts during an illness.

79 derived . . . loins : descendant of the Brutus who once freed Rome.
80 exorcist (ĕk'sôr sĭst) : one who calls up spirits.
81 mortified spirit : paralyzed energy.

82 Set on : advance.

WILLIAM SHAKESPEARE   **641**

Scene II. *Rome.* CAESAR's *house.*

Thunder and lightning. Enter CAESAR, *in his nightgown.*[1]

CAESAR. Nor heaven nor earth have been at peace tonight.
Thrice hath Calpurnia in her sleep cried out
"Help ho! They murther Caesar!" Who's within?[2]

Enter a SERVANT.

SERVANT. My lord?

5   CAESAR. Go bid the priests do present sacrifice,
And bring me their opinions of success.[3]
    SERVANT. I will, my lord.   *(Exit.)*

Enter CALPURNIA.

CALPURNIA. What mean you, Caesar? Think you to walk
   forth?
You shall not stir out of your house today.

10   CAESAR. Caesar shall forth. The things that threatened me
Ne'er looked but on my back. When they shall see
The face of Caesar, they are vanished.
    CALPURNIA. Caesar, I never stood on ceremonies,[4]
Yet now they fright me. There is one within,

15 Besides the things that we have heard and seen,
Recounts most horrid sights seen by the watch.
A lioness hath whelpèd in the streets,
And graves have yawned and yielded up their dead.
Fierce fiery warriors fought upon the clouds
20 In ranks and squadrons and right form of war,
Which drizzled blood upon the Capitol.
The noise of battle hurtled in the air,
Horses did neigh, and dying men did groan,
And ghosts did shriek and squeal about the streets.
25 O Caesar, these things are beyond all use,[5]
And I do fear them!

    CAESAR.   What can be avoided
Whose end is purposed by the mighty gods?
Yet Caesar shall go forth; for these predictions
Are to the world in general as to Caesar.
30   CALPURNIA. When beggars die there are no comets seen;
The heavens themselves blaze forth the death of princes.
    CAESAR. Cowards die many times before their deaths;
The valiant never taste of death but once.
Of all the wonders that I yet have heard,
35 It seems to me most strange that men should fear,
Seeing that death, a necessary end,
Will come when it will come.

Enter a SERVANT.

        What say the augurers?

Servant. They would not have you to stir forth today.
Plucking the entrails[6] of an offering forth,

6 entrails : inner parts.

40 They could not find a heart within the beast.
      Caesar. The gods do this in shame of cowardice.
Caesar should be a beast without a heart
If he should stay at home today for fear.
No, Caesar shall not. Danger knows full well

45 That Caesar is more dangerous than he.
We are two lions littered in one day,
And I the elder and more terrible,
And Caesar shall go forth.
      Calpurnia.   Alas, my lord!
Your wisdom is consumed in confidence.

50 Do not go forth today. Call it my fear
That keeps you in the house and not your own.
We'll send Mark Antony to the Senate House,
And he shall say you are not well today.
Let me upon my knee prevail in this.

55   **Caesar.** Mark Antony shall say I am not well,
And for thy humor[7] I will stay at home.

7 humor : whim.

Enter **Decius.**

Here's Decius Brutus; he shall tell them so.
      Decius. Caesar, all hail! Good morrow, worthy Caesar!
I come to fetch you to the Senate House.

60   **Caesar.** And you are come in very happy time[8]
To bear my greeting to the senators

8 in very happy time : at the right moment.

And tell them that I will not come today.
Cannot, is false; and that I dare not, falser:
I will not come today. Tell them so, Decius.

65   **Calpurnia.** Say he is sick.
      Caesar.   Shall Caesar send a lie?
Have I in conquest stretched mine arm so far
To be afeard to tell graybeards the truth?
Decius, go tell them Caesar will not come.
      Decius. Most mighty Caesar, let me know some cause,

70 Lest I be laughed at when I tell them so.
      Caesar. The cause is in my will: I will not come.
That is enough to satisfy the Senate;
But for your private satisfaction,
Because I love you, I will let you know.

75 Calpurnia here, my wife, stays[9] me at home.

9 stays : keeps.

She dreamt tonight she saw my statuë,
Which, like a fountain with an hundred spouts,
Did run pure blood; and many lusty Romans
Came smiling and did bathe their hands in it.

80 And these does she apply for warnings and portents

WILLIAM SHAKESPEARE   **643**

And evils imminent, and on her knee
Hath begged that I will stay at home today.

    DECIUS. This dream is all amiss interpreted;
It was a vision fair and fortunate.
85 Your statue spouting blood in many pipes,
In which so many smiling Romans bathed,
Signifies that from you great Rome shall suck
Reviving blood, and that great men shall press
For tinctures, stains, relics, and cognizance.[10]
90 This by Calpurnia's dream is signified.

    CAESAR. And this way have you well expounded it.

    DECIUS. I have, when you have heard what I can say;
And know it now. The Senate have concluded
To give this day a crown to mighty Caesar.
95 If you shall send them word you will not come,
Their minds may change. Besides, it were a mock
Apt to be rendered,[11] for some one to say
"Break up the Senate till another time,
When Caesar's wife shall meet with better dreams."
100 If Caesar hide himself, shall they not whisper
"Lo, Caesar is afraid"?
Pardon me, Caesar; for my dear dear love
To your proceeding[12] bids me tell you this,
And reason to my love is liable.[13]
105   CAESAR. How foolish do your fears seem now, Calpurnia!
I am ashamèd I did yield to them.
Give me my robe, for I will go.

Enter BRUTUS, CAIUS LIGARIUS, CASCA, TREBONIUS,
CINNA, *and* PUBLIUS.

And look where Publius is come to fetch me.

    PUBLIUS. Good morrow, Caesar.

    CAESAR.   Welcome, Publius.
110 What, Brutus, are you stirred so early too?
Good morrow, Casca. Caius Ligarius,
Caesar was ne'er so much your enemy[14]
As that same ague[15] which hath made you lean.
What is't o'clock?

    BRUTUS.   Caesar, 'tis strucken eight.
115   CAESAR. I thank you for your pains and courtesy.

Enter ANTONY.

See! Antony, that revels long a-nights,
Is notwithstanding up. Good morrow, Antony.

    ANTONY. So to most noble Caesar.

    CAESAR.   Bid them prepare within.
I am to blame to be thus waited for.
120 Now, Cinna. Now, Metellus. What, Trebonius;

10 cognizance : a badge to show that one is a subject of some nobleman (here of Caesar).

11 Apt to be rendered : ready to be spoken.

12 proceeding : advancement.

13 reason to my love is liable : What is reasonable or proper is subordinate to my love.

14 enemy : Caesar had just pardoned Ligarius for his support of Pompey.

15 ague (ā′gū) : illness.

I have an hour's talk in store for you;
Remember that you call on me today;
Be near me, that I may remember you.
    TREBONIUS. Caesar, I will. (*Aside.*) And so near will I be
125 That your best friends shall wish I had been further.
    CAESAR. Good friends, go in and taste some wine with me,
And we (like friends) will straightway go together.
    BRUTUS (*aside*). That every like is not the same,[16] O Caesar,
The heart of Brutus erns[17] to think upon.   (*Exeunt.*)

> 16. That every . . . same :
> that every seeming friend
> is not a true friend.
> 17 erns : sorrows.

Scene III. *Rome. A street near the Capitol.*

Enter ARTEMIDORUS, *reading a paper.*

    ARTEMIDORUS. Caesar, beware of Brutus; take heed of Cassius; come not near Casca; have an eye to Cinna; trust not Trebonius; mark well Metellus Cimber; Decius Brutus loves thee not; thou hast wronged Caius Ligarius. There is but one
5 mind in all these men, and it is bent against Caesar. If thou beest not immortal, look about you. Security gives way to conspiracy.[1] The mighty gods defend thee!
                          Thy lover,[2]
                           ARTEMIDORUS.

> 1 Security . . . conspiracy :
> Being unaware of danger
> makes way for plots against
> you.
> 2 lover : devoted friend.
> 3 suitor : one who makes a
> request.
> 4 emulation : envy.

10 Here will I stand till Caesar pass along
And as a suitor[3] will I give him this.
My heart laments that virtue cannot live
Out of the teeth of emulation.[4]
If thou read this, O Caesar, thou mayst live;
15 If not, the Fates with traitors do contrive.   (*Exit.*)

Scene IV. *Before the house of* BRUTUS.

Enter PORTIA *and* LUCIUS.

    PORTIA. I prithee, boy, run to the Senate House.
Stay not to answer me, but get thee gone!
Why dost thou stay?
    LUCIUS.   To know my errand, madam.
    PORTIA. I would have had thee there and here again
5 Ere I can tell thee what thou shouldst do there.
(*Aside.*) O constancy,[1] be strong upon my side,
Set a huge mountain 'tween my heart and tongue!
I have a man's mind, but a woman's might.
How hard it is for women to keep counsel![2]
Art thou here yet?
10   LUCIUS.   Madam what should I do?
Run to the Capitol and nothing else?
And so return to you and nothing else?

> 1 constancy : firmness.

> 2 counsel : a secret.

Portia. Yes, bring me word, boy, if thy lord look well,
For he went sickly forth; and take good note
15 What Caesar doth, what suitors press to him.
Hark, boy! What noise is that?
   Lucius. I hear none, madam.
   Portia.   Prithee listen well.
I heard a bustling rumor³ like a fray,⁴
And the wind brings it from the Capitol.
20   **Lucius.** Sooth,⁵ madam, I hear nothing.

               Enter the **Soothsayer.**

   Portia. Come hither, fellow. Which way hast thou been?
   Soothsayer. At mine own house, good lady.
   Portia. What is't o'clock?
   Soothsayer.   About the ninth hour, lady.
   Portia. Is Caesar yet gone to the Capitol?
25   **Soothsayer.** Madam, not yet. I go to take my stand,
To see him pass on to the Capitol.
   Portia. Thou hast some suit to Caesar, hast thou not?
   Soothsayer. That I have, lady, if it will please Caesar
To be so good to Caesar as to hear me:
30 I shall beseech him to befriend himself.
   Portia. Why, know'st thou any harm's intended towards
    him?
   Soothsayer. None that I know will be, much that I fear may
    chance.
Good morrow to you. Here the street is narrow.
The throng that follows Caesar at the heels,
35 Of senators, of praetors,⁶ common suitors,
Will crowd a feeble man almost to death.
I'll get me to a place more void⁷ and there
Speak to great Caesar as he comes along.   (*Exit.*)
   Portia. I must go in. Ay me, how weak a thing
40 The heart of woman is! O Brutus,
The heavens speed thee in thine enterprise!
Sure the boy heard me.—Brutus hath a suit
That Caesar will not grant.⁸—O, I grow faint.—
Run, Lucius, and commend me to my lord;⁹
45 Say I am merry.¹⁰ Come to me again
And bring me word what he doth say to thee.
                      (*Exeunt severally.*)

3 rumor : noise.
4 fray : fight.
5 Sooth : truly.

6 praetors : elected rulers.

7 void : empty.

8 Brutus . . . grant : spoken so that Lucius will not become suspicious.
9 commend me to my lord: Give him my love and best wishes.
10 merry : in good spirits (*not* gay).

The conspiracy scene in Julius Caesar *might have looked like this in Elizabethan times. Note the few props. Shakespeare usually is careful to indicate the time and place of his scenes through dialogue, but the lantern carried by one of the conspirators also indicates to the audience that it is night.*

WILLIAM SHAKESPEARE

Understanding the Play

ACT II

Scene i

1. Paraphrase Brutus's speech beginning with line 10. How successful has Cassius been in convincing Brutus?
2. Find in Brutus's lines his motives for joining the conspiracy against Caesar.
3. What is the purpose of the visit of the conspirators to Brutus?
4. What is the purpose of Brutus's speech beginning on line 114?
5. Where does Brutus first demonstrate his power over Cassius?
6. What other argument with Cassius does Brutus win?
7. Paraphrase Brutus's speech beginning with line 162. Why is Brutus so concerned about the way Caesar is executed and the appearance of the murder?
8. What do you learn about Brutus from his scene with Portia? What is on Portia's mind?
9. What do you learn about Brutus from his scene with Ligarius?
10. Do the final actions of the scene reveal a victory for Brutus's private life or for his public life? Explain.

Scene ii

1. What are Caesar and Calpurnia discussing? What do Caesar's remarks reveal about his attitude toward superstition?
2. How is Decius's part in this scene connected to his part in Act II, scene i? Why is Decius successful in his assignment? What does his success show about Caesar?
3. Contrast Calpurnia with Portia. Contrast Brutus's and Caesar's attitudes toward their wives.

Scene iii

1. What is the purpose of this scene?

Scene iv

1. What knowledge does Portia have in this scene that she did not have in Act II, scene i?
2. What is the dramatic purpose of again introducing the Soothsayer in this scene?

Act III

Scene I. *Rome. A street before the Capitol.*

Flourish. Enter Caesar, Brutus, Cassius, Casca, Decius, Metellus, Trebonius, Cinna, Antony, Lepidus, Artemidorus,
Popilius, Publius, *and the* Soothsayer.

Caesar. The ides of March are come.
Soothsayer. Ay, Caesar, but not gone.
Artemidorus. Hail, Caesar! Read this schedule.[1]
Decius. Trebonius doth desire you to o'erread
5   (At your best leisure) this his humble suit.
     Artemidorus. O Caesar, read mine first; for mine's a suit
That touches Caesar nearer. Read it, great Caesar!
     Caesar. What touches us[2] ourself shall be last served.
     Artemidorus. Delay not, Caesar! Read it instantly!
     Caesar. What, is the fellow mad?
10   Publius.   Sirrah,[3] give place.
     Cassius. What, urge you your petitions in the street?
Come to the Capitol.

      (Caesar *enters the Capitol, the rest following.*)

     Popilius. I wish your enterprise today may thrive.
     Cassius. What enterprise, Popilius?
     Popilius.   Fare you well.

       (*Advances to* Caesar.)

15   Brutus. What said Popilius Lena?
     Cassius. He wished today our enterprise might thrive.
I fear our purpose is discovered.
     Brutus. Look how he makes to Caesar. Mark him.
     Cassius. Casca, be sudden, for we fear prevention.
20 Brutus, what shall be done? If this be known,
Cassius or Caesar never shall turn back,
For I will slay myself.
     Brutus.   Cassius, be constant.[4]
Popilius Lena speaks not of our purposes;
For look, he smiles, and Caesar doth not change.
25   Cassius. Trebonius knows his time; for look you, Brutus,
He draws Mark Antony out of the way.

      (*Exeunt* Antony *and* Trebonius.)

     Decius. Where is Metellus Cimber? Let him go
And presently prefer his suit[5] to Caesar.
     Brutus. He is addressed.[6] Press near and second him.
30   Cinna. Casca, you are the first that rears your hand.
     Caesar. Are we all ready? What is now amiss
That Caesar and his Senate must redress?

1 schedule : document.

2 us : Caesar uses the royal
"we" although he had not
yet received the crown.

3 Sirrah : a contemptuous
form of *sir.*

4 constant : calm.

5 prefer his suit : make his
request.
6 addressed : ready.

WILLIAM SHAKESPEARE   **649**

METELLUS. Most high, most mighty, and most puissant[7] Caesar,

Metellus Cimber throws before thy seat

An humble heart. *(Kneels.)*

35 CAESAR.   I must prevent thee, Cimber.

These couchings and these lowly courtesies

Might fire the blood of ordinary men

And turn preordinance and first decree[8]

Into the law of children.[9] Be not fond[10]

40 To think that Caesar bears such rebel blood

That will be thawed from the true quality

With that which melteth fools—I mean, sweet words,

Low-crooked curtsies, and base spaniel fawning.

Thy brother by decree is banishèd.

45 If thou dost bend and pray and fawn for him,

I spurn thee like a cur out of my way.

Know, Caesar doth not wrong, nor without cause

Will he be satisfied.

METELLUS. Is there no voice more worthy than my own,

50 To sound more sweetly in great Caesar's ear

For the repealing of my banished brother?

BRUTUS. I kiss thy hand, but not in flattery, Caesar,

Desiring thee that Publius Cimber may

Have an immediate freedom of repeal.

CAESAR. What, Brutus?

55 CASSIUS.   Pardon, Caesar! Caesar, pardon!

As low as to thy foot doth Cassius fall

To beg enfranchisement for Publius Cimber.

CAESAR. I could be well moved, if I were as you;

If I could pray to move, prayers would move me:

60 But I am constant as the Northern Star,

Of whose true-fixed and resting quality

There is no fellow in the firmament.

The skies are painted with unnumbered sparks,

They are all fire, and every one doth shine;

65 But there's but one in all doth hold his place.

So in the world: 'tis furnished well with men,

And men are flesh and blood, and apprehensive;[11]

Yet in the number I do know but one

That unassailable holds on his rank,[12]

70 Unshaked of motion; and that I am he,

Let me a little show it, even in this—

That I was constant Cimber should be banished

And constant do remain to keep him so.

CINNA. O Caesar!

CAESAR.   Hence! Wilt thou lift up Olympus?[13]

DECIUS. Great Caesar!

---

7 puissant (pū'ə sənt) : powerful.

8 preordinance and first decree : Caesar's original decision.

9 law of children : law easily changed.

10 fond : foolish.

11 apprehensive : ruled by feelings.

12 holds on his rank : maintains his course.

13 lift up Olympus (ō lĭm'pəs) : change the minds of the gods.

JULIUS CAESAR

75 CAESAR.   Doth not Brutus bootless kneel?[14]
CASCA. Speak hands for me![15]
                    (*They stab* CAESAR—CASCA *first,* BRUTUS *last*).
CAESAR. Et tu, Brute?[16]—Then fall Caesar!   (*Dies.*)
CINNA. Liberty! Freedom! Tyranny is dead!
Run hence, proclaim, cry it about the streets!
80 CASSIUS. Some to the common pulpits[17] and cry out
"Liberty, freedom, and enfranchisement!"
BRUTUS. People and Senators, be not affrighted.
Fly not; stand still. Ambition's debt is paid.
CASCA. Go to the pulpit, Brutus.
DECIUS.   And Cassius too.
85 BRUTUS. Where's Publius?
CINNA. Here, quite confounded[18] with this mutiny.
METELLUS. Stand fast together, lest some friend of Caesar's
Should chance—
BRUTUS. Talk not of standing! Publius, good cheer.
90 There is no harm intended to your person
Nor to no Roman else. So tell them, Publius.
CASSIUS. And leave us, Publius, lest that the people,
Rushing on us, should do your age some mischief.
BRUTUS. Do so; and let no man abide[19] this deed
But we the doers.

                    Enter TREBONIUS.

95 CASSIUS.   Where is Antony?
TREBONIUS. Fled to his house amazed.
Men, wives, and children stare, cry out, and run,
As it were doomsday.
BRUTUS.   Fates, we will know your pleasures.
That we shall die, we know; 'tis but the time,
100 And drawing days out, that men stand upon.[20]
CASSIUS. Why, he that cuts off twenty years of life
Cuts off so many years of fearing death.
BRUTUS. Grant that, and then is death a benefit.
So are we Caesar's friends, that have abridged
105 His time of fearing death. Stoop, Romans, stoop,
And let us bathe our hands in Caesar's blood
Up to the elbows and besmear our swords.
Then walk we forth, even to the market place,
And waving our red weapons o'er our heads,
110 Let's all cry "Peace, freedom, and liberty!"
CASSIUS. Stoop then and wash. How many ages hence
Shall this our lofty scene be acted over
In states unborn and accents yet unknown!
BRUTUS. How many times shall Caesar bleed in sport,[21]
115 That now on Pompey's basis[22] lies along
No worthier than the dust!

WILLIAM SHAKESPEARE   **651**

14 Brutus bootless kneel :
If Brutus, my friend, kneels
in vain, why do you try to
change me?

15 Speak . . . me : Casca
has not spoken, but now
uses his hands to plant the
first dagger in Caesar.

16 Et tu, Brute?
(ĕt tū brōō′tĭ) : And you, too,
Brutus?

17 pulpits : platforms for
speakers.

18 confounded : confused.

19 abide : be punished for.

20 stand upon : find important.

21 sport : dramatic plays.
22 Pompey's basis : the
foot of Pompey's statue.

CASSIUS.   So oft as that shall be,
So often shall the knot of us be called
The men that gave their country liberty.
   DECIUS. What, shall we forth?
   CASSIUS.   Ay, every man away.
120 Brutus shall lead, and we will grace his heels
With the most boldest and best hearts of Rome.

                   Enter a SERVANT.

   BRUTUS. Soft! who comes here? A friend of Antony's.
   SERVANT. Thus, Brutus, did my master bid me kneel;
Thus did Mark Antony bid me fall down;
125 And being prostrate, thus he bade me say:
Brutus is noble, wise, valiant, and honest;
Caesar was mighty, bold, royal, and loving.
Say I love Brutus and I honor him;
Say I feared Caesar, honored him, and loved him.
130 If Brutus will vouchsafe that Antony
May safely come to him and be resolved²³   23 be resolved : receive an
How Caesar hath deserved to lie in death,   explanation.
Mark Antony shall not love Caesar dead
So well as Brutus living; but will follow
135 The fortunes and affairs of noble Brutus
Thorough the hazards of this untrod state²⁴   24 Thorough . . . untrod
With all true faith. So says my master Antony.   state : through the untried
   BRUTUS. Thy master is a wise and valiant Roman.   conditions of a new gov-
I never thought him worse.   ernment.
140 Tell him, so please him come unto this place,
He shall be satisfied and, by my honor,
Depart untouched.
   SERVANT.   I'll fetch him presently.   (*Exit.*)
   BRUTUS. I know that we shall have him well to friend.
   CASSIUS. I wish we may. But yet have I a mind
145 That fears him much; and my misgiving still
Falls shrewdly to the purpose.²⁵   25 my misgiving . . . pur-
                                                     pose : My misgivings usu-
                   Enter ANTONY.   ally fall unpleasantly near
                                                     the truth.
   BRUTUS. But here comes Antony. Welcome, Mark Antony.
   ANTONY. O mighty Caesar!²⁶ dost thou lie so low? 26 O mighty Caesar : On
Are all thy conquests, glories, triumphs, spoils,   seeing Caesar, Antony ig-
150 Shrunk to this little measure? Fare thee well.   nores the conspirators and
I know not, gentlemen, what you intend,   speaks first to the dead
Who else must be let blood, who else is rank.   body.
If I myself, there is no hour so fit
As Caesar's death's hour; nor no instrument
155 Of half that worth as those your swords, made rich
With the most noble blood of all this world.
I do beseech ye, if you bear me hard,
Now, whilst your purpled hands do reek and smoke,

Fulfill your pleasure. Live a thousand years,
160 I shall not find myself so apt[27] to die;
No place will please me so, no mean of death,
As here by Caesar, and by you cut off,
The choice and master spirits of this age.
    BRUTUS. O Antony, beg not your death of us!
165 Though now we must appear bloody and cruel,
As by our hands and this our present act
You see we do, yet see you but our hands
And this the bleeding business they have done.
Our hearts you see not. They are pitiful;
170 And pity to the general wrong of Rome
(As fire drives out fire, so pity pity)[28]
Hath done this deed on Caesar. For your part,
To you our swords have leaden points, Mark Antony.
Our arms in strength of malice, and our hearts
175 Of brothers' temper,[29] do receive you in
With all kind love, good thoughts, and reverence.
    CASSIUS. Your voice shall be as strong as any man's
In the disposing of new dignities.
    BRUTUS. Only be patient till we have appeased
180 The multitude, beside themselves with fear,
And then we will deliver you the cause
Why I, that did love Caesar when I struck him,
Have thus proceeded.
    ANTONY.   I doubt not of your wisdom.
Let each man render me his bloody hand.
185 First, Marcus Brutus, will I shake with you;
Next, Caius Cassius, do I take your hand;
Now, Decius Brutus, yours; now yours, Metellus;
Yours, Cinna; and, my valiant Casca, yours.
Though last, not least in love, yours, good Trebonius.
190 Gentlemen all—Alas, what shall I say?
My credit[30] now stands on such slippery ground
That one of two bad ways you must conceit me,[31]
Either a coward or a flatterer.
That I did love thee, Caesar, O, 'tis true!
195 If then thy spirit look upon us now,
Shall it not grieve thee dearer[32] than thy death
To see thy Antony making his peace,
Shaking the bloody fingers of thy foes,
Most noble! in the presence of thy corse?[33]
200 Had I as many eyes as thou hast wounds,
Weeping as fast as they stream forth thy blood,
It would become me better than to close
In terms[34] of friendship with thine enemies.
Pardon me, Julius! Here wast thou bayed,[35] brave hart;[36]

27 apt : ready.

28 so pity pity : so pity drives out pity.

29 Our arms . . . brothers' temper : Although our arms show hatred, our hearts receive you in brotherly kindness.

30 credit : reputation.
31 conceit me : regard me.

32 dearer : more keenly.

33 corse : corpse.

34 close in terms : come to terms.
35 bayed : brought to bay.
36 hart : a male deer.

205 Here didst thou fall; and here thy hunters stand,
Signed in thy spoil,[37] and crimsoned in thy lethe.[38]
O world, thou wast the forest to this hart;
And this indeed, O world, the heart of thee!
How like a deer, stroken[39] by many princes,
210 Dost thou here lie!
    CASSIUS. Mark Antony—
    ANTONY.   Pardon me, Caius Cassius.
The enemies of Caesar shall say this;
Then, in a friend, it is cold modesty.
    CASSIUS. I blame you not for praising Caesar so;
215 But what compact mean you to have with us?
Will you be pricked[40] in number of our friends,
Or shall we on, and not depend on you?
    ANTONY. Therefore I took your hands; but was indeed
Swayed from the point by looking down on Caesar.
220 Friends am I with you all, and love you all,
Upon this hope, that you shall give me reasons
Why and wherein Caesar was dangerous.
    BRUTUS. Or else were this a savage spectacle.
Our reasons are so full of good regard[41]
225 That were you, Antony, the son of Caesar,
You should be satisfied.
    ANTONY.   That's all I seek;
And am moreover suitor that I may
Produce his body to the market place
And in the pulpit, as becomes a friend,
230 Speak in the order of his funeral.
    BRUTUS. You shall, Mark Antony.
    CASSIUS.   Brutus, a word with you.
(*Aside to* BRUTUS.) You know not what you do. Do not consent
    sent
That Antony speak in his funeral.
Know you how much the people may be moved
235 By that which he will utter?
    BRUTUS (*aside to* CASSIUS). By your pardon—
I will myself into the pulpit first
And show the reason of our Caesar's death.
What Antony shall speak, I will protest[42]
240 He speaks by leave and by permission;
And that we are contented Caesar shall
Have all true rites and lawful ceremonies.
It shall advantage more than do us wrong.
    CASSIUS (*aside to* BRUTUS). I know not what may fall.[43] I
    like it not.
245 BRUTUS. Mark Antony, here, take you Caesar's body.
You shall not in your funeral speech blame us,

37 Signed in thy spoil :
marked with thy blood.
38 lethe (lē′thĭ) : death.
(Lethe was a river in Hades).
39 stroken : struck down.

40 pricked : counted.

41 full of good regard :
convincing.

42 protest : declare.

43 fall : happen.

But speak all good you can devise of Caesar;
And say you do't by our permission.
Else shall you not have any hand at all
250 About his funeral. And you shall speak
In the same pulpit whereto I am going,
After my speech is ended.

ANTONY.   Be it so.
I do desire no more.

BRUTUS. Prepare the body then, and follow us.

                        (*Exeunt all but* ANTONY.)

255   ANTONY. O, pardon me, thou bleeding piece of earth,
That I am meek and gentle with these butchers!
Thou art the ruins of the noblest man
That ever livèd in the tide of times.
Woe to the hand that shed this costly blood!
260 Over thy wounds now do I prophesy
(Which, like dumb mouths, do ope their ruby lips
To beg the voice and utterance of my tongue),
A curse shall light upon the limbs of men;
Domestic fury and fierce civil strife
265 Shall cumber44 all the parts of Italy;
Blood and destruction shall be so in use
And dreadful objects so familiar
That mothers shall but smile when they behold
Their infants quartered with the hands of war,
270 All pity choked with custom of fell deeds,45
And Caesar's spirit, ranging for revenge,
With Ate46 by his side come hot from hell,
Shall in these confines with a monarch's voice
Cry "Havoc!"47 and let slip48 the dogs of war,
275 That this foul deed shall smell above the earth
With carrion49 men, groaning for burial.

                    Enter a SERVANT.

You serve Octavius Caesar, do you not?
SERVANT. I do, Mark Antony.
ANTONY. Caesar did write for him to come to Rome.
280   SERVANT. He did receive his letters and is coming,
And bid me say to you by word of mouth—
O Caesar!
ANTONY. Thy heart is big. Get thee apart and weep.
Passion, I see, is catching; for mine eyes,
285 Seeing those beads of sorrow stand in thine,
Began to water. Is thy master coming?
SERVANT. He lies tonight within seven leagues of Rome.
ANTONY. Post back with speed and tell him what hath chanced.
Here is a mourning Rome, a dangerous Rome,

44 cumber : burden.

45 with custom of fell deeds : being accustomed to savage deeds.
46 Ate (ā′tǐ) : goddess of vengeance.
47 Havoc : Kill everyone.
48 let slip : release.
49 carrion : decaying.

WILLIAM SHAKESPEARE   655

290 No Rome of safety for Octavius yet.
    Hie hence and tell him so. Yet stay awhile.
    Thou shalt not back till I have borne this corse
    Into the market place. There shall I try
    In my oration how the people take
295 The cruel issue[50] of these bloody men;
    According to the which thou shalt discourse
    To young Octavius of the state of things.
    Lend me your hand.   (*Exeunt with* CAESAR's *body.*)

50 issue : deed.

Scene II. *Rome. The Forum.*[1]

Enter BRUTUS *and* CASSIUS, *with the* PLEBEIANS.

PLEBEIANS. We will be satisfied![2] Let us be satisfied!
BRUTUS. Then follow me and give me audience, friends.
Cassius, go you into the other street
And part the numbers.
5   Those that will hear me speak, let 'em stay here;
  Those that will follow Cassius, go with him;
  And public reasons shall be renderèd
  Of Caesar's death.
    1 PLEBEIAN.   I will hear Brutus speak.
    2 PLEBEIAN. I will hear Cassius, and compare their reasons
10 When severally[3] we hear them renderèd.

1 The Forum : the public square or market place.

2 satisfied : informed.

3 severally : separately.

        (*Exit* CASSIUS, *with some of the* PLEBEIANS.
           BRUTUS *goes into the pulpit.*)

    3 PLEBEIAN. The noble Brutus is ascended. Silence!
    BRUTUS. Be patient till the last.[4]
Romans, countrymen, and lovers,[5] hear me for my cause, and
be silent, that you may hear. Believe me for mine honor, and
15 have respect to mine honor,[6] that you may believe. Censure[7]
me in your wisdom, and awake your senses,[8] that you may the
better judge. If there be any in this assembly, any dear friend
of Caesar's, to him I say that Brutus' love to Caesar was no
less than his. If then that friend demand why Brutus rose
20 against Caesar, this is my answer: Not that I loved Caesar
less, but that I loved Rome more. Had you rather Caesar were
living, and die all slaves, than that Caesar were dead, to live
all freemen? As Caesar loved me, I weep for him; as he was
fortunate, I rejoice at it; as he was valiant, I honor him; but—
25 as he was ambitious, I slew him. There is tears for his love;
joy for his fortune; honor for his valor; and death for his ambition. Who is here so base that would be a bondman? if
any, speak; for him have I offended. Who is here so rude
that would not be a Roman? If any, speak; for him have I

4 the last : the end of my talk.
5 lovers : friends.
6 have respect to mine honor : Remember that I am an honorable man.
7 Censure : judge.
8 senses : thinking powers.

30 offended. Who is here so vile that will not love his country?
If any, speak; for him have I offended. I pause for a reply.

ALL. None, Brutus, none!

BRUTUS. Then none have I offended. I have done no more
to Caesar than you shall do to Brutus. The question of his
35 death is enrolled in the Capitol; his glory not extenuated,
wherein he was worthy; nor his offenses enforced,[9] for which
he suffered death.

Enter ANTONY and others, with CAESAR'S body.

Here comes his body, mourned by Mark Antony, who, though
he had no hand in his death, shall receive the benefit of his
40 dying, a place in the commonwealth,[10] as which of you shall
not? With this I depart, that, as I slew my best lover for the
good of Rome, I have the same dagger for myself when it
shall please my country to need my death.

ALL. Live, Brutus! live, live!

45   1 PLEBEIAN. Bring him with triumph home unto his house.

2 PLEBEIAN. Give him a statue with his ancestors.[11]

3 PLEBEIAN. Let him be Caesar.

4 PLEBEIAN.   Caesar's better parts[12]
Shall be crowned in Brutus.

1 PLEBEIAN. We'll bring him to his house with shouts and
clamors.

BRUTUS. My countrymen—

50   2 PLEBEIAN.   Peace! silence! Brutus speaks.

1 PLEBEIAN. Peace, ho!

BRUTUS. Good countrymen, let me depart alone,
And, for my sake, stay here with Antony.
Do grace[13] to Caesar's corpse, and grace his speech
55 Tending to Caesar's glories which Mark Antony,
By our permission, is allowed to make.
I do entreat you, not a man depart,
Save I alone, till Antony have spoke.   (Exit.)

1 PLEBEIAN. Stay, ho! and let us hear Mark Antony.

60   3 PLEBEIAN. Let him go up into the public chair.[14]
We'll hear him. Noble Antony, go up.

ANTONY. For Brutus' sake I am beholding to you.[15]
                                        (Goes up.)

4 PLEBEIAN. What does he say of Brutus?

3 PLEBEIAN.   He says for Brutus' sake
He finds himself beholding to us all.

65   4 PLEBEIAN. 'Twere best he speak no harm of Brutus here!

1 PLEBEIAN. This Caesar was a tyrant.

3 PLEBEIAN.   Nay, that's certain.
We are blest that Rome is rid of him.

2 PLEBEIAN. Peace! Let us hear what Antony can say.

9 The question . . . offenses
enforced : His death is a
matter of record; his glory
not understated nor his of-
fences emphasized.

10 a place in the common-
wealth : a citizen in a free
state.

11 his ancestors : the Brutus family that was instru-
mental in the early libera-
tion of Rome.

12 parts : qualities.

13 grace : honor.

14 public chair : speaker's
platform.

15 beholding to you :
obliged to you (for remaining to listen to me).

WILLIAM SHAKESPEARE   657

Antony. You gentle Romans—

All.   Peace, ho! Let us hear him.

70   **Antony.** Friends, Romans, countrymen, lend me your ears;
      I come to bury Caesar, not to praise him.
      The evil that men do lives after them;
      The good is oft interrèd[16] with their bones.
      So let it be with Caesar. The noble Brutus
75   Hath told you Caesar was ambitious.
      If it were so, it was a grievous fault,
      And grievously hath Caesar answered it.
      Here, under leave[17] of Brutus and the rest
80   So are they all, all honorable men),
      Come I to speak in Caesar's funeral.
      He was my friend, faithful and just to me;
      But Brutus says he was ambitious,
      And Brutus is an honorable man.
85   He hath brought many captives home to Rome,
      Whose ransoms did the general coffers[18] fill.
      When that the poor have cried, Caesar hath wept;
      Ambition should be made of sterner stuff.
90   Yet Brutus says he was ambitious;
      And Brutus is an honorable man.
      You all did see that on the Lupercal[19]
      Which he did thrice refuse. Was this ambition?
95   Yet Brutus says he was ambitious;
      And sure he is an honorable man.
      I speak not to disprove what Brutus spoke,
      But here I am to speak what I do know.
      You all did love him once, not without cause.
100   What cause withholds you then to mourn for him?
      O judgment, thou art fled to brutish beasts,
      And men have lost their reason! Bear with me.
      My heart is in the coffin there with Caesar,
      And I must pause till it come back to me.
105   1 **Plebeian.** Methinks there is much reason in his sayings.
      2 **Plebeian.** If thou consider rightly of the matter,
      Caesar has had great wrong.
      3 **Plebeian.**   Has he not, masters?
      I fear there will a worse come in his place.
      4 **Plebeian.** Marked ye his words? He would not take the
          crown;
110   Therefore 'tis certain he was not ambitious.
      1 **Plebeian.** If it be found so, some will dear abide it.[20]

3 PLEBEIAN. There's not a nobler man in Rome than An-
    tony.

    4 PLEBEIAN. Now mark him. He begins again to speak.

115   ANTONY. But yesterday the word of Caesar might
    Have stood against the world. Now lies he there,
    And none so poor to do him reverence.
    O masters! If I were disposed to stir
    Your hearts and minds to mutiny and rage,
120   I should do Brutus wrong, and Cassius wrong,
    Who, you all know, are honorable men.
    I will not do them wrong. I rather choose
    To wrong the dead, to wrong myself and you,
    Than I will wrong such honorable men.
125   But here's a parchment with the seal of Caesar.
    I found it in his closet;[21] 'tis his will.
    Let but the commons[22] hear this testament,
    Which (pardon me) I do not mean to read,
    And they would go and kiss dead Caesar's wounds
130   And dip their napkins[23] in his sacred blood;
    Yea, beg a hair of him for memory,
    And dying, mention it within their wills,
    Bequeathing it as a rich legacy
    Unto their issue.[24]
135   4 PLEBEIAN. We'll hear the will! Read it, Mark Antony.
    ALL. The will, the will! We will hear Caesar's will!
    ANTONY. Have patience, gentle friends; I must not read it.
    It is not meet[25] you know how Caesar loved you.
    You are not wood, you are not stones, but men;
140   And being men, hearing the will of Caesar,
    It will inflame you, it will make you mad.
    'Tis good you know not that you are his heirs;[26]
    For if you should, O, what would come of it?
    4 PLEBEIAN. Read the will! We'll hear it, Antony!
145   You shall read us the will, Caesar's will!
    ANTONY. Will you be patient? Will you stay awhile?
    I have o'ershot myself[27] to tell you of it.
    I fear I wrong the honorable men
    Whose daggers have stabbed Caesar; I do fear it.
150   4 PLEBEIAN. They were traitors. Honorable men!
    ALL. The will! the testament!
    2 PLEBEIAN. They were villains, murderers! The will! Read
    the will!
    ANTONY. You will compel me then to read the will?
    Then make a ring about the corpse of Caesar
155   And let me show you him that made the will.
    Shall I descend? and will you give me leave?
    ALL. Come down.

21 closet : study.

22 commons : general pub-
lic.

23 napkins : handkerchiefs.
(It was a custom to dip
cloths into the blood of
martyrs as relics.)

24 issue : children.

25 meet : proper.

26 you know not . . . heirs:
Antony discloses the main
fact about the will while
pretending not to read it.

27 o'ershot myself : gone
farther than I intended.

WILLIAM SHAKESPEARE

2 Plebeian. Descend.

3 Plebeian. You shall have leave.

(Antony comes down.)

160   4 Plebeian. A ring! Stand round.

    1 Plebeian. Stand from the hearse! Stand from the body!

    2 Plebeian. Room for Antony, most noble Antony!

    Antony. Nay, press not so upon me. Stand far off.

    All. Stand back! Room! Bear back!

165   Antony. If you have tears, prepare to shed them now.
You all do know this mantle.[28] I remember
The first time ever Caesar put it on.
'Twas on a summer's evening in his tent,
That day he overcame the Nervii.[29]

170 Look, in this place ran Cassius' dagger through.
See what a rent the envious Casca made.
Through this the well-beloved Brutus stabbed;
And as he plucked his cursèd steel away,
Mark how the blood of Caesar followed it,

175 As rushing out of doors to be resolved[30]
If Brutus so unkindly knocked or no;
For Brutus, as you know, was Caesar's angel.[31]
Judge, O you gods, how dearly Caesar loved him!
This was the most unkindest cut of all;

180 For when the noble Caesar saw him stab,
Ingratitude, more strong than traitors' arms,
Quite vanquished him. Then burst his mighty heart;
And in his mantle muffling up his face,
Even at the base of Pompey's statuë

185 (Which all the while ran blood) great Caesar fell.
O, what a fall was there, my countrymen!
Then I, and you, and all of us fell down,
Whilst bloody treason flourished over us.
O, now you weep, and I perceive you feel

190 The dint[32] of pity. These are gracious drops.
Kind souls, what weep you when you but behold
Our Caesar's vesture[33] wounded? Look you here!
Here is himself, marred as you see with traitors.[34]

    1 Plebeian. O piteous spectacle!

195   2 Plebeian. O noble Caesar!

    3 Plebeian. O woeful day!

    4 Plebeian. O traitors, villains!

    1 Plebeian. O most bloody sight!

    2 Plebeian. We will be revenged.

200   All. Revenge! About! Seek! Burn! Fire! Kill! Slay!
Let not a traitor live!

    Antony. Stay, countrymen.

    1 Plebeian. Peace there! Hear the noble Antony.

28 mantle : coat.

29 the Nervii : a warlike tribe in Gaul defeated by Caesar.

30 to be resolved : to find out for certain.

31 angel : dearest friend.

32 dint : effect.

33 vesture : clothing.

34 Look you . . . traitors : Antony removes the coat covering Caesar and reveals his wounds.

2 PLEBEIAN. We'll hear him, we'll follow him, we'll die
with him!

205   ANTONY. Good friends, sweet friends, let me not stir you up
To such a sudden flood of mutiny.
They that have done this deed are honorable.
What private griefs they have, alas, I know not,
That made them do it. They are wise and honorable,
210 And will no doubt with reasons answer you.
I come not, friends, to steal away your hearts.
I am no orator, as Brutus is,
But (as you know me all) a plain blunt man
That love my friend; and that they know full well
215 That gave me public leave to speak of him.
For I have neither wit, nor words, nor worth,
Action, nor utterance, nor the power of speech
To stir men's blood. I only speak right on.
I tell you that which you yourselves do know,
220 Show you sweet Caesar's wounds, poor poor dumb mouths,
And bid them speak for me. But were I Brutus,
And Brutus Antony, there were an Antony
Would ruffle up your spirits, and put a tongue
In every wound of Caesar that should move
225 The stones of Rome to rise and mutiny.
ALL. We'll mutiny.
1 PLEBEIAN.   We'll burn the house of Brutus.
3 PLEBEIAN. Away then! Come, seek the conspirators.
ANTONY. Yet hear me, countrymen. Yet hear me speak.
ALL. Peace, ho! Hear Antony, most noble Antony!
230   ANTONY. Why, friends, you go to do you know not what.
Wherein hath Caesar thus deserved your loves?
Alas, you know not! I must tell you then.
You have forgot the will I told you of.
ALL. Most true! The will! Let's stay and hear the will.
235   ANTONY. Here is the will, and under Caesar's seal.
To every Roman citizen he gives,
To every several man, seventy-five drachmas.[35]
2 PLEBEIAN. Most noble Caesar! We'll revenge his death!
3 PLEBEIAN. O royal Caesar!
240   ANTONY. Hear me with patience.
ALL. Peace, ho!
ANTONY. Moreover, he hath left you all his walks,
His private arbors, and new-planted orchards,[36]
On this side Tiber; he hath left them you,
245 And to your heirs forever—common pleasures,
To walk abroad and recreate yourselves.
Here was a Caesar! When comes such another?
1 PLEBEIAN. Never, never! Come, away, away!

35 seventy-five drachmas : Authorities have given this sum values ranging from ten to a hundred dollars.

36 orchards : gardens.

WILLIAM SHAKESPEARE   **661**

We'll burn his body in the holy place
250 And with the brands fire the traitors' houses.
Take up the body.

    2 PLEBEIAN. Go fetch fire!

    3 PLEBEIAN. Pluck down benches!

    4 PLEBEIAN. Pluck down forms,[37] windows, anything!

                (*Exeunt* PLEBEIANS *with the body.*)

37 forms : benches.

255 ANTONY. Now let it work. Mischief, thou art afoot,
Take thou what course thou wilt.

             Enter a SERVANT.

                How now, fellow?

SERVANT. Sir, Octavius is already come to Rome.

ANTONY. Where is he?

SERVANT. He and Lepidus[38] are at Caesar's house.

260 ANTONY. And thither will I straight to visit him.
He comes upon a wish.[39] Fortune is merry,
And in this mood will give us anything.

    SERVANT. I heard him say Brutus and Cassius
Are rid like madmen through the gates of Rome.

265 ANTONY. Belike[40] they had some notice of the people
How I had moved them. Bring me to Octavius.   (*Exeunt.*)

38 Lepidus : a supporter of
Caesar who entered Rome
with his army of soldiers
after Caesar's assassina-
tion.

39 He comes upon a wish :
I wanted him to come.

40 Belike : probably.

Scene III. *Rome. A street.*

Enter CINNA *the poet,*[1] *and after him the* PLEBEIANS.

CINNA. I dreamt tonight[2] that I did feast with Caesar,
And things unluckily charge my fantasy.[3]
I have no will to wander forth of doors,[4]
Yet something leads me forth.

5   1 PLEBEIAN. What is your name?

    2 PLEBEIAN. Whither are you going?

    3 PLEBEIAN. Where do you dwell?

    4 PLEBEIAN. Are you a married man or a bachelor?

    2 PLEBEIAN. Answer every man directly.

10   1 PLEBEIAN. Ay, and briefly.

    4 PLEBEIAN. Ay, and wisely.

    3 PLEBEIAN. Ay, and truly, you were best.[5]

    CINNA. What is my name? Whither am I going? Where do
I dwell? Am I a married man or a bachelor? Then, to answer
15 every man directly and briefly, wisely and truly: wisely I say,
I am a bachelor.

    2 PLEBEIAN. That's as much as to say they are fools that
marry. You'll bear me a bang[6] for that, I fear. Proceed—
directly.

1 Cinna the poet : This is
not Cinna the conspirator.

2 tonight : last night.

3 things . . . fantasy : My
thoughts are about bad
omens.

4 of doors : outside.

5 you were best : It would
be best for you.

6 You'll bear me a bang :
I'll hit you.

20 CINNA. Directly I am going to Caesar's funeral.

1 PLEBEIAN. As a friend or an enemy?

CINNA. As a friend.

2 PLEBEIAN. That matter is answered directly.

4 PLEBEIAN. For your dwelling—briefly.

25 CINNA. Briefly, I dwell by the Capitol.

3 PLEBEIAN. Your name, sir, truly.

CINNA. Truly, my name is Cinna.

1 PLEBEIAN. Tear him to pieces! He's a conspirator.

CINNA. I am Cinna the poet! I am Cinna the poet!

30 4 PLEBEIAN. Tear him for his bad verses! Tear him for his bad verses!

CINNA. I am not Cinna the conspirator.

4 PLEBEIAN. It is no matter; his name's Cinna! Pluck but his name out of his heart, and turn him going.

35 3 PLEBEIAN. Tear him, tear him! Come, brands, ho! firebrands! To Brutus', to Cassius'! Burn all! Some to Decius' house and some to Casca's; some to Ligarius'! Away, go!

(Exeunt all the PLEBEIANS *with* CINNA.)

Understanding the Play

ACT III

Scene i

1. How does Shakespeare build up suspense in this scene?
2. Paraphrase Caesar's speech beginning with line 35. In what way does this scene justify Brutus's fear of Caesar's use of power?
3. In Act II Brutus makes two basic decisions for the conspirators. What other important decision does Brutus make in this scene? What is Cassius's attitude toward this decision?
4. What evidence is there of Antony's true feelings toward the conspirators? How is he successful in hiding this feeling? Show that Cassius understood Antony better than Brutus did in view of scene ii.
5. Why did Brutus make errors in judgment? Why were Cassius's ideas sometimes wiser?
6. Paraphrase Antony's speech beginning with line 255. What major question remains unanswered at the end of this scene?

WILLIAM SHAKESPEARE

Shakespeare's company might have acted Caesar's assassination in this way. Note the mixture of Elizabethan and Roman costumes. Though often elaborate and sometimes very realistic, costumes were not bound by historical accuracy. Scenery was usually simple in comparison to modern staging.

Scene ii

1. To what motives in the crowd does Brutus appeal? To what motives does Antony appeal? Quote from each speech illustrations of this appeal.
2. Contrast the language (rhetorical devices) of Brutus's and Antony's speeches. Read illustrations of these devices from each speech. Which speech was most effective? Why?
3. What use does Antony make of Caesar's will?
4. What line following Brutus's speech shows that the Romans did not understand it?
5. How has Shakespeare earlier in the play prepared the audience for the Romans' change of heart?
6. Find quotations from Antony's speech in which he says the opposite from what he means. What effect does this have on the crowd? What are his reasons for these statements? Read them aloud in the tone the actor playing the part of Antony would probably use.
7. What characteristics of the crowd are revealed in this scene?

Scene iii

1. What happens in this scene? What is the purpose of the scene?

Scene I.[1] *Rome.* ANTONY's *house.*

Enter ANTONY, OCTAVIUS *and* LEPIDUS.[2]

ANTONY. These many, then, shall die; their names are
  pricked.[3]

OCTAVIUS. Your brother too must die. Consent you, Lepidus?

LEPIDUS. I do consent—

OCTAVIUS.   Prick him down, Antony.

LEPIDUS. Upon condition Publius shall not live,

5 Who is your sister's son, Mark Antony.

    ANTONY. He shall not live. Look, with a spot I damn him.

But, Lepidus, go you to Caesar's house.

Fetch the will hither, and we shall determine

How to cut off some charge[4] in legacies.

10 LEPIDUS. What? shall I find you here?

    OCTAVIUS. Or here or at the Capitol.   (*Exit* LEPIDUS.)

    ANTONY. This is a slight unmeritable man,

Meet to be sent on errands. Is it fit,

The threefold world divided, he should stand

One of the three to share it?

15 OCTAVIUS.   So you thought him,

And took his voice who should be pricked to die

In our black sentence and proscription.

    ANTONY. Octavius, I have seen more days than you;

And though we lay these honors on this man

20 To ease ourselves of divers sland'rous loads,[5]

He shall but bear them as the ass bears gold,

To groan and sweat under the business,

Either led or driven as we point the way;

And having brought our treasure where we will,

25 Then take we down his load, and turn him off

(Like to the empty ass) to shake his ears

And graze in commons.

    OCTAVIUS.   You may do your will;

But he's a tried and valiant soldier.

    ANTONY. So is my horse, Octavius, and for that

30 I do appoint him store of provender.[6]

It is a creature that I teach to fight,

To wind, to stop, to run directly on,

His corporal[7] motion governed by my spirit.

And, in some taste,[8] is Lepidus but so.

35 He must be taught, and trained, and bid go forth:

A barren-spirited fellow; one that feeds

On objects, arts, and imitations

Which, out of use and staled by other men,

1 Scene I : The scene takes place some time after Caesar's assassination.

2 Antony, Octavius, and Lepidus : Following the assassination of Caesar and the banishment of Brutus and Cassius, these three men now rule Rome as a triumvirate.

3 These . . . pricked : They have agreed on a list of names of men who must die because they oppose them politically.

4 cut off some charge : save money by not giving the people the money promised to them in the will Antony read at the funeral.

5 sland'rous loads : blame.

6 store of provender : plenty of food.

7 corporal : bodily.

8 taste : degree.

Begin his fashion.[9] Do not talk of him,
40 But as a property.[10] And now, Octavius,
Listen great things. Brutus and Cassius
Are levying powers.[11] We must straight make head.[12]
Therefore let our alliance be combined,
Our best friends made, and our best means stretched out;
45 And let us presently go sit in council
How covert matters may be best disclosed[13]
And open perils surest answerèd.[14]

    OCTAVIUS. Let us do so; for we are at the stake
And bayed about with many enemies;[15]
50 And some that smile have in their hearts, I fear,
Millions of mischiefs.   (*Exeunt.*)

Scene II. *The camp near Sardis. Before the tent of* BRUTUS.

    Drum. Enter BRUTUS, LUCILIUS, LUCIUS, *and the* ARMY.
        TITINIUS *and* PINDARUS *meet them.*

    BRUTUS. Stand ho!
    LUCILIUS. Give the word, ho! and stand!
    BRUTUS. What now, Lucilius? Is Cassius near?
    LUCILIUS. He is at hand, and Pindarus is come
5 To do you salutation from his master.
    BRUTUS. He greets me well. Your master, Pindarus,
In his own change, or by ill officers,[1]
Hath given me some worthy cause to wish
Things done undone; but if he be at hand,
I shall be satisfied.[2]
10   PINDARUS.   I do not doubt
But that my noble master will appear
Such as he is, full of regard and honor.
    BRUTUS. He is not doubted. A word, Lucilius,
How he received you. Let me be resolved.[3]
15   LUCILIUS. With courtesy and with respect enough,
But not with such familiar instances[4]
Nor with such free and friendly conference
As he hath used of old.
    BRUTUS.   Thou hast described
A hot friend cooling. Ever note, Lucilius,
20 When love begins to sicken and decay
It useth an enforcèd ceremony.
There are no tricks in plain and simple faith;
But hollow[5] men, like horses hot at hand,[6]
Make gallant show and promise of their mettle;
                        (*Low march within.*)

9 one that feeds . . . his fashion : He begins to copy the fashions of others after the fashion is already out of date.
10 a property : a tool we can use.
11 levying powers : collecting forces.
12 make head : organize an army.
13 covert . . . disclosed : the enemy's secret plans may best be discovered.
14 answered : met.
15 for we . . . many enemies : for we are in a dangerous position (similar to a bear tied to a stake in the Elizabethan game of bearbaiting).

1 In his own . . . ill officers : either by a change in his own feelings or by the acts of untrustworthy officers.
2 be satisfied : receive a full explanation.

3 resolved : told.

4 familiar instances : close friendship.

5 hollow : insincere.
6 hot at hand : full of spirit when reined in.

25 But when they should endure the bloody spur,
   They fall their crests, and like deceitful jades
   Sink in the trial.[7] Comes his army on?

     LUCILIUS. They mean this night in Sardis to be quartered.
   The greater part, the horse in general,
   Are come with Cassius.
30   BRUTUS.   Hark! He is arrived.
   March gently on to meet him.

        Enter CASSIUS *and his* POWERS.

   CASSIUS. Stand, ho!
   BRUTUS. Stand, ho! Speak the word along.
   1 SOLDIER. Stand!
35   2 SOLDIER. Stand!
   3 SOLDIER. Stand!
   CASSIUS. Most noble brother,[8] you have done me wrong.

8 brother : friend.

   BRUTUS. Judge me, you gods! wrong I mine enemies?
   And if not so, how should I wrong a brother?
40   CASSIUS. Brutus, this sober form[9] of yours hides wrongs;

9 sober form : serious appearance.

   And when you do them—
    BRUTUS.   Cassius, be content.[10]

10 content : calm.

   Speak your griefs softly. I do know you well.
   Before the eyes of both our armies here
   (Which should perceive nothing but love from us)
45 Let us not wrangle. Bid them move away.
   Then in my tent, Cassius, enlarge your griefs,
   And I will give you audience.
    CASSIUS.   Pindarus,
   Bid our commanders lead their charges[11] off

11 their charges : the troops.

   A little from this ground.
50   BRUTUS. Lucilius, do you the like; and let no man
   Come to our tent till we have done our conference.
   Let Lucius and Titinius guard our door.   (*Exeunt.*)

Scene III. *The camp near Sardis. Within the tent of* BRUTUS.

       Enter BRUTUS *and* CASSIUS.

1 noted : disgraced.

   CASSIUS. That you have wronged me doth appear in this:
   You have condemned and noted[1] Lucius Pella
   For taking bribes here of the Sardians;
   Wherein my letters, praying on his side,
5   Because I knew the man, were slighted off.
    BRUTUS. You wronged yourself to write in such a case.
    CASSIUS. In such a time as this it is not meet
   That every nice offense should bear his comment.[2]

2 That every . . . his comment : that every little fault should receive notice.

BRUTUS. Let me tell you, Cassius, you yourself
10 Are much condemned to have an itching palm,³
To sell and mart your offices for gold
To undeservers.
     CASSIUS.   I an itching palm?
You know that you are Brutus that speaks this,
Or, by the gods, this speech were else your last!
15 BRUTUS. The name of Cassius honors this corruption,
And chastisement⁴ doth therefore hide his head.
     CASSIUS. Chastisement?
     BRUTUS. Remember March; the ides of March remember.
Did not great Julius bleed for justice sake?
20 What villain touched his body that did stab
And not for justice? What, shall one of us,
That struck the foremost man of all this world
But for supporting robbers—shall we now
Contaminate our fingers with base bribes,
25 And sell the mighty space of our large honors
For so much trash⁵ as may be grasped thus?
I had rather be a dog and bay the moon⁶
Than such a Roman.
     CASSIUS.   Brutus, bait not me!
I'll not endure it. You forget yourself
30 To hedge me in.⁷ I am a soldier, I,
Older in practice, abler than yourself
To make conditions.⁸
     BRUTUS.   Go to! You are not, Cassius.
     CASSIUS. I am.
     BRUTUS. I say you are not.
35 CASSIUS. Urge⁹ me no more! I shall forget myself.
Have mind upon your health. Tempt me no farther.
     BRUTUS. Away, slight man!
     CASSIUS. Is't possible?
     BRUTUS.   Hear me, for I will speak.
Must I give way and room to your rash choler?¹⁰
40 Shall I be frighted when a madman stares?
     CASSIUS. O ye gods, ye gods! Must I endure all this?
     BRUTUS. All this? Ay, more! Fret till your proud heart break.
Go show your slaves how choleric you are
And make your bondmen tremble. Must I budge?
45 Must I observe you?¹¹ Must I stand and crouch
Under your testy humor? By the gods,
You shall digest the venom of your spleen,
Though it do split you; for from this day forth
I'll use you for my mirth, yea, for my laughter,
When you are waspish.
50 CASSIUS.   Is it come to this?

---

3 Let me tell . . . palm : Brutus here does not accuse Cassius of taking bribes, but he does point out that others accuse him of such action.

4 chastisement : punishment.

5 trash : money.

6 bay the moon : barking at the moon (a futile act).

7 To hedge me in : to tell me what to do.

8 make conditions : manage affairs.

9 Urge : irritate.

10 rash choler (kŏl′ər) **:** quick temper.

11 observe you : show you reverence.

BRUTUS. You say you are a better soldier.
Let it appear so; make your vaunting[12] true,
And it shall please me well. For mine own part,
I shall be glad to learn of noble men.
55 CASSIUS. You wrong me every way! You wrong me, Brutus!
I said an elder soldier, not a better.
Did I say "better"?
  BRUTUS.   If you did, I care not.
  CASSIUS. When Caesar lived he durst not thus have moved
    me.
  BRUTUS. Peace, peace! You durst not so have tempted him.
60 CASSIUS. I durst not?
  BRUTUS. No.
  CASSIUS. What, durst not tempt him?
  BRUTUS.   For your life you durst not.
  CASSIUS. Do not presume too much upon my love.
I may do that I shall be sorry for.
65 BRUTUS. You have done that you should be sorry for.
There is no terror, Cassius, in your threats;
For I am armed so strong in honesty
That they pass by me as the idle wind,
Which I respect not. I did send to you
70 For certain sums of gold, which you denied me;
For I can raise no money by vile means.
By heaven, I had rather coin my heart
And drop my blood for drachmas than to wring
From the hard hands of peasants their vile trash
75 By any indirection.[13] I did send
To you for gold to pay my legions,
Which you denied me. Was that done like Cassius?
Should I have answered Caius Cassius so?
When Marcus Brutus grows so covetous
80 To lock such rascal counters[14] from his friends,
Be ready, gods, with all your thunderbolts,
Dash him to pieces!
  CASSIUS.   I denied you not.
  BRUTUS. You did.
  CASSIUS. I did not. He was but a fool that brought
85 My answer back. Brutus hath rived my heart.
A friend should bear his friend's infirmities,
But Brutus makes mine greater than they are.
  BRUTUS. I do not, till you practice them on me.
  CASSIUS. You love me not.
  BRUTUS.   I do not like your faults.
90 CASSIUS. A friendly eye could never see such faults.
  BRUTUS. A flatterer's would not, though they do appear
As huge as high Olympus.

12 vaunting : boasting.

13 indirection : unjust means.

14 rascal counters : vile money.

670 JULIUS CAESAR

CASSIUS. Come, Antony, and young Octavius, come!
Revenge yourselves alone on Cassius.

95 For Cassius is aweary of the world:
Hated by one he loves; braved[15] by his brother;
Checked[16] like a bondman; all his faults observed,
Set in a notebook, learned and conned by rote[17]
To cast into my teeth. O, I could weep

100 My spirit from mine eyes! There is my dagger,
And here my naked breast; within, a heart
Dearer than Pluto's[18] mine, richer than gold.
If that thou be'st a Roman, take it forth.
I, that denied thee gold, will give my heart.

105 Strike as thou didst at Caesar; for I know,
When thou didst hate him worst, thou lov'dst him better
Than ever thou lov'dst Cassius.

BRUTUS.   Sheathe your dagger.
Be angry when you will; it shall have scope.[19]
Do what you will; dishonor shall be humor.[20]

110 O Cassius, you are yokèd with a lamb[21]
That carries anger as the flint bears fire;
Who, much enforcèd,[22] shows a hasty spark,
And straight is cold again.

CASSIUS.   Hath Cassius lived
To be but mirth and laughter to his Brutus

115 When grief and blood ill-tempered vexeth him?

BRUTUS. When I spoke that, I was ill-tempered too.

CASSIUS. Do you confess so much? Give me your hand.

BRUTUS. And my heart too.

CASSIUS.   O Brutus!

BRUTUS.   What's the matter?

CASSIUS. Have you not love enough to bear with me

120 When that rash humor[23] which my mother gave me
Makes me forgetful?

BRUTUS.   Yes, Cassius; and from henceforth,
When you are over-earnest with your Brutus,
He'll think your mother chides,[24] and leave you so.

Enter POET, *followed by* LUCILIUS, TITINIUS, *and* LUCIUS.

POET. Let me go in to see the generals!

125 There is some grudge between 'em. 'Tis not meet
They be alone.

LUCILIUS. You shall not come to them.

POET. Nothing but death shall stay me.

CASSIUS. How now? What's the matter?

130 POET. For shame, you generals! What do you mean?
Love and be friends, as two such men should be;
For I have seen more years, I'm sure, than ye.

CASSIUS. Ha, ha! How vilely doth this cynic rhyme!

15 braved : challenged.
16 Checked : rebuked.
17 learned and conned by rote : memorized.

18 Pluto : god of the underworld, and thus of wealthy mines.

19 scope : free play.
20 dishonor shall be humor: Your insults shall be considered the results of your bad disposition.
21 a lamb : that is, Brutus.
22 much enforcèd : given great cause.

23 rash humor : bad temper.

24 your mother chides : It is your inherited disposition.

WILLIAM SHAKESPEARE   671

BRUTUS. Get you hence, sirrah!25 Saucy fellow, hence!

135   CASSIUS. Bear with him, Brutus. 'Tis his fashion.

    BRUTUS. I'll know his humor when he knows his time.26
What should the wars do with these jigging27 fools?
Companion, hence!28

    CASSIUS.   Away, away, be gone!   (*Exit* POET.)

    BRUTUS. Lucilius and Titinius, bid the commanders

140 Prepare to lodge their companies tonight.

    CASSIUS. And come yourselves, and bring Messala with you
Immediately to us.   (*Exeunt* LUCILIUS *and* TITINIUS.)

    BRUTUS.   Lucius, a bowl of wine.   (*Exit* LUCIUS.)

    CASSIUS. I did not think you could have been so angry.

    BRUTUS. O Cassius, I am sick of many griefs.

145   CASSIUS. Of your philosophy29 you make no use
If you give place to30 accidental evils.

    BRUTUS. No man bears sorrow better. Portia is dead.

    CASSIUS. Ha! Portia?

    BRUTUS. She is dead.

150   CASSIUS. How scaped I killing when I crossed you so?
O insupportable and touching loss!
Upon what sickness?

    BRUTUS.   Impatient of my absence,
And grief that young Octavius with Mark Antony
Have made themselves so strong; for with her death

155 That tidings came. With this she fell distract,
And (her attendants absent) swallowed fire.31

    CASSIUS. And died so?

    BRUTUS.   Even so.

    CASSIUS.   O ye immortal gods!

      Enter LUCIUS, *with wine and tapers.*

    BRUTUS. Speak no more of her. Give me a bowl of wine.
In this I bury all unkindness, Cassius.   (*Drinks.*)

160   CASSIUS. My heart is thirsty for that noble pledge.
Fill, Lucius, till the wine o'erswell the cup.
I cannot drink too much of Brutus' love.   (*Drinks.*)

                          (*Exit* LUCIUS.)

      Enter TITINIUS *and* MESSALA.

    BRUTUS. Come in, Titinius! Welcome, good Messala.
Now sit we close about this taper here

165 And call in question32 our necessities.

    CASSIUS. Portia, art thou gone?

    BRUTUS.   No more, I pray you.
Messala, I have here received letters
That young Octavius and Mark Antony
Come down upon us with a mighty power,

170 Bending their expedition toward Philippi.

---

25 Get you hence, sirrah :
Brutus speaks in anger.
Unlike Cassius, he does
not have a sense of humor
about the situation.

26 knows his time : knows
when to be humorous.

27 jigging : rhyming.

28 Companion, hence : Fellow, go away.

29 your philosophy : As a
Stoic, Brutus believed that
a wise man should not be
ruled by his emotions and
should submit to unavoidable circumstances.

30 give place to : yield to.

31 fire : burning coals.
(This account of Portia's
death is found in several
ancient writers.)

32 call in question : discuss.

MESSALA. Myself have letters of the selfsame tenure.

BRUTUS. With what addition?

MESSALA. That by proscription and bills of outlawry
Octavius, Antony, and Lepidus
175 Have put to death an hundred senators.

BRUTUS. Therein our letters do not well agree.
Mine speak of seventy senators that died
By their proscriptions, Cicero being one.

CASSIUS. Cicero one?

MESSALA.   Cicero is dead,
180 And by that order of proscription.
Had you your letters from your wife, my lord?

BRUTUS. No, Messala.

MESSALA. Nor nothing in your letters writ of her?

BRUTUS. Nothing, Messala.

MESSALA.   That methinks is strange.
185 BRUTUS. Why ask you? Hear you aught of her in yours?

MESSALA. No, my lord.

BRUTUS. Now as you are a Roman, tell me true.

MESSALA. Then like a Roman bear the truth I tell;
For certain she is dead, and by strange manner.
190 BRUTUS. Why, farewell, Portia. We must die, Messala.
With meditating that she must die once,
I have the patience to endure it now.

MESSALA. Even so great men great losses should endure.

CASSIUS. I have as much of this in art[33] as you,   33 in art : in theory.
195 But yet my nature could not bear it so.

BRUTUS. Well, to our work alive. What do you think
Of marching to Philippi presently?

CASSIUS. I do not think it good.

BRUTUS.   Your reason?

CASSIUS.   This it is:
'Tis better that the enemy seek us.
200 So shall he waste his means, weary his soldiers,
Doing himself offense,[34] whilst we, lying still,   34 offense : harm.
Are full of rest, defense, and nimbleness.

BRUTUS. Good reasons must of force give place to better.
The people 'twixt Philippi and this ground
205 Do stand but in a forced affection;[35]   35 Do stand but in a forced
For they have grudged us contribution.   affection : are not our true
The enemy, marching along by them,   friends.
By them shall make a fuller number up,
Come on refreshed, new-added,[36] and encouraged;   36 new-added : reinforced.
210 From which advantage shall we cut him off
If at Philippi we do face him there,
These people at our back.

CASSIUS.   Hear me, good brother.

WILLIAM SHAKESPEARE   673

BRUTUS. Under your pardon. You must note beside
That we have tried the utmost of our friends,
215 Our legions are brimful, our cause is ripe.
The enemy increaseth every day;
We, at the height, are ready to decline.
There is a tide in the affairs of men
Which, taken at the flood, leads on to fortune;
220 Omitted,[37] all the voyage of their life
Is bound[38] in shallows and in miseries.
On such a full sea are we now afloat,
And we must take the current when it serves
Or lose our ventures.
　　CASSIUS.　　　　　Then, with your will,[39] go on.
225 We'll along ourselves and meet them at Philippi.
　　BRUTUS. The deep of night is crept upon our talk
And nature must obey necessity,
Which we will niggard[40] with a little rest.
There is no more to say?
　　CASSIUS.　　　　No more. Good night.
230 Early tomorrow will we rise and hence.[41]
　　BRUTUS. Lucius! (*Enter* LUCIUS.) My gown. (*Exit* LUCIUS.)
　　　Farewell, good Messala.
Good night, Titinius. Noble, noble Cassius,
Good night and good repose!
　　CASSIUS.　　　　　O my dear brother,
This was an ill beginning of the night!
235 Never come such division 'tween our souls!
Let it not, Brutus.

Enter LUCIUS, *with the gown.*

　　BRUTUS.　　　Everything is well.
　　CASSIUS. Good night, my lord.
　　BRUTUS.　　　　　Good night, good brother.
　　TITINIUS *and* MESSALA. Good night, Lord Brutus.
　　BRUTUS.　　　　　　　Farewell everyone.

(*Exeunt* CASSIUS, TITINIUS, *and* MESSALA.)

Give me the gown. Where is thy instrument?
　　LUCIUS. Here in the tent.
240 BRUTUS.　　　　What, thou speak'st drowsily?
Poor knave, I blame thee not; thou art o'erwatched.[42]
Call Claudius and some other of my men;
I'll have them sleep on cushions in my tent.
　　LUCIUS. Varro and Claudius!

Enter VARRO *and* CLAUDIUS.

245　VARRO. Calls my lord?
　　BRUTUS. I pray you, sirs, lie in my tent and sleep.
It may be I shall raise you by-and-by
On business to my brother Cassius.

37 Omitted : neglected.

38 bound : confined.

39 with your will : as you wish.

40 niggard : provide scantily.

41 hence : go.

42 o'erwatched : tired by the late hour.

VARRO. So please you, we will stand and watch your
    pleasure.
250 BRUTUS. I will not have it so. Lie down, good sirs.
It may be I shall otherwise bethink me.

                        (VARRO *and* CLAUDIUS *lie down.*)

Look, Lucius, here's the book I sought for so;
I put it in the pocket of my gown.
    LUCIUS. I was sure your lordship did not give it me.
255 BRUTUS. Bear with me, good boy, I am much forgetful.
Canst thou hold up thy heavy eyes awhile,
And touch thy instrument a strain or two?
    LUCIUS. Ay, my lord, an't[43] please you.   **43 an't : if it.**
    BRUTUS.   It does, my boy.
I trouble thee too much, but thou art willing.
260 LUCIUS. It is my duty, sir.
    BRUTUS. I should not urge thy duty past thy might.
I know young bloods look for a time of rest.
    LUCIUS. I have slept, my lord, already.
    BRUTUS. It was well done; and thou shalt sleep again;
265 I will not hold thee long. If I do live,
I will be good to thee.

            (*Music, and a song.* LUCIUS *falls asleep.*)

This is a sleepy tune. O murd'rous slumber!
Layest thou thy leaden mace[44] upon my boy,   **44 mace : club.**
That plays thee music? Gentle knave, good night.
270 I will not do thee so much wrong to wake thee.
If thou dost nod, thou break'st thy instrument;
I'll take it from thee; and, good boy, good night.
Let me see, let me see. Is not the leaf turned down
Where I left reading? Here it is, I think.   (*Sits.*)

                Enter the GHOST OF CAESAR.

275 How ill this taper burns![45] Ha! who comes here?   **45 ill . . . burns : It was a**
I think it is the weakness of mine eyes   **common belief that lights**
That shapes this monstrous apparition.   **grew dim when a ghost**
It comes upon me. Art thou anything?   **was near.**
Art thou some god, some angel, or some devil,
280 That mak'st my blood cold and my hair to stare?
Speak to me what thou art.
    GHOST. Thy evil spirit, Brutus.
    BRUTUS.   Why com'st thou?
    GHOST. To tell thee thou shalt see me at Philippi.
    BRUTUS. Well; then I shall see thee again?
285 GHOST. Ay, at Philippi.
    BRUTUS. Why, I will see thee at Philippi then.

                            (*Exit* GHOST.)

Now I have taken heart thou vanishest.
Ill spirit, I would hold more talk with thee.

WILLIAM SHAKESPEARE   **675**

Boy! Lucius! Varro! Claudius! Sirs! Awake!
290 Claudius!

  Lucius. The strings, my lord, are false.

  Brutus. He thinks he still is at his instrument.
Lucius, awake!

  Lucius. My lord?

295 Brutus. Didst thou dream, Lucius, that thou so criedest out?

  Lucius. My lord, I do not know that I did cry.

  Brutus. Yes, that thou didst. Didst thou see anything?

  Lucius. Nothing, my lord.

  Brutus. Sleep again, Lucius. Sirrah Claudius!

300 (To Varro.) Fellow thou, awake!

  Varro. My lord?

  Claudius. My lord?

  Brutus. Why did you so cry out, sirs, in your sleep?

  Both. Did we, my lord?

  Brutus.   Ay. Saw you anything?

305 Varro. No, my lord, I saw nothing.

  Claudius.   Nor I, my lord.

  Brutus. Go and commend me to my brother Cassius.
Bid him set on his pow'rs betimes before,
And we will follow.

  Both.   It shall be done, my lord.   (Exeunt.)

Understanding the Play

Act IV

Scene i

1. What do you discover about Antony's character in this scene?
2. What does this scene reveal of what has happened between Acts III and IV?

Scene ii

1. What has happened to the situations of Brutus and Antony since the assassination of Caesar?
2. How have the first three acts prepared you for a quarrel between Brutus and Cassius?

Scene iii

1. What do Brutus and Cassius argue about?
2. Paraphrase Brutus's speech beginning with line 218.
3. Again in this scene, Brutus makes a decision over the objection of Cassius. What is this decision? Explain the arguments of each.
4. What does the introduction of Caesar's ghost accomplish?

Act V.

Scene I. *Near Philippi.*

Enter Octavius, Antony, *and their* Army.

Octavius. Now, Antony, our hopes are answerèd.
You said the enemy would not come down
But keep the hills and upper regions.
It proves not so. Their battles[1] are at hand;
5 They mean to warn[2] us at Philippi here,
Answering before we do demand of them.
    Antony. Tut! I am in their bosoms[3] and I know
Wherefore they do it. They could be content[4]
To visit other places, and come down
10 With fearful bravery,[5] thinking by this face[6]
To fasten in our thoughts that they have courage.
But 'tis not so.

        Enter a Messenger.

    Messala. Prepare you, generals.
The enemy comes on in gallant show;
Their bloody sign of battle[7] is hung out,
15 And something to be done immediately.
    Antony. Octavius, lead your battle softly[8] on
Upon the left hand of the even field.
    Octavius. Upon the right hand I. Keep thou the left.
    Antony. Why do you cross me in this exigent?[9]
20   Octavius. I do not cross you; but I will do so.[10]
                                              (*March.*)
Drum. Enter Brutus, Cassius, *and their* Army; Lucilius,
        Titinius, Messala, *and others.*

    Brutus. They stand and would have parley.
    Cassius. Stand fast, Titinius. We must out and talk.
    Octavius. Mark Antony, shall we give sign of battle?
    Antony. No, Caesar,[11] we will answer on their charge.
25 Make forth. The generals would have some words.
    Octavius. Stir not until the signal.
    Brutus. Words before blows. Is it so, countrymen?
    Octavius. Not that we love words better, as you do.
    Brutus. Good words are better than bad strokes, Octavius.
30   Antony. In your bad strokes, Brutus, you give good words;
Witness the hole you made in Caesar's heart,
Crying "Long live! Hail, Caesar!"
    Cassius.   Antony,
The posture of your blows are yet unknown;
But for your words, they rob the Hybla[12] bees,
And leave them honeyless.

1 battles : armies.
2 warn : challenge.

3 I am in their bosoms : I understand their thoughts.
4 could be content : would like.
5 fearful bravery : cowardly bravado.
6 face : outward show.

7 bloody sign of battle : red flag on general's tent to signify immediate attack.
8 softly : slowly.

9 exigent (ĕk′sə jənt) : critical moment.
10 I do . . . do so : I am not opposing you; but I will do as I have said.

11 Caesar : Octavius Caesar.

12 Hybla : a place famous for honey.

35   ANTONY.   Not stingless too.

     BRUTUS. O yes, and soundless too!

For you have stol'n their buzzing, Antony,

And very wisely threat before you sting.

     ANTONY. Villains! you did not so when your vile daggers

40 Hacked one another in the sides of Caesar.

You showed your teeth like apes, and fawned like hounds,

And bowed like bondmen, kissing Caesar's feet;

Whilst damnèd Casca, like a cur, behind

Struck Caesar on the neck. O you flatterers!

45   CASSIUS. Flatterers? Now, Brutus, thank yourself!

This tongue had not offended so today

If Cassius might have ruled.[13]

     OCTAVIUS. Come, come, the cause! If arguing make us sweat,

The proof of it[14] will turn to redder drops.

50 Look,

I draw a sword against conspirators.

When think you that the sword goes up again?

Never, till Caesar's three-and-thirty wounds

Be well avenged, or till another Caesar[15]

55 Have added slaughter to the sword of traitors.[16]

     BRUTUS. Caesar, thou canst not die by traitors' hands

Unless thou bring'st them with thee.

     OCTAVIUS.   So I hope.

I was not born to die on Brutus' sword.

     BRUTUS. O, if thou wert the noblest of thy strain,

60 Young man, thou couldst not die more honorable.

     CASSIUS. A peevish schoolboy, worthless of such honor,

Joined with a masker and a reveler![17]

     ANTONY. Old Cassius still.

     OCTAVIUS.   Come, Antony. Away!

Defiance, traitors, hurl we in your teeth.

65 If you dare fight today, come to the field;

If not, when you have stomachs.[18]

(*Exeunt* OCTAVIUS, ANTONY, *and their* ARMY.)

     CASSIUS. Why, now blow wind, swell billow, and swim bark!

The storm is up, and all is on the hazard.

     BRUTUS. Ho, Lucilius! Hark, a word with you.

     LUCILIUS (*standing forth.*)   My lord?

(BRUTUS *and* LUCILIUS *converse apart.*)

     CASSIUS. Messala.

     MESSALA.   What says my general?

70   CASSIUS.   Messala,

This is my birthday; as this very day

13 If Cassius . . . ruled : Cassius had argued for Antony's death along with Caesar's.

14 proof of it : testing of it by battle.

15 another Caesar : Octavius.

16 Have added . . . of traitors : has been killed by the conspirators.

17 masker and a reveler : refers to Antony's fondness for games and parties.

18 stomachs : appetite for battle.

Was Cassius born. Give me thy hand, Messala.
Be thou my witness that against my will
(As Pompey was) am I compelled to set
75 Upon one battle all our liberties.
You know that I held Epicurus strong
And his opinion.¹⁹ Now I change my mind
And partly credit things that do presage.²⁰
Coming from Sardis, on our former ensign²¹
80 Two mighty eagles fell; and there they perched,
Gorging and feeding from our soldiers' hands,
Who to Philippi here consorted²² us.
This morning are they fled away and gone,
And in their steads do ravens, crows, and kites
85 Fly o'er our heads and downward look on us
As we were sickly prey. Their shadows seem
A canopy most fatal, under which
Our army lies, ready to give up the ghost.
        MESSALA. Believe not so.
        CASSIUS.   I but believe it partly;
90 For I am fresh of spirit and resolved
To meet all perils very constantly.²³
        BRUTUS. Even so, Lucilius.
        CASSIUS.   Now, most noble Brutus,
The gods today stand friendly, that we may,
Lovers in peace, lead on our days to age!
95 But since the affairs of men rest still²⁴ incertain,
Let's reason with the worst that may befall.
If we do lose this battle, then is this
The very last time we shall speak together.
What are you then determinèd to do?
100 BRUTUS. Even by the rule of that philosophy
By which I did blame Cato for the death
Which he did give himself—²⁵ I know not how,
But I do find it cowardly and vile,
For fear of what might fall, so to prevent
105 The time of life—²⁶ arming myself with patience
To stay²⁷ the providence of some high powers
That govern us below.
        CASSIUS.   Then, if we lose this battle,
You are contented to be led in triumph
Thorough the streets of Rome.
110 BRUTUS. No, Cassius, no. Think not, thou noble Roman,
That ever Brutus will go bound to Rome.
He bears too great a mind. But this same day
Must end that work the ides of March begun,
And whether we shall meet again I know not.
115 Therefore our everlasting farewell take.

WILLIAM SHAKESPEARE   **679**

19 held Epicurus
(ĕp ə kyoorʹəs) . . . opinion :
formerly followed the teachings of Epicurus, who did not believe in superstitious signs.
20 presage : predict the future.
21 former ensign : forward emblem carried on the top of a standard.
22 consorted : accompanied.

23 constantly : steadfastly.

24 rest still : remain always.

25 Lines 100-102 mean that Brutus had called Cato's suicide cowardly.
26 to prevent . . . life : to end life by suicide.
27 To stay : to await.

Forever and forever farewell, Cassius!
If we do meet again, why, we shall smile;
If not, why then this parting was well made.

CASSIUS. Forever and forever farewell, Brutus!
120 If we do meet again, we'll smile indeed;
If not, 'tis true this parting was well made.

BRUTUS. Why then, lead on. O that a man might know
The end of this day's business ere it come!
But it sufficeth that the day will end,
125 And then the end is known. Come, ho! Away!   (*Exeunt.*)

Scene II. *Near Philippi. The field of battle.*

Alarum.[1] *Enter* BRUTUS *and* MESSALA.

BRUTUS. Ride, ride, Messala, ride, and give these bills[2]
    Unto the legions on the other side.[3]   (*Loud alarum.*)
Let them set on at once; for I perceive
But cold demeanor in Octavius' wing,
5 And sudden push gives them the overthrow.
Ride, ride, Messala! Let them all come down.   (*Exeunt.*)

1 alarum : trumpet call to battle.
2 bills : instructions.
3 other side : other wing of the army of Brutus and Cassius.

Scene III. *Another part of the field.*

Alarums. Enter CASSIUS *and* TITINIUS.

CASSIUS. O, look, Titinius, look! The villains fly!
Myself have to mine own turned enemy.[1]
This ensign[2] here of mine was turning back;
I slew the coward and did take it from him.
5   TITINIUS. O Cassius, Brutus gave the word too early,
Who, having some advantage on Octavius,
Took it too eagerly. His soldiers fell to spoil,
Whilst we by Antony are all enclosed.

1 Myself have . . . turned enemy : I have become an enemy of my own men.
2 ensign : standard carrier.

Enter PINDARUS.

PINDARUS. Fly further off, my lord! fly further off!
10 Mark Antony is in your tents,[3] my lord.
Fly, therefore, noble Cassius, fly far off!

CASSIUS. This hill is far enough. Look, look, Titinius!
Are those my tents where I perceive the fire?

TITINIUS. They are, my lord.

CASSIUS.   Titinius, if thou lovest me,
15 Mount thou my horse and hide thy spurs in him
Till he have brought thee up to yonder troops
And here again, that I may rest assured
Whether yond troops are friend or enemy.

3 Mark Antony . . . tents : Mark Antony has captured your camp site.

Titinius. I will be here again with a thought. (*Exit.*)

20 Cassius. Go, Pindarus, get higher on that hill.
My sight was ever thick. Regard Titinius,
And tell me what thou not'st about the field.

(Pindarus *goes up.*)

This day I breathèd first. Time is come round,
And where I did begin, there shall I end.

25 My life is run his compass.[4] Sirrah, what news?

Pindarus (*above*).[5] O my lord!

Cassius. What news?

Pindarus (*above*). Titinius is enclosèd round about
With horsemen that make to[6] him on the spur.

30 Yet he spurs on. Now they are almost on him.
Now, Titinius!
Now some light. O, he lights too! He's ta'en. (*Shout.*) And
hark!
They shout for joy.[7]

Cassius.   Come down; behold no more.
O coward that I am to live so long

35 To see my best friend ta'en before my face!

Enter Pindarus *from above.*

Come hither, sirrah.
In Parthia did I take thee prisoner;
And then I swore thee, saving of thy life,
That whatsoever I did bid thee do,

40 Thou shouldst attempt it. Come now, keep thine oath.
Now be a freeman, and with this good sword,
That ran through Caesar's bowels, search this bosom.
Stand not to answer. Here, take thou the hilts;
And when my face is covered, as 'tis now,

45 Guide thou the sword. (Pindarus *stabs him.*)—Caesar, thou
art revenged
Even with the sword that killed thee. (*Dies.*)

Pindarus. So, I am free; yet would not so have been,
Durst I have done my will. O Cassius!
Far from this country Pindarus shall run,

50 Where never Roman shall take note of him. (*Exit.*)

Enter Titinius *and* Messala.

Messala. It is but change,[8] Titinius; for Octavius
Is overthrown by noble Brutus' power,
As Cassius' legions are by Antony.

Titinius. These tidings will well comfort Cassius.

Messala. Where did you leave him?

55 Titinius.   All disconsolate,
With Pindarus his bondman, on this hill.

Messala. Is not that he that lies upon the ground?

4 compass : circle; limits.

5 above : on the upper stage.

6 make to : approach.

7 Titinius is enclosèd . . . for joy : Pindarus misinterprets what he sees. Actually Titinius finds soldiers from their side, and they surround him in joy.

8 change : an exchange.

Titinius. He lies not like the living. O my heart!

Messala. Is not that he?

Titinius.   No, this was he, Messala,

60 But Cassius is no more. O setting sun,
As in thy red rays thou dost sink to night,
So in his red blood Cassius' day is set!
The sun of Rome is set. Our day is gone;
Clouds, dews, and dangers come; our deeds are done!

65 Mistrust of my success hath done this deed.

Messala. Mistrust of good success hath done this deed.
O hateful Error, Melancholy's child,
Why dost thou show to the apt[9] thoughts of men
The things that are not? O Error, soon conceived,

70 Thou never com'st unto a happy birth,
But kill'st the mother that engendered thee![10]

Titinius. What, Pindarus! Where art thou, Pindarus?

Messala. Seek him, Titinius, whilst I go to meet
The noble Brutus, thrusting this report

75 Into his ears. I may say "thrusting" it;
For piercing steel and darts envenomèd
Shall be as welcome to the ears of Brutus
As tidings of this sight.

Titinius.   Hie you, Messala,
And I will seek for Pindarus the while.   (*Exit* Messala.)

80 Why didst thou send me forth, brave Cassius?
Did I not meet thy friends, and did not they
Put on my brows this wreath of victory
And bid me give it thee? Didst thou not hear their shouts?
Alas, thou hast misconstrued everything!

85 But hold thee, take this garland on thy brow.
Thy Brutus bid me give it thee, and I
Will do his bidding. Brutus, come apace
And see how I regarded Caius Cassius.
By your leave, gods. This is a Roman's part.

90 Come, Cassius' sword, and find Titinius' heart.   (*Dies.*)

Alarum. Enter Brutus, Messala, Young Cato, Strato,
   Volumnius, *and* Lucilius.

Brutus. Where, where, Messala, doth his body lie?

Messala. Lo, yonder, and Titinius mourning it.

Brutus. Titinius' face is upward.

Cato.   He is slain.

Brutus. O Julius Caesar, thou art mighty yet!

95 Thy spirit walks abroad and turns our swords
In our own proper entrails.   (*Low alarums.*)

Cato.   Brave Titinius!
Look whe'r[11] he have not crowned dead Cassius.

---

9 apt : impressionable.

10 kill'st the . . . engendered thee : The error destroys the mind that conceived it.

11 whe'r : whether.

BRUTUS. Are yet two Romans living such as these?
The last of all the Romans, fare thee well!
100 It is impossible that ever Rome
Should breed thy fellow.[12] Friends, I owe moe[13] tears
To this dead man than you shall see me pay.
I shall find time, Cassius; I shall find time.
Come therefore, and to Thasos send his body.
105 His funerals shall not be in our camp,
Lest it discomfort us.[14] Lucilius, come;
And come, young Cato. Let us to the field.
Labeo and Flavius set our battles on.
'Tis three o'clock; and, Romans, yet ere night
110 We shall try fortune in a second fight.   (*Exeunt.*)

12 fellow : match.
13 moe : more.

14 discomfort us : dis-
hearten our troops.

Scene IV. *Another part of the field.*

Alarum. Enter BRUTUS, MESSALA,
YOUNG CATO, LUCILIUS, *and* FLAVIUS.

BRUTUS. Yet, countrymen, O, yet hold up your heads!
CATO. What bastard doth not? Who will go with me?
I will proclaim my name about the field.
I am the son of Marcus Cato, ho!
5   A foe to tyrants, and my country's friend.
I am the son of Marcus Cato, ho!

Enter SOLDIERS *and fight.*

BRUTUS. And I am Brutus, Marcus Brutus I!
Brutus, my country's friend! Know me for Brutus!   (*Exit.*)
                                        (YOUNG CATO *falls.*)
LUCILIUS. O young and noble Cato, art thou down?
10   Why, now thou diest as bravely as Titinius,
And mayst be honored, being Cato's son.
    1 SOLDIER. Yield, or thou diest.
    LUCILIUS.   Only I yield to die.
(*Offers money.*) There is so much that thou wilt kill me
    straight.
Kill Brutus[1] and be honored in his death.
15   1 SOLDIER. We must not. A noble prisoner!

1 Kill Brutus : Lucilius pretends to be Brutus.

Enter ANTONY.

    2 SOLDIER. Room ho! Tell Antony Brutus is ta'en.
    1 SOLDIER. I'll tell the news. Here comes the general.
Brutus is ta'en! Brutus is ta'en, my lord!
    ANTONY. Where is he?
20   LUCILIUS. Safe, Antony; Brutus is safe enough.
I dare assure thee that no enemy
Shall ever take alive the noble Brutus.

The gods defend him from so great a shame!
When you do find him, or alive or dead,
25 He will be found like Brutus, like himself.

ANTONY. This is not Brutus, friend; but, I assure you,
A prize no less in worth. Keep this man safe;
Give him all kindness. I had rather have
Such men my friends than enemies. Go on,
30 And see whe'r Brutus be alive or dead;
And bring us word unto Octavius' tent
How everything is chanced.   (*Exeunt.*)

Scene V. *Another part of the field.*

Enter BRUTUS, DARDANIUS, CLITUS, STRATO, *and* VOLUM-
NIUS.

BRUTUS. Come, poor remains of friends, rest on this rock.
CLITUS. Statilius showed the torchlight; but, my lord,
He came not back. He is or ta'en or slain.
BRUTUS. Sit thee down, Clitus. Slaying is the word.
5 It is a deed in fashion. Hark thee, Clitus.   (*Whispers.*)
CLITUS. What, I, my lord? No, not for all the world!
BRUTUS. Peace then. No words.
CLITUS.   I'll rather kill myself.
BRUTUS. Hark thee, Dardanius.   (*Whispers.*)
DARDANIUS.   Shall I do such a deed?
CLITUS. O Dardanius!
10 DARDANIUS. O Clitus!
CLITUS. What ill request did Brutus make to thee?
DARDANIUS. To kill him, Clitus. Look, he meditates.
CLITUS. Now is that noble vessel full of grief,
That it runs over even at his eyes.
15 BRUTUS. Come hither, good Volumnius. List a word.
VOLUMNIUS. What says my lord?
BRUTUS.   Why this, Volumnius.
The ghost of Caesar hath appeared to me
Two several[1] times by night—at Sardis once,   1 several : separate.
And this last night here in Philippi fields.
I know my hour is come.
20 VOLUMNIUS.   Not so, my lord.
BRUTUS. Nay, I am sure it is, Volumnius.
Thou seest the world, Volumnius, how it goes.
Our enemies have beat us to the pit.[2]   (*Low alarums.*)   2 pit : grave.
It is more worthy to leap in ourselves
25 Than tarry till they push us. Good Volumnius,
Thou know'st that we two went to school together.

Even for that our love of old, I prithee
Hold thou my sword-hilts whilst I run on it.
    VOLUMNIUS. That's not an office for a friend, my lord.
                                 (*Alarum still.*)
30   CLITUS. Fly, fly, my lord! There is no tarrying here.
    BRUTUS. Farewell to you; and you; and you, Volumnius.
Strato, thou hast been all this while asleep.
Farewell to thee too, Strato. Countrymen,
My heart doth joy that yet in all my life
35 I found no man but he was true to me.
I shall have glory by this losing day
More than Octavius and Mark Antony
By this vile conquest shall attain unto.
So fare you well at once; for Brutus' tongue
40 Hath almost ended his live's history.
Night hangs upon mine eyes; my bones would rest,
That have but labored to attain this hour.
               (*Alarum. Cry within: "Fly, fly, fly!"*)
    CLITUS. Fly, my lord, fly!
    BRUTUS.   Hence! I will follow.

       (*Exeunt* CLITUS, DARDANIUS, *and* VOLUMNIUS.)

I prithee, Strato, stay thou by thy lord.
45 Thou art a fellow of a good respect;[3]
Thy life hath had some smatch[4] of honor in it.
Hold then my sword and turn away thy face
While I do run upon it. Wilt thou, Strato?
    STRATO. Give me your hand first. Fare you well, my lord.
50 BRUTUS. Farewell, good Strato. Caesar, now be still.
I killed not thee with half so good a will.
              (*He runs on his sword and dies.*)

   Alarum. Retreat. Enter OCTAVIUS, ANTONY, MESSALA, LUCI-
            LIUS, *and the* ARMY.

    OCTAVIUS. What man is that?
    MESSALA. My master's man. Strato, where is thy master?
    STRATO. Free from the bondage you are in, Messala.
55 The conquerors can but make a fire of him;
For Brutus only overcame himself,
And no man else hath honor by his death.
    LUCILIUS. So Brutus should be found. I thank thee, Brutus,
That thou hast proved Lucilius' saying true.
60 OCTAVIUS. All that served Brutus, I will entertain them.[5]
Fellow, wilt thou bestow thy time with me?
    STRATO. Ay, if Messala will prefer[6] me to you.
    OCTAVIUS. Do so, good Messala.
    MESSALA. How died my master, Strato?
65 STRATO. I held the sword, and he did run on it.

3 respect : reputation.

4 smatch : taste.

5 entertain them : take them into my service.

6 prefer : recommend.

MESSALA. Octavius, then take him to follow thee,
That did the latest service to my master.

    ANTONY. This was the noblest Roman of them all.
All the conspirators save only he
70 Did that they did in envy of great Caesar;
He, only in a general honest thought
And common good to all,⁷ made one of them.
His life was gentle, and the elements
So mixed in him that Nature might stand up
75 And say to all the world, "This was a man!"

    OCTAVIUS. According to his virtue let us use him,
With all respect and rites of burial.
Within my tent his bones tonight shall lie,
Most like a soldier, ordered honorably.⁸
80 So call the field to rest, and let's away
To part⁹ the glories of this happy day.   (*Exeunt* ALL.)

7 in a general . . . good to
all : with honorable purpose
unselfishly did what he believed good for all Romans.

8 ordered honorably :
treated with all due honor.

9 part : share.

Understanding the Play

ACT V

Scene i

1. What is Cassius's attitude toward omens? What change in his attitude is revealed in this scene?
2. What is Brutus's attitude toward suicide? Paraphrase Brutus's speech beginning with line 110. What change in his attitude occurs during this scene?
3. Of what significance are these changes to the dramatic development of the play?

Scene ii

1. What plot exposition is given in this brief scene?

Scene iii

1. Explain the action in this scene that precedes Cassius's death.
2. How does Shakespeare develop sympathy for Cassius in this scene?

Scene iv

1. Why does Lucilius claim that he is Brutus?
2. Why did the soldiers not kill Lucilius?

Scene v

1. What does Brutus whisper in lines 5 and 8?
2. Give evidence from the scene that Brutus never wavered from his belief that what he had done was right.
3. What evidence can you discover in this scene as to why Shakespeare named this play *Julius Caesar* when actually Julius Caesar is not on stage nearly as much as other characters?
4. Paraphrase Antony's speech beginning with line 68.

Building Vocabulary Skills

1. Many of the words in this play have different meanings today than they did in Shakespeare's day. Below are quoted lines from the play. Substitute a word for the word italicized that would be more commonly used today. Explain how the meaning of the italicized word is different today from its former one.

(a)   What, know you not,
   Being *mechanical*, you ought not walk
   Upon a laboring day without the sign
   Of your profession? (I, i)
(b) Were I a common *laugher*, . . .
    . . . then hold me dangerous. (I, ii)
(c) What you would work me to, I have some *aim*. (I, ii)
(d) If I were Brutus now and he were Cassius,
    He should not *humor* me. (I, ii)
(e) *Repair* to Pompey's Porch, where you shall find us. (I, iii)
(f) The taper burneth in your *closet*, sir. (II, i)
(g)   . . . his means
   If he *improve* them, may well stretch so far
   As to annoy us all. (II, i)
(h) Send him but hither, and I'll *fashion* him. (II, i)
(i) Calpurnia here, my wife, *stays* me at home. (II, ii)
(j) I heard a bustling *rumor* like a fray,
    And the wind brings it from the Capitol. (II, iv)
(k) Cassius, be *constant*. (III, i)
(l) My credit now stands on such slippery ground
    That one of two bad ways you must *conceit* me,
    Either a coward or a flatterer. (III, i)
(m)   There shall I try
   In my oration how the people take
   The cruel *issue* of these bloody men. (III, ii)
(n) It is not *meet* you know how Caesar loved you. (IV, ii)
(o) Pluck down *forms*, windows, anything! (IV, ii)

2. Many expressions in everyday usage come to us from literary sources. The following lines from *Julius Caesar* are frequently quoted ones. Tell in what connection outside of the play *Julius Caesar* you have heard or read these passages or expressions based on them. What do the expressions mean as they are commonly used?

(*a*) Beware the ides of March.

(*b*) The fault, dear Brutus, is not in our stars,
But in ourselves, that we are underlings.

(*c*) It was Greek to me.

(*d*) Cowards die many times before their deaths;
The valiant never taste of death but once.

(*e*) Et tu, Brute?

(*f*) Cry "Havoc!" and let slip the dogs of war.

(*g*) Friends, Romans, countrymen, lend me your ears.

(*h*) This was the most unkindest cut of all.

(*i*) There is a tide in the affairs of men
Which, taken at the flood, leads on to fortune;
Omitted, all the voyage of their life
Is bound in shallows and in miseries.
On such a full sea are we now afloat,
And we must take the current when it serves
Or lose our ventures.

(*j*) O Julius Caesar, thou art mighty yet!

(*k*) Thy life hath had some smatch of honor in it.

(*l*) This was the noblest Roman of them all.
All the conspirators save only he
Did that they did in envy of great Caesar;
He, only in a general honest thought
And common good to all, made one of them.
His life was gentle, and the elements
So mixed in him that Nature might stand up
And say to all the world, "This was a man!"

Developing Language Skills

1. Several universal questions raised in the play *Julius Caesar* are listed below. In panel discussions or in short compositions, state the play's answers to these questions. Refer to the events in the play to substantiate your opinion.
   (*a*) Is loyalty to a person more important than dedication to the general good of society?
   (*b*) Can injustice be ended by murder?
   (*c*) Can force produce a peaceful society?
   (*d*) How can a skillful orator exert power over a mass audience?
   (*e*) Are men controlled by fortune more than by their own decisions and actions?
2. Comment on the following statement:
   Brutus was an idealist, but not a practical man. He often made errors in his evaluation of others.
3. Answer one of the following questions in two to five paragraphs:
   (*a*) What inner conflicts are faced by Brutus? by Caesar?
   (*b*) How does the historical figure of Caesar compare with the character of Caesar created by Shakespeare in this play? You should use the library for research on the historical Caesar before writing on this subject.
4. Professor Maynard Mack of Yale University states that Shakespeare gave Julius Caesar a double character:
   (*a*) "the human Caesar who has human ailments and is a human friend [and who] is the Caesar that can be killed," and
   (*b*) "the marmoreal Caesar, the everlasting Big Brother—the Napoleon, Mussolini, Hitler, Franco, Perón, Stalin, Khrushchev, to mention only a handful of his more recent incarnations—that Caesar is the one who must repeatedly be killed but never dies, because he is in you, and you, and you, and me."
   Write an essay in which you give evidence from the play to illustrate each of the two characters of Caesar. Be sure to include the ghost of Caesar in your analysis.
5. If you have read Dickens's *A Tale of Two Cities*, compare the result of the violent overthrow of power in the novel with the events in the play *Julius Caesar*.

Developing Oral Reading Skills

The unit on poetry in this book emphasized that poems were created to be read aloud rather than silently. The unit on drama pointed out that plays were written to be performed on a stage rather than read in a book. *Julius Caesar* is both poetry and drama and, therefore, doubly intended to be read aloud.

Before reading aloud speeches from the play, remember that your purpose is to interpret the meaning of the lines through your voice. Your listeners should better understand not only the literal meaning of the lines but also the feeling of the character speaking the lines because of the way you read them.

To interpret a passage, you must, of course, understand the meaning of the lines yourself. You must be familiar with the meaning of all the words, even if some of the words are now obsolete. You should also visualize the imagery, the picture described in the lines. For example, note how the meaning of the following lines depends on the images used:

> he doth bestride the narrow world
> Like a Colossus, and we petty men
> Walk under his huge legs and peep about
> To find ourselves dishonorable graves.

Not only must you see the imagery, but you must also understand the comparison to interpret lines orally. What things are being compared in the lines quoted above?

Once you thoroughly understand a passage, your task is to communicate your understanding through your voice to your listeners. The tempo or rate at which you read is one way of expressing meaning. The rhythm of the lines as well as the meaning will often indicate at what tempo to read. For example, read Antony's speech in Act III, scene i, lines 255-276. At what tempo should lines 255-259 be read as compared with lines 260-276?

The intonation (the rise and fall in pitch) with which you read helps to determine meaning, as does the emphasis placed on words. At Caesar's funeral in Act III, scene ii, lines 70-134, Antony uses the word *honorable* many times. As he gains courage and support, the intonation and emphasis he gives to this word changes. In what way do these changes affect the meaning of his oration?

One should be cautious in reading *Julius Caesar* aloud not to pause at the end of each line simply because it is the end of a line. Observe the marks of punctuation and pause where the meaning calls for a pause. One should also be careful not to let the rhythm of Shakespeare's iambic pentameter create a singsong reading. If you read to bring out the meaning and do not purposely try to emphasize the beat, the natural rhythm of the verse will add beauty and form to your oral presentation.

In addition to the lines referred to above, other passages particularly good for reading aloud in separation from the entire play are listed below.

Act I, scene ii, lines 135-161, Cassius.
                     lines 192-214, Caesar.

Act II, scene i, lines 10-34, Brutus.
                   lines 114-140, Brutus.
                   lines 162-183, Brutus.
                   lines 237-256, Portia.
Act II, scene ii, lines 8-37, Caesar and Calpurnia.
Act III, scene i, lines 255-276, Antony.
Act III, scene ii, lines 12-43, Brutus.
                   lines 70-255, Antony.
Act IV, scene iii, lines 1-123, Brutus and Cassius.
                   lines 213-224, Brutus.
Act V, scene v, lines 31-51, Brutus.
                   lines 68-75, Antony.

Author Biographies

AUDEN, WYSTAN HUGH (1907-   ). One of the most influential poets of the last thirty years, Auden was born in England, attended Oxford University, and taught school for a short time after graduating. He then became connected with a group of young liberal English poets, whose interest in politics and economics was often reflected in their poems. Later he became an American citizen and has taught and lectured at various colleges in addition to his writing. His poems display a mastery of technique; many are satirical or humorous in tone. They are available in a number of collections. He has also collaborated on plays—*The Dog Beneath the Skin* and *The Ascent of F.6*—and an opera libretto, *The Rake's Progress.*

BENÉT, STEPHEN VINCENT (1898-1943). Benét was born in Bethlehem, Pennsylvania, graduated from Yale in 1919, and then attended the Sorbonne in Paris. Here he met Rosemary Carr, whom he later married and with whom he collaborated in many writings, such as *A Book of Americans* (1933). Benét often based his stories and poems on figures from America's past, as in *John Brown's Body*, for which he won a Pulitzer prize in 1929. He also dealt with problems of modern American civilization in many works.

BIERCE, AMBROSE (1842-1914?). The question mark after Bierce's death date is a result of his disappearance after crossing the border to report the Mexican Revolution late in 1913. He was born in Ohio and fought throughout the Civil War as a Union volunteer. Most of his subsequent life was spent as a reporter, first in London and then for many years in California and Washington, D.C. In London he gained the nickname "Bitter Bierce" because of his biting style, which is exemplified in the satire of *The Devil's Dictionary.* Some of his best-known short stories, which often make use of the supernatural or gruesome, are found in the volume *In the Midst of Life.*

BISHOP, ELIZABETH (1911-   ). Born in Worcester, Massachusetts, Miss Bishop is a graduate of Vassar College and has traveled extensively. Her best-known book of poetry is *Poems, North and South*, which received a Pulitzer prize in 1956. The style of her poems might be described as direct and straightforward rather than emotional and rhetorical.

BROOKS, CHARLES S. (1878-1934). Born in Cleveland, Ohio, Brooks returned there after graduating from Yale University. He worked in his father's printing firm until 1915; after that he devoted himself to writing and the theater. He was a pioneer in the little theater movement and for years served as president of the Cleveland Playhouse. His collections of essays include *Chimney-Pot Papers, There's Pippins and Cheese to Come*, and *Journeys to Bagdad.*

BROWNING, ROBERT (1812-1889). Browning was born in a London suburb to a prosperous family and was given every educational advantage. Early in life he decided upon a poetical career, but the British public was slow in appreciating his verse, which was unconventional in its rhythm and content. From 1846 to 1861 Browning and his wife, Elizabeth Barrett Browning, herself a poet, spent a happy married life in Italy, where they had eloped to escape the rage of Elizabeth's domineering father. After returning to England following his wife's death, Browning published *Dramatis Personae* and *The Ring and the Book,* and his poetic genius was finally recognized. His development of the dramatic monologue was one of his major contributions to poetry.

BURNS, ROBERT (1759-1796). Probably the greatest of Scottish poets, Robert Burns lived his early life in poverty. His father, an unsuccessful small farmer, could not provide much schooling for his son, but Robert educated himself through wide reading. His first volume of poems, written for passage money to Jamaica, was a success on publication in 1786, and Burns decided to remain in England. He combined poetry-writing with farming and, then, government service for the rest of his short life. Burns was the last great poet to write in the native Scottish language. In his lyrics he captures the moods and melodies of Scottish history and peasant life.

BYRON, GEORGE GORDON, LORD (1788-1824). Lord Byron led a colorful life appropriate to a poet hailed as the genius of romance. The title "Stanzas Written on the Road Between Florence and Pisa" is a typical illustration of the many references in Byron's poetry to his extensive travels. Through Byron's *Childe Harold,* readers can glimpse the scenery, art, and customs of various European countries. Although an English poet, Lord Byron received his earliest recognition from continental Europe. Today, however, he is acclaimed by most English-language critics as a poet of exceptional power and vision.

CARRIER, CONSTANCE (1908-   ). Constance Carrier has had many of her poems published in *The Atlantic Monthly* and other leading American magazines. Her collection *Middle Voice* won the Lamont Award in 1954. She is a teacher in the Latin Department of the New Britain (Connecticut) Senior High School.

CHEKHOV, ANTON (1860-1904). (Pronounced: än tôn' chĕk'ôf; *Russian* chĕ'hôf.) Born into a family of tradesmen, Chekhov studied medicine in Moscow and practiced there for a short time, but he distinguished himself in writing rather than in medicine. When he died at forty-four of tuberculosis, he was recognized as one of Russia's greatest playwrights and, along with his French contemporary de Maupassant, as one of the most influential of the world's short-story writers. His short stories, which emphasize mood and form, have influenced many American and English writers. Chekhov's plays, which are often produced today, reflect the disintegration of Russian aristocracy. *The Three Sisters, The Cherry Orchard,* and *The Seagull* are three of his better-known dramas.

CHESTERTON, GILBERT KEITH (1874-1936). Poet, essayist, novelist, biographer, and writer of detective stories, Chesterton joined the staff of the *Illustrated London News* in 1905 and, with the exception of two issues, furnished a weekly essay for this publication for the next twenty-five years. Outstanding among his more than one hundred volumes are *Heretics* and *Tremendous Trifles,* essays; *The Victorian Age in Literature,* criticism; *The Man Who Was Thursday* and the *Father Brown* series, detective stories; and *Robert Browning, Charles Dickens,* and *George Bernard Shaw,* biographical studies.

CHUTE, MARCHETTE (1909-   ). Miss Chute was born and grew up in Minneapolis, Minnesota. Most of her writing has been in biography and children's verse. Her pleasant and readable style, as well as her careful research, is evident in *Geoffrey Chaucer of England, Shakespeare of London,* and *Ben Jonson of Westminster.*

COFFIN, ROBERT P. TRISTRAM (1892-1955). Coffin, who distinguished himself as Rhodes Scholar, Pierce Professor of English at Bowdoin College, and special lecturer at many universities, came from a family of whalers, fishermen, and farmers going back three hundred years in New England history. He says that he "cut his teeth on the Maine granite of Spruce Island (the last island between Maine and Spain)." Often based on Maine life, his books include *Ballads of Square-Toed Americans; Saltwater Farm; Kennebec, Cradle of Americans; Portrait of an American;* and *Strange Holiness,* which won the 1936 Pulitzer Prize for poetry.

COLERIDGE, SAMUEL TAYLOR (1772-1834). Coleridge was a famed English poet, critic, and philosopher. Through his poetry, based most often on supernatural subjects, Coleridge emphasized the importance of the imagination in unifying the reasoning and understanding powers of the mind. His most enduring and melodic poems are *The Rime of the Ancient Mariner,* "Christabel," and "Kubla Khan."

CONRAD, JOSEPH (1857-1924). Joseph Conrad (the name is taken from two of his given names) was born with the surname of Korzeniowski to Polish parents then living in the Ukraine. After his education in Poland, he decided, at the age of seventeen, to make a career of the sea. He joined first the French, and then the British, merchant marine; by 1886 he was commanding ships going to many parts of the world. He

also became proficient in the English language. While recuperating from a fever, Conrad met John Galsworthy, who urged him to go on with some writing that he had begun many years before. From that time on, writing replaced the sea as the central interest in his life. He produced many short stories, notable for their exotic atmosphere and character exploration, and such well-known novels as *Almayer's Folly, Lord Jim,* and *The Nigger of the Narcissus.*

CRANE, STEPHEN (1871-1900). Crane was born in Newark, New Jersey, the youngest of a minister's family of fourteen. He is best known for his novel *The Red Badge of Courage,* the forerunner of all modern war stories. This short novel, a detailed and unglamourous account of the fears and emotions of a private in the Civil War, was Crane's first literary success. Although he later distinguished himself as a war correspondent in Cuba and Greece, at the time when he wrote this realistic story Crane had no personal experience of war. Trained on the New York papers, the *Herald* and the *Tribune,* he wrote fiction that presented life as he knew it, a daily struggle for survival. At twenty-eight he died of tuberculosis.

CUMMINGS, EDWARD ESTLIN (1894-1962). American author and painter, e e cummings (as he preferred to write his name) is best known for his poetry, which appeared in unusual typographical styles. His methods of using punctuation, capitalization, and language are all a part of his point of view that glorifies the individualist. His poetry, published in such collections as *Poems 1923-1954,* became increasingly popular during the 1950's and 1960's.

DE LA MARE, WALTER JOHN (1873-1956). The world of English poet

Walter de la Mare is that of the imagination. He wrote of the twilight zone between the real and the unreal and often made a familiar scene become "suddenly strange." Surprisingly enough, he worked for many years as a bookkeeper; then a grant from the British government enabled him to spend his full time on writing. He is thought of primarily as a poet (*Collected Poems* and *Peacock Pie* are two of his best-known volumes), but he was also a gifted writer of prose, as shown by his novel *The Memoirs of a Midget*.

DICKINSON, EMILY (1830-1886). Emily Dickinson lived most of her life in Amherst, Massachusetts, except for the two terms of Congress when she lived in Washington, D.C., with her father, who had been elected a Massachusetts Representative. Her early life was gay and social until she was disappointed in love in her early twenties and withdrew from society. Few of her poems were published during her lifetime, for she shunned publicity and her style was too different from the popular style of the day. In 1955 all her poems were finally collected in a three-volume set, *Poems of Emily Dickinson.* The excellence of her poetry has been increasingly recognized in recent years.

DOS PASSOS, JOHN RODERIGO (1896-   ). Graduated from Harvard with honors in 1916, Dos Passos, who was studying in Spain when World War I broke out, immediately joined a French ambulance corps. His rebellion against established forms shows itself in his debunking war novels, his championing of the little man, and his original writing techniques. In recent years he has moved to a more conservative position. He has written biographies, essays, novels, plays, poetry, and travel books. His social commentary on post-World War I America, *USA,* from which "The Campers at Kitty Hawk" was taken, consists of three novels, *The 42nd Parallel, 1919,* and *The Big Money.*

DUNSANY, EDWARD JOHN MORETON DRAX PLUNKETT, LORD (1878-1957). (Pronounced: dŭn sā′nĭ.) Lord Dunsany, although he considered himself more an outdoorsman than a writer, was a prolific producer of plays, poems, and novels. His greatest success was in drama. He believed that people are better judges of the worth of a play than of any other literary genre because, he wrote, "all art is simply essence of life, but the drama is life itself." His plays are often concerned with the strange world of his imagination: he liked to write about "mysterious kingdoms where geography ends." "The Gods of the Mountain," "The Lost Silk Hat," and "A Night at the Inn" are among his more famous plays. Lord Dunsany, who was born in London of Irish parentage, maintained homes in both England and Ireland. He also traveled widely (making several lecture trips to the United States) and served in two world wars.

EINSTEIN, CHARLES (1926-   ). Born in Boston, Einstein grew up in New York City, and was graduated from the University of Chicago. His short stories have appeared in *The Atlantic Monthly* and *Harper's Magazine,* as well as in *This Week* and *The Saturday Evening Post.* His novel *No Time at All* was a best seller.

ELIOT, THOMAS STEARNS (1888-   ). In 1954 *Life* magazine called T. S. Eliot "the world's most distinguished living poet." Six years earlier he had won the Nobel Prize for literature, the highest honor an author can receive. Although he spent his entire childhood in St. Louis and as a young man attended

Harvard University, Eliot later moved to England, where he married and became a British subject. His poetry, though not widely read by the general population, is intensively studied in universities and colleges. Among his most famous works are the poems *The Waste Land* and "The Hollow Men" and the poetic dramas *Murder in the Cathedral* and *The Cocktail Party*. These works evidence not only his greatness as a poet but also his spiritual exploration of 20-century life.

EMERSON, RALPH WALDO (1803-1882). Born in Boston, Ralph Waldo Emerson lived most of his life in Massachusetts. He headed a group of writers and thinkers who expressed a new idealistic "Transcendental" philosophy. Henry Thoreau, Nathaniel Hawthorne, and Bronson Alcott were among the "Concord" authors connected with Emerson, who believed that man must reassert his dignity and obey his noble instincts. Although he was primarily noted as a lecturer and essayist, his poetry, which contains the essence of his philosophy, has received increasing attention.

EVANS, BERGEN (1904-   ). Evans was born in Ohio but spent part of his childhood in England, where his father served in the United States consular service. After returning to this country, he studied at Miami University in Ohio before going to England as a Rhodes Scholar at Oxford University, where he received a B.Litt. degree. He later received a Ph.D. from Harvard. He has been professor of English at Northwestern University since 1932 and became known to a wide television and radio audience as an informative and witty moderator of controversial language programs. In 1957, with his sister Cornelia Evans, he compiled *A Dictionary of Contemporary Usage*.

FINNEY, JACK (1911-   ). A native of Galesburg, Illinois, Finney was graduated from Knox College and worked in an advertising agency in New York City until his short stories began to sell. His stories are noted for their unusual plots and their flights into imagination. He has published three novels, *Five Against the House*, *The Body Snatchers*, and *The House of Numbers*, and one volume of short stories, *The Third Level*.

FISHER, DOROTHY CANFIELD (1879-1958). Daughter of the president of two great universities, Kansas and Ohio State, Mrs. Fisher earned her Ph.D. degree at Columbia University, and early distinguished herself as a linguist, translator, and author. She and her husband settled in rural Vermont, which is the locale of many of her works. In addition to writing short stories, novels, and scholarly papers, Mrs. Fisher served for years on the Vermont State Board of Education and as one of the judges of the Book-of-the-Month Club. Her works include *Hillsboro People*, *The Bent Twig*, and *Seasoned Timber*.

FOLLETT, WILSON (1887-1963). Born in North Attleboro, Massachusetts, Follett graduated from Harvard and taught at various colleges including Dartmouth, Brown University, and Radcliffe. He spent several years as an editor with publishing companies and frequently wrote magazine articles. He was the author of one novel, *No More Sea*, several books on the novel and novelists, and numerous short stories.

FORD, COREY (1902-   ). A graduate of Columbia University, Mr. Ford is a free-lance writer and a consultant to Dartmouth College. His writing, typified by his book *How to Guess Your Age*, is usually humorous or satirical.

FROST, ROBERT (1874-1963). Although Robert Frost was born in San Francisco, his parents were from a long line of New Englanders. After his father's death when Robert was ten, he and his mother moved to Massachusetts. Never happy or successful as a student in grammar school or college, he tried shoemaking, news reporting, farming, and teaching before moving to England at the age of thirty-eight. In the next two years his first two books were published, and his reputation as a poet was assured. After three years in England he returned to America, where he farmed in New England, lectured at many universities, and wrote his best poetry. He once said, "A complete poem is one where an emotion has found its thought and the thought has found the words." In recent years his poetry has received not only popular recognition but also critical acclaim. He won the Pulitzer Prize for poetry many times.

GALLICO, PAUL (1897-). Gallico was born in New York City, went through the city's public schools, and upon graduation from Columbia University joined the staff of the New York *Daily News* as a sports reporter. At thirty-nine he left the *Daily News* to devote all of his time to free-lance writing. Since that time he has traveled widely, served as a war correspondent during World War II for *Cosmopolitan* magazine, and written movie scripts, essays, novels, and short stories, of which the most famous is *The Snow Goose*.

GALSWORTHY, JOHN (1867-1933). For thirty-five years Galsworthy wrote a novel or a play a year, and he earned the Nobel Prize for literature the year before his death. An Oxford graduate, Galsworthy was deeply concerned with the social and economic changes going on in England between the end of the Victorian era and the mid-1920's. His most important work, *The Forsyte Saga*, is a monumental three-novel volume that begins with the Victorians and follows the fortunes of the Forsyte family through three generations. His great social dramas, *Justice*, *Strife*, and *Loyalties*, examine the code of the British upper classes.

GELSTED, OTTO (1888-). Otto Gelsted's homeland of Denmark was invaded by the Germans on April 9, 1940. He was a consistent opponent of Hitler, and in November of 1942 he was imprisoned by the Nazis "to make him harmless." Gelsted escaped to Sweden, where he opposed the Nazis through his war of words.

GLASPELL, SUSAN (1882-1948). Born and educated in Iowa, Susan Glaspell decided early in life that she wanted to be an author. The degree of her success is indicated by the fact that she is often called the mother of the American Little Theater. In 1915 with her husband, George Cram Cook, she founded the most influential of American community theaters, the Provincetown Players. It was for this group a year later that she wrote the one-act play "Trifles," to be produced on an old wharf that the Players had converted into a theater. She was also an actress and producer in the Provincetown Playhouse, the theater that introduced Eugene O'Neill's plays to the public. In addition to one- and three-act plays, she wrote many novels and a biography of her husband. In 1931 she won a Pulitzer prize for *Alison's House*, her full-length play based on the life of Emily Dickinson.

HENRY, O. (1862-1910). This was the pen name of William Sydney Porter, whose birthplace was Greensboro,

North Carolina. Porter was at different times reporter, ranch hand, and bank clerk. He fled in panic to Central America when accused of embezzling funds from the Texas bank in which he worked. His wife's illness led him to return several years later to stand trial. Although he declared he was innocent, Porter was sentenced to prison, where he began writing under the pen name O. Henry. He continued to use this name when he went to New York at the end of his five-year term and began writing a short story a week for the old *New York World*. His stories were collected under titles such as *Cabbages and Kings, The Four Million, Roads of Destiny*, and *Whirligigs;* many of them are famous for their surprise or "twist" endings.

HIGHET, GILBERT (1906-   ). Born in Glasgow, Scotland, Highet received a master's degree from the University of Glasgow in 1929, and went on to win scholastic honors at Oxford University and to teach there. In 1937 he began his career at Columbia University, where he became professor of Latin. He has also given popular radio talks on books and served as a Book-of-the-Month Club Editor. In 1951 he became a naturalized citizen of the United States. *The Classical Tradition, The Art of Teaching*, and *People, Places, and Things* are among his published works.

KIPLING, RUDYARD (1865-1936). Born to English parents living in Bombay, Kipling learned the native habits, language, and stories of India during his early childhood. He was educated in England but returned to India to work for a newspaper, for which he then traveled widely. In 1892 he married an American girl and lived in Vermont for five years. He and his family then settled in England, where Kipling spent the rest of his life. A prolific writer and a Nobel-prize winner, he turned out novels, short stories, children's stories, and verse. *The Light That Failed, The Jungle Book*, and *Captains Courageous* are three of his best-known books. His background of travel is shown in their varied settings, but he is usually thought of as a writer about India when it was a part of the British Empire.

LAMB, CHARLES (1775-1834). Although Lamb worked as a bookkeeper for the East India Company for more than thirty years, he found time to do considerable free-lance editing and criticism, to contribute his famous *Essays of Elia* to the *London Magazine*, and, with his sister Mary, to write *Tales from Shakespeare*. In spite of family burdens that included the care of his sister Mary, who was mentally disturbed most of her life, Lamb was connected with a literary circle made up of such famous English writers as Coleridge, Leigh Hunt, and Wordsworth.

LINDSAY, VACHEL (1879-1931). Vachel Lindsay grew up in Springfield, Illinois. After attending Hiram College in Ohio for three years, he studied art in Chicago and then in New York City, but he was unsuccessful in earning a living as an artist. Not wishing to go home a failure, he became a vagabond, trading poems for meals. This was the beginning of a lifelong career of lecturing and reciting his poems. Their sound, rhythm, and melody make them especially exciting when read aloud.

LONDON, JACK (1876-1916). Three years before his death, California-born London was the highest-paid author in the world. Much of his writing is based on personal experiences that include working as a common sailor, prospecting for gold in the Klondike, and serving as a war correspondent during the Russo-Japanese War. Although critics are inclined to neglect London because his work is uneven in quality, his novels *The Call of the Wild* and *The Sea Wolf* and his short stories "All Gold Canyon" and "To Build a Fire" insure him a place as one of America's best adventure writers.

MacLeish, Archibald (1892-   ). During the 1940's Archibald MacLeish filled several high governmental positions and also served as Librarian of Congress. Later he taught literature and creative writing courses at Harvard University for several years. A primary concern of his has been with the problem of man's relation to society, and his Broadway play *J.B.*, based on the Biblical book of Job, explores man's relationship to God. MacLeish's poetry has won two Pulitzer prizes.

Marquand, John (1893-1960). Marquand, whose novels are affectionately critical of Boston, was educated at Harvard and lived for some time in Massachusetts—in Cambridge and during the summers in the old sailing town of Newburyport. Following service in France with the A.E.F. during World War I, he joined the staff of the New York *Herald Tribune. The Late George Apley,* Pulitzer-prize novel of 1937, was published originally in *The Saturday Evening Post,* which also carried Marquand's Mr. Moto detective series and many of his short stories. His other novels include *Wickford Point, H. M. Pulham, Esq.,* and *Point of No Return.* Many of his books have been best sellers, and Marquand was undoubtedly one of the most financially successful of modern writers.

Marquis, Donald (1878-1937). Illinois-born Donald Robert Perry Marquis worked as an actor, news reporter, columnist, and magazine editor before becoming a novelist, poet, and dramatist. He is remembered more for his humorous and satirical works than for his serious dramas. He received early encouragement from Joel Chandler Harris, creator of Uncle Remus, and from novelist Christopher Morley. Although Marquis for a time was extremely successful as the author of the "Sun Dial" column in the New York *Sun,* he spent his last years in poverty and invalidism.

Maupassant, Guy de (1850-1893). (Pronounced: gē də mō på saN′.) The son of a Paris stockbroker, de Maupassant inherited a severe nervous disorder. He died at forty-two, hopelessly insane, but in his short life he had written more than two hundred stories. His newspaper experience and the influence of his literary master, Gustave Flaubert, helped him to write technically perfect stories in very few words. Most of his stories run under two thousand words. Considered France's most brilliant short-story writer, de Maupassant wrote about ordinary people in a pessimistic, often bitter, vein. "The Necklace," "A Piece of String," "Moonlight," and "A Coward" are among his masterpieces.

Millay, Edna St. Vincent (1892-1950). Edna St. Vincent Millay was born in Maine, where she attended elementary and high school. She was actively engaged in writing poetry during her college years at Barnard and Vassar. Her first long poem, "Renascence," was published when she was only twenty. Although it brought her wide recognition, her years in New York City's Greenwich Village were spent in the usual poverty of a struggling young author. In 1923 she married and moved to a country home where she continued her writing career. The same year as her marriage, she won the Pulitzer Prize for poetry for her volume *The Harp-Weaver*, containing, among other poems, twenty-two sonnets, the poetic form in which she did her finest work.

NASH, OGDEN (1902-   ). Born in Rye, New York, Ogden Nash is today one of the most widely read living American poets—an acknowledged master of humorous verse. Nash's subject matter is whatever takes his fancy in daily existence, and his wit sometimes contains a sharp sting for contemporary society. He follows his own poetic rules and often rearranges spelling to fit a particular rhyme. Both readers and critics, however, enjoy his unconventional verse, and he gives readings of his works throughout the United States. Some typical titles of his collections are *Versus* and *I'm a Stranger Here Myself.*

O'FLAHERTY, LIAM (1897-   ). (Pronounced: lē′əm ō flä′hər tĭ.) Novelist and short-story writer, Liam O'Flaherty is a native of Ireland's Aran Islands. He left University College in Dublin to join the Irish Guards and was injured in World War I. During his recuperation he became a world traveler. In 1925 he published his most famous novel, *The Informer*, the story of a man betrayed by a comrade. He now lives mostly in the United States but makes regular visits to Ireland.

PARKER, DOROTHY (1893-   ). In the 1920's Dorothy Parker was a book reviewer for *The New Yorker*, but when her first volume of verse was a phenomenal success, she resigned to become a free-lance poet and short-story writer. In those days she wrote for a critical and adoring public in an unconventional, close to flippant tone, establishing a reputation for wit and satire. Critic Alexander Woollcott described her as "so odd a blend of Little Nell and Lady Macbeth." She made so many delightfully outrageous statements and has been credited with so many more that her name is synonymous with the clever quip or the devastating phrase. Her vein of sophisticated bitterness shows through in the titles of her poetry volumes, *Enough Rope, Sunset Gun,* and *Death and Taxes,* and in her short-story collections, *Laments for the Living, After Such Pleasures,* and *Here Lies.*

PUSHKIN, ALEXANDER SERGEYEVICH (1799-1837). Alexander Pushkin was born in Moscow of aristocratic but poor parents. He was given an excellent education, but as a result of publishing a few political poems that displeased the Czar, Pushkin was exiled to southern Russia. There he read Byron, Walter Scott, and Shakespeare, and, as a result, opened the way through his own writing for a literary blending of European and Russian cultures. The poetry of Pushkin, which contains some of the most beautiful lyrics in the Russian language, had a great influence on his country's literature. His verse-novel, *Eugene Onegin,* is considered his masterpiece.

RATTIGAN, TERENCE (1911-   ). Terence Rattigan left Oxford and forfeited his claim to his father's money in order to write plays. Although judged by the critics to be without substance, his *French without Tears* and other early plays were tremendous box-office successes. *The Winslow Boy,* written while Rattigan was a gunner in the Royal Air Force during World War II, was the first of his plays to win the enthusiastic

AUTHOR BIOGRAPHIES

approval of the drama critics. *The Winslow Boy* won the Ellen Terry Award in London as the best play of 1946 and later the New York Critics' Circle award as the best foreign play of its season. Following the critical acclaim of *The Winslow Boy*, such plays as *The Browning Version, The Deep Blue Sea*, and *Separate Tables* have won for Rattigan the title of "master of the well-made play."

RICHTER, CONRAD (1890-   ). Richter was born in Pennsylvania, but his literary life is associated with Ohio and the Southwest, which he has dramatized in his stories of pioneering Americans. In 1928 he moved to New Mexico, where his interest in pioneer days was sharpened through his getting to know many of the men and women who had helped to settle the Southwest. Here he wrote his Ohio Trilogy: *The Trees, The Fields*, and *The Town*, the last of which won a Pulitzer prize in 1951.

ROETHKE, THEODORE (1908-1963). (Pronounced: rět'kě.) Roethke, a Harvard graduate, has been a professor of English at several leading American universities (also serving occasionally as varsity tennis coach). His writing is vigorous and imaginative. Among his principal collections are *The Lost Son and Other Poems* (1948) and *The Waking* (1953), for which he won the Pulitzer Prize for poetry.

SAINT-EXUPÉRY, ANTOINE DE (1900-1944). (Pronounced: äN twàn'də säN těg zY pě rē'.) An incredible Frenchman who made aviation history as a daring pilot and who won the Grand Prize of the French Academy for his stories of pilots and their planes, Saint-Exupéry disappeared during World War II on an operational flight over the Mediterranean while fighting with American forces in Africa. He distin-

guished himself as a pioneer professional pilot who helped to establish commercial air flights in France, Africa, and South America in the days when pilots were charting unknown countries in uncertain planes in weather that had yet to be patterned or predicted. His three books, *Wind, Sand, and Stars, Night Flight*, and *Flight to Arras*, have been collected in the one-volume *Airman's Odyssey*.

SANDBURG, CARL (1878-   ). Sandburg was born in Galesburg, Illinois, of Swedish immigrant parents. He left school at thirteen; and in the interval before he entered Lombard College, he worked as a barbershop porter, scene-shifter in a theater, and dishwasher in city hotels, as well as serving in the Spanish-American War. He later distinguished himself as a newspaperman, poet, historian, and biographer. For more than a generation, Sandburg's tall, erect figure, topped by a thatch of white hair falling over his forehead, has been the image of the rugged American individualist who excels in many fields. His publications include his six-volume biography, *Abraham Lincoln*, that won a Pulitzer prize in 1940, *The American Songbag, Remembrance Rock, Always the Young Strangers*, and *Steichen, the Photographer*, a biography of his famous brother-in-law. He has been praised and condemned for the racy, earthy language of his poetry, especially *Chicago Poems*, which helped to win the Pulitzer Prize for poetry for him in 1951.

SCHWARTZ, DELMORE (1913-   ). Poet, short-story writer, critic, and editor, Delmore Schwartz reflects the tragic view of life in his works. Born in Brooklyn, New York, Schwartz was graduated from New York University.

He has spent much of his adult life lecturing in American colleges, editing literary magazines, and writing poetry and motion-picture review columns for *The New Republic*.

SHAKESPEARE, WILLIAM (1564-1616). The greatest writer in the English language, William Shakespeare was born in Stratford-on-Avon, England, where he probably received a classical education in the local grammar school. He married at eighteen and about five years later arrived in London to begin his career as a poet and playwright. The first of his thirty-seven plays was performed when he was thirty. His popularity with the common people of his day was as great as his popularity among the literary scholars of our day. For a more detailed account of Shakespeare's career, see page 609.

SHAPIRO, KARL (1913-). Karl Shapiro, who was born in Baltimore, Maryland, is one of the most popular contemporary poets among young people. His poetry is clear and sharp; a single idea is imaginatively developed from the vivid images he creates in writing about a concrete experience. Some of Shapiro's best poetry was written during World War II while he served with the U.S. Army in the South Pacific. His collection *V-Letter* won a Pulitzer prize in 1945. Since the war, Shapiro has taught at various colleges and has edited the magazine *Poetry*.

SHELLEY, PERCY BYSSHE (1792-1822). In a short life marked by romantic adventure, Shelley wrote some of the finest English lyrics of the last two centuries. At the age of twenty-two he left England and spent most of his remaining eight years in Switzerland and Italy with his second wife and friends. His untimely death was by drowning in a mysterious boating mishap. Imagination, fragile beauty, melodious lyrics, and sublimity are among the chief characteristics of his poetry. A strong interest in social and political problems and a passion for freedom also mark many of his poems.

SOUTHEY, ROBERT (1774-1843). Born in England to a family of modest means, Robert Southey received only meager schooling. Through his own efforts, however, he was able to enter Oxford, first studying for a career in theology, then medicine, and later law. He was dissatisfied with these professions, and after meeting two British authors—Samuel Taylor Coleridge and Charles Lamb—he began a lifetime of writing. Southey married Coleridge's wife's sister, and the four lived together in the Lake District. Although at the age of thirty-nine he became poet laureate of England, today he is better remembered for his brilliant prose style, in the *Life of Nelson*, for example, than for his verse.

SPENCER, THEODORE (1902-1949). Pennsylvania-born poet Theodore Spencer received his undergraduate degrees from Princeton and from Cambridge, England, and his doctoral degree from Harvard University. He taught at Harvard much of his life, and is particularly known for his books on the Elizabethan Age and drama. His critical works include *Shakespeare and the Nature of Man* (1942); his poetry, which was small in quantity, includes *The Paradox in the Circle* (1941) and *An Acre in the Seed* (1949).

SPENDER, STEPHEN (1909-). Stephen Spender was born in London and educated in Oxford. As a young man he joined the anti-Fascist movement. A collection of his poetry, *Poems*, published when he was twenty-four, praised labor and denounced capital with conviction and power. He later became disillusioned with communism and rejected it completely. Besides poetry—his works have appeared as *Collected Poems*—Spender is also a critic and editor.

STEINBECK, JOHN (1902-   ). Steinbeck's best known writing concerns the economic depression of the 1930's and California's Salinas Valley; his characters are the indigent migratory workers, ranch hands, and fishermen on the Monterey Peninsula. Steinbeck knows these men first-hand from his experiences during the depression when he worked as fruit-picker, surveyor, and printer's helper in between occasional sessions at Stanford University. He had his first success as a writer in the late 1930's when *Of Mice and Men* became a best seller and *The Grapes of Wrath* won a Pulitzer prize. In 1962 he was awarded the Nobel Prize for literature.

STEPHENS, JAMES (1882-1950). Born in the slums of Dublin, James Stephens became a leading Irish poet, short-story writer, and novelist. A sense of fantasy and dreamlike delicacy characterize his style. Stephens was a well-known expert on Gaelic art, folk music, and stories; he made several visits to the United States, where he gave lectures about these interests. In later life he moved to London. *Kings and the Moon* is a collection of his poetry; and *The Crock of Gold* is a novel of fantasy.

STICKNEY, TRUMBULL (1874-1904). Although his parents were American, Trumbull Stickney spent most of his childhood and youth in Europe. He died at the age of thirty while serving as an instructor at Harvard. He published one volume of poems during his life; his friends William Vaughan

Moody and George Cabot Lodge compiled a second volume that Stickney had left uncompleted at the time of his death.

STROUT, RICHARD LEE (1898-   ). Strout was born in Cahoes, New York, and was graduated from Harvard in 1919. He served as a Second Lieutenant in World War I and as a war correspondent in World War II. He has been a member of the Washington Bureau of *The Christian Science Monitor* since 1921.

STUART, JESSE (1907-   ). Stuart lives on his own 723-acre farm in W-Hollow, Greenup County, Kentucky, near the one-room shack in which he was born. The first of his family to attend high school and college, Stuart fell in love with school in the first grade. After his study at Vanderbilt University, Stuart went back to his mountain home to teach and to write. His first book was a collection of poems, *Man with a Bull-Tongue Plow*. His poems, his short stories, and his novels are about his mountain friends and neighbors. *Taps for Private Tussie* and *Hie to the Hunters* are two of his better-known novels, and *The Thread That Runs So True* is his autobiography.

SULLIVAN, FRANK (1892-   ). A graduate of Cornell University, Frank Sullivan has been a contributor to newspapers and magazines. He is the author of humorous sketches collected under such titles as *Broccoli and Old Lace, A Rock in Every Snowball,* and *A Pearl in Every Oyster*. Many of Sullivan's sketches appeared originally in *The New Yorker*.

TEALE, EDWIN WAY (1899-   ). A graduate of Earlham College, Teale is a roving naturalist whose activities have included taking thousands of nature photographs, revising the insect-study program of the Boy Scouts of America, and writing for the *Popular Science Monthly* for many years. Since 1941 he has been a free-lance writer, a contributing editor of the *Audubon Magazine,* and a biographer (*The Wilderness World of John Muir*), as well as nature-book reviewer for the New York *Herald Tribune.* His books include *North with the Spring,* his most widely read book; *Autumn across America;* and *Journey into Summer.*

Teasdale, Sara (1884-1933). Sara Teasdale, born and educated in St. Louis, Missouri, traveled widely and eventually settled in New York. Through her early reading, especially of Christina Rosetti, she became interested in poetry, and she published her first volume in 1907. Her life was not a happy one—she had persistent health problems, her once happy marriage ended in divorce, and she had few close friends—yet her poetry is never bitter or cynical. Her simple lyric style is evident in such collections as *Rivers to the Sea, Dark of the Moon,* and *Strange Victory.*

Tennyson, Alfred, Lord (1809-1892). As poet laureate of England during most of Queen Victoria's reign, Tennyson more eloquently than any other writer voiced the thought of his age, reflecting the Victorian attitude toward life in his poetry. Tennyson's collection of poems published in 1842 established his genius as a lyric artist, but it was not until *Idylls of the King* was published seventeen years later that he achieved a wide and devoted readership. During the latter half of his life, he lived as a recluse; his son revealed in his biography of Tennyson that these years were spent in continual study to perfect his art. Tennyson is buried in the Poets' Corner of Westminster Abbey next to the grave of Robert Browning.

Thurber, James (1894-1961). Thurber had the good fortune to be born into a mildly eccentric family in Columbus, Ohio, whose activities he reported in his autobiography, *My Life and Hard Times.* He joined *The New Yorker* magazine as managing editor in 1926 but transferred to the "Talk of the Town" department, where he could continue writing. After giving up his formal association with *The New Yorker* in 1933, he was a free-lance contributor to the magazine until his death. The following titles of some of his many collections of essays suggest the off-beat quality of his writings: *The Middle-Aged Man on the Flying Trapeze, The Owl in the Attic and Other Perplexities,* and *The Seal in the Bedroom and Other Predicaments.* He often illustrated his stories with line drawings of melancholy dogs, frustrated men, and determined women. With Elliott Nugent, he coauthored *The Male Animal,* a play that is still a favorite with little theater and college drama groups. In 1960 he played himself briefly in the Broadway production of *A Thurber Carnival.*

Van Doren, Mark (1894-   ). The poetry of Mark Van Doren has often been compared to that of Robert Frost. The deceptively simple approach, the rural settings, and the "clean and chiseled" style are characteristic of both authors. Although Mark Van Doren spent much of his life in New York City, where he taught English at Columbia University, most of his writing has been done on his Connecticut farm. He has a wide reputation as a critic and lecturer, and he has published biography and fiction, as well as poetry. His *Collected Poems* won the Pulitzer Prize for poetry in 1940.

Weeks, Edward A. (1898-   ). Weeks

has been associated with *The Atlantic Monthly* editorial staff since 1924. When he succeeded the scholarly Ellery Sedgwick in 1938, he became ninth editor of the magazine that was founded in 1857 to champion the cause of antislavery. He studied at Cambridge University in England, following his graduation from Harvard University in 1922. He has edited various *Atlantic Monthly* publications and has published several volumes of essays including *This Trade of Writing*, *The Open Heart*, and *In Friendly Candor*.

WHITE, E. B. (1899-   ). Elwyn Brooks White was born in Mt. Vernon, New York, and was graduated in 1921 from Cornell, where he was editor of the college paper. Before joining *The New Yorker* magazine staff shortly after it was founded, he served as messboy on a trading ship to Alaska and worked for a New York advertising firm. When he moved from the city to the farm in Maine where he now lives and does free-lance writing, he celebrated his many trials and joys in a series of essays originally published in *Harper's Magazine*, and later in book form as *One Man's Meat*. He has collaborated on two books of essays with James Thurber (writer of "The Dog That Bit People," p. 303). Since White writes children's books as well as adult fare, readers are still arguing whether *Charlotte's Web* and *Stuart Little* are for adults or for children.

WHITE, LEE STROUT. *See* Strout, Richard Lee, and White, E. B.

WHITMAN, WALT (1819-1892). Born on Long Island and educated in Brooklyn, Walt Whitman spent his young manhood as a kind of vagabond journalist. During the Civil War when his brother lay wounded in a Washington, D.C., hospital, Walt went to care for him. Although his brother quickly recovered, Whitman had seen many soldiers suffering and, revealing his true concern for his fellow men, remained to dress the wounds of the injured and to read to them. After the war he worked as a government clerk and continued his writing. His *Leaves of Grass*, free verse first published in 1855 and later enlarged, was the most original work of poetry at that time created by an American. Considering himself the voice and prophet of democracy, Whitman contributed gusto and energy to American poetry through his new rhythms and sharp images.

WHYTE, WILLIAM H. (1917-   ). Whyte was born in West Chester, Pennsylvania, was graduated from Princeton, and served as captain in the U.S. Marines in World War II. He has been associated with *Fortune Magazine* since 1946 and is currently assistant managing editor. *The Organization Man* and *Is Anybody Listening?* (a series of articles examining our business culture) reflect his critical attitude toward the substitution of group standards for individual ones in today's business world.

YEATS, WILLIAM BUTLER (1865-1939). (Pronounced: yāts.) The world of William Butler Yeats is a mystic land ruled by unseen spirits. A leader in the Irish literary renaissance, Yeats is generally recognized as the greatest of all Irish poets. In addition to his poetry, he is well known for his plays written for the Abbey Theater, which he helped to found, and for his prose essays. In 1923 he was awarded the Nobel Prize for literature.

Literary Terms

Definitions for literary terms used in this book and also for certain fairly common terms not used in the text itself are given below. Page references in parentheses indicate that a term is further discussed on the pages listed. An asterisk after a word within a definition indicates that the word is defined under its own heading. A complete index to literary terms appears on page 752.

Abstract Terms: Terms that name ideas or qualities that cannot be known directly by the senses (for example, *goodness, knowledge, sportsmanship*). The meaning of an abstract term generally is made up of some characteristic that many objects, events, or actions have in common. For instance, the meaning of *sportsmanship* is based upon an intangible quality that many specific actions occurring in many different sports have in common, although no one of these actions is itself the meaning of the word. (See p. 473.)

Act: A major division in a play. Up until the late 19th century, plays were usually divided into five acts; today, serious plays frequently have three. There is no set number, however.

Allegory: A narrative* in which the characters and the setting* stand for abstract qualities and ideas. The writer of an allegory is not primarily trying to make his characters and their actions realistic, but to make them representative of ideas or truths (as the fact that Sir Evening-Star in "Gareth and Lynette" wears hardened skins is included in order to show that the habits of youth harden and become difficult to overcome as one grows old). Allegory is related to symbolism, but allegory usually makes a one-to-one equation between things; a symbol,* however, usually has a number of possible meanings.

Alliteration: *See* Sound Devices.

Allusion: A reference to a historical person or event or to a literary work or figure. The reference is usually to something well enough known so that a well-read person would be expected to recognize it (for example, "goat-footed / balloonMan" in the poem "in Just—" is an allusion to the Greek god Pan).

Anachronism (ə năk′rə nĭz′əm): Anything in a work of literature not existing at the time of the work's setting (for example, the appearance of Caius wearing a kerchief in *Julius Caesar* because he is sick: this was an Elizabethan, not a Roman, custom). Anachronisms may be used for humorous effect, as in Lamb's essay "A Dissertation upon Roast Pig."

Analogy: A comparison, usually for the purpose of making clearer something unfamiliar by likening it to something familiar. Analogy may also be used in argument to show that a certain thing which is true of one case will also be true of a similar second case. (See p. 375.)

Anecdote: A brief narrative account of an interesting incident. It is briefer than a short story,* does not have a complex plot,* and concerns only a single incident.

Anticlimax: Material that is of less importance or suspense than that which precedes it (when the reader has been led to expect material of greater importance or suspense). For example, in the typical detective story, the solving of the crime is the climax.* If this point were to be followed by a chapter of less interest to the reader, this last chapter would be anticlimactic.

Aphorism (ăf'ə riz'əm): A short pointed saying expressing some general truth (such as Emerson's statement that "A foolish consistency is the hobgoblin of little minds").

Aside: In drama, a character's private thoughts that are spoken by an actor while others are present on stage, but which supposedly are not overheard by the other characters.

Assonance: *See* Sound Devices.

Atmosphere: A pervading emotion or mood that contributes to the effect an author wants to achieve. He secures this effect chiefly by careful selection of details. For instance, in "The Damned Thing" Ambrose Bierce begins immediately to create an atmosphere appropriate to happenings that cannot be explained as fact by opening his story in a shadowy log cabin lit only by a single candle. (See p. 173.)

Autobiography: An account of a person's life written by that person.

Ballad:

Folk Ballad: A narrative poem* handed down by word of mouth. It usually has four-line stanzas,* and a refrain* often follows each stanza or is a part of it. The action in a ballad generally moves swiftly, and description is brief, only a few suggestive details usually being given. Folk ballads often have widely varying versions, since singers may modify the original words or some may be forgotten, replaced, or changed slightly as time goes on.

Literary Ballad: A narrative poem* based on the characteristics of a folk ballad but written down by its author and preserved by writing rather than by word of mouth. A literary ballad is more consciously artistic than a folk ballad, although not necessarily better literature; it is not apt to have the technical irregularities of many folk ballads. An example of a literary ballad is Auden's "O what is that sound," page 521.

Biography: The history of a person's life written by another person. It generally attempts to give a clear picture of its subject's personality and significance. (See pp. 377-382 and Fiction.)

Blank Verse: Unrhymed iambic pentameter. (See pp. 604-605.) It is used by Shakespeare in his plays and has been frequently used by other poets.

Cacophony: *See* Sound Devices.

Characterization: The means by which an author shows what a person is like. In fiction, the chief methods are description of a person, his actions, his words, his thoughts, or the comments and thoughts of others about him. In drama, a person is characterized chiefly through his actions and speech, and perhaps through the comments of other characters about him. His character also depends largely upon the actor playing him—the actor's gestures, appearance, facial expressions, and tone of voice.

Good characterization—that is, the creation of convincing and interesting characters—is usually regarded as the most essential quality in a novel, short story, or drama. (See pp. 7 and 150.)

Chronological Order: The relation of events in the order that they occurred in time.

Cliché (klē shā'): A trite or hackneyed expression; one that presented an original way of saying something when first used, but which has become stale through overuse (for example, "dead as a doornail"). (See p. 349.)

Climax: The moment of greatest suspense, or interest, in a literary work. *Climax* is often used as a synonym for *crisis,* and then means "the turning point of the conflict."

Complication: The part of a plot* that develops problems resulting from the basic conflict.* For example, imagine a story in which the basic conflict is between a boy and his parents. He runs away from home. The various problems he now encounters—perhaps getting hungry or lonely—make up the complication.

Concrete Terms: Terms that name things that can be experienced through the senses; the opposite of abstract terms.* Literature relies heavily on concrete language, because of its appeal to the senses and its greater vividness. (See p. 473.)

Conflict: The struggle upon which a novel, short story, drama, or sometimes a poem is based. There is usually one central conflict in a work of literature; but, particularly in longer works, several others are often present. Conflicts may be of many kinds: for instance, human beings may be in conflict with each other (either individually or as groups), an individual may be in conflict with his environment, or an individual may be in conflict with himself. A literary work usually first develops the nature of the conflict upon which the plot* is based, then shows the various reactions of the characters to the situation in which they find themselves, and concludes by showing the result of the conflict. When a writer handles a conflict skillfully, he arouses suspense* in the reader by making him want to know how the characters will react and how the conflict will finally turn out.

Connotation: The associations that a word or phrase may have beyond its accepted, literal definition. The phrase "imitation fur," for example, would generally sound better to people than "fake fur," although its meaning is the same. The difference would lie in the connotations of the two phrases, the feelings people associate with them because of past experiences. (See p. 172.)

Consonance: *See* Sound Devices.

Context: The words or passages which surround a term or passage in speech or writing. All words or longer portions of a piece of writing or of a speech can be accurately interpreted only in their context. For example, the phrase "a literary masterpiece" when lifted from such a sentence as "This book is hardly a literary masterpiece" does not represent the idea contained in the sentence at all.

Context can also be used to refer to conditions surrounding a person, action, or idea (as in the sentence "A writer's ideas should be examined within the *context* of his time").

Contrast: Setting off two things through opposing them to each other, as black and white together both set off and emphasize each other. An author may contrast characters (as in "The Heyday of the Blood"), environments (as in "The Third Level"), man and his environment (as in "All Gold Canyon"), abstract qualities (as in "On the Difference Between Wit and Humor"), images (as in the poem "When I Heard the Learn'd Astronomer"), and so on. An author frequently shows that he prefers one of the things he is contrasting to the other, and in this way defines his ideas about what is good and what is bad.

Couplet: Two lines of poetry that form a unit and rhyme (for example, the lines "A buck leaped out and took the tide/ With jewels flowing past each side" in "Crystal Moment," p. 471).

Crisis: The part of a plot* that decides the outcome of the conflict.* It is sometimes called the turning point, for after it the problems of the main character tend steadily to improve or to worsen. In short works of literature, the crisis is usually near the end. *Climax** is often used as a synonym for *crisis.* (See p. 195 and Plot.)

Definition: An expression that has the same meaning as the term being explained. As general rules, a definition should not contain the term being defined or any form of it, should not be a synonym, and should be put in more familiar terms than the word being defined. (See the dictionary entries on p. 376 for examples.)

Description: A piece of writing that describes something, as opposed to telling a story about it or explaining it. Almost all writing contains some description; very little is pure description.

Dialogue: Conversation between two or more characters. It can be used to reveal character, show conflicts between characters, give background information, and so on.

Diction: A writer's choice of words. Good diction is the selection of words that say accurately and precisely what one means. (See p. 545.)

Downstage: The front of a stage; the part nearest the audience. (See p. 150.)

Dramaturgy (drăm′ə tûr′jĭ): The art of writing plays.

End Rhyme: *See* Sound Devices.

Epic: A long narrative poem which generally recounts the heroic adventures of a legendary or historical person who was considered important in the history of his people. The *Iliad,* the *Odyssey,* the *Aeneid,* and the *Cid* are four of the best known epics in Western literature. The *Iliad* and the *Odyssey,* of Greek origin, tell of the Trojan War and the wanderings of Ulysses. The *Aeneid,* by Virgil, concerns the founding of Rome; the *Cid* relates the adventures of an 11th-century Spanish hero.

Epigraph (ĕp′ə grăf′): Lines appearing at the beginning of a book, chapter, poem, etc., which are separate from the actual story or stanzas. An epigraph is often a quotation which summarizes or suggests the main idea of what follows.

Episode: An incident. The plot* of a story or play is usually made up of several episodes which are closely related to each other.

Essay: *See* pages 263-264.

Euphony: *See* Sound Devices.

Exposition: The part of a plot* (usually occurring at the beginning of a story or drama) that gives the necessary background for understanding the characters and their conflicts. (See p. 7.) In essays, exposition is the explanation of an idea or thing. (See p. 335.)

Fable: A narrative* that uses animals, birds, etc., as characters. Although nonhuman, these characters represent certain types of persons or certain qualities (such as vanity) found in human beings. The purpose of a fable is usually to show some weakness or absurdity found in mankind. (See p. 499.)

Falling Action: The part of a play, following the crisis,* in which the working out and conclusion of the conflict* are shown.

Fantasy: A work of literature that deliberately employs unrealistic elements (for example, "The Third Level"). (See p. 75.)

Feminine Rhyme: *See* Sound Devices.

Fiction: This term is most often applied to short stories* and novels,* although actually *fiction* describes any narrative* that uses imaginary characters, events, or settings. When an author sets his work against historical events or uses historical personages as characters, the work is called HISTORICAL FICTION, or a HISTORICAL NOVEL. If an author writes a biography* but includes thoughts, conversations, or persons that he has invented himself, the work is called FICTIONAL BIOGRAPHY.

Figurative Language: Expressions which are not meant literally, but to some extent must be understood imaginatively. Figures of speech (for example, metaphor,* simile,* and personification*) are frequently based on a comparison. (See p. 486.)

Flashback: A sudden shifting backward in time. The flashback is usually accomplished in fiction* by having a character think back to some earlier time and what happened then. Its purpose is often to give information that is necessary for understanding the characters or plot. (See p. 88.)

Folk Ballad: *See* Ballad.

Folklore: Any song, tale, poem, or piece of knowledge handed down by word of mouth from generation to generation. While ballads,* tall tales,* fairy tales, and such stories are most often thought of as folklore, so, for example, would be the recipes handed down orally within a cultural group.

Foot: A rhythmical unit in a line of verse.* A foot usually contains one accented syllable and one or two unaccented syllables. (See pp. 509 and 604.)

Foreshadowing: An action, description, or comment that serves as a hint to prepare the reader for some later occurrence. For example, the soothsayer's warning to "Beware the ides of March" in the second scene of *Julius Caesar* foreshadows the coming assassination of Caesar.

Formal Essay: An essay that is serious in purpose and tone,* that generally tries to inform or to convince the reader of something, and that is generally clear and logical in its organization. (See p. 263.)

Free Verse: Poetry that has no regular pattern of rhythm* (for example, the poems of Walt Whitman and Carl Sandburg). (See p. 513.)

Generalization: A statement, usually a conclusion based on a number of specific instances, that has a widespread application. The statement "'The Cop and the Anthem' has a surprise ending" is a specific statement; the statement "O. Henry frequently uses surprise endings" is a generalization. A generalization, unless it is a widely known truth or a statement made by an authority you have no reason to doubt, should rarely be accepted as true without some proof.

Historical Fiction or **Novel:** *See* Fiction.

Iamb: A foot* consisting of an unaccented syllable followed by an accented syllable. (See pp. 509 and 604.)

Idyll: Originally, an idyll was a descriptive poem about the life of a simple country people—usually presenting their life in a rather rosy light. However, the term is applied to poems, like "Gareth and Lynette," which contain a great deal of description* and narrative.*

Image: Any sight, sound, smell, touch, or taste that an author's words suggest to the imagination; a sensory perception created through words. Images are important in description* or for the purpose of making an abstract idea concrete. (See p. 473.)

Imagery: The imagery of a literary work is made up of all the images* contained in it. The kind of imagery an author uses in connection with a character, setting, or idea frequently indicates his own attitude. (For example, Brooks uses contrasting images for wit and for humor in "On the Difference Between Wit and Humor," and the imagery connected with each suggests his attitude toward it.)

Imperfect Rhyme: *See* Sound Devices.

Informal Essay: An essay that is conversational in tone* and usually written to entertain as much as to inform. Style* is more important to its success than to that of the formal essay;* also, its organization is generally much looser than that of the formal essay. (See p. 263.)

Internal Rhyme: *See* Sound Devices.

Irony: There are several kinds of irony, but all generally involve some kind of contrast.* For example, there may be contrast between what a character or the reader thinks will happen and what actually happens (as in "The Cop and the Anthem"), a contrast between the nature of a subject and the language used to describe it (as in "A Dissertation upon Roast Pig" and "The Cop

and the Anthem"), or a contrast between what things seem to be and what they actually are (as in "The Necklace"). A skillful user of irony is rarely dull, for irony always involves something unexpected in a situation. (See p. 30.)

Legend: An account, usually in story form, handed down from the past. It is not unusual for legends to have as their basis some historical event or personage, although the true facts become greatly changed or lost as time goes by. (The stories of King Arthur and his knights, for example, were originally handed down as legends and eventually were used by many writers as the basis for their works.)

Light Verse: Poems in which the purpose is to entertain through a humorous treatment of the subject (even though the subject itself may be a serious one). The purpose of light verse may also be to satirize or to parody (as in the case of "Very Like a Whale").

Literal Language: Language in which the words are meant to be taken only at their face value. A literal statement, for example, could not be an understatement or an exaggeration; the words in it could not involve metaphor,* personification,* or any other figure of speech. Scientific or mathematical statements are good examples of literal speech. Literary works and most conversation are not often made up of completely literal language.

Literary Ballad: *See* Ballad.

Local Color: A term used mainly in reference to short stories,* and sometimes to novels.* It describes stories which are meant to bring out the particular features of a certain locality and its inhabitants. Although most realistic stories do this to some extent, their major purpose and emphasis is a different one. The local-color story, however, is apt deliberately to choose characters typical only in the region where the story takes place (for example, the old Yankee farmer of New England, or the rough gold miner of the California gold rush), to use dialect, and to describe habits of the people and features of their life peculiar to a certain region.

Lyric: A short poem which usually reveals the feelings or a personal experience of the writer; that is, it is personal (or subjective) poetry. An example is "Barter" (p. 485) by Sara Teasdale. The fact that the words to music are called *lyrics* indicates the songlike quality of much lyric poetry.

Masculine Rhyme: *See* Sound Devices.

Melodrama: A kind of play which generally has the following characteristics: (1) the characters are presented as either good or bad; their motivation* is not very convincingly or adequately developed; (2) the plot* often depends heavily on coincidence; (3) the ending is happy (the villain is defeated, the hero marries the heroine, etc.); (4) a strong appeal is made to the audience's emotions, although in a rather shallow way (that is, the audience is supposed to dislike, sympathize with, or pity the various characters intensely, although these characters are usually not very realistic).

Metaphor: An implied comparison between two things not usually thought of as being alike. For example, the phrase "a waltzing landscape" in "The Elements" compares the quickly shifting movements of a waltz to the appearance of a landscape seen from a storm-tossed plane. (See p. 488.)

Metaphorical: Figurative. (*Meta-*

phorical language is often used as a synonym for *figurative language.**)

Meter: A pattern of beats in poetry. (See pp. 508 and 604.)

Monologue: A work presented entirely through the speech of one person (as "The Waltz"). A monologue is usually in the form of a dramatic scene, a short-short story, or the kind of humorous narrative* comedians often use. A second person is assumed to be present, but what he says or does can be guessed at only through the words of the person delivering the monologue.

Motivation: The values, desires, or beliefs which cause a character to act as he does. Often, a character is clearly aware of his own motives (for example, in "Snake Dance" the boy lies to his mother because he desires her not to worry about him). But at other times, a character may not be aware of the true motives for his actions (for example, in "The Leader of the People" Jody is not aware of any reason for going on the mouse hunt apart from a vague feeling that it would be exciting; the reader, however, is aware that Jody wants to do this, in part, because it presents a chance for him to assert himself). For any character to be believable, it is important that his motivation be believable. (See p. 116.)

Myth: A story account of the actions and lives of gods and heroes. A myth may originate in an attempt to explain natural events (such as the cycle of the seasons or the origin of the earth) or to illustrate .and justify moral teachings (such as the belief that it is wrong to kill or that hospitality is a virtue). Although myths of the past are no longer believed in a literal sense, they still have literary importance as interesting stories and as symbolic statements of important ideas and truths.

LITERARY TERMS

Narrative: A story.

Narrative Essay: An essay which makes its point through telling a story (as the first half of "A Dissertation upon Roast Pig"). Many essays combine narration with description* or exposition.*

Narrative Poem: A poem which tells a story, such as "Gareth and Lynette." (See p. 557.)

Narrator: The person who tells a story. For example, in "Early Marriage" the author acts as narrator, but in "By the Waters of Babylon" John (the "I" of the story) is the narrator.

Nonfiction: Prose works based on fact or history (such as "The Old Gentleman" or "The Lobstering Man"), or works in which explanation of the author's ideas and opinions is the major purpose (such as "A Defense of Detective Stories").

Novel: A fictional narrative, longer than the short story,* but with no set length. Short novels (sometimes called *novelettes*) may have only thirty or forty pages. Like a short story, the novel organizes characters and their actions into some kind of plot.* A typical novel contains more characters than a short story, shows its characters in more depth than the short story, can contain more complicated action than the short story, and is more likely to introduce subplots.*

Novelette: *See* Novel.

Onomatopoeia: *See* Sound Devices.

Pace: The movement of narrative writing, determined by the author's method of telling his story. Summary statements reporting action move the fastest; conversation and fully reported scenes move more slowly but add vividness. (See p. 80.)

Parable: An illustration of some truth in story form. Plot* and character are less important than they are in the short story;* that is, the characters of a parable usually have little individuality, and the plot is determined by whatever the story is meant to illustrate rather than by the desire to arouse suspense* or to show what realistically might have happened. The New Testament contains many parables, such as that of the Prodigal Son (Luke 15:11-32).

Paradox: A statement which seems contradictory, but in which the two contradictory parts are both true. A paradox usually results from some words in a statement being used in an unusual or a figurative sense, or from the two contradictory parts having different levels of meaning. MacLeish's "Ars Poetica" (p. 556) contains many paradoxical statements, such as "A poem should be wordless."

Paraphrase: A restatement of a passage or poem which gives its meaning as accurately as possible but in different words. It is often used as a means of making difficult lines clearer or of testing a person's understanding of them.

Parody (păr'ə dĭ): An exaggerated imitation of a particular work or of a writer's style, written for the purpose of humor or ridicule.

Perfect Rhyme: *See* Sound Devices.

Personification: Giving the characteristics of a human being to an object or an abstraction (for example, "Old Father Time" or "the sighing wind"). (See p. 487.)

Plot: The series of actions which make up a work of fiction.* In a well-constructed plot, these actions are usually linked to one another through cause-and-effect in a way that brings out the author's meaning. As a very simple example, if an author presented one episode* in which a man bullied all those around him at work, and then followed with an episode in which the man was bullied by his family when he arrived home, the reader could easily see that the author was trying to show that a person compensates for his weaknesses in one area by asserting himself in another.

A typical plot (which an author may vary in one way or another) will: (1) open with a scene of exposition,* (2) introduce the conflict* either during or immediately after the exposition, (3) continue by developing the major conflict, and perhaps adding less important ones, (4) reach the crisis,* a decisive scene after which the conflict should logically turn out one way or the other, (5) show the action following the crisis (which may be very little or quite lengthy) and the final resolution* of the conflict.

Poetry: *See* pages 470-473.

Point of View: This term refers to the person through whose eyes the reader sees a story. The entire effect of a story depends largely upon the point of view from which it is told.

An author may act as narrator,* telling whatever is necessary in order to understand the characters and their actions and perhaps including his own opinions, theories, and philosophy (this is usually done only in older books). The OMNISCIENT (or all-knowing) AUTHOR POINT OF VIEW allows the reader to be told a great deal about the thoughts, feelings, and actions of many persons—more than any one character would know.

On the other hand, a character in a story may tell it: in that case, the reader must be aware of the kind of person that character is and how this affects his account. The FIRST PERSON POINT OF VIEW often gives great vividness to a story and makes it very convincing: it has the effectiveness of a first-hand account.

A variation that, in a sense, combines these two viewpoints, is one in which the story is told in the third person but is limited to describing what a single character can see and experience. This THIRD PERSON LIMITED POINT OF VIEW is a popular one today. (See pp. 21 and 26.)

Preface (prĕf´ĭs): An introduction of a book.

Prologue (prō´lôg): A section of a work that introduces what is to follow. It is most often used in connection with plays or poems.

Pun: A play upon words—either two words which sound alike (*soul* and *sole*, for example, form the basis for a pun in the first scene of *Julius Caesar*) or a single word with different meanings.

Punch Line: The last line of an anecdote* or joke which gives it point; it usually involves an unexpected twist of some sort.

Quatrain (kwŏt´rān): A four-line poem, or four-line stanza.*

Refrain: Lines repeated at certain intervals throughout a poem (sometimes the repetitions may vary slightly from one another). "A Kind of Good-bye" (p. 505) offers an example of a refrain with variations.

Resolution: The outcome of the plot;* the way the author ends the conflict.*

Rhyme: *See* Sound Devices.

Rhyme Scheme: The pattern of rhyme* used in a poem. To describe a rhyme scheme, the first rhyme is labeled *a*, the second *b*, etc. Thus, the rhyme scheme of the fourteen-line poem "Once by the Pacific" (p. 509) is *aabbccd-deeffgg*.

Rhythm: The beat, or tempo, of a poem. (See pp. 604-607.) *Rhythm* can also refer to the general speed of a work and the effect of this speed (as "a lively rhythm," "a dignified rhythm," or "a stately rhythm").

Rising Action: The part of a play up to the crisis:* the development of the conflict.*

Satire: A kind of writing in which the purpose is to expose through ridicule the evils or weaknesses of something (such as a law, social customs, or politics). A satirist frequently uses exaggeration, carrying certain types of characters or situations to an extreme in order to make the faults being criticized very clear. Although the result of this exaggeration is often humorous, the satirist's purpose is not primarily to entertain but to criticize. Irony* is a technique also frequently used in satire. It is important to remember in reading satire that the author rarely states his own beliefs directly: as in "You, Too, Can Write the Casual Style," the point is apt to be different from the one the author pretends to be making.

Scene: A division in the acts* of a play. A scene is generally marked by the drawing of the curtain or a brief darkening of the stage. Usually some time (even if a very brief amount) elapses between the end of one scene and the beginning of the next.

Scene can also be used to refer to an episode* or action in a short story* or novel.*

Script: The written version of a play, movie, radio, or television program, meant for use in production.

Selection of Detail: The author's selection of those details of setting, action, characters' appearances, and so forth, for inclusion in a literary work. Since an author cannot include everything that could be said about his characters, their daily lives, and their surroundings, his selection of detail is based on what he considers important about them.

Setting: The place and time of a story. Setting also includes any elements of a story that result from the place or time (such as the weather, historical events that affect the people in the story, or the kind of environment in which the characters live). (See p. 100.)

Short Story: A brief work of fiction,* ranging from a few hundred words in length (in which case, it is often called a SHORT-SHORT STORY) up to ten or twenty thousand. There is no set length, but the short story is often defined as one which can be read at a single sitting. It generally has few characters, and is more limited in scope than the novel.* (See the *Introduction to the Short Story*, pages 5-7, and the headnotes within the unit for further explanation.)

Simile: A figure of speech based on a comparison of two unlike things and introduced by *like* or *as* (or similar terms). For example, "Her eyes were black as night" is a simile, since it compares *eyes* and *night*, two unlike things. However, "Her eyes were as black as her sister's" is not a simile, since *her eyes* and *her sister's eyes* are like things. (See p. 486.)

Sketch: A brief description or explanation which attempts to suggest all the important features of its subject but not in complete detail.

Soliloquy: A stage convention* which allows an actor to express his inner thoughts in a speech. Although a person would not usually speak these thoughts, the soliloquy is useful as a means of showing a character's inner state of mind and of making his motives clear. (See Brutus's speech beginning IV, iii, 267, page 675, in *Julius Caesar*.)

Sonnet: A fourteen-line poem, usually in iambic pentameter and using rhyme.* There are many variations of this form, but two of the best-known are the Italian sonnet and the Shakespearean sonnet. The Italian sonnet is divided into groups of eight lines rhymed *abba,abba* and six lines rhymed *cdc,cdc* (the rhyme scheme of the last six lines sometimes differs from this). The Shakespearean sonnet is divided into three groups of four lines with a concluding couplet,* and is rhymed *abab,cdcd,efef,gg*.

Sound Devices: Musical techniques, used particularly in poetry. Some of the most common are listed below.

> **ALLITERATION:** The repetition of the same sound at the beginning of closely linked words or syllables (for example "play *b*aseball, *b*atting a *b*all" in the poem "All of us always turning away for solace"). (See p. 523.)

> **ASSONANCE** (ăs'ə nəns): A form of rhyme* in which the vowel sounds of two or more words are alike, but the consonants are different. For example: l*a*te and r*ai*d, h*o*ld and f*oa*m. Poets occasionally use assonance at the end of lines in place of the usual perfect rhymes; more frequently, assonance is used within lines simply for the musical effect of a repeated sound.

> **CACOPHONY** (kə kŏf'ə nĭ): The use of harsh or hard-to-pronounce sounds, particularly in poetry, and usu-

ally for the purpose of describing a harsh or unpleasant subject. (See p. 537.)

CONSONANCE (kŏn'sə nəns): A form of rhyme* in which the consonant sounds of the rhyming words are alike, but the vowels differ. For example, *lane* and *loan*, *like* and *lake*, *flower* and *flare*. It is used for the same purposes as assonance.

END RHYME: The use of rhyming words at the end of lines. Often end rhyme accentuates units of thought; for example, the rhyme at the end of the two lines in a couplet* ties the lines together by sound.

EUPHONY (ū'fə nĭ): The use of pleasing, generally easy-to-pronounce sounds, particularly in poetry. Liquid or soft sounds (for example, *l* and *s*) tend to be euphonious. (See p. 532.)

FEMININE RHYME: The rhyming of accented syllables followed by one or more rhyming unaccented syllables (for example, w*early* and dr*early*, w*alking* and t*alking*).

IMPERFECT RHYME: Rhyming words in which the last accented vowel and all sounds which follow are almost, but not quite, identical (for example, tr*uth* and pr*oof*, b*east* and l*eash*, p*aste* and h*aze*).

INTERNAL RHYME: The use of rhyme* within lines.

MASCULINE RHYME: The rhyming of single accented syllables (for example, h*unch* and l*unch*, des*ist* and enl*ist*).

ONOMATOPOEIA   (ŏn'ə măt'ə pē'ə): Words that suggest or imitate the sound of the action, object, or noise they stand for. Names of sounds are often onomatopoeic (for example, *snap, crack, swish*). Objects associated with a sound may also have onomatopoeic names (for example, *whip* and *tom-tom*). (See p. 527.)

PERFECT RHYME: Rhyming words in which the last accented vowel and all sounds which follow are identical (for example, c*are* and r*are*, fl*oor* and c*ore*, w*illow* and p*illow*).

RHYME: The repetition of similar sounds in words closely enough linked so that the ear catches the likeness.

Speaker: The person whose words or thoughts are given in a poem. Sometimes, particularly in lyric* poetry, this person is the poet himself. However, the speaker may be an imaginary person; for example, in "Dramatic Fragment" (p. 487) the reader should not assume that the "I" of the poem is the poet.

Stage Convention: A practice in the writing or performance of a play which is not realistic but which an audience is accustomed to accept (such as the soliloquy*).

Stanza: Each division of a poem which has repetitive units of lines. Each unit is generally similar to the others in number of lines, rhyme scheme,* and rhythm.* However, the stanzas may vary from each other in any of these ways. In a free-verse* poem that contains stanzas, a break between stanzaic units (shown by a blank space on the printed page) may simply show the beginning of a new unit of thought (like a paragraph in prose) and not the beginning of a repetition in form.

Stress: A heavy accent on a syllable in a line of poetry. A stress is usually indicated by a slant mark over the vowel of the accented syllable. The number and position of the stresses in a line determine its meter* (for example, "The líon cróuches thére! I sáw/ In bárren rócks his ámber éye!" is an example of iambic tetrameter).

Structure: The plan of a literary work; the organization of all its elements (such as plot,* characterization,* and description*) into a whole.

Style: A writer's characteristic manner of expression, determined largely through his arrangement of words, phrases, and sentences. Style, in a sense, expresses the writer's personality and way of thinking; it also reflects to a great extent the age in which he lives. A good style is one which is both suited to the subject matter and at the same time expresses the individual personality of the writer (or speaker). Thus, an oratorical style which might be suited to a political speech would not be suitable for dinner table conversation.

Subplot: A plot* that is subordinate to the main one. It usually centers around a character other than the central one. In a well-constructed work, a subplot is related to the main one in some way: for instance, it may provide a different treatment of the same theme. For example, the question of Catherine's marriage forms a subplot in *The Winslow Boy* and is connected with the main conflict.

Surprise Ending: An unexpected conclusion to a story, which may or may not be a logical outcome of previous events. (See p. 80.)

Suspense: The curiosity aroused in a reader as to the outcome of a situation. While the suspense is generally greatest as the reader nears the moment of crisis* and then follows its working out, an author can arouse suspense by the introduction of anything which interests the reader. For example, if the opening paragraph of a story describes a character interesting to the reader, he will want to read on and find out what happens to this person even though no conflict or problem has yet arisen.

Symbol: Something which is meaningful in its literal sense and which stands for something else at the same time. For example, in "A Brook in the City," the description of the brook and of what happens to it is meant literally: the poem is about a brook. However, the brook is also symbolical because it can stand for anything natural. In "The Coach of Life," on the other hand, the coach is not a symbol because the poem is not really about a coach or ride at all: these are only metaphorical* expressions for a description of life. (See pp. 125 and 494.)

Tall Tale: An exaggerated, usually humorous story, such as those about Paul Bunyan or Davy Crockett. A tall tale is nearly always told in a matter of fact way, in contrast to the obvious exaggeration.

Technique: A method or device for handling material. The devices used by Dos Passos in "The Campers at Kitty Hawk," page 395, illustrate the use of different techniques to achieve an intended effect.

Theme: The central idea of a literary work. A theme can generally be expressed as an abstract statement (such as: Right will prevail in the long run), although it usually is never put into such words in the story, drama, or poem. Such statements of theme vastly oversimplify the meaning of any work, but they can be useful as a means of indicating the main idea the work illustrates through its characters and plot,* its imagery* and figures of speech.

Essays and biographies, in which the author is more directly addressing the reader, frequently state their themes directly. (See p. 95.)

Tone: What corresponds in a literary work to the tone of voice a speaker uses. It results from the author's attitude toward his subject and characters, from the kind of approach toward his material he has decided upon, and sometimes from his attitude toward his readers. Identifying the tone of an author is one of the most difficult skills in literary analysis. One can recognize it partly from the author's choice of words and his selection of detail; but it is also necessary sometimes to take into account the cultural or social background against which the work was written. For example, the satirical tone of "You, Too, Can Write the Casual Style" is evident partly from what it says, partly from the way it says it, and partly from a reader's knowledge of certain trends in modern writing. (See p. 36.)

Topic Sentence: The sentence within a paragraph which states the central idea of the entire paragraph.

Transition: Anything which serves as a bridge connecting two parts of a work. A single word (such as *however*) or a phrase (such as *to conclude* or *as an example of this idea*) could serve as a transition between sentences or paragraphs. A paragraph could serve as a transition between explanations of two major ideas. In plays, a speech or some kind of physical action might serve as a transition between two episodes.* In short stories, the author might summarize what had happened between two scenes* as a means of transition. These are only a few of the possibilities, but—whatever means of bridging parts a writer uses—smooth transitions are important in helping the reader to follow ideas or actions.

Unity: The effect achieved when all parts of a literary work are chosen for the purpose of fulfilling the author's main goal (for example, to create a sense of horror, to develop a certain theme, to explore a certain character) and are successfully related to each other so as to accomplish this goal. (See p. 56.)

Upstage: The rear of a stage: the part farthest from the audience. (See p. 150.)

Usage: The customary use of words or phrases; the accepted forms of a language. Usage may vary somewhat in different parts of a country or in different social or economic groups. It will change slowly for an entire language as time goes on. In cases where a term is used differently by different groups, correct usage is thought of as the use made of it by well-educated speakers and good writers. (The essays "Sabotage in Springfield," p. 355, and "But What's a Dictionary For?" p. 365, both deal with questions of usage.)

Verse: Although this term is sometimes used as a synonym for poetry, it refers more specifically to the technical aspects of a poem. Thus, anything which employs rhythm* and rhyme* (for example, a nursery rhyme) can be regarded as a form of verse, but is not necessarily poetry. It is virtually impossible to define poetry, but generally it communicates an emotional experience, an idea, or a meaningful story as verse does not. Ogden Nash's poems would be examples of verse as opposed to poetry.

Glossary

The glossary is provided as a convenient means for looking up unfamiliar words used in this book. It may also be used in doing the *Building Vocabulary Skills* exercises. The words are defined according to their use in the book, although often additional meanings are also given. Words that are footnoted in the text have not usually been included in the glossary.

The order and kinds of information to be found in an entry are shown below. Reading this information will help in using the glossary quickly and accurately.

Information given in the entry:

1. The word to be defined, divided into syllables. Example: **ab·stract**.
2. Pronunciation of the entry. When two pronunciations are common for a word, both are usually given. Example: (ăb′străkt, ăb străkt′).
3. Part of speech and, when useful, information concerning the singular or plural form. Example: **al·gae** (ăl′jē), *n. pl.* (*sing.* **al·ga**, ăl′gə).
4. Restrictive labels. These may be usage labels (example: **redd** . . . *Colloq.*), geographical labels (example: **bar·ris·ter** . . . *England*), or special subject labels (example: **chro·mat·ic scale** . . . *Music*).
5. Definition of the entry. Where appropriate, examples may be given (as for *anachronism*), use of the word may be illustrated (as for *abstract*), or opposing concepts may be given (as for *analysis*).
6. Alternate spellings of the entry. Example: **ap·pall** . . . (Also, **appal**.)
7. Derivative parts of speech. A reasonably complete listing of the other parts of speech derived from an entry is usually given. Syllable division and accent marks for these derivative forms are always given; phonetic pronunciations are given whenever they would not be obvious. Example: **ab·stract** . . . —**ab·stract′ly**, *adv.* —**ab·strac′tion**, *n.*

The following abbreviations are used:

adj.	adjective	l.c.	lower case
adv.	adverb	n.	noun
cap.	capital	pl.	plural
Colloq.	colloquial	prep.	preposition
conj.	conjunction	pron.	pronoun
esp.	especially	sing.	singular
Fr.	French	U.S.	United States
Ger.	German	v.	verb

Pronunciation Key*

ă, act; ā, able; â, air; ä, art; b, back; ch, chief; d, do; ĕ, ebb, ē, equal; f, fit; g, give; h, hit; ĭ, if; ī, ice; j, just; k, kept; l, low; m, my; n, now; ng, sing; ŏ, box; ō, over; ô, order; oi, oil; ŏŏ, book; ōō, ooze; ou, out; p, page; r, read; s, see; sh, shoe; t, ten; th, thin; t͟h, that; ŭ, up; ū, use; û, urge; v, voice; w, west; y, yes; z, zeal; zh, vision; ə = a in *alone*, e in *system*, i in *easily*, o in *gallop*, u in *circus*; à as in Fr. *ami*; KH as in Ger. *ach*; N as in Fr. *bon*; œ as in Ger. *schon*; Y as in Ger. *uber*.

*The pronunciation system of *The American College Dictionary*, © Copyright 1947, 1963, Random House, Inc., New York. Used by permission.

a·ban·don (ə băn′dən), *n.* a surrender to one's feelings and impulses; letting oneself go.

a·base (ə bās′), *v.* to lower; degrade.

a·bash (ə băsh′), *v.* to embarrass.

ab·di·cate (ăb′də kāt′), *v.* to renounce a throne or some claim; relinquish a right, power, or trust. —**ab′di·ca′tion,** *n.*

ab·hor (ăb hôr′), *v.* to loathe.

ab·hor·rent (ăb hôr′ənt, ăb hŏr′ənt) *adj.* exciting horror; detestable.

a·bom·i·na·ble (ə bŏm′ə nə bəl), *adj.* detestable; loathsome. —**a·bom′i·na′tion,** *n.*

ab·ro·gate (ăb′rə gāt′), *v.* to abolish; annul by act of authority. —**ab′ro·ga′tion,** *n.*

ab·sorp·tion (ăb sôrp′shən), *n.* the state of being much interested.

ab·ste·mi·ous (ăb stē′mĭ əs), *adj.* moderate in the use of food and drink.

ab·stract (ăb′străkt, ăb străkt′), *adj.* thought of apart from particular instances or material objects; not concrete: as, *beauty is an abstract word.* —**ab·stract′ly,** *adv.* —**ab·strac′tion,** *n.*

ab·surd (ăb sûrd′, ăb zûrd′), *adj.* contrary to reason and common sense. —**ab·surd′i·ty,** *n.* —**ab·surd′ly,** *adv.*

a·byss (ə bĭs′), *n.* a bottomless, or deep immeasurable gulf.

ac·cli·mate (ə klī′mĭt, ăk′lə māt′), *v.* to become accustomed to a new environment or climate.

ac·cuse (ə kūz′), *v.* to bring a charge against. —**ac·cus′ive,** *adj.* (*Used by O. Henry*) tending to accuse.

ac·tin·ism (ăk′tə nĭz′əm), *n.* the action or the property of radiant energy by which chemical change is produced. —**ac·tin·ic** (ăk tĭn′ĭk), *adj.*

ad·duce (ə dūs′, ə dōōs′), *v.* to bring forward.

ad·junct (ăj′ŭngkt), *n.* 1. an addition that is not an essential part of the thing it is added to. 2. an assistant.

ad·mon·ish (ăd mŏn′ĭsh), *v.* 1. to caution or advise against something; to warn. 2. to reprove mildly for a fault. 3. to recall to duty. —**ad′mo·ni′tion,** *n.*

a·do·be (ə dō′bĭ), *n.* 1. sun-dried bricks used in dry regions. 2. a building constructed of sun-dried bricks.

ad·ver·sa·ry (ăd′vər sĕr′ĭ), *n.* an unfriendly opponent.

ad·vo·cate (ăd′və kāt′), *n. British.* one who pleads the cause of another in a court of law.

aerial perspective, *see* **perspective.**

aer·o·dy·nam·ics (âr′ō dī năm′ĭks), *n.* the branch of physics that deals with the forces (resistance, pressure, etc.) exerted by air or other gases in motion.

aer·o·naut·ics (âr′ə nô′tĭks), *n.* the science or art of flight.

af·fa·ble (ăf′ə bəl), *adj.* easy to talk to; polite; friendly. —**af′fa·bil′i·ty,** *n.*

af·fect (ə fĕkt′), *v.* to act on; produce an effect on.

af·fin·i·ty (ə fĭn′ə tĭ), *n.* a natural liking for, or attraction to, a person or thing.

af·fir·ma·tion (ăf′ər mā′shən), *n.* the assertion that something is true; the establishment or confirmation of a truth.

ag·a·ric (ăg′ə rĭk, ə găr′ĭk), *n.* a fungus.

ag·gres·sion (ə grĕsh′ən), *n.* the action of a state in violating the rights of another state, esp. its territorial rights.

ag·gres·sive (ə grĕs′ĭv), *adj.* 1. making the first attack. 2. energetic; vigorous.

ag·grieve (ə grēv′), *v.* to injure by injustice; to wrong.

a·ghast (ə găst′), *adj.* filled with sudden fright and amazed horror.

a·gue (ā′gū), *n.* 1. a malarial fever marked by successive hot, cold, and sweating fits. 2. a fit of shaking or shivering.

al·be·it (ôl bē′ĭt), *conj.* although.

al·bi·no (ăl bī′nō), *n.* 1. a person with a pale, milky skin, light hair, and pink eyes. 2. a plant or animal lacking normal coloration—that is, white, or nearly so, when normally it would have color.

al·gae (ăl′jē), *n. pl.* (*sing.* **al·ga,** ăl′gə), a group of plants, one or many-celled, containing chlorophyll but having no true root stem or leaf, found in water or damp places (for example, seaweeds or pond scum).

al·lay (ə lā′), *v.* to put at rest.

al·loy (ăl′oi, ə loi′), *n.* a substance made up of a mixture of two or more metals. —(ə loi′), *v.* 1. to mix by fusion—usually a valuable metal with a less valuable; hence, 2. to reduce in value by mixing.

ăct, āble, dâre, ärt; ĕbb, ēqual; ĭf, īce; hŏt, ōver, ôrder, oil, bŏŏk, ōōze, out; ŭp, ūse, ûrge; ə = a in *alone;* ch, chief; g, give; j, judge; ng, ring; sh, shoe; th, thin; th, that; zh, vision. See the full key at the beginning of this glossary.

al·lure·ment (ə loor'mənt), *n.* fascination; charm.

al·lu·sion (ə loo'zhən), *n.* a reference, either directly or by implication. **—al·lude'**, *v.*

am·ber (ăm'bər), *adj.* yellowish-brown. **—*n.*** a fossil resin, pale yellow, reddish or brownish, used in jewelry, etc.

am·bi·va·lence (ăm bĭv'ə ləns), *n.* *Psychology.* the coexistence of opposite and conflicting feelings about the same person or object.

am·bro·sia (ăm brō'zhə), *n.* the food of the gods, in classical mythology.

am·bro·sial (ăm brō'zhəl), *adj.* exceptionally delicious; worthy of the gods. (Also, **am·bro'sian.**)

a·nach·ro·nism (ə năk'rə nĭz'əm), *n.* something placed or occurring out of its proper time (for example, an automobile in an 18th-century story).

a·nal·o·gy (ə năl'ə jĭ), *n.* a partial similarity on which a comparison may be based.

a·nal·y·sis (ə năl'ə sĭs), *n.* separation of a whole, whether a material substance or a matter of thought, into its parts (as opposed to *synthesis,* the combination of parts into a whole). **—an'a·lyt'ic, an'a·lyt'i·cal,** *adj.* **—an'a·lyt'i·cal·ly,** *adv.*

an·a·lyze (ăn'ə līz'), *v.* to examine critically, so as to bring out the essential features of.

an·ar·chic (ăn är'kĭk), *adj.* 1. lawless. 2. tending to or advocating anarchy.

an·ar·chy (ăn'ər kĭ), *n.* 1. a state of society without government or law. 2. disorder.

a·ne·mi·a (ə nē'mĭ ə), *n.* deficiency of red blood corpuscles or of hemoglobin or both. **—a·ne'mic,** *adj.*

an·nals (ăn'əlz), *n. pl.* recorded history.

an·ten·na (ăn těn'ə), *n.* one of the jointed appendages occurring on the heads of insects, crustaceans, etc., often called feelers.

an·tic (ăn'tĭk), *adj.* odd, grotesque; capering.

an·ti·pa·thy (ăn tĭ'pə thĭ), *n.* strong dislike.

ap·a·thy (ăp'ə thĭ), *n.* lack of emotion; indifference.

ap·er·ture (ăp'ər chər), *n.* a hole, slit, crack, or other opening.

a·pex (ā'pěks), *n.* the tip or point.

aph·o·rism (ăf'ə rĭz'əm), *n.* a concise expression of some general truth, usually worded in a striking way.

ap·pall (ə pôl'), *v.* to overcome with fear; to fill with consternation and horror. (Also, **appal.**)

ap·per·tain (ăp'ər tān'), *v.* to relate or pertain to.

ap·pre·hen·sion (ăp'rĭ hěn'shən), *n.* dread of coming evil.

ap·pro·ba·tion (ăp'rə bā'shən), *n.* approval.

a·quat·ic (ə kwăt'ĭk), *adj.* 1. growing or living in or upon water. 2. pertaining to water.

ar·bi·tra·ry (är'bə trěr'ĭ), *adj.* 1. unreasonable. 2. subject to a single person's decision. **—ar'bi·tra'ri·ly,** *adv.* **—ar'bi·trar'i·ness,** *n.*

Ar·ca·di·a (är kā'dĭ ə), *n.* a mountainous region in ancient Greece, known for the simple life and contentment of its people.

arch (ärch), *adj.* sly; roguish.

ar·du·ous (är'joo əs), *adj.* laborious; difficult.

ar·id (ăr'ĭd), *adj.* dry; parched with heat. **—a·rid'i·ty,** *n.*

a·ro·ma (ə rō'mə), *n.* an odor, esp. an agreeable odor.

ar·ro·gant (ăr'ə gənt), *adj.* insolently proud and self-assertive. **—ar'ro·gance,** *n.* **—ar'ro·gant·ly,** *adv.*

ar·roy·o (ə roi'ō), *n.* (mainly used in southwest U.S. and parts of Spanish America) a small steep-sided watercourse or gulch, usually dry except after heavy rainfall.

ar·tic·u·late (är tĭk'yə lĭt), *adj.* 1. clear; distinct. 2. expressing oneself clearly, or capable of clear expression. **—**(är tĭk'yə lāt'), *v.* to utter clearly.

as·cet·ic (ə sět'ĭk), *adj.* self-denying. **—*n.*** a person who leads a life of self-denial.

as·sas·sin (ə săs'ĭn), *n.* one who undertakes to murder, esp. from fanaticism or for a reward.

as·sas·si·nate (ə săs'ə nāt'), *v.* to kill by sudden, or secret, premeditated assault. **—as·sas'si·na'tion,** *n.*

as·say (ə sā'), *v.* to judge the quality of.

as·sump·tion (ə sŭmp'shən), *n.* 1. act of supposing or taking for granted. 2. something taken for granted.

as·sur·ance (ə shoor'əns), *n.* confidence.

a·sun·der (ə sŭn'dər), *adj., adv.* 1. into pieces. 2. widely separated.

a·troc·i·ty (ə trŏs'ə tĭ), *n.* an act or quality of shocking cruelty or wickedness. **—a·tro·cious** (ə trō'shəs), *adj.* **—a·tro'cious·ly,** *adv.*

at·tar (ăt'tər), *n.* a perfume obtained from flowers, esp. damask roses.

at·test (ə těst'), *v.* to bear witness to; certify.

aug·ment (ôg měnt'), *v.* 1. to become larger. 2. to add to.

au·gu·ry (ô'gyə rĭ), *n.* an omen.

au·ra (ôr'ə), *n.* an invisible atmosphere supposedly arising from and surrounding a person or thing.

aus·pi·ces (ô'spə sĭz), *n. pl.* favoring influence; patronage.

aus·tere (ô stir'), *adj.* harsh, stern, forbidding; severely simple in appearance or way of life. —**aus·ter'i·ty,** *n.* —**aus·tere'ly,** *adv.*

au·then·ti·cate (ô thĕn'tə kāt'), *v.* to establish as genuine.

au·thor·i·tar·i·an (ə thôr'ĭ târ'ĭ ən), *adj.* favoring the principle of subjection to authority rather than that of individual freedom.

au·thor·i·ta·tive (ə thôr'ə tā'tĭv), *adj.* having due authority; having the weight of authority.

awe (ô), *n.* respectful or reverential fear, inspired by the grand or sublime. —*v.* to inspire with awe. —**aw'ful,** *adj.*

ba·bel (bā'bəl), *n.* **1.** a confused mixture of sounds. **2.** a scene of confusion.

bait (bāt), *v.* to torment: as, *a baited bull.*

bale (bāl), *n.* *Chiefly poetic.* **1.** evil; harm. **2.** woe.

bale·ful (bāl'fəl), *adj.* deadly; evil.

ba·nal (bā'nəl, bə nǎl'), *adj.* commonplace; stale. —**ba·nal'i·ty,** *n.* —**ba'nal·ly,** *adv.*

bar·ris·ter (bǎr'ĭs tər), *n.* **1.** *England.* a counselor admitted to plead at the bar in any court. **2.** *Colloq.* a lawyer.

bar·ter (bär'tər), *v.* **1.** to trade by exchange of commodities rather than by the use of money. **2.** to bargain away unwisely (used with *away*). —*n.* act of bartering.

bash (bǎsh), *n.* a word invented by Dunsany (author of "The Golden Doom") for a forgotten drug.

bas·tion (bǎs'chən, bǎs'tĭ ən), *n.* a fortified place.

be·hest (bĭ hĕst'), *n.* bidding.

be·lea·guer (bĭ lē'gər), *v.* to surround with enemy forces.

bel·lig·er·ent (bə lĭj'ər ənt), *adj.* warlike. —*n.* nation engaged in war.

bel·ly (bĕl'ĭ), *v.* to swell out, as a sail in a favorable wind.

be·nev·o·lent (bə nĕv'ə lənt), *adj.* desiring to do good for others; intended for benefits rather than for profits.

be·nign (bĭ nīn'), *adj.* **1.** kind. **2.** favorable. **3.** *Medicine.* not tending to produce death: as, *a benign tumor.*

ber·i·ber·i (bĕr'ĭ bĕr'ĭ), *n.* a disease common in the Far East, caused by vitamin deficiency.

bi·as (bī'əs), *n.* a mental leaning; preconceived opinion, prejudice.

big·ot (bĭg'ət), *n.* a bigoted person.

big·ot·ry (bĭg'ə trĭ), *n.* attachment to a particular creed, opinion, or practice so as to cause intolerance. —**big'ot·ed,** *adj.*

bilge (bĭlj), *n.* **1.** the more or less flat under part of a ship's hull. **2.** water that collects in the bilge.

bi·zarre (bĭ zär'), *adj.* singular in appearance, style, or character; odd.

blanch (blǎnch), *v.* to whiten; turn pale.

blast (blǎst), *v.* **1.** to cause to shrivel or wither. **2.** to ruin, destroy. **3.** to shatter by explosives.

bla·tant (blā'tənt), *adj.* loud-mouthed; in bad taste. —**bla'tan·cy,** *n.*

blight (blīt), *n.* **1.** a widespread, destructive plant disease, such as *chestnut blight.* **2.** any cause of destruction and ruin. —*v.* to wither and decay; to destroy.

bludg·eon (blŭj'ən), *n.* a short, heavy club with one end heavier than the other. —*v.* to strike with such a club.

bolt (bōlt), *n.* a block of timber to be sawed or cut.

book·mak·er (bŏok'mā'kər), *n.* a professional betting man who accepts bets of others. —**book'mak'ing,** *adj.* and *n.*

boor (bŏor), *n.* a clownish, rude, or unmannerly person.

boor'ish·ness, *n.* rude behavior. —**boor'ish,** *adj.*

botch (bŏch), *v.* to spoil by poor work. —*n.* a clumsy or poor piece of work.

bow (bō), *n.* one of the bent slats supporting the cover of a covered wagon.

bow (bou), *n.* the front or forward end of a ship, boat, or airplane.

bowd·ler·ize (boud'lə rīz'), *v.* to remove supposedly offensive passages from a book. [After Dr. Thomas Bowdler, who in 1818 published an edition of Shakespeare so treated.]

brand (brǎnd), *v.* **1.** to mark by stamping with a hot iron. **2.** to mark with infamy, disgrace.

brash (brǎsh), *adj.* **1.** hasty, rash. **2.** impertinent. —**brash'ness,** *n.*

bra·va·do (brə vä'dō), *n.* boasting, swaggering.

ăct, āble, dâre, ärt; ĕbb, ēqual; ĭf, īce; hŏt, ōver, ôrder, oil, bŏok, ōoze, out; ŭp, ūse, ûrge; ə = a in *alone*; ch, chief; g, give; j, judge; ng, ring; sh, shoe; th, thin; ŧħ, that; zh, vision. See the full key at the beginning of this glossary.

GLOSSARY   **723**

Bre·ton (brĕt'ən), *n.* a native of Brittany, a peninsula in northwest France. —*adj.* pertaining to Brittany, the Bretons, or their language.

brig (brĭg), *n.* a two-masted vessel square-rigged on both masts.

bro·gan (brō'gən), *n.* a coarse, stout shoe.

bro·mide (brō'mīd), *n.* *Slang.* 1. a bore, because speaking in platitudes. 2. a tiresome platitude. [These meanings derive from the use of certain bromides—chemical compounds—as sedatives.]

brood (brōōd), *v.* to dwell on in thought, often with morbid persistence.

brusque (brŭsk), *adj.* abrupt or blunt. —**brusque'ness**, *n.* —**brusque'ly**, *adv.*

Bru·tus (brōō'təs), *n.* Roman statesman, one of the assassins of Julius Caesar.

buck·board (bŭk'bôrd'), *n.* a light four wheeled carriage.

buf·foon (bə fōōn'), *n.* 1. one who amuses others by tricks, odd gestures and postures, jokes, etc. 2. one given to coarse or undignified joking.

buf·foon·er·y (bə fōō'nə rĭ), *n.* the antics of a buffoon.

bul·wark (bŏŏl'wərk), *n.* (usually *pl.*) *Nautical.* a solid part of a ship's side extending like a fence above the level of the deck.

buoy·ant (boi'ənt, bōō'yənt), *adj.* 1. tending to float. 2. not easily depressed; cheerful.

bu·reau (byŏŏr'ō), *n.* a division of a government department, or an independent administrative unit.

bu·reauc·ra·cy (byŏŏ rŏk'rə sĭ), *n.* 1. government by bureaus. 2. excessive red tape and routine.

bu·reau·crat (byŏŏr'ə krăt'), *n.* an official of a bureaucracy. —**bu'reau·crat'ic**, *adj.*

bur·ro (bûr'ō), *n.* a donkey.

butt (bŭt), *n.* the end of anything, esp. the larger, thicker end (as of a musket or fishing rod).

cab·i·net (kăb'ə nĭt), *n.* a group of ministers who help to manage the government of a nation.

ca·dav·er·ous (kə dăv'ər əs), *adj.* 1. of or like a corpse. 2. pale; ghastly.

cal·dron (kôl'drən), *n.* a large kettle or boiler. (Also, **cauldron**.)

cal·li·o·pe (kə lī'ə pē'), *n.* harsh musical instrument consisting of a set of steam whistles.

cal·lous (kăl'əs), *adj.* hardened; unsympathetic. —**cal'lous·ness**, *n.* —**cal'lous·ly**, *adv.*

ca·nal·ize (kə năl'īz, kăn'ə līz'), *v.* to divert into certain channels; to give a certain direction or provide a certain outlet for.

can·de·la·bra (kăn'də lä'brə), *n. pl.* (*sing.* **can'de·la'brum**), ornamental branched candlesticks. Also used as singular.

can·did (kăn'dĭd), *adj.* 1. frank; open. 2. honest. —**can'did·ly**, *adv.* —**can'did·ness**, *n.*

can·ker (kăng'kər), *n.* 1. a sore, usually in the mouth. 2. anything that corrupts, destroys, irritates. —*v.* 1. to infect with canker. 2. to corrupt; destroy slowly.

cant (kănt), *n.* 1. insincere statements, esp. pretense of enthusiasm for high ideals. 2. the special language of thieves, beggars, etc. 3. the vocabulary used by any special group.

Cape Horn (hôrn), *n.* a headland on a small island at the southern extremity of South America.

cap·i·tal (kăp'ə təl), *adj.* (when used as an exclamation) excellent, first-rate.

ca·price (kə prēs'), *n.* whim. —**ca·pri·cious**, (kə prĭ'shəs), *adj.*

cap·stan (kăp'stən), *n.* a device, resembling a windlass, for raising weights (as an anchor).

cap·tious (kăp'shəs), *adj.* faultfinding about trifles.

car·nage (kär'nĭj), *n.* the slaughter of a great number, as in battle; a massacre.

car·ni·val (kär'nə vəl), *n.* 1. an amusement show. 2. any merrymaking or noisy revelry. 3. the season preceding Lent, often a time of merrymaking.

cas·u·al (kăzh'ōō əl), *adj.* 1. happening by chance. 2. offhand; not planned for a purpose. —**cas'u·al·ly**, *adv.*

cat·a·pult (kăt'ə pŭlt'), *v.* to hurl with great force.

ca·tas·tro·phe (kə tăs'trə fĭ), *n.* 1. a sudden or widespread disaster. 2. a disastrous end.

cat·e·chism (kăt'ə kĭz'əm), *n.* 1. an elementary book containing the basic principles of the Christian religion, in the form of questions and answers. 2. a book of instructions, presented as questions and answers, in any subject.

cat·e·go·ry (kăt'ə gôr'ĭ), *n.* a division for purposes of classification, in any field of knowledge.

cay·use (kī ūs'), *n.* *Western U.S.* an Indian pony.

ce·les·tial (sə lĕs'chəl), *adj.* heavenly.

cer·e·bral (sĕr'ə brəl), *adj.* 1. pertaining to the brain. 2. intellectual.

cha·grin (shə grĭn′), *n.* a feeling of vexation or disappointment.

cham·ber·lain (chām′bər lĭn), *n.* **1.** the high steward of a nobleman or king. **2.** an official who manages the living quarters of a king or nobleman. **3.** an official who receives rents or revenues.

cha·os (kā′ŏs), *n.* **1.** utter confusion or disorder. **2.** the formlessness supposed to have preceded the existence of the ordered universe. —**cha·ot′ic**, *adj.* —**cha·ot′i·cal′ly**, *adv.*

char·ac·ter (kăr′ĭk tər), *n.* **1.** the sum of qualities that distinguishes one person or thing from another. **2.** good moral status; good repute. **3.** (in literature) a person represented in a story, drama, etc.

char·ac·ter·i·za·tion (kăr′ĭk tər ə zā′shən, kăr′ĭk trə zā′shən), *n.* creation and portrayal of fictitious characters.

char·ac·ter·ize (kăr′ĭk tə rīz′), *v.* to create and portray fictional characters.

char·lock (chär′lək), *n.* wild mustard.

cha·ry (châr′ĭ), *adj.* **1.** careful; wary. **2.** sparing (followed by *of*).

chasm (kăz′əm), *n.* a deep cleft in the earth's surface.

chas·tise (chăs tīz′), *v.* to punish, usually by beating. (Older spelling, *chastize*). —**chas·tise·ment** (chăs′tĭz mənt), *n.*

chig·ger (chĭg′ər), *n.* the parasitic larva of certain mites, which causes itching when attached to the skin.

chim·ney pot (chĭm′nĭ pŏt′), *n. British.* a pipe fitted on the top of a chimney to increase the draft and prevent smoking.

chiv·al·ry (shĭv′əl rĭ), *n.* **1.** the ideal qualifications of a knight, such as courtesy, generosity, courage. **2.** the rules and customs of medieval knighthood. —**chiv′al·rous, chiv′al·ric**, *adj.* —**chiv′al·rous·ly**, *adv.*

chop't (chŏpt), *adj. Archaic* for chapped; cracked. (Also **chopped, choppy**.)

chro·mat·ic scale (krō măt′ĭk), *Music.* a scale progressing by semitones (half steps).

chron·ic (krŏn′ĭk), *adj.* long-continued; constant.

chron·o·log·i·cal (krŏn′ə lŏj′ə kəl), *adj.* arranged in the order of time. —**chron′o·log′i·cal·ly**, *adv.*

chro·nom·e·ter (krə nŏm′ə tər), *n.* a time-keeper with special mechanism for ensuring accuracy, used for special purposes such as determining longitude at sea.

chuck·le·head (chŭk′əl hĕd′), *n. Colloq.* a blockhead. —**chuck′le·head′ed**, *adj.*

churl (chûrl), *n.* **1.** a peasant. **2.** a rude, boorish, or surly person. —**churl′ish**, *adj.* —**churl′ish·ness**, *n.* —**churl′ish·ly**, *adv.*

cinch (sĭnch), *U.S.* —*n.* **1.** a strong girth for a saddle or pack. **2.** *Slang.* something sure or easy. —*v.* **1.** to gird or bind firmly, as with a cinch. **2.** *Slang.* to make sure of.

cin·e·ma (sĭn′ə mə), *n.* a motion picture.

ci·pher (sī′fər), *n.* writing done in a secret code.

cis- (sĭs), a prefix meaning "this side of" or "on this side" when used of places or "subsequent to" when used of time.

cis·tern (sĭs′tərn), *n.* a large receptacle for storing water.

cit·a·del (sĭt′ə dəl, sĭt′ə dĕl), *n.* a stronghold.

clas·sic (klăs′ĭk), *n.* an author or a literary production of the first rank. —*adj.* **1.** of the highest class. **2.** serving as a standard or model.

clois·tered (klois′tərd), *adj.* retired from the world.

co·gent (kō′jənt), *adj.* convincing.

cog·i·tate (kŏj′ə tāt′), *v.* to think hard; ponder.

cog·ni·zance (kŏg′nə zəns), *n.* knowledge; notice; perception.

cog·ni·zant (kŏg′nə zənt), *adj.* aware (followed by *of*).

co·hort (kō′hôrt), *n.* **1.** one of the ten divisions in an ancient Roman legion. **2.** any group of warriors.

col·lab·o·ra·tion (kə lăb′ə rā′shən), *n.* working together; co-operating. —**col·lab′o·rate′**, *v.*

col·league (kŏl′ēg), *n.* an associate in professional work.

col·lec·tive (kə lĕk′tĭv), *adj.* pertaining to a group of individuals taken together.

collective behavior, *n.* the group behavior of individuals acting under the influence of one another.

col·lo·qui·al (kə lō′kwĭ əl), *adj.* suited to ordinary conversation, rather than to formal speech or writing. —**col·lo·qui·al·ism** (kə lō′kwĭ ə lĭz′əm), *n.*

ăct, āble, dâre, ärt; ĕbb, ēqual; ĭf, īce; hŏt, ōver, ôrder, oil, bŏŏk, ōōze, out; ŭp, ūse, ûrge; ə = a in *alone*; ch, chief; g, give; j, judge; ng, ring; sh, shoe; th, thin; th, that; zh, vision. See the full key at the beginning of this glossary.

col·lu·sion (kə lo͞o′zhən), *n.* a secret agreement for a fraudulent purpose. **col·lu′sive,** *adj.*

co·lo·ni·al·ism (kə lō′nĭ ə lĭz′əm), *n.* the policy of a nation seeking to extend or retain its authority over other peoples or territories.

com·mis·sa·ry (kŏm′ə sĕr′ĭ), *n.* **1.** a store that supplies food and equipment, esp. in an army, lumber camp, etc. **2.** *Military.* an officer of the commissariat, the department of an army charged with supplying provisions, etc.

com·mune (kə mūn′), *v.* to converse; to interchange thoughts and feelings.

com·pass (kŭm′pəs), *n.* **1.** an instrument for determining directions. **2.** space within limits; area.

com·pa·tri·ot (kəm pā′trĭ ət), *n.* a fellow countryman.

com·pla·cen·cy (kəm plā′sən sĭ), *n.* a feeling of quiet pleasure; self-satisfaction.

com·pla·cent (kəm plā′sənt), *adj.* pleased, esp. with oneself and one's own merits.

com·po·sure (kəm pō′zhər), *n.* calmness; a serene and collected state of mind.

com·pro·mise (kŏm′prə mīz′), *v.* **1.** to settle a difference by each yielding a part. **2.** to endanger; to involve unfavorably. —*n.* **1.** a settlement by adjustment. **2.** an endangering or involving unfavorably.

con·cept (kŏn′sĕpt), *n.* a general notion; an idea.

con·cep·tion (kən sĕp′shən), *n.* a mental image.

con·cise (kən sīs′), *adj.* expressing much in few words.

con·crete (kŏn′krēt, kŏn krēt′), *adj.* constituting an actual thing rather than an abstract idea. —**con·crete′ly,** *adv.* —**con·crete′ness,** *n.*

con·de·scend (kŏn′dĭ sĕnd′), *v.* to act as if conscious of stooping from a superior position or rank. —**con′de·scend′ing,** *adj.* —**con′de·scend′ing·ly,** *adv.* —**con′de·scen′sion,** *n.*

con·form·i·ty (kən fôr′mə tĭ), *n.* compliance; acting or believing in accord with conventional ideas or behavior.

con·jec·ture (kən jĕk′chər), *n.* an opinion formed without sufficient evidence for proof; a guess. —*v.* to form such an opinion.

con·junc·tion (kən jŭngk′shən), *n.* combination.

con·no·ta·tion (kŏn′ə tā′shən), *n.* implied or associated meanings (as distinguished from *denotation,* the literal meaning): as, *"house" has a literal meaning only; "home" has*

many connotations. —**con·note′,** *v.* —**con′·no·ta′tive,** *adj.*

con·serv·a·tive (kən sûr′və tĭv), *adj.* **1.** disposed to preserve existing conditions rather than to favor change. **2.** cautious or moderate. —**con·serv′a·tism,** *n.*

con·ster·na·tion (kŏn′stər nā′shən), *n.* paralyzing amazement and dread.

con·tem·plate (kŏn′ təm plāt′), *v.* to observe thoughtfully, with continued attention. —**con′tem·pla′tion,** *n.* —**con′tem·pla′tive, con·tem′pla·tive,** *adj.* —**con′tem·pla′tive·ly,** *adv.*

con·ti·gu·i·ty (kŏn′tə gū′ə tĭ), *n.* nearness.

con·tig·u·ous (kən tĭg′yo͞o əs), *adj.* **1.** touching; in contact. **2.** near.

con·ti·nu·i·ty (kŏn′tə nū′ə tĭ), *n.* state of being connected or uninterrupted.

con·tort (kən tôrt′), *v.* to twist out of shape. —**con·tor′tion,** *n.*

con·tour (kŏn′to͞or), *n.* the outline of a figure or body; the line that defines or bounds anything.

con·tri·tion (kən trĭsh′ən), *n.* a feeling of remorse for guilt. —**con·trite** (kən trīt′, kŏn′ trīt), *adj.*

con·tro·ver·sial (kŏn′ trə vûr′shəl), *adj.* subject to controversy; debatable.

con·tro·ver·sy (kŏn′trə vûr′ sĭ), *n.* a discussion of a question in which opposing opinions clash.

con·tu·sion (kən tū′zhən), *n.* an injury as from a blow with a blunt instrument; a bruise.

con·vene (kən vēn′), *v.* **1.** to assemble, usually for some public purpose. **2.** to cause to assemble.

con·ven·tion (kən vĕn′shən), *n.* **1.** an assembly. **2.** custom; usage.

con·ven·tion·al (kən vĕn′shən əl), *adj.* customary. —**con·ven′tion·al·ly,** *adv.*

con·verge (kən vûrj′), *v.* to tend to meet in a point or line. —**con·ver′gence,** *n.* —**con·ver′gent,** *adj.*

con·vo·lu·tion (kŏn′və lo͞o′shən), *n.* a coil; twist.

coo·lie (ko͞o′lĭ), *n.* (in India, China, etc.) an unskilled native laborer.

cor·nice (kôr′nĭs), *n.* a horizontal molded projection which crowns or finishes a wall, building, etc.

cor·pu·lent (kôr′pyə lənt), *adj.* large; bulky of body. —**cor′pu·lence,** *n.*

cor·ral (kə răl′), *n.* a pen or enclosure for cattle, horses, etc.

cor·rode (kə rōd′), *v.* to eat away gradually, esp. by chemical action. —**cor·ro′sion,** *n.* —**cor·ro′sive,** *adj.*

cos·mic (kŏz′mĭk), *adj.* **1.** of the cosmos. **2.**

immeasurably extended in time and space.

cos·mo·pol·i·tan (kŏz′mə pŏl′ə tən), *adj.* belonging to all parts of the world; at home all over the world. —*n.* one free from local prejudices; a citizen of the world.

cos·mos (kŏz′məs, kŏz′mŏs), *n.* the world or universe as a system of order and harmony (as opposed to *chaos*).

coun·sel (koun′səl), *n.* 1. advice. 2. a legal adviser.

coun·te·nance (koun′tə nəns), *v.* to approve; give support to.

course (kōrs), *n. Nautical.* the lowest square sail on any mast of a square-rigged ship.

cov·ert (kŭv′ərt), *adj.* 1. covered. 2. secret.

cow chip, *n.* a piece of dried cow manure.

coy (koi), *adj.* 1. demure. 2. pretending to be shy, often in a coquettish manner. —**coy′ly**, *adv.*

coy·o·te (kī ō′tĭ, kī′ōt), *n.* the prairie wolf.

cred·i·ble (krĕd′ə bəl), *adj.* believable. —**cred′i·bil′i·ty**, *n.* —**cred′i·bly**, *adv.*

creed (krēd), *n.* 1. an authoritative statement of the chief articles of Christian belief. 2. any system of belief or opinion.

cri·ter·i·on (krī tĭr′ĭ ən), *n.* (*pl.* **criteria**), a standard of judgment.

crit·ic (krĭt′ĭk), *n.* a person skilled in judging the qualities of some matter.

crit·i·cism (krĭt′ə sĭz′əm), *n.* act of passing judgment as to the merits and faults of anything. —**crit′i·cize**, *v.* —**crit′i·cal**, *adj.* —**crit′i·cal·ly**, *adv.*

crotch·et·y (krŏch′ĭt ĭ), *adj.* given to peculiar, stubborn notions; cantankerous.

cru·cial (krōō′shəl), *adj.* 1. decisive; involving a final decision. 2. trying; severe.

cruse (krōōz, krōōs), *n.* an earthen pot or bottle for liquids. —**widow′s cruse**, (Old Testament) a bottle which never became empty.

crus·ta·cean (krŭs tā′shən), *n.* a member of the class of invertebrates, generally aquatic, commonly having the body covered with a hard shell (for example, lobsters, crabs, shrimps).

cud·gel (kŭj′əl), *n.* a club. —*v.* 1. to beat. 2. **cudgel one's brains**, to think hard.

cu·li·na·ry (kū′lə nĕr′ĭ), *adj.* pertaining to cookery.

cull (kŭl), *v.* to pick, select. **cull out**, *Archaic.* pick out, select. —*n.* something picked out, esp. something rejected as not up to standard.

cul·ture (kŭl′chər), *n.* 1. enlightenment or refinement resulting from development by education or training. 2. *Sociology.* the sum total of ways of living built up by a group of human beings, and transmitted from one generation to another. —**cul′tu·ral**, *adj.*

culture change, *Sociology.* the process by which a culture is significantly modified (for example, by contact with another culture). (Also, **cultural change.**)

cul·vert (kŭl′vərt), *n.* a drain or channel crossing under a road.

cu·mu·lus (kū′myə ləs), *adj.* a cloud with summit made up of rounded heaps and with flat base.

cut·lass (kŭt′ləs), *n.* a short, heavy, slightly curved sword, formerly used at sea.

cyn·ic (sĭn′ĭk), *n.* 1. a sneering faultfinder. 2. one who doubts the goodness of human motives.

cyn·i·cal (sĭn′ə kəl), *adj.* distrusting the motives of others. —**cyn′i·cism**, *n.*

da·hoo·ri (də hōō′rĭ), *n.* a word invented by Dunsany for a game of ancient times.

de·bauch·er·y (dĭ bô′chə rĭ), *n.* excessive indulgence, usually in harmful pleasures; intemperance.

de·ca·dent (dĭ kā′dənt, dĕk′ə dənt), *adj.* falling into an inferior state; deteriorating. —**de·ca·dence** (dĭ kā′dəns, dĕk′ə dəns), *n.*

de·cant (dĭ kănt′), *v.* to pour gently, as liquor, from one container into another, without disturbing the sediment.

de·clin·a·tion (dĕk′lə nā′shən), *n.* a polite refusal.

ded·i·cate (dĕd′ə kāt′), *v.* to set apart and consecrate to a sacred purpose. —**ded′i·ca′tion**, *n.*

ded·i·ca·to·ry (dĕd′ə kə tōr′ĭ), *adj.* serving as a dedication.

def·er·ence (dĕf′ər əns), *n.* 1. yielding to the opinion, will, etc., of another. 2. courteous regard; respect. —**de·fer** (dĭ fûr′), *v.*

de·flect (dĭ flĕkt′), *v.* to bend or turn aside.

de·funct (dĭ fŭnkt′), *adj.* dead.

de·gen·er·ate (dĭ jĕn′ə rāt′), *v.* to decline in

ăct, āble, dâre, ärt; ĕbb, ēqual; ĭf, īce; hŏt, ōver, ôrder, oil, bŏŏk, ōōze, out; ŭp, ūse, ûrge; ə = a in *alone*; ch, chief; g, give; j, judge; ng, ring; sh, shoe; th, thin; th, that; zh, vision. See the full key at the beginning of this glossary.

physical, mental, or moral qualities. —(dĭ·
jĕn'ər ĭt), adj. having so declined. —de·
gen'er·a'tion, n.

de·grade (dĭ grād'), v. to lower in rank or
dignity; to debase.

de·jec·tion (dē jĕk'shən), n. depression; low-
ness of spirits.

de·lir·i·um (dĭ lĭr'ĭ əm), n. 1. a more or less
temporary disorder of the mental faculties,
as in fevers. 2. a state of violent excitement. —de·lir'i·ous, adj.

del·uge (dĕl'ūj), n. 1. flood; downpour. 2.
anything that overwhelms like a flood. —
v. to flood.

de·mean·or (dĭ mē'nər), n. outward behavior;
bearing.

dem·i·tasse (dĕm'ĭ tăs'), n. 1. a small cup for
serving black coffee after dinner. 2. the
coffee served in such a cup.

den·i·zen (dĕn'ə zən), n. inhabitant; resident.

de·nounce (dĭ nouns'), v. to assail with censure; to condemn openly.

de·nun·ci·a·tion (dĭ nŭn'sĭ ā'shən), n. open
and strong condemnation.

de·ple·tion (dĭ plē'shən), n. state of exhaustion due to loss of blood, undernourish-
ment, etc.

dep·re·cate (dĕp'rə kāt'), v. protest against,
—dep're·ca'tion, n.

de·pre·ca·to·ry (dĕp'rə kə tōr'ĭ), adj. expressing protest.

de·ride (dĭ rīd'), v. to laugh at mockingly.
—de·ri·sive (dĭ rī'sĭv), adj. —de·ri'sive·ly,
adv. —de·ri·sion (dĭ rĭzh'ən), n.

descriptive linguistics: see linguistics.

des·pi·ca·ble (dĕs'pĭ kə bəl), adj. deserving
scorn and contempt.

des·pot (dĕs'pət, dĕs'pŏt), n. an absolute
ruler.

des·pot·ism (dĕs'pə tĭz'əm), n. the exercise of
absolute authority. —des·pot'ic, adj. —
des·pot'i·cal·ly, adv.

de·tach (dĭ tăch'), v. to part; separate; withdraw.

de·tached (dĭ tăcht'), adj. 1. aloof; withdrawn; separate. 2. free from prejudice.
—de·tach'ment, n.

de·ter·i·o·rate (dĭ tĭr'ĭ ə rāt'), v. to make or
become lower in character or quality. —
de·te'ri·o·ra'tion, n.

dev·as·ta·tion (dĕv'ə stā'shən), n. destruction.
—dev'as·tate (dĕv'ə stāt'), v.

de·vi·ous (dē'vĭ əs), adj. 1. winding; rambling. 2. departing from the straight or
right way.

di·a·bol·i·cal (dī'ə bŏl'ĭk əl), adj. having the
qualities of a devil. (Also, di'a·bol'ic.)

dic·tion (dĭk'shən), n. 1. style of speaking or
writing resulting from choice of words. 2.
the degree of distinctness with which
speech sounds are uttered; enunciation.

die·hard (dī'härd'), n. one who opposes
something to the very last, esp. a conservative in politics.

dif·fi·dence (dĭf'ə dəns), n. lack of confidence
in one's own ability, worth, or fitness. —
dif'fi·dent, adj.

dif·fuse (dĭ fūz'), v. to scatter or spread
widely. —(dĭ fūs') adj. 1. widely spread.
2. wordy in speech or writing.

di·gress (də grĕs', dĭ grĕs'), v. to ramble.

di·gres·sion (dĭ grĕsh'ən), n. temporary departing from the main subject.

di·lem·ma (dĭ lĕm'ə), n. a situation calling
for a choice between equally undesirable
alternatives.

di·min·u·tive (dĭ mĭn'yə tĭv), adj. tiny.

di·plo·ma·cy (dĭ plō'mə sĭ), n. 1. the management by government officials of relations between nations. 2. tact. —dip'lo·mat'ic,
adj.

dirge (dûrj), n. a funeral song, or one of
mourning.

dis·as·trous (dĭs ăs'trəs), adj. ruinous; causing great injury or distress. —dis·as'trous·ly,
adv.

dis·con·cert (dĭs'kən sûrt'), v. to confuse, upset. —dis'con·cert'ed, adj.

dis·con·so·late (dĭs cŏn'sə lĭt), adj. unhappy;
without comfort. —dis·con'so·late·ly, adv.

dis·cred·it (dĭs krĕd'ĭt), v. to show to be un-
deserving of belief; to destroy confidence
in.

dis·crep·an·cy (dĭs krĕp'ən sĭ), n. inconsistency. —dis·crep'ant, adj.

dis·crim·i·nate (dĭs krĭm'ə nāt'), v. 1. to make
a distinction, as in favor of or against a
person or thing. 2. to observe differences
accurately. —dis·crim'i·na'tion, n.

dis·crim'i·nat·ing, adj. possessing the power
to make exact distinctions: as, a person of
discriminating taste or judgment.

dis·dain (dĭs dān'), n. scorn. —v. to treat
with contempt. —adj. dis·dain'ful.

di·shev·eled (dĭ shĕv'əld), adj. untidy.

dis·in·te·grate (dĭs ĭn'tə grāt'), v. to break up;
fall apart. —dis·in'te·gra'tion, n.

dis·par·age (dĭs pär'ĭj), v. to speak slightingly
of. —dis·par'age·ment, n.

dis·pas·sion·ate (dĭs păsh'ən ĭt), adj. free from
personal feeling; impartial; calm.

dis·sem·i·nate (dĭ sĕm'ə nāt'), v. to scatter (as
seed in sowing); to spread abroad (as a
rumor). —dis·sem'i·na'tion, n.

dis·si·pate (dĭs'ə pāt'), *v.* **1.** to scatter. **2.** to squander. **3.** to indulge extravagantly in pleasure. —**dis'si·pa'tion,** *n.*

dis·tort (dĭs tôrt'), *v.* **1.** to twist out of shape. **2.** to misrepresent. —**dis·tor'tion,** *n.*

dis·trac·tion (dĭs trăk'shən), *n.* **1.** a drawing of the thoughts in conflicting directions; confusion. **2.** anything that gives mental relaxation; amusement. —**dis·tract'ed,** *adj.* —**dis·tract'ed·ly,** *adv.*

di·vine (dĭ vīn'), *v.* to discover; find out by intuition; guess.

di·vulge (dĭ vŭlj'), *v.* to disclose or reveal something previously secret.

dod·der·y (dŏd'ər ĭ), *adj.* tottering; senile. (Also, **dod'der·ing.**)

dog·ma (dôg'mə, dŏg'mə), *n.* a system of principles or doctrines, as of a church.

dog·mat·ic (dôg măt'ĭk), *adj.* **1.** pertaining to doctrine. **2.** positive; opinionated.

dole·ful (dōl'fəl), *adj.* sorrowful; gloomy.

do·lor (dō'lər), *n.* *Chiefly poetic.* sorrow; grief.

do·main (dō mān'), *n.* **1.** a territory under rule. **2.** a field of action, thought, etc.

dom·i·nate (dŏm'ə nāt'), *v.* to rule over, control; tower above. —**dom'i·na'ting, dom'i·nant,** *adj.* —**dom'i·na'tion, do·min'ion,** *n.*

doom (dōōm), *n.* **1.** fate, especially if bad. **2.** ruin; death. **3.** a judgment, esp. an unfavorable one. —*v.* to condemn.

dooms·day (dōōmz'dā'), *n.* the day of the Last Judgment; the end of the world.

do·ry (dō'rĭ), *n.* a boat with a narrow, flat bottom, high ends, and flaring sides.

dow·er (dou'ər), *v.* to provide with a dowry.

dow·ry (dou'rĭ), *n.* the money, goods, or estate which a woman brings to her husband at marriage.

dowse or **douse** (dous), *v.* to plunge into water or other liquid; drench.

draft (drăft), *n.* **1.** act of drawing or pulling. **2.** a preliminary form of any writing, subject to revision.

draft animals, animals used or suited for drawing loads, as oxen, horses, etc.

draw (drô), *n.* *Physical geography.* a small natural drainway, usually the upper part of a stream valley.

droll·er·y (drō'lə rĭ), *n.* something amusingly queer or funny. —**droll** (drōl), *adj.*

drone (drōn), *n.* **1.** the male of the bee, stingless and making no honey. **2.** an idler, who lives on the labor of others.

drone (drōn), *n.* a continued dull, monotonous sound; a humming. —Also, *v.*

du·al (dū'əl), *adj.* twofold.

du·bi·ous (dū'bĭ ŭs), *adj.* doubtful.

dul·cet (dŭl'sĭt), *adj.* **1.** agreeable to the eye or ear. **2.** *Archaic.* sweet to the taste or smell.

dy·nam·ic (dī năm'ĭk), *adj.* active; forceful. (Opposed to *static.*)

dy·na·mo (dī'nə mō), *n.* a device for converting mechanical energy into electrical energy.

dy·nas·ty (dī'nəs tĭ), *n.* a sequence of rulers from the same family or stock.

e·clipse (ĭ klĭps'), *v.* to obscure, darken (as in a *solar eclipse,* when the light of the sun is cut off wholly or in part by the moon's coming between it and observers on earth).

e·co·nom·ic (ē'kə nŏm'ĭk, ĕk'ə nŏm'ĭk), *adj.* pertaining to the production, distribution, and use of income and wealth.

e·co·nom·ics (ē'kə nŏm'ĭks, ĕk'ə nŏm'ĭks), *n.* the science that deals with the production and consumption of wealth, and related problems.

ec·sta·sy (ĕk'stə sĭ), *n.* overpowering emotion; rapturous delight. —**ec·sta'tic,** *adj.*

ee·rie (ĭr'ĭ), *adj.* weird, strange, uncanny. —**ee'ri·ness,** *n.* —**ee'ri·ly,** *adv.*

ef·fect (ĭ fĕkt'), *n.* result, consequence. —*v.* to make happen.

ef·fec·tive (ĭ fĕk'tĭv), *adj.* producing the intended result. —**ef·fec'tive·ness,** *n.*

ef·fete (ĭ fēt'), *adj.* worn out; exhausted; having lost energy and vigor.

e·go·ist (ē'gō ĭst, ĕg'ō ĭst), *n.* a self-centered or selfish person. (Also, **e'go·tist.**) —**e'go·is'tic, e'go·tis'tic,** *adj.*

e·jac·u·la·tion (ĭ jăk'jə lā'shən), *n.* an exclamation. —**e·jac'u·late,** *v.*

e·lic·it (ĭ lĭs'ĭt), *v.* to draw out; bring out.

e·lude (ē lūd'), *v.* **1.** to avoid or escape; to slip away from. **2.** to escape the mind; baffle. —**e·lu'sive,** *adj.*

em·a·nate (ĕm'ə nāt'), *v.* to flow out or proceed from. —**em'a·na'tion,** *n.*

e·mit (ĭ mĭt'), *v.* to give out or forth.

ăct, āble, dâre, ärt; ĕbb, ēqual; ĭf, īce; hŏt, ōver, ôrder, oil, bŏŏk, ōōze, out; ŭp, ūse, ûrge; ə = a in *alone*; ch, chief; g, give; j, judge; ng, ring; sh, shoe; th, thin; t͟h, that; zh, vision. See the full key at the beginning of this glossary.

en·croach (ĕn krōch′), v. 1. to make gradual advances beyond proper limits. 2. to trespass upon someone else's property or rights. —**en·croach′ment,** n.

en·cum·ber (ĕn kŭm′bər), v. to burden or embarrass. (Also, **incumber.**)

en·fran·chise (ĕn frăn′chīz), v. 1. to admit to citizenship. 2. to liberate, as from slavery. —**en·fran·chise·ment** (ĕn frăn′chĭz mĕnt), n.

en·gross (ĕn grōs′), v. to occupy wholly, as the mind or attention.

e·nig·ma (ĭ nĭg′mə), n. something puzzling; a riddle.

en·ig·mat·ic (ĕn′ĭg măt′ĭk), adj. mysterious; puzzling.

en·join (ĕn join′), v. to tell a person to do something, esp. with authority.

e·nor·mi·ty (ĭ nôr′mə tĭ), n. something outrageous, as an offense.

en·thrall (ĭn thrâl′), v. to charm.

en·vi·ron·ment (ĕn vī′rən mənt), n. the sum of surrounding things, conditions, or influences.

ep·i·cure (ĕp′ə kyōōr′), n. one who cultivates a refined taste in eating and drinking.

ep·i·cu·re·an (ĕp′ə kyōō rē′ən), adj. fit for an epicure.

e·qui·lib·ri·um (ē′kwə lĭb′rĭ əm), n. state of rest; equal balance between forces that counteract each other.

e·ra (ē′rə), n. a period of time measured from some important occurrence or date: as, *the Christian era.*

e·rode (ĭ rōd′), v. to eat out or away. (Used esp. in geology, to denote the action of all the forces of nature that wear away the earth's surface.) —**e·ro′sion,** n.

er·rat·ic (ĭ răt′ĭk), adj. 1. deviating from the usual course in conduct or opinion; eccentric. 2. having no certain course; wandering.

er·ro·ne·ous (ə rō′nĭ əs, ĕ rō′nĭ əs), adj. mistaken; incorrect.

es·sen·tial (ə sĕn′shəl), adj. 1. being such by its very nature. 2. absolutely necessary.

es·tu·a·ry (ĕs′chōō ĕr′ĭ), n. an arm or inlet of the sea, esp. the wide mouth of a river, where the current meets the tide.

e·ther·e·al (ĭ thĭr′ĭ əl), adj. light, airy; extremely delicate or refined.

eth·ics (ĕ′thĭks), n. the science of the good and the nature of the right; the principles of morality.

Eu·clid (ū′klĭd), n. 1. Greek geometer at Alexandria, around 300 B.C. 2. the works of Euclid, especially his treatise on geometry. —**Eu·clid′e·an,** adj.

eu·lo·gize (ū′lə jīz′), v. to speak or write in praise of a person or thing, esp. of the dead. —**eu′lo·gy,** n.

e·vade (ĭ vād′), v. 1. to escape from by trickery. 2. to avoid doing or answering. —**e·va′sion,** n. —**e·vas′ive,** adj.

e·val·u·ate (ĭ văl′yōō āt′), v. to estimate; determine the value of. —**e·val′u·a′tion,** n.

e·van·es·cent (ĕv′ə nĕs′ənt), adj. 1. vanishing; fleeting. 2. scarcely perceptible.

e·voke (ĭ vōk′), v. to call up: as, *the scene evokes many memories.*

ex·cept (ĭk sĕpt′), v. to exclude; leave out.

ex·e·crate (ĕk′sə krāt′), v. 1. to detest completely. 2. to curse.

ex·ot·ic (ĭg zŏt′ĭk), adj. 1. foreign. 2. *Colloq.* strikingly unusual in color or appearance.

ex·pan·sive (ĭk spăn′sĭv), adj. 1. tending to expand. 2. having a wide range. 3. (of a person's character, speech, etc.) free, open, unrestrained.

ex·pa·ti·ate (ĭk spā′shĭ āt′), v. to write or talk at length upon a subject.

ex·pe·di·ent (ĭk spē′dĭ ənt), adj. 1. fit for a certain purpose. 2. advantageous; convenient. 3. useful for selfish advantage rather than for what is right or just. —*n.* a means to an end.

ex·plic·it (ĭk splĭs′ĭt), adj. definite; precise.

ex·tant (ĕks′tənt, ĭk stănt′), adj. in existence.

ex·tinct (ĭk stĭngkt′), adj. 1. no longer active, as a volcano. 2. having come to an end; without a living representative as a species.

ex·tol (ĭk stōl′, ĭk stŏl′), v. to praise highly.

ex·tra·ne·ous (ĭk strā′nĭ əs), adj. not belonging or proper to a thing; external.

ex·trem·i·ty (ĭk strĕm′ə tĭ), n. 1. the extreme terminal point; limit. 2. a condition of extreme need or distress.

ex·u·ber·ant (ĭg zōō′bər ənt), adj. overflowing with energy or high spirits.

ex·ult (ĭg zŭlt′), v. to show or feel triumphant joy. —**ex·ul·ta′tion, ex·ult′ance,** n. —**ex·ult′ant,** adj. —**ex·ult′ant·ly,** adv.

fa·ce·tious (fə sē′shəs), adj. 1. amusing. 2. trying to be amusing. —**fa·ce′tious·ly,** adv.

fa·cil·i·tate (fə sĭl′ə tāt′), v. to make easier.

fac·ul·ty (făk′əl tĭ), n. 1. an ability. 2. one of the powers of the mind, as memory or reason.

fain (fān), adv. *Poetic.* gladly; willingly. (Used with *would.*)

fair·way (fâr′wā′), n. *Golf.* that part of the links between tees and putting greens where the grass is kept short.

fal·si·fy (fôl′sə fī′), v. **1.** to make incorrect, esp. so as to deceive. **2.** to misrepresent. —**fal·si·fi·ca·tion** (fôl′sə fə kā′shən), n.

fal·ter (fôl′tər), v. **1.** to hesitate or waver. **2.** to speak hesitantly or brokenly.

fa·nat·ic (fə nǎt′ĭk), n. a person with extreme and unreasoning enthusiasm or zeal.

fa·nat·i·cism (fə nǎt′ə sĭz′əm), n. extreme and unreasoning spirit or conduct. —**fa·nat′i·cal**, adj.

fan·tas·tic (fǎn tǎs′tĭk), adj. **1.** odd; quaint; eccentric or grotesque. **2.** extravagantly fanciful; irrational. —**fan·tas′ti·cal·ly**, adv.

fan·ta·sy (fǎn′tə sĭ), n. **1.** wild, visionary fancy. **2.** a highly imaginative poem, play, etc. (Also, **phantasy.**)

far·row (fǎr′ō), n. a litter of pigs. —v. to produce a litter of pigs.

fas·tid·i·ous (fǎs tǐd′ĭ əs), adj. hard to please.

fa·thom (fǎth′əm), n. a unit of length equal to 6 feet, used principally in nautical or mining measurements. —v. **1.** to measure the depth of. **2.** to understand thoroughly.

fat·u·ous (fǎch′ŏŏ əs), adj. foolish, while pleased with oneself. —**fat′u·ous·ly**, adv.

fe·brile (fē′brəl), adj. feverish.

fed·er·al (fěd′ər əl), adj. of or designating a central government consisting of a union of states in which each member agrees to subordinate its power in common affairs to that of the central authority.

fed·er·al·ism (fěd′ər ə lĭz′əm), n. the federal principle of government.

fed·er·al·ist (fěd′ər əl ĭst), n. **1.** a person who believes in a federal form of government. **2.** (cap.) a person who favored union of the colonies after the War of Independence and adoption of the Constitution; a member of the Federal Party, a U.S. party of the 18th century.

feign (fān), v. to put on an appearance of (in order to deceive); to pretend.

fe·lic·i·ty (fĭ lĭs′ə tĭ), n. a state of great happiness.

fel·o·ny (fěl′ə nĭ), n. a serious crime.

fem·i·nism (fěm′ə nĭz′əm), n. the doctrine advocating the equality of women in social and political life. —**fem′i·nist**, n.

fe·tid (fět′ĭd, fē′tĭd), adj. having an offensive odor; stinking.

feu·dal (fū′dəl), adj. pertaining to or resembling the relations between rulers and subjects existing in the Middle Ages in Europe.

Feudal System, n. the organization of Europe in the Middle Ages.

fi·ber (fī′bər), n. a fine threadlike piece.

fi·brous (fī′brəs), adj. containing, consisting of, or resembling fibers.

fidg·et (fĭj′ĭt), v. to move about restlessly, uneasily, or impatiently. **fidg′et·y** (fĭj′ə tĭ), adj.

fiend (fēnd), n. **1.** Satan. **2.** any evil spirit. **3.** a diabolically cruel or wicked person.

fi·nal·ize (fī′nə līz′), v. Colloq. to put into final form.

fire·brand (fīr′brǎnd′), n. **1.** a piece of burning wood. **2.** a person who stirs up others to revolt or strife.

fix·a·tion (fĭk sā′shən), n. a fixed idea, one upon which attention is steadily focused.

fla·grant (flā′grənt), adj. glaring; scandalous.

flail (flāl), n. an instrument for threshing grain by hand consisting of a staff or handle to one end of which is attached a freely swinging stick or bar. —v. to strike with, or as if with, such an instrument.

flange (flǎnj), n. a projecting rim, collar, edge, etc., on an object for keeping it in place, attaching it to another object, etc.

flaw (flô), n. **1.** a defect. **2.** a sudden gust or brief sharp storm of wind.

flinch (flĭnch), v. to draw back; shrink from the painful or unpleasant.

flint (flĭnt), n. **1.** a hard kind of stone. **2.** a piece of this stone, esp. as used for striking fire.

foal (fōl), n. the young of the horse, donkey, or similar animal; a colt. —v. to bring forth, give birth to (a foal).

fo·gy (fō′gĭ), n. an old-fashioned or excessively conservative person.

fold (fōld), n. **1.** a pen for sheep. **2.** a flock of sheep; hence, **3.** any group with common interests, aims, etc. **4.** a safe place where such a group gathers.

folk·sy (fōk′sĭ), adj. **1.** of or like the common people. **2.** sociable.

fore-and-aft (fôr′ənd ǎft′), adj. Nautical. in line with the keel of a ship: as, a fore-and-aft sail.

ǎct, āble, dâre, ärt; ěbb, ēqual; ǐf, īce; hǒt, ōver, ôrder, oil, bǒǒk, ōōze, out; ǔp, ūse, ûrge; ə = a in alone; ch, chief; g, give; j, judge; ng, ring; sh, shoe; th, thin; **th**, that; zh, vision. See the full key at the beginning of this glossary.

fore·cas·tle (fōk'səl), *n.* the seamen's quarters in the forward part of a merchant vessel.

for·lorn (fôr lôrn'), *adj.* forsaken; desolate; miserable; hopeless. —**for·lorn'ly,** *adv.*

for·mal (fôr'məl), *adj.* 1. according to prescribed or fixed customs. 2. designed for use or wear at ceremonies, elaborate parties, etc. 3. *Speech and writing.* designating that level of language usage characterized by extensive vocabulary and exactness in form (as opposed to *informal, colloquial*).

for·ti·tude (fôr'tə tūd', fôr'tə tōōd'), *n.* patient courage; endurance.

fos·ter (fôs'tər, fŏs'tər), *v.* to promote the growth or development of; to further.

foul (foul), *adj.* grossly offensive; wicked; vile. —**foul'ly,** *adv.*

foun·der (foun'dər), *v.* 1. to fill with water and sink (of ships). 2. to break down or go lame (of horses).

frame (frām), *n.* the constructional system that gives a building, vessel, etc., its model and strength.

frame of reference, a system of laws, customs, or values which serve as background for an individual's behavior, attitudes, or understanding.

free·hold (frē'hōld'), *n. Law.* an estate held for life, and with the privilege of receiving or passing on by inheritance.

fret·work (frĕt'wûrk'), *n.* ornamental work in which the design is formed by perforation.

friv·o·lous (frĭv'ə ləs), *adj.* 1. of little importance or worth. 2. lacking seriousness. 3. given to trifling.

frus·trate (frŭs'trāt), *v.* 1. to make plans, efforts, etc., useless. 2. to disappoint or thwart (a person).

funk (fŭngk), *n. Colloq.* cowering fear. —*v.* to be terrified; to try to shirk.

fu·til·i·ty (fū tĭl'ə tĭ), *n.* uselessness. —**fu·tile** (fū'təl), *adj.*

gab·ble (gă'bəl), *v.* to jabber, talk rapidly and unintelligibly. —*n.* rapid, unintelligible talk.

ga·ble (gā'bəl), *n.* the end of a ridged roof and the triangular section of wall from the level of the eaves to the peak of the roof. —**ga'bled,** *adj.*

gal·lant (găl'ənt), *adj.* brave; high-spirited. —(gə lănt'), *adj.* polite and attentive to women. —**gal'lant·ly,** *adv.*

gal·lan·try (găl'ən trĭ), *n.* 1. polite, courtly attention to women. 2. heroic bravery.

gal·ley (găl'ĭ), *n.* 1. an early seagoing vessel propelled by oars or by oars and sails. 2. the kitchen of a ship.

galley slave, 1. a person condemned to work at the oar on a galley. 2. an overworked person.

gal·van·ize (găl'və nīz'), *v.* 1. to stimulate by or as by an electric current. 2. to coat (metal, esp. iron or steel) with zinc.

gam·bol (găm'bəl), *v.* to skip about; frolic. —*n.* a skipping about.

gam·ut (găm'ət), *n.* the whole scale or range.

gan·grene (găng'grēn), *n.* the dying of tissue, as from the interruption of circulation.

gant·let (gănt'lĭt, gônt'lĭt), *n.* (more commonly spelled **gauntlet**) a medieval glove with metal plates worn to protect the hand from injury in combat. —**to throw down the gauntlet,** to challenge. —**to take up the gauntlet,** to accept a challenge. —**to run the gauntlet,** to pass through many perils, as from watchful enemies.

gaol (jāl), *n. British.* jail. —**gaol'er,** *n.*

gar·ru·lous (găr'ə ləs, găr'yə ləs), *adj.* talkative, esp. about trifles.

gear (gēr). *n.* implements, tools, or apparatus used for a particular occupation.

ge·nus (jē'nəs), *n.* kind; class.

ges·tic·u·late (jĕs tĭk'yə lāt'), *v.* to use gestures in an excited manner. —**ges·tic'u·la'tion,** *n.*

ges·ture (jĕs'chər), *n.* movement of the body, head, arms, hands, or face expressive of an idea or emotion. —*v.* to make use of or express by gestures.

gib·ber (jĭb'ər, gĭb'ər), *v.* to speak rapidly and inarticulately.

gib·ber·ish (jĭb'ər ĭsh, gĭb'ər ĭsh), *n.* rapid, unintelligible talk.

gill (gĭl), *n. Chiefly Scottish.* 1. a brook. 2. a wooded glen with a stream flowing through it. (Also, **ghyll**.)

gin·ger·ly (jĭn'jər lĭ), *adv.* very cautiously.

glut (glŭt), *v.* to feed or supply in excess of need or demand.

glut·ton (glŭt'ən), *n.* one who eats to excess.

gorge (gôrj), *n.* a narrow cleft with steep, rocky walls, esp. one through which a stream runs. —*v.* to stuff with food.

graft (grăft, gräft), *n.* 1. act of taking advantage of one's position to gain money, property, etc., dishonestly. 2. anything acquired by such illegal methods.

Grain Coast, *n.* part of the west coast of Africa, now Liberia and Sierra Leone, once so called because "grains of Paradise," the pungent peppery seeds of a plant native to the region, were much in demand for use in the making of cordials and in veterinary medicine, and hence an important trade item.

gram·o·phone (grăm′ə fōn′), *n.* a phonograph.

graph·ic (grăf′ĭk), *adj.* lifelike; vivid.

griev·ous (grē′vəs), *adj.* 1. causing grief. 2. glaringly bad; atrocious. —**griev′ous·ly,** *adv.*

grog·gy (grŏg′ĭ), *adj.* 1. staggering, as from exhaustion or blows. 2. intoxicated. —**grog′gi·ly,** *adv.*

guer·ril·la (gə rĭl′ə), *n.* a member of a small, independent band of soldiers which harasses the enemy by surprise raids, etc. —*adj.* pertaining to such fighters or their warfare.

guise (gīz), *n.* 1. appearance; aspect. 2. assumed appearance.

gus·to (gŭs′tō), *n.* hearty enjoyment.

gy·ra·tion (jī rā′shən), *n.* circular or spiral motion.

gy·rate (jī′rāt), *v.* to whirl.

hag·gard (hăg′ərd), *adj.* having a drawn, worn look, as from prolonged sleeplessness, exertion, anxiety, or grief.

hair·brained (hâr′brānd′), *adj.* (usually spelled **harebrained**) reckless; giddy.

handle·bar mustache, *see* **mustache.**

hap·haz·ard (hăp′hăz′ərd), *adj.* determined by mere chance. —**hap′haz′ard·ly,** *adv.*

har·ass (hăr′əs, hə răs′), *v.* to disturb persistently; torment.

hard·bit·ten (härd′bĭt′ən), *adj.* tough; stubborn.

har·le·quin (här′lə kwĭn, här′lə kĭn), *n.* a droll character in early comedy, dressed in particolored spangled tights and carrying a wooden sword; a clown.

har·ry (hă′rĭ), *v.* to torment; worry with unreasonable demands.

haut·boy (hō′boi, ō′boi), *n.* oboe (a woodwind instrument).

ha·ven (hā′vən), *n.* 1. a harbor. 2. any place of shelter and safety.

haw·ser (hô′zər), *n. Nautical.* a small cable or large rope.

haw·sered (hô′zərd), *adj.* tied up with a hawser.

haz·ard (hăz′ərd), *n.* 1. a risk. 2. *Golf.* an

obstacle (such as a road or water) on the course. —*v.* to venture; risk. —**haz′ard·ous,** *adj.*

hei·nous (hā′nəs), *adj.* hateful; gravely blameworthy.

her·e·sy (hĕr′ə sĭ), *n.* an opinion or doctrine at variance with the accepted doctrine, esp. of a church or religious system.

her·e·tic (hĕr′ə tĭk), *n.* a member of a church who holds opinions contrary to his church or rejects doctrines prescribed by his church.

he·ro·ics (hĭ rō′ĭks), *n. pl.* extravagant language or sentiment.

hey·day (hā′dā′), *n.* the point of highest vigor.

hi·ber·na·tor·i·al (hī′bûr nə tōr′ĭ əl), *adj.* pertaining to winter.

hi·er·o·glyph·ic (hī′ər ə glĭf′ĭk), *adj.* 1. designating the writing system of the ancient Egyptians. 2. hard to decipher. —*n.* 1. a hieroglyphic symbol. 2. a figure or symbol with a hidden meaning. (Also, **hi′er·o·glyph′.**)

high·hand·ed (hī′hăn′dĭd), *adj.* overbearing.

hi·lar·i·ous (hĭ lâr′ĭ əs), *adj.* boisterously gay. —**hi·lar·i·ty** (hĭ lăr′ə tĭ), *n.*

his·tri·on·ic (hĭs′trĭ ŏn′ĭk), *adj.* 1. pertaining to actors or acting. 2. artificial; affected.

hob·ble (hŏb′əl), *v.* 1. to limp. 2. to fasten together the legs of a horse or other animal, to prevent free motion.

hob·ble·de·hoy (hŏb′əl dĭ hoi′), *n.* 1. an adolescent boy. 2. an awkward, clumsy boy.

holt (hōlt), *n. Chiefly poetic.* a wood.

hom·age (hŏm′ĭj), *n.* honor, respect; tribute.

home·ly (hōm′lĭ), *adj.* plain, unpretentious; lacking in elegance.

hor·o·scope (hôr′ə scōp′), *n.* the position of the planets with relation to one another at a given time (esp. the time of a person's birth), regarded by some as determining destiny.

hos·pi·ta·ble (hŏs′pĭ tə bəl, or, esp. *British,* hŏs pĭt′ə bəl), *adj.* giving a generous welcome to guests or strangers.

ho·ver (hŭv′ər, hŏv′ər), *v.* 1. to hang fluttering or suspended in the air. 2. to keep lingering about.

hu·mane (hū mān′), *adj.* merciful; kindhearted.

ăct, āble, dâre, ärt; ĕbb, ēqual; ĭf, īce; hŏt, ōver, ôrder, oil, bŏŏk, ōōze, out; ŭp, ūse, ûrge; ə = a in *alone*; **ch,** chief; **g,** give; **j,** judge; **ng,** ring; **sh,** shoe; **th,** thin; **t̶h,** that; **zh,** vision. See the full key at the beginning of this glossary.

hyp·no·sis (hǐp nō′sǐs), *n.* a sleeplike condition characterized by marked response to the suggestions of the hypnotist.

hy·poc·ri·sy (hǐ pǒk′rə sǐ), *n.* act of pretending to have a character, beliefs, etc., that one does not possess.

hyp·o·crite (hǐp′ə krǐt), *n.* a pretender; one who practices hypocrisy. —**hyp′o·crit′i·cal**, *adj.*

hy·poth·e·sis (hǐ pŏth′ə sǐs), *n.* an unproved theory.

hys·ter·i·a (hǐs tǐr′ǐ ə), *n.* morbid or senseless emotionalism; emotional frenzy.

hys·ter·i·cal (hǐs tĕr′ə kəl), *adj.* emotionally disordered. —**hys·ter′i·cal·ly**, *adv.*

ich·thy·ol·o·gy (ǐk′thǐ ŏl′ə jǐ), *n.* the branch of zoology (zō ŏl′ə jǐ) that treats of fishes. —**ich′thy·ol′o·gist**, *n.*

ig·no·ble (ǐg nō′bəl), *adj.* 1. low; base. 2. humble, not noble.

il·lim·it·a·ble (ǐl lǐm′ǐt ə bəl), *adj.* boundless.

il·lu·sion (ǐ lōō′zhən), *n.* something that deceives by producing a false impression.

il·lu·so·ry (ǐ lōō′sə rǐ), *adj.* unreal.

im·mac·u·late (ǐ măk′yə lǐt), *adj.* free from spot or stain; spotlessly clean; pure.

im·ma·te·ri·al (ǐm′ə tǐr′ǐ əl), *adj.* unimportant.

im·mi·nent (ǐm′ə nənt), *adj.* likely to occur at any moment; overhanging.

im·mo·bile (ǐ mō′bǐl, ǐ mō′bēl), *adj.* 1. immovable. 2. motionless. —**im′mo·bil′i·ty**, *n.*

im·pair (ǐm pâr′), *v.* to make or become worse; to diminish in value; weaken. —**im·pair′ment**, *n.*

im·pas·sive (ǐm păs′ǐv), *adj.* without appearance of emotion.

im·pec·ca·ble (ǐm pĕk′ə bəl), *adj.* faultless.

im·ped·i·men·ta (ǐm pĕd′ə mĕn′tə), *n.* 1. supplies carried with an army. 2. things hindering progress; encumbrances.

im·per·a·tive (ǐm pĕr′ə tǐv), *adj.* 1. not to be avoided. 2. commanding. —*n.* command.

im·per·cep·ti·ble (ǐm′pər sĕp′tə bəl), *adj.* very slight; not easy to perceive. —**im′per·cep′ti·bly**, *adv.*

im·per·son·al (ǐm pûr′sən əl), *adj.* 1. without reference to a particular individual. 2. not having personal qualities or a personality. 3. *Grammar.* a. (of a verb) having no real subject; as, *it is sunny.* b. (of a pronoun) indefinite; as, *one should not do that.*

im·plic·it (ǐm plǐs′ǐt), *adj.* 1. unquestioning; absolute. 2. suggested but not actually stated. —**im·plic′it·ly**, *adv.*

im·ply (ǐm plī′), *v.* to suggest without actually stating. —**im′pli·ca′tion**, *n.*

in-, *prefix,* sometimes means "not," and sometimes "in." Often takes other forms, such as *im,* and *il* (*impossible, illiterate*), depending on the sound which follows it.

in·cal·cu·la·ble (ǐn kăl′kyə lə bəl), *adj.* that cannot be forecast; uncertain.

in·can·ta·tion (ǐn′kăn tā′shən), *n.* 1. the chanting of words supposed to have magical power. 2. a spell or charm.

in·car·na·tion (ǐn′kär nā′shən), *n.* embodiment; appearance in human form. —**in·car′nate**, *v.*, *adj.*

in·con·gru·ous (ǐn kŏng′grōō əs), *adj.* out of keeping; inappropriate; out of harmony. —**in·con′gru·ous·ly**, *adv.*

in·con·sid·er·a·ble (ǐn′kən sǐd′ər ə bəl), *adj.* 1. small in size, value, etc. 2. not worth noting.

in·con·sist·ent (ǐn′kən sǐs′tənt), *adj.* self-contradictory. —**in′con·sist′en·cy**, *n.*

in·cred·i·ble (ǐn krĕd′ə bəl), *adj.* seeming too extraordinary to be possible; not believable.

in·cre·du·li·ty (ǐn′krə dū′lə tǐ), *n.* a refusal to believe; unbelief.

in·cred·u·lous·ly (ǐn krĕj′ə ləs lǐ), *adv.* in a manner indicating unbelief. —**in·cred′u·lous**, *adj.*

in·de·co·rum (ǐn′dǐ kōr′əm), *n.* unseemly behavior. —**in·dec·o·rous** (ǐn dĕk′ə rəs), *adj.* **in·dec′o·rous·ly**, *adv.*

in·de·fat·i·ga·ble (ǐn′dǐ făt′ə gə bəl), *adj.* incapable of being tired out. **in′de·fat′i·ga·bly**, *adv.*

in·de·ter·mi·nate (ǐn′dǐ tûr′mə nǐt), *adj.* not fixed in extent; indefinite.

in·dis·ci·pline (ǐn dǐs′ə plǐn), *n.* lack of discipline (a state of order maintained by training and control).

in·dis·cre·tion (ǐn′dǐs krĕsh′ən), *n.* 1. lack of sound judgment. 2. an act showing lack of sound judgment.

in·dom·i·ta·ble (ǐn dŏm′ə tə bəl), *adj.* that cannot be subdued or overcome; unconquerable. —**in·dom′i·ta·bly**, *adv.*

in·ert (ǐn ûrt′), *adj.* having no inherent power of action, motion, or resistance; of an inactive nature. —**in·ert′ness**, *n.* —**in·ert′ly**, *adv.*

in·er·tia (ǐn ûr′shə), *n.* a tendency to remain in a fixed condition without change—if at rest, to remain so; if moving, to continue in the same manner or direction.

in·ev·i·ta·ble (ǐn ĕv′ə tə bəl), *adj.* that cannot be avoided; sure to happen.

in·ex·or·a·ble (ǐn ĕk′sə rə bəl), *adj.* unyielding; not to be persuaded or moved. —**in·ex′or·a·bly**, *adv.*

in·ex·pli·ca·ble (ĭn ĕks'plə kə bəl), *adj.* unexplainable. —in·ex'pli·ca·bly, *adv.*

in·fer (ĭn fûr'), *v.* to draw conclusions from evidence.

in·fer·ence (ĭn'fər əns), *n.* 1. the act of drawing conclusions from evidence. 2. conclusion drawn from evidence.

in·fi·nite (ĭn'fə nĭt), *adj.* 1. immeasurably great. 2. unlimited; perfect. —in·fin'i·ty, *n.* —in'fi·nite·ly, *adv.*

in·fringe·ment (ĭn frĭnj'mənt), *n.* a breach or infraction as of a law, right, or obligation; violation. —in·fringe', *v.*

in·hu·man (ĭn hū'mən), *adj.* lacking natural human feeling or sympathy; brutal.

in·hu·mane (ĭn'hū mān'), *adj.* not merciful or kind.

in·hu·man·i·ty (ĭn'hū măn'ə tĭ), *n.* cruelty.

in·im·i·cal (ĭn ĭm'ə kəl), *adj.* hostile.

in·i·qui·tous (ĭ nĭk'wə təs), *adj.* grossly unjust.

in·iq·ui·ty (ĭ nĭk'wə tĭ), *n.* 1. gross injustice. 2. a violation of right or duty.

in·i·ti·ate (ĭ nĭsh'ĭ āt'), *v.* to begin; originate.

ink·ling (ĭngk'lĭng), *n.* a hint.

in·qui·si·tion (ĭn'kwə zĭsh'ən), *n.* act of inquiring; far-reaching investigation.

in·quis·i·tive (ĭn kwĭz'ə tĭv), *adj.* unduly curious; prying.

in·sa·ti·a·ble (ĭn sā'shə bəl, ĭn sā'shĭ ə bəl), *adj.* incapable of being satisfied. —in·sa'tia·bil'·i·ty, *n.* —in·sa'tia·bly, *adv.*

in·scru·ta·ble (ĭn skroo'tə bəl), *adj.* not yielding up its meaning even to close examination; impenetrable.

in·sen·si·ble (ĭn sĕn'sə bəl), *adj.* 1. incapable of feeling or perceiving. 2. unaware or unappreciative.

in·sen·si·tive (ĭn sĕn'sə tĭv), *adj.* 1. not readily affected by external agencies or influences. 2. not having acute mental or emotional perceptions and reactions.

in·sin·u·ate (ĭn sĭn'yoo āt'), *v.* to suggest or hint slyly.

in·sin·u·a·tion (ĭn sĭn'yoo ā'shən), *n.* a sly suggestion or hint of something not plainly stated. —in·sin'u·a'ting·ly, *adv.*

in·sol·ven·cy (ĭn sŏl'vən sĭ), *n.* state of being unable to pay debts; bankruptcy.

in·sol·vent (ĭn sŏl'vənt), *adj.* unable to pay debts; bankrupt.

in·sti·gate (ĭn'stə gāt'), *v.* to spur on to some action. —in'sti·ga'tion, *n.*

in·su·lar (ĭn'sə lər), *adj.* 1. pertaining to or situated on an island. 2. narrow; prejudiced (as islanders might be because not in close contact with the larger world).

in·tact (ĭn tăkt'), *adj.* sound; whole; uninjured.

in·tan·gi·ble (ĭn tăn'jə bəl), *adj.* 1. incapable of being perceived by the sense of touch. 2. hard to define.

in·te·gral (ĭn'tə grəl), *adj.* belonging as a part to the whole; necessary to the completeness of the whole.

in·teg·ri·ty (ĭn tĕg'rə tĭ), *n.* 1. soundness of character and principles. 2. state of being whole, entire.

in·tent (ĭn tĕnt'), *n.* purpose. —*adj.* having the gaze or thoughts firmly fixed on something. —in·tent'ly, *adv.*

in·ter·lude (ĭn'tər lood'), *n.* 1. an intervening episode, period, space, etc. 2. anything that fills time between two events: as, *an interlude of waiting between trains.*

in·ter·po·late (ĭn tûr'pə lāt'), *v.* 1. to alter, enlarge, or corrupt (a book, manuscript, etc.) by inserting new material. 2. to insert something additional between things.

in·ter·pret (ĭn tûr'prĭt), *v.* to set forth the meaning of. —in·ter'pre·tive, *adj.*

in·ter·pre·ta·tion (ĭn tûr'prə tā'shən), *n.* 1. an explanation. 2. *Theater.* the rendering of a part in a play so as to bring out one's particular conception of the playwright's meaning.

in·ter·vene (ĭn'tər vēn'), *v.* 1. to come, be, or lie between. 2. to come between as an influencing force; to modify, settle, or hinder some action, etc. —in·ter·ven·tion (ĭn'tər vĕn'shən), *n.*

in·tol·er·a·ble (ĭn tŏl'ə rə bəl), *adj.* not to be put up with; unbearable.

in·tol·er·ant (ĭn tŏl'ər ənt), *adj.* not willing to permit or put up with contrary opinions, or other differences.

in·tri·cate (ĭn'trə kĭt), *adj.* 1. perplexingly entangled. 2. complicated; hard to understand.

in·trin·sic (ĭn trĭn'sĭk), *adj.* belonging to a thing by its very nature.

in·trude (ĭn trood'), *v.* 1. to thrust or bring

ăct, āble, dâre, ärt; ĕbb, ēqual; ĭf, īce; hŏt, ōver, ôrder, oil, bŏŏk, ōoze, out; ŭp, ūse, ûrge; ə = a
in *alone*; **ch**, chief; **g**, give; **j**, judge; **ng**, ring; **sh**, shoe; **th**, thin; **ṯẖ**, that; **zh**, vision. See the full
key at the beginning of this glossary.

in without reason, permission, or welcome.
2. to come uninvited. —in·tru′sion, n. —
in·tru′sive, adj. —in·tru′sive·ly, adv.

in·trud′er, n. one who intrudes.

in·tu·i·tion (ĭn′tyoo ĭsh′ən, ĭn′too ĭsh′ən), n.
direct perception of truths, facts, etc., independent of any reasoning process. —in-
tu·i·tive (ĭn tū′ə tĭv), adj.

in·veigh (ĭn vā′), v. to attack violently with
words (followed by against).

in·vo·ca·tion (ĭn′vō kā′shən), n. act of calling
upon (a deity, a spirit) for aid, protection,
etc.

in·voke (ĭn vōk′), v. 1. to call upon earnestly,
as with prayer. 2. to call forth by an in-
cantation; conjure.

i·ras·ci·ble (ĭ răs′ə bəl), adj. easily angered.
—i·ras′ci·bil′i·ty, n. —i·ras′ci·bly, adv.

ir·rel·e·vant (ĭ rĕl′ə vənt), adj. 1. not applicable. 2. Law. having no bearing on the
case (in relation to evidence).

ir·re·triev·a·ble (ĭr′ĭ trē′və bəl), adj. not recoverable.

i·sin·glass (ī′zĭng glăs′), n. 1. a transparent
form of gelatin, often derived from the air
bladders of fish. 2. mica.

is·sue (ĭsh′oo), n. a point the decision of
which determines a matter. —v. to come
out; emerge.

ja·ded (jā′dĭd), adj. worn out.

ju·bi·lant (joo′bə lənt), adj. showing or feeling great joy. —ju′bi·lant·ly, adv. —ju′bi-
la′tion, n.

ju·di·cious (joo dĭsh′əs), adj. having or showing good judgment.

ju·ris·dic·tion (joor′ĭs dĭk′shən), n. the right,
power, or authority to administer justice.

jus·ti·fy (jŭs′tə fī), v. 1. to show (an act,
statement, etc.) to be just, right, warranted.
2. to defend or uphold as blameless, just, or
right. 3. to declare guiltless.

ken (kĕn), n. 1. range of sight. 2. knowledge; mental perception.

knell (nĕl), n. the sound made by a bell
rung slowly for a death or a funeral.

lab·y·rinth (lăb′ə rĭnth), n. 1. a maze of paths
or passages in which it is difficult to find
one's way or to reach the exit. 2. Greek
legend. such a maze constructed by King
Minos of Crete.

lac·er·ate (lăs′ə rāt′), v. to tear roughly;
mangle.

lac·er·a·tion (lăs′ə rā′shən), n. rough, jagged
tear.

la·goon (lə goon′), n. any small pondlike
body of water, esp. one communicating with
a larger body of water.

la·i·ty (lā′ə tĭ), n. 1. laymen, as distinguished
from clergymen. 2. the people outside a
particular profession, as distinguished from
those belonging to it.

land·fall (lănd′fôl′), n. 1. an approach to or
sighting of land. 2. the land sighted or
reached.

lan·guish (lăng′gwĭsh), v. 1. to become weak.
2. to lose activity and vigor; to droop. —
lan′guid, adj. —lan′guid·ly, adv.

lan·guor (lăng′gər), n. 1. physical weakness
or faintness. 2. indolence. 3. emotional
softness or tenderness. —lan′guor·ous, adj.

lar·ce·ny (lär′sə nĭ), n. theft, robbery. —petit
or petty larceny, theft of property of small
value. —grand larceny, theft of property of
considerable or great value.

lar·va (lär′və), n. 1. the young of any insect which undergoes metamorphosis. 2.
any animal in a similar immature form.

lay (lā), adj. 1. pertaining to the laity, as
distinguished from the clergy: as, a lay sermon. 2. not belonging to or proceeding
from a profession, esp. law or medicine: as,
a lay opinion.

lay·man (lā′mən), n. not a clergyman; not a
member of a particular profession.

lead (lēd), n. Journalism. a short summary
serving as an introduction to a news story
or article. —adj. principal; summarizing in
an introduction: as, the lead paragraph.

lead (lĕd), n. 1. a heavy, comparatively soft
bluish-gray metal. 2. bullets; shot. 3. a
mass of lead suspended by a line, for measuring depths (sounding) at sea. —to heave
lead, Nautical. to cast the lead for sounding.

lec·tern (lĕk′tərn), n. a reading desk, esp. in
a church.

le·git·i·mate (lĭ jĭt′ə mĭt), adj. 1. lawful. 2.
in accordance with established rules, principles, or standards.

legitimate drama, drama for production on
the stage (as opposed to motion pictures).

le·o·nine (lē′ə nīn′), adj. lionlike.

le·thal (lē′thəl), adj. deadly.

lev·er·age (lĕv′ər ĭj, lē′vər ĭj), n. 1. power
gained by using a lever. 2. increased
power of action.

li·bel (lī′bəl), n. any written or printed statement, sign, picture, etc., that unjustly tends
to expose a person to public ridicule or
contempt or to injure his reputation. —
li′bel·ous, adj.

lib·er·al (lĭb′ər əl), *adj.* favorable to progress or reform, as in religious or political affairs. —*n.* a person of liberal principles or views, esp. in religion or politics.

lib·er·tar·i·an (lĭb′ ər târ′ĭ ən), *n.* one who advocates liberty of thought or conduct.

li·bret·to (lĭ brĕt′ō), *n.* 1. the text or words of an opera or other long musical composition. 2. a book or booklet containing such a text.

lim·bo (lĭm′bō), *n.* (*Often cap.*) 1. a supposed region on the border of hell or heaven, the place of those barred from heaven through no fault of their own. 2. a place to which persons or things are said to be sent when they are cast aside, forgotten, or out of date. 3. prison; confinement.

lin·e·age (lĭn′ĭ ĭj), *n.* 1. line of descendants from an ancestor. 2. ancestry.

lin·guist (lĭng′gwĭst), *n.* 1. a person skilled in foreign languages. 2. a specialist in the science of language (linguistics). —**lin·guis′·tic**, *adj.*

lin·guis·tics (lĭng gwĭs′tĭks), *n.* the science of language. —**descriptive linguistics**, the branch which treats the classification and arrangement of the features of language.

list·less (lĭst′lĭs), *adj.* feeling no interest or inclination toward anything. —**list′less·ness**, *n.* —**list′less·ly**, *adv.*

lit·a·ny (lĭt′ə nĭ), *n.* a ceremonial form of prayer consisting of a series of petitions with responses.

lit·er·al (lĭt′ər əl), *adj.* 1. true to fact, often in an unimaginative way. 2. being the natural or strict meaning of a word or words. —**lit′er·al·ly**, *adv.*

lit·er·ate (lĭt′ər ĭt), *adj.* 1. educated. 2. having extensive knowledge, experience, or culture.

log (lŏg), *n.* *Nautical.* the official record of a ship's voyage. (Also, **log·book.**)

log·ic (lŏj′ĭk), *n.* 1. sound reason. 2. the science of sound reasoning.

log·i·cal (lŏg′ə kəl), *adj.* according to the principles of sound reasoning; reasonable.

lon·gev·i·ty (lŏn jĕv′ə tĭ), *n.* long life.

lon·gi·tu·di·nal (lŏn′jə tū′də nəl), *adj.* pertaining to longitude or length; lengthwise. —**lon′gi·tu′di·nal·ly**, *adv.* —**lon′gi·tude′**, *n.*

lore (lōr), *n.* the body of knowledge (esp. of a traditional or popular nature) on a particular subject.

loy·al·ist (loi′əl ĭst), *n.* 1. a supporter of the existing government, esp. in time of revolt. 2. one who remained loyal to the British government during the American Revolution.

lu·cra·tive (loo′krə tĭv), *adj.* profitable.

lu·di·crous (loo′də krəs), *adj.* ridiculous.

lu·gu·bri·ous (loo gū′brĭ əs, loo goo′brĭ əs), *adj.* mournful; dismal.

luke·warm (look′wôrm′), *adj.* 1. tepid. 2. showing little enthusiasm.

lu·pine (loo′pĭn), *adj.* wolfish; savage.

lus·ter (lŭs′tər), *n.* radiant brightness.

lus·trous (lŭs′trəs), *adj.* shining; bright.

mad·der (măd′ər), *n.* a climbing plant with groups of small yellowish flowers. Its root is used for making dyes (red and other colors).

ma·dro·ña, ma·dro·ño (mə drō′nyə, mə drō′nyō), *n.* an evergreen tree or shrub, the arbutus or strawberry tree, of western North America. —*Colloq.* **madroné**

mag·nan·i·mous (măg năn′ə məs), *adj.* 1. generous in forgiving; free from petty resentment or vindictiveness. 2. noble of mind. —**mag′na·nim′i·ty**, *n.*

mag·nil·o·quent (măg nĭl′ə kwĕnt), *adj.* expressed in a grandiose style.

ma·lev·o·lent (mə lĕv′ə lənt), *adj.* showing ill will. —**ma·lev′o·lent·ly**, *adv.*

mal·ice (măl′ĭs), *n.* desire to inflict injury or suffering on another. —**ma·li′cious**, *adj.* —**ma·li′cious·ly**, *adv.*

mal·nu·tri·tion (măl′nū trĭsh′ən), *n.* state resulting from lack of proper food.

ma·neu·ver (mə noo′vər), *n.* 1. a planned and regulated movement of troops, war vessels, etc. 2. an adroit move. —*v.* 1. to change the position of troops, etc., by a regulated plan. 2. to manipulate with skill.

man·i·fest (măn′ə fĕst′), *adj.* evident; plain.

man·i·fold (măn′ə fōld′), *adj.* numerous and varied.

man·na (măn′ə), *n.* 1. the food miraculously supplied the Israelites in the wilderness (Exodus 16:14-36). 2. divine or spiritual food.

ăct, āble, dâre, ärt; ĕbb, ēqual; ĭf, īce; hŏt, ōver, ôrder, oil, book, ooze, out; ŭp, ūse, ûrge; ə = a in *alone*; **ch**, chief; **g**, give; **j**, judge; **ng**, ring; **sh**, shoe; **th**, thin; **th**, that; **zh**, vision. See the full key at the beginning of this glossary.

man·ner·ism (măn′ə rĭz′əm), *n.* a habitual peculiarity of manner, either in a person or in a literary or other artistic work.

man·za·ni·ta (măn′zə nē′tə), *n.* any of several kinds of shrub of the western U.S.

Mar·i·po·sa lily (măr′ə pō′sə), a plant of the western U.S. and Mexico, having tuliplike flowers of various colors.

mar·mo·re·al (mär mōr′ĭ əl), *adj.* of or like marble.

mash·er (măsh′ər), *n. Slang of earlier times, now rare.* a man who attempts to flirt with strange women. —**mash,** *v.*

mat·tock (măt′ək), *n.* an instrument for loosening the soil in digging, shaped like a pickax, but having one end broad instead of pointed.

mean (mēn), *adj.* 1. inferior; low; of little importance. 2. stingy, miserly.

mel·o·dra·ma (měl′ə drä′mə), *n.* a play exaggerated in violence, sentiment, and passion. —**mel′o·dra·mat′ic,** *adj.* —**mel′o·dra·mat′i·cal·ly,** *adv.*

me·men·to (mĭ měn′tō), *n.* something that serves as a reminder of what is past.

mem·o·ran·dum (měn′ə răn′dəm), *n.* (*pl.* mem′o·ran′da), a note made of something to be remembered.

men·tor (měn′tər), *n.* a wise, trusted adviser.

me·sa (mā′sə; *Spanish,* mě′sä), *n.* a kind of tableland common in dry parts of southwestern U.S., having a flat top and bounded by steep rock walls.

met·a·phys·ics (mět′ə fĭz′ĭks), *n.* that branch of philosophy which treats of first principles, including the science of being, and the origin and structure of the universe.

mi·cros·co·pist (mī krŏs′kə pĭst, mī′krə skŏp′ĭst), *n.* an expert in the use of the microscope for investigation.

mi·cros·co·py (mī krŏs′kə pĭ, mī′krə skō′pĭ), *n.* investigation by means of the miscroscope.

mil·i·tant (mĭl′ə tənt), *adj.* combative; aggressive. —*n.* one engaged in active strife.

mil·li·me·ter (mĭl′ə mē′tər), *n.* a unit of length in the metric system, equivalent to 0.03937 inch, or one thousandth of a meter.

min·a·ret (mĭn ə rět′, mĭn′ə rět), *n.* a lofty slender tower attached to a mosque (Mohammedan temple) with one or more balconies from which the people are called to prayer.

min·ion (mĭn′yən), *n.* a favorite servant; a favorite (used only in a bad sense).

mi·nute (mī nūt′), *adj.* extremely small.

mi·rage (mĭ räzh′), *n.* an optical illusion due to atmospheric conditions by which reflected images of distant objects are seen, often inverted.

mis- (mĭs), a prefix meaning "ill," "mistaken," or "wrong."

mis·con·cep·tion (mĭs′kən sěp′shən), *n.* a mistaken notion.

mis·con·strue (mĭs′kən strōō′, mĭs kŏn′strōō), *v.* to misinterpret.

mi·ter (mī′tər), *n.* the official headdress of a bishop of the Western church, the outline of the front and back resembling that of a pointed arch.

mo·bile (mō′bəl, mō′bēl), *adj.* moving readily; changing easily in expression. —**mo·bil′i·ty,** *n.*

mo·bi·lize (mō′bə līz′), *v.* to put into readiness for action.

mon·o·cle (mŏn′ə kəl), *n.* an eyeglass for one eye.

mo·nop·o·list (mə nŏp′ə lĭst), *n.* one who has or advocates monopoly.

mo·nop·o·lize (mə nŏp′ə līz′), *v.* to obtain exclusive possession of; to keep entirely to oneself.

mo·nop·o·ly (mə nŏp′ə lĭ), *n.* 1. exclusive control of a commodity or service, making possible the manipulation of prices. 2. a company or the like having such control.

mon·strous (mŏn′strəs), *adj.* 1. huge. 2. shocking.

mo·sa·ic (mō zā′ĭk), *n.* 1. a picture or decoration made of small pieces of stone, glass, etc., of different colors, inlaid to form a design. 2. something resembling a mosaic in composition.

mot·ley (mŏt′lĭ), *adj.* 1. made up of many different or clashing elements: as, *a motley crowd.* 2. of many colors or patches of color. —*n.* the particolored garment of the old-time professional jester.

mud dauber, *n.* any of certain wasps which construct mud cells for their larvae and provision them with insects.

mud·dle (mŭd′əl), *v.* 1. to mix up or jumble together. 2. to render confused mentally, or unable to think clearly.

mun·dane (mŭn′dān), *adj.* worldly.

mu·nic·i·pal (mū nĭs′ə pəl), *adj.* of or pertaining to the local government of a town or city.

mus·sel (mŭs′əl), *n.* a kind of edible marine bivalve (having two shells hinged together, like the clam).

mus·tache (mŭs′tăsh, məs tăsh′), *n.* the hair growing on the upper lip. —**handle-bar mustache,** a mustache in the shape of the curved steering bar of a bicycle.

mu·ta·tion (mū tā′shən), *n.* change.

mu·ti·nous (mū′tə nəs), *adj.* 1. disposed to, engaged in, or involving revolt against constituted authority, esp. by soldiers or seamen. 2. rebellious.

myr·i·ad (mĭr′ĭ əd), *n.* an indefinitely great number.

mys·tic (mĭs′tĭk), *adj.* mysterious; beyond the bounds of ordinary knowledge. (Also, **mys′ti·cal.**)

na·ïve (nä ēv′), *adj.* simple; unsuspecting; unsophisticated.

na·ïve·té (nä ēv′tā′), *n.* artless simplicity.

na·per·y (nā′pə rĭ), *n.* table linen.

naugh·ty (nô′tĭ), *adj.* 1. disobedient; mischievous (esp. in speaking about children). 2. *Obsolete.* wicked, evil.

ne·gate (nĭ gāt′, nē′gāt), *v.* to deny.

neg·li·gence (nĕg′lə jəns), *n.* neglect.

neg·li·gi·ble (nĕg′lə jə bəl), *adj.* that may be disregarded.

neu·tral (nū′trəl), *adj. Electric magnetism.* neither positive nor negative; not electrified. **—neu′tral·ize,** *v.*

nig·gard·ly (nĭg′ərd lĭ), *adj.* stingy.

noc·tur·nal (nŏk tûr′nəl), *adj.* pertaining to the night.

non·cha·lant (nŏn′shə lənt, non′shə länt′), *adj.* coolly unconcerned. **—non′cha·lant·ly,** *adv.*

nos·tal·gia (nŏs tăl′jə), *n.* 1. homesickness or strong desire for family and friends. 2. a wistful desire to return to some past period. **—nos·tal′gic,** *adj.*

no·to·ri·ous (nō tōr′ĭ əs), *adj.* widely but unfavorably known. **—no·to·ri·e·ty** (nō′tə rī′ə tĭ), *n.* **—no·to′ri·ous·ly,** *adv.*

nov·ice (nŏv′ĭs), *n.* one who is new to the circumstances, work, etc., in which he is placed.

nox·ious (nŏk′shəs), *adj.* hurtful.

nu·ance (nū äns′, nōō äns′, nū′äns, nōō′äns; *French* nY äns′), *n.* a shade of color, expression, meaning, feeling, etc.

ob·jec·tive (əb jĕk′tĭv), *adj.* impartial; relying on evidence only (as opposed to personal feelings).

ob·jec·tiv·i·ty (ŏb′jĕk tĭv′ə tĭ), *n.* (in writing) portraying character and events through reporting externals (actions, appearance, facial expression, etc.), leaving the reader to draw his own conclusions about the thoughts and feelings of the persons involved.

ob·lig·a·to·ry (ə blĭg′ə tōr′ĭ, ŏb′lə gə tōr′ĭ), *adj.* 1. binding morally or legally. 2. required.

ob·lique (ə blēk′), *adj.* 1. diverging from a straight line. 2. indirect.

ob·lit·er·ate (ə blĭt′ə rāt′), *v.* to remove all traces of; destroy.

ob·liv·i·on (ə blĭv′ĭ ən), *n.* state of being forgotten.

ob·liv·i·ous (ə blĭv′ĭ əs), *adj.* unmindful; forgetful.

ob·nox·ious (əb nŏk′shəs), *adj.* offensive; detestable.

ob·scene (əb sēn′, ŏb sēn′), *adj.* indecent; repulsive; offensive to modesty. **—ob·scen·i·ty** (əb sēn′ə tĭ), *n.* **—ob·scene·ly** (əb sēn′lĭ), *adv.*

ob·scure (əb skyoor′), *adj.* 1. dim, dark. 2. uncertain of meaning; hard to understand. 3. unknown. **—ob·scu′ri·ty,** *n.* **—ob·scure′ly,** *adv.*

ob·so·lete (ŏb′sə lēt′), *adj.* no longer in use; out of date. **ob′so·les′cent,** *adj.* **—ob′so·les′cence,** *n.*

ob·ste·tri·cian (ŏb′stē trĭsh′ən), *n.* one skilled in obstetrics.

ob·ste·trics (əb stĕt′rĭks), *n.* the branch of medical science concerned with caring for and treating women before, in, and after childbirth.

ob·vi·ous (ŏb′vĭ əs), *adj.* open to view or knowledge; plain, evident, clear. **—ob′vi·ous·ly,** *adv.*

o·di·ous (ō′dĭ əs), *adj.* detestable.

Od·ys·sey (ŏd′ə sĭ), *n.* 1. Homer's epic poem on the ten years' wandering of Odysseus on his way home to Ithaca after the Trojan War. 2. (*l.c.*) any long series of wanderings.

o·le·ag·i·nous (ō′lĭ ăj′ə nəs), *adj.* having the nature or qualities of oil.

o·mi·nous (ŏm′ə nəs), *adj.* threatening; portending evil; of ill omen. **—om′i·nous·ly,** *adv.*

om·nis·cience (ŏm nĭsh′əns), *n.* all-inclusive knowledge.

om·nis·cient (ŏm nĭsh′ənt), *adj.* knowing all things.

o·paque (ō pāk′), *adj.* 1. not letting light pass

ăct, āble, dâre, ärt; ĕbb, ēqual; ĭf, īce; hŏt, ōver, ôrder, oil, bŏŏk, ōōze, out; ŭp, ūse, ûrge; ə = a in *alone*; ch, chief; g, give; j, judge; ng, ring; sh, shoe; th, thin; th, that; zh, vision. See the full key at the beginning of this glossary.

through; not transparent. **2.** dull or dark.

op·ti·mism (ŏp'tə mĭz'əm), *n.* disposition to hope for the best or to look on the bright side of things. —**op'ti·mis'tic,** *adj.*

op·u·lence (ŏp'yə ləns), *n.* riches; wealth.

or·a·cle (ôr'ə kəl), *n.* **1.** (in ancient Greece) an answer given by a priest or priestess at a shrine as the response of a god. **2.** any utterance made as infallible.

o·rac·u·lar (ō răk'yə lər), *adj.* uttered or delivered as if divinely inspired or infallible.

original sin, *see* **sin.**

os·cil·late (ŏs'ə lāt'), *v.* to swing to and fro as a pendulum does. —**os'cil·la'tion,** *n.*

out·rig·ger (out'rĭg'ər), *n.* a framework extended outboard from the side of a boat, esp. in South Pacific canoes, to prevent upsetting.

o·ver·state (ō'vər stāt'), *v.* to exaggerate. —**o'ver·state'ment,** *n.*

pa·cif·ic (pə sĭf'ĭk), *adj.* tending to make peace; conciliatory. —**pa·cif'i·cal·ly,** *adv.*

pall (pôl), *n.* **1.** a cloth, often of velvet, for spreading over a coffin. **2.** something that covers with gloom or darkness.

pal·lid (păl'ĭd), *adj.* pale.

palm·y (pä'mĭ), *adj.* glorious; prosperous; flourishing.

pal·try (pôl'trĭ), *adj.* trifling; worthless.

pam·per (păm'pər), *v.* to indulge to excess.

pan·el (păn'əl), *n.* a group of persons selected for a specific purpose, as discussing, judging, etc.

panel discussion, a discussion carried on by a selected group of speakers before an audience.

pan·ic (păn'ĭk), *n.* demoralizing terror.

pan·o·ra·ma (păn'ə răm'ə, păn'ə rä'mə), *n.* an unobstructed view over a wide area.

pan·to·mime (păn'tə mīm'), *n.* **1.** meaningful gesture without speech. **2.** a play in which the performers express themselves by mute gestures. —*Also v.*

pa·pa·cy (pā'pə sĭ), *n.* the office or jurisdiction of the Pope (of Rome).

pa·pal (pā'pəl), *adj.* of or pertaining to the Pope, the papacy, or the Roman Catholic Church.

papal titles, titles conferred by the Pope, representing the Church.

pa·pier-ma·ché (pā'pər mə shā'; *French* pä-pyĕ'mà shĕ'), *n.* a substance made of pulped paper mixed with glue and other substances, molded when moist to form various articles, and becoming hard and strong when dry.

par·a·dox (păr'ə dŏks'), *n.* a statement seemingly self-contradictory, and yet expressing a truth. —**par'a·dox'i·cal,** *adj.* —**par'a·dox'-i·cal·ly,** *adv.*

par·a·pet (păr'ə pĭt), *n.* a protective wall at the edge of a balcony, roof, bridge, or the like.

par·ley (pär'lĭ), *n.* a discussion; a conference. —*v.* to speak, talk, confer.

par·o·dy (păr'ə dĭ), *n.* a humorous imitation of a serious piece of writing. —*v.* to imitate in such a way as to ridicule.

par·ox·ysm (păr'ək sĭz'əm), *n.* **1.** a sudden attack or intensification of the symptoms of a disease. **2.** a sudden convulsion or outburst; spasm.

passing bell, *n.* a bell tolled to indicate a death.

pa·tent (păt'ənt, pā'tənt), *adj.* open to view or knowledge; evident. —**pa'tent·ly,** *adv.*

pa·thos (pā'thŏs), *n.* the quality in something experienced or observed which arouses feelings of pity, sympathy, or compassion.

pa·tri·arch (pā'trĭ ärk'), *n.* **1.** any of the earlier Biblical personages regarded as the fathers of the human race. **2.** the male head of a family or tribal line. —**pa'tri·ar'-chal,** *adj.*

pa·tri·cian (pə trĭsh'ən), *n.* **1.** a member of the original senatorial aristocracy in Rome. **2.** any noble or aristocrat. —*Also adj.*

peak·ed (pē'kĭd), *adj.* thin.

ped·ant (pĕd'ənt), *n.* one who makes an excessive show of learned exactness. —**pe·dan'tic,** *adj.*

pe·di·at·rics (pē'dĭ ăt'rĭks), *n.* the science of the medical and hygienic care of children. —**pe'di·at'ric,** *adj.*

per·ceive (pər sēv'), *v.* **1.** to become aware of through the senses. **2.** to grasp mentally.

per·cep·ti·ble (pər sĕp'tə bəl), *adj.* capable of being experienced through the senses.

per·cep·tion (pər sĕp'shən), *n.* **1.** the action or faculty of perceiving through the senses. **2.** insight or intuition, esp. in recognition of moral or aesthetic quality.

per·cep·tive (pər sĕp'tĭv), *adj.* of ready, intuitive insight.

per·en·ni·al (pə rĕn'ĭ əl), *adj.* **1.** lasting for an indefinitely long time. **2.** *Botany.* having a life cycle of more than two years.

per·func·to·ry (pər fŭngk'tə rĭ), *adj.* performed as a routine duty.

per·il·ous (pĕr'ə ləs), *adj.* dangerous, esp. great and immediate danger.

per·mis·sive (pər mĭs'ĭv), *adj.* permitting or allowing.

per·pe·tu·i·ty (pûr'pə tū'ə tĭ), *n.* endless or indefinitely long duration or existence. —**per·pet'u·ate**, *v.* —**per·pet'u·al**, *adj.* —**per·pet'u·al·ly**, *adv.*

per·spec·tive (pər spĕk'tĭv), *n.* 1. the art of picturing objects or a scene in such a way as to show them as they appear to the eye with reference to relative distance or depth. 2. the appearance of objects and scenes as determined by their relative distance and positions. 3. a distant view; vista. —**aerial perspective**, that branch of perspective which considers the expression of space in painting through variations of light, shade, color, etc.

per·turb (pər tûrb'), *v.* to disturb greatly; to agitate.

per·tur·ba·tion (pûr'tər bā'shən), *n.* mental disquiet or agitation.

pe·rus·al (pə rōō'zəl), *n.* a reading.

pe·ruse (pə rōōz'), *v.* to read through thoroughly.

per·vade (pər vād'), *v.* to go, pass, or spread throughout. —**per·va'sive**, *adj.*

per·verse (pər vûrs'), *adj.* wilfully determined to go contrary to what is expected or desired. —**per·ver'si·ty**, *n.*

per·vert (pər vûrt'), *v.* 1. to turn away from the right course. 2. to distort.

pes·si·mism (pĕs'ə mĭz'əm), *n.* disposition to take the gloomiest possible view.

pes·si·mist (pĕs'ə mĭst), *n.* one who looks on the gloomy side of things. —**pes'si·mis'tic**, *adj.*

petty cash, a small cash fund set aside to meet minor expenses.

pet·u·lant (pĕch'ə lənt), *adj.* impatiently irritable over trifles. **pet'u·lance**, *n.* —**pet'u·lant·ly**, *adv.*

phan·tasm (făn'tăz əm), *n.* a perception of something that has no physical reality, esp. a specter or ghost.

phan·tas·ma (făn tăz'mə), *n.* a phantasm.

phan·tom (făn'təm), *n.* an image appearing in a dream or formed in the mind.

phe·nom·e·non (fĭ nŏm'ə nŏn'), *n.* (*pl.* phenomena), 1. something observed or observable. 2. a remarkable thing or person. —**phe·nom'e·nal**, *adj.* —**phe·nom'e·nal·ly**, *adv.*

phi·lan·thro·py (fĭ lăn'thrə pĭ), *n.* love of mankind, esp. as shown in deeds of good will; charity. —**phil·an·throp·ic** (fĭl'ən thrŏp'ĭk), *adj.*

phi·lol·o·gy (fĭ lŏl'ə jĭ), *n.* 1. the study of written records, esp. literary texts, to establish their original form, etc. 2. the science of language.

phi·los·o·pher (fĭ lŏs'ə fər), *n.* 1. one versed in philosophy. 2. one who regulates his life by the light of reason. —**cracker-barrel philosophers**, village wiseacres. Derived from the use of the village store as a place to sit around in groups and exchange ideas. When there were not enough chairs, some sat on cracker barrels.

phi·los·o·phy (fĭ lŏs'ə fĭ), *n.* 1. the science of the truths underlying all knowledge. 2. a system of principles for guiding one's life. —**phil'o·soph'i·cal**, *adj.*

pho·net·ics (fō nĕt'ĭks), *n.* the science of speech sounds and their production.

phos·pho·res·cence (fŏs'fə rĕs'əns), *n.* 1. flamelike radiation, without heat. 2. property of giving out light without heat. 3. light so produced. —**phos'pho·res'cent**, *adj.*

phos·pho·rus (fŏs'fə rəs), *n.* *Chemistry.* a chemical element one of the properties of which is to be luminous in the dark.

pick·et (pĭk'ĭt), *n.* pointed stake used for purposes such as fencing.

piece·meal (pēs'mēl'), *adj.* piece by piece; gradually.

pinch (pĭnch), *n.* 1. as much as can be taken up between the finger and thumb. 2. a very small quantity. 3. a situation of special stress ("a tight place"). 4. *Slang.* a theft. —*v.* *Slang.* to steal.

pin·ion (pĭn'yən), *v.* 1. to cut off wing feathers to prevent a bird from flying. 2. to bind or hold fast.

pit (pĭt), *n.* a hole or cavity in the ground. —**bottomless pit**, the abode of evil spirits and lost souls; hell.

pith·y (pĭth'ĭ), *adj.* short and full of meaning.

pla·cate (plā'kāt), *v.* to appease, pacify, quiet the anger of.

plac·er (plăs'ər), *n.* *Mining.* 1. a superficial gravel or similar deposit containing particles of gold or the like. 2. a place where such a deposit is washed for gold.

plac·id (plăs'ĭd), *adj.* pleasantly calm or

ăct, āble, dâre, ärt; ĕbb, ēqual; ĭf, īce; hŏt, ōver, ôrder, oil, bŏŏk, ōōze, out; ŭp, ūse, ûrge; ə = a in *alone*; ch, chief; g, give; j, judge; ng, ring; sh, shoe; th, thin; th, that; zh, vision. See the full key at the beginning of this glossary.

peaceful; unruffled. —plac′id·ly, adv. —pla·cid′i·ty, n.

plain·tive (plān′tĭv), adj. mournful, sad. —plain′tive·ly, adv.

plan·e·ta·ry (plăn′ə těr′ĭ), adj. 1. pertaining to, or of the nature of, the planets. 2. wandering; erratic. 3. Machinery. pertaining to a form of transmission for varying the speed in automobiles.

plat·i·tude (plăt′ə tūd′, plăt′ə tōod′), n. a flat, dull, trite remark, esp. one uttered as if it were fresh and profound.

pla·za (plä′zə, plăz′ə), n. a public square in a city or town.

pleas·an·try (plěz′ən trĭ), n. pleasant humor in conversation.

pock·et (pŏk′ĭt), n. 1. a small bag inserted in a garment. 2. any pouchlike hollow or cavity. 3. a cavity in the earth, esp. one containing gold or other ore.

pomp (pŏmp), n. 1. stately display; splendor; magnificence. 2. a too showy, vain display.

pomp·ous (pŏm′pəs), adj. characterized by a pretentious show of dignity, learning, or importance.

poop (pōop), n. the stern of a ship.

port (pōrt), n. Nautical. the side of the ship to the left of a person facing the bow. (Opposite of starboard.) —adj. pertaining to, or on, the left side of a vessel as one faces the bow.

pos·te·ri·or (pŏs tĭr′ĭ ər), n. the hinder parts of the body. —adj. situated behind.

pos·ter·i·ty (pŏs těr′ə tĭ), n. succeeding generations; descendants.

pot·boil·er (pŏt′boi′lər), n. Colloq. a work of literature or art produced merely to earn money.

pre·car·i·ous (prĭ kâr′ĭ əs), adj. insecure. —pre·car′i·ous·ly, adv.

pre·cede (prē sēd′), v. to go before, as in place, rank, importance, or time.

pre·ced·ence (prĭ sē′dəns, prěs′ə dəns), n. priority in rank, importance, etc.

prec·e·dent (prěs′ə dənt), n. a preceding instance, esp. one serving as an example or justification in later cases.

pre·cip·i·tate (prĭ sĭp′ə tāt′), v. 1. to cast, plunge, hurl headlong. 2. to hasten; bring about in haste. —pre·cip′i·tan·cy, n.

pre·di·lec·tion (prē′də lěk′shən, prěd′ə lěk′-shən), n. a preconceived liking; preference.

pre·em·i·nence (prĭ ěm′ə nəns), n. state of being distinguished beyond others; superior to others. —pre·em′i·nent, adj.

pre·lude (prěl′ūd, prē′lōod), n. 1. an intro-duction to a principal event, action, performance, etc. 2. Music. a. an introductory section. b. since the 19th century, any short, romantic composition.

pre·med·i·tate (prĭ měd′ə tāt′), v. to plan beforehand.

pre·mo·ni·tion (prē′mə nĭsh′ən), n. a fore-warning. —pre·mon′i·to·ry, adj.

pre·na·tal (prē nā′təl), adj. previous to birth.

pre·oc·cu·pa·tion (prĭ ŏk′yə pā′shən), n. the state of being completely absorbed in thought, to the exclusion of immediate matters. —pre·oc′cu·py, v.

pre·pon·der·ance (prĭ pŏn′dər əns), n. supe-riority in weight, power, number, etc. —pre·pon′der·ant, adj. —pre·pon′der·ate, v.

pre·pos·sess (prē′pə zěs′), v. to impress favor-ably beforehand or at the outset. —pre′-pos·sess′ing, adj.

pre·pos·ter·ous (prĭ pŏs′tər əs), adj. contrary to nature, reason, and common sense; ab-surd.

pre·req·ui·site (prē rěk′wə zĭt), n. a thing re-quired beforehand. —adj. required before-hand.

pre·sen·ti·ment (prĭ zěn′tə mənt), n. a feel-ing of something about to happen, esp. something harmful.

pres·tige (prěs tēzh′), n. reputation or influ-ence arising from success, rank, etc.

pre·sump·tu·ous (prĭ zŭmp′chōo əs), adj. over-bold; taking too much for granted.

pre·ten·tious (prĭ těn′shəs), adj. 1. making exaggerated claims to dignity or impor-tance. 2. showy.

prime (prīm), adj. of the best quality. —v. to prepare or make ready.

pri·va·teer (prī′və tīr′), n. a privately owned and manned armed vessel, commissioned by a government at war to fight the enemy, esp. his commercial shipping.

priv·i·ly (prĭv′ə lĭ), adv. privately; secretly.

pro·di·gious (prə dĭj′əs), adj. extraordinary in size, amount, degree, etc.; wonderful. —pro·di′gious·ly, adv. —pro′di·gy, n.

pro·found (prə found′), adj. very deep.

pro·ject (prə jěkt′), v. 1. to throw. 2. to send forth in one's thoughts or imagina-tion. —pro·jec′tion, n.

pro·mo·tion (prə mō′shən), n. aid in organiz-ing (financial undertakings).

prone (prōn), adj. 1. having a tendency to-ward something. 2. lying face downward.

prop·a·gan·da (prŏp′ə găn′də), n. any sys-tematic, deliberate indoctrination; now of-ten used to imply deception or distortion.

prop·a·gan·dist (prŏp′ə găn′dĭst), n. one who

attempts to indoctrinate with a specific set of ideas.

prop·a·gate (prŏp'ə gāt'), *v.* to spread; extend.

prop·o·si·tion (prŏp'ə zĭsh'ən), *n.* something offered as a subject for discussion or argument.

pro·pri·e·ty (prō prī'ə tĭ), *n.* suitability to the occasion, in behavior or manners.

pro·sa·ic (prō zā'ĭk), *adj.* 1. dull; unimaginative. 2. having the character or spirit of prose rather than poetry.

pro·scribe (prō skrīb'), *v.* 1. to publish the name of a person condemned to death, with confiscation of property. 2. to outlaw. —**pro·scrip·tion** (prō skrĭp'shən), *n.*

pros·e·cu·tor (prŏs'ə kū'tər), *n.* 1. one who institutes and carries on legal proceedings in a court of law. 2. an officer charged with the conduct of such procedure in the interest of the public.

pro·to·plasm (prō'tə plăz'əm), *n. Biology.* a complex substance, the living matter of all vegetable and animal cells and tissues.

pro·tu·ber·ant (prō tū'bər ənt), *adj.* bulging out. —**pro·tu'ber·ance,** *n.*

prov·erb (prŏv'ərb), *n.* a short saying long in use, based on common sense, and putting some familiar truth or useful thought into expressive language: as, *a stitch in time saves nine.*

pro·voc·a·tive (prō vŏk'ə tĭv), *adj.* exciting; stimulating.

pseu·do·nym (sōō'də nĭm), *n.* a pen name.

psy·chi·a·trist (sī kī'ə trĭst), *n.* one who knows or practices the science of treating mental diseases.

psy·cho·log·i·cal (sī'kə lŏj'ə kəl), *adj.* pertaining to states and processes of mind and their influence on action.

psy·cho·lo·gy (sī kŏl'ə jĭ), *n.* the science of mind.

pug·na·cious (pŭg nā'shəs), *adj.* quarrelsome.

pun (pŭn), *n.* a play on words for humorous effect. —*v.* to make puns.

punc·til·i·o (pŭngt tĭl'ĭ ō'), *n.* 1. a fine point or detail in conduct, ceremony, etc. 2. exactness in the observance of forms. —**punc·til'i·ous,** *adj.*

pun·i·tive (pū'nə tĭv), *adj.* inflicting punishment.

pur·ga·to·ry (pûr'gə tōr'ĭ), *n.* 1. (in Roman Catholic belief) a condition or place of purification after death. 2. any situation of suffering.

pu·rism (pyōōr'ĭz əm), *n.* scrupulous or excessive insistence on purity of language, style, etc.

pur·ist (pyōōr'ĭst), *n.* an extremist in insisting upon purity of language.

pu·ri·tan·i·cal (pyōōr'ə tăn'ə kəl), *adj.* excessively strict and rigid.

putt (pŭt), *v. Golf.* to strike the ball gently and carefully so as to make it roll along the putting green into the hole.

quad (kwŏd), *n.* short for quadrangle. (Originally collegiate slang.)

quake (kwāk), *v.* to shake or tremble.

qualm (kwäm), *n.* 1. an uneasy scruple; a sudden misgiving. 2. a sudden sensation of nausea.

quarter boat, *Nautical.* any boat hung over a side along the quarter-deck.

quar·ter-deck (kwôr'tər dĕk'), *n. Nautical.* the upper deck between the mainmast and the stern.

qua·ver (kwā'vər), *n.* tremulous shake. —*v.* to quiver or tremble.

quib·ble (kwĭb'əl), *n.* a play on words for the purpose of evading the point. —*v.* to use words trickily; to evade the truth or the main point at issue.

quick (kwĭk), *adj.* 1. prompt; swift. 2. alive; vigorous. 3. *Archaic or Dialect.* endowed with life.

quin·tes·sence (kwĭn tĕs'əns), *n.* 1. the pure and concentrated essence of a substance. 2. the most perfect embodiment of something.

quirk (kwûrk), *n.* 1. a peculiarity. 2. a sudden twist.

quiz·zi·cal (kwĭz'ə kəl), *adj.* making fun of in a mild way, by an implied questioning; teasing: as, *a quizzical look.*

rad·i·cal (răd'ə kəl), *adj.* 1. going to the root. 2. extreme, esp. in the way of reform.

Rad·i·cal, *n.* one belonging to a political party favoring drastic reforms.

ram·part (răm'pärt), *n.* high fortification; barricade.

ăct, āble, dâre, ärt; ĕbb, ēqual; ĭf, īce; hŏt, ōver, ôrder, oil, bŏŏk, ōōze, out; ŭp, ūse, ûrge; ə = a in *alone;* **ch,** chief; **g,** give; **j,** judge; **ng,** ring; **sh,** shoe; **th,** thin; **th,** that; **zh,** vision. See the full key at the beginning of this glossary.

ran·cor (răng′kər), *n.* resentment; ill will.

rank (răngk), *adj.* **1.** growing too tall, coarse, and vigorous: as, *a rank growth of grass.* **2.** offensive.

ran·kle (răng′kəl), *v.* (of feelings and unpleasant experiences) to keep up bitter resentment within the mind.

rapt (răpt), *adj.* carried away by strong feeling.

rav·ish (răv′ĭsh), *v.* to fill with strong emotion, esp. joy.

re·ac·tion·ar·y (rĭ ăk′shə nĕr′ĭ), *n.* one who favors a reverse movement toward the past, particularly in the direction of political conservatism. —Also *adj.*

re·cep·tive (rĭ sĕp′tĭv), *adj.* quick to receive ideas. —**re′cep·tiv′i·ty,** *n.*

rec·ti·tude (rĕk′tə tūd′, rĕk′tə tōōd′), *n.* rightness of principle or practice.

redd (rĕd), *v. Colloq.* to put in order; tidy. (Usually followed by *up.*)

re·gale (rĭ gāl′), *v.* to entertain; delight.

re·lapse (rĭ lăps′), *v.* to fall back into a former state. —Also *n.*

rel·e·vant (rĕl′ə vənt), *adj.* pertinent; relating to the matter in hand.

re·luc·tant (rĭ lŭk′tənt), *adj.* unwilling. —**re·luc′tant·ly,** *adv.* —**re·luc′tance,** *n.*

rem·i·nis·cence (rĕm′ə nĭs′əns), *n.* **1.** the telling of a remembered experience. **2.** a mental impression retained and revived.

re·mon·strance (rĭ mŏn′strəns), *n.* a protest.

re·morse (rĭ môrs′), *n.* deep regret for wrongdoing.

re·morse·less·ness (rĭ môrs′lĭs nĕs), *n.* relentlessness; complete lack of pity. —**re·morse′·less,** *adj.* —**re·morse′less·ly,** *adv.*

ren·ais·sance (rĕn′ ə säns′, rĕn′ ə zäns′, rĭ nā′-səns; *French* rə nĕ säns′), *n.* **1.** a new birth; a revival. **2.** (*cap.*) the activity, spirit, or time of the great revival of art, letters, and learning in Europe during the 14th, 15th, and 16th centuries, marking the transition from the medieval to the modern world.

ren·e·gade (rĕn′ə gād′), *n.* one who deserts a party or cause for another.

re·nounce (rĭ nouns′), *v.* to give up voluntarily, often by a formal declaration.

rep·li·ca (rĕp′lə kə), *n.* a copy.

re·pu·di·ate (rĭ pū′dĭ āt′), *v.* to reject with condemnation. —**re·pu′di·a′tion,** *n.*

re·pug·nant (rĭ pŭg′nənt), *adj.* **1.** distasteful. **2.** contrary to one's nature or character.

re·search (rĭ sûrch′), *n.* diligent and systematic investigation, to discover facts or principles.

research ship, a ship equipped and used for research.

re·sil·i·ent (rĭ zĭl′ĭ ənt), *adj.* springing back; readily recovering. —**re·sil′i·ence,** *n.*

res·o·lute (rĕz′ə lōōt′), *adj.* determined.

res·o·lu·tion (rĕz′ə lōō′shən), *n.* **1.** firmness of purpose. **2.** solution or working out, as of a problem or the conflicts of a story.

re·solve (rĭ zŏlv′), *v.* **1.** to determine to do something. **2.** to solve (as a problem or the conflicts of a story).

res·o·nant (rĕz′ə nənt), *adj.* resounding.

re·spec·tive (rĭ spĕk′tĭv), *adj.* relating individually to two or more persons or things: as, *their respective destinations.*

re·spec·tive·ly (rĭ spĕk′tĭv lĭ), *adv.* with respect to two or more, in the order mentioned: as, *the first, second, and third seats of Row M were occupied by Mary, Kate, and Anna, respectively.*

res·pite (rĕs′pĭt), *n.* an interval of relief.

re·stric·tive (rĭ strĭk′tĭv), *adj.* **1.** tending to keep within limits. **2.** expressing so as to limit the application.

re·ten·tive (rĭ tĕn′tĭv), *adj.* having power to retain, hold, or keep in mind.

ret·i·cent (rĕt′ə sənt), *adj.* disposed to keep thoughts and feelings to oneself.

ret·i·na (rĕt′ə nə), *n.* the part of the eye which receives the image.

re·tract (rĭ trăkt′), *v.* to withdraw. —**re·trac′-tion,** *n.*

ret·ri·bu·tion (rĕt′rə bū′shən), *n.* a deserved punishment or (less commonly) reward. —**re·trib′u·tive, re·trib′u·to·ry,** *adj.*

re·trieve (rĭ trēv′), *v.* to recover.

ret·ro·spect (rĕt′rə spĕkt′), *n.* a looking back on past time or events.

rev·eil·le (rĕv′ə lĭ), *n.* a signal, as of a drum or bugle, to waken soldiers or sailors for the day's duties.

re·ver·sal (rĭ vûr′səl), *n.* **1.** act of turning upside down or inside out. **2.** a turning in the opposite direction from the usual or expected.

re·volt (rĭ vōlt′), *v.* **1.** to rebel. **2.** to turn away in horror and disgust (followed by *from*). —*n.* **1.** rebellion. **2.** feeling of complete disgust or horror.

rhap·so·dize (răp′sə dīz′), *v.* to speak or write rhapsodies. —**rhap·sod′i·cal·ly,** *adv.*

rhap·so·dy (răp′sə dĭ), *n.* an exalted or exaggerated expression of feeling or enthusiasm.

rhet·o·ric (rĕt′ə rĭk), *n.* the art or science of all specially literary uses of language, including the figures of speech.

rhe·tor·i·cal (rĭ tôr'ə kəl), *adj.* concerned with style and effect in expression.

ri·fle (rī'fəl), *v.* to ransack and rob.

rite (rīt), *n.* a ceremony; a customary religious act.

rit·u·al (rĭch'ōō əl), *n.* a prescribed code, form, or system, as in religious ceremonies.

Riv·i·er·a (rĭv'ī âr ə; *Italian* rē vyĕ'rä), *n.* a famous resort region along the Mediterranean coast.

role (rōl), *n.* a part played, as of an actor on the stage.

rove (rōv), *v.* dialect past tense of **rive**, to split or cleave.

roy·al·ty (roi'əl tĭ), *n.* 1. royal persons collectively. 2. a fixed portion of the proceeds of his work paid to an author, composer, etc.

rub·ble (rŭb'əl), *n.* rough broken stones, bricks, etc.

ru·di·men·ta·ry (rōō' də mĕn'tə rĭ), *adj.* elementary; undeveloped.

ru·mi·nate (rōō' mə nāt'), *v.* 1. to chew the cud. 2. to think over.

rum·pus (rŭm'pəs), *n. Colloq.* uproar.

runt (rŭnt), *n.* an undersized, stunted animal, person, or thing.

ruth·less (rōōth'lĭs), *adj.* without pity.

sab·o·tage (săb'ə täzh'), *n.* 1. malicious injury to work, tools, machinery, etc., or any underhand interference with production or business, by enemy agents in wartime or by employees during a trade dispute. 2. any malicious undermining of a cause. —*v.* to injure or attack in this manner.

sab·o·teur (săb'ə tûr'), *n.* one who practices sabotage.

sa·li·ent (sā'lĭ ənt), *adj.* prominent; conspicuous. —**sa'li·ence**, *n.* —**sa'li·ent·ly**, *adv.*

sal·ly (săl'ĭ), *n.* a sprightly remark.

sal·ver (săl'vər), *n.* a tray.

san·dal·wood (săn'dəl wood'), *n.* the fragrant heartwood of certain Asiatic trees, used for ornamental carving and burned as incense.

sar·don·ic (sär dŏn'ĭk), *adj.* bitterly ironical; sneering; scornful.

sa·rong (sə rông'), *n.* the principal garment for both sexes in the Malay Archipelago, consisting of a piece of cloth enveloping the lower part of the body like a skirt.

sat·ire (săt'īr), *n.* the use of irony, sarcasm, ridicule, etc., to expose vice, folly, etc., and to deride them. —**sat·i·rize** (săt' ə rīz), *v.* —**sat·i·rist** (săt'ə rĭst), *n.* —**sa·tir'i·cal**, *adj.* —**sa·tir'i·cal·ly**, *adv.*

sa·vor (sā'vər), *n.* 1. distinctive quality pleasantly affecting taste or smell. 2. power to excite or interest. —*v.* 1. to perceive with relish, esp. by taste or smell. 2. to give oneself over to the enjoyment of. —**sa'vor·y**, *adj.*

saw (sô), *n.* a saying; maxim; proverb.

scath·ing (skā'thĭng), *adj.* bitterly severe.

scoff (skŏf, skôf), *v.* to speak in mockery. —**scof'fer**, *n.* —**scoff'ing·ly**, *adv.*

scor·pi·on (skôr'pĭ ən), *n.* a small creature belonging to the same group as the spider (arachnids), found in warm regions, with a front pair of nipping claws and a slender jointed tail ending in a poisonous sting.

scourge (skûrj), *n.* a whip or lash. —*v.* to lash.

scribe (skrīb), *n.* 1. a penman; a copyist. 2. an official of ancient times who performed clerical duties. 3. *Jewish history.* one of a class of teachers who interpreted Jewish law to the people.

script (skrĭpt), *n. Theater.* the manuscript of a play or role.

scru·ple (skrōō'pəl), *n.* a feeling of hesitancy or doubt arising from difficulty in deciding what is right.

scru·pu·lous (skrōō'pyə ləs), *adj.* 1. having a strict regard for what is right. 2. extremely careful; exact to the smallest degree. —**scru'pu·lous·ly**, *adv.*

scud (skŭd), *v.* 1. to run quickly. 2. *Nautical.* to run before a gale. —*n.* clouds, spray, etc., driven by wind.

sear (sîr), *v.* to burn or char the surface of; to scorch.

se·di·tion (sĭ dĭsh'ən), *n.* incitement of discontent or rebellion against the government.

sen·si·bil·i·ty (sĕn'sə bĭl'ə tĭ), *n.* capacity for feeling; responsiveness.

sen·su·ous (sĕn'shōō əs), *adj.* pertaining to the senses; readily affected through the senses. —**sen'su·ous·ly**, *adv.*

sen·ti·ment (sĕn'tə mənt), *n.* 1. feeling. 2. refined or tender emotion.

ăct, āble, dâre, ärt; ĕbb, ēqual; ĭf, īce; hŏt, ōver, ôrder, oil, book, ōoze, out; ŭp, ūse, ûrge; ə = a in *alone*; **ch**, chief; **g**, give; **j**, judge; **ng**, ring; **sh**, shoe; **th**, thin; **th**, that; **zh**, vision. See the full key at the beginning of this glossary.

sen·ti·men·tal (sĕn′tə mĕn′təl), *adj.* weakly emotional; depending on feeling rather than reason. —sen′ti·men′tal·ism, *n.*

sep·ul·chre (sĕp′əl kər), *n.* tomb. (Also, sepulcher.)

ship·wright (shĭp′rīt), *n.* one employed in building or repairing ships.

shoal (shōl), *adj.* shallow. —*n.* 1. a place where the water is shallow. 2. a sand bar, esp. one which shows at low water. 3. a group of fish crowded close together. —*v.* to collect in a shoal.

shod·dy (shŏd′ĭ), *n.* 1. an inferior woolen material, made of rags. 2. anything inferior but pretentious. —*adj.* sham.

shy (shī), *v.* to start back or aside as in fear (used most often of a horse).

Si·a·mese twins (sī′ə mēz′), twins who are born joined together.

sib·i·lant (sĭb′ə lənt), *adj.* hissing.

sil·hou·ette (sĭl′ōō̆ĕt′), *n.* a dark image outlined against a lighter background. —*v.* to present such an image.

sil·i·ca (sĭl′ə kə), *n.* the dioxide of silicon, a hard, glassy mineral found in a variety of forms, as quartz, sand, etc. (The breathing of particles containing silica can cause a lung disease.)

sim·per (sĭm′pər), *v.* to smile in a silly, self-conscious way.

si·mul·ta·ne·ous (sī′məl tā′nĭ əs, sĭm′ əl tā′nĭ əs), *adj.* existing, occurring, or operating at the same time. —si′mul·ta′ne·ous·ly, *adv.*

sin (sĭn), *n.* an act thought of as contrary to the law of God. —original sin, 1. the sin of Adam and Eve in eating the forbidden fruit, in the story of the Garden of Eden. 2. an inborn tendency in all men to sin, inherited from Adam.

Si·nai (sī′nī), *n.* 1. a peninsula in northeast Egypt. 2. (Mount) the mountain from which the law (the Ten Commandments) was given to Moses.

sin·gu·lar (sĭng′gyə lər), *adj.* 1. remarkable. 2. odd; unusual. 3. being only one. — sin′gu·lar·ly, *adv.*

si·ren (sī′rən), *n.* 1. one of several sea nymphs, supposed to lure mariners to destruction by their singing. 2. an instrument for producing whistles, fog signals, etc.

skin (skĭn), *n. Slang.* a swindler. —*v. Slang.* to cheat by stripping of money or belongings.

skir·mish (skûr′mĭsh), *n.* a fight between small bodies of troops. —*v.* to take part in such a fight. —skir′mish·er, *n.*

slan·der (slăn′dər), *n.* a malicious, false, and defamatory statement or report. —slan′der·ous, *adj.*

sloth·ful (slōth′fəl, slôth′fəl), *adj.* lazy.

slov·en (slŭv′ən), *n.* one who is habitually negligent of neatness or cleanliness in dress, appearance, etc. —slov′en·ly, *adj.*

slug (slŭg), *n.* a snail-like creature, but without a shell.

sneer (snĭr), *v.* to smile or curl the lip in a manner that shows scorn, contempt, etc. —*n.* a look suggesting scorn.

snub (snŭb), *v.* 1. to treat with contempt. 2. to check or rebuke sharply. 3. to check (a boat, an unbroken horse, etc.) by means of a rope or line made fast to a fixed object.

snub·ber (snŭb′ər), *n.* a kind of automobile shock absorber which operates by restricting the action of the body springs.

so·cial·ism (sō′shə lĭz′əm), *n.* a theory of social organization which advocates government ownership and control of the means of production, etc.

so·cial·ist (sō′shəl ĭst), *n.* one who advocates or supports socialism.

so·lace (sŏl′ĭs), *n.* comfort; relief. —*v.* to give comfort or relief.

so·lic·i·tor (sə lĭs′ə tər), *n. England.* a member of the legal profession who advises clients, represents them before the lower courts, and prepares cases for barristers to try in the higher courts.

so·lic·i·tude (sə lĭs′ə tūd′, sə lĭs′ə tōōd′), *n.* concern; anxious care.

som·ber (sŏm′bər), *adj.* 1. gloomily dark. 2. depressing; dismal.

som·no·lent (sŏm′nə lənt), *adj.* drowsy. — som′no·lence, *n.* —som′no·lent·ly, *adv.*

so·no·rous (sə nôr′əs), *adj.* resonant; rich and full in sound.

sop (sŏp), *n.* 1. a piece of bread or the like dipped in liquid food. 2. something given to pacify or quiet, or as a bribe.

so·phis·ti·ca·ted (sə fĭs′tə kā′tĭd), *adj.* refined, by education or worldly experience or both, to the point of artificiality; worldly-wise. —so·phis′ti·ca′tion, *n.*

sor·cer·er (sôr′sər ər), *n.* a magician.

sor·cer·y (sôr′sə rĭ), *n.* magic, esp. that performed with the help of evil spirits.

sor·did (sôr′dĭd), *adj.* dirty; morally base; meanly selfish.

sound·ing (soun′dĭng), *n.* 1. process of measuring depth of water, as at sea. 2. (*pl.*) depths of water determined by means of lead and line, as at sea.

GLOSSARY

spas·mod·ic (spăz mŏd'ĭk), *adj.* sudden and violent, but brief; intermittent. —spasmod'i·cal·ly, *adv.*

spawn (spôn), *n.* the mass of eggs emitted by fish, crustaceans, etc. —*v.* to produce spawn.

spec·trum (spĕk'trəm), *n.* the series of colored bands diffracted (broken apart) and arranged in the order of their wave lengths by the passing of white light through a prism or other diffracting medium, and shading continuously from red (produced by the longest wave length visible) to violet (produced by the shortest).

spec·u·la·tion (spĕk'yə lā'shən), *n.* 1. engaging in business transactions involving considerable risk, with the chance of large gains. 2. consideration of possibilities; surmise. —spec'u·late', *v.*

spec·u·la·tive·ly (spĕk'yə lā' tĭv lĭ), *adv.* consideringly; with thoughtful surmise.

spell (spĕl), *v.* *Chiefly U.S.* to take the place of or relieve for a time.

sphinx (sfĭngks), *n.* 1. (ancient Egypt) a. a figure of an imaginary creature with the head of a man or an animal and the body of a lion. b. the huge stone figure of this kind near the pyramids of Gizeh. 2. (Greek mythology) a fabulous monster with the head and breast of a woman, the body of a lion or dog, and wings. It proposed a riddle to passers-by, killing those unable to guess it. When Oedipus solved the riddle, the sphinx killed itself.

sphinxlike, *adj.* presenting difficult questions; being of a mysterious nature.

spif·li·cate (spĭf'lə kāt), *v.* 1. to astonish; bewilder. 2. to beat; kill.

spit·toon (spĭ tōōn'), *n.* a bowl used as a receptacle for spit; a cuspidor.

spon·ta·ne·ous (spŏn tā'nĭ əs), *adj.* arising from internal forces; independent of anything external. —spon·ta'ne·ous·ly, *adv.*

spouse (spouz, spous), *n.* either member of a married pair in relation to the other; one's husband or wife.

spout (spout), *v.* *Colloq.* to declaim in an oratorical manner.

squeam·ish (skwē'mĭsh), *adj.* 1. easily shocked. 2. easily nauseated.

squid (skwĭd), *n.* a long slender sea mollusk

(the smaller varieties are used for food and for fish bait).

squire (skwīr), *n.* a country gentleman (esp. in England).

sta·ble (stā'bəl), *adj.* firm; steady. —sta·bil'i·ty, *n.* —sta'bil·ize, *v.*

stanch, *see* staunch.

star·board (stär'bōrd', stär'bərd), *n.* *Nautical.* the side of a ship to the right of a person looking toward the bow. —*adj.* pertaining to the right side of a ship.

stark (stärk), *adj.* 1. sheer; utter. 2. stiff or rigid. 3. rigid in death. 4. harsh, grim, desolate (used of places, etc.). —Also *adv.* —stark'ness, *n.*

stat·ic (stăt'ĭk), *adj.* in a fixed or stationary condition.

sta·tus (stā'təs, stăt'əs), *n.* 1. state of affairs. 2. standing (socially, professionally, etc.).

staunch or stanch (stänch, stănch), *adj.* firm or steadfast in principle, loyalty, etc. — stanch'ness, *n.* —stanch'ly, *adv.*

stead·fast (stĕd'făst'), *adj.* 1. firm in purpose; unwavering. 2. fixed in direction.

steel (stēl), *n.* 1. iron modified for strength, hardness, elasticity. 2. a piece of steel formerly used with flint for striking sparks to make fire.

ster·ile (stĕr'ĭl), *adj.* 1. free from living germs. 2. incapable of producing offspring. —ster'i·lize, *v.*

stick·ler (stĭk'lər), *n.* a person who insists on something unyieldingly. (Usually followed by *for.*)

stint (stĭnt), *n.* an allotted amount or piece of work: as, *to do one's daily stint.*

stip·u·late (stĭp'yə lāt'), *v.* to arrange or specify in the terms of an agreement.

sto·i·cal (stō'ə kəl), *adj.* calm and unflinching under suffering, bad fortune, etc. [From the Stoics, Greek philosophers who believed that all happenings, pleasant or unpleasant, being the result of divine will, should be taken calmly and courageously.] —sto'ic, *n.*

sto·lid (stŏl'ĭd), *adj.* not easily moved or stirred mentally; impassive, as from dullness or stupidity. —sto·lid·i·ty (stə lĭd'ə tĭ) *n.* —stol'id·ly, *adv.*

strat·a·gem (străt'ə jəm), *n.* a trick or scheme to deceive the enemy.

string (strĭng), *n.* 1. a set or number: as, *a*

ăct, āble, dâre, ärt; ĕbb, ēqual; ĭf, īce; hŏt, ōver, ôrder, oil, bŏŏk, ōōze, out; ŭp, ūse, ûrge; ə = a in *alone*; ch, chief; g, give; j, judge; ng, ring; sh, shoe; th, thin; th, that; zh, vision. See the full key at the beginning of this glossary.

string of race horses. **2.** any series of things arranged in a line or following closely one after another.

stripe (strīp), *n.* (in such expressions as *a man of quite a different stripe*) sort, kind.

sty (stī), *n.* a pen for swine.

styl·ize (stī'līz), *v.* to present according to a particular form or pattern, rather than in an individual way.

suave (swäv, swāv), *adj.* smoothly agreeable; polite. —**suave'ly**, *adv.*

sub·con·scious (sŭb kŏn'shəs), *adj.* **1.** existing or operating beneath or beyond consciousness. **2.** pertaining to mental activities of which the individual is unaware.

sub·jec·tive (səb jĕk'tĭv), *adj.* **1.** existing in the mind rather than in the object being thought about: as, *the poem was a subjective expression of his feelings toward the war.* **2.** affected by personal bias.

sub·jec·tiv·i·ty (sŭb'jĕk tĭv'ə tĭ), *n.* (*in writing*) portraying character and events through presenting the thoughts and feelings of the persons involved in addition to external evidence.

sub·li·mate (sŭb'lə māt'), *v.* to make nobler or purer.

sub·or·di·nate (sə bôr'də nāt'), *v.* to place in a lower order or rank; to make dependent. —Also *n.* and *adj.*

sub·or·di·nat·ing (sə bôr'də nā'tĭng), *adj.* (in some languages) introducing subordinate clauses—as *when, if,* etc., in English.

sub·side (səb sīd'), *v.* **1.** to sink. **2.** to become quiet.

sub·sist (səb sĭst'), *v.* to exist; to continue alive.

sub·sist·ence (səb sĭs'təns) *n.* means of supporting life.

sub·stand·ard (sŭb stăn'dərd), *adj.* **1.** below standard, esp. the minimum standard established by law. **2.** *Linguistics.* deviating from the standard language patterns of cultivated speakers and writers (for example, slang).

sub·stan·ti·ate (sŭb stăn'shĭ āt'), *v.* to prove by evidence.

sub·tle (sŭt'əl), *adj.* delicate; hard to perceive or interpret. —**sub·tle·ty** (sŭt'əl tĭ), *n.*

sub·ver·sion (səb vûr'shən), *n.* act of overthrowing, destroying, corrupting. —**subver'sive**, *adj.*

sub·vert (sŭb vûrt'), *v.* **1.** to overthrow. **2.** to undermine the principles of; corrupt.

suf·frage (sŭf'rĭj), *n.* the right of voting.

sul·try (sŭl'trĭ), *adj.* oppressively hot and close or moist. —**sul'tri·ness**, *n.*

su·per- (soo'pər), a prefix meaning "over," "above," "on top of," "greater than," etc.

su·per·a·bun·dant (soo'pər ə bŭn'dənt), *adj.* exceedingly or excessively abundant. —**su'per·a·bun'dant·ly**, *adv.*

su·per·car·go (soo'pər kär'gō), *n.* an officer on a merchant ship in charge of cargo and commercial concerns of the voyage.

su·per·cede, *see* **supersede.**

su·per·cil·i·ous (soo'pər sĭl'ĭ əs), *adj.* haughtily disdainful in expression, bearing, etc. —**su'per·cil'i·ous·ly**, *adv.*

su·per·fi·cial (soo'pər fĭsh'əl), *adj.* being at, on, or near the surface; shallow. —**su·per·fi·ci·al·i·ty** (soo'pər fĭsh'ĭ ăl'ə tĭ), *n.* —**su'per·fi'cial·ly**, *adv.*

su·per·flu·ous (soo'pûr'floo əs), *adj.* unnecessary; over and above what is sufficient or required. —**su·per'flu·ous·ly**, *adv.*

su·per·la·tive (sə pûr'lə tĭv), *adj.* surpassing all others. —*n.* something supreme, almost beyond words.

su·per·nat·u·ral (soo'pər năch'ə rəl), *adj.* being above or beyond what is natural; extraordinary. —**su'per·nat'u·ral·ly**, *adv.*

su·per·sede (soo'pər sēd'), *v.* (variant, **supercede**) **1.** to replace in power, use, etc., by another person or thing. **2.** to set aside in favor of something else (which is usually mentioned).

sup·port·a·ble (sə pôr'tə bəl), *adj.* endurable.

sup·press (sə prĕs'), *v.* **1.** do away with or put an end to by authority. **2.** keep in or repress. —**sup·pres'sion**, *n.*

sur·ly (sûr'lĭ), *adj.* boorishly rude. —**sur'li·ly**, *adv.* —**sur'li·ness**, *n.*

swath (swŏth, swôth), *n.* **1.** the space covered by the stroke of a scythe or the cut of a mowing machine. **2.** a strip, belt, or long and narrow extent of anything.

sym·bol·ize (sĭm'bə līz'), *v.* to stand for or represent. —**sym·bol'ic**, *adj.* —**sym·bol'i·cal·ly**, *adv.* —**sym'bol**, *n.*

sy·nod (sĭn'əd), *n.* **1.** a council of churches or church officials. **2.** any assembly or council.

syn·the·sis (sĭn'thə sĭs), *n.* *Chemistry.* the forming of compounds by the union of elements or the combination of simpler compounds.

syn·thet·ic (sĭn thĕt'ĭk), *adj.* pertaining to compounds formed by chemical reaction in a laboratory, as contrasted with those of natural origin.

tab·u·late (tăb'yə lāt'), *v.* to form into a table or scheme. —**tab'u·la'tion**, *n.*

tac·i·turn (tăs′ə tûrn′), *adj.* inclined to silence.

taint (tānt), *v.* 1. to modify as by a touch of something offensive. 2. to sully or tarnish. —*n.* 1. a touch of something offensive. 2. a trace of infection or contamination. 3. a touch of dishonor or discredit.

ta·pa (tä′pä), *n.* an unwoven cloth of the Pacific islands, made by steeping and beating the inner bark of a certain type of native tree.

tap·es·try (tăp′ĭs trĭ), *n.* 1. a wall-hanging consisting of a piece of hand-woven fabric, with a design. 2. a machine-woven reproduction of true tapestry.

tar·nish (tär′nĭsh), *v.* 1. to dull or discolor; to lose luster (as metal from oxidation). 2. to besmirch or sully (as a reputation).

tar·pau·lin (tär pô′lĭn), *n.* a waterproofed protective covering of canvas or other material.

taut·en (tô′tən), *v.* to draw tightly.

tech·nique (těk nēk′), *n.* method, esp. in artistic work.

tech·no·log·i·cal (těk′nə lŏj′ĭ kəl), *adj.* 1. relating to technology. 2. *Economics.* caused by technical advances in production methods: as, *technological unemployment.*

tech·nol·o·gy (těk nŏl′ə jĭ), *n.* the sciences of the industrial arts.

te·di·um (tē′dĭ əm), *n.* state of being wearisome through length and slowness. —**te′di·ous,** *adj.*

tem·per (těm′pər), *n.* the particular state of mind or feelings.

tem·per·a·ment (těm′pər ə mənt, těm′prə mənt), *n.* disposition, nature (of a person, consisting of the sum and mixture of his individual qualities).

tem′per·a·ment′al, *adj.* having a strongly marked individuality, with disinclination to submit to ordinary rules or restraints.

te·na·cious (tĭ nā′shəs), *adj.* 1. holding fast. 2. persistent. —**te·nac·i·ty** (tĭ năs′ə tĭ), *n.* —**te·na·cious·ly** (tĭ nā′shəs lĭ), *adv.*

ten·sion (těn′shən), *n.* strain; excitement; suspense.

ter·rain (tě rān′, těr′ān), *n.* a tract of land, esp. considered with reference to its natural features, military advantages, etc.

tes·ty (těs′tĭ), *adj.* irritably impatient. —**tes′ti·ly,** *adv.*

thatch (thăch), *n.* a covering of straw, palm leaves, etc., used in some countries for roofing, protecting grain stacks, etc. —*v.* to cover, as with thatch.

the·ol·o·gy (thē ŏl′ə jĭ), *n.* the science or study of divine things or religious truth.

the·sis (thē′sĭs), *n.* a proposition, esp. one to be discussed and proved or maintained against objections.

Thes·sa·ly (thěs′ə lĭ), *n.* a region in eastern Greece; a former division of ancient Greece.

three-di·men·sion·al (thrē′dĭ měn′shən əl), *adj.* having, or seeming to have, the dimension of depth in addition to those of length and width.

thun·der·struck (thŭn′dər strŭk′), *adj.* overcome with paralyzing dismay; astounded.

thwart (thwôrt), *v.* to oppose successfully; frustrate; baffle.

tick (tĭk), *n.* any of a large group of wingless bloodsucking insects or mites that infest man, cattle, or other animals.

tim·ber (tĭm′bər), *n.* 1. trees or wood suitable for building. 2. personal character or quality.

tin·der (tĭn′dər), *n.* material formerly used for catching the spark from a flint and steel struck together, for kindling fire.

tin′der·box′, *n.* box for holding tinder.

tip·pet (tĭp′ĭt), *n.* a scarf, usually of fur or wool, for covering the neck or the neck and shoulders, and usually having ends hanging down in front.

toll (tōl), *v.* to ring (a church bell) slowly with regularly repeated strokes for announcing a death.

tour·ni·quet (tŏŏr′nə kět′, tûr′nə kět′), *n.* a device for arresting bleeding, such as a bandage tightened by twisting.

trades (trādz), *n. pl.* the trade winds.

tra·duce (trə dūs′), *v.* slander; speak maliciously and falsely of.

tran·scen·den·tal (trăn′sěn děn′təl), *adj.* going above or beyond ordinary experience, thought, or belief. —**tran·scend′,** *v.*

trans·fix (trăns fĭks′), *v.* 1. to pierce through. 2. to fix fast. 3. to make motionless by means of some strong emotion.

ăct, āble, dâre, ärt; ĕbb, ēqual; ĭf, īce; hŏt, ōver, ôrder, oil, bŏŏk, ōōze, out; ŭp, ūse, ûrge; ə = a in *alone;* **ch,** chief; **g,** give; **j,** judge; **ng,** ring; **sh,** shoe; **th,** thin; **th,** that; **zh,** vision. See the full key at the beginning of this glossary.

tran·sient (trăn′shənt), *adj.* passing with time; not lasting.

tran·si·tion (trăn zĭsh′ən), *n.* passage from one position, state, stage, etc., to another. —**tran·si′tion·al**, *adj.*

trans·mis·sion (trăns mĭsh′ən, trănz mĭsh′ən), *n. Machinery.* 1. the transferring of motive force. 2. a device for this purpose, to vary rate of speed in automobiles.

trans·mute (trăns mūt′), *v.* to change, transform.

tran·splen·dent (trăn splĕn′dənt), *adj.* brilliant in appearance; gorgeous.

trav·ail (trăv′āl), *n.* physical or mental toil or exertion, esp. when painful.

trav·es·ty (trăv′ĭs tĭ), *n.* ridiculous imitation.

tree (trē), *n.* short form of saddletree (the frame of a saddle).

trek (trĕk), *n.* a migration. —*v.* to travel; migrate.

tri·lin·gual (trī lĭng′gwəl), *adj.* able to use three languages.

tril·o·gy (trĭl′ə jĭ), *n.* a series or group of three related dramas, operas, novels, etc.

trite (trīt), *adj.* hackneyed by constant use or repetition. —**trite′ness**, *n.*

truf·fle (trŭf′əl, trōō′fəl), *n.* an edible subterranean fungus, considered a great delicacy.

tryst (trĭst), *n.* an appointment to meet at a certain time and place.

trysting place, place of appointed meeting.

tu·le (tōō′lĕ), *n.* a kind of bulrush.

tur·bu·lent (tûr′byə lənt), *adj.* boisterous; unruly; disorderly. —**tur′bu·lence**, *n.* —**tur′bu·lent·ly**, *adv.*

tur·ret (tûr′ĭt), *n.* a small tower.

ty·phoon (tī fōōn′), *n.* a tropical cyclone or hurricane of the western Pacific area and the China seas.

ty·pog·ra·phy (tī pŏg′rə fĭ), *n.* 1. the art or process of printing with types. 2. the general character or appearance of printed matter. —**ty′po·graph′i·cal**, *adj.*

ul·te·ri·or (ŭl tĭr′ĭ ər), *adj.* beyond what is seen or avowed; intentionally kept concealed.

ul·ti·ma·tum (ŭl′tə mā′təm), *n.* a final statement of conditions, the rejection of which will involve breaking off relations with the individual or nation making the statement.

ul·ti·mate (ŭl′tə mĭt), *adj.* final; decisive; beyond which it is impossible to proceed.

ul·tra- (ŭl′trə), *prefix.* 1. beyond (in space or time): as, *ultraplanetary.* 2. excessively: as, *ultraconfident.*

un-, *prefix.* 1. not: as, *uncertain, unseen.* 2. the reverse of an action or state: as, *unfasten, uncork.*

un·a·bridged (ŭn′ə brĭjd′), *adj.* not shortened.

un·ac·count·a·ble (ŭn′ə koun′tə bəl), *adj.* not to be accounted for or explained. —**un′ac·count′a·bly**, *adv.*

un·al·loyed (ŭn′ə loid′), *adj.* pure; unmixed. —*see* **alloy**.

un·as·sert·ive (ŭn′ə sûr′tĭv), *adj.* not positive; not given to putting oneself forward boldly.

un·blem·ished (ŭn blĕm′ĭshd), *adj.* in perfect condition; without blemish.

un·bri·dled (ŭn brī′dəld), *adj.* 1. not having a bridle on (of a horse). 2. unrestrained.

un·con·ven·tion·al (ŭn′kən vĕn′shən əl), *adj.* not according to standard or accepted procedure or custom.

un·couth (ŭn kōōth′), *adj.* awkward, clumsy, or ill-mannered.

un·du·late (ŭn′dyə lāt′), *v.* to move in a wavelike manner. —**un′du·la′tion**, *n.*

un·in·hib·it·ed (ŭn′ĭn hĭb′ĭt əd), *adj.* unrestrained; not inhibited.

u·nique (ū nēk′), *adj.* 1. of which there is but one. 2. having no like or equal.

u·ni·ver·sal (ū′nə vûr′səl), *adj.* 1. characteristic of all. 2. applicable to many cases. 3. affecting all. —**u′ni·ver′sal·ly**, *adv.*

un·ob·tru·sive (ŭn′əb trōō′sĭv), *adj.* not thrusting oneself or itself forward.

un·or·tho·dox (ŭn ôr′thə dŏks′), *adj.* not approved; unconventional.

un·so·lic·it·ed (ŭn′sə lĭs′ĭt ĭd), *adj.* not requested; unsought for.

un·wield·y (ŭn wēl′dĭ), *adj.* of a size, shape, or weight that makes something awkward or hard to manage.

ur·ban (ûr′bən), *adj.* pertaining to a city or town.

u·su·rer (ū′zhə rər), *n.* one who lends money at an extremely high rate of interest.

u·surp (ū zûrp′), *v.* to seize and hold (office, position, power) by force or without right. —**u·surp′er**, *n.* —**u′sur·pa′tion**, *n.*

u·su·ry (ū′zhə rĭ), *n.* an exorbitant rate of interest, usually above the legal rate.

vac·il·late (văs′ə lāt′), *v.* to waver in mind; to be irresolute. —**vac′il·la′tion**, *n.* —**vac′il·la′ting**, *adj.*

vag·a·bond (văg′ə bŏnd′), *n.* 1. one who is without a fixed abode and wanders from place to place. 2. a tramp or vagrant. —*Also adj.*

val·iant (văl′yənt), *adj.* brave.

val·ue (văl′ū), *n.* **1.** worth. **2.** (*pl.*) the things regarded as most important by an individual or group (ideals, customs, institutions): as, *values of freedom and honesty.*

var·i·ant (vâr′ī ənt), *n.* a different form or spelling of the same word. —*adj.* **1.** tending to change. **2.** being an altered or different form of something.

vaunt (vônt), *v.* to boast, brag.

veer (vĭr), *v.* to shift to another direction, as the wind, or something moving with the wind.

ven·er·a·ble (vĕn′ər ə bəl), *adj.* commanding respect because of age and dignity of appearance.

ven·om (vĕn′əm), *n.* **1.** poison, esp. of snakes, spiders, etc. **2.** spite; malice.

ver·i·fy (vĕr′ə fī′), *v.* to prove to be true. —**ver′i·fi·ca′tion,** *n.*

ver·i·sim·il·i·tude (vĕr′ə sĭ mĭl′ĭ tūd′), *n.* the appearance of being true or real.

ves·tige (vĕs′tĭj), *n.* mark or trace of something no longer present.

vi·brant (vī′brənt), *adj.* **1.** moving to and fro rapidly. **2.** vigorous; pulsating with energy.

vin·di·cate (vĭn′də kāt′), *v.* to clear, as from a charge or suspicion. —**vin′di·ca′tion,** *n.*

vir·gin·al (vûr′jə nəl), *adj.* pure; fresh; untouched.

vir·tu·al (vûr′chŏŏ əl), *adj.* being something for most intents and purposes, but not actually being it in name, position, etc.: as, *although holding no office, he was the virtual ruler of the country.* —**vir′tu·al·ly,** *adv.*

vis·u·a·lize (vĭzh′ŏŏ ə līz′), *v.* to form a mental image of; to picture mentally.

vi·tal·i·ty (vī tăl′ə tĭ), *n.* vital force; power; vigor. —**vi′tal,** *adj.* —**vi′tal·ly,** *adv.*

vi·ti·ate (vĭsh′ī āt′), *v.* **1.** to impair the quality of. **2.** to corrupt; spoil.

vi·vac·i·ty (vī văs′ə tĭ, vĭ văs′ə tĭ), *n.* liveliness; animation.

vo·li·tion (vō lĭsh′ən), *n.* a determination by the will.

Vol·taire (vŏl târ′; *French* vôl tĕr′), French philosopher and writer, 1694-1778.

vol·un·tar·y (vŏl′ən tər′ĭ), *adj.* done of one's own accord.

vo·ra·cious (vō rā′shəs), *adj.* craving and de-vouring in large quantities (usually of food, but sometimes extended to other matters: as, *a voracious reader*).

vul·gar·i·ty (vəl găr′ə tĭ), *n.* coarseness; lack of good breeding, manners, or taste.

vul·ner·a·ble (vŭl′nər ə bəl), *adj.* **1.** liable to physical hurt. **2.** open to attack.

waist (wāst), *n. Nautical.* the central part of a ship; the part of the deck between the forecastle and the quarter-deck.

wal·low (wŏl′ō), *v.* to roll about, or lie, in mud, dust, water, etc.

wane (wān), *v.* **1.** (of the moon) to decrease after the full moon (opposite of *wax*). **2.** to decline in power, strength, etc. **3.** to draw to a close; approach an end. —Also *n.*

wan·ton (wŏn′tən), *adj.* malicious; uncalled for; deliberately disregardful of right, justice, humanity. —**wan′ton·ness,** *n.*

wa·ver (wā′vər), *v.* **1.** to sway to and fro; to become unsteady. **2.** to show doubt or indecision.

wax (wăks), *v.* **1.** to grow or become: as, *he waxed angry.* **2.** (of the moon) to increase in the extent of its illuminated portion before the full moon (opposite of *wane*).

weird (wĭrd), *adj.* uncanny.

weld (wĕld), *v.* to fuse; to bring into complete union.

wel·ter (wĕl′tər), *n.* **1.** a rolling or tumbling about. **2.** commotion; turmoil. —*v.* **1.** to roll or tumble about. **2.** to be drenched in something, esp. blood.

whelp (hwĕlp), *n.* **1.** the young of a dog, and of some other animals. **2.** (term of contempt) a youth.

whet (hwĕt), *v.* **1.** to sharpen (a knife, tool, etc.) by grinding or friction. **2.** to make keen or eager.

whim (hwĭm), *n.* an odd, fanciful notion.

whim·si·cal (hwĭm′zə kəl), *adj.* given to odd notions.

wile (wīl), *n.* trick; stratagem. —**wi′ly,** *adj.*

wince (wĭns), *n.* to shrink as from pain or a blow; to flinch.

wind·fall (wĭnd′fôl′), *n.* **1.** something blown down by the wind, as fruit. **2.** an unexpected piece of good fortune.

winding sheet, a sheet used to wrap a corpse for burial.

---

wise·a·cre (wīz'ā kər, wī'zə kər), *n.* (esp. in humorous or ironical use) one who possesses or affects to possess great wisdom.

withe (wĭth, wĭth), *n.* 1. a willow twig. 2. any tough, flexible twig or stem suitable for binding things together.

with·ers (wĭth' ərz), *n. pl.* the highest part of a horse's or other animal's back, behind the neck.

wiz·en (wĭz'ən), *v.* to dry up; wither.

wiz·ened (wĭz'ənd), *adj.* shriveled.

Woodchuck Day, February 2. According to superstition, if this day is clear, much more winter is ahead; if cloudy, spring is at hand. Supposedly, if the woodchuck comes out and sees his shadow on that day, he goes back for a long sleep; if not, he stays awake, in expectation of spring.

work·house (wûrk'hous'), *n.* 1. *U.S.* a house of correction; prison. 2. *Great Britain.* a poorhouse.

wot (wŏt), *v. Archaic.* part of an Old and Middle English verb meaning "to know."

wraith (rāth), *n.* an apparition; a visible spirit.

yeo·man·ry (yō'mən rĭ), *n.* a British volunteer cavalry force, originally composed largely of yeomen (farmers).

zeal (zēl), *n.* eager desire or endeavor; enthusiastic effort.

zeal·ous (zĕl'əs), *adj.* ardently active, devoted, or diligent. —zeal'ous·ly, *adv.*

ze·nith (zē'nĭth), *n.* 1. the point of the sun vertically above any place or observer. 2. highest point or state.

Index to Literary Terms

Page numbers in Roman type indicate that the term is defined or its use discussed on the page given. Page numbers in italics indicate a briefer discussion or mention of the term.

Index
of
Authors and Titles

The last number following an author's name indicates the page on which the biographical sketch of the author is found.

A B C D E F G H I J 069876543
PRINTED IN THE UNITED STATES OF AMERICA